LEOPOLD MOZART WITH HIS SON AND DAUGHTER (1763)

From a water-colour painting by Carmontelle
(Musée Condé, Chantilly)

THE
LETTERS OF MOZART
AND HIS FAMILY

*Chronologically arranged, translated and edited
with an Introduction, Notes and Indexes*

by

EMILY ANDERSON

W. W. NORTON & COMPANY

NEW YORK   LONDON

Published in Great Britain by
THE MACMILLAN PRESS LTD

Printed in Great Britain by
Redwood Burn Ltd, Trowbridge, Wiltshire

ISBN 0-393-02248-X

First American edition of 1985 revised edition
Published by
W. W. Norton & Company, Inc.,
500 Fifth Avenue,
New York
NY 10110

PUBLISHER'S PREFACE
TO THE THIRD EDITION

EMILY Anderson's translation of the Mozart family letters is one of the classics of the Mozart literature, indeed one of the classics of musical literature generally. Undertaken in the 1930s, it antedated any other complete version, in any language. Half a century has now passed since Miss Anderson undertook the main part of her work. It has been an active time in Mozart scholarship, in spite of the political vicissitudes that Europe has suffered and the consequent unavailability of much vital source material. A new edition of the Köchel catalogue of Mozart's works appeared in 1964, by which date Wolfgang Plath had already begun to publish the first results of his research on Mozart's handwriting and its chronology – research that continued to produce important results for 20 years, during the last ten of which it has been supplemented (and supported) by Alan Tyson's research on the papers that Mozart used. The new complete edition of Mozart's works (the Neue Mozart-Ausgabe), which was instituted in 1955, includes a number of publications not of music but of documentary material, among them the documentary biography prepared by Otto Erich Deutsch (1961) and, initiated by Deutsch but chiefly carried out by W. A. Bauer and J. H. Eibl, the seven-volume edition of the Mozart family correspondence (1962–75; including two volumes of detailed commentary and one of index).

Little of this material was available to Alec Hyatt King and Monica Carolan when they prepared the second edition of Emily Anderson's translation, for publication in 1966. In this third edition, an attempt has been made to provide new or revised annotations which, as far as possible, bring the information supplementary to the text in line with the most recent findings of scholarship. The text here is, of course, based on that of 1966 rather than the 1938 original.

It has from time to time been pointed out that Miss Anderson's text does not always fully reflect the quicksilver changes of mood and of tempo in Mozart's own literary style and provides it with a fluent literacy that is wanting in the original. More to the point, as far as the present revision is concerned, is the difference in scholarly approach between the 1930s and the 1980s. In her translations, Miss Anderson did not show where material was omitted in those letters which are printed in extract form (these include none from Mozart himself, it should be noted); we have indicated with a marginal asterisk the points at which there are such omissions, and have marked any substantially paraphrased passages with a bracket alongside the text. Miss Anderson's omissions rarely if ever concern any passage referring to music, musicians, performances or indeed Mozart himself; the omitted material generally treats of practical or trivial matters such as details of journeys, weather, ailments and news of or greetings from acquaintances. Where an asterisk appears alongside a letter written by Mozart himself, it indicates that a note added by someone else has been omitted. Miss Anderson generally standardized, and sometimes anglicized, name forms and spellings. Often she filled out dates and place names mentioned or implied in the text (thus 'the 12th' might be changed to '12 October'; or 'here' might be altered to 'Munich'). Occasionally she made minor adjustments to spellings of words in those passages not in the German language, and also in lists of names, though it was her general intention to leave these in their original forms. A few of her indications of which words are cyphered in letters

v

between members of the family are not strictly accurate. Very occasionally, Miss Anderson drew on material from Leopold Mozart's travel notes to help elucidate a passage; and sometimes she transferred sentences from one letter to another, usually also for that purpose. In the present edition, such passages have been adjusted, except those of a wholly trivial nature; anything that could be regarded as misleading or inaccurate in the light of recent findings has been corrected.

Mozart scholars have from time to time drawn attention to minor inaccuracies in the translations themselves. We are particularly grateful to Peter Branscombe for drawing attention to some of these, which have duly been corrected. A number of corrections have also been made to the dates of letters and to the identities of recipients (e.g. Letter 536*, which now seems likely to have been addressed to Count Wenzel Paar). A large number of footnotes have been revised to take into account the findings of recent research, both on the chronology of Mozart's works and on his contemporaries. For this we have drawn on a variety of sources, especially the documentary biography and, of course, the commentary volumes to the letters in the Neue Mozart-Ausgabe text. Some source locations have changed, and these are duly noted. Where an autograph source not used by Miss Anderson is now known, this is detailed in a footnote. It has, of course, been necessary to revise substantially the indexes of works and, in particular, persons: many figures referred to only casually in the text are now more exactly identified, and mistaken identifications are corrected. The process of editorial correction was planned by Stanley Sadie with Fiona Smart and carried out by Ms Smart.

The following abbreviations are used throughout the book. For full bibliographical details see Bibliography, p.979.

AMZ = *Allgemeine musikalische Zeitung* (1798/9)
MBA = *Mozart: Briefe und Aufzeichnungen* (1962–75)
MDB = *Mozart: die Dokumente seines Lebens, gesammelt und erläutert* (1961)
MM = *Mozarteums–Mitteilungen* (1918–21)
MMB = *Mitteilungen für die Mozartgemeinde in Berlin* (1895–1925)
WSF = *Wolfgang Amédée Mozart: sa vie musicale et son oeuvre* (1912–46)
ZMW = *Zeitschrift für Musikwissenschaft* (1918/19–1935)

PUBLISHER'S PREFACE TO THE
SECOND EDITION

THE first edition of Emily Anderson's *Letters of Mozart and his Family* was published in three volumes in 1938. Volume one went out of print in 1954 and volumes two and three in 1956. A selection of these letters, edited and introduced by the late Dr. Eric Blom with Miss Anderson's assistance, was first published by Penguin Books in 1956 under the title of *Mozart's Letters*. This was, of course, never intended to serve as more than a stopgap. Miss Anderson had long hoped to undertake the revision of the larger work and after her translation of *The Letters of Beethoven* was published in October 1961, she returned to Mozart, but her work was cut short by her sudden and much regretted death in October 1962.

By that date, she had finished a preliminary revision of the Mozart letters, in the course of which she had noted many passages which required checking for re-translation and footnotes which were to be emended or amplified. She had also marked various points in her text at which corrections and suggestions, sent to her over the years by Mozart scholars, were to be incorporated. It was likewise her intention to translate certain passages from the original German which she had omitted from the earlier edition. The only substantial change which she envisaged was that the letters of Constanze Mozart to Johann Anton André, translated and annotated by Dr. C. B. Oldman, were to be omitted, with his consent.

In the spring of 1963, the publishers engaged Miss Monica Carolan and Mr. A. Hyatt King to complete Miss Anderson's limited revision, to prepare the copy for the printer, read the proofs, compile new indexes and see the volumes through the press. Miss Carolan, who had assisted Miss Anderson throughout her work on the Beethoven letters, had also shared the preliminary revision of the Mozart letters. She was thus familiar with her system of annotation and knew how her accumulated papers could best be used. Mr. King had been a close friend of Miss Anderson for many years and had himself specialised in Mozart.

The revised edition includes seven Letters not in the 1938 edition, namely 273,[1] 425★★, 476★, 536★, 547★, 549★, 609★. Letters 96a and 273a are now published in a substantially expanded form from rediscovered autographs. (Letters 96a, 273a and 547★ had previously been published in the Penguin edition.)

The following points may also be noted:

In a few Letters, passages formerly ascribed to Mozart himself have been

---

[1] The letter numbered 273 in the 1938 edition has proved to be a postscript and is now numbered 273a.

vii

shown by Dr. Wilhelm Bauer and Professor Otto Erich Deutsch to be postscripts written by other members of his family. Here the necessary adjustment has been made. Certain changes have been made in the spelling of names in the text. The signatures of all Letters, whether abbreviated or not, are given exactly as in the originals.

The location of autographs or other sources has been brought up to date where possible.

Letters and passages in French have been kept in the original orthography.

The names of churches have been translated throughout.

In many autographs, the date is given with the writer's signature at the end. In these cases, the date has been repeated in square brackets at the head. Square brackets have also been used

(a) to enclose words or figures supplied in an incomplete original date,

(b) to enclose a conjectural date supplied to an undated letter.

Page-references to Köchel's *Chronologisch-thematisches Verzeichnis sämtlicher Tonwerke Wolfgang Amadé Mozarts* are to the sixth edition (1964). Traditional Köchel numbering has been retained with the numbers of the sixth edition added in square brackets.

With few exceptions, other references have been left as given in the 1938 edition, although the source referred to may now be available in a more comprehensive and easily accessible publication.[1]

We are confident that Miss Anderson would have wished us to express cordial thanks to Professor Otto Erich Deutsch. As an assiduous correspondent for two decades, he sent her a large quantity of corrections and suggestions, affecting both text and footnotes, which have been most gratefully incorporated.

Among Miss Anderson's regular correspondents during a long period were also the late Dr. Alfred Einstein and the late Professor Erich Hertzmann. The information which they gave her has likewise been gladly used. Much valuable advice and information has also been given by Dr. C. B. Oldman, who knew Miss Anderson well for nearly thirty years. Dr. Oldman has also kindly read the proofs and made various suggestions. Valuable assistance with proof-reading has also been given by Mr. H. C. Robbins Landon.

For permission to translate three previously unknown autograph letters our thanks are due to: the late Mr. S. L. Courtauld (Letter 425★★),

[1] For instance, the entries relevant to Mozart in Count Zinzendorf's diary, mentioned on p. 5, n. 1, partially printed in the *Mozarteums Mitteilungen* for 1919, have now been included by O. E. Deutsch in *Mozart. Die Dokumente seines Lebens*; and Leopold Mozart's *Reiseaufzeichnungen* (see p. 5, n. 4, and elsewhere), edited by Schurig in 1920 and now out of print, are given throughout volumes I and II of *Mozart. Briefe und Aufzeichnungen*. For general information, it may be noted that a list of important works on Mozart issued since 1938 is given on pp. xxxv, xxxvi.

Mr. Albi Rosenthal (Letter 273) and Mr. G. M. Schnitzler (Letter 549*). Mr. Rosenthal also kindly made available another autograph in his possession, Letter 273a, which was formerly known only in the extract quoted by Nissen. Thanks are also due to the late Mr. Richard Border, who owned the autograph of Letter 425* (previously known only from Nohl and thought to be a postscript) and brought it to Miss Anderson's attention.

We would finally express our gratitude to Bärenreiter Verlag, Kassel, for permission to make the above-mentioned adjustments of some post-scripts and for permission to publish translations of Letters 235a and 536* from the text given in:

Mozart. Briefe und Aufzeichnungen — *Gesamtausgabe*, herausgegeben von der Internationalen Stiftung Mozarteum Salzburg, gesammelt und erläutert von Wilhelm A. Bauer und Otto Erich Deutsch. Vier Textbände, ein Kommentar-, ein Register-Band (Bärenreiter-Verlag Kassel, Basel, Paris, London, New York 1962 ff.).

The editors of the second edition would like to express their thanks to Mr. H. Cowdell and Mr. T. M. Farmiloe, who have lavished much pains on these volumes at all stages of their production.

PREFACE TO THE FIRST EDITION [1938]

IT is impossible to acknowledge all the obligations I have incurred in the course of preparing this work, but I wish to thank in particular: Professor Ludwig Schiedermair of Bonn University, for allowing me to use his German edition of the Mozart family letters, for assisting me during the early stages of my undertaking and for supplying me from time to time with additional material; Mr. C. B. Oldman of the British Museum, for generously consenting to the inclusion in my edition of large portions of the unpublished letters from Mozart's widow to Johann Anton André, which are in his possession and which he has translated and edited for this purpose, and for constantly contributing from his wealth of information upon all matters relating to Mozart; Dr. Alfred Einstein, for most unselfishly placing at my disposal his immense knowledge of eighteenth-century music and the results of his research work on Mozart's musical MSS., which have now been embodied in the third edition (1937) of Köchel's catalogue of Mozart's works; Dr. Bernhard Paumgartner, Director of the Mozarteum, Salzburg, for granting me free access to its collection of autographs; Dr. Georg Schünemann, Director of the Music Department of the Prussian State Library, Berlin, for permission to consult its large collection of transcripts; the Public Library of Boston (Massachusetts), Herr Braus-Riggenbach (Basel), Dr. A. Einstein, Herr H. Eisemann (London), Dr. Elmer of the Library of Prague University, Frau Floersheim-Koch (Florence), Herr Karl Geigy-Hagenbach (Basel), Dr. Karl Geiringer of the Bibliothek der Gesellschaft der Musikfreunde (Vienna), Herr Paul Gottschalk (Berlin), Herr Otto Haas (London), Dr. Robert Haas of the Vienna National Library, Herr V. A. Heck (Vienna), Herr D. N. Heineman (Brussels), Herr Henri Hinrichsen (Leipzig), Mrs. Enid Lambart, Herr Rudolf Nydahl (Stockholm), Mr. C. B. Oldman, the Historical Society of Pennsylvania, the Pierpont Morgan Library (New York City), Dr. A. Rosenthal (London), Herr Scheurleer of the Gemeentemuseum (The Hague), Dr. Richard Strauss, Mr. W. Oliver Strunk of the Library of Congress (Washington), Herr Paul Wittgenstein (Vienna), for photostats or transcripts of autographs in their possession. I wish also to express my gratitude to Herr Ernst Boucke of the Prussian State Library (Berlin), Miss Muriel Clayton of the Victoria and Albert Museum, Herr Otto Erich Deutsch (Vienna), Herr Alfred Heidl of the Mozarteum (Salzburg), Mr. R. N. Carew Hunt, Dr. Georg Kinsky (Cologne), Mr. T. O. Mabbott (New York City), Mrs. H. S. M. Stuart, Frau Eva Thurner (Salzburg), Herr Stefan Zweig, for valuable information and assistance most generously given; to Professor Ludwig Schiedermair and Dr. Henry

G. Farmer, for kindly lending me printers' blocks for illustrations; to the Podestà of Bologna, Herr Max Hinrichsen of C. F. Peters Musikverlag (Leipzig), Herr Paul Hirsch (Cambridge), M. le Chef des Services Techniques et Commerciaux du Palais du Louvre (Paris), Städtisches Schlossmuseum (Mannheim), Mr. C. B. Oldman, J. Pierpont Morgan (New York City), Internationale Stiftung, Mozart Museum (Salzburg), Stift St. Peter (Salzburg), Städtisches Museum (Salzburg), for allowing me to reproduce portraits and engravings; to Dr. Alfred Einstein, Mr. C. B. Oldman and Mr. James Turner, for assistance in reading the proofs; and finally to Mr. Harold Macmillan, for his unfailing help and interest in the production of my edition.

EMILY ANDERSON

LONDON, 1938

INTRODUCTION TO THE
FIRST EDITION

IT should not be necessary to offer any apology for an English edition of the letters of Mozart and his family. The only existing translations—and those almost exclusively of the composer's letters—are to be found in two collections, one by Lady Wallace[1] and the other by M. M. Bozman.[2] But since the appearance of the former, over seventy years ago, more than a hundred letters of Mozart alone have come to light; and during the last quarter of a century the even more numerous and lengthy letters of his father, Leopold Mozart, have nearly all been collected and published in the original language. The present work is based upon the standard German edition of the Mozart family correspondence by Professor Ludwig Schiedermair, who spent many years collecting and copying the existing documents, i.e. autographs and transcripts in museums, libraries and private collections.[3] This *Gesamtausgabe*, a veritable boon to students of Mozart's life and works, completely superseded all previous texts, which apart from the one attempt of Nohl to produce a separate edition of Mozart's letters,[4] are to be found chiefly in the early biographies of the composer by Nissen,[5] Holmes,[6] Jahn,[7] in a more recent work by Schurig,[8]

---

[1] Ludwig Nohl, *Mozarts Briefe*, 1st edition, Leipzig, 1864, translated by Lady Wallace. Two volumes, London, 1865. This collection contains 268 letters of Mozart only.

[2] Hans Mersmann, *Mozarts Briefe in Auswahl*, Berlin, 1922, translated by M. M. Bozman. J. M. Dent and Sons, 1928. This selection contains only 141 letters of Mozart and a few extracts from those of his father.

[3] Ludwig Schiedermair, *Die Briefe Mozarts und seiner Familie*, four volumes, Munich and Leipzig, 1914. The first two volumes contain Mozart's letters, the third and fourth volumes those of his father, mother, sister, wife and cousin. The material covers the period from 1762 to 1791. A fifth volume contains reproductions of all the known portraits of Mozart and his family, of friends, statesmen, musicians and so forth, with whom he was associated, and of various places and documents of interest.

[4] See n. 1. Nohl brought out in 1877 a second edition, which has 282 letters, an addition of 14.

[5] Georg Nikolaus von Nissen, *Biographie W. A. Mozarts*, Leipzig, 1828. This biography, upon which Nissen, Constanze Mozart's second husband, was engaged at the time of his death in 1826, and for which he had full access to all the family letters and documents, was brought out by his widow with the help of a certain Dr. Feuerstein of Pirna near Dresden.

[6] Edward Holmes, *Life of Mozart*, London, 1845, 2nd edition, 1878. (Reissued by J. M. Dent and Sons in Everyman's Library, 1921.) This excellent short biography which, however, is little more than a rearrangement of Nissen's material, gives full extracts in a readable translation from the letters quoted in his work.

[7] Otto Jahn, *Wolfgang Amadeus Mozart*. Four volumes, Leipzig, 1856–1859; 2nd edition in two volumes, 1867; 3rd edition by Hermann Deiters, 1889–1891; 4th edition, 1905–1907. Jahn consulted the autographs in the Mozarteum at Salzburg and made full use of the immense collection of letters which had been copied for Aloys Fuchs (1799–1853) and which was then in Vienna. The second edition was translated into English by Pauline D. Townsend, three volumes, London, 1882.

[8] Arthur Schurig, *Wolfgang Amadeus Mozart*, two volumes, Leipzig, 1913. Schurig went to the original sources, chiefly in Salzburg and Berlin, and although his work does not profess to be an edition of the Mozart family correspondence, he in some cases gives longer extracts from Leopold Mozart's early letters (including those to his Augsburg publisher, J. J. Lotter)

and in the miscellaneous compilations of Nottebohm,[1] Nohl[2] and Leitzmann.[3] Here for the first time the reader was provided with material which enabled him to trace the development of a great composer from his earliest years (the first letter of Leopold Mozart is dated October, 1762, when his son was six) through his apprenticeship abroad to his triumphs and struggles and premature death in Vienna (Mozart's last letter is dated October, 1791).

But invaluable as is this contribution of Schiedermair to musical literature, a careful study of the correspondence and more particularly of the autographs soon led to the conviction that the proper arrangement of the material was one which would conform as far as possible to the order in which the letters were originally written. The present edition, therefore, observes a strictly chronological method, beginning with the first letters of Leopold Mozart from Vienna in 1762 and continuing up to Mozart's death in 1791.[4] Such a rearrangement has the following advantages. In the first place, as there are very few gaps in the correspondence, which covers almost the whole of Mozart's life, and forms, as it were, a continuous journal, the reader is presented with the primary sources for a biographical study. Secondly, as the Mozart family were inveterate letter-writers and indulged in a very full interchange of information and ideas (indeed most of Leopold Mozart's letters and some of Mozart's extend almost to the length of pamphlets), certain letters cannot be properly understood unless they are read in close connection with those to which they are the replies. Thirdly, as postage fees were at that time a heavy expense, Mozart, when travelling with his father or his mother, rarely troubled to write a separate

than does Schiedermair, and in many cases fuller notes. On the other hand, the spelling and punctuation are modernised, whereas in this respect Schiedermair's edition aims at an exact reproduction of the original documents. A second edition of Schurig's biography, in a smaller format, appeared in 1923.

[1] Gustav Nottebohm, *Mozartiana*, Leipzig, 1880. This little work is based upon unpublished material (not seen by Jahn) sent by Mozart's widow and sister in 1799 to the publishers Breitkopf and Härtel for a biography which was to have been written by Johann Friedrich Rochlitz (1769–1842), editor of the *Allgemeine Musikalische Zeitung*, who had met Mozart at Leipzig in 1789. It contains 42 new letters of Mozart, written chiefly during his last years in Vienna.

[2] Ludwig Nohl, *Mozart nach den Schilderungen seiner Zeitgenossen*, Leipzig, 1880. It contains one or two unpublished letters of Mozart and gives some long extracts from those of his father.

[3] Albert Leitzmann, *Mozarts Briefe*, Leipzig, 1910, a selection, based entirely on Jahn's copies of the letters in the Preussische Staatsbibliothek, Berlin. In 1926 Leitzmann brought out a work on Mozart (*Wolfgang Amadeus Mozarts Leben in seinen Briefen und Berichten der Zeitgenossen*, Leipzig, 1926), rather on the lines of Nohl's miscellany, for which he used Schiedermair's edition of the correspondence.

[4] It should be added that, like Schiedermair's edition, the present work is limited to the period of Mozart's life, 1756–1791. Thus none of Leopold Mozart's letters to J. J. Lotter of Augsburg, 1755–1756, regarding the publication of his *Versuch einer gründlichen Violinschule*, are included. For these the reader must be referred to the two editions of Schurig's biography (see p. xi, n. 8). On the other hand, as the title-page indicates, the present edition contains long extracts from letters written by Constanze Mozart to the Offenbach publisher, J. A. André, which are of special interest as dealing with the sale and publication of her late husband's musical manuscripts. [These letters have been omitted from the second edition. See p. v.].

letter, but either continued the letter which one of his parents had begun or added a postscript, or contented himself with scribbling a few lines inside the cover. Occasionally the reverse procedure was adopted; Mozart would begin the letter, and his father or his mother would finish it. Sometimes too, Mozart would take up the last words of the previous writer, use them as a theme for a variation [1] or even treat them as a peg on which to hang some comic remark.[2] In preparing this work one of the chief aims of the editor has been to present the letters as far as possible exactly as they were written.

It is hardly necessary to point out that the main purpose of this edition is to provide a complete collection of all the extant letters of Mozart himself, and that these have been treated with the same reverent care as one would treat the musical autographs of this great composer. The editor, therefore, has given every letter of Mozart in its entirety—in some cases for the first time.[3] At this point it may be appropriate to mention that Mozart's singularly outspoken letters to his cousin, Maria Anna Thekla, the so-called '*Bäslebriefe*', now appear in an unexpurgated form. Even in Germany an excessive prudishness or possibly a certain unwillingness to admit that the writer, formerly regarded as the Raphael or the Watteau of music, should have been capable of expressing himself with such grossness, has hitherto prevented their publication *in toto*. A study of the whole correspondence, however, shows clearly that it was not only when writing to his '*Bäsle*' that Mozart indulged in this particular kind of coarseness, but that on occasion he did so when writing to his mother[4] and to his sister; and that certainly his mother[5] and very probably the whole family and indeed many of their Salzburg friends were given to these indelicate jests.

In the case of Leopold Mozart's letters, however, a different method had to be adopted. Mozart's father was an indefatigable correspondent, a collector of information, a keeper of lists and diaries, who was forever exhorting his children to do likewise. Realising from the very first that his son was a genius and proposing some day to write his biography,[6] he not only kept so-called 'travel notes', most of which have been preserved,[7] but sent off to his landlord and later to his wife full descriptions of the

---

[1] e.g. Letters 212, 212a; 232, 232a; 249, 249a.   [2] e.g. Letters 79, 79a; 271b, 271c.

[3] For particulars of the hitherto unpublished letters or portions of letters see the List of Letters, p. xxi ff. In a few cases the only existing versions are those given by Nissen, whose ruthless manipulation of the autographs he used is well known to Mozart scholars. Facsimile no. 2 affords an example of this treatment. It is fortunate that the original documents handled by Nissen and showing the heavy strokes of his quill, are slowly coming to light.

[4] e.g. Letter 278, which is now published in its entirety. The only extant version is a copy made by Nottebohm, who must have received the autograph or perhaps only a transcript of the letter from Breitkopf and Härtel. See p. xii, n. 1.

[5] See especially Letters 209a, 214b, 219c.   [6] See Letter 51, p. 77.

[7] They have been edited by Arthur Schurig: *Leopold Mozarts Reiseaufzeichnungen, 1763–1771.* Dresden, 1920. The entries, a few of which were made by Mozart himself, have been transcribed and annotated, several being reproduced in facsimile.

countries he visited, the eminent persons he met and, not least, the triumphs of his two prodigies and of Wolfgang in particular.[1] It is possible, indeed, to trace four distinct periods in Leopold Mozart's correspondence. First of all, we have the very long letters to his landlord, Johann Lorenz Hagenauer, which give detailed accounts of his travels (1762–1768), of the courts at which his children performed, of the strange customs and habits of other nations, but which, apart from an occasional allusion to the feats of his children, couched in the language of the exultant showman, contain little matter of musical interest. Next, we have the letters written to his wife during the three journeys to Italy (1769–1773), letters which, as they were addressed to someone who shared these interests, give a most vivid description of the musical atmosphere and the social conditions prevailing in Rome, Bologna, Naples and Milan. Then a third period opens with his letters to his son, who, accompanied by his mother, has left Salzburg and gone off to seek his fortune elsewhere. These letters, particularly when they are read together with the replies from Mozart and his mother, are of very great interest. The reader finds himself at once absorbed in the most fascinating problem of the relations between father and son. In the first letters from Mozart we can almost hear his sigh of relief at having escaped from the oppressive atmosphere of the Archbishop's court and the cramping influence of an over-methodical, rather pedantic and perhaps a little too inquisitive parent; and we note his delight in his newly found freedom and his disinclination to trouble about the future. Very soon we detect in his father's letters an anxiety, a certain suspicion almost amounting to distrust, which, when he hears of his son's friendship with the Weber family, suddenly flares up in a blaze of bitter indignation and exasperation. Mozart, whose moral emancipation from his father is by this time almost complete, conceals nothing and continues to write with perfect frankness. Yet we see that a link has been broken and that behind his reluctance to accept an appointment in the Archbishop's service after his mother's death and his lamentable failure to establish himself in Paris, there lurks a kind of horror at the prospect of returning to his father's home. At the same time their all-absorbing interest in music provided a bond which was never broken. However much Mozart might feel that in other respects he was being misunderstood, in all matters relating to his art his father for many years continued to be his guide, philosopher and friend. Thus we have the illuminating correspondence about the composition of *Idomeneo*, (1780/81), which, as a revelation of a composer's method of dealing with his text and adjusting his work to the shortcomings of his singers, is almost unique in musical literature. And that he still regarded his father as a friend to whom he could always unburden himself about his

---

[1] By order of Leopold Mozart all his letters were kept and numbered, doubtless with a view to their being used for the biography he intended to write. See Letter 77, p. 108.

one passionate interest, is proved by his letters to him in regard to the composition of *Die Entführung aus dem Serail* (1781/82) and his struggles with Varesco's somewhat thankless libretto for *L'Oca del Cairo* (1783).[1] We now come to the fourth period of Leopold Mozart's correspondence (1784–1787), that is, the letters written to his daughter after her marriage.[2] These letters, while they throw much light on the worthy and rather lovable character of the writer and tell us a good deal about life in Salzburg and the comings and goings of its strange Archbishop, are on the whole of little value to the student of Mozart's life and works. For, after his final break with Salzburg and especially after his marriage to Constanze Weber in 1782, Mozart's relations with his father had become decidedly cool. The latter, it is true, still took an interest in his son's concerts, in the performances of his operas and above all in his latest compositions, some of which were duly sent off to Salzburg. But, partly on account of the estrangement which had arisen and partly owing to Mozart's own busy life which left him little time for letter-writing, Leopold Mozart, except when he encloses a letter or quotes a passage from one he has just received from Vienna, rarely refers to the doings of his son.

It soon became obvious to the editor that if Mozart was to form the centre of interest of this work and if the whole material was to be limited to three volumes, large portions of Leopold Mozart's letters, particularly of those belonging to the first and fourth periods, would have to be omitted.[3] At this point one important discovery in regard to the letters which Leopold Mozart wrote to his landlord while on his travels during the years 1762–1768, should be mentioned. As far as is known, the autographs of these letters have disappeared; but copies of them, apparently without any omissions, have been preserved in the Prussian State Library, Berlin. When checking these letters for the purpose of my edition, Herr E. Boucke, an assistant in the library, came upon the complete versions of long letters written by Leopold Mozart during the family's stay in Paris and London, 1763–1766, which appear to have been hitherto either unknown or entirely neglected. This is, to say the least, surprising, for the

[1] Leopold Mozart's letters to his son after the latter's removal to Vienna in March 1781 have not been preserved. Possibly they were lost during Mozart's many moves. It is highly improbable that, as has been frequently suggested, Constanze Mozart destroyed them on account of their supposed allusions to freemasonry. She carefully kept far more outspoken and compromising letters of Mozart, which she either bequeathed to her eldest son or sent to Breitkopf and Härtel. Moreover, the letters of Mozart's sister, who appears to have written to him pretty frequently during his first years in Vienna, have also not come down to us.

[2] These 125 letters, for the most part previously unpublished, have recently been edited by O. E. Deutsch and B. Paumgartner, *Leopold Mozarts Briefe an seine Tochter*, Salzburg and Leipzig, 1936.

[3] It will be seen that only extracts have been given of nearly all these letters. In performing this pruning operation, the principle followed has been that of removing all purely extraneous and irrelevant matter, such as local gossip, rather tiresome descriptions of illnesses, long lists of greetings and so forth.

London letters especially contain a most vivid and entertaining description of London life at that period, rivalling in its personal note the contemporary accounts of such well-known travellers as Pastor Moritz, Wendeborn and Grosley. Needless to say, it was with considerable reluctance that the editor decided to 'cut' this new material.[1]

In regard to the letters of Mozart's mother, all of which were written when she was accompanying him on his visits to Munich, Augsburg, Mannheim and Paris in search of work, it was thought advisable to give these in their entirety.[2] For, as will be seen, mother and son usually wrote on one sheet of paper; and hers are either hastily written postscripts or passages inserted in the body of Mozart's letters. Moreover, they are artless and often amusing; and their very outspokenness, verging occasionally on coarseness, throws fresh light on the home atmosphere in which Mozart grew up and explains to a certain extent a peculiar side of his nature which many readers of his letters have difficulty in connecting with the exquisite delicacy of his music.[3] On the other hand, some portions of the letters of Mozart's sister have been omitted. In the matter of letter-writing Nannerl proved to be an apt pupil of her father and, judging by the few letters which have been preserved, must have adopted his methods,[4] such as keeping a full diary of her own doings, drawing up lists of Salzburg theatrical performances and so forth.[5]

That Mozart wrote many more letters than we possess is evident from the leanness of certain years—notably the period from August 1784, the time of his sister's marriage and removal to St. Gilgen, to May 1787, the time of his father's death, for which many of the composer's letters are missing.[6] We know also, from references here and there, that other letters

---

[1] It is proposed to publish these letters in full in a separate volume, which will contain other interesting matter relating to the Mozarts' visit to England. [This proposal was never carried out.]

[2] Apart from a few sentences quoted in Eric Blom's biography of Mozart (Dent's Master Musicians series, 1935), pp. 70, 84 and 85, none of these letters have so far been translated into English.

[3] The following postscript (Letter 209a) is a specimen of Frau Mozart's grammar, spelling and punctuation: 'Von Neuigkeiten hat mir der wolfgang nichts übriggelassen, ich hoffe von dir bald einen brief zu bekomen, und mit freiden zu vernehmen, das du dich gesund befindest. wir seind gott lob wohlauf, und winschen michts andres als das du bey uns wehrest, welches mit der hilf gottes geschehen wird, sey nur indessen ohne sorgen, und schlage dir alle verdrüsslichkeiten aus dem Sinn, es wird schon alles recht werden, wann die hafftel daran Komen. wür führen ein charmantes leben, früh auf spath ins beth, den ganzen dag haben wür visiten, leben wie die fürsten Kinder, bis uns holt der Schinder. adio ben mio leb gesund, Rick den arsch zum mund. ich winsch ein guete nacht, scheiss ins beth das Kracht, es ist schon über einns. jezt kanst selber Reimen.

an meine liebe sallerl   MARIA ANNA MOZARTIN
Catherl, nanerl bimberl alles erdenkliches.'   [4] See Letter 222, pp. 317 f.
[5] See Letter 415, p. 751, where Mozart describes his sister as 'the living chronicle of Salzburg'.
[6] It is difficult to account for the disappearance of these documents, some of which Leopold Mozart enclosed in his own letters to his daughter, who carefully kept all her father's letters (now in the Mozarteum, Salzburg). Possibly she returned them after 1787 to her brother, who may have mislaid or even destroyed them during one of his numerous moves. See Abert, vol. ii, pp. 1035 f.

must have been written. For example, a letter sent to his wife from Berlin in May 1789 (Letter 565) mentions eleven letters to her, four of which have been lost. Again, the bibliography of Nissen's Life of Mozart (Appendix, p. 217) contains the startling entry: Mozarts Briefe an die Duschek, 1781. It is extremely probable too that Mozart corresponded with the singer Anna Storace after her return to London in March 1787, the more so as at that time he was seriously contemplating a visit to England. Then there are the 'two interesting letters to Frau von Trattner about music', which Constanze Mozart mentions in a letter to Breitkopf and Härtel of November 27th, 1799,[1]—truly an irreparable loss. Yet, as new letters of Mozart are slowly coming to light, there are grounds for hope that one day some of these hidden treasures may be recovered.

It should be mentioned that the present edition does not include two letters frequently ascribed to Mozart which are of very doubtful authenticity.

(1) A letter written in 1789 to a certain Baron von P., the autograph of which is supposed to have been in the possession of Moscheles, and in which Mozart describes his method of composition. It was first published by Friedrich Rochlitz in the *Allgemeine Musikalische Zeitung*, xvii, cols. 561 ff. of 1815, and soon made its appearance in English and French reviews. From internal evidence the letter is obviously a forgery. Jahn (1st ed., vol. iii, pp. 496 ff.) treats it as such; and Nohl, although he includes it in his edition of Mozart's letters (2nd ed., pp. 441 ff.), confesses that it is spurious. Holmes, who reproduces it in his *Life of Mozart* (Everyman edition, 1921, pp. 254 ff.), does not question its authenticity, which probably explains why it has been quoted *ad nauseam* in English popular biographies. It is not included in Schiedermair's edition of the letters.[2]

(2) A short letter in Italian which Mozart is supposed to have written in September 1791 to Lorenzo da Ponte. It is included in Schiedermair's edition, vol. ii, p. 350.[3] But after careful consideration the editor decided to reject this letter on the following grounds: (a) the only extant version is a transcript in the Prussian State Library, Berlin, which has no signature and mentions no addressee[4]: (b) the internal evidence, namely, the indication of extreme depression at a time when Mozart, though in poor health, was feeling unusually stimulated and exhilarated, is a strong argument against its being a genuine document.

A few words may be necessary in regard to the treatment of the text of Mozart's letters. As has already been stated, it has been the editor's aim to

[1] Quoted in Nottebohm, *Mozartiana*, p. 131. Frau von Trattner was Mozart's pupil on the piano. He dedicated to her his C minor Fantasia and Sonata (K. 475 and 457).
[2] See Schiedermair, vol. ii, p. 378, n. 308 [and O. E. Deutsch, 'Spurious Mozart Letters', *Music Review*, May 1964].
[3] Nohl in his edition of Mozart's letters (2nd ed., pp. 463 f.) prints it, undated, as being the last extant letter of the composer, adding that Ludwig von Köchel discovered it in London.
[4] The transcript has the following remark in the same handwriting: In the possession of Mr Young in London.

reproduce these as faithfully as possible. Several letters, however, contain rhymed passages, either written out as verse or concealed in prose, which, if the rhyming is to be retained and the full flavour of the original preserved, defy a literal translation. Here some sort of compromise was inevitable. Again, Mozart, who was a very spontaneous letter-writer and nearly always wrote in a great hurry, frequently indulges in colloquialisms and slang, which the editor, while avoiding passing fashions of speech of the present day, has endeavoured to render into the equivalent English phraseology. Mozart's extreme liveliness and haste are reflected too in his punctuation. Very often whole letters are a series of sentences strung together by dashes. As a slavish adherence in this respect to the originals would have produced pages wearisome to the eye of the reader, the letters have been punctuated more normally and the dashes retained only when the sense demands it. The same remark applies to Mozart's lavish use of brackets, which in many cases have been replaced by commas.

Another textual peculiarity, which characterises almost the whole correspondence, requires some explanation. After the accession of Hieronymus Colloredo to the Archbishopric of Salzburg in March 1772 (and indeed intermittently during the reign of his predecessor) the Mozart family made occasional use of a simple substitution cypher (certain letters of the alphabet being replaced by others) in order to be able to express their opinions freely.[1] They adopted this device because they had good reason for believing that before their letters were delivered, the Salzburg post office sent them to the Archbishop's residence for inspection.[2] In the present translation the words, phrases and passages which in the autographs are in cypher, have been enclosed in angular brackets.[3]

To the critic who may complain that there is too much annotation, the reply is that the fullness is due to the editor's desire to remedy a defect of the German *Gesamtausgabe*, that is, to throw more light on the circumstances of Mozart's life, to recapture as far as possible the atmosphere in which he composed and to revive the forgotten or only half-remembered musicians, singers, artists, writers and men and women of note, with whom he came in contact.[4]

As to the value of Mozart's letters, their spontaneousness, their wit, their extreme gaiety, their profound poignancy, their humanity and time-

---

[1] Facsimile no. 5 affords an example of this cypher, of which the key is: for the letters m, l, o, f, h, a, e, s, i, u substitute the letters a, e, s, i, u, m, l, o, f, h. In most cases Nissen has written the solution above the encyphered passage.

[2] That this suspicion was well founded is proved by an incident described in a letter from Leopold Mozart to his daughter, 19 January 1786. See Deutsch-Paumgartner, *Leopold Mozarts Briefe an seine Tochter*, 1936, pp. 241 ff.

[3] e.g. Letter 172, p. 228.

[4] For a criticism of Schiedermair's sparse annotation of the correspondence see A. Schurig in *Mozarteums Mitteilungen*, November 1919, pp. 7–9, and E. K. Blümml, *Aus Mozarts Freundes- und Familienkreis*, Leipzig, 1923, p. vii.

lessness, there is nothing fresh to say. But long association with Mozart as a letter-writer has not failed to open up certain trains of thought which it may be of interest to indicate. In the first place, there is the strange fact that, with few exceptions, nearly all Mozart's letters are addressed to members of his family, and that, as far as we know, he never wrote to any composer or musician.[1] Then, singular as the comparison may seem, in many of his letters Mozart, while expressing himself in words, seems in reality to be thinking in terms of music.[2] Thus when we come upon passages which are curiously involved, words written backwards, phrases reversed, and other similar oddities of expression, we remember his description of how on a certain occasion he extemporised fugues on a given theme in a minor key, playing all kinds of tricks with it, reversing it, turning it into the major and so forth.[3] Again, when we take up one of Mozart's autograph letters, many of which are untidily written, larded with erasures and splashed with ink-blots, and suddenly find him weaving delicate scrolls and fantastic flourishes round a capital,[4] we remember certain themes, upon which he has embroidered a wealth of variations, deliciously interlaced and flawless in texture.[5] Then again when he describes in such masterly fashion the Langenmantels, the Auernhammers, Wieland, Grimm, and gives us the long gallery of pen-portraits with which we are familiar, we remember that these are only the rough sketches for the Don Alfonsos, the Basilios and the Marcellinas which later on will be immortalised by his music. Indeed, though the letters we possess only make us wish for more, we have here the substance of what Mozart thought about music, his ideas on the training of a pianist, his profound knowledge of the art of the singer and, if we collect the relevant passages, some indication of his own method of composition. As an autobiography their value is, if anything, greater than that of the letters of other composers, such as Beethoven, Schumann and Wagner. Lastly, it is no exaggeration to say that from a psychological and personal point of view, Mozart's letters bear comparison with those of the great letter-writers of the world.

[1] Letter 529, addressed to Joseph Haydn, is simply the dedication of his six quartets.
[2] This statement is supported by Mozart's own account of how he composed the prelude while writing down the three-part fugue of K. 394 [383*a*]. See Letter 447.
[3] See Letter 228b, p. 339. [4] See Letter 236, p. 358, n. 1.
[5] e.g., the last movement of the piano concerto in C minor (K. 491), the Andante of the quintet in E♭ (K. 614), and the Andante of the divertimento in E♭ (K. 563).

LIST OF LETTERS

Owing to exigencies of space, in most cases extracts only have been given
of Leopold Mozart's letters.

VOLUME I

1762

1768

1769

1777

1777

1778

1779

1780

1781

1781

1782

1782

1783

1787

1789

1790

1791

LIST OF ILLUSTRATIONS

xlix

Mozart (1782)
From an unfinished portrait by Josef Lange.
Mozart Museum, Salzburg.

Letter from Mozart to his father (4 January 1783)

Constanze Mozart, *née* Weber (1782)
From a portrait by Josef Lange.
Hunterian Museum, University of Glasgow.

Marianne Mozart, Freifrau von Berchtold zu Sonnenburg (1785)
From a portrait by an unknown artist.
Mozart Museum, Salzburg.

Lorenzo Da Ponte
From a water-colour painting by an unknown artist.
Formerly in the possession of Signor Riccardo Rossi,
Vittorio Veneto.

Mozart (1789)
From a silver point drawing by Dora Stock.
Musikbibliothek der Stadt, Leipzig.

Emanuel Schikaneder
From an engraving by Löschenkohl.
Gesellschaft der Musikfreunde, Vienna.

TABLE OF MONEY VALUES

THIS table was compiled for the 1938 edition of this book from information in Muret-Sanders's German-English Dictionary, in W. H. Bruford's *Germany in the Eighteenth Century* (Cambridge, 1935), p. 329 f., and in the letters of Leopold Mozart, who frequently quotes the equivalent values of foreign coins and the fluctuating rates of exchange between the various German states. As there were several standards in common use for the minting of silver coins during the latter half of the eighteenth century, the values here given are of necessity only approximate. [Approximate 1985 values, in US dollars, are indicated in square brackets.]

GERMANY AND AUSTRIA

Taking the South German kreuzer (worth 4 pfennige, slightly more than the English farthing) as the standard, the following equivalent values of silver coins are obtained:

60 kreuzer (or 16 groschen) = 1 gulden, about 2 shillings. [$3.00]
90 kreuzer (or 24 groschen) = 1 reichsthaler, about 3 shillings. [$4.50]
120 kreuzer (or 32 groschen) = 1 laubthaler or federthaler, about 4 shillings. [$6.00]

The following gold coins were in common use in Germany and Austria:

1 ducat (used all over Europe) = 4½ gulden, about 9 shillings. [$13.50]
1 max d'or (used chiefly in Bavaria) = 6¼ gulden, about 13 shillings. [$18.75]
1 friedrich d'or (used chiefly in Prussia) = 8 gulden, about 16 shillings. [$24.00]
1 pistole (used all over Europe) = 7½ gulden, about 15 shillings. [22.50]
1 carolin (used chiefly in Southern Germany) = 9 gulden, about 18 shillings. [$27.00]
1 souverain d'or (used chiefly in Austria) = 13½ gulden, about 27 shillings. [$40.00]

FRANCE

4 liard = 1 sou = about half-penny. [$0.06]
20 sous = 1 livre, about eleven pence. [$1.25]
1 louis d'or = 24 livres, about twenty shillings. [$30.00]

ITALY

1 paolo (a silver coin of Tuscany, worth originally about 56 centesimi, and used as the equivalent of half a lira) = about sixpence. [$0.75]
1 cigliato (or, more commonly, gigliato) = a ducat, about 9 shillings. [$13.50]
1 zecchino (a Venetian gold coin) = about 9 shillings. [$14.00]
1 doppio = probably a doppio zecchino, about 20 shillings. [$30.00]

HOLLAND

1 rijder[1] = about 28 shillings. [$42.00]

[1] Leopold Mozart calls this coin a 'reitter'. See p. 62.

The first journey, undertaken without Frau Mozart, was to Munich, where Leopold Mozart performed with his two children before the Elector Maximilian III. They were absent about three weeks, from 12 January to the beginning of February 1762. There are no letters describing this visit.

The second journey of Leopold Mozart, this time with his whole family, was to Vienna and lasted from 18 September 1762 to 5 January 1763. The children performed several times at the Imperial Court and at concerts arranged specially for them by the Viennese nobility and foreign diplomats. This visit, towards the end of which the family also went briefly to Pressburg, is described in a series of letters from Leopold Mozart to his landlord, Lorenz Hagenauer. Letters 1-9.

(1) Leopold Mozart to Lorenz Hagenauer,[1] Salzburg

[Extract]   [Copy in the Staatsbibliothek Preussischer Kulturbesitz, West Berlin]

LINZ,[2] 3 October 1762

YOU have been thinking, haven't you, that we are already in Vienna? But we are still in Linz. Tomorrow, God willing, we shall go on to Vienna by the so-called ordinary boat. Indeed we should certainly have been there already, had we not been obliged against our will to spend five whole days in Passau. This delay, for which His Grace the Bishop of Passau was responsible, has made me lose eighty gulden, which I should have made here if I had arrived sooner, whereas I must now content myself with forty odd gulden, which *deductis deducendis*[3] remain from the concert we gave the day before yesterday. But what really took place in Passau I must postpone to a personal conversation, as it would be too lengthy to relate here. Suffice it to say that Wolfgang, but not my little girl, had the privilege of performing before His Grace and that for this he received one whole ducat, i.e. exactly four gulden, ten kreuzer. But don't tell that to anyone. Meanwhile we pray that our Archbishop[4] may live long. More when we meet.

Now let me describe our journey a little. The 20th of last month we arrived at Passau at five o'clock in the evening and left next morning with the Canon, Count Herberstein, reaching Linz at five o'clock in the evening of the same day. We are staying with people called Kiener and are very well looked after. They are two spinsters who, since the death of their parents, have taken charge of the house and who are so fond of my children that they do everything they possibly can for us. I should add that my children, the boy especially, fill everyone with amazement. Count Herberstein has gone on to Vienna and will spread in advance a sensational report about them. And yesterday Count von Schlick, Captain-General of this district, left with his wife for Vienna. Both were uncommonly gracious to us. They said that, as soon as we reached Vienna, we must go to see them; meanwhile they would speak to Count Durazzo[5] and make our arrival generally known there. To judge by appearances, everything ought to go well. May God keep us well and strong as hitherto. So far we

---

[1] Johann Lorenz Hagenauer (1712–1792), a Salzburg merchant, was Leopold Mozart's landlord, banker and correspondent. The Mozart family occupied the third floor of his house (since 1880 a Mozart museum) in the Getreidegasse no. 9, until they moved in 1773 to a house on their own in the Makartplatz (now Alter Markt no. 2).

[2] The Mozart family, Leopold Mozart and his wife, Nannerl and Wolfgang, had left Salzburg on 18 September.

[3] i.e. with the necessary deductions.

[4] Count Sigismund von Schrattenbach, Archbishop of Salzburg, 1753–1771.

[5] Manager of the Opera House, Vienna.

3

are still in good health, although I occasionally feel here and there some little twinges of gout. The children are merry and behave everywhere as if they were at home. The boy is as intimate with everyone, especially with the officers, as if he had known them all his life. I enclose my draft for this month. Please have it cashed; the tax on it, amounting to ten kreuzer, three pfennig, will have to be paid. Take your rent out of it. I should like your wife, to whom especially we send most obedient greetings, to arrange for four Masses to be said on our behalf at Maria-Plain[1] and that as soon as possible. My little girl sends greetings and would like your dear wife to know that she kept her promise at Mariahilf[2] in Passau. Yes, we all prayed for Herr Lorenz. Otherwise you are all well, I hope? That is our heart's wish. We shall soon write to you from Vienna. Perhaps

★ before we get there we shall have some news to send; so far there is none.

(2) *Leopold Mozart to Lorenz Hagenauer, Salzburg*

[*Extract*]   [*Autograph in the Mozarteum, Salzburg*]

[VIENNA, 16 *October* 1762]

On the feast of St. Francis[3] we left Linz at half past four in the afternoon by the so-called ordinary boat and reached Mauthausen after nightfall on the same day at half past seven. At noon on the following day, Tuesday, we arrived at Ybbs, where two Minorites and a Benedictine, who were with us on the boat, said Masses, during which our Woferl[4] strummed on the organ and played so well that the Franciscans, who happened to be entertaining some guests at their midday meal, left the table and with their company rushed to the choir and were almost struck dead with amazement. In the evening we reached Stein and on Wednesday at three in the afternoon arrived at Vienna; here at five o'clock we took our midday meal and supper at the same time. On the journey we had continual rain and a lot of wind. Wolfgang had already caught a cold in Linz, but in spite of our irregular life, early rising, eating and drinking at all hours, and

★ wind and rain, he has, thank God, kept well. When we landed, Gilowsky's servant, who was already there, came on board and brought us to our lodgings. But after leaving our luggage safely and tidily there, we soon hurried off to an inn to appease our hunger. Gilowsky himself then came to welcome us. Now we have already been here five days and do not yet know where the sun rises in Vienna, for to this very hour it has done nothing but rain and, with constant wind, has snowed a little now and then, so that we have even seen some snow on the roofs. Moreover it has been and still is very frosty, though not excessively cold. One thing I must

---

[1] Pilgrimage church, about one and a half hours' walk from Salzburg.
[2] Pilgrimage church outside Passau.   [3] 4 October.   [4] Pet name for Wolfgang.

make a point of telling you, which is, that we quickly got through the local customs and were let off the chief customs altogether. And for this we have to thank our Master Woferl. For he made friends at once with the customs officer, showed him his clavier, invited him to visit us and played him a minuet on his little fiddle. Thus we got through. The customs officer asked most politely to be allowed to visit us and for this purpose made a note of our lodgings. So far, in spite of the most atrocious weather, we have been to a concert given by Count Collalto.[1] Further, Countess Sinzendorf introduced us to Count Wilschegg[2] and on the 11th to His Excellency the Imperial Vice-Chancellor, Count Colloredo, where we were privileged to see and to speak to the leading ministers and ladies of the Imperial Court, to wit, the Hungarian Chancellor, Count Palffy, and the Bohemian Chancellor, Count Chotek, as well as Bishop Esterházy and a number of persons, all of whom I could not note. All, the ladies especially, were very gracious to us. Count Leopold Kühnburg's[3] fiancée spoke to my wife[4] of her own accord and told her that she is going to be married at Salzburg. She is a pretty, friendly woman, of medium height. She is expecting her betrothed in Vienna very shortly. Countess Sinzendorf is using her influence on our behalf, and all the ladies are in love with my boy. We are already being talked of everywhere; and when on the 10th I was alone at the opera,[5] I heard the Archduke Leopold[6] from his box say a number of things to another box, namely, that there was a boy in Vienna who played the clavier most excellently and so on. At eleven o'clock that very same evening I received a command to go to Schönbrunn[7] on the 12th. But the following day there came a fresh command to go there on the 13th instead, (the 12th being the Feast of Maximilian and therefore a very busy gala-day), because, I gather, they want to hear the children in comfort. Everyone is amazed, especially at the boy, and everyone whom I have heard says that his genius is incomprehensible. Baron Schell is using his influence on my behalf and is gratefully acknowledging the kindnesses he enjoyed at Salzburg. If you have an opportunity, please tell this to Herr Chiusolis with my respects. Count Daun[8] also has given me a note for Baron Schell and has filled me with hopes that I shall leave

---

[1] On 9 October. Deutsch: *Mozart, die Dokumente seines Lebens* (Kassel, 1961), p. 17, quotes a passage from Count Karl Zinzendorf's unpublished diary mentioning this concert: 'At eight o'clock in the evening I fetched Lamberg and we went together to Collalto where Madame Bianchi sang and a little boy of five and a half (Mozart) played the clavier'. See also *MDB*, p. 15.

[2] i.e. Wilczek.   [3] Chief Equerry in Salzburg.

[4] This passage disproves the statements made by Schurig, *L. Mozarts Reiseaufzeichnungen*, p. 11, and Abert, vol. i. p. 38, that Mozart's mother did not accompany her family to Vienna.

[5] Gluck's *Orfeo*.

[6] Later Leopold II, Holy Roman Emperor, [1790–1792].

[7] The Imperial summer residence outside Vienna, modelled on Versailles, where Maria Theresia preferred to live.

[8] A canon of Salzburg Cathedral.

Vienna fully satisfied. And so it seems, since the Court is asking to hear us before we have announced ourselves. For young Count Palffy happened to be passing through Linz as our concert was about to begin. He was calling on the Countess Schlick, who told him about the boy and persuaded him to stop the mail coach in front of the town hall and attend the concert with her. He listened with astonishment and spoke later with great excitement of the performance to the Archduke Joseph,[1] who passed it on to the Empress. Thus, as soon as it was known that we were in Vienna, the command came for us to go to court. That, you see, is how it happened.

I wrote the above on the 11th, fully intending to tell you on the 12th, after our return from Schönbrunn, how everything had gone off. But we had to drive from Schönbrunn straight to Prince von Hildburghausen, and six ducats were more important to us than the despatch of my letter. I have sufficient confidence in Frau Hagenauer[2] and trust enough to her kind friendship to know that she will accept even now our congratulations on her name-day and even in the short form of merely saying that we shall ask God to keep her and all her loved ones well and strong for many years to come and to invite us all in due course to play cards in Heaven. Now all that I have time for is to say in great haste that Their Majesties received us with such extraordinary graciousness that, when I shall tell of it, people will declare that I have made it up. Suffice it to say that Woferl jumped up on the Empress's[3] lap, put his arms round her neck and kissed her heartily. In short, we were there from three to six o'clock and the Emperor[4] himself came out of the next room and made me go in there to hear the Infanta[5] play the violin. On the 15th the Empress sent us by the Privy Paymaster, who drove up to our house in state, two dresses, one for the boy and one for the girl. As soon as the command arrives, they are to appear at court and the Privy Paymaster will fetch them. Today at half past two in the afternoon they are to go to the two youngest Archdukes[6] and at four o'clock to the Hungarian Chancellor, Count Palffy. Yesterday we were with Count Kaunitz,[7] and the day before with Countess Kinsky and later with the Count von Ulefeld. And we already have more engagements for the next two days. Please tell everybody that, thank God, we are well and happy. I send greetings and I am your old   MOZART

★

[1] Later Joseph II, Holy Roman Emperor, (1765–1790).
[2] Frau Maria Theresa Hagenauer (1717–1800). Her name-day was on 15 October.
[3] Maria Theresia.
[4] Francis I.
[5] Princess Isabella, daughter of Philip, Duke of Parma. She died on 27 November 1763, three years after her marriage to the Archduke Joseph.
[6] Archduke Ferdinand (1754–1806), later Governor-General of Milan, and Archduke Maximilian (1756–1801), later Elector of Cologne.
[7] Wenzel Anton von Kaunitz-Rietburg (1711–1794), Austrian Chancellor, 1753–1792. He was a great amateur of music.

(3) Leopold Mozart to Lorenz Hagenauer, Salzburg

[Extract]   [Copy in the Staatsbibliothek Preussischer Kulturbesitz, West Berlin]

VIENNA, 19 October 1762

You will have received my letter by the last post. This morning I was summoned to the Privy Paymaster, who received me with the greatest courtesy. His Majesty the Emperor wanted to know whether I could not remain in Vienna a little longer, and to this I replied that I was absolutely at His Majesty's disposal. The Paymaster then paid me a hundred ducats, adding that His Majesty would soon summon us again. From whatever point of view I consider it, I foresee that we shall hardly be home before Advent. But before then I shall send in my request for an extension of leave of absence.[1] For, even if I were able to leave here in two or three weeks, I must travel slowly on account of my children, so that they may rest now and then for a few days and not fall ill. I have put the Emperor's hundred ducats, as well as another twenty ducats, to your account with Herr Peisser.[2] If I can obtain a good carriage at a decent price, I have decided to purchase one in order to give the children greater comfort. Today we were at the French Ambassador's. Tomorrow we are invited to Count Harrach's from four to six, but which Count Harrach he is I do not know. I shall see where the carriage takes us to. For on every occasion we are fetched by a servant in the nobleman's carriage and are brought home again. From six or half past six to nine we are to perform for six ducats at a big concert which a certain rich nobleman is giving and at which the greatest virtuosi now in Vienna are going to perform. The nobles send us their invitations four, five, six to eight days in advance, in order not to miss us. For instance, the Chief Postmaster, Count Paar,[3] has already engaged us for next Monday. Woferl now gets enough driving, as he goes out at least twice a day. Once we drove out at half past two to a place where we stayed until a quarter to four. Count Hardegg then fetched us in his carriage and we drove in full gallop to a lady, at whose house we remained till half past five. Thence Count Kaunitz sent to fetch us and we stayed with him until about nine. I can hardly write, for both pen and ink are wretched and I must steal time to do so. I have absolutely no news to give you, as here they talk as little about the war,[4] as if there were no war. I have never in my life heard so little news or known as little as I have during these four or five weeks since I left Salzburg. I should like to hear some news from you; I hope at least that you will have something to tell me. Has His Grace[5] returned home already? I hope that

---

[1] At that time Leopold Mozart, second violin in the Archbishop's orchestra, was both instructor in the violin to the Kapellhaus and court composer.   [2] Banker in Vienna.
[3] Wenzel Johann Josef Paar (1719–1792), created Prince in 1769. His son Wenzel (1744–1812) was a friend and patron of Mozart during his last ten years in Vienna.
[4] The Seven Years' War (1756–1763).   [5] The Archbishop of Salzburg.

he is well. Is His Excellency Count Spaur[1] in Salzburg? He must be, I think. I wrote to him from Linz. How is our worthy Father Confessor?[2] When you can do so, please give him my most obedient greetings. I hope that your wife and all your dear ones are in excellent health. I send her my greetings. Do you know whom our Estlinger[3] came across? The innkeeper at Hellbrunn.[4] He had a long talk with him. But more important still, do you know where I am living? In the Fierberggassl, not far from the Hohe Brücke, on the first floor of the carpenter's house.[5] The room is a thousand feet long and one foot wide. You laugh? But it is no laughing matter for us when we tread on one another's corns. Still less is it a laughing matter when my boy throws me and the girl throws my wife out of our wretched beds or when they dig us in our ribs, as they do every night. Each of our beds is, I reckon, four and a half feet wide; and this amazingly palatial dwelling is divided by a partition into two parts for each of these large beds. But let us be patient! We are in Vienna. My wife would like to have her lined fur. But we think it would cost too much to send it by the mail coach and it might get spoilt in transit. It is in the chest in the little room. But, as I intend to have a new one made for her in Salzburg for the festival days, it would be better to buy something for her here, where there is plenty of choice. Would you like to know what Woferl's costume[6] is like? It is of the finest cloth, lilac in colour. The waistcoat is of moiré, and of the same shade as the coat, and both coat and waistcoat are trimmed with wide double gold braiding. It was made for the Archduke Maximilian.[7] Nannerl's[8] dress was the court dress of an Archduchess and is of white broché taffeta with all kinds of trimmings. It is a pity that we shall only be able to make a petticoat out of it. But it has a little bodice too. My paper is at an end and there is no more time. Give my greetings to everyone in Salzburg.

★

(4) *Leopold Mozart to Lorenz Hagenauer, Salzburg*

[*Extract*]   [*Copy in the Staatsbibliothek Preussischer Kulturbesitz, West Berlin*]

★
[VIENNA, 30 *October* 1762]

I was beginning to think that for fourteen days in succession we were far too happy. God has sent us a small cross and we must thank His infinite

---

[1] Count Ignaz Joseph Spaur, a canon of Salzburg Cathedral.
[2] Ferdinand Joseph Mayr, Father Confessor to Archbishop Schrattenbach until the latter's death in 1771.   [3] A music copyist in Salzburg.
[4] Schloss Hellbrunn, three miles to the south of Salzburg, was formerly the summer residence of the Archbishops.
[5] Leopold wrote 'Tischler-Hause', a corruption of the name of one Ditscher.
[6] Mozart was painted in this costume in 1763. The oil painting, in life size, probably by Pietro Lorenzoni, is now in the Mozart Museum, Salzburg. Archduke Maximilian (1756–1801) was the same age as Mozart.   [7] See p. 6.
[8] Pet name for Maria Anna, Mozart's only sister, born 30 July 1751. She too was painted in her costume.

goodness that things have turned out as they have. At seven o'clock in the evening of the 21st we again went to the Empress. Our Woferl, however, was not quite as well as usual and before we drove there and also as he was going to bed, he complained a good deal of his backside and his hips. When he got into bed, I examined the places where he said he had pain and found a few spots as large as a kreuzer, very red and slightly raised and painful to the touch. But they were only on his shins, on both elbows and a few on his posterior; altogether there were very few. He was feverish and we gave him a black powder [1] and a margrave powder; [2] but he had a rather restless night. On Friday we repeated the powders both morning and evening and we found that the spots had spread: but, although they were larger, they had not increased in number. We had to send messages to all the nobles, where we had engagements for the next eight days, and refuse for one day after another. We continued to give margrave powders and on Sunday Woferl began to perspire, as we wanted him to, for hitherto his fever had been more or less dry. I met the physician of the Countess von Sinzendorf (who happened to be away from Vienna) and gave him particulars. He at once came back with me and approved of what we had done. He said it was a kind of scarlet fever rash.

Thank God he is now so well that we hope that if not tomorrow, his name-day,[3] at least on the day after tomorrow he will get up for the first time. Also he has just cut a back tooth, which has made his left cheek swell. The nobles not only enquired most graciously every day about the condition of our boy, but talked about him a great deal to our physician; so that Dr. Bernhard (that is his name) could hardly be more attentive than he is. Meanwhile, this affair has cost me fifty ducats at least. But I am infinitely grateful to God that it has turned out so well. These scarlet fever spots, which are a fashionable complaint for children in Vienna, are dangerous and I hope that Woferl has now become acclimatized. For the change of air was the main cause of the trouble. Please give my most obedient respects to your wife and tell her that I must worry her again and ask her to be so kind as to arrange for three Masses to be said in Loreto[4] at the Holy Child and three Masses in Bergl[5] at S. Francisco de Paula.[6] I shall repay everything with thanks.

PS. I beg you to use every effort to ascertain what His Grace will do eventually and what hopes I may entertain of the post of Deputy

---

[1] *Pulvis epilepticus niger*, a common remedy at that time against all kinds of disorders.
[2] A remedy discovered by the German chemist Andreas Sigismund Marggraf (1709–1782).
[3] 31 October.
[4] Convent and church of St. Clara at Salzburg, founded in 1629.
[5] Pilgrimage church near Salzburg.
[6] St. Francis of Paula (1416–1508), Calabrian hermit and the founder of the Minims.

Kapellmeister.[1] I do not ask in vain; you are my friend. Who knows what I may do! If only I knew what the future will finally bring. For one thing is certain: I am now in circumstances which allow me to earn my living in Vienna also.

However I still prefer Salzburg to all other advantages. But I must not be kept back. Once more I beg you. For otherwise I myself don't know what I may let others persuade me to do.

★

(5) *Leopold Mozart to Lorenz Hagenauer, Salzburg*

[*Extract*]   [*Copy in the Staatsbibliothek Preussischer Kulturbesitz, West Berlin*]

VIENNA, 6 *November* 1762

I have safely received all your kind letters, and I realize fully how much I owe to your active exertions! But I know what your friendship means. You were born to render kind services to your fellow-creatures and to prove that you are a really true friend. From my last letter you will have gathered in what danger my Woferl was and in what anxiety I was on his account. Thank God, all is well again! Yesterday we rewarded our good Dr. Bernhard with a concert. He invited a number of friends to his house and sent his carriage for us. On the 4th, the festival of St. Charles, I took Woferl for the first time for a drive to St. Charles's Church[2] and the Josefstadt.[3] It was a most beautiful day. Since our arrival here we have hardly had three or four such days. Tell me, have you too had such dreadful rain in Salzburg? Here it has already begun to snow and today we are having real April weather. My wife and I send our greetings to your wife and thank her for all she has done. My wife will soon reply to her letter; and little Woferl sends most dutiful thanks for the kind remembrance of his name-day. He would have been happier, it is true, if he had not been obliged to spend it in bed, though he was better. Some of the nobles sent their congratulations and enquiries after his health; but that was all. We had enquiries from Count Ferdinand Harrach, Count Palffy, the French Ambassador, the Countess von Kinsky, Baron Pechmann, Baron Kurz and the Countess von Paar.[4] If he had not been at home for almost a fortnight, he would have come in for some presents. Well, well! Now we must see that things begin to move again. Until this

---

[1] Leopold Mozart was at this time second violinist and court composer in the Archbishop's service. G. F. Lolli had just been promoted to the post of Kapellmeister in place of J. E. Eberlin who had died in June 1762. In February 1763 Leopold Mozart was appointed Deputy-Kapellmeister.

[2] After St. Stephen's Cathedral, the most important church in Vienna. It was dedicated by Emperor Charles VI to St. Charles Borromeo after the cessation of the plague in 1713 and was completed in 1737. In the 18th century it stood in the open fields of the Wiental.

[3] A district of Vienna, then outside the walls.

[4] Antonia, née Countess Esterházy (1719–1771), wife of the Chief Postmaster.

trouble started, everything was going swimmingly.   ★

PS. If you would be so excessively kind as to go to Lauffen,[1] it is high time to do so. For usually His Excellency Count Spaur leaves Salzburg again on November 14th, that is, the day after the Paris Anniversary.[2] If a decision is not reached now,[3] through the intervention of His Excellency and the efforts of our Father Confessor,[4] it never will be. I shall then be obliged sooner or later to alter my plan. I already have addresses in Holland and France. But I shall tell you more when we meet.

Will you also be so kind and friendly as to make emphatic representations to His Excellency Count Spaur? I have written to him and to our Father Confessor, and furthermore to His Excellency the Chief Steward[5] about permission to remain in Vienna until Advent. Perhaps if you find an opportunity, for instance, after ten o'clock Mass in the Cathedral, you might just speak to him, though it would be even better if you could go and see him. You may also tell him quite plainly about the post of Deputy Kapellmeister, for he is very partial to me. You have no idea how advantageous it would be to me if I were to obtain this post while I am still here.

When I arrived in Vienna I found myself generally regarded as the Kapellmeister of Salzburg. Indeed when the Emperor himself wanted to take me in to hear the Infanta play the violin, he came out and called: "*Where is the Kapellmeister of Salzburg?*"

Latterly, I have not added the title on purpose, for people might think it an invention.[6] Almost every day occasions arise when I am obliged to contradict such statements, for far from me be all lies and bragging. Now you understand me. I trust to your friendship.

(6) *Leopold Mozart to Lorenz Hagenauer, Salzburg*

[*Extract*]   [*From the catalogue of Leo Liepmannssohn, Berlin*[7]]

[VIENNA, 10 *November* 1762]   ★
The enclosed poem[8] was handed to me by Count Collalto at the concert given yesterday by the Marquise von Pacheco. A certain Puffendorf wrote the lines while listening to my boy.   ★

[1] A small village, three miles from the famous health resort, Bad Ischl. The Archbishops of Salzburg often went there.
[2] 13 November was the anniversary of the election to the Archbishopric of Salzburg of Count Paris Lodron, who reigned from 1619 until 1653. He was one of the most famous ecclesiastical rulers of Salzburg. See H. Widmann, *Geschichte Salzburgs*, Gotha, 1914, vol. iii. p. 273 ff.
[3] Leopold Mozart again expresses his anxiety to obtain the post of Deputy-Kapellmeister. See p. 9.   [4] F. J. Mayr. See p. 8, n. 2.   [5] Count von Firmian.
[6] Possibly this rather obscure statement is an allusion to the form of address of letters directed to Leopold Mozart as 'maître de chapelle de S.A.R. l'archevêque de Salzbourg'.
[7] Autograph in the Pierpont Morgan Library, New York City.
[8] This short poem is quoted by Nissen, p. 27, and Abert, vol. ii. p. 928. See also *MDB*, p. 18f.

Master Woferl thanks you for your very kind remembrance of his name-day which he had to spend in Vienna and which gave him little pleasure.

★

We shall bring back plenty of new concertos. Ten have already been copied.

★

(7) *Leopold Mozart to Lorenz Hagenauer, Salzburg*

[*Extract*]   [*Copy in the Staatsbibliothek Preussischer Kulturbesitz, West Berlin*]

VIENNA, 24 *November* 1762

I have received your last letter. I would have done what you and the good friends we know of advised me, if I could have made up my mind immediately. And at last I have decided to do this on the next post-day. The causes which threw me into a certain sad state of indecision I shall tell you about later, but will it not by then be superfluous? Well, if this too fails, then I must hit on some other plan. And now for ourselves. Thank God, we are well, but we must wait patiently until we can direct our enterprise into its old successful path. For in Vienna the nobility are afraid of pockmarks and all kinds of rash. So my boy's illness has meant a set-back of about four weeks. For although since his recovery we have taken in twenty-one ducats, this is a mere trifle, seeing that we only just manage every day on one ducat, and that daily there are additional expenses. Apart from this we are in very good trim. The lady-in-waiting, the Countess Theresa von Lodron, recently conferred a great honour upon us. She gave us a box at the play (which is very difficult to get) and gave my Woferl shoe-buckles, which have little gold plates and look just like solid gold. On St. Elizabeth's day[1] we saw the gala table; and quite exceptional honours and kindnesses were bestowed on us there by the nobility. Suffice it to say that Her Majesty the Empress called out to me from the table and asked me whether my boy was now quite well. A description of St. Cecilia's Festival[2] I shall postpone until we meet. Indeed we shall need to have many long talks before we have discussed everything. On St. Cecilia's day we lunched with the Imperial Kapellmeister, von Reutter.[3] When we get home, I shall recite the menu to Frau Hagenauer. Yesterday we lunched with Herr von Wahlau and in the evening Dr. Bernhard took us to a box at the opera. And thus, God willing, one day after another passes. We have standing invitations to Herr Reutter and Herr von Wahlau. But my children's health might suffer. Moreover carriages cost

---

[1] 19 November.   [2] 22 November.
[3] Johann Adam Karl Georg Reutter (1708–1772) was Court and Cathedral Kapellmeister in Vienna, and a prolific composer. He was ennobled by Maria Theresia in 1740, and is best remembered for his connection with Haydn in the latter's early days.

me a good deal, for we usually take two, three and sometimes even four a day; and if we use the nobles' carriages, the tips for the coachman and the lacquey amount to as much. When shall we be home again? By Christmas or the New Year? I wish you and your wife and all your family much good fortune.   ★

(8) *Leopold Mozart to Lorenz Hagenauer, Salzburg*

[Extract]   *[Autograph formerly in the possession of Dr. Ludwig Schiedermair, Bonn]*

[VIENNA, 10 *December* 1762[1]]

On the 4th I wrote to His Grace and also to our Father Confessor and both letters were composed in the way my best friends suggested. I also added a lengthy apology for not being able to return to Salzburg at the prescribed time. To put it shortly, I cannot get home before Christmas or the New Year. The reasons I shall have to explain to you later when we meet. When you read this letter you will be reminded of our Court Sculptor.[2] But perhaps you have long ago come to the conclusion that *everyone who comes to Vienna, is charmed into staying here.* So it has almost been with us. But my reasons will solve the riddle for you.   ★

It is a good thing that we are not at home just now. We are trying to avoid smallpox; and it might find its way up to us.[3] Now you know the reason why we do not want to go home. I trust that all will turn out well. ★

Returning from Herr von Wahlau I have this moment received your letter of the 7th. I had really decided to leave at once and to reach Salzburg by the Feast of St. Thomas.[4] But when I saw Herr von Wahlau and told him about it, I left the matter for him to decide and he thereupon took the whole thing into his hands. He went so far as to assure me that His Grace would certainly grant an extension of a fortnight or three weeks, in order that I may fulfil the request of the Hungarian nobility. For you must know that for the last three weeks we have been worried to death with invitations to go to Pressburg[5] after the Feast of the Immaculate Conception.[6] And these became the more pressing when we met the greatest nobles of Hungary at the public banquet on the Emperor's

---

[1] Schiedermair (*Die Briefe Mozarts*, vol. iv, p. 394) suggests that this letter and the following one were written with a view to their being read out in Salzburg.

[2] Johann Baptist Hagenauer (1732–1810) was a distant relative of Lorenz Hagenauer, who helped him to pursue his art studies in Italy. In 1764 he was appointed Court Sculptor and Inspector of Galleries to the Archbishop of Salzburg. After the accession of Archbishop Hieronymus Colloredo in 1772 Hagenauer settled in Vienna, where he carried out certain commissions for the Emperor and eventually became Professor of Sculpture.

[3] Apparently the Hagenauer family had caught smallpox. See p. 3, n. 1.

[4] 21 December.

[5] Since 896 Pressburg (Pozsony) had belonged to Hungary, and was its capital from 1536 to 1784. In 1918 it passed to Czechoslovakia, and is now the chief Danubian port (Bratislava) of that country.   [6] 8 December.

birthday.¹ So tomorrow we are off to Pressburg. But I have not the slightest intention of staying there for more than a week. Herr von Wahlau who has taken the matter upon himself is writing in person to our Court about it. Otherwise I should have left immediately. For I really do not know whether I shall gain so very much in Pressburg. Meanwhile give my worthy and holy Father Confessor my most humble greetings and tell him that if by staying away I were to lose the favour of His Grace, I should be ready on the instant to leave by mail coach for Salzburg. At the moment there are still many things which might keep us here at least another month. For just think, Count Durazzo, who is Director of Music at this court, has not yet been able to arrange for us to play at his 'accademia' or public concert. If we agreed to do so, we could stay on until Lent and Easter and draw a nice sum every week. You will say that Vienna makes a fool of everyone. And indeed, when in certain respects I compare Salzburg with Vienna, I soon become confused. Well, if God keeps us in good health, I hope to wish you a happy New Year from my carriage. Meanwhile I wish a speedy recovery to Miss Ursula and Miss Francesca² and much patience to you and especially to your wife.

I am your honest friend

MOZART

(9) *Leopold Mozart to Lorenz Hagenauer, Salzburg*

[*Extract*]   [*Autograph formerly in the possession of Dr. Ludwig Schiedermair, Bonn*]

[VIENNA, 29 *December* 1762]

*Homo proponit, Deus disponit.*³ On the 20th I intended to leave Pressburg and on the 26th to take our departure from Vienna in order to reach Salzburg on New Year's Eve. But on the 19th I had unusually bad toothache. I repeat, *for me unusually bad toothache*; for I had pain in the whole row of the upper front teeth which are perfectly good and otherwise healthy. During the night my whole face swelled up and on the following day I really looked like the trumpeting angel; so much so that Lieutenant Winckler, the court drummer's brother, who called on us, did not recognise me when he entered the room and thought he had lost his way. In this sad circumstance I had to console myself with the thought that in any case we were held up by the extraordinarily fierce cold weather which had suddenly come; for the pontoon was removed and it was as much as they could do to get the post-bags across the Danube by means of small boats; and the postillion had then to proceed with a field-horse. Hence I had to

---

¹ 8 December.   ² Lorenz Hagenauer's daughters.
³ i.e. man proposes, God disposes.

wait for news that the March[1] (which is not a wide river) was frozen. So on Christmas Eve at half past eight in the morning I said good-bye to Pressburg and, travelling by a special route, reached our lodging in Vienna at half past eight in the evening. That day our journey was not very comfortable, for, though the road was frozen hard, it was indescribably bumpy and full of deep ruts and ridges.

Immediately after our return to Vienna our landlady told me that Countess Leopold Kinsky had daily enquired as to whether we had arrived. I called on her on Christmas Day and she said she had waited most anxiously for our return and had postponed a banquet which she wanted to give for Field-Marshal Daun, who would like to make our acquaintance. This banquet she therefore gave on Monday. Now I am most certainly leaving here on Friday morning, and with God's help will reach Linz on Sunday; and on the Vigil of the Epiphany, 5th January, 1763, I hope to stand in your room. I now ask you to add the following kindness ★ to those which you have already shown me in such numbers, and that is, to wish our gracious Father Confessor in my name the healthiest and happiest New Year and to ask him to continue his kind favours towards us. I would have written to him myself if I had not really hesitated to worry him so many times over with my letters. Give my New Year greetings too to Madame Robinig[2] and Fräulein Josepha *in optima forma*[3] and to all our excellent friends, including, of course, yourself, your wife and your whole household. Remember me also to Herr Reifenstuhl[4] and ask him to allow me to leave my carriage at his house for a few days until I find a place where I can store it. Meanwhile I trust that we shall all find one another in good health on January 5th. I am looking forward most ardently to telling you a host of things and to reminding you

that I am ever your true friend

MOZART

My wife and children send their greetings. If you could get the room heated for a few days, it would be well. Only a little fuel is necessary in the front stove.

[Written on the cover]

For the last few days it has been surprisingly cold here; and today it is quite extraordinarily so. Her Majesty the Empress has lost another Princess, the Princess Joanna,[5] aged thirteen, who, when we were at court, took my Woferl by the hand and led him through her rooms.

[1] The river Morava (or March), which now forms the frontier between Austria and Czechoslovakia, flows into the Danube about ten miles below Pressburg.

[2] Widow of a wealthy mine-owner in the Salzburg district. The Robinig family were very friendly with the Mozarts.   [3] i.e. in the best style.

[4] A Salzburg merchant, who kept a shop in the Getreidegasse.

[5] Princess Joanna, who died of typhus in December 1762, was Maria Theresia's eleventh child. She had already lost an infant daughter.

The third journey, the European tour, of Leopold Mozart and his wife and two children lasted from 9 June 1763 to 30 November 1766. The family visited the chief towns of Southern Germany and the Rhineland, remained a few weeks in Brussels, spent the first winter in Paris, almost a year and a half in London, the winter 1765-66 in Holland, and returned to Salzburg by way of Brussels, Paris, Geneva, Berne and Munich. The children performed at every court and frequently gave concerts. In Paris and London Mozart met and studied the works of those composers who for a considerable time influenced his own style of writing, i.e. Schobert and Eckardt in Paris and Johann Christian Bach in London. During the winter 1763-64 he wrote his first sonatas for the clavier and during the following summer, which his family spent in Chelsea, his first symphonies. The Mozarts' long tour is described very fully in letters from Leopold Mozart to his landlord, Lorenz Hagenauer. Letters 10-46.

(10) *Leopold Mozart to Lorenz Hagenauer, Salzburg*

[*Extract*]   [*Autograph in the Mozarteum, Salzburg*]

MONSIEUR,   WASSERBURG,[1] 11 *June* 1763

That was a snail's journey.[2] But it was not our fault. Two hours outside Wasserburg a back wheel broke in pieces and there we were stranded. Fortunately the weather was fine and bright, and still more fortunately there was a mill near by. The people came to our aid with a wheel which was too small and yet too long in the hub. We had to be thankful to have even that, although it meant hewing down a small tree to bind in front of the wheel, so that it should not run away. We broke up the smashed wheel in order to take away the iron with us, though we had to tie on the hoop under the carriage-box to do so. These are only the chief circumstances which kept us for an hour on the open road. Sebastian[3] and I covered the remainder of the distance with God's help *per pedes apostolorum*,[4] in order that our heavy bodies should not cause the wounded carriage any fresh casualty. Thus, while we might have reached Wasserburg at ten o'clock, we had to content ourselves with getting there at a quarter past twelve. The cartwright and the smith were forthwith summoned to produce a new wheel and it became necessary to feel the pulse of the other wheel as well. The *vota unanima* of the *consilium* were to effect that this wheel too was in an extremely dangerous condition and might collapse at a sudden jar. I was all the more ready to believe that it would, as the carriage doctors, even Dr. Niderl[5] himself, had foretold this the day before our departure.

We were told that the carriage would be restored to health early this morning, that is, in twenty-four hours. But the devil take it! Then we hoped to get away after lunch. In vain! The cartwright chopped and sawed, the smith singed and burnt and hammered hard. The latter would have set the patient on his legs again at once and made him walk, if the former could have handed him over more quickly. What were we to do now? We could only, most reluctantly, be patient! And we still have to do so, as I write. For the business will hardly be finished before this evening, so that we shall have to settle down here for another night. The most important side of the matter is the expense, for at least the honour of feeding the horses and the driver falls to me. Yet by Heaven it is better to lose ten wheels than a foot or a few fingers. We are well, thank God, as

---

[1] A small town in Bavaria, situated on the Inn. The Mozarts stayed at the inn 'Zum goldnen Stern'.

[2] The Mozart family, Leopold Mozart and his wife, Nannerl and Wolfgang, had left Salzburg on 9 June.

[3] Sebastian Winter, the Mozarts' man-servant.

[4] i.e. by means of the Apostles' feet.

[5] A Salzburg doctor and a friend of the Mozarts.

we hope that you both are and your whole household and all my good
★ friends, to whom I send greetings.

Our hired driver would be glad if you would tell his people that he
hopes to reach home next Tuesday evening; for tomorrow, God willing,
we look forward to being in Munich. Hence he will probably ride home
with the post-horses in two days. The latest news is that in order to amuse
ourselves we went to the organ and I explained to Woferl the use of the
pedal. Whereupon he tried it *stante pede*,[1] shoved the stool away and
played standing at the organ, at the same time working the pedal, and
doing it all as if he had been practising it for several months. Everyone was
amazed. Indeed this is a fresh act of God's grace, which many a one only
receives after much labour. We send our greetings and I am

your most devoted

MOZART

★

(11) *Leopold Mozart to Lorenz Hagenauer, Salzburg*

[*Extract*]   [*Copy in the Staatsbibliothek Preussischer Kulturbesitz, West Berlin*]

MUNICH, 21 June 1763

We are now in Munich. We arrived on Sunday evening, June 12th.
Monday was a gala-day on account of the Feast of St. Antony[2] and we
drove to Nymphenburg.[3] Prince von Zweibrücken, whose acquaintance
we had made in Vienna, saw us from the castle as we were walking in the
garden, recognised us and beckoned to us from the window. We went up
to him and, after talking to us for some time, he asked whether the
Elector[4] knew that we were here. We said, No. Whereupon he immediately sent off to the Elector a courtier who was standing beside him to ask
whether he would not like to hear the children? Meanwhile we were to
walk in the garden and wait for the reply. Soon afterwards a footman
arrived with a message bidding us appear at the concert at eight o'clock.
It was then four o'clock. So we walked through the garden and visited
Badenburg,[5] but were obliged by sudden rain and thunder to take shelter.
To be brief, Woferl was a great success. We did not get home until a
quarter past eleven, when we had some supper first and then got to bed
late. On Tuesday and Wednesday evenings we were invited to visit
Duke Clemens.[6] On Thursday we stayed at home in the evening on

---

[1] i.e. standing.   [2] St. Antony of Padua, 13 June.
[3] A suburb of Munich, with which it was incorporated in 1900, famous for its palace erected
by Elector Ferdinand Maria (1663–1676), and its park.
[4] Maximilian III, Elector of Bavaria. He had a marked talent for music, composed church
music and was a fine performer on the violoncello. The Mozarts had already performed before
him in January 1762.
[5] The Elector's bath-house, built 1718–1721.   [6] i.e. of Bavaria.

account of heavy rain. Now the question is how are we to get on, seeing that here the charming custom is to keep people waiting for presents for a long time, so that one has to be contented if one makes what one spends. Tomasini[1] has been here for three weeks and has only just been paid. Tell Wenzel[2] he can imagine how overjoyed we both were to meet here unexpectedly. He recognised me first, for he has grown tall, strong and handsome. He displayed sincere gratitude for the old friendship which I had shown him in Salzburg and this touched me and proved to me that he has a good heart. He too is going on to Stuttgart[3] and Mannheim and thence back to Vienna. The Elector lunched in town on the 18th and we ★ were at table with him. He and his sister and Prince von Zweibrücken talked to us during the whole meal. I got my boy to say that we were leaving the following day. The Elector said twice that he was sorry not to have heard my little girl. For when we were at Nymphenburg the time was too short, since the boy alone took up most of it by extemporizing and by playing a concerto for violin and clavier.[4] Two ladies sang and then the concert was over. So when the Elector said a second time: *I should have liked to hear her*, I could not but say *that it would not matter if we stayed on a few days longer*. So all that we can do is to drive over on Wednesday as quickly as possible to Augsburg. For yesterday there was hunting and today there is a French play, so that Nannerl cannot perform until tomorrow. I may thank God if I am paid on Tuesday. The Duke will not detain me; but he is waiting to see what the Elector is going to give me. Tomasini has reason to be dissatisfied with the Elector. He performed twice, had to wait for a long time and finally received eight max d'or. The Duke himself gave him a beautiful gold watch. Basta! I shall be glad if I receive what I have had to spend here and shall probably require for the journey to Augsburg. I can hardly wait for the hour to get away from Munich. I have no complaint to make about the Elector. He is most gracious and he said to me yesterday: 'Why, we are old acquaintances. We met nineteen years ago.' But the apostles only think of themselves and their purses. We lunched recently with Herr König, the Hamburg merchant, who was at our house in Salzburg. He too is lodging at Störzer's in the front part of the house, while we are two flights up in the new building. There I met a certain Johann Georg Wahler of Frankfurt, who lunched with us and gave me his address. He lives in the Römerberg[5] and is going to find private rooms for us in Frankfurt. On the same occasion

---

[1] The violinist Luigi Tomasini (1741–1808), Konzertmeister of Joseph Haydn's orchestra at Eisenstadt.
[2] Wenzel Hebelt, a Salzburg violinist who studied composition under Leopold Mozart.
[3] Leopold Mozart intended to visit Stuttgart. Cp. p. 23.
[4] The word 'clavier' is used when it is not certain what particular form of keyboard instrument is referred to.
[5] The centre of the old town, the market-place in front of the famous Römer, formerly the town hall of Frankfurt.

we met two Saxon councillors, De Bose and Hopfgarten, both most agreeable people. And all these persons we shall meet again, God willing, in Stuttgart or Mannheim, for they are travelling by the same route as we are.[1]

As I write a bit of this letter every day, it will be finished eventually. We leave tomorrow, June 22nd. Farewell. I remain etc.

PS.—We have now been paid and have received a hundred gulden from the Elector and seventy-five gulden from the Duke. But what our bill at the inn will be, we shall have the honour of hearing tomorrow. Herr Störzer has the reputation of giving good service, but also of writing letters and doing sums. Patience! Nannerl played before the Elector and the Duke and was warmly applauded. When we took our leave, both invited us to come again. Prince von Zweibrücken is to announce our arrival in Mannheim. He will soon be there. And Duke Clemens has provided us with a letter of recommendation to the Elector of the Palatinate.[2] Tell our friends that we are very well.

(12) *Leopold Mozart to Lorenz Hagenauer, Salzburg*

[*Extract*]   [*Autograph in the Mozarteum, Salzburg*]

LUDWIGSBURG,[3] 11 *July* 1763

I was kept in Augsburg for a long time[4] and gained little or nothing. For our takings had to be spent, as everything was uncommonly dear, although the landlord of the 'Drei Mohren', Herr Linay, the most charming man in the world, did me very well, as Herr Weiser will testify. The people who came to the concerts were almost all Lutherans. Apart from Herr Provino, who came all three times with Madame Berinet, and Herr Calligari, who appeared once *par réputation*, the only Catholic business man I saw was Herr Mayr, the master of Lisette Muralt. All the others were Lutherans. We left Augsburg on the 6th and reached Ulm[5]

---

[1] According to Leopold Mozart's *Reiseaufzeichnungen* the Mozarts met Baron de Bose and Baron Hopfgarten again in Augsburg, Ludwigsburg and Paris. See p. 42 f.

[2] Karl Theodor (1742–1799), who endeavoured at his court in Mannheim and Schwetzingen to imitate the manners and customs of the court of Louis XV at Versailles.

[3] The residence, with Stuttgart, of Duke Karl Eugen of Wurtemberg, who founded the Karlsschule, the famous military academy, where Schiller as a pupil wrote his play *Die Räuber*. The Mozarts stayed at the inn 'Zum goldnen Waldhorn'.

[4] Fifteen days. Augsburg was Leopold Mozart's native town and his two younger brothers, both bookbinders, were living there. The children gave three concerts, 28 and 30 June and 4 July, a report of which in the Salzburg *Europäische Zeitung* of 19 July 1763, is quoted by Nissen, p. 39, and Abert, vol. i. p. 43. They also met J. A. Stein, the organ builder and improver of the pianoforte, from whom Leopold Mozart bought a portable clavier (p. 28) and whom Mozart met again later (p. 315). See *MDB*, p. 23.

[5] The Mozarts stayed at the inn 'Zum goldnen Rad' and visited the Münster and its great organ.

in the evening, where we only stayed for that night and the following morning. We would not have spent the morning there had it not been that on account of horses we had difficulty in proceeding. And now for a piece of bad luck! When we arrived at the post-stage Plochingen, we heard that the Duke[1] had suddenly decided to go off on the night of the 10th to his hunting lodge Grafeneck, which is fourteen hours distant. So I quickly decided that, instead of going to Stuttgart, I would go straight to Ludwigsburg via Cannstatt in order to catch him. I arrived there late on the 9th and had just time to see a play at the French theatre. But not until the morning of the 10th was I able to see the Chief Kapellmeister Jommelli[2] and the Master of the Hounds, Baron von Pöllnitz, for both of whom I had letters from Count von Wolfegg.[3] In short, there was nothing to be done. Tomasini, who had been here a fortnight before I arrived, had not managed to get a hearing, and, as everyone tells me, the Duke has the charming habit of making people wait interminably before hearing them and then making them wait as long again before giving them a present. But I regard the whole business as the work of Jommelli, who is doing his best to weed out the Germans at this court and put in Italians only. He has almost succeeded too, and will succeed completely, for, apart from his yearly income of four thousand gulden, his allowances for four horses, wood and light, a house in Stuttgart and another one in Ludwigsburg, he enjoys to the full the favour of the Duke; and his wife is promised a pension of two thousand gulden after his death.[4] What do you think of that for a Kapellmeister's post? Furthermore, he has unlimited control over his orchestra and that explains its excellence. Indeed you can judge how partial Jommelli is to his country from the fact that he and some of his compatriots, who are ever swarming at his house to pay him their respects, were heard to say that it was amazing and hardly believable that a child of German birth could have such unusual genius and so much understanding and passion. *Ridete, amici!*[5] Well, I must get on. My prospects now seem all the worse, for the Duke has seized all the horses from the post and the hired coachmen. So I am forced to spend another day here. At the moment I am writing with constant interruptions, as I am endeavouring to beat up some horses and have sent messengers into every nook and corner of Ludwigsburg to find them. So you see that hitherto all I have gained is to have seen lands and towns and various people. ★

---

[1] Karl Eugen of Wurtemberg. The Mozarts were not invited to perform before him.

[2] Niccolò Jommelli (1714–1774) of Naples, a conspicuous representative of the Neapolitan School of operatic composers. From 1753 to 1768 he was Hofkapellmeister in Stuttgart.

[3] Count Anton Willibald Wolfegg, canon of Salzburg Cathedral.

[4] Schurig, vol. i. p. 124, note, quotes from the relevant document the conditions of Jommelli's appointment, and shows that Leopold Mozart's statement is exaggerated.

[5] i.e. Laugh, my friends.

Ludwigsburg is a very queer place. It is a town. Yet more than hedges and garden-trellises the soldiers form the walls of this town. When you spit, you spit into an officer's pocket or into a soldier's cartridge-box. In the streets you hear nothing but perpetual: '*Halt! Quick march! Right, Left*', etc., and you see nothing but arms, drums and war material. At the entrance to the castle there are two grenadiers and two mounted dragoons, with grenadier caps on their heads and cuirasses on their breasts, naked swords in their hands and overhead a fine large tin roof, instead of a sentry-box. In a word it would be impossible to find greater accuracy in drilling or a finer body of men. You see only men of the grenadier type, and every sergeant-major draws forty gulden a month. You will laugh; and really it is laughable. As I stood at the window, I thought I was looking at soldiers about to take their places in some play or opera. Just picture them to yourself. They are all exactly alike and every day their hair is done, not in ringlets but just like any petit-maître does his own— in innumerable curls combed back and powdered snow-white, with the beard greased coal-black. I shall write more from Mannheim. Now I must close. When you write, write to Mannheim and direct that the letter is to remain at the post till I fetch it. I received the music in Augsburg. If I were to write everything, I should have much more to say. But I must tell you that Wurtemberg is a very beautiful district. From Geislingen to Ludwigsburg you will see nothing to left or right but water, woods, fields, meadows, gardens and vineyards, and all these at once and mingled in the most charming fashion. Give my greetings to everyone in Salzburg and especially to our Father Confessor and Madame von Robinig and her family. Complimenti sopra complimenti. Addio!

I am your old

MOZART

My wife takes the greatest pleasure in the countryside in Wurtemberg.

[Written on the cover]

Tell Herr Wenzel that I have heard a certain Nardini[1] and that it would be impossible to hear a finer player for beauty, purity, evenness of tone and singing quality. But he plays rather lightly.

Herr Wodiska is still in service at Stuttgart but has not a good name on account of his childish behaviour. In Augsburg the choir master of St. Moritz, Herr Schuch, showed me a letter from Herr Meisner,[2] in which

---

[1] Pietro Nardini (1722–1793) of Tuscany, eminent violinist and composer, pupil of Tartini. Jommelli brought him in 1762 as solo violinist to the ducal court at Stuttgart, where he remained until 1765. In March 1770 he played with Mozart in Florence. See p. 125. Leopold Mozart in his *Reiseaufzeichnungen*, p. 22, mentions Nardini among the people he met in Augsburg. See *MBA*, No. 51.

[2] Joseph Meissner, a bass singer, composer and teacher of singing in Salzburg.

he signed himself Capellae Magister. I explained to him that he was 'magister' in singing, in order to excuse his childishness.[1]

(13) *Leopold Mozart to Lorenz Hagenauer, Salzburg*

[Extract]   *[Autograph in the Mozarteum, Salzburg]*

MONSIEUR!   SCHWETZINGEN,[2] 19 *July* 1763

As I was writing from Ludwigsburg, I did not dare to add that the soldiering there is driven to excess. For, in truth, twelve to fifteen thousand soldiers, who strut about every day dressed up to the nines, who can hardly walk on account of their tight gaiters and breeches made of the finest linen, all exactly alike, are too few to be taken seriously and too expensive to be joked about; consequently they are far too many. On the 12th at eight in the morning we at last got the coach-horses which had been promised us for four o'clock and, driving through Enzweihingen (entirely Lutheran and a wretched spot), we reached Bruchsal in the evening. On that day's journey we had pleasant views; and much pleasure was afforded us by a good friend, who coming from Augsburg happened to follow us. The Residenz in Bruchsal[3] is worth seeing. The rooms are in the very best taste; there are not many of them, but so noble, indescribably charming and elegant, that nothing pleasanter could be seen. Thence we drove, not to Mannheim, but straight to Schwetzingen, where the court always spends the summer. Apart from the letter of recommendation which I had brought with me from Vienna to the Director of Music, Baron Eberstein, we had already been introduced there by Prince von Zweibrücken; and in addition Prince Clemens of Bavaria had sent to the 'Drei Mohren' in Augsburg a letter of recommendation in his own hand for the Electress at Mannheim. Yesterday a concert, the second only to be held here since May, was arranged specially for us. It lasted from five to nine in the evening. Besides good male and female singers I had the pleasure of hearing an admirable flautist, Wendling[4] by name. The orchestra is undeniably the best in Germany. It consists altogether of people who are young and of good character, not drunkards, gamblers or dissolute fellows, so that both their behaviour and their playing are admirable.[5] My children have set all Schwetzingen talking. The Elector and his consort have shown indescribable pleasure and everyone has been

---

[1] At that time Giuseppe Francesco Lolli of Bologna was the Kapellmeister in Salzburg.

[2] About nine miles from Mannheim and the summer residence of the Electors. The Schloss was built by Elector Karl Ludwig in 1656 and the gardens laid out in 1753 by Elector Karl Theodor. The Mozarts arrived on 13 July and stayed at the inn 'Zum roten Haus'.

[3] An outstanding example of baroque, built 1722–1730.

[4] Johann Baptist Wendling (1723–1797), an eminent flautist, who frequently played in Paris and London. In 1751 or 1752 he joined the Mannheim orchestra and in 1778 followed the Elector to Munich.

[5] See p. 562, where Mozart expresses the same opinion on the Mannheim orchestra in almost the same words.

amazed. When we leave here we shall go to Frankfurt, where our address will be: *c/o Johann Georg Wahler, auf dem Römerberg.* And now I hope that you, my valued friend, and your dearest wife and all your dear ones are in excellent health; just as we all are. For, thank God, we have not been ill for a quarter of an hour. When circumstances arise which oblige us to follow certain customs of the country which are very different from our own, we often say: '*Now Frau Hagenauer should see us*'. For indeed we see many strange and quite unusual things which we should like you to see too. At present we are staying in places where there are four religions, Catholic, Lutheran, Calvinist and Jewish. Save for the court, which accounts for a large number of the inhabitants, Schwetzingen is chiefly Calvinist. It is only a village, but it has three churches, Catholic, Lutheran and Calvinist; and the whole of the Palatinate is like this. Strange to say, since we left Wasserburg, we have not had a holy water stoup in our rooms. For, even though the places are Catholic, such things are not to be found, because many Lutherans pass through, and therefore the rooms are so equipped that all religions can live in them together. In the bed-rooms too there are seldom any pictures save a few landscapes or the portrait of some old Emperor; there is hardly ever a crucifix. Fast-dishes one scarcely ever gets and they are very badly prepared, for everyone eats meat; and who knows what they have given us. Basta! It is not our fault. Our landlord here is a Calvinist. It is a good thing that this does not last long. Now I must close, for it is time to go to the French theatre, which could not be improved on, especially for its ballets and music.[1] I hope to find a letter from you in Frankfurt. I wish you good luck and good health and to all, left, right, behind and in front, I send my greetings, especially to our Father Confessor and to Madame Robinig. I am your old

MOZART

In the volume of music sent over by Madame Haffner[2] from Nuremberg there are six compositions, œuvres mêlées. Open it and give one of them to Adlgasser[3] with my compliments.

★

PS.—Money arrangements are surprisingly bad. In Bruchsal the Bavarian thaler already fetches only twenty-four kreuzer. The twenty-five groschen piece is twenty-four kreuzer and so on. The ducat is worth no more than five gulden. The Bavarian piece of twelve hardly fetches ten kreuzer, whereas in Augsburg the ducat fetches five gulden and twenty to twenty-four kreuzer. Herr Provino has excelled himself and has given me unasked the finest letters of credit to different places. So that thanks to him and to Herr Calligari I am well supplied with all that is necessary.

---

[1] For an excellent account of the French theatre and of French influences generally at the court of Karl Theodor up to 1770, see F. Walter, *Geschichte des Theaters und der Musik am Kurpfälzischen Hofe*, Leipzig, 1898.

[2] Wife of Johann Ulrich Haffner, musician and music publisher in Nuremberg.

[3] Anton Cajetan Adlgasser (1729–1777), court and cathedral organist in Salzburg.

(14) Leopold Mozart to Lorenz Hagenauer, Salzburg

[Extract]   [Copy in the Staatsbibliothek Preussischer Kulturbesitz, West Berlin]

MAINZ, 3 August 1763 ★

From Schwetzingen we drove to Heidelberg in order to see the castle and the great tun.[1] On the whole Heidelberg is very like Salzburg, that is to say, as to its situation. The fallen-in doors and walls in the castle, which are amazing to see, show the sad fruits of the late French wars.[2] In the Church of the Holy Ghost,[3] which is famous in history on account of the struggle between the Catholics and the Calvinists, which led the Electors to transfer their residence to Mannheim,[4] our Wolfgang so astonished everyone by his playing on the organ that by order of the Town Magistrate his name was inscribed with full particulars on it as a perpetual remembrance.[5] After receiving a present of fifteen louis d'or we came on from Schwetzingen through Worms to Mainz.[6]

In Mannheim a French colonel presented a little ring to Nannerl and a pretty toothpick case to little Wolfgang.   ★]

(15) Leopold Mozart to Lorenz Hagenauer, Salzburg

[Extract]   [Copy in the Staatsbibliothek Preussischer Kulturbesitz, West Berlin]

FRANKFURT,[7] 13 August 1763

The Elector[8] of Mainz was and still is suffering from a severe fever. People have been very anxious about him, as he has never yet been ill in his life. We lodged at the 'König von England' and during our stay gave a concert at the 'Römischer König'.[9] Then we left our carriage and some luggage at our lodgings and took the market boat to Frankfurt. We have been here a few days already. Next Thursday we shall give a concert, I

1 The monster cask, capable of holding 49,000 gallons of beer, constructed in 1751 under Elector Karl Theodor.
2 Begun in 1685, when Louis XIV laid claim to the Palatinate. In 1693 the castle was completely destroyed by Maréchal De Lorge.
3 Built at the beginning of the fifteenth century. In 1705 the nave was separated from the choir by a wall in order that the Catholics might worship in the latter and the Protestants in the former.
4 In 1720, owing to ecclesiastical differences with the Protestant citizens, Elector Karl Philipp moved his residence from Heidelberg (for five centuries the capital of the Palatinate) to Mannheim.
5 The organ was taken later to the Jesuit church and the inscription was removed.
6 The Mozarts spent eight days in Mainz and stayed at the inn 'Zum König von England'. According to a letter of Leopold Mozart of 7 December 1780 (p. 683, n. 1), they met there the famous violinist Karl Michael Esser, whom Mozart, then aged seven, rebuked for his careless playing. They also met Anna De Amicis, the famous operatic soprano, who ten years later sang in Milan in Mozart's Lucio Silla.
7 The Mozarts arrived at Frankfurt about 10 August and stayed at the inn 'Zum goldnen Löwen'.   8 Emmerich Joseph von Breidtbach.
9 The Mozarts gave three concerts in Mainz, which brought in 200 gulden. See p. 405.

think, and then return to Mainz, for the market boats ply daily between
★ Mainz and Frankfurt.

(16) *Leopold Mozart to Lorenz Hagenauer, Salzburg*

[*Extract*]   [*Copy in the Staatsbibliothek Preussischer Kulturbesitz, West Berlin*]

★   [FRANKFURT, 20 *August* 1763]
   We gave our concert on the 18th.[1] It went off splendidly. On the 22nd
and also on the 25th or 26th we are repeating it.[2] The Imperial Envoy the
Count von Pergen and his wife were there and everyone was amazed.
God is so gracious that, thanks be to Him, we are well and are admired
everywhere. Wolfgang is extraordinarily jolly, but a bit of a scamp as
well. And Nannerl no longer suffers by comparison with the boy, for she
plays so beautifully that everyone is talking about her and admiring her
execution. I bought a charming little clavier from Stein[3] in Augsburg,
★ which does us good service for practising on during our travels.
   Once since we started upon them, it was in Augsburg, I think, Wolfgang, on waking up in the morning, began to cry. I asked him the reason
and he said that he was sorry not to be seeing Herr Hagenauer, Wenzel,
Spitzeder, Deibl, Leutgeb, Vogt, Cajetan, Nazerl[4] and other good friends.
★   In Mainz Nannerl was given as presents an English hat and a galanterie
set of bottles (to the value of about four ducats). Here she has been given
a snuff-box of vernis martin[5] and a piece of Palatine embroidery, while
little Wolfgang has received a porcelain snuff-box.

(17) *Leopold Mozart to Lorenz Hagenauer, Salzburg*

[*Extract*]   [*Copy in the Staatsbibliothek Preussischer Kulturbesitz, West Berlin*]

                                                    [COBLENZ,[6] 26 *September* 1763]
   Before leaving Mainz I had to give another concert[7] to the nobles, after
★ which we came on to Coblenz. As early as the afternoon of the 18th we

----

[1] Goethe, aged fourteen, was present at this concert with his father, who noted in his diary
'4 gulden, 7 kreuzer pro concerto musicali duorum infantium'. In conversation with Eckermann, 3 February 1830, Goethe said, 'I still remember quite clearly the little fellow with his
wig and sword' (Eckermann, *Gespräche mit Goethe*, Leipzig, 1908, ii. p. 178).
[2] It was repeated too on 30 August. Abert, vol. i. p. 46, quotes the notice of this concert,
which describes enthusiastically the feats of Nannerl and Wolfgang.   [3] See p. 22, n. 4.
[4] The names enumerated are those of Lorenz Hagenauer himself and the Salzburg musicians
Wenzel Hebelt (violinist), Spitzeder (tenor), Deibl (oboist), Leutgeb (horn-player), Vogt
(violinist) and Hagenauer's sons Cajetan (see p. 52, n. 5) and Ignaz Joachim.
[5] A brilliant translucent varnish, giving the effect of lacquer. It was exploited, though not
invented, in the eighteenth century by four brothers Martin, and had an immense vogue for
sedan-chairs, tables, fans, boxes, etc.
[6] The Mozarts arrived on the 17th in Coblenz, where they spent about ten days. They
stayed at the inn 'Zu den drei Reichskronen'.   [7] See p. 27, n. 9.

performed here before the Elector,[1] and straight afterwards we received a present of ten louis d'or.

On the 19th and 20th we had the most atrocious rain. The 21st was an Ember Day, on which I did not want to travel. But in order that we should not spend our time to no purpose, the few nobles who are here arranged a concert, which was held on the 21st. It did not bring in much, but it was something, and I had no expenses in connexion with it. One of the reasons why I did not leave here immediately on the 19th or 20th was that Wolfgang had catarrh or a chill, which by the evening and the night of the 22nd had turned into a proper cold. So I am obliged to wait for a few days, especially as the weather is so bad. Thus we shall hardly leave before the 25th or 26th, for I must consider the health of my children before everything else. Here I met the Baron von Walderndorf and Kopp, a priest who was formerly a steward and is now an Ecclesiastical Commissioner. The Baron von Walderndorf and the Count von Pergen, Imperial Envoy, took my children by the hand to the Elector and introduced us, so that it was due to them that we were heard immediately. ★

We are a great deal with the family of Baron Kerpen, who is Electoral Privy Councillor and head of the nobility. He has seven sons and two daughters, nearly all of whom play the clavier and some of whom play the violin and the violoncello and sing. After this, you will not be surprized if you hear that since we left Salzburg, we have already spent 1068 ★ gulden. But other people have paid for this expenditure. Besides, to keep ★ our health and for the reputation of my court,[2] we must travel 'noblement'. Moreover we only associate with the nobility and distinguished ⌉ personages and receive exceptional courtesies and respect. ★

(18) *Leopold Mozart to Lorenz Hagenauer, Salzburg*

[*Extract*]   [*Copy in the Staatsbibliothek Preussischer Kulturbesitz, West Berlin*][3]

BRUSSELS,[4] 17 *October* 1763[5]

In Coblenz we took a private boat and leaving on September 27th at ★ ten in the morning we reached Bonn[6] that same evening in good time. Thence we travelled by mail coach through Brühl to Cologne, where we ★ arrived early in the evening of the 28th. We spent two days in that great old town. In the cathedral[7] there is a very ancient pulpit from which ★ ⌉

---

[1] Johann Philipp von Walderdorf, Elector of Trier.
[2] i.e. the Archbishop's court in Salzburg.   [3] Autograph in the Mozarteum, Salzburg.
[4] The Mozarts arrived on 4 October in Brussels, where they remained until 15 November. They stayed at the 'Hôtel d'Angleterre'.
[5] According to Leopold Mozart's statement, this letter was sealed and despatched on 4 November.
[6] Nissen, p. 44, adds: 'In Bonn the Elector (Maximilian Friedrich) was away'.
[7] In his *Reiseaufzeichnungen*, p. 26, Leopold Mozart mentions 'the dirty minster or cathedral'. See *MBA*, No. 65.

L   Martin Luther is supposed to have preached.

On September 30th we left Cologne by mail coach, travelling through
★ Aachen. It was the most awful road. Now as Aachen was the most expensive place which I had so far struck during our journey, I had the
honour of spending *nolens volens*[1] over seventy-five gulden there. Princess
Amalia,[2] sister of the King of Prussia, was there, it is true, but she herself
has no money, and her whole equipage and court retinue resembles a
physician's suite as closely as one drop of water another. If the kisses which
she gave to my children, and to Wolfgang especially, had been all new
louis d'or, we should be quite happy; but neither the innkeeper nor the
postmaster are paid in kisses. The most ridiculous thing seemed to me
that she tried by every means to persuade me to go not to Paris, but to
Berlin, and what is more she made to me proposals which I shall not write
down here, as nobody would believe them; for I did not believe them
★ myself, especially the particular one which she made to me.

From Aachen we drove on October 2nd to Liége, where we only
arrived at nine in the evening. We left early next morning—at about half
past seven. It was the most lovely day. From Liége to Paris—just think of
the amazing distance!—the post road is paved like the streets of a town
and planted on either side with trees like a garden walk. We spent the
night in Tirlemont. On the following day we reached Louvain early and
spent the morning there in order to see the town a little. The principal
church was the first building we visited. Here the valuable paintings of
the famous Netherland painters begin. I stood transfixed before a 'Last
Supper'.[3] On October 4th we reached Brussels early in the evening. We
★ are staying at the 'Hôtel D'Angleterre'. Quantities of white and black
marble and brass and the paintings of the most famous artists are to be
found here in the churches in great numbers. Day and night I have before
my eyes that picture by Rubens, in the big church, in which Christ in the
presence of the other apostles hands the keys to Peter. The figures are
★ life-size. In Prince Karl's[4] rooms I found not only beautiful Dutch tapes-
tries and paintings, but also a room with original Chinese statues, porcelain,
figures and various rare pieces; above all there was a room filled with an
indescribable quantity of all kinds of natural history specimens. I have
seen many such collections; but it would be difficult to find such a
quantity and so many species.

Prince Karl's present recreations are to lacquer, paint, varnish, eat,
drink and laugh heartily, so that he can be heard three or four rooms away.
The rules of the church are still taken fairly seriously here. You can see at

[1] i.e. willy nilly.
[2] Princess Amalia (1723–1787) was a lover and connoisseur of music.
[3] A famous triptych (c. 1464) by Dierick Bouts in the Église Saint-Pierre.
[4] Prince Charles of Lorraine, brother of Emperor Francis I and Governor of the Austrian
Netherlands. He died in 1780.

once that this is a country which belongs to Her Majesty the Empress. But rosaries are not usual and in the churches you never see anybody praying with one. They all pray out of books and at the elevation of the Host they never strike their breasts.[1] In all the churches no chairs are to be seen, but seats can be hired for a liard, in our coinage two pfennigs. ★

For you alone.   BRUSSELS, 4 *November* 1763 ★

We have now been kept in Brussels for nearly three weeks.[2] Prince Karl has spoken to me himself and has said that he will hear my children in a few days; and yet nothing has happened. Yes, it looks as if nothing will come of it, for the Prince spends his time hunting, eating and drinking, and in the end it appears that he has no money. Meanwhile in decency I have neither been able to leave nor to give a concert, since, as the Prince himself has said, I must await his decision. You can imagine that I shall in addition have a pretty bill to pay at the hotel; and for the journey to Paris I must have at least two hundred gulden in my pocket. ★

We have now received here, it is true, various handsome presents, which, however, I do not want to sell.

Little Wolfgang has been given two magnificent swords, one from Count von Frankenberg, Archbishop of Malines, the other from General Count De Ferraris. My little girl has received Dutch lace from the Archbishop, and from other courtiers cloaks, coats and so forth. With snuffboxes and étuis and such stuff we shall soon be able to rig out a stall. Indeed I hope that next Monday, when a big concert is being held, I shall haul in plenty of fat thalers and louis d'or. But as one must always be on the safe side, I beg you to be so good as to arrange through Herr Haffner or some other person that I receive another letter of credit for Paris. ★

If Salzburg has been surprised at my children, it will be completely amazed provided that God lets us return home. A propos, have you not yet received the portraits[3] of my children? ★

(19) *Leopold Mozart to Lorenz Hagenauer, Salzburg*

[*Extract*]   [*Copy in the Staatsbibliothek Preussischer Kulturbesitz, West Berlin*]

PARIS, 8 *December* 1763

After giving a fine concert in Brussels at which Prince Karl was present, we left at nine in the morning on my worthy name-day[4] with four post-horses, and after taking leave early of many good friends we reached Mons in the afternoon while it was still daylight. On the second day we

---

[1] Refers to the practice which still prevails in certain Catholic countries.
[2] Leopold Mozart surely means 'five weeks', as the Mozarts arrived on 4 October.
[3] Probably the portraits of Mozart and his sister in the costumes presented to them by the Empress Maria Theresia. See p. 8, n. 6 and n. 8.   [4] 15 November.

arrived just as early in Péronne and on the third in Gournay; on the fourth, November 18th, at half past three in the afternoon, we arrived at the Hôtel of the Count van Eyck[1] in Paris. Fortunately we found the Count and the Countess at home. They gave us a most friendly welcome and have provided us with a room in which we are living comfortably and happily. We have the Countess's harpsichord, because she does not need it. It is a good one and like ours has two manuals.

★

You would like to know perhaps how I like Paris? If I were to tell you this in circumstantial detail, neither the hide of a cow nor that of a rhinoceros would suffice. Buy yourself for forty-five kreuzer Johann Peter Willebrandt's *Historische Berichte und Pracktische Anmerkungen auf Reisen*, ★ *etc. Frankfurt und Leipzig* 1761. It will amuse you. The mourning for the Infanta[2] still prevents us from playing at court. Tomorrow we must go ★ to the Marquise de Villeroi and to the Countess Lillibonne.

(20) *Leopold Mozart to Lorenz Hagenauer, Salzburg*

[*Autograph in the Mozarteum, Salzburg*]

[VERSAILLES, *end of December* 1763[3]]

You may read the enclosed letter, make an extract of it, seal it up and deliver it to our Father Confessor with my most humble greetings and New Year wishes; or you may let him do the sealing himself.

Madame de Pompadour[4] is still a handsome woman. She is very like the late Frau Steiner, née Therese Freysauf,[5] and she has something of the appearance of the Austrian Empress, especially in her eyes. She is extremely haughty and still rules over everything. In Versailles[6] living is expensive; and it is very fortunate that at the present time it is almost as warm as in summer, for otherwise we should be hard put to it, as every log of wood costs five sous. Yesterday my boy got a gold snuff-box from Madame la Comtesse de Tessé[7] and today my little girl was given a small,

---

[1] Bavarian minister in Paris. His wife was a daughter of Count Georg Anton Felix Arco, Chief Chamberlain in Salzburg. They lived in the Hôtel Beauvais, rue St. Antoine (now rue de François-Miron, no. 68). According to a passage in his letter from Brussels here omitted, Leopold Mozart had taken rooms in the house where Christian von Mechel was living (see p. 33), but the Van Eycks invited the family to stay with them.

[2] Marie-Thérèse de Bourbon, the first wife of the Dauphin Louis, had recently died.

[3] The whole letter is written on a cover, which, according to a note on the autograph in Nissen's handwriting, contained a letter reporting on the Mozart's visit to Versailles, where they stayed from 24 December 1763 until 8 January 1764. No doubt the lost letter was to be given to the Archbishop.

[4] Mlle Jeanne Antoinette Poisson, later Mme le Normant d'Etioles, subsequently Marquise de Pompadour (1721–1764), had been established at Versailles since 1745 as 'maîtresse en titre'.

[5] The Freysauf family kept a shop in the Judengasse, Salzburg.

[6] At Versailles the Mozarts lodged 'Au Cormier, rue des Bons Enfants'.

[7] Lady-in-waiting to Madame la Dauphine. She kept a salon and was famous for her wit. Mozart's second printed work was dedicated to her.

transparent snuff-box, inlaid with gold, from the Princess Carignan, and Wolfgang a pocket writing case in silver, with silver pens with which to write his compositions; it is so small and exquisitely worked that it is impossible to describe it. My children have taken almost everyone by storm. But everywhere the results of the late war are to be seen. It is impossible to write down all that one would like to describe. Wish all my good friends a happy New Year. I should like to write to everybody if I had time and if every letter did not cost twenty or thirty sous. If I had written a longer letter to His Grace, I should certainly have had to pay five livres, for they charge according to the weight and the size or the shape. Did you send me an answer? Perhaps you did and I shall find it at our Hôtel in Paris when we get back. Farewell—à Dieu! Myself, my wife and children send our greetings and wish you, your wife and all your family a happy New Year. Thank God, we are all well. You should see Wolfgang in his black suit and French hat.

(21) *Leopold Mozart to Christian von Mechel*[1]

[Autograph in the Staatsbibliothek Preussischer Kulturbesitz, West Berlin]

MON AMI!   [Paris, *9 January* 1764]
We arrived back from Versailles yesterday evening at half past eight. I called at your quarters today after one o'clock and tried both entrances. To prove this I have written my name on your blackboard. We are hoping to see you soon. Farewell. My children send greetings to you.

MOZART

I even walked to your place, a very wonderful thing for me!

A Monsieur de Mechel,
    rue St. Honoré,
        chez M. le Noir, Notaire,
            vis à vis la rue d'Eschelle.

(22) *Leopold Mozart to Frau Maria Theresa Hagenauer*

[Extract]   *[Autograph in the Museum Carolino Augusteum, Salzburg]*

MADAME!   PARIS, 1 *February* 1764
One must not always write to men but must sometimes remember the fair and devout sex. I really cannot tell you whether the women in Paris are fair; for they are painted so unnaturally, like the dolls of

---

[1] Christian von Mechel (1737–1817), a native of Basel, lived from 1758 or 1759 to 1764 in Paris, where he studied copper-engraving under Wille and Delafosse. After a short stay in Italy he returned to Basel, where he founded a famous firm of art dealers.

Berchtesgaden,[1] that even a naturally beautiful woman on account of this detestable make-up is unbearable to the eyes of an honest German. As for piety, I can assure you that it is not difficult to get to the bottom of the miracles of the French women saints; the greatest of them are performed by those who are neither virgins nor wives nor widows, and they are all performed during their lifetime. Later on we shall speak more fully on this subject. But really it is extremely difficult to distinguish here who is the lady of the house. Everyone lives as he or she likes and, if God is not specially gracious, the French state will suffer the fate of the former Persian Empire.

I received safely your husband's two letters of December 20th and January 19th with the three enclosures. The most important and certainly to you the most pleasant piece of information I can give you is that, thank God, we are all well. And I too always look forward most eagerly to hearing that all of you are in good health. Since my last letter from Versailles[2] I would assuredly have written to you, only I kept on postponing this in order to await the result of our affair at Versailles and be able to tell you about it. But as everything here, even more so than at other courts, goes at a snail's pace, and since these matters have to be dealt with by the Menus Plaisirs,[3] one must be patient. If the recognition we receive equals the pleasure which my children have given this court, we ought to do very well. I should like to tell you that it is not the custom here to kiss the hand of royal persons or to disturb them with a petition or even to speak to them *au passage*, as they call it, that is to say, when they walk to church through the gallery and the royal apartments. Neither is it the custom here to do homage either by an inclination of the head or a genuflexion to the King or to members of the Royal Family. On the contrary, one remains erect and immovable, and, standing thus, one just lets the King and his family pass close by. Hence you can well imagine how impressed and amazed these French people, who are so infatuated with their court customs, must have been, when the King's daughters, not only in their apartments but in the public gallery, stopped when they saw my children, came up to them and not only allowed them to kiss their hands, but kissed them innumerable times. And the same thing happened with Madame la Dauphine.[4] But what appeared most extraordinary to these French people was that at the *grand couvert* on the evening of New Year's Day, not only was it necessary to make room for us all to go up to the royal table, but my Wolfgang was graciously

---

[1] A village in Bavaria, near Salzburg, famous for centuries for its painted carvings.

[2] Letter 20.

[3] Term given to certain Royal expenses regulated by a special administration, housed in the Hôtel des Menus Plaisirs, which dealt chiefly with the ceremonies, festivals and performances at court.

[4] Maria Josepha of Saxony, wife of the Dauphin Louis who died in 1765, and mother of Louis XVI.

privileged to stand beside the Queen[1] the whole time, to talk constantly to her, entertain her and kiss her hands repeatedly, besides partaking of the dishes which she handed him from the table. The Queen speaks as good German as we do and, as the King knows none, she interpreted to him everything that our gallant Wolfgang said. I stood beside him, and on the other side of the King, where M. le Dauphin and Madame Adélaïde[2] were seated, stood my wife and daughter. Now you must know that the King never dines in public, except on Sunday evenings when the whole Royal Family dine together. But not everyone is allowed to be present. When, however, there is a great festival, such as New Year's Day, Easter, Whitsuntide, the name-days and so forth, the *grand couvert* is held, to which all persons of distinction are admitted. There is not, however, very much room and consequently the hall soon gets filled up. We arrived late. So the Swiss Guards had to make way for us and we were led through the hall into the room close to the royal table, through which the Royal Family enter. As they passed us they spoke to our Wolfgang and we then followed them to table.

You can hardly expect me to describe Versailles to you. I can only tell you that we arrived there on Christmas Eve and attended Matins and three Masses in the Royal Chapel. We were in the Royal Gallery when the King came from Madame la Dauphine, to whom he had been breaking the news which he had just received of the death of her brother, the Elector of Saxony.[3] I heard good and bad music there. Everything sung by individual voices and supposed to resemble an aria was empty, frozen and wretched—in a word, French; but the choruses are good and even excellent. So every day I have been with my little man to the Mass in the Royal Chapel to hear the choir in the motet, which is always performed there. The Royal Mass is at one o'clock. But if the King goes hunting, his Mass is at ten o'clock and the Queen's Mass at half-past twelve. I shall tell you more about all this later. In sixteen days we were obliged to spend about twelve louis d'or in Versailles. Perhaps you think it too much and find it difficult to understand? But in Versailles there is no *carosse de remise* and no *fiacre*, only sedan-chairs. Thus for every drive one has to pay twelve sous. So now you will see that, as on many days, for the weather was always bad, we had to have at least two, if not three, sedan-chairs, they came to one laubthaler and sometimes more. If you now add four new black suits, you will not be surprised if our visit to Versailles has cost us twenty-six or twenty-seven louis d'or. Well, we must see what we shall get from the court in return. Apart from what we hope to receive, we have not taken in at Versailles more than twelve louis d'or. My Master

---

[1] Maria Leszczynska, daughter of the exiled King of Poland, who married Louis XV in 1725.
[2] Eldest daughter of Louis XV.
[3] Elector Frederick Christian, who died of smallpox, 17 December 1763.

Wolfgang, however, has received from Madame la Comtesse de Tessé *a gold snuff-box* and *a gold watch*, valuable on account of its smallness, the size of which I have traced here. Nannerl has been given an uncommonly beautiful, *heavy toothpick case of solid gold*. From another lady[1] Wolfgang has received a travelling writing case in silver and Nannerl an unusually fine tortoiseshell snuff-box inlaid with gold. Further, the number of our snuff-boxes has been increased by a red one with gold bands, by another

in some sort of glass material set in gold, and by a third in vernis martin, inlaid with the most beautiful flowers of coloured gold and various pastoral instruments. In addition we have received a small ring set in gold with an antique head, and a host of trifles which I do not value very highly, such as sword-bands, ribbons and armlets, flowers for caps, fichus for Nannerl and so forth. But I hope after four weeks to have a better story to tell of louis d'or, for it takes longer than to walk to Maxglan[2] before one is properly known in Paris. And I assure you that it does not require a telescope to see everywhere the evil results of the late war.[3] For the French insist on continuing their external magnificence and therefore only the fermiers are rich, while the lords are deep in debt. The bulk of the country's wealth is divided amongst about a hundred persons, a few big banquiers and fermiers généraux; and, finally, most money is spent on Lucretias, who do not stab themselves. All the same you can imagine that remarkably beautiful and precious things are to be seen here, and astonishing follies too. In winter the women wear not only fur-trimmed garments, but also neck ruffles or neckties of fur and instead of flowers even fur in their hair and fur armlets and so forth. But the most ridiculous sight is the type of sword-band, which is in fashion here, bound round and round with fine fur—an excellent idea, for the sword will not catch cold. And in addition to their idiotic 'mode' in all things, there is their extreme love of comfort, which has caused this nation to turn a deaf ear to the voice of nature. Hence everyone in Paris sends new-born children to be reared in the country. Persons of both high and low rank do this and pay a bagatelle for it. But you see the wretched consequences of this practice. For you will hardly find any other city with so many miserable and mutilated persons. You have only to spend a minute in a church or walk along a few streets to meet some blind or lame or limping or half-putrefied beggar, or to find someone lying on the street who has had his hand eaten away as a child by the pigs, or someone else who in childhood fell into the fire and had half an arm burnt off while the foster-father and his family were working in the

★

---

[1] Princess Carignan. See p. 33.
[2] A suburb of Salzburg, about half an hour's walk from the town.
[3] For French social life at this period see Hippolyte Taine, *L'Ancien Régime*, 1875, *passim*, and J. B. Perkins, *France under Louis XV*, 1897, vol. ii.

fields. And there are numbers of such people, whom disgust makes me refrain from looking at when I pass them. Now I am going to jump from the ugly to the charming and moreover to someone who has charmed a king. You surely would like to know what Madame la Marquise de Pompadour is like? She must have been very beautiful, for she is still good-looking. In figure she is tall and stately, stout, or rather well-covered, but very well-proportioned. She is fair and extremely like our former Therese Freysauf,[1] while her eyes are rather like those of Her Majesty the Empress.[2] She is extremely dignified and uncommonly intelligent. Her apartments at Versailles are like a paradise and look out on the gardens. In Paris she has a most splendid Hôtel, entirely rebuilt, in the Faubourg St. Honoré. In the room where the clavecin is (which is all gilt and most artistically lacquered and painted) hangs a lifesize portrait of herself and beside it a portrait of the King. Now for another matter! There is a perpetual war here between the Italian and the French music.[3] The whole of French music is not worth a sou. But the French are now starting to make drastic changes, for they are beginning to waver very much; and in ten to fifteen years the present French taste, I hope, will have completely disappeared. The Germans are taking the lead in the publication of their compositions. Amongst these Schobert,[4] Eckardt,[5] Honnauer[6] for the clavier, and Hochbrucker[7] and Mayr[8] for the harp are the favourites. M. Le Grand,[9] a French clavier-player, has abandoned his own style completely and his sonatas are now in our style. Schobert, Eckardt, Le Grand and Hochbrucker have all brought us their engraved sonatas and presented them to my children. At present four sonatas of M. Wolfgang Mozart are being engraved.[10] Picture to yourself the furore which

---

[1] A Salzburg acquaintance. See p. 32.

[2] Maria Theresia, Empress of Austria. See p. 32.

[3] Rousseau, who sided with the Italians, in his *Confessions*, Book 8, gives a most vivid account of this 'war'. See also his *Lettre sur la musique française*, published in 1753. See Abert, vol. i. p. 627 ff.

[4] Johann Schobert (*c.* 1735–1767), a native of Silesia, settled in Paris in 1760 in the service of the Prince de Conti. He was a famous player on the harpsichord and composed sonatas for clavier with violin accompaniment, of which the first set was published in Paris in 1764. For an excellent account of Schobert and his influence on Mozart, see WSF, vol. i. p. 65 ff.

[5] Johann Gottfried Eckardt (1735–1809), born in Augsburg. From 1758 he lived in Paris, where as a player on the harpsichord he was a rival to Schobert. He also composed for his instrument and was a painter of miniatures. Eckardt's *Six sonates pour le clavecin* were published in Paris in May 1763. According to WSF, vol. i. p. 41 ff., they influenced Mozart's first two sonatas, K. 6 and 8.

[6] Leonzi Honnauer (1717–1809), harpsichordist to Prince Louis de Rohan, spent most of his life in Paris, where a number of his harpsichord sonatas were published, 1760–1770.

[7] Christian Hochbrucker, born in Bavaria, was a virtuoso on the harp. In 1760 he settled in Paris, where some of his compositions were published. In 1792 during the Revolution he fled to London.

[8] Probably Philippe Jacques Meyer (1737–1819), a native of Strassburg, who was a famous performer on the harp. He came to England in 1772 and settled there in 1784.

[9] Le Grand was a popular harpsichord teacher and organist at St. Germain-des-Prés.

[10] K. 6, 7, 8, 9, with the title *Sonates pour le clavecin qui peuvent se jouer avec l'accompagnement de violon.* K. 6, 7. were dedicated to Madame Victoire, Louis XV's second daughter. K. 8, 9

they will make in the world when people read on the title-page that they have been composed by a seven-year-old child; and when the sceptics are challenged to test him, as he already has been, imagine the sensation when he asks someone to write down a minuet or some tune or other and then immediately and without touching the clavier writes in the bass and, if it is wanted, the second violin part.[1] In due course you will hear how fine these sonatas are; one of them has an Andante[2] in a quite unusual style. Indeed I can tell you, my dear Frau Hagenauer, that every day God performs fresh miracles through this child. By the time we reach home, God willing, he will be able to contribute to the court music. He frequently accompanies in public concerts. He even, when accompanying, transposes *a prima vista*;[3] and everywhere Italian or French works are put before him, which he plays off at sight. My little girl plays the most difficult works which we have of Schobert and Eckardt and others, Eckardt's being the most difficult, with incredible precision, and so excellently that *this mean Schobert* cannot conceal his envy and *jealousy* and is making himself a laughing-stock to Eckardt, who is an honest man, and to many others. Later on I shall tell you many things which would take too long to relate here. Schobert is not at all the man he is said to be. He flatters to one's face and is utterly false. But his religion is the religion in fashion. May God convert him! Now I have a very sad piece of news, something extremely distressing. We are all in great anxiety and very much upset. In a word, Countess Van Eyck is in a most dangerous condition, so much so that without the special grace of God she will hardly live. On Sunday we were with her before lunch, between twelve and one, and she was very cheerful. She had then been indoors for a few days owing to a cold, but that day she had been to church. As always, she talked a great deal to Wolfgang. During the night I heard a carriage enter the courtyard and then some disturbance in the house. In the morning I was told that the Countess ★ had suddenly fallen ill and had coughed up a quantity of blood. Imagine our distress, which is all the greater as I can only look on from a distance and may perhaps never speak to her or even see her again. My children pray and shed tears, as Wolfgang loves the Countess and she loves him to distraction. I am writing this on the evening of February 1st. God grant that tomorrow morning, before I close this letter, I may be able to write ★ more cheerfully. My wife can think of nothing else all day long but the poor Countess and indeed we are deeply concerned.

There is now little room left on this sheet of paper. I must add, however,

were dedicated to the Comtesse de Tessé. The engraver of both publications was Mme Vendôme.

[1] Grimm, *Correspondance Littéraire*, vol. iii. p. 365, has a letter dated Paris, 1 December 1763, describing the feats of these 'vrais prodiges'.

[2] WSF, vol. i. p. 82, suggest that Leopold Mozart is referring to the Adagio of the sonata K. 7, which was probably composed at Versailles.   [3] i.e. at first sight.

that the Archbishop of Paris has been cast out into the wilderness or, to put it mildly, has been exiled. He had a libellous pamphlet printed against the Parlement in favour of the Jesuits, which brought this punishment upon him.[1] As far as I hear, everyone blames him, for the King, who was informed that he was going to publish this piece of writing, tried in a friendly manner to dissuade him. However he persisted and thus deliberately dashed his head against the wall. The King hastened to exile him, otherwise the Parlement would have arrested him. *The secular arm is a bit too powerful here.* On the other hand the clergy go about the streets singly, lower their cowls below their shoulders, hold their hats in their hands and are absolutely indistinguishable from lay pedestrians. Farewell and thank God that I have finished writing—otherwise you would indeed have to put on your spectacles.[2] With greetings from myself, my children and my wife, I am your devoted

MOZART

How is our good Dellmor? Is he still in our neighbourhood? He will sometimes think of us when he sees nobody at our windows. Please give him my compliments and greetings from us all and especially from little Wolfgang. He is an honest man.[3]

(23) *Leopold Mozart to Lorenz Hagenauer, Salzburg*

[*Extract*]   [*Copy in the Staatsbibliothek Preussischer Kulturbesitz, West Berlin*]

MONSIEUR,   PARIS, 22 *February* 1764
The sun cannot always shine and clouds often gather, only however to be again dispersed. I did not make haste to send tidings of the sad death of Countess Van Eyck.[4] I thought it would be sufficient if I prepared the hearts of the people in Salzburg for this sad event, while leaving it to others to report the end. Nobody likes to die anywhere; but here it is doubly sad for an honest German if he falls ill or dies.

Soon afterwards a sudden and unexpected event plunged me into a certain embarrassment. My dear Wolfgang suddenly got a sore throat and a cold, so that on the 16th, the morning on which it started, he developed such an inflammation of the throat that he was in danger of choking. He also had a very high fever. After four days he got up and is now well again.

---

[1] Christophe de Beaumont, Archbishop of Paris, published in 1763 an *Apologie des Jésuites*, which was condemned by the Parlement. In January 1764 the King exiled him forty leagues from Paris. The *arrêt* of the Parlement suppressing the Jesuit order in France was issued in August 1762. In the previous year, 1761, their goods had been declared confiscated and their educational establishments closed. All the bishops, with one exception, were opposed to the suppression, which was, however, strongly supported by public opinion.
[2] The letter is so closely written.   [3] This paragraph is written on the cover.
[4] On February 6th.

As a precaution I wrote by local post to our friend the German Doctor Herrnschwand, who is the doctor of the Swiss Guards. But he did not have to come more than twice. Then I gave the boy a small dose of Vienna laxative water: now thank God he is well. My little girl too is ★ suffering from a cold, but is not feverish.

And now I beg you to have four Masses said as soon as possible at Maria-Plain and one at the Holy Child at Loreto. These we promised for the sake of our children, who were both ill. I hope that the other Masses will, as I asked, always continue to be said at Loreto, for as long as we are ★ away. The Duc d'Ayen[1] has arranged that in a fortnight at latest we shall drive out again to Versailles, in order that we may present to Madame Victoire, the King's second daughter, to whom it has been dedicated, the Œuvre 1er of the engraved sonatas of the great M. Wolfgang.[2] The Œuvre 2e will be dedicated, I think, to Madame la Comtesse de Tessé.[3] Within three or, at most, four weeks important things will have happened, if God wills. We have tilled the soil well and now hope for a good harvest. But one must take things as they come. I should have had at least twelve louis d'or more, if my children had not had to stay at home for a few days. Thank God, they are better. Do you know what people here are always wanting? They are trying to persuade me to let my boy be inoculated with smallpox.[4] But as I have now expressed sufficiently clearly my aversion to this impertinence, they are leaving me in peace. Here ★ inoculation is the general fashion. But, for my part, I leave the matter to the grace of God. It depends on His grace whether He wishes to keep this prodigy of nature in the world in which he has placed it, or to take it to Himself. I shall certainly watch over it so well that it is all one whether we are in Salzburg or in any other part of the world. But it is this watching ★ which makes travelling expensive.

Mr d'Hébert, Trésorier des Menus Plaisirs du Roi, has handed to Wolfgang from the King fifty louis d'or and a gold snuff-box.[5]

(24) *Leopold Mozart to Lorenz Hagenauer, Salzburg*

[*Extract*]   [*Copy in the Staatsbibliothek Preussischer Kulturbesitz, West Berlin*]

PARIS, 4 *March* 1764

On the 3rd our servant Sebastian Winter[6] left here with the country coach via Strassburg for Donaueschingen. He has entered the service of

---

[1] Brother of the Comtesse de Tessé.
[2] K. 6, 7. This was Mozart's first printed work.   [3] K. 8, 9.
[4] From the middle of the eighteenth century the inoculation of healthy persons from smallpox subjects was very common. But it was not until 1796 that Jenner discovered and applied his discovery of vaccine.   [5] The original of this sentence occurs in Nissen p. 59.
[6] See p. 19, n. 3.

Prince von Fürstenberg [1] as friseur. I have taken on another friseur, called Jean Pierre Potivin, who speaks good German and French, for he was born at Zabern in Alsace. Now I have to buy his clothes, again a heavy expense.

MADAME!

You will think perhaps that we are taking part in quite extraordinary carnival festivities? Oh, you are very much mistaken. It has never occurred to me to attend balls, which only begin after midnight. Here there are balls in every quarter; but you must know that they are for thirty or forty people and that one or, at most, two violins without a violoncello play the minuets; and what sort of minuets? Why, minuets which were danced already in the time of Henry IV; and in the whole town there are about two or three favourite minuets, which must always be played, because the people cannot dance to any save those particular ones during the playing of which they learned to dance. But, above all, contredanses[3] or what we call English dances, are danced! All this I know from hearsay only, for so far I have not seen them.

I ought to have finished writing long ago, but the things I have had to do for some days and shall have to do until the 10th in order to make sure that between six and nine on the evening of that day I shall pocket seventy-five louis d'or, have, as you will understand, prevented me.

(25) *Leopold Mozart to Lorenz Hagenauer, Salzburg*

[*Extract*]   [*Copy in the Staatsbibliothek Preussischer Kulturbesitz, West Berlin*]

PARIS, 1 *April* 1764

We are all well and we thank God from the bottom of our hearts. And now I have the pleasure of informing you that I hope in a few days to lodge with the bankers Turton et Baur 200 louis d'or, to be entrusted to safe hands and in due course sent off to Salzburg. On April 9th I shall again have to stand the shock which I had on March 10th. But I doubt very much whether this one will be as great as the first, for at the concert on March 10th I took in one hundred and twelve louis d'or. But fifty to sixty louis d'or are not to be despised either and, if there are more, one simply pockets them. Not a farthing is paid at the door. But whoever is without a ticket is not admitted, no matter who he is. My friends sell the tickets a week beforehand, each for a laubthaler or a federthaler, four of

[1] Joseph Wenzeslaus, Prince von Fürstenberg, himself a performer on the clavier and violoncello, collected his own Kapelle, which Franz Anton Martelli conducted, 1762–1770.
[2] The word is a corruption of the English 'country dance'. Mozart wrote a number of contredanses, especially during the years 1788, 1789 and 1791, for the masked balls at the Viennese court.

which make a louis d'or; and they collect the money. But most of the tickets, in blocks of twelve and twenty-four, are given to ladies, who sell them the more easily, as out of politeness one cannot refuse to buy them. *Est modus in rebus*[1], or, in our language, *Frenchmen like to be fooled*. On the billet (which is written on a card and bears my seal) there are only these words: Au Théâtre de M. Félix, rue et Porte St. Honoré, ce lundi 9 avril à six heures du soir. That is a hall in the house of a distinguished gentleman, in which there is a small theatre where the nobles often act and produce plays among themselves; and I got this room through Madame de Clermont, who lives in the house. But the permission to hold the two concerts there is something quite exceptional and is directly against the privilege which the King has given to the Opera, the Concert Spirituel[2] and the French and Italian theatres; and this permission had to be obtained from M. de Sartine, Lieutenant-General of Police, by the Duc de Chartres, Duc de Duras, Comte de Tessé and many of the leading ladies who sent messengers and wrote applications in their own hand.[3]

I beg you to have a Mass said for us every day for eight days after April 10th. You can distribute them as you like, provided that four are said at Loreto at the Holy Child and four at an altar of Our Lady. I only ask you to observe for certain the days I mention. Should this letter not arrive until after April 12th, though I think it will arrive before, please see that the Masses are begun on the following day. There are important reasons.[4]

And now it is time to tell you something about my two friends from Saxony, Baron von Hopfgarten and Baron von Bose.[5] They left here for Italy about two months ago and were bound for Vienna via Carinthia or Salzburg. I gave them a short letter for you, mentioning what I now write. If they travel through Salzburg, please assist them, so that they may not only see the sights of the place but also have due honour shown to them at court. For I myself have witnessed the great honours which these gentlemen received at the courts of the Elector of Bavaria, at Ludwigsburg, at the Palatine Court at Schwetzingen, at Mainz, at Brussels from Prince Karl and here at Versailles. They have been our loyal travelling companions. Sometimes they ordered our lodgings, sometimes we ordered theirs. Here you will find two men who have everything which honest men should have in this world; and, although they are both Lutherans,

---

[1] i.e. there is a limit in things.

[2] A great French musical institution, founded under Louis XV in 1725, which came to an end during the Revolution. As the Opera House was closed on important religious festivals, A. D. Philidor (1681–1728) obtained permission to arrange concerts on these days, pledging himself to perform neither French nor operatic music. The number of concerts in the year never exceeded twenty-four. The 'Concert Spirituel' formed the model for other public concerts and from it the history of concert-giving in the eighteenth century developed.

[3] See Leopold Mozart's letter no. 284b, in which he goes over this incident for the benefit of his son, who is on his way to Paris.

[4] Possibly refers to the Mozarts' approaching journey to London, during which they would cross the sea for the first time.   [5] See p. 22.

yet they are Lutherans of a different type and men from whose conversation I have often profited much. When parting, Baron von Bose gave Wolfgang as a remembrance a beautiful book containing spiritual thoughts in verse,[1] and wrote the following lines in front:

> Take this book, little seven-year-old Orpheus, from the hand of your admirer and friend! Read it often—and feel its divine songs and lend them (in these blissful hours of emotion) your irresistible harmonies; so that the heartless despiser of religion may read them—and pause—may hear them—and fall down and worship God.
>
> FRIEDRICH KARL, Baron von Bose

These two gentlemen can tell you a hundred things about our journey, and their company will afford you a thousand pleasures. If they go to Salzburg they will turn up after the Ascensa[2] in Venice. The taller of the two is Baron Hopfgarten and the little one is Baron von Bose.

We have by this time made the acquaintance of all the foreign envoys in Paris. The English Ambassador, Mylord Bedford, and his son are very partial to us; and the Russian Prince Galitzin[3] loves us as if we were his children. In a few days the sonatas will be ready, which little Master Wolfgang has dedicated to the Comtesse de Tessé. They would have been ready before; but the Countess absolutely refused to accept the dedication written by our best friend, M. Grimm.[4] So it had to be altered; and as she is usually in Versailles, we have had to wait all this time for an answer. It is a pity that this dedication was not allowed to be engraved. But the Countess refuses to be praised; and in this dedication both she and my boy are very vividly described. The Comtesse de Tessé has given Wolfgang another gold watch and Nannerl a gold box.[5]

But now you must know who this man is, this great friend of mine, to whom I owe everything here, this M. Grimm. He is secretary to the Duc d'Orléans and he is a man of learning and a great friend of humanity. All my other letters and recommendations brought me nothing; even those from the French Ambassador in Vienna, the Imperial Ambassador in Paris and all the letters of introduction from our Minister in Brussels, Count Cobenzl, Prince Conti, Duchesse d'Aiguillon and all the others, a whole litany of whom I could write down. M. Grimm alone, to whom I had a letter from a Frankfurt merchant's wife, has done everything. He

---

[1] Nissen, p. 61, mentions Gellert's *Geistliche Oden und Lieder* (1757) as the book, Gellert being the outstanding Protestant writer of sacred poems.

[2] The period around Ascension Day, one of the principal musical seasons in Venice.

[3] Dimitri Alexeivich Galitzin (1734–1803), Russian Ambassador to France (1763) and Holland (1769) and an intimate friend of Voltaire and Diderot.

[4] Friedrich Melchior Grimm (1723–1807) was the son of a German pastor in Regensburg. He studied in Leipzig, came to Paris in 1749, and in 1755 became secretary to the Duc d'Orléans. He was a friend of Diderot, d'Alembert, Rousseau, etc. He founded the famous *Correspondance Littéraire*, which survived till 1790.

[5] This sentence is paraphrased from Leopold Mozart's travel notes (*MBA* No. 76).

brought our business to court. He arranged for the first concert and he paid me on his own account eighty louis d'or, that is to say, he got rid of three hundred and twenty tickets. In addition he paid for the lighting, as more than sixty large wax candles were burnt. Well, this M. Grimm secured permission for the first concert and is now arranging for the second, for which one hundred tickets have already been sold. So you see what a man can do who has good sense and a kind heart. He comes from Regensburg. But he has been in Paris for over fifteen years already and knows how to launch everything in the right direction, so that it is bound to turn out as he wishes.

★

[*Written on the cover*]   [*Autograph in the Mozarteum, Salzburg*]

My children and my wife send their greetings to all. M. de Mechel,[1] a copper-engraver, is working himself to death to engrave our portraits, which M. de Carmontelle (an amateur)[2] has painted excellently well. Wolfgang is playing the clavier, I am standing behind his chair playing the violin, Nannerl is leaning on the clavecin with one arm, while in the other hand she is holding music, as if she were singing.

(26) Leopold Mozart to Lorenz Hagenauer, Salzburg

[*Extract*]   [*Copy in the Mozarteum, Salzburg*]

LONDON, 25 *April* 1764[3]

Thank God, we have safely crossed the Maxglanerbach.[4] Yet we have not done so without making a heavy contribution in vomiting. I, however, had the worst time of it. But we saved money which would have been spent on emetics; and, thank God, we are all well. Whoever has too much money should just take a journey from Paris to London; for his purse will certainly be lightened. We had the honour of spending four louis d'or in Calais,[5] although we did not take a single meal at home, but took them with the Procureur du Roi et de l'Amirauté, with whom we also left our carriage. As soon as you arrive at Dover, it is even worse; and when you land from the boat, you find yourself surrounded by

---

[1] See p. 33, n. 1. Possibly Mechel engraved the Carmontelle portrait under the direction of J. B. Delafosse, who signed it.

[2] L. C. de Carmontelle (1716–1806), painter and writer. He was a protégé of the Duc d' Orléans. See illustration no. 2.

[3] According to Nissen, p. 65, the Mozarts left Paris on 10 April. In his *Reiseaufzeichnungen* (*MBA* No. 99) Leopold Mozart states that they arrived in London on 23 April. For an account of their stay of fifteen months in England see C. F. Pohl, *Mozart und Haydn in London*, Vienna, 1867, Part II. p. 93 ff.

[4] i.e. the English Channel. The allusion is to a tiny stream at Maxglan, a suburb of Salzburg. See p. 36, n. 2.

[5] Under Calais Nannerl noted in her diary (reproduced in Leopold Mozart's *Reiseaufzeichnungen*, p. 59): 'I saw how the sea runs away and comes back again'. See *MBA*, No. 95.

thirty to forty people who are all 'your most obedient servant' and who want to snatch your luggage from your own servants in order to carry it to the inn, after which they must be paid what they demand. I had to pay three louis d'or for the crossing, for I took a boat for my family, for which one has to pay five louis d'or. I therefore took with me four other passengers, who each paid half a louis d'or. To be landed in a small boat at ✳ Dover from the large boat each person has to pay half a federthaler. So I had to pay six small or three large laubthaler, for I had two servants with me and had taken seven post-horses as far as Calais, as one servant rode. The second servant was an Italian called Porta, who has done this journey eight times already, so that all my friends in Paris advised me to take him with me. It was a very good thing too, for he arranged everything well and did all the bargaining. In London everyone seems to me to be in fancy dress; and you cannot imagine what my wife and my little girl look like in English hats and I and our big Wolfgang in English clothes. My next letter will tell you more. We greet you.

MOZART

My address is:
> À Monsieur Mozart, at the house of Mr. Cousin,
>> haircutter in Cecil Court,
>>> St. Martin's Lane,
>>>> at
>>>>> London.[1]

(27) Leopold Mozart to Lorenz Hagenauer, Salzburg

[Extract]   [Copy in the Staatsbibliothek Preussischer Kulturbesitz, West Berlin]

MONSIEUR!   LONDON, 28 May 1764

You know that the farther away an object is, the smaller does it seem to the eye; and so it is with my letters. My handwriting becomes smaller according to the distance I am from Salzburg. If we were to sail over to America, my letters would probably become quite illegible. For a mere letter without a cover the cost from here to Germany is a shilling and another shilling for the cover, so that a letter with a cover costs two shillings. A guinea is 21 shillings and is equal in value to the louis d'or, for at Dover the banker Miné, who had been recommended to me in Paris, gave me 12 guineas for 12 louis d'or. French money is not accepted here. You can work out, therefore, the value of a shilling. In her letter to Paris our most gracious Frau Hagenauer suggested: 'Perhaps even to England and Holland?' When I left Salzburg I had not quite decided to come to

---

[1] The Mozarts spent the first night at the coach-inn 'The White Bear' in Piccadilly (*Reiseaufzeichnungen*, p. 33), and then moved to their lodgings. See *MBA*, No. 99.

England. But as everybody, in Paris particularly, urged us to go to London, I made up my mind to do so. And now by the help of God we are
★ here. But we shall not go to Holland, that I can assure everyone.[1] We still do not know how we shall fare. We really ought to have come here in winter.

On April 27th we were with the King and Queen[2] in the Queen's Palace[3] in St. James's Park; so that by the fifth day after our arrival we were already at court.[4] The present was only twenty-four guineas, which we received immediately on leaving the King's apartment, but the graciousness with which both His Majesty the King and Her Majesty the Queen received us cannot be described. In short, their easy manner and friendly ways made us forget that they were the King and Queen of England. At all courts up to the present we have been received with extraordinary courtesy. But the welcome which we have been given here exceeds all others. A week later we were walking in St. James's Park. The King came along driving with the Queen and, although we all had on different clothes, they recognized us nevertheless and not only greeted us, but the King opened the window, leaned out and saluted us and especially
★ our Master Wolfgang, nodding to us and waving his hand.

In addition to all his kindnesses M. Grimm, our sworn friend, who did everything for us in Paris, gave Nannerl on our departure a gold watch and Wolfgang a fruit-knife such as is used in Paris with glacé fruits, the handle of which is of mother-of-pearl set in gold. It has two blades, one
★ of gold and the other of silver. I intended to send off this letter a week ago. I was, however, not only prevented from doing so, but I wanted to wait for some news. But I have nothing more to tell, except that on May 19th we were again with the King and Queen from six to ten in the evening, when the only other people present were the two princes, who are the King's brothers, and another, the brother of the Queen. When we left the room we were again handed twenty-four guineas. If this happens every three or four weeks, we can put up with it! Now we are going to give on June 5th[5] a so-called benefit concert or *concerto al nostro profitto*. It is really not the time to give such concerts and little profit is to be expected from them, for the season is over and the expenses of an undertaking of this kind

---

[1] Leopold Mozart, pressed to do so by the Dutch minister in London (see p. 58), took his family to Holland in September 1765. They remained there until the end of April 1766.

[2] George III, then twenty-seven years old, who since 1761 had been married to Charlotte Sophie von Mecklenburg-Strelitz, then twenty-one. Both were devoted to music and the Queen sang and played on the clavier tolerably well.

[3] Buckingham House, built in 1703 by the Duke of Buckingham, and bought by the Crown in 1720.

[4] Nannerl and Wolfgang performed at court on 27 April, 19 May and 25 October. See Leopold Mozart's *Reiseaufzeichnungen*, p. 33, and *MBA*, No. 99.

[5] The *Public Advertiser* announced a concert on 17 May, in Hickford's Room, Brewer Street, Golden Square, at which Master Mozart was to appear. This concert was postponed until 22 May, and even then Mozart, who was indisposed, did not perform. See *MDB*, p. 33 f.

amount to forty guineas. But since the King's birthday is on the 4th, many of the nobility will come up to town from the country. So we must take the risk and make use of this opportunity to become known. Each person pays half a guinea and, if it were winter, I could certainly count on six hundred persons, that is, three hundred guineas. Now, however, they all go to the pleasure gardens and into the country. Basta! Everything will certainly succeed, if with God's help we keep well and if He only keeps our invincible Wolfgang in good health. The King placed before him not only works of Wagenseil,[1] but those of Bach,[2] Abel[3] and Handel,[4] and he played off everything *prima vista*. He played so splendidly on the King's organ that they all value his organ-playing more highly than his clavier-playing. Then he accompanied the Queen in an aria which she sang, and also a flautist[5] who played a solo. Finally he took the bass part of some airs of Handel (which happened to be lying there) and played the most beautiful melody on it and in such a manner that everyone was amazed. In short, what he knew when we left Salzburg is a mere shadow compared with what he knows now. It exceeds all that one can imagine. He greets you from the clavier, where at the moment he is seated, playing through Kapellmeister Bach's trio.[6] We also send you greetings. Not a day passes without Wolfgang's talking at least thirty times of Salzburg and of his and our friends and patrons. He has now continually in his head an opera which he wants to produce there with several young people. I have already had to count up all the players whom he has noted down for his orchestra, among whom Kolb and Ranftl are often mentioned.

(28) *Leopold Mozart to Lorenz Hagenauer, Salzburg*

[*Extract*]   [*Copy in the Staatsbibliothek Preussischer Kulturbesitz, West Berlin*]

MONSIEUR!   LONDON, 8 *June* 1764

With the greatest pleasure in the world I received on June 6th your letter of May 21st, which therefore must have been wafted over by a

---

[1] Georg Christoph Wagenseil (1715–1777) of Vienna, composer to the Imperial court and music-master to the Empress Maria Theresia and her children.

[2] Johann Christian Bach (1735–1782), the youngest son of Johann Sebastian Bach, was trained by his brother Philipp Emanuel Bach in Berlin, then went to Milan and Bologna, where he studied under Padre Martini. In 1762 he came to London, where his operas *Orione* and *Zanaïda* were performed in 1763 and a third one, *Adriano in Siria*, in 1765.

[3] Karl Friedrich Abel (1723–1787), perhaps a pupil of J. S. Bach, had entered the Dresden court orchestra by 1743. He visited London in 1759 and in 1765 was appointed chamber musician to Queen Charlotte. He was a distinguished performer on the viola da gamba and founded in 1765 with J. C. Bach, with whom he lived, the famous Bach-Abel subscription concerts, fifteen concerts a year, an undertaking which lasted until 1781.

[4] George III's favourite composer.

[5] Probably Tacet, a frequent performer at the Bach-Abel concerts. See Leopold Mozart's *Reiseaufzeichnungen*, p. 34 and MBA, No. 99.

[6] WSF, vol. i. p. 104, suggest that this was one of the trios in J. C. Bach's Op. 2, *Six sonates pour le clavecin, accompagnées d'un violon ou flute traversière et d'un violoncelle*, published in London in 1763.

favourable wind. I am infinitely glad that my first letter reached you safely and I trust that the second one, which I sent off on the 20th, has arrived in the meantime.

★

I have had another shock, that is, the shock of taking in one hundred guineas in three hours. Fortunately it is now over. I have already told you that everyone is at present out of town. June 5th was the only day on which a concert could be attempted, because the King's birthday was on the 4th, and the reason why we gave it then was in order to become known. We had a week, or rather two or three days only, in which to distribute the 'billets', for before that date there was hardly anyone in London. But, although for this kind of concert four to eight weeks are usually necessary for the distribution of the 'billets', which here they call 'tickets', to the amazement of everyone there were present more than a couple of hundred persons, including the leading people in all London; not only all the ambassadors, but the principal families in England attended it and everyone was delighted. I cannot say whether I shall have a profit of one hundred guineas, as I have not yet received the money for thirty-six tickets from Mylord March[1] and for forty tickets from a friend in town and from various others; and the expenses are surprisingly great. But the profit will certainly not be less than ninety guineas. Now listen to a few details about the expenses. The hall without lighting and music-stands costs five guineas. Each clavier, of which I have had to have two on account of the concerto

★ for two claviers, costs half a guinea. The first violin gets three guineas and so on; and all who play the solos and concertos three, four and five guineas. The ordinary players receive each half a guinea and so forth. But, fortunately for me, all the musicians as well as the hall and everything else only cost me twenty guineas, because most of the performers would not accept anything. Well, God be praised, that is over and we have made

★ something.

My greetings to Herr Schachtner[2] and please thank him from me and from my wife and children for his friendly remembrances. I cannot send him any details other than what he will find in the newspapers, in the letters which I have written to you, and especially in my last one. What it all amounts to is this, that my little girl, although she is only twelve years old, is one of the most skilful players in Europe, and that, in a word, my boy knows in this his eighth year what one would expect only from a man

---

[1] William Douglas (1724–1810), 3rd Earl of March, succeeded his cousin as fourth Duke of Queensberry in 1778. He was a well-known man about town and a great patron of the turf and the opera. Later in life he was known as 'old Q', under which name he is constantly referred to by Horace Walpole.

[2] Johann Andreas Schachtner (1731–1795) had been court trumpeter in Salzburg since 1754. He was closely connected later with Mozart as the translator into German of the Italian libretto of Idomeneo and the author of the text of Zaide. After Mozart's death he wrote to Nannerl the famous letter of April 1792, describing her brother's childhood. See Abert, vol. i. p. 26 ff. and MBA, No. 1210.

of forty. Indeed only he who sees and hears him can believe it. You your-self and all our Salzburg friends have no idea of Wolfgang's progress; for he is quite different now.

I must close, for the post is going.
I am
your obedient servant

MOZART

PS.—My wife and I, Nannerl and our all-powerful Wolfgang send greetings to you, to your whole household and to all Salzburg.

(29) *Leopold Mozart to Lorenz Hagenauer, Salzburg*

[*Extract*]   [*Copy in the Staatsbibliothek Preussischer Kulturbesitz, West Berlin*]

MONSIEUR!   LONDON, 28 *June* 1764

I have much pleasure in informing you that I have again deposited ✷ with the bankers Loubier et Tessier a small sum of 100 guineas, which I could arrange to be paid to someone at Salzburg who might wish to use it in this country.

At the end of next week we are going to Tunbridge,[1] about thirty ✷ English miles from London, a distance which can be covered by the mail coach in three or four hours, for an English mile is not more than a German quarter of an hour. There are wells there and it lies in a corner between the east and the south. In July and August many of the nobility assemble in Tunbridge, for now nobody who has means and leisure re-mains in London.

On Friday, June 29th, that is, on the Feast of St. Peter and St. Paul, ✷ there will be a concert or benefit at Ranelagh in aid of a newly established Hôpital de femmes en couche,[2] and whoever wishes to attend it must pay five shillings entrance. I am letting Wolfgang play a concerto on the organ at this concert[3] in order to perform thereby the act of an English patriot who, as far as in him lies, endeavours to further the usefulness of this hospital which has been established *pro bono publico*. That is, you see, one way of winning the affection of this quite exceptional nation.

I send greetings, and so do my wife and Nannerl and little Wolfgang, ✷ who is always thinking of Salzburg.

I am
your old

MOZART ✷

[1] Owing to Leopold Mozart's illness this plan was not carried out.
[2] Probably the Lying-in Hospital (Surrey), the foundation-stone of which was laid in 1765.
[3] The notice of this concert in the *Public Advertiser* of June 26th described Mozart as 'the most extraordinary prodigy and most amazing genius that has appeared in any age', and stated that this boy of seven years (Mozart was then eight and a half) would perform on the harpsichord and organ works of his own composition. See *MDB*, p. 36 f.

(30) Leopold Mozart to Lorenz Hagenauer, Salzburg

[Extract]   [Copy in the Staatsbibliothek Preussischer Kulturbesitz, West Berlin]

MONSIEUR,   LONDON, 3 August 1764

Do not be frightened! But prepare your heart to hear one of the saddest events. Perhaps you will have already noticed my condition from my handwriting. Almighty God has visited me with a sudden and severe illness [which I contracted after a chill caught on my way home from a concert held at Mylord Thanet's], [1] and which I feel too weak to describe. Well! I have been clystered, purged and bled too on account of a severe inflammation of my throat. That is all over now and the doctors declare that I have no fever and tell me to eat. But I feel like a child. My stomach does not fancy anything and I am so frail that I can hardly think sensibly.

9 August 1764 [2]

I congratulate you on your name-day. I intended to write to you immediately after I received your welcome letter. But I was far too weak. I am now in a spot outside the town, [3] where I have been carried in a sedan-chair, in order to get more appetite and fresh strength from the good air. It has one of the most beautiful views in the world. Wherever I turn my eyes, I only see gardens and in the distance the finest castles; and the house in which I am living has a lovely garden.

It depends on the grace of God whether He will preserve my life. His most holy will be done.

(31) Leopold Mozart to Lorenz Hagenauer, Salzburg

[Extract]   [Copy in the Staatsbibliothek Preussischer Kulturbesitz, West Berlin]

CHELSEA near LONDON, 13 September 1764

MONSIEUR,

I notice that our letters have usually taken 16 to 17 days, for up to the present I have always received one from you on the 17th, or at any rate early on the 18th day. I thank you most humbly for having carried out so

---

[1] This clause is paraphrased from Letter 31. See the description on p. 51.

Sackville Tufton, 8th Earl of Thanet (1733–1786), had succeeded to the title in 1753. C. F. Pohl, *op. cit.* p. 103, n. 2, states that the Tufton family were devoted to the arts, mentioning the fact that in 1732 six cantatas by H. Carey appeared with a dedication to the father of the eighth Earl.   [2] This letter was finished in Chelsea.

[3] Chelsea was then a village two miles from London, proverbial for its healthy situation. The Mozart family took a house belonging to a Dr. Randal in Fivefields-Row (now 180 Ebury Street), where, according to the *Reiseaufzeichnungen*, p. 34 (*MBA*, No. 99), they spent seven weeks. It was here that Mozart composed his first symphonies, probably K. 16, 19, App. 223 [19a], App. 222 [19b], etc.

accurately my request for Masses. I now state that every day, although my progress is slow, I am feeling a little better, so that I am confident that I have no internal disorder. So that you may know, however, how my illness started, I must tell you that in England there is a kind of native complaint, which is called a '*cold*'. That is why you hardly ever see people wearing summer clothes. They all wear cloth garments. This so-called '*cold*' in the case of people who are not constitutionally sound, becomes so dangerous that in many cases it develops into a '*consumption*' as they call it here; but I call it '*febrem lentam*';[1] and the wisest course for such people to adopt is to leave England and cross the sea; and many instances can be found of people recovering their health on leaving this country. I caught this '*cold*' unexpectedly and in the following way. On July 8th at six in the evening we were to go to Mylord Thanet's.[2] Before six I sent out to the stands where carriages are to be found, but not one was to be had. It was Sunday, so all had been hired. It was an exceedingly fine and very hot day. I sent for a sedan-chair, put my two children into it and walked behind, as the weather was unusually lovely. But I had forgotten how fast the bearers stride along here; and I soon had a taste of it. I can walk fairly quickly, as you know, and my stoutness does not prevent me from doing so. But, before we arrived at Mylord Thanet's I often thought that I should have to give up; for London is not like Salzburg. And I perspired as profusely as it is possible for a man to do. I had only a silk waistcoat on, though I was wearing a cloth coat, which I buttoned up immediately on arriving at Mylord Thanet's. But it was to no purpose. The evening was cool and all the windows were open. We stayed until eleven o'clock and I at once felt ill and engaged a second sedan-chair to take me home. Yet until the 14th, although I did not feel well, I went about and tried to cure myself by perspiring, which is the remedy generally adopted here. But it was no good.

My wife and children send their greetings. My wife has had a great deal to do lately on account of my illness, and, as you may imagine, she has had a great many anxieties. In Chelsea we had our food sent to us at first from an eating-house; but as it was so poor, my wife began to do our cooking and we are now in such good trim that when we return to town next week we shall continue to do our own housekeeping. Perhaps too my wife, who has become very thin, will get a little fatter.

You yourself will have probably gathered that I shall certainly spend at least the whole winter here, and that, God willing, I shall make in London my chief profit of some thousands of gulden. I am now in a city which no one at our Salzburg court has ever yet dared to visit and which perhaps

---

[1] i.e. a slow fever.
[2] Leopold Mozart in his *Reiseaufzeichnungen*, p. 35, mentions Mylord Thanet, Grosvenor Square. See *MBA*, No. 99.

no one will ever visit in future. *Aut Caesar, aut nihil.*[1] We have come to our long journey's end. Once I leave England, I shall never see guineas again. So we must make the most of our opportunity. If only God in His graciousness grants us good health, we need not worry about the guineas. I am only sorry that I am obliged to spend what I might have saved. But it was God's will. Both in Salzburg and in London we are in His hands. He knows how good my intentions are. During the coming months I shall have to use every effort to win over the aristocracy and this will take a lot of galloping round and hard work. But if I achieve the object which
★ I have set myself, I shall haul in a fine fish or rather a good catch of guineas.

(32) *Leopold Mozart to Lorenz Hagenauer, Salzburg*

[*Extract*]   [*Copy in the Staatsbibliothek Preussischer Kulturbesitz, West Berlin*]

MONSIEUR!   LONDON,[2] 27 *November* 1764

Do not be surprised that I am rather late in replying. I have more to do than most people would imagine, although the nobility are not in town and Parliament, contrary to usage, is not assembling until January 10th of next year[3] and therefore guineas are not yet flying about and I am still living on my purse. Yet it will soon be high time for me to fill it up again, for since the beginning of July I have spent over one hundred and seventy guineas. In addition I have the heavy expense of having six sonatas[4] of our Master Wolfgang engraved and printed, which (at her
★ own request) are being dedicated to the Queen of Great Britain.

I and all my family send you and your wife millions of congratulations on the beginning of the new career of your son Cajetan.[5] I have a very good opinion of him and, since you are ever a good and sensible father, you will certainly welcome him with open arms and a smiling face when he comes home. As he has always been a quiet and placid boy, he will only do what is most wholesome for his spiritual welfare. On that account, he is doing his novitiate. Little Wolfgang wept when I read out this portion

    1 i.e. Either Caesar or nothing.
    2 On their return to town about September 25th the Mozarts took lodgings at Mr. Thomas Williamson's, 15 Thrift Street (now Frith Street), Soho. The house, which was rebuilt in 1858, occupied the site of the present no. 21, on the east side of the street. See F. G. Edwards, *Musical Haunts in London*, 1895, p. 46.
    3 The Parliament of 1765, which passed the Stamp Act, was opened by the King on January 10th.
    4 K. 10-15. They were called *six sonates pour le clavecin qui peuvent se jouer avec l'accompagnement de violon ou flaute traversière*, and the date of dedication was 18 January 1765. They were engraved at Leopold Mozart's expense. Wolfgang received from the Queen 50 guineas and the work was on sale at their lodgings from March 20th.
    5 Dominicus (Cajetan) Hagenauer entered the monastery of St. Peter at Salzburg in 1764 and in 1786 became abbot of the monastery. A Latin diary which he kept in 1769 mentions Mozart frequently. For the first Mass which Father Dominicus celebrated in October 1769, Mozart wrote his mass K. 66 (the Pater Dominicus Mass).

of your letter and, when he was asked why, he said that he was grieved, as he believed that he would never see him again. But we told him that it would not be so. He remembered that your son had often caught a fly for him and that he used to blow the organ and bring him his air-gun. As soon as he returns to Salzburg he is going to St. Peter's[1] and Mr. Cajetan is to catch a fly for him and shoot with him. So he has donned the garb of his order and entered upon his novitiate on the same day on which about seventeen years ago[2] I joined the order of patched trousers and made my profession at Aigen[3] with my wife. ✵

(33) *Leopold Mozart to Lorenz Hagenauer, Salzburg*

[*Extract*]   [*Copy in the Staatsbibliothek Preussischer Kulturbesitz, West Berlin*]

MONSIEUR!   LONDON, 3 *December* 1764

You will have received my letter of November 27th.[4] Here is the letter accompanying the sonatas.[5]

Whoever wants to buy these sonatas will have to pay forty-five kreuzer for each part, that is, one gulden, thirty kreuzer for both parts or for all four sonatas (since each part consists of two sonatas). Will you please see that a detailed notice about them is put in the Salzburg papers? In Paris the price of each part is four livres, four sous, as you will see on the title-page; a great difference from the price of forty-five kreuzer. In Frankfurt each part is being sold at one gulden, thirty kreuzer. I regret that a few mistakes have remained in the engraving, even after the corrections were made. The woman who engraved them and I were at too great a distance; and, as everything was done hurriedly, I had no time to obtain a revised proof. That is the reason why especially in Œuvre IIe in the last trio you will find three consecutive fifths in the violin part,[6] which my young gentleman perpetrated and which, although I corrected them, old Madame Vendôme left in. On the other hand, they are a proof that our little Wolfgang composed them himself, which, perhaps quite naturally, everyone will not believe. Well, it is so, all the same. My little Wolfgang sends greetings to you all and especially to Herr Spitzeder and asks him to perform these sonatas before His Grace, Wenzel playing the violin part. ✵

1 The famous Abbey of St. Peter in Salzburg, which was founded by St. Rupert in 696, and where the Archbishops lived until 1110.
2 Leopold Mozart and his wife were married on 21 November 1747.
3 A village about seven miles from Salzburg.
4 Letter 32.
5 Œuvre I (K. 6, 7) and Œuvre II (K. 8, 9), which had been engraved in Paris.
6 It was in the second minuet of the fourth sonata (K. 9) that Mozart displayed his lack of experience. In subsequent editions this succession was replaced by a succession of sixths.

On October 25th, the King's Coronation Day,[1] we were with the King and Queen from six to ten.[2]

(34) *Leopold Mozart to Lorenz Hagenauer, Salzburg*

[*Extract*]   [*Copy in the Staatsbibliothek Preussischer Kulturbesitz, West Berlin*]

MONSIEUR,   LONDON, 8 *February* 1765

★   On the evening of the 15th we are giving a concert, which will probably bring me in about one hundred and fifty guineas. Whether I shall still make anything after that and, if so, what, I do not know. By postponing the summoning of Parliament (which usually assembles two months earlier) the King has dealt upon the whole a severe blow at all arts and sciences.[3] To explain this would take too long.

This winter, nobody is making much money except Manzuoli[4] and a few others in the opera. Manzuoli is getting 1500 pounds sterling for this season and the money has had to be guaranteed in Italy, as the previous impresario De Giardini[5] went bankrupt last year; otherwise Manzuoli would not have come to London. In addition he is giving a benefit,[6] that is, an evening recital for himself, so that this winter he will be drawing more than 20,000 German gulden. He is the only person whom they have had to pay decently in order to set the opera on its feet again. On the other hand, five or six operas are being performed. The first was 'Ezio',[7] the second 'Berenice',[8] both so-called pasticci of different masters, the third 'Adriano in Syria', newly composed by Signor Bach.[9] And I know that a

---

[1] C. F. Pohl, *op. cit.* p. 109, draws attention to a slip of Leopold Mozart, inasmuch as it was the anniversary, not of the King's coronation (which took place on 22 September 1761), but of his accession to the throne in 1760.

[2] Although the Mozarts did not leave London until 24 July 1765, this was the last time the children performed at court.

[3] See p. 52.

[4] Giovanni Manzuoli, born *c.* 1720 in Florence, after Farinelli the most famous male soprano of his day. He sang in Madrid and Vienna and came to London for the opera season 1764–1765. Mozart took singing lessons from him and met him later in Florence.

[5] Felice de Giardini (1716–1796), born in Turin, eminent violinist. He first appeared in London in 1750. In 1755 he undertook the management of the Italian opera at the King's Theatre, Haymarket, suffered great financial losses, but retained it till 1765. Contrary to Leopold Mozart's statement, he was manager during the season 1764–1765.

[6] Manzuoli produced for his benefit Giardini's opera *Il Rè pastore* on 7 March 1765, and according to the *Gentleman's Magazine*, March 1765, made a profit of 1000 guineas. Ten years later Mozart set the same text to music.

[7] Performed 24 November 1764, a pasticcio consisting of pieces by several composers, a form of opera very common in the eighteenth century. For a repetition of *Ezio* Mozart composed his first aria 'Va, dal furor portata' (K. 21 [19c]).

[8] Performed 1 February 1765, a pasticcio of music by seven composers, including J. C. Bach, Galuppi, Vento, Abel.

[9] By Johann Christian Bach, performed 26 January 1765, 'by command of Their Majesties', and repeated seven times.

newly composed 'Demofoonte' by Vento[1] is coming, and then a few more pasticci. I shall tell you about all this later on.

I am writing this letter (to be followed by another very soon) solely in order not to miss the opportunity of sending a few sonatas[2] to Augsburg and Nuremberg. So I beg you to send thirty copies of each part, that is, sixty copies in all, to Herr Johann Jacob Lotter,[3] and the same number to Herr Haffner, lute-player in Nuremberg.[4] You will note that each part has ★ been sold at the price of one gulden, thirty kreuzer, but, as they are a bit of a rarity, I shall let them go to the natives of Salzburg half price. Please have this inserted in our local newspapers, adding that the little composer wants to let his fellow townsmen have each part for forty-five kreuzer, or both parts for one gulden, thirty kreuzer, in order to encourage the young people of Salzburg to study music with zest.

We send our greetings to all. Oh, what a lot of things I have to do. ★ The symphonies at the concert will all be by Wolfgang Mozart.[5] I must copy them myself, unless I want to pay one shilling for each sheet. Copying music is a very profitable business here. Our Estlinger[6] would laugh. I send him my congratulations. Addio.

★

(35) *Leopold Mozart to Lorenz Hagenauer, Salzburg*

[*Extract*]   [*Copy in the Staatsbibliothek Preussischer Kulturbesitz, West Berlin*]

MONSIEUR!   LONDON, 19 *March* 1765

I am certain that my last short letter reached you before the end of Salzburg's Lent market and that therefore it arrived in time.[7]

My concert, which I intended to give on February 15th, did not take place until the 21st, and on account of the number of entertainments (which really weary one here) was not so well attended as I had hoped. Nevertheless, I took in about one hundred and thirty guineas. As, however, the expenses connected with it amounted to over twenty-seven

---

[1] Mateo Vento (1735–1776), born in Naples, a famous operatic composer. He was brought by De Giardini in 1763 to London, where he composed a number of operas. His *Demofoonte* was performed on 2 March 1765, and was repeated thirteen times.

[2] Mozart's Œuvre I and Œuvre II (K. 6-9).

[3] Johann Jacob Lotter, music publisher in Augsburg. He published in 1756 Leopold Mozart's *Violinschule*. Leopold Mozart corresponded frequently with him. Schurig, vol. i. pp. 58-66, gives a selection of these letters; those surviving appear complete in *MBA*.

[4] Johann Ulrich Haffner, music publisher in Nuremberg.

[5] The concert was postponed to February 18th and again to February 21st, when it was held in the Little Theatre, Haymarket, at 6 P.M. 'in order to allow the nobility to attend other assemblies'. The notice added that 'all the ouvertures (i.e. symphonies) are by this amazing composer, who is only eight years old'. Mozart was then nine. See *MDB*, pp. 40–42. The symphonies which were performed could have been K. 16, K. 19, K. App. 223 [19a] (rediscovered in 1981) and K. App. 222 [19b]. See p. 50, n. 3.

[6] A Salzburg music copyist.

[7] Probably refers to Letter 34 and to the opportunity of sending copies of Mozart's first printed works to Augsburg and Nuremberg.

guineas, I have not made much more than one hundred guineas.[1]

I know, however, what the reason is, and why we are not being treated more generously, although since our arrival in London we have made a few hundred guineas. I did not accept a proposal which was made to me. But what is the use of saying much about a matter upon which I have decided deliberately after mature consideration and several sleepless nights and which is now done with, as I will not bring up my children in such a dangerous place (where the majority of the inhabitants have no religion and where one only has evil examples before one). You would be amazed if you saw the way children are brought up here; not to mention other
★ matters connected with religion.

I must ask you to reply to this letter as soon as possible, for, as it is quite likely that I shall leave London at the beginning of May, I must have an
★ answer by the end of April.

The Queen has given our Wolfgang a present of fifty guineas for the
★ dedication of the sonatas.

Please ask our dear friend Spitzeder to forgive me for not yet replying to his very welcome letters. He will surely realise how much a man has to do, who is keeping his whole family in a town where, even with the strictest economy, it costs him 300 pounds sterling a year to do so, and where, in addition, he ought to be saving a little. Has Herr Adlgasser not yet returned to Salzburg? We send him our greetings. Why, of course we
★ know Mr. Bach. I must close, for the post is going.

(36) *Leopold Mozart to Lorenz Hagenauer, Salzburg*

[*Extract*]   [*Copy in the Staatsbibliothek Preussischer Kulturbesitz, West Berlin*]

MONSIEUR!   LONDON, 18 *April* 1765

I was delighted to receive your letter. You have made most excellent
★ arrangements. At the moment I have very little news to send you.

As for my departure, I have no more definite news; and any sensible person must realize that it is not an easy matter to decide. It will take us all our time to get away from here. The very sight of the luggage we have to pack makes me perspire. Just think! We have been in England for a whole year. Why, we have practically made our home here, so that to take our departure from England requires even more preparation than when we
★ left Salzburg.

<hr>

[1] The next and last concert was held on 13 May 1765. On March 11th the *Public Advertiser* had a notice that the 'prodigies of nature' were giving in six weeks a last concert before their departure from England and that every day from 12 to 3, visitors could come to Mr. Mozart's lodgings in Thrift Street, hear the prodigies perform in private, test them and buy concert tickets, now reduced to five shillings each. Leopold Mozart took the opportunity of selling copies of Mozart's sonatas and engravings of the Carmontelle painting. See *MDB*, p. 43 ff.

(37) Leopold Mozart to Lorenz Hagenauer, Salzburg

[Extract]   [Copy in the Staatsbibliothek Preussischer Kulturbesitz, West Berlin]

Monsieur!   London, 9 July 1765

No doubt you will all be thinking that we have long ago swum over the sea. But it has been impossible to get away. We are now in London and once we leave we cannot return to England in three days. So I simply ⋆ cannot hurry.   ⋆

I beg you when you receive this letter to arrange immediately for six Masses to be said, two at the Holy Child at Loreto, two in the Parish and two at Maria-Plain. These are to prepare our way over the sea.[1]   ⋆

I thought when I left Paris that I had requested my friend M. Grimm to send a number of the portrait engravings[2] to you at Salzburg. As I heard nothing more about this, I enquired recently from him and he replied that I had never said anything about it. I have therefore asked him to send you a large supply, so that if a parcel arrives you will know what it is. Please present a copy to our most gracious lord.[3] These copper engravings were done immediately after our arrival in Paris, when my boy was seven and my little girl eleven. Grimm was responsible for this. In Paris each engraving is sold for twenty-four sous.   ⋆

(38) Leopold Mozart to Lorenz Hagenauer, Salzburg

[Extract]   [Copy in the Staatsbibliothek Preussischer Kulturbesitz, West Berlin]

The Hague,[4] 19 September 1765

You are receiving a letter from the Haag, but not from the Haag[5] near Munich, nor from the Haag which is near Lambach[6] in Austria. No! It is from the Haag in Holland. That will indeed seem very strange to you, the more so as you may have hoped, even if you did not think it, that maybe we were not so far away. We would have been, if not near you, nevertheless already out of Holland, had not an indisposition which first affected my little Wolfgang in Lille and then myself kept us back for four weeks. But now you are going to hear all about the accident which has brought us here, seeing that I had decided to go not to Holland,[7] but to

---

[1] Leopold Mozart was proposing to leave England. The last notice in the *Public Advertiser*, July 11th, stated that the children would play every day from 12 to 3 in the 'Swan and Hoop' tavern, Cornhill, admittance 2s. 6d., and that they would play together on one clavier with the keyboard covered. See *MDB*, p. 45 f.

[2] See p. 44, n. 2.   [3] The Archbishop.

[4] The Mozarts arrived at The Hague on September 11th and stayed at the inn 'La Ville de Paris', described in Leopold Mozart's *Reiseaufzeichnungen*, p. 41, as 'une très mauvaise auberge'. See *MBA*, No. 105.

[5] A village 33 miles from Munich, on the road to Salzburg.

[6] A village about thirty miles from Linz, on the road to Salzburg.   [7] See p. 46.

Milan and home through Venice. The Dutch Envoy in London several times begged us to visit the Prince of Orange at The Hague. But I let this go in by one ear and out by the other. We made preparations for our departure; and so little did I think of going to Holland that I sent *all our furs* and other things in a trunk to Paris. But when on July 24th we had actually left and had driven out of London, we spent a day in Canterbury and then stayed until the end of the month at the country home of an English gentleman[1] in order to see the horse-racing. On the very day of our departure the Dutch Envoy drove to our lodgings and was told that we had gone to Canterbury for the races and would then leave England immediately. He turned up at once in Canterbury and implored me at all costs to go to The Hague, as the Princess of Weilburg,[2] sister of the Prince of Orange, was extremely anxious to see this child, about whom she had heard and read so much. In short, he and everybody talked at me so insistently and the proposal was so attractive that I had to decide to come, the more so as you know that one should not refuse anything to a woman
★ in pregnancy. So I left England on August 1st, and sailed from Dover at ten in the morning. We had most beautiful weather and such a good wind that in three and a half hours we landed at Calais port and took our midday meal with a healthy stomach, as we had not been sick during the crossing. Our plan now was to spend the month of August in Holland, to reach Paris towards the end of September and then move gradually homewards until we should come in sight of the Untersberg.[3]

In Calais we made the acquaintance of the Duchesse de Montmorency
★ and the Prince de Croy; thence I went to Dunkerque. We then drove to Lille, whither the Chevalier de Mezziers, Commandant in Dunkerque,
★ had persuaded us to go. Now we have another proof that our human plans count for nothing. In Lille Wolfgang contracted a very bad cold
★ and when after a few weeks it had improved somewhat, my turn came. This put us back four weeks and I was not very well when I left Lille[4] and was not much better when we arrived in Ghent, where we only stayed a day. Ghent is a large but not a populous town. In the afternoon Wolfgang played on the new organ at the Bernardines. In Antwerp we remained two days on account of Sunday and there Wolfgang played on the big organ in the Cathedral. I should mention that good organs are to be found in Flanders and Brabant. But a great deal could be said here

---

[1] Leopold Mozart's travel notes (*MBA*, No. 99, lines 138–9) refer to 'Mr Horatio Man Esqr.: at Bourn near Canterbury, Kent:' Bourne Place, seven miles south-east of Canterbury, was the mansion house of the manor of Bishopsbourne and, according to Hasted, *History of Kent*, 1790, vol. iii. p. 746, n. (x), Sir Horace Mann resided there for several years, presumably by some arrangement with the owner, Mr. Stephen Beckington. This Horace Mann (1744–1814) was the nephew of Sir Horace Mann, British Minister in Florence and the friend and correspondent of Horace Walpole.
[2] Princess Caroline of Nassau-Weilburg.
[3] The most conspicuous mountain near Salzburg, about 6500 ft.   [4] On September 4th.

about the best of the pictures. Antwerp especially is the place for these. We have been to all the churches and I have never seen more black and white marble and such a wealth of excellent paintings, especially by Rubens, as I have seen here and in Brussels; above all, his 'Descent from the Cross' in the great church in Antwerp surpasses everything one can imagine. I left my carriage in Antwerp and hired one from the post-master to drive as far as Moerdijk. There we crossed a small arm of the sea. On the other side there are coaches ready to drive one as far as Rotterdam, where one then gets into a small boat and is taken almost to the inn. It was a good day's journey from Antwerp to Rotterdam, as it took from half past six in the morning until eight o'clock in the evening. We only spent half a day in Rotterdam, as we left in the afternoon on a trekschuit[1] for The Hague and were already there at seven o'clock. I must confess that I should have been very sorry if I had not seen Holland; for in all the towns of Europe which I have visited, everything for the most part seems to be the same, whereas both the Dutch towns and villages are quite different from all others in Europe. It would take too long to describe them, but I must say that I very much appreciate their cleanliness (which to many of us appears excessive). I should also like to add that I enjoyed seeing the statue of the famous Erasmus of Rotterdam in the square of that city. We have now been eight days at The Hague and have been twice with the Princess and once with the Prince of Orange, who had us fetched and sent home in his carriage. My daughter, however, was not with us. For now her turn has come and she has a very heavy cold on the chest, which is only now beginning to loosen. As soon as she is better, we have to go again to the Prince of Orange, the Princess of Weilburg and the Duke of Wolfenbüttel. The journey here has been paid for. But I shall have to see who is going to pay for the return journey. For I should prefer not to touch the money which is lying in wait for me at Amsterdam.

In Lille on August 26th we heard of the death of the Emperor.[2]

(39) *Leopold Mozart to Lorenz Hagenauer, Salzburg*

[*Extract*]   [*Copy in the Staatsbibliothek Preussischer Kulturbesitz, West Berlin*]

THE HAGUE, 5 *November* 1765

Yes, yes! Most certainly! *Homo proponit, Deus disponit.*[3] I have a sure proof of this. Man cannot escape his fate.

I had to come to Holland against my inclination and though I have not lost my daughter, I have seen her lying well-nigh *in extremis*. Yet who

---

[1] Dutch for a 'barge'.
[2] Francis I, Holy Roman Emperor, died on 18 August 1765.
[3] A favourite quotation of Leopold Mozart. See p. 14.

urged us to come to Holland more than my daughter? Indeed she had the greatest desire to go whither her fate was driving her. You will remember that in my first letter which I wrote from here I told you that she had caught a cold on September 12th, the second day after our arrival. At first it appeared to be of no consequence and even seemed to be getting better, so she did not go to bed. But on the evening of the 26th she suddenly started to shiver and asked to lie down. After the shivering she had fever and I saw that her throat was inflamed. The following day she was no better and I sent for a doctor. To cut a long story short, at four o'clock on the evening of the 28th she was bled; and although her pulse improved somewhat, she still was a little feverish.

★

The doctor himself had given up hope and my poor child, feeling how weak she was, partly realised the danger. I prepared her to resign herself to God's will and not only did she receive Holy Communion but the priest found her in such a serious condition that he gave her the Holy Sacrament of Extreme Unction, for she was often so weak that she could hardly utter what she wanted to say. Whoever could have listened to the conversations which we three, my wife, myself and my daughter, had on several evenings, during which we convinced her of the vanity of this world and the happy death of children, would not have heard it without tears. Meanwhile little Wolfgang in the next room was amusing himself with his music. On October 21st, the same day on which I had the Holy Sacrament given to her at five o'clock in the afternoon, I arranged for a consultation at half past one (which they call here before mid-day). The honest old Professor Zwenke[1] (who no longer attends anybody and whom the Princess of Weilburg sent to me) showed at once that he understood the case much better. First of all he took the child's hand and felt her pulse thoroughly. He put on his glasses and examined her eyes, her tongue and her whole face. Then he had to be told the *statum morbi*.[2] This was the first time that I had especial reason to be grateful for my knowledge of the Latin tongue, for if I had not known that language, Herr Professor would have been told of quite different symptoms. For after the doctor had already been convicted by his conscience that he had made a complete blunder, he had of course to explain and describe the case in such a way as to justify the remedies he had used. But whenever he said anything which was not accurate, I contradicted him as I had already done every time he talked of the lesions, boils, pocks on the lung (or whatever he preferred to call them) which he had diagnosed. He declared more particularly that she was in pain and could not lie on both sides, which was not true and which I contradicted every time he said it.

★

[1] Thomas Zwenke, Director of the School of Anatomy and private physician to the Stadt-holder. See Scheurleer, *Mozarts Verblijf in Nederland*, 's Gravenhage, 1883, p. 76.
[2] i.e. the state of the illness.

All this time, whether asleep or awake, she was delirious and kept talking in her sleep, now in English, now in French, and now in German; and as our travels had given her plenty to chatter about, we often had to laugh in spite of all our distress. This did something to remove the sadness which Wolfgang was feeling on account of his sister. ★

Now it depends upon whether God will graciously allow her to recover her strength or whether some other accident will send her into eternity. We have always trusted to the Divine Will and even before we left Salzburg we prayed to God earnestly to prevent or to bless our intended journey. If my daughter dies, she will die happy. If God grants her life, then we pray to Him to send her later such an innocent and blessed death as she would have now. I hope for the latter. For on that same Sunday when she was very ill, I read the Gospel *'Domine, descende'*. 'Come, Lord! before my daughter dies.' And now on this Sunday the Gospel was: *'Thy daughter slept: thy faith hath helped thee'*. You will find it, if you look it up in the Gospel. But you can easily imagine what a time we have been having, and that all my plans have been suddenly upset. We could not and would not entrust our child to strangers, so for a long time my wife has not been going to bed until six in the morning, when I get up and look after my daughter till noon. Thus my wife and I have divided the time until midday, each of us sleeping about five or six hours. And how long will it be until my daughter, if she is to recover, will be in a fit state to travel? This is the worst season and the weather is getting more severe. Our furs were sent from Calais to Paris, for, according to my reckoning, we should have already left Holland by now. You are always asking me by what route I shall travel home. Did I not write to you that I sent a trunk from Calais to Paris? And you know that I have already left a lot of luggage there. It follows therefore that I must travel through Paris, as I want to do. I shall not lose by it. It was my intention to spend the three months, August, September and October, in Brabant, Holland and Flanders, to stay in Paris during November and to travel home in December so that I should certainly be home *ad Festum S. Thomae.*[1] Now God has upset my calculations and it no longer depends on what I wish, but on the condition of my daughter; and any reasonable person will see that, if God spares her, I cannot expose her capriciously to the obvious danger of losing her life through an inopportune journey. It is easy to understand that I have derived no advantage, but the greatest loss from this accident. And I think that there is sufficient cause for wonder (if one considers it well) how I am in a position to stand these tours and especially in the style in which we travel. For France, England and Holland are countries where one talks, not about pieces of twelve and pennies, but only about louis

---

[1] St. Thomas's day, December 21st.

d'or, guineas, ducats and reitters.[1] Perhaps you do not know what a reitter is? It is a Dutch coin—a whole reitter being worth fourteen Dutch gulden, half a reitter seven Dutch gulden. I shall show them to you. My present expenses are perfectly dreadful, for here one must pay for everything. Everyone knows of course what Holland is. So heavy inroads are made on my purse. Basta! After all, what is money, if only I get away again safe and sound with my family?

Please arrange for a Mass to be said for my daughter at Maria-Plain, one at the Holy Child at Loreto, one in honour of St. Walpurgis[2] and two at Passau on the Mariahilfberg. My little girl has been thinking too of pious Crescentia[3] and has been wanting to have a Mass said in her honour as well. But, as we are not entitled to do this until our Church has come to a decision about this pious person, I leave it to your dear wife to hold a Consistorium about this with some Franciscan fathers, and so to arrange the matter that my daughter shall be satisfied and the ordinances of God and of our church shall not be offended.[4]

★ I have not yet been to Amsterdam. But as soon as my daughter is well enough for me to leave my wife alone with her, I am going to drive there with Wolfgang, but only to spend a few days. By the mail coach it is only a journey of six or seven hours, though it takes longer by water. These are all very curious facts and I shall talk to you about them later on. I shall not fail to do what you want in Amsterdam. In conclusion I hope that you do not think from the circumstances of my daughter's illness and treatment that I took the first doctor I could get. No indeed! He is Dr. Hayman, Physician to the Imperial, Portuguese, Spanish, French and Neapolitan Envoys, all of whom recommended him to me.

★

(40) *Leopold Mozart to Lorenz Hagenauer, Salzburg*

[*Extract*]   [*Copy in the Staatsbibliothek Preussischer Kulturbesitz, West Berlin*]

THE HAGUE, 12 *December* 1765

That you may be relieved at the outset of all anxiety, I now tell you that, thank God, we are all alive. Yes, I can almost say that we are all well.

---

[1] i.e. rijder.

[2] St. Walpurgis, born in Sussex *c*. 710, went to Germany *c*. 750 with some nuns at the request of St. Boniface of Mainz. In 754 she became Abbess of the Benedictine Nunnery of Heidenheim and on the death of her brother Wunnibald, Abbot of the monastery of Heidenheim, she succeeded to his charge and governed the joint community until her death *c*. 779. In 871 her relics were removed to Eichstätt, where a church was built which became a place of pilgrimage. Her festival was celebrated at various times of the year and particularly on May 1st. Walburga was Nannerl's third Christian name. See Jahn, vol. i. p. 26, n. 1.

[3] St. Crescentia. Little is known about her. It is said that a tumulus with a stone containing an inscription about her death originally existed near Paris.

[4] St. Crescentia had not yet been canonised.

For our dear little Wolfgang has at last, with the help of God, survived his horrible struggle and is on the road to recovery.

My daughter was scarcely a week out of bed and had just begun to walk across the bedroom floor by herself, when on November 15th little Wolfgang contracted an illness which in four weeks has made him so wretched that he is not only absolutely unrecognizable, but has nothing left but his tender skin and his little bones and for the last five days has been carried daily from his bed to a chair. Yesterday and today, however, we led him a few times across the room so that gradually he may learn to use his feet and stand upright by himself. You would like to know what was wrong with him? God knows! I am tired of describing illnesses to you. It began with a fever. Our night vigils were shared, as they were ★ during my daughter's illness; so that it is owing to the great grace of God that we, especially my wife, have been able to stand all this. But patience! What God sends must be endured. Now all that I can do is to await the time when it will please the Almighty to give my Wolfgang sufficient strength to enable us to undertake such an important journey at this season. Expense must not be considered. The devil take the money, if one only gets off with one's skin! But I will not describe to you the other circumstances in which we have found ourselves for the last three months. Had it not been for God's quite extraordinary grace, my children would not have survived these severe illnesses nor we these heavy blows.

Please have the following Masses said soon: three at the Holy Child at Loreto, one at Maria-Plain and one at Passau on the Mariahilfberg, two at St. Anne in the Parish Church of the Franciscans, one in honour of St. Walpurgis and one in honour of St. Vincent Ferrer,[1] in all nine Masses. My daughter is now so well that no trace of her illness is to be seen. I hope to God that our dear Wolfgang will also recover in a few weeks; for youth soon regains strength. I owe replies to letters from Adlgasser and Spitzeder which I shall repay in a few days. My present circumstances will excuse me. Please give our compliments to all. My children's illness, especially our Wolfgang's, has saddened not only us, but all our friends here. My daughter is not yet known in Holland, for she fell ill the day after our arrival.[2] But I cannot count my friends in this place, for people might think it boastful.   ★

---

[1] St. Vincent Ferrer (1355–1419) was a Spanish Dominican and the most famous preacher of his generation. He was appointed by Benedict XIII master of the Sacred Palace and he played an important part at the Council of Constance (1415), where he proposed the simultaneous deposition of the three rival popes. He was canonised by Calixtus III in 1455.

[2] Mozart had performed at court alone on September 12th and 18th. On September 30th he had given a concert alone, at which all the ouvertures (symphonies) were of his composition and at which musicians were invited to give him new music to read.

(41) Leopold Mozart to Lorenz Hagenauer, Salzburg

[Extract]   [Copy in the Staatsbibliothek Preussischer Kulturbesitz, West Berlin]

PARIS,[1] 16 May 1766

You will undoubtedly be more surprised than usual at not having received a letter from me for so long, and I should not have left you without any news of our condition if I had not been assured that you had heard about us at least twice from Herr Kulmann in Amsterdam. The illness of my children is the only reason why I have not yet sent you and my friends as exact a description of Holland as I have done of France and England. From Amsterdam[2] we returned to The Hague for the festival of the Prince of Orange (which took place on March 11th[3] and lasted some time), on which occasion our little composer was asked to turn out six sonatas for the clavier with violin accompaniment,[4] for the Prince's sister, Princess von Nassau-Weilburg. These were at once engraved. In addition he had to compose something for the Prince's concert and also arias for the Princess and so forth. On our arrival home you shall see them all. I have asked Herr Kulmann to send a little box to you at Salzburg. As soon as it arrives, please open it and look for the small wide parcel, which is unsealed and on which 'Music' is written. In it you will find two copies of the sonatas engraved at The Hague. Take one copy with the violin part and get the clavier and violin parts bound separately and see that these are presented most humbly to His Grace on our behalf. In the same parcel there are two sets of variations, one of which little Wolfgang had to compose on an air,[5] written on the occasion of the majority and installation of the Prince; the other set he dashed off hurriedly on another melody[6] which everybody all over Holland is singing, playing and whistling. They are trifles! But if you want to add a copy of each, you may do so, as they are unusual. I shall have the honour of showing you my 'Violinschule' in the Dutch language.[7] This book these Dutch gentlemen translated and

---

[1] The Mozarts arrived on May 10th in Paris, where they stayed until July 9th, lodging 'chez M. Brie, baigneur, rue traversière'. They spent four days, May 28th to June 1st, in Versailles.

[2] After giving a second concert at The Hague, on January 22nd, at which both Nannerl and Wolfgang performed, Leopold Mozart took his family to Amsterdam, where the children gave concerts on January 29th and February 20th. At both concerts, at which only Mozart's compositions were performed, they played works for four hands on one clavier and at the second concert works for two claviers. Probably the symphony B♭ (K. 22), composed at The Hague, was performed at one of these concerts.

[3] The correct date was March 8th. Abert, vol. i. p. 71, suggests that March 11th was the day on which the Mozarts appeared at court.

[4] K. 26–31, announced in the 's–Gravenhaegse Woensdagse Courant, 16 April 1766.

[5] K. 24, harpsichord variations on an air composed for the installation of the Stadtholder by C. E. Graf or Graaf (1723–1804), Kapellmeister to the Prince of Orange.

[6] K. 25, harpsichord variations on the old national anthem of Holland, Wilhelmus van Nassouwe. The fugue of the 'Galimathias musicum' (K. 32) which Mozart, with his father's assistance, also composed for the festival, is on the same air.

[7] A Dutch translation of Leopold Mozart's Versuch einer gründlichen Violinschule, Augsburg, 1756. The copy which was presented to William V is in the Royal Library at The Hague.

produced in the same format as the original. It was dedicated to the Prince and presented to him in my presence at the festival of his installation. The edition is an uncommonly fine one, even finer than my own. The publisher (or rather, the printer in Haarlem) came to me and handed me the book in a respectful manner. He was accompanied by the organist who invited our little Wolfgang to play on the great organ in Haarlem, which is so famous. This took place on the following morning from ten to eleven. It is an extremely fine instrument with 68 stops, entirely of pewter, be it noted, for wood does not last in this damp country.

It would take too long to describe our journey from Holland through Amsterdam, Utrecht,[1] Rotterdam, across the Maas, and then across an arm of the sea at Moerdijk to Antwerp. Still more impossible would it be to describe the present sorry state of the formerly great commercial town of Antwerp and to enumerate the causes thereof.[2] Later on we shall talk about this. We travelled through Malines, where we visited our old acquaintance, the Archbishop,[3] to Brussels, where we only rested for a day and, leaving by the mail coach at nine in the morning, arrived in Valenciennes at half past seven in the evening.   ★

In Cambrai I saw the tomb of the great Fénelon and his marble bust. He has made himself immortal by his 'Télémaque', his book on the education of girls, his dialogues of the dead, his fables, and other sacred and secular works. Then without stopping anywhere we travelled on to Paris and went to the lodgings which our friend M. Grimm had engaged for us. Thank God, we found our luggage in good condition.   ★

As we are now dressed again in black, one can see how my children have grown. We are all well. When we get back to Salzburg nobody, ★ at first, will recognize little Wolfgang. It is a long time since we left and meanwhile he has seen and got to know many thousands of people.   ★

My very dear Hagenauer, we met in Amsterdam a native of Salzburg who owing to certain circumstances had become a Calvinist. My most urgent desire was to lead him back to the right path. I made every effort. That brought me back to Amsterdam[4] and kept me longer in Holland.   ★

---

[1] The Mozarts gave another concert in Amsterdam on April 16th and one in Utrecht.
[2] The main decline of Antwerp was in the sixteenth century. About 1540 it was at the height of its importance. Then came very unhealthy speculations, leading to serious bankruptcies and unsettlement; and the political troubles made many prominent citizens take refuge in Holland. From 1580 onwards it was in decline and Amsterdam soon passed it in importance. In the eighteenth century it suffered from the closing of the Scheldt (ever since the Treaty of Münster) and it was sacked by the French in 1746. In 1780 its population was only *c.* 40,000, 12,000 of whom were living on alms.
[3] See p. 31.
[4] Probably refers to his second visit to Amsterdam in the middle of April when his children gave their third concert.

(42) Leopold Mozart to Lorenz Hagenauer, Salzburg

[Extract]   [Copy in the Staatsbibliothek Preussischer Kulturbesitz, West Berlin]

★
PARIS, 9 June 1766

Next week we are to go again to Versailles, where twelve days ago we spent four whole days.

★
I have not told you what our next route will be, for I think it will be more interesting if the superscription on my next letter tells it to you. Meanwhile we have had the pleasure of a visit from His Highness the Hereditary Prince of Brunswick,[1] a very agreeable, handsome and friendly gentleman. On entering the room he asked me whether I was the author of the book on the violin, and so on. He is soon to leave Paris, visit en passant forts of Metz, Strassburg and the rest, and then travel via Geneva to Turin, and so through Italy.

★

(43) Leopold Mozart to Lorenz Hagenauer, Salzburg

[Extract]   [Copy in the Staatsbibliothek Preussischer Kulturbesitz, West Berlin]

LYONS, 16 August 1766

Do not be shocked that I am writing to you from Lyons. By the time that you receive this letter we shall have had, with the help of God, a sufficiently long opportunity of discovering what Geneva and the Genevan pocket watches are like, for in two or three days we leave here for that city. We went from Paris to Dijon[2] in Burgundy, where we spent a fortnight. We did this on account of the Prince de Condé, who had invited us there on the occasion of the assembly of the Burgundian states, which only takes place every three years.

★
We shall probably stay at least a fortnight in Geneva. Then we shall travel through Switzerland by way of Lausanne and Berne. But whether we shall leave Switzerland on the right by Zürich or on the left by Basel, I do not know. Thence we shall go straight through Ulm to Dischingen[3] to His Highness Prince Taxis, as we arranged with M. Beecke,[4] whom we met in Paris, and who will also be there. Further, I hope to meet the Bishop of Augsburg either in Dillingen or in Augsburg and, after paying

---

[1] Karl Wilhelm Ferdinand, Hereditary Prince of Brunswick, who was a distinguished violinist.

[2] Leopold Mozart's *Reiseaufzeichnungen* has the entry 'Dijon', p. 40, before the second entry 'Paris', p. 47. In Dijon the Mozarts met Charles de Brosses (1709–1777), famous later for his *Lettres familières, écrites d'Italie*, 1739–40. He was a great lover of music, had associated with Hasse, Tartini, etc., and translated into French Metastasio's dramas. Leopold Mozart's criticism of the violinists in the Dijon orchestra is 'asini tutti' (all fools). See *MBA*, No. 110.

[3] A small village about thirteen miles from Dillingen, where Schloss Taxis is.

[4] The pianist and composer Ignaz von Beecke, of Wallerstein. See p. 305, n. 1.

our brief respects to His Highness the Elector of Bavaria and Duke Clemens, to congratulate Frau Hagenauer on her name-day.[1] But all this with the help of God! People have been trying hard to persuade us to ★ proceed to the French ports of Marseilles, Bordeaux, etc. And don't you think it very heroic and magnanimous of us to have decided to abandon a trip to Turin, which lies almost in front of us? Don't you think that its proximity, our circumstances, the general encouragement to do so and our own interest and love of travel ought to have induced us to follow our noses and go to Italy and then, after witnessing the Festival of the Ascension in Venice, return home through the Tyrol? Surely you will agree that now is the time when my children on account of their youth can arouse the admiration of everyone. However, I have taken my decision. I have promised to go home and I shall keep my word.   ★

(44) *Leopold Mozart to Lorenz Hagenauer, Salzburg*

[*Extract*]   [*Copy in the Staatsbibliothek Preussischer Kulturbesitz, West Berlin*]

MUNICH, 10 *November* 1766

As far as I remember, my last letter was from Lyons, which we left after a stay of four weeks. We then went on to Geneva, where we found everything still in flames after the civil war. This, however, did not prevent us from staying three weeks. Perhaps you know that immediately ★ outside Geneva the famous Voltaire has a castle called Ferney, where he is living.

Whoever wishes to go to Berne must travel through Lausanne. We had only intended to spend half a day there; but when we alighted from our carriages, the servants of Prince Ludwig of Wurtemberg,[2] of Madame d'Aulbonne, of Madame Hermenche, of M. de Sévery and others came up, and I had to let these distinguished personages persuade me to spend five days in Lausanne. The above-mentioned Prince was with us when we got ★ into our carriage and, upon shaking hands with him, I had to promise to write to him very often and send him news of ourselves. From Lausanne we went to Berne and thence to Zürich. In the former town we only spent eight, in the latter fourteen days.[3] In both places we had an opportunity of getting to know men of learning; and at Zürich the two Gesners,[4] both learned persons, made our stay very pleasant and our

---

[1] Leopold Mozart hoped to be home by October 15th.
[2] Brother of Duke Karl Eugen.
[3] Probably from September 28th to October 10th. They gave two concerts there.
[4] Johannes Gessner, physicist, and Salomon Gessner (1730–1788), poet. The latter gave the Mozarts, amongst other works, a copy of his poems with a dedication, quoted by Nissen, p. 116. Nissen adds that Salomon Gessner's wife gave the Mozarts a copy of Wieland's poetical works and her brother a German translation of Samuel Butler's *Hudibras*. See *MDB*, p. 60.

departure very sad. We took away tokens of their friendship.

Thence we proceeded through Winterthur to Schaffhausen. Here too our four days' stay was a very pleasant one and we found on our arrival in Donaueschingen Herr Meisner, who came to welcome us and helped us and our luggage out of the carriage! He remained on in Donaueschingen with us for four days longer.

His Highness the Prince welcomed us with extraordinary graciousness. It was not necessary to announce our arrival, for we were already being eagerly awaited, as Herr Meisner can testify. The Director of Music, Martelli, came at once to welcome us and to invite us to court. Well, we were there for twelve days. On nine days there was music in the evening from five to nine and each time we performed something different. If the season had not been so advanced, we should not have got away. The Prince gave me twenty-four louis d'or and to each of my children a diamond ring. Tears flowed from his eyes when we took leave of him, and truly we all wept at saying good-bye. He begged me to write to him often. Indeed our departure was as sad as our stay had been agreeable. Then we travelled at terrific speed through Messkirch to Ulm, Günzburg and Dillingen, where we only stayed two days, picked up two rings from the Prince [1] and, after spending a day in Augsburg, came to Munich where we arrived the day before yesterday and where we are staying at Störzer's. Yesterday, Sunday, we visited His Highness the Elector at table and were most graciously received. Wolfgang had at once to compose, standing beside the Elector, a piece for which His Highness hummed the beginning, or rather a few bars of the theme, and he then had to play it for him after dinner in the music room. You can easily guess how surprised everyone was to see and hear this.

That night, however, I noticed that Wolfgang was not well. He was restless and I have had to keep him in bed today, as I shall perhaps have to do for a few days more. With this weather and with the stove heating to which we have now to accustom ourselves, it is not surprising that such a delicate frame should have to suffer a little.

The arrangements which we must make for our home are worrying me very much.[2] You yourself will understand this to some extent, and after our safe arrival (which God grant!) you will see it for yourself. God, who has been far too good to me, a miserable sinner, has bestowed such talents on my children that, apart from my duty as a father, they alone would spur me on to sacrifice everything to their successful development. Every moment I lose is lost for ever. And if I ever guessed how precious for youth is time, I realize it now. You know that my children are accustomed

---

[1] Joseph I, Prince-Bishop of Augsburg.

[2] Probably refers to Leopold Mozart's intention to move into a house of his own.

to work. But if with the excuse that one thing prevents another they were to accustom themselves to hours of idleness, my whole plan would crumble to pieces. Habit is an iron shirt. And you yourself know how much my children and especially Wolfgang have to learn. But who knows what plans are being made for us after our return to Salzburg? Perhaps we shall be received in such a way that we shall be only too glad to shoulder our bundles and clear out. But at least, God willing, I am going to bring back my children to their native town. If they are not wanted, it is not my fault. But people shall not get them for nothing. Well, I rely entirely on your sensible judgment and true friendship. Conversation will give us more pleasure. Farewell.   ★

(45) *Leopold Mozart to Lorenz Hagenauer, Salzburg*

[*Extract*]   [*Copy in the Staatsbibliothek Preussischer Kulturbesitz, West Berlin*]

MUNICH, 15 *November* 1766

If things had gone as I intended, my last letter would have begun as follows: *Here you have a letter from Regensburg*—for I should now be there, in response to the insistent request of Prince Ludwig of Wurtemberg, Prince von Fürstenberg and Prince Taxis. From here it is a stone's throw and we should have gone straight home through Landshut and Alt-Ötting. This indeed is the route which we shall take on our journey and we shall doubtless still meet His Grace in Lauffen. But whether we shall now travel by way of Regensburg, I very much doubt, as I must wait until our little Wolfgang has completely recovered, and only then shall I know how soon we can get away from here. Meanwhile the weather is getting worse and worse. Our dear Frau Hagenauer will remember that after our return from Vienna[1] little Wolfgang fell ill and was very sick, so that we dreaded smallpox; and that finally the trouble settled in his feet where he complained of pains and so forth.

Now he has had a similar attack. He could not stand on his feet or move his toes or knees. No one could come near him and for four nights he could not sleep. This pulled him down a great deal and caused us all the more anxiety, since the whole time, and especially towards evening, he was very hot and feverish. Today he is noticeably better; but it will certainly be a week more before he is quite restored to health. In God's name, a hundred gulden soon disappear. I am now accustomed to this bad business.   ★

[1] January 1763.

(46) Leopold Mozart to Lorenz Hagenauer, Salzburg

[Extract]   [Copy in the Staatsbibliothek Preussischer Kulturbesitz, West Berlin]

MUNICH, 22 November 1766

Now I myself am impatient. Until now Wolfgang has been unwell. He went out yesterday for the first time and today the Elector is giving a concert at which we have to appear. This impatience of mine is due to the very tiresome custom which prevails at this court, of making people wait for a very long time.[1]

★

[1] The Mozarts had been in Munich since November 8th and arrived in Salzburg on November 29th or 30th. Nissen, p. 120, adds that at Biberach Mozart competed on the organ with Sixtus Bachmann (1754–1818), later Father Sixtus of the Monastery of Marchthal, who was two years older than himself.

The fourth journey of Leopold Mozart and his wife and two children was to Vienna (their second visit), presumably in order to take part in the celebrations connected with the forthcoming marriage of the Archduchess Maria Josepha to King Ferdinand of Naples. But owing to the death of the bride in October 1767 and the prolonged court mourning, nearly all musical activities ceased for a time. Nevertheless the Mozarts remained in Vienna until January 1769. At the Emperor Joseph's suggestion Mozart wrote an opera buffa La Finta Semplice, *which however, was not performed. On the other hand, his operetta* Bastien und Bastienne *was produced at the private theatre of the famous Dr. Anton Mesmer. The visit to Vienna is described in a series of letters from Leopold Mozart to his landlord, Lorenz Hagenauer. Letters 47-70.*

(47) Leopold Mozart to Lorenz Hagenauer, Salzburg

[Extract]   [Copy in the Staatsbibliothek Preussischer Kulturbesitz, West Berlin]

VIENNA,[1] 22 September 1767

On the first day we drove to Vöcklabruck; on the second in the morn- ★
ing to Lambach (where we took lunch in the monastery). In the evening
we went on to Linz where we stayed at the 'Grüner Baum', an inn outside
the town. On Sunday we did no more than walk up the Strengberg. On
Monday morning we drove to Melk, where after lunch we went up to the
monastery[2] and were shown the rooms. We did not disclose our identity
until, when visiting the church and its organ, we gave the organist the
opportunity of recognizing or rather guessing from his playing who little
Wolfgang was. Immediately afterwards, however, we got into our
carriage and drove to St. Pölten and on the morning of the following day
to Purkersdorf and Vienna.   ★

His Majesty[3] has only just returned from Hungary and during these
days the Empress has her monthly devotions in memory of the death of
the late Emperor.[4] So far I have nothing to report about our arrangements
here. But every day there is either an opera seria or an opera buffa or a play. ★

(48) Leopold Mozart to Lorenz Hagenauer, Salzburg

[Extract]   [Copy in the Staatsbibliothek Preussischer Kulturbesitz, West Berlin]

VIENNA, 29 September 1767

I have nothing to tell you except that, thank God, we are all well; and
that news is quite certainly worth the postage.

Hasse's[5] opera is beautiful, but the singers, be it noted, are nothing out ★
of the ordinary for such a festive occasion.[6] Signor Tibaldi[7] is the tenor

---

[1] The Mozarts left Salzburg on September 11th and arrived in Vienna on September 15th
and took rooms in the house of a goldsmith.
[2] The famous Benedictine abbey and church.   [3] Joseph II.   [4] See p. 59, n. 2.
[5] *Partenope*, text by Metastasio, produced on 9 September 1767. The composer, Johann
Adolph Hasse (1699–1783), born in Hamburg, was first a tenor. In 1724 he went to Naples to
study composition under A. Scarlatti and possibly Porpora, and there wrote his first operas.
Owing to his personal charm and popularity, he was known in Italy as 'Il caro Sassone'. In
1730 he married Faustina Bordoni, the famous soprano, and became Kapellmeister in Dresden.
After the siege of Dresden in 1760 he and his wife moved to Vienna, where he soon became
the rival of Gluck.
[6] The celebrations in connection with the betrothal of the Archduchess Maria Josepha to
King Ferdinand of Naples.
[7] Giuseppe Luigi Tibaldi, a famous tenor, born 1719 in Bologna. He was a pupil of Padre
Martini and during the years 1760–1772 was a leading operatic singer.

and Signor Rauzzini[1] from Munich, the leading castrato. The prima donna is Signora Teiber,[2] the daughter of a violinist at the Viennese court. But the dances are excellent, the leading dancer being the famous Frenchman Vestris.[3]

★

(49) *Leopold Mozart to Frau Maria Theresa Hagenauer, Salzburg*

[*Extract*]   [*Copy in the Staatsbibliothek Preussischer Kulturbesitz, West Berlin*]

★ MADAME!   VIENNA, 14 *October* 1767[4]

I left Herr Estlinger certain symphonies to copy, which I hope are now ready. These are the symphonies which I have to send to Donaueschingen.[5] By the next post I shall send you a letter for the Prince which should be enclosed with the symphonies and should be sent off by the mail coach. I hope that Herr Estlinger understood what I wanted. The concertos for two claviers should be sent to Herr Gesner[6] at Zürich. The symphonies should go to Donaueschingen, and the clavier concertos, which Herr Spitzeder gave Herr Estlinger to copy, should, when copied, be delivered by him to Herr von Menhofer, who will thereupon pay him ★ for them.

For Herr Hagenauer alone.

Do not be surprised if we draw four hundred or even five hundred gulden. *Aut Caesar aut nihil*; but not in Wenzel Hebelt's manner. Perhaps in one single day I shall pay it all back. So far we have played nowhere, for we have not yet performed at court. Later on I shall tell you some extra-★ ordinary things.

(50) *Leopold Mozart to Lorenz Hagenauer, Salzburg*

[*Extract*]   [*Copy in the Staatsbibliothek Preussischer Kulturbesitz, West Berlin*]

VIENNA, 17 *October* 1767

The Princess bride has become a bride of the Heavenly bridegroom.[7] What an amazing change!

[1] Venanzio Rauzzini (1746–1810), born in Rome, went to Munich in 1766, He was an eminent teacher of singing and also an operatic composer.

[2] Elizabeth Teiber, who was one of a large family of musicians in Vienna. Her sister Therese Teiber, also a famous soprano, married later the tenor Ferdinand Arnold.

[3] Vestris, a large family of Italian musicians and dancers, originally Vestri from Florence. The one mentioned here was Gaëtan Apolline Balthasar (1729–1808), who had worked under Noverre. In Paris in 1778 he danced in Mozart's ballet, written for Noverre, *Les petits riens* (K. App. 10 [299b]).

[4] A short letter from Leopold Mozart, dated 7 October 1767, says: '. . . That Princess Josepha, the bride of the King of Naples, has contracted smallpox, also upsets our plans to some extent. . . .' See *MBA*, No. 118.

[5] The Prince von Fürstenberg had ordered six symphonies by Leopold Mozart.

[6] Salomon Gessner. See p. 67, n. 4.

[7] Princess Josepha died of smallpox on October 15th.

We see a good deal of the Duke de Braganza,[1] Prince Kaunitz, M. De L'Augier,[2] and Baron Fries.[3]

Another strange thing is that the second opera was the story of the Greek fable of Psyche. The title was: Amor e Psiche.[4]

Do not forget to pray for us, for if God did not watch over us, we should certainly be in a sorry plight, as you shall hear later on.

(51) *Leopold Mozart to Lorenz Hagenauer, Salzburg*

[*Extract*]   [*Copy in the Staatsbibliothek Preussischer Kulturbesitz, West Berlin*]

OLMÜTZ,[5] 10 *November* 1767

Te Deum Laudamus!
Little Wolfgang has got over the smallpox safely!
And where?—In Olmütz!
And where?—At the residence of His Excellency Count Podstatzky.[6]
You will have already observed from my previous letter that everything in Vienna has gone topsy-turvy. Now I must give you a few particulars which concern us alone; and from them you will see how Divine Providence links everything together, so that, if we trust to it completely, we cannot go wrong.

The elder son of the goldsmith with whom we were living, caught smallpox immediately after our arrival. We only heard of this after he had almost got over it and after the two younger children had caught it too. In vain did I search quickly for another lodging which would take us all. I was forced to leave my wife and daughter where they were and to run off with Wolfgang to a good friend. The servant remained with my wife. The only subject of conversation in Vienna was the smallpox. Of ten children whose names were put on the death register, nine had died of this disease. You can easily imagine how I felt. Whole nights were spent without sleep and during the day we had no rest.

I had decided immediately after the death of the Princess bride to go to Moravia, until the first mourning in Vienna should be over. But it was impossible to get away. For His Majesty the Emperor talked about us so often that we could never be certain when it would occur to him to

---

[1] Duke Johann Carl de Braganza, a famous traveller and patron of the arts.
[2] Physician to the Viennese court, at whose home scholars and artists were entertained.
[3] Baron Johann von Fries (1719–1785), a wealthy business man and banker in Vienna.
[4] An opera by F. L. Gassmann (1729–1774), who was a native of Bohemia and studied under Padre Martini of Bologna. In 1764 he was invited to Vienna as ballet composer and in 1771 was appointed Hofkapellmeister. Salieri was his pupil.
[5] The Mozarts were in Olmütz from October 26th to December 23rd. Mozart's illness lasted from October 26th to November 10th.
[6] Count Leopold Anton von Podstatzky, Dean of the Cathedral at Olmütz. His brother was a Canon of the Cathedral at Salzburg.

summon us. As soon, however, as the Archduchess Elizabeth fell ill, I let nothing more stop me, and I could scarcely wait until the hour came when I could get my little Wolfgang out of Vienna (which was by this time thoroughly infected) and into a different atmosphere.

On the afternoon of October 23rd we drove off and reached Brünn [1] on Saturday 24th. I took little Wolfgang to His Excellency Count von Schrattenbach [2] and Countess von Herberstein. They talked about a concert with a view to hearing my children and everything was already arranged. But I had a certain inner presentiment which I could not shake off and which impelled me all of a sudden to go on at once to Olmütz and hold the concert in Brünn on my return. So on Sunday evening I ex-
★ plained this to His Excellency, who agreed that I was acting wisely. We therefore quickly packed up our things and on Monday the 26th we left
★ Olmütz and soon arrived there.

We put up at the 'Schwarzer Adler' and, to our annoyance, we had to take a wretched damp room, because the few other rooms were occupied. We were therefore obliged to have it heated, another cause for annoyance, because the stove smoked so that we were almost blinded and at ten o'clock little Wolfgang was complaining of his eyes. I noticed that his head was warm, that his cheeks were hot and very red, but that his hands were as cold as ice. Moreover his pulse was not right. So we gave him some black powder and put him to bed. During the night he was rather restless and in the morning he still had the dry fever. At this point we were given two better rooms, so we wrapped Wolfgang up in furs and took him into the other suite. As the fever increased we gave him some margrave powder and some black powder. Towards evening he began to rave, and all night long and during the morning of the 28th he was delirious. After church I went to His Excellency Count Podstatzky, who received me most graciously. When I told him that my small boy had fallen ill and that I feared that he might have smallpox, he told me that he would take us in, as he was not at all nervous of the disease. He sent immediately for the steward, ordered him to get two rooms ready and
★ sent for a doctor to visit us at the 'Schwarzer Adler'. At four o'clock in the afternoon little Wolfgang was packed up in leather wrappings and furs and lifted into the carriage, and I drove with him to the Cathedral Deanery. On the 29th we saw a few little red pocks, but all the same we were not certain whether it was the smallpox, for he was no longer very
★ ill. He took nothing but a powder every six hours and always scabious tea afterwards.

On the 30th and the 31st, his name-day, the smallpox came out com-
★ pletely. As soon as this happened, the fever disappeared altogether and,

---

[1] The capital of Moravia, about ninety miles from Vienna.
[2] Count Franz Anton von Schrattenbach, brother of the Archbishop of Salzburg.

thank God, he was still right in his head. He was very much inflamed and as he had swollen to a surprising extent and had a thick nose, when he looked at himself in the mirror, he said: 'Now I am like little Mayr',[1] meaning the musician. Since yesterday the spots have been falling off here and there and two days ago all the swelling disappeared.

You will have already realised the truth of my motto: In te, Domine, speravi, non confundar in aeternum.[2] I leave it to you to consider in what a wonderful way our fate took us to Olmütz and how extraordinary it was that Count Podstatzky of his own accord took us in with a child who was to develop smallpox. I shall not mention with what kindness, graciousness and liberality we were waited on in every way. But I should really like to know how many people there are who would receive into their house, as he did, a whole family with a child in such a condition, and this from no other motive than fellow-feeling. This deed will do Count Podstatzky no little honour in the biography of our little one which I shall have printed later on. For from a certain aspect there begins here a new period of his life.

I am sorry that I shall have to return to Salzburg later than I intended. But at this time of the year we cannot make an early departure without ★ endangering Wolfgang's health.

I have received your letter with the enclosure from M. Grimm in Paris. ★ You will have seen in his letter what he has to say about the Russian Court and the Hereditary Prince of Brunswick;[3] also how and in what kind of company Herr Schobert[4] went into eternity.

Here is a reply to Herr Joseph which Wolfgang has written in bed.[5] ★

I still have one anxiety, which weighs heavily upon me, which is, lest my little girl should also get smallpox; for who knows whether the few pocks which she had were the real ones?

[Written on the cover]   *[Autograph in the Mozarteum, Salzburg]*
★

For you alone.

The six symphonies, which Estlinger has copied,[6] should be rolled up well and given to the mail coach with the address: A son Altesse Sérénissime Le Prince de Fürstenberg etc. à Donaueschingen. I shall write a letter to the Prince from here. The concerto for two claviers by Wagenseil should be added to the other printed sonatas,[7] which are to be sent to Herr Gesner in Zürich. But you will see now how topsy-turvy everything has been and how when we thought that all had gone wrong, God bestowed

---

[1] Andreas Mayr, a member of the Salzburg court orchestra.
[2] The opening words of Psalm 71.   [3] See p. 66, n. 1.
[4] See p. 37, n. 4. Schobert died on 28 August 1767, from eating some fungi which he had gathered near Paris and which poisoned his family, his cook and three friends. His death is described by Grimm in his *Correspondance Littéraire*, vol. vii. p. 422.
[5] A letter, which is evidently lost, addressed to Joseph Hagenauer. See p. 91, n. 1
[6] See p. 74.   [7] Mozart's sonatas, K. 6–9, K. 10–15 and K. 26–31.

upon us His infinite grace and allowed our dear Wolfgang to make a good recovery from his illness. But I do not mind anything so long as this ★ is safely over. What do you say to Count Podstatzky's treatment of us? Does not such a deed deserve some sort of expression of approval, if not of thanks from His Grace, made, if not in person, at least through his brother in Brünn or through Count von Herberstein, or, at the very least, conveyed in the form of a letter from our Father Confessor, or from the Court Chancellor? I beg you to try to get something of this sort done.

(52) *Leopold Mozart to Lorenz Hagenauer, Salzburg*

[*Extract*]   [*Copy in the Staatsbibliothek Preussischer Kulturbesitz, West Berlin*]

OLMÜTZ, 29 *November* 1767

I have this moment received your letter.
Iterum Iterumque
Te Deum Laudamus!

My daughter has got over the smallpox safely—a proof that the few pocks which she had in childhood were not the genuine article, as I had already suspected. She survived her attack so well that you will not notice on her ★ any marks whatever and only a few on Wolfgang. Now I must tell you a few other things. For instance, before leaving Vienna, I wanted to let you know that Herr Haydn,[1] Herr Leutgeb,[2] Herr Franz Drasil[3] and also Herr Küffel[4] called on us. At that time I was too busy to tell you that we returned the visits of Haydn and of the above-mentioned gentlemen and that we met Theresa, Herr Haydn's lady-love.[5]

★ Little Wolfgang. was overjoyed to receive the letter in verse from Sallerl[6] and read it out to the Count.
★

(53) *Leopold Mozart to Lorenz Hagenauer, Salzburg*

[*Extract*]   [*Copy in the Staatsbibliothek Preussischer Kulturbesitz, West Berlin*]

VIENNA, 12 *January* 1768

★   That we spent a fortnight in Brünn, where we arrived on Christmas

[1] Johann Michael Haydn (1737–1806), a younger brother of Joseph Haydn and a composer of note. In 1762 on Eberlin's death he was appointed Konzertmeister of the Salzburg court orchestra, and in 1777 after Adlgasser's death he became organist at the churches of Holy Trinity and St. Peter. In August 1768 he married the Salzburg court singer Maria Magdalena Lipp, daughter of the second organist of the Cathedral.
[2] Joseph Leutgeb, horn-player in the Salzburg court orchestra, and later a close friend of Mozart. In 1777 he opened a cheesemonger's shop in Vienna, where he died in 1811.
[3] Franz Drasil was a horn-player in the Salzburg court orchestra. See A. J. Hammerle, *Mozart und einige Zeitgenossen*, Salzburg, 1877, p. 35.
[4] Ignaz Küffel, a cellist in the Salzburg court orchestra. See p. 93 and p. 95, n. 1.
[5] A portion of this letter which has been omitted contains an amusing description of the lady, who was the daughter of a Viennese hosier. Michael Haydn did not marry her.
[6] Rosalie Joly, a chambermaid in the household of Count Felix Arco. She was a friend of the Mozart children.

Eve, will certainly be known in Salzburg from the letters of Her Excellency Countess von Herberstein. The kindnesses which we received in the home of Count Schrattenbach[1] and the special consideration shown to us by His Excellency and by the whole aristocracy of Brünn I shall not fail later on to extol in detail to His Grace, our most gracious overlord.[2] We left Brünn on the 9th. With four post-horses we succeeded in reaching Poysdorf at six o'clock on the same evening and this in spite of snow and storm. Here, however, we took six horses and on Sunday the 10th we drove off at eight in the morning and were already on the Tabor by five o'clock in the evening.[3]

                ★

(54) *Leopold Mozart to Lorenz Hagenauer, Salzburg*

[*Extract*]   [*Copy in the Staatsbibliothek Preussischer Kulturbesitz, West Berlin*]

VIENNA, *23 January* 1768

The latest news which I have to report (apart from the fact that, thank God, we are all well) is that on Tuesday the 19th we were with Her Majesty the Empress from half past two to half past four in the afternoon. His Majesty the Emperor[4] came out into the anteroom where we were waiting until Their Majesties had taken coffee, and brought us in himself. In addition to the Emperor and the Empress, Prince Albert of Saxony[5] and all the Archduchesses were present; but apart from these royal personages there was not a soul. It would take too long to describe to you all that was said and done there. I shall only say that you cannot possibly conceive with what familiarity Her Majesty the Empress conversed with my wife, talking to her partly of my children's smallpox and partly of the events of our grand tour; nor can you imagine how she stroked my wife's cheeks and pressed her hands. Meanwhile His Majesty the Emperor talked to little Wolfgang and to me about music, and many other things too, which often made Nannerl blush. Later on I shall tell you more personally. For you know me. I hate to write about things which many a puffed-up 'Gogelkopf'[6] (that is a Swabian expression), sitting behind the stove, would regard as lies. But from this extraordinary friendliness you must not conclude that we are going to be paid in proportion. I at least cannot form a favourable opinion, judging from what I see here and from the

---

[1] See p. 76, n. 2.
[2] The Archbishop of Salzburg. Count Franz Anton von Schrattenbach was his brother. See p. 76, n. 2.
[3] On their return from Brünn the Mozarts took rooms in a house on the Hohe Brücke. See p. 817, n. 2.
[4] Joseph II, since 1765 co-regent with his mother, the Empress Maria Theresia.
[5] Duke Albert of Saxe-Teschen, Governor of the Austrian Netherlands, who was married to Maria Theresia's daughter, Maria Christina.
[6] An idiot. Nissen, p. 128, adds: 'a Swabian and Bavarian expression'.

present conditions in Vienna. But these are things which time must show
and about which we can talk more easily.

★

(55) *Leopold Mozart to Lorenz Hagenauer, Salzburg*

[*Extract*]   [*Copy in the Staatsbibliothek Preussischer Kulturbesitz, West Berlin*]

VIENNA, 30 *January*–3 *February* 1768 [1]

For you alone.

It is now time to give you a fuller and clearer report of our circumstances, I know not whether they are fortunate or unfortunate, and to hear
your friendly opinion. If money makes the sole happiness of man, then
we are doubtless to be pitied now, seeing that, as you know, we have
spent so much of our capital that there is little apparent hope of our being
able to recover it. If, on the other hand, health and versatility in knowledge are a man's greatest possession, then, God be praised, we are still well
off. We have weathered the biggest and most dangerous storm. By the
grace of God we are all well and my children have certainly not only forgotten nothing, but, as you will see, have made great progress.

I know that what must strike you as most incomprehensible is why it is
that our affairs do not improve more rapidly. I shall explain this to you as
well as I can. At the same time I must omit certain things which cannot be
entrusted to my pen. That the Viennese, generally speaking, do not care
to see serious and sensible performances, have little or no idea of them,
and only want to see foolish stuff, dances, devils, ghosts, magic, clowns,
Lipperl,[2] Bernardon,[3] witches and apparitions is well known; and their
★ theatres prove it every day. That is the first and main reason. The household organisation at court, which I cannot describe here, is an element
involving many consequences, which it would take too long to explain
and to illustrate by examples. That is the second reason. These two lead to
countless strange things, for everything depends on chance and blind
fortune and more often on some detestable meanness, which fortunately
does not characterize everyone, or even on some very impudent and
daring piece of bluff. To come now to our own affairs, I must tell you that
many other adverse events have taken place. On our arrival, the first thing
we had to do was to obtain an entry at court. But Her Majesty the
Empress no longer[4] has concerts in her apartments, nor does she go either
to the opera or to the play; and her manner of life is so removed from the
world that it would be impossible for me to describe it adequately. She

---

[1] This long letter was finished and sent off on 3 February 1768.
[2] A diminutive of Philip and the name of a clown on the Viennese stage.
[3] A clown's part invented by the Viennese actor Joseph Felix von Kurz (1717–1783).
[4] Since the death of Francis I on 18 August 1765.

directed us to the Emperor. But as this gentleman positively abhors everything that might entail any expenditure, it was a very long time before he made up his mind; and in the meantime there occurred the sad death of the Princess bride and all the events of which my letters have already informed you. After our return from Moravia we met the Royal Family sooner than we expected. For hardly had the Empress been told of what had happened to us in Olmütz and that we had returned, when we were informed of the day and the hour when we should appear. But what was the use of all this amazing graciousness and this indescribable friendliness? What effect did it produce? None whatever, save a medal, which is, it is true, beautiful, but so worthless that I do not even care to mention its value. She leaves everything else to the Emperor, who enters it in his book of oblivion and believes, no doubt, that he has paid us by his most gracious conversations. Now you will ask me what the other nobles in Vienna do? What do they do? They all cut down their expenses, as far as possible, in order to please the Emperor. If the chief is extravagant, everyone lets things rip. But if the chief economizes, everyone wants to have the most economical household.   ★

The members of the aristocracy are our patrons. Prince Kaunitz, the Duke de Braganza, Fräulein von Guttenberg, who is the left eye of the Empress, the Chief Equerry Count Dietrichstein, who is all-powerful with the Emperor, are our friends. But what bad luck! So far we have not been able to speak to Prince Kaunitz,[1] because his weakness is that he is so afraid of smallpox that he even avoids persons whose faces still show red spots. Hence, as little Wolfgang has still many red spots on his face, which are, it is true, small but which come out in cold weather, he merely sent us a message through our friend De L'Augier that during Lent he would look after our interests, but that just now during the carnival, the nobles could not be assembled for a function. But as I was considering this matter as carefully as I could and thinking of how much money I had already spent and that if I were now to go home without waiting for anything more, it would perhaps be extremely foolish, something quite different occurred. For I was told that all the clavier-players and composers in Vienna were opposed to our advancement, with the sole exception of Wagenseil, who, however, as he was ill at home, could not help us or contribute anything to our advantage. The chief maxim of these people was to avoid most carefully every occasion of seeing us and of admitting little Wolfgang's skill. And why? So that on the many occasions on which they might be asked whether they had heard this boy and what they thought of him, they could always say *that they had not heard him and that it could not possibly be true; that it was all humbug and foolishness; that it was all*

---

[1] Nissen, p. 131, inserts 'this time', as during their first visit to Vienna in 1762 he was one of the chief patrons of the Mozarts. See pp. 6 and 7.

pre-arranged; that he was given music which he already knew; that it was ridiculous to think that he could compose, and so forth. That, you see, is why they are keeping out of our way. For he who has seen and heard cannot talk in such a manner without exposing himself to the danger of thereby losing his honour. But I caught one of these people nicely. We had arranged with someone to inform us quietly when the man in question would be there. Our friend was then to hand this person a most extraordinarily difficult concerto, which was to be put before little Wolfgang. So we turned up and the fellow had the opportunity, therefore, of hearing his concerto played off by little Wolfgang as if he knew it by heart. The amazement of this composer and clavier-player, his expressions and the remarks he made in giving vent to his admiration, made us all realize what I have already said above. Finally he declared: *All I can say as an honest person is that this boy is the greatest man now living in the world. It was impossible to believe it.* But in order to convince the public of what it really amounts to, I decided to do something entirely out of the ordinary, that is, to get Wolfgang to write an opera for the theatre. Can you not imagine what a turmoil secretly arose amongst those composers? What? Today we are to see a Gluck [1] and tomorrow a boy of twelve seated at the harpsichord and conducting his own opera? Yes, despite all those who envy him! I have even won Gluck over to our side, though, I admit, only to the extent that, though he is not quite whole-hearted, he has decided not to let it be noticed; for our patrons are his also. In order to make our position safe in regard to the actors, who usually cause the composer most annoyance, I have taken the matter up with them, and one of them has given me all the suggestions for the work. But, in reality it was the Emperor himself who first gave me the idea of getting little Wolfgang to write an opera. For he asked the boy twice whether he would like to compose an opera and conduct it himself? Wolfgang said, Yes. But more than this the Emperor could not suggest, since the operas are the concern of Affligio. [2] The consequences of this undertaking, if God helps us to carry it out, are so enormous, but so easy to visualize, that they require no explanation. But now I must spare no money, for it will come back to me today or tomorrow. Never venture, never win. I must show what we can do. We must succeed or fail. And where is my boy more likely to succeed than in the theatre? But of course the opera will not be performed until after Easter. I shall soon write for permission to stay here longer. It is not an opera seria, however, for no operas of that kind are being given now; and moreover people do not like them. So it is an opera buffa, but not a

---

[1] Since 1755 Gluck had been living almost entirely in Vienna. His operas *Alceste* (1767) and *Paride ed Elena* (1770) embodied his ideas on the reform of the opera.
[2] Giuseppe Affligio was manager of the Burgtheater and the Theater am Kärntner Tor during the years 1767–1770.

short one, for it is to last about two and a half or three hours.[1] There are no singers here for serious operas. Even Gluck's serious opera, 'Alceste',[2] was performed entirely by opera buffa singers. He too is now writing an opera buffa,[3] for there are excellent singers here for works of this kind, such as Signori Caribaldi, Caratoli, Poggi, Laschi, Polini, Signorina Bernasconi,[4] Signorina Eberhardi, Signorina Baglioni.

What do you think? Is not the reputation of having written an opera for the Viennese theatre the best way to enhance one's credit not only in Germany but also in Italy? Farewell.

(56) *Leopold Mozart to Lorenz Hagenauer, Salzburg*

[*Extract*]   [*Copy in the Staatsbibliothek Preussischer Kulturbesitz, West Berlin*]

VIENNA, 13 *February* 1768 ★

I should very much like to have here the bound copy of my 'Violin-schule'[5] which is standing or lying about amongst my books. When the Salzburg delegates come here, the copy could easily come with them. I even ought to have a few more unbound copies as well. But Heaven knows where the copper-plates are, though I think they are below, in the chest with the glasses. The table is probably with each book, and whatever copper-plates belong to it, will be seen from the bound copy. It ought to be possible to find the errata-sheet and the directions to the bookbinder. If so, all the better, but if not, just send me, if you please, the bound copy. It may also be that I have already inserted the copper-plates into the few copies which are still there. I cannot remember. Send it open, not sealed. ★
I have no news to give you, except that as in Salzburg we are having operas, redoutes, balls, plays and so forth; but at these balls some of those who attend are without masks, while others wear some disguise but no dominos. Wolfgang herewith sends this riddle[6] to Herr Adlgasser, since ★
we were so dense as not to be able to solve his riddle. We send greetings to all our good friends.

[1] Mozart's *La finta semplice*. The libretto was written by Marco Coltellini, who had lived in Vienna since 1758 and succeeded Metastasio as 'poeta cesareo'.
[2] *Alceste* was first performed on 26 December 1767.
[3] As far as is known Gluck never carried out this plan.
[4] Antonia Bernasconi, of German extraction, stepdaughter and pupil of Andrea Bernasconi, Kapellmeister at the Munich court. She first appeared in Vienna in Gluck's *Alceste*, 1767. In 1770 she sang at Milan in Mozart's *Mitridate* and in 1783 was still singing in Vienna.
[5] Leopold Mozart's treatise on the playing of the violin, called *Versuch einer gründlichen Violinschule*, published in 1756 by J. J. Lotter, Augsburg, won him fame during his lifetime. A considerable number of letters written to his publisher, 1755–1756, while the work was being printed, show his love of accuracy and his painstaking interest in the work. It went through new editions in 1770, 1787, 1791 and 1804 and was translated into Dutch (1766), French (1770) and Russian (1804). A selection was published in English in *c.* 1812 and a complete version by Editha Knocker appeared in 1948.
[6] Mozart was fond of sending riddles and puzzles to his friends.

(57) Leopold Mozart to Lorenz Hagenauer, Salzburg

[Extract]   [Copy in the Staatsbibliothek Preussischer Kulturbesitz, West Berlin]

VIENNA, 30 March 1768

★ We are all in good health and, thank God, in good circumstances. The ice is broken! Not only on the Danube, but also in our affairs. Our enemies are beaten! Note well, *here in Vienna*. Nothing can happen at once. By *phlegma* I have transformed beasts into men and left them to their own confusion. The chief reason for this present letter is that I am asking you to tell Herr Wenzel Hebelt [1] to hand in to His Grace the report on the instruction in the Kapellhaus, which, in the past, I have always entrusted to him. Furthermore I ask you to explain to our Father Confessor, with the humble greetings of myself and my family, that I still hold the appointment as instructor in the violin to the Archbishop's Kapellhaus, [2] but that for the last five years, that is, since my first journey to Vienna, [3] I have left this work to Herr Wenzel. But since on account of my absence I can receive nothing from the Archbishop's exchequer, the authorities should be informed, so that someone else may be appointed *pro instructione*. [4]

Thank you for the copies of my 'Violinschule' which you sent. As the copper-plates have turned up, I should very much like to have two or three more copies of the book with the missing copper-plates and also two
★ more copper-plates of the portrait, [5] as these are very dirty.

Last week a big concert was given for us at the house of His Highness Prince von Galitzin, [6] the Russian Ambassador. The Dean of the Cathedral and Count von Wolfegg [7] were there. The opera is getting on well. But it will probably not be performed until after the Emperor's return from Hungary.
★

(58) Leopold Mozart to Lorenz Hagenauer, Salzburg

[Extract]   [Copy in the Staatsbibliothek Preussischer Kulturbesitz, West Berlin]

VIENNA, 20 April 1768

★ We had the honour and pleasure of beginning the *Salzburg wedding festivities* here. At my suggestion we held a concert and entertained the

[1] See p. 21, n. 2.
[2] Since 1744 Leopold Mozart, who was appointed in 1743 fourth violinist in the Hofkapelle, had been entrusted with the teaching of the violin to the boys in the Kapellhaus.
[3] September 1762.   [4] i.e. as an instructor.
[5] Leopold Mozart's book on the violin contains a portrait of himself. A facsimile of the first edition of the *Violinschule*, edited by Bernhard Paumgartner, was published in 1922 by Carl Stephenson, Vienna.
[6] Prince Dimitri Mihalovich Galitzin (1720–1794), Ambassador to the Court of Vienna from 1762.   [7] See p. 23, n. 3.

wedding guests for a whole evening to the pleasure and satisfaction of everybody. We call it the beginning of the Salzburg wedding festivities, because we are natives of Salzburg.

His Majesty the Emperor has now left for Hungary or rather for the Turkish frontiers. Hence the opera will be performed in June after his return.

(59) *Leopold Mozart to Lorenz Hagenauer, Salzburg*

[*Extract*]   [*Autograph in the Mozarteum, Salzburg*]

For you alone.   VIENNA, 11 *May* 1768

I have duly congratulated His Grace on his esteemed name-day in a letter which I have just sent off. I have also written to the Chief Steward about the Archbishop's Kapellhaus. So Herr Meisner is going away? And where to? That my pay would stop at the end of March I told you already. It may be true, as people are telling me in their letters, that through the influence of His Grace's brother[1] I could once more obtain my salary as violin instructor to the Prince's Kapellhaus and as first violinist, if I were to beg for it. His brother knows this nice story, for I told it to him here. But how can I in fairness and honour obtain by begging something which I am not earning? For I am not performing my services in Salzburg, as I feel pretty sure most of the courtiers in Salzburg are saying. On the other hand this is what makes it easy for me to get permission to make a journey to Italy, a journey which, taking all the circumstances into consideration, can now be postponed no longer and for which I have received from the Emperor himself all the necessary introductions for Florence, the Imperial States and Naples. Or should I perhaps sit down in Salzburg with the empty hope of some better fortune, let Wolfgang grow up, and allow myself and my children to be made fools of until I reach the age which prevents me from travelling and until he attains the age and physical appearance which no longer attract admiration for his merits? Is my child to have taken the first step with this opera for nothing, and is he not to hurry on with firm steps along the road which is now so broad and easy to follow?

Here is the copy of the letter from the Chief Steward:

> Per espresso comando di S.A. Rma: devo far sapere a V.S. qualmente il Clement^mo Principe P^re. niente abbia in contrario, che il Sgr: Mozart se ne possi restar fuori a suo piacimento sin tanto che vuole, ed inoltre gli passerà ancora questo mese di marzo il suo salario; ma in avvenire, quando non sii

---

[1] Count von Schrattenbach. See p. 76, n. 2.

attualmente presente in Salisburgo, sarà bensì mantenuto come prima nel suo servizio, ma durante la sua assenza non gli lascierà più correre il solito salario. Di tanto ho voluto rendere avvisato V: S: etc.[1]

You see, how gracious!—I can remain away as long as I like, provided I do not ask to be paid. I am quite satisfied. At least I can stay away without further reproaches. But I shall not be able to leave here for Salzburg before the end of July.[2] Our furs are now becoming a nuisance to us and I shall send them back shortly by some driver. On the other hand I must—yes, I must ask you to do me a favour. The heat is getting more and more intense, and I am becoming ashamed of appearing at my hosts' houses in cloth garments. Wolfgang too needs a lighter costume. So I beg you to send me by the next mail coach my silk suit from Lyons, my red cloth suit (which I need for the return journey) and Wolfgang's light grey camlet suit, my wife's and daughter's Persian silk dresses and a lady's hat with a veil in front, which is to be found in the large round hat-box. Please put in with the rest of the parcel pieces for patching Wolfgang's red and cherry-coloured suit and my English red-brown suit.

One thing more! I wonder if you would speak to Herr Alterdinger[3] about something? I once asked him whether he would not undertake to translate my 'Violinschule' into Italian? If he would like to do this, I will pay what he asks. He should begin with the *Preface* and the *Introductions* and then tell me candidly what he thinks I ought to pay him. But, as I wrote it in three months, I hope that it will not be difficult for him to finish the translation in the same time. You will easily guess my purpose.[4] Only I should like to remind you that, as it is a manual of instruction, it ought not to be translated in a highflown style, but, as it is in German and for the man in the street, in a style which is clear and intelligible.

I thought indeed that Herr Hartmayr would soon devise some other plan, if the redoutes were not allowed. I should still like that house; but, if God does not wish it, no more do I.[5] If I had security for my children, I could take some decision. My dear Frau Hagenauer and your family, keep well and in good health. We all send you greetings and I am

your old

MOZART

---

[1] By express command of His Most Reverend Highness I inform you that our most gracious Prince has no objection to Herr Mozart's staying away as long as he likes and will pay him his salary for the month of March, but that in future when he is not actually in Salzburg he will be retained as before in the Archbishop's service but during his absence will not be paid his usual salary. I have to acquaint you with this decision, etc.

[2] The Mozarts did not return to Salzburg until January 1769.

[3] Rochus Alterdinger, administrator of the Archbishop's household.

[4] i.e. Leopold Mozart's projected visit to Italy with his son. As far as is known, his *Violinschule* was never translated into Italian.

[5] Leopold Mozart was trying to find a house for his family. See p. 69 f.

(60) *Leopold Mozart to Lorenz Hagenauer, Salzburg*

[*Extract*]   [*Copy in the Staatsbibliothek Preussischer Kulturbesitz, West Berlin*]

VIENNA, 4 *June* 1768 ★

Herr Spitzeder writes that he has had two arias copied. I should like to know how many arias Madame Wodiska sent from Munich. *There ought to be three of them in manuscript; and in addition a book with arias engraved or printed in London with the title 'Orione'.*[1] If she has not sent these, she has done me out of several arias, and this I should not like at all. That is what happens if one is *bonae voluntatis,* and cannot refuse people anything. ★

(61) *Leopold Mozart to Lorenz Hagenauer, Salzburg*

[*Extract*]   [*Copy in the Staatsbibliothek Preussischer Kulturbesitz, West Berlin*]

VIENNA, 29 *June* 1768 ★

I could tell you a very long story of all sorts of the most deeply laid plots and malicious persecutions. But I am too tired to go over these in my mind and would rather save them up *for our conversation, which we shall have shortly.*

Well, thank God, we are all in good health; although envy assails us ★ from all sides. You know, however, that I hold fast to my old motto: *In te, Domine, speravi. Fiat voluntas tua.*[2] ★

(62) *Leopold Mozart to Lorenz Hagenauer, Salzburg*

[*Extract*]   [*Copy in the Staatsbibliothek Preussischer Kulturbesitz, West Berlin*]

VIENNA, 30 *July* 1768

You have made everything all right again! We were only afraid, lest perhaps someone in your house should be unwell. On this score we are all the more happy, as we see that the cause of this silence was rather that you were very well and were enjoying the garden. Yet with regard to another matter, that is, our very long stay in Vienna, we are extremely displeased. Indeed, only our honour keeps us here! Otherwise we should have been in Salzburg long ago. But would you like everyone in Vienna to say that little Wolfgang had not been able to compose the opera; or that it turned out such poor stuff that it could not be produced; or that it was not he who

---

[1] *Orione ossia Diana vendicata,* Johann Christian Bach's first opera performed in England, was produced at the King's Theatre on 19 February 1763, and ran for nearly three months. The 'Favourite Songs' were published by Walsh in that year.
[2] A mixture of quotations from Psalm 71 and the Lord's Prayer.

wrote it, but his father? Would you wish us to look on in cold blood while such defamations should be circulated in all countries? Would this redound to our honour, nay, to the honour of our most gracious Prince? You will ask: '*What does His Majesty the Emperor say to it?*' Here I can only touch on the matter briefly, for it cannot be described in detail. But you will grasp it. Had I known all that I know now and could I have foreseen the events which have taken place, little Wolfgang would certainly never have written a note, but would have been at home long ago. The theatre is farmed out, or rather entrusted to a certain Affligio,[1] who has to pay some 1000 gulden a year to people whom the court would otherwise have to pay. The Emperor and the whole Imperial Family pay nothing for their boxes. Consequently the court cannot say a word to this Affligio, for everything is undertaken at his risk; and he is really now in danger of getting into trouble, as you shall soon hear.

His Majesty asked our Wolfgang whether he would not like to write an opera and said that he would very much like to see him at the clavier conducting it. He gave Affligio to understand that he would like this, and Affligio thereupon made a contract with us for one hundred ducats. At first the opera was to be performed at Easter. But the poet[2] was the first to prevent this, for, on the pretext of making here and there certain necessary alterations, he kept on delaying, so that by Easter we had received from him only two of the amended arias. Next, the opera was fixed for Whitsuntide and then for the return of His Majesty from Hungary. But at this point the mask fell from the face. For in the meantime all the composers, amongst whom Gluck is a leading figure,[3] undermined everything in order to prevent the success of this opera. The singers were talked over, the orchestra were worked up and every means was used to stop its performance. The singers who, moreover, hardly know their parts and one or two of whom have to learn everything entirely by ear, were now put up to say that they could not sing their arias, which they had nevertheless previously heard in our room and which they had approved of, applauded and described as quite suitable for them. The orchestra were now to say that they did not like a boy to conduct them, and a hundred similar things. Meanwhile some people spread the report that the music was not worth a fig; others said that it did not fit the words, or was against the metre, thus proving that the boy had not sufficient command of the Italian language. As soon as I heard this, I made it quite clear in the most eminent quarters that Hasse, the father of music, and the great Metastasio had stated that the slanderers who spread this report should go to them and hear out of their own mouths that thirty

---

[1] See p. 82, n. 2.   [2] Marco Coltellini. Cp. p. 83, n. 1.
[3] Undoubtedly an exaggerated statement, as Schiedermair, vol. iv. p. 396, and Abert, vol. i. p. 123, point out.

operas have been performed in Vienna, which in no respect can touch this boy's opera which they both admire in the very highest degree. Then it was said that not the boy, but his father had written it. But here too the credit of the slanderers began to fall. For they dropped *ab uno extremo ad aliud*[1] until they were in the soup. I asked someone to take any portion of the works of Metastasio, open the book and put before little Wolfgang the first aria which he should hit upon. Wolfgang took up his pen and with the most amazing rapidity wrote, without hesitation and in the presence of several eminent persons, the music for this aria for several instruments. He did this at the houses of Kapellmeister Bonno,[2] Abbate Metastasio, Hasse and the Duke de Braganza and Prince von Kaunitz. Meanwhile arrangements have been made for another opera and, as no more objections can be raised, little Wolfgang's is to be performed immediately afterwards. Hundreds of times I have wanted to pack up and go off. If this opera had been an opera seria, I should have left immediately and at the very first moment, and should have laid it at the feet of His Grace. But, as it is an *opera buffa*, and, what is more, an opera which demands certain types of *persone buffe*, I must save our reputation in Vienna, cost what it may. The honour of our most gracious Prince is also involved. His Grace has no liars, charlatans and deceivers in his service, who with his foreknowledge and permission go to other towns in order, like conjurers, to throw dust in people's eyes. No, he sends honest men, who to the honour of their Prince and of their country announce to the world a miracle, which God has allowed to see the light in Salzburg. I owe this act to Almighty God, otherwise I should be the most thankless creature. *And if it is ever to be my duty to convince the world of this miracle, it is so now, when people are ridiculing whatever is called a miracle and denying all miracles.* Therefore they must be convinced. And was it not a great joy and a tremendous victory for me to hear a Voltairian[3] say to me in amazement: '*Now for once in my life I have seen a miracle; and this is the first!*' But because this miracle is too evident and consequently not to be denied, they want to suppress it. *They refuse to let God have the honour.* They think that it is only a question of a few years and that thereafter it will become natural and cease to be a Divine miracle. So they want to withdraw it from the eyes of the world. For how could it be more visibly manifested than at a public show and in a large and populous town? But why should we be surprised at persecutions away from home, when almost the same thing has taken place in this child's native town? What a disgrace! What inhumanity! You may wonder perhaps why Prince Kaunitz and other great people, indeed His Majesty the Emperor himself, do not command

---

[1] i.e. from one extreme to another.
[2] Giuseppe Bonno (1710–1788), born in Vienna, son of one of the Imperial footmen, studied composition in Naples. In 1739 he was appointed Court Composer in Vienna, and in 1774, on the death of Gassmann, Court Kapellmeister.   [3] Probably Grimm.

that the opera be performed. First of all, they cannot command it, for it solely concerns the interest of Signor Affligio (whom some call Count Affligio). In the second place, they might perhaps command him to produce it at some other time. But it was Prince Kaunitz who, against the will of His Majesty, persuaded Affligio to bring to Vienna French players who are costing him more than 70,000 gulden a year and who are ruining him (as they are not drawing the crowds which were hoped for). So now Affligio is throwing the blame on Prince Kaunitz and because the latter, on the other hand, hoped to induce the Emperor to take an interest in the French theatre and thus defray his (Affligio's) expenses, His Majesty has not appeared at any performance for many weeks. Now you know the annoying circumstances, all of which arose simultaneously and helped to persuade Affligio to reject little Wolfgang's opera and keep his hundred ducats in his pocket. On the other hand these same circumstances prevented everyone from speaking to Affligio in a sharp, commanding and emphatic manner for fear they should have to compensate him for the 70,000 gulden. All this, of course, happened behind our backs. Affligio blamed the singers for the postponement of the opera and said that they could not and would not sing it. The singers, on the other hand, blamed Affligio and made out that he had not only said that he would not produce it, but had himself told them so. Whereas, of course, the truth is that they could always have this or that passage altered, if they so desired. So it is going to be performed. But if, as we shall soon see, some fresh obstacle begins to loom, I shall send my complaint to Their Majesties the Emperor and the Empress and demand such satisfaction as will save our honour before all Vienna and the whole honest world. For it would be no honour for us and no honour for our Salzburg court, if we were simply to allow ourselves to be driven away by persecuting envy and thus, after our departure, enable the wicked to make out to the ignorant public (as they have already done) that little Wolfgang never managed to write the opera at all or that it turned out such poor stuff that it simply could not be performed, and so forth. You see how one has to fight one's way through the world. If a man has no talents, he is unhappy enough; but if he has, envy pursues him in proportion to his ability. Moreover, in addition to all I have just told you, one of the singers, Signorina Bernasconi, has just caught a bad cold, and Signorina Baglioni is not very well. This again holds us up and will delay the business for at least three weeks. So that with extreme annoyance, such as I never elsewhere experienced on our travels, I have to await the result of this hateful affair. All sensible people must with shame agree that it is a disgrace to our nation that we Germans are trying to suppress a German, to whom foreign countries have done justice by their great admiration and even by public acknowledgments in writing. But by patience and perseverance one must convince people that our adversaries are wicked liars, slanderers and envious creatures, who would laugh in their sleeves if we were to get frightened or tired out and, by going off in a huff, give them the victory. Now, I think, you know my circumstances, although I have only described them in a general way. I should also have reported to our most gracious lord what has happened, if I had not felt some hesitation at disturbing him with such a long story in the midst of more important affairs. We all send our greetings to our Father Confessor and beg him to lay them at the feet of His Grace. Your Joseph [1] will see from this report that my enemies in Salzburg wish us well, since they are spreading the news that little Wolfgang has received 2000 gulden for the opera.

(63) *Leopold Mozart to Lorenz Hagenauer, Salzburg*

[*Extract*]   [*Copy in the Staatsbibliothek Preussischer Kulturbesitz, West Berlin*]

VIENNA, 6 *August* 1768

I should never have dreamt that on the Feast of St. Laurence [2] I should still be in Vienna. My last letter explained to you very fully why I must ★ still remain on here and what irritation it causes me.

I should be sick of the annoying circumstances which are keeping me here, if I did not know by experience that in the end many an affair takes quite a different turn from what one could ever have hoped. How often has Divine Providence clearly compelled me to go forward or has kept ★ me back!

(64) *Leopold Mozart to Lorenz Hagenauer, Salzburg*

[*Extract*]   [*Copy in the Staatsbibliothek Preussischer Kulturbesitz, West Berlin*]

VIENNA, 13 *September* 1768

It was a year ago the day before yesterday, September 11th, that we left Salzburg. Could I ever have dreamt then that I should stay a year in Vienna? But who can oppose Fate! I am so annoyed that I could foam at the mouth. The only good thing to be said is that we all, thank God, are well. But I only wish that I could let you know the happy day of our departure! ★

It is impossible for me to describe our affairs as fully as I should like. I have neither the time nor the patience. You will hear it all when we meet

---

[1] A son of Lorenz Hagenauer.   [2] August 10th.

and indeed some amazing things. As soon as our business is over we shall leave immediately.

★

We sometimes lunch with Father Parhammer[1] and we happened to be with him when the Emperor was laying the foundation stone for the new church.[2] On that occasion His Majesty asked Wolfgang how far he had got with his opera, and talked to him for a long time. Several people heard him do this.

★

(65) *Leopold Mozart to Lorenz Hagenauer, Salzburg*

[*Extract*]   [*Copy in the Staatsbibliothek Preussischer Kulturbesitz, West Berlin*]

VIENNA, 14 *September* 1768

I have this very moment received your letter of the 10th. Here is my reply! The reason for my silence was as Madame Wynne has stated. I know Countess von Rosenberg and her sister-in-law. The Countess does not belong to the most select aristocracy, for she is the sister of a wealthy gentleman of private means, a Mr. Wynne,[3] a London acquaintance of mine, whose name I will show you on my list.

The brother of this Mr. Wynne fell in love with a German lady, Cronemann by name, the same who has been singing at Salzburg. Her father was a musician in Holland and her father's brother with several sons is still in Amsterdam. One son is a musician in the service of Prince Conti in Paris and came to see us with Schobert. The mother of this singer attached herself to an Italian Kapellmeister, Paradies,[4] who, after the death of her husband, took entire charge of the children. When I was in London he married off this one to Mr. Wynne, and another to Signor Paolo Mazzinghi,[5] a London violinist.

★

---

[1] Ignaz Parhammer (1715–1786), a famous Jesuit Father, who after the emigration of the Protestants from Salzburg in 1733 took an active part in restoring the Catholic faith. In 1758 he became Father Confessor to the Emperor Joseph and in 1759 took over the management of the Waisenhaus (Orphanage), where he introduced the teaching of music on the model of the Venetian schools of music.

[2] In summer 1768 the Emperor laid the foundation stone of the new Orphanage Church on the Rennweg.

[3] Richard Wynne, the father of Elizabeth, chief author of the Wynne diaries, edited by Anne Fremantle, London, 1935. He is not mentioned in the *Reiseaufzeichnungen* of Leopold Mozart, who must refer to some other list. His eldest sister Giustiniana married on 17 January 1758 Count Orsini von Rosenberg, Imperial Ambassador to the Venetian Republic, who died in 1765. A portion of this letter which has been omitted contains a long account of Richard's younger brother William, the 'wicked uncle' of the Wynne diaries.

[4] Pietro Domenico Paradies (Paradisi), 1710–1792, born at Naples, was trained by Porpora and made a reputation as a teacher and composer for the harpsichord. He came in 1746 to London, where he lived for many years. According to C. F. Pohl, *Mozart in London*, pp. 176–177, he married off his pupil Miss Cassandra Frederick to Thomas (*sic*) Wynne, a wealthy landowner in South Wales, and her sister to Tommaso Mazzinghi.

[5] Not Paolo, but Tommaso Mazzinghi, violinist at Marylebone Gardens, who died in 1775. He is mentioned in Leopold Mozart's *Reiseaufzeichnungen*, p. 36 (*MBA*, No. 99).

As for Wolfgang's opera all I can tell you is that, to put it shortly, the whole hell of musicians has arisen to prevent the display of a child's ability. I cannot even press for its performance, since a conspiracy has been formed to produce it, if it must be produced, extremely badly and thus ruin it. I have had to await the arrival of the Emperor. Otherwise the 'bataille' would have commenced long ago. Believe me, I shall leave nothing undone which may be necessary to save my child's honour. I knew how it would be long ago and have suspected it even longer. I even spoke to His Excellency Count von Zeill. The latter, however, believed that all the musicians were in favour of Wolfgang, because he too judged by appearances and knew nothing of the inner wickedness of these beasts. Patience! Time will clear up everything and God lets nothing happen to no purpose.

Farewell to you all. I am your old

MOZART

(66) *Leopold Mozart to Lorenz Hagenauer, Salzburg*

[*Extract*]   [*Copy in the Staatsbibliothek Preussischer Kulturbesitz, West Berlin*]

VIENNA, 24 *September* 1768

I wrote today to His Grace the Archbishop. I hope that there is no foundation for the 'bruit' which you reported to me.[1] But if God has some other purpose for us, then it will not be in our power to alter it. I hope, however, that you will not leave me in ignorance for a single moment. On the morning of the 21st I had an audience with His Majesty the Emperor and handed to him my complaints about the theatrical impresario Affligio.[2] His Excellency Count Spork[3] has already been entrusted with the investigation and Affligio has been ordered to give an explanation; in addition to the hundred ducats for the opera, I am demanding repayment of the expenses which I have incurred here during all this time. But patience! We shall soon know the result. The Emperor was most gracious and promised us full justice.

Today I have had to draw money again. Heaven will repay everything. ★

Herr Küffel has entered the service of Prince Esterházy at Eisenstadt, ★]
where Herr Joseph Haydn is Kapellmeister.

---

[1] Possibly a rumour that, on account of his prolonged absence, Leopold Mozart would be asked to resign his appointments in the Archbishop's service.

[2] The autograph of Leopold Mozart's 'Species facti', a formal complaint to the Emperor Joseph II, is in the Zavertal Collection of Mozart relics at Glasgow University and was published by Farmer and Smith, *New Mozartiana*, Glasgow, 1935, pp. 113–119. The petition was quite unsuccessful. See also *MBA*, No. 139, and *MDB*, p. 80 f.

[3] Johann Wenzel Spork (1724–1804), Austrian statesman and a connoisseur of music. In 1764 Maria Theresia appointed him Director of Court and Chamber Music.

(67) Leopold Mozart to Lorenz Hagenauer, Salzburg

[Extract]   [Copy in the Staatsbibliothek Preussischer Kulturbesitz, West Berlin]

VIENNA, 12 November 1768

★   The new church of Father Parhammer's orphanage will be blessed on the Feast of the Immaculate Conception. For this Feast Wolfgang has composed a solemn mass,[1] an offertorium[2] and a trumpet concerto for a boy,[3] and has dedicated them to the orphanage. Presumably Wolfgang himself will conduct this music.[4] There are reasons for everything.

★

(68) Leopold Mozart to Lorenz Hagenauer, Salzburg

[Extract]   [Copy in the Staatsbibliothek Preussischer Kulturbesitz, West Berlin]

VIENNA, 14 December 1768

★   Only now have we been able to conclude our affairs.

★   The Mass, which was produced by little Wolfgang on December 7th at Father Parhammer's orphanage in the presence of the Imperial Court and which he himself conducted, has restored that reputation which our enemies, by preventing the performance of the opera, intended to destroy, and, as the throng was amazing, has convinced the court and the public of the wickedness of our adversaries. I shall give you more details when we meet.[5] And, what is more, Her Majesty the Empress has sent us a beautiful present.

★

(69) Leopold Mozart to Archbishop Sigismund von Schrattenbach

[Autograph in the Landesarchiv, Salzburg]

[SALZBURG, before 8 March 1769]

YOUR GRACE, MOST WORTHY PRINCE OF THE HOLY ROMAN EMPIRE, MOST GRACIOUS PRINCE AND LORD!

When Your Grace was recently pleased to allow me most graciously to remain a few months longer in Vienna, you gave orders, however, that

---

[1] Perhaps K. 139 [47a]. See Köchel, pp. 73, 74.
[2] Sometimes identified with K. 117 [66a], 'Benedictus sit Deus'.
[3] This has not been preserved.
[4] Conducting with a baton was then the custom for church music, whereas operas and orchestral works were generally conducted from the harpsichord. See G. Schünemann, *Geschichte des Dirigierens*, 1913, p. 154 f.
[5] The Mozarts arrived back in Salzburg on 5 January 1769.

until my return my pay should be withheld.[1] As my stay in Vienna has nevertheless taken place against my will and to my disadvantage and as I could not leave Vienna before without loss of my own honour and that of my child; and as, in addition, both my son and I have composed various works for the Church, and especially for use in the Cathedral,[2] I now most humbly beg Your Grace not only to pay me for the past month, but as a special favour to give your most gracious order that the sum which has been withheld should also be paid to me. The greater this favour is, the more shall I endeavour to render myself worthy of it and to pray God for Your Grace's welfare.

I and my children send our most humble greetings to Your Grace, our Prince and Lord.

Your most obedient
LEOPOLD MOZART,
Deputy-Kapellmeister[3]

(70) *Mozart to a Girl Friend*

[*Copy in the Staatsbibliothek Preussischer Kulturbesitz, West Berlin*]

DEAR FRIEND, [SALZBURG, 1769[4]]

Forgive me for taking the liberty of plaguing you with a few lines but as you said yesterday that you could understand everything, no matter what Latin words I might choose to write down, curiosity has got the better of me and I am writing down for you a few lines made up of various Latin words. When you have read them, please do me the favour of sending me your answer by one of Hagenauer's maids, for our Nannie cannot wait. But you must send me a letter too.

Cuperem scire de qua causa, a quam plurimis adolescentibus otium usque adeo aestimatur, ut ipsi se nec verbis, nec verberibus, ab hoc sinant abduci,[5]

WOLFGANG
MOZART

[1] See p. 85 n. 4. Schurig, vol. i. p. 188, quotes the order to the Court Pay Office, dated 18 March 1768, to the effect that 'if the court musicians, Mozart, Meisner and Küffel do not turn up in April, they are not to receive any more pay'.

[2] Mozart's recent sacred works included two masses written for Vienna, K. 139 [47a] and K. 49 [47d], and one for Salzburg, K. 65 [61a].

[3] The result of this application was that the 'applicant was granted his pay for the months of January and February'.

[4] The recipient is unknown. The indefinite date is an addition in a strange handwriting. This is the first letter of Mozart's which has been handed down.

[5] 'I should like to know for what reason idleness is so popular with most young people that it is impossible to draw them from it either by words or by punishments.'

Leitzmann, *W. A. Mozarts Leben*, Leipzig, 1926, p. 471 n., suggests that this Latin passage was extracted from some Latin grammar or reading-book at which Mozart was then working. And Schiedermair points out, vol. i. p. 295, n. 1, that probably Mozart was engrossed in Latin studies, seeing that in 1768 and 1769 he composed his first three masses in G major (K. 49 [47d]), D minor (K. 65 [61a]) and C major (K. 66).

Mozart's fifth journey was a visit to Italy with his father, who took him to Rovereto, Verona, Milan, Parma, Bologna, Florence, Rome, Naples, and other towns. On their return journey they spent three months in Bologna, where Mozart studied counterpoint under the learned Padre Martini, and nearly four months in Milan, where he carried out a commission to write the first opera Mitridate, Rè di Ponto *for the 1770-71 carnival season. In Italy Mozart heard several operas and made the acquaintance of the leading Italian singers. He composed too during this time several operatic arias, an oratorio* La Betulia liberata, *and his first string quartet. This tour, the first Italian journey, lasted from 13 December 1769 to 28 March 1771. It is described in letters from Leopold Mozart to his wife, Mozart occasionally adding letters or postscripts of varying length. Letters 71-137.*

(71) *Leopold Mozart to his Wife*

[*Autograph in the Mozarteum, Salzburg*]

[WÖRGL, 14 *December* 1769[1]]

We reached Kalterl at one o'clock and had for our lunch a piece of preserved veal accompanied by a most fearful stinking smell. With this we drank a few draughts of good beer, for the wine was a laxative. We reached Lofer after seven. When I had ordered our supper, we went to call on the prefect who was very much annoyed with us for not having gone at once to his house. So, as we had already ordered our meal in the inn, we had it brought to the prefect's house, where we supped, gossiped until ten o'clock and were given a fine room and a good bed. In the morning I drank chocolate and Wolfgang had some excellent soup. We drove until midday to St. Johann and arrived this evening at Wörgl, where I sent an invitation to the Vicar, Herr Hartmann Kehlhammer of Chiemsee. He has just come and sends you greetings. It is now ten o'clock and we must go to bed, for to morrow I have to be up at five. In spite of the roads which were, as I had been told, very bad, I slept soundly, for I saw that we had a very good driver. In these parts, especially from Lofer to St. Johann, there is an extraordinary amount of snow. Keep well and cheerful! I shall write immediately from Innsbruck.

MZT.

(71a) *Mozart to his Mother*

[*Autograph in the Pierpont Morgan Library, New York City*]

DEAREST MAMMA!   [WÖRGL, 14 *December* 1769[2]]

My heart is completely enchanted with all these pleasures, because it is so jolly on this journey, because it is so warm in the carriage and because our coachman is a fine fellow who, when the road gives him the slightest chance, drives so fast. Papa will have already described the journey to Mamma. The reason why I am writing to Mamma is to show her that I know my duty and that I am with the deepest respect her devoted son

WOLFGANG MOZART

[1] The information given in the letters written by Leopold Mozart and his son during their first journey to Italy is supplemented by notes kept by Mozart himself during their stay in Innsbruck, Bozen, Rovereto and Naples. The autograph of these notes, which were published by A. Sandberger, *Jahrbuch der Musikbibliothek Peters*, 1901, is in the Bavarian State Library. These notes, together with those kept by Leopold Mozart in the other Italian towns they visited, are also reproduced in A. Schurig, *Leopold Mozarts Reiseaufzeichnungen*, 1920, pp. 49–54, and in *MBA*.

[2] The Mozarts left Salzburg on 13 December 1769.

[3] A postscript to his father's letter.

(71b) *Mozart to his Sister*

[Autograph in the Pierpont Morgan Library, New York City]

MY DEAREST SISTER,   [WÖRGL, 14 *December* 1769[1]]

Thank God, we have arrived safely at Wörgl. To tell the truth, I must say that travelling is very jolly, that it is not at all cold and that it is as warm in our carriage as in a room. How is your sore throat? Surely our Signore Seccatore[2] turned up the very day we left? If you see Herr von Schiedenhofen,[3] tell him that I am always singing 'Tralaliera, Tralaliera' and that I need not put sugar in my soup now that I am no longer in Salzburg. At Lofer we supped and slept in the house of Herr Helmreich, who is prefect there. His wife is an excellent lady. She is the sister of Herr Moll. I am hungry. I am longing to eat something. Meanwhile, farewell. Addio.

PS.—My compliments to all my good friends, to Herr Hagenauer (the merchant), his wife, his sons and his daughters, to Madame Rosa[4] and her husband, to Herr Adlgasser and Herr Spitzeder. As for Herr Hornung,[5] ask him from me whether he has again made the mistake of thinking that I was in bed instead of you.

WOLFGANG MOZART

(72) *Leopold Mozart to his Wife*

[Autograph in the Mozarteum, Salzburg]

[INNSBRUCK, 15 *December* 1769]

Friday, at six o'clock in the evening

We have been here half an hour already. At noon we were in Schwaz. The country near Innsbruck seemed to me to resemble somewhat the road towards Hallein near Kaltenhausen; and Innsbruck itself is similarly situated. Otherwise so far I have nothing to tell. Thank God, we are well. We are lodging at the 'Weisses Kreuz'. If you have anything to write to me, you can send the letter here. If in the meantime I depart, I shall first leave a message at the Post Office that letters should be forwarded to Bozen. You have only to address your letters:

à Mr: Mozart, Maître de Chapelle de la Musique de S:A:S: Le Prince Archevêque de Salzbourg.

---

[1] A second postscript, written in Italian, to his father's letter.

[2] i.e. Mr. Boring, obviously some Salzburg acquaintance.

[3] Joachim Ferdinand von Schiedenhofen (1747–1823) was a friend of Mozart's. He became later Court Councillor at Salzburg.

[4] Rosa Barducci, a portrait painter, who in 1764 married Johann Baptist Hagenauer, Court Sculptor in Salzburg, whom she had met in Florence. See p. 13, n. 2.

[5] Joseph Hornung, a bass singer in the service of the Salzburg court.

In a fit of absentmindedness I took away with me on my watch the key of our clavichord. I return it herewith, as it is unnecessary to carry it about with me so far. See that it is not lost. Farewell! Farewell to all! Wolfgang and I kiss you and Nannerl, and I am your old

MZT.

I am giving this letter now to the Vienna post.

(73) *Leopold Mozart to his Wife*

[*Autograph in the Mozarteum, Salzburg*]

[INNSBRUCK] 17 *December* [1769]
Sunday night, December 17th, I think, for
I no longer possess a calendar of this year.

His Excellency Count Spaur,[1] the brother of our Salzburg member of the Cathedral Chapter, on my announcing my arrival through my servant, not only sent his servant immediately to welcome me and to tell me that his carriage would fetch us on Saturday at two o'clock and drive us to his house, but with his wife received me most graciously and offered to place his carriage at our service, an offer which I accepted. Early on Sunday morning I received a note from him inviting us to a concert at five o'clock, which was to take place at the house of Count Leopold Künigl. Meanwhile I made use of the carriage, drove twice to Herr von Kalckhammer, then to Baron Christiani, where I chatted for three quarters of an hour about all sorts of things, then to His Excellency Baron Enzenberg, and finally at five o'clock to the concert. Wolfgang was presented with a very beautiful concerto which he played there at sight. As usual we were received with all honours and were brought home later by Count Spaur in person. In short, we are perfectly satisfied. Tomorrow I intend to pack up my things, which will not take long, as I did not unpack much, and on Tuesday, God willing, I propose to leave. Please give Herr von Schiedenhofen my obedient thanks both for the letter of recommendation which he sent me and for the kind apology which he made in my stead and which is really justified. Please ask him to give my thanks and my greetings to Herr Major. I shall write to Herr von Schiedenhofen myself as soon as I have time. I hope that you are all well. I shall write again from Bozen. You must keep all our letters. I purposely left at home the various parts of the opera,[2] even the violin parts, and only took the

---

[1] Count Johann Nepomuk Spaur (1724–1793), governor of the Tyrol.
[2] *La finta semplice*, written in Vienna 1768, and performed in Salzburg 1769.

score with me. But we forgot to take a few arias for Wolfgang. It does not matter, however, for we shall get enough arias. A certain Count Attems, who spoke to us here, is going to Salzburg with his wife. He studied there many years ago and he is an old acquaintance of mine. He will perhaps call on you in order to hear Nannerl play something to him. We kiss you and Nannerl a thousand times. Farewell to all! I am your old   MOZART

⟨The present was twelve ducats.[1]⟩

(74) *Leopold Mozart to his Wife*

[Autograph in the Mozarteum, Salzburg]

BOZEN, 22 *December* 1769

We arrived safely at Bozen[2] yesterday evening. Today I took my two letters to the post and lunched with Herr Kurzweil. Tomorrow at midday we are invited to Herr Stockhammer, to whom Herr Ranftl gave us an introduction, and this evening we are going to Herr Antoni Gummer. I myself do not yet know whether we shall stay here over Christmas or leave tomorrow evening. Meanwhile, I think that you had better write to me at Rovereto, where I shall call at the post. In addition, I am leaving instructions at all Post Offices and my name as well, which is as well known everywhere as a bad half-penny. We are, thank God, in good health. Here is a sheet from the Innsbruck paper.[3] I hope that you are both well. Good-bye! Our greetings to all our good friends. I write in haste and I am your old

MZT.

I and Wolfgang kiss you a thousand times.
Herr Kurzweil sends you his greetings.

(75) *Leopold Mozart to his Wife*

[Extract]   *[Autograph in the Mozarteum, Salzburg]*

VERONA,[4] 7 *January* 1770

I am very sorry not to have received your first letter, which is probably lying at the Bozen Post Office. I shall make enquiries, for it will have been forwarded there from Innsbruck. *Thank God, we are well!* Let me tell you so at the outset. It would have been helpful if you had told me

---

[1] Passages in angular brackets are in cypher in the original. See p. xviii.
[2] In Bozen the Mozarts stayed at the inn 'Zur Sonne'.
[3] Quoted by Nissen, p. 157; translated in *MDB*, p. 101.
[4] The Mozarts arrived at Verona on December 27th and stayed at the 'Due Torri'.

how many letters you have received from me, for I sent you one from Wörgl, one by the hired coachman, one from Innsbruck by post and one from Bozen.[1] We only spent a day and a half in Bozen. We had hardly ★ arrived at Rovereto[2] when a certain Christiani, who took the woman's part in the play 'The Child of Cato' at the Collegio Rupertino, turned up at once and on behalf of his brother invited us to lunch on the following day. And who was this brother? That very same Nicolaus Christiani who was Ecclesiastical Commissioner in Salzburg and my pupil on the violin, and who is now the chief man in Rovereto and the whole district, that is, Lieutenant of the County representing Her Majesty the Empress. You will remember him. As soon as we entered his house, he said that Wolf- ★ gang was like you, for he remembered your appearance quite well. The ★ nobles gave a concert in the house of Baron Todeschi. And who was this Baron Todeschi? That same person whom Herr Giovanni once brought to us in Vienna. You will perhaps remember him. It is hardly necessary to mention how greatly Wolfgang has been doing himself credit. In the afternoon of the following day we went to the organ of the principal church, and, although only six or eight of the leading people knew that we were coming, we found all Rovereto assembled there and some very strong fellows had to go ahead and make way for us to the choir, where we then had to wait for over five minutes before we could reach the organ, as everyone wanted to get close to us. We spent four days in Rovereto. We have standing invitations here from Marchese Carlotti and ★ also from Signor Locatelli.[3] We have lunched twice with Marchese Car- lotti and also with Count Carlo Emily and twice with Count Giusti, who has a beautiful garden and picture-gallery. You will perhaps find them mentioned in Keyssler's Reisebeschreibung.[4] We dined yesterday with Signor Locatelli and today there was absolute confusion, which I must describe to you in greater detail. We were invited to the house of a certain honest fellow, Signor Ragazzoni. Signor Lugiati,[5] the Receiver- General of Venice, had asked some courtiers to request me to allow Wolfgang to have his portrait painted.[6] Yesterday morning he had the first sitting and today after church he was to have the second one and we were to dine there too. Signor Lugiati himself went to Signor Ragazzoni

[1] Letters 71, 72, 73 and 74.
[2] The Mozarts arrived at Rovereto on December 24th and stayed at the inn 'Zur Rose'.
[3] Not the famous violinist Pietro Locatelli (1693-1764), as Abert, vol. i. pp. 177 and 331, seems to suggest, but Michelangelo Locatelli, a merchant.
[4] Johann Georg Keyssler, Neueste Reise durch Deutschland, Böhmen, Ungarn, die Schweiz, Italien und Lothringen, Hanover, 1740-1741. The Baedeker of the eighteenth century.
[5] Pietro Lugiati (1724-1788), a famous connoisseur and patron of music. Nissen, p. 197 f., quotes an Italian letter, dated 22 April 1770, which Lugiati wrote to Frau Mozart about her son, describing him as 'un portente di Natura nella musica'. See MBA, No. 178.
[6] This oil painting for which Mozart sat on 6 and 7 January 1770, was done by a Saverio dalla Rosa, a nephew of the Cignaroli mentioned in Leopold Mozart's Reiseaufzeichnungen, p. 50 (MBA, No. 154). See illustration no. 3.

and begged him to leave us to him, to which the latter had to agree, though most reluctantly, because Lugiati is very powerful in Venice. So this morning after church we were to go to his house to sit once more for the painter before we went on to lunch. But again an even greater person appeared, to wit, the Bishop of Verona, of the house of Giustiniani, who sent us, through Signor Locatelli, an invitation not only to call on him after church, but to lunch with him. On hearing, however, that Wolfgang's portrait was being painted and that we wanted to leave, he let us lunch with Signor Lugiati, but kept us until after one o'clock. Progress was then made with the portrait and we did not sit down to lunch until three o'clock. Afterwards we drove to St. Thomas's Church in order to play on the two organs there; and although we only decided to do this while we were at table and although only a few tickets had been sent to Marchese Carlotti and Count Pedemonte, nevertheless such a crowd had assembled that we had hardly room to get out of the coach. The crush was so great that we were obliged to go through the monastery. But in a moment so many people had rushed up to us that we should not have been able to proceed at all, if the Fathers, who were already waiting for us at the monastery doors, had not taken us into their midst. When the performance was over, the throng was even greater, for everyone wanted to see the little organist. As soon as we were seated in our carriage, I told the coachman to drive us home, where we have locked ourselves in our room and I have begun to write this letter. But I have had to tear myself away, for they would not have left us in peace long enough to finish it. We are driving out tomorrow with Signor Locatelli to see the Amphitheatre and other rare sights of the town. Then we shall lunch with him and drive round afterwards to pay farewell calls. The day after tomorrow we shall pack and on Wednesday evening, God willing, we shall travel to Mantua which, although it is near, is almost a winter day's journey on
★ account of the filthy road. Now my paper is at an end. Farewell. I am your old

MZT.

(75a) *Mozart to his Sister*

[Copy in a private collection]

DEAREST SISTER!   VERONA, 7 *January* 1770

    I have had an aching feeling, because I have been so long waiting in vain for an answer. I have had good reason too, because I have not yet received your letter. Here ends the German booby and the Italian one begins. Lei è più franca nella lingua italiana di quel che mi ho imaginato. Lei mi dica la cagione perchè lei non fu nella commedia che hanno giocato i cavalieri? Adesso sentiamo sempre opere: una è titolata: il Ruggiero.[1] Oronte, il padre di Bradamante, è un principe (fa il signor Afferi), un bravo cantante, un baritono, ma [2] forced when he sings falsetto, but not as much as Tibaldi in Vienna. Bradamante, figlia di Oronte, innamorata di Ruggiero (she is to marry Leone, but she does not want him), fa una povera Baronessa, che ha avuto una gran disgrazia, ma non so che. Recita under an assumed name, but I do not know it, ha una voce passabile, e la statura non sarebbe male, ma distona come il diavolo. Ruggiero, un ricco principe, innamorato di Bradamante, un musico, canta un poco in the manner of Manzuoli ed ha una bellissima voce forte ed è gia vecchio, ha cinquantacinque anni ed ha una flexible throat. Leone, who is to marry Bradamante, is very rich, but whether he is rich off the stage, I do not know. Fa una donna, la moglie di Afferi. Ha una bellissima voce, ma è tanto susurro nel teatro che non si sente niente. Irene fa una sorella di Lolli,[3] del gran violinista, che abbiamo sentito a Vienna. She has a muffled voice and always sings a semiquaver too late o troppo a buon' ora. Ganno fa un signor, che non so come egli si chiama, è la prima volta che lui recita.[4] After each act there is a ballet. There is a good dancer here called Monsieur Ruesler. He is a German and dances very well. One of the last times we were at the opera (but not the very last time) we asked M. Ruesler to come up to our palco (for we have a free entrance to the palco of Marchese Carlotti, as we have the key) and there we had a talk with him. A propos, everyone is masked now and it is really very convenient when you wear your mask, as you have the advantage of not having to take off your hat when you are greeted and of not having to address the person by name. You just say, 'servitore umilissimo, Signora Maschera'. Cospetto di Bacco, what fun! But the funniest thing of all is that we go to bed between seven and half past seven. Se lei indovinasse questo, io dirò certamente che lei sia la madre di tutti indovini.[5]

---

[1] Probably, as Schiedermair, vol. i. p. 4, n. 2, suggests, the opera by Pietro Guglielmi (1727–1804), which had already been performed in Venice.

[2] You are more fluent in Italian than I had imagined. Please tell me the reason why you did not go to the play which the courtiers acted? At present we are always hearing operas. One of them is 'Ruggiero'. Oronte, father of Bradamante, is a prince. Signor Afferi takes this part. He is a fine singer, a baritone, but, . . .

[3] Antonio Lolli (c. 1730–1802), a famous violinist who after touring with Nardini became leader at Stuttgart and subsequently at St. Petersburg. His sister is described in the *Reiseaufzeichnungen*, p. 50, as a singer and the wife of Signor Amelli, a dancer. See *MBA*, No. 154.

[4] Bradamante, daughter of Oronte, is in love with Ruggiero, . . . Her part is sung by a poor Baroness, who has had a great misfortune, but I don't know what it was. She is singing, . . . Her voice is tolerably good and she has not a bad presence, but she sings devilishly out of tune. The part of Ruggiero, a rich prince, who is in love with Bradamante, is sung by a castrato, who sings rather in the manner of Manzuoli and has a very fine powerful voice and is already old. He is fifty-five and has, . . . His part is sung by a woman, Afferi's wife. She has a most beautiful voice, but there is so much whispering in the theatre that you can't hear anything. Irene's part is sung by a sister of Lolli, the great violinist, whom we heard in Vienna. . . . The part of Ganno is taken by someone whose name I do not know. He is singing for the first time.

[5] If you guess this I shall certainly say that you are the mother of all guessers.

Kiss my mother's hand for me. I kiss you a thousand times and assure you that I shall always remain

your sincere brother

WOLFGANG MOZART

Portez-vous bien et aimez-moi toujours.

(76) *Leopold Mozart to his Wife*

[*Extract*]   [*Autograph in the Mozarteum, Salzburg*]

MANTUA,[1] 11 January 1770

We arrived here yesterday evening and went to the opera[2] an hour later, at six o'clock. Thank God, we are well. Wolfgang looks as if he had been through a campaign, for his face is reddish-brown, especially about the nose and mouth, for instance, just like the face of His Majesty the Emperor. This is due to the air and to the open fires. My beauty has not yet suffered, or I should be in despair. I have not yet anything to write
★ about from here. Tomorrow we are invited to lunch with Count Francesco Eugenio D'Arco and then I shall be able to let you know more about this town. Meanwhile I must tell you something about Verona. We have seen the Amphitheatre and the Geological Museum, which you will read about in Keyssler's Reisebeschreibung. I am bringing back a book on the antiquities of Verona. Herr von Helmreich, to whom I send greetings, will surely lend you the other two parts of Keyssler, so that, although you are not with us, you can at least travel at home in imagination. I should make the letters too heavy and too dear, if I were to send along the newspaper notices which have appeared about Wolfgang in Mantua and other places. But I enclose this one,[3] in which there are two mistakes, for it says 'the present *Kapellmeister*' and 'not yet thirteen years old', instead of fourteen. But you know how it is; journalists write as it occurs to them and whatever comes into their minds. I could send you along other comments too, for in Verona the poets vied with one another in composing verses about him. Here is a copy of a sonnet which a learned dilettante jotted down in our presence.[4] Kapellmeister Daniele Barba also sang extempore the most beautiful verses about Wolfgang.

On the 16th in the Hall of the Accademia Filarmonica there will be the usual weekly concert to which we are invited.[5] Then we shall leave im-

---

[1] The Mozarts reached Mantua on January 10th and stayed at the 'Ancora Verde'.

[2] For Mozart's account of the opera, which was Hasse's *Demetrio*, see p. 110.

[3] Nissen, pp. 169–170, reproduces this cutting from a Mantuan newspaper of January 9th. See also *MDB*, p. 105.

[4] For this sonnet by Zaccaria Betti, described in the *Reiseaufzeichnungen*, p. 50 (*MBA*, No. 154), as 'poeta dilettante', together with a poem addressed to Mozart by Meschini, see Nissen, pp. 162–163, and *MDB*, pp. 103–104.

[5] For the programme of this concert and for the comment of a Mantuan newspaper, see Nissen, pp. 170–174 and *MDB*, pp. 106–108. Rudolf Lewicki in *MM*, Nov. 1920, p. 30, gives the Italian text of the latter.

mediately for Milan and, if the weather is cold and the roads are frozen, we shall travel through Cremona.[1] If it is mild and the roads in consequence bad, we must go through Brescia. It is very quiet here and one never hears a word about anything. It is just like being in Germany. By my honour I swear I have hardly time to write this letter, and on account of it we have had to miss the opera today. As soon as we reach Milan I shall write to you again; and you must write to me at Milan. You may add below: per ricapito del Signor Troger, Segretario di S. Eccellenza il Signor Conte Carlo di Firmian.[2] Now I must go to bed. Farewell to you and Nannerl. We kiss you a thousand times. We drink your health every day. Wolfgang never forgets to do this. Good-bye. I am your old

MZT.

All kinds of greetings to all our good friends. I cannot write to anybody, for I am hustled to death. Nothing but dressing and undressing, packing and unpacking, and withal no warm room, so that one freezes like a dog. Everything I touch is as cold as ice. And if you were to see the doors and locks in the rooms! just like prisons! Post the enclosed letter to Herr Friederici[3] at Gera, so that it may be forwarded quickly and safely. It is an order for a harpsichord.

(77) *Leopold Mozart to his Wife*

[*Extract*]   [*Autograph in the Mozarteum, Salzburg*]

MILAN, 26 *January* 1770

I have received from Herr Troger your letter of the 12th. We reached Milan[4] at noon on the 23rd. On the 24th your letter arrived and with it your first note which, at my request, Herr Antoni Gummer called for at the Bozen Post Office and forwarded to me. You complain that for three weeks you have had no word from me. But I wrote to you from Verona and from Mantua.[5] You ought to have received my first letter from Verona, as I posted it there on January 7th. The second letter cannot have reached Salzburg yet, for I only posted it in Mantua on the 15th. At midday on the 10th we left Verona and reached Mantua in the evening, as I believe I have already told you. I wish you could see the hall where the

---

[1] The Mozarts took this route. See *Reiseaufzeichnungen*, p. 50, and *MBA*, No. 156.

[2] Count Carlo di Firmian (1718–1782), who had been Governor-General of Lombardy since 1759, was a native of Deutschmetz in the province of Trent.

[3] Christian Ernst Friederici (1709–1780), a well-known manufacturer of claviers and the first to make upright instruments. Equally famous was his son Christian Gottlob Friederici (1750–1805).

[4] The Mozarts stayed at the Augustinian monastery of San Marco.

[5] Letters 75 and 76.

concert took place, the so-called Teatrino della Accademia Filarmonica. In all my life I have never seen anything more beautiful of its kind; and as *I hope that you are carefully collecting all our letters*, I shall describe it to you later when we meet. It is not a theatre, but a hall built with boxes like an opera house. Where the stage ought to be, there is a raised platform for the orchestra and behind the orchestra another gallery built with boxes for the audience. The crowds, the general shouting, clapping, noisy enthusiasm and cries of 'Bravo' and, in a word, the admiration displayed by the listeners, I cannot adequately describe to you.

Meanwhile some reports will doubtless have reached Salzburg not only from Rovereto but also from Verona and Mantua.

Herewith I enclose another poem composed by a lady, Signora Sartoretti, who entertained us in Mantua. On the following day her servant brought us on a beautiful plate an exceedingly fine bouquet with red ribbons below and a large piece of four ducats entwined in the ribbons; above was the poem, a copy of which I enclose.[1] I can assure you that everywhere I have found the most charming people and that in all towns we have had our particular friends, who have been with us until the last moment before our departure and have done everything to make our stay a pleasant one. I enclose a Mantuan newspaper, which we only received in Milan. Among other things you will find in it the programme of the music which was performed at the concert.[2] You must know, however, that neither this concert in Mantua nor the one in Verona were given for money, for everybody goes in free; in Verona this privilege belongs only to the nobles who alone keep up these concerts; but in Mantua the nobles, the military class and the eminent citizens may all attend them, because they are subsidised by Her Majesty the Empress. You will easily understand that we shall not become rich in Italy and you will admit that we shall do well enough if we earn our travelling expenses; and these I have always earned. But I assure you that although there are only two of us, the expenses are not small, and I fear that we have paid out about seventy ducats. It is already six weeks since we left Salzburg. Even if you live *a pasto* in Italy and hardly ever lunch at home, yet supper, room, firewood and so forth are all so dear, that after nine to eleven days in an inn you seldom get away with a bill for less than six ducats. I often thank God that I left you at home. Firstly, you would not have been able to stand the cold. Secondly, it would have cost us a great deal of money and we should not have been so free to live the way in which we now do; for here *we are staying at the Augustinian monastery of S. Marco*; not that we do so free, by any means! But we can live here comfortably and safely and we are near His Excellency Count Firmian. We have three large guest rooms. In the first we have a fire, take our meals and give audiences;

---

[1] For this poem see Abert, vol. ii. p. 932, and *MDB*, p. 108 f.   [2] See p. 106, n. 3.

in the second I sleep and we have put our trunk there; in the third room Wolfgang sleeps and there we keep our other small luggage. We each sleep on four good mattresses and every night the bed is warmed, so that Wolfgang, when he goes to bed, is always quite happy. We have a brother, Frater Alfonso, especially for our service and we are very well looked after. But I cannot tell you how long we shall stay here. His Excellency the Count is suffering from a cold. He wanted very much to give a concert in his house and to invite the Duke of Modena. So I have not been able to deliver the other letters of introduction, because this concert must take place first, as I think it will, on Tuesday or Wednesday next, for His Excellency is already better. I told you that Wolfgang had got red hands and a red face from the cold and the open fires. He is quite well now. Madame Sartoretti in Mantua gave him some skin cream to rub on his hands every evening, and in three days they were all right; and now he looks as he did before. *Otherwise, thank God, we have always been well*; and the change of air only gave Wolfgang a kind of dry cough which he shook off long ago. We shall hardly hear Herr Meisner sing in Florence, for not only will our stay here be a rather long one, but, as Turin is so near, we shall undoubtedly take a trip there. We are also proposing to spend a short time in Parma and Bologna, and thus we shall not reach Florence until the beginning of Lent.

Address all your letters in future to Mr. Troger, as you have been doing ★ lately. I am your old faithful

L. MZT

We kiss you both a thousand times.

(77a) *Mozart to his Sister*

[*Autograph in a private collection*]

[MILAN, 26 *January* 1770[1]]

I rejoice with my whole heart that you had such a good time during that sleigh-drive and I wish you a thousand opportunities of amusement so that you may spend your life very merrily. But one thing distresses me, and that is, that you have made Herr von Mölk[2] sigh and suffer so frightfully and that you did not go sleigh-driving with him, so that he might have upset you. How many handkerchiefs will he not have used that day, weeping on your account. No doubt he will have previously taken an ounce of tartar, which will have purged his wretchedly dirty

---

[1] This letter was probably sent in the same cover as Letter 77.

[2] One of the sons of Court Chancellor Felix von Mölk, probably Joseph. He was a friend of Mozart and in love with Nannerl.

body. I have no news except that Herr Gellert, the poet,[1] has died at Leipzig and since his death has written no more poetry. Just before I began this letter I composed an aria[2] from 'Demetrio',[3] which begins:

> Misero tu non sei:
> tu spieghi il tuo dolore,
> e, se non desti amore,
> ritrovi almen pietà.
>
> Misera ben son io
> che nel segreto laccio
> amo, non spero e taccio,
> e l' idol mio nol sa.

The opera at Mantua was charming. They played 'Demetrio'. The prima donna sings well, but very softly; and when you do not see her acting, but only singing, you would think that she is not singing at all. For she cannot open her mouth, but whines out everything. However, we are quite accustomed to that now. The seconda donna looks like a grenadier and has a powerful voice too, and, I must say, does not sing badly, seeing that she is acting for the first time. The primo uomo, il musico, sings beautifully, though his voice is uneven. His name is Caselli. Il secondo uomo is already old and I do not like him. His name is——. As for the tenors, one is called Otini.[4] He does not sing badly, but rather heavily like all Italian tenors, and he is a great friend of ours. I do not know the name of the other one. He is still young, but not particularly good. Primo ballerino—good. Prima ballerina—good, and it is said that she is not hideous, but I have not seen her close to. The rest are quite ordinary. A grotesco was there who jumps well, but cannot write as I do, I mean, as sows piddle. The orchestra was not bad. In Cremona it is good. The first violin is called Spagnoletto. The prima donna is not bad; she is quite old, I should say, and not good-looking; she acts better than she sings and she is the wife of a violinist called Masi, who plays in the orchestra. The opera was: La Clemenza di Tito.[5] Seconda donna, young, not at all bad on the stage, but nothing out of the ordinary. Primo uomo, musico, Cicognani—a delightful voice and a beautiful cantabile. The other two castrati, young and passable. The tenor's name is: non lo so.[6] He has a pleasant way with him, and resembles as though he were his natural son, Leroy in Vienna, who came to Geneva.

Ballerino primo, good. Ballerina prima, good but very plain. There

---

[1] Christian Fürchtegott Gellert (1715–1769), who since 1751 had been Professor of Philosophy at Leipzig University, enjoyed in his day a great reputation as a poet and man of letters. He died on 13 December 1769.

[2] This composition has not been preserved.

[3] Hasse's opera on a text by Metastasio which was performed at Mantua.

[4] Appears in the *Reiseaufzeichnungen*, p. 50 (*MBA*, No. 156), as 'Uttini'.

[5] Opera by J. A. Hasse.   [6] I don't know it.

was a woman dancer there, who did not dance badly and, what is very remarkable, was not bad-looking on the stage and off it. The others were quite ordinary. A grotesco was there too, who whenever he jumped let off a fart. As for Milan I really cannot tell you very much. We have not yet been to the opera, but we have heard that it has not been a success. Aprile,[1] primo uomo, sings well and has a beautiful even voice. We heard him in a church, when there happened to be a great festival. Madame Piccinelli from Paris, who sang at our concert, is acting in the opera. Monsieur Pick,[2] who danced in Vienna, is dancing here too. The opera is called: 'Didone abbandonata'.[3] This opera will soon come to an end and Signor Piccinni,[4] who is writing the next opera, is here. I have heard that his is called: 'Cesare in Egitto'.[5] Here there are also feste di ballo which begin as soon as the opera is over. The wife of Count von Firmian's steward is a Viennese. Last Friday we dined there and we are dining there again next Sunday. Farewell. Kiss my mother's hands a thousand times in vece mia.[6] I remain, true till death, your brother

WOLFGANG DE MOZART
The Honourable Highdale,
Friend of the Counting-house.

(78) Leopold Mozart to his Wife

[Extract]   [Autograph in the Mozarteum, Salzburg]

MILAN, 3 February 1770

I thought that you would receive my letters gradually. I hope that by this time my letter from Mantua too and the one from Milan will have reached you. This then is my eighth letter. I have nothing to say, save that, thank God, we are well; that our hands, especially Wolfgang's, are quite all right again; that the steward's wife made the skin cream for us very successfully and according to your recipe; that yesterday we were at the dress rehearsal of the new opera, 'Cesare in Egitto'; that this opera is excellent and that we both saw and spoke to Maestro Piccinni and Madame Piccinelli; that for the last fortnight we have had the most

---

[1] Giuseppe Aprile (1732–1813), a male contralto, was trained in Naples and from 1763 onwards sang in all the principal theatres of Italy and Germany.

[2] His real name was Le Picq.

[3] The composer of this opera was Ignazio Celionat of Turin.

[4] Niccolò Piccinni (1728–1800) was for a time the most popular of Italian operatic composers. His first successes were in Naples, but he achieved a veritable triumph in Rome in 1760 with his opera buffa La Cecchina, ossia la buona figliuola. He moved in 1776 to Paris, where his first French opera Roland, produced in July 1778, brought him a crowd of admirers who ranged themselves against Gluck and his partisans.

[5] Abert, vol. i. p. 181, n. 2, points out that the original score of Piccinni's opera bears the title Cesare e Cleopatra.   [6] On my behalf.

beautiful weather; that every day Wolfgang looks forward to his well-warmed mattresses; that he cannot write a letter to you because he is composing two Latin motets [1] for two castrati, one of whom is fifteen and the other sixteen years old, who asked him to compose them, and to whom, as they are friends of his and sing beautifully, he could not refuse anything; that it is very distressing to me to see and hear these boys and to know that I cannot take them back to Salzburg; that I foresee that we shall stay longer in Milan than I expected; that His Excellency Count Firmian has not yet completely recovered from his cold; that during the last few days I have again found an account in the papers of how the in-
★ habitants literally waylaid us in Bozolo, and about Wolfgang's skill and so forth; that Wolfgang sends you his thanks for your congratulations;
★ that I and Wolfgang kiss you and Nannerl a thousand times and that I am ever your

faithful husband

MOZART

★ Have our two guns been cleaned? Is Nannerl practising the harpsichord regularly?
★

(79) Leopold Mozart to his Wife

[Extract]   [Autograph in the Nationalbibliothek, Vienna]

MILAN, 10 February 1770

You will, I hope, have received my letters of January 27th and February 3rd, and also my letter from Mantua. [2] What I certainly foresee is that we shall remain here until the end of the carnival. His Excellency Count von Firmian is now better and on Wednesday, February 7th, we had the honour of lunching with him for the first time. After lunch he presented Wolfgang with the nine volumes of Metastasio's works, the Turin edition, one of the most beautiful, and very handsomely bound. You can well imagine that this present is very welcome to me as well as to Wolfgang. His Excellency is much impressed by Wolfgang's skill and marks us out for his special courtesies and distinctions. It would take too long to describe in detail the evidence of his knowledge which Wolfgang has given in the presence of Maestro Sammartini [3] and of a number of the most brilliant people, and of how he has amazed them. You know how it is on these occasions, for you have seen it often enough.
★ Meanwhile we have had the opportunity of hearing various kinds of

---

[1] These have not been preserved.

[2] Letters 77 (dated January 26th), 78 and 76.

[3] Giovanni Battista Sammartini (1700 or 1701–1775) was a prolific composer for instruments and voices and became maestro di cappella to more than half the churches in Milan, for which he furnished masses on all the great festivals.

church music and yesterday we listened to the High Mass or Requiem for old Marchese Litta, who to the annoyance of his enormous family died during the carnival, although they would have gladly allowed him to go on living until Lent. The Dies Irae of this Requiem lasted about three quarters of an hour. At two o'clock in the afternoon it was all over and we lunched about half past two.

You must not expect me to give you a description of the church services here. I am far too irritated to do so. They merely consist of music and of church adornment. Apart from these the most disgusting licentiousness prevails.

This very moment I have come in from a vesper service, which lasted over two hours, so that I have only had time to fetch this letter and finish writing it in the steward's quarters of Count Firmian's house. I also wanted to see whether there was not a letter from you. But I found nothing. You are very lazy. We have been here a long time and although this is the third letter which I have written from Milan, I have so far had no reply. All that I can do is not write to you for a few weeks. Wolfgang looks forward from post-day to post-day to a letter from you and yet nothing arrives. Addio. I am your old

MZT

★

(79a) *Mozart to his Mother and Sister*

[Autograph in the Nationalbibliothek, Vienna]

[MILAN, 10 *February* 1770[1]]

Talk of the devil and he will appear. Thanks and praise be to God, I am quite well and I can scarcely await the hour when I shall receive an answer from you. I kiss Mamma's hand and to my sister I send a pockmark of a kiss and I remain the same old . . . old what? . . . the same old buffoon,

WOLFGANG in GERMANY, AMADEO in ITALY,

DE MOZARTINI

(79b) *Leopold Mozart to his Wife*

[Autograph in the Nationalbibliothek, Vienna]

[MILAN, 10 *February* 1770[2]]

I kiss you and Nannerl, but only once, because you do not write. Herr Troger sends greetings to you. Tell Mlle Troger that I am very much obliged to her brother for having found us such comfortable

[1] A postscript to his father's letter.   [2] A postscript added after Mozart's.

quarters, where we are well looked after and have a brother specially chosen to serve us.[1]

(80) *Leopold Mozart to his Wife*

[Extract]   [*Autograph in the Gemeentemuseum, The Hague*]

MILAN, 17 *February* 1770

⋆ Praise be to God, we are both well. That the winter, as you say, is not so dangerous in Italy as the summer, I can well believe. So we hope that God will spare us. And if one does not ruin one's health by irregular living and unnecessary stuffing and swilling and if one has otherwise no natural weakness, there is nothing to fear, for everywhere we are in God's hands. Wolfgang will not spoil his health by eating and drinking. You know how he controls himself; and I can assure you that I have never seen him take such care of himself as he does in this country. Whatever does not seem right to him he leaves and often he eats very little, yet none the
⋆ less he is fat and cheerful and gay and jolly all day long.

The tailor has just called with cloaks and cowls which we have had to order. I looked at myself in the mirror, as we were trying them on, and thought of how *in my old age I too have had to take part in this tomfoolery*. The costume suits Wolfgang amazingly well. After having had to make this foolish expenditure, my only consolation is that one can use these costumes again for all sorts of things and can make linings, kitchen cloths and so forth, out of them.

Tomorrow the Duke and the Princess of Modena, the future bride of the Archduke Ferdinand,[2] are coming to Count Firmian's to hear Wolfgang play. In the evening we are driving en masque to the gala opera and afterwards we shall attend the ball. Then we shall drive home with our great friend, Signor Don Ferdinando,[3] who is steward to the Count. Next Friday there will be a concert for the general public and we shall then see
⋆ what profit we shall make. But on the whole we shall not earn much in Italy. The main thing is that there is the greatest enthusiasm and understanding here and that the Italians see how much Wolfgang knows. Otherwise one must generally accept admiration and bravos as payment. In this connexion I must tell you that everywhere we have been received with the greatest courtesy imaginable and that on all occasions we have
⋆ been asked to meet the leading nobles. Wolfgang kisses most humbly the hands of Her Excellency the Countess von Arco[4] and thanks her for the
⋆ kiss she sent, which is far more precious to him than many young ones.

---

[1] Frater Alfonso. See p. 109.

[2] Mozart was commissioned later by the Empress Maria Theresia to compose a dramatic serenata *Ascanio in Alba* for the marriage of the Archduke Ferdinand in October 1771.

[3] Don Fernando Germani, steward to Count Firmian.

[4] Probably the wife of Count Georg Anton Felix von Arco, Chief Chamberlain to the Archbishop of Salzburg.

(80a) *Mozart to his Sister*

[*Autograph in the Gemeentemuseum, The Hague*]

[MILAN, 17 *February* 1770 [1]]

Here I am, now you have me. Dear little Marianne, with all my arse I rejoice that you had such a frightfully good time. Tell Nurse Ursula, the one, I mean, with the cold arse, that I still maintain that I sent back all her songs to her. But *in any case* if, engrossed in my high and important thoughts, I swept the song off to Italy, I shall not fail, should I find it, to stuff it into a letter. Addio. Farewell, my children. I kiss Mamma's hands a thousand times and send you a hundred kisses or smacks on your marvellous horseface. Per fare il fine,[2] I am your, etc.[3]

★

(81) *Leopold Mozart to his Wife*

[*Autograph in the Mozarteum, Salzburg*]

MILAN, *Shrove Tuesday*[4] 1770

Last Saturday we had to drive unexpectedly to the opera and ball with the steward,[5] so I was not able to write to you. Our concert, which took place on Friday,[6] went off in the same way as our concerts have done everywhere, and therefore no further description is necessary. We are well, God be praised, and although we are not rich, yet we always have a little more than what is barely necessary. On Monday or Tuesday of the second week in Lent, with God's help we shall leave Milan for Parma. We should like to go off sooner, but Count Firmian wants to give a big concert for the ladies in his house in the first week of Lent;[7] and other things will have to be arranged. Here the inhabitants will still be eating meat tomorrow and on Thursday; every day operas and balls will still take place; and on Saturday the last ball will be held. This is according to the Use of St. Ambrose, which the whole town follows.[8] In the monasteries, however, they observe the Roman customs and begin Lent on Ash Wednesday. But on that day and on Thursday all the priests run out of the monasteries to their acquaintances in the town and invite themselves to eat meat. What do you think of that? Oh, later on I shall tell you a hundred nice stories of the same kind, which are not at all edifying but extremely annoying. I am quite delighted that Salzburg is so gay now and

---

[1] A postscript to his father's letter.   [2] To conclude.
[3] The autograph breaks off here.   [4] 27 February.
[5] Don Fernando Germani.   [6] 23 February.
[7] This concert was given on 12 March and is described on p. 118.
[8] In the liturgical year according to the Ambrosian rite, fasting began on the first Sunday in Lent and not on Ash Wednesday.

that you too have some entertainment. Give my best greetings every-where. Before I leave here I shall write to the Chief Steward.¹ Go on enclosing the letters to Herr Troger even if I have left Milan, for he will certainly forward them. Farewell, I must close. Wolfgang is busy com-posing two arias.² I kiss you and Nannerl a thousand times and I remain

your old

MZT.

Basil's³ accident not only distressed us very greatly, but cost Wolfgang many tears. You know how sensitive he is. God grant that Basil may recover. I wish it from my heart and send him our greetings.

(81a) *Mozart to his Mother and Sister*

[Autograph in the Mozarteum, Salzburg]

[MILAN, *Shrove Tuesday* 1770⁴]

And I kiss Mamma and you. I am utterly confused with all the things I have to do. It is impossible for me to write more.

(82) *Leopold Mozart to his Wife*

[*Extract*]   *[Autograph in the Mozarteum, Salzburg]*

MILAN, 3 *March* 1770

Today, March 3rd, is the last day of carnival. Every day during the week whole companies of masqueraders have paraded through the town. Of these the most important were: firstly, the facchinata or facchin-maschera; secondly, the mascherata of the petits-maîtres; and finally, the mascherata of the so-called chicchera, which took place today and which is only another procession of the petits-maîtres, but this time they all ride either in carriages or on horseback. It was not at all a bad show. Further, there were today a number of carriages with cavaliers en masque; and a great many other masked persons were to be seen in the streets. In a word, everyone is either in the street or at a window.

Recently I had to miss a post-day and now the day of our departure is drawing near. But you will certainly receive one more letter from me from Milan, as we shall not get away from here before the 12th, 13th or 14th. You will understand that I have unpacked all our belongings and must now pack everything again. The luggage has, moreover, increased

---

¹ Count von Firmian, brother of Count Carlo di Firmian, Governor of Lombardy.
² Probably two of the four arias which Mozart composed for Count Firmian's concert. See p. 118, n. 1.
³ Basilius Amann (1756–1785), son of Privy Councillor Franz Anton von Amann of Salzburg, was a friend of Mozart.   ⁴ A postscript to his father's letter.

a good deal and I should like to send home a few things. When we left Mantua it was bitterly cold and we bought two fine foot-bags, which cost five ducats. We had to take these, as cheaper ones were not to be had. They are of grey cloth, lined with wolf's fur and trimmed with fine laces and tassels. They have done us excellent service and without them we should have fared badly in the Italian sedia.

Now I must close. Farewell. I kiss you both. My greetings to all Salzburg.

I am your old

MZT

(82a) *Mozart to his Sister*

[Autograph in the Library of Congress, Washington]

Cara Sorella mia,   [Milan, 3 *March* 1770]
Indeed I rejoice with my whole heart that you have had such a good time. But perhaps you think that I have not been having a good time. Indeed I have, and I cannot remember how often, but I think we have been to the opera six or seven times and then to the festa di ballo which, as in Vienna, begins after the opera, but with this difference that there the dancing is more orderly. We have also seen the facchinata and the chiccherata. The facchinata is a mascherata, a beautiful sight, so called because people dress up as facchini or valets. There was a barca with a number of people in it, and many persons went on foot, and there were four to six bands of trumpeters and drummers and a few companies of fiddlers and of players on other instruments. The chiccherata which we saw today is also a mascherata. *Chiccheri* is the Milanese word for the people we call petits-maîtres or, let us say, coxcombs. They all rode on horseback and it was a charming affair. I am now as heartily glad that Herr von Amann[1] is better as I was grieved when I heard of his accident. What sort of mask did Madame Rosa wear and also Herr von Mölk and the Prince and Herr von Schiedenhofen? If you know, please write and tell me and you will do me a great favour. Today Count Firmian's steward has invited us to celebrate our last day with him, and we shall have much to chatter about. Addio. Farewell. Next post-day I shall write you a Milanese letter.

I am, etc.

Wolfgang Mozart

3 *March* 1770
PS. Kiss Mamma's hands for me 1000000000000 times. Greetings to all our good friends and a thousand greetings to you from Catch-me-quick-and-then-you-have-me and from Don Cacarella, especially from behind and[2]

(83) *Leopold Mozart to his Wife*

[*Extract*]   [*Autograph in the Mozarteum, Salzburg*]

MILAN, 13 *March* 1770

It was impossible for me to write last Saturday, because Wolfgang had to compose for the concert held yesterday at Count Firmian's, three arias and a recitative with violins,[1] and I had to copy the violin parts myself and then have them duplicated, so that they should not be stolen. Over one hundred and fifty members of the leading nobility were present, the most important of them being the Duke, the Princess and the Cardinal. We have now decided to leave Milan, God willing, on Thursday, that is, the day after tomorrow. But as we are not leaving until midday and as we are travelling in a vettura, we shall not reach Parma until Saturday morning. You will realize that I have an amazing number of things to do, the more so as on account of our long stay the whole trunk has had to be unpacked. Between this evening and tomorrow another matter has to be decided. For Wolfgang has been asked to write the first opera here for next Christmas.[2] If this is settled, you will be glad, for then, as far as we can judge, we shall certainly reach home sooner than we should otherwise have done. Indeed it will take us all our time to reach Rome for Passion week. You know that Rome is a place where one simply must stay. Then we shall go on to Naples, which is such an important centre that even if a scrittura[3] does not bring us back to Milan to write the opera, some circumstance may easily arise to keep us there during the whole of next winter. For if the scrittura is concluded, the libretto will be sent to us. Wolfgang can then think things out a little and, travelling via Loreto, we can be back in Milan by Advent. Further, as the composer is not obliged to stay on after the opera has been staged, we can then get home via Venice within a year. But I leave it all to Providence and to the ordering of God.

As this is my most strenuous week, I beg you to make excuses for me and to give my congratulations to all who are called Joseph.[4] You know how tedious, sad and trying a departure is. Please give especially my respectful greetings and apologies to our Father Confessor.[5]

Continue to address your letters, as you have done hitherto, to Herr Troger who will forward them to me safely.

As soon as I reach Bologna or Florence I shall write to you, and perhaps also from Parma.

Tomorrow we are having a farewell dinner with His Excellency,[6] who

---

[1] K. App. 2 [73A] and K. 88 [73c] (on texts from Metastasio's *Demetrio* and *Artaserse*) and K. 77 [73e] (on a text from Metastasio's *Demofoonte*), an aria in the grand style with an accompanied recitative.   [2] *Mitridate, Rè di Ponto.*
[3] A written contract.
[4] 19 March being St. Joseph's Day.
[5] Ferdinand Joseph Mayr.   [6] Count Firmian, Governor of Lombardy.

is giving us letters of introduction for Parma, Florence, Rome and Naples. I cannot tell you how gracious he has been to us during the whole period of our stay. I would have written before now to the Chief Steward,[1] if I had not had to wait until tomorrow in order to do so more fully. I kiss you ★ and Nannerl a thousand times and I am your old

MZT

(83a) *Mozart to his Mother and Sister*

[*Autograph in the Mozarteum, Salzburg*]

[MILAN, 13 *March* 1770[2]]

I send greetings and kiss Mamma and my sister millions of times, and, thank God, I am well. Addio.

(84) *Leopold Mozart to his Wife*

[*Extract*]   [*Autograph in the Mozarteum, Salzburg*]

[BOLOGNA], 24 *March* 1770

We arrived today at Bologna[3] with your last letter, which we found at the post, as Herr Troger forwarded it with some others from Count Firmian. Thank God, we are well and we live in hopes that God will keep us so. We shall not stay here more than four days and we shall only spend about five or six days in Florence. So with God's help we shall reach Rome at the latest on Tuesday or Wednesday in Passion Week; and we shall certainly see the Functiones on Holy Thursday.

I wrote from Parma to the Chief Steward, thanking him for the favours we had enjoyed in the house of Count Firmian and requesting him to tell His Grace that Wolfgang is to write the opera for Milan and asking that he should obtain leave of absence for me. I wrote to His Grace by today's post, sending him my most humble wishes for election day and asking for leave of absence on account of Wolfgang's opera. So find out whether these two letters have arrived safely. The scrittura has already been drawn up and exchanged between both parties; so all that is now required is His Grace's permission. Actually the contract was drawn up in Count Firmian's house. We are to receive 100 cigliati and free lodging. The opera is to begin in the Christmas holidays. The recitatives must be sent to Milan in October and we must be there by November 1st so that

---

[1] Count Firmian of Salzburg. No doubt Leopold Mozart was writing to ask for an extension of leave of absence, as his son had been commissioned to write the next opera for Milan.
[2] A postscript to his father's letter.
[3] The Mozarts left Milan on 15 March and travelled to Bologna by way of Lodi, Piacenza, Parma and Modena. At Lodi Mozart composed his first string quartet, K. 80 [73f].

Wolfgang may write the arias. The prima donna and seconda donna are
Signora Gabrielli[1] and her sister.[2] The tenor is Signor Ettore,[3] who is now
Cavaliere Ettore, as he wears a certain order. The primo uomo and the
others have not yet been chosen. Perhaps Manzuoli will sing. Signora
Gabrielli is known throughout Italy to be an extremely conceited fool
who besides squandering all her money does the most idiotic things. We
shall meet her on our travels in Rome or Naples, as she is coming up
from Palermo, and we shall then do homage to her as a queen and praise
her to the skies, as that is the way to curry favour. In Parma Signora
Guari,[4] who is also called Bastardina or Bastardella, invited us to dinner
and sang three arias for us. I could not believe that she was able to reach
C sopra acuto, but my ears convinced me. The passages which Wolfgang
has written down[5] occurred in her aria and these she sang, it is true, more
softly than her deeper notes, but as beautifully as an octave stop in an
organ. In short, she sang the trills and the passages exactly as Wolfgang
has written them down, note for note. Further, she has a good deep alto
down to G. She is not beautiful, and yet not ugly, but occasionally she has
a wild look in her eyes, like that of people who are subject to epilepsy,
and she limps with one foot. Otherwise she has a good presence, a good
character and a good reputation. Count Firmian gave Wolfgang a snuff-
★ box set in gold containing twenty cigliati.

This is the most expensive place which we have so far struck in Italy.
We are staying, it is true, at the best inn, the 'Pellegrino', but we have also
the honour of paying a ducat a day. The prices here have risen, because
there are more people in the town than there were a few years ago. Of
expelled Jesuits alone there are more than a thousand. Farewell! I am glad
that Nannerl is working hard. But she must not sing more than she thinks
is good for her chest. We both kiss you millions of times. Addio. I am
your old

★   MZT

(84a) *Mozart to his Sister*

[*From Nissen, pp.* 184-186]

Oh you busy thing!   [BOLOGNA], 24 *March* 1770
As I have been idle for so long, I have been thinking that it would not
be a bad idea if I did some work again for a short while. Every post-day,
when letters arrive from Germany, I enjoy eating and drinking far more

---

[1] Catterina Gabrielli (1730–1796) was born in Rome and studied under Garcia and Porpora.
She was a famous prima donna of her time, and toured Europe with her sister Francesca as
seconda donna.   [2] Francesca Gabrielli (b. *c.* 1735).

[3] Guglielmo d'Ettore, a member of the Munich opera, who was appearing in Venice and
Padua with great success.

[4] Lucrezia Agujari (1743–1783) was born at Ferrara as the natural child of a nobleman, and
was always announced in the playbills as La Bastardina or Bastardella. She was celebrated for
the unusual extent of her vocal range.   [5] See pp. 121, 122.

than usual. Please write and tell me who is singing in the oratorios and let me know their titles as well. Tell me also how you like Haydn's[1] minuets and whether they are better than his earlier ones. I rejoice from my heart that Herr von Amann has recovered. Please tell him to take good care of himself and to avoid violent exercise. Please do not forget this. But tell him also that I often think of him and of how in Triebenbach[2] we used to play at workmen and of how he acted the name Schrattenbach[3] by means of a bag of shot and by making the sound *sh*. Tell him also that I often remember his saying to me: 'Shall we split ourselves up?' and how I always replied: 'Good Gracious, no!' I shall soon send you a minuet which Mr. Pick danced in the theatre and which everyone danced to afterwards at the feste di ballo in Milan, solely in order that you may see how slowly people dance here. The minuet itself is very beautiful. It comes, of course, from Vienna and was most certainly composed by Deller or Starzer.[4] It has plenty of notes. Why? Because it is a stage minuet which is danced slowly. The minuets in Milan, in fact the Italian minuets generally, have plenty of notes, are played slowly and have several bars, *e.g.*, the first part has sixteen, the second twenty or twenty-four.

In Parma we got to know a singer and heard her perform very beautifully in her own house—the famous Bastardella[5] who has (1) a beautiful voice, (2) a marvellous throat, (3) an incredible range. While I was present she sang the following notes and passages:

[1] Michael Haydn.
[2] A suburb of Salzburg.
[3] An allusion to the Counts von Schrattenbach, one of whom, Sigismund, was Archbishop of Salzburg from 1753 to 1772, and another of whom, Franz Anton, the Mozarts had met at Brünn in 1767.
[4] Florian Deller (1729–1773) and Joseph Starzer (1726 or 1727–1787) were well-known composers of ballet music in Vienna.
[5] Lucrezia Agujari. See p. 120, n. 4.

(85) *Leopold Mozart to his Wife*

[*Extract*]   [*Autograph in the Mozarteum, Salzburg*]

BOLOGNA, 27 *March* 1770

From Parma I wrote to the Chief Steward and from here on the 24th I wrote to His Grace and to you. I await your reply as to whether all these letters have arrived safely. There was a concert yesterday at the house of Count Pallavicini, to which His Eminence the Cardinal[1] and the leading nobles were invited. I have already introduced to you Count Carl von Firmian; and now I should like you to know Count Pallavicini also. They are two gentlemen who in all respects have the same outlook, friendliness, magnanimity, placidity and a special love for and insight into all branches of knowledge. On Sunday I was privileged to pay my respects to Count Pallavicini and to hand him the letter from Count Firmian. As soon as he heard that I intended to be in Rome in Holy Week he immediately said that he would try to arrange to have the pleasure tomorrow not only of hearing this extraordinary young virtuoso himself but of granting the

---

[1] Cardinal Legate Antonio Colonna Branciforte.

same privilege to the leading nobles of the town. I shall not describe all the circumstances, nor how, for instance, we were fetched in His Excellency's carriage and waited upon; I shall only say that about one hundred and fifty members of the leading nobility were present. The famous Padre Martini[1] was also invited and, although he never goes to concerts, he came nevertheless to this one, which began at about half past seven and lasted until half past eleven, because the nobles refused to break up the party. Signor Aprile and Signor Cicognani sang. We are leaving the day after tomorrow, Thursday the 29th, and shall arrive in Florence on Friday evening, where we shall stay until the 5th and then continue our journey to Rome, which we hope to reach at midday on the 11th, if God places no obstacle in our way.

What especially pleases me is that we are extraordinarily popular and that Wolfgang is admired here even more than he has been in all the other towns of Italy; the reason is that Bologna is the centre and dwelling-place of many masters, artists and scholars. Here too he has been most thoroughly tested, and the fact that Padre Martini, the idol of the Italians, speaks of him with great admiration and has himself set him all the tests, has increased his reputation all over Italy. We have visited him twice and each time Wolfgang has worked out a fugue, for which the Padre had only written down with a few notes the *ducem* or *la guida*. We have also visited Cavaliere Broschi[2] or the so-called Signor Farinelli, on his estate outside the town. Here we have met Spagnoletta,[3] who is to be the prima donna in the opera, which is being performed in May, that is, instead of Gabrielli, who is still in Palermo and has let down the people of Bologna, just as she probably will let down the people of Milan also.

We have met here Signor Manfredini,[4] the castrato, who, travelling with Herr Panter from Russia by way of Vienna, came to see us in Salzburg.

A certain old Signor Abbate Zanardi sends his greetings to Herr Andrino. A few people have been asking for Kapellmeister Lolli.[5] Herr Brinsecchi and many persons have been asking for our Court Statuarius.[6]

---

[1] Giovanni Battista Martini (1706–1784), a Franciscan Father, was one of the most important scholarly musicians of the eighteenth century. In 1725 he became maestro di cappella of the church of San Francesco at Bologna, where he spent the rest of his life teaching and writing. Scholars from all parts of the world came to Bologna to consult him. In 1774–1775 he published a work on counterpoint, and at the time of his death he was working at the fourth volume of his great *Storia della musica*.

[2] Carlo Broschi, called Farinelli (1705–1782), born in Andria, was the most famous male soprano of his day. He was trained by Porpora and, after a series of triumphs in all the theatres of Italy, in Vienna and in London, and a prolonged stay at the court of Philip V of Spain, he retired in 1762 to his villa near Bologna.   [3] Giuseppa Useda, La Spagnoletta.

[4] He was brother to the famous Vincenzo Manfredini (1737–1799), maestro di cappella and author of the *Difesa della musica moderna*.

[5] Giuseppe Francesco Lolli of Bologna was Kapellmeister in Salzburg from 1763 until 1778.

[6] Johann Baptist Hagenauer, a relative of the Hagenauer family, was architect and sculptor to the Salzburg court. He had studied in Florence and Bologna.

All send their greetings along with mine.

We have been to the Instituto and have admired the fine statues of our Court Statuarius. What I have seen in Bologna surpasses the British Museum. For here one can see not only the rarities of nature but *everything that deserves the name of science*, preserved like a dictionary in beautiful rooms and in a clean and orderly fashion. Indeed you would be amazed. I refuse to say anything about the churches, the paintings, the fine architecture and the furnishings of the various palaces, for indeed I can hardly write for drowsiness, as it is past one o'clock. Wolfgang has been snoring for a long time and I fall asleep as I write.

I kiss you and Nannerl a thousand times. My greetings to all Salzburg. I am your faithful and sleepy husband

MZT.

It was not at all a bad idea to send the ball minuet to catch us at Bologna to be arranged for the clavier, as there is no one in Salzburg who could do this. Indeed Wolfgang was exceedingly pleased and thanks Herr von Schiedenhofen and Nannerl. He will write very soon himself. I wrote this letter yesterday after he had gone to bed and I am adding a few lines today while he is still asleep, for the post leaves almost immediately. Herewith he sends the minuet which Mr. Pick danced in the theatre in Milan. Again we send our greetings to all our good friends and I beg Herr von Schiedenhofen, Herr von Mölk and others who have written to me not to take it amiss that I do not reply. I hope they will bear in mind how much a traveller has to do, especially as I am single-handed. *Kommabit aliquando zeitus bequemus schreibendi. Nunc kopfus meus semper vollus est multis gedankibus.*[1] Wolfgang kisses you and Nannerl a thousand times.

(86) *Leopold Mozart to his Wife*

[Extract]   [*Autograph in the Mozarteum, Salzburg*]

FLORENCE, 3 *April* 1770

We arrived safely in Florence[2] on the evening of March 30th. On the 31st we spent the whole day indoors and Wolfgang stayed in bed until lunch, as he had caught a slight cold from the rain and the violent wind through which we drove in the mountains. I made him take tea and violet juice and he perspired a little. On the morning of April 1st we drove at ten o'clock to Count von Rosenberg,[3] who received us immediately,

---

[1] Sometime there will come a convenient time for writing. At present my head is always full of many thoughts.   [2] The Mozarts stayed at the 'Aquila'.
[3] Franz Xaver Wolf Orsini-Rosenberg (1723–1796) was Obersthofmeister at the court of Tuscany from 1766 to 1772. In 1776 he was appointed Chief Chamberlain to the Viennese court and Director of the Court Theatres, and subsequently played an important part in Mozart's life.

although more than fifty people were in the antechamber, and this because we brought a letter from Count Firmian and because he had already heard about us from the Count Joseph von Kaunitz,[1] who reached Florence the day before our arrival and is staying with him. He had dined with us in Bologna at the house of Count Pallavicini. Count Rosenberg at once sent us to the Duca de Salviati at the court with a message that he was to present us to the Grand Duke.[2] We heard the sermon and Mass in the chapel and after the service we had an audience. The Grand Duke was uncommonly gracious, asked at once for Nannerl, said that his wife was very anxious to hear Wolfgang play, and spoke to us for a full quarter of an hour. Yesterday evening, April 2nd, we were fetched and driven to the castle outside the town, where we remained until after ten o'clock. Everything went off as usual and the amazement was all the greater as Marchese Ligniville,[3] the Director of Music, who is the finest expert in counterpoint in the whole of Italy, placed the most difficult fugues before Wolfgang and gave him the most difficult themes, which he played off and worked out as easily as one eats a piece of bread. Nardini, that excellent violinist, accompanied him. This afternoon we are going to see Manzuoli, whom we met yesterday in the street and who sends you his greetings. The castrato Nicolini who was with Guadagni[4] in Vienna is here too. I am very sorry that we have to leave on Friday in order to reach Rome in time. I should like you to see Florence itself and the surrounding country and the situation of the town, for you would say that one should live and die here. During these few days I shall see all that there is to be seen. I must close, for the post is leaving. Wolfgang and I send our greetings to all; we kiss you a thousand times and I am your old

MOZART

(87) *Leopold Mozart to his Wife*

[*Extract*]   [*Autograph in the Nationalbibliothek, Vienna*]

ROME, 14 *April* 1770

We arrived here safely on the 11th at noon.[5] I could have been more easily persuaded to return to Salzburg than to proceed to Rome, for we had to travel for five days from Florence to Rome in the most horrible

---

[1] Imperial Ambassador successively in Stockholm, St. Petersburg and Madrid.
[2] Subsequently Emperor Leopold II, 1790–1792. He had heard the Mozart children perform in Vienna in 1762. See p. 5.
[3] Marchese Eugenio De Ligniville, Duca di Conca, who was Director of Music at the court of Tuscany from 1765 to 1790.
[4] Gaetano Guadagni (*c.* 1725–1792), one of the most famous male contraltos of the eighteenth century. From 1748 to 1753 he sang in London in Handel's oratorios.
[5] The Mozarts, after spending a few days in an uncomfortable lodging-house, took rooms in the house of the Papal Courier Steffano Uslenghi in the Piazza del Clementino. See p. 129.

rain and cold wind. I am told here that they have had constant rain for four months and indeed we had a taste of it, for we went on Wednesday and Thursday in fine weather to St. Peter's and to the Sistine Chapel to hear the Miserere during the Mass, and on our way home were surprised by such a frightful downpour that our cloaks have never yet been so drenched as they then were. But I will not give you a long description of that dreadful journey. Picture to yourself a more or less uncultivated country and the most horrible, filthy inns, where we got nothing to eat save here and there eggs and broccoli; while on fast-days they sometimes made a fuss about giving us the former. Fortunately we had a good supper at Viterbo and slept well. There we saw St. Rosa of Viterbo, whose body like that of St. Catherine at Bologna can be seen in a well-preserved condition.[1] From the former saint we took away as a remembrance a fever antidote and relics, from the latter a belt. On arriving here on the 11th, we went to St. Peter's after lunch and then to Mass. On the 12th we were present at the Functiones, and when the Pope[2] was serving the poor at table we were quite close to him, as we were standing beside him at the top of the table. This incident was all the more amazing as we had to pass through two doors guarded by Swiss guards in armour and make our way through many hundreds of people. And moreover you must note that we had as yet no acquaintances. But our fine clothes, the German tongue, and my usual freedom of manner which led me to make my servant order the Swiss guards in German to make way for us, soon helped us through everywhere. They took Wolfgang for some German courtier, while some even thought that he was a prince, which my servant allowed them to believe; I myself was taken for his tutor. Thus we made our way to the Cardinals' table. There Wolfgang happened to be standing between the chairs of two Cardinals, one of whom was Cardinal Pallavicini, who made a sign to him and said: '*Will you be so good as to tell me in confidence who you are?*' And Wolfgang told him. The Cardinal showed the greatest astonishment and said: '*Ah, you are the famous boy, about whom so many things have been written to me*'. Whereupon Wolfgang asked him: '*Are you not Cardinal Pallavicini?*' The Cardinal replied: '*Yes, I am, but why?*' Then Wolfgang told him *that we had letters to deliver to His Eminence and that we were going to pay him our respects*. The Cardinal appeared to be delighted, remarked that Wolfgang spoke Italian very well and among other things added: '*Ik kann auck ein benig deutsch sprecken*'. When we were leaving, Wolfgang kissed his hand and the Cardinal took off his berretta and

---

[1] The body of St. Rosa (*d.* 1252), who incited the people to rise against the Emperor Frederick II, is preserved in a side-chapel of the Church of Santa Rosa at Viterbo. That of St. Catherine Vigri (*d.* 1463), Abbess of the Poor Clares, is in the chapel which bears her name in the Church of Corpus Domini at Bologna.

[2] Clement XIV (1705–1774), formerly Cardinal Ganganelli. He became Pope in 1759 and his reign was rendered famous by the dissolution of the Jesuit order.

bowed very politely. You have often heard of the famous Miserere [1] in Rome, which is so greatly prized that the performers in the chapel are forbidden on pain of excommunication to take away a single part of it, to copy it or to give it to anyone. *But we have it already.* Wolfgang has written it down and we would have sent it to Salzburg in this letter, if it were not necessary for us to be there to perform it. But the manner of performance contributes more to its effect than the composition itself. So we shall bring it home with us. Moreover, as it is one of the secrets of Rome, we do not wish to let it fall into other hands, *ut non incurramus mediate vel immediate in censuram Ecclesiae.* [2] We have already examined St. Peter's church thoroughly and we shall certainly not neglect anything that should be seen in Rome. Tomorrow, God willing, we shall see His Holiness pontificate. You cannot conceive how conceited the clergy are here. Any priest who has the slightest association with a Cardinal, thinks himself as good as he, and as each Cardinal, when on business connected with His Holiness, drives with a cortège of three or four carriages, each of which is filled with his chaplains, secretaries and valets, I am looking forward to tomorrow, when we shall walk past all these proud gentlemen and leave them in ignorance as to our identity. For we have not yet presented ourselves anywhere, because the Functiones are now taking place. On Monday we shall begin to deliver our twenty letters of introduction.

Though I am glad that neither of you undertook this journey with us, yet I am sorry that you are not seeing all these Italian towns, and especially Rome. It is useless and quite impossible to describe it in a few words. Once more I advise you to read Keyssler's *Reisebeschreibung.* Two hours after our arrival we went en passant into the German College and found there Herr von Mölk[3] in excellent health and other acquaintances also. Out of regard for him I am going to let Wolfgang perform before the whole College, since they would like to hear him. With the help of Abbate Marcobruni we immediately took a lodging in a private house. But as there is only one room here and we must have two rooms in order to receive callers, we are going to move this evening into more spacious quarters. Today and yesterday I have been a bit of an invalid, for I have taken three digestive powders; but, thank God, I feel well. Wolfgang is splendid and sends herewith a contredanse.[4] He would like Herr Cirillus Hofmann[5] to make up the steps for it; when the two violins play as

---

[1] The Miserere of Gregorio Allegri (1582–1652). Abert, vol. i. p. 189, n. 2, draws attention to a slight exaggeration on the part of Leopold Mozart, inasmuch as according to Burney the Pope had had this beautiful Miserere copied for the Emperor Leopold I, the King of Portugal and Padre Martini, and Burney himself was handed copies in Rome and Florence. See Burney, *Present State of Music in France and Italy,* 2nd edition, 1773, p. 285 ff.

[2] i.e. so that we shall not incur the censure of the Church now or later.

[3] Albert von Mölk, a son of Franz Felix von Mölk. At the time he was a student at the German College in Rome.

[4] K. 123 [73g].   [5] Dancing master at the Salzburg court.

leaders, only two persons should lead the dance; but whenever the orchestra comes in with all the instruments, the whole company should dance together. It would be by far the best arrangement if it were danced by five couples. The first couple should begin the first solo, the second dance the second and so on, as there are five solos and five tutti passages.

★   Pray earnestly to God Almighty for our good health. We shall certainly do our share, for I can assure you that we take all possible care and that Wolfgang pays as much attention to his health as if he were the most grown up person. May God keep you both likewise in good health. I am your old

MZT.

Wolfgang and I kiss you and Nannerl a thousand times.

(87a) *Mozart to his Mother and Sister*

[Autograph in the Nationalbibliothek, Vienna]

[ROME, 14 *April* 1770][1]

Praise and thanks be to God, I and my wretched pen are well and I kiss Mamma and Nannerl a thousand or 1000 times. I only wish that my sister were in Rome, for this town would certainly please her, as St. Peter's church and many other things in Rome are *regular*. The most beautiful flowers are now being carried past in the street—so Papa has just told me. I am a fool, as everyone knows. Oh, I am having a hard time, for in our rooms there is only one bed and so Mamma can well imagine that I get no sleep with Papa. I am looking forward to our new quarters. I have just now drawn St. Peter with his keys and with him St. Paul with his sword and St. Luke with my sister and so forth. I have had the honour of kissing St. Peter's foot in St. Peter's church and as I have the misfortune to be so small, I, that same old dunce,

WOLFGANG MOZART

had to be lifted up.

(88) *Leopold Mozart to his Wife*

[Extract]   *[Autograph in the Mozarteum, Salzburg]*

ROME, 21 *April* 1770

Your letters of the 2nd and the 6th are, I presume, the replies to my two letters from Bologna. Meanwhile you will have received a letter from Florence and my first one from Rome, in which I gave you a hasty description of the bad weather we had and of our tiresome journey, but

[1] A postscript to his father's letter.

forgot to mention that we arrived at noon amid thunder and lightning and that the weather at a good hour's distance from Rome received us with crackling and flashes and thus accompanied us to our destination in the same way as great men are welcomed by the firing of big guns. So far we have had rain all the time and today is the first on which we have been able to visit one or two places in safety. We have met a great many Englishmen here and amongst others Mr. Beckford,[1] whose acquaintance we made at Lady Effingham's[2] in London, and with whom as well as with some other Englishmen we walked for a couple of hours this morning in the garden of the Villa Medici, which belongs to the Grand Duke of Florence. We have moved out of our first lodging and Herr Marcobruni, *who sends you his greetings*, has brought us to the house of the Papal courier, Signor Uslenghi, in the Piazza del Clementino. Here we are very comfortable and the wife and daughter of the landlord vie with one another in waiting upon us. The husband is in Portugal and so they treat me as if I were the master of the house. We all dine together and we have a large room which, as it gets the morning sun, is very healthy. When friends come to see us, all the other rooms are at our disposal and, as the daughter is beginning to learn the clavier, we have a harpsichord too. I send special greetings to Herr von Schiedenhofen and I am much ★ obliged to him for making Nannerl play often upon the harpsichord. I shall certainly write to him soon myself. I cannot tell you anything about our affairs, for I am tired; the further we have penetrated into Italy, the greater has been the general amazement. Moreover Wolfgang's knowledge does not stand still, but increases from day to day; so that the greatest connoisseurs and masters are at a loss for suitable words to express their admiration. Two days ago we were at the house of a Neapolitan Prince San Angelo. Yesterday we were at the house of Prince Chigi, where amongst others were present the so-called King of England or Pretender,[3] and the Secretary of State Cardinal Pallavicini. Before long we are to be presented to His Holiness. But before I close I must describe a charming incident.

In Florence we came across a young Englishman, who is a pupil of the famous violinist Nardini. This boy,[4] who *plays most beautifully* and who is the same age and the same size as Wolfgang, came to the house of the

---

[1] William Beckford, of Somerley, the historian of Jamaica. This William (not to be confused with either the author of *Vathek* or with the Lord Mayor) was in Rome in the summer of 1770. See Burney, *op. cit.*, p. 268 : see also C. B. Oldman, 'Beckford and Mozart,' *Music and Letters*, 1966.

[2] Elizabeth, Countess of Effingham, a sister of William Beckford, the famous Lord Mayor of London and the father of the author of *Vathek*.

[3] Charles Edward, the young Pretender (1720–1788). He was then living in Rome under the name of Count of Albany.

[4] Thomas Linley (1756–1778), eldest son of Thomas Linley, composer and singing master at Bath, at an early age displayed extraordinary skill on the violin. He studied under Nardini in Florence, and on his return to England became leader and solo-player at his father's concerts

learned poetess, Signora Corilla,[1] where we happened to be on the introduction of M. De L'Augier. The two boys performed one after the other throughout the whole evening, constantly embracing each other. On the following day the little Englishman, a most charming boy, had his violin brought to our rooms and played the whole afternoon, Wolfgang accompanying him on his own. On the next day we lunched with M. Gavard, the administrator of the grand ducal finances, and these two boys played in turn the whole afternoon, not like boys, but like men! Little Tommaso accompanied us home and wept bitter tears, because we were leaving on the following day. But when he heard that our departure would not take place until noon, he called on us at nine o'clock in the morning and gave Wolfgang with many embraces the following poem, which Signora Corilla had to compose for him on the previous evening.[2] Then he accompanied our carriage as far as the city gate. I should like you to have witnessed this scene. I now close with devoted greetings to all our friends and I am your old

MZT

We kiss you both a thousand times.

(88a) *Mozart to his Sister*

[*Autograph formerly in the possession of D. Salomon, Berlin*]

CARA SORELLA MIA!   [ROME, 21 *April* 1770]

I am delighted that you liked the minuet I sent you from Bologna,[3] I mean, the one which Signor Pick danced at Milan. I hope that you have received the contredanse which I enclosed in my first letter from Rome.[4] Do tell me quite frankly how you like it.

Please try to find the arithmetical tables. You know that you wrote them down yourself. I have lost my copy and so have quite forgotten them. So I beg you to copy them out for me with some other examples in arithmetic and send them to me here.

Manzuoli is negotiating with the Milanese to sing in my opera. With that in view he sang four or five arias to me in Florence, including some

in Bath and composed sacred and operatic music. He was drowned at the age of twenty-two. Burney, *op. cit.* p. 255, has the following remarks about Linley and Mozart: 'My little country-man, Linley, who had been two years under Signor Nardini, was at Florence when I arrived there and was universally admired. The *Tommasino*, as he is called, and the little Mozart are talked of all over Italy as the most promising geniuses of this age.'

   [1] The assumed name of Maddalena Morelli, a famous poetess of her day, who was crowned on the Capitol in 1776. Burney, *op. cit.* p. 259 f., praises also her musical gifts and adds in a footnote, 'She has almost every evening a *conversazione* or assembly, which is much frequented by the foreigners and men of letters at Florence'.
   [2] For this poem see Nissen, p. 195, Abert, vol. ii. p. 934, *MBA*, No. 175, and *MDB*, p. 115 f.
   [3] See p. 124.   [4] K. 123 [73g]. Cp. p. 127.

which I had to compose in Milan,[1] in order that the Milanese, who had heard none of my dramatic music, should see that I am capable of writing an opera. Manzuoli is demanding a thousand ducats. It is not known for certain whether Gabrielli will come. Some say that De Amicis will sing. We are to meet her in Naples. I should like her and Manzuoli to take the parts. Then we should have two good acquaintances and friends. The libretto has not yet been chosen. I recommended to Don Ferdinando and Herr von Troger a text by Metastasio.[2]

At the moment I am working at the aria: Se ardire, e speranza.[3]

(89) *Mozart to his Sister*

[*Autograph in the Library of the Historical Society of Pennsylvania, Philadelphia*]

MY DEAR SISTER, [ROME, 25 *April* 1770[4]]

I assure you that every post-day I look forward with an incredible eagerness to receiving some letters from Salzburg. Yesterday we were at San Lorenzo and heard vespers, and this morning the Mass which was sung, and in the evening the second vespers, because it is the festival of Our Lady of Good Counsel. During the last few days we have been to the Campidoglio and have seen several fine things. If I were to write down all that I have seen, this small sheet would not suffice. I have played at two concerts and tomorrow I am playing at another. This evening we saw a contralto singer, a castrato, who was very like Signor Meisner, whom by the way we shall have the honour of meeting at Naples. Immediately after lunch we play boccia. That is a game which I have learnt in Rome. When I come home, I shall teach it to you. Tell Signor Mölk that I am delighted and rejoice with him that his father is in better health and that I ask him to be so kind as to convey my respects to his father, his mother, his sister, his brother and his cousins and to all his relatives. Please do what I asked you to do the last time I wrote to you and please send me a reply about this. When I have finished this letter I shall finish a symphony which I have begun.[5] The aria is finished.[6] A symphony[7] is being copied (my father is the copyist), for we do not wish to give it out to be copied, as it would be stolen. My greetings to all

[1] See p. 118, n. 1.
[2] The text which was ultimately chosen was one by Vittorio Amadeo Cigna-Santi, a poet of Turin. It was a free adaptation of Parini's translation of Racine's *Mithridate* and had already been set to music by Quirino Gasparini and performed at Turin in 1767.
[3] K. 82 [73 o]. The words were taken from Metastasio's *Demofoonte*.
[4] This letter is in Italian.
[5] Probably K. 95 [73n] or K. 97 [73m] or, perhaps, K. 81 [73l] or K. 73.
[6] K. 82 [73 o].
[7] See above, n. 5.

my friends and please kiss Mamma's hands for me, for I am (Tra la liera)

WOLFGANGO in GERMANIA
and AMADEO MOZART in ITALIA

ROMA caput mundi,
  April 25th, 1770,
  and next year 1771.
    Behind as in front
    And double in the middle.   I kiss you both.[1]

(89a) *Mozart to Herr von Schiedenhofen*

[Autograph in the Library of the Historical Society of Pennsylvania, Philadelphia]

[ROME, 25 *April* 1770[2]]

For Signor von Schiedenhofen

Please forgive me for never writing to you, but as I had no time, I could not do my duty. Here is a minuet which *Signor Pick* danced at Milan.

(90) *Leopold Mozart to his Wife*

[Extract]   *[Autograph in the Mozarteum, Salzburg]*

★

ROME, 28 *April* 1770

It is still cold, not as cold as in Salzburg, but not as warm as it ought to be in Rome, for there are always bitter winds and dull clouds. But as soon as the sun peeps out it is very hot.

We have been at the house of Principessa Barbarini, where we met Prince Xaver of Saxony[3] and, for the second time, the Pretender or so-called King of England, and Cardinal Pallavicini, and amongst others a courtier who knew us in our Paris days. Today at the house of the Ambassadore di Malta[4] we met a courtier who knew us when we were in Vienna, the Swedish envoy who met us in London and Count von Wallerstein. The Duca di Bracciano has sent us an invitation for tomorrow to the concert which is being held by the Duca di Altemps. We are

---

[1] This sentence is in Leopold Mozart's hand.   [2] This letter is in Italian.

[3] Prince Xaver of Saxony (1730–1806), who since 1769 had been living in France and Italy under the name of Comte de la Lusace, was the second son of King August of Saxony and had been Regent of Saxony from 1763 to 1768.

[4] Probably Cavaliere Santarelli, Cappellano di Malta and maestro di cappella to Pope Clement XIV. When Burney visited him in 1770 he was engaged in writing a history of church music, which, however, was never published. See Burney, *op. cit.* p. 277 ff.

lunching on Monday with the Augustinians, the same order which also has a house in Salzburg. The General will be present.[1]

With God's help we shall leave on May 12th by the procaccio[2] for ★ Naples, where we have already ordered a lodging. For the last fortnight the roads thither have been very unsafe and a merchant has been killed. But the sbirri[3] and the bloodthirsty Papal soldiers were immediately sent out from Rome and we hear that a skirmish has already taken place in which five sbirri and three robbers were killed, four robbers taken prisoner and the rest dispersed. But they have now drawn nearer the Neapolitan borders and, if it is true that they have killed a Neapolitan courier on his way to Spain, every effort will be made from Naples to clear up the roads. I shall not leave here until I know that they are safe; and in the procaccio one is in a large company.   ★

Thank God, Wolfgang is in good health except for a slight toothache ★ on one side of his face as usual.   ★

We kiss you and Nannerl a thousand times and I am your old

MZT.

(90a) *Mozart to his Mother and Sister*

[Autograph in the Mozarteum, Salzburg]

[ROME, 28 *April* 1770[4]]

I kiss my sister's face and Mamma's hands. I have not yet seen any scorpions or spiders nor do people talk or hear anything about them. Mamma will surely recognise my handwriting? She ought to let me know this quickly, or I shall sign my name underneath.

(91) *Leopold Mozart to his Wife*

[Extract]   *[Autograph in the Mozarteum, Salzburg]*

ROME, 2 *May* 1770 ★

The latest news is that Herr Meisner arrived from Naples at midday and is off again in two days to Florence and thence straight on to Salzburg; so he will turn up there shortly. He sends his greetings to you all. I have already written to His Grace. You want to know whether Wolfgang still sings and plays the fiddle? He plays the fiddle, but not in public. He sings, but only when some text is put before him. He has grown a little. I am neither fatter nor thinner; and we have got accustomed to Italian food.

---

[1] His name, Padre Vasquez, appears in the *Reiseaufzeichnungen*, p. 53. See *MBA*, No. 183.
[2] A form of stage-coach.   [3] The police.   [4] A postscript to his father's letter.

We are leaving sooner than I expected, because I have the opportunity of travelling to Naples with four Augustinians. So we shall be off on May 8th. Otherwise I have nothing to write about. I trust that God will keep both you and Nannerl well and allow us not only to reach Naples in good health and return here but also to reach home safely later on. I shall not stay longer than about five weeks in Naples; then I shall travel through Loreto to Bologna and Pisa and those parts; and so spend the hottest

★ season in the coolest and healthiest spot. We kiss you and Nannerl a thousand times and I am your old

MZT

★ Herr Meisner and Wolfgang performed today in the German College.[1]

(91a) *Mozart to his Mother and Sister*

[Autograph in the Mozarteum, Salzburg]

ROME, [2 *May*] 1770[2]

Praise and thanks be to God, I am well and kiss Mamma's hand and my sister's face, nose, mouth, neck and my bad pen and arse, if it is clean. WOLFGANGO MOZART. ROME, 1770

(92) *Leopold Mozart to his Wife*

[Extract]   *[Autograph in the Mozarteum, Salzburg]*

NAPLES, 19 *May* 1770

You will have received my last letter from Rome, dated May 2nd. I am sorry that I had to leave you without letters for such a long time, for in the meantime you will both have been very anxious. We left Rome on May 8th at ten o'clock in the morning together with three other sedie or two-seated carriages and we had a light lunch at one o'clock in the Augustinian monastery at Marino. On the evening of the 11th we were again well fed in an Augustinian monastery at Sessa and at noon on the 12th we arrived at the Augustinian monastery at Capua, intending to reach Naples in the evening. It happened, however, that on that Sunday, the 13th, the veiling of a lady was to take place in the convent, where one of my travelling companions, Padre Segarelli, had been confessor some years previously. He was to be present at this veiling and begged us to remain there too. Thus we saw the ceremony, which was very magnificent and for which a Kapellmeister with three or four carriages of virtuosi arrived

---

[1] The autograph of this letter has a short postscript added by Meisner.
[2] A postscript to his father's letter.

on the evening of the 12th and began the proceedings with symphonies and a Salve Regina. They all stayed in the Augustinian monastery, so you can imagine that on that evening we went to bed very late. The veiling, or rather the service, did not take place, however, until noon on Sunday, and the whole affair was over at about three o'clock. Apart from the ladies and gentlemen who were intimate friends no one save us two was invited to table in the convent. It would be impossible to describe everything that took place. We slept until ten o'clock next morning and after lunch we drove to Naples, where we arrived early in the evening and spent two nights in a house belonging to the Augustinian monastery of S. Giovanni a Carbonara. But we are now lodging in a house where we pay ten ducati d'argento or four ducats a month in our money. We drove yesterday to Portici to call on the minister, Marchese Tanucci,[1] and we shall drive out there again tomorrow. We had dreadful roads and a very cool breeze. We have left our fine cloth suits in Rome and have had to put on our two beautifully braided summer costumes. Wolfgang's is of rose-coloured moiré, but the colour is so peculiar that in Italy it is called colore di fuoco or flame-coloured; it is trimmed with silver lace and lined with sky-blue silk. My costume is of the colour of cinnamon and is made of piquéd Florentine cloth with silver lace and is lined with apple green silk. They are two fine costumes, but, before we reach home, they will look like old maids. Yesterday evening we called on the English ambassador, Hamilton,[2] a London acquaintance of ours, whose wife[3] plays the clavier with unusual feeling and is a very pleasant person. She trembled at having to play before Wolfgang. She has a valuable instrument, made in England by Tschudi,[4] which has two manuals and a pedal, so that the two manuals can be disconnected by the action of the foot. We found at Hamilton's house Mr. Beckford and Mr. Weis, also London acquaintances. We lunched on the 16th with Tschudi,[5] who had been in Salzburg and requested me to convey his greetings to Count Spaur and to all his good friends and very many compliments to you especially and to Nannerl. He embraced us constantly, particularly on our arrival and departure, and offered us his services on all occasions. The day before yesterday

---

[1] The Marchese Bernardo Tanucci (1698–1783), Prime Minister of the Kingdom of Naples, was famous for his long struggle against the power of the Vatican and for his active influence in securing the dissolution of the Jesuit Order in 1773. The marriage of Ferdinand IV to Caroline of Austria proved, however, his undoing. He attempted to oppose her influence and was deprived of his office in 1776. He was a man of wide interests and was responsible for the first excavations of Pompeii and Herculaneum.

[2] Sir William Hamilton (1730–1803), diplomatist and antiquarian, had been Ambassador to the Court of Naples since 1764.

[3] Sir William Hamilton's first wife, Miss Barlow, whom he married in 1758, was a gifted musician. She died in 1782. Burney, *op. cit.* p. 333, praises her performance.

[4] Burkhardt Tschudi (1702–1773), famous harpsichord-maker and founder of the house of Broadwood. The Mozarts had known him in London. See *Reiseaufzeichnungen*, p. 38, and *MBA*, No. 99.

[5] Baron Fridolin Tschudi.

we met in the street M. Meurikofer[1] from Lyons, who was looking everywhere for us; he had left a card for us with his address at the Augustinian monastery and at last had run into us by chance. He came back with us to our lodging and then took us to his house. We were to have lunched with him tomorrow, but as we have to drive to Portici, we have had to cancel this arrangement. He sends cordial greetings to you all. He is in partnership here with a friend and both have offered their services to me in all eventualities. You will surely remember him, a dark young man, who often had to sing that Italian song for Wolfgang with his spectacles on his nose. I cannot yet say how long we shall stay here. The matter is entirely out of my hands. It may be five weeks or five months, but I think that it will be five weeks. It all depends on circumstances.

On the Feast of St. Philip and St. James[2] while I was hearing High Mass in the Church of the Holy Apostles in Rome, I saw before me a well-known face. Its owner came up; and who do you think he was? Why, our former servant Porta. He was neatly dressed, with lace cuffs, a gold watch and so forth. He had been with the French troops in Corsica. On the following day, just as Herr Meisner was coming in, he came to offer me his services. I refused to have anything to do with him and turned a deaf ear. Ask Herr Meisner, for he saw him. The fellow is an adventurer.

On reading the article about the Miserere, we simply burst out laughing. There is not the slightest cause for anxiety. Everywhere else far more fuss is being made about Wolfgang's feat. All Rome knows and even the Pope himself that he wrote it down. There is nothing whatever to fear; on the contrary, the achievement has done him great credit, as you will shortly hear. You will see to it that the letter is read out everywhere, so that we may be sure that His Grace hears what Wolfgang has done. If the portraits are good likenesses, you may pay the painter whatever you like.

Now I must close, for we are off to the Imperial Ambassador the Count von Kaunitz. Farewell, we kiss you and Nannerl 1000 times and

I am your old

MZT

I trust that your cold left you long ago.

(92a) *Mozart to his Sister*

[*Autograph in the Mozarteum, Salzburg*]

CARA SORELLA MIA,   NAPLES, 19 *May* 1770

Alla vostra lettera non saprei veramente rispondere, perchè non avete scritto niente quasi. I menuetti del Signor Haydn[3] vi manderò

---

[1] A Swiss merchant in Lyons.   [2] May 1st.   [3] See p. 78, n. 1.

quando avrò più tempo, il primo già vi mandai. Ma ⟨I don't understand. You say that they have been stolen. Did you steal them? Or what do you mean?⟩

Vi prego di scrivermi presto e tutti i giorni della posta. Io vi ringrazio di avermi mandato questi arithmetical business, e vi prego, se mai volete avere mal di testa, di mandarmi ancora un poco di questi feats. Perdonatemi che scrivo si malamente, ma la ragione è perchè anche io ebbi un poco mal di testa.[1] I very much like the twelfth minuet of Haydn, which you have sent me; and you have set the bass to it exceedingly well and without the slightest mistake. You must try your hand at such things more often.

Mamma must not forget to see that both our guns are cleaned. Tell me, how is Mr. Canary? Does he still sing? And still whistle? Do you know what makes me think of him? Because there is a canary in our front room which makes a noise just like ours. A propos, I suppose Herr Johannes[2] has received the letter of congratulation which we intended to write to him? But if by any chance he has not received it, I shall tell him myself when I get back to Salzburg what would have been in it. Yesterday we put on our new clothes and we were as beautiful as angels. But I fear that they are the only beautiful things we shall bring home. Addio. Farewell. Remember me to our Nannie and tell her to pray for me earnestly.

I am

WOLFGANG MOZART

The opera, which Jommelli is composing, will begin on the 30th.[3] We saw the King and Queen at Mass in the court chapel at Portici and we have seen Vesuvius too. Naples is beautiful, but it is as crowded as Vienna and Paris. And of the two, London and Naples, I do not know whether Naples does not surpass London for the insolence of the people; for here the lazzaroni have their own general or chief, who receives twenty-five ducati d'argento from the King every month, solely for the purpose of keeping them in order.

De Amicis is singing in the opera. We have been to see her.[4] Cafaro[5]

---

[1] I really don't know how to reply to your letter, because you wrote almost nothing. When I have more time, I shall send you Herr Haydn's minuets. I have already sent you the first one. But, . . . Please write to me soon and write every post-day. Thanks for sending me that arithmetical business and, if you ever want to have a headache, please send me a few more of these feats. Forgive me for writing so badly, but the reason is that I too have had a slight headache.

[2] Johann Baptist Hagenauer. See p. 13, n. 2.

[3] Niccolò Jommelli (1714–1774), who had been Court Kapellmeister in Stuttgart from 1753 to 1768, had returned to Italy and settled in his native village, Aversa, near Naples. The opera to which Mozart refers was *Armida abbandonata*, the first one which Jommelli composed on his return to Naples and which was performed on 30 May 1770, at the Teatro San Carlo.

[4] The autograph has 'and she recognised us at once', which Mozart struck out.

[5] Pasquale Cafaro (1706–1787), a well-known Neapolitan composer of operas and oratorios. His *Antigono* was performed in Naples on 13 August 1770.

is composing the second opera and Ciccio di Majo the third.[1] It is not yet known who is composing the fourth. Go regularly to Mirabell[2] to hear the Litanies and to listen to the Regina Coeli or the Salve Regina and sleep soundly and do not have any bad dreams. Give Herr von Schiedenhofen my fiercest greetings, 'Tralaliera, Tralaliera', and tell him to learn to play on the clavier the repeating minuet, so that he *does* not forget it. He must *do* so soon, so that he may *do* me the pleasure of accompanying him one day. *Do* remember me to all my good friends, and *do* keep well and *do* not die, so that you may *do* another letter for me and that I may *do* another for you and that we may keep on *doing* until we are *done*. For I am the man to go on *doing* until there is nothing more to *do*.

Meanwhile I *do* remain

WOLFGANG MOZART

(93) *Leopold Mozart to his Wife*

[Extract]   [Autograph in the Mozarteum, Salzburg]

NAPLES, 22 May 1770

In the meantime you will have received my letter of the 19th. Two days ago we went for a walk on the Molo and whom do you think we met? Why, our good friend, Mr. Donker,[3] tall, handsome Donker of Amsterdam, who for the last three years has been living here with the French consul. This consul was present on the evening when we dined with Donker in Amsterdam. We lunched with him yesterday and in the afternoon we called on the wife of the Imperial Ambassador, Countess von Kaunitz, née Princess von Öttingen. We shall soon have finished paying visits. Marchesa Tanucci, the Prime Minister's wife, sent her steward to me yesterday with a message that the latter was to be at my disposal to take us round everywhere and show us all the rare sights of Naples. This distinction amazes everyone, as this Prime Minister is really a king and has enormous influence. Yesterday Herr Meurikofer took us to the opera buffa, which is excellent. Old Principessa di Belmonte[4] saw us at once and greeted us most cordially, although our box was a good distance from hers.

★   I write in haste. I kiss you and Nannerl 1000 times. Herr Donker sends
★ cordial greetings to you and to Nannerl and I am your old

MZT

[1] Francesco (Ciccio) di Majo (1732–1770), son of Giuseppe di Majo (1698–1772), had been a pupil of Padre Martini and from 1759 onwards had been composing operas regularly. *Eumene*, the last one on which he was working, was completed by Insanguine and was performed at Naples on 20 January 1771.

[2] Schloss Mirabell, built in 1606 by Archbishop Wolf Dietrich, was remodelled in a baroque style during the years 1721–1727. It is now divided up into private dwellings. The gardens are still kept in the style of the eighteenth century.

[3] Donker appears in Leopold Mozart's *Reiseaufzeichnungen*, p. 45 (*MBA*, No. 105).

[4] Principessa di Belmonte-Pignatelli, famous for her friendship with Metastasio.

(93a) *Mozart to his Mother and Sister*

[*Autograph in the Mozarteum, Salzburg*]

[NAPLES, 22 *May* 1770[1]]

Praise and thanks be to God, I am well and kiss Mamma's hands and kiss you both a thousand times.

(94) *Leopold Mozart to his Wife*

[*Extract*]   [*Autograph in the Mozarteum, Salzburg*]

NAPLES, 26 *May* 1770

This is the third letter which I am writing to you from Naples. The situation of this town pleases me more and more every day and Naples itself is on the whole not ugly. But I only wish that the natives were not so godless and that certain people, who do not for a moment imagine that they are fools, were not so stupid as they are.[2] And the superstition! Here it is so deeply rooted that I can say with certainty that heresy now rules supreme and that everyone treats this state of affairs with indifference. I shall explain this to you later on. I hope to bring back copper engravings of the views and rare sights of Naples, such as I already possess of Rome. God be praised, we are both well. The tailor has in hand two costumes, which I chose with the assistance of M. Meurikofer. Mine is of Pompadour, or rather, dark red shot moiré, lined with sky-blue taffeta and trimmed with silver buttons. Wolfgang's is of apple-green shot moiré, with silver buttons and lined with rose-coloured taffeta.

On Monday we are giving a concert, which the Countess von Kaunitz, the Imperial Ambassador's wife, Lady Hamilton, Principessa Belmonte, Principessa Francavilla, Duchessa Calabritta are organising and which, I think, will bring us in at least one hundred and fifty zecchini. Indeed we need money, for, if we leave, we shall have a long journey during which we shall not be able to earn anything and, if we remain, we shall have to hold out for five months. It is true that here we should always be able to earn enough for our needs, but I am still determined to leave in three weeks. We hope to be presented to the King and Queen next week. ★

Farewell to you and Nannerl. We kiss you both and I am your old

MZT

My greetings to the whole of Salzburg.

---

[1] A postscript to his father's letter.
[2] Abert, vol. i. p. 191, n. 1, suggests that 'certain people' is an allusion to the King and Queen of Naples.

(95) *Leopold Mozart to his Wife*

[*Extract*]   [*Autograph in the Mozarteum, Salzburg*]

NAPLES, 29 *May* 1770

I am probably writing far too often and you will be surprised to see a letter from me every post-day! But this is a precaution on my part, lest perhaps some letter should go astray. We are rather far from one another and a letter from Salzburg to Naples takes fourteen days. This is my fourth letter from here. I still intend to leave Naples on June 16th, if nothing prevents us. Yesterday we gave our concert, which was a great success and brought us in a considerable sum. The court returns to town tomorrow, May 30th, to celebrate the King's name-day with an opera and other festivities. If we leave here on the 16th we shall go to Marino and stay at the Augustinian monastery, as the Prior has begged us to do. For he wants to accompany us to Genazzano and show us the miraculous image of Our Lady of Good Counsel.[1] As it is not a long journey, I have accepted his offer in order to see this sacred image. Thus we can spend six or seven days with our friends in Rome and then start on our journey to Loreto. By leaving here at the time I have stated we shall see, so to speak, the whole of Italy. For, if we feel inclined, we shall travel on through the country beyond Loreto to Bologna or even to Florence and thence to Pisa, Lucca and Leghorn and spend the two hot months in the most suitable spot, probably going on to Milan via Genoa. If Wolfgang had not already the scrittura for the opera in Milan, he would have obtained one for Bologna, Rome or Naples, for he has received offers from all these places. So far we have not had to endure great heat, as it has been raining the whole time. Yesterday we had violent wind and heavy rain; and it is quite unusual for Naples not to have greater heat. All the same we shall return home fairly well tanned, for the air has that effect, and, as soon as the sun appears, you notice at once that you are in Naples. You yourself know that Wolfgang is always longing to be brown.

I must close, for this very moment a footman has come from the Principessa di Francavilla with an invitation to drive to her house, as she wants to see us. My greetings to all Salzburg. We kiss you and Nannerl 1000 times and I am your old

MZT

Wolfgang can hardly wait for the post-days and he begs you to write sometimes twice a week, especially if there is anything new to tell. But in Salzburg it does not take long to jot down news.

Vesuvius has not yet given me the pleasure of appearing to burn or

[1] Genazzano, 30 m. S.E. of Rome, is noted for its pilgrimage chapel of Our Lady of Good Counsel.

rather, to spit fire. Very occasionally you see a little smoke. But one of these days we shall inspect it at close quarters.

(95a) *Mozart to his Sister*

[Autograph in the Mozarteum, Salzburg]

MY DEAREST SISTER,   [NAPLES, 29 *May* 1770 [1]]

The day before yesterday we were at the rehearsal of Signor Jommelli's opera, which is well composed and which I really like. He himself spoke to us and was very polite. We have also been to a church to hear some music composed by Signor Ciccio di Majo, which was most beautiful. He too spoke to us and was most gracious. Signora De Amicis sang marvellously well. Thank God, we are in very good health, and I am especially so when a letter comes from Salzburg. I beg you to send me a letter every post-day, even if you have nothing to write about. I should like to have one merely in order to receive some letter every time the post comes in. I hope that you received my letter which contained passages in another language, which you will surely have understood or made out.[2] It would not be a bad plan if sometimes you were to send me a little note in Italian. I have nothing more to write to you about, except to ask you to give my greetings to all my friends, male and female, and especially to Herr von Schiedenhofen, who no doubt has already received the letter which my father wrote to him. Please give my greetings to Herr von Amann and ask him how he is and then let me know. Addio.
29 May 1770.

WOLFGANGO AMADEO MOZART

Kiss my mother's hand for me.

(96) *Leopold Mozart to his Wife*

[Extract]   *[Autograph in the Mozarteum, Salzburg]*

NAPLES, 5 *June* 1770

I only received today—June 5th—your letter of May 18th. You will ★ have received by now my first four letters from here.[3] Our concert went off very well, but I cannot write anything yet about the court. The Principessa di Francavilla has given us a handsome present and we are hoping for a few more trifles. You will be very much disappointed that I do not send you more details about our takings, but I refrain from doing

---

[1] This letter is in Italian.
[2] No doubt Mozart is referring to his letter of 19 May, which has passages in Italian. See pp. 136, 137.   [3] Letters 92–95.

so on purpose, because in Salzburg only the earnings are considered and the expenses ignored and because there are very, very few people who realize what travelling costs. Let it suffice if I tell you that, thank God, we lack nothing that is necessary to enable us to continue our travels in an honourable fashion. One of the finest sights is the daily passeggio, when in a few hundred carriages the nobles go out driving in the afternoon until Ave Maria to the Strada Nuova and the Molo. The Queen too goes out driving very often, always on Sundays and on holidays. As she drives along the sea coast, guns are fired off on the ships, and on the right and on the left the carriages stop and their occupants salute her as she passes them. As soon as it is twilight, the flambeaux are lighted on all the carriages and produce a sort of illumination. Since we drive there daily and always in a carriage belonging to some lord, I have two flambeaux, that is, the servant of the lord who has sent his carriage has one and our servant has the other. However, that is no great expense, as flambeaux are very cheap here. One sees several carriages with four flambeaux carried by four footmen. Her Majesty the Queen always greets us with quite exceptional friendliness. On Whit Sunday we were at the great ball given by the French Ambassador on the occasion of the betrothal of the Dauphin.[1] Two invitation cards had been sent to us. I am still determined to leave Rome on the 16th with the procaccio, or possibly on the 20th, if I secure a private sedia in which I shall travel with the Imperial Ambassador Count Kaunitz.

I kiss you and Nannerl 1000 times and I am your old

MZT

(96a) *Mozart to his Sister*

[Autograph sold by J. A. Stargardt, Marburg, 1–2 February 1977]

CARA SORELLA MIA,   NAPLES, 5 *June* 1770

Vesuvius is smoking furiously today. Thunder and lightning and all the rest. We gorged ourselves today with Herr Doll.[2] He is a German composer and a fine fellow.[3] Now I shall begin to describe my way of life. Alle nove ore, qualche volta anche alle dieci mi sveglio, e poi andiamo fuor di casa, e poi pranziamo da un trattore, e dopo pranzo scriviamo, e poi sortiamo, e indi ceniamo, ma che cosa? Al giorno di grasso, un mezzo pollo, ovvero un piccolo boccone d'arrosto; al giorno di magro, un piccolo pesce; e di poi andiamo a dormire.[4] Est-ce que vous avez compris? Let us

---

[1] Louis (later Louis XVI) to Marie Antoinette of Austria.

[2] Joseph Doll was 'secondo maestro' at the Conservatorio di Sant' Onofrio in Naples, where he died in August 1774. See S. di Giacomo, *Il Conservatorio di Sant' Onofrio*, 1924, p. 159 f.

[3] These first sentences and others in this letter are in Salzburg dialect.

[4] I wake up at nine, sometimes even at ten, and then we go out, and then we lunch at an eating-house, and after lunch we write, and then we go out, and then we have supper, and what do we eat? On ordinary days half a chicken or a small slice of roast meat; on fast days a little fish; and then we go to bed.

talk Salzburgish for a change, for it is more sensible. Thank God, we are well, my father and I.

I hope that you too are well and Mamma also. If Fräulein Aloysia von Schiedenhofen comes to see you again, give her my compliments. Naples and Rome are two sleepy towns. What a beautiful handwriting mine is, is it not?

Write to me and do not be so lazy. Altrimenti avrete qualche bastonata da me.[1] Quel plaisir! Je te casserai la tête. I am already looking forward to the portraits, and I am anxious to see what they are like. If I like them I shall have similar ones done of my father and myself. Tell me, little girl, where have you been, eh? Yesterday we were in the company of Herr Meurikofer who sends his regards to you and Mamma. The opera here is one of Jommelli's; it is beautiful, but too serious and old-fashioned for the theatre. De Amicis sings amazingly well and so does Aprile, who sang in Milan. The dances are wretchedly pompous. The theatre is beautiful. The King has had a rough Neapolitan upbringing and in the opera he always stands on a stool so as to look a little taller than the Queen. She is beautiful and gracious, and on the Molo (that is a drive) she bowed to me in a most friendly manner at least six times. Every evening the nobles send us their carriages to drive out with them to the Molo. We were invited on Sunday to the ball given by the French Ambassador. I can't write anything more. My compliments to all our kind friends. Farewell.

WOLFGANG MOZART

I kiss Mamma's hand.

(97) *Leopold Mozart to his Wife*

[*Extract*]   [*Autograph in the Mozarteum, Salzburg*]

NAPLES, 9 *June* 1770

We shall hardly receive a letter from you here in reply to my first letter from Naples, for it is still definitely fixed that we leave either on the 16th with the procaccio or on the 20th with the mail coach. So I shall get your letters in Rome. If you write as soon as you receive this one, I can still pick up your reply in Rome or Herr Marcobruni can forward it. Before I leave here I shall write once or twice and tell you where to send your letters. In some respects it is a pity that we cannot stay longer in Naples, for during the summer there are many pleasant things to be seen and there is a perpetual variety of fruits, vegetables and flowers from week to week. The situation of the town, the fruitfulness of the country, the liveliness of the people, the rare sights and a hundred beautiful things make me sorry

---

[1] Otherwise I shall give you a whipping.

to leave. But the filth, the crowds of beggars, the hateful and godless populace, the disgraceful way in which children are brought up, the incredible frivolity even in the churches, make it possible quite calmly to leave behind what is good. Not only shall I bring back all the rare sights in several beautiful copper engravings, but Herr Meurikofer has given me a fine collection of Vesuvius lava, not of the lava which everyone can obtain easily, but choice pieces with a description of the minerals which they contain, rare and not easy to procure. If God permits us to return ★ home in good health, you will see many beautiful things. Keep well, both of you. We kiss you both 1000 times and I am your old

MOZART

Our servant has brought news this very moment that the sedia which we hoped to get is at my service. So I shall leave with the mail coach on the 20th and reach Rome in twenty-six hours; whereas with the procaccio I should have to spend four and a half days on the road, which, although it is very beautiful, has the most abominable inns. Our remembrances to Herr Meisner, who can describe these inns to you. The sedia belongs to the General of the Augustinian Fathers. We are lunching tomorrow at the Augustinian monastery of S. Giovanni a Carbonara, where a great feast ★ is being held.

During the coming week we shall visit Vesuvius, the two buried cities, where ancient rooms are being excavated, then Caserta and so forth, in short, all the rare sights, of which I already possess engravings.
★

(98) *Leopold Mozart to his Wife*

[*Extract*]   [*From Nissen, pp. 211–212*[1]]

★
NAPLES, 16 *June* 1770
We cannot leave after all on the 20th, as Count Kaunitz will not be
★ ready by that date. On the 13th we drove in a carriage to Pozzuoli, and then took ship to Baia, where we saw the baths of Nero, the subterranean grotto of Sibylla Cumana, Lago d'Averno, Tempio di Venere, Tempio di Diana, Sepolcro d'Agrippina, the Elysian fields, the Dead Sea, where Charon was ferryman, la Piscina Mirabile, the Cento Camerelle, and so forth. On the return journey we visited many old baths, temples, underground rooms, Monte Nuovo, Monte Gauro, Molo di Pozzuoli, Colosseo, Solfatara, Astroni, Grotta del Cane, Lago d'Agnano, but especially the ★ Grotto di Pozzuoli and Virgil's grave. We lunched today with the Carthusians on the hill of San Martino and visited all the sights and rarities of the place and admired the view. On Monday and Tuesday we are going

[1] Autograph in the Museum Carolino Augusteum, Salzburg.

to Vesuvius, Pompeii, Herculaneum and its excavations, Caserta and Capo di Monte. All this is going to cost money.

(98a) *Mozart to his Mother and Sister*

[From Nissen, p. 212[1]]

[NAPLES, 16 *June* 1770[2]]

I too am still alive and always merry as usual and I simply love travelling. I have now been on the Mediterranean[3] too. I kiss Mamma's hand and Nannerl 1000 times and am your Simple Simon of a son and Jack Pudding of a brother.

1770

(99) *Leopold Mozart to his Wife*

[Extract]   *[Autograph in the Mozarteum, Salzburg]*

ROME, 27 *June* 1770

We reached Rome yesterday evening at eight o'clock, having done in twenty-seven hours with the mail coach the same journey which previously took us four and a half days with the vettura. But indeed we flew. Count Kaunitz only arrived today. I thought it wise to travel by ourselves, as one often does not find enough horses at the post-stages, and thus one is given the pleasure of sitting and waiting half a day for their return. So we left Naples by ourselves and I announced everywhere that I was the steward of the Imperial Ambassador, because in these parts the stewards of such personages are very highly respected. Thus not only did I ensure a safe journey, but I was given good horses and quick service; and at Rome it was not necessary for me to go to the Customs Office for the usual examination, for at the gate I was received with a deep bow, and was simply told to drive on to my destination, at which I was so pleased that I threw a few paoli in their faces. As we had only slept for two out of the twenty-seven hours of our journey and had only eaten four cold roast chickens and a piece of bread in the carriage, you can well imagine how hungry, thirsty and sleepy we were. Our good hostess—Signora Uslenghi—gave us some nice well-cooked rice and we just ate two lightly boiled eggs each. As soon as we got to our bedroom, Wolfgang sat down on a chair and at once began to snore and to sleep so soundly that I completely undressed him and put him to bed without his showing the least sign of waking up. Indeed he went on snoring, although now and then I had to raise him and

---

[1] Autograph in the Museum Carolino Augusteum, Salzburg.
[2] A postscript to his father's letter.
[3] The original text has 'Merditeranischen' in allusion to a characteristic joke in the Mozart family.

put him down again and finally drag him to bed sound asleep. When he awoke after nine o'clock in the morning, he did not know where he was nor how he had got to bed. Almost the whole night through he had lain in the same place. God be praised, we are well.

While we were in Naples the impresario Signor Amadori, who met and heard Wolfgang at Jommelli's house, made him an offer to write an opera for the Teatro Reale San Carlo, which, on account of our Milan engagement, we could not accept. Whereupon the impresario said that he quite understood that it would not be worth our while to travel as far as Naples for one single opera, but that he hoped that Wolfgang would soon write an opera in Bologna or Rome. He begged us to inform him if this should be possible, so that he might immediately send us the scrittura for the Teatro Reale. Hornung has asked us for arias. You can give him whatever he wants. You can also give Spitzeder anything he may desire. They can choose and take what they like, provided they return them eventually. You and Nannerl are well, we hope. We kiss you both 1000 times. I am

your old

MOZART

(100) *Leopold Mozart to his Wife*

[Extract]   [Autograph in the Mozarteum, Salzburg]

ROME, 30 *July* [*recte June*] 1770

You ask whether Wolfgang has begun his opera? Why, he is not even thinking of it. You should ask us again when we have reached Milan on November 1st. So far we know nothing either about the cast or about the libretto. But now we do know who will be the primo uomo and the tenor. Santorini, who sang during the last carnival in Turin, will be the primo uomo and Ettore will be the tenor. We found Santorini here; he called on us yesterday and said that he believed that the first opera would be 'Nitteti'.[1] Basta! We still have plenty of time.

You ask whether we played before the King of Naples? No, indeed! We did not get beyond the stock compliments which the Queen paid us wherever she met us. She has no influence and what sort of a fellow the King is it is perhaps wiser to speak of than to write about. You can easily imagine what kind of place the court is. The young violinist, Lamotte,[2] who is in the service of the Empress and has come to Italy at her command and at her expense, spent a long time in Naples and stayed on for an extra

---

[1] Composed by Johann Adolf Hasse. See Letter 106.
[2] Franz Lamotte (*c.* 1751–1781), born in Vienna, at the age of twelve played a violin concerto before the Empress, who sent him to Italy to study, and on his return in 1772 took him into the court service.

three weeks, because he was given to understand that the King and Queen would hear him. But they never did. Later on I shall tell you several amusing things about that court and you shall see the King's portrait.

I hope to be able to let you know soon what we are going to do here. I have been obliged either to stay indoors or to limp about very slowly. So I have not yet been able to pay my respects to princes and cardinals. In my first letter I did not mention this, but as the limb is now improving I shall describe my unfortunate accident. You know that two horses and a postillion are equal to three beasts. During the last stage to Rome the postillion kept on lashing the horse which was between the shafts and therefore supporting the sedia. Finally the horse reared, stuck fast in the sand and dirt which was more than half a foot deep, and fell heavily on one side, pulling down with him the front of the two-wheeled sedia. I held back Wolfgang with one hand, so that he should not be hurled out; but the plunge forward pulled my right foot so violently to the centre bar of the falling dashboard that half the shin-bone of my right leg was gashed to the width of a finger. I should mention that the dashboard could not be attached and had thus fallen back. On the following day my injury seemed rather serious, as my foot was very much swollen; and I have spent the greater part of yesterday and today in bed. But now, as I write, my leg is much better and the wound, though it is very long, looks healthy; it has almost ceased to suppurate and, what is more, I have no pain. I have only used the white ointment and shall apply nothing else. Perhaps this accident had to happen, for otherwise you would have packed the ointment and lint to no purpose. I am only sorry that there is so little plaster. By the next post please tell me how it is made. You must not ★ worry, for with God's help the leg will heal. I am only annoyed at having to stay longer in Rome than I intended; not on account of Rome itself, which I like very much, but on account of the journey which is still before us. But God will protect us, and the great heat has not yet come. ★

Farewell to you and Nannerl. I kiss you both 1000 times and I am your old

MZT ★

(101) *Leopold Mozart to his Wife*

[*Extract*]   [*Autograph in the Mozarteum, Salzburg*]

ROME, 4 *July* 1770

I have nothing to write to you about except that, thank God, my foot is well. On the other hand I have slight rheumatism in my left shoulder. In eight or ten days at the latest we shall travel to Bologna by way of Loreto. This very moment a servant of Cardinal Pallavicini has invited us to lunch with His Eminence tomorrow. We are dining on Friday with

His Excellency the Tuscan Ambassador, Baron Sant' Odile. Tomorrow we are to hear a piece of news which, if it is true, will fill you both with amazement. For Cardinal Pallavicini is said to have been commanded by the Pope to hand Wolfgang the cross and diploma of an order.[1] Do not say much about this yet. If it is true, I shall write to you next Saturday. When we were at the Cardinal's house a few days ago he once or twice called Wolfgang 'Signor Cavaliere'. We thought that he was joking, but now I hear that it is true and that this is behind tomorrow's invitation. Addio! Farewell! I must hurry, for the post is going. Wolfgang cannot send you a letter, as he is writing to the son of Field-marshal Pallavicini in Bologna. We kiss you 1000 times.

MZT

Wolfgang grew noticeably in Naples.

(102) *Leopold Mozart to his Wife*

[*Extract*]   [*From Nissen, p.* 215[2]]

ROME, 7 July 1770

What I wrote the other day about the cross of an order is quite correct. It is the same order as Gluck's and is worded as follows: *te creamus auratae militiae equitem.*[3] Wolfgang has to wear a beautiful gold cross, which he has received. You can imagine how I laugh when I hear people calling him 'Signor Cavaliere' all the time. Tomorrow we are to have an audience with the Pope.

(102a) *Mozart to his Sister*

[*Autograph sold by J. A. Stargardt, Marburg, 28 November* 1979]

CARA SORELLA MIA!   [ROME, 7 July 1770[4]]

I am amazed to find how well you can compose. In a word, the song is beautiful. Try this more often. Send me soon the other six minuets by Haydn,[5] I beg you, Farewell.

WOLFGANG MOZART

PS.—My compliments to all my good friends. I kiss Mamma's hand: Mademoiselle, j'ai l'honneur d'être votre très humble serviteur e frere.

CHEVALIER DE MOZART

Rome 7 July 1770 Addio. Keep well, and shit in your bed make a mess of it.[6]

---

[1] The Order of the Golden Spur, which Pope Clement XIV conferred on Mozart on 8 July 1770.   [2] Autograph sold by J. A. Stargardt, Marburg, 28 November 1979.
[3] 'We create you a Knight of the Golden Spur'.   [4] A postscript to his father's letter.
[5] Michael Haydn. See p. 78.   [6] This sentence is in Italian.

(103) *Leopold Mozart to his Wife*

[*Extract*]   [*Autograph in the Pierpont Morgan Library, New York City*]

BOLOGNA, 21 *July* 1770

We congratulate you on your common name-day [1] which is just past, and we wish you both good health and more especially the grace of God. For that is all we need. Everything else comes of its own accord.

We heard Mass in Città Castellana, and afterwards Wolfgang played on the organ. The day on which we performed our devotions in Loreto happened to be the 16th. I bought six little bells and various other trifles. In addition to other relics I am bringing back from Rome a piece of the Holy Cross. We visited the fair in Sinigaglia. We arrived here yesterday, having left Rome on the 10th. Count Pallavicini has offered us everything we require, and I have accepted his carriage.

If Wolfgang continues to grow as he is doing, he will be quite tall by the time we get home.

(103a) *Mozart to his Mother*

[*Autograph in the Pierpont Morgan Library, New York City*]

[BOLOGNA, 21 *July* 1770 [2]]

I congratulate Mamma on her name-day and I hope that she may live many hundreds of years and enjoy good health. I always ask this of God and pray for this every day and I shall always pray every day for both of you. It is impossible for me to send presents, but I shall bring home a few little bells from Loreto and candles and bonnets and fleas. Meanwhile, farewell, dear Mamma. I kiss Mamma's hands a thousand times and remain till death

her faithful son
WOLFGANG MOZART

(103b) *Mozart to his Sister*

[*Autograph in the Pierpont Morgan Library, New York City*]

CARA SORELLA MIA,   [BOLOGNA, 21 *July* 1770]

I hope that God will always grant you good health and will let you live another hundred years and will let you die when you have reached a

---

[1] July 16th.
[2] This note and the following one are postscripts to his father's letter. The one to his sister is in Italian.

thousand. I hope that you will get to know me better in the future and that then you will decide how much you like me. I have no time to write much. My pen is not worth a fig nor is he who is holding it. We do not yet know the title of the opera which I have to compose in Milan. Addio. Our hostess in Rome gave me as a present the 'Arabian Nights' in Italian. It is very amusing to read.[1]

★

(104) *Leopold Mozart to Lorenz Hagenauer, Salzburg*

[*From Nohl, 'Mozart nach den Schilderungen seiner Zeitgenossen', pp.* 112–113[2]]

BOLOGNA, 28 *July* 1770

If I were to observe punctiliously the rules of good behaviour, I should indeed be ashamed to appear before you with such a wretched scrap of paper. But as I am certain that you are accustomed to judge people not by their outward appearance but by their inner and true worth, I do not hesitate to wish you from an honest heart, even on this small piece of paper, thousands of pleasures, years without number and, above all, constant good health, not only on your name-day[3] but at all times. And united with all my dear ones in your friendship, which is so precious to us, I send my best greetings. God keep you for the consolation and happiness of your excellent wife, to whom I send special greetings, and for the support of your dear children, who in the future will surely bring you nothing but honour, joy and pleasure. Again, united to you and your beloved wife in friendship, I send my wishes and remain your most

obediently devoted and at the moment

limping friend

MOZART

(104a) *Mozart to Lorenz Hagenauer, Salzburg*

[*Autograph in the Staatsbibliothek Preussischer Kulturbesitz, West Berlin*]

[BOLOGNA, 28 *July* 1770[4]]

I too slip in amongst the number of friends who are congratulating you and confirm all my father's cordial wishes and present my compliments to you and to dear Frau Hagenauer.

Your most obedient servant

WOLFGANGO AMADEO MOZART

---

[1] According to Nissen, pp. 216–217, the last two sentences were written on the cover, which is lost.

[2] Copy in the Staatsbibliothek Preussischer Kulturbesitz, West Berlin.

[3] **August 10th.**

[4] A postscript to his father's letter.

(105) *Leopold Mozart to his Wife*

[*Extract*]   [*Autograph in the possession of Dr. Myron Prinzmetal, Beverley Hills*]

BOLOGNA, 28 *July* 1770

You will have received my first letter from Bologna, dated July 21st. I have now been nine days here and have not left my room, but have been either in bed or sitting up with my foot resting on a chair. But I hope that by the time you read this letter I shall have been out walking a few times. Well, this joke will cost me twelve ducats. For it is no fun being ill ⋆ in an inn. If I had taken in a thousand doppi in Naples I could have got over this expense. All the same I still have more money than we need, and ⋆ so we are content and praise God.

We received yesterday the libretto and the list of the singers. The title ⋆ of the opera is: *Mitridate, Rè di Ponto,* and the text is by a poet of Turin, Signor Vittorio Amadeo Cigna-Santi. It was performed there in 1767.[1] The characters are:

Mitridate, Rè di Ponto	Il Signor Guglielmo d' Ettore
Aspasia, promessa sposa di Mitridate	Signora Antonia Bernasconi, prima donna
Sifare, figlio di Mitridate, amante d' Aspasia	Signor Santorini, soprano, primo uomo[2]
Farnace, primo figlio di Mitridate, amante della medesima Aspasia	Signor Cicognani, contra alto
Ismene, figlia del Rè dei Parti, amante di Farnace	Signora Varese, seconda donna, soprano
Arbate, governatore di Ninfea	Soprano
Marzio, tribuno romano	Tenore[3]

We knew Signora Bernasconi already. Signor Santorini sang for us in Rome. Cicognani is here and is a good friend of ours. Ettore is also here.

We like the two portraits[4] very much; but, in order to appreciate them, ⋆ one must not look at them closely, but from a distance. For pastels are not like miniatures. They are rather oily; but at a distance much of the roughness disappears. Besides, we are satisfied, so that is enough. Wolfgang thanks you and his sister and all his good friends for the good wishes. We kiss you both a thousand times and I am

your old

MZT.

---

[1] Set to music by Abbate Quirino Gasparini (1721–1778), who was maestro di cappella of Turin Cathedral from 1760 until his death.

[2] Nissen, p. 218, in his version of this letter adds the remark 'who sang for the first time during the last carnival in Turin'. Actually the part of Sifare was taken by Pietro Benedetti. See Köchel, p. 120.

[3] Eventually the parts of Arbate and Marzio were filled by Pietro Muschietti and Gasparo Bassano respectively.   [4] These portraits have disappeared.

You can imagine what our household is like, now that I cannot get about. You know what Wolfgang is.

(105a) Mozart to his Sister

[*Autograph in the possession of Dr. Myron Prinzmetal, Beverley Hills*]

MY DEAREST SISTER,   [BOLOGNA, 28 *July* 1770 [1]]
I must confess that I am frightfully pleased that you have sent us the portraits, which I like very much. I have no more news to send you. Kiss my mother's hand a thousand times for me. I kiss you 1000000 times and remain your most humble servant

WOLFGANG AMADEO MOZART

(106) Leopold Mozart to his Wife

[*Extract*]   [*Autograph in the Mozarteum, Salzburg*]

BOLOGNA, 4 *August* 1770
I am still writing from my bed. Not that my right foot is still dangerously disabled. No, thank God, it is better, though the skin is now peeling and the leg looks as if I had had chicken-pox. But apart from my desire to spare this right foot and so prevent any fresh inflammation, I cannot get about on account of my left foot, as, during the night, I had severe pain and slight inflammation in my big toe and in the other toes of that foot, a pain rather like gout, which prevents me from walking. I shall hardly get away from this inn under twenty ducats, if that does the trick! Well, in God's name, let the devil take the money, if only one escapes with one's skin!
★ We have not yet had any heat and I am glad, for otherwise I should have lost heart at having to remain on my bed all this time.
★ During the last few days Mysliwecek [2] came to see me and so did Manfredini, the castrato, who visited us in Salzburg on his way home from Russia. His brother, Kapellmeister Manfredini,[3] has also been to see us, and a certain Schmidt, who gave a concert in Berne, whom Schulz [4]

[1] A postscript in Italian to his father's letter.
[2] Joseph Mysliwecek (1737–1781) was born near Prague, studied in Italy and composed several operas for Naples, Bologna and Munich. The Italians called him 'Il divino Boëmo':
[3] Vincenzo Manfredini (1737–1799), maestro di cappella in Bologna and author of a famous work, *Difesa della musica moderna*, and many other treatises on music.
[4] There were two brothers of this name, both bassoon-players in the Salzburg court orchestra. See A. J. Hammerle, *op. cit.* p. 34.

(to whom we send our greetings) will remember well. Mysliwecek has obtained the scrittura for the first opera of the 1772 carnival in Milan, that is, a year after our Wolfgang's opera. My last letter gave you details about the first opera in Milan and the singers. The second is to be 'Nitteti'. Farewell. We kiss you a thousand times and I am at the moment your old impatient, gouty, bedridden

MZT

★

(106a) *Mozart to his Sister*

[*Copy formerly in the Musikhistorisches Museum von W. Heyer, Cologne*]

[BOLOGNA, *4 August* 1770 [1]]

I am heartily sorry that Jungfrau Martha is so ill and I pray every day that she may recover. Tell her from me that she should not move about too much and that she should eat plenty of salt meats.

A propos! Did you give my letter to my dear Sigmund Robinig? [2] You say nothing about it. If you see him, please tell him not to forget me altogether. It is impossible for me to write a better hand, for this pen is for writing music and not for letters. My fiddle has now been restrung and I play every day. But I add this simply because Mamma wanted to know whether I still play the fiddle. More than six times at least I have had the honour of going alone to a church and to some magnificent function. In the meantime I have composed four Italian symphonies, [3] to say nothing of arias, of which I must have composed at least five or six, [4] and also a motet. [5]

Does Deibl [6] often visit you? Does he still honour you with his entertaining conversation? And the Honourable Karl von Vogt? [7] Does he still deign to listen to your unbearable voice? Schiedenhofen must help you to write lots of minuets; otherwise—not a single lump of sugar for him.

If I had the time, I ought to plague both Mölk and Schiedenhofen with a few lines. But, as this most necessary condition is lacking, I beg them to forgive my slackness and to allow me to postpone this honour to some future date.

---

[1] A postscript to his father's letter.
[2] Sigmund Robinig (1760–1823), son of Georg Joseph Robinig von Rottenfeld (1711–1760), a wealthy mine-owner in the district of Salzburg. He was a friend of Mozart's.
[3] Probably K. 81 [73l], 84 [73q], 95 [73n], 97 [73m]. See Köchel, pp. 104, 105.
[4] K. 77 [73e], 78 [73b], 79 [73d], 82 [73 o], 88 [73c].
[5] Possibly K. 117 [66a]. See WSF, vol. i. p. 285 f.
[6] Franz de Paula Deibl (? –1783), oboist and violinist in the Salzburg court orchestra. See A. S. Hammerle, *op. cit.* p. 35.
[7] Karl Vogt, violinist in the service of the Salzburg court. He is described in Hammerle, *op. cit.* p. 29, as 'a serious performer, who can produce a full and powerful tone'.

Opening bars of various *Cassations*:[1]

There, I have granted your request. I hardly think that it can be one of my compositions, for who would dare to pass off as his own a composition by the Kapellmeister's son, whose mother and sister are in Salzburg?[2] Addio! Farewell. My sole amusement at the moment consists in dancing English steps and in pirouetting and cutting capers. Italy is a sleepy country! I am always drowsy! Addio! Farewell.

4 August 1770.   WOLFGANG MOZART

My greetings to all my good friends! I kiss Mamma's hand!

---

[1] K. 63, 99 [63a], 62. 'Cassation', 'divertimento', 'serenade' and 'Finalmusik' are terms used to describe a kind of composition, often consisting of eight or ten movements, which was performed at court functions, at celebrations and out of doors. The derivation of the word 'cassation' has been much discussed. WSF, vol. i. p. 201, maintain that 'cassation' is connected with 'casser', that is to say, that it was used originally for music, the movements of which need not be played in sequence, but a connection with the German word 'Gasse' (street) is more probable.

[2] Evidently Nannerl had written to say that some Salzburg composer had passed off one of Mozart's compositions as his own.

(107) *Leopold Mozart to his Wife*

[*Extract*]   [*Autograph in the Mozarteum, Salzburg*]

A country house outside BOLOGNA, 11 *August* 1770

On the 4th, that is, the day after you wrote to me, you will have received a letter from me dated July 28th; and in the meantime my letter of August 4th will also have reached you. After hearing Mass in Bologna we arrived yesterday about noon at this country house, which is situated almost the same distance from the town as Maria-Plain is from Salzburg. At last we have now slept our fill. I need not send you a description of all the fine things here, for you can picture to yourself the rooms and the beds. Our sheets are of finer linen than many a nobleman's shirt, everything is of silver, even the bedroom sets, and the nightlights and so forth. Yesterday evening we went for a drive in two sedias, that is, Wolfgang, the Countess and the young Count in one, and I and His Excellency the Field-marshal[1] in the other. We have two servants to wait on us, a footman and a valet. The former sleeps in our anteroom in order to be at hand in case of necessity. The latter has to dress Wolfgang's hair. His Excellency has put us into the first rooms, which in Salzburg we should call the ground floor. Since in summer the upper rooms get all the heat, these are the best rooms, as we do not feel the slightest heat the whole day long nor particularly during the night. In addition to our rooms we have the *sala terrena* where we take our meals and where everything is fresh, cool and pleasant. The young Count, who is about Wolfgang's age and is sole heir to the property, is very talented, plays the clavier, speaks German, Italian and French and has five or six masters every day for lessons in various sciences and accomplishments. He is already Imperial Chamberlain. You can well believe that this young lord and Wolfgang are the best of friends. We shall remain here some time, but I do not know for how long; perhaps for the rest of the month, till the great heat is over. And my foot? Thank God, it is well. The wound has healed up completely and the skin is gradually peeling off. But since I have to use the foot during the day, however much I try to avoid doing so, the lower part, near the ankle, becomes slightly swollen by the evening. During the night, however, the swelling always disappears and it becomes less noticeable every day. My host and hostess never let me stand, but insist on my remaining seated with my foot propped up on another chair. Why, even at Mass today two chairs were put ready for me in the chapel. We have Mass daily at about noon and the young Count serves. After Mass the Rosary, the litany, the Salve Regina and the De Profundis are said.

We invite you to partake of the finest figs, melons and peaches! I am delighted to be able to tell you that, thank God, we are well. Give my ★

---

[1] Count Pallavicini.

greetings to Kapellmeister Lolli and tell him that I shall certainly deliver his messages and that I have already spoken to some old acquaintances of his.[1] We forgot to congratulate Nannerl on her name-day. When I was laid up with my foot my old melancholy thoughts came to me very often. It is sad to hear that living is becoming dearer in Salzburg. Are no means being devised to meet the rise in prices? Give special greetings to Schiedenhofen and his gracious mother. I shall soon reply to his letter. I must stop, for His Excellency's letters are being sent to town and this one must go with them. We kiss you and Nannerl a thousand times. Wolfgang has just now gone out driving with the Countess. We send greetings to all and I am your old

MZT.

(108) *Leopold Mozart to his Wife*

[*Extract*]   [*Autograph in a private collection, U.S.A.*]

BOLOGNA, 21 *August* 1770

Thank God, my foot is now quite well.

We are still alla Croce del Biacco, the country house which belongs to Count Bolognetti, but which Count Pallavicini has taken for a few years. The great annual festival, which the members of the Bologna Philharmonic Society celebrate most magnificently with Vespers and High Mass, takes place on the 30th. We are going to hear it, and then we shall probably leave Bologna.

★

(108a) *Mozart to his Mother and Sister*

[*Autograph in a private collection, U.S.A.*]

[BOLOGNA, 21 *August* 1770[2]]

I too am still alive and, what is more, as merry as can be. I had a great desire today to ride on a donkey, for it is the custom in Italy, and so I thought that I too should try it. We have the honour to go about with a certain Dominican, who is regarded as a holy man. For my part I do not believe it, for at breakfast he often takes a cup of chocolate and immediately afterwards a good glass of strong Spanish wine; and I myself have had the honour of lunching with this saint who at table drank a whole decanter and finished up with a full glass of strong wine, two large slices of melon, some peaches, pears, five cups of coffee, a whole plate of birds and two full saucers of milk and lemon. He may, of course, be following some sort of diet, but I do not think so, for it would be too much; more-

---

[1] See p. 123, n. 5.   [2] A postscript to his father's letter.

over he takes several little snacks during the afternoon. Addio. Farewell.
Kiss Mamma's hands for me. My greetings to all who know me.

WOLFGANG MOZART, 1770

PS. We have made the acquaintance of a certain German Dominican,
called Pater Cantor, who has asked me to give his kind regards to Herr
Hagenauer, the sculptor,[1] at Salzburg. He tells me that when Hagenauer
was in Bologna he always confessed to him. Addio.

(109) *Leopold Mozart to his Wife*

[*Extract*]   [*Autograph in the Mozarteum, Salzburg*]

BOLOGNA, 25 *August* 1770

I wrote to you on the 21st, and I suppose that, if letters to Germany are
delayed in Innsbruck as long as letters from Germany are, you will receive
two letters at once. We are still in the country and, thank God, we are
well. So I have no news whatever for you. You must not worry if my
letters do not arrive punctually, for, as we are out of town, it often happens
that there is no opportunity either of writing letters or of posting them.
Meanwhile continue to address yours to Bologna, although when you
receive this letter it is possible that we shall be about to leave. The weather
is beautiful, neither too warm nor too cold. As there is a Dominican
Father here, a German from Bohemia, to whom our Court Statuarius
used to confess, we performed our devotions today in the Parish Church,
which was all the more convenient as this Father accompanied us. We
were quite alone there, for the peasants attend Mass early in the morning.
We confessed and received Communion and then, having performed
together the Stations of the Cross, we returned to the castle, which is only
two hundred feet away, and where the Dominican said Mass and the ★
Rosary for my host. So you ought to have two fine gold halos made for
us in Salzburg; for we shall certainly return home as saints.   ★

Thank God my foot, or rather, my feet, are well. I still keep a small
protection on the ankle of my wounded foot, more as a precaution than
as a necessity, for it still swells slightly every evening. But that is not
surprising, as during the journey I was not able to take care of it; and then
for three whole weeks it was never used and the skin had almost completely peeled off. I do not desire a repetition of this joke, especially when
travelling; indeed it was the very last thing I wanted.

I am trying hard to devise a means of lightening my luggage, which is
getting more and more bulky, for in Milan I shall be picking up a great

---

[1] Johann Baptist Hagenauer (1732–1810). See p. 13, n. 2.

many things which we left behind. If I can send a few articles from here to
Bozen, I shall certainly do so. But I am not sure that I can. Above all,
books and music, which are always accumulating, cause me much inconvenience. As soon as I reach Milan, I shall have to have nearly all Wolfgang's cravats and shirts altered. He will have to wait until then, for Frau
Theresa, the wife of Count Firmian's steward,[1] can do me this service.
Everything he wears is rather tight for him and he has removed all the
silk threads which were wound round his diamond ring, which however
still has a little wax in it. But you must not think that he has grown very
tall. It is only that his limbs are becoming bigger and stronger. He has no
longer any singing voice. It has gone completely. He has neither a deep
nor a high voice, not even five pure notes. He is most annoyed, for he can
no longer sing his own compositions, which he would sometimes like to
do.

The book, my 'Violinschule,' has not yet arrived in Bologna. Perhaps
Brinsecchi is to receive it in a bale of linen? Find this out from Haffner, to
whom I send greetings. If it reaches me in Bologna, I shall have the
pleasure of handing it to Padre Martini in person. Now I must stop, so
as not to miss the post. We kiss you and Nannerl a thousand times and I
am your old

L. MOZART

★

(110) *Leopold Mozart to his Wife*

[*Extract*]   [*Autograph in the Mozarteum, Salzburg*]

BOLOGNA, 1 *September* 1770

You will have received my letter of August 25th. Not only are we still
in the country as the guests of His Excellency Count Pallavicini, but we
shall very probably remain here for some time and then proceed straight
to Milan via Parma. I am very sorry to have to miss Leghorn, but I still
have hopes of seeing Genoa. If we have time and if I feel inclined, we can
do so from Milan.

My foot has kept me for a long time in Bologna; and now it will soon
be time to think rather of the recitatives for the opera than of a protracted
journey and of visits to various towns. For, when you are moving from
place to place, and have little or no time, you really cannot do anything.
Moreover this is the season when everyone goes into the country and
none of the gentry are to be found in town. So we shall arrive in Milan a
little earlier, perhaps by a month, than we are due. Meanwhile, continue
to write to Bologna. His Excellency arranged for us to be driven into

---

[1] Don Fernando Germani.

town on the 30th in order to hear the Mass and Vespers of the Accademia ★
Filarmonica, which had been composed by ten different masters; that is
to say, one wrote the Kyrie and Gloria, another the Credo, and so forth.
Thus each psalm of the vespers was set to music by a different Kapellmeister, who in each case conducted his own composition. But they all
had to be members of the Academy.[1] We lunched with Brinsecchi who
did us very well. Please give my greetings to Haffner and tell him how
excellently we were entertained. The weather is very mild and the great
heat is over. A few days ago we had a thunderstorm and amazingly heavy
rain. It was so steamy that one could hardly breathe. That was the end of
the heat. I am very sorry to hear that prices are still rising in Salzburg.
What will happen to all of us who have to live on our monthly pay? ★

Wolfgang read Nannerl's long story with much pleasure, but as he has
gone out driving with the Countess, he cannot write. I have stayed indoors to write this letter and I must send one to Milan also. So I must stop.
We kiss you both a thousand times and I am your old

LEOP MOZART ★

(111) *Leopold Mozart to his Wife*

[Extract]　　　　　　　　　　　　　　[Autograph in the Mozarteum, Salzburg]

BOLOGNA, 8 September 1770

I have received your letter of August 24th and I hope that my letters of
August 21st and 25th and September 1st have now reached you. Brinsecchi
has not yet received my 'Violinschule'. ★

I shall reply later on about the other matters you mention. We are still
in the country and, thank God, we are well. I have written to Milan to
find out whether our rooms there are available and to ask that they be got
ready, for we shall arrive there a month earlier than we expected, that is,
by the beginning of October at latest, instead of at the beginning of
November. And, as I have not been able to visit Leghorn, I shall take a
short trip from Milan to the Borromean Islands, which are not far off and
are well worth seeing. ★

We both kiss you a thousand times and I am your old

LEOP MOZART ★

---

[1] Burney, *op. cit.* p. 230 ff., gives a lengthy description of this performance. Petronio Lanzi,
President of the Academy, had composed the Kyrie and Gloria, and Lorenzo Gibelli, a pupil
of Padre Martini, the Credo. Burney goes on to say: 'I must acquaint my musical reader that
at the performance just mentioned, I met with M. Mozart and his son, the little German whose
premature and almost supernatural talents so much astonished us in London a few years ago,
when he had scarce quitted his infant state'.

(111a) *Mozart to his Sister*

[*Autograph in the Mozarteum, Salzburg*]

[BOLOGNA, 8 *September* 1770¹]

In order not to fail in my duty, I will add a few words myself. Please write and tell me to what Brotherhoods I belong and let me know what prayers I must offer for them. I am this moment reading 'Télémaque' and have already got to the second part. Meanwhile, farewell.

WOLFGANG MOZART

I kiss Mamma's hand.

(112) *Mozart to Thomas Linley, Florence*

[*From Giulio Piccini Jarro, 'L'origine della maschera di Stentorello', 1898, pp. 5-6*]

MY DEAR FRIEND,   [BOLOGNA, 10 *September* 1770²]

Here is a letter at last! Indeed I am very late in replying to your charming letter addressed to me at Naples, which, however, I only received two months after you had written it. My father's plan was to travel to Loreto via Bologna, and thence to Milan via Florence, Leghorn and Genoa. We should then have given you a surprise by turning up unexpectedly in Florence. But, as he had the misfortune to gash his leg rather badly when the shaft-horse of our sedia fell on the road, and as this wound not only kept him in bed for three weeks but held us up in Bologna for another seven, this nasty accident has forced us to change our plans and to proceed to Milan via Parma.

Firstly, we have missed the suitable time for such a journey and, secondly, the season is over, for everyone is in the country and therefore we could not earn our expenses. I assure you that this accident has annoyed us very much. I would do everything in my power to have the pleasure of embracing my dear friend. Moreover my father and I would very much like to meet again Signor Gavard and his very dear and charming family, and also Signora Corilla and Signor Nardini, and then to return to Bologna. This we would do indeed, if we had the slightest hope of making even the expenses of our journey.

As for the engravings you lost, my father remembered you; and his order arrived in time for two other copies to be kept for you. So please

---

¹ A postscript to his father's letter.
² This letter and its postscript are in Italian. Jarro states that he copied them from the autograph in the possession of Novello. No doubt this is the letter to which Edward Holmes refers in his *Life of Mozart*, 1845 (reprinted by J. M. Dent, 1921, p. 54, n. 1), where he states that the late Rev. Ozias Linley, of Dulwich College, possessed a letter written by Mozart to his brother Thomas in Italian and esteemed this document, in the handwriting of the composer of *Don Giovanni*, beyond all price. The autograph has since been rediscovered and was sold by J. A. Stargardt, Marburg, 2–3 December 1975.

let me know of some means of sending them to you. Keep me in your friendship and believe that my affection for you will endure for ever and that I am your most devoted servant and loving friend

AMADEO WOLFGANGO MOZART

(112a) *Leopold Mozart to Thomas Linley, Florence*

[*From Giulio Piccini Jarro, 'L'origine della maschera di Stentorello', 1898, p. 6*]

[BOLOGNA, 10 *September* 1770 [1]]

Please give our greetings to all our friends.

LEOPOLDO MOZART

(113) *Leopold Mozart to his Wife*

[*Extract*]   [*Autograph formerly in the Mozarteum, Salzburg*]

BOLOGNA, 18 *September* 1770 ★

Baron Riedheim who arrived in Bologna on the 15th left today. As I only heard this yesterday and could not go myself, I sent the footman into Bologna. Riedheim wrote a note to me and I hope to see him in Milan. We like the minuets very much. Wolfgang has no time at the moment to write to his sister, but he will do so as soon as he can. We send you both ★ many millions of kisses and I am your old

MZT.

If you are so keen to travel to Italy, we invite you to the opera at Milan.

(114) *Leopold Mozart to his Wife*

[*Extract*]   [*Autograph in the Theatersammlung, Hamburg University*]

BOLOGNA, 22 *September* 1770

We are still in the country, but we shall certainly return to town tomorrow or Thursday. Send your next letter to Milan and to the same address, à Mr: Leopolde Troger Secretaire de la Chancellerie, intime de L:L:M:M:Imp:Roy:& apost:dans leur Lombardie à Milan.   ★

Both here and in Rome we have been hearing lately of a great movement, the object of which is to suppress the religion of the Jesuits. The House of Bourbon absolutely refuses to be pacified and both Spain and France are still most insistently urging the Pope to dissolve the order.

---

[1] A postscript to Mozart's letter.

Furthermore a violent book has appeared in Naples, the author of which is a certain Marchese Spiriti. It is a refutation of a Papalist theologian, Father Mamachi, a Dominican, who some time ago wrote a very powerful book in favour of the clergy, that is to say, on behalf of the Immunitas Ecclesiae and the right of the Church to possess property; and in it he attacked the ruling lords and their ministers rather sharply. Now this Marchese Spiriti wrote against this book in a very satirical vein, doubtless at the instigation of the Spanish, Portuguese and Neapolitan courts.[1]

★   Today I am not at all disposed to write as I am suffering from a pain in my shoulder, which is just as if someone had run a knife through my shoulder-blade. You and Nannerl must keep well. We send you many thousands of kisses o o o o o o o; and I am your old

MZT

(114a) *Mozart to his Sister*

[Autograph in the Theatersammlung, Hamburg University]

[BOLOGNA, 22 *September* 1770[2]]

I hope that my Mamma is well, and you too; and I should like you to answer my letters more carefully in future, for it is surely far easier to reply to questions than to make up something for onself. I like Haydn's[3] six minuets better than the first twelve. We have often had to perform them for the countess.[4] We should like to be able to introduce the German taste in minuets into Italy, where they last nearly as long as a whole symphony. Excuse my wretched writing. I could do better, but I am in a hurry. We should like to have two small calendars for next year. Addio.

C: W: MOZART

I kiss Mamma's hand.

(115) *Leopold Mozart to his Wife*

[Extract]   *[Autograph in the Koch Collection, Basel]*

BOLOGNA, 29 *September* [1770]

★   God willing, we shall leave Bologna on October 6th or 8th. Both
★ Wolfgang and I are dreadfully distressed about good little Martha. God give her strength! What is to be done? We cannot get her out of our

---

[1] Tommaso Maria Mamachi (1713–1792) was a great Dominican scholar and historian of Christian antiquities. His principal work was his *Originum et antiquitatum Christianorum libri XX*, Rome, 1749–1755. The writing to which L. Mozart here refers was his *Del diritto libero della Chiesa d'acquistare e di possedere beni temporali*, Rome, 1769. Mamachi was an active controversialist and his polemical writings gained him many enemies. Among these was the Marchese Spiriti, who attacked him in his *Mamachiana, per chi vuol divertirsi*, 1770.
[2] A postscript to his father's letter.   [3] Michael Haydn.
[4] Wife of Count Pallavicini.

minds all day long. Wolfgang began the recitatives for the opera today. ★
We kiss you both 1000,000,000 times.

You will have already heard that relations between the Pope and Portugal are again on a friendly footing. But people are very much afraid that the Jesuit order will be dissolved. For Bishop Palafox,[1] who in his day was so grievously persecuted by the Jesuits, is to be beatified. I could tell you about several disputes of this kind, but they would hardly interest you. It is a great misfortune that now-a-days in Catholic countries, even in Italy, the most disgraceful pamphlets are being published against the authority of the Pope and the immunity of the clergy.   ★

(115a) *Mozart to his Mother*

[*Autograph in the Koch Collection, Basel*]

[BOLOGNA, *29 September* 1770[2]]

To make the letter a little fuller, I will also add a few words. I am sincerely sorry to hear of the long illness which poor Jungfrau Martha has to bear with patience, and I hope that with God's help she will recover. But, if she does not, we must not be unduly distressed, for God's will is always best and He certainly knows best whether it is better for us to be in this world or in the next. She should console herself, however, with the thought that after the rain she may enjoy the sunshine. I kiss Mamma's hands. Farewell. Addio.

WOLFGANG MOZART

(116) *Leopold Mozart to his Wife*

[*From Mitteilungen für die Mozartgemeinde in Berlin, October* 1910, *pp.* 230–231[3]]

BOLOGNA, *6 October* 1770

I received today your letter of September 14th, although I rather expected one dated the 28th. It is the fault of the Tyrolese and Italian posts that letters are delayed for a week or a fortnight. We have now been back in town for five days and have witnessed the festival of St. Petronius,

---

[1] Jean de Palafox de Mendoza (1600–1659), Spanish theologian, after serving as a layman on the Council of the Indies, took orders and was appointed in 1639 Bishop of Puebla-de-los-Angeles (Angelopolis) in Mexico, where he had certain differences with the Jesuits. The question was submitted to Pope Innocent X, and Palafox returned to Europe in 1643 to plead his cause. The King of Spain, satisfied with his conduct, gave him in 1653 the bishopric of Osma. He died a few years later, leaving a great reputation for piety. In 1694 the first steps were taken to procure his beatification. The case was not, however, introduced until 1726, when, in spite of the strong support of the Spanish Government, it was decided that this honour should not be conferred upon one who had been the declared enemy of the Jesuits.
[2] A postscript to his father's letter.   [3] Autograph in a private collection, Brunswick.

which was celebrated here most magnificently and on the occasion of which there was performed in the huge church of St. Petronius a musical work in which all the musicians of Bologna took part. We intended to leave for Milan on Monday or Tuesday. But something is keeping us here until Thursday, *something* which, if it really happens, will do Wolfgang extraordinary honour.[1] I have a great deal to do and that is the reason why I cannot write to Frau Hagenauer for her name-day, as I had intended. So I must ask you to convey our greetings. I hardly have time to scrawl this letter; and now for the next few post-days you will have no letters until you receive one from Milan.

Padre Martini has already received the book.[2] We are the best of friends. The second part of his own work is now ready.[3] I shall bring back both parts. We are at his house every day and have long discussions on the history of music.

So you have had three concerts? Well, three cheers! And you did not invite us? We should have appeared in a trice and then flown away again. We kiss you both many ten thousand millions of times and I am

your old

MZT.

(116a) *Mozart to his Sister*

[*From Mitteilungen für die Mozartgemeinde in Berlin, October* 1910, *pp.* 230–231[4]]

[BOLOGNA, *6 October* 1770[5]]

We received your letter too late, but it does not matter, as the Italian post is extremely irregular. I rejoice from my heart that you enjoyed yourself so much and I wish that I had been there. I hope that Jungfrau Martha is better. I played the organ today in the Dominican Chapel. Congratulate Frau Hagenauer and Theresa from me and tell them that I wish from my heart that they may live to celebrate the anniversary of Father Dominic's ordination[6] and that we may all live together again very happily. It looks as though you did not receive the letter in which I enclosed a note for Sigmund,[7] for I have not had a reply. Addio. Farewell. I kiss Mamma's hand and I send congratulations to all Theresas, and greetings to all other friends in our house and elsewhere. I hope that I shall

---

[1] Leopold Mozart is referring to the prospect of his son's admission to membership of the Accademia Filarmonica of Bologna.

[2] Leopold Mozart's *Violinschule*, published in 1756. According to Köchel, p. 110, the autograph of Mozart's minuet K. 122 [73t], composed probably at Bologna in August 1770 and sent to Salzburg, contains a few lines in his father's handwriting, asking Frau Mozart to send him a copy of his treatise, which he wished to present to Padre Martini.

[3] Padre Martini's *Storia della Musica*, the first volume of which had appeared in 1757.

[4] Autograph in a private collection, Brunswick.   [5] A postscript to his father's letter.

[6] Dominicus Hagenauer, a son of the Mozarts' landlord, had entered the monastery of St. Peter in Salzburg, of which he became Abbot in 1786.

[7] Sigmund Robinig. see p. 153, n. 2.

soon hear those Pertl chamber symphonies and perhaps blow a little trumpet or play on a little pipe by way of accompaniment.[1] I have heard and seen the great festival of St. Petronius in Bologna. It was beautiful, but very long. They had to fetch trumpeters from Lucca for the salvo, but they played abominably.

Addio.   WOLFG. MOZART

(117) *Leopold Mozart to his Wife*

[Extract]   [*Autograph in the Mozarteum, Salzburg*]

MILAN, 20 *October* 1770

We arrived in Milan, thank God, safe and sound at five o'clock in the evening of the 18th. We had to spend a whole day in Parma, as the surprisingly heavy rains had made the rivers rise so high that no one could cross them. We drove during the whole afternoon of the 14th through a terrific thunderstorm and frightfully heavy rain; yet my luggage did not get wet, for I had covered it well with double waterproof cloth. For nearly three weeks I had had very painful rheumatism in my right arm; and this pain I took with me on the journey. But so far from getting worse, it is, on the contrary, noticeably better, although I have not yet got rid of it completely. But note that I am not, nor have I been, treating it in any way. It will have to go as it came. The motion of the sedia did not do it any good. But I said to myself, evil must banish evil. So owing to the thunderstorm and heavy rain it was a rather unpleasant journey, and with my bad arm a rather painful one.

We left Bologna a few days later than we had intended, for by a unanimous vote the Accademia Filarmonica received Wolfgang into their society and awarded him the diploma of Accademico Filarmonico. He won this honour under all the normal conditions and after a previous examination. For on October 9th he had to appear in the Hall of the Academy at four o'clock in the afternoon. There the Princeps Accademiae and the two Censores, who all three are old Kapellmeisters, put before him, in the presence of all the members, an antiphon taken out of an antiphoner, which he had to arrange for four parts in an anteroom, into which the Bedellus led him, locking the door behind him. When Wolfgang had finished it, it was examined by the Censores and all the Kapellmeisters and Compositores. Then a vote was taken, which was done by means of white and black balls. As all the balls were white, Wolfgang was called in and all the members clapped their hands as he entered and congratulated him, and the Princeps Accademiae informed him, on behalf of the company, that he had passed the examination. He thanked them and

[1] Mozart is referring to the informal concerts in his Salzburg home, to which his father alludes in the last paragraph of his letter. Frau Mozart's maiden name was Anna Maria Pertl.

then the ceremony was over. Meanwhile Brinsecchi and I were locked in the library of the Academy on the other side of the hall. All the members were surprised that Wolfgang had finished his task so quickly, seeing that many candidates had spent three hours over an antiphon of three lines. For I must tell you that it is not at all an easy task, for in this kind of composition many things are not allowed and of these Wolfgang had been told previously. Yet he had finished it in less than half an hour.[1] Later the Bedellus brought the certificate to our house. It is in Latin and contains among others the following words:—*testamur Dominum Wolfgangum Amadeum etc.—sub die 9 mensis octobris anni 1770 inter academiae nostrae magistros compositores adscriptum fuisse, etc.*[2] This distinction does Wolfgang all the more credit for the Accademia Bonnoniensis is more than a hundred years old[3] and, apart from Padre Martini and other eminent Italians, only the most distinguished citizens of other countries are members of it.[4]

★

Farewell to both. We kiss you 100000 times and I am your old

★

MOZART

(117a) *Mozart to his Mother*

[*Autograph in the Mozarteum, Salzburg*]

MY DEAR MAMMA,   [MILAN, 20 October 1770[5]]

I cannot write much, for my fingers are aching from composing so many recitatives. Mamma, I beg you to pray for me, that my opera may go well and that we may be happy together again. I kiss Mamma's hand a thousand times and I have many things to say to my sister, but what? God and I alone know. If it is God's will, I shall soon, I hope, be able to tell them to her myself. Meanwhile I kiss her 1000 times. My greetings to all my good friends. We have lost our good little Martha, but with God's help we shall meet her in a better place.

★

(118) *Leopold Mozart to his Wife*

[Extract]   [*Autograph in the Bibliothèque du Musée, Mariemont*]

MILAN, 27 October 1770

You will have received my first letter from Milan, dated October 20th. By the same post I wrote to the Archbishop. Tell me whether he received

---

[1] Köchel, p. 112, points out that the autograph of Mozart's work (K. 86 [73v]) contains certain corrections made by Padre Martini and that the register of the Bologna Academy states that Mozart finished it 'in less than an hour'.
[2] We witness that Master Wolfgang Amadeus etc.—has been enrolled among the master composers of our academy on the 9th day of October 1770; etc. Nissen, p. 226, reproduces the text of the diploma of the Bologna Academy, dated 10 October 1770. See *MDB*, p. 127.
[3] The Bologna Academy was founded in 1666.
[4] The statutory conditions were that the candidate for membership should be not less than 20 years old and should have spent a year in the junior class of singers and players. These conditions were waived in the case of Mozart.   [5] A postscript to his father's letter.

my letter, for no doubt you will hear about it soon. Thank God, we are well. As the heavy rain has continued, we have been out of the house very little. Spagnoletta, whom you saw in Lyons, is here and is to sing in Verona during the carnival. She tells us that the tenor is coming from Germany and is in the service of a court not far from Bavaria. Perhaps it is Meisner? For I know that Meisner could have got a contract for the theatre in Verona, and I presume therefore that it is he. Let me know this at once. God willing, we shall leave here after the middle of January and travel to Venice by way of Brescia, Verona, Vicenza and Padua, in order to see the end of the carnival, which this year is very short, and to hear some of the concerts given in Lent, which, as everyone tells me, is the best season for performances. I am only sorry that afterwards we shall have a filthy and perhaps even a dangerous journey home, as it is no joke travelling through the mountains in spring, when the snow is melting. I am still thinking of leaving Italy through Carinthia, for I have now seen the Tyrol and, unless there is some necessity for it, it is no fun, I think, for me to cover the same route twice after the fashion of dogs. Meanwhile please ask Johann and Joseph Hagenauer to let me know whether I can find private rooms in some comfortable house in Venice. On my way through I shall certainly stay for a short time in Brescia, Verona and the other places which I have mentioned, in order to see the operas; and therefore I shall not arrive in Venice until February, and perhaps not even until the beginning of the week after Candlemas.

Herr Haffner, to whom I send warmest greetings, promised me to send us letters of introduction for Venice. If he still would like to do so, he could send them in advance to a friend there, so that I may find them when I arrive. When we were in Bologna Mysliwecek visited us very often and we constantly went to see him. He often mentioned Johannes Hagenauer and, of course, Herr Cröner.[1] He was writing for Padua an oratorio,[2] which he has probably finished by now. He is then going to Bohemia. He is an honest fellow and we became intimate friends.

Our lodgings here are not far from the theatre. They consist of a large room with a balcony, three windows and a fireplace, and of a bedroom about the same size with two large windows but no fireplace. So, provided we do not freeze to death, we shall be sure not to smell, for we have enough air. The bed is about nine feet wide. We are rather a long way from Count Firmian's house, but this time we have to be near the theatre.

We wish you both good health and, above all, cheaper living, as your letters always contain the sad news that prices are going up. What will become of Salzburg, if some means are not devised of establishing a sound

---

[1] Possibly one of the large family of Bavarian musicians who served the Electoral court at Munich.

[2] Mysliwecek's oratorio *Giuseppe riconosciuto*, on a text by Metastasio, which was performed in Padua in 1771.

régime? With the small pay we get we shall in time all be beggars. The poor court servants have hardly enough to satisfy their hunger; and their children who learn nothing, because there is no money, will grow up to be idlers, and in about twenty years the town will be full of useless people living in misery, a burden both to the court and to the whole community. In a few years' time others will have to admit that what I say is true. If everyone is to be allowed to marry and if a population is required for a town, it should be known beforehand how the means of subsistence is to be found for all these people.

⋆ We kiss you 100,000,000 times and I am your old

⋆   MOZART

(118a) Mozart to his Sister

[*Autograph in the Bibliothèque du Musée, Mariemont*]

DEAREST SISTER!   [MILAN, 27 October 1770 [1]]
    You know what a great chatterbox I am—and was, when I left you. But at the moment I am talking in signs, as the son of the house is deaf and dumb from birth. Now I must work at my opera. I am heartily sorry that I cannot let you have the minuets you asked for, but, God willing, you may perhaps have them at Easter—and me too. I cannot write anything more, and I do not know what to write about, as there is no news. Farewell and pray for me. I kiss Mamma's hand, and I send greetings to all my acquaintances, and I am, as always, your brother

WOLFGANG MOZART

(119) Leopold Mozart to his Wife

[*Extract*]   [*From Nissen, pp. 230–231 [2]*]

MILAN, 3 November 1770
⋆ Wolfgang thanks you for your congratulations on his name-day [3] and hopes that, if God in His goodness allows us to meet again, he will be able
⋆ to reward you for all your good wishes by giving you joy and pleasure.
    I cannot think of anything to write to you about, except that, thank God, we are well and wish that New Year's Day or at least Christmas were here already. For until then there will always be something to do or to think about, perhaps some small worry to make one foam at the mouth and have an unpleasant time. But patience! Thanks be to God that this great undertaking is nearly over, and, God be praised, once more in honourable fashion. With His help, we shall nibble our way through these unavoidable annoyances which every Kapellmeister has to face with
⋆ this canaille of virtuosi.

[1] A postscript to his father's letter.
[2] Autograph in the Museum Carolino Augusteum, Salzburg.   [2] October 31st.

(119a) *Mozart to his Sister*

[*Autograph in the Museum Carolino Augusteum, Salzburg*]

DEAREST DARLING LITTLE SISTER, [MILAN, 3 *November* 1770[1]]
I thank Mamma and you for your sincere good wishes and I burn
with eagerness to see you both in Salzburg soon again. To return to your
congratulations I must say that I almost suspected that it was Martinelli
who composed those Italian wishes. But as you are always such a clever
sister and as you managed to arrange it so deftly by adding immediately
under your Italian wishes Martinelli's greetings in the same handwriting,
I simply could not detect it and said at once to Papa: 'Ah! If only I were
so clever and smart!' And Papa said: 'Yes, I agree'. Then I said: 'I am
sleepy'. And he said—just this very moment: 'Stop writing'. Addio. Pray
to God that my opera may go well. I kiss Mamma's hand and I send
greetings to all my friends and am, as always, your brother
WOLFGANG MOZART, whose fingers are
tired from writing.

(120) *Leopold Mozart to his Wife*

[*Extract*] [*Autograph in the Mozarteum, Salzburg*]

MILAN, 10 *November* 1770
I have received the miscellany which our good friends have sent us and
we are both of us very glad that you had such a good time in Triebenbach.
If our excellent friends sometimes add a joke to your letters, they will be ★
doing a good deed, for Wolfgang is now busy with serious matters and is
therefore very serious himself. So I am delighted when he occasionally
gets hold of something really funny. By the way, I ask my friends to
excuse me for not writing to anyone. I now feel less inclined to write than
ever and later on you will be astounded to hear what a storm we have
been through, to weather which presence of mind and constant thought
were necessary. God be praised, we have won the first battle and have
defeated an enemy, who brought to the prima donna's house all the arias
which she was to sing in our opera and tried to persuade her not to sing
any of Wolfgang's. We have seen them all and they are all new, but
neither she nor we know who composed them. But she gave that wretch
a flat refusal, and she is now beside herself with delight at the arias which
Wolfgang has composed to suit her. So also is her maestro, Signor
Lampugnani,[2] who is rehearsing her part with her and who cannot

---

[1] A postscript to his father's letter.
[2] Giovanni Battista Lampugnani (1706–*c.* 1784), a prolific composer of operas.

sufficiently praise them; for when we called on her today, she happened to be studying her first aria with him. But a second storm, which we can already see in the distance, is gathering in the theatrical sky. Yet with God's help and if we conduct ourselves bravely we shall fight our way through. Do not worry, for these are unavoidable accidents which befall the greatest masters. If only we keep well and do not get constipated, little else matters. We must not take things too much to heart. You will hear everything in due course. It still rains here most of the time and we have thick mists, which, after one fine day, then settle down upon us.

We both kiss you a million times and I remain your old

LEOP MOZART

I cannot remember whether I told you that Kreusser Junior[1] looked us up in Bologna, that is, young Kreusser of Amsterdam, whose brother is first violin there and who came to see us constantly and wanted to travel with us. He asked for us in Rome and Naples, but each time we had already left. He is now returning to Holland through Turin and Paris and he sends greetings to you both.

I have this very moment received your letter of November 2nd. Dr. Bridi[2] of Rovereto is himself a good performer on the clavier. Count Castelbarco I know well. I am writing this letter in the steward's quarters of Count Firmian's house.

(121) *Leopold Mozart to his Wife*

[*Extract*]   [*Autograph in the Mozarteum, Salzburg*]

MILAN, 17 November 1770

In my last letter, dated November 10th, I asked you to thank all our good friends for their very kind congratulations.[3] I have no reason to thank you and Nannerl, for you conveyed, it is true, the good wishes of others, but your own stuck in your pen; and Nannerl, I suppose, could not think of a motto, for she too wrote nothing, though in the last letter but one which she wrote, she promised her brother that she would con-
★ gratulate him in her next letter. Indeed it would not have killed Nannerl if she had written to me. Why, now I come to think of it, yes, she did

---

[1] Georg Anton Kreusser (1746–1810), violinist and composer. After studying in Italy he returned in 1773 to Germany and became Konzertmeister to the Elector of Mainz. His elder brother, Adam Kreusser (1732–1791), a famous horn-player and violinist, became Konzertmeister at Amsterdam, where the Mozarts made the acquaintance of both brothers. See Leopold Mozart's *Reiseaufzeichnungen*, p. 45, and *MBA*, No. 105.

[2] Probably Antonio Giacomo Bridi (1721–1799). His nephew, Giuseppe Antonio Bridi, sang in the Vienna performance of *Idomeneo* in 1786 and published in 1827 a volume of *Brevi notizie intorno ad alcuni compositori di musica*, which mentions Mozart.

[3] Referring to a passage in his last letter, which for lack of space has been omitted.

send her brother an Italian congratulation; now I do remember. When you have several other things in your head, it is quite impossible to bear everything in mind.

Thank God, we are well. During the last few days Wolfgang has had an abscess in a tooth with a slight inflammation on one side of his face. The prima donna is infinitely pleased with her arias. The primo uomo is to arrive next week.

We have now weathered a second storm and, although a few more incidents will probably occur, I trust that with God's help all will go well. For that an opera should win general applause is a stroke of luck which in Italy is very rare, because there are so many factions and because an indifferent, indeed even a bad solo dancer has her supporters who combine to shout 'Bravo' and to make a great noise. However, we have overcome many difficulties and with God's help this undertaking too will meet with success.

You asked me lately whether we are living far from Herr Troger. It takes a quarter of an hour to Count Firmian's house and there is hardly a day that we do not walk out there after lunch for the sake of exercise, for unless it is absolutely necessary I do not want Wolfgang to compose after his midday meal. This evening we are going with Herr Troger into the country, about as far as Plain[1] is from Salzburg, and we are staying there till Monday. He has bought a vineyard and fields out there and next spring he is going to build a house on this property. Meanwhile he has rented one there. Now I have no more news for you. We kiss you both ten million times and I am your old   LEOP MOZART

(122) *Leopold Mozart to his Wife*

[*Extract*]   [*Autograph in the Mozarteum, Salzburg*]

MILAN, 24 *November* 1770

I have nothing to tell you, except that, thank God, we are both well. I am writing this letter in great haste at Count Firmian's house. Wolfgang has his hands full now, as the time is getting on and he has only composed one aria for the primo uomo,[2] because the latter has not yet arrived and because Wolfgang refuses to do the work twice over and prefers to wait for his arrival so as to fit the costume to his figure. I have this moment received your letter and I have read with great delight of your merry-makings.

Addio. We kiss you a hundred thousand times and I am your old

MZT.

[1] i.e. Maria-Plain.
[2] Pietro Benedetti, a male soprano, who sang the part of Sifare. He did not arrive in Milan until December 1st.

(123) *Leopold Mozart to his Wife*

[*Extract*]   [*Autograph in the Mozarteum, Salzburg*]

MILAN, 1 *December* 1770

I have received your letter of November 16th. I wrote on November 24th in a great hurry and so forgot to tell you that I received your letter of November 9th, filled with congratulations from you and Nannerl. When Wolfgang read it, he became rather sad and said: '*I am truly sorry for Mamma and Nannerl, because in his last letter Papa wrote such cutting remarks in jest*'. I told him that you would certainly realize that I would receive your letter very soon, which I did in fact, a few hours after mine had been handed to the post. So I send you my most solemn thanks. In the evening of November 24th, the day on which I sent you my last letter, Baron Riedheim and his tutor came to see us, and on Monday, the 26th, we met at the concert held in Count Firmian's house. He offered to take a letter for us, but, as I write every Saturday, I declined with thanks. I did intend to give him some trifles for you, which he could have easily taken, such as pieces of the Sacred Cross, some relics or a few snuff-boxes. But it has been raining so hard and the weather has been so abominable that I shall have to pay my return visit to Baron Riedheim in Salzburg. By the time you read this letter, you will have already spoken to him and heard from him that we are well. He will have told you also what a wretched orchestra performed at that concert. For these good people have all gone off to the country with their patrons and it will be eight or twelve days before
★ they return for the rehearsals of the opera. You think that the opera is already finished, but you are greatly mistaken. If it had depended on our son alone, two operas would have been ready by now. But in Italy everything is quite mad. You will hear all about this later on, for it would take too long to tell you everything. At the time I write, the primo uomo has not yet arrived, but he will certainly arrive today. Farewell. We kiss you both a hundred thousand million times and I am your old

MZT

(123a) *Mozart to his Sister*

[*Autograph in the Mozarteum, Salzburg*]

DEAREST SISTER,   [MILAN, 1 *December* 1770 [1]]

As I have not written for so long, I thought I might moderate your annoyance or disappointment with these few lines. Papa will have already informed you that we had the honour of making the acquaintance of

---

[1] A postscript to his father's letter.

Baron Riedheim. At present I have a lot of work and writing to do in connexion with my opera. I hope that with God's help all will go well. Addio. Farewell. I am, as always, your faithful brother

WOLFGANG MOZART

PS. Kiss Mamma's hands for me, my greetings to all good friends.

(123b) *Leopold Mozart to his Wife*

[*Autograph in the Mozarteum, Salzburg*]

[MILAN, 1 *December* 1770]

As we were leaving the house yesterday, we heard something which you will think incredible and which I never imagined that I should hear, *above all in Italy.* We listened to two beggars, a man and a woman, singing together in the street and they sang the whole song together in *fifths*, and without missing a note. I have never heard this in Germany. At a distance I thought that they were two persons, each of whom was singing a different song. But when we came up we found that they were singing together a beautiful duet in perfect fifths. I immediately thought of the late Herr Wenzel, and of how, if these two beggars were to sing on his grave, he would undoubtedly rise from the dead.

(124) *Leopold Mozart to his Wife*

[*Extract*]   [*Autograph in the Mozarteum, Salzburg*]

MILAN, 8 *December* 1770

The second rehearsal of the recitatives is taking place today after the Angelus. The first went so well that only once did I take up my pen to alter a single letter, and that was, *della* to *dalla.* This achievement does the copyist great credit and has provoked general surprise, seeing that, as everyone says, an amazing number of words and notes have usually to be altered all through the text. I hope that it will be the same with the instrumental rehearsals, which, by the time you receive this letter, will perhaps have already begun. As far as I can judge without a father's partiality I consider that Wolfgang has written the opera well and with great intelligence. As the singers are good, all will depend upon the

orchestra, and ultimately upon the caprice of the audience. Thus, as in a
★ lottery, there is a large element of luck. I write this in haste. We kiss you
ten million times and I am your old

★   MOZART

(125) Leopold Mozart to his Wife

[Extract]   [From Nissen, pp. 235-236]

MILAN, 15 December 1770

The first rehearsal with instruments took place on the 12th, but there
were only sixteen players, and this rehearsal was held in order to discover
whether the score had been copied correctly. On the 17th we shall have
the first rehearsal with the full orchestra, which will consist of fourteen
first and fourteen second violins, twenty-eight violins in all, two
claviers, six double basses, two violoncellos, two bassoons, six violas,
two oboes and two flutes (who, if there are no flutes, always play as four
oboes), four horns and two trumpets etc, sixty players in all.

Before the first rehearsal with the small orchestra took place, there were
plenty of people who cynically described the music beforehand as miserable immature stuff and thus prophesied its failure, because, as they maintained, it was impossible for such a young boy, and, what is more, a
German, to write an Italian opera or, great virtuoso though he might be,
to grasp and apply the *chiaro ed oscuro* which is necessary for the theatre.
But since the evening of the first short rehearsal all these people have been
silent and have not uttered a syllable. The copyist is absolutely delighted,
which is a good omen in Italy, where, if the music is a success, the copyist
by selling the arias sometimes makes more money than the Kapellmeister
does by his composition. The singers are quite satisfied and indeed altogether delighted, and especially the prima donna and the primo uomo,
who are simply enchanted with their duet. The primo uomo has actually
said that if this duet does not go down, he will let himself be *castrated*
again. Basta! Everything now depends on the fancy of the public. Apart
from the honour, which is a small vanity, the whole business does not
interest us very much. In this strange world we have already undertaken
many things and God has always assisted us. We now stand on the brink
of this enterprise and there are a few circumstances which do not make it
★ easy for us. Yet this time too God will be on our side.

On St. Stephen's day, a good hour after Ave Maria, picture to yourselves Maestro Don Amadeo seated at the clavier in the orchestra and
myself a spectator and a listener in a box up above; and do wish him a
★ successful performance and say a few paternosters for him.

(126) *Leopold Mozart to his Wife*

[*Extract*]　　　　　　　　　[*Autograph in the Library of Congress, Washington*]

MILAN, 22 *December* 1770

A Happy New Year!

The first rehearsal in the sala di ridotto was on the 17th and the first
rehearsal in the theatre was on the 19th. The latter, thank God, went off
very well. Yesterday evening we had a rehearsal of the recitatives, today
after Ave Maria there will be a second rehearsal in the theatre, and on
Monday the dress rehearsal will take place.

As for the 26th, the day of the performance, my one consolation is that
both the singers and the orchestra are evidently quite satisfied; and, thank
God, I too still have ears to hear. During the rehearsal I placed myself in
the main entrance right at the back in order to hear the music at a distance;
but possibly my ears were too partial! Meanwhile we hear that our good
friends are hopeful and delighted and indeed they congratulate my son
with genuine pleasure; on the other hand the malevolent are now silent.
The greatest and most distinguished Kapellmeisters of this town, Fioroni [1]
and Sammartini, are our true friends; and so are Lampugnani, Piazza,
Colombo and others. Thus the envy, or rather the distrust and the wicked
prejudices which some cherished in regard to our son's composition, will
not be able to injure him very much. I hope at least that Wolfgang will
not have the bad luck of Signor Jommelli, whose second opera at Naples [2]
has failed so miserably that people are even wanting to substitute another;
and Jommelli is a most celebrated master, of whom the Italians make a
terrible fuss. But it was really rather foolish of him to undertake to compose in one year two operas for the same theatre, the more so as he must
have realized that his first opera (which we saw) was not a great success.
You now know that from the 26th we shall be in the opera house every
evening from an hour after Ave Maria until eleven or twelve o'clock,
with the exception of Fridays. In about a fortnight I shall be able to inform
you of our departure for Turin, whence we shall proceed at break neck
speed in order to be able to spend the last days of spring in Venice.
Farewell. We kiss you several 100000 times and I am ever your old

MOZART

Picture to yourselves little Wolfgang in a scarlet suit, trimmed with
gold braid and lined with sky-blue satin. The tailor is starting to make it
today. Wolfgang will wear this suit during the first three days when he is

---

[1] Giovanni Andrea Fioroni (1704–1778) was maestro di cappella at Milan Cathedral from
1747 until his death. He was an important composer of church music.
[2] Jommelli's second opera at Naples, performed on 4 November 1770, was *Demofoonte*,
which had been produced at Stuttgart in 1759. His first opera at Naples was *Armida abbandonata*,
performed on 30 May 1770.

seated at the clavier. The one which was made for him in Salzburg is too
short by half a foot and in any case is too tight and too small.

(126a) *Mozart to his Sister*

[*Autograph in the Library of Congress, Washington*]

Sinfonia   [MILAN, 22 *December* 1770]

Find out whether they have this symphony of Mysliwecek's in Salzburg.
If not, we shall bring it back with us.

(127) *Leopold Mozart to his Wife*

[*Extract*]   [*Autograph in the Nationalbibliothek, Vienna*]

MILAN, 29 *December* 1770

God be praised, the first performance of the opera took place on the
26th and won general applause; and two things, which have never yet
happened in Milan, occurred on that evening. First of all, contrary to the
custom of a first night, an aria of the prima donna was repeated, though
usually at a first performance the audience never call out 'fuora'. Secondly,
after almost all the arias, with the exception of a few at the end, there was
extraordinary applause and cries of: 'Evviva il Maestro! Evviva il
Maestrino!'

On the 27th two arias of the prima donna were repeated. As it was
Thursday and there was Friday to follow, the management had to try to
cut down the encores; otherwise the duet would also have been repeated,
for the audience were so enthusiastic. But most of the listeners wanted to
have some supper at home, and it so happens that this opera with its three
ballets lasts six good hours. The ballets, however, are now going to be
shortened, for they last two hours at least. How we wished that you and
Nannerl could have had the pleasure of seeing the opera!

Within living memory there has never been such eagerness to see the
first opera as there has been this time. But there was a very great difference
of opinion beforehand and whenever two persons said that it would be a
fine one, ten persons at once said that they knew that it was ridiculous
stuff, others that it was a horrible mixture, and others again that the music
was German and barbarous. In Italy patronage does not in any way help
the good reception of an opera, for everyone who goes in wants to talk,

shout and criticise it as much as he likes, as he has paid for his seat. But this time protection did help us and was really necessary in order to ensure that the composition should not be rejected, or a spoke put in the wheel of our maestro while he was writing it or even during the rehearsals. Further, we had to see that he was not hindered and that no malevolent members of the orchestra or disagreeable singers should play him any tricks. I write this letter in haste, as the third performance is taking place today. You know that in Italy everyone is given a different name. For instance, Hasse is called Sassone, Galuppi [1] is called Buranello, and so forth. They have christened our son Il Signor Cavaliere Filarmonico.

We kiss you both a hundred thousand times and I am your old

MOZART

(128) *Leopold Mozart to Padre Martini, Bologna*

[Autograph in the Nationalbibliothek, Vienna]

MILAN, 2 January 1771 [2]

MOST REVEREND PADRE MAESTRO,
MOST ESTEEMED PADRE,

While wishing you a very happy New Year I must inform you that my son's opera has been received most favourably in spite of the great opposition of his enemies and detractors, who, before hearing a single note had spread the rumour that it was a barbarous German composition, without form and content, and impossible for the orchestra to perform, so that they led half the town of Milan to wonder whether it would be anything more than a patchwork. One person had the brilliant idea of bringing the prima donna all her arias, and the duet as well, all of which had been composed by Abbate Gasparini of Turin,[3] with a view to persuading her to insert those arias and not to accept anything composed by this boy, who would certainly never be capable of writing a single good one. But the prima donna said that she would like first of all to try my son's arias; and having tried them she declared that she was satisfied and more than satisfied. Nevertheless the caluminators kept on spreading most evil reports. But the first rehearsal with instruments so effectively stopped the mouths of those cruel and barbarous backbiters that not a word more was heard. All the leading players in the orchestra swore that the opera was clear and straightforward and easy to play; and all the singers declared that they were content. It is usually the misfortune of the first opera in

---

[1] Baldassare Galuppi (1706–1785) was born on the island of Burano, near Venice. He was a successful composer of opere buffe.

[2] This letter is in Italian.

[3] See p. 151, n. 1. Gasparini's opera *Mitridate* had been performed at Turin in 1767.

Milan either to fail completely or at least to draw very few spectators, as everybody is waiting for the second one. But during the six performances which have so far taken place, the theatre has always been full and every evening two arias have had to be repeated, while most of the others have been warmly applauded.

My very dear Signor Padre Maestro, we hope to have news of your good health and we still trust that we shall receive the promised Miserere, your most excellent composition, and your work for sixteen performers. Signor Giuseppe Brinsecchi will not fail to refund the expenses of having them copied. And as soon as I reach home, which will be about Eastertide, I shall not fail to send you everything which I think may please you. My son most humbly kisses your hands and, united with him in all reverence and esteem for you, I am, Reverend Father,

your most devoted and grateful servant

LEOPOLDO MOZART

(129) *Leopold Mozart to his Wife*

[Extract]   [*Copy in the Staatsbibliothek Preussischer Kulturbesitz, West Berlin*]

MILAN, 5 January
behind as before and double in the middle (1771)

I can hardly find time to write to you, for every day we go to the opera and this means going to bed at half past one or even two o'clock in the morning, as we must have something to eat after the performance. So we get up late, and the day, which is short enough as it is, becomes, in consequence, even shorter. We have so many visits to pay that we do not know how we shall ever work them off. We lunched on Thursday with Madame D'Aste, née Marianne Troger, who fed us most magnificently on liver dumplings and sauerkraut, which Wolfgang had asked for, and on other good things, which included a fine capon and a pheasant. Yesterday there was a small concert at Count Firmian's, where Dr. Bridi sang a cantata and then put before Wolfgang a new and difficult concerto, which was a very beautiful one. He delivered your greetings, told us all the news and praised Nannerl very highly. Today we are again lunching with His Excellency. On the 11th or 12th we are off to Turin, but we shall only stay there for about eight days, when we shall return to Milan, pack up everything and go on to Venice. Our second stay here will not exceed four days, but we shall see a performance of the second opera. Our son's opera is still running, is still winning general applause and is, as the Italians say, *alle stelle*! Since the third performance we two have been listeners and spectators, sometimes in the parterre and sometimes in the boxes or palchi, where everyone is eager to speak to the Signore Maestro and see him at close quarters. During the performance we walk about here and there, wherever we like. For the Maestro was obliged to conduct the opera from the orchestra only on the first three evenings, when Maestro Lampugnani accompanied at the second clavier.[1] But now, as Wolfgang is no longer conducting, Lampugnani plays the first clavier and Maestro Melchior Chiesa[2] the second one. If about fifteen or eighteen years ago, when Lampugnani had already composed so much in England and Melchior Chiesa in Italy, and I had heard their operas, arias and symphonies, someone had said to me that these masters would take part in the performance of my son's composition, and, when he left the clavier, would have to sit down and accompany his music, I should have told him that he was fit for a lunatic asylum. So we see what the Almighty Power of God can make of us human beings, if we do not bury the talents which he has most graciously bestowed upon us.   ★

I enclose the local newspapers which I have just received. You will find the opera mentioned right at the end.[3] My greetings to the whole of Salzburg. We kiss you a million times and I am your old

MOZART

Please send these newspapers to His Grace the Prince. You need only take them to His Excellency the Chief Steward.

(130) *Leopold Mozart to his Wife*

[Autograph in the Mozarteum, Salzburg]

MILAN, 12 *January* 1771

We are not leaving for Turin until next Monday. I must tell you that I received yesterday from Signor Pietro Lugiati the news that our son has been made a member of the Accademia Filarmonica of Verona and that the Cancelliere dell'Accademia is about to draft his diploma.[4] Thank God, the opera is drawing so well that every day the theatre is full. I remind you once more to buy some linen with which to make shirts, for I am having Wolfgang's sleeves lengthened, so that we may carry on with his little shirts until we get home. Herr Wider has written to me from Venice and I have already replied. Count Firmian has left for Parma and, as Herr Troger is with him and we are now off to Turin, we shall probably receive your letters after considerable delay. We kiss you both many million

[1] During the first three performances Mozart, as the custom was, conducted whilst playing the first clavier.

[2] Very little is known about Chiesa. Burney, *op. cit.* p. 113, remarks, 'Chiesa and Monza seem and are said to be the two best composers for the stage here at present'.

[3] For an article from a Milan paper of 2 January 1771 see Nissen, p. 240 f., and *MDB*, p. 130 f.

[4] For the text of the diploma see Nissen, p. 241 ff., and *MDB*, p. 131 f.

times. I have nothing to write about and I have a great deal to do, as I have to send off letters to half the world.

I am your old

MOZART

(130a) *Mozart to his Sister*

[*Autograph in the Mozarteum, Salzburg*]

DEAREST SISTER,   [MILAN, 12 *January* 1771 [1]]

I have not written for a long time, for I was busy with my opera, but as I now have time, I will be more attentive to my duty. The opera, God be praised, is a success, for every evening the theatre is full, much to the astonishment of everyone, for several people say that since they have been in Milan they have never seen such crowds at a first opera. Papa and I, thank God, are well, and I hope that at Easter I shall be able to tell you and Mamma everything with my own lips. Addio. I kiss Mamma's hand. A propos! Yesterday the copyist called on us and said that he had orders to transcribe my opera for the court at Lisbon. Meanwhile farewell, my dear Mademoiselle sister. I have the honour to be and to remain from now to all eternity

your faithful brother

(131) *Leopold Mozart to his Wife*

[*Extract*]   [*Autograph in the Mozarteum, Salzburg*]

MILAN, 2 *February* 1771

I have received four letters from you and you will have had nothing from me for two post-days. But you will have gathered that our journey to Turin prevented us from writing. From that very beautiful town, where we saw a magnificent opera,[2] we returned here on January 31st. You will hear everything in due course. Address your letters in future to Herr Wider in Venice. We lunched today with Count Firmian. I have hardly time to write, as I must pack.

Francesco di Majo, the Kapellmeister, has died at Naples [3] and Caratoli [4] has travelled from Pisa into the next world.

★ Dr. Bridi has not said a word about the two concertos. So there is no

---

[1] A postscript to his father's letter. The signature has been cut off the autograph.

[2] WSF, vol. i. p. 332, n. 1, suggest that this opera was either Platania's *Berenice* or Paisiello's *Annibale in Torino*, both of which were performed at Turin early in 1771. A third possibility is Pugnani's *Issea*, which was performed there in the same year.

[3] He died on 17 November 1770.

[4] Caratoli (1705–1772), a famous basso buffo in his day, was chosen for the part of Cassandro in Mozart's *La finta semplice*, which was to have been performed in Vienna in 1768. The report which Leopold Mozart mentions was false, as Caratoli died in Vienna in 1772.

hope of seeing anything of them until he returns in July from his travels for he has gone off with Count Wolkenstein to Naples or Rome.

We hope to arrive in Salzburg for the Feast of St. Joseph[1] or at latest in Passion Week. Our greetings to the whole town. We kiss you ten thousand times and I am your old

MZT.

(132) *Leopold Mozart to his Wife*

[*Extract*]   [*Autograph in the Mozarteum, Salzburg*]

VENICE, 13 *February* 1771

Owing to shocking weather and a violent gale we only reached Venice early on Carnival Monday.[2] In the afternoon we managed to find Herr Wider, who, with his wife, accompanied us to the opera. On Tuesday we lunched with him and went to the opera, which began at two and went on until seven. We dined with him afterwards and about eleven or twelve o'clock by German time we were on the Piazza San Marco on our way to the Ridotto. We said to one another that at that moment both of you would probably be with Herr Hagenauer and would be little thinking that we were talking about you on the Piazza San Marco. The weather was horribly wet, but today, Ash Wednesday, it is most beautiful. God be praised, we are well. Whom do you think we met in Brescia? We were on our way to the opera buffa and ran into Signora Angelica Maggiori, prima donna, who is married to a tenor, who was also singing. She was very much surprised to see us. Tell Spitzeder that if he wants to meet his former impresario Crosa, he can find him in Milan, where he goes about begging, miserably clad and with a long beard. Thus it is that God punishes deceivers! You will have heard of the deaths of Caratoli and Laschi.[3] I have received your letter with the note from Herr von Vogt. Farewell, I must hurry. We kiss you a hundred thousand times and I am your old

MOZART ★

(132a) *Mozart to his Sister*

[*Autograph in the Mozarteum, Salzburg*]

DEAREST SISTER,   [VENICE, 13 *February* 1771[4]]

Papa will have already told you that I am well. I have nothing to write except that I kiss Mamma's hand. Farewell.

[1] 19 March.
[2] 11 February. The Mozarts remained in Venice until 12 March.
[3] A famous basso buffo, for whom Mozart wrote the part of Fracasso in *La finta semplice*, 1768.
[4] This note and the following one are postscripts to his father's letter. The second note is in Italian.

(132b) *Mozart to Johann Nepomuk Hagenauer*[1]

[*Autograph in the Mozarteum, Salzburg*]

AL SIGNORE GIOVANNI.

[VENICE, 13 *February* 1771]

The particularly splendid pearl[2] and all the other pearls too admire you very greatly. I assure you that they are all in love with you and that they hope that like a Turk you will marry them all, and make the whole six of them happy. I am writing this in Herr Wider's house. He is a fine fellow, just as you told me in your letter. Yesterday we wound up the carnival at his house, dined with him and then danced and went with the pearls to the new Ridotto, which I liked immensely. When I am at Herr Wider's and look out of the window, I can see the house where you lived when you were in Venice. I have no news for you. I am charmed with Venice. My greetings to your father, mother, sisters, brothers and to all my friends. Addio.

13 February 1771   WOLFGANGO AMADEO MOZART

(133) *Leopold Mozart to his Wife*

[*Extract*]   [*Autograph in the Mozarteum, Salzburg*]

VENICE, 20 *February* 1770 [*recte* 1771]

Thank God, we are in good health. Since your letter of February 1st I have received nothing from you, so I do not know whether you have written or not. I am writing this letter again at Herr Wider's, where I wrote my first one, which you will have received. We have lunched with him four times already and his daughters are at the moment engaged in washing and mending my lace cuffs. The elder daughter has presented Wolfgang with a beautiful pair. It is impossible for me to say too much about the honesty of this family, all of whom send their greetings to you and especially to the whole Hagenauer household. If Johannes is always saying nice things about the Widers, I assure you that he can never say enough. I too have had some experience of people in this world, but I have met few, indeed very few, like them. For besides being willing, sincere, absolutely honest and full of human kindness, they are also courteous, they have excellent manners and are not at all puffed up by the kindnesses which they perform. We shall not get away from here before the beginning of next month. But I am still determined to be back in Salzburg if not at the Feast of St. Joseph, at any rate in Passion Week and,

---

[1] This postscript was previously thought to be to Johann Baptist Hagenauer. Johann Nepomuk Hagenauer, a son of Lorenz Hagenauer, had stayed with the Wider family in Venice, 1767–1768.

[2] One of Herr Wider's six daughters, perhaps Catarina.

with God's help, by Eastertide. Otherwise I have nothing more to write ★
to you about, except that we kiss you both ten million times and that I
live in hopes of seeing you soon and telling you by word of mouth that
I am your old

MOZART

We shall soon have had enough of gondolas. During the first days the
whole bed rocked in our sleep and the whole time I was thinking that I
was in one of them. We have lunched with the brother of Signor Lugiati.
Tomorrow we are lunching with Her Excellency Catarina Cornaro, on
Sunday with the Patriarch, on Monday with His Excellency Dolfino, and
so forth. Next week we shall be lunching for the most part with nobles.[1]

(133a) *Mozart to his Sister*

[*Autograph in the Mozarteum, Salzburg*]

[VENICE, 20 *February* 1771[2]]

God be praised, I too am still alive and well. De Amicis sang here at San
Benedetto. Tell Johannes that Wider's pearls, especially Mademoiselle
Catarina, are always talking about him, and that he must soon come back
to Venice and submit to the *attacco*, that is, have his bottom spanked when
he is lying on the ground, so that he may become a true Venetian. They
tried to do it to me—the seven women all together—and yet they could
not pull me down. Addio. I kiss Mamma's hand and we both send greetings to all our good friends. Farewell. Amen.

(134) *Leopold Mozart to his Wife*

[*Extract*]   [*Autograph in the Mozarteum, Salzburg*]

VENICE, 1 *March* 1771

Thank God, we are well, and we are always being invited out, now
here and now there. So the gondolas of our hosts are constantly in front
of our house and every day we ride on the Grande Canal. We shall leave
Venice eight days later than I had intended, and we shall have to spend
two or three days in Vicenza, for the Bishop, who belongs to the house of
Cornaro, will not let us pass through without lunching, or as he would
prefer, spending at least two days with him. Then we shall stay three days
in Verona, perhaps even four. Nevertheless, unless something untoward
should happen to us, which God forbid, we shall be in Salzburg before

---

[1] The last three sentences of this postscript follow 133a.
[2] A postscript to his father's letter.

Easter. I am sorry that during our journey we shall have dismal fast-days all the time. Perhaps we shall reach Reichenhall on Good Friday and hear the usual Passion Play. Later on I shall tell you in detail how I like the Arsenal, the churches, the ospedali[1] and other things, in fact Venice as a whole. Meanwhile I shall content myself with saying that beautiful and unusual things are to be seen here. My pen and ink will tell you that I am writing at the Wider's, where I have this moment received your letter with Adlgasser's enclosure. We send our greetings to him and to his wife. I shall do all he wants and answer his note by word of mouth. As for the opera, we shall not be able to bring it with us, for it is still in the hands of the copyist and he, like all opera copyists in Italy, will not let it out of his hands, as long as he can make his profit. When we left Milan, he had to make five complete copies, one for the Impresa,[2] two for Vienna, one for the Duchess of Parma and one for the Lisbon court, to say nothing of individual arias. And who knows whether the copyist has not received some more orders in the meantime. Even then he told me that I must not expect to see it before Easter, by which time I hope to be in Salzburg; but

★ it will be sent home from Milan. We are again lunching today with Wider who, when we are not invited elsewhere, always entertains us. He and his whole family send their greetings. Indeed I owe him many kindnesses. Next Tuesday we shall give a big concert and on the Sunday before we

★ shall be at the house of the Imperial Ambassador. Addio. Farewell to both. We kiss you many hundred thousand times. I am your old

MOZART

★

(135) *Leopold Mozart to his Wife*

[Extract]   [Autograph in the Mozarteum, Salzburg]

VENICE, 6 March 1771

You have to thank Wider for this letter, for he has made me write to you, as it is after lunch and I have nothing to do for a little; and besides today is post-day. Yesterday we gave a fine concert and during the last few days we have been so horribly pestered that I do not know who will win the race to secure us. So I cannot get away before Monday, the day I have now fixed for our departure. You must not think, however, that we shall not be in Salzburg by Easter. The extra days which I spend here I shall deduct from the time which I am to spend at other towns, where there will not be so much to detain us, indeed hardly anything. Thank God, we are well and are only sorry that we cannot remain here longer. It is indeed a pity, for we have got to know the whole nobility very well; and every-

---

[1] These were homes for orphans or illegitimate children, which were often great schools of music. Burney, *op. cit.* p. 145 ff., describes his visit to four famous ospedali in Venice.

[2] i.e. the management of the Ducal Theatre at Milan.

where, at parties, at table, and, in fact, on all occasions we are so overwhelmed with honours that our hosts not only send their secretaries to
fetch us and convey us home in their gondolas, but often the noble himself
accompanies us on our return; and this is true of the greatest of them, for
instance, the Cornaro, Grimani, Mocenigo, Dolfino, Valieri and so forth.
We have had some beautiful days; but today it is raining hard. I hope that ★
this will not continue, or we shall have a dreadful drive from Padua to
Vicenza. Basta! One must take things as they come; and these are matters
which never disturb my peaceful sleep, if only we are in good health.
After this letter you will hardly have time to send me another, unless perhaps you write to Innsbruck, where I shall call at the post.   ★
   Farewell. We kiss you ten thousand times and I am your old

                                                          MOZART ★

(136) *Leopold Mozart to his Wife*

[*Extract*]   [*Autograph in the Mozarteum, Salzburg*]

                                          VICENZA, 14 *March* 1771 [1]

On Monday the —— no, on Tuesday the 12th we left Venice, but we
let everybody think that we were off on Monday, in order to have one
day free in which to pack in peace. Nevertheless the truth leaked out and
we had to lunch with Her Excellency Catarina Cornaro, where we were
given as presents for our journey a beautiful snuff-box and two pairs of
precious lace cuffs. So we sailed away on the 12th. I took a barcello for
ourselves and Wider, his wife and his two daughters, Catarina and Rosa;
and the Abbate too came with us as far as Padua. They brought food and
drink and all other necessaries and we cooked and ate on board. We spent
the 13th in Padua and stayed in the Palazzo of the nobleman Pesaro. On
the 14th we came on to Vicenza, and they returned to Venice. We saw as
much of Padua as can be seen in a day, as there too we were not left in
peace and Wolfgang had to play at two houses. Moreover he has received
a commission to compose an oratorio for Padua, which he can do at his
leisure. [2] We called on Padre Maestro Vallotti [3] at the church of St.
Anthony and then on Ferrandini, [4] at whose house Wolfgang had to play.
Finally he performed on the excellent organ in the wonderful church of
San Giustino. We are spending tomorrow, the 15th, in Vicenza, and not
without good reason. On the 16th, God willing, we shall go on to Verona,

---

   [1] This letter, which is dated 14 March, was sent off from Verona on 18 March.
   [2] *La Betulia liberata*. The text was by Metastasio. During the spring of 1771 Florian Gassmann
composed an oratorio on the same text. In 1784 Mozart, hoping to have his oratorio performed
in Vienna, added two numbers to his original score. See p. 881.
   [3] Padre Francesco Antonio Vallotti (1697–1780), a Franciscan, was the greatest organist in
Italy of his day and was maestro di cappella in Padua from 1728 until his death.
   [4] Giovanni Ferrandini, a well-known composer and teacher, had just settled in Padua.

where we shall certainly remain for three days and therefore shall not get away before the 20th, when I intend to leave for Rovereto and make for home as quickly as possible. So on Good Friday we shall visit the sacred graves at Reichenhall and then hurry on to Mülln; and we shall certainly sing Alleluja with you on Easter Saturday. But if nothing occurs to hold us up on our journey, we may arrive on Thursday. Perhaps I shall be able to send you more definite news from some stage on our route. I have received your letter with the large seal. Before I saw it I heard that this letter was waiting for me and a thousand ideas occurred to me, for I suspected that it might be a communication from some important quarter.[1]

VERONA, 18 *March* 1771

We arrived here in the evening of the day before yesterday and we shall leave the day after tomorrow. Thus on account of one or two delays we shall not arrive until the afternoon or evening of Good Friday. Today I received from Venice, together with a letter from Wider, your letters with the enclosure from Schiedenhofen. We had a talk yesterday with young Kerschbaumer,[2] who sends greetings to his dear parents. He is well and happy. He came with us to Signor Lugiati's house where we are staying, saw the fine company which had assembled to hear Wolfgang perform and, being thus present, heard him play as well. He is going on to Venice and if I may advise Herr Kerschbaumer, to whom I send my greetings, he ought to entrust his son too to Johann Wider. This is the advice of an honest man. I know what is good and what is bad for young people, especially in Venice, the most dangerous place in all Italy. Yesterday I received a letter from Milan, alluding to one from Vienna, which I am to receive in Salzburg, and which will not only fill you with amazement but will bring our son imperishable honour.[3] The same letter contained another very pleasant piece of news. Farewell to all. We kiss you many hundred thousand times and I am ever your old

MZT

(137) *Leopold Mozart to his Wife*

[Extract]   [Copy in the Staatsbibliothek Preussischer Kulturbesitz, West Berlin]

INNSBRUCK, *Monday*,
25 *March* 1771

We arrived here this evening in a violent gale, in snow and horribly cold weather. God willing, we shall leave tomorrow. I hope to arrive in

---

[1] Leopold Mozart refers to the commission described below (n.3), or perhaps to the Archbishop of Salzburg.
[2] Son of a Salzburg merchant, who kept a shop in the Marktplatz.
[3] The Empress Maria Theresia had commissioned Mozart to compose a dramatic serenata to be performed at Milan in October 1771 on the occasion of the marriage of her son, the Archduke Ferdinand, to Princess Maria Beatrice Ricciarda of Modena.

Salzburg on Thursday afternoon. Addio. Farewell. I must hurry, for the post is leaving.

Your old

MZT ★

(137a) *Mozart to his Mother and Sister*

[*Copy in the Staatsbibliothek Preussischer Kulturbesitz, West Berlin*]

[INNSBRUCK, 25 *March* 1771[1]]

I kiss Mamma's hand and I kiss Nannerl thousands of times. Thank God, I am well and I hope to see and talk to you both very soon. My greetings to all my good friends.

WOLFGANG MOZART

[1] A postscript to his father's letter.

Mozart's sixth journey was to Milan, where he carried out a commission from the Empress Maria Theresia to compose a dramatic serenata, Ascanio in Alba, *for the marriage of her son, the Archduke Ferdinand, to Princess Maria Beatrice Ricciarda of Modena. He was accompanied by his father. This visit, the second Italian journey, which lasted from 13 August to 15 December 1771, is described in joint letters from father and son to Frau Mozart and Nannerl. Letters 138–158.*

LEOPOLD MOZART (*c*. 1765)
From a portrait by an unknown artist
(Mozart Museum, Salzburg)

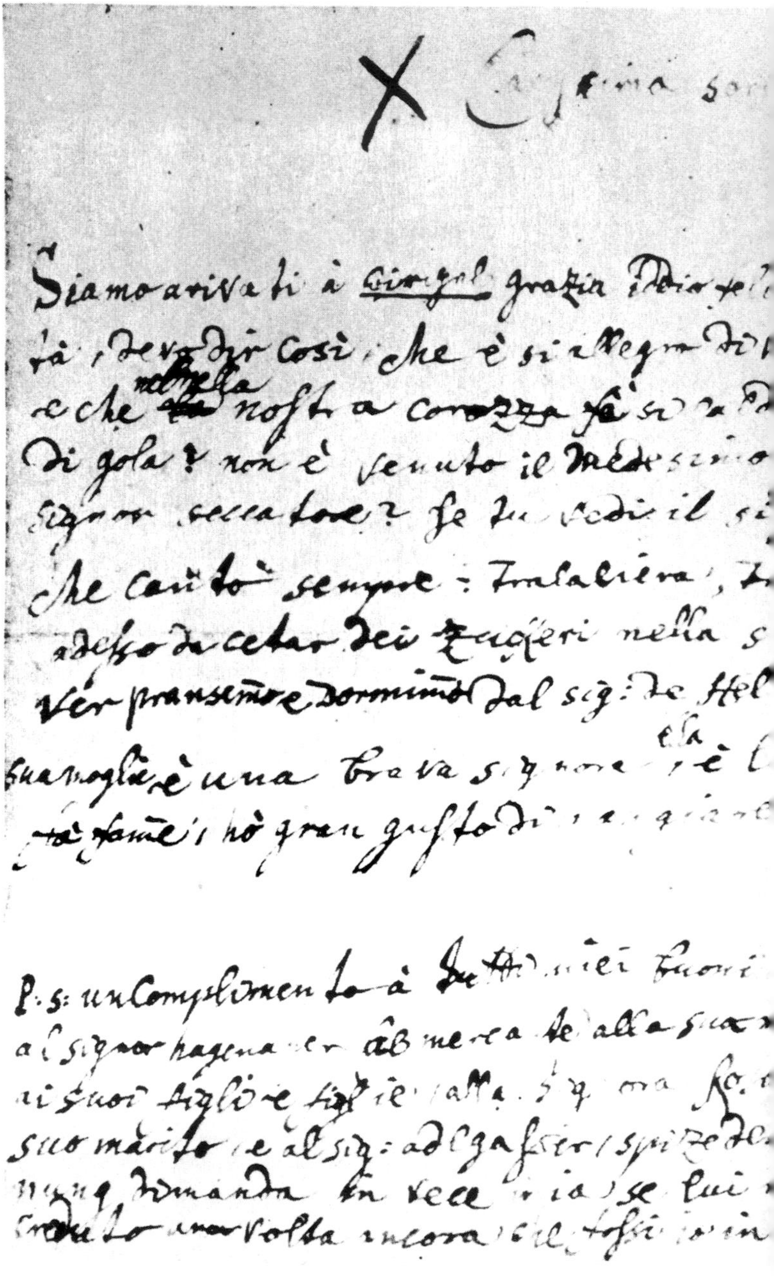

X Carissima sor

Siamo arivati à Wirgel grazia Idio fel
tà, devo dir così, che è si allegra di
e che nella nostra carozza fà si
di gola? non è venuto il medesimo
signor seccatore? se tu vedi il si
che cantò sempre: Tralaliera, t
adesso di cetar dei Zuccheri nella s
ver pransenore dormimo dal sig: de Hel
sua moglie è una brava signora, ella è l
tà fame, i hò gran gusto di

P.S: un complimento à tutti miei buoni
al signor hagenauer mercante alla sua
ai suoi figli e figlie, alla sig. ora
suo marito, e al sig: adlgasser, spitzede
domanda in vece se lui
creduto una volta ancora, che fossi io in

POSTSCRIPT FROM MOZART TO HIS SISTER (14 December 1769)

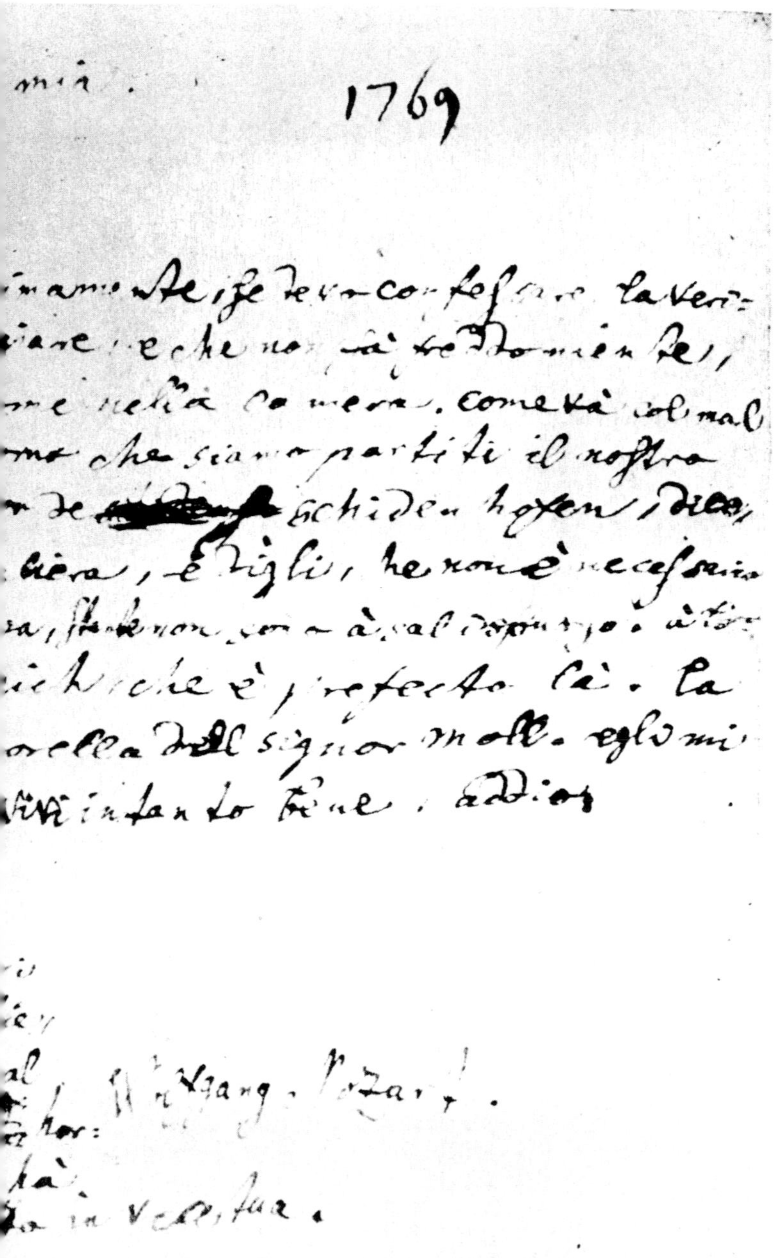

Autograph in the Pierpont Morgan Library, New York City

MOZART (1770)
From a portrait by Saverio dalla Rosa
(private collection)

PADRE MARTINI

From a portrait by an unknown artist (*c.* 1775)
Civico Museo Bibliografico Musicale, Bologna.

Bologna d 29 Febr: 1770.

LETTER FROM LEOPOLD MOZART TO HIS WIFE, WITH POSTSCRIPT FROM MOZART

(29 September 1770)

Autograph in the Koch Collection, Basel

MOZART, WEARING THE ORDER OF THE GOLDEN SPUR (1777)

From a portrait by an unknown artist
Civico Museo Bibliografico Musicale, Bologna.

(138) *Leopold Mozart to his Wife*

[*Autograph in the Mozarteum, Salzburg*]

BOZEN, 16 *August* 1771[1]

It is now striking twelve o'clock. We have had a light lunch and are about to start off in order to reach Trento this evening. Thank God, we are both like two deer, but, I should add, we are not in heat! Farewell to all. We kiss you ten thousand times.

MOZART

(138a) *Mozart to his Mother and Sister*

[*Autograph in the Mozarteum, Salzburg*]

[BOZEN, 16 *August* 1771[2]]

I haven't time to write much. We send our greetings to all our good friends. I kiss Mamma and Nannerl many ten thousand times. Addio.

WOLFGANG MOZART

(139) *Leopold Mozart to his Wife*

[*Extract*]   [*Autograph in the Mozarteum, Salzburg*]

VERONA, 18 *August* 1771

You will have received my short note from Bozen and now I am going to write to you more fully. The first day of our journey was a regular scramble. At Kaltern the postillion gave the horses some hay and while he was doing so, we ate without sitting down a few slices of boiled beef and with these we drank a measure of very good strong beer. When we reached Waidring we took some soup and some St. Johann's sherbet, which was not at all bad. We had supper at St. Johann and on the 14th we lunched at the post-station at Kundl and had supper at Innsbruck. On the 15th we lunched at Steinach and had supper at Brixen. On the 16th we lunched at Bozen and had supper at Trento. At nine o'clock in the morning of the 17th we arrived at Rovereto, intending to be in Verona that night and at noon on the following day to reach Ala, where we were to give the two Signori Piccinni a surprise. We should have done this if, firstly, we had not spent too much time with Baron Pizzini[3] in Rovereto (where Dr. Bridi also turned up immediately) and thus only left at eleven o'clock and, secondly, we had not met with so many hindrances on the way. For, first of all Lolli, the famous violinist,[4] came to see us; then the

---

[1] The Mozarts left Salzburg on 13 August.   [2] A postscript to his father's letter.
[3] Probably a relative of the Piccinni (Pizzini) family of Ala, mentioned above.
[4] Antonio Lolli. See p. 105, n. 3.

postillions had to change their horses; and the peasants' carts kept on holding us up in the narrow roads. So we did not reach the Piccinnis' house in Ala until one o'clock in the afternoon; and long before our arrival I had decided to spend the night there, as I did not dare to go on to Verona, where the gates are closed at Ave Maria. Moreover the heat was intense and we could go to church in our travelling clothes more easily in Ala than in Verona. There too we passed the time with music, or rather, we entertained our hosts and we did not leave until seven this morning for Verona, where we arrived at Signor Lugiati's house at half past twelve and lunched at one o'clock. After lunch everyone has gone off to sleep and I am making use of the time to scribble this letter with a miserable pen and in very hot weather. With some difficulty I persuaded Wolfgang to sleep too, but he only did so for half an hour. I must tell you that in my hurry I forgot to take with me some clavier sonatas and trios for a good friend in Milan, who has rendered us many services. When Troger goes to Salzburg, ask him to take them and in the meantime get them ready. Nannerl should pick out two trios, one by Joseph Haydn in F with violin and violoncello,[1] one in C by Wagenseil (with variations, please remember) and also Adlgasser's in G; also the little Cassation by Wolfgang in C[2] and some good sonatas by Rutini,[3] for instance, in Eb, in D and so on. If Nannerl wants to play them, she has other copies, for they are amongst the sonatas by Rutini which were engraved in Nuremberg. Give our greetings to Troger and ask him to introduce you to Count Firmian, to whom you should pay your respects, for we owe him a great deal. So do not forget to do this.

I shall write from Milan as soon as possible. Keep well. We kiss you a hundred thousand times and

I am your old

MZT

What beautiful handwriting mine is!

(139a) *Mozart to his Sister*

[*Autograph in the Mozarteum, Salzburg*]

DEAREST SISTER,   [VERONA, 18 *August* 1771[4]]
    I have only slept half an hour, for I do not care much about sleeping after a meal. You may trust, believe, opine, hold the opinion, cherish the

---

[1] Probably Op. IV, no. 1, composed in 1766.   [2] There is no trace of this composition.
    [3] Giovanni Marco Rutini (1723–1797), born in Florence, where after a prolonged residence in Germany and Austria he became maestro di cappella to the court. He wrote a number of operas, clavier sonatas and some church music. Seven collections of his clavier works had already been published. According to Einstein the sonatas mentioned by Leopold Mozart are Nos. 6 and 2 of Op. VI.   [4] A postscript to his father's letter.

constant hope, consider, imagine, think and be confident that we are well, but I can assure you of the fact. Well, I must hurry. Addio. My greetings to all our good friends. Wish Herr von Hefner[1] from me a prosperous journey and ask him if he has seen anything of Annamiedl? Addio. Keep well. I kiss Mamma's hand. What beautiful handwriting mine is!

WOLFGANG

(140) *Leopold Mozart to his Wife*

[Extract] [Autograph in the Mozarteum, Salzburg]

MILAN, 24 *August* 1771

We reached Milan safely on Wednesday, August 21st, after seven in the evening, having spent the whole of Monday with Signor Lugiati in Verona, whence I wrote to you. You will no doubt have received my letter. I ought to tell you that we have not yet received from Vienna the ★ text[2] which everyone is awaiting with great anxiety, for until it arrives the costumes cannot be made, the stage arranged nor other details settled. On October 15th the Archduke[3] will arrive in Milan, alight from his carriage at the Cathedral, enter it and get married. There will be kissing of hands and afterwards a grand supper and then good night! On the following day the celebrations will begin, which I shall describe later on. Meanwhile I have seen twenty thousand pounds of wax candles, waiting to illuminate the Cathedral, the Court and other places on October 15th. ★

Keep well, both of you. We kiss you many hundred millions of times and I am your old ★

MOZART

(140a) *Mozart to his Sister*

[Autograph in the Mozarteum, Salzburg]

DEAREST SISTER, [MILAN, 24 *August* 1771[4]]

We suffered greatly from the heat on our journey and the dust worried us most impertinently the whole time, so that we should certainly have been choked to death, if we had not been too clever for that. Here it has not rained for a whole month (or so the Milanese say). Today it began to drizzle a little, but now the sun is shining and it is very hot again. What you promised me (you know what, you dear one!) you will surely

---

[1] Heinrich Wilhelm von Hefner, a son of the town magistrate, Franz von Hefner. According to Hammerle, *op. cit.* p. 8, n., he must have been slightly older than Mozart.

[2] The text *Ascanio in Alba* was by Abbate Giuseppe Parini (1729–1799), a celebrated poet and satirist of the day, who held the chair of rhetoric at Milan University. The text had to be submitted to the Viennese court for its approval.

[3] Archduke Ferdinand (1754–1806), son of the Empress Maria Theresia.

[4] A postscript to his father's letter.

do and I shall certainly be most grateful to you. The Princess[1] had an attack of diarrhœa the other day. Apart from that I have no news. Do send me some. My greetings to all our good friends, and I kiss Mamma's hand. I am simply panting from the heat! So I am tearing open my waistcoat. Addio. Farewell.

WOLFGANG

Upstairs we have a violinist, downstairs another one, in the next room a singing-master who gives lessons, and in the other room opposite ours an oboist. That is good fun when you are composing! It gives you plenty of ideas.

(141) *Leopold Mozart to his Wife*

[*Extract*]   [*Autograph in the Mozarteum, Salzburg*]

MILAN, 31 August 1771

This is the fourth letter which you are receiving from me. I must now praise my sedia, which stood this journey very well. For although we rattled along the Venetian roads from Verona and even from Peri at a terrific pace and over the biggest stones, I did not feel the slightest dis-
★ comfort. Until we reached Bozen the weather was mild, but from Bozen to Innsbruck it was rather cold. The sun, which came out now and then, drew up in places mists, which collected and came down in rain, so that during our first night at St. Johann I took my flannel jerkin out of our night-bag and put it on, taking it off again at noon at our first stage outside Bozen, while the horses were being changed. Since then it has been warm. My only fear is that it may rain heavily during the marriage, and bad weather on the occasion of such festivities is certainly very inconvenient. The text has arrived at last, but so far Wolfgang has only written the overture, that is, a rather long Allegro, followed by an Andante, which has to be danced, but only by a few people. Instead of the last Allegro he has composed a kind of contredanse and chorus, to be sung and danced at the same time. He will have a good deal of work during the coming month. Hasse arrived yesterday and we are now going out to call on him.[2] We have paid our respects to Her Royal Highness the Princess, who was so gracious that she not only spoke to us for a long time and was most friendly, but, strange to say, rushed up when she saw us, took off her

---

[1] Princess Maria Beatrice Ricciarda of Modena, daughter of the hereditary Prince Ercole Rainaldo.
[2] Hasse had been commissioned to write the opera seria for this festive occasion. His *Ruggiero*, on a text by Metastasio, was performed on October 16th, the day after the Royal wedding.

glove, held out her hand and began to talk before we had time to address her.   ★

Farewell. We kiss you many million times and I am your old

MOZART

(141a) *Mozart to his Sister*

[*Autograph in the Mozarteum, Salzburg*]

DEAREST SISTER,   [MILAN, 31 *August* 1771 [1]]

Praise and thanks be to God, we are well. I have already eaten lots of good pears and peaches and melons for you. My only amusement is to talk the deaf and dumb language, and that I can do to perfection.[2] Hasse arrived yesterday and we are calling on him today. The libretto for the serenata only reached us last Thursday. There is little to write about. I beg you to remember the other matter, if there is nothing else to be done.[3] You know what I mean. Compliments from Herr Germani and especially from his wife who is longing to meet you, from Madame D'Aste and from her husband and from me too. My greetings to all our good friends. I kiss Mamma's hand. Addio.

WOLFGANG

(142) *Leopold Mozart to his Wife*

[*Extract*]   [*Autograph in the Mozarteum, Salzburg*]

MILAN, 7 *September* 1771

Heaven has refreshed us at last with a little rain which has fallen for a few days in succession. At the moment we are up to the eyes in work, for ★ the libretto arrived late and then remained until two days ago in the poet's hands, because this passage and that had to be altered. I hope it will be a success. Wolfgang is now very busy composing, as he has to write the ballet which links together the two acts or parts.[4]   ★

I hope you are both well. I trust that Nannerl is still taking her soup of herbs, now that she has discovered that it does her good. If Secretary Troger is still in Salzburg, give him a few boxes of Hansl Spielmann pills, which I really need, for I know that they do me good when owing to ★ constipation I get my old giddiness. Since I left Salzburg I have had it a

---

[1] A postscript to his father's letter.
[2] The Mozarts had evidently taken rooms in the same house where they stayed during their second visit to Milan. See p. 168.
[3] Nissen, p. 253, n., mentions the fact that 'a young lady, of whom Mozart was fond, was about to get married'.
[4] Abert, vol. i. p. 276, n. 1, points out that usually the entr'acte ballets were written by some other composer.

good deal, but not so violently as to have to vomit or to be obliged to go to bed. I have only been taking the pills for three days and I notice already that my head is much clearer. But unfortunately I have only eight of them left. We kiss you many million times and I am

your old

L. MOZART

★ As Nannerl has not written, neither is Wolfgang writing. Have you received my pay for the month of August?

(143) Leopold Mozart to his Wife

[From Nissen, pp. 254-255]

MILAN, 13 September 1771

In twelve days Wolfgang, with God's help, will have completely finished the serenata, which is really an *azione teatrale* in two parts. All the recitatives with and without instruments are ready and so are all the choruses, eight in number, of which five are danced as well as sung. Today we saw the rehearsal of the dances and we greatly admired the hard work of the ballet masters, Pick and Fabier. The first scene is Venus coming out of the clouds accompanied by genii and graces.

The Andante of the symphony is danced by eleven women, that is, eight genii and three graces, or eight graces and three goddesses. The last Allegro of the symphony, which has a chorus of thirty-two voices, eight sopranos, eight contraltos, eight tenors and eight basses, is danced by sixteen persons at the same time, eight men and eight women.

Another chorus is made up of shepherds and shepherdesses, sung by different performers. Further, there are choruses of shepherds alone, tenors and basses, and of shepherdesses alone, sopranos and contraltos. In the last scene all the singers and dancers appear, genii, graces, shepherds and shepherdesses, and they dance the last chorus together. This does not include the solo dancers, Mr. Pick, Madame Binetti, Mr. Fabier and Mlle Blache. The short solo dances, which take place during the choruses, sometimes for two sopranos, sometimes for alto and soprano and so forth, are interspersed with solos for male and female dancers.

The singers in the cantata are:

La Venere,	Signora Falchini, seconda donna
Ascanio,	Signor Manzuoli, primo uomo
Silvia,	Signora Girelli,[1] prima donna

---

[1] Maria Antonia Girelli-Aguilar had been singing in Gluck's operas.

Aceste, sacerdote,   Signor Tibaldi, tenore
Fauno, pastore,   Signor Solzi, secondo uomo.

I am already making arrangements about Venice 1773.[1]

(143a) *Mozart to his Sister*

[From Nissen, p. 256]

DEAREST SISTER,   [MILAN, 13 *September* 1771[2]]

I am only writing in order to—write. But writing is indeed most tiresome, because I have a very heavy cold and a bad cough. Tell Fräulein W. von Mölk[3] that I am indeed longing to be back in Salzburg if only in order to receive once more for the minuets such a present as I was given at her concert. She will know what I mean.

(144) *Leopold Mozart to his Wife*

[Extract]   *[Autograph in the Mozarteum, Salzburg]*

MILAN, 21 *September* 1771

After the Angelus today there will be the first instrumental rehearsal of the opera by Signor Hasse, who, thank God, is very well; and towards the end of next week the serenata will be rehearsed. The first rehearsal of the recitatives will take place on Monday and on the following days the choruses will be rehearsed. On Monday or Tuesday at the latest Wolfgang will have finished his work. Signor Manzuoli often comes to see us, but we have only been to see him once. Signor Tibaldi comes almost every day at about eleven o'clock and remains seated at the table till about one, while Wolfgang is composing. Everyone is extremely kind and has the greatest respect for Wolfgang. Indeed we have not experienced any unpleasantness whatsoever, for all these famous singers are most excellent and sensible people. The serenata is really a short opera; indeed, as far as the music is concerned, it is very short and is only lengthened by the two grand ballets which are performed after the first and second acts, each of which will last three quarters of an hour.

There is no room on this sheet to describe the elaborate preparations for

---

[1] Soon after his arrival at Milan Mozart was commissioned to compose the second opera of the 1773 carnival season for the Teatro San Benedetto in Venice. Probably owing to his previous contract with the Ducal Theatre in Milan to write an opera for the same season, this commission was not carried out. The contract for Venice, signed by the impresario Michele Dall' Agata, and dated 17 August 1771, is given in Nissen, pp. 255–256, and *MDB*, p. 135.   [2] A postscript to his father's letter.

[3] Anna Barbara (Waberl) von Mölk (1752–1823), daughter of Court Chancellor Felix von Mölk. Mozart was then in love with her.

these festivities. All Milan is astir, the more so as a great deal, in fact most of the work has been postponed to the last minute. Consequently everyone is now at work. Some are getting the theatre ready, as the whole building requires to be renovated and redecorated. Others are busy preparing for the reception of His Highness, engaging lodgings and rooms, illuminating and adorning the Cathedral, obtaining garments and liveries for the servants, and horses and carriages and so forth for the balls. There are, in fact, a hundred things to do and I cannot keep them all in my mind. So everyone is frightfully busy! A few days ago Miss Davies[1] arrived here and drove past our house in the mail coach. I recognized her and she saw us, for we happened to be standing on the balcony. A few hours later I went to call on her at the 'Three Kings', which is not very far off, as I guessed that she would be staying there, since it is the most respectable inn. She, her sister, her father and her mother could hardly express their joy. I told their servant where Herr Hasse was staying and very soon his daughter appeared, who also was beside herself with delight, for they have been most cordial friends since they met in Vienna. They all asked for you at once and they send you their greetings. You will surely remember Miss Davies with her armonica? Did you see the rope-dancers when they were in Salzburg? They are now on their way here and ought to arrive very soon. Great work is in progress, for an extraordinarily large hut is being erected for them. The Italian plays came to an end two days ago, for the theatre must now be kept free for rehearsals and the painters must not be prevented from working day and night. These Italian players were uncommonly good, especially in character-plays and tragedies.

Whoever now comes to Milan to attend these wedding festivities will certainly see some fine things. A carriage for four persons would not eat up much money, but the rooms would be a very heavy item. Of course I could take one room for both of us. In the circumstances we should have
★ to camp like soldiers for a short time and have our meals cooked at home.

I have received this very moment your letter of September 13th. In your previous letter you said that many persons have already gone crazy and now you tell me that many have died of dysentery. That is very unfortunate. For when people are attacked both in their heads and in their arses, their condition is indeed dangerous. I must have caught this disease in Salzburg, for I still have frequent attacks of giddiness. But this is not surprising, for evidently the air was already infected, and it is easy to catch

---

[1] Marianne Davies (1744–1792) first became proficient on the harpsichord and from 1762 onwards won a great reputation for her skill on the armonica or 'musical glasses', an instrument which had been much improved by Benjamin Franklin. In 1768 she and her sister Cecilia, an excellent singer, left England and settled for three years in Vienna, lodging in the same house as Hasse and instructing the daughters of the Empress Maria Theresia. From Vienna the sisters went to Milan, where Cecilia appeared in Hasse's opera *Ruggiero* in 1771. In 1773 they returned to London.

a complaint. That is why I wrote to you about the pills, for I want my arse to cure my head.

We kiss you both 10,000,000 times and I am your old

LP MOZART

(144a) *Mozart to his Sister*

[Autograph in the Mozarteum, Salzburg]

[MILAN, 21 September 1771 [1]]

Praise and thanks be to God, I am well. I cannot write much, firstly, because I have nothing to say, and secondly, because my fingers ache so from composing. Farewell. I kiss Mamma's hand. I often let off my whistle, but not a soul answers me. There are now only two arias of the serenata to compose and then I shall be finished. My greetings to all my good friends. I no longer want to go home to Salzburg, for I am afraid that I might go crazy too.[2]

WOLFGANG ★

(145) *Leopold Mozart to his Wife*

[*Extract*]   [*Autograph in the Mozarteum, Salzburg*]

MILAN, 28 September 1771

This month has simply flown by with amazing rapidity, as we had first of all to wait for the text, and when it arrived, there was always something to do. Our holidays and recreation have now begun, or rather they began last Tuesday, for Wolfgang had already finished everything by Monday,[3] and so on Tuesday we resumed our walks. The first rehearsal with the whole orchestra takes place today. The choruses were rehearsed yesterday, but without the instruments. Give our greetings to Herr Spitzeder and tell him that among our choral singers is a bass, Bianchi by name, whose wife is the leading soprano. This man has twice been to see us in order to press his claims, for he takes a bass part in the Cathedral choir and would very much like to join our Archbishop's Kapelle. But as far as I know, the vacancies for voices have already either been filled or bespoken. You will be pleased to hear that I have good hopes that Wolfgang's work will win great applause; firstly, because both Signor Manzuoli and all the other singers are not only immensely pleased with their arias, but are looking forward even more than we are to hearing the serenata performed this evening with all the instruments; and secondly, because I know how good Wolfgang's work is and what an impression it will make, for it is

---

[1] A postscript to his father's letter.
[2] Mozart is alluding to the last paragraph of his father's letter. [3] September 23rd.

more than certain that his composition is excellently adapted both to the
★ singers and to the orchestra.

Thank God, we are well. The weather is still lovely and a few very
violent storms have satisfied our longing for rain. Everyone is now happy,
but we are all wishing that it may keep fine during the wedding. Please
tell me in all your letters what sort of weather you are having.[1] Farewell.
We kiss you both ten thousand million times and I am your old

MOZART

Our greetings to the whole of Salzburg.

(146) *Leopold Mozart to his Wife*

[Extract]   [Autograph in the Mozarteum, Salzburg]

MILAN, 5 *October* 1771

Count Firmian arrived last Tuesday about eight o'clock in the evening
and will leave tomorrow for Mantua to meet His Highness the Prince and
★ accompany him to Milan. I hear too that Count Sauerau is to arrive here
shortly and also the Duke of York, who was Duke of Gloucester when
we were in England and on his brother's death succeeded to his present
title. He is now either in Genoa or in Turin. Yesterday we had a second
rehearsal of Wolfgang's cantata, and today the opera is being rehearsed.
Then we shall have two days' rest and on Tuesday the cantata will be
rehearsed again. The theatre is full from eight o'clock in the morning to
eleven o'clock at night, for the dancers are always there. Chaplain Troger,
when handing me the pills, told me that you and Nannerl would have
liked to come with us. If this was your real feeling, it was very wrong of
you not to tell me so quite frankly, though the expense of the outward and
return journeys alone would have meant a difference to me of at least
sixty ducats. But really you need not feel any regrets, for you would have
had to put up with a heat which is incredibly trying. It is true that arrangements are being made for some remarkable entertainments, but they are
all shows which you have already seen better performed elsewhere and,
on account of the crowd, you would only see them here at great inconvenience and, if you insisted on seeing every bit of the trash, at the risk of
your life.

Perhaps some day you will have an opportunity of hearing operas in
Italy; and indeed any carnival opera in Milan would be more spectacular
than this one is going to be, for apart from the dances Wolfgang's has no
embellishment whatsoever. I hope that I shall not need the pills. Thank
God, my head is better. The trouble was simply a dreadful stuffiness which

[1] Nissen, p. 259, adds the remark: 'He himself always wrote about the weather at great
length'.

started in my head while I was on the journey and which was brought on by the great heat. The result was that in six weeks I scarcely used three handkerchiefs, because all the moisture in my brain dried up and stuck fast, thus causing a perpetual giddiness. Foot-baths, inhaling the steam from boiling tea, and finally the change in the weather and the cool damp air have cured me. We have sunshine again and we hope that there will be no rain during the festivities. Farewell. We kiss you many hundred thousand times and I am your old

MOZART ★

(146a) *Mozart to his Sister*

[*Autograph in the Mozarteum, Salzburg*]

[MILAN, 5 October 1771[1]]

Praise and thanks be to God, I too am quite well, but always sleepy. We have been twice to see Count Castelbarco and he was present at my first rehearsal in the theatre. I have no news except that next Tuesday we shall have another rehearsal. What I was going to tell you Papa has snatched from my pen, I mean, he has already written to you. Signora Gabrielli is here and we shall very soon call on her, so that we may get to know all the leading women singers. Addio. Farewell. My greetings to all our good friends.

WOLFGANG

(147) *Leopold Mozart to his Wife*

[*Extract*]   [*Autograph in the Mozarteum, Salzburg*]

MILAN, 12 October 1771

Chaplain Troger has made your mouth water for Italy far too much and I agree that for people who have not seen as much of the world as you have, there are many strange things to be seen here. But for you they would not be very wonderful, and Italy can always be visited.   ★

Yesterday the fourth rehearsal of the serenata took place; tomorrow there will be the seventh rehearsal of Signor Sassone's[2] opera and on Monday the last rehearsal of Wolfgang's.

Baron Dupin tells us that he accompanied Nannerl on the violin. The Duke of York has already arrived and also a prince of Saxe-Gotha. The Hereditary Princes, that is, the father and the mother of the Princess bride, have also arrived. Count Sauerau too is here. The crowds are enormous and people will have to see everything in the greatest discomfort. Admirable regulations have been issued, as, for instance, that commoners may

---

[1] A postscript to his father's letter.   [2] i.e. Hasse.

not bear swords or any other arms, that everyone must be identified at the gates and that all householders must hand in to a specially appointed committee a description of their tenants. No one may go about the streets at night without a light. Soldiers and sbirri patrol the town and hussars its outskirts. Everyone must have tickets for the opera, the serenata, the ball, the court banquet and all other festivities and so on.

I must close, for we have to check the two copies of the serenata, which were made in a hurry for His Majesty the Emperor and for the Archduke, and which must now be bound; and there is a great deal to correct, for Italian copyists make shocking mistakes. We kiss you both many hundred thousand times and I am your old

MOZART

Our greetings to all.

The Archduke will arrive in the evening of the 15th and the wedding will then take place. After it is over, there will be the kissing of hands at court, followed by two hours of music and a banquet. On the 16th there will be the opera, the 17th the serenata, on the 18th, 19th and 20th nothing on account of the anniversary of the death of His Majesty the Emperor.[1] On Monday the serenata will be repeated and so forth.

(148) *Leopold Mozart to his Wife*

[*Extract*]　　　　　　　　　　　　　　　[*Autograph in the Mozarteum, Salzburg*]

MILAN, 19 *October* 1771

Marcobruni sends greetings to you. He is with me and we are just off to the theatre. For on the 16th the opera was performed and on the 17th Wolfgang's serenata, which was such an extraordinary success that it has to be repeated today. The Archduke recently ordered two copies. We are constantly addressed in the street by courtiers and other persons who wish to congratulate the young composer. It really distresses me very greatly, but Wolfgang's serenata has killed Hasse's opera more than I can say in detail. In my next letter I shall reply to your last one and to Nannerl's postscript. You will both see Italy more pleasantly later on than you would now during this horrible rush. Addio. We kiss you both many ten thousand times. I am

your old

MZT

★　Pray to God and thank Him!

Troger sends his greetings, especially to you and to Nannerl who is sighing so deeply for Milan.

---

[1] The Emperor Charles VI, who died on 20 October 1740.

(149) *Leopold Mozart to his Wife*

[*Extract*]   [*Autograph in the Mozarteum, Salzburg*]

MILAN, 26 *October* 1771

I have received your letter from Triebenbach and I am delighted that you both had a good time. Perhaps some report will have reached Salzburg ★ of the tremendous applause which Wolfgang's serenata has won; for young Kerschbaumer, who is here for a few days, both saw and heard in the theatre how on October 24th, the day before yesterday, Their Royal Highnesses the Archduke and Archduchess not only caused two arias to be repeated by applauding them, but both during the serenata and afterwards leaned over from their box towards Wolfgang and showed their gracious approval by calling out '*Bravissimo, maestro*' and clapping their hands. Their applause was taken up each time by the courtiers and the whole audience.

Today there is the opera, but yesterday, being Friday, there was no performance. Tomorrow and the day after we shall have the serenata again. The Archduke and his wife are well and very happy. This will give ★ great pleasure to Her Majesty the Empress, for some anxiety was felt lest he should not have been pleased with his bride, because she is not beautiful. On the other hand she is unusually friendly, agreeable and virtuous, and greatly beloved by everyone; and she has completely won over the Archduke, for she has the best heart and the most pleasant manners in the world. Take care of yourselves. We kiss you a hundred million times and I am ever your faithful

MZT
★

If you need some clothes, get what is necessary made for you, for neither you nor Nannerl must do without necessities. What must be, must be. And do not buy inferior materials, since to buy shoddy stuff is no economy. Have a handsome dress made for festivals and put on every day the clothes which were made for you in Vienna. But do not buy woollen material, which is not worth a fig.

(149a) *Mozart to his Sister*

[*Autograph in the Mozarteum, Salzburg*]

DEAREST SISTER,   [MILAN, 26 *October* 1771[1]]

Praise and thanks be to God, I too am well. As my work is now finished, I have more time to write letters. But I have nothing to say, for Papa has told you everything already. I have no news except that numbers 35, 59,

---

[1] A postscript to his father's letter.

60, 61, 62 were drawn in the lottery; and so, if we had taken these numbers, we should have won. But as we did not take any tickets, we have neither won nor lost, but we have had our laugh at other people who did. The two arias which were encored in the serenata were sung by Manzuoli and by the prima donna, Girelli, respectively. I hope you will have a good time at Triebenbach and get some shooting and walking too, if the weather permits. We are now off to the opera. My compliments to all our good friends. Baron Dupin is a frequent visitor at the house of the Mademoiselle who plays the clavier,[1] and so we often meet him. I kiss Mamma's hand. Farewell. I am, as always, your faithful brother

WOLFGANG

PS. Excuse this shocking writing, but I am in a hurry.

(150) *Leopold Mozart to his Wife*

[Autograph in the Mozarteum, Salzburg]

MILAN, 2 *November* 1771

We are delighted that you had a good time at Triebenbach and that you reached home again safe and well. I am staying indoors for a few days, because I have had very bad rheumatism all over me, which I have almost altogether steamed away simply by drinking elderberry tea. Among our medicines we had only one single black powder. Fortunately Signora d'Aste has quantities of them. As we had only one digestive powder left, she sent off the prescription, which luckily she happened to have, to the chemist and procured some more for me. This is a silly story, I admit, for when you read it, I hope that I shall not only be perfectly well, but soon quite ready to leave. So when you receive this letter, you may write to Verona, al Signor Lugiati. I have already told you that the serenata has won the day. Farewell. We kiss you both many hundred million times and I am your old

MOZART

I still have to write an answer to His Excellency Count Pallavicini, who has sent me an extremely courteous letter.

(150a) *Mozart to his Mother and Sister*

[From Nissen, pp. 261-262]

[MILAN, 2 *November* 1771[2]]

Papa says that Herr Kerschbaumer has undoubtedly made good use of his travels and kept his eyes open, and we can assure you that he has be-

---

[1] Possibly Marianne Davies. See p. 198, n. 1..

[2] A postscript to his father's letter. Nissen, p. 261, adds that the first portion of this postscript, which he omits, is a description of all the festivities which have taken place.

haved very sensibly. He will certainly be able to tell you more about his tour than some of his friends, one of whom could not see Paris properly, because the houses there are too high. There is a performance of Hasse's opera today, but as Papa is not going out, I cannot be there. Fortunately I know nearly all the arias by heart and so I can see and hear it at home in my head.

(151) *Leopold Mozart to his Wife*

[Autograph in the Mozarteum, Salzburg]

MILAN, 9 *November* 1771

I write in great haste to say that I have received your congratulations and the whole parcel of letters. Wolfgang will express his own thanks, God willing, at the end of this month or during the first days of December. Thank God, I am quite well again. We lunched yesterday with Count Firmian in the company of Hasse. Both he and Wolfgang have received beautiful presents for their compositions. Apart from the money they have got, Hasse has been given a snuff-box and Wolfgang a watch set in diamonds. I have already told you in my last letter not to send any more letters to Milan, but to write to Verona, whence you will shortly receive letters from me, telling you whether we shall go for a few days to Padua or travel straight home. Should a post-day pass without a letter from me, then you will know that I am en route and can no longer write. Addio. We kiss you many ten million times and I am ever your old

MOZART

(151a) *Mozart to his Sister*

[Autograph in the Mozarteum, Salzburg]

DEAREST SISTER,   MILAN, 9 *November* 1771 [1]

I kiss Mamma's hand and send greetings to all our friends. Meanwhile I send my thanks in great haste to all who have congratulated me.[2] I shall thank them better when I see them. Farewell.

WOLFGANG

(152) *Leopold Mozart to his Wife*

[Extract]   *[Autograph in the Mozarteum, Salzburg]*

MILAN, 16 *November* 1771

I have received your letter of November 8th. I hoped to leave for certain on the 18th, but His Royal Highness the Archduke now wishes to

---

[1] A postscript to his father's letter.
[2] Probably on his name-day, October 31st, as well as on the success of *Ascanio in Alba*.

205

speak to us when he returns from Varese in a week's time. So our stay here will have to be prolonged for more than ten days. Patience! God willing, we shall soon meet again.

★   Thank all our good friends for their cordial congratulations. I owe Herr von Hefner an answer; but in the meantime give him my sincere thanks and greetings. My head is full and I have more things to think of than you can guess. That the serenata was extremely successful is quite true, but I very much doubt whether, if a paid appointment is vacant, His Grace will remember Wolfgang.[1] Now I must close, for I still have to write a letter to Verona. Send your letters there, addressed to Signor Pietro Lugiati, who will give them to me. Farewell. We kiss you both ten thousand million times and I am your old

MOZART.

(153) *Leopold Mozart to his Wife*

[*Autograph in a private collection, Switzerland*]

MILAN, 24 or 23 *November* 1771

We are still here and we shall probably stay on for another week, for the Archduke is not returning from Varese until Tuesday, when he will receive us. Yet, God willing, we shall reach home during the first fortnight of December, for, even if we break our journey on the way, we shall cover the ground from here to Salzburg in a week. Thank God, we are well. Address your next letter to Verona and I think it ought to be your last, if in the meantime you do not receive another one from me. The weather here is still cold, but very fine and it has not rained for a long time. Marcobruni, in whose room I am writing, sends his greetings to you both, and so do the Trogers and Signor and Signora d'Aste. Mysliwecek, who arrived yesterday and is writing the first opera,[2] was with us today. Herr von Mayr and Herr Chiusole also send their greetings. We often meet them, and we had music for several hours yesterday in Mayr's rooms. We kiss you a hundred thousand times and I am your old

MOZART

[1] Mozart had been appointed Konzertmeister to Archbishop Sigismund on 27 November 1769, but, possibly owing to the former's frequent absences from Salzburg, the appointment, to which an annual salary of 150 gulden was attached, did not take effect until April 1772, after the installation of the new Archbishop, Hieronymus Colloredo.

[2] Mysliwecek's opera *Il gran Tamerlano*, on a text by Agostino Piovene, was performed on 26 December 1771.

(153a) *Mozart to his Sister*

[*Autograph in a private collection, Switzerland*]

MILAN, 24 *November* 1771 [1]

Herr von Alphen [2] is here and is just the same as he was at Vienna and Paris. I have some more news too. Manzuoli, who up to the present has been generally looked upon as the most sensible of the castrati, has in his old age [3] given the world a sample of his stupidity and conceit. He was engaged for the opera at a salary of five hundred cigliati, but, as the contract did not mention the serenata, he demanded another five hundred for that, that is, one thousand cigliati in all. The court only gave him seven hundred and a fine gold snuff-box (quite enough, I think). But he like a true castrato returned both the seven hundred cigliati and the snuff-box and went off without anything. I do not know how it will all end—badly, I expect. I have no other news. I kiss Mamma's hand. I send greetings to all my good friends. Addio. Farewell. I am your true and faithful brother

WOLFGANG

(154) *Leopold Mozart to his Wife*

[*Extract*]   [*Autograph in the Mozarteum, Salzburg*]

MILAN, 30 *November* [1771]

I never thought that at the end of November I should still be in Milan, but circumstances have detained me. Moreover, it is Advent and in Salzburg no concerts are held at court. So the arrangement still stands that I shall arrive home during the first fortnight of December. Yes, even if I leave here on December 2nd or 3rd, I can easily reach Salzburg on the 9th or 10th. Thank God, we are well, and that is the best news I can send you. The weather here is extraordinarily cold, but very fine. I shall find your letters in Verona, if you have written; for now you may certainly go on doing so. Hoping to see you soon, we kiss you many ten million times and I am your old

MOZART

(154a) *Mozart to his Mother and Sister*

[*Autograph in the Mozarteum, Salzburg*]

[MILAN, 30 *November* 1771 [4]]

Lest you should think that I am unwell I am sending you these few lines. I kiss Mamma's hand. My greetings to all our good friends. I have

[1] A postscript to his father's letter.
[2] Eusebius Johann Alphen (1741–1772), born in Vienna, made his mark as a miniature-painter. Abert, vol. ii. p. 1037, n. 3, suggests that during the Mozart's second visit to Paris in 1766, Alphen may have done the small ivory miniature of Wolfgang and Nannerl which is now in the Mozart Museum, Salzburg.
[3] He was about forty-six.   [4] A postscript to his father's letter.

seen four rascals hanged here in the Piazza del Duomo. They hang them just as they do in Lyons.

WOLFGANG

(155) *Leopold Mozart to his Wife*

[*Autograph in the Mozarteum, Salzburg*]

ALA, 8 *December* 1771

At four o'clock in the afternoon of today we arrived here and we shall spend the night with the Piccinnis and then go on tomorrow to Trento. There we shall spend the day, for I have to carry out some commissions from Milan. I think that when you read this letter we shall be driving towards Salzburg, where we shall arrive in the evening, if not earlier. As soon as you receive it, open the small room, so that on our arrival it may not be quite cold. For as Wolfgang will sleep there and not in the back room, you should leave the door open so that the air may be warmed up. The question which you asked me in one of your four letters which I found in Verona, I shall answer when we meet. All that I can now say is that the affair is not quite hopeless. Farewell. We kiss you many million times and I am your old

MZT.

(156) *Leopold Mozart to his Wife*

[*Autograph in the Mozarteum, Salzburg*]

BRIXEN, 11 *December* 1771

We shall not arrive until Monday, as Count Spaur, who is keeping us here and sends you a thousand greetings, refuses to let us go. Moreover the days are short and the roads are bad, so that we really cannot leave.[1] We kiss you many hundred thousand times and I am your old

MZT.

(157) *Leopold Mozart to the Cathedral Chapter of the Archbishopric of Salzburg*

[*Autograph in the Landesarchiv, Salzburg*]

[SALZBURG, 16 *December* 1771]

MY LORDS PROVOST, DEAN, SENIOR AND
    THE WHOLE CATHEDRAL CHAPTER OF THE
        ARCHBISHOPRIC OF SALZBURG,
Your Excellencies will be aware that Her Imperial Majesty was

---

1 The Mozarts reached Salzburg on December 15th.

graciously pleased to summon my son to Milan to compose a dramatic serenata for performance on the occasion of the wedding festivities there, and that His Excellency Count Firmian in a letter to his brother the Chief Steward endeavoured to obtain from the late Archbishop[1] permission for me to accompany my son to Italy. His Grace gave us leave to travel but at the same time suspended my salary which, as it is, amounts only to 28 gulden, 30 kreuzer a month, and which, through an oversight, I was permitted to draw for a further month and a half.

His Excellency the Count von Sauerau wrote, however, to the Court Chancellor and sent him the pleasant news of the unanimous applause and the honour which my son had won for himself. Whereupon His Grace immediately gave me leave to retain the sum already paid.

I am submitting, therefore, to Your Excellencies and most gracious Lords my most humble request that the small amount deducted, that is, 59 gulden for the months of October and November, be paid to me in full.

I remain

Your Excellencies' most
obedient servant

LEOPOLD MOZART
Deputy-Kapellmeister

(158) *Leopold Mozart to J. G. I. Breitkopf, Leipzig*

[*Extract*]   [*Copy in the Staatsbibliothek Preussischer Kulturbesitz, West Berlin*]

[SALZBURG, 7 *February* 1772]

We arrived back from Milan on December 15th. As my son has again won great honour by his composition of the dramatic serenata, he has been asked to write the first opera for the coming carnival in Milan[2] and immediately afterwards the second opera for the Teatro San Benedetto in Venice.[3] We shall therefore remain in Salzburg until the end of September and then travel to Italy for the third time.

Should you wish to print any of my son's compositions, this intervening period would be the best time to order them. You have only to state what you consider most suitable. He can let you have clavier compositions or trios for two violins and violoncello, or quartets for two violins, viola and violoncello, or symphonies for two violins, viola, two horns, two oboes or transverse flutes, and double bass. In short, my son will write whatever

---

[1] Count Sigismund von Schrattenbach, who had been Archbishop of Salzburg since 1753, had died that day. He was succeeded on 14 March 1772, by Hieronymus Joseph Franz von Paula, Count Colloredo, who had been Bishop of Gurk. Mozart was commissioned to write the festival opera *Il sogno di Scipione* to celebrate his formal installation on 29 April 1772.

[2] Nissen, pp. 264–265, quotes this contract, dated 4 March 1771, and signed by Federico Castiglione, manager of the Ducal Theatre. See also *MDB*, p. 133.

[3] See p. 197, n. 1.

kind of composition you may consider most profitable to yourself, provided you let us know in good time.

Your obedient servant

LEOPOLD MOZART

Salzburg, 7 February 1772

Have you had any news from our friend M. Grimm? Have you sold any copies of the portraits and the sonatas?

Mozart's seventh journey was again to Milan, where he carried out a commission to write the first opera Lucio Silla for the 1772–1773 carnival season. During his short stay in Italy Mozart composed six string quartets. This visit, the third Italian journey, which lasted from 24 October 1772 to 13 March 1773, is described in joint letters from father and son to Frau Mozart and Nannerl. Letters 159–176.

(159) *Leopold Mozart to his Wife*

[*Extract*]   [*Autograph in the Mozarteum, Salzburg*]

BOZEN, 28 *October* 1772

Have we not travelled a great distance, seeing that we are now in Bozen? We reached St. Johann on the first day before eight o'clock in the evening,[1] but as on the following day, which was Sunday, there was no Mass earlier than six o'clock matins, we only got away at seven o'clock, and did not reach Innsbruck until about ten o'clock. We spent Monday there and in the afternoon drove to Hall to visit the Royal Convent, where Countess Lodron, the sister of the wife of our Chief Steward,[2] showed us everything and Wolfgang played on the organ in the church. We got as far as Brixen yesterday and arrived in Bozen today at noon; and here we are staying, as otherwise we should have to drive to Trento very late at night and in the most drenching rain which began this after-noon. Nor is there on the road any convenient lodging for the night. So with God's help we shall move on there tomorrow morning at five o'clock. We called on Frater Vincenz Ranftl in the Dominican monastery of this gloomy town. He is very well and sends his greetings to the whole of Salzburg.

Thank God, my health is now more or less restored, in spite of our   ★
irregular way of living. If travelling is necessary for it, I shall try to obtain a post as courier or perhaps become a mail coach conductor. Wolfgang is well too and at the moment is writing a quartet[3] to while away the time. He sends greetings to everyone.

Farewell. We kiss you many thousand times and I am your old   ★

MZT.

(159a) *Mozart to his Sister*

[*Autograph in the Mozarteum, Salzburg*]

[BOZEN, 28 *October* 1772[4]]

We have already reached Bozen. Already? I mean, at last. I am hungry, thirsty, sleepy and lazy, but I feel well. In Hall we visited the Convent and I played on the organ. If you see Nannerl Nader, tell her I have spoken to Herr Brindl, her beloved, who sends greetings to her. I hope that you have kept your word and that ⟨last Sunday you went to see D.N.⟩ Farewell. Let me have some news. Bozen—this pigsty.

---

[1] The Mozarts left Salzburg on Saturday, October 24th.   [2] Count Firmian.
[3] Probably K. 155 [134a].   [4] A postscript to his father's letter.

Here is a poem about someone who became wild and enraged with Bozen.

> If to Bozen I must come,
> Faith, I'd rather cut my thumb.

(160) *Mozart to his Mother*

[Autograph in the Bibliothèque Municipale, Lille]

MILAN, 7 *November* 1772

Do not be alarmed at seeing my handwriting instead of Papa's. The reasons are as follows: (1) We are at Signor d'Aste's [1] and Baron Cristani is here and they all have so much to talk about that Papa simply cannot get time to write; and (2) He is too lazy. We arrived here on the 4th at noon and we are well. All our good friends are in the country or at Mantua except Signor d'Aste and his wife, who have asked me to send their greetings to you and to my sister. Mysliwecek is still here. There is no truth in the report which is being so vigorously discussed in Germany of an Italian war or of the fortifying of the castle at Milan. Excuse my wretched handwriting. When you write to us, do so direct, for it is not the custom here, as it is in Germany, for people to carry letters about, but they have to be fetched at the post and so we go there every post-day to get them. There is no news here, but we are waiting for some from Salzburg. We hope that you received our letter from Bozen. Well, I cannot think of anything else, so I shall close. Our greetings to all our good friends. We kiss Mamma 100,000 times (I did not bring any more noughts with me) and I kiss Mamma's hands and prefer to embrace my sister in person rather than in imagination.

(160a) *Mozart to his Sister*

[Autograph in the Bibliothèque Municipale, Lille]

DEAREST SISTER,   [MILAN, 7 *November* 1772 [2]]

I hope that you have been to see the lady—⟨you know who. If you see her,⟩ please give her ⟨my compliments.⟩ I hope, and indeed I do not doubt, that you are in good health. I forgot to tell you that we have run across Signor Belardo here, the dancer, whom we knew at The Hague and at Amsterdam. It was he who attacked the dancer, Signor

---

[1] The Mozarts arrived at Milan on November 4th and stayed with the d'Astes.
[2] This letter is in Italian.

Neri,[1] with his sword, because he thought that it was owing to the latter that he had been refused permission to dance in the theatre.

Addio. Do not forget me. I am ever your

faithful brother
AMADEO WOLFGANGO
MOZART

(160b) *Leopold Mozart to his Wife*

[Autograph in the Bibliothèque Municipale, Lille]

[MILAN, 7 November 1772[2]]

We spent Wolfgang's name-day[3] very cheerfully at Ala with the two brothers Piccinni and we also stayed at Verona. We then came on to Milan. The weather is always fine here, and indeed the only rain we have had during our journey was in the afternoon of the day after St. Simon and St. Jude.[4] That was all. Keep well! Addio!

In Verona and here too we have seen comic operas.

(161) *Leopold Mozart to his Wife*

[Autograph in the Mozarteum, Salzburg]

[*Extract*]

MILAN, 14 November 1772

You will have received our first letter from Milan. After three days of ★ travelling my health is so good that I am really surprised, for we have been living very irregularly, especially on the journey from Verona to Milan. Yet now that I have been here for almost a fortnight, some trifling disorders have begun to plague me again; indeed I drop into thinking about Salzburg and, without noticing it, I go on brooding for some time. However, I quickly banish these thoughts or at least try to do so, just as I used to drive out all those wicked ideas which in my youth the devil suggested to me.

Not one of the singers has arrived yet except Signora Suarti, who sings ★ the part of the secondo uomo, and the ultimo tenore.[5] The primo uomo, Signor Rauzzini, is expected shortly. But Signora De Amicis will not be here until the end of this month or the beginning of December. Meanwhile Wolfgang has got much amusement from composing the choruses, of which there are three, and from altering and partly rewriting the few

---

[1] Neri appears in the *Reiseaufzeichnungen*, p. 45, under 'Amsterdam'. See *MBA*, No. 105.
[2] A postscript to Mozart's letter.   [3] October 31st.   [4] October 28th.
[5] The second tenor, Giuseppe Onofrio.

recitatives which he composed in Salzburg. For the poet[1] sent the libretto to Abbate Metastasio in Vienna for his approval and the latter, after correcting and altering a good deal, added a whole scene in the second act. Wolfgang has now written all the recitatives and the overture. So Herr Leutgeb[2] wants to go to Rome? And I am to write and tell him whether there is an opening here? That is most difficult! If he were here during the first few days of December, there would be some hope of his being asked to accompany an aria in the opera. But, once they are written, it is too late. He ought to travel via Brescia, where he could call on Count Lecchi, who is a first-rate violinist and a great connoisseur and amateur of music, with whom we have promised to stay on our return journey. It is not so easy to give a public concert here and it is scarcely any use attempting to do so without special patronage, while even then one is sometimes swindled out of one's profits. Apart from this he would lose nothing and he could live with us and would therefore have no expenses for light and wood. I hear that M. Baudace, the Frenchman, will soon be here with his French horn. Basta! Leutgeb will not lose anything; but he will have to be here in good time if he wants to get work in the opera. So he ought to leave with the mail coach at the very beginning of December, so that he may arrive here in time; for the opera is to be produced on December 26th. What about his leave of absence?

★ Farewell. We kiss you many hundred million times and I am your old

L MZT

★ The variations are in my writing-case, where I usually write; but Nannerl must not give them away, for there are some mistakes in them.

(162) *Leopold Mozart to his Wife*

[Extract] *[Autograph in the possession of Dr. F. Salzer-Wittgenstein, New York]*

MILAN, 21 *November* 1772

Thank God, we are well and strong and like fish in water, for it has ★ rained heavily for the last week. Today is the anniversary of our wedding day. It was twenty-five years ago, I think, that we had the sensible idea of getting married, one which we had cherished, it is true, for many years. All good things take time!

The primo uomo, Signor Rauzzini, has just arrived; so now there will be more and more to do and things will become increasingly lively. But

---

[1] The libretto of *Lucio Silla* had been written by Giovanni De Gamerra (1743–1803) of Leghorn, who first became a priest and then a soldier. He wrote a number of dramas and even attempted to establish a national theatre at Naples.

[2] See p. 78 note 2.

there will also be no lack of those charming incidents which are usual in the theatre. However, they are of little importance. The figs which Wolfgang was given when he left Salzburg have been as miraculous as the loaves and fishes in the Gospel, for they have lasted until now.

Yes indeed, there is a great deal to do at the moment. Even if it is not work, all sorts of arrangements have to be made.

(162a) *Mozart to his Sister*

[*Autograph in the possession of Dr. F. Salzer-Wittgenstein, New York*]

[MILAN, 21 *November* 1772 [1]]

I thank you, you know for what. I ask Herr von Hefner to forgive me for not yet replying to his letter, but it has been and still is impossible to do so, for as soon as I get home, there is always something to write; often something is already lying on the table; and out of doors, in the street, I can't possibly write. If you see him, let him read the following and tell him that he must content himself with it for the present. I shall not take it amiss that my paltry friend has not replied to me. As soon as he has time, he will surely, without doubt, doubtless, certainly, and undeniably send me an answer. My greetings to all my good friends. I kiss Mamma's hands. Well fare and news me soon some send. The Germany from post has not yet arrived.

Milano à, 2771, November 12 the. Oidda.

I usual as am

MOZART WOLFGANG

(163) *Leopold Mozart to his Wife*

[*Extract*]

[*Autograph in the Mozarteum, Salzburg*]

MILAN, 28 *November* 1772

I have received today your letter of the 20th. You want me to write very fully, but what is there to write about? Our best news is that, thank God, we are both well. There is no news here, for almost everyone is in the country and will not return to Milan until Christmas, when the festivities will begin with the re-opening of the theatre. Even the Archduke is out of town. As for my headache, I do not get it very often and it is only occasionally that I am seized for a few moments by my old giddiness which comes on when I turn over or raise myself in bed at night. At the same time I have a perfectly healthy appetite. But we only eat once a day, at two o'clock in the afternoon. In the evening we have an apple and a slice of bread and we drink a small glass of wine.

[1] A postscript to his father's letter.

217

I am writing in the house of Madame d'Aste, who sends her greetings to you. Monsieur d'Aste asks me to tell you that he is very much disappointed that you did not send greetings to him also. For I opened your
★ last letter in their house and read it aloud. Signora De Amicis is to leave Venice today and will therefore be here in a few days; then the work will be really enjoyable. Up to the present very little has been done. Wolfgang has only composed the first aria for the primo uomo, but it is superlatively beautiful and he sings it like an angel. Addio. Farewell. We kiss you many hundred thousand times and I am your old

MZT

(163a) *Mozart to his Sister*

[Autograph in the Mozarteum, Salzburg]

[MILAN, 28 November 1772 [1]]

We both send congratulations to Herr von Amann. Please tell him from me that I am vexed that he always made a secret of it, whenever I said anything to him about his fiancée. I should have thought that he was more sincere. I have greetings to deliver from Herr and Frau von Germani. They too are sorry that they cannot be with you. One thing more. Please tell Herr von Amann that if he intends his wedding to be the real thing, he should be so kind as to wait until our return in order that what he promised me may come true, that is, that I should dance at his wedding. Farewell. I kiss Mamma's hand. My greetings to all our good friends. ⟨Tell Herr Leutgeb to take the plunge and come to Milan, for he will certainly make his mark here.⟩ But he must come soon. Do not forget to tell him this, for I am very anxious that he should come. Adieu.

(164) *Leopold Mozart to his Wife*

[Autograph in the Mozarteum, Salzburg]

[Extract]

MILAN, 5 December 1772

★ Signora De Amicis, who sends greetings to you both and also to Adlgasser, turned up very late last night. Her journey from Venice to Milan by mail coach with six horses took a week, as the roads were so flooded and muddy. Unfortunately poor Cordoni, the tenor, is so ill that he cannot come. So the Secretary to the Theatre has been sent off by special post-chaise to Turin and a courier has been despatched to Bologna to find some other good tenor, who, as he has to play the part of Lucio Silla, must not only sing well, but be a first-rate actor and have a hand-

---

[1] A postscript to his father's letter.

some presence. As the prima donna only arrived yesterday and as it is not yet known who the tenor will be, you will realize that the major and most important portion of the opera has not yet been composed; but now great strides will be made.

Does Kapellmeister Lolli still conduct in the Cathedral?

We both send greetings to all our good friends in the promised land of Salzburg. We kiss you ten million times through the damp air, for here the weather is rainy, and I am

your old

MZT

(164a) Mozart to his Sister

[Autograph in the Mozarteum, Salzburg]

[MILAN, 5 December 1772 [1]]

I still have fourteen numbers to compose and then I shall have finished. But indeed the trio and the duet might well count as four. It is impossible for me to write much, as I have no news and, moreover, I do not know what I am writing, for I can think of nothing but my opera and I am in danger of writing down not words but a whole aria. I have greetings to deliver from Herr and Frau von Germani to Mamma, to you and to Adlgasser. I have learnt a new game here in Milan, called: *Mercante in fiera*, and as soon as I come home, we shall play it. I have also learnt from Frau d'Aste a new language which is easy to speak, but troublesome though not impossible to write; it is a little bit childish, but it will do for Salzburg. Addio. Farewell. Remember me to our beautiful Nannie and to the canary, for these two and you are the most innocent creatures in our house. I suppose Fischietti [2] will soon be setting to work at an opera buffa, which, when translated, means 'crazy opera'. Addio. I kiss Mamma's hand.

(165) Leopold Mozart to his Wife

[Extract]

[Autograph in the Mozarteum, Salzburg]

MILAN, 12 December 1772

I received today your letter of December 4th. Thank God, we are well, myself especially. During the coming week, while this letter is wending its way to Salzburg, Wolfgang will have his heaviest work. For these blessed theatrical people leave everything to the very last minute. The tenor [3] who

---

[1] A postscript to his father's letter.
[2] Domenico Fischietti, born ?1725 at Naples, was Kapellmeister at Dresden from 1765 until 1772, when he was appointed Kapellmeister at Salzburg, a post which he held until 1783. He composed many comic operas and also oratorios.
[3] Bassano Morgnoni, who was from Lodi, not from Turin.

is coming from Turin belongs to the King's Cappella. He is expected about the 14th or 15th and not until he arrives can his four arias be composed for him. Signora De Amicis sends greetings to you both. She is very well satisfied with the three arias which she has had so far. Wolfgang has introduced into her principal aria [1] passages which are unusual, quite unique and extremely difficult and which she sings amazingly well. We are very friendly and intimate with her. I am writing with a wretched pen and very poor ink, as Wolfgang, who is composing at another table, has the good ★ ink. The first rehearsal of the recitatives took place this morning. The second rehearsal will be held when the tenor arrives.

For some time now we have had constant rain here, but during the last three days the weather has been very fine and not at all cold, so that we have not yet had a fire in our hearth. That Wolfgang did not give the minuets to Fräulein Waberl [2] was an oversight which she will surely forgive, when she remembers that he is a careless fellow, who easily forgets things. But why he found it easier to remember Fräulein Barisani, [3] can be explained quite naturally and it is not necessary to give the reason.

We send our cordial greetings to all our good friends and we kiss you both as often as you like it and I assure you most sincerely that until death I shall ever be your admirer

L MZT

How is Mlle Zezi? [4] Does she still take lessons and does Nannerl spend much time with her? I send greetings to Nannerl and a message urging her to practise hard and to teach little Zezi conscientiously. I know well that she herself will benefit if she accustoms herself to teaching someone else very thoroughly and patiently. I am not writing this without a motive.

(166) *Leopold Mozart to his Wife*

[Extract]   [*Autograph in the Mozarteum, Salzburg*]

MILAN, 18 *December* 1772

My greetings to all our good friends. We kiss you both many ten thousand times and I remain your old

MZT.

I am writing this letter today, Friday the 18th, for tomorrow we shall hardly have time to write anything, because we are to have the first

---

[1] Probably Giunia's aria (no. 11) 'Ah se il crudel periglio'.
[2] See p. 197, n. 3.
[3] Probably Therese von Barisani, a daughter of Dr. Sylvester von Barisani (1719–1810), private physician to the Archbishop of Salzburg.
[4] Barbara Zezi, whose father kept a grocer's shop in the Getreidegasse.

rehearsal with all the instruments at half past nine in the morning. During the last few days we have had three rehearsals of the recitatives. The tenor arrived only yesterday evening and Wolfgang composed today two arias for him and has still two more to do. The second rehearsal takes place on Sunday the 20th, the third on Tuesday the 22nd, and the dress rehearsal on Wednesday the 23rd. On Thursday and Friday there will be no rehearsals; but on Saturday the 26th, the very day on which you will receive this letter, we shall have the first performance of the opera. I am writing to you at eleven o'clock at night and Wolfgang has just finished the second aria for the tenor. We shall celebrate Christmas Eve at supper with Herr and Frau von Germani, who send you greetings and who wish that you were here. We are lunching tomorrow with Herr von Mayr and after lunch I shall still be able to write a few words. Addio. Farewell.   ★

(166a) *Mozart to his Sister*

[*Autograph formerly in the Mozarteum, Salzburg*[1]]

[MILAN, 18 *December* 1772[2]]

I hope that you are well, my dear sister. When you receive this letter, my dear sister, that very evening my opera will have been performed, my dear sister. Think of me, my dear sister, and try as hard as you can to imagine that you, my dear sister, are hearing and seeing it too, my dear sister. That is hard, I admit, as it is already eleven o'clock. Otherwise I believe and do not doubt at all that during the day it is brighter than at Easter. We are lunching tomorrow, my dear sister, with Herr von Mayr, and why, do you think? Guess! Why, because he has asked us. The rehearsal tomorrow is at the theatre, but Signor Castiglione, the impresario, has begged me not to tell anyone about it; otherwise a whole crowd of people will come running in, and we do not want this. So, my child, I beg you not to mention it to anyone, my child, otherwise too many people will come running in, my child. That reminds me. Have you heard what happened here? I will tell you. We left Count Firmian's today to go home and when we reached our street, we opened the hall door and what do you think we did? Why, we went in. Farewell, my little lung. I kiss you my liver, and remain as always, my stomach, your unworthy

{ frater
{ brother   WOLFGANG

Please, please, my dear sister, something is biting me. Do come and scratch me.

---

[1] Copy in the Staatsbibliothek Preussischer Kulturbesitz, West Berlin.
[2] A postscript to his father's letter. In the autograph every other line is written upside down.

(167) *Leopold Mozart to his Wife*

[*Extract*]   [*Autograph in the Mozarteum, Salzburg*]

MILAN, 26 *December* 1772

We have just this moment risen from table at Madame d'Aste's, with whom we have been lunching and at whose house I am now writing. She sends you greetings. The opera is to begin in about two or three hours' time. May God be gracious! The dress rehearsal the day before yesterday went off so well as to give us reason to hope for the greatest success. The music alone, without the ballets,[1] lasts for four hours. We received your letter today and enjoyed all your news. By this post I am also writing to the Chief Steward and *to the Archbishop and I am enclosing the opera text.* With regard to the ⟨letter to Florence⟩[2] there has been a serious misunderstanding. Abbate Augustini took away with him to Rome the whole parcel[3] which he should have handed to Herr Troger here. The result has been that all these things, which have only now come back from Rome, have just been sent off to ⟨Florence⟩. Count Firmian ⟨added a good, strong covering letter, and now we must await the reply⟩. On the evenings of the 21st, 22nd and 23rd there were great parties in Count Firmian's house, at which all the nobles were present. On each day they went on from five o'clock in the evening until eleven o'clock with continuous vocal and instrumental music. We were among those invited and Wolfgang performed each evening. On the third day, in particular, Wolfgang was called upon to perform, at the request of Their Royal Highnesses, immediately after their arrival. Both of them spoke to us for a long time. On all three evenings the greatest houses of the town were illuminated with enormous torches, the bells of the churches near Count Firmian's house played melodies like the carillons in the Netherlands, and in the street there was music with trumpets and drums. This festival was held to celebrate the raising of His Eminence the Bishop of Passau to the dignity of Cardinal.

De Amicis is our best friend. She sings and acts like an angel and is extremely pleased because Wolfgang has served her extraordinarily well. Both you and the whole of Salzburg would be amazed if you could hear her. We kiss you many ten thousand times and in haste I remain

your old

MZT.

---

[1] Mozart is believed to have composed for *Lucio Silla* the unfinished ballet *Le gelosie del serraglio*, K. App. 109 [K. 135a].

[2] Leopold Mozart had applied to the Archduke Leopold of Tuscany, who in 1791 became Emperor Leopold II, for an appointment for his son.

[3] This contained a copy of *Lucio Silla*, intended for the Archduke.

(168) *Leopold Mozart to his Wife*

[*Autograph in the Mozarteum, Salzburg*]

A Happy New Year!   MILAN, 2 *January* 1773

I forgot the other day to wish you a happy New Year, because I was not only in a hurry, but in a condition of absolute confusion. I was preoccupied and absent-minded and at that very moment we were going off to the theatre. The opera was a great success, although on the first evening several very distressing incidents took place. The first hitch was that the performance, which was due to begin one hour after the Angelus, started three hours late, that is—about eight o'clock by German time. Thus it did not finish until two o'clock in the morning. It was only just before the Angelus that the Archduke rose from his midday meal and he then had to write with his own hand five letters of New Year greetings to Their Majesties the Emperor and Empress; and, I ought to mention, he writes very slowly. Picture to yourself the whole theatre which by half past five was so full that not another soul could get in. On the first evening the singers are always very nervous at having to perform before such a distinguished audience. But for three hours singers, orchestra and audience (many of the latter standing) had to wait impatiently in the overheated atmosphere until the opera should begin. Next, the tenor, who was engaged as a stop-gap, is a church singer from Lodi who has never before acted on such a big stage, who has only taken the part of primo tenore a couple of times, and who moreover was only engaged a week before the performance. At the point where in her first aria the prima donna expected from him an angry gesture, he exaggerated his anger so much that he looked as if he was about to box her ears and strike her on the nose with his fist. This made the audience laugh. Signora De Amicis, carried along by her own enthusiasm, did not realise why they were laughing, and, being thus taken aback, did not sing well for the rest of the evening. Further, she was jealous, because as soon as the primo uomo[1] came on the stage, the Archduchess clapped her hands. This was a ruse on the part of that castrato, who had arranged that the Archduchess should be told that he would not be able to sing for nervousness in order that he might thus ensure that the court would encourage and applaud him. To console Signora De Amicis the court summoned her at about noon on the following day and she had an audience with their Royal Highnesses which lasted a whole hour. Only then did the opera begin to go well; and although in the case of a first opera the theatre is usually very empty, on the first six evenings (today is the seventh) the hall was so full that it was hardly possible to slip in. Further, the prima donna is still having it all her own way and her arias have to be repeated. Madame d'Aste, at whose house I am writing,

---

[1] Venanzio Rauzzini.

sends greetings and wishes for a happy New Year. We kiss you many millions of times and I am your old

MZT.

Wolfgang sends special greetings to everyone. Thank God, we are well.

(169) *Leopold Mozart to his Wife*

[Extract]   [*Autograph in the Mozarteum, Salzburg*]

MILAN, 9 *January* 1773

That you received no letter from me on one post-day must be due to a mistake at some post office, for I have written to you, as usual, every post-day. So you need not worry, for it may well happen that one letter goes
★ astray. Thank God, the opera is an extraordinary success, and every day the theatre is surprisingly full, although people do not usually flock in large numbers to the first opera unless it is an outstanding success. Every evening arias are repeated and since the first night the opera has gained daily in popularity and has won increasing applause. Count Castelbarco has presented my son with a gold watch to which is attached a beautiful
★ gold chain with a gold chaise and a gold lantern. You never told me that Prince Colloredo was so ill in Vienna. For over a week we have been told here that he was dying, but now we hear that he is somewhat better. People have doubtless kept quiet about this in Salzburg in order not to upset the arrangements for the concerts and the operas.

I am surprised that Leutgeb did not leave Salzburg sooner, if he really intended to do so. Up to the present there is no thought of our leaving here. We may do so at about the end of this month, for we want to hear the music of the second opera.[1] Thank God, we are both well, and for some time my head has been better. It began to freeze a little two days ago and now we have most beautiful weather. Monsieur and Madame d'Aste and Herr von Troger, Herr Germani and his wife and Signor Maestro Mysliwecek send greetings, and they all long to meet you. Count Castel-
★ barco has given me special messages for both of you. We kiss you many ten million times and I am your old

MZT.

⟨I hear from Florence that the Grand Duke has received my letter, is giving it sympathetic consideration and will let me know the result. We still live in hopes.⟩[2]

---

[1] Paisiello's *Il Sismano nel Mogol.*
[2] This postscript follows Mozart's postscript to his sister.

(169a) *Mozart to his Sister*

[*Autograph in the Mozarteum, Salzburg*]

[MILAN, 9 January 1773 [1]]

When you see Madame d'Aste, Herr Troger, Herr Germani and his wife, please give them my regards. I have greetings for you from Herr von Schiedenhofen, Herr Hefner and from other good friends of blood and bone and especially from the wife of the Court Chancellor. I have no news except that Count Sauerau has been made Dean of the Cathedral.[2] Addio.

(170) *Leopold Mozart to his Wife*

[*Extract*]   [*Autograph in the Mozarteum, Salzburg*]

MILAN, 16 January 1773

His Grace the Archbishop has replied most favourably and has asked me to bring him back a few articles, which I am now procuring and about which I shall write to him by the next post.

Wolfgang's opera has now been performed seventeen times and will be performed about twenty times in all. It was arranged that the second opera was to begin on January 23rd. But as things are going so well and as the management, who at first had contracted for five hundred ducats, have now received more than a thousand, the second opera will not be produced until about the 30th. I must write quickly and only very little, because I have other letters to send off today. I am your old

LE MZT:

Monsieur and Madame d'Aste send greetings and so do Signor and Signora Germani. Herr Mysliwecek kisses Nannerl's expert hands. That was the message for her which he gave Wolfgang. Greetings too from De Amicis and her little Giuseppina, for she has been married for over five years.[3]

⟨There is little hope of what I wrote to you. God will help us. But do save money and keep cheerful, for we must have means, if we want to undertake a journey. I regret every farthing which we spend in Salzburg. Up to the present no reply has come from the Grand Duke, but we know from the Count's letter to Troger that there is very little likelihood of our getting work in Florence. Yet I still trust that at least he will recommend us.⟩ Farewell. We must go out for a drive and the carriage is at the door.

---

[1] A postscript to his father's letter. A nonsensical note, imitating perhaps the last short one he had had from Nannerl.
[2] i.e. of Salzburg.   [3] She married Buonsolazzi, a Neapolitan official.

(170a) *Mozart to his Sister*

[*Autograph in the Mozarteum, Salzburg*]

[MILAN, 16 January 1773[1]]

I for have the primo a uomo[2] motet compose which to tomorrow at Church the Theatine performed be will. Keep well, I you beg. Farewell. Addio. I[3] sorry to any My to our friends, am not have news. greetings all good male and Fare I Mamma's I you a female. well. kiss hand. kiss too thousand times am always faithful at and as your brother Milan.

(171) *Leopold Mozart to his Wife*

[*Extract*]   [*Autograph in the Mozarteum, Salzburg*]

MILAN, 23 *January* 1773

I am writing in bed, for during the last week I have been plagued with acute rheumatism and have had to lie up. The pain began in the joint of the left thigh, moved down after a few days to the left knee and has now settled in the right knee. The only remedy I have tried is burr root tea, three or four large glasses of which I drink every day. I have to lie on the mattress, for the room is often even colder than the street outside. The most distressing circumstance is that I have to cover these painful thighs with cloaks, furs and so forth in order to keep warm and perspire, because I have only been given one or two single blankets. So I am lying wrapped in my dressing-gown and furs in order to keep warm, and you can imagine how heavy they are on my feet and how uncomfortable it is for me when I want to move. After you receive this letter, do not write to Milan any more, because with God's help I hope to be able to leave during the first week of February, unless the copyists detain me for the music which has to be copied for His Grace and which they cannot undertake at present, as they are busy with work for the theatre. For the second opera does not

★ begin until January 30th. Wolfgang is sorry that Leutgeb will arrive too late to hear his work. The theatre is extraordinarily crowded and the opera is being performed twenty-six times. The remaining performances will be kept for the second opera. On Fridays and on one or two holy days there are no performances. ⟨I have sent Wolfgang's opera to the Grand Duke in Florence. Even if there is no hope of obtaining anything from him, I trust that he will recommend us. But if it is all in vain, we shall not go

---

[1] A postscript to his father's letter.
[2] Mozart composed for Rauzzini the motet 'Exsultate, jubilate', K. 165 [158a].
[3] The solution of Mozart's jumble is as follows: write 'I' over 'am', 'sorry' over 'not', 'and' over 'female', 'a' over 'thousand', 'times' over 'and' and then read up and down.

under, for God will help us. I have already thought out some plans.⟩ ★
We kiss you both many tens of thousands of times and I am your old
MZT.

(171a) *Mozart to his Sister*

[*Autograph in the Mozarteum, Salzburg*]

[MILAN, 23 *January* 1773[1]]

Signor and Signora d'Aste, Signor and Signora Germani, Signor
Mysliwecek and Signora De Amicis have asked me to send you their
compliments and regards. I beg you to tell Johann Hagenauer from me
not to doubt that I will certainly visit that armourer's shop and see whether
they have anything he wants and that, if I find it, I shall not fail to bring it
home with me. I am vexed that Leutgeb left Salzburg too late to see a
performance of my opera; and perhaps he will miss us too, unless we
meet on the way. The first orchestral rehearsal of the second opera took
place yesterday evening, but I only heard the first act, since, as it was late,
I left at the beginning of the second. In this opera there are to be twenty-
four horses and a great crowd of people on the stage, so that it will be a
miracle if some accident does not happen. I like the music, but I do not
know whether the public will like it, for only people connected with the
theatre have been allowed to attend the first rehearsal. I hope that my
father will be able to go out tomorrow. This evening the weather is very
bad. Signora Teiber[2] is now at Bologna. She is singing at Turin during the
coming carnival and the following year she will go and sing at Naples.
My compliments to all my friends. Kiss my mother's hands for me. I have
no more news. Farewell. Excuse my bad writing, but my pen is not worth
a straw.

(172) *Leopold Mozart to his Wife*

[*Extract*]　　　　　　　　　　　[*Autograph in the Mozarteum, Salzburg*]

MILAN, 30 *January* 1773

We have received no letter today, unless the courier from Rome who
passes through Mantua happens to deliver something—for he sometimes
brings with him letters from Germany which have been left behind in
Mantua. If not, your letter, assuming that you wrote one, will arrive about
Wednesday. You will see from my handwriting that I am scrawling this
in bed, as I am still laid up with this accursed rheumatism and am suffering
like a dog. Patience is the patron saint of all cowards. The pious proverb

---

[1] This letter is in Italian.
[2] Elisabeth Teiber (1744–1816), one of a large family of Viennese musicians, who were the
children of Matthäus Teiber (*c.* 1711–1785), a famous violinist in the service of the Austrian
court.

says: Better here than there. But I say—better there than here, because a rheumaticky person who is perspiring in bed cannot appreciate a cold room, which is even colder than the street. Though indeed I should not like an overheated room either. Today the second opera is being performed for the first time, and I am very unhappy not to be able to hear it. I am sending Wolfgang to Herr Germani's box and in the meantime I myself shall have to mope at home. We have had dreadful rainy weather for some days. But yesterday, January 29th, the most beautiful weather returned and now it is more warm than cold. If my health had allowed me to do so, I should have left here during the first days of February. But now I must count myself lucky if I get away on the 10th or 12th, for this is the most dangerous season for my illness, as in the Tyrol I shall meet with more

★ snow and fresh air than I require. Wolfgang is well, and this very moment, as I write, he is turning one somersault after another. We kiss you many hundred thousand times and I am your old

MZT.

★

⟨I have received no further reply from the Grand Duke in Florence. What I wrote about my illness is all quite untrue. I was in bed for a few days, but now I am well and am off to the opera this evening. You must, however, spread the news everywhere that I am ill. You should cut off this scrap of paper so that it may not fall into the hands of others.⟩[1]

(173) *Leopold Mozart to his Wife*

[Extract]   [Autograph in the Mozarteum, Salzburg]

MILAN, 6 February 1773

I had certainly hoped to leave here at the beginning of next week and thus to see you before the end of the carnival. But this accursed rheumatism has settled in my right shoulder and, as I cannot do anything for myself, I am making no progress. So you can imagine how I feel, the more so as the weather is now frightfully cold and there is a bitter wind that goes through you. We have no means of heating our room, not even a fireplace. I can only try to keep myself warm in a bed covered with fur and clothes, on which even our footbags are piled up. Nevertheless I shall endeavour, if it is possible, to leave at the end of next week and hope to be in Salzburg for the last three days of the carnival. I say, *if it is possible*, for, if my rheumatism is not completely cured, I must not attempt in this cold weather to start on so long a journey, which will take us through the Tyrol, where the cold will undoubtedly be bitter and where I must run

---

[1] Frau Mozart did not do so.

the risk of having possibly to lie up in some wretched inn on the way. Meanwhile I presume that this will be my last letter from Milan. I should ★ like you to find an opportunity of speaking to the Chief Steward, to Count Sauerau or to Countess von Arco[1] and of informing them, with my most humble greetings, of my indisposition. This is the more important as enquiries have been made about our arrival. I shall certainly leave Milan as soon as I can.

Wolfgang is composing a quartet,[2] and I am relieved that I have written this letter. We kiss you many hundred million times and I am your old disabled

MZT

★

⟨Thank God, we are well. I cannot start on my journey, as I must await the arrival of a courtier from Florence. Leutgeb has not yet reached Milan. Meanwhile you must cultivate our friendship with Count Sauerau.⟩

(174) *Leopold Mozart to his Wife*

[Extract]   *[Autograph in the Mozarteum, Salzburg]*

MILAN, 13 February 1773 ★

My rheumatism which moved to my right shoulder has settled down ★ there much more obstinately than when I had it in my thighs and knees. Nor have I been able to treat it so well, for in an icy cold room it is easier to keep one's feet warm in bed than one's shoulders. I was in constant dread lest I should suffer again as dreadfully as I did ten years ago when for fourteen whole weeks I had these cruel pains in both shoulders. Thank God, I trust that this attack will not be so bad, for the pains have already become less acute. But I cannot use my right arm and, as Wolfgang is not able to do much for me or even for himself, you can realize what fun we are having. I would have written to the Chief Steward and humbly requested him to apologize to His Grace for our belated return to Salzburg, but I can assure you that it is impossible for me to compose a single line of good sense without getting feverish and that I cannot even write a few words neatly. So please find an opportunity of laying our humble request before His Excellency and of assuring him that we shall leave as soon as possible.

Leutgeb arrived late one evening a week ago and on the following ★ Sunday he came to call on us. I have not seen him for the last two days,

---

[1] Wife of Count Georg Anton Felix von Arco, Chief Chamberlain to the Archbishop.
[2] Probably K. 157 or 158.

for he is staying with the painter Martin Knoller,[1] a good quarter of an hour from this house. He pays nothing for his lodging. So far he has arranged his affairs pretty well and he will make quite a fortune here, for he is extraordinarily popular. If the concert takes place which the courtiers want to arrange for him, I wager that he will get one hundred cigliati on the spot. The Archduke too wants to hear him.

I am tired of holding my pen, and though my hands and feet are cold, ★ my head is hot. So I must close. We kiss you many thousand times and I am your old

MZT

★

We are showering sugared words on the copyist to encourage him to finish the score of Wolfgang's opera, so that we may take it home with us. But we do not yet know whether we shall be so lucky.

(175) *Leopold Mozart to his Wife*

[*Extract*] [*Autograph in the Mozarteum, Salzburg*]

MILAN, 20 *February* 1773

Alas, we are still in Milan! I sent a letter today to the Chief Steward and I found it difficult to write legibly. My rheumatism now makes me impatient. We shall have to travel through the Tyrol where I hear that the snow is very thick and I fear that we may be overwhelmed by an avalanche, as milder weather is coming. So you can understand that as soon as my ★ health permits I shall leave. I have no more news for you except that, ★ thank God, Wolfgang is well. I am your old

MZT

★

(176) *Leopold Mozart to his Wife*

[*Extract*] [*Autograph in the Mozarteum, Salzburg*]

MILAN, 27 *February* 1773

I can only write a few words today, for it is the last day of carnival and Lent begins tomorrow. So it is just as if everyone here were going mad. We are leaving in two or three days and I am sending you this letter as an enclosure in one to Spitzeder, so that you may say that you have received

---

[1] Martin Knoller (1725–1804) was born at Steinach in Tyrol, studied in Italy and in 1765 settled in Milan, where he made a great reputation as a painter of portraits and historical subjects. He became court painter to Count Firmian, Governor-General of Lombardy, and, with the exception of a short visit to Vienna in 1790, remained in Milan for the rest of his life. It is possible that he painted the ivory miniature of Mozart, which was formerly in the possession of the latter's sister and is now in the Mozart Museum, Salzburg.

no word from me and that therefore you think that we have probably left already. We must, and we want to arrive in Salzburg on the evening of Election day, March 13th.[1] As for the affair you know of there is nothing to be done.[2] I shall tell you all when we meet. God has probably some other plan for us. You cannot think into what confusion our de- ★ parture has thrown me. Indeed I find it hard to leave Italy.

M. and Mme d'Aste send their greetings. We kiss you many 100,000 times and I am your old

MZT

I shall write to you on our journey.

[1] The first anniversary of the election of the new Archbishop, Hieronymus Colloredo.
[2] Leopold Mozart is alluding to his application to the Archduke Leopold of Tuscany.

Mozart's eighth journey was to Vienna, whither, owing to the absence from Salzburg of Archbishop Hieronymus Colloredo, his father accompanied him in the hope of obtaining for him an appointment at the Viennese court. This hope was not realized. During his two months' stay in Vienna, Mozart composed a second series of six string quartets. This visit, which lasted from 14 July to 26 September 1773, is described in joint letters from father and son to Frau Mozart and Nannerl. Letters 177-188.

(177) *Leopold Mozart to his Wife*

[*Extract*]   [*Autograph in the Mozarteum, Salzburg*]

VIENNA, 21 *July* 1773[1]

When we arrived in Vienna old Frau Fischer happened to be at table, for they take their supper at six o'clock. Her daughter and her son-in-law were at Baden[2] and only returned last Monday. She knew nothing whatever about our arrival, for the letter had been written to her daughter and lay there unopened, because so far she had had no opportunity of forwarding it to her. But the old lady was extraordinarily pleased to see us and was only sorry that you and Nannerl had not come too. She and her daughter send their greetings and, together with our own wishes, 100,000 wishes for your and Nannerl's name-day.[3] We shall drink the health of Your Highness and celebrate your name-day in the Landstrasse.[4] We have fine rooms here and everything we require. We lunched on Sunday ★ with young Mesmer[5] in the company of Herr von Heufeld.[6] Nobody recognized Wolfgang, for each time I let him go in alone. You can picture to yourself their joy in the Landstrasse at seeing us. Everywhere it has been the same. We found Fräulein Franzl[7] in bed. She is really very much emaciated and if she has another illness of this kind, she will be done for! Herr von Bosch[8] has got a post in the War Department in Brünn. Mme von Mesmer has lost her mother-in-law.[9] She can use the interest on the whole property, but she can neither sell houses nor touch the capital. The Mesmers are all well and in good form as usual. Herr von Mesmer,[10] at whose house we lunched on Monday, played to us on Miss Davies's armonica or glass instrument and played very well. It cost him about fifty ducats and it is very beautifully made. His garden is extremely fine, with views and statues, a theatre, an aviary, a pigeon-loft and, at the top, a belvedere looking right over the Prater. We dined with them on Saturday and also on Monday. They all send their greetings. I must close, for I have ★

---

[1] The Mozarts left Salzburg on 14 July.   [2] A watering-place near Vienna.
[3] 26 July.
[4] i.e. with Dr. Mesmer's family. They lived in a magnificent house in the Landstrasse, which belonged to his wife whose first husband was Herr von Bosch.
[5] Joseph Mesmer, a relative of Dr. Mesmer, who founded the Vienna Reform School.
[6] Franz von Heufeld (1731–1795), a well-known dramatist and writer, who since 1769 had been manager of the Deutsches Theater in Vienna.
[7] Franziska von Osterling, who later married Mesmer's stepson, Franz de Paula von Bosch.
[8] Dr. Mesmer's stepson.   [9] Frau von Eulenschenk.
[10] Dr. Franz Anton Mesmer (1734–1815), born at Iznang on Lake Constance, was educated at the Jesuit College of Dillingen and proceeded to study medicine at the Universities of Ingolstadt and Vienna. In 1768 he married a wealthy widow, Frau von Bosch, and settled in her mother-in-law's house in the Landstrasse. He soon made a tremendous reputation for cures by magnetism.

still time to write a few lines to young Herr von Andretter[1] and to send
★ him the beginning of the Finalmusik.[2] We kiss you both many 10,000,000
times and I am your old

MZT

(178) *Leopold Mozart to his Wife*

[*Extract*]   [*Autograph in the Mozarteum, Salzburg*]

VIENNA, 12 *August* 1773

I have received all your letters.

Her Majesty the Empress was very gracious to us, but that was all. I am
saving up a full account until our return, for it is impossible for me to give
★ it in writing. His Grace[3] returns today from Laxenburg. He will spend a
few days with his father in Sierndorf and then go back to Salzburg. But
he will hardly leave before next Saturday or Sunday, and thus will not
arrive in Salzburg until next week. You will hear by the next post when
★ we shall leave. If we do not leave next Monday, we shall not get home
before the beginning of September. I shall know today or tomorrow.
Meanwhile Fräulein Franzl has again been dangerously ill and blisters had
to be applied to her arms and feet. She is so much better now that she has
knitted in bed a red silk purse for Wolfgang which she has given him as a
remembrance. She sends greetings, as they all do, the whole litany of the
Landstrasse, the two Frau Fischers and Herr Fischer, the Bonnos and so on.
Young Mesmer's boy is really talented, so much so that if only he were
my son or at least lived with me, he would get on. As for the girl, she is
none other than the daughter of Dr. Auenbrugger, or rather his elder
daughter. Both of them, and in particular the elder, play extraordinarily
well and are thoroughly musical. We dine with them occasionally.
The family, however, do not draw a subsidy from the Empress. Young
Mesmer has a good appointment. He is in charge of the organisation of
the Normalschulen of all the Imperial hereditary dominions, the governor
of which is a nobleman. Do you know that Herr von Mesmer[4] plays
Miss Davies's armonica unusually well? He is the only person in Vienna
who has learnt it and he possesses a much finer glass instrument than Miss
Davies does. Wolfgang too has played upon it. How I should like to have
one! On the feast of St. Cajetan[5] the Fathers invited us to luncheon and
to the service; and, because the organ was not good enough for an organ
concerto, Wolfgang borrowed from Herr Teiber[6] a violin and a concerto
which he was impudent enough to play. In the octave of the feast of St.

---

[1] Judas Thaddäus von Andretter, a son of Johann Ernst von Andretter, War Councillor at the
Salzburg court.
[2] K. 185 [167a], probably performed about August 1st as 'Finalmusik' for Salzburg University.
[3] The Archbishop of Salzburg.   [4] Dr. Franz Anton Mesmer.   [5] 7 August.
[6] Probably Matthäus Teiber (see p. 227, n. 2) or his son Friedrich (1748–1829).

Ignatius[1] one of Wolfgang's masses, the Dominicus mass,[2] was performed at the Jesuits, Auf Dem Hof. I conducted it and it was very well received. We are delighted that the Finalmusik[3] went off well.

Wolfgang will express his thanks to Herr Meisner later on. Meanwhile we send him our greetings.

Now I have sent you a great deal of news. We kiss you many 100000 ★ times and I am your old

MZT

(178a) *Mozart to his Sister*

[*Autograph in the Mozarteum, Salzburg*]

[VIENNA, 12 *August* 1773[4]]

Hodie nous avons begegnet per strada Dominum Edelbach,[5] welcher uns di voi compliments ausgerichtet hat, et qui sich tibi et ta mère empfehlen lässt. Addio.

W. M.

Landstrasse 12 August

Stephanie Junior[6] and his pretty wife send their greetings.

(179) *Leopold Mozart to his Wife*

[*Extract*] [*Autograph in the Mozarteum, Salzburg*]

VIENNA, 14 *August* 1773

I received today your letter of the 10th. On Tuesday His Grace will leave Sierndorf, where he is staying with his father, and will arrive here on Wednesday evening or early on Thursday. You ask when we shall return? Not yet, for His Grace has given us permission to stay on here. Von Mesmer's cousin, who is also called Mesmer, is a travelling cook in the service of the Archbishop. He arrived in Salzburg about a fortnight before the departure of the latter, and left with him at once for Vienna. He was commissioned by Herr and Frau von Mesmer to visit us in Salzburg and to deliver a thousand kind messages, but he has now excused himself on the ground that he called on us and found nobody at home. This time he will go to see you at once, as he is the bearer of innumerable messages from us all. You will notice that he is rather like young Mesmer,

---

[1] An 'octave' is the week following a feast-day.

[2] K. 66, the Mass which Mozart wrote in 1769 for his friend, Cajetan (Dominicus) Hagenauer who had just entered the monastery of St. Peter and had to conduct his first service. [3] K. 185 [167a].

[4] A postscript to his father's letter. 'Today we met in the street Herr Edelbach who has given us your compliments, and who asks to be remembered to you and to your mother. Farewell.'

[5] Benedikt Schlossgängl von Edelbach (1748– ?), a son of Franz Josef Schlossgängl von Edelbach, Professor of Law at Salzburg University.

[6] Gottlieb Stephanie, an actor and dramatist in Vienna. See p. 725, n. 2. (This note is added in Stephanie's hand.)

that he is very refined, has an aristocratic bearing and for a cook is rather
proud.

★   After a great deal of rain we now have fine weather at last and during
these few days it has been extraordinarily warm. The Mesmers and all that
★ gang send their greetings; likewise the two Frau Fischers and Herr Fischer.
We kiss you many hundred thousand times and I am your old

MZT

The whole families of Martinez[1] and Bonno send their greetings to you,
weather permitting.[2]

(179a) *Mozart to his Sister*

[Autograph in the Mozarteum, Salzburg]

[VIENNA, 14 *August* 1773[3]]
I hope, my queen, that you are enjoying the highest degree of health
and that now and then or rather, sometimes, or, better still, occasionally,
or, even better still, qualche volta, as the Italians say, you will sacrifice for
my benefit some of your important and intimate thoughts, which ever
proceed from that very fine and clear reasoning power, which in addition
to your beauty, and although from a woman, and particularly from one
of such tender years, almost nothing of the kind is ever expected, you
possess, O queen, so abundantly as to put men and even greybeards to
shame. There now, you have a well-turned sentence. Farewell.

WOLFGANG MOZART

(180) *Leopold Mozart to his Wife*

[Extract]   *[Autograph in the Mozarteum, Salzburg]*

VIENNA, 21 *August* 1773
A good friend of Herr Fischer has invited him and ourselves to Baden.
As we have never seen that part of the world, we are lunching today with
Herr Fischer and are driving out there after lunch, returning tomorrow
(Sunday) evening. We have hired two carriages, one of which will take
Herr Fischer, his wife and our two selves, and the other, Herr Teiber[4]
and his family.

★   I could not write by the last post as we had a big concert in the garden

---

[1] The family of Niccolò Martinez, master of ceremonies to the Papal Nuncio in Vienna.
During his long stay in Vienna, from 1730 to 1782, Metastasio lived with this family. One of
the daughters, Marianne Martinez, became an accomplished musician, whose talents are
enthusiastically described by Burney, *Present State of Music in Germany, etc.*, 2nd edition, 1775,
vol. i. p. 310 ff.
[2] The last two words are an addition in Mozart's handwriting.
[3] A postscript to his father's letter.
[4] Matthäus Teiber (*c.* 1711–1785), violinist in the service of the Viennese court and father of
Anton Teiber, violinist, Franz Teiber, organist, and the singers Elisabeth and Therese Teiber.

of the Landstrasse. Fräulein Franzl has now had a second relapse from which she has again recovered. It is amazing how she can stand so much bleeding and so many medicines, blisters, convulsions, fainting fits and so forth, for she is nothing but skin and bone. Herr von Mesmer is adding ★ three new rooms on the ground floor in order that he may be able to live downstairs during the winter, since although an enormous amount of wood is burnt upstairs, the rooms never get warmed up. You probably did not write last post-day, as I received no letter. Today's post has not yet arrived. Let me know when the Archbishop leaves Salzburg. We kiss ★ ★ you many 100000 times and I am your old

MZT

I have this moment received your letter.[1] If I had known Frau von Mesmer's[2] circumstances which, as you know, *were very doubtful*, I could have brought you both with us. But not only was it impossible for me to know them, but there were other difficulties. Both the Mesmers in the Landstrasse and Frau Fischer wanted to have you as their guests; but how should we have got home? You could have come to Vienna by water, or more quickly, but rather inconveniently, by mail coach. But how could you have returned? And what a fearful sensation this would have made in Salzburg! You can rest assured that your visit would have given great pleasure to us and to all our good friends in Vienna. But now it is no longer worth while and we are not in a position to meet any great expenditure. If we had had some prospects or if we had made some money, I should certainly have written to you to come. But there are many matters about which one cannot write. Moreover we must avoid anything which might create a stir or provoke any suspicion either here or, in particular at Salzburg, or which might give someone an opportunity to put a spoke in our wheel.

We do not know ourselves when we shall leave. It may be soon, but there may be some delay. It depends on circumstances which I may not enumerate. God willing, we shall certainly be home by the end of September. Things must and will alter. Be comforted and keep well! God will help us!

Should the Archbishop stay away for a long time, we shall not hurry home.

(180a) Mozart to his Sister

[Autograph in the Mozarteum, Salzburg]

[VIENNA, 21 August 1773[3]]

If one considers the favour of Time and if at the same time one does not forget completely the respect due to the sun, then it is certain that, praise

---

[1] This postscript follows Letter 180a.   [2] i.e. Dr. Mesmer's wife, who was wealthy.
[3] A postscript to his father's letter.

and thanks be to God, I am well. But the second sentence is quite different, if for 'sun' we put 'moon' and for 'favour' we put 'art'. In this case anyone who is blessed with a little common sense will conclude that I am a fool, because you are my sister. How is Miss Bimbes?[1] Please give her all sorts of messages from me. My greetings to all my good friends. I have to deliver greetings too from Herr and Frau von Mesmer, Brean, Grill, Saliet, Steigentesch, Stephanie, Sepherl and Fräulein Franzl to Mamma and to you and to Herr von Schiedenhofen. I have all sorts of messages too from Mr. Greibich,[2] whose acquaintance we first made at Pressburg and later in Vienna, and from Her Majesty the Empress, Frau Fischer and Prince Kaunitz.

Oidda. Gnagflow Trazom.

Anneiv, Tsugua, ts12, 3771

(181) *Leopold Mozart to his Wife*

[*Extract*]   [*Autograph in the Mozarteum, Salzburg*]

VIENNA, 25 *August* 1773

I am astonished to hear that Madame Rosa has left for Vienna. I have not yet seen her, as I do not know where she is living; presumably with Hofvergolter. Herr von Mölk, whom I went to see today, knew as little about her as I did. But did no shimmer of an idea occur to you, prompting you to make use of this convenient opportunity to send a cloth travelling coat of mine down the river? You could have sent, for instance, my English redbrown coat with the golden paillettes and Wolfgang's grey ★ coat. I am writing in a great hurry at young Mesmer's house, where we lunched today to celebrate the eighth anniversary of their wedding day and where we drank your healths. The Mesmers went off today to the Rotmühle. We shall visit them if we have time, and we shall bring the Teibers with us, for the daughter sings and the son plays the violin. All that Nannerl writes about corselets, caps and so forth I shall see to as far as possible, but my purse is getting emptier. As my figure becomes stouter, my purse becomes thinner, for you may well believe that I am getting ★ visibly fatter. Take care of yourselves. We kiss you many 100000000 times and I am your old

MZT

★

At the moment Wolfgang is playing the clavier, so he cannot write. We returned from Baden on Monday in time for lunch. All our friends there send their greetings to you. Fräulein Franzl has now recovered.

★

[1] Bimbes or Bimperl was the Mozarts' fox-terrier bitch.
[2] Perhaps Franz Kreibich, who was first violin in the Emperor Joseph II's string quartet.

(182) *Leopold Mozart to his Wife*

[*Extract*]   [*Autograph in the Mozarteum, Salzburg*]

VIENNA, 28 *August* 1773

We met Madame Rosa on Thursday evening on the Bastei, where we happened to be with Herr von Mölk. The good lady treated us very distantly, as she was arm in arm with a certain Rosa, painter of animals and inspector of picture galleries. We often go to see Mr. De L'Augier, who ★ sends greetings to both of you. Baden is a tiny town, where there are very many baths, like those of Gastein, but built more conveniently. Most of the houses are constructed so as to have rooms which can be let to visitors who want board and lodging. Frau Schultz, whose husband, poor old blind fellow, died in Baden, and who then married some good-natured idiot, is the principal comic actress at the theatre and now acts very well, although in her youth she was very mediocre. The Mesmers are at the ★ Rotmühle,[1] where Fräulein Franzl will probably fall ill again and possibly die. Not only she but also her sister are constantly at the Mesmers'. We ★ kiss you many 100,000,000 times and I am your old

MZT

★

Tomorrow we are lunching with Herr Noverre.[2] Herr Backer, the flautist, also sends his regards.

(183) *Leopold Mozart to his Wife*

[*Extract*]   [*Autograph in the Mozarteum, Salzburg*]

VIENNA, 4 *September* 1773

Now it is all up with the poor Jesuits! I call them poor, for only those who were the leaders, I mean, the rabbis and *corpus religionis*[3] as a whole, could be called rich. The ordinary members had nothing. The Jesuit monastery Auf Dem Hof must be cleared out by September 16th. The church treasure, their wine-cellars and, in fact, their entire property have already been sealed up, for the Jesuit Order has been suppressed. But they may dress as secular priests and it is said that each priest will have three hundred gulden a year, which is not so bad. If he gets Masses as well, a young Jesuit can find a pretty room and a nice housekeeper, for otherwise he will not have very much to do, as they will no longer be allowed to

---

[1] In Rannersdorf, near Schwechat.

[2] Jean Georges Noverre (1727–1810), a famous dancer and leader of the ballet at the Opéra-Comique in Paris. From 1753 he toured in France, Germany and Italy until finally in 1776 he settled for good in Paris as maître des ballets en chef at the Paris opera. He considerably improved the ballet by introducing dramatic action. See H. Abert, *Noverre und sein Einfluss auf die dramatische Ballettkomposition*, Jahrbuch Peters, 1908.   [3] i.e. religious order.

preach or to hear confession. The public is very much distressed. I hear that a Papal Brief is to be published to the effect that on pain of excommunication no one is to write or even speak a word against their suppression. On the other hand, many good Catholics are of the opinion that except in matters of faith His Holiness the Pope has no right to command and that it may truly be said that they would not have been interfered with if they had been as poor as the poor Capuchins. For in Rome they have already begun to appropriate Jesuit property *ad pias causas;*[1] but that was an easy matter, for even if the Pope takes it for himself, it is being used *ad causas pias.* The Viennese Court would not accept the first Papal Brief,[2] because, as I hear, it contained the statement, *that the possessions of the Jesuits should be used ad causas pias.* Well, as the Court refused to have laws dictated to it, His Holiness has given His Majesty a free hand to use the possessions of the Jesuits as he likes. Everything is still in great confusion and no one knows who will get the churches and the schools. And, be it noted, the same thing applies to all the Imperial territories.[3]

Herr Gassmann[4] has been ill, but is now better. I do not know how this will affect our stay in Vienna. Fools everywhere are but fools![5] We and all the others send greetings, and I am your old

MZT

We shall not stay here much longer. By the next post I shall write more about our plans. I must close. Wolfgang has no time to scribble anything, for we are almost missing the post.

(184) *Leopold Mozart to his Wife*

[Extract]   [Autograph in the Mozarteum, Salzburg]

VIENNA, *8 September* 1773

I am very much obliged to the citizens of Salzburg who are so anxious for my return. In that case I shall go back with greater pleasure and shall walk about the whole night in the illuminated town, so that the lights may not burn in vain. At least I shall find the lock in the hall door more easily, for I suppose that the illuminations will be so arranged that we shall have the good fortune to find a lantern at the street corner.

---

[1] i.e. for religious causes.

[2] Probably Leopold Mozart is referring to the famous Papal Brief 'Dominus ac Redemptor' of 21 July 1773.

[3] For a full account of the attitude of the Austrian court to the dissolution of the Jesuit order, see Ludwig Freiherr von Pastor, *Geschichte der Päpste*, 1932, vol. xvi., section 1, p. 191 ff.

[4] Florian Leopold Gassmann (1729–1774), who since 1772 had been Kapellmeister to the Viennese court, died on 20 January, 1774. His successor was Giuseppe Bonno (1710–1788).

[5] Leopold Mozart is alluding to the suspicions of some people in Salzburg who were connecting his son's visit to Vienna with Gassmann's illness.

God willing, I shall leave at the end of next week. But as I have often done this journey and have never been to Mariazell, it may be that I shall return home through that village and through St. Wolfgang,[1] in order to show our Wolfgang the pilgrimage church of his patron saint, which he has not yet seen, and St. Gilgen,[2] the famous birthplace of his mother. But whether we shall do this or not you will learn from my next letters. So, whatever happens, we shall arrive, God willing, during the week of September 24th or 25th.

★

(184a) *Mozart to his Mother*

[Autograph in the Mozarteum, Salzburg]

[VIENNA, 8 *September* 1773]

Little Wolfgang has no time to write, for he has nothing to do. He is walking up and down the room like a dog with fleas.

Concerto
per violino obbligato
e stromenti
del sig. Giuseppe Mysliwecek
detto il Boemo
= Basso =

That is what my writing-pad looks like.

(184b) *Leopold Mozart to his Wife*

[Autograph in the Mozarteum, Salzburg]

[VIENNA, 8 *September* 1773]

We both send greetings to all our good friends at home and elsewhere and we kiss you many 10000000 times and I remain your old

MZT

There will be some delay over the departure of the Jesuit Fathers until everything has been arranged. It is said that they may still act as Court preachers and so forth, provided that they go about as lay priests. I shall bring with me a printed copy of the Bull. The millions which the Church is getting from the Jesuits will whet its appetite and make it lay hands on the revenues of a few other religious orders.

---

[1] A small village on the Wolfgangsee, about 30 miles from Salzburg.
[2] Another village on the Wolfgangsee, where Nannerl went to live after her marriage in 1784.

(185) Leopold Mozart to his Wife

[Extract]   [Autograph in the Mozarteum, Salzburg]

VIENNA, 11 September 1773

The Jesuits are beginning to leave their monasteries. The Court Fathers, those who preached in the Stefanskirche, and six confessors left yesterday and will perform their duties next Sunday as usual, but in lay priests' clothes; for the order which has been issued to the higher Jesuits is that no one in the garb of a Jesuit may either hear confession or preach. Today I am too much out of humour and too stupid to write any more.[1] We kiss you many 100000 times and I am your old

MZT

(186) Leopold Mozart to his Wife

[Extract]   [Autograph in the Mozarteum, Salzburg]

VIENNA, 15 September 1773

The weather here is now becoming rather cool, especially in the morning and in the evening. On the whole, wine, fruit and vegetables have had a surprisingly good season and wine is actually being sold at six kreuzer per measure, solely in order to get empty vats. In Hungary there has been a glut of wheat, but the hay has been much poorer than usual. The Jesuit Fathers are already going about as lay priests in long black robes and cloaks with Italian collars.

His Majesty the Emperor, travelling from Poland through Moravia, arrived here last Monday morning shortly after seven o'clock. It was in a way a surprise, as he was not expected until October. It is a fact that the Russians have been thoroughly beaten a few times by the Turks, so that they now want to recall their troops in Poland.[2] Meanwhile the Prussians are to occupy the Russian portion of Poland. We and all our friends here send greetings to all of you, both at home and elsewhere. So far I have not been out to the Rotmühle, although the Mesmers have been there for a long time and Fräulein Franzl nearly died there again. We kiss you a million times and I am your old

MZT

---

[1] The first portion of this letter, which has been omitted, describes in detail the death of Dr. Niderl, a Salzburg doctor and a friend of the Mozart family, which Leopold Mozart felt very deeply.
[2] In 1773 Catherine the Great ordered Rumiantzov to cross the Danube, which he did, unwillingly, in June. He besieged Silistria but was obliged to retire and, harassed by the Turks, barely escaped disaster while recrossing the river. There is, however, no evidence for Leopold Mozart's statement that the Russians were obliged to withdraw their troops from that part of Poland which they were occupying as a result of the First Partition of 1772.

(186a) *Mozart to his Sister*

[*Autograph in the Mozarteum, Salzburg*]

[VIENNA, 15 *September* 1773[1]]

Praise and thanks be to God, we are quite well. Although we are busy, we are snatching some of our time to write to you. We hope that you are well too. Dr. Niderl's death made us very sad and indeed we wept, howled, groaned and moaned. Our regards to all good souls who praise the Lord God, and to all our good friends. We remain, yours graciously,

WOLFGANG

From our Residence, Vienna.[2]
15 September 1773.

(186b) *Mozart to Herr von Hefner*

[*Autograph in the Mozarteum, Salzburg*]

[VIENNA, 15 *September* 1773[3]]

To Herr von Hefner

I hope that we shall still find you in Salzburg,
                                        my friendly slug.
I hope that you are well and are not an enemy spi-
-der, for if so I'll be an enemy fly
or even a friendly bug.
So I strongly advise you to write better rhymes, for
if not, our Salzburg Cathedral will see me no more.
For I'm quite *capax*[4] to go off to Constant-
-inople, that city whose praises all chant.
And then you won't see me again nor I you; yet
when horses are hungry, some oats they get.

Farewell, my lad,	I'm ever to infinity
or else I'll go mad.	from now to all eternity.

(187) *Leopold Mozart to his Wife*

[*Extract*]   [*Autograph in the Mozarteum, Salzburg*]

VIENNA, 18 *September* 1773

For reasons which you will hear about on our arrival, we shall not be able to leave here before next Wednesday or Thursday. Thank God, we

---

[1] A postscript to his father's letter.
[2] Mozart is probably poking fun at the Salzburg Archbishop.
[3] An enclosure in his father's letter.   [4] i.e. able.

★ are well. The enclosure you sent me was from Mysliwecek in Naples. Nearly all the Jesuit Fathers have left their monasteries. Some brothers are already going about in lay apparel and have found employment as domestic servants. One has gone as butler to a convent, a few cleverer ones have become stewards and chamberlains, and the hunchbacked Jesuit apothecary is now apothecary in the Spanish hospital, where he is paid seven hundred gulden and is given full board.

★ We have not yet been able to go to the Rotmühle and I hardly think that we shall have time to do so. We kiss you many 10000000 times and I am your old

★   MZT

Wolfgang is composing something most enthusiastically.[1]

(188) *Leopold Mozart to his Wife*

[*Extract*]   [*Autograph in the Mozarteum, Salzburg*]

VIENNA, 22 *September* 1773

I see that I shall not be able to leave before Friday, or perhaps even Saturday. Today at last we drove out to the Rotmühle at about half past eleven in the morning and returned after seven in the evening. So it will be impossible to make all our arrangements tomorrow. Hence I shall probably leave on Saturday. All our friends send you their greetings! I cannot think of anything else to tell you. I am writing in great haste at the house of young Herr Mesmer, with whose wife we went to the Rotmühle.

Farewell to you all! I am hurrying so as not to miss the post. This will

★ be my last letter. We kiss you many 10000000 times and I am your old

                                                                                    MZT

[1] Either his string quartet K. 172 or, more probably, the choruses for Baron von Gebler's drama *Thamos, König von Ägypten*, K. 345 [33ba], a work which Mozart took up again in Salzburg in 1779. See WSF, vol. ii. p. 98 ff.

Mozart's ninth journey was to Munich, where he carried out a commission to write an opera buffa, La finta giardiniera, *for the 1774–1775 carnival season. His father accompanied him, and his sister Nannerl joined them three weeks later in order to see the first performance. This visit, which lasted from 6 December 1774 to 8 March 1775, is described in joint letters from father and son to Frau Mozart. Letters 189–203.*

(189) *Leopold Mozart to his Wife*

[*Extract*]   [*Copy in the Staatsbibliothek Preussischer Kulturbesitz, West Berlin*]

[MUNICH, 9 *December* 1774]

We reached Wasserburg at nine in the evening and, although we only left at eight o'clock next morning, we arrived safely in Munich on the following day, Wednesday, at about half past three in the afternoon.[1] Our lodging is small but quite comfortable. Herr von Pernat[2] shows us indeed more courtesy and honour than we deserve and it is quite evident that out of real friendship he is in many ways sacrificing his convenience to us. So far I have nothing to tell you about the opera.[3] We only made the acquaintance today of the people connected with it, all of whom, and in particular Count Seeau,[4] were very kind to us. Thank God, we are well. As to Nannerl, to whom I send greetings, I have nothing to write to you. Up to the present I have no prospect of finding a lodging for her. Besides we have been here too short a time. We kiss you both and I am your old

MOZART

★

(190) *Leopold Mozart to his Wife*

[*Extract*]   [*Autograph in the Mozarteum, Salzburg*]

MUNICH, 14 *December* 1774 ★

Thank God, we are well. I have not yet been able to find a suitable lodging for Nannerl, for one has to be very careful in Munich. Another difficulty has arisen, and in this respect Munich resembles Salzburg. An opera, for which the public has to pay, cannot be performed here more than twice in succession, for otherwise the attendance would be poor. So for two or three weeks other operas have to be performed and then the first one may be trotted out again, just as is done in the case of plays and ballets. Thus the singers know the parts of at least twenty operas which are performed in turn, and at the same time they study a new one. So Wolfgang's will not be produced before Christmas and probably the first performance will be on the 29th.[5] So it is possible that Nannerl may

---

[1] The Mozarts had left Salzburg on 6 December.

[2] The Mozarts were lodging with Johann Nepomuk von Pernat, canon of the Frauenkirche in Munich, who lived in Bellvall's house.

[3] Mozart's opera buffa *La finta giardiniera*, on a text thought to have been prepared by Marco Coltellini (see p. 83, n. 1) after Ranieri de' Calzabigi, Gluck's famous librettist. The libretto had already been set to music by Pasquale Anfossi and performed in Rome in 1774.

[4] Joseph Anton, Count von Seeau, Privy Councillor, was at that time Intendant or Controller of operatic and dramatic performances at the Electoral Court. From 1778 until his death in 1799 he was manager of the Munich National Theatre.

[5] *La finta giardiniera* was not performed until 13 January 1775.

not see it at all. For once the carnival is in full swing, only light and short operettas are performed on a small stage, which is rigged up in the Salle de Redoute. Here people gather in masks, here there are numbers of gambling tables and there is perpetual noise, conversation and gambling. Nothing sensible is ever performed there, because no one pays any attention. I shall tell you more about this later on. Please look up the two Litanies De Venerabili Altaris Sacramento, which are performed in the Hours. There is one of mine in D major (the score will surely be with it), a recent one which begins with the violin and double bass staccato (you know the one I mean); at the Agnus Dei the second violin has triplet notes the whole time. Then you will find Wolfgang's great Litany.[1] The score is with it, bound in blue paper. Make quite sure that all the parts are there, for these two Litanies are to be performed here in the Hours on New Year's Day. You should hand them in at the post on Saturday evening, for the mail coach leaves on Sunday. Write this address on the parcel:

À

Monsieur Jean Nepomuc de Pernat chanoine e
grand Custos de Notre Dame
à Munic

We kiss you many 1000 times and send greetings to everybody everywhere and I am your old

MZT.

(191) *Leopold Mozart to his Wife*

[*Extract*]   [*Autograph in the Mozarteum, Salzburg*]

MUNICH, 16 *December* 1774

I have now found a lodging for Nannerl, and where do you think it is? With Madame, or rather Widow von Durst, formerly the wife of a salt merchant at Reichenhall, whom Herr von Mölk drove over to visit so often and whom we frequently heard him mention. She is a young woman of about twenty-six or twenty-eight, a brunette, with dark eyes, very retiring, sensible and well read. She does not care for the society of philanderers and she is very courteous and pleasant. And who do you think helped me to find this lodging? Herr von Dufresne.[2] He asked me why I had not brought Nannerl with me and I told him that she would indeed have an opportunity of coming over to Munich with Madame von Robinig, but that, as we were now living with Herr von Pernat, I did not

---

[1] K. 125. Litaniae de venerabili altaris sacramento, composed in March 1772. It was modelled on his father's Litany.
[2] Franz Dufresne, a Munich Court Councillor.

know where to put her. He thought it over and finally said that he knew of a room in the house of Frau von Durst, that he would discuss it with her at the next opportunity and hear what she had to say, and that he was very hopeful, seeing that she lived quite alone and only received visits from her best friends and from his own parents. He then brought me the news that all would be well and that Madame Durst's only fear was lest Nannerl's presence might bring Herr von Bellvall back to her house, as she knew that he used to visit us in Salzburg; she did not mind his visiting Nannerl, but she was afraid that he might make it an excuse to start sitting on her doorstep later on. Her objection is quite justified; a young widow should not receive frequent visits from a man who is not living with his wife.

I went to see her myself today. Nannerl is to have a room of her own to sleep in, which, it is true, is rather dark, but she will spend the rest of the time in Frau von Durst's room, which looks out on the big market-place and where a harpsichord will be put for her.

Now I suppose that Nannerl will realise how silly it is not to be able to put on one's cap or make up one's face or perform other necessary duties by oneself. For one cannot always count on the services of other people. I very much suspect that Frau von Durst is accustomed to dress her own hair. So Nannerl must acquire the habit of putting on a négligé cap very neatly and of making up her face. She should also practise the clavier most diligently, especially the sonatas of Paradisi[1] and Bach,[2] and Lucchesi's[3] concerto and so forth. There is still no letter from you. We kiss you both and send greetings to all and I am your old

MZT

How is Miss Bimbes? Madame von Durst too has a small lap-dog, called, I think, Finette.

(191a) *Mozart to his Sister*

[Autograph in the Mozarteum, Salzburg]

[MUNICH, 16 *December* 1774[4]]

I have toothache.
Johannes Chrysostomus Wolfgangus Amadeus Sigismundus Mozartus

---

[1] Pietro Domenico Paradisi (*c.* 1710–1792). His twelve *Sonate di gravicembalo* had already been printed. Cp. p. 92, n. 4.
[2] Johann Christian Bach.
[3] Andrea Lucchesi (1741–1801), a Venetian, came in 1771 to Bonn, where he was appointed Kapellmeister in 1774. He composed eight operas, some church music, symphonies and violin sonatas.
[4] A postscript to his father's letter.

Mariae Annae Mozartae matri et sorori, ac amicis omnibus, praesertimque pulchris virginibus, ac freillibus, gratiosisque freillibus

S.P.D.[1]

(191b) *Leopold Mozart resumes writing*

[*Autograph in the Mozarteum, Salzburg*]

December 17th, in the morning

Wolfgang stayed at home yesterday as he had toothache, and he is staying indoors today as his cheek is swollen.

Nannerl should find an opportunity of telling Count Sauerau that she would like to go to Munich with Madame von Robinig and Herr Gschwendner. It is important that he should know of our arrangements. Addio. I hope that I shall have a letter from you today.

★

(192) *Leopold Mozart to his Wife*

[*Extract*]   [*Autograph in the Mozarteum, Salzburg*]

MUNICH, 21 *December* 1774

I have today received both your letter enclosing the two Litanies and another one from you. Nannerl must certainly have a fur rug for the journey, or she will not be able to stand the cold in a half-open coach. She must wrap up her head well and she must protect her feet with something more than her felt shoes only, which after a time do not keep out the cold. She ought therefore to slip on the fur boots which she will find in the trunk under the roof. Perhaps Herr Gschwendner will also be kind enough to put a little hay in the bottom of the coach. You remember how thoroughly we protected ourselves. Just think of the quantities of clothes which we wore. I had felt shoes over my boots and we had foot-bags and even so we should not have been able to stand the cold if at the third stage, Frabertsham, I had not had a large bundle of hay put into the coach and had our foot-bags completely surrounded and covered with it. For when the journey lasts a whole day, the cold goes right through one. In addition to the sonatas of Bach and Paradisi, Nannerl might also bring copies of Wolfgang's sonatas[2] and variations[3] and any other sonatas she likes, for they do not take up much room. She need not bring many concertos, for we have Wolfgang's concerto[4] here, and if she brings a few others, that

[1] Johannes Chrysostomus Wolfgang Amadeus Sigismund Mozart sends many greetings to Maria Anna Mozart, his mother and his sister, and to all his friends, and especially to pretty girls and Fräuleins and gracious Fräuleins. Salutem plurimam dicit.

[2] Recent research suggests that the five clavier sonatas, K. 279–283 [189d–h], which were thought to be referred to here, date from early 1775. See W. Plath, *Acta Mozartiana*, xxi (1974), p. 26. No more recent sonatas are known than K. App. 199–202 [K.33d–h].

[3] The two sets of clavier variations, K. 179 [189a] and K. 180 [173c], composed in 1774 and 1773 respectively.

[4] Probably K. 175, Mozart's first clavier concerto, which he composed in December 1773.

will be quite sufficient, for who knows whether she will use them at all. She must try to pack everything in one box, for she will not need many clothes for twelve days; and she will probably have to bring a hat-box, though indeed the latter will be a little inconvenient. However, one advantage is that women's clothes can be folded into a very small space. Wolfgang's swelling is now much better. Tomorrow, God willing, he will go out for the first time after spending six days indoors. We kiss you both and send greetings to all. Take care of yourselves. I am your old

MZT ★

In the writing case in the middle drawer above the desk (the drawer which does not close) you will find, I think, a little sheet of small music manuscript, on which are written only a few notes in Alle Breve time and here and there *pagina* and so on. The sheet contains a shortened form of the fugue *Pignus Futurae Gloriae* from Wolfgang's Litany.[1] If you find it, enclose it in a letter by the very next post. If you cannot find it in the drawer where the toy coach and horse are, then I do not know where it is.

I had a letter today from the Chief Steward about the commission which I received from His Grace and regarding which I have myself already written to him. The Archduke,[2] who is now in Paris, will hardly come to Munich before the end of March. The reference to Count Saurau was only if Nannerl should meet him, for I thought that he might pay you a visit. Perhaps she will come across him by chance. For that very reason no secret should be made of her visit, and you should say that Frau von Durst, widow of the salt merchant at Reichenhall, has invited her to stay with her.

(193) *Leopold Mozart to his Wife*

[*Extract*]   [*Autograph in the Mozarteum, Salzburg*]

[MUNICH, 28 December 1774]
On Holy Innocents' Day in the evening,
for the post leaves tomorrow at noon.

A Happy New Year!

On the very same day that you were both with Count Saurau, the first rehearsal of Wolfgang's opera took place at ten in the morning and was so well received that the first performance has been postponed until January 5th in order that the singers may learn their parts more thoroughly and thus, knowing the music perfectly, may act with greater confidence

---

[1] K. 125. See p. 250, n. 1.
[2] The Archduke Maximilian, the youngest son of the Empress Maria Theresia, in honour of whose visit to Salzburg in April 1775 Mozart was commissioned to write his opera *Il rè pastore*, on a text after Metastasio.

and not spoil the opera. To have got it ready by December 29th would have meant a fearful rush. As a musical composition it is indeed amazingly popular, and everything now depends on the stage production, which will, I trust, be a success, for the actors are not unfavourable to us. So it was a very fortunate occasion on which to inform Count Sauerau of Nannerl's journey and I am glad of this. I quite believe that these people are all very polite, for it is their policy to be so; but undoubtedly they suspect all sorts of things. You or Nannerl must go to Herr Hagenauer and ask him to give her a letter of credit for me to one of his agents in Munich. For even if a money present is given, it often does not come for some time and one cannot go on waiting for it. Even a present is sometimes not sent until later on. So I am not counting on getting anything, for all the arrangements here are very slow and there is often great confusion. You have only to explain this to Herr Joseph with my compliments. You will find in a leaden box some Spanish tobacco, with which Nannerl might fill a small snuff-box which she could bring with her, for my supply is coming to an end. In Wolfgang's drawer you will see an oval tobacco box, which she could use for this purpose. I again urge her to have a good fur rug and plenty of hay round her feet. Wolfgang has had to stay at home for six days with a swollen face. His cheek was swollen inside and outside and his right eye also. For two days he could only take some soup. So it is necessary to protect one's face and ears, for when you drive against the wind in a half-open coach, the air nips your face the whole time. And if you get into the coach without having your feet very warm, it is impossible to get them warm for the rest of the day. Nannerl will probably get in at Gschwendner's. So on the day before they leave, her felt boots should be brought to his house and hung up beside the stove, in order that they may be well warmed. She can then put them on when she gets into the coach. She should take some money with her for emergencies. Should anything further occur to me, you will hear it on Monday before her departure. But I cannot at the moment think of anything else. Farewell. We kiss you both and with greetings to all I am your old

MOZART

★

(193a) *Mozart to his Sister*

[Autograph in the Mozarteum, Salzburg]

[MUNICH, 28 December 1774[1]]

MY DEAREST SISTER,

I beg you not to forget to keep your promise before you leave, I mean, to pay the call we both know of . . . for I have my reasons. I beg

---

[1] A postscript to his father's letter.

you to convey my greetings there—but in the most definite way—in the most tender fashion—and—oh, I need not be so anxious, for of course I know my sister and how extremely tender she is. I am quite certain that she will do her utmost to do me a kindness—and for her own advantage too—but that is rather nasty. But we shall quarrel about this in Munich. Farewell.

(194) *Leopold Mozart to his Wife*

[*Autograph in the Mozarteum, Salzburg*]

MUNICH, 30 *December* 1774

When you read this letter Nannerl will have almost finished packing. So I must tell you quickly that there is something else which she will have to bring, but it is a trifle and the only condition is that it should lie flat. For I should like to have five or six copies of the copper engraving of our Paris portrait.[1] Herr von Pernat insists on having one, and so do one or two other good friends. You will find them in the drawer with all the other engravings, on the right hand side and almost on the top. But they must lie perfectly flat and not become bent. I forgot to mention too that Nannerl ought to bring a fancy dress, even if it is only a Salzburg peasant dress. I am sorry that I did not think of this sooner, but she would only be able to get a domino here. Perhaps, however, you have seen to this. We were with the Imperial Ambassador today, who was very friendly and gracious to us. You have probably sent off some New Year cards. I hope you have not forgotten Count Sauerau and Countess von Lodron. I have written to the Archbishop to wish him a happy New Year. Nannerl will arrive just in time for the opera, for she will get here on Wednesday afternoon and it is being performed on Thursday.[2] If Herr von Mölk comes too, he will see it; but if he postpones his visit, he will not do so until Easter, for after January 5th no more operas will be performed in the theatre. In the Salle de Redoute only operettas, or rather intermezzi,[3] are given, during which, however, hundreds of masks stroll around, chatter, jest and gamble at the different tables. Thus no serious work can be performed. You must know that this time last year Maestro Tozzi,[4] who this year is writing the opera seria, wrote an opera buffa, and contrived to write it so well that it killed the opera seria written by Maestro Sales.[5] Now it so happens that Wolfgang's opera is being performed

[1] The Carmontelle portrait of the Mozart family, painted in the autumn of 1763.
[2] 5 January. Actually Mozart's opera was not performed until 13 January.
[3] i.e. opere buffe in one or two acts.
[4] Antonio Tozzi was Kapellmeister at the Munich court. His opera seria for 1775 was *Orfeo ed Euridice*. In Einstein's opinion Tozzi's opera buffa for 1774 was probably *La serva astuta*.
[5] Pietro Pompeo Sales (c. 1729–1797), born at Brescia, was first in the service of the Bishop of Augsburg and in 1768 became Kapellmeister to the Elector at Coblenz. He composed operas, oratorios, church music, symphonies and concertos. His opera seria for 1774 was *Achille in Sciro*.

before Tozzi's, and when people heard the first rehearsal, they all said that Tozzi was being paid back in his own coin, for Wolfgang's opera would certainly kill his. I do not like these bickerings. I try as far as possible to suppress such remarks and I keep on protesting. But the whole orchestra and all who have heard the rehearsal say that they have never listened to a finer composition, for it is one in which all the arias are beautiful. And wherever we go, the same thing is said. Basta! God will make everything right. Farewell. I wish Nannerl a good journey. We kiss you both, send our greetings to all and I am your old

MOZART

(194a) *Mozart to his Sister*

[Autograph in the Mozarteum, Salzburg]

[MUNICH, 30 *December* 1774[1]]

I present my compliments to Roxelana, and invite her to take tea this evening with the Sultan. Please give all sorts of messages to Jungfrau Mitzerl,[2] and tell her that she must never doubt my love. I see her constantly before me in her ravishing négligée.[3] I have seen many pretty girls here, but have not yet found such a beauty. My sister must not forget to bring with her Eckardt's variations sur le menuet d'Exaudet[4] and my variations on Fischer's minuet.[5] I went to the theatre yesterday to see the 'Mode nach der Haushaltung',[6] which was very well acted. My greetings to all my good friends. I hope that you will—farewell—I see you soon in Munich to hope. I have compliments to deliver to you from Frau von Durst. Is it true that Hagenauer has been appointed Professor of Sculpture in Vienna?[7] Herr von Mölk said so in a letter to Father Wasenau and the letter read out Father Wasenau to me. My mother's hand I kiss, the rest she'll have to miss. I beg you to keep very warm on the journey, or else for a fortnight at home you'll sit and beside the stove perspire a bit and

---

[1] A postscript to his father's letter.

[2] Fräulein Maria Raab, the elderly owner of the Mozarts' house in the Makartplatz, into which they had moved in 1773. She lived next door.

[3] Mozart means 'with her hair undressed'.

[4] These variations had been engraved in Paris in 1764.

[5] K. 179 [189a]. These twelve variations were composed in 1774 on a theme from the last movement of an oboe concerto written by Johann Christian Fischer (1733–1800), a famous oboist, who, after prolonged tours on the Continent, finally settled in London. He married Gainsborough's daughter. Mozart heard him play in Holland in 1765 (see Leopold Mozart's *Reiseaufzeichnungen*, p. 42, *MBA*, No. 105), and again in Vienna in 1787. See p. 907, n. 3.

[6] Mozart is referring in jest to *Die Haushaltung nach der Mode, oder Was soll man für eine Frau nehmen?*, a comedy written in 1765 by Franz von Heufeld (1731–1795), who in 1769 became manager of the German theatre in Vienna. Possibly Mozart had already seen this comedy during his family's visit to Vienna in 1768.

[7] Johann Baptist Hagenauer, court sculptor in Salzburg, had moved in 1774 to Vienna, where he did some work for the Schönbrunn Palace and was appointed Professor of Sculpture.

not a soul will protect you one whit. But I simply refuse to have a fit; and now the lightning's beginning to spit.

Your Munich
brother, the 1774th day of Anno 30, Decembre.

(195) *Leopold Mozart to his Wife*

[*Autograph in the Mozarteum, Salzburg*]

MUNICH, 5 *January* 1775

Nannerl reached Munich yesterday before two in the afternoon quite safely, but we could not be there when she arrived, as we were the guests of Herr von Gilowsky at Störzer's, where lunch is not served until half past one. So we first saw the Robinigs, who came to Störzer's just as we were having our meal. But I had already sent out Herr von Pernat's servant who was waiting for them at the bridge in the Thal¹ and brought them straight to Frau von Durst, at whose house Herr von Dufresne had already turned up. That evening we were with Nannerl until eight o'clock and today I sent the servant to fetch her for coffee with us. She is drinking some with Wolfgang this very moment, and I have been drinking my tea. Then I am sending her back, as Frau von Durst goes to church with her and wants to take her to a different church every day. You will have heard from Herr Schulz that Wolfgang's opera is not being performed until the 13th. There is a rumour here that the Archbishop is coming over to Munich, and even Count Seeau told me this. Otherwise I have no news. Lock up the rooms carefully so that nothing may be stolen, for when you go out something might easily happen. My greetings to Jungfrau Mitzerl and to everybody. We all three kiss you and I am your old

MOZART

(195a) *Nannerl Mozart to her Mother*

[*Autograph in the Mozarteum, Salzburg*]

[MUNICH, 5 *January* 1775²]

I have arrived safely in Munich and was so well cared for during the entire journey that it was impossible to feel cold. I slept with Fräulein Louise³ in Frau von Robinig's bedroom and we had lunch and supper en

---

¹ A street in Munich between the Isarthor and the Rathaus.
² A postscript to her father's letter.   ³ A daughter of Frau Robinig.

compagnie with Frau von Robinig. Meanwhile I hope that Mamma is well. I kiss Mamma's hand and with my brother, that blackguard,

I am

your most obedient daughter

MARIE ANNE MOZART

(196) *Mozart to his Mother*

[*Autograph in the Mozarteum, Salzburg*]

MUNICH, 11 *January* 1775

Thank God, all three of us are quite well. It is impossible for me to write a long letter, as I am off this very moment to a rehearsal of my opera. Tomorrow we are having the dress rehearsal and the performance takes place on Friday, the 13th. Mamma must not worry; it will go off quite well. I am very much distressed that Mamma should suspect ⟨Count Seeau,⟩ for he is certainly a charming and courteous gentleman and has more savoir vivre than many of his class in Salzburg. We were at the masked concert yesterday. Herr von Mölk was so astounded and crossed himself so often as he listened to the opera seria, that we were absolutely ashamed of him, for everyone could see quite clearly that he had never been anywhere but to Salzburg and Innsbruck. Addio. I kiss Mamma's hands.

WOLFGANG

(196a) *Leopold Mozart to his Wife*

[*Autograph in the Mozarteum, Salzburg*]

[MUNICH, 11 *January* 1775[1]]

I hope that you are quite well. I have nothing to write about except to send our greetings to everyone. We are off now to the rehearsal of the opera. It is true that the Archbishop informed the Elector that he would come, but no one knows when this will be, whether now or in the spring. Farewell. We kiss you many 10,000 times and I am your old

MZT

Up to the present it seems that there is every likelihood that Wolfgang will compose the grand opera here this time next year.

---

[1] A postscript to Mozart's letter.

(197) *Mozart to his Mother*

[Autograph in the Mozarteum, Salzburg]

MUNICH, 14 *January* 1775

Thank God! My opera was performed yesterday, the 13th, for the first time and was such a success that it is impossible for me to describe the applause to Mamma. In the first place, the whole theatre was so packed that a great many people were turned away. Then after each aria there was a terrific noise, clapping of hands and cries of 'Viva Maestro'. Her Highness the Electress and the Dowager Electress (who were sitting opposite me) also called out 'Bravo' to me. After the opera was over and during the pause when there is usually silence until the ballet begins, people kept on clapping all the time and shouting 'Bravo'; now stopping, now beginning again and so on. Afterwards I went off with Papa to a certain room through which the Elector and the whole Court had to pass and I kissed the hands of the Elector and Electress and Their Highnesses, who were all very gracious. Early this morning His Grace the Bishop of Chiemsee[1] sent me a message, congratulating me on the extraordinary success of my opera. I fear that we cannot return to Salzburg very soon and Mamma must not wish it, for she knows how much good it is doing me to be able to breathe freely.[2] We shall come home soon enough. One very urgent and necessary reason for our absence is that next Friday my opera is being performed again and it is most essential that I should be present. Otherwise my work would be quite unrecognizable—for very strange things happen here. I kiss Mamma's hands 1000 times. My greetings to all my good friends. My compliments to M. Andretter and I beg him to forgive me for not yet replying, but it has been impossible for me to find the time. However, I shall do so very soon. Adieu. 1000 kisses to Bimberl.

(197a) *Leopold Mozart to his Wife*

[Autograph in the Mozarteum, Salzburg]

[MUNICH, 14 *January* 1775[3]]

You must have received two letters from me and one from Nannerl. I do not yet know how Nannerl will return to Salzburg nor whether she

---

[1] Count Ferdinand Christoph von Zeill (1719–1786), Bishop of Chiemsee. He was a candidate for the Archbishopric of Salzburg in 1772, but retired in favour of Hieronymus Colloredo, Bishop of Gurk. He was a connoisseur and patron of music and was very partial to Mozart.

[2] Mozart is alluding to the tyrannical attitude of the Archbishop.

[3] A postscript to Mozart's letter.

can travel with Frau von Robinig. Perhaps she will wait and come back with us. Farewell. We kiss you many 1000000 times and I am your old

MOZART

I have received all your letters.
My greetings to all.

(198) *Leopold Mozart to his Wife*

[*Extract*] [*Autograph in the Mozarteum, Salzburg*]

MUNICH, 18 *January* 1775

My last letter and other letters which must have been written to Salzburg will have told you that the opera has won general applause; and you will now have heard it from Herr Gschwendner in person. Picture to yourself the embarrassment of His Grace the Archbishop at hearing the opera praised by the whole family of the Elector and by all the nobles, and at receiving the enthusiastic congratulations which they all expressed to him. Why, he was so embarrassed that he could only reply with a bow of the head and a shrug of the shoulders. We have not yet spoken to him, for he is still too much taken up by the compliments of the nobility. He arrived about half past six in the evening just as the grand opera had begun and entered the Elector's box. It would take too long if I were to describe all the other ceremonies. The Archbishop will not hear Wolfgang's opera buffa, because, as all the other days are already filled up, it will be given on a Friday. But it cannot be performed on this coming Friday, as it is the anniversary of the death of the late Bavarian Emperor.[1] And who knows whether it can be performed on the following Friday, the 27th, as the second woman singer[2] is very ill. I am sorry that so many people have come over from Salzburg for what one may call nothing, but at least they will have seen the grand opera. It is not known yet whether the Archbishop will leave tomorrow or will stay on until next Tuesday. Addio. We kiss you many 1000000 times and I am your old

MOZART

I understand that there will be a big concert in the Kaisersaal on Saturday and that the Archbishop will probably stay on here until Monday or Tuesday.

---

[1] Emperor Charles VII, who died on 20 January 1745. He was the father of the reigning Elector Maximilian III.
[2] Probably Teresina Manservisi.

(198a) *Mozart to his Sister*

[*Autograph in the Mozarteum, Salzburg*]

MY DEAR SISTER!   [MUNICH, 18 *January* 1775[1]]

Is it my fault that it has just struck a quarter past seven? It is not Papa's fault either. Mamma will hear more news from my sister. But now there is no pleasure in travelling because the Archbishop is not staying here for long. It is even said that he will remain on until he leaves again. I am only sorry that he will not see the first Ridotto. My compliments to Baron Zemen and to all my good friends. I kiss Mamma's hands. Farewell. I shall fetch you very soon.

Your faithful
FRANCIS WITH THE BLEEDING NOSE

Milan, 5 May 1756.[2]

(199) *Leopold Mozart to his Wife*

[*Extract*]   [*Autograph in the Mozarteum, Salzburg*]

MUNICH, 21 January 1775

That the gentlemen of Salzburg are gossiping so much and are convinced that Wolfgang has entered the service of the Elector, is due to our enemies and to those whose conscience tells them that if he had done so, it would have been with good reason. You know well that we are accustomed to these childish stories and that such talk leaves me quite cold. So you can tell that to everyone. His Grace will certainly not leave before next Wednesday. The two Dukes of Zweibrücken and the Elector of the ★ Palatinate are coming over to Munich, so we must stay on until the opera has been performed a second time. This morning Nannerl and a valet of ★ the Elector, accompanied by Barbara Eberlin and a few others, drove off in a court carriage to Nymphenburg to see the castle rooms. They are lunching there. Then at three o'clock Nannerl is coming with me to the Court to see the rooms, the jewels and so forth. The Hagenauers will, no doubt, have heard something from Munich about Wolfgang's opera. Go and see them and give them my greetings. All possible honours are being showered on the Archbishop and his retinue. Thank God, we are well and we hope and trust that you are also. We kiss you many 1000000 times and send our greetings to all and I am your old

MOZART

---

[1] A postscript to his father's letter.
[2] This postscript with its nonsensical date was really intended for his mother, as Nannerl was still in Munich.

They rightly fear in Salzburg lest one bird after another may fly away, since Hagenauer Statuarius[1] has also taken another appointment. Addio. Farewell. Tell me everything you hear, and we shall have something to laugh about, for we know these fools.

(200) *Leopold Mozart to his Wife*

[*Extract*]   [*Autograph in the Mozarteum, Salzburg*]

MUNICH, 8 *February* 1775

★   Thank God, we are well. Herr Kempfer left yesterday for Augsburg after performing before the Elector and spending a week in Munich. A few rascals have been here too. One was a teacher of English, born in Silesia, Schwarz by name. He was here for almost a year and then decamped with watches and clothes, leaving many debts behind him. The other made out that he was the son of Schmittmeyer, the rich banker in Vienna, and spent a few weeks here. But he cleared out when it was discovered that he was the son of an innkeeper of Nikolsburg in Moravia. He is probably now under arrest in Augsburg. We all kiss you. Farewell. I am your old

MOZART

We send greetings to all.
Count Wolfegg is here too and the two young Counts von Zeill.

(201) *Leopold Mozart to his Wife*

[*Extract*]   [*Autograph in the Mozarteum, Salzburg*]

MUNICH, 15 *February* 1775

★   Thank God, all three of us are well, but I shall be glad when this
★   carnival is over. We shall probably travel home on Ash Wednesday. A short Mass by Wolfgang was performed last Sunday in the Court chapel and I conducted it. Next Sunday another is to be performed.[2] Yesterday we had extraordinary weather, just like April, now fine now rainy. At one o'clock there was a fire alarm, for the fire was coming out of the chimney and was already very fierce. But it was put out at once by the crowd. We are not going to the Redoute today, as we really must rest. It is the first one that we have missed. Yesterday Nannerl wore the dress of an Amazon, which suited her very well. As a daily diary is being kept, you

---

[1] See p. 256, n. 7.
[2] K. 192 [186f] and, probably, K. 194 [186h], which were composed in 1774.

will have everything read out to you in due course.[1] Farewell. We all kiss you many 100000 times and send greetings to everyone, and I am your old

MOZART

(202) *Leopold Mozart to his Wife*

[Extract]   [*Autograph in the Mozarteum, Salzburg*]

MUNICH, 21 *February* 1775

I shall be delighted when this carnival is over. I am really tired out, for it is lasting far too long. Signor Tozzi,[2] who composed the opera 'Orfeo', has decamped. He had a prolonged love affair with Countess von Seefeld, whose brother, Count Sedlizky, was in the know, as was also an Italian tenor, Signor Guerrieri. The Countess left Munich six weeks ago on the pretext of visiting her estates, but what she really did was to run away from her husband and children, taking a great deal of money and jewelry with her. Thank God, we are well, and hope to be in Salzburg on the ★ first Sunday in Lent. Farewell. We send greetings to all, kiss you many 10000000 times and I am your old

MZT

The first masked Redoute in Salzburg will have gone off well. You simply must go to one! Addio.

(202★) *Nannerl Mozart to her Mother*

[*Autograph in the Mozarteum, Salzburg*]

[MUNICH, *end of February* 1775[3]]

Thank God we are quite well. I hope that Mamma too is very well.

A propos, are the canary, the tomtits and the robin redbreast still alive, or have they let the birds starve? We shall come home at the end of the carnival. Meanwhile my pupils must go on practising, and perhaps Herr Schulz would be so kind as to go to Barbara Zezi a few times a week, and, if he will, to Fräulein Andretter, and hear them play their pieces.

---

[1] There is clear evidence that the keeping of diaries was a habit of the Mozart family. For instance, we have Nannerl's *Reisetagebuch*, kept during their grand tour, 1763–1766, and fragments of diaries kept jointly by Nannerl and Wolfgang from 1775–1777, 1779–1780 and 1783. All this material is in *MBA*.

[2] See p. 255, n. 4.

[3] This and the following note were previously thought to have been sent with Letter 202, but must date from the end of February, the approximate date of the performance mentioned by Leopold Mozart in Letter 202a.

(202a) *Leopold Mozart to his Wife*

Some people have come to see us, so I can only write to you in a great hurry that I and, thank God, we all are well. I am sorry for poor Marschall.[1] Wolfgang's opera has been performed again, but on account of the woman singer who was ill, it had to be cut short. I could write a great deal about this singer, who was absolutely wretched, but I shall tell you all about her when I see you. Farewell. Do go to the ball in the Town Hall. We kiss you many 10000 times. My greetings to all. I am your old

                                                                    MZT

We hope to leave here in about a fortnight. We are never at home the whole day long.

(203) *Leopold Mozart to his Wife*

[*Extract*]   [*Autograph in the Mozarteum, Salzburg*]

                                                          Ash Wednesday
                                                   [MUNICH, 1 *March*] 1775

Thank God, the carnival is over. We have now fixed our departure for Monday, the 6th, so we shall arrive in Salzburg rather late in the evening of Tuesday the 7th, for on the first day we are only travelling as far as Wasserburg. Should our arrival be postponed for a day, you will receive a letter on Tuesday or perhaps even on Monday morning. We are to bring with us from Munich a young lady, who would like to stay with us for three or four months and improve her harpsichord playing. Up to the present I have refused this. But in the meantime you might think out where we could get some bedding, for, if necessary, we shall have to put up a bed near the door in Nannerl's room, where the red sofa stands; and the sofa will have to be placed in front of the stove between your clothes-chest and the bed, so that we can put things on it. But I hope that nothing will come of this; and what I am saying is only by way of warning. If it has to be, as I hope it will not, I shall write to you by the next post. I am very much pleased that Herr Lotter has sent me something, for there is now a big hole in my purse. Otherwise, thank God, we are well; and we all three hope to see you and kiss you with delight. You may tell everyone the story of Tozzi and Countess Seefeld, so that people may realize that Italians are knaves the world over. For the last few days we have had most beautiful weather. Wolfgang's opera is to be performed on Thursday. Farewell. We all three kiss you many millions of times and I am your old

                                                                    MZT

---

[1] Jakob Anton Marschall, a cellist in the Salzburg court orchestra, who died in February 1775. See Hammerle, *op. cit.* p. 33.

(204) Leopold Mozart to J. G. I. Breitkopf, Leipzig

[Extract]   [Autograph in the Staatsbibliothek Preussischer Kulturbesitz, West Berlin]

[SALZBURG, 6 October 1775] ★

As I decided some time ago to have some of my son's compositions
printed, I should like you to let me know as soon as possible whether you
would like to publish some of them, that is to say, symphonies, quartets,
trios, sonatas for violin and violoncello, even solo sonatas for violin or
clavier sonatas. In regard to the latter perhaps you would like to print
clavier sonatas in the same style as those of Carl Philipp Emanuel Bach
'mit veränderten Reprisen'? These were printed by Georg Ludwig Winter
in Berlin,[1] and this type of sonata is very popular. I must ask you again to
let me know as soon as possible and, what is more, on what conditions you
would undertake to publish them, so that we may not engage in a long
correspondence about a trifling business and so that, if nothing comes of
my suggestion, I may apply to some other firm. I shall be very grateful if
you will send me a list of all the works of Carl Philipp Emanuel Bach ★
which you can supply.

Your obedient servant

LEOPOLD MOZART

Do you ever hear from our friend Herr Grimm in Paris? I have not had
a letter from him for over a year. Have you sold the sonatas which my
son composed as a child and the portraits?

(205) Mozart to Padre Martini, Bologna

[MS in the Nationalbibliothek, Vienna]

[SALZBURG, 4 September 1776[2]]

MOST REVEREND PADRE MAESTRO, MY ESTEEMED PATRON,

The regard, the esteem and the respect which I cherish for your
illustrious person have prompted me to trouble you with this letter and to
send you a humble specimen of my music, which I submit to your
masterly judgment. I composed for last year's carnival at Munich an
opera buffa, 'La finta giardiniera'. A few days before my departure the
Elector expressed a desire to hear some of my contrapuntal compositions.

---

[1] C. P. E. Bach's *Sechs Sonaten fürs Clavier mit veränderten Reprisen* were published by Georg
Ludwig Winter, Berlin, 1760.
[2] This letter is in Italian, in the hand of Leopold Mozart (see W. Plath, *Mozart-Jahrbuch
1960/1*, p. 84).

I was therefore obliged to write this motet¹ in a great hurry, in order to have time to have the score copied for His Highness and to have the parts written out and thus enable it to be performed during the Offertory at High Mass on the following Sunday. Most beloved and esteemed Signor Padre Maestro! I beg you most earnestly to tell me, frankly and without reserve, what you think of it.² We live in this world in order to learn industriously and, by interchanging our ideas, to enlighten one another and thus endeavour to promote the sciences and the fine arts. Oh, how often have I longed to be near you, most Reverend Father, so that I might be able to talk to and have discussion with you. For I live in a country where music leads a struggling existence, though indeed apart from those who have left us, we still have excellent teachers and particularly composers of great wisdom, learning and taste. As for the theatre, we are in a bad way for lack of singers. We have no castrati, and we shall never have them, because they insist on being handsomely paid; and generosity is not one of our faults. Meanwhile I am amusing myself by writing chamber music and music for the church,³ in which branches of composition we have two other excellent masters of counterpoint, Signori Haydn⁴ and Adlgasser.⁵ My father is in the service of the Cathedral and this gives me an opportunity of writing as much church music as I like. He has already served this court for thirty-six years and as he knows that the present Archbishop cannot and will not have anything to do with people who are getting on in years, he no longer puts his whole heart into his work, but has taken up literature, which was always a favourite study of his. Our church music is very different from that of Italy, since a mass with the whole Kyrie, the Gloria, the Credo, the Epistle sonata,⁶ the Offertory or Motet, the Sanctus and the Agnus Dei must not last longer than three quarters of an hour. This applies even to the most Solemn Mass said by the Archbishop himself. So you see that a special study is required for this kind of composition. At the same time, the mass must have all the instruments—trumpets, drums and so forth. Alas, that we are so far apart, my very dear Signor Padre Maestro! If we were together, I should have so many things to tell you! I send my devoted remembrances to all the members of the Accademia Filarmonica.⁷ I long to win your favour and

¹ K. 222 [205a], 'Misericordias Domini', performed in Munich on 5 March 1775.
² In his reply, dated 18 December 1776, Padre Martini praises highly Mozart's composition, adding that 'it has all the qualities which modern music demands, good harmony, rich modulation, etc.' See Köchel, p. 228.
³ During the year 1776 Mozart composed several divertimenti, church sonatas, a Litany (K. 243) and three masses (K. 257, 258, 259).
⁴ See p. 78, n. 1.   ⁵ See p. 26, n. 3.
⁶ While the priest read the Epistle, the organist played softly a sonata with or without violin accompaniment. This practice, which prevailed in Italian church services, was first introduced into Austria during the reign of the Emperor Joseph II.
⁷ The Accademia Filarmonica of Bologna, of which Mozart had been made a member in October 1770.

I never cease to grieve that I am far away from that one person in the world whom I love, revere and esteem most of all and whose most humble and devoted servant, most

Reverend Father, I shall always be.

WOLFGANGO AMADEO MOZART

If you condescend to write to me, please address your letter to Salzburg via Trento.

● (206) *Mozart to Archbishop Hieronymus Colloredo*

[*MS in the Landesarchiv, Salzburg*[1]]

[SALZBURG, 1 *August* 1777]

YOUR GRACE, MOST WORTHY PRINCE OF THE HOLY ROMAN EMPIRE!

I will not presume to trouble Your Grace with a full description of our unhappy circumstances, which my father has set forth most accurately in his very humble petition[2] which was handed to you on March 14th, 1777. As, however, your most gracious decision was never conveyed to him, my father intended last June once more most respectfully to beg Your Grace to allow us to travel for a few months in order to enable us to make some money; and he would have done so, if you had not given orders that in view of the imminent visit of His Majesty the Emperor your orchestra should practise various works with a view to their performance. Later my father again applied for leave of absence, which Your Grace refused to grant, though you permitted me, who am in any case only a half-time servant, to travel alone. Our situation is pressing and my father has therefore decided to let me go alone. But to this course also Your Grace has been pleased to raise certain objections. Most Gracious Prince and Lord! Parents endeavour to place their children in a position to earn their own bread; and in this they follow alike their own interest and that of the State. The greater the talents which children have received from God, the more are they bound to use them for the improvement of their own and their parents' circumstances, so that they may at the same time assist them and take thought for their own future progress. The Gospel teaches us to use our talents in this way. My conscience tells me that I owe it to God to be grateful to my father, who has spent his time unwearyingly upon my education, so that I may lighten his burden, look after myself and later on be able to support my sister. For I should be sorry to think that she should have spent so many hours at the harpsichord and not be able to make good use of her training.

---

[1] This letter is in Leopold Mozart's hand.
[2] Not extant.

Your Grace will therefore be so good as to allow me to ask you most humbly for my discharge, of which I should like to take advantage before the autumn, so that I may not be obliged to face the bad weather during the ensuing winter months. Your Grace will not misunderstand this petition, seeing that when I asked you for permission to travel to Vienna three years ago,[1] you graciously declared that I had nothing to hope for in Salzburg and would do better to seek my fortune elsewhere. I thank Your Grace for all the favours I have received from you and, in the hope of being able to serve you later on with greater success, I am

your most humble and obedient servant
WOLFGANG AMADE MOZART[2]

[1] Mozart is probably referring to his visit to Vienna in the summer of 1773.

[2] The Archbishop's minute, dated 28 August 1777, is as follows: 'To the Court Chamberlain with my decision that in the name of the Gospel father and son have my permission to seek their fortune elsewhere'. Leopold Mozart, however, was retained in his appointment. See p. 281.

In September 1777 Mozart, who, owing to his strained relations with the Archbishop of Salzburg, Hieronymus Colloredo, saw no prospect of advancement in his native town, set off with his mother on a tour of the musical centres of Southern Germany in the hope of securing commissions or possibly obtaining a permanent appointment at some court. Their first visit was to Munich, where Mozart soon realized that there was no opening for him. They left for Augsburg on October 11th. Letters 207–220.

(207) *Mozart to his Father*

[*Autograph in the Mozarteum, Salzburg*]

[WASSERBURG], 23 *September* 1777

MON TRÉS CHER PÉRE,

Praise and thanks be to God, we arrived safely at Waging, Stein, Frabertsham and Wasserburg. Now for a brief account of our journey. When we reached the town gates we had to wait for nearly a quarter of an hour until they were opened for us, for some work was being done there. Outside Schinn we came across a herd of cows, one of which was most remarkable—for she was *lop-sided*, a thing we had never seen before. At Schinn we saw a carriage which was at a standstill and behold—our postillion shouted out: 'We must change here'. 'As you like', said I. As Mamma and I were chatting, a fat gentleman, whose *symphony*[1] I recognised immediately, came up to our carriage. He was a merchant from Memmingen.[2] He looked at me for some time and finally said: 'You are Herr Mozart, are you not?' 'At your service', I replied. 'I know you too, but cannot remember your name. I saw you a year ago at a concert in Mirabell.' Whereupon he told me his name, but, thank Heaven, I have forgotten it. But I have retained one which is much more important. For when I saw him at Salzburg he had a young man with him, and on this occasion he was travelling with that young man's brother, who comes from Memmingen and is called Herr von Unhold. This young gentleman pressed me to go to Memmingen, if it were possible. We asked them to deliver 100000 compliments to Papa and to my brute of a sister, which they promised to do. This change of carriages was very inconvenient for me, for I should have liked to give a letter to the postillion to take back from Waging. After we had eaten something there, we then had the honour of continuing our journey as far as Stein with the same horses with which we had already driven for an hour and a half. At Waging I was alone for a moment with the priest, who was amazed to see us, for he had heard nothing whatever about our story.[3] From Stein we travelled with a postillion who was a perfectly dreadful phlegmaticus—*as a driver, I mean*. We thought we should never reach the next stage, but we got there eventually. As I write this letter, Mamma is already half asleep. From Frabertsham to Wasserburg everything went well. Viviamo come i principi.[4] Only one person is wanting—and that is Papa. Ah well, it is God's will. All will yet be well. I hope that Papa is well and as happy as I

---

[1] i.e. ensemble, or Mozart perhaps means his demeanour.
[2] Herr von Krimmel, as will be seen later. See p. 291, n. 2.
[3] i.e. the strained relations between the Archbishop and Mozart and his father.
[4] We are living like princes.

am. I am most attentive to my duty. I am quite a second Papa, for I see to everything. I have begged Mamma to let me pay the postillions, for I can deal with these fellows better than she can. At the Stern here they do you extraordinarily well. Why, I am sitting here as if I were a prince. Half an hour ago (Mamma happened to be in the closet) the porter knocked at the door and asked me about all sorts of things, and I answered him with my most serious air, looking just as I do in my portrait.[1] Well, I must stop. Mamma has now finished undressing. We both of us beg Papa to take care of his health, not to go out too early and not to worry, but to laugh heartily and be merry and always remember, as we do, that our Mufti H.C.[2] is an idiot, but that God is compassionate, merciful and loving. I kiss Papa's hands 1000 times and embrace my brute of a sister as often as I have already taken snuff today. I believe I have left my diplomas[3] at home? Please send them to me as soon as you can.

Early in the morning, about half past six on
            September 24th.
                Your most obedient son
                        WOLFGANG AMADÉ MOZART

PS.—My pen is rough and I am not polite.
    Wasserburg, 23 September 1777.
        undecima hora nocte tempore.[4]

(208) *Leopold Mozart to his Wife and Son*

[Extract]   [*Autograph in the Mozarteum, Salzburg*]

MY TWO DEAR ONES!   SALZBURG, 25 *September* 1777

I received dear Wolfgang's letter this morning with the greatest pleasure; and just now Bullinger[5], who sends his greetings, has read it and laughed most heartily: When you are well I am extremely happy, and, thank Heaven, I myself am now very much better. After you both had left, I walked up our steps very wearily and threw myself down on a chair. When we said good-bye, I made great efforts to control myself in order not to make our parting too painful; and in the rush and flurry I forgot to give my son a father's blessing. I ran to the window and sent my blessing after you; but I did not see you driving out through the gate and so came to the conclusion that you were gone already, as I had sat for

---

[1] During the summer of 1777 a portrait of Mozart was painted by an unknown artist in Salzburg. Mozart looks very serious and rather ill. A copy of this portrait was sent to Padre Martini at Bologna. See illustration No. 5.
[2] Archbishop Hieronymus Colloredo.
[3] The diplomas of membership of the Academies of Bologna and Verona, awarded to Mozart in October 1770 and January 1771.   [4] i.e. at 11 o'clock at night.
[5] Abbé Joseph Bullinger, tutor to the family of Count Arco and a lifelong friend of the Mozarts.

a long time without thinking of anything. Nannerl wept bitterly and I had to use every effort to console her. She complained of a headache and a sick stomach and in the end she retched and vomited; and putting a cloth round her head she went off to bed and had the shutters closed. Poor Bimbes lay down beside her. For my own part, I went to my room and said my morning prayers. I then lay down on my bed at half past eight and read a book and thus becoming calmer fell asleep. The dog came to my bedside and I awoke. As she made signs to me to take her for a run, I gathered that it must be nearly noon and that she wanted to be let out. I got up, took my fur cloak and saw that Nannerl was fast asleep. The clock then showed half past twelve. When I came in with the dog, I woke Nannerl and ordered lunch. But she had no appetite, she would eat nothing and went to bed immediately afterwards, so that, when Bullinger had left, I passed the time lying on my bed, praying and reading. In the evening she felt better and was hungry. We played piquet and then had supper in my room. After that we had a few more games and, with God's blessing, went off to bed. That is how we spent that sad day which I never thought I should have to face. On Wednesday Nannerl went to early Mass and in the afternoon we had our shooting.[1] Bullinger won for Sallerl,[2] for he shot for both her and Mamma. So Mamma has won eleven kreuzer, but Wolfgang has lost four. Bullinger and Katherl[3] played with us until six; and that dreadful day ended with the Rosary, which I say for you daily. This morning I asked Herr Glatz of Augsburg to come and see me and we agreed that when you are in Augsburg, you should stay at the 'Lamm' in the Heiligkreuzgasse, where the tariff is thirty kreuzer for lunch, where the rooms are comfortable and where the most respectable people, both Englishmen and Frenchmen, put up. From there it is quite a short distance to the Church of the Holy Cross; and my brother, Franz Aloys,[4] also lives near by in the Jesuitengasse. So you should not say anything to Herr Albert,[5] for the 'Drei Mohren'[6] is far too expensive; the landlord asks an outrageous price for his rooms and every meal works out at about forty-

---

[1] One of the favourite recreations of the Mozart family and their friends was 'Bölzel-schiessen', i.e. shooting at targets with air-guns. These shooting matches usually took place on Sunday afternoons. The 'Schützencompagnie' or company of marksmen, met at different houses, each member in turn providing a pictorial target, which had to be topical in subject and embellished with verses. The company kept a cash-box and members were allowed to shoot for absent relatives and friends.   [2] Rosalie Joly.

[3] Maria Anna Katharina Gilowsky (1750–1802), daughter of Wenzel Andreä Gilowsky von Urazowa, who held an appointment in the Archbishop's household. She was a great friend of Nannerl's.

[4] Leopold Mozart's two younger brothers, Joseph Ignaz Mozart (1725–1796) and Franz Aloys Mozart (1727–1791), were bookbinders in Augsburg. The latter, the more prosperous of the two, was the father of Maria Anna Thekla, the 'Bäsle'.

[5] Albert was the landlord of the 'Schwarzer Adler' in the Kaufingerstrasse, Munich. On account of his interest in literature and music he was nicknamed 'der gelehrte Wirt'.

[6] The Mozart family, when starting on their European Tour in 1763, had spent a fortnight at this inn at Augsburg, evidently on the recommendation of Herr Albert. See p. 22.

five or even forty-eight kreuzer a head. If you do go to Augsburg, Wolfgang should be taken at once to the organ-builder Stein[1] who will hardly recognize him, as he has not seen him since he was seven. He can tell him that he has come from Innsbruck with a commission to see his instruments. Glatz tells me that Stein, Bioley and Fingerle are in a position to arrange a very fine concert. You must also call on Christoph von Zabuesnig, a merchant and a scholar, who composed that fine German poem about you when he was in Salzburg.[2] He might get some suitable and flattering
★ notice put into the Augsburg paper. My brother or his daughter will certainly take you to the magistrate Von Langenmantel, to whom you should deliver my very humble regards. Mamma knows that we are old acquaintances, for we travelled together to Salzburg on the occasion when Von Hefner's father[3] was also with us. When you are at Courts you must not wear the cross of your order,[4] but in Augsburg you should wear it every day, for there it will win you esteem and respect, as it will in all towns where there is no reigning lord. If you care to visit the monasteries of the Holy Cross and St. Ulrich, you should do so and try their organs. Stein will probably take you to his organ at the Franciscan Church.[5] *Hülber's*[6] *son is in the monastery of St. Ulrich.* By the way, a certain organist and composer is now in Augsburg, of whom they make a great fuss, but whose name I have forgotten. Wherever you stay, you will always, will
★ you not, get the servant to put the boot-trees into your boots?

I intended to get up at nine o'clock this morning, but Glatz found me in bed and then Clessin,[7] the sergeant-major, came in, so that I could not get up till eleven. They all admire Wolfgang's portrait.[8] Clessin was under the impression that you were returning very soon, and so was Schiedenhofen, who was with us yesterday evening from five to seven; and indeed so is everybody. If you should leave Munich without being able to let me know, you should send a note to the Post Office saying: *If letters should arrive with the following address:* à M: Wolfgang Amadé Mozart maître de musique, please forward them to Augsburg, c/o Landlord of the Lamm, in the Heiligkreuzgasse.

You have left behind you the trousers of your pike-grey suit. If I find

[1] Johann Andreas Stein (1728–1792), a famous organ-builder and harpsichord maker. See p. 22, n. 4.
[2] For this poem, written in 1769, see Abert, vol. ii. pp. 929–930 and *MDB*, pp. 86–87.
[3] The Salzburg magistrate Franz von Hefner, who had died in 1769. He was the father of Mozart's friend Heinrich Wilhelm von Hefner.
[4] The order of the Golden Spur, conferred on Mozart by Pope Clement XIV. See p. 148.
[5] Where Stein was organist and had built the instrument.
[6] Joseph Hülber, violinist and flautist in the Salzburg court orchestra.
[7] Johann Dominicus Clessin von Königsklee, sergeant-major and later captain in the Archbishop's body-guard.
[8] The so-called Bologna portrait, painted in the summer of 1777 by an unknown artist in Salzburg. The original has disappeared, but the copy sent to Padre Martini is in the Library of the Liceo Musicale, Bologna. Mozart is wearing the cross of his order. See illustration no. 5.

no other opportunity, I shall give them, together with the music for Andretter,[1] some contredanses, the Adagio and Rondo which you composed for Brunetti,[2] and anything else I may find, to the messenger who, should he miss you, can send them on to my brother in Augsburg. I believe that he does not arrive until noon on Monday.

Haydn[3] and Kapellmeister Rust[4] have had a row. The horn concerto, which has been performed once already, was to be rehearsed again after Vespers and Ferlendis[5] and Brunetti had not turned up. Haydn became very angry and said that the rehearsal was quite unnecessary and why should they wait for those Italian asses? Rust maintained that it was for him to give orders and so forth. The service lasted until a quarter to eleven and an Agnus Dei by Haydn was performed again, because Rust was not ready. The sonata was one of Wolfgang's.[6]

While you are in Munich, do not forget to ask for letters of recommendation, and especially for a letter from the Bishop of Chiemsee.[7] Count Sensheim could give you one for Würzburg, where his father's brother is bishop. Nannerl and I send greetings to Mamma and we kiss you and her millions of times.

Addio.

MOZART

(209) *Mozart to his Father*

[*Autograph in the Mozarteum, Salzburg*]

MON TRÉS CHER PÉRE,   MUNICH, 26 *September* 1777

We arrived here on the 24th at half past four in the afternoon. The first piece of news we heard was that we had to drive to the customs house accompanied by a grenadier with a fixed bayonet. And the first acquaintance we met on the way was Signor Consoli,[8] who recognized me at once and whose joy at seeing me cannot be described. He called on me the very next day. Words fail me to express the delight of Herr Albert, who is indeed a thoroughly honest man and our very good friend. After my arrival I played on the clavier till supper-time, for Herr Albert had not yet come in. But he soon turned up and we went down to supper, where

---

[1] K. 185 [167a]. See p. 236, n. 1.
[2] Antonio Brunetti was first violin and soloist in the Salzburg court orchestra. The works referred to are K. 261 and 269 [261a], both composed in 1776.   [3] Michael Haydn.
[4] Jakob Rust, who was Kapellmeister in Salzburg during the years 1777–1778.
[5] Giuseppe Ferlendis was oboist in the Salzburg court orchestra.
[6] Mozart wrote at least six church sonatas during the years 1776 and 1777.
[7] Count Ferdinand Zeill. See p. 259, n. 1.
[8] Tommaso Consoli (1753– ?) joined the Munich Kapelle in 1773 and was an excellent male soprano. He sang in Mozart's *Il rè pastore*, which was performed in April 1775 at Salzburg in honour of the visit of the Archduke Maximilian.

I met Mr. Sfeer and some kind of secretary, a very good friend of his, who both send their greetings to you. We got to bed late and were very tired after our journey; but all the same we got up at seven the next morning, the 25th. My hair, however, was so untidy that I did not reach Count Seeau's until half past ten and when I got there I was told that he had already gone out hunting. Patience! I then asked to be taken to Pernat, the choirmaster—but he had gone off with Baron Schmidt to his estates. I found Herr Bellvall, but he was very busy. He gave me 1000 greetings for you. During lunch Rossi made his appearance and at two o'clock Consoli turned up, and at three o'clock Becke and Herr von Bellvall. I called on Frau von Durst who is now living near the Franciscans and at six o'clock I went for a short walk with Becke. There is a certain Professor Huber here (perhaps you will remember him better than I do) who tells me that he saw me during our last visit to Vienna and that he heard me play at young Herr von Mesmer's house. He is neither very tall nor very small, pale, with whitish grey hair, and in features he somewhat resembles our Salzburg Equerry. He is a Deputy-Intendant at the theatre; his job is to read through the plays sent in for production, improve, spoil, expand them or cut them down. He comes to Albert's every evening and often has a talk with me. I was at Count Seeau's today, Friday the 26th, at half past eight in the morning. This is what happened. I walked into the house and Madame Niesser, the actress, who was just coming out, asked me: 'I suppose you want to see the Count?' 'Yes', I replied. 'Well, he is still in his garden and goodness knows when he will return.' I asked her where the garden was. 'Well,' she said, 'I too want to see him, so let us go together.' We had hardly passed the lodge gates before the Count came towards us; and when he was about twelve paces from us, he recognized me, addressed me by name, and was extremely polite. He was already acquainted with my story.[1] As we mounted the steps together very slowly, I disclosed to him very briefly the object of my visit. He said that I should ask immediately for an audience with His Highness the Elector and that if for any reason I was unable to see him, I should put my case before him in writing. I begged him to keep the whole thing secret and he promised me to do so. When I remarked that a first-rate composer was badly needed here, he said: 'I am well aware of it'. After this I called on the Bishop of Chiemsee and was with him for half an hour. I told him everything and he promised me to do his best in the matter. He was going to Nymphenburg at one o'clock and promised to speak to Her Highness the Electress without fail. The Court returns to Munich on Sunday evening. We lunched today at Rasco's with Herr von Bellvall. Rasco and his wife, Herr von Cori, Bellvall and Passauer send you their greetings. Then we went to Frau von Durst, who lives three flights up in Burgomaster

[1] See p. 271, n. 3.

Schmadl's house, where Herr von Cori lodges on the second floor. Thence Herr Siegl (who has now been married for two months) fetched us and we all went together to Frau von Hofstetten, whose husband is away but will soon return. Franz Dufresne is now Court Chancellor, but up to the present *sine auro*.[1] Afterwards Siegl took Mamma home, for she had promised Becke to go with him to the theatre, and I accompanied Frau von Durst to her lodgings and then on to the theatre, where we all met again. The play was: *Henriette, oder Sie ist schon verheiratet*.[2] This morning at half past eleven Becke and I called on the beautiful Fräulein von Seeau. Fräulein von Tosson has made a very good match. Her husband's name is Hepp and he is said to be extremely rich. Herr Johannes Cröner,[3] by being amazingly blunt, has been made Deputy-Konzertmeister. He produced two symphonies (Dio mene liberi)[4] of his own composition. The Elector asked him: 'Did you really compose these yourself?' 'Yes, Your Highness.' 'Who taught you then?' 'Oh, a schoolmaster in Switzerland. People make such a fuss about composing, but that schoolmaster told me more than all our composers here could tell me.' Count Schönborn and his wife, the Archbishop's sister,[5] arrived here today when I happened to be at the theatre. In conversation with them Herr Albert mentioned that I was here and told them that I was no longer in the Archbishop's service. They were both amazed and absolutely refused to believe that (oh, blessed memory!) my whole salary used to be twelve gulden, thirty kreuzer a month.[6] They were only changing horses, or they would have been delighted to have had a word with me; as it was, I missed them. Now at last please let me enquire after your health and condition. I hope, and so does Mamma, that you are both quite well. I am always in my very best spirits, for my heart has been as light as a feather ever since I got away from all that humbug; and, what is more, I have become fatter. Herr von Wallau spoke to me at the theatre today and I called on Countess La Rosée in her box. Well, I must leave Mamma a little room. Please deliver compliments to the whole worshipful company of marksmen from three of its members, that is, Mamma, myself and M. Novac, who comes to Albert's every day. Meanwhile farewell, my dearest Papa. I kiss your hands countless times and embrace my brute of a sister.

WOLFG: AMADÉ MOZART.

---

[1] i.e. without money.
[2] A comedy by G. F. W. Grossmann.
[3] Cröner was the name of a large family of musicians who all served the Electors of Bavaria and were nearly all violinists. The Deputy-Konzertmeister to whom Mozart refers was Johannes Nepomuk von Cröner, who after the death of Elector Maximilian III in 1777 was pensioned off and died in 1785.
[4] God save me from them.
[5] Maria Theresa (1744– ?), Princess Colloredo, was the second wife of Eugen Franz Erwein, Count Schönborn (1727–1801).
[6] Mozart's annual salary as Konzertmeister to the Archbishop was 150 gulden.

(209a) *Maria Anna Mozart to her Husband*

[*Autograph in the Mozarteum, Salzburg*]

[MUNICH, 26 September 1777[1]]

Wolfgang has left me no news to tell. I hope that I shall soon get a letter from you and hear with delight that you are well. Thank God, we are in good trim and only wish that you were with us, which, with God's help, will happen some day. Meanwhile do not worry and shake off all your troubles. Everything will come right in the end, when the hooks and eyes have been put on. We lead a most charming life—up early—late to bed, and visitors all day long. Addio, ben mio. Keep well, my love. Into your mouth your arse you'll shove. I wish you good-night, my dear, but first shit in your bed and make it burst. It is long after one o'clock already. Now you can go on rhyming yourself.

MARIA ANNA MOZART

All sorts of messages to
    my dear Sallerl, Katherl, Nannerl,
        Bimberl.

(210) *Leopold Mozart to his Wife and Son*

[*Extract*]   [*Autograph in the Mozarteum, Salzburg*]

SALZBURG, 27 September 1777

You will have received my letter. As yet we have had no news of you from Munich, probably because you were not able to write until Saturday. I feel somewhat better, but my cough will not leave me. I have not gone out yet, and shall not do so until tomorrow, when I shall go to the half past ten Mass in the Church of the Holy Trinity; but if I do not feel quite well, I shall not stir out. Young Herr von Unhold from Munich has just been to see me, so I had to stop writing and talk to him; and Nannerl had to play a sonata for him. My dear Wolfgang, I beg you not to write any more jokes about our Mufti. Remember that I am in Salzburg and that one of your letters might get lost or find its way into other hands. Herr von Moll spent four hours with me yesterday. He is going home on Tuesday or Wednesday of next week, and is delighted to leave Salzburg, for he has come to hate being here. In the bag containing the trousers you will find a steel button for your green summer suit and various pieces of cloth for patching, all of which I presume you will still receive in Munich, for it is possible that things may go better there than we supposed. You mention something about your diplomas, but I scarcely think that you need them. If any difficulty should arise, I can always send them and I can enclose as well a full account of the whole affair. It does our Prince no

---

[1] A postscript to Mozart's letter.

credit that he gave you such a poor salary, and it does you little honour that you served him so long for that bagatelle. If anyone asks you what pay you received, *it would be better for you to say quite frankly that you only stayed in Salzburg to please your father and until you were a little older, because the pay is usually only three or four hundred gulden, except in the case of Italians, whom the Prince now remunerates more handsomely.* I trust that you have called on Woschitka[1] and flattered him. You should make friends with everybody. I wrote that sentence in the dark, but now I have a light! Yesterday little Victoria Adlgasser[2] did Nannerl's hair and this afternoon Katherl combed it out and dressed it. We played in the afternoon with Bullinger, *who always sends you his greetings.* Then Seelos,[3] who greets you, came to call on me, and Nannerl took Bimperl, who also greets you, for a walk.

My affair is again on the old footing. What is contained in my diploma, which the Privy Chancery sent to me today, is so long that I shall copy it out word for word in my next letter, which I hope to write the day after tomorrow. For I must close now and send off the parcel today to be put in tomorrow's mail coach. The reply to my petition is really comical; it is most polite and perfectly ridiculous, for it dodges the point. Mitzerl, Tresel[4] and all Salzburg send their greetings to you. Nannerl has tidied up everywhere. She sends greetings to you and kisses you and Mamma a million times. And I?—Ah, but you surely know that my whole heart is with you. God keep you in good health! My very life depends on yours. I am your old deserted father and husband

MOZART

My greetings to our good friends in Munich. Provided that both of you are well I am as gay as a lark.

★

(211) *Leopold Mozart to his Wife and Son*

[Extract]   [Autograph in the Mozarteum, Salzburg]

SALZBURG, 28 *September* 1777

I went out for the first time today, and to Mirabell, to hear the last Mass, and I sat up in the side oratory. During the service I saw Herr von Gilowsky with Frau von Riedel on his arm and Herr Grenier with Herr von Riedel walking into the courtyard to look at the rooms. So, when Mass was over, I crossed the landing and went there to greet them. They were very much surprised when I told them that you were both in Munich and had perhaps even left. They promised to come and see us on Monday.

[1] Franz Xaver Woschitka (1728–1796), leading cellist in the Munich court orchestra.
[2] Daughter of Anton Cajetan Adlgasser, court and cathedral organist in Salzburg.
[3] Jakob Seelos, tenor in the Salzburg court choir.
[4] Therese, the Mozarts' maid-of-all-work.

After lunch the marksmen came and the Paymaster contributed the target, which Bullinger won. But I won the second and, as I shot for Mamma, I made seven kreuzer for her. Wolfgang, for whom Bullinger shot, has won thirteen. Afterwards Kassl and Katherl played with us until the dress rehearsal of the French play at five o'clock, when they all three went off to the theatre. I then took Bimperl for a walk of about 100 yards from our front door and having brought her home, went on myself to the dress rehearsal. The actors were in full dress, but no other people were allowed in. Five hundred tickets are being distributed for Tuesday. The Archbishop went off to Weidwirth for a few days, but, as Count Guntacker[1] and his wife arrived this morning, he returned this evening. We are having the most lovely, warm weather and today, thank God, I am very well and have hardly coughed at all, sometimes not even three times in two hours. But I am still taking medicine to make me perspire and I shall have to speak about my health to Dr. Barisani,[2] as I have got very thin. I trust that with God's help I shall get well, for now I am more placid than I used to be and I shall take great care of myself in every way. But I beg you, dear Wolfgang, not to indulge in any excesses, for from your youth up you have been used to a regular life. And you must avoid heating drinks, for you know that you soon get hot and that you prefer cold to warmth, which is a clear proof that your blood, which has a tendency to heat, immediately boils up. Strong drinks therefore and too much wine of any kind are bad for you. Picture to yourself in what unhappiness and distress you would plunge your dear mother in a far distant country, not to mention myself. I have written very circumstantially to M. Duschek,[3] and I have added that on your journey you will find an opportunity of writing to him. Madame Duschek[4] has replied to my letter and tells me that she too has heard of our worries in Salzburg, that they both sympathize very deeply and long to see our merits rewarded and that Wolfgang, who, she supposes, must now be more of a scamp than ever, should come directly or indirectly to Prague, where he will always be given a very warm welcome. Now I must copy out for you the reply to my petition. You will see how hard they must have worked—if only to put it together.

[1] Count Guntacker Colloredo, brother of the Archbishop of Salzburg.

[2] Dr. Sylvester von Barisani (1719–1810), born in Castelfranco, was private physician to the Archbishop. His two sons, Franz and Sigmund, became doctors, the one in Salzburg, the other in Vienna.

[3] Franz Xaver Duschek (1731–1799), born at Chotebor in Czechoslovakia, studied music in Prague and later in Vienna under Wagenseil. He settled in Prague as a teacher of music and performer on the clavier, for which he wrote a number of compositions.

[4] Josepha Duschek (1753–1824), *née* Hambacher, was born in Prague, where she became a pupil of Franz Duschek, whom she married. She became a famous singer and was called 'Bohemia's Gabrielli'. She and her husband met Mozart at Salzburg in August 1777, when he wrote for her the scena and aria 'Ah, lo previdi' from Paisiello's *Andromeda*, K. 272. An interesting account of the Duscheks, who played a praiseworthy part in Mozart's later years, is to be found in Procházka, *Mozart in Prag* (Prague, 1892), chap. i.

Ex Decreto Cels^{mi}. Principis, 26 Sept., 1777.

To signify to the petitioner that His Grace desires that there should be real harmony amongst his musicians. In gracious confidence therefore that the petitioner will conduct himself calmly and peaceably with the Kapellmeister and other persons appointed to the court orchestra, His Grace retains him in his employment and graciously commands him to endeavour to render good service both to the Church and to His Grace's person.

Did you ever in your life read such a rigmarole of nonsense? Whoever reads the petition and then the reply will be obliged to think that the Chancery Clerk attached this document to the wrong petition. Fortunately no one but Bullinger has read it, and probably nobody else will do so, for the Paymaster asked me today to send for my salary. He did not want to read anything and in any case he would not have objected to sending me the money, as he had not received any definite authority to strike me off his pay-sheet. Last Friday Herr Kolb gave a grand concert to the foreign merchants, at which Ferlendis, Ferrari,[1] Kassl, Stadler,[2] Pinzger,[3] etc. were present. He played on the fiddle your concerto[4] and your Nachtmusik[5] and, as the music was so much praised and won extraordinary acclamation and applause, he announced 'You have been hearing the compositions of a good friend who is no longer with us'. Whereupon they all cried out: 'What a pity that we have lost him!' The concert took place in Eizenberger's hall. When it was over, they all got drunk and shouldered one another in processions round the room, knocking against the lustres or rather, against the large chandelier which hangs from the middle of the ceiling, so that they smashed the centre bowl and other pieces, which will now have to be sent to Venice to be replaced. I sent off this morning the parcel with the trousers, so I hope that you have received them. If you have not, you should enquire, for parcels often go to the customs house. That was why I wrote on mine: *one worn pair of trousers and some music.*

Monday morning, September 29th

I have this moment received your first letter from Munich. Perhaps all will go well. Possibly you could get things working if you could find an ★ opportunity of showing the Elector everything you can do, especially in fugues, canons and counterpoint compositions. You must play up all you can to Count Seeau and tell him what arias and ballets and so forth you

---

[1] Cellist in the Salzburg court orchestra.   [2] Matthias Stadler, a violinist.
[3] Andreas Pinzger (c. 1742–1817) was a violinist in the Salzburg court orchestra.
[4] During the year 1775 Mozart wrote five violin concertos, i.e. K. 207, 211, 216, 218, 219.
[5] Probably one of the virtuoso movements from Mozart's Haffner serenade (K. 250 [248b]), written for performance on the eve of the wedding of Marie Elizabeth Haffner to F. X. Späth, 22 July 1776.

are prepared to compose for his theatre, and this without asking for remuneration. You must be excessively polite to the courtiers, for each one has a finger in that pie. Consoli could sing the new scena you wrote for Madame Duschek[1] and you could speak to Count Seeau about her. Perhaps you could give a concert in Count Seeau's garden. If there is a ray of hope in all this, you will have to stay on in Munich. Make good friends with Woschitka, for he can always speak to the Elector and he is in great favour. Should the Elector require you to write a piece for the viol da gamba, Woschitka could tell you what it should be like and could show you the works which he prefers, so that you may get some idea of his taste. If you have not spoken and cannot speak to him and are thus obliged to apply to him in writing, Herr von Bellvall will tell you who ought to draft the letter. In conversation and in writing you may state quite frankly both to the Elector and to Count Seeau that in regard to your knowledge of counterpoint His Highness need only consult Padre Maestro Martini of Bologna and Herr Hasse in Venice and hear what they think. If you really must have them, I will send you your two diplomas which state that when you were only fourteen you were appointed maestro di cappella of the Academies of Bologna and Verona. I am now quite happy; and I am delighted that Mamma, whom I kiss 1000 times, is
★ in good form and I can well believe that you feel lighthearted. The story about Albert (to whom we send greetings) and Countess von Schönborn is really killing. Our greetings to all our friends and acquaintances. So Herr Siegl too has taken the plunge? I congratulate him most cordially!
★ I kiss you both most affectionately and remain the old deserted hermit with his housekeeper

MOZART

I send you herewith the two diplomas and Padre Martini's testimonial.[2] See that the Elector reads them. Count Seeau should read them too and make the Elector do so. What a sensation they will make! I mean, the fact that seven years ago you were made maestro di cappella of both Academies.

(211a) *Nannerl Mozart to her Mother and Brother*

[*Extract*]   [*Autograph in the Mozarteum, Salzburg*]

[SALZBURG, 29 *September* 1777[3]]
I am delighted to hear that Mamma and Jack Pudding are cheerful and in good spirits. Alas, we poor orphans have to mope for boredom and

---

[1] K. 272. 'Ah, lo previdi', composed in Salzburg, August 1777. See p. 280, n. 4.
[2] Nissen, p. 227 f., gives the text of Padre Martini's testimonial, dated 12 October 1770. In a footnote he adds the remark that 'it is not known why this testimonial was ever asked for and granted'. See also *MDB*, p. 127 f.   [3] A postscript to her father's letter.

fiddle away the time somehow or other. That reminds me, Bimperl, please be so good as to send me soon a short preambulum. But write one this time from C into B♭, so that I may gradually learn it by heart.

I have no good news to send you from home. So I kiss Mamma's hands and to you, you rascal! you villain! I give a juicy kiss and I remain Mamma's obedient daughter and your sister who is living in hopes—

MARIE ANNE MOZART

Miss Pimpes too is living in hopes, for she stands or sits at the door whole half-hours on end and thinks every minute that you are going to come. All the same she is quite well, eats, drinks, sleeps, shits and pisses.

(212) *Maria Anna Mozart to her Husband*

[*Autograph in the Mozarteum, Salzburg*]

MUNICH, 29 *September* 1777

Thank God, we are well and are still here. Wolfgang went today to see the Bishop of Chiemsee and tomorrow he is to pay his respects to the Elector. He was not able to do so before. Herr Woschitka had supper with us yesterday and lunched with us today and was very civil. We must wait and see how we get on. We have very many good friends who would like us to remain here.

(212a) *Mozart to his Father*

[*Autograph in the Mozarteum, Salzburg*]

[MUNICH, 29-30 *September* 1777[1]]

True enough! Any number of good friends, but unfortunately most of them can do little or nothing. I was with Count Seeau yesterday morning at half past ten and found him much more serious and not so frank as he was the first time. But it was only in appearance. Then today I called on Prince Zeill, who said to me in the most polite manner: 'I am afraid that we shall not accomplish very much here. When we were at table at Nymphenburg I had a few words in private with the Elector. He said: "It is too early yet. He ought to go off, travel to Italy and make a name for himself. I am not refusing him, but it is too soon."' So there we are! Most of these great lords are downright infatuated with Italy. Zeill advised me, however, to go to the Elector and put my case before him all the same. I had a private talk at table today with Woschitka, who told me to call at nine o'clock tomorrow morning, when he will certainly procure an audience for me. We are good friends now. He wanted absolûment to

---

[1] Mozart's letter is really a continuation of the one begun by his mother.

know who the person was,[1] but I just said: 'Rest assured that I am your friend and ever will be, and that I too am convinced of your friendship. That must suffice'. Now to return to my story. The Bishop of Chiemsee also had a word in private with the Electress, who, however, shrugged her shoulders and said that she would do her best, but was very doubtful. Now to go back to Count Seeau. When Prince Zeill had told him the whole story, he said: 'Do you know whether Mozart gets enough money from home to enable him with a small subsidy to remain on here? I should very much like to keep him.' 'I do not know', replied the Bishop, 'but I very much doubt it. However, you have only to ask him.' So that was why on the following day he was so thoughtful. I like Munich and I am inclined to think, as many of my friends do, that if only I could stay here for a year or two, I could win both profit and honour by my work and therefore would be sought after by the Court instead of having to canvass them. Since my arrival Herr Albert has thought out a scheme, which, I believe, would not be impossible of execution. It amounts to this. He wants to collect ten good friends, each of whom would fork out one ducat a month, thus making ten ducats or fifty gulden a month, or 600 gulden a year. Then if I could get 200 gulden a year from Count Seeau, I should have 800 gulden. Now what does Papa think of this idea? Is it not a proof of friendship? And should I not accept it, provided, of course, that the proposal is serious? It seems perfectly satisfactory to me. I should be near Salzburg, and if you, my dearest Papa, should feel inclined (as I heartily wish that you may) to leave Salzburg and end your days in Munich, the plan would be delightful and quite simple. For if we have had to live in Salzburg on 504 gulden, surely we could manage in Munich on 600 or 800?

Countess La Rosée has asked me to send you 100000 compliments. What a charming woman she is! and a very good friend of ours. Herr von Dufresne told me the other day that the two of them often squabbled about us with the 'Presidentess'.[2] Papa is in high favour with the Countess. She says that for a long time she has not met a man of such good sense and that you can see it in his face! I go to her every day. Her brother is not here.

(212b) *Maria Anna Mozart resumes writing*

[*Autograph in the Mozarteum, Salzburg*]

We lunched on Friday with Herr Bellvall and then called on Frau von Durst and went to the theatre with her. She sends greetings to you and

[1] Mozart is probably alluding to someone who was trying to disturb the good relations between Woschitka and himself.

[2] Perhaps Madame la Présidente, a lady of fashion in Munich, whose performance on the harpsichord Burney describes in *The Present State of Music in Germany, etc.*, 2nd edition, 1775, vol. i. p. 172.

Nannerl. Herr Becke went off to the country today with Countess Seeau. I am quite happy in Munich, but I should like to be able to divide myself, so that I could also be with you in Salzburg. Do take care of your health, do not go out until you are quite well again and do not let any gray hairs grow. With God's help, all will come right, as it surely must. Greetings to all my friends, that is, Frau von Moll, Frau von Gerlichs,[1] Mamsell Katherl and especially to my dearest Sallerl and Herr Bullinger, Frau Hagenauer, Jungfer Mitzerl, in a word to all who like to hear from us. I kiss Bimperl on her little tongue; but she will probably have forgotten me. Nannerl ought to look very smart indeed, as she has two lady's maids. Write and tell us all that has happened since in Salzburg. A German operetta is being performed tomorrow and we shall see it, because it is making such a sensation. It is said to be very fine. I send plenty of greetings to Thresel also. She must not feel lonely till I return and she must take out Bimbes regularly and make her perform. My greetings also to the birds. I simply cannot write much, for my pen is wretched and I cannot write at all with my gold pen. So I kiss you both many million times. Live together happily and keep well. I pray for both of you every day. Addio.

MARIA ANNA MOZART

(212c) *Mozart resumes writing*

[Autograph in the Mozarteum, Salzburg]

At nine o'clock today, the 30th, I went as arranged with M. Woschitka to Court. Everyone was in hunting dress. Baron Kern was acting chamberlain. I might have gone there yesterday evening, but I did not want to tread on the toes of M. Woschitka, who of his own accord had offered to procure me an audience with the Elector. At ten o'clock he showed me into a little narrow room through which His Highness was to pass on his way to hear Mass before going to hunt. Count Seeau went by and greeted me in the most friendly fashion, saying: 'How do you do, my very dear Mozart!' When the Elector came up to me, I said: 'Your Highness will allow me to throw myself most humbly at your feet and offer you my services'. 'So you have left Salzburg for good?' 'Yes, your Highness, for good.' 'How is that? Have you had a row with him?' 'Not at all, Your Highness. I only asked him for permission to travel, which he refused. So I was compelled to take this step, though indeed I had long been intending to clear out. For Salzburg is no place for me, I can assure you.' 'Good Heavens! There's a young man for you! But your father is still in Salzburg?' 'Yes, your Highness. He too throws himself most humbly at your

---

[1] Anna Maria von Gerlichs, widow of the Salzburg Privy Councillor Gerhart von Gerlichs, who died in 1763.

feet, and so forth. I have been three times to Italy already, I have written three operas, I am a member of the Bologna Academy, where I had to pass a test, at which many maestri have laboured and sweated for four or five hours, but which I finished in an hour. Let that be a proof that I am competent to serve at any Court. My sole wish, however, is to serve your Highness, who himself is such a great——' 'Yes, my dear boy, but I have no vacancy. I am sorry. If only there were a vacancy——' 'I assure your Highness that I should not fail to do credit to Munich.' 'I know. But it is no good, for there is no vacancy here.' This he said as he walked away. Whereupon I commended myself to his good graces. Herr Woschitka has advised me to put in an appearance at Court as often as I can. This afternoon I went to see Count Salern.[1] The Countess, his daughter, is now a maid of honour. She had gone out hunting with the rest. Ravani and I were in the street when the whole company passed by. The Elector and the Electress greeted me in a most friendly manner. Countess Salern recognised me at once and waved her hand to me repeatedly. Baron Rumling, whom I saw beforehand in the antechamber, has never been so *civil* to me as he was on this occasion. How I got on with Salern I shall tell you in my next letter. It was quite satisfactory. He was very polite—and frank. I do beg you to take great care of your health. I kiss Papa's hands 100000 times and always remain your most obedient son

Wolfgang Amadé Mozart

PS. Ma très chère sœur. I shall send you very soon a letter all for yourself. My greetings to A.B.C.M.R. and more letters of the alphabet of that kind. Addio.

Someone built a house here and wrote on it:

> To build a house is good fun, 'tis true.
> That 'twould cost so much I never knew.

During the night someone scrawled underneath:

> That to build a house would cost so much brass
> You ought to have known, you silly ass.

(213) *Leopold Mozart to his Son*

[*Extract*]   [*Autograph in the Mozarteum, Salzburg*]

Salzburg, [30 *September*] 1777

Mon trés cher Fils!

There was a rehearsal in the theatre this morning. Haydn[2] had to provide entr'acte music for 'Zaïre.'[3] At nine o'clock already one performer

---

[1] Count Joseph von Salern (1718–1805), chief manager of the opera in Munich.
[2] Michael Haydn.   [3] Incidental music for a performance of Voltaire's *Zaïre*.

after the other began to turn up; the rehearsal started at ten and they were not finished until about half past eleven. Of course the Turkish music was included and a march too. Countess von Schönborn came to the rehearsal driven in a chaise by Count Czernin.[1] The music is supposed to suit the action very well and to be very fine. Although it was entirely for stringed and wind-instruments, the court harpsichord had to be brought over and Haydn played on it. On the previous evening Hafeneder's[2] Finalmusik was performed at the back of the pages' garden, where Madame Rosa used to live. The Archbishop had supper in Hellbrunn and the play began after half past six. We saw from our window the attendance, which,   ★ however, was not so large as I had expected, for almost half the ticket-holders had stayed away.[3] People say that it is to be performed very often, so I shall be able to hear the music whenever I like. I have seen the dress rehearsal. The play was already over by half past eight, so that the Prince and all the company had to wait half an hour for their carriages. Half a company of grenadiers were parading in the square and the Prince walked up and down the garden.

October 1st. Is not Baron Dürnitz[4] in Munich? Then he is probably on his   ★ estates. What is Herr von Dufraisne, the priest, doing? Yesterday I received quite unexpectedly a letter from Mysliwecek, which I am quoting for you.

> Diversi ordinari sono ch'io ricevei avviso da Napoli che per diversi impegni fortissimi hanno dovuto prendere un certo Maestro Valentini[5] per l'opera di carnevale, nonostante però s'accorderanno cigliati 100 al Signor figlio per un' opera l'anno venturo. Ma vogliono l'impresario, cioè, il signor *Don Gaetano Santoro,* che V.S. gli scriva che per meno di 100 cigliati non può venire, ma con i 100 d'esser pronto di accettar l'opera che si destinerà. Io sono tanto tormentato da cotesti impresari che assolutamente vogliono ch'io ne scriva due l'anno venturo: e a momenti aspetto la scrittura. Già a me toccheranno gli siti più cattivi, non importa. Io in Napoli sono conosciuto, e ne scrissi sei. Perchè so che vogliono che io scrivessi la prima, e probabilmente la terza. Io consiglio sempre, per maggior sicurezza, l'opera del carnevale. Dio sa, se ci potrò andare, ma già che vogliono così, accetterò la scrittura, se non potrò, la rimanderò. V.S. dunque da me sarà avvisato quali opere me deveno toccare. Ed allora potrà Lei scrivere al Signor Don Gaetano Santoro circa il prezzo e circa l'opera

---

[1] Count Johann Rudolf Czernin, brother of the Countess Lützow and nephew of the Archbishop.

[2] Joseph Hafeneder, violinist and composer, was a member of the Salzburg court orchestra.

[3] The Mozarts' house in the Makartplatz had a good view of the Salzburg theatre.

[4] Baron Thaddäus von Dürnitz (? –1803), a well known-patron of music and a good performer on the clavier and the bassoon. He commissioned Mozart after the latter's arrival in Munich in December 1774 to write various works, including the clavier sonata, K. 284 [205b], for which, however, he never paid him.

[5] There were several operatic composers of this name in the latter half of the eighteenth century, chief of whom were Giovanni Valentini and Michael Angelo Valentini.

addirittura, ovvero mandarmi la lettera, che io l'invierò. Frattanto mille saluti a tutta la stimatissima famiglia e mi do l'onore, etc., etc.[1]

You see from this letter that I cannot answer it at once, because I still have to wait to hear from him what operas he is going to compose. Moreover, he does not seem to have the faintest idea that you are in Munich. So I am waiting for a letter from you, which I hope to receive tomorrow morning, and then I shall be able to take a decision; for one must be guided by circumstances. The journey to Naples is too far and too expensive, especially if you decide to go beyond Munich. Our object is now quite a different one; and should you have the good fortune, which is hardly likely, to get an appointment in Munich, you could not run away during the first year. But in that case you could draft the letter to Santoro to the effect that the offer brings you honour and ensures a contract for an opera in Naples for some other year, when it would be more convenient and practicable. If in the meantime Mysliwecek hears or has heard that you are in Munich, your excuse, if you do not wish to visit him, will have to be that your Mamma forbids you to do so and that other people have persuaded you, and so forth. It is indeed a pity. But, if he is sensible, he will appreciate the point and will not nourish a grievance against a mother. Even if he does manage to reach Naples, what sort of figure will the poor fellow, who is now without a nose, cut in the theatre? But *propriâ culpâ haec acciderunt*.[2] Where does the blame lie, but on himself and on the horrible life he has led? What a disgrace he is before the whole world! Everybody must fly from him and loathe him. It is indeed a real calamity, which he has brought on himself.

Thursday, October 2nd. I was at the Thursday service today, where I heard that the play is to be repeated on Saturday, and that on Sunday there will be a ball, probably a subscription affair. Haydn's interlude was so good that the Archbishop honoured him by saying at table *that he never would have thought that Haydn was capable of composing such music and that instead of beer he ought always to drink burgundy*. What kind of talk is that!

---

[1] Some posts ago I received the news from Naples that owing to several important commitments the authorities have had to engage a certain Maestro Valentini for the carnival opera. Nevertheless they will undertake to pay 100 cigliati to your son for an opera for next year. But the impresario Don Gaetano Santoro would like you to write, refusing to allow your son to go for less than 100 cigliati, but stating that for this sum he will compose whatever opera is allotted to him. Indeed I am worried to death by those impresarios who insist on my writing two operas next year; and at the moment I am awaiting the contract. I shall have the worst of the bargain, but no matter. I am well known in Naples and have written six operas. So I know that they will want me to write the first and probably the third. For greater safety I always advise the carnival opera. Heaven knows whether I shall be able to go to Naples, but as they wish it, I shall accept the contract. If I cannot go, I shall return it. I will inform you in due course what operas have been allotted to me. Then you may write to Don Gaetano Santoro about the fee and the opera itself, or send me your letter which I shall forward to him. Meanwhile, a thousand greetings to your whole most esteemed family, and I have the honour, etc., etc.   [2] i.e. but this happened through his own fault.

After the service I went straight home, as I was expecting a letter from you. But although it is now midday, no letter has arrived yet. Meanwhile I must tell you that I feel very much better, but that I still have a slight cough and a stinking expectoration. Moreover, two days ago a slight ★ rheumatism developed in my left shoulder; but I have kept warm and yesterday afternoon I went for a walk with Nannerl and Pimperl in the hot sun. I let it grill me, got some fresh air and felt so well that I longed to be able to get into a coach and clear out of Salzburg. As it is now past ★ four o'clock and too late for your letter to come, I shall close mine and go for a walk with Nannerl and Pimpes! Everybody sends greetings, especially Frau Hagenauer, to whom I have just been talking in the street and who sends us invitations every day or invites herself to our house. Nannerl and I kiss you millions of times, we wish you luck 1000 times and especially good health; and, hoping to receive a letter tomorrow, I am the old grass widower, bereft of wife and child,

MOZART

If you can perform something before the Elector, you will—or you may—at least get a present, that is, if there is nothing else for you to do.

(214) *Mozart to his Father*

[Autograph in the Mozarteum, Salzburg]

[MUNICH, 2 October 1777]

Yesterday, October 1st, I called on Count Salern again and today, the 2nd, I actually lunched there. During the last three days I have had quite enough playing, I think, but I have thoroughly enjoyed it. Papa must not suppose that I like to go to Count Salern's on account of——. Not at all, for unfortunately, she is in service at Court and therefore is never at home. But about ten o'clock tomorrow morning I shall go to Court with Madame Hepp, née Tosson, and shall then see her. For the Court leaves on Saturday and will not return until the 20th. I am lunching tomorrow with Frau and Fräulein De Branca,[1] who is now half my pupil, as Siegl seldom turns up and Becke, who usually accompanies her on the flute, is not here. At Count Salern's during those three days I played several things out of my head, and then the two Cassations I wrote for the Countess[2] and finally the Finalmusik with the Rondo,[3] all from memory. You cannot imagine how delighted Count Salern was. But he really understands music, for all the time he kept on shouting 'Bravo', where

---

[1] Wife and daughter of Privy Councillor De Branca. Frau De Branca was a Frenchwoman.
[2] K. 247 and 287 [271H], two Divertimenti written in 1776 and 1777 for Countess Antonia Lodron.
[3] Perhaps K. 250 [248b], the Haffner serenade, composed in 1776.

other noblemen would take a pinch of snuff, blow their noses, clear their throats—or start a conversation. I said to him that I only wished that the Elector could be there, for then he might hear something. As it is, he knows nothing whatever about me. He has no idea what I can do. Why do these gentlemen believe what anyone tells them and never try to find out for themselves? Yes, it is always the same. I am willing to submit to a test. Let him get together all the composers in Munich, let him even summon a few from Italy, France, Germany, England and Spain. I undertake to compete with any of them in composition. I told Salern what I had done in Italy and I begged him, whenever the conversation should turn on me, to trot out these facts. He said: 'I have very little influence, but what I can do, I will do with my whole heart'. He too is strongly of the opinion that if I could stay on here for a time, the problem would solve itself. If I were here alone, it would not be impossible for me to manage somehow, for I should ask for at least 300 gulden from Count Seeau. As for food, I should not have to worry, for I should always be invited out, and whenever I had no invitation, Albert would only be too delighted to have me at table. I eat very little, drink water, just at dessert I take a small glass of wine. I should draw up a contract with Count Seeau (all on the advice of my good friends) on the following lines: to compose every year four German operas, some *buffe*, some *serie*; and to be allowed a *sera* or benefit performance of each for myself, as is the custom here. That alone would bring me in at least 500 gulden, which with my salary would make up 800 gulden. But I should certainly make more, for Reiner,[1] the actor and singer, took in 200 gulden on the occasion of his benefit; and I am *very popular* here. And how much more popular I should be if I could help forward the German national theatre? And with my help it would certainly succeed. For when I heard the German sing-spiel, I was simply itching to compose. The leading soprano is called Mlle Kaiser.[2] She is the daughter of a cook by a count here and is a very attractive girl; pretty on the stage, that is; but I have not yet seen her near. She is a native of the town. When I heard her, it was only her third appearance. She has a beautiful voice, not powerful but by no means weak, very pure and her intonation is good. Valesi[3] has taught her; and from her singing you can tell that he knows how to sing as well as how to teach. When she sustains her voice for a few bars, I have been astonished at the

[1] Franz von Paula Reiner (1743–?) lived from 1767 to 1778 in Munich, where he introduced the operetta.

[2] This singer performed in Munich until 1784 and later moved to Vienna.

[3] Johann Evangelist Wallishauser (1735–1811), a Bavarian, had at first great successes as a singer. The Duke of Bavaria sent him to study in Padua, where he adopted the name of Valesi, and in 1771 he sang in opera at Florence, and subsequently in all the leading theatres of Italy. In 1776 he returned to Munich for good, and eventually devoted himself entirely to training singers. Two of his most distinguished pupils were Valentin Adamberger and Carl Maria von Weber.

beauty of her *crescendo* and *decrescendo*. She still takes her trills slowly and I am very glad. They will be all the truer and clearer when later on she wants to trill more rapidly, for it is always easier to do them quickly in any case. People here are delighted with her—and I am delighted with them. Mamma was in the pit. She went in as early as half past four in order to secure a seat; but I did not turn up until half past six, as I have the entrée to all the boxes, for I am so well known. I was in the Brancas' box and I kept my opera-glasses on Mlle Kaiser and she often drew a tear from me. I kept on calling out 'Brava, Bravissima', for I could not forget that it was only her third appearance on the stage. The play was 'The Fisher-maiden', a very good translation of Piccinni's opera.[1] As yet they have no original plays. They would like to produce a German opera seria soon, and they are very anxious that I should compose it. Professor Huber, whom I have already mentioned, is one of the people who want this. Now I must go to bed, for I have come to an end of my tether. It is ten o'clock sharp.

Baron Rumling paid me a compliment the other day by saying: 'I *love* the theatre, good actors and actresses, good singers, and, last but not least, a first-rate composer like yourself'. Only words, it is true, and it is very easy to talk. But he has never spoken to me before in such a flattering manner. I wish you good night—tomorrow, God willing, I shall have the honour of talking to you again, my dearest Papa, in writing.

October 2nd. Number four on the second floor.

(214a) *Maria Anna Mozart to her Husband*

[*Autograph in the Mozarteum, Salzburg*]

[MUNICH, 2 *October* 1777]

Wolfgang is lunching today with Madame Branca and I have lunched at home; but as soon as three o'clock strikes I am going to Frau von Tosson, who is sending someone to fetch me. Herr von Krimmel[2] turned up again yesterday with Herr von Unhold. He is a good friend of ours and is trying hard to persuade us to go to Memmingen and to give a first-class concert, as he assures us that we shall make more there than at a court. I quite believe it, for, as hardly anybody goes to such a place, the people there are glad when they can get anyone at all. Now how is your health? I am not really satisfied with your letters. I don't like that cough, which is lasting far too long. You ought not to have anything wrong with you at all. I beg you to use the sago soon, and the sooner the better, so that you may regain your strength as quickly as possible. We received the parcel

---

[1] Piccinni's *La Pescatrice*, produced in 1766. Burney saw it in Florence in 1770. See Burney, *Present State of Music in France and Italy*, 2nd edition, 1773, p. 241 ff.

[2] See p. 271, n. 2.

by the mail coach and the other one too by the ordinary post. I send greetings to Nannerl. Please tell her not to get cross with you and to take good care that you have no worries and to help you to pass the time so that you do not get melancholy. Bimperl, I trust, is doing her duty and making up to you, for she is a good and faithful fox terrier. I send greetings to Tresel also and should like you to tell her that it is all one whether

(214b) *Mozart resumes writing*

[*Autograph in the Mozarteum, Salzburg*]

I shit the muck or she eats it. But now for something more sensible.

I am writing this on October 3rd. The Court is leaving tomorrow and will not return until the 20th. If it had stayed, I should have kept on hammering and I should have stayed on myself for some time. As it is, I hope next Tuesday to continue my journey with Mamma, but the position is this: in the meantime the company, about which I wrote to you the other day, will be formed; so that, when we are tired of travelling, we shall have a safe place to return to. Herr von Krimmel was with the Bishop of Chiemsee today; he had a good many things to settle with him, including that matter of the salt. Von Krimmel is a curious fellow. Here they call him 'Your Grace', I mean, the flunkeys do. He would like nothing better than that I should remain here, and spoke about me very warmly to the Prince.[1] He said to me: 'Just leave it to me. I shall talk to the Prince. I know how to deal with him, as I have often been of service to him.' The Prince promised him that I would *certainly* be taken into the Court service, but added that things could not be done quite so quickly. As soon as the Court returns, he will speak most seriously and earnestly to the Elector. At eight o'clock this morning I saw Count Seeau. I was very brief and merely said: 'I have come, Your Excellency, solely in order to explain myself and produce my credentials. It has been cast up at me that I ought to travel to Italy. Why, I have spent sixteen months in Italy and, as everyone knows, I have written three operas. My other achievements Your Excellency will learn about from these papers.' I then showed him my diplomas and added: 'I am showing these to Your Excellency and I am telling you all this so that, if ever my name is mentioned and any injustice should be done to me, you may be justified in taking my part'. He asked me if I was now going to France. I replied that I was staying on in Germany. But he thought I meant Munich and asked with a pleasant smile: 'What? So you are staying on here?' 'No', I said, 'I should have liked to; and, to tell the truth, the only reason why I should have been glad of a

[1] i.e. the Bishop of Chiemsee.

subsidy from the Elector is that I might have been able to serve Your Excellency with my compositions and without asking for anything in return. I should have regarded it as a pleasure.' At these words he actually raised his skull-cap. At ten o'clock I was at Court with the Countess Salern, who has already received the arias. The Robinigs just say, of course, whatever comes into their heads. Afterwards I lunched with the Brancas. Privy Councillor von Branca had been invited to the French Ambassador's, and so was not at home. He is addressed as 'Your Excellency'. His wife is a Frenchwoman, who hardly knows a word of German, so I spoke French to her all the time, and I talked quite boldly. She told me that I did not speak at all badly and that I had one good habit, that is, of talking slowly, which made it quite easy to understand me. She is an excellent woman with the most charming manners. Her daughter plays quite nicely, but her time is still poor. I thought at first that it was due to her own carelessness or that her ear was at fault, but I can now blame no one but her teacher, who is far too indulgent and is satisfied with anything. I made her play to me today. I wager that after two month's lessons from me she would play quite well and accurately. She asked me to send her greetings to you and to the whole Robinig family. She was at the convent at the same time as Fräulein Louise. Later in the day a certain Fräulein Lindner, who is now at Count Salern's as governess to the two young countesses, also requested me to send all sorts of messages to the Robinigs and to Fräulein Louise von Schiedenhofen, with whom she was at the same convent. At four o'clock I went to Frau von Tosson, where I found Mamma and Frau von Hepp. I played there until eight o'clock and then we went home. About half past nine in the evening a small orchestra of five players, two clarinets, two horns and one bassoon, came up to the house. Herr Albert (whose name-day is tomorrow) had ordered this music in his and my honour. They did not play at all badly together. They were the same people who play in Albert's dining-hall during the meals. But you can tell at once that Fiala[1] has trained them. They played some of his compositions and I must say that they were very pretty and that he has some very good ideas.

Tomorrow we are going to have a little scratch-concert among ourselves, but, I should add, on that wretched clavier. Oh! Oh! Oh! Well, I wish you a very restful night and I improve on this good wish by hearing to hope soon that Papa is well quite. I forgiveness your crave for my disgraceful handwriting, but ink, haste, sleep, dreams and all the rest. . . . I Papa your, my hands kiss, a thousand times dearest, and my embrace, the

---

[1] Joseph Fiala (1748 or 1754–1816), born in Bohemia, was an oboist in the Kapelle of Prince Kraft Ernst von Oettingen-Wallerstein from 1774 to 1777, when he joined the orchestra at Munich. From 1778 onwards he was an oboist at Salzburg where he became friendly with the Mozart family. He was also a noted performer on the cello and viola da gamba.

heart, sister I with all my brute of a, and remain, now and for ever, amen,

WOLFGANG most obedient your
AMADÉ MOZART son

Munich, 3 October 1777.

To all good friends, to all bad friends, good friends, bad friends, all sorts of messages.

(215) *Leopold Mozart to his Son*

[Extract]   [Autograph in the Mozarteum, Salzburg]

MON TRÈS CHER FILS!   SALZBURG, 4 October 1777
    I have no great hopes of anything happening in Munich. Unless there is a vacancy, the Elector is bound to refuse to take anyone and, moreover, there are always secret enemies about, whose fears would prevent your getting an appointment. Herr Albert's scheme is indeed a proof of the greatest friendship imaginable. Yet, however possible it may seem to you to find ten persons, each of whom will give you a ducat a month, to me it is quite inconceivable. For who are these philanthropists or these music-lovers? And what sort of undertaking or what kind of service will they require from you in return? To me it seems far more likely that Count Seeau may contribute something. But unless he does, what you may expect from Albert would only be a mere trifle. If he could make the arrangement even for a year—that is all I will say for the moment—then you could accept an offer from Count Seeau. But what would he demand!—perhaps all the work which Herr Michl[1] has been doing? Running about and training singers! That would be a dog's life and quite out of the question! In short, I cannot see where these ten charming friends are to come from. Further, Albert may not be able to see them at once, as some of them are perhaps out of town. Moreover, I should prefer merchants or other honest persons to these courtiers, for a great deal would depend on whether they would keep their word and for how long. *If the arrangement is immediately practicable, well and good, and you*

---

[1] Joseph Michl (1745–after 1815), a nephew of another Bavarian composer of the same name, was trained in Munich. In 1776 he became composer of chamber music to the Bavarian court, but lost this appointment after the Elector's death in 1777. He wrote a great many compositions solely for performance in Munich. Burney heard one of his works performed in 1772. See Burney, *Present State of Music in Germany, etc.*, 2nd edition, 1775, vol. i. p. 172.

ought to accept it. But if it cannot be made at once, then you simply must not lounge about, use up your money and waste your time. For in spite of all the compliments and shows of friendship which you are receiving, you cannot hope to make a farthing in Munich. So, if the whole scheme cannot be set going now, then let Albert and our other good friends continue their efforts and do you continue your journey and wait until you hear from him. For the rage for these Italians does not extend very much further than Munich and practically comes to an end there. In ★ Mannheim, for instance, everyone except a few castrati is already German, and in Trier at the court of His Royal Highness the Elector, Prince Clement of Saxony, you will only find Maestro Sales; all the rest are Germans. In Mainz they are all Germans, and in Würzburg I only know of Fracassini,[1] a violinist, who is now Konzertmeister, I think, or perhaps Kapellmeister. But these posts he obtained through his German wife, a singer and a native of Würzburg. At the courts of all the less important Protestant Princes you will not find a single Italian. I am writing in haste, for Herr Lotter wants to take my letter. I am enclosing the chorale melodies, which here or there you may find useful and perhaps even necessary, for one should aim at knowing everything. I have just been to see the Chief Steward, who is paying me a special visit one of these days in order that I may tell him everything in detail. For there is no peace at his house; someone is always being announced or else his Countess comes rushing in. He loves you with his whole heart. Before he heard our story, he had already bought four horses and was looking forward to the pleasure he would give you by turning up with one of them for you to ride on. When, however, he heard about our affair, he simply could not express his annoyance. He was paying his respects one day to the Archbishop, who said to him: '*Now we have one man less in the orchestra*'. Firmian replied: '*Your Grace has lost a great virtuoso*'. '*Why?*' asked the Prince. The reply was: '*Mozart is the greatest player on the clavier whom I have ever heard in my life; on the violin he rendered very good services to Your Grace; and he is a first-rate composer*'. The Archbishop was silent, for he had nothing to say. Now I must close because I have no more room. When writing you should at least mention *whether you have had such and such a letter.* You must surely have received by now the parcel containing the roll with the diplomas and Padre Martini's testimonial. We kiss you millions of times and I am your old

MOZART

Be careful not to lose Padre Martini's testimonial.

---

[1] Aloisio Lodovico Fracassini (1733–1798), a pupil of Tartini, became solo violinist to the Bishop of Bamberg in 1757. The Bishop's court was sometimes in Würzburg and sometimes in Bamberg. In 1764, two years after his marriage to the soprano singer of the Würzburg Hofkapelle, Anna Katharina Boyer, Fracassini became Konzertmeister in Würzburg.

(215a) *Nannerl Mozart to her Mother and Brother*

[*Extract*] [*Autograph in the Mozarteum, Salzburg*]

[SALZBURG, 4 October 1777[1]]

DEAREST MAMMA AND DEAREST BROTHER!

I am very glad that you are both well and in good trim. Since you left I have not yet sent you an account of my daily routine; so I shall begin today. [The day you left, September 23rd, I spent chiefly in bed, for I was vomiting and had a horrible headache. On the 24th, at half past seven I went to early Mass in Holy Trinity. In the afternoon we had a shooting match. Papa will have told you who won.

On the 25th I went to the half past ten Mass. Herr Glatz and Herr Clessin came to see us in the morning and Herr Bullinger in the afternoon.

On the 26th little Victoria Adlgasser dressed my hair in the morning and Barbara Eberlin was with us. I went to the half past ten Mass and in the afternoon from four to five I took Pimperl for a walk. Then Herr Moll spent the evening with us and stayed until nine o'clock.

On the 27th I went to the half past eleven Mass in Mirabell and in the afternoon I went to market with Katherl Gilowsky. Afterwards we played cards until four o'clock with Abbé Bullinger. Then Katherl combed my hair and I took Pimperl for a walk. Later in the day Herr

★ Unhold came to see us and delivered messages from you.

Today, October 4th, Victoria did my hair. I went to the half past ten Mass and now I shall take Pimperl for a walk and then go to the play with

★ Papa.] Keep well. I kiss Mamma's hands and I beg you not to forget me.

MARIA ANNA MOZART

(216) *Leopold Mozart to his Wife and Son*

[*Extract*] [*Autograph in the Mozarteum, Salzburg*]

SALZBURG, 6 October 1777

I received your letter of October 3rd at a quarter to ten this morning, while I was still in bed, for we were at the ball last night until half past twelve. I quite agree that if you were alone, you could live in Munich. But it would do you no honour, and how the Archbishop would laugh! *You can live in that way anywhere, not only in Munich. You must not make yourself so cheap and throw yourself away in this manner, for indeed we have not yet come to that.* Mamma must make her mind easy, for I am much

---

[1] A postscript to her father's letter. The sections enclosed in square brackets were copied by Nannerl from her diary. For lack of space the entries from September 28th to October 3rd are omitted.

better and this afternoon I am going to take some sago, which has just been got ready. I went to the ball for the sake of some recreation and got a great deal of fun out of it, for nobody recognised me and I quizzed people most dreadfully. With God's help you will now continue your journey. When you reach Augsburg, stay at the 'Lamm' in the Heiligkreuzgasse, which all the merchants from that town have recommended so highly. Everything else I have already written to you. If anything further should occur to you which you would like to have, I can still send it to Augsburg, as it is not too far. I understand that the Bishop of Chiemsee is to be here tomorrow evening. He will therefore be leaving Munich this evening. He has to take a confirmation at Werfen and it is impossible to say whether he will return to Munich in the immediate future, for the Archbishop does not like him to be there. On Saturday I was at the play. As there was a French epilogue, Brunetti had to play a concerto while the actors were changing dresses, and he played your Strassburg concerto [1] most excellently. But in the two Allegros he played wrong notes occasionally and once nearly came to grief in a cadenza. Haydn's intermezzi [2] are really beautiful. After the first act there was an Arioso with variations for violoncello, flute, oboe and so forth; and incidentally, preceding a variation which was piano, there was one on the Turkish music, which was so sudden and unexpected that all the women looked terrified and the audience burst out laughing. Between the third and fourth acts there was a cantabile movement with a continuous recitative for the cor anglais. Then the Arioso came in again, which, together with the preceding sad scene with Zaïre and the following act, affected us very much. I must add that the orchestra performed your concerto amazingly well. I hear that one more oboist is coming from Italy as secundarius, but nothing more is being said about the castrato. The Chief Steward has had to tell Meisner, who could not sing on one or two occasions because of a cold, that he must sing and perform regularly in the church services or else he will be dismissed. Such is the great favourite's reward! I kiss you both millions of times, with my whole heart I am ever with you, and I remain your old husband and father

MOZART

You say nothing about Mysliwecek, as though he were not in Munich. How then am I to reply to his letter? I suppose that he will have heard that you are there. *Please give Herr Albert my most cordial and sincere greetings and my thanks for all his kindnesses to you, for his friendly support, his interest and his efforts. Indeed I urge him most insistently to care as a true friend for your*

---

[1] Mozart's violin concerto in D major (K. 218), composed in 1775, the last movement of which has a theme reminiscent of a Strassburg dance. See Köchel, p. 243.
[2] The incidental music which Michael Haydn wrote for Voltaire's *Zaïre*. See p. 302, n. 3.

welfare. Basta! He is one of the most honest men and the lover of mankind which I have always thought him to be. What grieves me now and then is that I no longer hear you playing on the clavier or the violin; and whenever I enter our house a slight feeling of melancholy comes over me, for, as I approach the door, I think that I ought to be hearing you play.

Our maid Tresel finds it extraordinarily funny that Nannerl should be for ever poking her nose into the kitchen and scolding her daily about its dirty condition. For Nannerl does not overlook the least thing; and when Tresel tells a lie, Nannerl at once points out to her that it is an untruth. In short, Tresel's eyes are getting wider and wider, for Nannerl says everything to her without mincing matters, though indeed she becomes quite calm again after it is all over.

Addio, keep well! But do take care of your health, for illness would be the worst thing that could befall you. And save as much money as you can, for travelling is expensive.

★

(216a) *Nannerl Mozart to her Mother and Brother*

[*Extract*]   [*Autograph in the Mozarteum, Salzburg*]

SALZBURG, 5 *October* 1777[1]

Today, October 5th, we had shooting in our house. Papa supplied the target. I shot for Mamma, who has lost nine kreuzer. Katherl shot for you
★ and won the most. Barbara Eberlin is with me at the moment and sends you her greetings. She wants to take me off to her garden. So farewell. I kiss Mamma's hands and am

your old grandmother

MARIA ANNA MOZART

It would not do you any credit to stay on in Munich without an appointment. It would do us far more honour if you could succeed in obtaining a post under some other great lord. You will surely find one.
★

(217) *Mozart to his Father*

[*Autograph in the Mozarteum, Salzburg*]

MON TRÉS CHÉR PÉRE   MUNICH, 6 *October* 1777

Mamma cannot begin this letter; firstly, because she won't be bothered; and secondly, because she has a headache! So I have to rise to the occasion. I shall be going off in a moment with Professor [Huber] to call on Mlle Kaiser. Yesterday, Sunday, October 5th, we had a religious

---

[1] A postscript to her father's letter.

wedding or *altum tempus ecclesiasticum*[1] in this house and there was dancing. I only danced four minuets and by eleven o'clock I was back in my room, for among fifty ladies there was only one who could keep in time; and that was Mlle Käser, a sister of the secretary of that Count Perusa who was once in Salzburg. The Professor has been kind enough to let me down. So I have not been able to go to Mlle Kaiser, as I do not know her address.

(217a) *Maria Anna Mozart to her Husband*

[Autograph in the Mozarteum, Salzburg]

MUNICH, 6 *October* 1777

Herr Lotter brought us your letter today and assured us that you are well, news which greatly delighted us. We have received safely all your letters and the parcels. This I wrote in my last letter. I don't know whether we shall stay on here for the rest of the week, but we shall know this in three or four days' time. Herr Albert is making great efforts and he hopes to arrange something, if he can only get the people together. He has eight subscribers already. Every week, that is, every Saturday, there is a concert in his hall. Herr von Dürnitz has also put in an appearance and some other good people. They all want us to stay on for the winter at least, and Prince Zeill would also like it. The latter is going off to Salzburg the day after tomorrow, but he will only stay there for a day. He too is taking an interest in Wolfgang and has already spoken to Count Sensheim and Count Bergheim, who have promised him to do their very best. He is exceptionally popular here and can do a great deal. One must just be a little bit patient. That is why Herr Albert thinks that if we could only hold out for this winter, we should not have to spend our capital; for the concerts begin next month, on November 1st, and go on until May. So far he is not at all anxious, for all his friends have not yet turned up. I send greetings to Nannerl and by the next post I shall send her the silks. My compliments to Sallerl and to Herr Bullinger, Frau Hagenauer and Herr Gött[2] and other good friends, Mlle Katherl, Tresel, Pimperl and so forth.

I remain your miserable grass widow
MARIA ANNA MOZART

(217b) *Mozart resumes writing*

[Autograph in the Mozarteum, Salzburg]

The day before yesterday, Saturday the 4th, on the solemn festival of the name-day of His Royal Highness Archduke Albert[3] we had a little

---

[1] i.e. an old religious occasion.

[2] A nickname for godfather. Frau Mozart refers to Mozart's godfather Johann Gottlieb Pergmayr.

[3] i.e. the landlord of the 'Schwarzer Adler'. See p. 273, n. 5.

concert here, which began at half past three and finished at about eight. M. Dupreille,[1] whom Papa will probably remember, was also present. He was a pupil of Tartini. In the morning he was giving a violin lesson to Albert's youngest son Carl, when I happened to come in. I had never thought much of Dupreille, but I saw that he was taking great pains over the lesson, and when we started to talk of the fiddle as a solo and orchestral instrument, he made quite sensible remarks and always agreed with me, so that I went back on my former opinion and was convinced that I should find in him an excellent performer and a reliable orchestral player. I asked him therefore to be so good as to come to our little concert in the afternoon. We first played Haydn's two quintets,[2] but to my dismay I found that I could hardly hear him. He could not play four bars in succession without going wrong. He could not find his fingering and he knew nothing whatever about short rests. The best one can say about him is that he was very polite and praised the quintets; apart from that—Well, I said nothing at all, but he kept on exclaiming: 'I beg your pardon. I have lost my place again! It's ticklish stuff, but very fine.' I kept on replying: 'Do not worry. We are just among ourselves.' I then played my concertos in C, B♭ and E♭,[3] and after that my trio.[4] There indeed I had a fine accompaniment! In the Adagio I had to play his part for six bars. As a finale I played my last Cassation in B♭.[5] They all opened their eyes! I played as though I were the finest fiddler in all Europe. On the following Sunday at three o'clock we called on a certain Herr von Hamm. I have simply no time to write more, otherwise Herr von Kleinmayr[6] will not be able to take the letter. The Bishop of Chiemsee left today for Salzburg. I send my sister herewith six duets for clavicembalo and violin by Schuster,[7] which I have often played here. They are not bad. If I stay on I shall write six myself in the same style, as they are very popular here.[8] My main object in sending them to you is that you may amuse yourselves à deux. Addio.

[1] Charles Albert Dupreille (1728–1796), violinist in the Munich court orchestra.
[2] Probably two quintets composed by Michael Haydn in 1773, Perger 108 and 109.
[3] K. 246, 238, 271. The first two clavier concertos were composed in 1776, the third in 1777.
[4] K. 254, a clavier trio, composed in 1776.
[5] K. 287 [271H]. See p. 289, n. 2.
[6] Johann Franz Thaddäus von Kleinmayr (1733–1805), Secretary to the Salzburg Court Council.
[7] Joseph Schuster (1748–1812), a native of Dresden. In 1765 he and his friend Franz Seydelmann went with Naumann to Italy to study composition, and remained there until 1768. In 1772 both were appointed church composers to the Elector of Saxony. Schuster wrote several Italian and German operas, oratorios, symphonies and chamber music. It has not yet been discovered to which works of Schuster Mozart is referring. See Köchel, pp. 297, 298 and 887.
[8] Mozart carried out his intention at Mannheim, where he composed the five sonatas for violin and clavier, K. 296, 301–303, 305 [293a–d]. Abert, vol. i. pp. 623–626, points out how greatly Mozart's sonatas show the influence of Schuster's. See also Saint-Foix, vol. iii. p. 38 ff.

I kiss your hands 1000 times. And I beg you, Nannerl, to wait patiently a little longer.[1]

I am your most obedient son
WOLFGANG AMADÉ MOZART

Munich, 6 October 1777.[2]

(218) *Leopold Mozart to his Son*

[*Extract*] [*Autograph in the Mozarteum, Salzburg*]

MON TRÈS CHER FILS! SALZBURG, 9 *October* 1777

As I assume that you have now left Munich, I am writing to Augsburg and am enclosing a letter for Herr Stein, in which I urge him very strongly to arrange one or two concerts and tell him that you will inform him in person of the atrocious treatment which we have been receiving in Salzburg.[3] Do yourself credit on his organ, for he values it very highly; and, moreover, it is a good one. Write and tell me *what instruments he has*. When you were in Munich, you probably did not practise the violin at all? But I should be sorry to hear this. Brunetti now praises you to the skies! And when I was saying the other day that after all you played the violin *passabilmente*, he burst out: 'Cosa? Cazzo! Se suonava tutto! Questo era del Principe un puntiglio mal inteso, col suo proprio danno.'[4] Herr Glatz will bring you a pair of white silk stockings, which I have picked out for you. I put them on for the ball and found them far too tight. You will find too a book of small music paper, which I have put in, in case you should care to write a preambulum for your sister, for this kind of paper is thinner and more convenient for enclosing in a letter. When you talk to Herr Stein, you must not mention our instruments from Gera, for he is jealous of Friederici. But if this is impossible, you should say that I took over the instruments belonging to Colonel Count Prank, who left Salzburg on account of his epilepsy. You should add that you know nothing about the other instruments, as you were too young to notice ★ such things. The Archbishop goes off to Lauffen today and will be away for about a fortnight. Countess Schönborn has left and has taken with her the present for your sonatas. I am still finding one or two little things which you need, so you will be glad when you are further away, for if I am always sending you something, your luggage will become more and more bulky. There is a whole music score for the wind-instruments of

---

[1] Mozart is referring to the composition she had asked for. See p. 283.
[2] The autograph of this letter has the following postscript by the Munich musician Siegl, first published in *MM*, Nov. 1920, p. 32: 'I, Siegl, now a thoroughly trained husband, send my most humble greetings to the Papa of the cher fils!'. See *MBA*, No. 345.
[3] Leopold Mozart is referring to their strained relations with the Archbishop.
[4] What? Nonsense! Why, he could play anything! That was a mistaken idea the Prince persisted in, to his own loss. See Letter 266.

the Court orchestra and the score of the Adagio you wrote specially for
Brunetti, because he found the other one too artificial.[1] Perhaps I shall
copy it out on small paper and send it bit by bit. I do not know whether
you will be able to arrange more than one concert in Augsburg, for the
natives there have had an overdose of them. I read in a paper the other day
that Baumgartner, the cellist,[2] and four other musicians gave a concert
there together. When you perform something, and especially if it is a
clavier concerto, take care to see, when the concert is over, that you have
collected all the parts, since you have no scores with you. If you find that
you cannot give more than one good concert in Augsburg, it would be as
well not to stay there too long. I must close, for the post will soon be
going. We did not expect a letter today, for the Munich people always
give theirs to the Reichenhall post, which does not arrive until tomorrow.
Keep well! We are in good health and I seem to get better every day. I
sleep fairly well, my cough is disappearing and I look better. Ah, but
you and Mamma are ever in my mind. We both kiss you many
10000000000000 times and I am your old faithful, honest husband and
father

MOZART

I hear that for his fine composition[3] Haydn only received from the
Archbishop six Bavarian thalers (che generosità!)[4]

(219) Mozart to his Father

[Autograph in the Mozarteum, Salzburg]

MON TRÉS CHER PÉRE!   [MUNICH, 11 October 1777]
    Why have I said nothing so far about Mysliwecek? Because it was a
relief not to have to think of him for a while. For whenever he was
mentioned, I was obliged to hear how highly he has been praising me and
what a good and true friend of mine he is! At the same time I felt pity and
sympathy for him. People described his appearance to me and I was nearly
distracted. Was I to know that Mysliwecek, so good a friend of mine, was
in a town, even in a corner of the world where I was and was I not to see
him, to speak to him? Impossible! So I resolved to go and see him. But on
the previous day I went to the Governor of the Ducal Hospital and asked
him whether he could not arrange for me to talk to Mysliwecek in the
garden, since, although everyone, even the doctors had assured me that
there was no longer any danger of infection, I did not want to go to his

---

[1] K. 261, an Adagio written in 1776 to replace the original Adagio of K. 219, Mozart's
violin concerto in A major, composed in 1775.
  [2] Johann Baptist Baumgartner (1723–1781), born in Augsburg, was a member of the Stockholm court orchestra in 1775.
  [3] i.e. the incidental music for Voltaire's Zaïre.   [4] How generous!

room, as it was very small and smelt rather strongly. The Governor said that I was perfectly right and told me that Mysliwecek usually took a walk in the garden between eleven and twelve and that if I did not find him there, I was to ask whether he would not come down. I went therefore on the following day with Herr von Hamm, Secretary for War, (about whom I shall have something to say later on) and with Mamma to the hospital. Mamma went into the church and we walked into the garden. Mysliwecek was not there; so we sent him a message. I saw him coming across the garden towards us and recognised him at once by his walk. I should say here that he had already sent me his compliments through Herr Heller,[1] the cellist, and had begged me to be so kind as to visit him before my departure. When he came up to me, we shook hands in the most friendly fashion. 'You see', he said, 'how unfortunate I am!' These words and his appearance, which Papa already knows about, as it has been described to him, so wrung my heart that all I could say half sobbing was: 'With my whole heart I pity you'. *'My dear friend'*, he said, for he saw that I was moved and began at once to speak more cheerfully, *'do tell me what you are doing. I was told that you were here, but I could hardly believe it. Was it possible that Mozart was in Munich and had not visited me all this time?'* I replied: 'Indeed I must crave your forgiveness. I have had so many calls to pay. I have so many true friends here.' *'I am sure that you have very true friends here, but none so true as I, that I can assure you.'* He asked me whether I had not heard from Papa about a letter—'Yes', I interrupted, 'he wrote to me (I was so distracted and trembled so in every limb that I could hardly speak), but not in detail.' Mysliwecek then told me that Signor Gaetano Santoro, the Naples impresario, had been obliged owing to *impegni* and *protectione*[2] to give the carnival opera this season to a certain Maestro Valentini, but that next year he would have three to distribute, one of which would be at his disposal. *'So'*, said Mysliwecek, *'as I have already composed six times for Naples, I have not the slightest objection to taking on the less important opera and giving you the better one, I mean, the one for the carnival. God knows whether I shall be able to travel. If I cannot, then I shall just return the scrittura. The cast for next year is excellent; they are all singers whom I have recommended. My credit in Naples, you see, is so high that when I say, 'Engage this man', they engage him at once.'* The primo uomo is Marchesi,[3] whom he praises very highly and so does the whole of Munich. Then there is Marchiani, a good prima donna, and, further, a tenor, whose name I have forgotten, but who, as Mysliwecek says, is now the

---

[1] Gaudenz Heller (1750– ?), born at Politz in Czechoslovakia, became a famous cellist. He first held an appointment under the Bavarian Elector, and in 1780 settled in Bonn.

[2] i.e. obligations and patronage.

[3] Ludovico Marchesi (1755–1829), of Milan, was a famous male soprano. He made his début in Rome about 1773 and in 1776 entered the service of the Elector of Bavaria. After the latter's death in 1777 Marchesi returned to Italy, had a two years' engagement at the Teatro San Carlo in Naples, and continued to sing until 1805.

best tenor in Italy. '*I implore you*', he urged, '*go to Italy. There one is really esteemed and valued.*' And I am sure he is right. When I think it over carefully, I have to admit that in no country have I received so many honours, nowhere have I been so esteemed as in Italy; and certainly it is a real distinction to have written operas in Italy, especially for Naples. He told me that he would draft a letter to Santoro for me, and that I was to come to him on the morrow and copy it. But I could not possibly bring myself to go to his room; and yet if I wanted to copy it, I should have to do so, for I could not write in the garden. So I promised him to call without fail. But on the following day I wrote to him in Italian saying, *quite frankly*, that it was impossible for me to come to him, that I had eaten nothing and had only slept for three hours, and in the morning felt like a man who had lost his reason, that he was continually before my eyes, and so forth— all statements which are as true as that the sun can shine. He sent me the following reply:

> Lei è troppo sensibile al mio male. Io la ringrazio del suo buon cuore. Se parte per Praga, gli farò una lettera per il Conte Pachta.[1] Non si pigli tanto a cuore la mia disgrazia. Il principio fu d'una ribaltata di calesse, poi sono capitato nelle mani dei dottori ignoranti. Pazienza Ci sarà quel che Dio vorrà.[2]

He has sent me the following draft of a letter to Santoro:

> La brama ch'ebbi già da tanto tempo di servire V.S. Ill. e codesto rispettabilissimo pubblico di Napoli, colle mie debolezze di produrmi in codesto Real Teatro, è il motivo ch'io (non riguardando il lungo e dispendioso viaggio) condiscendo e mi contento di scriver l'anno venturo in codesto Regio Teatro una opera per 100 cigliati, pregandola però se possibile fosse che mi fosse confidata l'ultima, cioè, quella del carnevale, perchè i miei interessi non mi permetteranno di poter accettare una opera prima di quel tempo. Già tanto spero dalla sua grazia ed, avendo l'approvazione Reale per me, prego di mandar la scrittura al Maestro Mysliwecek, che così mi sarà sicuramente ricapitata. Frattanto anzioso d'imparar a conoscere persona di tanto merito, mi do l'onore di protestarmi per sempre etc.[3]

---

[1] Count Johann Pachta belonged to the Prague nobility, and was a devoted lover of music. During his first visit to Prague in 1787 Mozart was commissioned by him to compose some country dances, and wrote for him six German dances (K. 509).

[2] You feel my suffering too keenly. I am grateful for your good heart. If you go to Prague, I shall give you a letter for Count Pachta. Do not take my misfortune so much to heart. My illness began as the result of a carriage accident and then I fell into the hands of ignorant doctors. Patience, God's will will be done.

[3] The longing I have had for a considerable time to serve your illustrious person and that most worthy public of Naples by appearing with my humble works in your Royal Theatre, is the reason why (disregarding the long and expensive journey) I agree and am willing to compose an opera next year for the Royal Theatre for 100 cigliati. But, if possible, I should like to have the contract for the last one, I mean, the carnival opera, because my interests will not allow me to accept a commission before that time. I trust that you will be so gracious as to agree and that, when you have received the Royal approval, you will send the written contract to Maestro Mysliwecek, through whom I shall safely receive it. Meanwhile, longing to make the acquaintance of such a distinguished person, I have the honour to assure you that I am ever, etc.

Mysliwecek showed me too some letters in which my name was frequently mentioned. I am told that he has expressed great surprise when people here have talked about Beecke [1] or other clavier-players of the same kind, and has always exclaimed: 'Make no mistake. No one can play like Mozart. In Italy, where the greatest masters are to be found, they talk of no one but Mozart. When he is mentioned, everyone is silent.' I can now write the letter to Naples when I choose, but the sooner the better. First, however, I should like to have the opinion of that very wise Court Kapellmeister, Herr von Mozart!

I have an inexpressible longing to write another opera. It is a long way to go, it is true, but it would be a long time before I should have to write it. Many things may happen before then. But I think that I ought to accept it. If in the meantime I fail to secure an appointment, eh bien, then I can fall back on Italy. I shall still have my certain 100 ducats at the carnival and once I have composed for Naples, I shall be in demand everywhere. Moreover, as Papa is well aware, there are also opere buffe here and there in the spring, summer and autumn, which one can write for practice and for something to do. I should not make very much, it is true, but, all the same, it would be something; and they would bring me more honour and credit than if I were to give a hundred concerts in Germany. And I am happier when I have something to compose, for that, after all, is my sole delight and passion. And if I secure an appointment or if I have hopes of settling down somewhere, then the scrittura will be an excellent recommendation, will give me prestige and greatly enhance my value. But all this is only talk—talk out of the fulness of my heart. If Papa can prove conclusively that I am wrong, well, then I shall acquiesce, although unwillingly. For I have only to hear an opera discussed, I have only to sit in a theatre, hear the orchestra tuning their instruments—oh, I am quite beside myself at once.

Tomorrow Mamma and I are taking leave of Mysliwecek in the garden. For only the other day, when he heard me say that I had to fetch my mother in the church, he said: 'If only I were not such a sight, I should very much like to meet the mother of such a great virtuoso'. I implore you, my dearest Papa, to reply to Mysliwecek. Write to him as often as you have time. You can give him no greater pleasure. For the man is completely deserted and often no one goes to see him for a whole week. 'I assure you', he said, 'it seems very strange that so few people come to see me. In Italy I had company every day.' If it were not for his face, he would be the same old Mysliwecek, full of fire, spirit and life, a little thin, of course, but otherwise the same excellent, cheerful fellow. All Munich is talking about

[1] Ignaz von Beecke (1733–1803) was adjutant and music director to Prince Kraft Ernst von Öttingen-Wallerstein. He was an excellent pianist and composed a wide range of vocal and instrumental works. See p. 345, n. 1.

his oratorio 'Abramo ed Isacco', which he produced here.[1] He has now finished, except for a few arias, a cantata or serenata for Lent. When his illness was at its worst he composed an opera for Padua.[2] But nothing can help him. Even here they all say that the Munich doctors and surgeons have done for him. He has a fearful cancer of the bone. The surgeon Caco, that ass, burnt away his nose. Imagine what agony he must have suffered. Herr Heller has just been to see him. When I wrote that letter to him yesterday, I sent him my serenata which I composed in Salzburg for Archduke Maximilian;[3] and Heller gave it to him with the letter.

Now for something else.

(219a) *Maria Anna Mozart to her Husband*

[Autograph in the Mozarteum, Salzburg]

[MUNICH, 11 *October* 1777]

There is a Secretary for War here, Herr von Hamm by name, about whom Wolfgang has already written to you. He has a daughter who plays the clavier but who has not been well taught. He would like to send her to you in Salzburg for a year in order that she might perfect her playing. She is thirteen and, as she is an only child, she has been brought up rather indulgently. He is spending a lot of money on her. He is going to write to you himself, so we have had to give him your address. He is the most honest man in the world. He is completely wrapt up in his daughter. I have only written this to you so that you may know about it in advance and decide what you want to do. We are travelling from here to Augsburg tomorrow, October 11th, so I am busy packing, and this gives me a great deal of trouble, for I am doing it all by myself, since Wolfgang cannot help me the least little bit. He and I were with Mysliwecek today from eleven until half past twelve. He is indeed to be pitied. I talked to him as if I had known him all my life. He is a true friend to Wolfgang and has said the kindest things about him everywhere. Everyone has told us so.

(219b) *Mozart resumes writing*

[Autograph in the Mozarteum, Salzburg]

Herr von Hamm's address is as follows:

A Monsieur Monsieur de Hamm, secretaire de guerre de
S.A.E. Sérénissime de Baviére, à Munic.

Immediately after lunch yesterday I went with Mamma to a coffee

---

[1] It was written in 1776 for Florence.
[2] Probably his *Atide*, produced at Padua in 1774.
[3] *Il rè pastore*, composed in 1775 on the occasion of a visit of the Archduke Maximilian, Maria Theresia's youngest son.

party at the two Fräulein Freysingers'. Mamma, however, drank no coffee, but had two bottles of Tyrolese wine instead. She went home at three o'clock to put a few things together for our journey. I went with the two young ladies to the said Herr von Hamm, where the three ladies each played a concerto and I played one of Eichner's[1] at sight and then went on improvising. Miss Simplicity von Hamm's teacher is a certain clergyman of the name of Schreier. He is a good organist, but no cembalist. He kept on staring at me through his spectacles the whole time. He is a dry sort of fellow, who does not say much: but he tapped me on the shoulder, sighed and said: 'Yes—you are—you know—yes—that is true—you are first-rate'. A propos. Does Papa not recall the name Freysinger? The Papa of the two beautiful young ladies whom I have mentioned says that he knows Papa quite well, and was a student with him. He still remembers particularly Wessobrunn, where Papa (this was news to me) played on the organ amazingly well. *'It was quite terrifying'*, he said, *'to see how rapid your Papa was with his feet and hands. Indeed he was absolutely amazing. Ah, he was a great fellow. My father thought the world of him. And how he fooled the clerics to the top of their bent about becoming a priest!*[2] *You are the very image of him, as he then was, absolutely the very image. But when I knew him, he was just a little shorter.'* A propos. Now for something else. A certain Court Councillor, Öfele by name, who is one of the best Court Councillors here, sends his most humble greetings to Papa. He could have been Chancellor long ago, but for one thing—his love of the bottle. When I first saw him at Albert's, I thought, and so did Mamma, 'Goodness me, what a superlative idiot!' Just picture him, a very tall fellow, strongly built, rather corpulent, with a perfectly absurd face. When he crosses the room to go to another table, he places both hands on his stomach, bends over them and hoists his belly aloft, nods his head and then draws back his right foot with great rapidity. And he performs the same trick afresh for every person in turn. He says he knows Papa infinitely well. I am now off to the theatre for a while. Later on I shall write more. I simply cannot do so now, for my fingers are aching horribly.

(219c) *Maria Anna Mozart resumes writing*

[*Autograph in the Mozarteum, Salzburg*]

[MUNICH, 11 *October* 1777]

And I am sweating so that the water is pouring down my face, simply from the fag of packing. The devil take all travelling. I feel that I could

---

[1] Ernst Eichner (1740–1777), born in Mannheim, was a distinguished violinist and bassoon player. He lived for a time in Paris and in London and then went to Potsdam, where he entered the service of the Prussian Crown Prince. His compositions are typical of the Mannheim school.

[2] Leopold Mozart was intended for the Church, but after two years' study at the University of Salzburg he decided to take up music as a profession.

shove my feet into my mug, I am so exhausted. I hope that you and Nannerl are well. I send most cordial greetings to my dear Sallerl and Monsieur Bullinger. Please tell Nannerl not to give Bimperl too much to eat, lest she should get too fat. I send greetings to Thresel. Addio. I kiss you both millions of times.

MARIA ANNA MOZART

Munich, [October] 11th, at eight o'clock in the evening, 1777.

(219d) *Mozart resumes writing*

[Autograph in the Mozarteum, Salzburg]

MUNICH, 11 October [1777]

I am writing this at a quarter to twelve at night. I have just been to the Lipperl Theatre.[1] I only went to see the ballet, or rather pantomime, which I had not yet seen. It was called: *Das von der Fée girigaricanarimanarischaribari verfertigte Ei.* It was excellent and very good fun. We are off to Augsburg tomorrow, for Prince Taxis is not at Regensburg, but at Dischingen. At the moment, it is true, he is at one of his summer residences, but it is not more than an hour from Dischingen. In Augsburg I shall follow Papa's instructions to the letter. I think it would be best if Papa were now to write to us at Augsburg and direct his letters to be delivered at the 'Lamm'. I shall write again as soon as we decide to move on. What a clever suggestion that is, isn't it? Herr von Bellvall, who came to see us this evening at Albert's, sends 100000 greetings to Papa and to my sister. I enclose four praeambula[2] for her. She will see and hear for herself into what keys they lead. I hope that you received the Schuster duets. My greetings to all my good friends, especially to young Count Arco,[3] to Miss Sallerl, and to my best friend Herr Bullinger, whom I will get you to ask to be so good as to make at the eleven o'clock concert next Sunday an authoritative pronouncement in my name, presenting my compliments to all the members of the orchestra and exhorting them to be diligent, lest I be proved a liar one of these days. For I have extolled these concerts everywhere and shall continue to do so. I kiss Papa's hands and I am his most obedient son

WOLFGANG MOZART

---

[1] Probably the Kasperle-Theater, a popular playhouse near the Isartor.
[2] There is no trace of these works.
[3] Count Leopold Arco, son of Count Georg Anton Felix von Arco, Chief Chamberlain at the Salzburg Court. Abbé Bullinger had been his tutor.

(220) *Leopold Mozart to his Son*

[*Extract*]   [*Autograph in the Mozarteum, Salzburg*]

MON TRÈS CHER FILS!   SALZBURG, 12 *October* 1777
    I hope that both you and Mamma are very well and that you have
received the letter which I enclosed to my brother Franz Aloys. Thank
God, we are both in excellent health. As the weather is fine, we take an
early walk every day with our faithful Bimperl, who is in splendid trim
and only becomes very sad and obviously most anxious when we are both
out of the house, for then she thinks that because she has lost you two,
she is now going to lose us as well. So when we went to the ball and she
saw us masked, she refused to leave Mitzerl, and, when we got home, she
was so overjoyed that I thought she would choke. Moreover, when we
were out, she would not stay on her bed in the room, but remained lying
on the ground outside the porter's door. She would not sleep, but kept on
moaning, wondering, I suppose, whether we should ever return.
    People here are gossiping and saying that you have got such a handsome ★
present from the Elector that you have enough money with which to
travel for a whole year and that as soon as there is a vacancy he will take
you into his service. Well, I prefer that people should say something
amiable and flattering rather than something unpleasant—especially on
account of the Archbishop! I suppose that the Bishop of Chiemsee's
household have been spreading rumours of this kind in order to spite the
Archbishop. How I hope that the weather will remain as fine as it is for
your journey.

                                                    October 13*th*
    We received, not, as we had hoped, from Augsburg, but once more
from Munich, your letter which says that you were going to Augsburg on
Saturday the 11th; and by mistake you both dated your letter the 11th
instead of, as it should have been, the evening of the 10th. But by Heaven,
if you stayed so long, almost three weeks, in Munich, where you could
not hope to make a farthing, you will indeed get on well in this world!
That Prince Taxis is at Dischingen and not at Regensburg was no news
to me. But you must find out at the Head Post Office in Augsburg, where
my brother's daughter¹ is very well known, how long he is staying at
Dischingen, for to go off to Regensburg would mean a very considerable
détour. He will probably return to Regensburg after All Saints'; so you
should arrange your stay at Augsburg accordingly. Not far from Dischingen and close to Donauwörth is the famous Imperial Monastery of

---

¹ Maria Anna Thekla (1758–1841), the only surviving child of Leopold Mozart's brother,
Franz Aloys. See p. 273, n. 4. For an account of Mozart's 'Bäsle', see *MMB*, March 1904,
p. 245 ff., and Abert, vol. ii. pp. 959–975.

Kaysersheim,[1] whose Abbot, I hear, is a great patron of virtuosi and where you will receive all kinds of honours. But you must do yourself credit and set a high price on your talent. You will find out all this in Augsburg and Herr Stein will be an excellent guide and will obtain letters for you to various places. I do not know whether you would do better to go first to Wallerstein or to Kaysersheim; I mean, of course, after you have been to Prince Taxis. Kaysersheim lies to the right and Wallerstein to the left, so I think you should go first to Kaysersheim and then the Abbot could let his horses take you to Wallerstein. Prince von Öttingen-Wallerstein will perhaps be in his castle at Hohenaltheim, which is close to Wallerstein. You can find all this out in Augsburg and later on in Dischingen. You will remember that *the Prince, who was that handsome young gentleman in Naples, invited you to visit him*; and you can make this the reason why you are paying him your respects. It used to be possible to get work at the Margrave's in Anspach and with the Commandant at Mergentheim or Mergenthal. Thus your journey to Würzburg should be so arranged as to take in Anspach and Mergentheim on your way. You will easily ascertain whether these places are still good for your purpose. But you must not believe every ass, for even if here and there many people are not very highly esteemed and have therefore become discontented, yet great virtuosi are regarded quite differently. If at some particular place the whole orchestra, I say, *the whole orchestra* have been dismissed, that, I admit, is a sign that no more money is to be made there, and if you can find no players to accompany you, of course it would be impossible to perform. From Würzburg to Mannheim you go through Heidelberg. Other places worth visiting are Darmstadt, Frankfurt, Mainz and Coblenz. Now that it occurs to me, I must remind you (as you pay little attention to these things) that the Pope, who conferred that order on you, was the famous Pope Ganganelli, Clement XIV. You must wear your cross in Kaysersheim. What you write about the opera in Naples *I myself thought of long ago*. Did Mysliwecek give you Don Santoro's address? You may now send him the letter from Augsburg or enclose it to me; it does not matter, provided it is written clearly and intelligibly. If you have not got his address, then you must send me the letter. I will correspond with Mysliwecek and set things going; but everything depends on the address. Meanwhile what could I have written to Mysliwecek when I did not know whether you had seen him or not? Moreover, I could not send you my opinion upon the matter, as I did not know what might lie behind it. For I was convinced that Mysliwecek knew that you were in Munich, since you both arrived there on the 22nd[2] and he did not write to me until the 28th. About the whole history of his illness I shall write more fully

---

[1] Kaysersheim (now Kaisheim), a Cistercian monastery, founded in 1134 by Count Heinrich von Lechsmünd.   [2] In fact the Mozarts arrived on September 24th.

some other time. He is indeed to be pitied! Only too well do I understand your fright and your terror, when you saw him. I should have felt exactly the same. You know how tender-hearted I am!

Mamma writes about the daughter of War Secretary von Hamm. It is quite possible that he may write to me; and, if he does, I shall be exceedingly embarrassed. First of all, you know that we live very frugally and that these people are used to good living. But that is not the main reason. You both say that she has had a very stupid upbringing. So I presume that she has little talent for music, and, if this is so, she would not do me any credit. The wrong position of her hands is not very important, for that can be remedied. But if she has no ear and therefore no sense of time, then I must humbly refuse the honour. In order to find this out, you should give her a short test, which would be quickly done. You have only to play two simple bars to her and see whether she can play them *a tempo*, that is, whether, once she knows the notes of the two bars, she can imitate the time also. So write by the next post and say whether she has any ear or not; for at present it is very difficult for me to decide. It is quite true that Herr Freisinger was a fellow-student of mine; but I never knew that he heard me play the organ so admirably in Wessobrunn monastery. So nothing can be kept secret. You know how often I have said to you: *Murder will out.* You ask whether I know Court Councillor Öfele? Do I not? He was married to the handsome daughter of Lepin, a merchant, in the Abbot's chapel and by the Abbot himself, and I, being then a descanter in the monastery of St. Ulrich, sang a cantata at the Nuptial Mass. His wife not only sang well but was a good performer on the harpsichord and she brought him a dowry of 30,000 gulden. I saw him afterwards in Munich quite frequently when he had become a Court Councillor. *Sic transit gloria mundi!*[1] Drink has been the ruin of him. His excessive devotion to music has undoubtedly contributed to it.

I well believe that dear Mamma finds packing a troublesome job. Oh, how gladly would I do it for her and relieve her. I kiss her many million times and wish her health and patience. It is more difficult for me to be patient. Nannerl thanks you for the praeambula. The whole company of ★ marksmen, Hagenauer, Schiedenhofen and so forth, Mitzerl and all Salzburg send their greetings. We kiss you both most cordially and I am your old

MOZART

You ask whether we received Schuster's duets? Not a trace of them! Could you not have added 'which I sent by Tom, Dick or Harry'? Where are we to make enquiries? Who was to deliver them? Indeed I must say that you are sometimes very slap-dash! ★

---

[1] i.e. so passes the glory of the world.

At Augsburg, his father's native town, Mozart gave a concert which, however, brought in very little money. After a fortnight's stay, during which he tried for the first time the new Stein pianoforte and made the acquaintance of his cousin, Maria Anna Thekla, Mozart and his mother left for Mannheim. Letters 221-231.

(221) *Maria Anna Mozart to her Husband*

[*Autograph in the Mozarteum, Salzburg*]

AUGSBURG, 14 *October* 1777

We left Munich on the 11th at noon and arrived safely in Augsburg at nine in the evening; and this journey we did in nine hours with a hired coachman who, moreover, fed his horses for an hour.

(221a) *Mozart continues the letter*

[*Autograph in the Mozarteum, Salzburg*]

[AUGSBURG, 14 *October* 1777]

So we did not make a mistake about the date; for we wrote in the morning; and we shall be off again, I think, next Friday, that is, the day after tomorrow. For just hear how kind and generous these good Augsburg gentlemen have been! In no place have I been overwhelmed with so many marks of honour as here. My first visit was to the magistrate, Longotabarro.[1] My uncle, a most excellent and lovable man and an honourable townsman, accompanied me and had the honour of waiting upstairs on the landing like a lackey until I should come out of the Arch-Magistrate's room. I did not forget to deliver at once my Papa's most humble respects. He was so good as to remember our whole history and asked me: '*How has he fared all this time?*' Whereupon I at once replied: 'Very well, thanks and praise be to God. And I trust that you too have fared very well?' After that he began to unbend, and addressed me in the second person, while I continued to address him as 'Your Highness', as I had done from the very first. He would not let me go and I had to follow him upstairs to his son-in-law (on the second floor); and meanwhile my uncle had the honour of waiting, seated on a stool in the lobby. I had to restrain myself, most manfully, otherwise I should have said something quite politely, of course. Upstairs I had the honour of playing for about three quarters of an hour upon a good clavichord by Stein in the presence of the dressed-up son and the long-legged young wife and the stupid old lady. I improvised and finally I played off at sight all the music he had, including some very pretty pieces by a certain Edelmann.[2] They were all exceedingly polite and I too was very polite. For it is my custom to treat

---

[1] Von Langenmantel. See p. 274.

[2] Johann Friedrich Edelmann (1749–1794), born in Strassburg, went to Paris with his pupil Baron Dietrich and became a popular clavier-player and composer. When Baron Dietrich became Mayor of Strassburg, Edelmann returned with him to his native town, where both were guillotined during the French Revolution.

people as I find them; it pays best in the end. I told them that after lunch I was going to see Stein. The young gentleman of his own accord offered to take me there. I thanked him for his kindness and promised to call again at two o'clock, which I did. We all set off together, accompanied by his brother-in-law, who looked the perfect student. Although I had asked them to keep my identity a secret, yet Herr von Langenmantel was so thoughtless as to say to Herr Stein: 'I have the honour of introducing to you a virtuoso on the clavier', and began to snigger. I at once protested and said that I was only an unworthy pupil of Herr Siegl in Munich, who had asked me to deliver 1000 compliments to him. He shook his head— and said finally: 'Is it possible that I have the honour of seeing Herr Mozart before me?' 'Oh, no,' I replied, 'my name is Trazom and I have a letter for you.' He took the letter and wanted to break the seal at once. But I did not give him time to do so and asked: 'Surely you do not want to read that letter now? Open the door, and let us go into your room. I am most anxious to see your pianofortes.' 'All right,' he said, 'just as you wish. But I feel sure that I am not mistaken.' He opened the door and I ran straight to one of the three claviers which stood in the room. I began to play. He could scarcely open the letter in his eagerness to make sure. He only read the signature. 'Oh,' he cried and embraced me. He kept crossing himself and making faces and was as pleased as Punch. I shall tell you later on all about his claviers. He then took me straight to a coffee-house. When I entered I thought that I should drop down, overcome by the stink and fumes of tobacco. But with God's help I had to stand it for an hour; and I pretended to enjoy it all, though to me it seemed as if we were in Turkey. He then talked a great deal about a certain composer, called Graf, who, however, has only written flute concertos. He said 'Now Graf [1] is something quite exceptional', and all that kind of *exaggerated* talk. I was sweating with fright, my head, my hands and my whole body. This Graf is a brother of the two who live at The Hague[2] and at Zürich respectively. My host would not let me off, but took me to him at once. Graf is indeed a most noble fellow. He had a dressing-gown on, which I should not be ashamed to be seen wearing in the street. His words are all on stilts and he generally opens his mouth before he knows what he wants to say; and often it shuts again without having done anything. After many compliments he performed a concerto for two flutes. I had to play the first violin part. This is what I think of it. It is not at all pleasing to the ear, not a bit natural. He often plunges into a new key far too brusquely and it is all quite devoid of charm. When it was

---

[1] Friedrich Hartmann Graf (1727–1795), born in Rudolstadt, went to Hamburg in 1759 as a flute virtuoso and toured as flautist and conductor until 1772, when he became music director in Augsburg. In his day he was regarded as a composer of outstanding merit, who did not write only for the flute, as Mozart's description would seem to imply.

[2] See p. 64, n. 5.

over, I praised him very highly, for he really deserves it. The poor fellow must have taken a great deal of trouble over it and he must have studied hard enough. At last a clavichord, one of Stein's, was brought out of the inner room, an excellent instrument, but covered with dust and dirt. Herr Graf, who is Director here, stood there transfixed, like someone who has always imagined that his wanderings from key to key are quite unusual and now finds that one can be even more unusual and yet not offend the ear. In a word, they were all astounded. Now I must close, or else I shall miss the post which leaves at four o'clock. The next time I shall tell you the whole story about Augsburg. I kiss your hands 1000 times and

I am

WOLFGANG MOZART

(221b) *Mozart to his Father*

[*Autograph in the Koch Collection, Basel*]

[AUGSBURG, 14 October 1777[1]]

I gave the Schuster duets to Herr von Kleinmayr to take with him to Salzburg, and with them I also wrote a letter in which I explained that he was taking charge of them. My greetings to all my good friends, especially to Herr Bullinger. Please send me the Bishop of Chiemsee's address. Do not forget it!

(221c) *Maria Anna Mozart to her Husband*

[*Autograph in the Koch Collection, Basel*]

[AUGSBURG, 14 October 1777][2]

All sorts of messages from me to all my good friends.

MARIA ANNA MOZART

(222) *Leopold Mozart to his Son*

[*Extract*]　　　　　　　　　　　　　[*Autograph in the Mozarteum, Salzburg*]

MON TRÉS CHER FILS!　　　　　　　　SALZBURG, 15 October 1777

Including the letter which I enclosed to my brother, this is the third which you will receive from me in Augsburg. I foresee that you may

---

[1] A postscript to the above letter.
[2] A postscript to Mozart's letter.

not be able to give a concert before next Sunday, as it has always to be announced a week in advance. I must remind you of something which you can make use of, if circumstances permit. If you find that you are warmly applauded and are very highly esteemed, I should like *a special article, praising your gifts, to appear in the Augsburg papers, after you have left*, an article which my brother could perhaps dictate to Herr Stein or which Herr Glatz could draft and Herr Stein could arrange to have published. You know why! It would make someone here very angry,[1] but Herr Stein and some other Evangelicals would get a lot of fun out of it. You know, of course, that the Lutherans should be called *Evangelicals*, for they do not like to be called Lutherans. Thus, for instance, you should talk of an *Evangelical Church* and not of a *Lutheran Church*; similarly the Calvinists like to be called *Protestants* and not Calvinists. It has just occurred to me that I ought to tell you this, for no more than a single wrong word may often lead to an unpleasant experience with some irritable person, though, of course, sensible people pay no attention to such formalities. Now for your journey. I quite agree with what you say about the opera in Naples, that is, that you should endeavour to obtain the scrittura. Yes; and if the Naples plan does not come off, I am quite prepared to approach Michele Dall'Agata[2] once more, for it is always well to have a contract in the offing. You both stayed in Munich far too long, so you must now give one or two concerts in Augsburg in order to earn something, *be it ever so little*. Flattering words, praises and cries of 'Bravissimo' pay neither postmasters nor landlords. So as soon as you find that there is no more money to be made, you should try to get away at once. There is usually an opera in Mannheim on November 4th, the Feast of St. Charles; and the question now is, whether you propose to be there by that date? Why, it is almost impossible! Prince Taxis and Prince von Öttingen-Wallerstein sometimes go there to see the opera; and, fortunately, neither of them live very far from Augsburg. So, unless you find that it is clearly to your advantage to do so, you must not stay on there for a minute longer than is absolutely necessary. The opera which is being performed in Mannheim for the Feast of St. Charles *will be repeated during the carnival*. So, if you can win the favour of Prince Taxis, you ought not to hurry away to Mannheim, *for you can see the operas there later on*. Moreover, if you want to be in Mannheim by November 4th, it is quite out of the question to go on to Würzburg from Wallerstein. No, you would have to travel straight to Mannheim, which is a good distance from Wallerstein, about twenty miles, or a two days' journey. *Mamma will find the route on the postal maps.* A great deal, of course, depends on whether the roads are good and on

---

[1] Archbishop Hieronymus Colloredo.
[2] Michele Dall'Agata, impresario of the Teatro San Benedetto in Venice. He did not reply to Leopold Mozart's two applications.

whether the route is circuitous. From Wallerstein to Würzburg is a stretch of only fifteen miles and the distance from Würzburg to Mannheim is the same. The days are now beginning to get shorter. So you should always try to leave *early in the morning* in order not to have to travel late at night. You can get fuller information about all this from our good friends in Augsburg and especially, I believe, from the Director of the Post Office, who knows my brother's daughter very well and who will perhaps give you letters of introduction to the Court of Prince Taxis. When talking to strangers who happen to be staying at your inn, you should not be too outspoken about your journey, for there are many rascals and adventurers about. Be sure to remember to ask *Prince Taxis and Prince von Öttingen-Wallerstein for letters of introduction to Mannheim.*

When you were leaving, there were a thousand necessary matters which I simply could not talk over with you, because I was ill, confused, out of humour, depressed and very sad; because, moreover, speaking hurt my chest very much, and because the packing and hoisting of your luggage on the coach in the early morning gave me a number of things to think about. Had this not been so, I should have told you that immediately after your arrival in Munich, you should try to find a copyist and that you should do this wherever you stay for any length of time. For you must really endeavour to get ahead with your composition, and that you can do if you have in readiness copies of symphonies and divertimenti to present to a Prince or to some other patron. The copying should be arranged so that *the copyist writes out at your lodgings and under your supervision at least the violino primo or some other leading part.* The rest he can copy out at home. It is absolutely essential that you should have something ready for Prince Taxis and you should therefore give the oboe-, horn- and viola-parts of six *good symphonies* at once to one or, better still, to *several copyists* (in order to speed up matters). You would thus be in a position to present to the Prince the whole score of a symphony and still have the duplicated violin and bass parts to be used on some other occasion, as, for example, at Würzburg, to which you would only have to add the parts for oboe, horn and viola. The divertimenti can be copied very quickly, even though it is true that yours have a number of parts and are rather long. Basta! Wherever you are, you must look about immediately for a copyist, or else you will lose a great deal! For if you do not do this, of what use to you will be all the music which you have taken away? You really cannot wait until some patron has them copied; and, now that I come to think of it, he would thank you for allowing him to do so and would not pay you a farthing. It is far too laborious to have your compositions copied from the score, and a thousand mistakes will creep in unless the copyist works the whole time under your supervision. But he could come *for a few mornings*, when you happen to be in, copy out *the chief parts*

★ and then write out the remainder at home. *Your main object, however, should now be to have something ready for Prince Taxis*; and, if you had a copy of your oboe concerto,[1] Perwein[2] might enable you to make an honest penny in Wallerstein. Further, the Abbot of Kaysersheim would certainly reward you well for your music; and there you would have the no small advantage of not having to pay anything for food, drink and the rest, in respect of which landlords' bills usually make heavy inroads on one's purse. Now you understand me. *These steps are really necessary and are to your interest.* All the compliments, visits and so forth are only incidental and should not be taken seriously. For you must not lose sight of your main object, which is to make money. All your endeavours should thus be directed to earning money, and you should be very careful *to spend as little as possible*, or you will not be able to travel in an honourable fashion, and may even have to remain rooted to one spot and there run up debts. After all, you can find copyists everywhere. You should get the copyist first of all to show you a specimen of his writing, and also the kind of paper he uses, which should resemble that which you have already used. In a word, it is necessary to take thought for everything, so that no fatal mistake is made; and this it is possible to do, if you have your head screwed on. And another idea occurs to me. You took with you the big Latin prayer book, which you will find very useful, not only because it has all the Psalms and other Church texts,—Mamma has the German version of the Psalms in her big service-book—, but also because it will help you *to keep up your Latin*. You should sometimes for a change say your morning and evening prayers out of it. These are easy to understand

★ and you might add some confession and communion prayers.

My brother will gladly bind for you the scores which are still on loose sheets, but you should remind him that *the edges must not be clipped.* He need only look at the other bound scores. When you are in Augsburg, my brother or his daughter or his wife (to all of whom I send my greetings) will certainly help you to pack. Baron Dürnitz[3] was in Munich, was he not? You could easily have used that money for the journey. *How much had you to pay at Albert's?*

The preludes[4] which you sent Nannerl are superlatively beautiful and she kisses you a million times in gratitude for them. She plays them very well already. I shall write by the next post to Venice and see whether you cannot secure the opera for Ascension. Mysliwecek has informed me with

---

[1] Köchel (p. 295, 296) suggests that Leopold Mozart is referring to an oboe concerto which his son had composed for Giuseppe Ferlendis and which he rewrote later in Mannheim as a flute concerto for De Jean (K. 314 [285d]).

[2] An oboist in the Archbishop's service who in 1777 joined the orchestra of Prince von Öttingen-Wallerstein.

[3] He owed Mozart a fee for composing the clavier sonata, K. 284 [205b], and possibly some other works. See p. 287, n, 4.

[4] See p. 283.

the greatest delight that, although he never expected it, he had the pleasure of seeing both you and Mamma, *la quale*, he writes, *è veramente una signora di garbo, degna del Signor Mozart*.[1] He tells me that he has now sent twelve symphonies and six quintets with oboe obbligato to the Archbishop and he asks me to arrange for their performance and to endeavour to make the Archbishop remember him for his earlier music and this present contribution: *producir di rammentar al Principe la musica vecchia e moderna che gli mando, per interesse mio. Sono viaggiatore* and so forth.[2] He adds at the end: *Alla signorina figlia manderò delle suonate per cembalo*.[3] I shall be very curious to hear what will happen about the Naples scrittura which we are hoping to obtain, while in the meantime we must try to secure the contract for Ascension. You must think ahead and aim at getting on. Should you obtain a good appointment in Mannheim or in some other centre, this will not prevent you from undertaking a journey to Italy, for every great lord, who really loves music, regards it as a personal honour if someone in his service makes a reputation for himself. I shall send my next letter franco to my brother's address in Augsburg. He will be able to forward it, if you have left, as he will know your route. I am inclined to think, however, that it will still catch you in Augsburg. You really should not worry about the opera in Mannheim, for you can see it during the carnival. *But you must make a point of visiting Prince Taxis on his estates;* and when you are there, you will have to be guided by circumstances. How you should set things going I shall let you know some other time. We have not yet received the Schuster duets, but perhaps they will come by today's mail coach. Thank God, we are well; and I should be even better, if I were one of those light-hearted fathers who can forget their wives and children in three weeks. That I could not do in a hundred years, nay, even during my lifetime. Nannerl and I kiss you a million times and, alive and dead, I am your old honest husband and father

MOZART

Many of my questions receive no answer; on the other hand, you will notice that I reply to all yours. Why? Because when I have written to you about all sorts of important items, I then put your letter before me—read it through and, whenever you ask a question, I answer it then and there. Furthermore, I always keep a slip of paper on my table, and whenever anything occurs to me, which I want to tell you about, I jot it down in a few words. Thus when I begin writing, it is impossible for me to forget anything. I am sending you this rather long letter with some music, for I

---

[1] Who is truly a charming lady, worthy of Herr Mozart.
[2] Endeavour to remind the Prince in my interest of my earlier music and the compositions which I am now sending him. I am a traveller and so forth.
[3] I shall send some cembalo sonatas to your daughter.

could not refrain from letting you have these works.[1] Sometimes an opportunity occurs of composing in the same style; and these are still very good models.

The Hagenauers (yesterday all the Theresas received shoals of congratulations), Fräulein Sallerl, Count Arco, our ever faithful Bullinger, who came to see us yesterday evening at half past six when Nannerl and I were practising the clavier as usual, Fräulein Mitzerl, Ferlendis and Ferrari, Mme Gerlichs, Court Councillor von Mölk, who did not even know that Mamma was away, and Tresel, who is just the same as ever, except that, instead of sitting in the kitchen in the evenings, she now has to spin, and last Friday had to do in one day what she has taken two days to get through up to the present (however, she is in good form and is better tempered than she used to be)—all of the above and many others, whom I cannot think of at the moment, send their greetings. Addio!

(224)[2] Mozart to his Father

[Autograph in the Mozarteum, Salzburg]

[AUGSBURG, 16 October 1777]

MON TRÉS CHER PÉRE,

All that I can say about the daughter of Hamm, the Secretary for War, is that she undoubtedly must have a gift for music, as she has only been learning for three years and yet can play several pieces really well. But I find it difficult to give you an idea of the impression she makes on me when she is playing. She seems to me so curiously affected. She stalks over the clavier with her long bony fingers in such an odd way. It is true that she has not yet had a really good teacher, and if she stays in Munich she will never, never become what her father is so anxious that she should be: and that is, a first-rate performer on the clavier. If she comes to Papa at Salzburg, her gain will be twofold; both in musical knowledge and in intelligence, which is not exactly her strong point at present. She has made me laugh a great deal already at her expense and you would certainly get plenty of entertainment for your pains. She would not eat much, for she is far too simple. You say that I ought to have tested her playing. Why, I simply could not do so for laughing. For whenever, by way of example, I played a passage with my right hand she at once exclaimed Bravissimo!

---

[1] According to Köchel, p. 768, this collection (K. App. 109ᵛᶦ [A. 71-88]) is a copy made by Leopold Mozart of eighteen church works by Ernst Eberlin and Michael Haydn. It is now in the British Museum.

[2] The letter formerly numbered 223 is in fact a postscript to No. 225; see p. 330.

in a tiny mouse-like voice. I will now finish the account of my Augsburg
adventures as briefly as I can. Herr von Fingerle, to whom I delivered
Papa's compliments, was also present at Director Graf's. Everyone was
extremely polite and talked the whole time of getting up a concert.
They all declared: 'It will be one of the most brilliant concerts we have
ever had in Augsburg. Your acquaintance with our magistrate Langenmantel will be a great point in your favour. Besides, the name of Mozart
carries great weight here.' We parted in very good spirits. Now Papa
must know that at Herr Stein's young Herr von Langenmantel had
declared that he would undertake to get up a concert in the Stube [1] for
the patricians alone, as a special honour for me. You can scarcely imagine
how earnestly he spoke and with what enthusiasm he promised to take
up the matter. We arranged that I should call on him the next day and
hear the decision. I went. This was October 13th. He was very polite,
but said that he could not tell me anything definite yet. I played to him
again for about an hour and he invited me to lunch on the following day,
the 14th. In the morning he sent a message asking me to come at eleven
o'clock and bring some music, as he had invited some of the orchestra and
they would like to play something. I sent him some music at once and
arrived myself at eleven o'clock. He mumbled a whole string of excuses
and remarked quite coolly: 'Look here, a concert is quite out of the
question. Oh, I assure you, I lost my temper yesterday on your account.
The patricians told me that their funds were very low and that you were
not the type of virtuoso to whom they could offer a souverain d'or.'
I smiled and said 'I quite agree'. *He is Intendant of the orchestra at the Stube
and his old father is the magistrate!* But I did not let it worry me. We went
up to lunch. The old man was also at table; he was very polite, but did
not say a word about the concert. After lunch I played two concertos,
improvised something and then played the violin in one of Hafeneder's
trios. I would gladly have done some more fiddling, but I was accompanied so badly that it gave me the colic. He said to me in a very friendly
manner: 'You must spend the day with us and we will go to the play and
then you will come back to supper with us'. We were all very merry.
When we got back from the theatre, I played again until we went to
supper. He had already questioned me in the morning about my cross
and I had explained quite clearly how I had got it and what it was. [1] He
and his brother-in-law kept on saying: 'We must get our crosses too, so
that we may belong to the same body as Mozart'. But I took no notice.
They also addressed me repeatedly: 'Hallo, you fine gentleman, Knight
of the Spur'. I said nothing; but during supper things really got beyond a
joke. They asked me 'About how much does it cost? Three ducats? Must

---

[1] A local term for the large hall in the Augsburg Rathaus.
[2] See p. 148, n. 1.

one have permission to wear it? Does this permission cost something too? We really must send for our crosses.' A certain Baron Bagge, an officer, who was there, called out: 'Come! You ought to be ashamed of yourselves. What would you do with the cross?' That young ass, von Kurzenmantel,[1] winked at him. I saw him and he knew it. Then we had a little peace. He offered me snuff and said: 'There, take a pinch'. I still said nothing. At last he began again in a jeering tone: 'Well, tomorrow I shall send someone to your inn and perhaps you will be so kind as to lend me the cross just for a moment. I shall return it immediately. I only want to have a word with our goldsmith. He is quite a character and I am sure that if I ask him what its value is, he will say: 'About a Bavarian thaler'. And it is not worth more, for it is not gold at all, only copper. Ha! Ha!' 'You are wrong there', I said, 'it is tin. Ha! Ha!' I was burning with anger and rage. 'But do tell me', he said, 'I suppose that, if necessary, I can leave out the spur?' 'Oh, yes,' I replied. 'You do not need one, for you have one in your head already. I have one in mine too, but of a very different kind, and indeed I should not care to exchange it for yours. Here, take a pinch of snuff.' I offered him some. He turned rather pale, but began again: 'The other day—your order looked fine on that grand waistcoat of yours'. I said nothing. At length he called out to the servant: 'Hi, there, you will have to show more respect to my brother-in-law and myself when we wear the same cross as Herr Mozart. Here, take a pinch of snuff.' 'That is really very strange,' I began, as though I had not heard what he said, 'but it would be easier for me to obtain all the orders which it is possible for you to win than for you to become what I am, even if you were to die twice and be born again. Take a pinch of snuff on that.' With that I stood up. They all got up too and were exceedingly embarrassed. I took my hat and sword and said: 'I shall have the pleasure of seeing you tomorrow'. 'Oh, I shall not be here tomorrow.' 'Well, then, the day after, if I am here myself.' 'Why, you surely do not mean to——' 'I mean nothing. You are a lot of mean pigs. Good-bye for the present.' And off I went. The next day, the 15th, I told the whole story to Herr von Stein, Herr Geniaux[2] and Director Graf—not about the cross, but how utterly disgusted I was that such fine promises had been made to me about a concert and that nothing had come of them. 'That is what is called playing the fool with people and letting them down', I said. 'I am heartily sorry that I ever came here. I should never in my life have believed that in Augsburg, my father's native town, his son would have been so insulted.' You cannot imagine, dear Papa, how sorry and angry the three of them

---

[1] Another pun of Mozart's on the name Langenmantel. See p. 315.

[2] Christof Gignoux, an Augsburg organ-builder. He appears in the *Reiseaufzeichnungen*, p. 22 (*MBA* No. 51), after Stein, as Gingeoux. So the Mozarts met him in 1763. See *ZMW*, Jan. 1934, p. 43.

were. 'Oh,' they said, 'you really must give a concert here. We can do without the patricians.' But I stuck to my decision, and said: 'Well, I shall give a small farewell concert at Herr von Stein's for my few good friends here, who are connoisseurs'. The Director was quite distressed. 'It is abominable,' he cried, 'it is a scandal. Who would have thought it of Langenmantel? Pardieu, if he had really wanted it, it would have gone off well'. We parted. The Director in his dressing-gown accompanied me downstairs to the front door. Herr Stein and Herr Geniaux, who sends greetings to Papa, walked home with me. They urged us to decide to stay here for a while, but we were adamant. Now Papa must know that yesterday young Herr von Langenmantel, after coolly stammering out his nice bit of news about my concert, told me that the patricians had invited me to their concert on the following Thursday. 'I shall come and listen', I replied. 'Oh, but you will give us the pleasure of hearing you play?' *'Well, who knows? Why not?'* But after being so grossly insulted on the following evening, I resolved never to go to him again but to let the whole company of patricians lick my arse and to leave the place. On Thursday, the 16th, I was called out from table and found one of Langenmantel's servants, who had brought a message asking whether I was going along with him to the concert, and, if so, would I please go to him immediately after lunch. I sent him my humble regards, but said that I was not going to the concert and that I could not go to him, as I was already engaged, *which was in fact the case,*—but that I would call on the morrow to take my leave of him, as I should be leaving Augsburg on Saturday at the latest. Meanwhile Herr von Stein had rushed off to the other patricians of the Evangelical persuasion and had given them such a fearful talking-to that these gentlemen were quite uneasy. 'What,' they said, 'are we going to let a man who does us so much honour go away without even hearing him? Herr von Langenmantel thinks no doubt that because he has heard him, that is enough.' Enfin, they became so excited about it that our good young Herr von Kurzenmantel himself had to look up Herr von Stein and entreat him on behalf of all the patricians to do his utmost to persuade me to attend the concert, but to add that I was not to expect anything first-rate and so forth. So after much hesitation I went along with him. The leading nobles were very polite to me, especially a certain Baron Relling, an officer, who is also a Director or some such animal. He himself unpacked my music. I had brought a symphony too, which was performed and in which I played the fiddle. But the Augsburg orchestra is enough to give one a fit. That young puppy von Langenmantel was quite polite, though he still had a sneer on his face. 'I really thought you would slip away from us', he said; 'I even thought that perhaps you might have taken offence at our joke the other day.' 'Not at all', I said, 'you are still very young. But I advise you to be more careful in future. I am not used to such jokes. And the subject you were joking about does you no honour at all, and has served no purpose, for I still wear my cross. It would have been better to have tried some other joke.' 'I assure you', he said, 'it was only my brother-in-law who——' 'Well, let us say no more about it', I said. 'We were nearly deprived of the pleasure of seeing you', he added. 'Yes', I said, 'if it had not been for Herr von Stein, I should certainly not have come. And, to tell you the truth, I have only come so that you, gentlemen of Augsburg, may not be laughed at in other countries, when I tell people that I spent a week in the town where my father was born without anyone taking the trouble to hear me.' I played a concerto which, save for the accompaniment, went very well. Finally I played another sonata.[1] Baron Relling, on behalf of the whole company, thanked me most politely, asked me to take the will for the deed and gave me two ducats. They have not yet left me in peace, for they want me to give a public concert before next Sunday. Perhaps I will. But I have already had such a sickener of it that I can hardly express what I feel. I shall be honestly glad to go off again to a place where there is a court. I may say that if it were not for my good uncle and aunt and my really charming cousin, I should have as many regrets at having come to Augsburg as I have hairs on my head. I must now say a few words about my dear little cousin. But I shall save that up until tomorrow, for one must be in very good spirits if one wants to praise her as she deserves.

On the morning of this day, the 17th, I write and declare that our little cousin is beautiful, intelligent, charming, clever and gay; and that is because she has mixed with people a great deal, and has also spent some time in Munich. Indeed we two get on extremely well, for, like myself, she is a bit of a scamp. We both laugh at everyone and have great fun. I beg you not to forget the address of the Bishop of Chiemsee. I shall probably send off to Mysliwecek today the letter for Gaetano Santoro, as we arranged. He has already given me his address. I beg you to write soon to poor Mysliwecek, because I know that your letter will give him great pleasure. Next time I shall give you an account of Stein's pianofortes and organs and tell you about the concert in the Stube. A great crowd of the nobility was there: the Duchess Smackbottom, the Countess Makewater, to say nothing of the Princess Dunghill with her two daughters, who, however, are already married to the two Princes Potbelly von Pigtail. Farewell to all. I kiss Papa's hands 100000 times and I embrace my brute of a sister with a bearish tenderness and remain your most obedient son

WOLFGANG AMADÉ MOZART

Augsburg, 17 October 1777.

---

[1] K. 283 [189h]. See p. 329, n. 2.

(224a) *Maria Anna Thekla Mozart, the 'Bäsle', to her Uncle*

[*Autograph in the Mozarteum, Salzburg*]

[AUGSBURG 16 *October* 1777[1]]

MY PARTICULARLY LOVABLE UNCLE,

It is impossible for me to express the great pleasure which we have felt at the safe arrival of my aunt and of such a dear cousin and indeed we regret that we are losing so soon such excellent friends, who show us so much kindness. We are only sorry that we have not had the good fortune to see you here with my aunt. My parents send their humble greetings to you both, my uncle and my cousin Nannerl, and they hope that you are well. Please give my greetings to my cousin Nannerl and ask her to keep me in her friendship, since I flatter myself that I shall one day win her affection. I have the honour to send you my greetings and I remain with much respect

your devoted servant and niece
M. A. MOZART

Augsburg, 16 October 1777.

My father cannot remember whether he informed you that on 31 May, 1777, he gave Herr Lotter four copies of your 'Violinschule', and two more on 13 August 1777.

(225) *Mozart to his Father*

[*Autograph in the Mozarteum, Salzburg*]

[AUGSBURG, 17 *October* 1777]

MON TRÉS CHER PÉRE!

This time I shall begin at once with Stein's pianofortes. Before I had seen any of his make, Späth's[2] claviers had always been my favourites. But now I much prefer Stein's, for they damp ever so much better than the Regensburg instruments. When I strike hard, I can keep my finger on the note or raise it, but the sound ceases the moment I have produced it. In whatever way I touch the keys, the tone is always even. It never jars, it is never stronger or weaker or entirely absent; in a word, it is always even. It is true that he does not sell a pianoforte of this kind for less than

---

[1] A separate letter sent in the same cover as Mozart's.

[2] Franz Jakob Späth (1714–98), a famous manufacturer of organs and claviers at Regensburg. Like·Stein he also made pianofortes, and Mozart evidently possessed one of these.

three hundred gulden, but the trouble and the labour which Stein puts into the making of it cannot be paid for. His instruments have this special advantage over others that they are made with escape action. Only one maker in a hundred bothers about this. But without an escapement it is impossible to avoid jangling and vibration after the note is struck. When you touch the keys, the hammers fall back again the moment after they have struck the strings, whether you hold down the keys or release them. He himself told me that when he has finished making one of these claviers, he sits down to it and tries all kinds of passages, runs and jumps, and he shaves and works away until it can do anything. For he labours solely in the interest of music and not for his own profit; otherwise he would soon finish his work. He often says: 'If I were not myself such a passionate lover of music and had not myself some slight skill on the clavier, I should certainly long ago have lost patience with my work. But I do like an instrument which never lets the player down and which is durable.' And his claviers certainly do last. He guarantees that the sounding-board will neither break nor split. When he has finished making one for a clavier, he places it in the open air, exposing it to rain, snow, the heat of the sun and all the devils in order that it may crack. Then he inserts wedges and glues them in to make the instrument very strong and firm. He is delighted when it cracks, for he can then be sure that nothing more can happen to it. Indeed he often cuts into it himself and then glues it together again and strengthens it in this way. He has finished making three pianofortes of this kind. Today I played on one again.

We lunched today, the 17th, with young Herr Gassner, a handsome young widower, who has lost a pretty young wife. They had only been married two years. He is a very fine, polite young fellow. We were most royally entertained. At lunch there was also a colleague of Abbé Henri, Bullinger, and Wishofer, an ex-Jesuit, who is now Kapellmeister in the Augsburg Cathedral. He knows Herr Schachtner very well, for he was his choir-master at Ingolstadt. His name is Pater Gerbl, and he asked me to send his greetings to Herr Schachtner. After lunch Herr Gassner, one of his sisters-in-law, Mamma, our little cousin and I went to see Herr Stein. At four o'clock the Kapellmeister turned up and so later on did Herr Schmittbauer, organist at St. Ulrich, a nice, oily, old gentleman. There I just played at sight a sonata by Beecke, which was rather hard and *miserabile al solito*.[1] Really I cannot describe the amazement of the Kapellmeister and the organist, who kept crossing themselves. Here and at Munich I have played all my six sonatas by heart several times.[2] I played the fifth, in G,[3] at that grand concert in the Stube. The last one in D,[4]

[1] Wretched as usual.
[2] K. 279-284 [189d-h, 205b], of which the last one was written for Baron von Dürnitz. See p. 287, n. 4.   [3] K. 283 [189h], composed in 1774.
[4] K. 284 [205b], the so-called 'Dürnitz sonata', composed in 1775.

sounds exquisite on Stein's pianoforte. The device too which you work with your knee is better on his than on other instruments. I have only to touch it and it works; and when you shift your knee the slightest bit, you do not hear the least reverberation. Well, tomorrow perhaps I shall come to his organs—I mean, I shall come *to write about them*; and I am saving up his little daughter for the very last. When I told Herr Stein that I should very much like to play on his organ, as that instrument was my passion, he was greatly surprised and said: 'What? A man like you, so fine a clavier-player, wants to play on an instrument which has no douceur, no expression, no piano, no forte, but is always the same?' 'That does not matter', I replied. 'In my eyes and ears the organ is the king of instruments.'

'Well,' he said, 'as you like.' So off we went together. I noticed at once from what he said that he thought that I would not do much on his organ; that I would play, for instance, in a thoroughly pianistic style. He told me that he had taken Schubart[1] at his own request to this same organ. 'I was rather nervous,' he said, 'for Schubart had told everyone and the church was pretty full. For I thought of course that this fellow would be all spirit, fire and rapid execution, qualities which are not at all suited to the organ. But as soon as he began I changed my opinion. All I said to Stein was: 'Well, Herr Stein, do you think that I am going to canter about on your organ? 'Ah, you, he replied, 'that is quite another matter.' We reached the choir and I began to improvise, when he started to laugh; then I played a fugue. 'I can well believe', he said, 'that you like to play the organ, when you play so well.' At first the pedal seemed a bit strange to me, as it was not divided. It started with C, and then D and E followed in the same row. But with us D and E are above, as E♭ and F♯ are here. But I soon got the hang of it. I have also been to St. Ulrich to play on the old organ there. The staircase there is perfectly dreadful. I begged them to get someone to play on the organ, saying that I should like to go down and listen, for up above it produces no effect whatever. But I could form no opinion, for the young choirmaster, a priest, rushed up and down the keyboard in such a fashion that one could not get the least idea of anything. And when he wanted to play a few chords, the result was simply discords, for the notes did not harmonize. Afterwards we had to go off to a wine-shop, as my Mamma, my little cousin and Herr Stein were with us. A certain Father Emilian, a conceited ass and a sorry wit of his profession, was very sweet on my little cousin and wanted to jest with her, but she made fun of him—finally when he was a bit tipsy, which soon happened, he began to talk about music and sang a canon, saying: 'In my

---

1 Christian Friedrich Daniel Schubart (1739–91), a Swabian by birth, who from 1769 to 1773 was organist at Ludwigsburg. He later moved to Augsburg, where he founded in 1774 the *Deutsche Chronik*, and for his revolutionary opinions was imprisoned for ten years, 1777–87, at Hohenasperg. See *ZMW*, Jan. 1934, p. 43.

life I have never heard anything more beautiful'. I said: 'I am sorry that I cannot join in, but nature has not bestowed on me the gift of intoning'. 'That does not matter', he said. He began. I took the third voice, but I invented quite a different text, i.e., 'Pater Emilian, oh, you idiot, you, lick my arse. I beg you'. All this, *sotto voce*, to my cousin. Then we laughed together for another half-hour. He said to me: 'If only we could be together longer, I should like to discuss composition with you'. 'Then', I replied, 'we should soon have dried up.' *On the scent, Towser.* To be continued in my next.

W: A: Mozart

[*Written on the cover*[1]]   [*Autograph in the possession of Max Reis, Zürich*]

Mr. Novac, who arrived here today, sends greetings to all and especially to Mlle Katherl. I shall write a more amusing letter next time. Next Wednesday I am giving a sort of a concert in Count Fugger's drawing-room.[2] My dear cousin also sends you her love. The three of us are now going to Herr Stein's where, we are lunching. The only thing I have to worry about is how I shall be accompanied at my concert, for the orchestra here is execrable. I must close now, for it is already eleven o'clock. I kiss Papa's hands 10000 times and embrace my sister in a manner most bold,

and I am, behold,

neither warm nor cold,

your most obedient son

W: A: Mozart

Our compliments
a tutti, tutti, tutti.

(226) Leopold Mozart to his Son

[*Extract*]   [*Autograph in the Mozarteum, Salzburg*]

Salzburg, 18 *October* 1777

Mon très cher Fils!

I received yesterday your letter from Augsburg, dated October 14th, which must have been sent off on the 15th. First of all, *with regard to October 11th, I must finish my case for the prosecution.* I know that I am right and that you made a mistake, for the letter was signed by my dear spouse

---

[1] This postscript was formerly thought to be a separate letter (No. 223).
[2] Probably the famous Fuggerhaus in Augsburg, the town house of Prince Fugger von Babenhausen, built 1512–15.

with these unmistakeable words—'*Munich, October 11th, at eight o'clock in the evening*'. Then my son and heir steps in and writes the following words: '*Munich, October 11th. I am writing this at a quarter to twelve at night, and so on*'.[1] So you were then already in Augsburg? Who is right now? I guessed, of course, that the letter did not leave Munich until midday on Saturday, at the same time that you did. *Toot, toot!* We did not receive the Schuster duets until yesterday evening, for Herr von Kleinmayr's luggage only came by the last mail coach. We lit our candles at once and to my delight Nannerl played them off, yes, to my great astonishment, without the slightest hesitation and on the whole performed her part in the Adagio with taste and expression. Herr Bullinger, who was with Abbé Henri, came in just as we were unpacking them and we were glad that you mentioned in the letter you enclosed that Herr von Kleinmayr was bringing them, or we should never have believed the servant who delivered them. Oh, how Herr Bullinger laughed! I am glad that you danced at the *altum tempus ecclesiasticum*[2] and I am only sorry that owing to the lack of good partners you had such a poor time. It is quite possible that the Bishop of Chiemsee has spoken to Counts Sensheim and Bergheim and, if so, no harm has been done. *Non si deve lasciare strada intentata*,[3] and so on. The Bishop went off at once to a confirmation in Werfen; he is then going to his bishopric for a visitation and later on to Bischofshofen to see the new building. As soon as he returns I shall pay my respects to him. The concert on Albert's name-day must have sounded very strange with a violinist like Dupreille, who is so sure of his time! Count Seeau probably knows all about him, which explains why he asked Joseph Cröner[4] to lead the orchestra for your opera buffa.[5] I am not surprised that when you played your last Cassation they all opened their eyes. You yourself do not know how well you play the violin, if you will only *do yourself credit and play with energy, with your whole heart and mind, yes, just as if you were the first violinist in Europe*. You must not play carelessly, or people will think that from some foolish conceit you consider yourself to be a great player, seeing that many people do not even know that you play the violin, since you have been known from childhood as a clavier-player. So whence could you draw the grounds for such conceit and presumption?—Say these words first: '*I really must apologize, but I am no violinist*'. Then play with your whole mind and you will overcome all difficulties. Oh, how often you will hear a violinist play, who has a great reputation, and feel very sorry for him! What you tell me about Augsburg and your visit to the Magistrate Longotabarro is precisely what I expected. That letter of yours made me and all of us laugh very heartily, and not least Herr

---

[1] See p. 308.   [2] See 299, n. 1.   [3] We must leave no avenue unexplored.
[4] See p. 277, n. 3.
[5] *La finta giardiniera*, which Mozart composed for the Munich carnival season, 1775.

Bullinger. Whenever I thought of your journey to Augsburg, Wieland's Abderiten[1] occurred to me. How often does one not experience in real life some circumstance of which one has read and which at the time seemed utterly impossible! Herr Longotabarro was extraordinarily clever at his studies, but he never got beyond Salzburg and Innsbruck, where he was obliged to continue them and where he became Juris Utriusque Doctor. He was then immediately appointed to the lowest post in the magistracy, served through all the grades in the Augsburg municipality, and finally became Magistrate, which is the highest rung in the ladder. He has therefore seen nothing of the world. You may have thought it strange that my brother had to wait in the lobby, but he will not have thought so. All the citizens of Salzburg, even the leading merchants, must appear in their cloaks at the Town Syndicate, and the Syndic makes them, and particularly the ordinary citizens, wait for hours in the lobby; yet, after all, the Syndic is only a syndic and not the reigning prince. On the other hand the Magistrate of Augsburg is their little king. Moreover the natives are accustomed to treatment of this kind, for they have the most extraordinary respect for their Syndic, because they have no greater lord.

★

Monday, October 20th
I have just received your letter of the 17th and I am very curious to read the continuation of the Augsburg story. Everyone knows about the beggarliness of the patricians and every honest man there laughs about it. That is why they are *in the pay of the rich merchants*, who can get anything for money from their hungry superiors. As for young Herr von Longotabarro, he has not had to go in search of his love of quizzing and jeering, for his cher père was also given to it. It is thus due to his upbringing; and indeed this is the sole privilege which the young patricians have ever claimed and still do claim—to jeer at others, whenever an opportunity presents itself. Therein consists their great nobility. But the effect of anyone lowering himself to their vulgar level is at once to make them drop into their jeering habits, which they usually adopt only towards people of their own class. You made yourself too cheap with that fellow. You went to the theatre together! You were merry! You were not sufficiently reserved, you were far too familiar! In short, you were far too free and easy with such a *puppy*, and he thought, of course, that he could make fun of you. Let that serve as a lesson to you *to associate freely and naturally with grown-up people* rather than with such ill-bred, unfledged boys whose only boast is that their father is the magistrate of the town. *Such fellows should always be kept at arm's length; their society should be*

---

[1] Christoph Martin Wieland (1733–1813), a native of Wurtemberg, enjoyed a great reputation in his day as a poet and man of letters. He published in 1774 *Die Abderiten, eine sehr wahrscheinliche Geschichte*, an admirable satire on German provincialism and one of his most attractive prose writings.

avoided and, still more so, their intimate companionship. One thing is quite certain—*they would have had great difficulty in dragging me to their beggarly concert.* Basta! You did it to please Herr Stein and I take it that by now you will have given a public concert and have left Augsburg or at least be about to leave it. I sent off to you by the last post a very big letter franco, in which there is a collection of good scores, and which by this time you will have received.

I have told you that I wrote to Mysliwecek. When you reach Mannheim, ★
the principal person, and one whom you can trust absolutely, is *Signor Raaff*,[1] an honest *God-fearing* man, who loves German musicians and can give you very valuable help and counsel. Would that he could arrange for the Elector[2] to retain you for the winter in order to find out what you know and to give you an opportunity of displaying your powers! Anyhow, Signor Raaff can give you the best advice and you should ask for a special interview with him. Herr Danner,[3] the violinist, who is an old friend and acquaintance of ours, will introduce you to him. But you must say no word of your intentions to anyone but Signor Raaff, who will tell you whether you should have an audience with the Elector, and who can perhaps arrange one for you himself. *At first you should only endeavour to get a hearing. Afterwards you should have an audience and set things going.* Even if nothing more can be done, you will still get some fine present. *When you have given your performance, you should present one of your compositions to the Elector, and finally you yourself should ask him to test you more thoroughly and give you an opportunity of showing your ability in all kinds of composition, especially in church music.* You must make a point of going to the chapel and observing the style employed there—length, shortness and so forth. For these lords always consider the one style to which they are accustomed to be the best. *Consuetudo est altera natura*[4]! I believe that there is in Mannheim a better composer of church music than in Munich, probably some good old fellow. In Mannheim, too, there is an opportunity of writing for the German stage. But see to it that you do not confide in anybody. For many a one says: '*I should like you to remain here*', in order to worm your intention out of you and then work against you. Basta! Common sense! And reserve! May God give you good

---

[1] Anton Raaff (1714–1797), one of the most famous tenors of the eighteenth century. He was born at Holzem, near Bonn, where the Elector Clemens August had him trained as a singer. Raaff studied at Bologna under Bernacchi, and returned to Germany in 1742. He then had long residences abroad, 1752–1755 in Lisbon, 1755–1759 in Madrid under Farinelli and 1759–1769 in Naples. He again returned to Germany in 1770 and took an appointment at Mannheim under the Elector Karl Theodor. His last public performance was in 1781 in Mozart's *Idomeneo*. The remaining years of his life were spent in retirement in Munich. For a full account of his career, see Heinz Freiberger, *Anton Raaff*, Bonn, 1929.

[2] Karl Theodor, Elector of the Palatinate.

[3] Johann Georg Danner (1722–1803). According to Leopold Mozart's *Reiseaufzeichnungen*, p. 22, the Mozarts met the Danner family at Schwetzingen in 1763. See *MBA*, No. 57.

[4] Custom is second nature.

health. I, thank God, am a hundred per cent better; my cough has gone and with God's help I hope to come in for what will be better times for poor fools like ourselves. Hold fast to God, I beg you, Who will see to everything. For all men are villains! The older you become and the more you associate with people, the more you will realize this sad truth. Just think of all the promises, flatteries and the hundred circumstances we have already experienced, and draw for yourself the conclusion as to how much one can build on human aid, seeing that in the end everyone always finds, or invents some plausible excuse for throwing the failure of his good intentions on the shoulders of a third person. I kiss Mamma, wish her patience and urge her to protect herself well against the cold. I kiss you and beg you to think over courageously everything you are about to do and not to give your friendship and your full confidence to every flatterer so readily. God bless you on your journey, and, while I kiss you both a million times, I am your old

MOZART

(226a) *Nannerl Mozart to her Brother*

[Extract]   [Autograph in the Mozarteum, Salzburg]

DEAREST BROTHER!   [SALZBURG, 20 October 1777 [1]]

I am glad that, praise and thanks be to God, and you Mamma are well. I am sorry that I cannot write more often; but firstly, I have no time, and secondly, when I have leisure to do so, Papa always happens to be writing. I thank you for the Schuster duets, which are very pretty and attractive. Who gave them to you? Must we copy them and return them to you? ★ We had some shooting yesterday at home. Next Sunday Mamma is to provide the target and, as you told me to let you know when your turn would come, I should like you to write at once and give me your idea for a target. Then I could let the others know immediately and it could be ★ got ready in a fortnight. I kiss Mamma's hands and I embrace you.

(226b) *Leopold Mozart resumes writing*

[Autograph in the Mozarteum, Salzburg]

Greetings from us both to my dear brother, to my sister-in-law and to your little cousin. I am altogether delighted to hear that my niece is beautiful, sensible, charming, clever and gay, and so far from having any objection to make, I should like to have the honour of meeting her.

[1] A postscript to her father's letter.

Only it seems to me that she has too many friends among the priests. If I am mistaken, I shall be charmed to beg her pardon on bended knee. But I only say: *it seems to me.* For appearances are deceptive, particularly at such a distance as Augsburg is from Salzburg, and particularly at this season when mists are falling so thickly that it is impossible to see further than thirty feet. Now you can laugh as much as you like! I am quite pleased to hear that she is a bit of a scamp, but these ecclesiastical gentlemen are often far worse. I am waiting for the continuation of your story about Stein's instruments and the Duchess Smackbottom and the rest.

(227) *Leopold Mozart to his Wife*

[Extract]   [*Autograph in the Mozarteum, Salzburg*]

MY DEAR WIFE!   SALZBURG, 23 *October* 1777 ★
 Tell Wolfgang that the Court Baker's saucer-eyed daughter who danced with him at the Stern, who often paid him friendly compliments and who ended by entering the convent at Loreto, has returned to her father's house. She heard that Wolfgang was going to leave Salzburg and probably hoped to see him again and to prevent him from doing so. Will Wolfgang be so kind as to refund to her father the money which the pomp and all the fine preparation for entering her convent cost him! You are still in Augsburg? Bravissimo! My last letter to you was enclosed in one to my brother, as I thought that you might by now have cleared out over hedges and ditches. I see however that you will not get away before the 24th or 2;th, and that you are therefore staying for a fortnight. Of course, if you want to give a concert, you must make it known several days in advance. I only hope that it may be profitable! Though I doubt whether it will bring in much. Everyone who comes will probably pay one gulden, twelve kreuzer; but will a great many turn up? *I am very curious to hear all about it.* I knew already that the orchestra was very poor; it is indeed disappointing. *Herr Hagenauer has just sent me the news sheet and Frau von Gerlichs has this moment brought the paper; both contain an announcement of your concert.* It is all to the good that you have left two items free.[1] The concert is very well announced. So you are going to play the clavier concerto for three harpsichords?[2] Perhaps Herr Stein's little daughter is going to play? Perhaps she will play on the first harpsichord, you on the second and Father Stein on the third? This is only guess-work on my part! By the time you read this letter the concert will be over *and I hope to have*

[1] Leopold Mozart means that no works are mentioned. Probably Mozart intended to improvise.
[2] K. 242, composed in 1776 for the Countess Antonia Lodron and her two daughters Aloisia and Josepha.

a few words of news as to how it went off. I am glad that Herr Stein's piano-fortes are so good, but indeed they are expensive. Herr Gasser (not Gassner) has only just lost his pretty young wife, as I read in a letter which he sent a short time ago to Herr Hagenauer. So he entertained you in princely fashion? He is indeed an uncommonly helpful and pleasant man. You have also called on Herr von Zabuesnig, for he mentioned it in a letter to Johannes Hagenauer, adding that he would gladly have invited you to his home, had not his wife been approaching her confinement, but that he would be delighted to go to your concert. Now do not forget to make careful preparations for your departure, for the cold is becoming more

★ and more bitter. Thank God I am well. I have neither a pain in my chest nor a cough and I have made a complete recovery. By this time you will probably have become more accustomed to walking than you were in Salzburg, as you have now to walk for a quarter, or as much as half an hour when you go to St. Ulrich or when you visit Herr Stein, that is, if he still lives on the Lech, outside the town. With all this exercise I trust that you are well. God keep you both. I am your old

MOZART

MON TRÈS CHER FILS!

I am to wish you happiness on your name-day! But what can I now wish you that I do not always wish you? And that is, the grace of God, that it may follow you everywhere, that it may never leave you. And this it will never do, if you are diligent in fulfilling the duties of a true Catholic Christian. You know me. I am no pedant and no praying Peter and still less am I a hypocrite. But surely you will not refuse the request of a father, that you should take thought for your soul's welfare so that in the hour of his death you may cause him no anxiety, and that in that dread moment he may have no reason to reproach himself for not having watched over your soul's salvation. Farewell! Be happy! Be sensible! Honour and care for your mother, who in her old age is having much anxiety. Love me as I love you. Your truly affectionate father

LEOP. MOZART

★

(227a) *Nannerl Mozart to her Brother*

[Extract]   [Autograph in the Mozarteum, Salzburg]

DEAREST BROTHER!   [SALZBURG, 23 October 1777 [1]]

I wish you all happiness and blessings and that God may ever keep you in good health. When things fare well or badly with you, think of us, who are obliged to live sadly here, separated from you both. I only wish that

---

[1] A postscript to her father's letter.

what Herr Cassel[1] came to congratulate us about were true, that is, that you and Papa were appointed to Munich and were to draw 1600 gulden. I am sure that it is Haydn's wife[2] and her vulgar set who concoct these lies. For they would like to see Papa leave Salzburg, so that her husband might be certain of the post of Kapellmeister.

Katherl Gilowsky sends her greetings to Mamma and congratulations to you on your name-day. As the Chamberlain is back again, she never has time to visit us except on Sundays. Tresel and Bimperl also send you their congratulations. Farewell and keep in good health. I kiss Mamma's hands and I give you a smacking kiss.

★

(228) *Mozart to his Father*

[Autograph in the Mozarteum, Salzburg]

[AUGSBURG, 23 *October* 1777]

MON TRÉS CHER PÉRE!

My concert duly took place yesterday, Wednesday, the 22nd. Count Wolfegg[3] was very active in connection with it and brought several highborn elderly ladies with him. During the first days of our stay I called at his lodgings to pay my respects to him, but he was away. He returned a few days ago and when he heard that I was here, he did not wait for me to call on him, but came in at my door just as I was taking my hat and sword to visit him. But before I come to the concert, I must give you some account of our first few days. As I have already written, I went last Saturday to St. Ulrich. A few days before, my uncle had taken me to see the Abbot[4] of the Holy Cross Monastery, an excellent, honest old man, and on the Saturday before my visit to St. Ulrich I again went to the Holy Cross Monastery with my cousin, as the Dean and the Procurator were not there on the former occasion and my cousin said that the latter was such a jolly fellow.

(228a) *Maria Anna Mozart to her Husband*

[Autograph in the Mozarteum, Salzburg]

[AUGSBURG, 23 *October* 1777]

Today, the 23rd, Wolfgang is lunching again at the Holy Cross Monastery and I too was invited, but as the cold has given me pains in

---

[1] Joseph Thomas Cassel played the violin (and occasionally the double bass) in the Salzburg court orchestra.

[2] Maria Magdalena, wife of Michael Haydn. She was the daughter of Franz Ignaz Lipp, organist in the Salzburg Cathedral, and was a singer.

[3] Count Anton Willibald Wolfegg, canon of Salzburg Cathedral.

[4] Bartholomäus Christa was Abbot of the Holy Cross Monastery from 1760 to 1780. Mozart gave him copies of his masses, K. 192 [186f] and K. 220 [196b].

my belly, I have stayed at home. Is it as cold at Salzburg as it is here, where everything is frozen hard just as if it were midwinter? If nothing prevents us, we intend to leave for Wallerstein[1] on the day after tomorrow Saturday. The concert here was an amazing success. The papers will tell you more. Herr Stein took infinite trouble and rendered us many kindnesses. You must write him a letter and thank him. I hope that you and Nannerl are in good health, but somehow I am dreadfully anxious lest you should be unwell, as we have not had a line from you this week. Do write to me soon and relieve me of my anxiety. I am very much surprised that you have not received the Schuster duets—

(228b) *Mozart resumes writing*

[*Autograph in the Mozarteum, Salzburg*]

Why, of course he has received them.

Mamma. Not at all, he has kept on writing that he has not yet received them.

Wolfgang. I detest arguing. He has certainly got them and that's an end of it.

Mamma. You are wrong, Wolfgang.

Wolfgang. No, I am right. I will show it to Mamma in black and white.

Mamma. Where then?

Wolfgang. There, read that.

Mamma is reading your letter now. Last Sunday I attended Mass in the Church of the Holy Cross and at ten o'clock I went to Herr Stein. That was on the 19th. We rehearsed a few symphonies for the concert. Afterwards I lunched with my uncle at the Holy Cross Monastery. During the meal we had some music. In spite of their poor fiddling I prefer the monastery players to the Augsburg orchestra. I performed a symphony and played Vanhall's violin concerto in Bb,[2] which was unanimously applauded. The Dean, who is a cousin of Eberlin,[3] by name Zeschinger, is a fine, jolly fellow and knows Papa quite well. In the evening at supper I played my Strassburg concerto,[4] which went like oil. Everyone praised my beautiful, pure tone. Afterwards they brought in a small clavichord and I improvised

---

[1] A small suburb of Nördlingen, and the residence of Prince Kraft Ernst of Öttingen-Wallerstein, an enthusiastic patron of music.

[2] Johann Baptist Vanhal or Wanhal (1739–1813) was born in Czechoslovakia of Dutch extraction. About 1761 he went to Vienna where he was trained as a violinist by Dittersdorf. After a prolonged stay in Italy he settled in Vienna. He was a most prolific and popular composer of symphonies, string quartets and all kinds of church music.

[3] Johann Ernst Eberlin (1702–62), a former court organist and Kapellmeister in Salzburg and an eminent composer of sacred music.

[4] K. 218. See p. 297, n. 1.

and then played a sonata[1] and the Fischer variations.[2] Then the others whispered to the Dean that he should just hear me play something in the organ style. I asked him to give me a theme. He declined, but one of the monks gave me one. I put it through its paces and in the middle (the fugue was in G minor) I started off in the major key and played something quite lively, though in the same tempo; and after that the theme over again, but this time arseways. Finally it occurred to me, could I not use my lively tune as the theme for a fugue? I did not waste much time in asking, but did so at once, and it went as neatly as if Daser[3] had fitted it. The Dean was absolutely staggered. 'Why, it's simply phenomenal, that's all I can say,' he said. 'I should never have believed what I have heard. You are a first-rate fellow. My Abbot told me, it is true, that he had never in his life heard anyone play the organ so smoothly and so soundly.' (For he had heard me a few days before, when the Dean was away.) At last someone produced a sonata in fugal style and wanted me to play it. But I said: 'Gentlemen, this is too much. Let me tell you, I shall certainly not be able to play that sonata at sight.' 'Yes, that I can well believe', said the Dean very pressingly, for he was my strong supporter. 'It is too much to expect. No one could tackle that.' 'However,' I said, 'I should like to try it.' I heard the Dean muttering behind me all the time: 'Oh, you little villain, oh, you rascal, oh, you——!' I played until eleven o'clock, for I was bombarded and besieged with themes for fugues. When I was at Stein's house the other day he put before me a sonata by Beecke—I think that I have told you that already. That reminds me, now for his little daughter.[4] Anyone who sees and hears her play and can keep from laughing, must, like her father, be made of stone.[5] For instead of sitting in the middle of the clavier, she sits right up opposite the treble, as it gives her more chance of flopping about and making grimaces. She rolls her eyes and smirks. When a passage is repeated, she plays it more slowly the second time. If it has to be played a third time, then she plays it even more slowly. When a passage is being played, the arm must be raised as high as possible, and according as the notes in the passage are stressed, the arm, not the fingers, must do this, and that too with great emphasis in a heavy and clumsy manner. But the best joke of all is that when she comes to a passage which ought to flow like oil and which necessitates a change of finger, she does not bother her head about it, but when the moment arrives, she just leaves out the notes, raises her hand

---

[1] Probably one of his clavier sonatas, K. 279-284 [189d-h, 205b].

[2] K. 179 [189a]. See p. 256, n. 5.　　　　　　　　　[3] A Salzburg tailor.

[4] Maria Anna (Nanette) Stein (1769-1833) was the infant prodigy of Augsburg, where she had given her first recital in 1776, at the age of seven. After her father's death in 1792 she managed his business. In 1794 she married Johann Andreas Streicher, a piano-maker from Stuttgart, famous for his friendship with Schiller. The Streichers moved to Vienna, where they established a piano factory and where in later years Nanette proved a staunch friend to Beethoven.　　　　　[5] Mozart puns on the word 'Stein', which means 'stone'.

and starts off again quite comfortably—a method by which she is much more likely to strike a wrong note, which often produces a curious effect. I am simply writing this in order to give Papa some idea of clavier-playing and clavier-teaching, so that he may derive some profit from it later on. Herr Stein is quite crazy about his daughter, who is eight and a half and who now learns everything by heart. She may succeed, for she has great talent for music. But she will not make progress by this method—for she will never acquire great rapidity, since she definitely does all she can to make her hands heavy. Further, she will never acquire the most essential, the most difficult and the chief requisite in music, which is, time, because from her earliest years she has done her utmost not to play in time. Herr Stein and I discussed this point for two hours at least and I have almost converted him, for he now asks my advice on everything. He used to be quite crazy about Beecke; but now he sees and hears that I am the better player, that I do not make grimaces, and yet play with such expression that, as he himself confesses, no one up to the present has been able to get such good results out of his pianofortes. Everyone is amazed that I can always keep strict time. What these people cannot grasp is that in tempo rubato in an Adagio, the left hand should go on playing in strict time. With them the left hand always follows suit. Count Wolfegg and several other passionate admirers of Beecke, publicly admitted at a concert the other day that I had wiped the floor with him. The Count kept running about in the hall, exclaiming: 'I have never heard anything like this in my life'. And he said to me: 'I really must tell you, I have never heard you play as you played today. I shall tell your father so too as soon as I return to Salzburg.' Now what does Papa think that we played immediately after the symphony? Why, the concerto for three claviers.[1] Herr Demmler[2] played the first, I the second and Herr Stein the third. Then I gave a solo, my last sonata in D, written for Baron Dürnitz,[3] and after my concerto in B♭.[4] I then played another solo, quite in the style of the organ, a fugue in C minor and then all of a sudden a magnificent sonata in C major, out of my head, and a Rondo to finish up with. There was a regular din of applause. Herr Stein was so amazed that he could only make faces and grimaces. As for Herr Demmler, he couldn't stop laughing. He is a quaint fellow, for when he likes anything very much, all he does is to burst into fits of laughter. In my case he even started to curse. Addio. I kiss Papa's hands and embrace my sister with my whole heart. I am your most obedient son

WOLFGANG AMADÉ MOZART

24 October, 1777. Augusta Vindelicorum.

---

[1] K. 242, composed in 1776.
[2] Johann Michael Demmler (1748–1785), organist at Augsburg Cathedral.
[3] K. 284 [205b]. See p. 287, n. 4.   [4] K. 238, a clavier concerto composed in 1776.

(229) *Mozart to his Father*

[*Autograph in the Mozarteum, Salzburg*]

[AUGSBURG, 25 *October* 1777[1]]

The concert, before expenses were deducted, brought in ninety gulden. So, adding the two ducats I was given in the Stube, we have now taken in one hundred gulden. The expenses of the concert amounted to about sixteen gulden, thirty kreuzer. I had the hall for nothing; and many of the performers, I think, will have given their services *free*. *Altogether* we are now twenty-six or twenty-seven gulden out of pocket; which is not too bad. I am writing this letter on Saturday, the 25th. I received this morning your letter containing the sad news of the death of the wife of the Chief Purveyor.[2] Fräulein Tonerl can now point her snout—and perhaps she will have to open it very wide—and then close it without having snatched *anything*. As for the Court Baker's daughter, I have no objection whatever to raise. I saw all this coming long ago and that was the reason why I was so reluctant to leave home and why I felt our departure so keenly. But I hope the story is not known all over Salzburg? I implore Papa most earnestly to keep it quiet as long as possible and for Heaven's sake to refund on my behalf the expenses which her father incurred in connection with her magnificent entry into the convent; pending my return to Salzburg when (like Father Gassner in his little monastery) quite naturally and without any sorcery I shall make the poor girl first ill and then well again and restore her to her convent for life. I kiss Papa's hands and thank him most humbly for his congratulations on my name-day. Papa must not worry, for God is ever before my eyes. I realise His omnipotence and I fear His anger; but I also recognize His love, His compassion and His tenderness towards His creatures. He will never forsake His own. If it is according to His will, so let it be according to mine. Thus all will be well and I must needs be happy and contented. I too will certainly endeavour to follow most strictly your counsel and the advice which you have been good enough to give me. I thank Herr Bullinger 1000 times for his congratulations. I shall write to him soon and express my gratitude. Meanwhile I can only assure him that I know of and possess no better, no more sincere or faithful friend than he is. To Sallerl, whom I also thank most humbly, I shall enclose in my letter to Herr Bullinger some verses of thanks. I also thank my sister, who, by the way, may keep the Schuster duets and must not worry about anything in future. I wrote Gassner as the merchant's name and not Gasser on purpose, for everyone here calls him by that name. In his first letter Papa says that I made myself cheap

---

[1] This letter has been found to be a continuation of Letter 228.

[2] Leopold Mozart's letter of 23 October contains a full account of her fatal illness, which for reasons of space has had to be omitted.

with that young von Langenmantel. Not at all. I was just natural, that was all. I think Papa imagines that he is still a boy. Why, he is twenty-one or twenty-two and a married man. Is it possible to remain a boy when one is married? Since that episode I have not gone near them; but today as a parting message I left two cards at the house and apologized for not going up, explaining that I had too many important calls to pay. Now I must close, for Mamma insists *absolument* on our going to table and then packing. Tomorrow we shall travel straight to Wallerstein. I think it will be best if Papa continues to address his letters to my uncle, until we have settled down somewhere, but not in prison, of course.[1] My dear little cousin, who sends greetings to you both, is not at all *infatuated with priests.* Yesterday, to please me, she dressed up as a Frenchwoman. When she does so, she is five per cent prettier. Well, addio. I again kiss Papa's hands and embrace my sister and send greetings to all my good friends; and now off to the closet run I, where perchance shit some muck shall I, and ever the same fool am I.

WOLFGANG and AMADEUS MOZARTY

Augsburg, 25 Octobery, seventeen hundred and seventy-seveny.

(230) *Nannerl Mozart to her Mother and Brother*

[Extract]   [*Autograph in the Mozarteum, Salzburg*]

[SALZBURG, 27 October 1777]

MY DEAREST MAMMA AND MY DEAR BROTHER,

Not a single letter! And we were looking forward to hearing how the concert had gone off. We hope that you are both in good health. Thank God, we are well.

A castrato,[2] who happened to be passing through, sang yesterday at Court. Papa was there and heard him, but he did not like his singing particularly, for he has a rather nasal voice and is a long-legged fellow with a long face and a low forehead. All the same, he sings far better than Madame Duschek. As the Archbishop is of the same opinion, perhaps he will take him into his service, for Signor Caselli,[3] who was offered 2000 gulden but no leave of absence during the carnival, is not coming. Otherwise I have no news. We hope to hear something from you soon. By the way, do not forget your target. I kiss Mamma's hands and wish you both good health and great success.

I am
your devoted sister
MARIE ANNE MOZART

---

[1] Mozart is playing upon the two meanings of the word *sitzen.*
[2] Francesco Ceccarelli. He was appointed soon afterwards to the Archbishop's service for six years at an annual salary of 800 gulden.
[3] Probably Vincenzo Caselli, a male soprano, whom the Mozarts met at Mantua in 1770. See Leopold Mozart's *Reiseaufzeichnungen*, p. 50, and *MBA*, No. 156.

(230a) *Leopold Mozart to his Wife and Son*

[Autograph in the Mozarteum, Salzburg]

[SALZBURG, 27 October 1777[1]]

It is never more necessary to write than when one is about to leave a place, even if the note consists only of two lines. We had not the slightest doubt that we would have received a letter from you today; yet nothing has come. If you have left Augsburg, my brother could or ought to have told us so. You are most fortunate in having very fine weather. Today, the 27th, it is most beautifully warm. I do not yet know the name of the castrato,[2] but I gather that Rust wrote to him in confidence that he ought to come for an audition, for he now praises him and shoves him forward on every possible occasion. He sings rather through his nose, and produces some notes in his throat, and his voice is not at all strong; but if he does not cost much, he is quite good enough. The choral singer Egger has died.[3] Probably Hofstettner will take his place as tenor in the Church of the Holy Trinity. You must always leave a note at post offices, so that letters may be forwarded; otherwise they will be lost. This is the third letter which I am addressing to my brother. You will have received, no doubt, the parcel containing the scores of Eberlin's works, which I sent to the landlord of the Lamm. If you are in good health, all is well. God keep you! Lately dear Mamma has added nothing to your letters. I hope that the exercise which this journey involves will be good for her. Did she not buy herself some felt shoes in Augsburg? She has left her knickers behind as well. I, of course, was ill at the time, or I should have attended to a hundred things. You should examine your carriage very carefully and particularly the wheels; and, if there is little rain, you should often have them wetted. You ought to have *a second coachman* at your disposal, for if you lose one on the way, *there you are high and dry*! And this can happen to you any moment, for from now on you will have bad roads. Be sure *not to travel late at night*; it is far better to get up early in the morning, and, if you can avoid doing so, never mention at the inns *whither* and *when* you are travelling; for sometimes some bad fellow overhears these remarks and makes use of the information. Now I must close. I kiss you both a million times and, while I am always wishing to be with you, I assure you from the bottom of my heart that I am until death

your old husband and father

LEOPOLD MOZART

I must tell you that in everything which has to do with the house Nannerl is extraordinarily industrious, hard-working and amazingly

---

[1] The continuation of Nannerl's letter.   [2] See p. 342, n. 2.

[3] Georg Anton Egger, a tenor in the Salzburg Cathedral choir.

attentive; besides which she plays as much as she can and is an excellent accompanist. Every evening we practise for two, or two and a half hours at least. Addio.

(231) *Leopold Mozart to his Son*

[*Extract*]   [*Autograph in the Mozarteum, Salzburg*]

MON TRÉS CHER FILS!   SALZBURG, 29 *October* 1777

Up to the present I have written to you by every post and although I read in Mamma's letter of October 23rd that she was anxious because she had received no letter from me that week, I hope and, judging by what you wrote about that Langenmantel boy, I assume that my letter, which I sent off from Salzburg on October 20th, has by this time reached you. Actually I have already addressed three letters to my brother and this is the fourth. I trust that you will write from every town you stay in and inform me, if possible, when you leave. If it is not possible to do so, then you must leave the name of the place on a card at the Post Office and thus no letter will be lost. The above is an extremely necessary precaution and you should make a point of doing this in person, for we have known of hundreds of instances of hired servants and valets who intercept letters when they arrive and open them in the hope of finding a credit note or draft; and of innumerable letters, which were to have been taken to the post, but were kept back by the servant who pocketed the six kreuzer which he should have paid for the postage. This last is a very common trick. God be thanked that your concert in Augsburg went off so well. I long from my heart to read an account of it in tomorrow's papers, and I may say that all Salzburg is of the same mind. *You know, of course, why.* The whole town was delighted when they read the notice, which was worded so nicely, and after the concert everyone was anxious to see Thursday's and Friday's papers, which arrived here on Sunday, for they thought that something further would have been published in them, which, of course, was impossible. In Wednesday's paper there was only a notice at the foot of the page to the effect that the concert would begin at six o'clock. I know only too well that the Dean at Holy Cross is a gay fellow. He ought to have put before you his little galanterie pieces for the clavier which he had printed by Lotter eighteen or nineteen years ago. Then you would have found out the name of the author, who was such a sly rascal that he published his works under the name of Reschnezgi.[1]

As for Herr Stein's little daughter, I am glad that her father is becoming sensible and that all who are in favour of making grimaces are beginning to think better of it. I suggested her for the first clavier, because you had

[1] i.e. Zeschinger. See p. 338.

not said very much about her; so I thought that perhaps she played very well. If you have an opportunity, try to find out ⟨who Herr Beecke's father was. He was born at Wallerstein or somewhere in that district and his father was a schoolmaster or an organist.[1] Tell me also how Beecke behaves to you⟩.

October 30th. This very moment, at half past eleven in the morning, I have received four letters—one from your little cousin, one from Herr Stein, one from Herr von Hamm and the fourth from Mysliwecek. Your cousin is very sad at your departure, for her distress at parting from Mamma will not have been anything out of the ordinary. Moreover she solemnly protests against the accusation of being *too friendly with priests.* Herr Stein's letter is full of your praises and he even maintains that I myself never heard you play as you played at that concert. Tell me whether I shall find more about it in the papers and whether you left on Sunday and whether your parting from your cousin was very sad and distressing. Herr von Hamm writes from Munich that he would like to send me his daughter in the spring. Herr Mysliwecek sends me six short clavier pieces for Nannerl, and his letter is *in forma ostensiva*[2] a polite and concise reminder about the music which he sent some time ago to the Archbishop. So I shall show this letter to the Countess.[3] *I had advised him to adopt these tactics.* If the Countess refuses to deal with the matter, then I shall take it up with the Chief Steward. I should like Mysliwecek to be paid decently. The letter is drafted quite clearly; he mentions that the copying and binding of both batches of musical scores cost him about ten ducats.

I have just received a paper which contains a splendid article about your concert. I gather from your letter that from Wallerstein you will go straight to Mannheim; and Herr Stein tells me the same. I suppose therefore that Prince Taxis has already gone to Regensburg; and I imagine that you have been given a letter to his Director of Music,[4] as you have mentioned nothing more about Dischingen. Thus owing to your long stay in Munich and Augsburg you have used up over 100 gulden, while, if you had remained for a shorter time in Munich, you would now have a surplus. But we can get over that, as something has been set going there— although really all you got there was *flattery* and expressions of good intentions. To some extent Augsburg has made up for your losses. Now you must be well on your guard, for Mannheim is a dangerous spot as far as money is concerned. Everything is very dear. You will have to move heaven and earth to obtain a hearing, then wait interminably for a

---

[1] Ignaz von Beecke (1733–1803) was born at Wimpfen im Tal on the Neckar. His father was warden of the Military College. See L. Schiedermair, 'Die Blütezeit der Öttingen-Wallersteinschen Hofkapelle' in *Sammelbände der Internationalen Musikgesellschaft,* IX, 107 f.
[2] i.e. in a presentable form.   [3] Countess Lodron, the Archbishop's sister.
[4] Joseph Riepel (1708–1782), music director to Prince Thurn and Taxis at Regensburg. He composed church music, operas, chamber music and wrote works on the theory of music. See Burney, *Present State of Music in Germany, etc.,* 2nd edition, 1775, vol. ii. p. 320.

present and in the end receive at most ten carolins—or 100 gulden, a sum which by that time you will have probably spent. The Court is packed with people who look on strangers with suspicion and who put spokes in the wheels of the very ablest. Economy is most necessary. If Herr Danner or some other friend could take you from your inn to a private lodging, you would save half your money. You must consider carefully whether you ought to offer your services to the Elector, with a view, that is, to obtaining an appointment. For my part, I should say no! since he only offers a miserable remuneration. But if it can be arranged that the Elector shall test your knowledge and if no one in the orchestra thinks that you are looking for an appointment or trying to fly over the heads of others, then something may be arranged; and this you should discuss in confidence with the Elector, telling him frankly *that you are coming straight to him, because you are well aware that through other channels matters are frequently represented to the reigning lord in an unfavourable light and that the talents of the young are almost invariably kept back.* Now I must close. God keep you

★ well. We kiss you both most cordially. Take care of your health. We are well. Do not leave us without letters. If you cannot do so, for you have to run about a great deal, perhaps Mamma could undertake to write to

★ me when you arrive at some destination. Nannerl and I, alive and dead, are the old faithful, abandoned orphan and grass widower and everything that is sad.

MOZART

★

Mozart and his mother spent the next four months at Mann-heim, which possessed one of the finest orchestras in Europe and where German opera was being gradually established. Here Mozart formed friendships with Cannabich, the two Wendlings and the Weber family, and met Vogler, Holzbauer, Raaff and Wieland. But all his efforts to interest the Elector in his future met with no response. His position soon became precarious and his prospects of making both ends meet very uncertain. Urged by his exasperated father, who was obliged to run up debts in order to provide money for the travellers and was beginning to doubt his son's capacity to meet life's responsibilities, Mozart reluctantly decided to try his luck in Paris. During his stay at Mannheim Mozart's chief compositions were two flute quartets and a flute concerto written to order, two clavier sonatas, four violin sonatas and three arias. Letters 232–297.

(232) *Maria Anna Mozart to her Husband*

[*Autograph in the Mozarteum, Salzburg*]

MY DEAREST HUSBAND,   MANNHEIM, 31 *October* 1777

Thank God, we both arrived here safe and sound yesterday, the 30th, at six o'clock in the evening. We left Augsburg last Sunday, the 26th, lunched at Donauwörth and drove in the afternoon to Nördlingen. At seven o'clock we reached Hohenaltheim, where the Prince of Wallerstein is staying and where we lodged in a wretched inn. We would have started off again on the following day, had I not caught a heavy cold which obliged us to spend two nights and one whole day there. Herr Perwein was with us most of the time. The Prince of Wallerstein is greatly to be pitied, for he is in the deepest melancholy and cannot look at anybody without bursting into tears. Wolfgang had a talk with him, but the Prince is so absent-minded that he asked him four or five times about the same thing. He refuses to listen to music and spends all his time with his child. We therefore left for Nördlingen on Tuesday, the 28th, St. Simon and St. Jude's day, at seven in the morning. Captain Beecke had given us our route, a horrible road to Ellwangen, and so through Schwäbisch-Hall and Heilbronn to Heidelberg and Mannheim. But the postmaster in Ellwangen strongly advised us not to go by this route, which, he said, nobody ever took when driving, but only if they were going on horseback. We thereupon drove from Ellwangen, to Aalen, Schwäbisch-Gmünd, Schorndorf, Cannstatt, Enzweihungen, Kündlingen, Bruchsal, Wagheussel, Schwetzingen and thence to Mannheim, this route being longer by only one stage and a half. Wolfgang has gone to see young Herr Danner, who is already married, although he is a year younger than my son. Old Herr Danner is not here, but will return from his estate in the country on Monday. Meanwhile his son is taking Wolfgang to meet Messieurs Raaff and Cannabich.[1] We were only a few yards from Bruchsal yesterday when Herr von Schmidt, who was coming from Speyer, met us on the road. He recognised us, as Wolfgang did him. He got out of his coach at once and, shouting out 'Halt', came up to our carriage and spoke to us. He was uncommonly glad to see us and was sorry not to be in Mannheim. He also advised us to take rooms at the 'Pfälzischer Hof', where he always

---

[1] Christian Cannabich (1731–1798), born in Mannheim, was trained as a violinist by Johann Stamitz, a pioneer of the famous Mannheim school. He studied in Italy under Jommelli and in 1759 became leader of the Mannheim orchestra, and in 1775 director of instrumental music. In 1778 he followed the Elector Karl Theodor to Munich. Cannabich was a composer of note, but his chief merit lies in his work as leader of the Mannheim orchestra, solo violinist and teacher. In his day he trained nearly all the violinists of the Mannheim orchestra. According to Leopold Mozart's *Reiseaufzeichnungen*, p. 47, the Mozart family met Cannabich in Paris during their second visit in May 1766. See *MBA*, No. 110.

stays. So we are there and not at the 'Prinz Friedrich', which is much dearer. If we find that we have to stay on for a good while, we shall go to some private house, for living in inns is far too expensive. I hope that you and Nannerl are well. And what is my Bimperl doing? I have not heard anything of her for a long time. I am sorry from my heart that the Chief Purveyor's wife died so suddenly. Fräulein Tonerl's mouth will probably water. Wolfgang is writing today to my brother-in-law in Augsburg to tell him to forward the letters he has received, for we told him to keep them until we should send him our address. So Wolfgang will hardly be able to write to you today, for he is at the rehearsal of the oratorio, moreover the post goes at six o'clock and it is already half past four. So you will have to put up with my humble self.

(232a) *Mozart to his Father*

[Autograph in the Mozarteum, Salzburg]

[MANNHEIM, 31 *October* 1777]

And please put up with my very mediocre self. I went with Herr Danner today to M. Cannabich, who was exceedingly courteous. I played to him on his pianoforte, which is a very good one, and we went together to the rehearsal. I thought I should not be able to keep myself from laughing when I was introduced to the people there. Some who knew me by repute were very polite and fearfully respectful; others, however, who had never heard of me, stared at me wide-eyed, and certainly in a rather sneering manner. They probably think that because I am little and young, nothing great or mature can come out of me; but they will soon see. Herr Cannabich himself is taking me tomorrow to Count Savioli,[1] the Intendant of the orchestra. It is a good thing that the Elector's name-day falls very soon. The oratorio, which is being rehearsed, is by Handel,[2] but I did not stay to hear it, for, before it came on, they rehearsed a Psalm—a Magnificat—by Vogler,[3] the Deputy-Kapellmeister

---

[1] Count Louis Aurèle de Savioli.

[2] Handel's *Messiah*, Part I, was performed on 1 November. Vogler conducted it. Berlin and Hamburg had already given performances of this oratorio.

[3] Abt Georg Joseph Vogler (1749–1814), born in Würzburg, was the son of a violin-maker. He first studied law and theology and in 1772 became Court Chaplain at Mannheim, but in 1773 the Elector Karl Theodor provided him with funds to study music under Padre Martini at Bologna. Vogler proceeded instead to Padua and became a pupil of Vallotti. He was ordained a priest in Rome. In 1775 he returned to Mannheim as the Elector's vice-Kapellmeister and spiritual counsellor and became a famous teacher. Owing to his peculiarities he made many enemies as well as devoted friends. In 1784 Vogler followed the Electoral Court to Munich, where he trained the celebrated singer Aloysia Weber-Lange. He soon set out, however, on his many travels abroad, which included a visit to England in 1790. He was a prolific composer and writer of books on musical theory, but his fame rests on his success as a teacher of famous composers, such as Weber and Meyerbeer. See Schafhäutl, *Abt Georg Joseph Vogler*, Augsburg, 1888.

here, and it lasted almost an hour. Now I must close, for I have still to
write to my little cousin. I kiss Papa's hands and my sisterly beloved I
embrace shortly and sweetly, as is proper.

JOANNES*** CHRISOSTOMUS SIGISMUNDUS**
WOLFGANG* GOTTLIEB MOZART

*Today is my name-day! **That is my confirmation name!
***January 27th is my birthday!

Our greetings to all our acquaintances, and particularly to Count
Leopold Arco, Herr Bullinger, Mlle Katherl and the whole company of
shitters.

À Mademoiselle Rosalie Joli
A thousand thanks, dear Sally, for your wishes.
Now in your honour I shall drink whole dishes
Of coffee, tea, and even lemonade,
Dipping therein a sticklet of pomade,
And also—Oh! It's striking six o'clock!
Whoe'er denies it, well, he's just a—block.

To be continued in my next.

(233) *Mozart to his Cousin, Maria Anna Thekla Mozart, Augsburg*

[*Autograph formerly in the possession of Richard Strauss*]

[MANNHEIM, 31 *October* 1777[1]]

50 *October* 1777.[2]

How very odd! I am to write something sensible and not one sensible
idea occurs to me. Do not forget to remind the Dean to send me that
music soon. Do not forget your promise; I shall certainly not forget mine.
How can you doubt me? I shall send you very soon a whole letter in
French, which you can then get the Postmaster to translate for you. I
hope that by this time you have started to learn French? Well, I have too
little space left to jot down any more sensible remarks. Besides, too much
sense gives one a headache. In any case my letter is full of sensible and
learned stuff, as you must acknowledge if you have read it; and if you
have not yet read it, please do so quickly, for you will draw a great deal
of profit from it and some lines in it will make you shed bitter tears.

---

[1] The version of this letter is that given in Nottebohm, *Mozartiana*, p. 71.
[2] A nonsensical date was one of Mozart's favourite jokes. See p. 261.

(234) *Leopold Mozart to his Son*

[*Extract*]   [*Autograph in the Mozarteum, Salzburg*]

MON TRÈS CHER FILS!   SALZBURG, 1 *November* 1777

I have this moment come in from the Cathedral service, during which Haydn's oboe mass[1] was performed, he himself conducting it. He had also composed the offertory and, instead of a sonata, he had set to music the words of the graduale, which the priest has to say. The mass was rehearsed yesterday after Vespers. The Prince did not conduct the service, but Count Friedrich Lodron took his place, as the Bishop of Chiemsee, Breuner and Dietrichstein are in Augsburg for the All Saints Peremptorio and were therefore not available. I liked the whole mass very much, as there were six oboists, three double basses, two bassoons and the castrato *who has been taken on for six months at one hundred gulden a month*.[2] Ferlendis and Sandmayr played the oboe solos. The oboist at Lodron's, a certain student, the chief watchman and Oberkirchner[3] were the oboists in the orchestra. Cassel and the choirmaster Knozenbry were the double basses, seated near the organ and beside the trombones; Estlinger was there with his bassoon; Hofner and Perwein were seated beside the oboists on the violinists' platform. What I particularly liked was that, since oboes and bassoons resemble very much the human voice, the tutti seemed to be a very strongly supported chorus of voices, as the sopranos and altos, strengthened by the six oboes and the alto trombones, admirably balanced the number of tenor and bass voices; and the pieno was so majestic that I could have easily done without the oboe solos. The whole affair lasted an hour and a quarter and I found it far too short, for it is really an excellent composition. It all flows along naturally; the fugues, and particularly the Et vitam etc. in the Credo, the Dona Nobis and the Hallelujah in the offertory are worked out in a masterly fashion, the themes being most natural and without any exaggerated modulations or too sudden transitions. The graduale, which was performed instead of the sonata, is a piece of pure counterpoint throughout *in pieno*.[4] The voice of the castrato did on the whole good service here. If some time or other I can obtain this mass, I shall certainly send it to you. I should mention that Brunetti stood behind Ferlendis, Wenzl Sadlo[5] behind the bassoon-players and Hafeneder behind the other oboists. They watched Haydn throughout the performance and beat time on their shoulders; otherwise it would have really gone higgledy-piggledy in places and particularly in the fugues and in the

[1] Michael Haydn's mass which Leopold Mozart praises so highly is his so-called Hieronymus mass in C major, finished on 14 September 1777.

[2] Francesco Ceccarelli. See p. 342, n. 2.

[3] Perhaps Johann Michael Oberkirchner, a native of Donauwörth. See Hammerle, *op. cit.* p. 35.   [4] i.e. in full.

[5] Wenzl Sadlo played the horn in the Salzburg court orchestra. See Hammerle, *op. cit.* p. 35.

running bass-accompaniments. The result may be at last an appointment as Cathedral Kapellmeister or Deputy-Kapellmeister, for which Haydn has been working for so many years. But there are great difficulties. For you must know that Rust[1] is in wretched health; so much so that Dr Barisani has told him that he must leave Salzburg as soon as possible unless he wants to leave his bones here this winter.

Sunday, November 2nd. The graduale was not by Haydn but by an Italian. Haydn had got it from Reutter[2] some time or other. I was with Countess von Lodron today from a quarter to eleven until after noon. She was, of course, very polite and said that she had read in the papers that you were in Augsburg and that she was sure that you would go to Mannheim not only on account of its great opera but because German operas are always performed there and the Elector values people of talent. This, it should be noted, tallies with a remark which she made at lunch yesterday and which Abbé Henri passed on to me: '*Mozart*', she said, '*will go to Mannheim and, whatever happens, I am persuaded that the Elector will retain him.*' She talked a great deal and, upon her asking me about Stein's pianoforte, I told her what you had written to me about it. She said that you were right, judging by the approval of Countess Schönborn,[3] who had told her that she had travelled through Augsburg on purpose in order to see these instruments and, finding them infinitely better than Späth's, had ordered one for herself at the cost of 700 gulden. I am surprised that Herr Stein said nothing to you about this. When we came to speak of Haydn's mass, I mentioned what I have just told you, and she immediately interrupted me: '*Yes*,' she said, '*that was precisely the Archbishop's opinion. Haydn did not understand him properly. He told me so the first time the Kyrie and Gloria were rehearsed, but he added; 'I did not want to say anything more to him, so as not to make him confused and out of humour, as he has begun it like that'*.' The Countess tried to get me to allow Nannerl to pay her a visit in order that she should play the clavier rondo which Mysliwecek has sent her. The object of my visit was in fact mainly on account of Mysliwecek's letter. She assured me that by the last post the Archbishop had sent to him at Munich a draft for twenty-five or thirty ducats. She invited me several times to visit her more often and she ended by asking me to send you her greetings. Then Count Potbelly[4] and their son and heir Sigerl both shouted out: 'From me too! From me too!' She even asked me how Count Leopold Arco was getting on, a thing she has never yet done, and I praised him in appropriate fashion. By the way, Abbé Henri came to congratulate you on your name-day. You promised to write to him and you should do so when you get a free moment.

---

[1] See p. 275, n. 4.   [2] See p. 12, n. 3.
[3] Countess von Lodron and Countess Schönborn were sisters of the Archbishop.
[4] Count Ernst Lodron, Marshal of the district of Salzburg. Sigmund Lodron was his only son.

Monday, November 3rd. I have this moment come in from the Requiem, in which Signor Ceccarelli sang, as it was Festum Praepositum. He lives
★ in the wig-maker's house, where Ferrari used to live at first. He is a good sight-reader and his method is excellent. He asked me all about you and said that he was sorry to have missed meeting a virtuoso, of whom he had heard such extraordinary accounts both in Italy and at Salzburg. I have
★ invited him to see your portrait. Now I have something to tell you which will certainly infuriate you, for it has annoyed me very much. It is hardly believable, but on the day on which you gave your concert, our best friend, M. Grimm, arrived at the 'Drei Mohren', next to the Concert Hall. I have read in the Augsburger Intelligenzblatt that *Herr von Grimm, envoy of Saxe-Gotha, was due to arrive from Saxony by the mail coach on the 22nd and would stay at the 'Drei Mohren'.* Is it not maddening? I presume that he arrived late in the evening and left again on the following morning; otherwise he would have read the announcement or would have heard people talking about you. Where on earth is he now? God knows. Perhaps you will run into him somewhere. Well, now you know at any rate that he is travelling. How delighted this man would have been and both you and Mamma also, if he had arrived *a tempo* and had been present
★ at the concert. We had our usual shooting yesterday. Next Sunday we shall have as a target the sad parting of two persons dissolving in tears, Wolfgang and the 'Basle'. Where will you be reading this letter? Probably in Mannheim. For this is the second post-day on which we have received no letters. I hope that you will get something to do in Mannheim, where they are always performing German operas. Perhaps you will get a contract to compose one. If you do, you know that I need not urge you to imitate the natural and popular style, which everyone easily understands. The grand and sublime style is suited to grand subjects. Everything in its place. I hope that you are both well. That is our first wish and it should be your principal care. I am always a little bit worried about Mamma. You, dear Wolfgang, should keep to your usual diet, which is very important for your health. I need not be anxious about Mamma, if she only keeps warm. Now farewell. God preserve you, God bless you. Nannerl and I kiss you both a million times and I am your old

TRAZOM

★

(235) *Mozart to his Father*

[*Autograph in the Mozarteum, Salzburg*]

[MANNHEIM, 4 *November* 1777]

MONSIEUR MON TRÉS CHER PÉRE,

We wrote the day before we left Augsburg. It looks as though you haven't received the letter yet.[1] I shall be sorry if it is lost, for it is a long

[1] Letter 228.

one and in it I described my concert very fully. It also contains something about Stein's daughter, and, further, my thanks for the congratulations on my name-day. But I hope that by now you have received it. This is my second letter from Mannheim. I am with Cannabich every day. Mamma too came with me today to his house. He is quite a different person from what he used to be and the whole orchestra say the same thing. He has taken a great fancy to me. He has a daughter who plays the clavier quite nicely;[1] and in order to make a real friend of him I am now working at a sonata for her, which is almost finished save for the Rondo.[2] When I had composed the opening Allegro and the Andante I took them to their house and played both to them. Papa cannot imagine the applause which this sonata won. It so happened that some members of the orchestra were there, young Danner, a horn-player called Lang,[3] and the oboist[4] whose name I have forgotten, but who plays very well and has a delightfully pure tone. I have made him a present of my oboe concerto,[5] which is being copied in a room at Cannabich's, and the fellow is quite crazy with delight. I played this concerto to him today on the pianoforte at Cannabich's, and, although *everybody knew that I was the composer*, it was very well received. Nobody said that it was not *well composed*, because the people here do not understand such matters—they had better consult the Archbishop, who will at once put them right.[6] I played all my six sonatas[7] today at Cannabich's. Herr Kapellmeister Holzbauer[8] himself took me today to Count Savioli, the Intendant, and Cannabich happened to be there. Herr Holzbauer spoke to the Count in Italian, suggesting that the Elector ought to grant me the favour of a hearing. He added that I had been here fifteen years ago, when I was seven, but that now I was older and more developed in music as well as in body. 'Ah,' said the Count, 'that is——' Goodness knows who he thought I was. But Cannabich stepped in at once, and I pretended not to hear and fell into conversation with some other people. I noticed, however, that he was speaking to the Count about me with an earnest expression. The latter then said to me: 'I hear that you play the clavier quite passably'. I bowed.

Now I must tell you about the music here. On Saturday, All Saints' Day, I was at High Mass in the Kapelle. The orchestra is excellent and very strong. On either side there are ten or eleven violins, four violas, two

---

[1] Cannabich's eldest daughter Rosa.
[2] K. 309 [284b]. For the identification of this clavier sonata see Köchel, p. 289.
[3] Either Franz Lang (1751– ?) or his younger brother, Martin Lang (1755–1819). Both were horn-players in the Mannheim orchestra.
[4] Friedrich Ramm (1744–?1811) was appointed in 1759 oboist in the Mannheim orchestra, which he followed to Munich in 1778.
[5] K. 314 [285d]. See p. 320, n. 1.   [6] This is ironical.   [7] K. 279–284 [189d–h, 205b].
[8] Ignaz Holzbauer (1711–1783), born in Vienna, became Kapellmeister at Mannheim in 1753 and held this appointment until the Elector's death in 1777. He composed eleven Italian operas, a famous German opera *Günther von Schwarzburg*, produced at Mannheim in 1777, oratorios, symphonies, masses and a great deal of church music.

oboes, two flutes and two clarinets, two horns, four violoncellos, four bassoons and four double basses, also trumpets and drums. They can produce fine music, but I should not care to have one of my masses performed here. Why? On account of their shortness? No, everything must be short here too. Because a different style of composition is required? Not at all. But because, as things are at present, you must write principally for the instruments, as you cannot imagine anything worse than the voices here. Six sopranos, six altos, six tenors and six basses against twenty violins and twelve basses is just like zero to one. Is that not so, Herr Bullinger? The reason for this state of affairs is that the Italians are now in very bad odour here. They have only two castrati, who are already old and will just be allowed to die off. The soprano would actually prefer to sing alto, as he can no longer take the high notes. The few boys they have are miserable. The tenors and basses are like our funeral singers. Deputy-Kapellmeister Vogler, who had composed the mass which was performed the other day, is a dreary musical jester, an exceedingly conceited and rather incompetent fellow.[1] The whole orchestra dislikes him. But today, Sunday, I heard a mass by Holzbauer, which he wrote twenty-six years ago, but which is very fine. He is a good composer, he has a good church style, he knows how to write for voices and instruments, and he composes good fugues. They have two organists here who alone would be worth a special visit to Mannheim.[2] I have had an opportunity of hearing them properly, for it is not the custom here to sing the Benedictus, but during that part of the service the organist has to play the whole time. On the first occasion I heard the second organist and on the second, the first organist. But in my opinion the second is even more distinguished than the first. For when I heard him, I enquired: 'Who is playing the organ?' I was told, the second organist. He played abominably. When I heard the other one, I asked: 'Who is playing now?' I was told, our first organist. He played even more wretchedly and I think that if they were thrown together, something even worse would be the result. To watch these gentlemen is enough to make one die of laughing. The second, when seated at the organ, is like a child at stool, for his face tells you what he can do. The first, at any rate, wears spectacles. I went and stood at the organ and watched him in the hope of learning something from him. At every note he lifts his hands right up in the air. His forte is to play in six parts, but chiefly in five and eight parts! He often leaves out the right hand for fun and plays with the left hand alone. In short, he can do just what he likes, for he is completely master of his instrument. Mamma asks me to tell Nannerl that the lining for the coat is at the very bottom of the large box on the right hand side. She will find all sorts of bits for patching,

---

[1] Mozart had already sided with Vogler's opponents. For a good account of Mozart's relations with Vogler see Abert, vol. ii. p. 982 ff.

[2] Nikolaus Bayer and Anton Marxfelder. The latter was in Mannheim from 1745 to 1778.

black, white, yellow, brown, red, green, blue and so forth.

Mamma sends her greetings to all. It is impossible for her to write, for she still has to say her office, as we were very late getting home from the rehearsal of the grand opera. The cotton is not in skeins, but in a ball, wrapped up in a blue cloth. Yes, that is how it is and not otherwise! After High Mass tomorrow I have to go to that stern Electress, who *insists* on teaching me to knit. I am dreadfully nervous, as both she and the most honourable Elector want me to knit in public at the grand gala concert on Thursday evening. The young princess here, who is a natural child of the Elector, also knits very nicely. The Duke and Duchess of Zweibrücken arrived here punctually at eight o'clock. A propos, Mamma and I beg Papa very earnestly to be so good as to send a souvenir to our dear cousin, for we both regretted that we had nothing with us to give her; but we promised to write to Papa and to ask him to send her something, or rather two things, one from Mamma, a double fichu like her own, and one from myself, a trinket, such as a box or toothpick case, or whatever you like, so long as it is pretty, for she deserves it. She and her father took a great deal of trouble and wasted much time in our company. Moreover my uncle took in the money at my concert. Addio. Baccio le mani di vostra paternità ed abbraccio con leggiertà la mia sorella e facendo i miei complimenti da per tutto sono di tutto cuore.[1]

WOLFGANGO AMADEO MOZART

Mannheim, li 4 di novembre 1777.

(235a) *Postscript written by Maria Anna Mozart to her Husband on the cover*

[*Autograph in the possession of Frau Ruth Weiss, Fellbach, Stuttgart*]

A certain Signor Gervasio and his wife, who knew you in Holland, send their congratulations to your son the virtuoso. He plays the mandolin and she sings: they gave a concert to-day. Our greetings to the whole of Salzburg, Herr Bullinger, Jungfrau Sallerl.

(235b) *Postscript written by Mozart on the cover*

[*Autograph in the possession of Frau Ruth Weiss, Fellbach, Stuttgart*]

Gilowski Katherl, fr: v: Gerlisch, h: von Heffner, fr: v: Heffner, fr: v: Schidenhofen, h: Geschwendner, h: Sandner and all who are dead. As for the targets, if it is not too late, this is what I would like. A short man with fair hair, shown bending over and displaying his bare arse. From his mouth come the words: 'Good appetite for the meal'. The other man to be shown booted and spurred with a red cloak and a fine

---

[1] I kiss my father's hands and embrace my sister tenderly. I send greetings to everyone and remain with all my heart. . . .

fashionable wig. He must be of medium height and in such a position
that he licks the other man's arse. From his mouth come the words: 'Oh,
there's nothing to beat it'. So, please. If not this time, another time.

(236) Mozart to his Cousin, Maria Anna Thekla Mozart, Augsburg

[Autograph in the Stefan Zweig Collection, British Library, London]

DEAREST COZ FUZZ!   [MANNHEIM, 5 November 1777[1]]

I have received reprieved your dear letter, telling selling me that my
uncle carbuncle, my aunt can't and you too are very well hell. Thank God,
we too are in excellent health wealth. Today the letter setter from my
Papa Ha! Ha! dropped safely into my claws paws. I hope that you too
have got shot the note dote which I wrote to you from Mannheim. If so,
so much the better, better the much so. Now for some sense. I am very
sorry to hear that the Abbot rabbit has had another stroke so soon moon.
But I trust that with God's cod's help it will have no serious consequences
excrescences. You say lay that you will keep the compromise[2] which you
made me before I left Augsburg and that you will do so soon boon. Well,
that will certainly be a shock to me. You write further, you pour out,
disclose, divulge, notify, declare, signify, inform, acquaint me with the
fact, make it quite clear, request, demand, desire, wish, would like, order
me to send lend you my portrait. Eh bien, I shall certainly despatch
scratch it to you. Oui, par ma foi. I shit on your nose and it will run down
your chin. A propos. Have you got that Spuni Cuni business? Do tell me!
Do you still love me? I am sure you do! If so, so much the better, better
the much so!

Well, so it is in this world, I'm told. One has the purse and another has
the gold. Whom do you hold with? Surely with me—I am certain you
do. But now things are more difficult. A propos. Would you not like to
go and see Herr Goldschmidt again soon? . . . But, you ask, what for?
What for?—Why, nothing at all—beyond asking about that Spuni Cuni
business. Well, well; that's all right. Long live all those who . . . how does
it go on? Well, I wish you good night, but first shit into your bed and
make it burst. Sleep soundly, my love, into your mouth your arse you'll
shove. Now I'm off to fool about and then I'll sleep a bit, no doubt.
Tomorrow we'll talk sensibly for a bit vomit. I tell a things of lot to have
you, you imagine can't simply how have I much say to; but hear all
tomorrow it will you. Meanwhile, good-bye. Oh, my arse is burning
like fire! What on earth does it mean?—Perhaps some muck wants to come

---

[1] The autograph of this letter, a facsimile of which was published for private circulation
by Herbert Reichner, Vienna, 1931, shows a tremendous flourish round the first letter of
'Allerliebstes Bäsle Häsle'.

[2] Mozart uses instead of Versprechen (promise) the word Verbrechen (crime).

out? Why yes, muck, I know, see and smell you . . . and . . . what is that?
—Is it possible . . . Ye gods!—can I believe those ears of mine? Yes indeed,
it is so—what a long melancholy note! Today letter the writing am 5th
this I. Yesterday I had to talk with the formidable Electress and tomorrow,
the 6th, I am playing at the great gala concert; and afterwards I am to play
again to her in private, as she herself told me. Now for some real sense.

No. 1. A letter or letters addressed to me will reach you, which I must
ask you to—to what? Why, a fox is no hare, well . . . Now, where was
I . . . Yes, of course, at reach. Yes, they will reach you—well, what will?
—Why, now I remember. Letters, why, letters will reach you . . . But
what sort of letters?—Why, of course, letters addressed to me, which I
must ask you to forward without fail. I shall let you know where I go on
to from Mannheim.

Now for No. 2. I must ask you, why not?—I must ask you, dearest
dunce, why not?—if you happen to be writing to Madame Tavernier at
Munich, to send my regards to the two Misses Freysinger, why not?—
Strange!—Why not? And say that I beg the youngest one, Fräulein
Josepha, to forgive me, why not?—Why should I not beg her to forgive
me? Strange! Why should I not? Say that she must forgive me for not
having yet sent her the sonata[1] I promised her and that I shall send it as
soon as possible. Why not?——What?—Why not?—Why should I not
send it?—Why should I not despatch it?—Why not?—Strange! I don't
know why I shouldn't—Well then—you will do me this favour.—Why
not?—Why should you not do it?—Why not?—Strange! I shall do the
same for you, when you want me to. Why not? Why should I not do it
for you? Strange! Why not?—I can't think why not?

Do not forget also to send my compliments to the Papa and Mamma of
the two young ladies, for it is a gross fault to forget must shall will have
one's duty to father and mother. When the sonata is finished, I shall send
it to you and the letter as well; and you will be good enough to send it on
to Munich. Now I must close, though it makes me morose. Dear Uncle,
let us go at once to the Holy Cross Monastery and see if anyone is still
up? We shall not stay long, we shall just ring the bell, that is all. Now I
must tell you of a sad thing which has happened just this very moment.
As I was doing my best to write this letter, I heard something on the
street. I stopped writing—I got up—went to the window . . . and . . . the
sound ceased. I sat down again, started off again to write—but I had
hardly written ten words when again I heard something. I got up again—
As I did, I again heard a sound, this time quite faint—but I seemed to
smell something slightly burnt—and wherever I went, it smelt. When I
looked out of the window, the smell disappeared. When I looked back

---

[1] Saint-Foix, vol. iii. p. 18, suggests that this clavier sonata is K. 311 [284c], begun in
Munich and finished in Mannheim.

into the room, I again noticed it. In the end Mamma said to me: 'I bet you have let off one'. 'I don't think so, Mamma', I replied. 'Well, I am certain that you have', she insisted. Well, I thought 'Let's see', put my finger to my arse and then to my nose and—Ecce, provatum est. Mamma was right after all. Well, farewell. I kiss you 1000 times and remain, as always, your little old piggy wiggy

WOLFGANG AMADÉ ROSY POSY

A thousand compliments from us two travellers to my aunt and uncle. My greetings bleatings to all my good friends sends. Addio, booby looby.

♡ 333 to the grave, if my life I save.
Miehnnam, Rebotco eht ʰᵗ5, 7771.

(237) *Leopold Mozart to his Wife and Son*

[*Extract*]   [*Autograph in the Mozarteum, Salzburg*]

SALZBURG, 6 *November* 1777

MY DEAR WIFE AND MY DEAR SON!

Thank God that you have arrived safely in Mannheim! I do not know, it is true, and I very much doubt whether Wolfgang will find there all those things which he has imagined and the great advantages which several people may perhaps have described to him. That long journey from Augsburg to Mannheim will have made heavy inroads on your purse and Mannheim will hardly fill it again. Basta! You are there, however. Herr Beecke will indeed be glad that neither Prince Taxis nor the Abbot at Kaysersheim heard you play. Thus he is still cock of the walk in his country and the clavier-god of his admirers. Herr Vogler is the person who, as far as I know, has published a treatise on musical composition.[1] He is well versed in counterpoint and in algebra and he has ★ under his control the school of music or academy for young people. If, as is usually the case with courts of that kind, you are likely to be kept waiting, arrange for some other lodgings. Perhaps Wolfgang will be able to obtain from the Elector a commission to write a German opera. *I am indeed anxious*, for Mannheim is an expensive place. You know how we are placed at the moment. I hope that Herr Danner, to whom I send most polite greetings, will assist and guide you and I trust that Wolfgang will endeavour by ingratiating politeness to make friends of everybody. Deputy-Kapellmeister Vogler must be a very clever man, for the Elector thinks very highly of him. I am anxious to hear whether you gain the favour of Herr Raaff, to whom I send my humble greetings. He has always been praised to me as a very honest Christian. I wrote to Mysli-

[1] *Tonwissenschaft und Tonsetzkunst*, Mannheim, 1776.

wecek and asked him to write to Raaff about you. Now I hope that you
are both well and that Mamma's cold is better. Thank God, we are both
in good health and Pimperl is too, for she has never been so fresh as she is
now. Keep well. We both kiss you a million times and I am your old.

MOZART ★
★

(238) *Maria Anna Mozart to her Husband*

[*Autograph in the Mozarteum, Salzburg*]

MY DEAREST   MANNHEIM, 8 *November* 1777
      We have received safely your last letter of October 29th and all the
others; but it is absolutely impossible to answer all your questions as
accurately as we should like to, for we can only steal the time and we
generally write at night. We never get to bed before one o'clock, we get
up late the following morning and we are just ready in time for lunch.
After lunch we go to Herr Director Cannabich and at nine o'clock we
come home to supper. The gala days are now over. On the first there was
a service at eleven o'clock, during which cannons and rockets were fired
off. Afterwards Wolfgang had to go to the Electress to whom the Intendant, Count Savioli, had introduced him. She remembered that he had
been here fourteen years ago, but she did not recognize him. After that
there was a splendid banquet and during the evening a magnificent
reception. On the second day the grand German opera, entitled 'Günther
von Schwarzburg', was performed.[1] It is very beautiful and the music is
incomparably fine. There was also a marvellously beautiful ballet.[2] On
the third day there was a grand concert at which Wolfgang played a
concerto; then, before the final symphony, he improvised and gave them
a sonata. He won extraordinary applause from the Elector and Electress
and from all who heard him. On the fourth day there was a gala play,
which we went to see with Monsieur and Madame Cannabich. We both
lunched with Herr Cannabich on the day of the concert, and my son is
lunching alone with him today, as immediately after their meal he is
going with him to the ⟨Elector's children⟩. He was there yesterday and
the ⟨Elector⟩ was present the whole time. There are four children and two
of them play the clavier.[3] ⟨The Elector is immensely attached to them,⟩
and commanded the Intendant to arrange that Wolfgang should be taken
to them. He is to play once more quite alone, for the Electress has
promised this, so we must wait until she sends a command. Meanwhile,
my dear husband, I wish you 1000 happinesses for your coming name-
day, and I hope that you may enjoy everything beneficial to your soul

---

[1] The text was by Professor Anton Klein and the music by Ignaz Holzbauer.
[2] The ballet was designed by Lauchéry and set to music by Cannabich.
[3] They were the four children, one son and three daughters, of Countess Haydeck, née
Seuffert, who had been an actress. The son later became Prince von Bretzenheim.

and body, and constant good health. Above all I wish I were with you to congratulate you in person. But, as this is not possible now, we shall drink your health in a good Rhine wine (which we only wish from our hearts that you had) and we shall always think of in the most pleasant hope of meeting again, if it be God's will, and then remaining together. I send my greetings to Nannerl. Please ask her whether her cousin has already sent her the silks, for she promised me to forward them to her at once. Baron Schafmann[1] and Herr Döhl called on us yesterday morning and left today for Wetzlar.

(238a) *Mozart to his Father*

[Autograph in the Mozarteum, Salzburg]

I wrote out at Cannabich's this morning the Rondo to the sonata for his daughter, with the result that they refused to let me go. The Elector, the Electress and the whole Court are very much pleased with me. At the concert, on both occasions when I played, the Elector and the Electress came up quite close to the clavier. After the concert Cannabich arranged for me to speak to them. I kissed the Elector's hand. He remarked: 'I think it is about fifteen years since you were here last'. 'Yes, Your Highness, fifteen years since I had the honour of——' 'You play admirably.' When I kissed the Princess's hand she said to me: 'Monsieur, je vous assure, on ne peut pas jouer mieux'. I went yesterday with Cannabich on the visit Mamma has already referred to and there I talked to the Elector as to an old friend. He is a most gracious and courteous gentleman. He said to me: 'I hear that you have written an opera at Munich'. 'Yes, your Highness,' I replied, 'I commend myself to Your Highness's good graces. My dearest wish is to write an opera here. I beg you not to forget me utterly. Thanks and praise be to God, I know German too',[2] and I smiled. 'That can easily be managed', he answered. ⟨He has a son and three daughters. The eldest girl and the young Count⟩ play the clavier. The Elector put some questions to me in confidence about his ⟨children⟩, and I expressed myself quite frankly, but without disparaging their ⟨teacher⟩. Cannabich too was of my opinion. On leaving, the Elector thanked me very graciously. After lunch today at about two o'clock I went with Cannabich to Wendling, the flautist.[3] There they were all extremely polite to me. The daughter,[4] ⟨who was at one time the Elector's mistress⟩, plays the clavier very charmingly. I then played myself. I was in such excellent spirits

---

[1] Balthasar von Schafmann, Baron von Hammerles and Kanösowitz, Chief Magistrate of the Abtenau district.
[2] Mozart's Munich opera *La finta giardiniera* was on an Italian text.
[3] The Mozarts had heard Wendling play in 1763 when they visited Schwetzingen, the summer residence of the Elector. See p. 25, n. 4.
[4] Augusta Wendling, who was then twenty-five.

today—words fail me to describe my feelings. I improvised and then I played three duets with violin accompaniment which I had never seen and the composer of which I had never even heard of. They were all so delighted that I had to kiss the ladies. In the daughter's case this was no hardship, for she is not at all bad-looking. Afterwards we went back ⟨to the Elector's natural children⟩. There I played again with my whole heart. I played three times. The Elector himself kept on asking me for more. He sat down each time beside me and did not move a inch. I also asked a certain Professor to give me a theme for a fugue which I proceeded to develop. Now for my congratulations:—

DEAREST PAPA!

I cannot write in verse, for I am no poet. I cannot arrange the parts of speech with such art as to produce effects of light and shade, for I am no painter. Even by signs and gestures I cannot express my thoughts and feelings, for I am no dancer. But I can do so by means of sounds, for I am a musician. So tomorrow at Cannabich's I shall play on the clavier a whole congratulatory composition in honour of your name-day and of your birthday. All I can do today is to wish you, mon très cher Père, from the bottom of my heart what I wish you every day, both morning and evening; health, long life and good spirits. I hope too that you have now less cause for annoyance than when I was in Salzburg. For I must admit that I was the sole cause of it. They treated me badly and I did not deserve it. You naturally sympathised with me—but too feelingly. Believe me, that was the chief and most important reason for my leaving Salzburg in such a hurry. I hope too that my wishes have been fulfilled. I must now conclude with a musical congratulation. I wish you as many years of life as years will be needed until nothing new can be produced in music. Now farewell. I beg you most humbly to go on loving me just a little and in the meantime to put up with these poor congratulations until I get new drawers made in my small and narrow brain-box, into which I can put that wisdom which I intend yet to acquire. I kiss Papa's hands 1000 times and remain until death, mon trés cher Pére,

your most obedient son
WOLFGANG AMADÉ MOZART

Mannheim, 8 November 1777.

(239) *Leopold Mozart to his Son*

[Extract]   [*Autograph in the Mozarteum, Salzburg*]

MON TRÉS CHER FILS!   SALZBURG, 10 *November* 1777

In the greatest hurry I write to say that I received your letter of November 4th on my way to the service at the Cajetans, as today is the Feast of

St. Andrew Avellino. I lunched there; and then I had to run to Vespers in the Cathedral on account of St. Martin,[1] and now I have an hour left in which to write, for the post goes at five o'clock.

★

I should like you to win the Elector's favour and to be able to show what you can do *on the organ and in composition.* Indeed they need a good organist in Mannheim. I hope that you will send *your sister the sonata, which you have composed for Mlle Cannabich, copied out on small paper.* Did I not tell you recently that the Italians are not in favour at Mannheim? Why, I knew it! I hear that Vogler is a musical theorist, so he may well be ⟨a *fool* or a comedian⟩. I have not seen any of his compositions. Herr Holzbauer was always an excellent, honest fellow. Please give my compliments to him and to Cannabich. You tell me nothing whatever about the grand opera and the theatre. Perhaps you will do so in your next letter. Are there no actors in Mannheim? Are German operas being performed? If you get an opportunity of really showing what you can do, then you have hopes of remaining there; for just to play a concerto and nothing else is something which anyone can do who has practised it. I am sorry that we are now so far from one another. By the time I write to you about any matter, it is all over as far as you are concerned. Have you not tried to leave your inn and get private rooms and cheaper board? Herr

★

Cannabich will surely advise and help you. I shall certainly send your cousin something and I shall write to her today about it in the letter to her which I began yesterday. We two and Bimperl and Theresa are well, as

★

I hope and trust that you both always are. We kiss you both a million times and I am your old husband and son

MOZART

(240) *Leopold Mozart to his Son*

[*Extract*]   [*Autograph in the Mozarteum, Salzburg*]

MON TRÈS CHER FILS!   SALZBURG, 13 *November* 1777

I think that I have told you that Mysliwecek wrote a letter to me *in forma ostensiva*[2] (as I had asked him to, in order that I might show it to the person in question), in which he urged me to find out whether the music he sent both some years ago and again recently had been delivered to the Archbishop. As a result, he was sent a draft for twenty-five ducats. He now informs me that he received it on November 8th and that on his doctor's advice he will remain a while longer in Munich for the benefit of his health, which is improving, and so that he may be able to travel in

---

[1] 11 November.   [2] See p. 345, n. 2.

greater safety. He adds that he is going to present to the Elector a cantata (*Enea negl'Elisi*) which, he feels sure, will be performed together with Monza's opera,[1] as the Elector has ordered the score to be copied immediately. He tells me, further, that, as I requested, he has written to Signor Raaff, that he has received his own scritture for the operas for May 30th and November 4th and that he is now waiting for the scrittura for you, which, however, cannot arrive for another month. As soon as he receives it, he will forward it to me at Salzburg. To tell the truth I am really not counting on this contract, for you know what excuses these Italians make and what tangles of wires there are at Naples. I heard today that the Archbishop commissioned Brunetti yesterday to write to Mysliwecek and order some concertoni, which may or may not be included in the twenty-five ducats. The graduale in counterpoint which I liked so much was by the famous Maestro Lotti, who died a long time ago.[2] As for your resignation from the Archbishop's service, Herr ★ Duschek has been strongly suspected of having influenced both yourself and the rest of us, and this suspicion has now been extended to Counts Hardik and Lützow. Duschek told me this himself. Certainly, if you had gone to Prague, the Archbishop would have been convinced that his suspicions were justified! But, as it is, he is simply being made a fool of. On St. Martin's Day I lunched in the priests' house and the healths of both of you were drunk. Nannerl invited herself that day to old Hagenauer's and he has told her that whenever I lunch out, she must take her meal with them.

My dear Wolfgang, in your last letter of November 4th, signed on St. Charles's day, there is so much confusion that it is impossible for me to know when this and that took place. You keep on saying, '*Today I played my six sonatas at Cannabich's. Herr Holzbauer took me today to Count Savioli. But today, being Sunday, I heard the mass by Holzbauer. Mamma cannot write—we got home very late from the rehearsal of the opera. Tomorrow after High Mass I have to go to the Electress'*—and all this, *according to your signature, happened, it seems, on November 4th, St. Charles's day.* Surely the opera, and not the rehearsal took place on that day? So my common sense tells me that you did not write the letter on November 4th, but only closed it on that day. Why can you not do as I do? When I break off writing and go on the next day, I set down whether it is Sunday or Monday. It is then possible to tell in what order things have happened; and it may sometimes be important to have this information. Meanwhile

---

[1] *Attilio Regolo*, by Carlo Monza (*c.* 1735–1801), who in 1787 became maestro di cappella in Milan Cathedral, and was already an operatic composer of note. According to the *Reiseaufzeichnungen*, p. 51, the Mozarts had met him Milan in 1770. See *MBA*, No. 166.

[2] Antonio Lotti (1667–1740), an eminent Venetian composer, who in 1704 became organist at St. Mark's, Venice. He wrote a number of operas, one of which, *Giustino*, was produced in Venice when he was 16. After 1719 he only composed church music.

★ I had already written to Herr Pfeil and Herr Otto in Frankfurt to find out about winter concerts and whether you could not obtain a well-paid appointment there, such as Meisner and Reiner used to have. I received an answer at once, written on November 4th, which arrived at the same time as your letter, and in which, in the most sincere and friendly manner and to his great regret, Herr Pfeil informed me on behalf of old Otto that

★ nothing could be done. He added that of course you could give a private concert on your own, but that the music-lovers were so apathetic and so few in number that you would run the risk of not even making your expenses. Thus, much as he would like to have you, he would not advise you in your own interest to make a special journey to Frankfurt. But if your tour were to bring you there, your visit would give him infinite pleasure, and he said that you would find at his house a collection of instruments which would mean for you an embarrassment of choice. He mentioned that in addition to his large Friederici harpsichord with two manuals like our own, he had a perfectly new and very large forte-piano in mahogany, which he described at length and with the greatest enthusiasm. Further, he has a clavichord also in mahogany, which he would not sell for 200 gulden, as he says that this instrument simply has not got its equal; that the descant sounds like a violin being played softly, and the bass notes like trombones. In addition, he has a number of fortepianos all made by Friederici, as he deals in these. He regrets that his large collection of clavier music contains no composition of yours. As far as I can see, most of it comes from Lang in Coblenz, to whom he offers to give you letters of introduction. He closes with the remark: 'How are your dearest wife and your daughter? Tell your son that if he is travelling through Frankfurt, he must not forget me, for I shall show him how much I loved him as a child and how much I love him still.' So in this direction

★ little or nothing can be done. I am really at a loss as to how to advise you, for, if there is no prospect of your remaining in Mannheim, you will surely go on to Mainz, and from there it is only a short trip to Frankfurt. Returning, you could then go on to Coblenz and call on the Elector of Trier, who is Prince Clement of Saxony. You will remember that seated at table between him and the Elector of Bavaria you once wrote a composition in pencil when we were passing through Munich on our way back from England.[1] But whither could you go after that? To the Elector of Cologne, at Bonn, where Lucchesi is still Kapellmeister? That visit would not even pay the expenses of your journey and, besides, it would take you too far to the right of the direct route to Holland through the Netherlands—and so to Paris? What a fearful distance! Where on earth would you raise the money for such a journey? Indeed I did not think that you would decide on going to Mannheim immediately, as you never

---

[1] See p. 68.

even mentioned it to me, which you ought to have done from Augsburg, the more so as I wrote to you on purpose, saying that I would send you my considered opinion as to what steps you should take there. I know well that I wrote to you very fully, but I was proposing to send you a written statement, a document which you could have handed to the Elector.

You say that after the service you were summoned to the Electress. There you had an opportunity of ingratiating yourself and, if circumstances permitted, of making a beginning with the plan you have in mind. But why should I trouble to write at length! Who knows whether this letter will reach you in Mannheim? And even if you are still there, I do not know how things are in that town. Mannheim has poor organists. If there is no hope of your getting an appointment there, the Elector might keep you for a year, or at least for this winter, the more so as *you could give as a good excuse to the Electress your mother's age and the strain of a winter journey, which would be very uncomfortable indeed for an elderly woman.* If you have to stay there, you will not lack opportunities of showing what you can do in every branch of music and of making yourself popular. Then, if you must leave in the spring or summer, you have only to go to Spa, which is swarming with English people. In a word, if you do not ask for a *permanent* appointment, an Elector who so loves and values talents, will give you an opportunity for a short time at least of displaying your genius at his Court, that famous Court, whose rays, like those of the sun, illumine the whole of Germany, nay even the whole of Europe. Herr Cannabich would gain a great deal if you were to help his daughter *without getting in the way of her teacher.* But everything will depend on your audience with the Elector and the Electress and on the skill with which you address them. Women sympathize with one another, and Her Highness knows what old age means. Count Savioli must not be pushed aside, but by treating him respectfully you should make a friend of him, which is your duty and at the same time good diplomacy. All this is neither intrigue nor deception, but is the way which will enable you to gain sufficient time to display your gifts in all directions. For your youth and your appearance prevent people from realizing the wealth of the Divine grace which has been bestowed on you in your talents. You have left behind you many places, where people never got to know half of what you can do. I have nothing more to say, as I have received no letter today, and so I do not know how you are getting on. Perhaps, as has often happened already, I shall receive a letter tomorrow by the extra post. But in that case I cannot reply until Monday. I repeat, however, that I do not doubt but that the Elector will keep you for the winter and perhaps even longer, if Mamma represents to the Electress the discomfort of a journey. ⟨If you do spend a winter there, I feel sure that you will be appointed permanently and with a good salary.⟩ I hope that you are both well, as, thank God, we are. Nannerl and

I kiss you cordially a million times. I shall write every post-day, as I have always done, and I am your old husband and father

MOZART

I repeat that *on your departure you should leave at the post office a note stating to what address your letters should be forwarded.* Herr Bullinger and all Salzburg send their greetings. I am exceedingly anxious to hear whether this letter reaches you in Mannheim. We are now separated by a very great distance, for a letter takes six days, and if you do not write every post-day, we have no idea where you are or what you are doing. Do but write '*we are well*', nothing more—and surely my dear wife, who will sometimes be alone at home, can do that.

(241) *Mozart to his Father*

[*Autograph in the Mozarteum, Salzburg*]

[MANNHEIM, 13 *November* 1777]

MON TRÉS CHER PÉRE!

We have received your last two letters dated October 29th and November 6th. I must now answer all your questions. I did not get the letter in which you asked me to find out ⟨about Beecke's parentage⟩, until I had reached Mannheim, consequently too late for me to do so. It would never have occurred to me to do anything of the sort, as it really does not concern me in the least. Well, would Papa like to know how Beecke received me? Why, very favourably and most politely. He asked me where I was going. I said that, as far as I knew, it was to Paris. He then gave me a good deal of advice, remarking that he had just been there himself. 'You will make heaps of money by giving lessons,' he added, 'for in Paris they are very fond of the clavier.' He at once arranged for me to be taken to the officers' mess and took steps to secure me an audience with the Prince.[1] He expressed great regret that he himself happened to have a sore throat (which was perfectly true) and that he could not therefore take me out himself, and entertain me. He was sorry too that he could not arrange some music in my honour, but on that very day most of the performers had taken a holiday and gone out walking to some place or other. At his request I had to try his clavichord, which is a very good one. He frequently exclaimed, 'Bravo!' I improvised and played my sonatas in B♭ and D.[2] In short, he was very polite and I was the same, but perfectly serious. We fell to talking of various things, amongst others of Vienna, and how the Emperor was no great lover of music. 'That is true,' he said; 'he knows

---

[1] Prince Kraft Ernst von Öttingen-Wallerstein. Mozart is describing their visit to Hohenalt-heim, of which his mother had already written a short account. See p. 349.

[2] Probably K. 281 [189f], 284 [205b].

something about counterpoint, but that is all. I can still remember (here he rubbed his forehead) that when I had to play to him, I had not the least idea what to play. So I started to play fugues and such-like foolery, and all the time I played I was laughing up my sleeve.' When I heard this, I was scarcely able to contain myself and felt that I should love to say to him: 'Sir, I well believe that you laughed, but surely not as heartily as I should have done, had I been listening to you'. He then went on to say (something which is quite true) that music is performed in the Imperial apartments which would drive a dog away. I remarked that whenever I heard that kind of music and could not get away from it, it always gave me a headache. 'Oh, it does not affect me at all', he retorted. 'Bad music never gets on my nerves; on the other hand, beautiful music does; and then I sometimes do get a headache.'. Once more I thought to myself: 'Yes, a shallow pate like yours no doubt begins to ache when it hears something which it cannot understand'.

Now for some news from Mannheim. Yesterday I had to go with Cannabich to Count Savioli, the Intendant, to fetch my present. It was just as I had expected. No money, but a fine gold watch. At the moment ten carolins would have suited me better than the watch, which including the chains and the mottoes has been valued at twenty. What one needs on a journey is money; and, let me tell you, I now have five watches. I am therefore seriously thinking of having an additional watch pocket on each leg of my trousers so that when I visit some great lord, I shall wear both watches (which, moreover, is now the 'mode') so that it will not occur to him to present me with another one. I see from Papa's letter that he has not seen Vogler's book.[1] I have just read it, as I borrowed it from Cannabich. Let me give you a short history of Vogler. He came here, absolutely down and out, performed on the clavier and composed a ballet.[2] People took pity on him and the Elector sent him to Italy.[3] When the Elector happened to be in Bologna,[4] he asked Padre Vallotti about him and received this reply: 'O altezza, questo è un gran uomo!'[5] He also asked Padre Martini, who informed him: 'Altezza, è buono; ma a poco a poco, quando sarà un poco più vecchio, più sodo, si farà, si farà, ma bisogna che si cangi molto'.[6] When Vogler returned to Mannheim, he took orders and was immediately made Court chaplain.[7] He produced a Miserere which, everyone tells me, simply cannot be listened to, for it sounds all wrong. Hearing that his composition was not receiving much praise, Vogler went to the Elector and complained that the orchestra were

[1] See p. 360, n. 1.   [2] Probably his *Jagdballett*, 1772.   [3] Early in 1773.
[4] The Elector Karl Theodor went to Italy in 1774. The conversation must have taken place in Padua, where Vallotti had been maestro di cappella since 1730.
[5] Oh, Your Highness, he is a great man!
[6] Your Highness, he is good; and gradually, as he becomes older and surer of himself, he will improve. But he will have to change considerably.
[7] Vogler had actually held this post before leaving for Italy. See p. 350, n. 3.

369

playing it badly on purpose. In a word, he was so clever at pulling strings (he had had more than one naughty little affair with women, who were useful to him) that he was appointed Deputy-Kapellmeister. But he is a fool, who imagines that he is the very pitch of perfection. The whole orchestra, from A to Z, detest him. He has caused Holzbauer a great deal of annoyance. His book is more useful for teaching arithmetic than for teaching composition. He says he can turn out a composer in three weeks and a singer in six months, but so far no one has seen him do it. He disparages the great masters. Why, he even belittled Bach[1] to me. Bach has written two operas here, the first of which was more popular than the second, 'Lucio Silla'. Now, as I too had composed a 'Lucio Silla' in Milan, I wanted to see Bach's opera and I had heard from Holzbauer that Vogler possessed a copy. So I asked him for it. 'Delighted,' he said. 'I shall send it to you tomorrow. But you will not make head or tail of it.' When he saw me a few days later, he asked me with an obvious sneer: 'Well, do you find it beautiful? Have you learnt anything from it?—It has one fine aria. Let me see, what are the words?' He turned to somebody who happened to be standing beside him. 'What sort of aria?' asked his companion. 'Why, of course, that hideous aria by Bach, that filthy stuff— yes, yes, *Pupille amate*,[2] which he certainly wrote in his cups.' I thought I should have to seize his front hair and pull it hard, but I pretended not to hear him, said nothing and walked off. He has had his day with the Elector. My sonata for Mlle Rosa Cannabich is now finished. Last Sunday I tried the organ in the chapel for fun. I came in during the Kyrie and played the end of it, and, when the priest had finished intoning the Gloria, I played a cadenza. As my performance was so different from what they are accustomed to here, they all looked round, especially Holzbauer. He said to me: 'If I had known this I should have put on another mass'. 'Yes,' I replied, 'so that you could have caught me out!' The elder Toeschi[3] and Wendling were standing beside me all the time. The people were splitting with laughter. Now and then the music was marked pizzicato and each time I just touched the keys very lightly. I was in my very best spirits. Instead of a Benedictus the organist has to play here the whole time. So I took the theme of the Sanctus and developed it as a fugue. Whereupon they all stood gaping. Finally, after the *Ita missa est*, I played a fugue. The pedal there is different from ours, which put me out a bit at first; but I soon got the hang of it. Now I must close. Papa should continue to write to us at Mannheim. It is safer. I shall see that we get his letters all right. I

---

[1] Johann Christian Bach, whose operas *Temistocle* and *Lucio Silla* had been performed at Mannheim in 1772 and 1774.

[2] The aria 'Pupille amate' in *Lucio Silla*.

[3] Carl Joseph Toeschi (1731–1788), a pupil of the great Johann Stamitz, became a violinist in the Mannheim orchestra in 1752, and in 1759 Konzertmeister in Mannheim. He was a prolific composer in all branches of orchestral and chamber music.

know what Mysliwecek's sonatas are like, for I played them at Munich.
They are quite easy and pleasing to the ear. I should advise my sister, to
whom I send my most humble greetings, to play them with plenty of
expression, taste and fire, and to learn them by heart. For they are sonatas
which are bound to please everyone, which are easy to memorize and very
effective when played with the proper precision. I kiss Papa's hands and
remain his obedient son

WOLFGANG AMADÈ MOZART

Mannheim, 13 November 1777.

(241a) *Maria Anna Mozart to her Husband*

[Autograph in the Library of the University of Prague]

[MANNHEIM, 13 *November* 1777[1]]

Today, the 13th, we received your letter of November 1st, which
therefore arrived a post-day later than your last letter. Thank God, we
are well. Wolfgang has received from the Elector a watch of the finest
workmanship, small but beautifully designed. The day before yesterday,
being the feast of St. Martin, we lunched with old Herr Danner and
yesterday with young Herr Danner. We and especially my son have also
lunched very often with Herr Cannabich. I too am with them every day
and they are extremely courteous to us. Herr Danner sends you his
greetings and longs to see you. Wolfgang wants to know whether the
Bishop of Chiemsee has arrived in Munich, for he would like to write to
him. *I must close, for Wolfgang must go out and he has to write the address and
take the letter to the post.* I kiss you and Nannerl many 1000 times and I send
greetings to the whole of Salzburg. I remain your faithful wife

MARIA ANNA MOZART

(242) *Mozart to his Cousin, Maria Anna Thekla Mozart, Augsburg*

[Autograph in the Heinemann Collection, Pierpont Morgan Library, New York City]

[MANNHEIM, 13 *November* 1777]

Now do send her a sensible letter for once. You can make jokes in it all
the same. But tell her that you have received all your letters which she
forwarded, so that she may no longer worry and fret.[2]

---

[1] A postscript to Mozart's letter on the cover.
[2] The autograph of this letter begins with this apparently disconnected sentence. Mozart
evidently jotted down what his mother happened to say to him.

Ma trés chére Niéce! Cousine! fille! Mére, Sœur, et Épouse!

Bless my soul, a thousand curses, Croatians, damnations, devils, witches, sorcerers, hell's battalions to all eternity, by all the elements, air, water, earth and fire, Europe, Asia, Africa and America, Jesuits, Augustinians, Benedictines, Capuchins, Minorites, Franciscans, Dominicans, Carthusians and Brothers of the Holy Cross, Canons regular and irregular, all slackers, knaves, cowards, sluggards and toadies higgledy-piggledy, asses, buffaloes, oxen, fools, nit-wits and dunces! What sort of behaviour is that, my dears —four smart soldiers and three bandoliers? . . . Such a parcel to get, but no portrait[1] as yet! I was all eagerness—in fact, I was quite sure—for you yourself had written the other day that I was to have it soon, very, very soon. Perhaps you doubt that I shall keep my word? Surely you do not doubt me? Well, anyhow, I implore you to send me yours—the sooner, the better. And I trust that you will have it done, as I urged you, in French costume.

How do I like Mohmheim?[2] As well as I could like any place without my little cousin. Forgive my wretched writing, but the pen is already worn to a shred, and I've been shitting, so 'tis said, nigh twenty-two years through the same old hole, which is not yet frayed one whit, though I've used it daily to shit, and each time the muck with my teeth I've bit.

On the other hand, I hope that, however that may be, you have received all my letters, that is, one from Hohenaltheim[3] and two from Mannheim; and this one, however that may be, is my third letter from Mannheim, but the fourth in all, however that may be. Now I must close, however that may be, for I am not yet dressed and we are lunching this very moment, so that after that we may shit again, however that may be. Do go on loving me, as I love you, then we shall never cease loving one another, though the lion hovers round the walls, though doubt's hard victory has not been weighed and the tyrant's frenzy has crept to decay; yet Codrus, the wise philosopher, often eats soot instead of porridge, and the Romans, the props of my arse, have always been and ever will be— half-castes. Adieu. J'espère que vous aures déjà pris quelque lection dans la langue française, et je ne doute point que—céoutes—que vous saures bientôt mieux le français, que moi; car il y a certainement deux ans que je n'ai pas écrit un môt dans cette langue. Adieu cependant. Je vous baise vos mains, votre visage, vos genoux, et votre—enfin, tout ce que vous me permettes de baiser. Je suis de tout mon cœur

votre tres affectionné Neveu et Cousin

WOLFG: AMADÉ MOZART

Mannheim, le 13 Nomv: 1777.

[1] The 'Bäsle' sent Mozart her portrait in February 1778. It is a pencil drawing, which is now in the Mozart Museum, Salzburg. See illustration no. 7.
[2] i.e. Mannheim.   [3] This letter is lost.

(243) *Maria Anna Mozart to her Husband*

[*Autograph in the Mozarteum, Salzburg*]

MOHMHEIM, 14 *November* 1777
DOMMSCHLEIM [1]

MY DEAR HUSBAND,

I sent you off a letter only yesterday and I am begining another one again today. You asked in yours whether Wolfgang has gained the favour of Herr Raaff. Well, all I can tell you is that Raaff is a good, honest fellow, but all the same he can do nothing. He's been singing in the opera here. You can see that he must have been a good singer in his time; but he is packing up like Herr Meisner, to whom by the way I much prefer to listen. But Raaff is the most honest fellow in the world. I spoke to him at the concert and he congratulated me on my son's ability and seemed to be absolutely amazed at him; likewise Herr Kapellmeister Holzbauer, who has a great opinion of my son.

(243a) *Mozart to his Father*

[*Autograph in the Mozarteum, Salzburg*]

[MANNHEIM, 14 *November* 1777]

I, Johannes Chrysostomus Amadeus Wolfgangus Sigismundus Mozart, hereby plead guilty and confess that yesterday and the day before (not to mention on several other occasions) I did not get home until midnight; and that from ten o'clock until the said hour at Cannabich's house and in the presence and company of the said Cannabich, his wife and daughter, the Treasurer,[2] Ramm and Lang I did frequently, without any difficulty, but quite easily, perpetrate—rhymes, the same being, moreover, sheer garbage, that is, on such subjects as muck, shitting and arse-licking—and that too in thoughts, words—but not in deeds. I should not have behaved so godlessly, however, if our ringleader, known under the name of Lisel (Elisabetha Cannabich),[3] had not egged me on and incited me; at the same time I must admit that I thoroughly enjoyed it. I confess all these sins and transgressions of mine from the bottom of my heart and in the hope of having to confess them very often, I firmly resolve to go on with the sinful life which I have begun. Wherefore I beg for the holy dispensation, if it can be easily obtained; if not, it's all one to me, for the game will go on all the same. *Lusus enim suum habet ambitum,*[4] as the late Meisner, the singer, says (chap. 9, p. 24); so does Saint Ascenditor too, patron of burnt soup coffee, musty lemonade, almondless milk of almonds and, more particularly, of strawberry ice full of bits of ice, as he himself is a great connoisseur and artist in ices. As soon as I can, I shall have the

---

[1] This word is in Mozart's hand.
[2] Gres, who appears to have held an official appointment at the Mannheim court.
[3] Cannabich's second daughter.   [4] For the game has its own bounds.

sonata which I have written for Mlle Cannabich copied out on small paper and shall send it to my sister. I began to teach it to Mlle Rosa three days ago. We finished the opening Allegro today. The Andante will give us most trouble, for it is full of expression and must be played accurately and with the exact shades of forte and piano, precisely as they are marked. She is very smart and learns very easily. Her right hand is very good, but her left, unfortunately, is completely ruined. I can honestly say that I often feel quite sorry for her when I see her struggling, as she so often does, until she really gets quite out of breath, not from lack of skill but simply because she cannot help it. For she has got into the habit of doing what she does, because no one has ever shown her any other way. I have told her mother and I have told her too that if I were her regular teacher, I would lock up all her music, cover the keys with a handkerchief and make her practise, first with the right hand and then with the left, nothing but passages, trills, mordants and so forth, very slowly at first, until each hand should be thoroughly trained. I would then undertake to turn her into a first-rate clavierist. For it's a great pity. She has so much talent, reads quite passably, possesses so much natural facility and plays with plenty of feeling. They both said that I was right. Now for the opera, but quite briefly. Holzbauer's music is very beautiful. The poetry doesn't deserve such music. What surprises me most of all is that a man as old as Holzbauer should still posses so much spirit; for you can't imagine what fire there is in that music.[1] The prima donna was Mme Elizabeth Wendling, not the flautist's wife, but the fiddler's.[2] She is always indisposed and, what is more, the opera was not written for her, but for a certain Danzi, who is at present in England;[3] consequently it is not suited to her voice but is too high for her. On one occasion Raaff sang four arias, about 450 bars in all, in such a fashion as to call forth the remark that his voice was the strongest reason why he sang so badly. Anyone who hears him begin an aria without at once reminding himself that it is Raaff, the once famous tenor, who is singing, is bound to burst out laughing. It's a fact. I thought to myself: 'If I didn't know that this was Raaff, I should double up with laughing'. As it is, I just pull out my handkerchief and hide a smile. Moreover, he has never been, so people here tell me, anything of an actor; you'd only have had to hear him, without even looking at him; nor has he by any means a good presence. In the opera he had to die, and while dying sing a very very very long aria in slow time; well, he died with a grin on his face, and towards the end of the aria his voice gave out so

---

[1] Holzbauer was sixty-six when he composed his opera *Günther von Schwarzburg*, which was performed on 5 January 1777, and was still running.
[2] Elizabeth Augusta Wendling, *née* Sarselli (1746–1786), wife of Franz Anton Wendling, brother of Johann Baptist Wendling and a violinist in the Mannheim orchestra.
[3] Franziska Danzi (1759–1791), daughter of the Mannheim cellist, Innocenz Danzi, became a famous prima donna. In 1778 she married the Mannheim oboist, Ludwig August Le Brun.

badly that one really couldn't stand it any longer. I was sitting in the orchestra beside Wendling the flautist. He had objected beforehand that it was unnatural for a man to keep on singing until he died, as it was too long to wait. Whereupon I remarked: 'Have a little patience. He'll soon be gone, for I hear it.' 'So do I', he said and laughed. The second female singer is a certain Mlle Strasser (but not one of the Strasser sisters) who sings very well and is an excellent actress.[1] There is a permanent German National Theatre here as in Munich. German Singspiele are performed occasionally, but the singers in them are wretched. I lunched yesterday with Baron and Baroness von Hagen. The Baron is Master of the Hunt. Three days ago I went to see Herr Schmalz, the merchant, to whom I had a letter of introduction from Herr Herzog, or rather from Nocker and Schiedl. I expected to find a very amiable and honest man. I handed him the letter. He read it through, made me a slight bow and— said nothing. At length (after many apologies for not having paid my respects to him long ago) I mentioned the fact that I had played before the Elector. 'Really?'—*altum silentium!*[2] I said nothing. He said nothing. At last I said: 'I shall not trouble you any longer. I have the honour——' At this point he interrupted me: 'If I can be of any service to you, please——' 'Before I leave I shall take the liberty of asking you——' 'For money?' 'Yes, if you will be so kind as to——' 'Oh! that I cannot do. There is nothing in the letter about money. I cannot give you any money. But if there's anything else——?' 'But there is *nothing else* you can do for me, nothing whatever that I know of. I have the honour to take my leave of you.' Yesterday I wrote the whole story to Herr Herzog in Augsburg. We must now wait for an answer. Consequently Papa can go on writing to Mannheim. Please remember me to all my good friends. I kiss Papa's hands 100,000 times and embrace my sister with all my heart, and I am your young brother and father,

WOLFGANG GOTTLIEB MOZART

because Papa wrote in his last letter 'I am your old husband and son'.

On this day, the 16th, I finished this letter, this letter, otherwise Papa will not know when it was sent off. Have you finished it?—the letter? . . . Yes, Mamma, it's finished now, the letter.[3]

(244) *Leopold Mozart to his Wife and Son*

[*Extract*]   [*Autograph in the Mozarteum, Salzburg*]

SALZBURG, 17 *November* 1777

MY DEAR WIFE! AND MY DEAR SON!

I received only today, November 17th, your letter of the 8th. So it

---

[1] Barbara Strasser. She married later Johann Ignaz Ludwig Fischer, one of the most celebrated bass singers of his day and the original Osmin in Mozart's *Entführung aus dem Serail.*
[2] Profound silence.   [3] Mozart jots down the remarks he is exchanging with his mother.

must have been sent to the post too late or have been left lying there. I thank you both for your congratulations and wish you both good health and happiness and that we shall meet again joyfully—and possibly over a glass of Rhine wine! Anyone who reads your letters of congratulation and this reply of mine, would think that we are constantly handling full glasses, as we talk so glibly about Rhine wine. Meanwhile you will have received my letters of the 3rd, the 6th, the 10th and the 13th. In the last one I was a little bit peevish, as I had had no news from you. I sent you my views about Mannheim, but perhaps they will arrive too late. I admit that your letter of the 8th, to which I am now replying, raises my hopes, as ⟨you are going to have an opportunity of speaking to the Elector and also, if necessary, of playing to him.⟩ If you can only remain there for six months and ⟨show what you can do in all styles of music, you will certainly be appointed—especially if there are such wretched organists there⟩. Have you not played ⟨the organ⟩ as well? My dear spouse complains that the only time she can write is at night. I can believe it, as I know only too well how it is on journeys, especially when you want to write a letter at a moment's notice—anywhere if need be. But if every evening you write down, just as Wolfgang used to do at home, what has happened on that day, even a few words, then on the post-day you need only finish the letter and everything has been put in. Do not be annoyed with me, my dear ones. For tell me, what entertainment have Nannerl and I in Salzburg now, except—the post-days! As it is, I am never sure whether a letter will reach you in the same place. We are very far apart and I think I can and ought to hope that you will be able to stay in ⟨Mannheim⟩. Basta! God in His most holy providence will guide both you and ourselves along the

★ true path. Herr Wolfgang Mozart contributed a charming target to our shooting yesterday. An Augsburg maiden stood on the right and handed a parting bouquet to a young man in riding boots and about to leave; in the other hand she held an enormous linen cloth which trailed along on the ground and with which she was drying her weeping eyes. The young dandy was dragging a similar linen sheet with which he was doing the same, and in the other hand he held his hat containing the bull's eye, which could be spotted there more easily than on the bouquet. Above were the words:

    Adieu, my pretty cousin!
    Adieu, my gallant cousin!
I wish you good luck on your journey, good health and fine weather!
We have spent very nicely and gaily a fortnight together.
'Tis this that makes parting so sad for us twain.
These dear ones we welcomed must leave us again.
    Hateful Fate! Now I weep bitter tears, but in vain!

★   The weather was dreadful, so we stayed at home and played cards until five o'clock with Katherl Gilowsky and Cajetan Andretter, who send their greetings to you. The rest of the evening we two spent at the clavier as usual. We are alone every day and if we go on practising during the winter, Nannerl will be able to accompany everything, figured or unfigured, in the easiest or the most difficult keys, and, what is more, with the most unexpected changes of key. For in this respect your compositions afford her ample opportunity to perfect herself. Moreover we always choose the most difficult ones and especially your works in C major and F major with the minor movements,[1] which we often pick out to practise. ★

As for Hagenauer,[2] the architect, things are now moving forward a bit. He wants to get away, but the Prince keeps on trying to detain him by offering him all kinds of jobs and by flattering him. So nothing has been decided. When I hear these things, it always pleases me to think that you are far away from this worry. You are quite right. I did feel the greatest annoyance at the mean treatment you had to put up with. It was that which gnawed at my heart, which kept me awake at night, which was ever on my mind and finally consumed me. My dear son, if you are happy, then I am too and your mother, and your sister and all of us. And you must be so, I trust, if you rely, as I do, on God's grace and on your own sensible behaviour. Thank God, we are well. I trust that you are both in good health. If so, all is well. What will and must be will happen. It is enough if with your common sense you contribute your quota to your own happiness. I for my part shall never cease to care for the welfare of my children, teach them what I can and, as I have done hitherto, use all my efforts on their behalf until I die.

Your old faithful husband and father

MOZART

Francesco von Barisani,[3] who is sitting beside me, sends his greetings to you both. ⟨The Elector's natural children may be a fortunate circumstance for you.⟩

★

(244a) *Nannerl Mozart to her Mother and Brother*

[*Autograph in the Mozarteum, Salzburg*]

[SALZBURG, 17 *November* 1777[4]]

I kiss Mamma's hands and I embrace you. I am glad that you are both in good health. Thank God, we too are well. Pimperl, who is quite fit and jolly, curls herself up at the feet of both of you and so does Theresa. Barbara Eberlin, the Adlgassers, the Hagenauers, Katherl Gilowsky, the Andretters, Bawanzky and all Salzburg send their greetings to you both.

---

[1] Mozart's clavier sonatas K. 279 [189d] and K. 280 [189e], the slow movements of which are in minor keys.
[2] Johann Georg Hagenauer, who like his brother Johann Baptist Hagenauer was an architect.
[3] Son of Dr. von Barisani, the Archbishop's private physician. He too became a doctor.
[4] A postscript to her father's letter.

(245) *Mozart to his Father*

[*Autograph in the Mozarteum, Salzburg*]

MANNHEIM, 20 *November* 1777

MON TRÉS CHER PÉRE

I must be quite brief today, as I have no more paper in the house. Yesterday, Wednesday, the 19th, the gala began again. I went to the service, brand new music composed by Vogler. I had already been to the afternoon rehearsal the day before yesterday, but went off immediately after the Kyrie. I have never in my life heard such stuff. In many places the parts simply do not harmonize. He modulates in such a violent way as to make you think that he is resolved to drag you with him by the scruff of the neck; not that there is anything remarkable about it all to make it worth the trouble; no, it is all clumsy plunging. I will not say anything about the way in which the ideas are worked out. I will only say that it is impossible that a mass of Vogler's should please any composer who is worthy of the name. To put it briefly, if I hear an idea which is not at all bad—well—it will certainly not remain *not at all bad* for long, but will soon become—beautiful? God forbid!—bad and thoroughly bad; and that in two or three different ways. Either the idea has scarcely been introduced before another comes along and ruins it; or he does not round it off naturally enough to preserve its merit; or it is not in the right place; or, finally, it is ruined by the instrumentation. That's Vogler's music. Cannabich is now a much better composer than he was when we knew him in Paris.[1] But what Mamma and I noticed at once about the symphonies here is that they all begin in the same manner, always with an introduction in slow time and in unison. I must now tell Papa something about the Holy Cross Monastery in Augsburg, which I have kept on forgetting to mention.

I received a great many kindnesses there and the Abbot is the best man in the world, an excellent old dunce, who, however, is likely to pop off at any moment, as he is very short of breath. For instance, he had a stroke quite recently, in fact on the very day we left. He, the Dean and the Procurator made us swear that if ever we came to Augsburg again we would drive straight to the Monastery. The Procurator is a jolly fellow like Father Leopold at Seeon. My cousin had told me beforehand what he was like, and so at our first meeting we were on as good terms as if we had known one another for twenty years. I left with them there my mass in F, the first of the short masses in C and my contrapuntal Offertory in D minor.[2] My cousin is acting agent-in-chief for me. I have got back safely the Offertory, which I asked to be returned first. Now they have all plagued me, including the Abbot, to give them a litany *De Venerabili.*

---

[1] In 1766, when Mozart was ten years old. See p. 349, n. 1.

[2] K. 192 [186f], 220 [196b], 222 [205a].

I told them that I hadn't one with me; and as a matter of fact I was not quite sure whether I had. I looked for it, but couldn't find it. But they wouldn't leave me in peace, they thought I was just trying to put them off. So I said: 'Look here, I haven't got it with me, it's at Salzburg. Write to my Papa. It's for him to decide. If he sends it to you, well and good. If not, I can do nothing.' So I expect that a letter from the Dean to Papa will soon make its appearance. Do just as you like. If you want to send them one, send them my last one, in E♭.[1] For they can provide the full forces needed, since a great many performers turn up at that time. They even engage them, as it is their chief festival. Adieu. I kiss Papa's hands 100,000 times and embrace my sister with all my heart and remain your most obedient son

WOLFGANG AMADÉ MOZART

(245a) *Maria Anna Mozart to her Husband*

[*Autograph sold by J. A. Stargardt, Marburg,* 11 *June* 1980]

[MANNHEIM, 20 *November* 1777[2]]

Our greetings to all our acquaintances, especially to Herr Bullinger, Jungfer Sallerl, Jungfer Mitzerl, Katherl Gilowsky, Herr Gött. I send greetings too to Theresa. Thank God, we are well. Today the grand opera is being performed again. Yesterday, on the feast of St. Elizabeth Wolfgang and I lunched with Herr and Madame Wendling, I mean, the flautist. Wolfgang is a tremendous favourite with them. They have an only daughter who is very beautiful and whom that Bach[3] in England wanted to marry. She has been delicate for more than a year and a half as she never recovered completely from a fever. It is a pity about the creature. Addio. Take care of yourselves. I kiss you and Nannerl several thousand times and remain your faithful

old wife

FRAU MOZART

(246) *Leopold Mozart to his Son*

[*Extract*]   [*Autograph in the Mozarteum, Salzburg*]

MON TRÈS CHER FILS!   SALZBURG, 20 *November* 1777

As much as your letter of November 8th filled me with a certain hope and delighted all of us, especially Herr Bullinger, so much were we distressed by your letter of the 13th, which to our great surprise we received on the evening of the 18th, that is on the fifth day after its dispatch, whereas all the others took six days at the very least. It would

---

[1] K. 243, composed in 1776.
[2] A postscript to Mozart's letter, written inside the cover.
[3] Johann Christian Bach.

have been very much better, I admit, if you had received fifteen louis
d'or instead of a watch, which you say has been valued at twenty louis
d'or, since for travelling money is very necessary, indeed indispensable.
Where will you read this letter, I wonder? Probably in Mainz. For the love
of Heaven, ⟨you really must try to get some money⟩. You will not have
received my letter of the 13th in Mannheim, as probably you had left
already. I had planned everything in advance, and in regard to Frankfurt
I reported to you in detail what Leopold Heinrich Pfeil wrote to me.
What earthly use was all the information I made a point of sending you!
However, what is done cannot be helped. Further, I was never privileged
to hear why you had to hurry off immediately to Mannheim. I presume
that it was at the urgent persuasion of various people who thought they
knew better, and possibly in order not to miss the fine German opera.
But indeed your journey was not a direct one, for Herr Beecke *in his
malevolence* sent you off on a roundabout track, since, as Bullinger says,
everyone there knows that the way to Mannheim is by Cannstatt and
Bruchsal and *not by the other route*, which people sometimes choose. And,
pray, has Herr Beecke himself never travelled to Mannheim? That tiresome journey to Ellwangen was all to no purpose; and again you have to
thank Herr Beecke's kindness for this unnecessary expenditure. And had
Prince Taxis already returned to Regensburg? Well! It can't be helped!
But now you must see to it not only that the *Elector of Mainz* hears you
play but that you receive a present of money and, if it is at all possible,
give a concert in the town as well. For Mainz is the centre of a great
aristocracy and the seat of the government, which is not true of Mannheim,
as the government and people of importance there reside in Dusseldorf.
Konzertmeister Kreusser is the best person to help you in all these matters
and to arrange everything. For in regard to your first object, he himself
knows as a traveller that money is necessary; and when you have played
before the Elector, you can tell him everything quite frankly, the more
so as in Mannheim you only received a galanterie. As for your concert,
Kreusser can do a great deal, for he is popular in Mainz. If he is not there,
then the leading singer, Franziska Ursprünger, to whom I send most
devoted greetings, will tell you to whom you should apply—perhaps to
the cellist Schwachhofen junior, to whom I send my regards, who could
also introduce you to Prince von Biberach who lives close by and takes
lessons from him. I am talking at random about Mainz, simply because I
presume that you are there, although you do not say a single word about
where you are going to. But Mainz is the nearest Court; and to reach it
may have cost you ten to eleven gulden in coach fares and tips. There you
will have an opportunity of presenting Choirmaster Stark with clavier
compositions, which, after simplifying their difficult passages, he can
then hand on to his pupils. Why did you not make a point of giving the

Elector of Mannheim some of your compositions? I sent you that enclosure not only *for your own purpose* but in order that *you should make your compositions known*, for there is such an excellent orchestra there. Well, probably you had no time to think of this. Where are you going to now? To Paris? What route will you take? Are you making for Paris without any introductions? What route will you choose so as to be able to make some money on the way? You must make some, for you doubtless appreciate what a sum will be necessary for this terrific journey. And when you reach Paris, to whom will you apply? Surely you must have enough money in your pocket to enable you to live until you have made the necessary acquaintances who will help you to earn something? You can do a great deal in Paris by giving lessons. That is quite certain. But no one obtains pupils at once; and are people going to dismiss their own teachers immediately and take a stranger who has only just arrived? A great deal of money can be made by having your compositions engraved and sold. Yes, but for all these schemes it is necessary to have some patron, a friend or two, a subscription list; and does not all this presuppose that you have already made a number of acquaintances?—Well, let us drop this for the moment. It is quite certain that the journey and the first period of your stay in Paris will necessitate a well-filled purse. ⟨You know that we owe Herr Bullinger three hundred gulden and Herr Weiser more than a hundred. I forget how much we owe Kerschbaumer, but it probably amounts to forty gulden. In the New Year I shall be getting bills from the dressmaker and the tailor, not to mention other trifling accounts *of a few gulden* and our daily unavoidable expenses. Food does not cost much, but there are many other expenses, *especially now in the winter, what with wood, candles* and many other small items, so that I have to rack my brains to fit them all in.⟩ Nevertheless I am willing, if you really wish to go to Paris, to arrange for you to draw there *an advance of twenty or thirty louis d'or* in the hope that this sum will come back to me doubled and trebled. But is our good friend Grimm there now? Why would ill luck have it that you were both quite close to one another in Augsburg without knowing it? Perhaps he is in Paris? Perhaps when he was in Augsburg he was about to leave for Paris? But who knows? How would it be if Wolfgang were to write now to M. Grimm, Envoyé de S. A. Sérénissime, Le Duc de Saxe-Gotha, à Paris? In this letter he could tell him about his journey and express his regret that they should have been so close to one another in Augsburg, where Wolfgang's concert took place on the very evening when Grimm turned in to the 'Drei Mohren'. You must send him an address to reply to, possibly Coblenz or wherever you may be going to. And, as a note left behind at the Post Office on your departure will ensure that your letters are forwarded, you will certainly have a reply from him, if he is in Paris. If not, it does not matter if the letter is lost, as there will be nothing compromising in it. It would be wiser, however, not to put your signature too low down or to leave too much empty space, for, if a letter of this kind were to fall into unknown and evil hands, some rascal might cut óut the name and write in the space above a demand for a few louis d'or. I have already reminded you twice that by means of a note left behind giving your address, you are sure to receive your letters, for it is in the interest of the Post Office to forward to its destination *a letter which has not yet been paid for*. Good friends, whom you might ask to do this, might forget it. So when you arrive at some town, you must enquire several times at the Post Office. What I have said about a money advance in Paris ⟨*cannot be arranged, if you now proceed to draw money in Frankfurt*⟩. Therefore you really must *endeavour to obtain a present of money*⟩ or at any rate see that some lady shall undertake ⟨*to exploit*⟩ your ⟨*watch*⟩ among the nobility, as Lamotte did in Prague with all the galanteries he had received there. Herr von Dalberg's[1] handsome wife could do that for you. Herr Kreusser knows best how to arrange it. But that is not all! When I ask Mamma about the journey to Paris, she will say: 'But how shall we travel?' *Why, you must take the same old road as we took many years ago.* Mamma will remember that there are thirty-four stages. But I must remind you that you cannot use our chaise any longer, since four horses and two postillions are necessary. I beg you to send me your ideas as to how you are really thinking of continuing your journey.

The Prince of Chiemsee has had an attack of gout at Zeill in Swabia. Otherwise he would have been in Munich long ago. But if you write to him now at Munich, he will certainly have got there by this time. You seem to like Munich better than Mannheim. I too should prefer Munich, in spite of the fact that the orchestra in Mannheim is excellent. But Mannheim has no singers and every year they make changes in the singers and maestri at the opera. Would you not write to Prince Zeill and ask him to suggest to the Elector and Count Seeau that they should take you on for a year or two, as the latter usually does with his castrati? Say that you will not ask for a certificate of appointment, that you are a young man who is not yet trying to get established, but has still time to make his fortune in the world—but that you have a great desire to serve the Elector for any period of time he may choose. You could write *a separate letter* to the Prince, mentioning that His Excellency Count Seeau would not lose by this arrangement, seeing that you would undertake to touch up his German Singspiele and that you would give an assurance, perhaps even a written undertaking, that you will not beseech or worry the Elector to retain you any longer than the period arranged for, unless of course he himself wishes to do so. What I feel is that if you were in

---

[1] Baron Friedrich Christoph Anton von Dalberg, director of music at the court of Mainz.

Munich, you would be nearer Italy. Then, if you obtained a scrittura, he would let you go and your salary would continue. And even if you do not obtain a scrittura now, your work in Munich would be the best way to obtain one eventually and, in addition, a hundred other things which I need not mention. There are an amazing number of castles of the nobility and monasteries in the neighbourhood of Munich and, once you are known, there will always be plenty of amusement to be had, what with hunting, riding and driving. There will also be countless opportunities to compose for the church and the theatre, besides more entertainments in winter than in any other place I know of. I must close. We both kiss dear Mamma and yourself and I am your old husband and father

MOZART

We had no letter from you today. Perhaps we shall get one by Friday's post. About that German opera you mentioned, who composed it? Who sang and how? *Not a word!* And that concert you mentioned, who played, sang, blew and whistled? Was the music good? *Not a word!* You are nice people indeed! Ah yes, Mamma *did say that the music of the opera was fine.* That is so—but for the rest—we may whistle for it! What sort of people played the violin concertos there? Herr Fränzl?[1] We may whistle! And what about that ancient philosopher and mummified Raaff? We may whistle indeed!

(247) *Mozart to his Father*

[*Autograph in the Mozarteum, Salsburg*]
MANNHEIM, 22 *November*, 1777
In the evening, or rather, *nocte tempŗris,*
Puncto and *accurat* on the stroke of ten.

MON TRÉS CHER PÉRE!
(I nearly dropped into the feminine.)

First of all I must inform you that my most truthful letter to Herr Herzog in Augsburg, puncto Schmalzii,[2] has had a very good effect. He has written a most polite letter to me in reply and expressed his annoyance that I got such a cold reception from the said Herr Butter. He sent me the other day a sealed letter for Herr Milk, together with a draft for 150 gulden on the said Herr Cheese. You must know that although I had only spoken to Herr Herzog on one single occasion, I couldn't refrain from

---

[1] Ignaz Fränzl (1736–1811), a famous violinist, who became a member of the Mannheim orchestra in 1747 and its leader in 1774. When the court was transferred to Munich in 1778, Fränzl remained in Mannheim and was musical director of the Nationaltheater from 1790 to 1803.

[2] On the subject of Herr Schmalz see p. 375. Mozart proceeds to pun on his name, which means 'lard'.

asking him in my letter to be so kind as to send me a draft on Herr Schmalz, alias Butter, Milk, Cheese or on anyone else he chose. A ça, apparently the joke came off. So there's no need to knock and offer sympathy. This morning, the 21st, we received your letter of the 17th. I was not at home but at Cannabich's, where Mr. Wendling was rehearsing a concerto which I had scored for him. At six o'clock today the gala concert took place. I had the pleasure of hearing Herr Fränzl (who is married to a sister of Mme Cannabich) play a concerto on the violin. I like his playing very much. You know that I am no great lover of difficulties. He plays difficult things, but his hearers are not aware that they are difficult; they think that they could at once do the same themselves. That is real playing. He has too a most beautiful, round tone. He never misses a note, you can hear everything. It is all clear cut. He has a beautiful staccato, played with a single bowing, up or down; and I have never heard anyone play a double trill as he does. In a word, in my opinion he is no wizard, but a very sound fiddler. If I could only get rid of this habit of slanty writing! I am very sorry that I was not in Salzburg during Madame Adlgasser's sad experience, so that I might have consoled her.[1] For I'm very good at that—especially with such a pretty woman as Mme Nadlstrasser.[2] All that you write about ⟨Mannheim⟩ I know already— but I never like to write about anything prematurely. Everything will be all right. In my next letter I may perhaps be able to tell you something *very good* for you, but only *good* for me, or something *very bad* in your eyes, but *tolerable* in mine; or it may be something *tolerable* for you, but *good, precious and valuable* for me! Rather in the style of an oracle, is it not? Well, it is obscure, yet intelligible. Remember me to Herr Bullinger. I feel ashamed, whenever I get a letter from you, as there is generally some message from him in it; and when I think that I have not yet written to the man who is my best and truest friend, and who has shown me so much kindness and sympathy! But—I shall make no excuses—No. I shall ask him instead to make my excuses for me as far as he can and I promise to write to him as soon as I feel *settled*. Up to the present I have never been so. For as soon as I know that as likely as not and in all probability I shall have to leave a place, then I simply cannot settle down. And although I now have just a faint hope, I still can't feel settled until I know where I am. Part of the oracle must come to pass. I think it will be either the middle section or the third. It's all the same to me. For it's all one at all times whether I gobble up the dirt or Papa chews it. Bother, I can't say it properly! I meant to say: it's all one whether Papa chews the dirt or I gobble it up. Well, I would rather chuck it. I can see it's no use. A propos. Did you reply to Herr von Hamm at Munich? Are you taking on his

---

[1] Mozart refers to a story in his father's letter of 17 November, which for lack of space has had to be omitted.   [2] Mozart is punning on the name Adlgasser.

daughter? I hope I told you that Holzbauer's grand opera is in German? If not, I am telling you now. It is entitled 'Günther von Schwarzburg', but not our worthy Herr Günther, Barber and Councillor of Salzburg. During the next carnival 'Rosemunde' will be performed, a new text by Wieland with new music by Schweitzer.[1] Both of them are coming here. I have already seen some of the opera and played it on the clavier, but I will not say anything about it yet. The target you had painted for me as Master of the Shoot is superb and the verses are incomparable. Well, there's nothing left for me to write except to wish you all a thoroughly good rest and that you will all sleep soundly until I wake you up with this present letter. Adieu. I kiss Papa's hands 100000000 times and embrace my sister, that darling blister, with all my heart, until I smart, just a little or not at all, and remain your most obedient son, hoping away you will not run,

WOLFGANG AMADÉ MOZART

Knight of the Golden Spur and, as soon as I marry, of the Double Horn, Member of the Grand Academies of Verona, Bologna. Oui, mon ami!

(247a) *Maria Anna Mozart to her Husband*

[*Autograph in the Mozarteum, Salzburg*]

MY DEAR HUSBAND,   MANNHEIM, [23 *November* 1777[2]]

We have received all your letters safely and, thank God, we are well, and I am glad that you are both in good health. We are still in Mannheim and you may go on sending all our letters here. If we leave, we shall certainly make arrangements to have them forwarded. I am very sorry for poor Martinelli[3]. What on earth will Lenerl do now, for the inheritance will probably not be very large? You do not tell us very much about Salzburg. Are there no players there? Are no operas being performed? Is Dr. Barisani still out of favour? Does our Chief Purveyor still pay attention to Fräulein Tonerl? I should like to know all these things in detail. We send special greetings to Mlle Sallerl and M. Bullinger. Please tell them that we think of them every day. This very moment Nannerl will please lay aside whatever she is doing and give Bimperl a kiss on her little paws and make it smack so loudly that I can hear it in Mannheim.

---

[1] Anton Schweitzer (1735–1787) was first Kapellmeister of Seyler's theatrical company in Hildburghausen, which performed German singspiele. After studying in Italy he became musical director at the Ducal Theatre in Weimar, for which he composed *Alceste*, on a text by Wieland. This opera was performed at Mannheim in 1773, and he and Wieland were commissioned by the Elector to write an opera for the 1778 carnival.

[2] A postscript to Mozart's letter.

[3] Frau Mozart is referring to a passage in her husband's letter of 17 November, which for lack of space has had to be omitted.

Remember me to the Hagenauers, Robinigs, Frau von Gerlichs, the Barisanis, Jungfer Mitzerl, Katherl Gilowsky, to whom we send congratulations on her coming name-day. Remember us too to Theresa. Now I think I have sent greetings to all and our compliments and thanks. Keep well, both of you, and think of us, as we do of you. Then we and you shall all be happy. Addio. I kiss you and Nannerl many 100 000 000 000 times without number, and remain your faithful wife,

both in body and soul,

FRAU MARIA ANNA MOZART

(248) *Leopold Mozart to his Son*

[*Extract*]   [*Autograph in the Mozarteum, Salzburg*]

MON TRÈS CHER FILS!   SALZBURG, 24 *November* 1777

Indeed I do not know what to say to you. I am so amazed at your last letter of November 16th, in which you inform me *with the greatest sans-gêne* that Herr Schmalz, probably the father, brother or friend of Herr Schmalz of the leather-shop at Munich, or possibly even he himself, excused himself by saying that he had no instructions to provide you with money. That I can well believe and he was quite right. You ought to have asked Herr Herzog or somebody in the firm of Nocker and Schiedl to arrange for you to have a small credit elsewhere, *as I used to do.* For these people had no orders from Hagenauer to extend this credit to other houses, and no true business man exceeds his literal orders. But they would have done so if you had asked them beforehand. This incident, however, was described to me as frankly and coolly as if I had chests full of money and as if I were going to be horribly annoyed that payment had not been made to you at once. I shall not waste time with a lengthy description of our circumstances, for you yourself know them and so does Mamma. In my letter of the 20th I enumerated our chief debts and even so forgot to mention a ⟨*rather large sum which we owe*⟩ to Hagenauer, and which at the moment ⟨*we are not reducing by a single farthing.*⟩ What astonished me most of all in your last letter was that all of a sudden you trotted out this story, without mentioning a word about it in your previous one, in which you just said that for your journey money would be more necessary and more welcome than a present, although you both knew at the time that financially you were in very low water. So, if Herr Schmalz had obliged you, I should have been saddled with a bill, *without having received the slightest warning from you beforehand, and that too at a time when it was the last thing I expected.* Very nice of you, indeed! I leave it to you to think over, bearing in mind all my circumstances. You wrote to me from Augsburg that you were only 27 gulden on the wrong side. I have now worked out that if you were 30 gulden on the wrong side, you would still have 170 gulden; and if that silly trip to Mannheim through Wallerstein cost you 70 gulden, you should still have 100 gulden. Even if it cost you more, *have you still not enough* to take you both to Mainz? There you would be near Frankfurt and, if it were absolutely necessary, you could draw a little with your second letter of credit from Herr Bollongari. Then you would only have to apply to some merchant in Mainz who is in touch with Herr Bollongari and who would undertake to send him the letter of credit and give you the sum you require. Would that not be more sensible than to sit down in Mannheim and use up your money to no purpose, particularly as with this sum you could meet the expenses of the journey which costs only about 15 to 16 gulden? For the distance to Worms is only 1¼ stages, to Oppenheim 2 and to Mainz 1, that is, only about 3¾ stages in all. And if on your arrival you had little or no money, we have acquaintances there who would stand by you; and no gentleman need be ashamed if he has not a farthing in his pocket, provided he can produce a letter of credit. For to be short of money can happen to the wealthiest and most respectable people. Why, it is even a maxim when travelling, only to carry, if possible, the sum that is absolutely necessary. I keep on talking at random about Mainz, all pure supposition, as you have not done me the honour of telling me in a single letter where you are thinking of going. You wrote to me from Augsburg at the very last moment: 'We are off to Wallerstein tomorrow'; and Herr Stein wrote to me: 'They left for Wallerstein and Mannheim at 7.30 on Sunday'. Surely you should let me know your arrangements some time beforehand, as now and then I might make useful preparations and send reminders, as I endeavoured to do for Frankfurt by writing to Otto and Pfeil.—But indeed your journey does not concern me! Is it not so? As it is, you could have taken quite a different route from Mannheim, I mean, to Würzburg, and thence to the Margrave of Darmstadt and on to Frankfurt and Mainz. But how can I fathom your intentions, or make any suggestions, seeing that I am never consulted and was never told how things were progressing in Manheim? On the contrary I got a different impression from your letter ⟨in which you mentioned an opportunity of a heart-to-heart talk with the Elector⟩, and thought that you would be staying there for a long time. All your plans and views, inclinations, intentions and so forth, whatever they may be, you ought to have reported candidly and in good time, as even by the quickest and safest route it takes *twelve days* to receive a letter from you and answer it. This too, however, you did not take the trouble to consider, seeing that in your last letter, dated the 16th, you told me *that I could go on writing to Mannheim*, although you could only receive this letter after 12 days at the earliest that is, not before the 28th. But I did not receive your letter until

Friday, 21st, as a present on *our wedding day*, and thus could not reply before the 24th. So you will read this letter—God knows where, on the 1st or 2nd of December. You must not think that I do not realise how many incidental expenses crop up on journeys and how money disappears, especially if one is too generous or too kind-hearted. My dear wife prided herself on getting up early, on not dawdling and on doing everything briskly and economically. *But 16 days in Munich, 14 days in Augsburg,* and now, to judge by your last letter of November 16th, 17 *days in Mannheim,* which, if you await the reply from Augsburg, will be prolonged to three weeks—that is lightning speed, in truth! You have now been away eight weeks, that is, two months, and have already reached Mannheim! How amazingly quick! When we travelled to England we spent nine days in Munich, where we performed before the Elector and Duke Clemens and had to wait for a present. We spent a fortnight in Augsburg, but we gave three concerts there, on June 28th and 30th and July 4th. We left Salzburg on June 9th and only arrived in Munich on the 12th, because in Wasserburg we had to have new wheels put on our carriage. Yet we reached Schwetzingen on July 13th, although we stopped at Ulm, Ludwigsburg and Bruchsal. So you see that your long and quite unnecessary sojourn has ruined all your prospects; the most beautiful autumn within living memory has gone by and so far you have just had a holiday and have spent the time in enjoyment and amusement. Now the bad weather, short days and the cold have arrived and these conditions will become worse, while our prospects and purposes become more costly and more distant. You cannot go on travelling the whole winter, and if you want to make a stay, you ought to do so in a large town where there is a society and where merit has hopes and opportunities of being rewarded—and where is there such a place abroad? Nowhere except Paris. But if you want to live in Paris, you must adopt quite a different manner of living and an entirely different outlook. There must be attention and daily concentration on earning some money and you must cultivate extreme politeness in order to ingratiate yourself with people of standing. I shall write more about this in my next letter, in which I shall put forward my ideas about another
★ route which you could take in order to reach Paris more quickly. Meanwhile, whatever route you take, see that you get letters of recommendation to Paris from anyone who will give them, merchants, courtiers and so forth. And is there no French Ambassador or Resident in Mainz or Coblenz? No, I think not. You have no letters of introduction—whereas I had lots of them. These are absolutely essential if you want to procure patrons and acquaintances at once. A journey of this kind is no joke. As yet you have had no experience of it. You should have more important things in your mind than practical jokes; you should be endeavouring to arrange a hundred things in advance, or you will find yourself suddenly

in the soup, and without money—and where there is no money, friends
are no longer to be found, and that too even if you give a hundred lessons
for nothing, compose sonatas and, instead of occupying yourself more
profitably, play the fool every evening from ten o'clock until midnight.
Then ask for money credit! Suddenly jokes will cease, and in a moment
the most laughter-raising countenance will certainly become serious. I
do not blame you at all for putting the Cannabich household under an
obligation to you by your friendly kindness. That was a sensible thing to
do. But you might have devoted a few idle hours in the evening to your
father who is so anxious about you and you might have sent him not
just a rigmarole dashed off in a hurry, but a proper, confidential and
detailed report of the expenses incurred on your journey, of the money
you still have in hand, a few particulars about the journey you are going
to undertake and about your intentions with regard to Mannheim; and
then you would have had advice from him. I hope that you yourself will
have the good sense to see this. For in the long run everything recoils on
your poor old father. As I said above, I received your letter on the 21st,
but I could not reply to it before today. Yesterday, the 23rd, I made my
confession at Holy Trinity and with weeping eyes recommended you
both to the protection of Almighty God. Bullinger, who sends you his   ★
greetings, was rather surprised at your letter and, in view of our serious
circumstances, did not appear to relish your joke about your open confession. At 5.30 I went to see Hagenauer to ask *that if Nocker and Schiedl*
did not inform him by post that they had given you a draft, he might have a letter
to this effect sent by today's post to Augsburg. This morning I again went to
the shop and saw Herr Joseph and found that, although they had had
letters from Nocker and Schiedl, no mention had been made of you. He
promised me to write today. Now I have seen to everything and trust
that in the meantime you will have got some money. The firm of Nocker
and Schiedl will not report until they know how much money you have
drawn. Remember, it is always better, whenever you draw money, to do
so, not in guldens, but piecemeal, for instance, six or seven louis d'or,
carolins or whatever the coinage may be. I have now unburdened my
whole heart to you and in the light of truth, such as is pleasing to God.
Experience will teach you that it is no joke to undertake such a journey
and to have to live on whatever sums you happen to make, and that above
all you must pray earnestly to God for good health, protect yourself carefully against wicked people and earn money by every means you know
of and can use, and spend it with the greatest economy. I prefer when
travelling that a man to whom I have perhaps given very little and whom
I may never see again in this life, should say of me that I am a skinflint,
rather than that he should laugh at me behind my back for giving him
too much. The page is full and I am tired, my eyes especially. Nannerl

and I wish you the best of health and kiss you cordially a million times and I am your old husband and father, but not your son

MOZART

I hope that you received my letter of the 20th in which I told you to write to M. Grimm in Paris, and also what you ought to write to the Prince of Chiemsee in Munich. By the next post I shall send you particulars of all the stages to Paris and my ideas and so forth, and also the list of our former acquaintances there. Addio.

(249) *Maria Anna Mozart to her Husband*

[Autograph in the Mozarteum, Salzburg]

MY DEAR HUSBAND,   MANNHEIM, 26 *November* 1777

You want to know why we came here in such a hurry? Well, first of all, I must tell you that Prince Taxis was no longer at Dischingen and that some time before he left, he sent off his orchestra to Regensburg. Then, when we were in Hohenaltheim, Prince Taxis was staying with some other noble family on their estate. So where should we have gone? Perhaps to Würzburg? But the Bishop was then in Bamberg. And when we left Würzburg we should have had to travel through the Forest of Spessart. So we preferred to come to Mannheim.

(249a) *Mozart continues the letter*

[Autograph in the Mozarteum, Salzburg]

And, moreover, everyone who knows it, the gentry included, advised me to come to Mannheim. The reason why we are still here, is that I am thinking of staying on for the winter. I am only waiting for a reply from the Elector. Count Savioli, the Intendant, is a very honest gentleman, and I told him to be so kind ⟨as to tell the Elector that, as in any case the weather is at present bad for travelling, I should like to stay here and teach the young Count.⟩ He promised me to do his best, but begged me to have patience until the gala days were over. All this took place with the knowledge and at the *instigation* of Cannabich. When I told him that I had been to Savioli and what I had said to him, he remarked that he would sooner believe that it would happen than that it would not. Cannabich had himself mentioned the matter even before ⟨the Count spoke to the Elector.⟩ I must now wait and see. Tomorrow I shall draw my 150 gulden from Herr Schmalz, as I have no doubt that our landlord would rather hear the sound of money than of music. I never imagined I should get a watch for a present here, but such is the case. I should have left long ago if they hadn't all said: 'Where will you spend the winter then?—It's a very bad time of the year for travelling. Stay where you are.' Cannabich is very anxious for me to stay on. So I have now put out a feeler, and, as a affair of this sort cannot be hurried up, I must just wait patiently. I hope soon to be able to send you really good news. I already have two pupils in view (not counting my Archpupil),[1] who will most probably give me a louis d'or each per month. But without the Arch-one, it is true, it can't be managed. Now do let me drop all that, how it is and how it will be. What is the use of needless speculation? What will happen we know not—and yet we do know! It is God's will. Cheer up then, Allegro, non siate sì pegro.[2] If after all we do leave Mannheim, we shall go straight to—where do you think?—to Weilburg or whatever the place is called, to the Princess, the sister of the Prince of Orange, whom we knew so well à la Haie.[3] And there we shall remain, that is to say, as long as the officers' table is to our taste; and we shall get at least six louis d'or. Herr Sterkel[4] came here from Würzburg a few days ago. The day before yesterday, the 24th, Cannabich and I lunched again with Herr von Hagen, Chief Master of the Hunt, and I spent the evening at Cannabich's *al solito*.[5] Sterkel came in. He played five duets, but so fast that it was hard to follow them, and not at all clearly, and not in time. Everyone said the same. Mlle Cannabich played the sixth and, to tell the truth, better than Sterkel. Now I must close as I have no room for more, for I can't write in bed, and it is an effort to stay up, as I'm so sleepy. I shall write more the next time, but I can't today, for lack of space, I mean. I will have a large supply of paper for my next letter. Adieu. Confound it! There's still some more to write. I kiss Papa's hands and embrace my sister with all my heart and am ever

your faithful son
WOLFGANG AMADÉ MOZART

Mannheim, 26 November 1777.

If I could find some more room, I would send 100,000 compliments from us 2, I mean, from us two, to all our good friends: particularly to the A's:—the Adlgassers, Andretters and Arco (Count); B's:—Herren Bullinger, Barisani and Berantzky; C's:—Czernin (Count), Cusetti and

---

[1] i.e. the young Count. [2] Don't be so lazy.
[3] Princess Caroline von Nassau-Weilburg, to whom Mozart dedicated in 1766 his clavier sonatas, K. 26–31.
[4] Abt Johann Franz Xaver Sterkel (1750–1817) born at Würzburg, was a distinguished clavier-player and a very prolific and popular composer. In 1778 he became chaplain and organist to the Elector of Mainz, in whose service he remained until 1805.
[5] i.e. as usual.

the three organ blowers (Calcanten); D's:—Herren Daser, Deibl and Dommeseer; E's:—Mlle Barbara Eberlin, Herr Estlinger and all the asses (Eseln) in Salzburg; F's:—Firmian (Count and Countess and their little molly-coddle), young Franz and the Freihof of St. Peter's; G's:—Mlle, Mme and the two MM. Gilowsky and the Councillor too; also Herren Grétry and Gablerbrey; H's:—the Haydns, Hagenauers, Theresa Höllbrey: J's:—Joli (Miss Sallerl), Herr Janitsch the fiddler and Hagenauer's Jakob; K's:—Herr and Frau von Küsinger, Count and Countess Kühnburg and Herr Kassel; L's:—Baron Lehrbach, Count and Countess Lützow, Count and Countess Lodron; M's:—Herren Meisner, Medlhammer and Moserbrey; N's:—Nannerl, our Court ninny, Father Florian, and all night watchmen; O's:—Count Oxenstirn, Herr Overseer and all the oxen in Salzburg; P's:—the Prexes, Count Prank, the Lord High Cook, and Count Perusa; Q's:—Herren Quilibet, Quodlibet and all quakers; R's:—Father Florian Reichsigel, the Robinigs and Maestro Rust; S's:—Herren Suscipe, Seiffert and all the sows in Salzburg; T's:—Herr Tanzberger, our butcher, Theresa and all trumpeters; U's:—the towns of Ulm and Utrecht and all the clocks (Uhren) in Salzburg, especially if you put an H in at the beginning;[1] W's:—the Weisers, Hans the Wurst-maker and Woferl; X's:—Xantippe, Xerxes and all whose names begin with an X; Y's:—Herr Ypsilon, Herr Ybrig and all whose names begin with a Y; and, lastly, Z's:—Herr Zabuesnig, Herr Zonca and Herr Zezi[2] at the Castle. Addio. If I had room I would write something more, at least my compliments to my good friends. But it is impossible, for I don't know where I could work them in. I can't write anything sensible today, as I am rails off the quite. Papa be annoyed not must. I that just like today feel. I help it cannot. Warefell. I gish you nood-wight, Sound sleeply. Next time I'll sensible more writely.

(250) *Leopold Mozart to his Son*

[Extract]   [Autograph in the Mozarteum, Salzburg]

MON TRÉS CHER FILS!   SALZBURG, 27 *November* 1777

I received on the 25th, five days after its despatch, your letter of the 20th, written on a scrap of paper, *as you had no more in the house*. But, as usual, there was not a word in it as to whether in the meantime you had had a letter from me, although you must have received the one I wrote on the 13th, seven days previously. Besides I have already told you that up to the present I have written every post-day; and as you are aware that

[1] Mozart's joke is that by prefixing an H to 'U(h)ren', one obtains the word 'Huren' (whores).
[2] The personal names in this list are partly those of persons known to the Mozart family, partly those of persons not known to them, and partly those of imaginary persons.

the Salzburg post goes on Mondays and Thursdays only, you may know for certain whether you have received all my letters; and surely it is not much trouble for you to mention at the beginning of yours: 'I have received your letter of the ——'. Further, there is *not a word* about where you are going to or what plans you are thinking of making. Although I keep on hoping from one letter to another, yet every time there is— *nothing—not a single word!* The object of your journey, the very necessary object was and is and must be, to obtain ⟨an appointment or to make money.⟩ So far I see little prospect of the one or the other; unless, of course, it has to be kept a secret from me. You sent me from Munich most detailed news about everything. Thus I knew how matters stood, and up to the present I have still been able to arrange things and think out what measures you might adopt in order to get something done. From Augsburg too you sent me a full report—my only objection being that both in Munich and Augsburg you stayed too long—but at least ⟨*something to your credit appeared in the papers.*⟩ I was expecting, however, a reply to my suggestions about your journey, to know whither you were travelling, and why this plan—and not that—but—not a word—and then you write to me from Mannheim ⟨about a watch and no money.⟩—A pretty kettle of fish; and yet not a syllable about your plans for your next journey. I keep on racking my brains—and write myself blind. I do want to arrange things in advance. You, however, make light of everything, you are indifferent, you tie my hands when I want to advise and help, since you do not say a word about where you are going to next. I shall give you a clear instance of an unpardonable piece of thoughtlessness on your part. As you do not mention anything ⟨about your wish to remain in Mannheim⟩ or that ⟨you have told the Elector⟩ or that you have taken any further steps on these lines, I am driven to think that you are planning another journey. So, as I mentioned in previous letters, you will probably be thinking of going on to Paris. Now, whatever route you choose, *you cannot hope to earn enough money* on the way to defray the expenses of this costly journey. Did it never occur to you both that at some point on this long route a credit would have to be arranged? ⟨*You have only reached Mannheim*⟩ and you are already in that predicament. When you leave Mainz, you cannot draw any more money in Frankfurt. If you draw some now in Mannheim, then, in the name of Heaven, you must not draw any more in Frankfurt, where, to be sure, you cannot make any. So it is to be hoped that in Mainz, Coblenz and Bonn you will make enough money out of the three Electors to take you to Brussels. During our grand tour we travelled from Bonn to Cologne through Jülich to Aachen, from Aachen to Liège; thence through Tirlemont to Brussels. Aachen and Liège are expensive places and in the winter the former is empty. I see on my map, *on which all the routes are marked*, that your most direct one is from Cologne straight to Maastricht, a distance of 14 German miles at most. From Maastricht the route proceeds through Tongres (or Tongern in German)—St. Trond—Tirlemont—and Louvain direct to Brussels. From Maastricht to Brussels is a distance of not more than 14 German miles. Hence the whole route from Cologne to Brussels is 28 German miles, that is, 3 miles more than from Salzburg to Augsburg, which is 25 miles. So there is not much difference. As you are travelling by post-chaise and can stop wherever you like, Maastricht and Louvain are two places, especially the latter, which is a well-populated town with a great University, where you could perhaps give a concert. It could be arranged in this way. First find out from your landlord who is the *Kapellmeister or Music Director* of the place, or, if there is none, *who is its leading musician.* Arrange to be taken to him, or, if he is not too grand a person, ask him to call on you. You will then know at once whether giving a concert there is an expensive business, whether you can count on having a good harpsichord, whether an orchestra is available and whether there are many lovers of music. Perhaps you might be introduced to someone who from a love of music would interest himself in your undertaking. In short, you must find out quickly whether something can be done or not—and you should do this on your arrival and without unpacking anything: just put on a few fine rings and so forth, in case when you call you should find a harpsichord there and be asked to perform. As great violinists are rarely to be found in towns of that size, you might play a violin concerto which can be easily accompanied. *But no doubt your violin is having a rest!* That I can well imagine. I should be more inclined to count on Louvain, where we turned in at the 'Wilder Mann' and were very well done; I only paid 2 gulden 30 kreuzer for lunch for five people. I don't think that there is much to be made in Maastricht.

To return to our discussion about a credit. You ought to have written to me about continuing your journey—for you surely realize that you must get credit in Brussels, since it is impossible to foretell all eventualities and the distance is extraordinarily great. It might not be possible to arrange to give a concert quickly and you would then run the risk of having to sit there for two or three weeks and spend money to no purpose. *I dare not advise you to* choose the other route through Trier and Luxemburg, which I mentioned the other day, for things might not turn out well and, moreover, I do not know whether money is to be made in either of these centres; whereas on the Rhine route you will find *three Electors*; and in Brussels and Louvain perhaps something might be done. A little thought and common sense thought and common sense should convince you that it is most necessary to think things out and to take these wearisome and constant precautions and that fruitless over-anxiousness is not prompting me to write as I do, nor timorous melancholy imaginings, but simply experience. I am longing to hear where you are and to know whither you are going, so that I may make further arrangements. My dear wife always writes very little; but as she does tell us where she is being invited to lunch, we know at least that she is in good health. God bless you and keep you well! We too are flourishing, thank God, and jog along as well as we can. Nannerl attends to everything and I spend my day, partly with my numerous services in the churches, and partly with my pupils, with writing to you and sitting with Nannerl at the clavier from 5.30 to 8.30 in the evening. All our friends send their greetings, and so do Bullinger and Gött, who are with me at the moment; and also Jungfer Sallerl, Mitzerl, the Hagenauers, Andretters, Katherl Gilowsky, Frau Moshammer, I mean, Marianne, the wife of the Contrôleur, who did not even know that you had left Salzburg. We kiss you a million times and I am ever your old husband and father

MZT ★

The copy of your portrait, which is a splendid likeness, is being sent to Bozen by Herr Triendl on December 3rd or 4th and thence to Bologna.[1] Your portrait has already been framed in a black frame with thick gold beading.

★

(251) *Mozart to his Father*

[*Autograph in the Mozarteum, Salzburg*]

MANNHEIM, 29 *November* 1777
In the evening

MON TRÉS CHER PÉRE!

Your letter of the 24th reached me safely this morning. I see from it that you would never be able to adapt yourself equally to good fortune or bad fortune, if perchance some adversity should befall use. Up to the present all four of us, as things are, have been neither fortunate nor unfortunate, and I present all four of us, as things are, have been neither fortunate nor unfortunate, and I thank God for that. You make many reproaches to us both—all quite undeserved. We spend nothing beyond what is necessary; and what is necessary when travelling you know as well as we do and even better. That we stayed so long in Munich was entirely due to *me*; and if I had been alone, I should most certainly be there still. Why did we spend a fortnight in Augsburg? I am almost driven to think that you never received the letters I sent from there. I wanted to give a concert. I was let down. In this way I lost a week. I wanted absolument to leave. They wouldn't let me. They wanted me to give a concert. I wanted them to

---

[1] i.e. the copy sent to Padre Martini. See p. 272, n. 1.

press me to do so; which they did. I gave a concert. That accounts for that fortnight. Why did we make straight for Mannheim? That I answered in my last letter. Why are we still here? Well—do you really believe that I would stop anywhere without a reason? But I might have told my father —very well, you shall hear the reason and, what is more, the whole course of events. But God knows that I did not want to say anything about it, simply because I could give you no details (any more than I can now) and because I know you well enough to realize that a *vague* account would only cause you worry and anxiety; and this I have always tried to avoid. But if you attribute it to my negligence, thoughtlessness and laziness, I can only thank you for your good opinion of me and sincerely regret that you do not know your own son.

I am not careless, I am simply prepared for anything and am able, in consequence, to wait patiently for whatever may come, and endure it— provided that my honour and the good name of Mozart are not affected. Well, as it must be so, so let it be. But I must beg you at the outset not to give way prematurely to joy or sadness. For come what may, all is well, so long as a man enjoys good health. For happiness consists—simply in imagination. Last Tuesday week, November 18th, the day before St. Elizabeth's Day, I went to Count Savioli in the morning and asked him whether it wasn't possible ⟨that the Elector might keep me here this winter? I would like to teach the young Count.⟩ He said: 'Yes, I will ⟨suggest it to the Elector;⟩ and, if it rests with me, it will certainly be arranged'. In the afternoon I was at Cannabich's. As I had gone to the Count on his advice, he asked me at once whether I had been there. I told him everything. He then said: 'I should very much like you to ⟨stay with us for the winter,⟩ but I should like it still more ⟨if you could get a permanent post'.⟩ I replied that it was my dearest wish to be near them always, but that I really did not know how it would be possible for me to be so ⟨permanently.⟩ I added: 'You have ⟨two Kapellmeisters⟩ already, so I don't know ⟨what I could be.⟩ I shouldn't like to be subordinate to ⟨Vogler'.⟩ 'That you shan't', he rejoined. 'None of the ⟨musicians⟩ here are inferior to the ⟨Kapellmeister,⟩ or even to the ⟨Intendant. Why, the Elector could make you his chamber composer.⟩ Just wait, I will ⟨discuss it with the Count.'⟩ On the following Thursday there was a grand concert. When ⟨the Count⟩ saw me, he apologized to me for not having yet mentioned the matter: ⟨the gala⟩ was still in progress, but as soon ⟨as it was over,⟩ that is on Monday, he would ⟨certainly put in a word.⟩ I waited for three days and, as I had heard nothing whatever, I went to him to inquire. That was yesterday, Friday. 'My dear Mr. Mozart,' he said, 'there was a ⟨hunt⟩ on today, ⟨so it was not possible for me to speak to the Elector.⟩ But this time tomorrow ⟨I shall certainly be able to give you an answer.'⟩ I begged him not to forget. To tell the truth I was rather annoyed when I left him and I decided to take my six easiest variations on Fischer's minuet [1] (which I had copied out here expressly for this purpose) ⟨to the young Count⟩ in order to have an opportunity ⟨of speaking to the Elector in person.⟩ You can hardly imagine how delighted ⟨the governess⟩ was to see me. I was received most courteously. When I pulled out the variations and told her that ⟨they were for the Count,⟩ she said: 'Oh, that is good of you; but have you something for ⟨the Countess too?'⟩ 'Not yet,' I said, 'but if I stay here long enough to have time to compose something, then I shall——' 'A propos', she said, 'I am glad to hear ⟨that you are staying for the winter.'⟩ 'What? That is the first I have heard of it!' 'You surprise me. How very strange. ⟨The Elector told me so himself⟩ the other day, "A propos," he said, ⟨"Mozart is staying here for the winter." '⟩ 'Well, if you heard it from him, you heard it from the one person who has the right to say it. For without ⟨the Elector⟩ I naturally ⟨cannot stay here.'⟩ I then told her the whole story. We arranged that the next day (that is today) I should come some time after four o'clock and bring with me something for ⟨the Countess.⟩ In the meantime ⟨she would speak to the Elector,⟩ who would ⟨still be there when I came.⟩ I went there today, but he had not arrived. But I shall go again tomorrow. I have composed a Rondo [2] for ⟨the Countess.⟩ Now, tell me, have I not reason enough to stay here and await the result? Should I go off now, just when I have taken the most important step? I now have the chance of ⟨speaking to the Elector in person.⟩ I shall in all probability ⟨stay here for the winter. For the Elector likes me, thinks highly of me and knows what I can do.⟩ In my next letter I hope to be able to give you some good news. But once more I beg you neither to rejoice nor worry too soon, and to take no one but Herr Bullinger and my sister into your confidence. I send her herewith the Allegro and Andante of the sonata for Mlle Cannabich. [3] The Rondo will follow the next time. It would have made the packet too thick to send them all together. You must put up with the original. You can have it copied for six kreuzer the sheet more easily than I can for twenty-four. Don't you think that's dear? Adieu. I kiss your hands 100,000 times and embrace my sister with all my heart and remain your most

obedient son

WOLFGANG AMADÉ MOZART

You may have heard something of my sonata, for at Cannabich's it is sung, strummed, fiddled or whistled at least three times a day! only *sotto voce*, of course!

---

[1] K. 179 [189a], composed in 1774.   [2] There is no trace of this composition.
[3] K. 309 [284b].

(251a) *Maria Anna Mozart to her Husband*

[Autograph in the Mozarteum, Salzburg]

MY DEAR HUSBAND,   [MANNHEIM, 29 *November* 1777 [1]]
I kiss you and Nannerl many 1000 times and beg you to give our greetings to all our acquaintances. I shall write more the next time. But now it is midnight already. Addio. I remain your faithful wife

MARIA ANNA MOZART

(252) *Leopold Mozart to his Son*

[Extract]   *[Autograph in the Mozarteum, Salzburg]*

★ MON TRÉS CHER FILS!   SALZBURG, 1 *December* 1777
Yesterday, Friday, in the morning old Fräulein von Küfstein passed over into eternity, and in the afternoon, when Bullinger was with us as usual, we received your letter of the 23rd. *Blast your oracular utterances and all the rest!* I hinted in my last letter that there must be secrets which I am not allowed to know. You are perfectly right. Whether they turn out well or ill, I shall hear them soon enough. In the same letter I could only write in pure supposition and as cautiously as possible: and I must confess that as I could not find any facts in your letters except your approaching journey and your ⟨lack of money,⟩ I was naturally extremely anxious. Moreover as I know the world better than either of you, and how few, yes, most certainly, how few ⟨true friends⟩ are to be found, my hope hangs by ⟨a very slight thread.⟩ Still you must ⟨have found a friend in Herr Cannabich, for on account of his daughter, it is to his interest⟩ to be one. Really I do not know ⟨what to say.⟩ But if in this instance ⟨nothing should come⟩ of it all? Well, let us leave ⟨it to Almighty God!⟩
★ What you wrote about the Litany for the Church of the Holy Cross you could have done without so much circumlocution, *ad captandam benevolentiam.*[2] Besides I should not have been opposed to it, as I know that usually they choose this kind of Litany. But as for engaging people to play in the orchestra, I know perfectly well that *that is not so.* I was a descanter there myself for a while and used to sing, standing on the steps beside the organ. They engage the *town musicians* and the *court trumpeters,*
★ when the latter happen to be there. So far I have heard nothing from Augsburg. I should prefer to send them a copy of the parts rather than the

---

[1] A postscript to Mozart's letter, written on the cover.
[2] For the sake of winning goodwill.

score in your handwriting, for many years ago the Dean, who was then organist, held on to one of my scores for three years, before I could get it back. Besides I could have it copied here much more satisfactorily than they would, if they let their students play about with it and smudge it. Moreover you are aware that to one who is not in the habit of reading your scores, many passages in them are difficult to make out. So I prefer to have it copied neatly and without untidy corrections and possibly fresh errors.

I had a letter some time ago from Herr von Hamm, Secretary for War, and sent him a reply, asking him to state what he would be willing to pay me for boarding and teaching his daughter. He then wrote again to say that he hoped I would be content with 150 gulden a year inclusive, that is, 12 gulden 30 kreuzer a month; but he did not forget to mention that her daily breakfast should consist of a small bowl of coffee and a white roll. I have not yet replied, as I have not had time. Besides there is no hurry, for in his first letter he said that he would not send his daughter until next spring and repeated this in his second letter, in which he talked about travelling in winter and added that first of all she would have to be well supplied—or rather equipped with everything. So I take it that her trousseau has to be collected first. Perhaps I am even to marry her! In accordance with her father's proposal I should thus have the honour of giving Fräulein von Hamm for 25 kreuzer a day her board and drink, breakfast, lodging and instruction in every subject. I shall write to him soon again and point out carefully that it is impossible for me to take her under 200 gulden a year. Well, before next spring there will have been many a snowstorm and much water will have flowed under the bridges. Herr Leutgeb, who has now bought in a suburb of Vienna a cheese-monger's shop (the size of a snail's shell), wrote to us both after your departure, promised to pay me in due course, and asked you for a concerto. But he must know by now that you are no longer in Salzburg. Mme Duschek wrote to me the other day. She and her husband want to know where you are and how you are getting on. In conclusion, I should like to hear whether Baron Dürnitz paid you in Munich? or whether you made him a present of your composition?[1]—or whether you or I ought not to remind him? I think that is all. Nannerl is at the Hagenauers at the moment and is then going on to the Robinigs where I shall join her, as Fräulein Louise wants to hear us play Schuster's duets. Keep in as good health as we are. We kiss you both many 100000000000 times and I am ever, like those innocent angels who puff along without joy and sorrow, your husband and father

MZT

[1] Probably K. 284 [205b], the clavier sonata written for Baron Thaddäus von Dürnitz. See p. 287, n. 4.

(253) *Mozart to his Father*

[*Autograph in the Mozarteum, Salzburg*]

MANNHEIM, 3 *December* 1777

MONSIEUR MON TRÉS CHER PÉRE,

I can still write nothing definite about my position here. Last Monday, after going for three days in succession, morning and afternoon, ⟨to his natural children,⟩ I had at last the good fortune to meet ⟨the Elector.⟩ We all thought indeed that once more our efforts were to be in vain, as it was then quite late. ⟨But at last we saw him coming. The governess⟩ at once told ⟨the Countess⟩ to seat herself at the clavier and I placed myself beside her and gave her a lesson; and that was how ⟨the Elector found us when he came into the room. We stood up but he told us to go on.⟩ When the Countess had finished playing, the governess was the first to speak and said that I had composed a very fine Rondo. I played it and he liked it very much. At length he asked: 'But will she be able to learn it?' 'Oh yes,' I replied. 'I only wish ⟨that I might have the good fortune to teach it to her myself.' He smiled and said: 'I should like it too. But would not her playing be spoilt if she had two different masters?' 'Oh no, Your Highness', I replied. 'All that matters is whether she has a good one or a bad. I hope Your Highness will not doubt—and will have confidence in me.'⟩ 'Oh, most certainly', ⟨he replied. The governess then said:⟩ 'See, Herr Mozart has also written some variations on Fischer's minuet for ⟨the young Count'.⟩ I played them and ⟨he liked them⟩ very much. He then began to jest ⟨with the Countess.⟩ I thanked him ⟨for his present.⟩ He said: 'Well, ⟨I shall think it over. How long are you going to stay here?'⟩ *My reply:* ⟨'As long as your Highness commands. I have no engagements whatsoever: I can stay as long as Your Highness requires.'⟩ That was all. I went there again this morning. I was told that yesterday ⟨the Elector⟩ had again remarked: ⟨Mozart is staying here for the winter'.⟩ Well, we are now in the thick of it and I am bound to wait. Today, for the fourth time, I lunched with Wendling. Before we sat down, Count Savioli came in with Kapellmeister Schweitzer, who had arrived the night before. Savioli said to me: ⟨'I spoke to the Elector again yesterday, but he hasn't yet made up his mind'.⟩ I told him that I should like to have a word with him, and we went to the window. I told him about ⟨the Elector's⟩ hesitation and complained that things were dragging on so long. I said that ⟨my expenses here were already heavy⟩ and I begged him ⟨to persuade the Elector to grant me a permanent appointment,⟩ as I feared that ⟨he would give me so little during the winter that I should probably not be able to stay on.⟩ 'He ought', I said, ⟨'to give me some work. I like work.'⟩ Savioli said that ⟨he would certainly suggest it to the Elector⟩ but that he could not do so this evening, ⟨because the Elector is not going to Court today;⟩ but he promised to give me ⟨a definite answer tomorrow.⟩ Well, I'm prepared for anything now. ⟨If he does not retain me, I shall press for a *contribution towards my travelling expenses*, for I don't intend to make him a present of the Rondo and the Variations.⟩ I assure you that it is because I am convinced that, whatever happens, things will certainly turn out well that I am so calm about it all. I have resigned myself entirely to the will of God.

We received yesterday your letter of November 27th. I hope you got the Allegro and Andante of my sonata! Here is the Rondo. Herr Kapellmeister Schweitzer is a good, worthy, honest fellow, dry and smooth like our ⟨Haydn,⟩ but better-spoken. There are some very beautiful passages in his new opera and I do not doubt that it will be a real success. His 'Alceste',[1] which is not half as fine as 'Rosemunde',[2] was very popular. The fact that it was the first German Singspiel had, of course, a lot to do with it. It no longer makes so strong an impression on people who are only carried away by novelty. Herr Wieland, who wrote the libretto, is also coming here this winter. I should like to meet him. Who knows? Perhaps—by the time Papa reads this, it will all, with God's will, be settled. ⟨If I stay here, I am to go to Paris in Lent⟩ in the company of Wendling, Ramm, who plays very beautifully, and Lauchéry, the balletmaster.[3] Wendling assures me that I shall never regret it. He has been twice to Paris and has only just returned. He maintains that it is still the only place where one can make money and a great reputation. He said: 'Why, you are a fellow who can turn your hand to anything. I will tell you the way to set about it. You must compose all sorts, opera seria, opéra comique, oratorio, everything, in fact. Once a man has written a couple of operas in Paris, he is sure of a settled yearly income. Then there is the *Concert Spirituel* and the *Académie des Amateurs*, which pay five louis d'or for a symphony. If you take pupils, the usual fee is three louis d'or for twelve lessons. Further, you can get sonatas, trios and quartets engraved *par souscription*. Cannabich and Toeschi send a great deal of their music to Paris.' Wendling is an experienced traveller. Please let me have your views about this scheme, which strikes me as being useful and sensible. I shall be travelling with a man who knows Paris (present-day Paris, for it has changed considerably) thoroughly. My expenses will

---

[1] *Alceste*, for which Wieland had written the text, was performed at Weimar on 28 May 1773, with tremendous success, and soon found its way to other theatres. The Elector Karl Theodor had it performed in Schwetzingen on 13 August 1775.

[2] After the successful performance of *Alceste* in Mannheim, the Elector commissioned Wieland to write a new German opera, for which Schweitzer was to compose the music. *Rosemunde* was to have been performed on 11 January 1778, but, owing to the death of the Bavarian Elector on 30 December 1777, and the immediate departure of the Elector Karl Theodor for Munich, the performance was dropped. The opera was given in Mannheim on 20 January 1780. See F. Walter, *Geschichte des Theaters und der Musik am Kurpfälzischen Hofe*, Leipzig, 1898, p. 246 ff.

[3] Étienne Lauchéry, who since 1774 had been maître de ballet at the Mannheim theatre.

be no greater. Indeed I don't think that I shall spend half as much, as I shall only have myself to pay for, since Mamma would stay here, probably with the Wendlings. Herr Ritter,[1] a fine bassoon-player, is off to Paris on December 12th. Now if I had been alone, this would have been an excellent opportunity for me. He mentioned it to me himself. Ramm, the oboist, is a very good, jolly, honest fellow of about 35, who has already travelled a great deal, and consequently has plenty of experience. The chief and best musicians here are very fond of me and show me great respect. They never call me anything but 'Herr Kapellmeister'. I may say that I very much regret not having a copy of at least one mass with me. I should have certainly had one performed, for I heard one of Holzbauer's recently and it is quite in our style. If only I had the 'Misericordias'[2] copied out. But it cannot be helped now. There's no altering it. I would have decided to have one copied, but copying is much too expensive here and I might not have got as much for the mass as it would have cost me to have it copied. They are not very generous here. Now please remember me to all my good friends, especially Count Arco, Mlle Sallerl, Herr Bullinger and the whole company of marksmen. I kiss Papa's hands 100000 times and embrace my sister with all my heart and hope that my sonata will please you, my sister and Herr Bullinger and all who hear it as much as it has pleased all who have heard it here. Adieu. I am your most obedient son

WOLFGANG AMADÉ MOZART

(253a) *Maria Anna Mozart to her Husband*

[Autograph in the Mozarteum, Salzburg]

MY DEAR HUSBAND,   [MANNHEIM, 3 *December* 1777[3]]
You see that I can't write very much to you, as Wolfgang has left me no room. In any case he has told you all there is to tell, so that I have no more news for you about our affairs. Often I just wish that I could spend at least one day with you, so that I could talk to you about all the things we cannot write about. To do so is quite impossible, for the letters would be far too long. We write to you twice every week, so you ought to get as many letters as we do. Addio. Keep well. I kiss you both many 100000 times and remain your faithful wife

MARIA ANNA MOZART

All sorts of messages to all our acquaintances.

---

[1] Georg Wenzel Ritter (1748–1808), bassoon-player, was appointed in 1768 to the Mannheim orchestra, which he followed to Munich in 1778. In 1788 he took an appointment under King Frederick William II of Prussia.   [2] K. 222 [205a], composed in 1775.
[3] A postscript to Mozart's letter, written on the cover.

(254) *Mozart to his Cousin, Maria Anna Thekla Mozart, Augsburg*

[*Copy in the Mozarteum, Salzburg*]

[MANNHEIM, 3 *December* 1777]

MA TRÈS CHÈRE COUSINE!

Before I write to you, I must go to the closet. Well, that's over. Ah! At last I feel lighter, a weight is off my heart; and now I can guzzle again. Oh, oh, when you've emptied yourself, life is far more worth living. Your letter of November 25th would have reached me safely, if you hadn't written that you had had pains in your head, throat and arms; but as you say that now, at the moment, for the present, for the nonce, at this instant you feel no more pains, I have safely received your letter of November 26th. Yes, yes, my dearest Miss Cousin, thus has it been since days of old, Tom has the purse and Dick has the gold; and what do you hold it with? with your ☜, don't you? Huzza, copper-smith, come, be a man, catch if you can, lick my arse, copper-smith. Yes, and true it is that whosoever believes it, is happy and whosoever does not, will go to Heaven, but straight, and not in the way I am writing. You see now that I can write just as I like, both fair and untidy, both straight and crooked. The other day I was in a bad humour and I wrote a fair, straight and serious hand; today I am in good spirits and I am writing an untidy, crooked and jolly one. So all depends now on what you prefer. You must make the choice (I have no medium article to offer you) between fair and untidy, straight and crooked, serious and jolly, the three first or the three last. I expect to hear your decision in your next letter. My decision is taken; when it's necessary, I go somewhere; but it all depends on circumstances. If I have diarrhœa, I run: and if I can't contain myself any longer, I shit into my trousers. God preserve thee, foot, on the window-sill lies the hamstring. I am much obliged to you, my dear Miss Cousin, for the compliments from your Fräulein Freysinger, which your dear Fräulein Juliana has been so kind as to send me. You say: 'I could tell you a great deal more, but too much is more than enough'. In *one* letter it is too much, I admit, but one can write a great deal by instalments. You see what I mean? As for the sonata,[1] she must possess herself in patience for a little longer. If it had been for my dear coz, it would have been finished long ago. Who knows whether Mlle Freysinger hasn't forgotten all about it? All the same I'll get it done as soon as possible, write a letter to accompany it and beg my dear coz to deliver them safely. A propos, since I left Augsburg, I have not taken off my trousers, except at night before going to bed. What will you think when you hear that I am still in

---

[1] See p. 359, n. 1.

Mannheim, dug in? It is due to my not having left and gone somewhere else! But now I think that I shall soon leave Mannheim. Yet Augsburg, through you, can continue to write to me and address letters to Mannheim until further notice. My uncle, my aunt and my cousin send their greetings to my Mamma and to me. They were very anxious about us and thought that we must be ill, as they had received no letter from us for so long. But at last to their delight they received the day before yesterday our letter of November 26th, and today, December 3rd, they have had the pleasure of replying to me. So I am to keep my promise to you? Ah, you are glad to hear this. Be sure you don't forget to compose the Munich for sonata, for what one has once performed, one must promise, one must always be a word of one's man. Well, let's be serious.

I must tell you something very briefly. I did not lunch at home today, but with a certain Mr. Wendling. Now you must know that he always takes his lunch at two o'clock, that he is married and has a daughter who, however, is always ailing. His wife is singing in the new opera and he plays the flute. Well, can you believe it, but when it was half past one we all, except the daughter who stayed in bed, we all, I say, sat down to table and began to eat.

Please give a whole arseful of greetings from us both to all our good friends. Our remembrances to your parents will be found on Page 3, line 12. Well, I've no more news to give you, save that an old cow has shit some new muck. So now adieu, Anna Maria Schlosser, née Schlüsselmacher. Take care of yourself and continue to love me. Write without delay, for it is cold today and keep your promise too or else forsooth I'll spue. Adieu, mon Dieu, I send you a great dollop of kisses, slap bang wollop!

Mannheim	Ma très chère cousine,
without slime,	Were you never in Berlin?
The 3rd of December,	Your cousin of virtues rare
Today's not an Ember,	In weather foul or fair
1777 in dark obscurity,	W. A. MOZART,
From now to all eternity	Who shits without a fart.
Amen.	

(255) *Leopold Mozart to his Wife and Son*

[*Extract*]   [*Autograph in the Mozarteum, Salzburg*]

SALZBURG, 4 *December* 1777

MY DEAR WIFE AND DEAR SON!

That you have had to await the result of what you wrote to me about I quite understand. Further, you need not have troubled to describe all that happened contrary to what I was expecting and to what would have been to our advantage, as it is all over now and can no longer be remedied. But that you, my son, should tell me *that all planning is needless and useless, since after all we do not know what is going to happen*, argues indeed a scattered brain; and you must have written that quite thoughtlessly. No sensible man, I need hardly say, no Christian will deny that *all things will and must happen in accordance with the will of God*. But does it follow therefore that on all occasions we are to act blindly, ever live carelessly, make no plans and merely wait until something drops down from the sky of its own accord? Does not God himself and do not all sensible folk require that in all our actions we should consider, as far as our human reason enables us to, their consequences and their result, and should endeavour to see as far ahead as we can? Now if this is essential in all our actions, how much more necessary is it not in your present circumstances and on a journey? Surely you have already experienced some of the consequences of your actions? Or do you really think that it is enough to have made that démarche ⟨*to the Elector with a view to spending the winter in Mannheim?*⟩ Surely you must think out, as you ought to have done long ago, a plan which you can adopt, if this present business should not come off. And surely you ought to have told me about it long ago and obtained my views. And now you write—what? 'If after all we do leave Mannheim we we shall go straight to Weilburg, to the Princess of Nassau-Weilburg (for whom you wrote the sonatas in Holland).[1] And there we shall remain as long as the ⟨*officers' table*⟩ is to our taste,'[2] What sort of a yarn is that? Those are the words, as are indeed all the remarks which precede them, of a man ⟨who has lost his reason⟩ and who is trying to delude himself and me. But ⟨you still hope⟩ to get six louis d'or, and that will make everything right. I should now like to enquire whether you know for certain that the Princess is there; if she is, there must be a special reason, seeing that her consort, on account of his military profession, has to reside at The Hague. Surely you ought to have told me this long ago? There is another question—whether you would not do better to go to Mainz— and thence to Weilburg via Frankfurt; for if you now go straight to Weilburg, you will strike the road to Frankfurt; and as you are not staying in Weilburg for good, the road to Mainz will take you back through Frankfurt. But if you go to Mainz first and from there to Weilburg, you will have a short distance to go from Weilburg to Coblenz via Nassau. But perhaps you want to give up Mainz, where we have so many good friends and where we took in from three concerts 200 gulden, although we did not play before the Elector, who happened to be ill. Tell me, my dear son, do you really think now that these are useless

---

[1] K. 26–31, six sonatas for the clavier with violin accompaniment, written for and dedicated to the Princess Caroline of Nassau-Weilburg in 1766.   [2] See p. 391.

speculations? Our dear good Mamma promised: 'I shall keep a careful account of our expenses'. Excellent! I do not ask and have never dreamt of asking you to produce detailed statements of your expenditure. But when you reached Augsburg, you might have written to say, 'We paid out so much at Albert's in Munich, and so much slipped away in travelling expenses, so that we now have such and such a sum'. You wrote to me from Augsburg that in spite of what you took in at your concert you were about twenty gulden on the wrong side. You ought to have told me at least in your second letter from Mannheim that the journey cost you so much and that now you stood as follows . . . and then I should have made arrangements in time. But perhaps you think that my plan to provide you with a letter of credit for Augsburg was also an unnecessary precaution? Do you imagine that Herr Herzog, *who is a good friend of mine*, would in response to all your letters from Mannheim have provided you with money? Far from it! The most he might have done would have been to make enquiries from me first. Why was I not to hear from you that you needed money, until you were absolutely down and out? ⟨*You wanted to wait and see what the Elector would give you.*⟩ Your object in acting thus was to prevent me from worrying. But it would have cost me far less anxiety if I had been told everything quite frankly and in good time. For I know even better than you do that on such journeys a man must be prepared for all emergencies, if he is not to be unpleasantly embarrassed at some moment when he is least expecting it. In such moments all one's *friends* disappear! *One should be cheerful and enjoy oneself, I admit*. But at other times *one should be serious*; and travelling is a serious occupation, during which not a day should be wasted. The days which at this season are short and moreover cost money in an inn, slip away rapidly. Good God! You ask me not to plan ahead, although ⟨*it is solely on your account that I am in debt to the extent of 450 gulden;*⟩ and you think perhaps to put me in a good humour by sending me a hundred silly jokes. I am delighted when you are in good spirits; but instead of the greetings you sent in the form of an alphabet,[1] I should have been better pleased if you had sent me the reasons for your proposed journey to

★ ★ Weilburg. In a word, this is not unnecessary circumspection. Whoever acts otherwise is a stupid, careless fellow who, particularly *in the world as it is today*, with all his cleverness will always be left behind, and may even meet disaster, the more so as he is sure to be taken in by flatterers, fawners and back-biters. Mark well, my son, that *to find one man in a thousand*, who is your true friend from unselfish motives, is to find *one of the greatest wonders of this world*. Think of all those who call themselves or seem to be your friends and you will surely detect some reason why they act thus. If they are not self-interested themselves, then probably they are professing

[1] See pp. 391, 392.

friendship in the interest of some other friend, who is necessary to them;
or they keep up their friendship with you in order by picking you out, to
cause a third person annoyance. If this letter does not reach you in Mann-   ★
heim, that is, if you are in Weilburg already, I cannot help you. But if you
are still at Mannheim and have to leave, then Mamma will see on the map
that your best move is to go to Mainz first, or else Mainz will have to be
omitted or you will have to come back a bit on your route. Remember
that in Weilburg, where everyone is ⟨either Lutheran or Calvinist,⟩ you
will not find ⟨a Catholic church.⟩ So I do not want you ⟨to stay there too
long.⟩

And who informed you, pray, that from Würzburg to Mannheim would
take you through the Forest of Spessart, which, as everyone knows, is
near Aschaffenburg and between Fulda and Frankfurt? It was probably
Herr Beecke who told you that cock and bull story. Why, Aschaffenburg
and Würzburg are ten miles apart.   ★

You must now seriously consider how you are going to deal with your
present difficulties, travel with all possible economy and make sensible
plans. Under no circumstances must you sell our chaise. God keep you
both and myself. Nannerl and I kiss you many 100000000 times and I am
your old husband and father

MZT

Count Czernin asks me to send you his greetings. There was a rumour
the other day that the Archbishop was not only sending Haydn to Italy
but that he had wanted to send him off to Bozen with Triendl, who,
however, had got out of it. My dear Wolfgang, I beg you to think out
your plans and to give up writing to me about matters which are over
and done with. Otherwise we shall all be most unhappy.

(256) *Mozart to his Father*

[*Autograph in the Mozarteum, Salzburg*]

MANNHEIM, 6 *December* 1777

MON TRÉS CHER PÉRE!

I can still tell you nothing more. I'm beginning to get sick of this joke.
I am only curious now as to how it will end. ⟨Count Savioli⟩ has already
spoken three times ⟨to the Elector and each time his reply has been⟩ a
shrug of the shoulders and the remark that he would certainly ⟨give me
an answer, but that he had not yet made up his mind.⟩ My good friends
quite agree with me that all this hesitation and reserve is rather a good
sign than a bad one. ⟨For if the Elector had no intention of taking me on

407

at all, he would have said so at once; as it is,⟩ I attribute this delay to—
⟨denari siamo un poco scrocconi.⟩[1] Moreover I know for a fact that ⟨the
Elector likes me.⟩ A buon conto, we must just wait a little longer. I may
say at once that I should be glad ⟨if the affair turned out well,⟩ as otherwise I should regret ⟨having sat about here for so long and wasted our
money.⟩ However, come what may, it can never be bad, if it is in accordance with God's will; and that it may be so is my daily prayer. Papa is
right in his guess as to the chief reason ⟨for Herr Cannabich's friendship.⟩
But there is one other little matter for which ⟨he can make use of me.⟩
He has to produce selections of all ⟨his ballet music,⟩ but these must be
arranged for ⟨the clavier.⟩ He is quite unable to transcribe them in such a
way as to render them effective and at the same time easy. So he finds me
very handy ⟨for this,⟩ as he did on one occasion already when I arranged
a contredanse for him.[2] He has been away hunting for the last eight days
and doesn't return until next Tuesday. Such things, of course, contribute
⟨a good deal to a close friendship,⟩ but all the same I do not think, to say
the least, that he ⟨would work against me;⟩ for he has altered considerably.
When a man reaches a certain age and sees his children growing up, his
ideas are bound to change a little. His daughter who is fifteen, his eldest
child, is a very pretty and charming girl. She is very intelligent and steady
for her age. She is serious, does not say much, but when she does speak,
she is pleasant and amiable. Yesterday she again gave me indescribable
pleasure; she played the whole of my sonata—excellently. The Andante
(which must *not be taken too quickly*) she plays with the utmost expression.
Moreover she likes playing it. I had already finished the Allegro, as you
know, on the day after my arrival, and thus had only seen Mlle Cannabich
once. Young Danner asked me how I thought of composing the Andante.
I said that I would make it fit closely the character of Mlle Rosa. When I
played it, it was an extraordinary success. Young Danner told me so
afterwards. It really is a fact. She is exactly like the Andante. I hope that
you received the sonata safely. Your letter of December 1st reached us
this morning. Today I lunched with Wendling for the sixth time and
with Schweitzer for the second. Tomorrow for a change I shall lunch
there again. I go there regularly for meals. But now I must go to bed.
I wish you both good night.

(256a) *Maria Anna Mozart to her Husband*

[*Autograph in the Mozarteum, Salzburg*]

[MANNHEIM, 7 *December* 1777]
    Wolfgang is lunching with Herr Wendling today, December 7th. So
I am at home alone, as I usually am, and have to put up with the most

---

[1] We are a little stingy with the cash.   [2] There is no trace of these compositions.

horrible cold. For even if they light a small fire, they never put any more coal on it, so that when it burns out, the room gets cold again. A little fire of this kind costs twelve kreuzer. So I make them light one in the morning, when we get up, and another in the evening. During the day I have to put up with dreadful cold. As I write I can hardly hold my pen, I am freezing so. You must not be so accommodating about Herr Hamm. As it is, 200 gulden is little enough, for that will include her laundry. You must bear in mind all our expenses. In a convent she would have to pay 100 gulden for food and drink alone, and that would not include a teacher and other extras. So charge him what is right and see that you make some profit for your trouble. Only death costs nothing—and even that's not true. I am really delighted that you have given Jungfer Sandl[1] that room, for she is a good girl and will not give you much trouble. Up to the present we have not been to any balls and only to one gala play, for the tickets are very expensive. You have to pay 45 kreuzer in the parterre and 1 gulden in the cheaper boxes, and besides you have to get there early, if you want to be sure of a good seat. So we have not bothered. No one gets in free. Everyone has to pay, both performers in the orchestra and those connected with the theatre, for the Elector pays them all and gives them large salaries. The leading actor in the theatre, Herr Marchand,[2] gets 3000 gulden a year, and the most wretched singer, even a beginner, gets 600. In the orchestra too they get fine salaries. Herr Cannabich as Director now draws 1800 gulden, Herr Fränzl as Konzertmeister 1400 gulden, Kapellmeister Holzbauer almost 3000 gulden, and in addition they get presents for any new compositions. Rather different this from ⟨Salzburg.⟩ It makes your mouth water. We are now relying on that God who, if it is His divine will, will see to it that the ⟨Elector⟩ will retain us. Things are moving a bit slowly. We must just wait and see, and be grateful for the time being that he has not refused altogether.

(256b) *Mozart resumes writing*

[Autograph in the Mozarteum, Salzburg]

I have just this moment come back from Wendling's. As soon as I have taken this letter to the post I shall run off there again, for they are going to rehearse the opera[3] *in camera caritatis*.[4] At 6.30 I am going on to Cannabich's to give my usual daily lesson on the clavier.

A propos. I must correct a statement I made. I told you yesterday that Mlle Cannabich was 15; she is, however, only 13, though she is getting

---

[1] Sandl Auer was a poor cap-mender to whom Leopold Mozart had offered a room at the back of his house. He had mentioned this in Letter 252 (portion omitted).

[2] Theobald Marchand. See p. 582, n. 2.

[3] Schweitzer's *Rosemunde*.   [4] i.e. between ourselves.

on for 14. Our greetings to all our good friends, especially to Herr Bullinger. Mamma is burning with indignation, rage and jealousy at the thought that all that Papa has to do is to move the chest and open the door in order to get to that pretty young chambermaid.[1] I assure you that I deeply regret that I am away from Salzburg, as this would have been a splendid opportunity for me to forget all my troubles in the arms of such a beautiful, charming, blue-nosed maiden. But so it had to be. I must just console myself with the thought that there are many women quite as fair. Now I must close, or else I shall miss the post. Hoping (for the third time!) that in my next letter I really shall have some news to tell you, whether it means a fulfilment of our hopes or not, I kiss your hands 1000 times and remain, as always,

your {most obedient son / faithful wife

WOLFG:AMADÉ MOZART
MARIA ANNA MOZART[2]

My sister,
Who sleeps at Sylvester,
I do embrace with all my might
In Lent as well as on Carnival night.

(257) *Leopold Mozart to his Son*

[Extract]   [*Autograph in the Mozarteum, Salzburg*]

MON TRÈS CHER FILS!   SALZBURG, 8 *December* 1777

It is evident that we have not understood one another. The step you took was, in my opinion, well taken and my letters told you so. But did you write to tell me whether you had made any plans or not? And as to whether the step you took led to anything? Not a single word! But suddenly I get your letter, saying: ⟨'*The present was a gold watch. In view of our journey I should have much preferred some money.*'⟩ Then you go on to say: 'I called on Herr Schmalz ⟨*who excused himself by remarking that he had orders to give me money*'.⟩ What else could I gather from these statements but that ⟨you wanted to leave and could not do so for lack of money?⟩ Surely you must understand my astonishment at having news like this dumped on me when I was least expecting it, and particularly as you had never prepared me for it. How?—What?—Why?—Whither? If you had only said that you were staying on, ⟨that you were *intending to spend the winter in Mannheim*, that you had *approached* the Elector or were proposing to do so,⟩ then Nannerl, Bullinger and I would have understood

---

[1] Sandl Auer, see p. 409, n. 1.   [2] This signature is in Mozart's handwriting.

everything quite clearly and would not have been anxious. At the same time I was aware that a prolonged stay in any one centre meant money. So naturally I was plagued by a thousand thoughts and I had to write a great many things to you which I otherwise should not have written.

You are convinced that I should *never be able to adapt myself equally to good fortune or bad fortune.* True, for there is only one occasion when I *can* adapt myself, and that is, when in spite of all the preparations which I have made, ill luck comes upon me. Then I have nothing with which to reproach myself. When I was dangerously ill in England,[1] I had thought out already the arrangements for entrusting you to safe hands in the event of my death. And during the dangerous illnesses of yourself and Nannerl at The Hague[2] and at Olmütz,[3] Mamma and I managed to comfort one another. But the fact remains that in all our misfortunes we always knew where to get money. However, my mind is now at rest and ★
I am prepared for any eventuality. Your anxiety that your affairs should be kept secret is quite unnecessary. For do you imagine for one moment that I would give ⟨the *Archbishop, who seems to hear everything, an opportunity of laughing at us,*⟩ if nothing should come of your scheme? Can you believe this of me? I have not yet told you that after you left, everybody kept on asking me, *where you were going to?* I always replied, as I still do, that I did not know myself. Indeed I could say so truthfully, as at the time I did not know. They read about Augsburg in the papers and Baron Schafmann wrote about Mannheim. When people ask me with a significant look why you are still in Mannheim, I always say that I myself do not know whether you are still there. You stayed on there for the Elector's name-day and perhaps you may not leave now until after his birthday, which is December 12th. For, if I remember rightly, he was born on 10 or 12 December, 1724.[4] Well, enough of this. But nothing makes my heart so heavy or makes me feel so restless as *ignorance and doubt* and anxiety for those who are more precious to me than *life itself.* I should like you to remain in Mannheim for the winter, particularly as a long journey at this time would not be very suitable for Mamma. So I have been wondering what better arrangement could be made. ⟨*If you are appointed to instruct the young Count,*⟩ you will have ample opportunity ⟨*of ingratiating yourself with the Elector;*⟩ and I need hardly tell you ⟨*that you must make a good friend of the governess too.*⟩ The last point in your letter about which I have something to say is your wild statement that *happiness consists only in imagination.* I quite agree. But would you apply your dictum so universally that, for instance, a traveller who is ⟨stranded in an inn or a post-house without money with which to proceed on his journey⟩ and who is exposed, in consequence, to the rude taunts ⟨of a landlord or a postmaster,⟩

---

[1] In 1764.　　　　　[2] In 1765.　　　　　[3] In 1767.
[4] The Elector Karl Theodor was born on 1 December 1724.

ought to console himself with the thought that happiness consists only in imagination?—My dear Wolfgang, this dictum is a moral saw only applicable to people who are perpetually discontented. Most of us, nay almost all of us, are never content, and everyone considers his neighbour to be more fortunate than himself. So this saying is to instruct, guide, and remind us that everyone should be content with his station in life and should not envy his neighbour, whom he probably never would envy, if he were thoroughly well acquainted with the private circumstances of the latter. For we always judge by appearances, and most people are careful to hide their real misfortunes.

★ There is a rumour that a handsome winter suit has been ordered in the guardarobba for Herr Haydn on the occasion of his journey to Italy. How I should like to hear him talking to the Italians in Italy! They will certainly
★ exclaim: 'Questo è un vero tedesco!'[1] Now I must close, for the sheet is really covered, quite seriously—not, as it was in your case, to provide a joke. If you stay on in Mannheim, I shall send you the two sonatas a quattro mani,[2] copied out on small paper for your two pupils. We kiss you both with all our hearts and wish you good health and so forth and along with Nannerl I am your young husband and father

MZT

★ Greetings upon greetings!—you must imagine them yourselves, for there are so many of them that I have not been able to make a note of them, remember them and write them down. Bimperl is barking and drowning them all with the row she is making at the moment.[3]

(257a) *Nannerl Mozart to her Mother and Brother*

[Autograph in the Mozarteum, Salzburg]

[SALZBURG, 8 December 1777[4]]

I am really delighted that, thank God, you are both well. We are as fit as one can be in this dull Salzburg. Thanks for the first movement and the Andante of your sonata which I have already played through. The Andante requires indeed great concentration and exactness in playing. But I like the sonata very much. One can see from its style that you composed it in Mannheim. I am now looking forward to the Rondo. The wife of Anton Lodron, the Marshal of the Court, has died. There is no other news. I do hope that you will be able to stay in Mannheim for the winter, as it would be too trying for Mamma to have to travel at this

---

[1] He's a real German!
[2] Probably K. 381 [123a] and 358 [186c], composed in 1772 and 1773–1774.
[3] This postscript follows Nannerl's letter.   [4] A postscript to her father's letter.

time of the year. Keep well, both of you, and do think of us very often.
I kiss Mamma's hands and embrace my brother.

(258) *Mozart to his Father*

[*Autograph in the Mozarteum, Salzburg*]

MANNHEIM, 10 *December* 1777

MON TRÉS CHER PÉRE!

There's nothing to be hoped for at present ⟨from the Elector⟩. The
day before yesterday I went to the concert at Court to get ⟨his answer.
Count Savioli⟩ studiously avoided me, but I made my way up to him.
When he saw me, he shrugged his shoulders. What,' I said, 'no answer
yet?' 'Please forgive me,' he replied, 'unfortunately none.' '*Eh bien,*' I
said, 'the Elector might have told me so before.' 'True,' he said, 'but he
would not have made up his mind even now, if I had not prodded him
and pointed out that you had been hanging on here for such a long time
and were using up all your money at the inn.' 'That's what worries me
most of all', I retorted. 'It's not at all nice. However, I am very much
obliged to you, Count (we don't address him as Your Excellency), for
having taken such an interest in me, and I beg you to thank ⟨the Elector⟩
on my behalf for his gracious though belated reply and to say that I can
assure him that he would never have regretted it if he had taken me on.'
'Oh,' he replied, 'I am surer of that than you think.' I then told Wendling
about the decision. He went quite red in the face and remarked very
angrily: 'We must find some way out. You must stay here, at least for
the next two months until we can go to Paris together. Cannabich returns
from his hunting tomorrow. We can then discuss the matter further.'
Whereupon I left the concert and went straight to Madame Cannabich.
Our Treasurer came with me. He is an excellent fellow and a good friend
of mine. On the way I told him what had happened. You cannot imagine
how wild the fellow became. When we entered the room, he burst out
at once: 'Well, here's another who has been favoured with the usual nice
treatment they deal you out ⟨at Court.⟩' 'What,' exclaimed Madame,
'so nothing has come of it?' I told them the whole story. They then told
me about all kinds of pretty pranks which have been played on people
here. Mlle Rosa was three rooms off and busy with the laundry at the
time. When she had finished she came in and said to me: 'Are you ready
to begin?' For it was time for our lesson. 'I am at your service', I replied.
'But we must have a really serious lesson today', she said. 'We certainly
must,' I rejoined, 'for we shan't have the chance much longer.' 'Why?
What's this?' She went up to her mother who told her. 'What?' she said,

'is it really true? I can't believe it.' 'Yes, yes, quite true', her mother said. Thereupon Mlle Rosa played my sonata very seriously. I assure you, I couldn't keep from weeping. In the end the mother, the daughter and the Treasurer all had tears in their eyes. For she had been playing my sonata, which is the favourite of the whole house. 'I say', said the Treasurer, 'If the Kapellmeister (they never call me anything else here) leaves us, he will make us all weep.' I must say that I have some very kind friends here. Indeed it is at times like these that one gets to know their worth. For they are friends not only in words but in deeds.

Let me tell you just one thing more. The other day I went to lunch at Wendling's as usual. 'Our Indian', he said, meaning a Dutchman,[1] a gentleman of means and a lover of all the sciences, who is a great friend and ⟨admirer⟩ of mine, 'our Indian is really a first-rate fellow. He is willing to give you 200 gulden if you will compose for him three short, simple concertos and a couple of quartets for the flute. Through Cannabich you can get at least two pupils who will pay well. You can compose duets for clavier and violin here and have them engraved *par souscription*. Your lunch and supper you can always have with us. You can lodge at the Privy Court Councillor's.[2] All that will cost you nothing. For your mother we shall find some cheap lodging for the next two months until you have written home about all our plans. Your Mamma can then travel home and we can go on to Paris.' Mamma is quite satisfied with this arrangement and it only remains for you to give your consent. I am so certain of it that if it were now the time to travel, I should go off to Paris without waiting for an answer. For no other answer could be expected from a father who is so sensible and has shown himself up to the present so anxious for the welfare of his children. Herr Wendling who sends you his compliments is a bosom friend of our bosom friend Grimm. The latter, when he was here, said a good deal about me to Wendling, I mean, when he came here after seeing us in Salzburg. As soon as I get your reply to this letter I shall write to him, for I have it from a stranger, whom I met at table here, that he is now in Paris. As we shall not be leaving before March 6th, I should also be glad if, through Herr Mesmer in Vienna or somebody or other, you could possibly arrange for me to get a letter to the Queen of France—but only if there's no difficulty about it; it's really of no great importance, though undoubtedly it would be better to have it. This was also a suggestion of Herr Wendling's'. I can magine that what I have written will seem strange to you, living as you are in a town where one is accustomed to having stupid enemies or weak and silly friends who, because ⟨Salzburg's⟩ stodgy bread is indispensable to them, are always toadying and are consequently one thing one day and

---

[1] Ferdinand De Jean (or Dechamps), a German by birth, who was a surgeon with the Dutch East India Co. and an amateur flautist.   [2] Serrarius.

another the next. You see, that was just the reason why I have kept on writing childish nonsense and jokes to you and have rarely been serious. I wanted to wait for the upshot of the whole affair here in order to save you from worry and to spare my good friends, on whom (though they are quite innocent) you are perhaps throwing all the blame, as though they had been working against me in secret. That is certainly not the case. I know well enough who was the cause! However, your letters have compelled me to tell you the whole story. But I implore you, for Heaven's sake do not upset yourself about it; God willed it so. Bear in mind this only too certain truth that it is not always possible for a man to do what he proposes. He often thinks—'This would be very pleasant, and that would be very bad and undesirable'; and when it comes about, he often finds it is just the opposite. Well, I must go to bed now. I shall have quite enough to write during the next two months, three concertos, two quartets, four or six duets for the clavier. And then I have an idea of writing a new grand mass and presenting ⟨it to the Elector.⟩ Adieu. Please reply at once to all my questions. I kiss your hands 100000 times and embrace my sister with all my heart and remain your most obedient son

WOLFGANG AMADE MOZART

Baron Dürnitz was not in Munich when I was there. I shall write to Prince ⟨Zeill⟩ on the next post-day and ask him to ⟨push on with⟩ my Munich scheme. If you would write to him too, I should be very glad. But be short and to the point; and let there be ⟨no cringing,⟩ for I cannot bear that. One thing is quite certain, if he wants to, he can ⟨fix it up;⟩ for all ⟨Munich⟩ told me so.

(258a) *Maria Anna Mozart to her Husband*

[Autograph in the Koch Collection, Basel]

[MANNHEIM, 11 December 1777]

MY DEAR HUSBAND,

You insist on knowing how much we have spent on our journey. We told you about Albert's account and that our bill in Augsburg was 300 gulden. Wolfgang told you that we were 24 gulden on the wrong side; but he forgot to include the expenses of the concert, which were 16 gulden, and also our landlord's account. Thus by the time we got to Mannheim we had only about 60 gulden in all. So if we had gone off again after a fortnight, we should not have had much left. For travelling expenses have gone up a lot since everything has become so dear. It is not anything like what it used to be, you would be surprised. As for Wolfgang's journey to Paris, you must think it over and let us know if you approve. At this time of the year Paris is the only place where there is anything doing. Monsieur Wendling is an honest fellow, as everybody knows. He has travelled far and wide and has been to Paris thirteen times already. He knows every stick and stone there; and then our friend Herr Grimm is his best friend and has done a lot for him. So make up your mind and whatever you decide will suit me. Herr Wendling has assured me that he will be a father to Wolfgang, whom he loves as if he were his own son; and Wolfgang will be looked after as well as if he were with me. As you may imagine, I myself do not like to let him go, nor do I like to have to travel home alone, it is such an awful distance. I can't bear to think of it. But what can we do? I am too old to undertake such a long journey to Paris and besides it would cost too much. To travel à quatre is much cheaper than to meet all one's expenses oneself. I shall write more next post-day. Today I have a headache and I think I am in for a cold. It is bitterly cold here. I am so frozen that I can hardly hold my pen. Wolfgang has gone out to look at lodgings. The cheap ones are very scarce here, but there are plenty of expensive ones. Tell Nannerl that people do not wear jackets here except indoors. Out-of-doors they wear chiefly cloaks and capes. The caps they wear are much prettier than what we wear in Salzburg and quite different—their frisure is quite wonderful, nothing piled up at all. The women are very smartly dressed. If it were not such a distance, I would send Nannerl a cap and a Palatine. Addio. Keep well, both of you. I kiss you many 1000000 times and remain your faithful wife

11 December 1777   MARIA ANNA MOZART

All sorts of messages to all our good friends, especially to Bullinger, Jungfer Sallerl, Katherl Gilowsky, the Andretters, Hagenauers, Robinigs, Frau von Gerlichs, the Schiedenhofens, Mölks, Jungfrau Mitzerl, Herr Gött, Jungfrau Sandl, Theresa.

A kiss for Bimperl.

(259) *Leopold Mozart to his Son*

[*Extract*]   [*Autograph in the Mozarteum, Salzburg*]

SALZBURG, 11 *December* 1777

MON TRÉS CHER FILS!

I received safely on the 9th your letter of the 3rd. It is a great pity that all your letters reach us on *Tuesdays and Fridays*, since we cannot reply to them before Thursdays and Mondays. Nannerl plays your whole sonata[1] excellently and with great expression. If you leave Mannheim, *as I now presume you will*, I shall have it copied and enclose a small sheet in every

---

[1] Probably K. 309 [284b].

letter, so that you may have it again. Your sonata is a strange composition. ★
It has something in it of the *rather artificial* Mannheim style, but so very
little that your own good style is not spoilt thereby. I am assuming that
you will leave Mannheim, for you ⟨told Count Savioli⟩ that you feared
that the Elector ⟨would give you so little during the winter that it would be
impossible for you to stay.⟩ But though he does not intend ⟨to appoint you
permanently,⟩ he may be wondering whether you may not stay on after
all and he may therefore be hesitating to take a decision. So the logical
conclusion ⟨is that *he is not going to retain you.*⟩ Basta! Well, it is all over
now and God knows where you will be reading this letter. Your next one
which I am expecting tomorrow will surely tell me. If you had thought ★
things out a bit beforehand, you would have taken with you your
testimonials and so forth from Padre Martini and shown them to the
Elector. You must surely know that he thinks the world of Padre Martini
and that he sent Herr Ritschel,[1] whom he afterwards appointed his
Deputy-Kapellmeister, to be trained by him, and after Ritschel's death,
Vogler also. Besides you surely know that Martini dedicated Part II of
his book to the Elector?[2] You ought at least to have shown Count Savioli
your diplomas from the Academies and your testimonials, the more so as
Italians are always impressed by these public tributes from their fellow-
countrymen. For even though you may have convinced all the leading
musicians in Mannheim of your knowledge of composition, does it
follow that the Elector is aware of it? Have these gentlemen an opportunity
of telling him? *And would they want to tell him?* The Elector knows that
you are a *competent clavier-player*, but he has had no opportunity of
hearing *what you can do* in the way of composition. I am not going to say
anything more about having your works copied, which you ought to
have arranged during your long visits to Munich and Augsburg, since
the farther you travel the more expensive does copying become. You
will remember, however, that I was very much against your taking so
many symphonies with you. I just picked out a good number of them,
but I naturally thought that you would leave some of them behind. Yet
instead of putting several aside, you added to them others, and thus made
such an enormous pile that you could not pack any of your church music.
If I had not been so ill that I could hardly speak, I should not have let you
take more than about four or six symphonies with the parts doubled for
concert use, and all the others in single parts or in their original scores.
Could you not have performed in Mannheim your Haffner music,[3] your
concertone[4] or one of your Lodron serenades?[5] I suppose that the Elector

---

[1] Johannes Ritschel, who was deputy Kapellmeister at Mannheim from 1764 until his death
in 1766.
[2] Part II of his *Storia della musica*, published in 1770.   [3] K. 250 [248b], written in 1776.
[4] K. 190 [186E], for two violins and orchestra, written in 1774.
[5] K. 247 and 287 [271H]. See p. 289, n. 2.

never has music except when there is a gala concert—and that Herr
Cannabich has already provided for such occasions.

If you have left Mannheim, I trust that before your departure you got
Herr Wendling *to give you a few letters of introduction or some addresses in
Paris*—and that you have found out from him where *he lived*—and where
he used to lunch. If you have not done so, write to him at once and ask him
⌐   *for all these.* You must make a point of getting hold of some honest person
who will direct you immediately to a comfortable and inexpensive
lodging, so that you may not have to stay at an inn nor, if possible, even
★ have to put up at one at all. Your conscience, if you will hear its voice,
must be reminding you that you have kept on postponing many things
which you ought to have done. For example, you ought to have had
your 'Misericordias'[1] copied, as soon as it was returned to you from
Augsburg, since it is not a big work; you ought to have enquired whether
the court copyist would not copy one of your masses for the Elector, as
was done with your 'Misericordias' in Munich; you ought to have hit on
the idea ⟨*about his natural children, your variations and your Rondo*⟩[2] much
earlier and immediately after you received his present—and indeed many
other things which the above remarks and my frequent questions must
★ recall to your mind. Your idea about travelling to Paris with Herr
Wendling is not to be rejected entirely. There is time to think it over. It
★ all depends where you will be in Lent. I fully realize how much money
can be made in Paris and told you this in my last letter. If M. Grimm is
there, then your fortune is made. If not, no doubt you will make fresh
★ acquaintances. If you have left Mannheim, you ought to go straight to
Paris and I shall fire off at once a letter to M. Grimm and send you
particulars of all our old acquaintances there. If you are in Mainz, you will
know from one of my letters what you can do there. I now close with the
hope that God may keep you in good health, for which I pray to Him
constantly, and with the earnest reminder that you must take the greatest
care of it. For a break-down would be our most crushing misfortune and
would plunge us all into the deepest misery. I dare not remember that I
⟨now owe more than six hundred gulden⟩—or else—

Nannerl and I kiss you millions of times. We both send you our
greetings and I remain your old husband and father

MZT

★   The castrato[3] is now living at the fencing-master's and goes to Varesco[4]
for his meals. Addio!

¹ K. 222 [205a]. See pp. 378 and 402.
² This rather obscure passage is an allusion to Mozart's Letter 251, in which he tells his
father that he made a present of these two compositions to the Elector's children.
³ Francesco Ceccarelli.
⁴ Abbate Giambattista Varesco, who since 1766 had been court chaplain in Salzburg. He
wrote the Italian libretti for Mozart's opera seria *Idomeneo*, 1781, and for his unfinished opera
buffa *L' oca del Cairo*, 1783.

MY DEAR WIFE,

I am delighted to hear that you are well, but I am rather anxious as to whether you have really left Mannheim, for travelling in winter must be very uncomfortable for you. You must protect yourself from the cold as well as you can and it would be better to buy another large fur. You did not take a foot-bag with you, although we have two. You say that if you were to tell me everything, your letters would be too long. But you see that I take a whole sheet, and that I write all over it and only leave room for the seal. I do this simply in order to tell you a great many things, and I write twice as much as you write to me—and yet I only pay six kreuzers. I trust that you too only pay six kreuzers for my very long letters. You see that I do not use separate covers and that I fill in all the empty spaces with writing. Indeed I too should like to talk to you. Oh, sometimes I cannot get you out of my head the whole day long, especially when I think of you, travelling in this cold weather—and of other things—which ought to have turned out very differently. God, however, will provide! But we human beings must also take thought; and in this world it is impossible by honest expedients only, to get on at Court. All sorts of ways and means have to be adopted. I well know how expensive a journey can be, and my oft-repeated reminders that you ought to look about for private rooms will have told you that I foresaw that your stay in Mannheim would be a long one. I realized what you wanted to do and suspected at the same time that the fulfilment of your plan might be delayed and perhaps in the end come to nothing. Inns are expensive, especially if you take supper there, though indeed, if you are frequently invited to a late lunch at a good table, you can content yourself with soup at night. As it is, these landlords ask quite enough for a room and so forth. Farewell. I try to comfort myself as well as I can and I remain your

honest husband

MZT

(260) *Maria Anna Mozart to her Husband and Daughter*

[*Autograph in the Mozarteum, Salzburg*]

MANNHEIM, 14 *December* 1777

MY DEAR HUSBAND AND NANNERL,

Thank God, we have left the inn at last and have a nice room now with two fine beds and an alcove in the house of a Privy Court Councillor.[1] I don't yet know his name. He has an excellent wife and a Mademoiselle of fifteen, who has been playing the clavier for eight years already and to

---

[1] Serrarius. See p. 414.

whom Wolfgang has to give lessons. For this we get free lodging, including wood and light. Wolfgang has his meals at Monsieur Wendling's
and I go for mine to young Herr Danner's, who in return for this takes
lessons in composition from my son. That is our present arrangement.
Wolfgang has such an awful lot to do that he really doesn't know whether
he is standing on his head or his heels. He lunched today with the wealthy
Dutchman[1] who is giving him 200 gulden for some compositions. He
hasn't come back yet and if he doesn't soon, I shan't be able to send off
this letter. It is almost four o'clock now. I could not write before, as I
was not lunching at home. I have not yet got our landlord's account. You
cannot imagine in what high favour Wolfgang is here both with the
orchestra and with other people. They all say that there is no one to
touch him. They absolutely idolize his compositions. Often I do not see
him all day long. I am at home alone most of the time, for on account
of the cold and wet weather I cannot go out much, as I have no umbrella
to put up when it snows or rains. The old and young Herren Danner
send their greetings to you; and Wolfgang and I send our compliments
to the whole population of Salzburg. I wish I could be with you just for
one day so that I could have a chat with you, for in a letter it is impossible
to describe everything in detail. Well, I shall close this letter, for Wolfgang
will not be able to write a great deal today. The post will be off in a
moment. Addio. I kiss you and Nannerl many 1000 times and remain
your faithful wife

MARIANNA MOZART

(260a) *Mozart to his Father*

[*Autograph in the Mozarteum, Salzburg*]

[MANNHEIM, 14 *December* 1777]

I can only write a few words. I did not get home until four o'clock,
and had to give a lesson at once to the daughter of the house.[2] It is almost
half past five now and therefore time to close this letter. I shall tell Mamma
always to start writing a few days in advance, so that I shan't have a dozen
things to do at once. For it's no longer easy for me to see to this; what
little time I have for writing I must devote to composition, as I have a lot
of work before me. As for my journey to Paris I implore you to let me
have an answer quickly. I played through my concertone[3] to Herr
Wendling on the clavier. He remarked that it was just the thing for Paris.

---

[1] De Jean (or Dechamps). See p. 414.   [2] Therese Pierron Serrarius.
[3] K. 190 [186E], composed in 1774.

When I play it to Baron Bagge,[1] he's quite beside himself. Adieu.

A fine handwriting and a glorious rigmarole, eh? I kiss your hands 100000 times and embrace my sister with all my heart and remain your most obedient son

WOLFGANG AMADÉ MOZART

My greetings to everyone in Salzburg and especially to Herr Bullinger.

(261) *Leopold Mozart to his Son*

[*Extract*]   [*Autograph in the Mozarteum, Salzburg*]

MON TRÈS CHER FILS!   SALZBURG, 15 *December* 1777

In the name of Heaven! Patience! For I too have nothing to say. Surely your business must be over by now—not at the moment of writing, but by the time you read this letter, which will be about the 21st. Almighty God grant that in accordance with His most holy will everything has turned out well. ⟨*If you have not been retained then you will have surely received a handsome sum for your travelling expenses.*⟩ I take it that you used your ⟨expenses in the inn⟩, your *total* expenses, as an excuse? ⟨*It would have pleased me best of all if you had been able to settle in Mannheim.*⟩ If I had been in your shoes, ⟨I should have *gone on teaching the Rondo and the variations to the children.* For, even if the Elector had not *given you a large salary now*, he would *soon have raised it.*⟩ Enough! We must resign ourselves to the will of God. But we must always do our best, and for that reason must always ⟨*take thought.*⟩ Have you ⟨*finished composing the ballets for Herr Cannabich?*⟩[2] I should have left myself plenty of time for that. From the very first moment when you told me of this business, I formed the opinion, and still hold it, that the only way to achieve success was ⟨through the children, or rather through the governess, and by thus *obtaining the opportunity of speaking to the Elector himself.* For although *Count Savioli*⟩ may mean well as far as you are concerned (a thing about which one can never be too sure in this wicked world), yet ⟨he may *not have the opportunity*⟩ of raising the matter very often or even have the courage to do so. Now I have nothing more to write about. I pity you, my dear wife, ★ for having to suffer so from the cold, although you pay 24 kreuzer a day for heating. And it must be even worse now, as we too have been having for some time the most extraordinarily cold weather. If I were you, I should look up and visit somebody who has a warm room, and whenever

---

[1] Baron Karl Ernst von Bagge (1718–1791), whose musical salon in Paris was famous. The Mozart family had met him in Paris in 1764. See the *Reiseaufzeichnungen*, p. 29 (*MBA*, No. 74). For a study of Baron Bagge see G. Cucuel, 'Le Baron de Bagge et son temps', in *L'Année Musicale*, no. 1, 1912.   [2] See p. 408.

I had to be at home, I should get into bed, rest my back against the pillows and cover myself up to the waist and then read or knit or sew or even play cards, or tell my fortune with the cards. If anyone should chance to call, you could say that you have a slight headache or make some other excuse. I should certainly do this rather than suffer from cold. You have both been away now for three months, that is, a quarter of a year. To me it already seems a year.

Is it necessary for me to ask whether Wolfgang is not getting a little lax perhaps ⟨about confession?⟩ God must come first! From His hands we receive our temporal happiness; and at the same time we must think of our eternal salvation. Young people do not like to hear about these things, I know, for I was once young myself. But, thank God, in spite of all my youthful foolish pranks, I always pulled myself together. I avoided all dangers to my soul and ever kept God and my honour and the consequences, the *very dangerous consequences* of foolishness, before my eyes. We have no news at all. We and all our good friends send you our greetings. We kiss you millions of times and while awaiting news from you constantly—and patiently, I remain your husband and father

MZT

Your daughter and sister

NANNERL

Nothing more is being said about Haydn's journey. We still have time to
★ wish you a Happy New Year.

A propos!—Is Wolfgang's beard going to be cut off, singed off, or
★ shaved off?

(262) *Leopold Mozart to his Son*

[*Extract*]   [*Autograph in the Mozarteum, Salzburg*]

MON TRÉS CHER FILS!   SALZBURG, 18 *December* 1777

The news contained in your letter of the 10th about the unfavourable result of your famous affair did not find me quite unprepared, for I had already hinted as much to Bullinger and your sister, and indeed I never expected anything else. You too will have gathered this from my letters. It is true that I should have been glad if you had been successful, for you could have undertaken other journeys from Mannheim from time to time just the same. Further you will have noticed in all my letters that I have been keeping my eye on Paris. I must now write to you very fully. You know that for many years certain people[1] in Salzburg have been trying our patience and you know how often you and I have longed to clear out. No doubt you still remember what objections I used to raise

---

[1] i.e. the Archbishop.

to our doing this, and how I would point out that it would be impossible for us all to leave. You now realize these difficulties, that is, the great expenses of travelling and the impossibility of making enough money to defray them, especially with a whole family. I could not let you travel alone, because you were not accustomed to attend to everything or to be independent of the help of others and because you knew so little about different currencies and nothing whatever about foreign money. Moreover you had not the faintest idea about packing nor about the innumerable necessary arrangements which crop up on journeys. I used to point out to you that, even if you were to remain in Salzburg until you were a little over twenty, you would not necessarily be wasting your time, which you could spend in dipping into other useful branches of knowledge and in training your reason by reading good books in several languages. Further, I used to remind you that it takes time for a young man, even one of such extraordinary gifts that he surpasses all other masters, to win the esteem which he deserves. Indeed several years are necessary; and as long as the young man is under twenty, his enemies and persecutors will certainly attribute his possible lack of success to his youth and slight experience. Have you the slightest doubt that such considerations were put forward to ⟨*the Elector in regard to the instruction of his natural children?*⟩ I am indeed as little fond of cringing as you are; and you will remember that while you were in Munich, I told you that you should not make yourself *so cheap*; and that all those attempts to collect ten persons who would so arrange matters that you might stay on there, seemed to me *far too cringing*. But kind-hearted and well-meaning friends persuaded you to do so—fires of straw, I call them, which quickly flare up—and end in smoke. Yet doubtless it was well meant! It is true that I should like you to have an appointment, but only one, such as you might find in Munich or Mannheim, which would enable you to travel from time to time. And I think too that you should not make a contract for life. Now for your ★ journey to Paris, where indeed I wish you were already. This was precisely my objection to your disastrously long stay at Mannheim. It is only natural that the gentlemen with whom you are going to travel to Paris should not let you go on without them. They need a fourth; and where will they get such *a fourth* as you are? That Herr Wendling is your friend, that he means well, that he knows Paris, that he will take great care of you —all that I do not doubt for a moment. And that he will try to arrange for you to be supported in Mannheim until March, I do not doubt that either. For it is very important that he should have your company. All friendships have their motives. If this Dutch gentleman[1] gives you 200 gulden, then you can keep going in Mannheim, especially if you go to Wendling's for lunch. Supposing Mamma spends 3 gulden a week for

[1] De Jean (or Dechamps).

food, that is 12 gulden a month; or perhaps Cannabich or Wendling would feed her at the rate of 4 gulden a week, which would be 16 gulden a month—then how much does a room cost by the month? If you get 200 gulden from your Dutchman and together you spend 50 gulden a month, that is, 100 gulden in two months; and if you can get a couple of pupils, you will still have 100 gulden to spare; and if you have free board, how can you each spend 50 gulden a month? In short! I quite approve of your present arrangement. But that you should be living with a Court Councillor[1]—whose name you do not seem to know—and that Mamma should have to live alone, *that I simply will not have*. As long as Mamma is in Mannheim, you and she must live together. *You should not and must not leave Mamma alone and at the mercy of other people*, as long as she is with you. However small her room may be, space can surely be found for a bed for you—and in any case why not take a larger room? It will cost a couple of gulden more, of course, but that is no great expense for two months and will certainly be only half the amount that you were paying at the inn. If only you had done what I told you in my letters to Augsburg and in subsequent ones, that is, that on reaching Mannheim *you should look for a private room at once*, you would have saved a good deal

★ of money. Mamma ought to remember how we travelled long ago. I never used to stay at inns in towns where I thought we were going to make a long sojourn. For instance, I know nothing about inns in Paris, London, Vienna, or even Brünn. You will realize that Mamma cannot leave Mannheim now that really cold weather is setting in. Besides, I must think out the easiest and most convenient way to bring her home. In the meantime be sure you stay with her and care for her, so that she may lack nothing, for indeed she cares for you. But if the 200 gulden, which the Indian[2] is going to give you, have turned out to be only another fire of straw which has flamed up in the first excitement of friendship and has already ended in smoke, then pack up and go. But if they are genuine gulden, then set to and carry out his commission; and I agree that it would be a very good thing if you were to write a new grand mass for the Elector. So during the next two months you will have to be methodical with your time. ⟨It would be well for you to write to Prince Zeill and say that you are not asking the Elector to give you a permanent appointment, but that *you would like him to take you on for a couple of years*, so that you might have the opportunity and the privilege of serving him and giving him proofs of your *talent*.⟩ I shall write also by the next post. Then you must write to Herr Grimm as I shall too. Herr Bullinger and all our good friends send their greetings. Nannerl and I kiss you millions of times and I am your devoted father

MZT

---

[1] Serrarius.   [2] De Jean (or Dechamps).

We send our regards to the whole Cannabich and Wendling households.

MY DEAR WIFE!

My letter above contains my reply about the question of this journey to Paris with Herr Wendling. But I want you and Wolfgang to live together, provided that it is all right about the 200 gulden. If there is any uncertainty, however, and no guarantee, then pack up and go off to Mainz at once. On your arrival in Mannheim you ought with the help of young Herr Danner or someone else to have looked about at once for private rooms. You ought to have done this and disregarded the objections of other people. I mentioned it so often—and yet you did not do it and as a result it has been to our loss. You say that you sent me Albert's account. *Not a trace of it!* It is quite evident from your letters that you both always scribble them off in a hurry, at night and when you are half asleep, and that you just jot down whatever occurs to you at the moment. Probably you yourself, therefore, do not remember what you have written, and I wager that you hardly ever read a letter which Wolfgang has written to me. By Heaven! You are nice folk! I can well believe that the price of food has gone up with the general rise; but postal fees have remained the same. I myself had already worked out that you must have spent a great deal of money. Well, well! If you had read my letters carefully, you would have known what to do, even if you had arrived in Mainz without a farthing. However, it can't be helped. ⟨*Nobody worked against Wolfgang more than Vogler.*⟩ I said so long ago to Bullinger and Nannerl. If it is true that you are to get 200 gulden from the Dutchman, then I shall have to think out how you can come home later on. For you could not do so now; it would be far too cold for you, particularly as the cold generally becomes most severe at Christmas and Twelfth Night. Besides, how are you going to travel? In our chaise? And quite alone? This all requires very careful consideration. Once you reach Augsburg, it will be easy. Do you think that Wolfgang will now attend to his affairs? I hope he has got accustomed to doing this and that his head is not always full of music. Farewell to you both. I am

your old husband

MZT

★

(263) *Maria Anna Mozart to her Husband*

[*Autograph in the Mozarteum, Salzburg*]

MY DEAR HUSBAND,   MANNHEIM, 18 *December* 1777

We have received all your letters safely and up to the present have not missed a single one. But the postage fee here is much higher than in

Salzburg. We have to pay twelve kreuzers for every letter we receive or send, and eighteen kreuzers if it is a large one. Since our arrival we have already spent more than six gulden on postage. For things are done here in the French style. We now have a perfectly splendid room with two beautiful beds and full service. The Privy Court Councillor's name is Serrarius. His wife is very charming to us. I have supper with them every evening and chat to the wife and daughter until half past ten. They would like me to spend every afternoon with them. I cannot tell you what a high opinion they have of my son. They only regret that he cannot spend all his time with them. A distinguished Lutheran came to see us today and has invited Wolfgang most courteously to try the new organ in the Lutheran church. All the Kapellmeisters who are in Mannheim are to be present. He is to try it at three o'clock this afternoon. He has so much to do that he really doesn't know whether he is standing on his head or his heels; what with composing and giving lessons he hasn't time to visit anybody. So you see we can stop here for the winter quite comfortably, and all this is due to Monsieur Wendling, who loves Wolfgang as his own son. The inkeeper's bill, which has pretty well emptied our purses, amounted to 111 gulden, and I gave 3 gulden in tips to the waiters and maids. It would have been better, of course, if we had taken rooms sooner, but they are very dear here. A furnished room alone costs three to four gulden a week and on top of that other necessities have to be purchased. And our affairs have always been so unsettled that we have never known from one day to another whether we are leaving or staying on. It would not have been worth our while to move out for three or four days. All this time I have been worried and anxious about living in this uncertainty and being bottled up in an inn. Every day I wanted to go to some other house. We still have 72 gulden left of our whole capital. We drew 150 gulden from Herr Schmalz; otherwise we could not have paid our landlord. With this sum and what Wolfgang is going to make during the winter we must meet our travelling expenses. For, as you are already aware, one needs a lot of money in Paris. Even here our expenses are quite heavy enough, and that too although we have free board and lodging. For there is our laundry, which is very expensive in Mannheim shoes, hair powder, pomade and other trifles which I cannot recall at the moment, but all of which cost money, so that the whole time one has to keep forking out. I really don't know how I could live more economically. Since I left Salzburg I have only had one cap made and not a single pair of shoes. I never took wine at the inn unless Wolfgang was having a meal there, and then we had a glass together. Yet our account has mounted up to such a figure. The room, fire and candles alone came to 30 gulden for the six weeks; and our room was under the roof and had two wretched beds; my feet were never warm the whole day long and I used to sit in my fur and my felt shoes. So you can imagine how happy I am to be able to lie in comfort for once and to have a fine warm room, praise and thanks be to God. I trust that Almighty God who has ordered everything so well will give us all the other things we desire, if they are good for us. Everything has been arranged so satisfactorily—when we were least thinking that it would. I promised a Holy Mass at the Holy Child of Loreto, and also in Maria-Plain, which I beg you to have said, perhaps at the Child of Loreto at once and later on in Maria-Plain when the weather is warmer, so that Nannerl can go out there. Both of these are for my protection on our journey and I put my whole trust in them, for I shall certainly not be forsaken. I have no other news beyond what you must know already, that is, that the English have suffered a crushing defeat at the hands of the Americans and that a whole regiment has been captured.[1] Schweitzer's new opera[2] is being rehearsed every day. Wolfgang does not like it at all. He says there is nothing natural about it, that it is all exaggerated and that it is not composed to suit the singers. We must wait and see whether the performance will be a success. I wish you and Nannerl a happy Christmas and New Year. I have to write in good time, since you always get our letters so late. Keep well and cheerful until our next joyful meeting. Please give my compliments to all our good friends, especially to Monsieur Bullinger and Mlle Sallerl. I have greetings to deliver from our acquaintances here, some of whom you know and some of whom you do not. Addio. I kiss you both many 10000 times and remain as always your faithful wife until death

MARIANNA MOZART

I send warm greetings to Theresa.

Pimperl, I suppose, is still quite well. Has she never been snarly since we left? Has she never had an attack of hydrophobia? I was indoors all day today, as I had a heavy cold and could only take some soup, which Herr Danner sent in to me. I hope to get out tomorrow, if it is God's will. Addio. I kiss you both again.

(263a) *Mozart to his Father*

[Autograph in the Mozarteum, Salzburg]

[MANNHEIM, 18 December 1777]

At top speed and in the greatest hurry. The organ in the Lutheran church which has just been tried today is very good, both in the full and

---

[1] Probably a reference to Burgoyne's unsuccessful operations against Gates in September and October, which led to the surrender of the former at Saratoga on 17 October 1777. The French immediately concluded a treaty with the revolted colonies, which was, however, not signed until 6 November 1778.   [2] *Rosemunde*.

in single stops. Vogler played it. He is, to put it bluntly, a trickster pure and simple. As soon as he tries to play maestoso, he becomes as dry as dust; and it is a great relief that playing upon the organ bores him and that therefore it doesn't last long. But what is the result? An unintelligible muddle. I listened to him from a distance. He then began a fugue, in which one note was struck six times and presto. Whereupon I went up to him. Indeed I would much rather watch him than hear him. There was a whole crowd of people there, including many of the musicians, Holzbauer, Cannabich, Toeschi and so forth. I shall soon have finished one quartet[1] for the Indian Dutchman,[2] that true friend of humanity. A propos, Herr Wendling told me yesterday that he had written to you by the last post. Addio. My greetings to everyone in Salzburg. I kiss your hands 100000 times and embrace my sister with all my heart. Oh what a fine handwriting! I am your most obedient son

WOLFGANG AMADÉ MOZART

I had to conduct the opera[3] at Wendling's the other day with a few violins, in place of Schweitzer who was indisposed.

(264) *Maria Anna Mozart to her Husband*

[Autograph in the Mozarteum, Salzburg]

MY DEAR HUSBAND,   MANNHEIM, 20 *December* 1777

I have received this very moment your letter of the 15th and am delighted to hear that you are both well. Thank God, we are too. Wolfgang is out and therefore will not read your letter until eleven o'clock tonight when he gets home. I wrote to you on the 10th that all was well with us. These last two days I have not been out of doors, for the weather has been both wet and cold. Wolfgang and I are lunching, tomorrow, Sunday, with our landlord, Privy Court Councillor Serrarius; so that is why I am writing today. If I left it until tomorrow, we might get away too late for us to write, for the post leaves at six o'clock in the evening. What you say about confessing, we already did at the Feast of the Immaculate Conception. We rarely hear Mass during the week, I must admit, for daylight is so late now that it is impossible for us to get out in time and the last Mass is at eleven o'clock and the church is a good distance from this house. But on Sundays and Holy days we can go to the Pfarrkirche. Indeed Wolfgang goes every Sunday to High Mass at the Hofkirche in order to hear the music. I have no news whatever for you, for during the last two days nothing has happened. From now on I

---

[1] Probably K. 285.   [2] De Jean (or Dechamps).   [3] Schweitzer's new opera *Rosemunde*.

shall write once a week, which is much more sensible, because every letter, big or small, costs twelve kreuzers; and moreover the post-days, which are Thursday and Saturday, are so close together that it is much simpler to write once only. We have not yet called in the barber to deal with Wolfgang's beard: we have just been cutting it with scissors. But this will not do much longer and the barber will soon have to tackle it. We send all sorts of messages to Sallerl and to our best friend Herr Bullinger.

(264a) *Mozart to his Father*

[Autograph in the Mozarteum, Salzburg]

[MANNHEIM, 20 *December* 1777]

I wish you, dearest Papa, a very happy New Year, and hope that every day your health, which is so precious to me, may get better and better, to the advantage and delight of your wife and children, to the satisfaction of your true friends and to the vexation and annoyance of your enemies! I beg you during the coming year to love me with the same fatherly affection as you have shown me hitherto! I for my part shall endeavour to my utmost to deserve more and more the love of so excellent a father. Your last letter, dated December 15th, gave me the greatest pleasure, as it told me that, praise and thanks be to God, you are quite well. We two, God again be thanked, are in excellent health. I can't help being so, for I certainly get enough exercise. I am writing this at eleven o'clock at night, for it is the only time I am free. We can't get up before eight o'clock, for until half past eight there is no daylight in our room, which is on the ground floor. I dress in haste and at ten I sit down to compose until about twelve or half past twelve. Then I go to Wendling's, where I again compose a little until half past one, when we have lunch. Thus the time passes until three, when I go off to the Mainzischer Hof (an inn) to a Dutch officer[1] to give him a lesson in galanterie and thoroughbass, for which I receive, if I am not mistaken, four ducats for twelve lessons. At four I must be home again to instruct the daughter of the house. We never begin our lesson before half past four, as we have to wait for the lights. At six I go to Cannabich's and give Mlle Rosa her lesson. I stay there to supper, after which we talk or occasionally someone plays. If it is the latter, I always take a book out of my pocket and read—as I used to do in Salzburg. I have just said that your last letter gave me great pleasure. That is true! But one thing upset me a little bit—your enquiry as to whether I wasn't perhaps getting a little lax about confession. I have nothing to say to this; but just let me ask you one thing, and that is, not

---

[1] De La Pottrie.

to have such a bad opinion of me. I like to enjoy myself, but rest assured that I can be as serious as anyone else can. Since I left Salzburg (and even in Salzburg itself) I have come across people who, although they are ten, twelve and thirty years my senior, have talked and behaved in such a way as I should blush to imitate. So once more I beg you most humbly to think better of me. Please give my greetings to Herr Bullinger, my very best friend, and convey to him my heartiest wishes for the New Year. Remember me to all my good friends, and particularly to Father Dominic.[1]

My dearest Rosie, O sweetheart mine,
My dearest Nan, O sister mine.
Angel, a thousand thanks for your excellent wishes.
And here is one from Mozart, that queerest of fishes.
Good luck and happiness, if such things be, to you.
I trust you will love me, as Woferl loves you too.
And truthfully I tell you that you he does admire
And, if you were to ask him, would rush into the fire.
Exactly as he says them, his words do I impart,
And I see it all so clearly, that passion in his heart
For his sweet Rosie Joli and his dear sister Nan.
Ah, come away, you darlings! A dance for maid and man!
Long life to all you dear ones, Papa and my Mamma,
My sister and her brother! Hey sassa! Houp sassa!
And Woferl too and also the mistress of his heart.
And this for evermore, my dears, as long as he can fart,
As long as he can piddle and shit it with the best,
So long will he and Rosie and Nan and all be blest—
A charming crew! Alas, to bed I now must creep,
For I hear it striking midnight, when we all should be asleep.

WOLFGANG AMADÈ MOZART
MARIA ANNA MOZART[2]

(265) *Leopold Mozart to his Wife and Son*

[*Extract*]   [*Autograph in the Mozarteum, Salzburg*]

SALZBURG, [21]-22 *December* 1777

MY DEAR WIFE AND DEAR SON!

I sent you in my last letter my views about your journey to Paris. I am delighted to see from your letter of December 14th that you have left

---

[1] Dominicus Hagenauer, who in 1764 had become a priest and for whom Mozart wrote in 1769 his mass K. 66.
[2] Her signature is in Mozart's handwriting.

the inn and are now well provided for on the whole for the next two months. Herr Wendling, to whom I was going to write by this post, has anticipated me. I had no time to write to him last post-day, as I had to write to Padre Maestro Martini, to tell him about the portrait which I had already dispatched.[1] ★

I wrote the above yesterday, Sunday, December 21st, on my return home after the Horary Service, when your mass in B flat major[2] was performed, in which the castrato[3] sang most excellently. In the evening ★ Johannes Hagenauer came to tell me that Count Castelbarco had arrived at the 'Schiffwirth' that very moment. I went off there at once, but was told that he had just gone out and would be leaving again in an hour to join his brother, the officer, in Schwanenstadt, but that he would be back again in Salzburg in five or six days, when he would be staying for some time. The servant, on hearing my name, which I was asked to leave, exclaimed: 'Oh, lo conosco, il padre di quel giovane che ha scritto tre opere in Milano. Non manchèro di presentare i suoi rispetti ed attenzioni al mio padrone.'[4] ★

Adlgasser, who died today, is to be buried tomorrow night, and on the 24th there will be a service at St. Sebastian's.[5] Who will be the new organist, I wonder? Who will teach in the Kapellhaus? And who will instruct the Countess's[6] daughters? I am thankful that neither Nannerl nor I have had anything to do with them. She will probably try to find an opportunity of speaking to me. His Excellency the Chief Steward[7] sent for me today after my lesson at Arco's.[8] He wanted to see me, because he likes you so much and was wondering whether he ought not to put your name forward to the Archbishop for the post of organist. I thanked him for his kind proposal, which I declined, and said that it was quite out of the question and explained a good deal to him. He replied that he was very much relieved and that he now had a load off his mind. You will both understand that *I must postpone my answer to Herr Wendling, to whom I send my most humble greetings*. The Adlgasser incident has prevented me. I must now go off to their house, help these people and make arrangements about the music for the service. God protect you. Mamma ought to write a good deal to us, but Wolfgang only a little, because he has so much to

[1] Leopold Mozart's letter to Padre Martini about his son's portrait is dated 22 December. See letter 266. He may refer to another letter which has been lost, but this is not likely.

[2] K. 275 [272b], composed in 1777.

[3] Francesco Ceccarelli.

[4] Oh, I know you, for you are the father of the youth who wrote three operas at Milan. I shall certainly present your respects and regards to my master.

[5] This postscript follows Letter 265a. A portion of Letter 265, which has been omitted, contains a long description of Adlgasser's fatal seizure while playing the organ during a Vesper Service in the cathedral.

[6] Countess Lodron, the Archbishop's sister.

[7] Count von Firmian.

[8] Leopold Mozart taught the violin to Count Leopold Arco, son of Count Georg Anton Felix Arco, Chief Chamberlain to the Archbishop.

do. Nannerl plays his sonata[1] with the greatest expression. We kiss you millions of times and I am your old

MZT

★

(265a) *Nannerl Mozart to her Mother and Brother*

[Autograph in the Mozarteum, Salzburg]

[SALZBURG, 22 December 1777[2]]

Since you have now become so distinguished and your time is so much taken up that you cannot write to me, probably you will have no time to read a few lines from me either. So with your permission I shall take the liberty of talking quite alone to Mamma. Besides it is going to be women's chat. I trust that you are both well and happy. Mamma was kind enough to tell me that the frisures and caps they wear in Mannheim are much prettier and that the women dress much more smartly than in Salzburg. That I can well believe. And if I am going to be fortunate enough to have my Mamma back here in two months, then I should like to ask her to be so good as to watch closely how that frisure is made and to bring a toupee cushion with her and whatever else is necessary for it and, if possible, a cap in the very latest fashion and anything else she may like to bring. If only I could make money by giving lessons as I did some time ago, I should love to have my garnet-red gown made into a Bolognese and trimmed with lawn. In that case, I might perhaps find a cheaper lawn in Mannheim. But I must banish all thoughts of new fashions like these. I am delighted that you now have a comfortable room and I trust that Mamma no longer suffers from the cold as she did at the inn. I must stop now, otherwise Papa will have no more room. I wish you both continual good health and I kiss Mamma's hand and embrace my brother.

(266) *Leopold Mozart to Padre Martini, Bologna*

[Autograph formerly in the Preussische Staatsbibliothek, Berlin]

[SALZBURG, 22 December 1777[3]]

MOST REVEREND PADRE MAESTRO,
    MOST ESTEEMED FATHER,
    Tandem aliquando![4] For the last year my son has owed you a reply to your very kind letter of 18 December 1776, in which you were good enough to express your approval of his motet for four voices[5] and at the same time your desire to have a portrait of him and of myself. So far I

---

[1] K. 309 [284b], written for Rosa Cannabich.   [2] A postscript to her father's letter.
[3] This letter is in Italian.   [4] At last!
[5] K. 222 [205a], composed early in 1775 at Munich. See p. 266, n. 1.

have hesitated to send you these for lack of a competent artist, such as is not to be found in this part of the world. I kept on postponing it in the hope that, as sometimes happens, some good painter would pass through Salzburg. In the end, however, I had to make up my mind quickly and commission one of our own painters to carry out the work. Now listen to our story. For the last five years my son has been serving our Prince for *a miserable pittance* in the hope that his efforts and his slight knowledge coupled with his very great zeal and uninterrupted studies would in time be appreciated. But we were wrong! I refrain from giving you a full description of the manner in which our Prince prefers to think and act. Suffice it to say that he was not ashamed to declare that *my son knew nothing and that he ought to betake himself to some conservatorio of music at Naples and study music*. And why? Simply in order to make it quite clear that a young man in a subordinate position should not be so foolish as to feel convinced that he deserved better pay and more recognition, since he had heard that decisive statement from the lips of a Prince. The rest of the story will gradually find its way to Italy, where possibly it may be known already. This disappointment made me decide to allow my son to resign from the service and go off elsewhere. So he left Salzburg on September 23rd and after spending a short time at the Electoral Court of Munich he proceeded to Mannheim, where he is at present and in excellent health and whence he sends you his most devoted regards. He will remain there until the beginning of March, that is, until the carnival is over; and, God willing, he will be in Paris at the beginning of Lent. This is the reason which determined me to have the portrait painted before his departure and thereby to serve our dear Signor Padre Maestro. If with your usual goodness of heart you would be so kind as to send to His Highness the Elector a true account and a favourable description of my son, you would be performing a very fine act, the more so as two words from you are worth more than the warmest recommendation from a king. I flatter myself that possibly you may do so, when you are writing to Mannheim for the New Year. But, if the painting has not yet reached you, you will ask, where is the portrait? I gave it to the firm of Sigmund Haffner, merchant of Salzburg, who took it on the occasion of the Fair of St. Andrew to Bozen, whence he will endeavour to send it to you, addressed probably to Signor Brinsecchi at Bologna. The painting is of no great value as a work of art, but I assure you that it is an excellent likeness. My son is exactly like that. I have jotted down at the back of the portrait his name and his age. I now have another idea, and that is, to send you the beginnings of my son's compositions, starting with the cembalo sonatas written for Madame Victoire[1] and engraved in Paris *when he was seven years old*; then the sonatas he composed *when he was*

---

[1] K. 6, 7.

eight for the Queen of England,[1] which were engraved in London; then those he composed *at the age of nine* for the Princess of Nassau-Weilburg,[2] which were engraved in Holland, and so forth. To these I might add a short account of his travels and any noteworthy incidents. As for my portrait, I do not think that my snout deserves to be placed in the company of men of talent. If, however, you desire it, I shall endeavour to fulfil your wish, but solely on account of this one merit of mine, namely, that I have done my duty in the matter of cultivating the talent which God in his goodness has bestowed on my son. I beg you to continue to grant us your favour and protection, to take great care of your health and to remember that I am ever at your command and that I remain, most Reverend Padre, your command and that I remain, most Reverend Padre, your most humble, devoted and grateful servant

LEOPOLD MOZART

Salzburg, 22 December 1777.

I have mentioned the New Year and have almost forgotten to send you my wishes. But what would you like me to say? *I wish you good health*—that is all you need. May God say: Amen!

(267) *Mozart to his Father*

[Autograph in the Mozarteum, Salzburg]

MANNHEIM, 27 December 1777

MON TRÈS CHER PÉRE!

Fine paper this, isn't it? Indeed, I only wish I could produce something better! But it's too late now to get any other. You know already from our previous letters that Mamma and I now have excellent lodgings. I never intended that she should take rooms apart from me. But when Privy Court Councillor Serrarius was so kind as to offer to house us, *I naturally thanked him*; but that was all. I didn't accept. The other day I called on him with Herr Wendling and M. Dechamps, the valiant Dutchman, and just waited until he should start the subject again. At length he renewed his proposal and I thanked him and replied as follows: 'I realize how kind it is of you to honour me with an invitation to lodge with you, but I regret that unfortunately I cannot accept your generous offer. You will not take it amiss if I tell you that I do not like my Mamma to be separated from me without good cause, and, as things are, I know no reason why she should live in one part of the town and I in another. If I were to go to Paris, it would naturally be a very great advantage for me if she were not with me. But for the two months we shall be here, a few

[1] K. 10-15.   [2] K. 26-31.

gulden more or less will make no difference.' With this speech I achieved a *complete* fulfilment of my wishes, that is, that board and lodging for the two of us should not make us a penny the poorer. Well, I must now hurry upstairs to supper. We have been playing cards until this very minute, that is, half past ten. I went the other day with M. De La Potrie, the Dutch officer, who is my pupil, to the Reformed Church, and played on the organ for an hour and a half. I put my whole heart into it. Some time soon we, that is, the Cannabichs, Wendlings, Serrariuses and Mozarts, are going to the Lutheran church, where I shall have some good fun on the organ. I tried the full organ before during that test, about which I wrote to you, but didn't play much, only a prelude and a fugue. I have now added Herr Wieland to the list of my acquaintances.[1] But he doesn't know as much about me as I know about him, for he has never heard any of my compositions. I had imagined him to be quite different from what I found him. He strikes you as slightly affected in his speech. He has a rather childish voice; he keeps on quizzing you over his glasses; he indulges in a sort of pedantic rudeness, combined occasionally with a stupid condescension. But I am not surprised that he permits himself such behaviour here, even though he may be quite different in Weimar and elsewhere, for people stare at him as if he had dropped from Heaven. Everyone seems embarrassed in his presence, no one says a word or moves an inch; all listen intently to every word he utters; and it's a pity they often have to wait so long, for he has a defect of speech that makes him speak very slowly and he can't say half a dozen words without stopping. Apart from that, he is what we all know him to be, a most gifted fellow. He has a frightfully ugly face, covered with pock-marks, and he has a rather long nose. In height he is, I should say, a little taller than Papa. You must have no doubt about the Dutchman's 200 gulden. Well, I must close now, as I want to go on composing for a little while. One thing more. I suppose I had better not write to ⟨Prince Zeill⟩ just yet? You probably know the reason already, since Munich is nearer to Salzburg than to Mannheim, and therefore you must have heard ⟨that the Elector is dying of smallpox.⟩ It is quite true. This is bound to upset things a bit. Now, farewell. As for Mamma's journey home, I think it could most easily be arranged during Lent and in the company of some merchants. That's merely what I think; what I know beyond all question is that what meets with your approval will be the best for us, for you are Court Kapellmeister and a paragon of intelligence! Madame Robinig has said so. I kiss Papa's hands—you know Papa?—1000 times and embrace my sister with all my heart and in spite of my scratchy writing I remain your most obedient son and true and faithful brother

WOLFGANG AMADÉ MOZART

[1] Wieland arrived at Mannheim on 21 December.

(267a) *Maria Anna Mozart to her Husband*

[*Autograph in the Mozarteum, Salzburg*]

MANNHEIM, 28 *December* [1777]
I have received this very moment your letter of December 22nd. I am truly sorry about Herr Adlgasser's sad and rapid death, which was indeed very sudden and gave me a great shock.[1] The poor wife and children are greatly to be pitied. She will be inconsolable, for I know her, as you do too, and also the reason why she will be inconsolable.[2] We did not write to you last post-day. The last time I told you that, thank God, we were very well. I usually spend the whole afternoon with the wife of the Privy Court Councillor and have supper with them every evening. Everyone thinks the world of Wolfgang, but indeed he plays quite differently from what he used to in Salzburg—for there are pianofortes here, on which he plays so extraordinarily well that people say they have never heard the like. In short everyone who has heard him says that he has not got his equal. Although Beecke has been performing here and Schubart too, yet everyone says that Wolfgang far surpasses them in beauty of tone, quality and execution. And they are all positively amazed at the way he plays out of his head and reads off whatever is put before him. Please tell Nannerl that lawn is not at all cheap in Mannheim and also that no coloured lawn is worn, only white. I shall see whether I can bring the cap with me. The trimming here is very charming and will certainly please her. Greetings to all our acquaintances and friends, especially to Herr Bullinger and Jungfer Sallerl, from myself and Wolfgang. I send greetings to Theresa and my compliments too to Herr Gött. And once more I wish you a happy New Year, a better one than the last, and especially that you, my dear husband, may keep well and live happily, and that we may have a joyful meeting in the coming year. Addio. I kiss you many 1000 times and I remain as always your faithful wife

MARIA ANNA MOZART

(268) *Leopold Mozart to his Wife and Son*

[*Extract*]   [*Autograph in the Mozarteum, Salzburg*]

SALZBURG, 29 *December* 1777

MY DEAR WIFE AND DEAR WOLFGANG,
We both wish you a very happy New Year! God grant that the year 1778 may bring us more happiness than the last. We trust to God's grace

---

[1] See p. 431, n. 5.
[2] Obviously a reference to the small pension which Frau Adlgasser would receive from the Archbishop.

and mercy and to the talent, industry and intelligence, but particularly to the good heart, of our dear Wolfgang, who will certainly do his utmost to win glory, honour and money in order to help us and to save his father from the scornful mockery and sneers of certain persons, whose names I dare not mention, but whose ridicule would, as you know, most certainly send me to my grave. Wolfgang's good fortune and success will be our sweetest revenge, of which, as you will see, we are already tasting a little. Count Starhemberg[1] happened to be with Count Arco the other day. The conversation turned on Adlgasser's death. *Count Arco.* You are in a fix, are you not? Young Mozart would now have rendered you good service. *Count Starhemberg.* Very true. He ought to have had patience a little longer. *Count Arco.* Patience? How absurd! Who could have foreseen this sudden death—and besides, what would you have given him apart from his few dirty gulden? It is a good thing for him that he has cleared out. You have all treated him abominably quite long enough. *Count Starhemberg.* Yes, I admit, he was treated very badly. Everyone allows that he is the most competent clavier-player in Europe. But all the same he could have waited a little longer. *Count Arco, very heatedly.* Well, let's chuck it! He is quite happy in Mannheim, where he has found good companions with whom he is going off to Paris. You will never get Mozart back again. And serve you right! You will have precisely the same experience with Hagenauer.[2] *Count Starhemberg.* Hagenauer is to have a salary from the beginning of next year. *Count Arco.* A fine salary it'll be, to be sure—and even if he gets one, you have made sport of him and led him by the nose quite long enough. Then the conversation turned on myself—in which connexion Count Starhemberg declared that he believed *that no more competent teacher could be found.* You will notice that Count Arco kept on saying 'You—you—' that is, he lumped Count Starhemberg and company together in order not to have to mention the Prince.   ★

Who do you think has been made organist at Holy Trinity? Herr Haydn! Everybody is laughing. He will be an expensive item, as after every Litany he swills a quart of wine and sends Lipp,[3] who is also a tippler, to do the other services. Meanwhile Spitzeder is to instruct the chapel boys in the clavier until something definite has been decided. We now kiss you millions of times, the sheet is full and I am your   ★
old

MZT

[1] Count Josef Starhemberg, canon of Salzburg Cathedral.
[2] Johann Georg Hagenauer. See p. 377, n. 2.
[3] Franz Ignaz Lipp, second organist in the Cathedral and father-in-law of Michael Haydn.

(268a) *Nannerl Mozart to her Mother and Brother*

[*Autograph in the Mozarteum, Salzburg*]

[SALZBURG, 29 December 1777[1]]

I wish Mamma and my dearest brother a joyful New Year, good health and happiness. I hope that Mamma will soon return to us in good health; and as for you, my dear brother, I wish that, wherever you may go, you may be successful and also enjoy good health; and as for myself, I should like to have the pleasure of seeing you soon again, provided it is not in Salzburg. I send greetings to Mamma as her obedient daughter and to my brother as his faithful sister and friend. Katherl Gilowsky sends New Year wishes to you both. We had our shooting yesterday. Bullinger contributed the target which the Paymaster won. On New Year's Day Mamma is to provide the target. As cashier for us both I should state that I am quite satisfied with my cash-box, for until Mamma returns, her losses will not have been very great. Please forgive me for not writing more often or more fully; but, as you see, Papa hardly leaves me any room and, when he does, it is only a tiny bit.

(269) *Maria Anna Mozart to her Husband*

[*Autograph in the Mozarteum, Salzburg*]

MANNHEIM, 3 *January* 1778

I received yesterday, January 2nd, the letter you enclosed to Herr Wendling and was delighted to hear that you are both well. Thank God, we also are in good health. But on account of the death of the Elector of Bavaria[2] everyone here is in the deepest mourning; there are no operas (for which I am truly sorry); all plays, balls, concerts, sleigh-drives, music, everything has been stopped. The courier arrived from Munich at seven o'clock on the evening of the 31st with the sad news that the Elector had died at one o'clock on the previous afternoon. Our Elector left for Munich at ten o'clock on the evening of New Year's Day and has arrived there long since. God grant that everything may turn out well and that no troubles may come. I wish it with all my heart, for he is a very good ruler. Here it is deadly quiet and thoroughly boring, and in Munich it must be even more so. That I can well imagine. Salzburg will be a much jollier place this winter, for the carnival will last a long time. Well, how is Frau Adlgasser? Remember me to her. I sympathise with her with my whole heart. Those poor children are to be pitied. Victoria

---

[1] A postscript to her father's letter.
[2] The Elector Maximilian III had died on 30 December 1777.

will probably not stay with her, and indeed who could blame her? *Today, Sunday, January 4th.* I received yesterday evening your letter of December 29th and was delighted to read how old ⟨Count Arco⟩ gave Count ⟨Starhemberg⟩ such a fine dressing-down. He really wishes us well, I believe. It does my heart good to hear that they are realizing at last what they have lost in Wolfgang. It was ⟨very mean⟩ of Herr Haydn to take the post of organist at Holy Trinity. I thought he went to Italy in order to become a Kapellmeister. What is Kapellmeister Rust doing? Is he still in Salzburg? Has he recovered or not? Is Herr von Schiedenhofen not getting married this carnival to Fräulein Nannerl and Herr von Mölk to Fräulein Josepha? Is Franz Barisani still in Salzburg? Give him our best regards. People are anxiously awaiting today a courier from Bavaria to hear whether the Elector arrived safely and what is happening there. God grant that everything may turn out well. I wish it with all my heart. Please give Katherl Gilowsky my New Year wishes and greetings and the same to all my other good friends. It would indeed be a very good thing if you could arrange for a letter of introduction from someone in Vienna to the Queen.[1] I have no more news to send you, for I am not very well known here, and there is very little in Mannheim that could interest you. But I know everyone and everything in Salzburg. So you can write and tell me all that is happening; and there is far more news there than here. Addio. Keep well, both of you. I kiss you many 100000 times and remain as always your old faithful wife

MARIANNA MOZART

Wolfgang has not come home yet. Whether he will get back in time to add a few lines I really don't know. He has a lot of composing to do, time simply flies and he has, as it were, to steal it. For how can it be otherwise when he must go to one place for his meals, to another to compose and give lessons, and to yet another when he wants to sleep?

(269a) *Mozart to his Father*

[*Autograph in the Mozarteum, Salzburg*]

[MANNHEIM, *January* 4 1778]

I hope that you are both quite well. I am in excellent health, thank God. As you may readily imagine, I am greatly distressed at the death of the Elector of Bavaria. All that I hope is that the Elector here will succeed to the whole of Bavaria and move to Munich. I think that you too would be quite satisfied with such an arrangement. At noon today Karl Theodor was proclaimed here at court Duke of Bavaria. In Munich

[1] Marie-Antoinette.

too, immediately after the death of the Elector, Count Daun, the Chief Equerry, claimed allegiance on behalf of our Elector and got the dragoons to ride round the whole town with trumpets and drums, shouting 'Long live our Elector Karl Theodor'. If all goes well, as I hope it will, Count Daun will get a rather pretty present. His adjutant, a certain Lilienau whom he sent here with news of the death, got 3000 gulden from the Elector. Now farewell. I kiss your hands 1000 times and embrace my sister with all my heart and remain

WOLF: MOZART

A tous mes amis des compliments.

(270) Leopold Mozart to his Son

[Extract]   [Autograph in the Mozarteum, Salzburg]

★ MON TRES CHER FILS!   SALZBURG, 5 January 1778

On the 30th the Elector of Bavaria passed over into eternity. In the afternoon of the same day His Highness the Elector of Mannheim was proclaimed Duke of Bavaria, and on the following day all government
★ departments and the army had to take the oath of allegiance. Meanwhile news has come that on Friday, January 2nd, the Elector of Mannheim arrived in Munich very quietly and quite alone, that is to say, accompanied only by a courtier, Count or Baron Vieregg. You can easily imagine that here too people are wishing that things may remain as they are. I had to laugh very heartily today, for it was rumoured in town that the Elector was going to appoint you Kapellmeister in Munich, as old Bernasconi[1] is no longer able to perform his duties. It is said here that news has come from Vöcklabruck that the 〈Imperial soldiers〉 who are encamped there and also near Wels, have received orders to 〈get ready to march:〉 moreover, Trumpeter Schwarz's son is said to have written something to the same effect from Bohemia. God preserve us! that would be a nice business![2] But we shall soon know. In regard to Mamma's return journey I have been thinking for some time that the most convenient way would be for her to travel in one of the empty coaches which come to fetch merchants in Salzburg. But the problem is, *how is she to travel from Mannheim to Augsburg?* If she could find some suitable means, our chaise could be sold

---

[1] Andrea Bernasconi (1706–1784) had been Kapellmeister at the Munich court since 1755. He was the stepfather and teacher of the famous singer Antonia Bernasconi.

[2] The outcome of these events was the war of the Bavarian Succession. As the Bavarian line of Electors had died out, Karl Theodor, as head of the elder dynasty of the House of Wittelsbach and in consequence of certain agreements, became the lawful heir to the Bavarian territories. He came to an agreement with the Emperor Joseph II (the Pact of Vienna, signed on 15 January 1778), which Frederick the Great regarded as an infringement of his rights. With Saxony as his ally, Frederick invaded Bohemia in July 1778. After the Peace of Teschen, May 1779, the Pact of Vienna was annulled.

in Mannheim. If not, she will have to travel in the chaise to Augsburg and leave it at the Holy Cross Monastery until my brother finds an opportunity of selling it. For, as you will be four people on your journey to Paris, you will not be able to use it. At the same time it would fetch a better price in Mannheim, where everything is dear. From Augsburg Mamma will be able to reach Salzburg in three days. Some of the hired coachmen leave there on March 9th, some on the 10th, to fetch the merchants; and she could travel very comfortably in a closed glass-windowed coach for four. I once did the journey home for a max d'or. If she prefers to travel with the merchants when they come to Salzburg, it may be a little difficult to arrange, as they generally make up parties of four. But whatever she chooses, I can in any case settle it through my brother. The main question, however, is, *which is the best way for her to travel from Mannheim to Augsburg?* The other portion of the journey I can arrange, provided we think about it in good time. *Time flies*; and I should much prefer her to make the fourth in a party travelling to Salzburg. *I could then let you know at what date she ought to be in Augsburg.* As for the chaise, I paid *about* 80 *gulden* for it, but you will surely find some friend to value it for you; and if Mamma cannot use it, mind you sell it as advantageously as possible. In Mannheim, at least, people surely cannot buy much of a carriage for eight louis d'or. If, however, Mamma has no suitable opportunity of travelling to Augsburg, then some *honest* traveller might perhaps be glad to accompany her in her comfortable chaise and she could charge him his post-chaise fare. But you would, of course, have to know something about him. Further, if, as I wish and hope, the Elector remains in peaceful possession of his new dukedom, somebody will be travelling from time to time from Munich to Mannheim, whom she could accompany; and once she is in Munich, she can then hire a coachman and drive home. But everything depends on how you think that she can get to Augsburg, since the remainder of the journey will have to be arranged accordingly. Only I must remind you not to leave anything to the last moment. Mamma should make a list of *your linen, stockings and so forth*, in good time, and indeed of *all your clothes, so that you may know what you have with you.* That reminds me, what are you going to do about the trunk? Possibly one of you can make use of it. But I think that it would be too big for either of you. These points must be settled in good time. If Mamma prefers to bring it back, she could of course fill it up with straw, as her clothes take up so little space. *Wolfgang could more easily use it. Basta! Be sure and settle these matters well in advance.*

　　When Adlgasser died, I said to Nannerl: 'You bet that the Archbishop ★ will get the Countess[1] to write to Joseph Arco, the Bishop of Königgrätz, to get his organist, that grubby Hasse or Hass, or whatever he is called,

---

[1] The Countess Lodron.

to come'. You will remember that the Countess once mentioned this to
you? He is the dirty old fellow who tested you at Prince Pugiatowsky's in
Vienna with the theme of Scarlatti's fugue. And it really is a fact that the
Archbishop has already written about him. Meanwhile I have been twice
already to the Lodron ladies. On New Year's Eve the Countess sent her
manservant to ask me to come. She informed me with her usual insincere
friendliness that she had a request to make, which, however, if it was
inconvenient to me, I was to refuse quite frankly, as she did not wish to
embarrass me; which, to my mind, was as much as to say that she fully
realized that I was under no obligation to her. She then asked me to take
on the teaching of her daughters, though she was well aware that I had
very little time and did not like to be bothered. I made a few objections
and finally said that I would come on one day at eleven in the morning
and on the next at four in the afternoon. Whereupon she was delighted,
talked a lot and said a number of nice things about you both. She was in
★ the room on Friday when I came to teach the young ladies. I have just
received your letter of December 27th. *I did not write to you on New Year's
Day*, for on the eve and on the day itself I was busy with congratulations.
I am positively delighted that you are now in such a comfortable house,
that you are in good health and that you, my dear wife, have a nice warm
room. The portrait you sketched of ⟨Wieland⟩ for my benefit I too could
almost have given you, although I have never seen him. For M. Grimm
and the two Romanzows gave me a most minute description of him
during a walk which we all took together over the Mönchsberg. Philo-
sophical birds of his type usually have something odd about them. You
must not be in the least distressed that I enquired about your ⟨confession.⟩
I shall answer your question another time. But surely you will be able to
supply the answer yourself, if you will just put yourself in my place, or
indeed in the place of any father. Could Mamma bring with her a Mannheim Court calendar? And I should very much like to know the title of
Vogler's book[1] *and how much it costs*? If Wolfgang can remember how I
set to work about these things, he will procure both very cheaply. He
must not laugh, however, but preserve a very serious expression. I must
★ certainly close now, for the paper is becoming blacker and blacker. Do take
care of your health. Nannerl and I kiss you a million times and I am
your old   MZT

★   (271) *Maria Anna Mozart to her Husband*

[*Autograph in the Mozarteum, Salzburg*]

MY DEAR HUSBAND,   MANNHEIM, 10 *January* 1778
    I received today your letter of the 5th and am delighted to hear that
you are both well. Eternal thanks be to God, we too are in good health.

––––––––––
[1] *Tonwissenschaft und Tonsetzkunst*, Mannheim, 1776.

We had heard some of your news about Bavaria, but not in such detail. People here are not suspecting any action on the part of ⟨Austria,⟩ but some folks are rather afraid of ⟨Prussia.⟩ Indeed there is a frightful lot of talk, mostly lies and nothing definite to report. Everyone is absolutely silent about the real truth, whatever it may be. God grant that everything may remain peaceful. I wish it with all my heart. As for my return journey, do not worry, for we shall think out the easiest way to arrange it. I am quite willing to travel in the company of merchants, if it can be arranged. But it is not so easy to settle from Mannheim that I should be in Augsburg at the very time that they would want to leave. If we still have peace, then it is quite probable that somebody may be going from here to Munich. We must make lots of enquiries so that we do not get in too late. I shall probably have to bring home the trunk with me, for it is too big for Wolfgang to use, since there will be four of them, each with his luggage, and the trunk would be far too heavy. But all this we shall find out when the time comes. May God but grant us the blessing of peace.

(271a) *Mozart to his Father*

[*Autograph in the Mozarteum, Salzburg*]

[MANNHEIM, 10 *January* 1778]

Indeed, I wish it with all my heart. What I really should like to see, you will have already gathered from my last letter. As for Mamma's journey home it is high time that we began to think about it; for although there have been rehearsals of the opera all the time, it is not at all certain whether it will be performed;[1] if it isn't, we shall probably leave on February 15th. If there weren't so many preparations to make, it would be easy enough. I shall make full enquiries. I shan't want the big trunk. My idea is to take as little luggage with me as possible and to leave all the things I don't want, such as that stack of symphonies, etc., and a few clothes besides, with the Privy Court Councillor here, where they are sure to be well looked after. Then again, as soon as I have heard your advice about this, I shall follow the opinion and practice of my travelling companions and have a black suit made for me, as they have done, and keep for Germany my braided clothes, which in any case are no longer the fashion in Paris. In the first place, a black suit is an economy (which is my chief consideration on my journey to Paris), and, secondly, it looks well and is suitable for both country and drawing-room wear; with a black coat you can go anywhere. The tailor has just brought Herr

---

[1] *Rosemunde*, which was to have been performed on 11 January 1778, was not given in Mannheim until 20 January 1780.

Wendling his suit today. The clothes I intend to take with me are my brown puce-coloured Spanish coat and the two waistcoats. Please tell me in your next letter whether I ought to do so. Well, let's change the subject. Now that he has heard me twice, Herr ⟨Wieland⟩ is quite enchanted with me. The last time after showering compliments on me he said: 'It is a real piece of good fortune that I have found you here', and he pressed my hand. Today there was a rehearsal of 'Rosemunde' in the theatre. It is—good, but ⟨nothing more.⟩ If it were bad, they couldn't produce it, could they?

Just as one can't sleep without lying in bed! Yet there's no rule without an exception. I myself have come across some instances of this. So good-night!

(271b) *Maria Anna Mozart resumes writing*

[Autograph in the Mozarteum, Salzburg]

[MANNHEIM, 11 *January* 1778]
I lunched today, [January] 11th, with Herr Danner as usual. They both asked me to send their most devoted greetings to you and Nannerl. They are both excellent people and are exceedingly kind to me. I am not at all pleased that you have taken on the ⟨Countess's daughters.⟩ She isn't worth so much trouble on your part and doesn't deserve such a return for her deceitfulness.

(271c) *Mozart resumes writing*

[Autograph in the Mozarteum, Salzburg]

[MANNHEIM, 11 *January* 1778]
Particolarmente per un zecchino il mese.[1] Now for some sensible talk. I know for a fact that ⟨the Emperor⟩ is proposing to ⟨establish German opera in Vienna⟩ and that he is making every effort ⟨to find a young Kapellmeister⟩ who understands the ⟨German language,⟩ is talented and is capable of striking out a new line. ⟨Benda[2] of Gotha⟩ is applying, but ⟨Schweitzer⟩[3] is determined to get it. I think it would ⟨be a good thing for me⟩—provided, of course, that ⟨the pay⟩ is good. ⟨If the Emperor will give me a thousand gulden, I will write a German opera for him: if he won't have me,⟩ it's all the same to me. Please write to all ⟨our friends in Vienna⟩ you can think of and tell them ⟨that it is in my power

---

[1] Particularly for a zecchino a month.
[2] Georg Benda (1722–1795), the most distinguished member of a family of Czech musicians, was Kapellmeister to the Duke of Gotha from 1750 until 1778. He composed sacred and instrumental music and several operettas. His fame, however, rests on his two duodramas *Ariadne auf Naxos* and *Medea*, 1775.
[3] Anton Schweitzer had been musical director of the Seyler theatrical company in Gotha since 1774.

to do honour to the Emperor.⟩ If he won't take me on any other terms, then let him ⟨try me with an opera⟩—after that he can do what he likes for all I care. Adieu. But please set the ball rolling *at once*, or ⟨someone may forestall me.⟩ I kiss your hands 1000 times and embrace my sister with all my heart and remain

WOLFGANG MOZART

(271d) *Maria Anna Mozart resumes writing*

[Autograph in the Mozarteum, Salzburg]

[MANNHEIM, 11 *January* 1778]

Wolfgang is now composing six new trios[1] and is going to have them engraved by subscription. When they are finished he'll send you six copies, so that you may sell them in Salzburg. Addio. Keep well. I remain as always your wife faithful unto death

MARIANNA MOZART

All sorts of messages to all our acquaintances.
My kindest regards to Bimperl.

(272) *Leopold Mozart to his Wife and Son*

[Extract]   *[Autograph in the Mozarteum, Salzburg]*

MY DEAR ONES!   SALZBURG, 12 *January* 1778

I didn't write to you last post-day and I too shall write only once a week, unless something special happens. I have received your letter of the 3rd and am delighted that you are well. We too are in good health, except that Nannerl has had a cold in her head for some days and I am not letting her go out. We have had no more letters from Munich. ★ Perhaps my correspondent[2] has no definite information—or perhaps he does not dare to write. All that people know here is that the new Imperial Ambassador to Munich is the Imperial envoy Baron Lehrbach, District Commandant of Ellingen, and an uncle of our Lehrbach here. An officer and 28 men of the Taxis regiment have moved into Reichenhall. Cornet Andretter has written home for money, but doesn't yet know where he has been ordered to. Otherwise everything is quiet and I trust that it may remain so. Mysliwecek has written to say that at the Prince's request he composed two concertoni which he sent to Brunetti, but has had no

---

[1] K. 301-306 [293a-c, 300c, 293d, 300l], six sonatas for clavier and violin, four of which Mozart composed in Mannheim. They were published in November 1778 by Sieber in Paris and were dedicated to the Electress Marie Elizabeth of the Palatinate. Frau Mozart calls them trios, as they could be performed with a cello obbligato.

[2] Leopold Mozart's correspondent was Johann Baptist Becke, flautist in the Munich court orchestra.

reply. I have written to tell him that he will get nothing for them, as they were probably included in the former payment, but that he ought to go on reminding Brunetti until the latter gets tired of paying the six kreuzer ★ postal fee and sets things going. We are to have only five or six balls at the Town Hall. The actors are wretched, are drawing very small audiences and are much to be pitied. We have not yet seen any of their performances. They say that after Easter the Archbishop would like to bring over the opera buffa from Munich and pay the company 50 ducats a month out of ★ his own pocket. His Excellency the Chief Steward has just told me that His Grace commanded him to ask *Haydn and me* whether we knew of a *very good organist* who must, however, be a *first-rate clavierist*, and at the same time *of good appearance and presence, as he will be giving lessons to the ladies.* 'What?' I asked, 'did His Grace mention me too?' 'Yes, you in particular', he replied and laughed. I said: 'I know nobody who has all these qualities. *If there is such a person in Mannheim, then he can make his fortune.*' The Prince booked Walter's room at the Andretters for a new Italian secretary and had it heated for a week. But the latter having only got as far as Rovereto, already began to sniff the air of Salzburg, and this brought on such a violent fever that he turned back home, and although he had only been away for three days, he looked so ill that, as letters ★ about him state, he was absolutely unrecognizable. Wolfgang will laugh when he hears that Fehlacher of Lauffen has applied for the post of ★ Court Organist. Rust never goes out now. He is setting the 'Parnasso confuso'[1] to music for the consecration of the new Bishop of Olmütz. But, as Spitzeder and the copyists tell me, he is for the most part using ★ arias taken from his own scores. I must close now. We kiss you both a million times. Nannerl is better—and we are your old

MZT

All—Herr Bullinger especially, send you their greetings. Addio! I am enclosing only one page of your sonata,[2] so that the letter may not be too bulky. I shall return it bit by bit.[3]

(273) *Maria Anna Mozart to her Husband*

[Autograph in the possession of A. Rosenthal, London]

MANNHEIM, 17 January 1778

MY DEAR HUSBAND,

I was delighted to receive today your letter dated the 12th. I am sorry that so many people are ill. No doubt this is due to the bad weather. Here

---

[1] A text by Metastasio.
[2] K. 309 [284b], written for Rosa Cannabich, which Leopold Mozart was having copied in Salzburg.   [3] These last two sentences are written on the wrapper.

we have had a lot of rain and now it is rather warm for the season and very unhealthy. One never hears any news here and everything is very quiet. There has already been a rumour that the Imperial soldiers have marched into Bavaria. But no one really knows anything for certain. I think that if the Emperor were planning something against the Elector, the Elector would not stay so long in Munich but would return to Mannheim. We know, of course, that Baron Lehrbach is the Imperial envoy and we know him quite well. He is an excellent gentleman and he has been here. We had a letter to him from the Baron Lehrbach at Salzburg. Wolfgang handed him the letter here at our inn. May God but grant that everything may remain peaceful. My journey home would not be at all enjoyable if there were soldiers round about. God protect me from such a thing. I should certainly die of fright. Meanwhile I live in hopes that events will very soon show what turn they are going to take.

(273a) *Mozart to his Father*

[*Autograph in the possession of A. Rosenthal, London*]

[MANNHEIM, 17 *January* 1778]
Next Wednesday I am going for a few days to Kirchheim-Bolanden to visit the Princess of Orange.[1] People here have said such nice things to me about her that I have at last decided to go. A Dutch officer,[2] a good friend of mine, got a terrible scolding from her for not bringing me with him when he went to offer her his New Year wishes. I shall get eight louis d'or at least, for, as she is passionately fond of singing, I have had four arias copied for her and, as she has a nice little orchestra and gives a concert every day, I shall also present her with a symphony. Moreover the copying of the arias will not cost me much, for it has been done by a certain Herr Weber,[3] who is accompanying me there. I don't know whether I have already written about his daughter[4] or not—She sings indeed most admirably and has a lovely, pure voice. The only thing she lacks is dramatic action; were it not for that, she might be the prima

---

[1] Princesse Caroline of Nassau-Weilburg, sister of William of Orange. See p. 391, n. 3.
[2] Probably De La Pottrie.
[3] Fridolin Weber (1733–1779), uncle of Karl Maria von Weber, composer of *Der Freischütz*, was first a notary. In 1765 he accepted an ill-paid post as bass singer at the Mannheim court and manged to eke out an existence by prompting and copying. He and his family followed the Electoral Court to Munich in 1778, but soon moved to Vienna, where his second daughter, Aloysia, had obtained an appointment at the Opera. He died in October 1779. For a full account of the Weber family see Schurig, vol. ii. pp. 463–465; E. K. Blümml, *Aus Mozarts Freundes- und Familienkreis*, 1923; F. Hefele, *Die Vorfahren Karl Maria von Webers*, 1926.
[4] Aloysia (*c.* 1760–1839), Fridolin Weber's second daughter. She was then about seventeen.

donna on any stage. She is only sixteen. Her father is a thoroughly honest German who is bringing up his children well, and for that very reason the girl is persecuted with attentions here. He has six children, five girls and one son.[1] He and his wife and children have been obliged to live for fourteen years[2] on an income of 200 gulden and because he has always attended carefully to his duties and has provided the Elector with a very talented singer, who is only sixteen, he now gets in all—400 gulden. She sings most excellently my aria written for De Amicis with those horribly difficult passages[3] and she is to sing it at Kirchheim-Bolanden. She is quite well able to teach herself. She accompanies herself very well and she also plays galanterie quite respectably. What is most fortunate for her at Mannheim is that she has won the praise of all honest people of good will. Even the Elector and the Electress are only too glad to receive her, provided it doesn't cost them anything. She can go to the Electress whenever she likes, even daily; and this is due to her good behaviour.

Do you know what I should like to ask you to do?—To send me whenever you have an opportunity, *but as soon as possible*, let us say, bit by bit, the two sonatas for four hands[4] and the Fischer variations![5]—For I could make good use of them in Paris.

I think that we shall leave here on February 15th at latest, as there is no opera here. Now for something else. Last Wednesday there was a big party at our house to which I too was invited. There were fifteen guests and in the evening the young lady of the house[6] was to play the concerto[7] I had taught her. About eleven in the morning the Privy Councillor came to see me and brought Herr Vogler who by the way wanted absolument to make my closer acquaintance. I just can't tell you how often he had bothered me to go to him. At last he overcame his pride and paid me the first visit. Besides, people tell me that he is now quite different, since he is no longer so much admired; for at first they made an idol of him. So we at once went upstairs together, the guests began to arrive by degrees and did nothing but chatter. After dinner, however, he sent to his house for two claviers, tuned to the same pitch, and also for his tedious engraved sonatas. I had to play them while he accompanied me on the other clavier. At his urgent request I had to send for my sonatas also.[8] I should mention that before dinner he had scrambled through my concerto[9] at sight (the one which the daughter of the house plays—written for Countess Lützow[10]). He took the first movement *prestissimo*, the Andante *allegro* and the Rondo, believe it or not, *prestississimo*. He

---

[1] We only know of four daughters, Josefa Hofer, Aloysia Lange, Konstanze Mozart and Sophie Haibel.   [2] Twelve years. Fridolin Weber had moved from Zell to Mannheim in 1765.
[3] Giunia's aria no. 11, 'Ah, se il crudel', in Mozart's opera *Lucio Silla*, composed 1772.
[4] K. 358 [186c] and K. 381 [123a].   [5] K. 179 [189a].   [6] Therese Pierron Serrarius.
[7] K. 246.   [8] Probably K. 279-284 [189d-h, 205b].   [9] K. 246.
[10] Wife of Count von Lützow, commandant of the castle Hohensalzburg.

generally played the bass differently from the way it was written, inventing now and then quite another harmony and even melody. Nothing else is possible at that pace, for the eyes cannot see the music nor the hands perform it. Well, what good is it?—That kind of sight-reading and shitting are all one to me. The listeners (I mean those who deserve the name) can only say that they have *seen* music and piano-playing. They hear, think and—feel as little during the performance as *the player himself*. Well, you may easily imagine that it was unendurable. At the same time I could not bring myself to say to him, *Far too quick!* Besides, it is much easier to play a thing quickly than slowly: in passage-work you can leave out a few notes without anyone noticing it. But is that beautiful?—In rapid playing the right and left hands can be changed without anyone seeing or hearing it. But is that beautiful?—And wherein consists the art of playing *prima vista*? In this: in playing the piece in the time in which it ought to be played, and in playing all the notes, appoggiaturas and so forth, exactly as they are written and with the appropriate expression and taste, so that you might suppose that the performer had composed it himself. Vogler's fingering too is wretched; his left thumb is just like that of the late Adlgasser and he does all the treble runs downwards with the thumb and first finger of his right hand. In my next letter I shall tell you more about this. For in the meantime Vogler has invited me to a musical party. So after all I must stand high in his favour. Addio. I kiss your hands 100,000 times and embrace my sister with all my heart. Our best regards to all our good friends and especially to Herr Bullinger and Mlle. Sallerl.

WOLFGANG AMADÈ MOZART

Please copy out for me a beautifully written A B C with both capital and small letters, and send it to me.

(274) *Leopold Mozart to his Son*

[Extract]   [Autograph in the Mozarteum, Salzburg]

SALZBURG, 19 *January* 1778

You say that on your journey to Paris you intend to take as little luggage as possible. That is very sound. But it would be a mistake to leave anything behind in Mannheim. I have had experience of this and have a thousand times regretted that I have left things behind, thus obliging me to return to the place or to have them sent òn at great risk and expense or perhaps abandon them altogether. I should never have made our second journey to Paris from England, if I had not left a number of things there, and I should have saved a great deal of money in Holland, if I had not sent our furs and other things from Calais to Paris. For how could I foresee that my children would fall ill in Holland and that I should be forced to remain there and buy a lot of things over again

★ at a very high price? So you must take your clothes with you. You cannot and must not do the same as your travelling companions, for your circumstances are very different from theirs. These gentlemen are only going to Paris for a short time, so it is to their interest not only to take very little luggage, but to save up their fine clothes for the gala-days in Mannheim. They can't go about in Paris in an ordinary everyday costume, such as they wear at home, just as we used to wear daily in other places the clothes which we wore in Salzburg on Sundays. If they were to wear their fine clothes every day in Paris, they would be faced with the sad necessity of having to purchase more fine clothes with which to appear at Court at home. Now as the attire which does one most honour in Paris and elsewhere is a black suit with a richly worked waistcoat for special occasions, it is quite true that their preparations are perfectly sound. But your circumstances are quite different. It would be very foolish for you to travel to Paris merely in order to put in an appearance and then return to Mannheim with these gentlemen. I well believe that they all want to have you back. I need not tell you the reason, for you know it. But as you must now endeavour to make greater strides, to win for yourself, as far as in you lies, glory, honour and a great name, and thus make money also, you have a purpose which cannot be achieved in a few months, still less in a few weeks. So to my mind economy demands

★ that you should take your clothes with you. As for your music, you must
★ leave nothing behind you in Mannheim. Carriers will surely be going to Paris. You could pack everything into a small box (but not your principal scores) and send them on to Paris. *Write on the box the address at which it should be delivered and that it contains music.* You will be able to make use of it all in Paris. If this doesn't work (though if it were myself, it would *have* to work!), then Mamma must bring home your music. Nothing must be left in Mannheim. I shall write about everything else next time.

I sent off at once full details of what ⟨*you told me about the Emperor's German opera*⟩ to Heufeld,[1] and begged him most urgently to send ⟨*a petition to the Emperor and Empress immediately.*⟩ I am writing by the next post to the Chief Equerry Count Dietrichstein, to the wife of Dr. Vaugg and to a few other people who, I think, can do something. All our Salzburg friends send their greetings to you both, and Nannerl and I kiss you many 1000 times and I remain ever your old

MZT

---

[1] Franz von Heufeld, who had great influence in the theatrical world in Vienna. Leopold Mozart's letter is lost.

★

I shall write again by the next post and enclose a little more of your
sonata; to do so now would make this letter too bulky. By that time I
shall have more to say ⟨about the prospects of a war.⟩

★

(275) *Maria Anna Mozart to her Husband*

[*Autograph in the Mozarteum, Salzburg*]

MY DEAR HUSBAND,   MANNHEIM, 24 *January* 1778
    I was delighted to receive today your letter of the 19th, and the news
it contains has given me much pleasure. For one hears nothing at all here;
it is as quiet as if one were no longer in the world. People only sigh and
long to have ⟨the Elector⟩ back. His absence means a great loss to the
town, for no visitors come here, as there is nothing to see. The townspeople have generally made their biggest profits during the carnival,
when they are able to fleece visitors properly; but this year their prospect
of doing so is spoiled. Wolfgang went off yesterday morning with Herr
Weber and his daughter to Kirchheim-Bolanden to visit the Princess of
Weilburg.[1] I hardly think that she will let them go before the week is out,
for she is a passionate lover of music and plays the clavier and sings.
Wolfgang took with him a supply of arias and symphonies to present to
her. The place is only a ten hours' drive from here, that is, a short day's
journey. The Princess is nearly always there and only goes to Holland
for about two months of the year in order to visit her brother. Meanwhile
I have persuaded Wolfgang to change his mind about his clothes, which
he is now going to take with him; and I shall persuade him to take the
big trunk, for if he packs into it all his clothes and all his music, which
made up three huge parcels, it will certainly be full enough; and as I hear
that they are going to travel by the mail coach (which, by the way, starts
from here and does not travel at night), it is much better for him to have
all his luggage together in one trunk. You have not yet had a reply from
Herr von Grimm. I think you would have done better to send your letter
to his old address, for if he has left it, the people would doubtless know
where he has moved to. It was a good plan to write those letters to
Vienna, but I ought to remind you that it would do no harm if you were
to write to Count Thun also, who has so much influence ⟨with the
Emperor⟩ and had such a liking for Wolfgang. There is a singer at the
opera here, Hartig[2] by name, who is so affectionate and friendly with us
that he never calls me anything but his dear Mamma. Without knowing
you he sends you his warmest greetings. He called on me today to see

---

[1] See p. 447.
[2] Franz Christian Hartig (1750–1819), a tenor at the Mannheim opera. He was being
trained by Raaff.

how I was getting along without Wolfgang. When he heard that I was writing home, he at once asked me to convey his most devoted compliments.

Our hostess, the wife of the Privy Court Councillor, also sends you her greetings. She is indeed an excellent woman. I have to spend the whole afternoon and evening until half past ten with them. As soon as I get home after lunch, the young lady comes to our room and makes me go upstairs to them. We do needlework until it gets dark and after supper we play 'fire and murder' (which I have taught them) at twenty counters for a kreuzer. So you can work out how much we can lose. Addio. Keep well, both of you. I kiss you both 1000 times and remain as always your faithful wife

MARIA ANNA MOZART

Please give my best greetings to all our good friends, especially to Monsieur Bullinger and Mlle Sallerl.
A kiss for Bimperl.

(276) *Leopold Mozart to his Wife and Son*

[*Extract*]   [*Autograph in the Mozarteum, Salzburg*]

MY DEAR ONES!   SALZBURG, 26 [*recte* 25] *January* 1778
My last letter, a very long one, was dated the 19th and I did not write on the 22nd. I have received your letter of the 17th. Thank God that you are well. We too are in good health. Padre Maestro Martini has replied, but he had not yet received the portrait which was packed with other goods and will have travelled very slowly by carriers. He sends Wolfgang a thousand greetings and says that he is going to write to Signor Raaff and ask him to say on his behalf all sorts of nice things to the Elector
★ about you and your merits. Herr Janitsch,[1] the violinist, and a cellist[2] from Wallerstein have arrived in Salzburg and came to see me at once. They brought a letter for Count Kühnburg from Beecke, who has gone on to Vienna. The Archbishop is not going to hear them play at Court. He said that if they liked they could give a concert, but he did not offer to go to it. The upshot of all this and the information which I have got from them I shall tell you next time I write. Beecke must be very jealous of Wolfgang, for he tries to belittle him as much as possible. I have sent

---

[1] Anton Janitsch (1753–1812), a member of the orchestra of Prince Kraft Ernst von Öttingen-Wallerstein. See p. 338, n. 1.
[2] Joseph Reicha (1746–1795), a Czech, was a cellist in the Wallerstein orchestra and in 1785 was appointed musical director to the Elector of Cologne. His nephew was the well-known Czech composer, Anton Reicha (1770–1836).

off my second letter to Vienna about that matter and a letter to the wife of Dr. Vaugg, which contains the fullest and most vivid description of our affair. People of his type generally get a thing done more easily than the very great, with whom you can never be sure as to whether they are not already interested in someone else. I put forward most insistently my requests—⟨both about the *German opera* and about the *recommendation to Paris.*⟩ By the next post I shall write to a different quarter. Grimm has not yet replied, which is rather disappointing for me. I shall send you the sonatas for four hands[1] and the variations.[2] Mysliwecek wrote again the other day to say that he was hoping to receive shortly your scrittura from Naples. But I regard it as an excuse, for he only makes an announcement like this when he wants me to do something for him. By the way, I stick to my opinion that Wolfgang should leave nothing behind him in Mannheim. It is high time that Mamma got ready for her journey, for a ★ good opportunity may perhaps present itself for her to reach Augsburg or even Munich. Ah, my dear Wolfgang, I must not brood on the whole business, for if I do, the heaviest sadness comes over me. Nannerl sends you greetings and kisses Mamma's hands. We kiss you a million times and I am your old

MZT

Wolfgang will have returned from Kirchheim by now. Mlle Weber and her father will have had the same experience as others. *Propheta non acceptus in patria!*[3]

The two gentlemen from Wallerstein[4] insisted on hearing Nannerl play. It emerged that their sole object in so doing was that they might guess from her style of playing what yours was like; and they were particularly anxious to hear one of your compositions. She played your Mannheim sonata[5] most excellently and with all the necessary expression. They were amazed at her performance and at the composition, saying that they had never heard any of your works and that this one had some entirely new and original ideas; and Reicha, the cellist, who is an excellent clavierist and who had previously been playing on our harpsichord very smoothly and in the style of the organ, remarked several times that *it was a very sound composition.* After that they accompanied Nannerl most excellently in your clavier trio in B♭.[6] ★

I have just this moment heard that Count Daun, canon of our Cathedral, has stated that the Elector is to remain in Munich and that he is going to have his orchestra brought over after Easter. The first is quite possible, for

---

[1] K. 381 [123a] and K. 358 [186c]. See p. 412, n. 2.
[2] The variations are K. 179 [189a], twelve variations on a minuet by Fischer. See p. 256, n. 5.
[3] A prophet has no honour in his own country.
[4] Anton Janitsch and Joseph Reicha.   [5] K. 309 [284b].   [6] K. 254, composed in 1776.

he must himself take stock of the government, introduce law and order and wrest it from the claws of those vultures, a task which he can entrust to no one else. The second may be a natural consequence of the first. What do you think of this letter? Have I left a single white spot uncovered?

Addio.

(277) *Leopold Mozart to his Son*

[*Extract*]   [*Autograph in the Mozarteum, Salzburg*]

MON TRÉS CHER FILS!   SALZBURG, 29 *January* 1778

Here is Herr von Heufeld's letter.[1] To tell the truth, I did not expect much from the whole business, ⟨for the Emperor⟩ seems to me to be like our Archbishop, that is to say, he declares, '*I must have something very good but as cheaply as possible*'. I don't want the letter back, so Mamma may keep it. Enclosed with it was a note from Director Mesmer,[2] which runs as follows:

DEAREST FRIEND,

I cannot understand how it is that you have not had a reply to your letter to me, for I certainly wrote to you after my illness, though rather late, it is true. I wonder whether my wife, who was very anxious at the time about her Joseph, could have forgotten to post my letters? My cousin, Dr. Mesmer, who is leaving one of these days for Paris and intended to introduce my son to you on the way through, was to have reproached you with the same kind of slackness. Well, the plan has been dropped, as your son is no longer in Salzburg. You may rest assured that I have a warm affection for you and take an interest in everything which concerns your family. Why did you not send your son straight to Vienna? And why are you not sending him now? I promise you faithfully that he can have free board, lodging and everything else with us as long as he likes, and that all your friends in Vienna, myself included, will endeavour to obtain some good appointment for him. But unless he comes here, it is impossible to do anything for him. There is plenty of room in Vienna for a great talent, but these things cannot be arranged in a trice. With the help of good friends, however, it would be possible for him to achieve his object; and, after all, Vienna is the best place to live in. You know all about your Swabian friends and the advantages of this capital. So choose—and let me know. I remain your old friend

MESMER

[1] Heufeld's letter, which gives an interesting account of theatrical conditions in Vienna, is printed in *MBA*, No. 407, and translated in *MDB*, pp. 169–171. Heufeld held out little hope of an appointment for Mozart, but suggested that he should compose a German opera, send it to the Emperor and, if possible, come to Vienna. He mentioned the advantage of having the support of Wieland, who, however, had strongly recommended Schweitzer.
[2] See p. 235.

If our good Mesmer had replied or if his wife had not kept back the letters, I should doubtless have considered sending you to Vienna, for you would have been very well treated in his house. If you decide to take this path, it is still open to you. You will see that Herr von Heufeld, who, as we know, is not a very ardent Christian, says nevertheless that he trusts you to hold to the good principles inculcated by your parents and to guard yourself against evil company. Count Kühnburg, Chief Equerry, who, as is well known, lays no claim to saintliness, talked to me a few days ago in the same vein and expressed extreme anxiety about Paris, which he knows thoroughly. He said that you should be on your guard against its dangers and that you should refrain from all familiarity with young Frenchmen, and even more so with the women, who are always on the look-out for strangers to keep them, who run after young people of talent in an astonishing way in order to get at their money, draw them into their net or even land them as husbands. God and your own good sense will preserve you. Any such calamity would be the death of me! Janitsch and Reicha went off to Linz this morning by the mail coach. They will have taken in about 70 gulden at their concert, although the Archbishop only forked out eight. They are both very fine players; they have an extraordinary facility and lightness in their bowing, sure intonation and a beautiful tone, and they play with the greatest expression. Reicha is a first-rate fellow. Janitsch plays in the style of Lolli,[1] but his adagio playing is infinitely better. Indeed I am no lover of excessively rapid passages, where you have to produce the notes with the half tone of the violin and, so to speak, only touch the fiddle with the bow and almost play in the air. On the other hand his cantabile playing is very poor, for he is inclined to make sharp jerks and to indulge in allegro fireworks which to an understanding listener are really most offensive. Reicha has a better cantabile. Both, however, have Beecke's[2] fault of dragging the time, of holding back the whole orchestra by a nod and then returning to the original tempo. They ended by playing a duet in *contrattempo*[3] and with the most astounding execution and precision. But the tempo of their playing was altogether in the manner of the two Besozzi[4] of Turin,

---

[1] The famous eighteenth-century violinist and teacher, Antonio Lolli (*c.* 1730–1802).

[2] The pianist Ignaz von Beecke, also a Wallerstein musician. See p. 305, n. 1, and p. 345, n. 1.

[3] Leopold Mozart may mean 'broken time', which he discusses fully in his *Violinschule*, chap. xii. § 16. (See facsimile edition by B. Paumgartner, Vienna, 1922, p. 26.) Certainly the expression can be used to indicate either 'with syncopation' or 'in florid counterpoint', i.e. with one part playing rapid passages while the other proceeds steadily.

[4] The Besozzi were an Italian family of distinguished wind-instrument players. The two brothers to whom Leopold Mozart refers were probably Alessandro (1702–1793), a remarkable oboist, who in 1731 joined the court orchestra at Turin, and Paolo Girolamo (1704–1778), a famous bassoon-player. Paolo Girolamo was the special associate of Alessandro, and their beautiful duet performances aroused Burney's enthusiasm (*Present State of Music in France and Italy*, 1773, p. 69).

who by the way are both dead now.[1] Reicha and Janitsch spent the wholeofyesterdayafternoonuntilsixo'clockatourhouse. Yoursisterhad to play your clavier concertos[2] from the original score and some other pieces. We played their violin parts. They liked your compositions immensely. Reicha played a concerto of his own which was quite good, ★ with some new ideas and rather after your style. Haydn liked it too. If you are really leaving on February 15th, then I have only two more ★ post-days left. So, in order to let you have all the music, I must send a rather heavy letter each time. It will be expensive for you, but you really need the sonatas for four hands and the variations.[3] Who will comb Wolfgang's hair now? Is his head ⟨free of lice?⟩ Oh, indeed I have a great many things to think of ! If only Herr Grimm had replied; that would have taken a heavy load off my heart. All send their greetings. Nannerl and I kiss you millions of times and I am your old

MZT

(278) *Mozart to his Mother at Mannheim*

[Copy in the Mozarteum, Salzburg]

[WORMS, 31 January 1778]

Oh, mother mine!
Butter is fine.
Praise and thanks be to Him,
We're alive and full of vim.
Through the world we dash,
Though we're rather short of cash.
But we don't find this provoking
And none of us are choking.
Besides, to people I'm tied
Who carry their muck inside
And let it out, if they are able,
Both before and after table.
At night of farts there is no lack,
Which are let off, forsooth, with a powerful crack.
The king of farts came yesterday
Whose farts smelt sweeter than the may.
His voice, however, was no treat
And he himself was in a heat.
Well, now we've been over a week away
And we've been shitting every day.
Wendling, no doubt, is in a rage
That I haven't composed a single page;

---

[1] Paolo Girolamo died in 1778, but Alessandro was still living.
[2] Perhaps K. 175, 238, 246 and 271.   [3] See p. 453.

But when I cross the Rhine once more,
I'll surely dash home through the door
And, lest he call me mean and petty,
I'll finish off his four quartetti.[1]
The concerto[2] for Paris I'll keep, 'tis more fitting.
I'll scribble it there some day when I'm shitting.
Indeed I swear 'twould be far better fun
With the Webers around the world to run
Than to go with those bores, you know whom I mean,
When I think of their faces, I get the spleen.
But I suppose it must be and off we shall toddle,
Though Weber's arse I prefer to Ramm's noddle.
A slice of Weber's arse is a thing
I'd rather have than Monsieur Wendling.
With our shitting God we cannot hurt
And least of all if we bite the dirt.
We are honest birds, all of a feather,
We have summa summarum eight eyes together,
Not counting those on which we sit.
But now I really must rest a bit
From rhyming. Yet this I must add,
That on Monday I'll have the honour, egad,
To embrace you and kiss yours hands so fair.
But first in my pants I'll shit, I swear.

Adieu Mamma

Worms, January 1778th   Your faithful child,
    Anno 31.   With distemper wild.

TRAZOM

(279) *Maria Anna Mozart to her Husband*

[*Autograph in the Mozarteum, Salzburg*]

MY DEAR HUSBAND,   MANNHEIM, 1 *February* 1778

I have received your letter of the 25th and am delighted to hear that you are well. Wolfgang has not yet returned from Kirchheim and will probably not come back until next Wednesday. Herr Weber has written to his wife that the Princess will not let them go before then. So I too must be content, I suppose. But about his journey to Paris, I am every bit as anxious as you are. If only Monsieur Grimm were there, I shouldn't

---

[1] Wendling had obtained for Mozart a commission to write three easy flute concertos and two flute quartets for De Jean. See pp. 414, 481.

[2] Mozart composed one flute concerto, K. 313 [285c], in Mannheim and probably rewrote for De Jean his oboe concerto, K. 314 [285d], written in 1778 for Ferlendis. See p. 320, n. 1.

worry at all, for he could perhaps take him into his house or help him to make his fortune in some way or another. Grimm has certainly been a true friend to us and one on whom we can rely. I have just this moment had a letter from Wolfgang, who is in Worms and will get back here tomorrow. How glad I shall be to see him again. The Privy Court Councillor invariably copies out the news which you send me from Salzburg and the articles about the war, and always looks forward most eagerly to my getting your letter, for everything is kept very quiet here and the rumours we hear are lies. Thus whatever you tell us we regard as articles of faith. The people of the Palatinate say that ⟨the Elector⟩ cannot possibly remain ⟨in Munich⟩. In short, they consider ⟨Mannheim and the Palatinate to be far superior to and finer than Bavaria and Munich.⟩ It is all right for you to house the opera-singers, provided they do not spoil the stove in our new room by heating it too much, and that they do not behave like a lot of pigs as Italians generally do.[1] You need not worry about Wolfgang taking all his things with him. He must take everything and the big trunk as well. I shall see that he does. A smaller trunk will do for me. The list of marksmen will be shorter when the two gentlemen from Wallerstein go off again.[2] I can well believe that Captain Beecke is trying to belittle Wolfgang, for up to the present he has been looked up to as a god in his own district and in the neighbourhood of Augsburg. But when people heard Wolfgang, they immediately exclaimed: 'Why, he knocks Beecke into a cocked hat. You simply can't compare them.' All sorts of messages to all our good friends, and especially to Monsieur Bullinger and Mlle Sallerl. I kiss you both a million times and remain your faithful wife

MARIANNA MOZART

I wanted very much to write more. But they have already sent for me to go upstairs, for I have to spend the whole day with them and never get back to my room until half past ten. Addio. Once more, do keep well.

(280) *Leopold Mozart to his Wife*

[Extract]   [Autograph in the Mozarteum, Salzburg]

MY DEAR WIFE!   SALZBURG, 2 *February* 1778

I have received your letter of January 24th. Wolfgang will have long since returned and I hope that he has received a handsome present. You will need money for the journey. I have just received two New Year ⟨accounts from tailors,⟩ I mean, from Daser and Amman. The first, for Wolfgang's suit and waistcoats, amounts to 15 gulden, the second, for

---

[1] Frau Mozart is referring to a passage in her husband's letter of 25 January, which for lack of space has had to be omitted.

[2] Anton Janitsch and Josef Reicha had joined the Mozarts' shooting parties.

yourself, amounts to 6 gulden 24 kreuzer. ⟨I don't know how I am going to pay them⟩ and they will ⟨have to be paid⟩ before our Salzburg fair. ⟨Moreover, Theresa wants her wages⟩ to buy things for herself. Then there is our ⟨house rent,⟩ though that sum I shall be able to raise; but, by Heaven, I do not know how I am going to meet the other bills. Mannheim will probably have to sigh and groan, for not only now, when circumstances require his presence, but in the future too, the Elector will assuredly spend most of his time in Munich. You will have gathered from Herr von Heufeld's letter that introductions, especially from the great ones of this world, sometimes do more harm than good. But Dr. Vaugg's wife, to whom I wrote a most pressing letter, will certainly be able to make use of the fact that people have not forgotten our Wolfgang. I have now fired off replies to the Honourables Heufeld and Mesmer. If Wolfgang were to go to Vienna today, he knows of one safe haven into which he can turn. Please give my most devoted greetings to the wife of the Privy Court Councillor, her husband and daughter, to Herr Hartig, Herr Wendling and all the other gentlemen. I know that you will have done so very often even if I did not mention it, just as I always deliver greetings here from you. *Bring back with you any old stockings, silk or otherwise, and anything else belonging to Wolfgang which he doesn't want; also any old linen of his or other articles,* for no doubt he will require a supply of new things. You and I can make use of some of his old clothes. When I close the letter, I ★ shall *probably* put in all the music which I have to send to Wolfgang. I ★ have bought something for his cousin, but I have not yet found a safe means of dispatching it to her. She has sent Wolfgang her portrait, for which he was always asking her.[1] Why did he put her to this expense? After all it is probably a miniature and possibly not even a good likeness. Nannerl kisses your hands and embraces her brother with all her heart. I am your old

MZT

How are you going to travel home? I shall write another letter to Herr Grimm and address it: rue Neuve Luxembourg. Nannerl asks you not to forget to bring her *the kind of cap that is in fashion.*

(281) *Mozart to his Father*

[*Portions of autograph in the Mozarteum, Salzburg, and in the Library of the Paris Conservatoire*]

MONSIEUR [MANNHEIM, 4 *February* 1778]
    MON TRÉS CHER PÉRE!

I simply cannot wait as I usually do until Saturday, because it is too long already since I have had the pleasure of talking to you in a letter.

[1] See p. 371, n. 2.

The first thing I want to tell you about is how I and my good friends got on at Kirchheim-Bolanden. Well, it was just a holiday trip—nothing more. We set off from here at eight o'clock on Friday morning, after I had breakfasted with Herr Weber. We had a smart covered coach which held four and we reached Kirchheim-Bolanden at four o'clock. We had to send a list of our names at once to the castle. Early next morning Herr Konzertmeister Rothfischer[1] called on us. He had already been described to me in Mannheim as a most honest fellow; and I found him so. In the evening, Saturday evening, we went to Court, where Mlle Weber sang three arias. I say nothing about her singing—only one word, excellent! I wrote to you the other day about her merits; but I shall not be able to close this letter without telling you something more about her, for only now have I got to know her properly and as a result to discover her great powers. We had to dine afterwards at the officers' table. We were obliged to walk a good distance to church next day, for the Catholic church is rather far off. That was Sunday. We lunched again with the officers, but they had no concert in the evening, as it was Sunday. So they have only 300 concerts in the year. We could have dined at Court in the evening, but we did not wish to do so, preferring to remain in the inn by ourselves. We would have unanimously and with heartfelt gladness done without the meals at Court, for we never enjoyed ourselves better than when we were alone. But we had to think a little about economy—for, as it was, we had quite enough to pay for. The following day, Monday, we again had a concert, and also on Tuesday and Wednesday. Mlle Weber sang thirteen times in all and played the clavier twice, for she does not play at all badly. What surprises me most is her excellent sight-reading. Would you believe it, she played my difficult sonatas[2] at sight, *slowly* but without missing a single note! On my honour I would rather hear my sonatas played by her than by Vogler! I played a dozen times in all, and once by request on the organ in the Lutheran church. I presented four symphonies to the Princess and received ⟨only seven louis d'or in silver,⟩ mark you, and my poor dear Mlle Weber only ⟨five.⟩ Really it was the last thing I expected. I was not hoping for much, but at least I thought that each of us would receive ⟨eight louis d'or.⟩ Basta! We have lost nothing by it, however, for I still have a profit of 42 gulden and moreover the inexpressible pleasure of making the acquaintance of a thoroughly honest, good Catholic Christian family. I am truly sorry that I did not get to know them long ago. I am now coming to an important point, about which I want you to reply at once.

Mamma and I have talked the matter over and are agreed that we do not like the sort of life the Wendlings lead.

---

[1] Paul Rothfischer, a violinist in the service of the Princess of Nassau-Weilburg.
[2] Probably the clavier sonatas of the series K. 279–284 [189d–h, 205b].

Wendling is a thoroughly honest, excellent fellow, but unfortunately he has no religion whatever; and the whole family are the same. It is enough to say that his daughter has been somebody's ⟨mistress.[1]⟩ Ramm is a decent fellow, but a libertine. I know myself, and I am positive that I have enough religion never at any time to do anything which I could not do openly before the whole world; but the mere idea of being, even though it is only on a journey, in the society of people whose way of thinking is so entirely different from my own (and from that of all honourable people), horrifies me. But of course they can do as they please. I have not the heart to travel with them, I should not have a single happy hour, I should not know what to talk about. For, in a word, I do not fully trust them. Friends who have no religion cannot be our friends for long. I have already given them a slight hint in advance by saying that during my absence three letters have arrived, about which all that I can tell them is that it is unlikely that I shall be able to travel with them to Paris, but that perhaps I shall follow them—or perhaps go elsewhere; and that they must not count on me. My idea is as follows:

I propose to remain here and finish entirely at my leisure that music for De Jean, for which I am to get 200 gulden. I can stay here as long as I like and neither board nor lodging costs me anything. In the meantime Herr Weber will endeavour to get engagements here and there for concerts with me, and we shall then travel together. When I am with him, it is just as if I were travelling with you. The very reason why I am so fond of him is because, apart from his personal appearance, he is just like you and has exactly your character and way of thinking. If my mother were not, as you know, too *comfortably lazy* to write, she would tell you the very same thing! I must confess that I much enjoyed travelling with them. We were happy and merry; I was hearing a man talk like you; I had nothing to worry about; I found my torn clothes mended; in short, I was waited on like a prince.

I have become so fond of this unfortunate family that my dearest wish is to make them happy; and perhaps I may be able to do so. My advice is that they should go to Italy. So now I should like you to write to our good friend Lugiati, and the sooner the better, and enquire what are the highest terms given to a prima donna in Verona—the more the better, one can always climb down—perhaps too it would be possible to obtain the Ascensa in Venice.[2] As far as her singing is concerned, I would wager my life that she will bring me renown. Even in a short time she has greatly profited by my instruction, and how much greater will the improvement be by then! I am not anxious either about her acting. If our

---

[1] See p. 362, n. 4.
[2] i.e. the contract to sing in the opera performed about the time of the Festival of the Ascension.

plan succeeds, we, M. Weber, his two daughters[1] and I will have the honour of visiting my dear Papa and my dear sister for a fortnight on our way through Salzburg. My sister will find a friend and a companion in Mlle Weber, for, like my sister in Salzburg, she has a reputation for good behaviour, her father resembles my father and the whole family resemble the Mozarts. True, there are envious folk, as there are in Salzburg, but when it comes to the point, they have to speak the truth. Honesty is the best policy. I can say that I shall look forward immensely to going to Salzburg with them, if only that you may hear her sing. She sings superbly the arias which I wrote for De Amicis, both the bravura aria and 'Parto, m'affretto' and 'Dalla sponda tenebrosa'.[2] I beg you to do your best to get us to Italy. You know my greatest desire is—to write operas.[3]

I will gladly write an opera for Verona for 50 zecchini, if only in order that she may make her name; for if I do not compose it, I fear that she may be victimized. By that time I shall have made so much money on the other journeys we propose to undertake together, that I shall not be the loser. I think we shall go to Switzerland and perhaps also to Holland. Do write to me soon about this. If we stay anywhere for long, the eldest daughter will be very useful to us; for we could have our own ménage, as she can cook. A propos, you must not be too much surprised when you hear that I have only 42 gulden left out of 77. That is merely the result of my delight at being again in the company of honest and like-minded people. I paid one half of the expenses, for I could not do otherwise, but I shall not do so on our other journeys and I have already told them so; I shall then pay only for *myself*. After we left, we stayed five days at Worms, where Weber has a brother-in-law, who is the Dean of the Monastery. I should add that he is terrified of Herr Weber's sarcastic quill. We had a jolly time there and lunched and dined every day with the Dean. I may say that this little journey gave me fine practice on the clavier. The Dean is an excellent and sensible man. Well, it is time for me to stop. If I were to write all I think, I should have no paper left. Send me an answer soon, I beg you. Do not forget how much I desire to write operas. I envy anyone who is composing one. I could really weep for vexation when I hear or see an aria. But Italian, not German; seriosa, not buffa. You should not have sent me Heufeld's letter, which caused me more annoyance than pleasure. The fool thinks that I shall write a comic opera; yes, and write one on chance and at my own risk. I think too that he would not have disgraced his title of 'Honourable',[4] if he had written 'der Herr Sohn'

---

[1] Josefa and Aloysia.

[2] Arias sung by De Amicis, who took the part of Giunia in *Lucio Silla*, composed in 1772. See p. 448, n. 3.

[3] The autograph in the Mozarteum, Salzburg, ends here. The autograph of the remaining portion of this letter is in the library of the Paris Conservatoire.

[4] Franz von Heufeld had recently received from the Emperor the Austrian title of 'Edler'.

and not 'Ihr Sohn'. But what is he after all but a Viennese booby; or perhaps he thinks that people remain twelve years old for ever? I have now written all that is weighing on my heart. My mother is quite satisfied with my ideas. It is impossible for me to travel with people—with a man—who leads a life of which the veriest stripling could not but be ashamed; and the thought of helping a poor family, without injury to myself, delights my very soul. I kiss your hands a thousands times and remain until death your most obedient son

WOLFGANG AMADÉ MOZART

Mannheim, 4 February 1778.

My greetings to all our good friends, and particularly to my best friend—Herr Bullinger.

(281a) *Maria Anna Mozart to her Husband*

[Copy in the Staatsbibliothek Preussischer Kulturbesitz, West Berlin[1]]

MY DEAR HUSBAND! MANNHEIM, 5 *February* [1778]
You will have seen from this letter that when Wolfgang makes new acquaintances, he immediately wants to give his life and property for them.
True, she sings exceedingly well; still, we must not lose sight of our own interests. I never liked his being in the company of Wendling and Ramm, but I never ventured to raise any objections, nor would he ever have listened to me.
But as soon as he got to know the Webers, he immediately changed his mind. In short, he prefers other people to me, for I remonstrate with him about this and that, and about things which I do not like; and he objects to this. So you yourself will have to think over what ought to be done. I do not consider his journey to Paris with Wendling at all advisable. I would rather accompany him myself later on. It would not cost so very much in the mail coach. Perhaps you will still get a reply from Herr Grimm. Meanwhile we are not losing anything here. I am writing this quite secretly, while he is at dinner, and I shall close, for I do not want to be caught. Addio.
I remain your faithful wife MARIA ANNA MOZART

(282) *Leopold Mozart to his Son*

[*Extract*] [*Autograph in the Mozarteum, Salzburg*]

MY DEAR SON! SALZBURG, 5 *February* 1778
As in all probability this will be the last letter which will reach you at Mannheim, it is addressed to you alone. My heart is heavy indeed, now

---

[1] Autograph in the Library of the Paris Conservatoire.

that I know that you will be still farther away from me. True, you can realise this to some extent, but you cannot feel the burden of grief which is weighing down my heart. If you will take the trouble to remember what I undertook with you two children in your tender youth, you will not accuse me of cowardice, but will admit, as others do, that I always have been and still am a man who has the courage to dare all. Yet I managed everything with the greatest caution and consideration that was humanly possible—for no one can prevent accidents—as only God knows what the future will bring. Up to the present, it is true, we have been neither happy nor unhappy; things have been, thank God, half and half. We have done everything to make you happier and through you to bring happiness to ourselves and to set your future at least on a firm footing. But Fate has willed that we should not achieve our purpose. As you are aware, owing to our last step I am now in very deep waters. As you know, ⟨*I am now in debt* to the extent⟩ of about 700 gulden and ⟨*haven't the faintest idea how I am going to support myself, Mamma and your sister on my monthly salary;*⟩ for as long as I live I cannot now hope ⟨*to get another farthing from the Prince.*⟩ So it must be as clear as noonday to you that the future of your old parents and of your good sister who loves you with all her heart, is entirely in your hands. Since you were born or rather since my marriage it has been very difficult for me to ⟨*support*⟩ a wife, seven children,[1] two maids and Mamma's own mother ⟨*on my monthly pay* of about 20 gulden⟩, and ⟨*to meet the expenses*⟩ of child-births, deaths and illnesses. If you think it over, you will realise that not only have I never spent a farthing on the smallest pleasure for myself but that without God's special mercy I should never have succeeded in spite of all my efforts ⟨*in keeping out of debt;*⟩ and yet ⟨*this is the first time I have got into debt.*⟩ When you were children, I gave up all my time to you in the hope that not only would you be able to provide later on for yourselves, but also that I might enjoy a comfortable old age, be able to give an account to God of the education of my children, be free from all anxiety, devote myself to the welfare of my soul and thus be enabled to meet my death in peace. But God has ordained that I must now take on again the *wearisome task* of giving lessons and that too in a town where this heavy work is so wretchedly paid that it is impossible to ⟨*earn enough each month to support oneself and one's family;*⟩ yet one has to be thankful to have any work, though one has to talk oneself hoarse if one is ⟨*to make even a pittance.*⟩ My dear Wolfgang, not only do I not distrust you in the very slightest degree; on the contrary, I place all my trust and confidence in your filial love. Our future depends on your abundant good sense, if

[1] Jahn, vol. i. p. 26, and Abert, vol. ii, p. 904, give particulars of Leopold Mozart's seven children, only two of whom survived, i.e. Nannerl, the fourth, born in 1751, and Wolfgang, the youngest, born in 1756.

you will only hearken to it, and on more fortunate circumstances, which, it is true, we cannot command. You are going off now to an entirely different world. Please do not think that prejudice makes me regard Paris as a very dangerous place; au contraire—from my own experience I have no reason whatever to think Paris so very dangerous. But my situation then and your present one are entirely different. On our first visit we stayed at the house of an ambassador and the second time in a self-contained lodging.[1] I had a certain position and you were children. I avoided all acquaintances and, mark you, *particularly all familiarity with people of our own profession*; you will remember that I did the same in Italy. I made the acquaintance and sought only the friendship of people of position—and, what is more, among these I associated with older people, never with young fellows, not even if they were of the highest rank. I never invited anyone to visit me constantly in my rooms, as I wanted to be quite free. Besides I thought it was more sensible to visit others when it suited me. For if I do not like the man or if I have work or business to do, I can stay away; whereas if people come to see me and don't know when to leave, it is difficult to get rid of them; and a person who is otherwise a welcome visitor may well hinder me when I have work on hand which must be done. You are but a young man of twenty-two; so you cannot have that settled gravity which might discourage any young fellow, of whatever rank he may be, an adventurer, jester or deceiver, old or young, from seeking your acquaintance and friendship in order to draw you into his company and then by degrees bend you to his will. One drifts imperceptibly into these traps and then one cannot get out. I shall say nothing about women, for where they are concerned the greatest reserve and prudence are necessary, Nature herself being our enemy. Whoever does not use his judgement to the utmost to keep the necessary reserve with them, will exert it in vain later on when he endeavours to extricate himself from the labyrinth, *a misfortune, which most often ends in death*. But how blindly we may often be led on by seemingly meaningless jests, flatteries and fun, for which Reason, when she reawakens later, is compelled to blush, you yourself may perhaps have learnt a little by experience. However, I do not want to reproach you. I know that you love me, not merely as your father, but also as your truest and surest friend; and that you understand and realize that our happiness and unhappiness, and, what is more, my long life or my speedy death are, if I may say so, apart from God, in your hands. If I have read you aright, I have nothing but joy to expect from you, and this alone must console me when I am robbed by your absence of a father's delight at hearing you, seeing you and folding you in his arms. Live like a good Catholic. Love and fear God. Pray most ardently to Him in true devotion and put

[1] Leopold Mozart is referring to their visits to Paris in 1763 and 1766.

your trust in Him; and lead so Christian a life that, if I should see you no more, the hour of my death may be free from anxiety. From my heart I give you my paternal blessing and remain until death your faithful father and your surest friend

LEOPOLD MOZART

Here is a list of our Paris acquaintances, who will all be delighted to ★ see you.[1]

(282a) *Leopold Mozart to his Wife*

[*Extract*]   [*Autograph in the Mozarteum, Salzburg*][2]

MY DEAR WIFE,   [SALZBURG, 5 *February* 1778]
As you will receive this letter on the 11th or 12th and as I doubt whether a letter will still reach Wolfgang in Mannheim, I will say good-bye to him with this enclosure! I write this with tears in my eyes. Nannerl kisses her dear brother Wolfgang a million times. She would have added a few words of farewell to him, but the paper was already filled up and, besides, I did not let her read my letter. We entreat Wolfgang *to take great care of his health and too keep to the diet he has been accustomed to at home.* If not, he will *have to be bled* as soon as he arrives in Paris. All *heating food* disagrees with him. He will surely take with him *our big Latin prayer-book,* which contains all the psalms in the full office of Our Lady. If he decides to buy the German version of this office of Our Lady in Mannheim, he ought to try to get a copy in the very smallest format. The Latin psalms are difficult to read and a German translation would be helpful. Learned contrapuntal settings of the psalms are performed at the Concert Spirituel; and one can acquire a great reputation by this means. Perhaps Wolfgang could have his 'Misericordias'[3] performed there as well. You have received, I hope, the two sonatas for four hands, the Fischer variations and the Rondo,[4] which were all enclosed in one letter? Farewell. We kiss you millions of times.

MZT.

(283) *Maria Anna Mozart to her Husband*

[*Autograph in the Mozarteum, Salzburg*]

MY DEAR HUSBAND,   MANNHEIM, 7 *February* 1778
You will have seen from Wolfgang's last letter of February 4th that he is quite determined not to go to Paris with ⟨Wendling.⟩ He has told you the reasons, and it is true that those fellows would be ⟨bad company

---

[1] Leopold Mozart encloses a long list, which is almost the same as the lists entered in his *Reiseaufzeichnungen,* pp. 29–32, 47–48. See *MBA,* Nos. 74 and 84.
[2] This undated Postscript is written on the cover of Letter 282.   [3] K. 222 [205a].
[4] K. 358 [186c], 381 [123a], 179 [189a], and probably the rondo of Mozart's clavier sonata, K. 309 [284b], which Leopold Mozart was having copied and returning bit by bit.

for him and might lead him astray.⟩ But do write all the same to Herr von Grimm, whom Wolfgang trusts absolutely. He can always go to Paris later on and meanwhile he is losing nothing by staying here, for it is costing him nothing he can finish his compositions, which he ought not to hurry over.[1] As far as news is concerned, I must tell you that next week the plays and balls are to begin again, for the townspeople would lose far too heavily if the mourning were to last any longer. I can well believe that things are in a sad state in Salzburg; if this goes on, ⟨the whole country will probably be ruined. I pity all good folks who have to live there under such a monster.⟩ I wish Herr von Schiedenhofen a thousand happinesses and blessings on his marriage; and indeed he will need them. Does not Fräulein Louise come to see us any more and is Nannerl Kranach still at home? How is our Chief Purveyor and does he still pay attention to Fräulein Antonia and Herr von Mölk to his Josepha?

(283a) *Mozart to his Father*

[Portions of autograph in the Mozarteum, Salzburg, and in the possession of A. Rosenthal, London]

[MANNHEIM, *7 February* 1778]

Herr von Schiedenhofen might have let me know long ago through you that he was getting married soon, and I should have composed new minuets for the occasion.[2] I wish him joy with my whole heart; but his, I daresay, is again one of those money matches and nothing else. I should not like to marry in this way; I want to make my wife happy, but not to become rich by her means. So I shall let things be and enjoy my golden freedom until I am so well off that I can support a wife and children. Herr von Schiedenhofen was obliged to choose a rich wife; his title demanded it. People of noble birth must never marry from inclination or love, but only from interest and all kinds of secondary considerations. Again, it would not at all suit a grandee to love his wife after she had done her duty and brought into the world a bouncing son and heir. But we poor humble people can not only choose a wife whom we love and who loves us, but we may, can and do take such a one, because we are neither noble, nor highly born, nor aristocratic, nor rich, but, on the contrary, lowly born, humble and poor; so we do not need a wealthy wife, for our riches, being in our brains, die with us—and these no man can take from us unless he chops off our heads, in which case—we need nothing more. We received safely your letter of February 2nd. I had already told you in my previous letter my chief reason for not going to Paris with those people. My second reason is that I have thought over carefully what I should have

---

[1] The works ordered by De Jean. See p. 414.
[2] Mozart's friend, Joachim Ferdinand von Schiedenhofen (1747–1823), married Anna Daubrawa von Daubrawaick (1759–1818), the daughter of the Chief Magistrate of Salzburg.

to do there. I could not get on at all without pupils, which is a kind of work that is quite uncongenial to me—and of this I have an excellent example here. I could have had two pupils. I went three times to each, but finding one of them out, I never went back. I will gladly give lessons as a favour, particularly when I see that my pupil has talent, inclination and anxiety to learn; but to be obliged to go to a house at a certain hour —or to have to wait at home for a pupil—is what I cannot do, no matter how much money it may bring me in. I find it impossible, so must leave it to those who can do nothing else but play the clavier. I am a composer and was born to be a Kapellmeister. I neither can nor ought to bury the talent for composition with which God in his goodness has so richly endowed me (I may say so without conceit, for I feel it now more than ever); and this I should be doing were I to take many pupils, for it is a most unsettling métier. I would rather, if I may speak plainly, neglect the clavier than composition, for in my case the clavier with me is only a side-line, though, thank God, a very good one. My third reason is that I do not know for certain whether our friend Grimm is in Paris. If he is, I can always follow in the mail coach; for a capital one goes from here through Strassburg. We had intended in any event to have gone by it. They too are travelling in this way. Herr Wendling is inconsolable at my not going with them, but I believe that this proceeds more from self-interest than from friendship. In addition to the reason which I gave him (about the three letters that had come during my absence), I also told him about the pupils and begged him to procure something *certain* for me, in which case I should be delighted to follow him to Paris (for I can easily do so)—especially if I am to write an opera. Writing operas is now my one burning ambition; but they must be French rather than German, and Italian rather than either. The Wendlings, one and all, are of the opinion that my compositions would be extraordinarily popular in Paris. I have no fears on that score, for, as you know, I can more or less adopt or imitate any kind and any style of composition. Shortly after my arrival I composed a French song[1] for Mlle Gustel (the daughter), who gave me the words; and she sings it incomparably well. I have the honour to enclose it to you. At Wendlings it is sung every day, for they are positively crazy about it. Now here is a satire which was written in Munich. I do not know whether you know it or not, but at any rate here it is:—

THE KIND AUSTRIANS

Our frontiers to powerfully defend,
But not to do us any harm,
Good Joseph his soldiers doth send

---

[1] K. 307 [284d], an arietta, 'Oiseaux, si tous les ans', written for Augusta Wendling, daughter of the flautist Johann Baptist Wendling.

That obstreperous Fritz to alarm.
From eastwards these neighbours have come
And as friends they have filed through our gates,
Both outposts and guards; and no sum
In return our good Joseph awaits.
Our hearths and our homes he's protecting,
So let's give him full use of our land
And, no evil purpose suspecting,
Our welfare entrust to his hand.
But if they too long should remain
And if, after all, 'twere deceit,
The intruders we'll drive out again,
For us no impossible feat.
'Tis true, we possess few soldati,
They're rather a costly affair;
But look at our dancers, castrati,
And of clerics we've more than a pair,
Not to mention those companies grand,
Money-lenders—and huntsman and hound.
Why, Joseph, if these made a stand,
They'd surely dash you to the ground.
Some generals too we possess,
More numerous perhaps than your own,
The piper you'll pay, you confess;
Then leave us in peace and alone.
We hope it—we're just sitting tight.
Oh, do keep those Prussians away!
We hate them, but don't want to fight.
Guardian angel, protect us, we pray.[1]

Joseph's declaration follows in the cover:

> Joseph's declaration
> In a tone of exaltation.
>
> Bavaria, keep calm! I come to defend,
> But what I defend, I'll grab in the end.

In my last letter I forgot to mention Mlle Weber's greatest merit, which is her superb cantabile singing. Please do not forget about Italy. I commend this poor, but excellent little Mlle Weber to your interest with all my heart, *caldamente*[2], as the Italians say. I have given her three of De

---

[1] The autograph in the Mozarteum, Salzburg, ends here. The autograph of the remaining portion of this letter, written inside the cover, is in the possession of A. Rosenthal, London.
[2] i.e. warmly.

Amicis's arias,[1] the scena I wrote for Madame Duschek[2] (to whom I shall be writing soon) and four arias from 'Il Rè pastore'.[3] I have also promised her to have some arias sent from home. I hope you will be kind enough to send them to me, but send them *gratis*, I beg you, and you will really be doing a good work! You will find the list of them on the French song which her father has copied out, and the paper is part of a present from him; but indeed he has given me much more. Now I must close. I kiss your hands a thousand times and embrace my sister with all my heart. Our compliments to all our good friends, especially to Herr Bullinger. Addio. I am your most obedient son

WMZT

Thanks for the sonatas for four hands and the Fischer variations.

(284) *Leopold Mozart to his Wife*

[Extract]   [*Autograph in the Mozarteum, Salzburg*]

MY DEAR WIFE!   SALZBURG, 9 *February* 1778

People in Mannheim will know enough by this time about conditions in Bavaria, since the Austrian manifestoes have appeared in the papers. Wolfgang ought to be in Munich at the moment, for he could have a word with Baron Zemen, who was and perhaps still is Saxon envoy to Bavaria.

★ So far I have not heard a word about the preparations for your journey, but perhaps your next letter will tell me something. Here is another sheet of music for Wolfgang, which I trust will still reach him. If, however he has left already, you had better keep it until he has sent you his address in Paris. Possibly, however, Madame Wendling knows it, and, if so, you can send a letter along with the music. But I hope he will not have left before this letter reaches you. Commend our son to Herr Wendling once more and most warmly, and may God protect him! I felt sure that your last letter would have something more to tell, but as Wolfgang wrote to
★ you from Worms, you had naturally nothing new to report. It would have been well if Wolfgang could have found an opportunity of getting someone to remind the Elector about him. However, there is time enough for that. Farewell. We kiss you both millions of times and I remain your old

MZT

---

[1] Giunia's arias in *Lucio Silla*. See. p. 448, n. 3.   [2] K. 272.
[3] Probably nos. 2, 3, 8 and 10.

(284a) *Nannerl Mozart to her Mother and Brother*

[Autograph in the Mozarteum, Salzburg]

[SALZBURG, 9 *February* 1778[1]]

Papa never leaves me room enough to write to Mamma and yourself. I hope to see her soon and I beg her not to forget me when she is leaving Mannheim. I wish you a pleasant journey to Paris and the best of health. I do hope, however, that I shall be able to embrace you soon. But God alone knows when that will happen. We are both longing for you to make your fortune, for that, I know for certain, will mean happiness to us all. I kiss Mamma's hands and embrace you and trust that you will always remember us all and think of us. But you must only do so when you have time, say, for a quarter of an hour when you are neither composing nor teaching.

(284b) *Leopold Mozart to his Son*

[Extract]   *[Autograph in the Mozarteum, Salzburg]*

MY DEAR SON!   SALZBURG, 9 *February* 1778

You will have received no doubt the small scores, which I made up in a neat parcel, and also my letter with the list of our acquaintances in Paris. The most important people are M. Grimm and Madame la Duchesse de Bourbon, formerly Mademoiselle d'Orléans, with whom we found Paisible[2] on the two occasions when we visited her in the convent, and who dedicated to you a little piece for the clavier, which she had composed herself. Her husband is the son of Prince Condé and is only 22, whereas she is 28. ⟨She is not happily married; and I believe that they are not living together.⟩ Her brother, the Duc de Chartres, is about 31. It was he who got permission from M. de Sartine, then Lieutenant de la Police, for us to give those two concerts which brought us in so much money. Then there is Madame la Comtesse de Tessé, to whom you dedicated your sonatas,[3] and who is a great patroness of all branches of knowledge. She took a great fancy to you and gave you the little watch and your sister the gold toothpick case. I hope she has returned to Paris. She and her husband, who have been travelling a great deal, were in Italy some time ago and in Sicily too, I understand. You must make a point of finding out

---

[1] A postscript to her father's letter.
[2] Louis Henri Paisible (*c.* 1745–1782), born in Paris, was a famous violinist. He was a pupil of Gaviniès, through whose influence he became a member of the orchestra of the Concert Spirituel and one of the musicians attached to the household of the Duchesse de Bourbon. He soon threw up these posts and started travelling in the Netherlands, Germany and Russia, where, disheartened by failure, he shot himself in St. Petersburg. He composed a few works for the violin.   [3] K. 8 and 9.

whether the Duc de Braganza may not perhaps be in Paris. He left Vienna last autumn in order to return to Lisbon, where as a result of the death of the King of Portugal there is now a government more favourable to him. I know that he broke his journey in Paris, but possibly he has left by this time. He would be a useful person for you to know. I must not forget Madame d'Épinay,[1] a very intimate friend of M. Grimm, who gave Mamma that beautiful fan. That reminds me, the Comtesse de Tessé would procure you, I am sure, through her father the Duc d'Ayen, who took us to Versailles, an introduction to Madame Victoire, who would be only too glad to see you, as she was so gracious and friendly to you when you were a child. I should mention too Madame la Duchesse d'Enville, La Duchesse d'Aiguillon, La Duchesse de Mazarin, La Comtesse de Lillebonne, Madame de St. Julien, Madame la Princesse de Robeck, Madame la Comtesse de Wall. In short! All the people on that list are people of rank, who are sure to remember you and on whom you must not hesitate to call and, with a certain dignified courtesy and ease of manner, ask for their protection. I assure you that this will be no easy task for any one like your self, who is not always associating with the aristocracy; but it is of the utmost importance that you should do so. This politesse is extraordinarily efficacious in winning over the French and will at once secure for you the friendship of all these great ones and their many acquaintances. *Mark you, you must do this at once*, and you must let nothing put you off. As it is, you are arriving in Paris rather late, too late in fact, for in the summer everyone goes into the country. Grimm, if he is there, will endorse my views and give you all the help you require. You can tell him all that I have written to you. If he is not in Paris, Madame d'Épinay will assist you in every way or introduce you to one of her friends, that is, if you can manage to find her at once. Meanwhile Baron Bagge will probably be able to give you the addresses of one or two people. Herr Wendling or somebody else will be able to tell you how

★ much you should pay for a fiacre. Whenever you walk, be very careful, for in wet weather the paving-stones in Paris, which are rather like rounded squares, are extremely slippery, so that one is constantly tripping. Well, I had better send you a few more names of other people whom we knew long ago, namely, M. l'Abbé Gauzargue,[2] Kapellmeister in the Royal Court Chapel at Versailles, a most worthy man, with whom we had lunch; M. Eckardt, clavierist; M. Gaviniés,[3] violino; Hockbrucker,

---

[1] Louise Tardieu d'Esclavelles d'Épinay (1726–1783), a French writer, well known on account of her *liaisons* with Rousseau and Grimm and her friendships with Diderot, d'Alembert and other French men of letters. Her *Mémoires*, a sort of autobiographical romance, were published in Paris in 1818.

[2] Abbé Charles Gauzargue (*c.* 1725–1799). He wrote a *Traité de composition*, Paris, 1797.

[3] Pierre Gaviniès (1728–1800), an eminent violinist, called the French Tartini. He appeared in 1741 at the Concert Spirituel, which he subsequently directed, 1773–1777; and when the Paris Conservatoire was founded in 1795, he was appointed to a professorship of the violin.

harpist. The latter, as you know, is a cheerful fool, but *you must avoid having anything to do with him*, for he has *a very bad reputation* on account of his dissolute life; moreover, he is a coarse fellow and runs up debts. M. du Borde,[1] a very conceited violoncellist; M. le Tourneur,[2] court organist; M. Molitor, who plays the French horn at Versailles; M. Haranc,[3] violino; M. Besson, violino; M. le Grand, clavierist; M. Jélyotte,[4] chanteur au théâtre; M. Mayer, harpist; M. Henno, who plays the French horn at Prince Conti's; M. Duni,[5] maître de chapelle, who has written some comic operas; M. Canévas,[6] violoncellist, whose daughter married Herr Cramer and died at Mannheim; M. le Duc,[7] violino; Mlle Fel,[8] an old singer in the French theatre; M. Cahaut,[9] joueur de la lute chez le Prince Conti; M. Honnauer, clavecin; M. Philidor,[10] compositeur, and so forth. I need hardly tell you, for you know this quite well yourself, that with *very few exceptions* you will gain nothing by associating with these people, and that to be intimate with them may even do you harm. If Gluck and Piccinni are there, you will avoid their company as much as possible; and you must not form a close friendship with Grétry.[11] De la

[1] Jean Pierre Duport (1741–1818), one of two brothers who were eminent violoncellists. He was in the orchestra of Prince Conti until 1769, then paid several visits to London, travelled to Spain in 1771 and finally, on the invitation of Frederick the Great, settled in Berlin as first violoncellist in the king's orchestra, his pupil being the future king, Frederick William II.

[2] In Leopold Mozart's *Reiseaufzeichnungen*, p. 30, le Tourneur is described as 'claveciniste de la cour'. See *MBA*, No. 76.

[3] Louis André Haranc (1738–1805) became in 1770 first violin in the court orchestra and in 1775 Director of the court music to the Queen.

[4] Pierre de Jélyotte (1713–1797), a French tenor and composer. He was trained at Toulouse, first appeared in the Paris opéra in 1733, soon took part in all the important productions and continued to sing until 1779. The Mozarts had met him in Paris in 1764. Leopold Mozart's entry in his *Reiseaufzeichnungen*, p. 32, is 'chanteur renommé en France, c'est-à-dire, pour leur goût'. See *MBA*, No. 84.

[5] Egidio Romoaldo Duni (1709–1775), composer of Italian and French light operas. He was born and studied in Naples and had his first triumph in Rome with his opera *Nerone*. After several travels abroad he was appointed tutor to the court of Parma. At the Duke's suggestion he composed a French opera *Ninette à la cour*, which was so popular that in 1757 he settled in Paris, where he wrote twenty operas, most of which were outstanding successes. He is regarded as the founder of the French opéra-comique.

[6] Canavas. In his *Reiseaufzeichnungen*, p. 32, Leopold Mozart adds the remark 'Sa femme et sa fille qui joue du clavecin fort bien et qui chante bien'. See *MBA*, No. 84.

[7] Simon Le Duc l'Aîné (before 1748–1777), a soloist in violin concertos at the Concert Spirituel and a well-known music publisher.

[8] Marie Fel (1716–1794), a famous high soprano, who made her début in 1734 at the opera and the Concert Spirituel, but had to retire in 1759 owing to bad health.

[9] Joseph Kohaut (1738–1793). He also wrote operas for the Comédie-Italienne. A second entry in the *Reiseaufzeichnungen* has the remark 'honnête homme'. See *MBA*, No. 418.

[10] François André Danican Philidor (1726–1795), an eminent composer and a distinguished chess-player. He at first supported himself in Paris by giving lessons and copying music. He then travelled and wrote books on chess. Diderot and other friends brought him back to Paris, where he started to compose sacred and operatic music and from 1759 onwards won great successes with his comic operas. He is generally regarded as Duni's successor.

[11] André Ernest Modeste Grétry (1741–1813), born at Liège, an eminent composer of operas. He very soon discovered that comic opera was his true vocation and from 1768 onwards won outstanding successes in Paris. He has been called the 'Molière of music'. His literary activity too was very great, though the value of his works as contributions to the study of music is small.

politesse et pas d'autre chose. *You can always be perfectly natural* with people of high rank; but with everybody else *please behave like an Englishman.* You must not be so open with everyone! You should not let a friseur or any other domestique see your money, rings or watch; still less should you leave them lying about. ⟨Even your friends should not know when you receive money or how much you have in hand.⟩ If you have any cash, take it to the bankers Turton et Baur. I only kept out what I really needed and gave them the remainder, for which they handed me a receipt. Thus I could be sure that my money would not be stolen, while, if anyone wanted to borrow from me, I could make the excuse that I had sent off my earnings to Salzburg. Never go out walking at night. And finally, remind yourself every day what you owe to God, who has bestowed such extraordinary talents upon you. Do not get annoyed with me for telling you this so often. Surely you realise my responsibility as a father? You were vexed when I reminded you the other day ⟨about confessing.⟩ But put yourself in my place and then tell me whether it is my duty to do so or not? Oh, Heaven! When shall I see you again? I kiss you millions of times and remain your surest and truest friend and father

L:MZT

(285) *Leopold Mozart to his Son*

[Extract]   [Autograph in the Mozarteum, Salzburg]

MY DEAR SON!   SALZBURG, [11]–12 *February* 1778

I have read your letter of the 4th with amazement and horror. I am beginning to answer it today, the 11th, for the whole night long I was unable to sleep and am so exhausted that I can only write quite slowly, word by word, and so gradually finish what I have to say by tomorrow. Up to the present, thank God, I have been in good health; but this letter, in which I only recognise my son by that failing of his which makes him believe everyone at the first word spoken, open his kind heart to every plausible flatterer and let others sway him as they like, so that he is led by whimsical ideas and ill-considered and impracticable projects to sacrifice his own name and interests, and even the interests and the claims of his aged and honourable parents to those of strangers—this letter, I say, depressed me exceedingly, the more so as I was cherishing the reasonable hope that certain circumstances which you had had to face already, as well as my own reminders, both spoken and written, could not have failed to convince you that not only for the sake of your happiness but in order that you may be able to gain a livelihood and attain at length the desired goal in a world of men in varying degrees good and bad, fortunate and unfortunate, it was imperative for you to guard your warm heart by the strictest reserve, undertake nothing without full consideration and never let yourself be carried away by enthusiastic notions and blind fancies. My dear son, I implore you to read this letter carefully—and take time to reflect upon it. Merciful God! those happy moments are gone when, as child and boy, you never went to bed without standing on a chair and singing to me *Oragna fiagata fa*,[1] and ending by kissing me again and again on the tip of my nose and telling me that when I grew old you would put me in a glass case and protect me from every breath of air, so that you might always have me with you and honour me. Listen to me, therefore, in patience! You are fully acquainted with our difficulties in Salzburg—you know my wretched income, why I kept my promise to let you go away, and all my various troubles. The purpose of your journey was twofold—either to get a good permanent appointment, or, if this should fail, to go off to some big city where large sums of money can be earned. Both plans were designed to assist your parents and to help on your dear sister, but above all to build up your own name and reputation in the world. The latter was partly accomplished in your childhood and boyhood; and it now depends on you alone to raise yourself gradually to a position of eminence, such as no musician has ever obtained. You owe that to the extraordinary talents which you have received from a beneficent God; and now it depends solely on your good sense and your way of life whether you die as an ordinary musician, utterly forgotten by the world, or as a famous Kapellmeister, of whom posterity will read,—whether, captured by some woman, you die bedded on straw in an attic full of starving children, or whether, after a Christian life spent in contentment, honour and renown, you leave this world with your family well provided for and your name respected by all. You took that journey to Munich—with what purpose you know—but nothing could be done. Well-meaning friends wanted to keep you there and you wished to remain. Someone hit on the idea of forming a company—but I need not recapitulate everything in detail. At the time you thought the scheme practicable. I did not. Read the letter I sent you in reply. You have a sense of honour. Would it have done you honour, assuming that the scheme had been carried out, to depend on the monthly charity of ten persons? At that time you were quite amazingly taken up with the little singer[2] at the theatre and your dearest wish was to forward the cause of the German stage; now you declare that you would not even care to write a comic opera! No sooner had you left the gates of Munich behind you than (as I prophesied) your whole company

---

[1] For the melody, which, as Abert (vol. i, p. 28, n. 1) points out, is a variation of an old Dutch folk-song 'Willem von Nassau', see Leitzmann, p. 12. In the material which Nissen collected for his biography of Mozart, and which is now in the Mozarteum, Salzburg, there is a statement that Mozart often hummed a tune to the nonsensical words 'Nannetta Nanon, puisque la bedetta fa, Nannetta, inevenedetta fa Nanon'. See *MM*, November 1919, p. 30.

[2] Mademoiselle Kaiser. See p. 290, n. 2.

of subscribers had forgotten you. What would be your lot were you in Munich now?—In the end one can always see the providence of God. In Augsburg too you had your little romance, you amused yourself with my brother's daughter, who now must needs send you her portrait. The rest I wrote to you in my first letters to Mannheim. When you were at Wallerstein[1] you caused the company great amusement, you took up a violin, and danced about and played, so that people described you to absent friends as a merry, high-spirited and brainless fellow, thus giving Herr Beecke the opportunity of disparaging your merits although your compositions and your sister's playing (for she always says '*I am only my brother's pupil*') have since made these two gentlemen regard you in another light, so that they now have the very highest opinion of your art and are indeed more inclined to run down Herr Beecke's poor compositions. When you were in Mannheim you did well to win the good graces of Herr ⟨*Cannabich*⟩. But you would have gained nothing, had he not been seeking a double advantage therefrom. I have already written to you about the rest. Next, Herr ⟨Cannabich's⟩ daughter was smothered in praises, her temperament was recorded in the Adagio of a sonata, in short, *she* was now the reigning favourite. Then you made the acquaintance of Herr Wendling. *He* was now the most honourable friend—and what happened next, I need not repeat. Suddenly you strike up a new acquaintanceship—with Herr Weber; all your other friends are forgotten; now *this family* is the most honourable, the most Christian family and the daughter is to have the leading role in the tragedy to be enacted between your own family and hers! In the transports into which your kind and too open heart has thrown you, you think all your ill-considered fancies as reasonable and practicable as if they were bound to be accomplished in the normal course of nature. You are thinking of taking her to Italy as a prima donna. Tell me, do you know of any prima donna who, without having first appeared many times in Germany, has walked on to the stage in Italy as prima donna? In how many operas did not Signora Bernasconi sing in Vienna, and operas too of the most passionate type, produced under the very severe criticism and direction of Gluck and Calzabigi?[2] In how many operas did not Mlle Teiber[3] sing in Vienna under Hasse's direction and taught by that old singer and very famous actress, Signora Tesi,[4] whom you saw at Prince Hildburghausen's[5] and whose negress

[1] Leopold Mozart had evidently heard an account of his son's doings from Anton Janitsch and Joseph Reicha.

[2] Raniero da Calzabigi (1715–1795), famous in musical history as the librettist of Gluck's three great Italian operas, *Orfeo ed Euridice* (1762), *Alceste* (1767) and *Paride ed Elena* (1770).

[3] Elizabeth Teiber. See p. 74, n. 2.

[4] Vittoria Tesi-Tramontini (1700–1775), a celebrated singer. She was born in Florence and in her youth sang chiefly in Italy. In 1747 she settled in Vienna where she opened a school of singing.

[5] Prince Joseph Friedrich von Sachsen-Hildburghausen, Imperial Field-marshal, famous in musical history as the patron of Gluck.

you kissed as a child?[1] How many times did not Mlle Schindler[2] appear in Italian opera at Vienna, after making her début in a private production at Baron Fries's country seat under the direction of Hasse and Tesi and Metastasio? Did any of these people dare to throw themselves at the head of the Italian public? And how much patronage, what powerful recommendations did they not need before they were able to attain their object? Princes and counts recommended them, famous composers and poets vouched for their ability. And now you want me to write to Lugiati! Your proposal is to compose an opera for fifty ducats, although you know that the Veronese have no money and never commission a new opera. I am now to remember the Ascensa, although Michele Dall' Agata has not even replied to my two previous letters. I am quite willing to believe that Mlle ⟨Weber⟩ sings like a Gabrielli; that she has a *powerful voice* for the Italian stage; that she has the build of a prima donna and all the rest; but it is absurd of you to vouch for her capacity to act. Acting calls for more than these qualities. Why, old Hasse's childish, albeit most kindly meant and good-natured efforts on behalf of Miss Davies[3] banished her for ever from the Italian stage, where she was hissed off on the first night and her part given to De Amicis. Even an experienced male actor, let alone a female, may well tremble during his first appearance in a foreign country. And do you think that is all?—By no means!—Ci vuole il possesso del teatro.[4] This is particularly true of a woman, who has in addition to consider the way in which she dresses and adorns herself. You yourself know all this, if you will but think it over. I know that serious reflection on all these points will convince you that, kindly as your plan is meant, it needs *time* and *much preparation* and must be approached in a very different way if it is ever to be carried out. What impresario would not laugh, were one to recommend him a girl of sixteen or seventeen, who has never yet appeared on a stage! As for your proposal (I can hardly write when I think of it), your proposal to travel about with Herr ⟨Weber⟩ and, be it noted, his two daughters—it has nearly made me lose my reason! My dearest son! How can you have allowed yourself to be bewitched even for an hour by such a horrible idea, which must have been suggested to you by someone or other! Your letter reads like a romance. For could you really make up your mind to go trailing about the world with strangers? Quite apart from your reputation—what of your old parents and your dear sister? To expose me to the mockery and ridicule of the Prince and

---

[1] During Mozart's first visit to Vienna in 1762.

[2] Anna Maria Elisabeth Schindler, (1757–1779), a well-known singer at the Italian opera in Vienna who in 1775 married the actor Josef Lange. Lange's second wife was Aloysia Weber.

[3] Cecilia Davies (1738–1836), the younger sister of Marianne Davies, the armonica-player. She was an excellent singer and was fairly successful in Italy, where she was called 'L'Inglesina'. In 1771 she appeared in Hasse's opera *Ruggiero* in Milan.

[4] One must have the stage presence.

of *the whole town which loves you?* Yes, to expose me to mockery and yourself to contempt, for in reply to repeated questions, I have had to tell everyone that you were going to Paris. And now, after all, you want to roam about with strangers and take your chance? Surely, after a little reflection you will give up all idea of doing so! But that I may convince you of your rash precipitancy, let me tell you that the time is now coming when no man in his senses could think of such a thing. Conditions are now such that it is impossible to guess where war may break out, for everywhere regiments are either on the march or under marching orders. —To Switzerland?—To Holland? Why, there is not a soul there the whole summer; and at Berne and Zürich in winter one can just make enough not to die of starvation, but nothing more. As for Holland they have things to think of there besides music; and in any case half one's takings are eaten up by Herr Hummel[1] and concert expenses. Besides, what will become of your reputation? Those are places for lesser lights, for second-rate composers, for scribblers, for a Schwindel,[2] a Zappa,[3] a Ricci[4] and the like. Name any one great composer to me who would deign to take such an abject step! *Off with you to Paris!* and that soon! Find your place among great people. *Aut Caesar aut nihil.* The mere thought of seeing Paris ought to have preserved you from all these flighty ideas. *From Paris the name and fame of a man of great talent resounds throughout the whole world. There the nobility treat men of genius with the greatest deference, esteem and courtesy; there you will see a refined manner of life, which forms an astonishing contrast to the coarseness of our German courtiers and their ladies; and there you may become proficient in the French tongue.* As for the company of ⟨Wendling⟩ and his friends, you do not need it at all. You have known them for a long time—and did your Mamma not realize what type of men they were? Were you both blind?—Nay, but I know how it was. You were set upon it, and she did not dare to oppose you. It angers me that both of you should have lacked the confidence and frankness to give me circumstantial and detailed information. You both treated me in the same way over that matter of the ⟨Elector,⟩ and yet in the end it all had to come out. You want to spare me anxiety and in the end you suddenly overturn a whole bucketful of worries on my head, which almost kill me! You know, and you have a thousand proofs of it, that God in his goodness

---

[1] Johann Julius Hummel (1728–1798), a music publisher at Amsterdam (from *c.* 1754) and Berlin (from 1770), who published many important works. The business was dissolved in 1822.

[2] Friedrich Schwindel (1737–1786) was a skilful player on the violin, flute and clavier. As a composer he was a follower of the Mannheim school. From 1765 onwards his numerous symphonies, quartets and trios were performed in Amsterdam, Paris and London.

[3] Francesco Zappa of Milan was a famous violoncellist in his day and composed several works, chiefly for his instrument.

[4] Abbate Pasquale Ricci (1732–1817) was born in Como, where he eventually became maestro di cappella of the cathedral. He travelled widely. Many of his numerous compositions were published and were well received in other countries.

has given me sound judgement, that I still have my head screwed on, and that in the most tangled circumstances I have often found a way out and foreseen and guessed aright. What has prevented you then from asking my advice from always acting as I desired? My son, you should regard me rather as your most sincere friend, than as a severe father. Consider whether I have not always treated you kindly, served you as a servant his master, even provided you with all possible entertainment and helped you to enjoy all honourable and seemly pleasures, often at great inconvenience to myself! I presume that Herr ⟨Wendling⟩ has left already. Though half-dead, I have managed to think out and arrange everything connected with your journey to Paris. Herr Arbauer, a well-known merchant of Augsburg and Frankfurt, is now there with his German agent and is staying for the whole of Lent. I shall send off a letter to him on the 23rd and by the same post I shall write to you very fully and tell you what you have to do and how much approximately the journey will cost you; and I shall enclose an open letter which you must deliver to Herr Arbauer (I understand that he was at your Augsburg concert), who will be expecting it. This wretched business has cost me a couple of sleepless nights. As soon as you receive this letter, I want you to write and tell me *how much money you have in hand*. I trust that you can count for certain on those 200 gulden. I was amazed to read your remark that you would now finish that music for M. De Jean at your leisure. It seems then that you have not yet delivered it. Yet you were thinking of leaving on February 15th?—You even went on a trip to Kirchheim—even taking Mlle ⟨Weber⟩ with you, with the result that of course you received less money, as the Princess had two people to reward, a present which otherwise you might have had for yourself. However, that does not matter. But, Good God! Suppose Herr ⟨*Wendling*⟩ were now to play a trick on you and M. De Jean were ⟨to break his word,⟩ for the arrangement was that you were to wait and travel with them. Do send me news by the next post, so that I may know how things are. Well, I am going to tell you what you *can* do for Mlle Weber. Tell me, who are the people who give lessons in Italy? Are they not old maestri, and generally *old tenors*? Has Signor Raaff heard her sing? Have a word with him and ask him to hear her perform your arias. *You could say that you would like him to hear a few of them*. In this way you could use your influence with him later on her behalf. However he may sing now, he knows his job, and if she impresses him, she can count on making a good impression on all the Italian impresarios who knew him in his prime. Meanwhile she could surely find an opportunity of getting on the stage in Mannheim where, even if it is unpaid work, she would be gaining experience. Your desire to help the oppressed you have inherited from your father. But you really must consider first of all the welfare of your parents, or else your soul will go to the devil. Think of me as you saw me when you left us, *standing beside the carriage in a state of utter wretchedness*. Ill as I was, I had been packing for you until two o'clock in the morning, and there I was at the carriage again at six o'clock, seeing to everything for you. Hurt me now, if you can be so cruel! Win fame and *make money* in Paris; then, *when you have money to spend*, go off to Italy and get commissions for operas. This cannot be done by writing letters to impresarios, though I am prepared to do so. Then you could put forward Mlle ⟨Weber's⟩ name, which can be the more easily done if you do so personally. Write to me by the next post without fail. We kiss you both a million times and I remain your old honest husband and father

MZT

Bullinger sends his greetings.

Nannerl has wept her full share during these last two days. Addio.[1]

* Mamma is to go to Paris with Wolfgang, so you had better make the necessary arrangements.

(286) *Maria Anna Mozart to her Husband*

[Autograph in the Mozarteum, Salzburg]

My dear Husband,   MANNHEIM, 13 *February* 1778

We know only too well what the situation is in Bavaria. But as for the Electress of Saxony's claims we have not yet heard anything about them. That would really be too much. In the end the Elector would have nothing left of his whole inheritance. Everything is very quiet here and there seems to be nothing but secrets. The papers only talk about matters of indifference; there is not a single thing about Bavaria. As for my journey to Salzburg I do hope that we shall hit on something suitable, for the weather is still too cold and raw for me to sit all day in an open carriage. Really it would be too uncomfortable. And after all if I had wanted to travel in winter, it would not have been necessary for us to stay here so long. Moreover, when the weather gets milder, we shall more easily find some opportunity for me to travel in company. I do not mind a bit, provided I have not got to travel alone to Augsburg. I am not at all nervous about the journey on to Salzburg. I shan't forget Nannerl. In the meantime I send my greetings to her, and also to all our good friends. Addio. Keep well, both of you. I kiss you both many 100000 times and remain your faithful wife

MARIANNA MOZART

In the meantime you will have received our letter and decided what is to be done.

---

[1] This word and the following sentence are the conclusion of a passage written on the cover.

(286a) *Mozart to his Father*

[*Autograph in the Mozarteum, Salzburg*]

MONSIEUR   [MANNHEIM, 14 *February* 1778]
MON TRÉS CHER PÉRE!

I see from your letter of February 9th that you have not yet received my last two letters. Herr Wendling and Herr Ramm are leaving early tomorrow morning. If I thought that you would be really displeased with me for not going to Paris with them, I should regret having stayed here; but I hope it is not so. The road to Paris is still open. Herr Wendling has promised to make enquiries immediately about M. Grimm and to send me information at once. If I have such a friend in Paris, I shall certainly go there, for he will assuredly arrange something for me. The main cause of my not going with them is that we have not yet been able to arrange about Mamma returning to Augsburg. How on earth could she have stayed here in the house without me? I do implore you just to give a little thought to her journey from Augsburg to Salzburg; once I know about this, I shall arrange for her to get to Augsburg comfortably. If there is no other way, I shall take her there myself. We can lodge at the Holy Cross Monastery. But the essential thing to know is whether she will be then travelling home with one or more persons? And whether, if they are only two, there will be a chaise there already, or whether she ought to use ours? This last we can settle quite well later on. The main thing is to get her safely on the road from Augsburg to Salzburg. The journey to Augsburg will not cost much, for no doubt there are drivers here who can be engaged at a cheap rate. By that time, however, I hope to have made enough to pay for Mamma's journey home. Just now I really do not know how it would be possible. M. De Jean is also leaving for Paris tomorrow and, because I have only finished two concertos[1] and three quartets[2] for him, has sent me 96 gulden (that is, 4 gulden too little, evidently supposing that this was the half of 200); but he must pay me in full, for that was my agreement with the Wendlings, and I can send him the other pieces later. It is not surprising that I have not been able to finish them, for I never have a single quiet hour here. I can only compose at night, so that I can't get up early as well; besides, one is not always in the mood for working. I could, to be sure, scribble off things the whole day long, but a composition of this kind goes out into the world, and naturally I do not want to have cause to be ashamed of my name on the title-page. Moreover, you know that I become quite powerless whenever I am obliged to write for an instrument which I cannot bear. Hence as a

---

[1] K. 313 [285c] and 314 [285d]. See p. 457, n. 1.
[2] K. 285 and 285a. There is no trace of a third quartet for De Jean. K. App. 171 [K. 285b], which was thought to date from 1778, was probably written in 1781 or 1782. See R. Leavis, *Music and Letters*, xliii (1962), p. 48 ff. See p. 457.

diversion I compose something else, such as duets for clavier and violin,[1] or I work at my mass.[2] Now I am settling down seriously to the clavier duets, as I want to have them engraved. If only the Elector were here, I should very quickly finish the mass. But what can't be, can't be. I am much obliged to you, my dear Papa, for your fatherly letter; I shall put it by among my treasures and always refer to it. Please do not forget about my mother's journey from Augsburg to Salzburg and let me know the precise time; and please remember the arias I mentioned in my last letter. If I am not mistaken, there are also some cadenzas which I once jotted down and at least one aria cantabile with coloratura indications.[3] I should like that first of all, for it would be good practice for Mlle Weber. I only taught her the day before yesterday an Andantino Cantabile by Bach,[4] the whole of it. Yesterday there was a concert at Cannabich's, where all the music was of my composition, except the first symphony, which was his own. Mlle Rosa played my concerto in B♭,[5] then Herr Ramm (by way of a change) played for the fifth time my oboe concerto written for Ferlendis,[6] which is making a great sensation here. It is now Ramm's cheval de bataille. After that Mlle Weber sang most charmingly the aria di bravura of De Amicis.[7] Then I played my old concerto in D major,[8] because it is such a favourite here, and I also extemporized for half an hour; after which Mlle Weber sang De Amicis's aria 'Parto, m'affretto'[9] and was loudly applauded. Finally my ouverture to 'Il Rè pastore' was performed. I do entreat you most earnestly to interest yourself in Mlle Weber; I would give anything if she could only make her fortune. Husband, wife and five children on an income of 450 gulden! —On my own account too, don't forget about Italy. You know my great longing and my passion. I hope that all will go well. I have placed my trust in God, Who will never forsake us. Now farewell, and don't forget all my requests and recommendations. I kiss your hands 100000 times and remain your most obedient son

WOLFGANG GOTTLIEB MOZART

Mannheim, 14 February 1778.

I embrace my sister with all my heart. My greetings to all our good friends and especially to Herr Bullinger. A propos, how do you like the French aria?[10]

[1] The violin sonatas K. 301-306 [293a–c, 300c, 293d, 300l], two of which, K. 304 [300c] and 306 [300l], were written in Paris. The series was engraved in 1778 by Sieber in Paris and dedicated to the Electress Marie Elizabeth of the Palatinate.

[2] Probably K. 322 [296a], a Kyrie composed in 1778, was intended to form part of this mass. Otherwise there is no trace of it.   [3] See p. 494, n. 2, and Köchel, pp. 300, 301.

[4] Johann Christian Bach.   [5] K. 238.

[6] Probably K. 314 [285d], which Mozart rewrote as a flute concerto for De Jean. See Köchel, p. 295, 296.   [7] See p. 448, n. 3.

[8] K. 175, composed in 1773, Mozart's first clavier concerto.

[9] From Mozart's opera Lucio Silla.   [10] K. 307 [284d]. See p. 468, n. 1.

(287) *Leopold Mozart to his Wife and Son*

[*Extract*]   [*Autograph in the Mozarteum, Salzburg*]

SALZBURG, 16 *February* 1778

MY DEAR WIFE AND MY DEAR SON!

I have received your letter of February 7th with the French aria[1] which was enclosed; and my letter of the 12th, written in pain and fear, will have reached you by this time. I began a second letter yesterday, which, however, I do not feel able to finish today. I am saving it up for some other post-day. Your aria has made me breathe a little more easily, for here is one of my dear Wolfgang's compositions and something so excellent that I am sure that it was only some very persuasive tongue which must for the moment have driven you to prefer a knock-about existence to the reputation which you might acquire in a city so famous and so profitable to the talented as Paris. Everyone is right who says that your compositions will be very popular in Paris; and you yourself are convinced, as I am too, that you are able to imitate all styles of composition. It was a good thing that you did not travel with those fellows. But you had long since detected the ⟨*evil streak in their characters*;⟩ and yet all that long time when you ⟨*were associating with them*,⟩ you did not sufficiently trust your father (who is so anxious about you) to write to him about it and ask him for his advice: and it horrifies me to think that your mother did not do so either. My son! You are hot-tempered and impulsive in all your ways! Since your childhood and boyhood your whole character has changed. As a child and a boy you were serious rather than childish and when you sat at the clavier or were otherwise intent on music, no one dared to have the slightest jest with you. Why, even your expression was so solemn that, observing the early efflorescence of your talent and your ever grave and thoughtful little face, many discerning people of different countries sadly doubted whether your life would be a long one. But now, as far as I can see, you are much too ready to retort in a bantering tone to the first challenge—and that, of course, is the first step towards undue familiarity, which anyone who wants to preserve his self-respect will try to avoid in this world. A good-hearted fellow is accustomed, it is true, to express himself freely and naturally; none the less it is a mistake to do so. And it is just your good heart which prevents you from detecting any shortcomings in a person who showers praises on you, has a great opinion of you and flatters you to the skies, and who makes you give him all your confidence and affection; whereas as a boy you were so extraordinarily modest that you used to weep when people praised you overmuch. The greatest art of all is *to know oneself* and then, my dear son, to do as I do, that is, *to endeavour to get to know others through and through*. This, as you

[1] K. 307 [284d].

know, has always been my study; and certainly it is a fine, useful and indeed most necessary one. As for your giving lessons in Paris you need not bother your head about it. *In the first place*, no one is going to dismiss his master at once and engage you. *In the second place*, no one would dare to ask you, and you yourself would certainly not take on anyone except possibly some lady, who is already *a good player and wants to take lessons in interpretation*, which would be easy work for good pay. For instance, would you not have gladly undertaken to give Countess von Lützow and Countess Lodron two or three lessons a week at a fee of two or three louis d'or a month, the more so as such ladies also put themselves to a great deal of trouble to collect subscribers for the engraving of your compositions? In Paris everything is done by these great ladies, many of whom are devoted lovers of the clavier and in some cases excellent performers. These are the people who can help you. As for composition, why, you could make money and gain a great reputation by publishing *works for the clavier, string quartets and so forth, symphonies* and possibly a collection of *melodious French arias* with clavier accompaniment like the one you sent me, and finally operas. Well, what objection have you to raise now? But you want everything to be done at once, before people have even seen you or heard any of your works. Read my long list of the acquaintances we had in Paris at that time. All, or at least most of them, are the leading people in that city and they will all be both delighted and interested to see you again. Even if only six of them take you up (and indeed one single one of the most influential of them would be enough), you would be able to do whatever you pleased, I shall have the arias which you want for Mlle Weber copied, and I shall send what I can find. I enclose herewith two unsealed letters of recommendation, which you must keep safely and, when you reach Paris, present to Herr Joseph Felix Arbauer, the big dealer in fancy goods. Mr. Mayer, in whose house Count ★ Wolfegg lived, is Arbauer's agent. I must close. Nannerl and I kiss you both 100000 times and I remain your faithful husband and father

MZT

Grassl Martini, who was Prince Breuner's attendant, was buried today. Wolfgang will remember that he composed for him a little piece for the French horn.[1]

★

(288) Mozart to his Father

[Autograph in the Mozarteum, Salzburg]

MONSIEUR   MANNHEIM, 19 *February* 1778
  MON TRÉS CHER PÉRE!

I hope you received my last two letters safely. In the last one I discussed my mother's journey home, but I now see from your letter of the

---

[1] There is no trace of this composition. See Köchel, p. 47.

12th that this was quite unnecessary. I always thought that you would disapprove of my undertaking a journey ⟨with the Webers,⟩ but I never had any such intention—I mean, of course, *in our present circumstances.* I gave them my word of honour, however, to write to you about it. Herr Weber does not know how we stand—and I shall certainly never tell anyone. I wish my position were such that I had no cause to consider anyone else and that we were all comfortably off. In the intoxication of the moment I forgot how impossible it is at present to carry out my plan, and therefore also—to tell you what I have now done. The reasons why I have not gone off to Paris must be sufficiently evident to you from my last two letters. If my mother had not first raised the point, I should certainly have gone with my friends; but when I saw that she did not like the scheme, then I began to dislike it myself. For as soon as people lose confidence in me, I am apt to lose confidence in myself. Those days when, standing on a chair, I used to sing to you *Oragna fiagata fa* and finish by kissing you on the tip of your nose, are gone indeed; but do I honour, love and obey you any the less on that account? I will say no more. As for your reproach about the little singer in Munich,[1] I must confess that I was an ass to tell you such a palpable lie. Why, she does not yet know what *singing* means. It is true that for a person who had only been studying for three months she sang surprisingly well, and she had, in addition, a very pleasing and pure voice. Why I praised her so much may well have been because I was hearing people say from morning to night 'There is no better singer in all Europe' and 'Who has not heard her, has heard nothing'. I did not dare to contradict them, partly because I wanted to make some good friends, and partly because I had come straight from Salzburg, where we are not in the habit of contradicting anyone; but as soon as I was alone, I never could help laughing. Why then did I not laugh at her when writing to you? I really cannot tell.

What you say so cuttingly about my merry intercourse with your brother's daughter has hurt me very much; but since matters are not as you think, it is not necessary for me to reply. I don't know what to say about Wallerstein. I was very grave and reserved at Beecke's; and at the officers' table also I maintained a very serious demeanour and did not say a word to anyone. Let us forget all that; you only wrote it in a temper.

What you say about Mlle Weber is all perfectly true; and at the time I wrote that letter I knew quite as well as you do that she is still too young and that she must first learn how to act and make frequent appearances on the stage. But with some people one must proceed—by degrees. These good people are as tired of being here as—you know whom and where;[2] and they think that every scheme is practicable. I promised them to write everything to my father; but when the letter was on its way to Salzburg,

[1] Mlle Kaiser. See p. 475.   [2] Mozart and his father in Salzburg.

I kept on telling them: 'She must be patient a little longer, she is a bit too young yet, etc.' They do not mind what I say to them, for they have a high opinion of me. On my advice the father has engaged Madame Toscani (an actress) to give his daughter lessons in acting. Everything you say about Mlle Weber is true, except one thing—that 'she sings like a Gabrielli'; for I should not at all like her to sing in that style. Those who have heard Gabrielli are forced to admit that she was an adept only at runs and roulades; she adopted, however, such an unusual interpretation that she won admiration; but it never survived the fourth time of hearing. In the long run she could not please, for people soon get tired of coloratura passages. Moreover she had the misfortune of not being able to sing. She was not capable of *sustaining* a breve properly, and, as she had no *messa di voce*,[1] she could not dwell on her notes; in short, she sang with skill but without understanding. Mlle Weber's singing, on the other hand, goes to the heart, and she prefers to sing cantabile. Lately I have made her practise the passages in my grand aria,[2] because, if she goes to Italy, she will have to sing bravura arias. Undoubtedly she will never forget how to sing cantabile, for that is her natural bent. Raaff himself (who is certainly no flatterer), when asked to give his candid opinion, said 'She sang, not like a student, but like a master'. So now you know all. I still commend her to your interest with all my heart; and please don't forget about the arias, cadenzas and the rest. Farewell. I kiss your hands 100000 times and remain your most obedient son

WOLFGANG AMADÉ MOZART

I can't write any more for sheer hunger. My mother will display the contents of our large cash-box. I embrace my sister with all my heart. Tell her she must not cry over every silly trifle, or I shall never go home again. My greetings to all our good friends, especially to Herr Bullinger.

(288a) *Maria Anna Mozart to her Husband*

[*Autograph in the Mozarteum, Salzburg*]

MY DEAR HUSBAND   [MANNHEIM, 19 *February* 1778]
    I hope that this letter may find you well again. We are both awfully sorry that our letter horrified you so. On the other hand, your last letter of the 12th distressed us greatly. I implore you with all my might not to take everything to heart in the way you do, for it is bad for your health. Why, everything can be made right again and we have lost nothing but ⟨bad⟩ company. We shall do our very best to make arrangements for

---

[1] i.e. sustained voice.   [2] From *Lucio Silla*. See p. 448, n. 3.

our journey to Paris. Our whole capital now consists of 140 gulden. We shall try to sell the carriage, but I should say that we shall hardly get more than 60 or 70 gulden for it; only the other day someone bought a fine glass carriage with four seats for nine louis d'or. We shall pack all our things into two trunks and travel by mail coach, which will not be very expensive. Quite respectable people travel in this way. But we ought to have rooms engaged, so that we need not stay at the inn for long. If that merchant you told us about would be so kind as to help us to find them, it would be splendid. Meanwhile I am longing for your next letter, so that we may make arrangements in accordance with what you want us to do. Addio. Keep well, both of you. I kiss you both several 10000 times and remain your faithful wife

MARIA ANNA MOZART

All sorts of messages to all our good friends.
What a horrible pen and ink.

(289) *Mozart to his Father*

[*Autograph in the Mozarteum, Salzburg*]

MONSIEUR [MANNHEIM, 22 *February* 1778]
MON TRÉS CHER PÉRE,

I have been confined to the house for two days and have been taking antispasmodics, black powders and elderberry tea to make me sweat, as I have had catarrh, a cold in the head, headache, a sore throat, pains in my eyes and earache. But, thank God, I am better now and I hope to go out tomorrow, as it is Sunday. I received your letter of the 16th and the two unsealed letters of introduction for Paris. I am glad that you like my French aria. Please forgive my not writing much now, but really I cannot —I am afraid of bringing back my headache, and besides I feel no inclination to write today. It is impossible to put on paper all that we think—at least I find it so. I would rather say it than write it. My last letter will have told you just how things stand. Please believe what you like of me, but not anything bad. There are people who think that no one can love a poor girl without having evil designs; and that charming word maîtresse, wh—e in our tongue, is really much too charming! But I am no Brunetti! no Mysliwecek! I am a Mozart, and a young and clean-minded Mozart. So you will forgive me, I hope, if in my eagerness I sometimes get excited,— if that is the expression I should use, though indeed I would much rather say, if I sometimes write naturally. I have much to say on this subject, but I cannot, for I find it impossible to do so. Among my many faults I have

also this one, a persistent belief that my friends who know me, really do know me. Therefore many words are not necessary: for if they do not know me, oh, then where could I ever find words enough? It is bad enough that one needs words at all—and letters into the bargain. All this, however, is not intended for you, my dear Papa. No, indeed! You know me too well and besides you are too good-natured thoughtlessly to rob anyone of his good name. I only mean those people—and they know that I mean them—who believe such a thing. I have made up my mind to stay at home today, although it is Sunday, because it is snowing so hard. To-morrow I must go out, for our house nymph, Mlle Pierron, my highly esteemed pupil, is to scramble through my concerto (written for the high and mighty Countess Lützow)[1] at the French concert which is held every Monday. I too, prostitution though it be, shall ask them to give me some-thing to strum and shall contrive to thump it out *prima fista*. For I am a born wood-hitter and all I can do is to strum a little on the clavier. Now please let me stop, for I am not at all in the humour for writing letters today, but feel far more inclined to compose. Once more, please don't forget to do what I asked you in my previous letters about the cadenzas and the aria cantabile with coloratura indications. I am obliged to you already for having had the arias I asked for copied so quickly. That proves that you have confidence in me and that you believe me when I suggest something to you. Well, good-bye. I kiss your hands 1000 times and embrace my sister with all my heart and remain your most obedient son
                                        WOLFGANG AMADÉ MOZART
Mannheim, 22 February 1778.

My greetings to all good friends and especially to my dearest friend Herr Bullinger.

(289a) *Maria Anna Mozart to her Husband*

[Autograph in the Mozarteum, Salzburg]

MY DEAR HUSBAND   [MANNHEIM, 22 *February* 1778]
    You say that we have no confidence in you and that we ought to have told you at once about Herr ⟨Wendling's⟩ way of living. The reason why we didn't do so is that for a long time we knew nothing about it. For at first all his friends praised him to us and said that we could not do better than let Wolfgang travel with him; and it is perfectly true that Herr Wendling is the best fellow in the world, only the whole household knows nothing about religion and does not value it. The mother and the daughter never go to church from one end of the year to the other, never go to confession and never hear Mass. On the other hand they are always going

---

[1] K. 246, composed in 1776.

off to the theatre. They say that a church is not healthy. We have heard all this bit by bit partly from their own friends and partly from what Wolfgang himself has seen and heard. I prayed every day that God might prevent this journey and, thank Heaven, He has done so. Most people here have no religion and are out-and-out free-thinkers. No one knows that this is the reason why Wolfgang has not gone off with them, for, if it were known, we should be laughed at. Even our Privy Court Councillor, who is a bird of the same feather, does not know it. We have given him another reason, that is, that Wolfgang has been waiting for letters from Vienna and can't leave until they arrive. They are delighted in the house here that Wolfgang hasn't left, for thus their daughter can make further strides. Thank God, I am well, and I trust that you are the same. Wolfgang has had to stay at home for three days as he had a severe cold and sore throat. But now, thank God, he is well again and is going out tomorrow. I do hope that Wolfgang will make his fortune in Paris quickly, so that you and Nannerl may follow us soon. How delighted I should be to have you both with us, for nothing could be better. If it is God's will, He will arrange it. Living must be getting harder and harder in Salzburg, and in such circumstances it must be very wretched for everybody. Addio. Keep well, both of you. I kiss you both many 100000 times and remain as always your faithful wife

MARIA ANNA MOZART

Our greetings to all our acquaintances, especially to Monsieur Bullinger, Jungfer Sallerl, Katherl Gilowsky, Herr Deibl, Jungfrau Mitzerl, Frau von Gerlichs. A kiss for Bimperl, who will by this time have forgotten me and will no longer recognize me.

(290) *Leopold Mozart to his Son*

[Extract]   [Autograph in the Mozarteum, Salzburg]

MON TRÉS CHER FILS!   SALZBURG, 23 *February* 1778

In order to convince me that in all matters you are careless and in-attentive, you say at the beginning of your letter of the 14th that you see from my letter of the 9th that I have not yet received your last two letters. So on the 9th I should have replied to your wild letter sent off on the 5th, which almost killed me, although you ought to know from my long cor-respondence with you since you have been in Mannheim, that a letter of mine takes six days to reach you, and although I have told you already that your letters always arrive on *Tuesdays or Fridays,* so that you cannot have a reply from me under a fortnight. But alas! What is the use of all my ★

precise thinking, all my care, all my consideration and my paternal efforts
in pursuance of a most important and necessary enterprise, if (when faced
with an apparently serious obstacle which Mamma perhaps may have
perceived long ago) you fail to give your father your full confidence and
only change your mind when, caught between two fires, you can neither
advance nor retreat? Just when I am thinking that things are now on a
better footing and taking their proper course, I am suddenly confronted
with some foolish, unexpected fancy of yours or else it appears that matters
were different from what you represented them to me. So once more I
have guessed aright! You have only received 96 gulden instead of 200—
and why?—because you finished only two concertos and only three
quartets for your client.[1] How many were you to have composed for him,
then, since he would only pay you half? Why do you *lie* to me, saying
that you had only to compose three short easy concertos and a couple of
quartets? And why did you not listen to me when I said *expressly: You
ought to satisfy this gentleman as quickly as you possibly can.* Why did I tell
you to do so? So that you would be sure of getting those 200 gulden, for
indeed I know people better than you do. Have I not guessed everything?
It seems that I, who am at a distance, see more and judge better than you
do with these people under your very nose. You must be ready to believe
me, when I mistrust people, and to act as prudently as I direct. Indeed you
have bought experience lately at a somewhat heavy cost to us all. True,
you have arranged with Herr Wendling that the sum in question is to be
paid to you later and that you will send on your compositions. Yes—and
if Wendling can advantageously dispose of what you have now delivered
to flautist friends in Paris, then he will try to get a little more. One party
has to pay; the other gets the profit. Further, you wrote to me about a
couple of pupils and in particular about the Dutch officer,[2] who would pay
you three or, as you were inclined to believe, four ducats for twelve
lessons. And now it appears that you could have had these pupils, but that
you gave them up, simply because on one or two occasions you did not
find them at home. You would rather give lessons as a favour.—Yes, of
course you would! And you would rather, I suppose, leave your poor old
father in need! The effort is too great for a young man like yourself, however good the pay may be; and, no doubt, it is more seemly that your old
father of fifty-eight should run round from house to house for a miserable
fee, so that he may earn the necessary means of support for himself and
his daughter by the sweat of his brow and, *instead of paying off his debts,*
support you with what remains over, while you in the meantime can
amuse yourself by giving a girl lessons for nothing! My son, do reflect and
listen to your common sense! Just think whether you are not treating me

---

[1] The works ordered by De Jean. See p. 481, notes 1 and 2.
[2] De La Pottrie. See p. 429.

more cruelly than does our Prince. From him I have never expected anything, but from you I have expected all. From him I take everything as a
favour, but from you I can hope to receive all by virtue of your duty as
my child. After all, he is a stranger to me, but you are my son. You know
what I have endured for more than five years—yes—and what a lot I have
had to swallow on your account. The Prince's conduct can only bend me,
but yours can crush me. He can only make me ill, but you can kill me.
Had I not your sister and Bullinger, that true friend of ours, I should
probably not have the strength to write this letter which I have been
penning for the last two days. I have to conceal my anxiety from the whole
world; they are the only two persons to whom I can tell all, and who comfort me. I believed that everything you were writing was the truth; and as
everyone here is genuinely delighted when things go well with you and
as people were always asking about you, I, in my joy, gave them a *full
account* of how you were making money and would then go off to Paris.
And as you know how everyone takes delight ⟨in annoying the Archbishop,⟩ a good many people used my story for that purpose. Old Herr
Hagenauer was very sorry that you had to draw 150 gulden in Mannheim,
for these business people naturally want us to earn some money. But when
I told him what you had written, namely, that you had free board and
lodging, that you would be getting 200 gulden and that you had pupils as
well, he was very well pleased. Of course I had to ask him to wait a little
for the repayment of the 150 gulden. Whereupon he replied: '*Don't
mention it! I have every confidence in your Wolfgang. He will do his duty as a
son. Let him get off to Paris and don't worry.*' Well, consider these words and
our present circumstances and tell me whether I can stand any more,
seeing that as an honourable man I cannot leave you in your present
situation, cost what it may. You may rest assured that not a soul knows
that we sent those 150 gulden to Mannheim, for the Hagenauers would
never, never give ⟨the Archbishop⟩ that pleasure. But how disappointed
these friends will be that once more I have to send you money to help you to
get to Paris! All the same, I shall prove to you that you must abide by this
decision. Your proposal to go travelling about, particularly in the present
critical state of Europe, cannot be considered for a moment; very often
you would not even make your travelling expenses; the whole time you
would have to be making enquiries and begging and seeking patrons, so
that your concerts should bring in money; the whole time you would
have to be trying to get letters of introduction from one place to another,
asking for permission to give a concert and facing a hundred incidental
unpleasant circumstances; and in the end you would hardly get enough
money to pay the innkeeper and to meet your travelling expenses, so that
you would have to use your own capital (if you had any) or pawn or even
sell your clothes, watch and rings. Of the former I have had experience.

I had to draw 100 gulden from Herr Ollenschläger in Frankfurt and immediately after my arrival in Paris a further 300 gulden from Turton and Baur, of which, it is true, I used very little, as we soon began to make money. But first of all we had to become known by delivering letters of introduction, etc., and in a large city that takes time, for it is not always possible to meet acquaintances. My dear Wolfgang, all your letters convince me that you are ready to accept, without due consideration and reflection, the first wild idea that comes into your head or that anyone puts there. For example, you say, 'I am a composer. *I must not bury* my talent for composition, etc.' Who says that you ought to do so? But that is precisely what you would be doing, were you to roam about in gipsy fashion. If you want to make your name as a composer, you must be either in Paris, or Vienna or Italy. You are now nearest Paris. The only other question is: 'Where have I most hope of getting on?' *In Italy*, where in *Naples alone* there are at least three hundred maestri and where, from one end of the country to the other, the maestri have contracts (very often two years in advance) with those theatres that pay well? or in Paris, where perhaps two or three are writing for the stage, and other composers may be counted on one's fingers? The clavier must bring you your first acquaintances and make you popular with the great. After that you can have something engraved by subscription, which is slightly more profitable than composing six quartets for an Italian gentleman and getting a few ducats, and perhaps a snuff-box worth three, for your pains. Vienna is even better in that respect, for at least it is possible to get up a subscription for music to be copied for private circulation. You and others have had experience of both. In short, if I could instill into you greater stability and more reflection when these wild ideas occur to you, I should make you the happiest man in the world. I realize, however, that time alone will teach you this, though indeed, as far as your talent is concerned, everything came before its time, while in all branches of knowledge you have always grasped everything with the greatest ease. Why then should it not be possible for you to learn to know people, to fathom their intentions, to close your heart to the world and in every case to think things over carefully, so that you do not always see only the good side of a question or that side which is most flattering to you or which furthers some momentary whim? My dear son, *God has given you excellent judgment*, which (as far as I can see) *only two things* prevent you from using properly. For thanks to me you have learned how to use it and how to know your fellow-creatures. When in the past I used always to guess aright and often foresee the future, you used to say in fun: '*Next to God comes Papa*'. Now what, do you think, are these two things? Examine yourself, my dear Wolfgang, learn to know yourself, and you will discover them. First of all, you have a little too much *pride and self-love*; and secondly, you immediately make yourself too *cheap* and open your heart to everyone; in short! wishing to be unconstrained and natural, you fall into the other extreme of being too unreserved. True, the first failing ought to check the second, for whoever has pride and self-love will not readily descend to familiarity. Your pride and self-love, however, are only touched when you do not at once get the appreciation you deserve. You think that even those who do not know you, ought to see by your face that you are a man of genius! But when it comes to flatterers who, in order to bend you to their selfish purposes, praise you to the skies, you open your heart with the greatest ease and believe them as you do the Bible. Please do not think that I mistrust your ★ filial love; the purpose of all my remarks is to make you an honourable man. Millions have not received the tremendous favour which God has bestowed upon you. What a responsibility! And what a shame if such a great genius were to founder! And that can happen in a moment! You are confronted with far more dangers than those millions who have no talent, for you are exposed to many more ordeals and temptations. Mamma must go with you to Paris and you must confide in her, just as you must confide in me when you write to me. By the next post I shall send you full particulars, as well as all the addresses you require and also letters to Diderot, d'Alembert and the rest. I must close. Nannerl and I kiss you ★ many thousand times and I am your old

MZT

All send greetings, and especially Herr Bullinger.

By the next post I shall get details, I hope, of the amount of money you have in hand.

By that time our chaise will have been sold, I suppose.

(291) *Leopold Mozart to his Wife and Son*

[*Extract*]   [*Autograph in the Mozarteum, Salzburg*]

SALZBURG, 25 and 26 *February* 1778

MY DEAR WIFE AND MY DEAR SON!

Thank God, I feel somewhat better, though I am still troubled from time to time with nervous palpitations. This is, however, only natural, for I cannot shake off my worries. But indeed, I am never depressed by care, if it is merely due to some misfortune and if I am told everything frankly, fully and immediately, so that I may contrive and advise; for then I can think out calmly how to help, propose a remedy and suggest a way out. But if . . . Well, let us forget it . . . I have told you already, my son, that you were very wise not to travel to Paris ⟨in that company. A father who thus sacrifices his daughter⟩ from self-interest is loathsome.[1] How could

[1] Wendling, whose daughter Augusta had been the Elector's mistress.

★ you rely on his friendship? Meanwhile I shall do my best for Mlle Weber.
I suggest that she should keep on very good terms with Signor Raaff and
make sure of his support, which will most certainly help her to achieve
her object, for he has a tremendous reputation in Italy and has many
★ acquaintances among eminent people there, professors and impresarios. I
at once sent for the two copyists to copy those arias which you asked for,
so that they might be ready for the Munich mail coach on the 22nd, but
to get the work done in time was out of the question. All three copyists
have been busy day and night copying Rust's serenata. 'Il Parnasso confuso', as he wants to get away and the serenata has still to be rehearsed
under his direction, so that Herr Haydn, who plays the clavier, can conduct
it in his absence. However, after a good deal of hunting I found the three
arias: *Il tenero momento*; the scena, *Fra i pensieri più funesti di morte*; and
Pupille amate;[1] and with these I have had to be content. I have also found
Bach's aria *Cara*, etc.,[2] but neither the coloratura passages, which your
sister copied, nor the various cadenzas which at one time were copied
out neatly on small paper. The latter used to be with the little scores.
When you were leaving, you bundled everything together in a great
★ hurry, so that it is quite possible that you took them with you. The
arias ought to arrive in Mannheim by mail coach during the first week of
★ March. If I had not made the necessary enquiries about the departure of
the mail coach, I should not have been able to send them until March 1st,
and even then only as far as Munich, *'Learning comes before doing'*, as
Kessler, our learned trumpeter, declares. I am sending you also five grand
arias of Bertoni,[3] Monza, Gasparini, Grétry and Colla.[4] So I have the
honour ⟨to make you a present⟩ of five arias and ⟨to pay the expense of
having⟩ three of them ⟨copied and posted⟩ to Augsburg, though, by
Heaven, I myself ⟨do not possess a farthing. I look like poor Lazarus. My
dressing-gown is so shabby⟩ that if somebody calls in the morning, ⟨I
have to make myself scarce. My old flannel jerkin⟩, which I have been
wearing morning and evening for years, ⟨is so torn that⟩ I can hardly
⟨keep it⟩ on any longer and I cannot afford ⟨to have either a new dressing-
gown or a new jerkin made.⟩ Since your departure I haven't had ⟨a single
pair of new shoes,⟩ nor have I any ⟨black silk stockings⟩ left. On Sundays
I wear ⟨old white stockings⟩ and during the week ⟨black woollen Berlin
stockings,⟩ which I bought for 1 gulden 12 kreuzer. If someone had told

[1] From Mozart's *Lucio Silla*, nos. 2, 22 and 21.
[2] 'Cara la dolce fiamma', an aria from J. C. Bach's opera *Adriano in Siria*. The coloratura
cadenzas K. 293e which Mozart wrote for this and two other arias of J. C. Bach have been
preserved. See Köchel, p. 300, 301, and W. Plath, *Mozart-Jahrbuch 1960/61*, p. 106 and 1971/72,
p. 20.
[3] Ferdinando Giuseppe Bertoni (1725–1813), a famous operatic composer in his time. He
was trained by Padre Martini and became organist and subsequently maestro di cappella at
St. Mark's, Venice.
[4] Giuseppe Colla (1731–1806), was maestro di cappella to the Duke of Parma. He married
in 1780 Lucrezia Agujari, the famous coloratura soprano. He wrote several successful operas.

me a few years ago that I should have to wear ⟨woollen stockings⟩ and that, when the weather is dry and frosty, I should be glad of your old ⟨felt shoes⟩ to pull on over my ⟨old ones,⟩ and that in order to protect myself from the cold I should have to put on two or three ⟨old⟩ waist-coats—would I ever have believed him? ⟨Plays⟩ and balls are ⟨out of the question⟩ for us. Such is our life, cares within and cares without; and, to make things worse, I have no wife or son with me, and God knows whether—or when—we shall meet again! My one great delight—to hear your compositions—is gone! Everything around me is dead! Your sister alone is now my support, and I try to banish the cares which seem to overwhelm me by a very quiet form of entertainment, which is, to play through on the violin from six to eight every evening, arias, symphonies, masses, vespers, and so forth, while your sister plays the figured bass and gets practice in accompanying. To my amazement she has made such progress that she plays off at sight everything I bring back from the Cathedral, however difficult the fugues may be. By degrees we shall soon have finished playing the contents of the Cathedral chest. Each time I only bring home the organ and violin parts of a few compositions. By means of this practice which she has kept up since your departure, she has acquired such perfect insight into harmony and modulations that not only can she move from one key into another, but she extemporizes so successfully that you would be astounded. And do you know what has inspired her with this determination and terrific industry? *My death!* She realizes and foresees the misery into which she would be plunged, were I suddenly to breathe my last. In that case what do you think would be the future of your Mamma and your sister? Adlgasser's three children have been given 8 gulden a month for one year only. The ⟨*Prince*⟩ would give my women-folk nothing whatever, for you went off on your own and at the same time he ⟨dismissed⟩ me.[1] He would say that you should support your mother and that your sister should go into domestic service, as he now makes all daughters do who have lost their fathers. So your sister was not crying over a silly trifle, when she wept over your letter: and yet when you told us that you had not got the 200 gulden, she just said: '*Thank God it's no worse!*' Up to the present we have always thought Nannerl rather stingy. But she agrees that to help you both, her own savings must be sacrificed. For how could I, without blushing for shame, ⟨approach⟩ Herr Hagenauer again ⟨for money⟩, without offering him some security? And your sister is doing this willingly and cheerfully, although she knows that if I were to die today she would be absolutely stranded. She gets up daily at six o'clock and goes to Holy Trinity, where she prays so ardently that several people have already spoken to me about it. My dear Wolfgang,

---

[1] Leopold Mozart is referring no doubt to the Archbishop's reply to his son's application for his discharge in the summer of 1777. See p. 268, n. 2.

you are young and you do not worry much, for so far you have never
had to bother about anything; you banish all serious thoughts, you have
long since forgotten the Salzburg cross, on which I am still hanging;
you only listen to praises and flatteries and thus are becoming by degrees
insensible and unable to realize our condition or to devise some means of
relieving it. In short, you never think of the future. The present alone
engulfs you completely, and sweeps you off your feet, although if you
would only ponder the consequences of your actions and face them in
★ good earnest, you would I know, be horrified. You will receive this letter
on March 4th, and on the 8th you will get another one with particulars
about your board and lodging in Paris. We kiss you millions of times and
I who still hover between fear and hope, remain your old

MZT

I suppose you know that Noverre is master of the ballet at the Paris
★ opera. Rust has gone away, so once more I am the only Kapellmeister.
Ferlendis wants to go off travelling in the spring or he may even leave
altogether. Ferrari still wants to get married or to leave Salzburg. Brunetti
is in a terrible fix. St. Peter's house, where Haydn lives, used to be his
headquarters. But he has now to support Judith[1] and the child, and he has
debts amounting to 600 gulden; so people are beginning to think that all
of a sudden it will be: Where is Brunetti? The great Luz and Brunetti now
take their meals at Spitzeder's, which has become the headquarters of the
Italians and a regular gambling den. Addio. Get ready for your journey,
so that you may leave as soon as you receive my next letter. The French
diligences are not at all draughty and very well sprung. Try to sell our
chaise soon for as high a price as possible.

(292) *Mozart to his Father*

[*Autograph in the Mozarteum, Salzburg*]

MONSIEUR,   [MANNHEIM, 28 *February* 1778]
MON TRÉS CHER PÉRE!

We have received your letter of February 23rd. I hope I shall get the
arias next Friday or Saturday, although in your last letter you said nothing
more about them, so that I don't know whether you sent them off by the
mail coach on the 22nd. I hope you did, for before I leave I should like to
play and sing them to Mlle Weber. I was at Raaff's yesterday and brought
him an aria which I composed for him the other day.[2] The words are: '*Se
al labbro mio non credi, bella nemica mia*', etc. I don't think that Metastasio

---

[1] Judith Lipp, a daughter of the organist Franz Ignaz Lipp, and the mistress of Brunetti.
[2] K. 295.

wrote them.[1] He liked it enormously. One must treat a man like Raaff in a particular way. I chose those words on purpose, because I knew that he already had an aria on them: so of course he will sing mine with greater facility and more pleasure. I asked him to tell me candidly if he did not like it or if it did not suit his voice, adding that I would alter it if he wished or even compose another. 'God forbid,' he said, 'the aria must remain just as it is, for nothing could be finer. But please shorten it a little, for I am no longer able to sustain my notes.' 'Most gladly,' I replied, 'as much as you like. I made it a little long on purpose, for it is always easy to cut down, but not so easy to lengthen.' After he had sung the second part, he took off his spectacles, and looking at me with wide-open eyes, said: 'Beautiful! Beautiful! That is a charming *seconda parte.*' And he sang it three times. When I took leave of him he thanked me most cordially, while I assured him that I would arrange the aria in such a way that it would give him pleasure to sing it. For I like an aria to fit a singer as perfectly as a well-made suit of clothes.[2] For practice I have also set to music the aria '*Non so d'onde viene,*' etc.[3] which has been so beautifully composed by Bach.[4] Just because I know Bach's setting so well and like it so much, and because it is always ringing in my ears, I wished to try and see whether in spite of all this I could not write an aria totally unlike his. And, indeed, mine does not resemble his in the very least. At first I had intended it for Raaff; but the beginning seemed to me too high for his voice. Yet I liked it so much that I would not alter it; and from the orchestral accompaniment, too, it seemed to me better suited to a soprano. So I decided to write it for Mlle Weber. Well, I put it aside and started off on the words '*Se al labbro*' for Raaff. But all in vain! I simply couldn't compose for the first aria kept on running in my head. So I returned to it and made up my mind to compose it exactly for Mlle Weber's voice. It's an Andante sostenuto (preceded by a short recitative); then follows the second part, *Nel seno a destarmi,* and then the sostenuto again. When it was finished, I said to Mlle Weber: 'Learn the aria yourself. Sing it as you think it ought to go; then let me hear it and afterwards I will tell you candidly what pleases and what displeases me.' After a couple of days I went to the Webers and she sang it for me, accompanying herself. I was obliged to confess that she had sung it exactly as I wished and as I should have taught it to her myself. This is now the best aria she has; and it will ensure her success wherever she goes. Yesterday at Wendling's I sketched the aria which I had promised his wife, adding a short recitative. She had chosen the words herself—from 'Didone',

---

[1] The words of the aria were taken from Hasse's opera *Artaserse*, the text of which may have been by Antonio Salvi.
[2] The autograph of the aria shows corrections and cuts which Mozart made to suit Raaff.
[3] K. 294, recitative and aria on a text from Metastasio's *Olimpiade*, written for Aloysia Weber. In 1787 Mozart set the same words to music for the famous bass singer, J. I. L. Fischer (K. 512).   [4] Johann Christian Bach. See p. 551, n. 2.

'*Ah, non lasciarmi, no*'.[1] She and her daughter are quite crazy about it. I have also promised the daughter some more French ariettas, and began one today.[2] When they are ready I shall send them to you on small paper as I did my first aria. I still have two of the six clavier sonatas to compose,[3] but there's no hurry, for I can't have them engraved here. Nothing is done in this place by subscription; it is a miserly spot, and the engraver will not do them at his own expense, but wants to go halves with me in the sale. So I prefer to have them engraved in Paris, where the engravers are delighted to get something new and pay handsomely and where it is easier to get a thing done by subscription. I would have had these sonatas copied and sent to you long ago; but I thought to myself: 'No, I prefer to send them to him when they have been engraved.' I am looking forward most particularly to the Concert Spirituel in Paris, for I shall probably be asked to compose something for it. The orchestra is said to be so excellent and strong: and my favourite type of composition, the chorus, can be well performed there. I am indeed glad that the French value choruses highly. The only fault found with Piccinni's new opera 'Roland',[4] is that the choruses are too meagre and weak, and that the music on the whole is a little monotonous; otherwise it was universally liked. To be sure, they are accustomed to Gluck's choruses in Paris. Do rely on me. I shall do my very best to bring honour to the name of Mozart and I have not the slightest fear. My last letters will have given you full particulars as to *how things are now*, and as to *what my intentions are*. I do entreat you never to allow the thought to cross your mind that I can ever forget you, for I cannot bear it. My chief purpose was, is and ever shall be to endeavour to bring about our speedy and happy reunion! But we must be patient. You yourself know even better than I do how often things go awry—but they will soon go straight—only do have patience! Let us place our trust in God, Who will never forsake us. I shall not be found wanting. How can you doubt me? Surely it is to your interest that I should work as hard as I can, so that I may have the joy and happiness (the sooner the better too) of embracing with all my heart my most beloved and dearest father? There—you see! Nothing in this world is wholly free from self-interest! If war should break out ⟨in Bavaria⟩, follow us at once, I beg you. I have full confidence in three friends, all of them powerful and invincible, God, your head and mine. Our heads, I admit, are very different, but each in its own way is good, serviceable and useful, and I hope that in time mine will by degrees equal yours in those branches in which it is now inferior. Well, good-bye! Be merry and cheerful. Remember that you have a son who has never,

---

[1] K. 486a [295a], recitative and aria on a text from Metastasio's *Didone abbandonata*, written for Dorothea Wendling.   [2] K. 308 [295b], 'Dans un bois solitaire'.

[2] K. 301, 302, 303 and 305 [293a–d] were composed at Mannheim, K. 304 [300c] and 306 [300l] in Paris.

[4] *Roland*, the first opera which Piccinni wrote for Paris, was performed on 27 January, 1778.

knowingly, forgotten his filial duty to you, who will endeavour to become
more and more worthy of so good a father and who will remain unchangingly your most obedient

WOLFGANG MOZART

I embrace my sister with all my heart!

My greetings to all my good friends, and particularly to Herr Bullinger.
If you have not yet sent off the arias, please do so as soon as possible and
you will make me really happy. Ah, if only ⟨the Elector of Bavaria had
not died!⟩ I would have finished the mass[1] and produced it and it would
have made a great sensation here. I was in excellent humour for composing
it when the devil had to trot out that accursed Doctor Sanftl![2]

(292a) *Maria Anna Mozart to her Husband*

[Autograph in the Mozarteum, Salzburg]

MY DEAR HUSBAND,   [MANNHEIM, 28 *February* 1778]
     We are now preparing gradually for our departure. I should be glad
to pocket a good price for the carriage, but indeed I doubt whether we
shall get much for it. However, we shall do our best and keep on until we
get at least 50 gulden. These people simply won't value it at more than 4
carolins and keep on finding all sorts of flaws in it. It is always the way
when you want to sell an article; and here particularly there are so many
selfish people who keep on trying to make double or treble profits and
won't do the smallest kindness without pay. I shall be delighted to be out
of this and am longing for the day to arrive, which, if it is God's will, will
certainly be in a fortnight at latest. Meanwhile I am so looking forward to
your letters and to what you have to say to us. Rest assured that everything
will be done in accordance with what you want and prescribe. Keep well,
both of you. I kiss you both many 10000 times and remain as always your
faithful wife

MARIA ANNA MOZART

All sorts of messages to all our good friends.

(293) *Mozart to his Cousin, Maria Anna Thekla Mozart, Augsburg*

[Autograph in the Stefan Zweig Collection, British Library, London]

[MANNHEIM, 28 February 1778]

MADEMOISELLE MA TRÉS CHÉRE COUSINE!
     Perhaps you think or are even convinced that I am dead? That I have
pegged out? Or hopped a twig? Not at all. Don't believe it, I implore you.

---

[1] See p. 482, n. 2.
[2] The Elector's death was generally considered to be due to the carelessness of his private
physician, Dr. Sanftl.

For believing and shitting are two very different things! Now how could I be writing such a beautiful hand if I were dead? How could that be possible? I shan't apologize for my very long silence, for you would never believe me. Yet what is true is true. I have had so many things to do that I had time indeed to think of my little cousin, but not to write, you see. So I just had to let things be. But now I have the honour to inquire how you are and whether you perspire? Whether your stomach is still in good order? Whether indeed you have no disorder? Whether you still can like me at all? Whether with chalk you often scrawl? Whether now and then you have me in mind? Whether to hang yourself you sometimes feel inclined? Whether you have been wild? With this poor foolish child? Whether to make peace with me you'll be so kind? If not, I swear I'll let off one behind! Ah, you're laughing! Victoria! Our arses shall be the symbol of our peacemaking! I knew that you wouldn't be able to resist me much longer. Why, of course, I'm sure of success, even if today I should make a mess, though to Paris I go in a fortnight or less. So if you want to send a reply to me from that town of Augsburg yonder, you see, then write at once, the sooner the better, so that I may be sure to receive your letter, or else if I'm gone I'll have the bad luck, instead of a letter to get some muck. Muck!—Muck!—Ah, muck! Sweet word! Muck! chuck! That too is fine. Muck, chuck!—muck!—suck—o charmante! muck, suck! That's what I like! Muck, chuck and suck! Chuck muck and suck muck!

Now for something else. When the carnival was on, did you have some good fun? One can have far more fun at this time in Augsburg than here. How I wish I were with you so that we could run about together. Mamma and I send our greetings to your father and mother and to you, little cousin, and we trust all three of you are well and in good spirits. Praise and thanks be to God, we are in good health. Don't believe it. All the better, better the all. A propos, how are you getting on with your French? May I soon send you a whole letter in French? You would like one from Paris, would you not? Do tell me whether you still have that Spuni Cuni business? I'm sure you have. Well, I must tell you something before I close, for I must really stop soon, as I am in a hurry, for just at the moment I have nothing whatever to do; and also because I have no more room, as you see; the paper will soon be at an end; and besides I am tired and my fingers are twitching from so much writing; and finally even if I had room, I really don't know what I could tell you, apart from this story which I am proposing to relate. Now listen, it happened not very long ago, it all took place here and it made a great sensation too, for it seemed almost unbelievable; and, between ourselves, no one knows how the affair is going to turn out. Well, to make a long story short, about four hours from here—I have forgotten the name of the place—at some village or other—and indeed it is all one, whether the village was Tribsterill, where muck runs into the sea, or Burmesquik, where the crooked arse-holes are manufactured—in short, it was a village. Now in that village there was a peasant or shepherd, who was well advanced in years, but was still hale and hearty. He was unmarried and very comfortably off and he led a jolly life. But, before I finish my story, I must tell you that when he spoke he had a dreadful voice, so that whenever he said anything, people were always terrified of him. Well to make a long story short, you must know that he had a dog called Bellot, a very fine large dog, white with black spots. Now one day the shepherd was walking along with his sheep, of which he had eleven thousand, and was carrying in his hand a stick with a beautiful rose-coloured ribbon. For he always carried a stick. It was his habit to do this. Well, let's get on. After he had walked for a good hour or so, he got tired and sat down near a river and fell asleep, and dreamt that he had lost his sheep. He awoke in terror, but to his great joy found all his sheep beside him. So he got up and walked on, but not for very long; for he had hardly walked for half an hour before he came to a bridge, which was very long but well protected on both sides in order to prevent people from falling into the river. Well, he looked at his flock and, as he was obliged to cross the river, he began to drive his eleven thousand sheep over the bridge. Now please be so kind as to wait until the eleven thousand sheep have reached the other side and then I shall finish my story. I have already told you that no one knows how the affair is going to turn out. But I hope that before I send you my next letter the sheep will have crossed the river. If not, I really don't care very much; as far as I am concerned, they could have remained this side of the water. So you must just be content with this instalment. I have told you all I know; and it is much better to stop than to make up the rest. If I did so, you would not believe any of the story; but as it is, you will surely believe—not even half of it. Well, I must close, though it makes me morose. Whoever begins must cease, or else he gives people no peace. My greetings to every single friend, and whoever doesn't believe me, may lick me world without end, from now to all eternity, until I cease to be a nonentity. He can go on licking for ever, in truth, why, even I am alarmed, forsooth, for I fear that my muck will soon dry up and that he won't have enough if he wants to sup. Adieu, little cousin. I am, I was, I should be, I have been, I had been, I should have been, oh that I were, oh that I might be, would to God I were, I shall be, if I should be, oh that I should be, I shall have been, oh that I had been, would to God that I had been, what?—a duffer. Adieu, ma chère cousine, where have you been? I am your same old faithful cousin

WOLFGANG AMADÉ MOZART

Mannheim, 28 February 1778.

(294) Leopold Mozart to his Wife and Son

[Extract]   [Autograph in the Mozarteum, Salzburg]

SALZBURG, 28 February: 1 and 2 March 1778

MY DEAREST WIFE AND DEAREST SON!

I have received your letter of February 22nd. Thank God that Wolfgang is better again. When you are travelling, your main concern should be your health. If Mamma has not got enough black powders with her, she will probably get some in Mannheim more easily than in Paris. I am trying to recall the name of the German doctor who is, I think, physician to the Swiss Guard, and who came to see us on the night Wolfgang got his dangerous cold. As far as I can recollect, it was something like 'Herrschwand'.

★ Well, I must give Wolfgang a description of Baron Bache or Bagge (for I don't know how he spells his name). As far as I know, he was a poor Baron from Prussia or somewhere in those parts, who married the daughter of a wealthy Paris hatter. As time passed by, all sorts of quarrels arose between them and, after we returned to Salzburg, husband and wife drifted into a situation which was followed by a lawsuit, and she is supposed to have entered a convent. He is a passionate lover of music and used to give concerts in his house, as he may still do, for all I know. Further, he always kept a few musicians, such as two players on the French horn (Henno[1] was one), two oboists, a double bass and so forth, to whom he paid a small salary, which they were glad to receive, as it was permanent. Apart from them he did what he could with the help of the foreign virtuosi who came to him for advice and to obtain that opportunity which his house provided, of making acquaintances in a foreign city. Even Parisian virtuosi often go there, some to perform their new compositions, and others to hear foreign music, for Bagge is always on the look-out for new stuff; and finally people go there to listen to these same foreign virtuosi. All that he did for us long ago was to sell some tickets for our first concert, about which Herr von Grimm had badgered him; and for our last concert he sent us his musicians and charged us nothing, so that we had only to pay the singer, Mme Piccinelli, and M. Gaviniés, though indeed in the end the latter refused to take anything. What I noticed about Bagge was that what he liked above all was to pay for a good composition. So, my dear Wolfgang, when first you go to Baron Bagge's, you ought to be rather reserved and you should begin by producing only your very best music, so that you may at once gain credit for yourself. Io Victoria! Now I need not write anything more! Baron Grimm is in Paris! I have this moment received a letter from him, which again contains evidence of

---

[1] Schurig in his note to Leopold Mozart's entry in his *Reiseaufzeichnungen*, p. 69, maintains that this is Heina, who was also a music publisher in Paris. See *MBA*, No. 84.

your usual carelessness. True, Wolfgang was busy and is short-sighted; but did not Mamma see our friend Grimm at the concert at Augsburg?—for it seems that he placed himself in your line of vision. I will quote his letter, or rather the particular passage in German, which is as follows:

> I received only the other day your letter of December 25th; and just as I was about to reply to it, your second letter of January 9th arrived. It is perfectly true that I was in Augsburg when Herr Amadeo gave his concert. I was on the point of leaving again at once—but as a matter of fact I went to his concert, where I so placed myself that he and Madame Mozart could see me. But neither recognized me, and as I was in a great hurry to leave and as everyone told me that the Mozarts were on their way to Paris, I decided to remain unrecognized, as we should be sure to meet there. I shall be delighted to see him again; but I am very sorry that he is coming without his father. I see from your letter that he is now on his way; so I may hope to see him any day, and shall then hear everything and decide what I can do for him. He is certainly in good hands with M. Wendling, who can render him most useful services. But no one can take the place of a father (mais personne ne peut remplacer un pére). I returned from my travels three months ago and do not yet know whether my recent journey from Russia will be my last. Il serait temps de songer au repos. Je vous envoie ci-joint mon adresse, pour que vos lettres ne risquent plus de s'égarer. Je suis accablé d'affaires et d'écritures et par conséquent bien mauvais correspondant, mais lorsque M. votre fils sera ici, il sera mon sécrétaire et nous vous tiendrons au courant; en attendant n'ayez point d'inquiétude. Je crois votre fils d'une conduite assez sage pour ne pas redouter pour lui les dangers de Paris. S'il était enclin au libertinage, il pourrait sans doute courir quelques risques; mais s'il a de la raison, il se garantira de tout inconvénient sans mener pour cela la vie d'un ermite, etc. Je suis bien fâché que vous soyez cloué a Salzbourg. Adieu, Monsieur, vous connaissez les sentiments que je vous ai voués. Je vous prie de les regarder comme invariables. Paris, le 21 février, 1778.

He enclosed a card with his address.

> Monsieur le Baron de Grimm, Ministre Plénipotentiaire de Saxe-Gotha, rue de la Chaussée d'Antin, près le Boulevard.

In the circumstances I think you ought to drive straight to the Lion d'Argent and, if you arrive late, call on Baron Grimm on the following morning. Who knows but that you might perhaps be able to live quite close to him? I cannot at the moment find the rue de la Chaussée d'Antin. I shall reply, of course, to Baron Grimm at once. I have made arrangements for you to draw four or five louis d'or from Herr Schmalz in Mannheim. So even if you sell our chaise for only five louis d'or, you will have 100 German gulden. When you wrote to me on February 19th, you had only

140 gulden. I gather therefore that Wolfgang has earned nothing by giving lessons and that all that was, as usual, only soap-bubbles. I strongly advise you to leave very soon and hope to hear about this in your next

★ letter. Twice I have been informed that Wolfgang is going to publish clavier duets by subscription; *but whether at Mannheim or Paris I have not yet been told.* He had better do it in Paris. As soon as he gets there, I shall send him from my travelling accounts an item quoting the cost. Addio. We kiss you millions of times. Nannerl and I wish you a pleasant journey. God keep you. Addio.

★
                                                                                MZT

(295) *Leopold Mozart to his Wife and Son*

[*Extract*]   [*Autograph in the Mozarteum, Salzburg*]

                                                    SALZBURG, 5 *March* 1778

MY DEAR WIFE AND MY DEAR SON!

As you will not receive my letter of March 2nd until the 7th or 8th, I am thinking that you will not be able to leave before the 15th, for I take it that the mail coach leaves once a week. *But you must leave on the 15th.* So I am writing once more, as you will still get this letter on the 11th. In my last I told you that Baron Grimm had written to me and I gave you the contents of his letter. I told you also that I had had a letter sent to Herr Herzog, to enable you still to draw four or five louis d'or in Mannheim. You will probably have sold our chaise by this time for as high a price as you have been able to get. But if once again you have left everything to the last minute—it is your own fault; for indeed I reminded you about everything in good time, that is, about your luggage, the trunks, the mail coach and all your other expenses. You really must think of nothing but your own affairs, do everything immediately and not let yourself be put off by anyone. One important point must not be forgotten, and that is, *to take no other money with you but louis d'or and laubthaler,* for this is the only

★ money that is accepted on the route from Strassburg into France. For Heaven's sake don't waste a moment in getting everything fixed up, for if you reach Paris too late in the season, very little can be done. Besides, it takes time to make acquaintances, as it is such a big place and people are constantly going off to the country. So you must hurry up and make your acquaintances, while people are still in town. If you do not, your prospects will be ruined and we shall have the same story over again of your pulling to pieces whatever plans I have tried to make for you, while your own schemes, which I have done my best to further, have turned out to be impracticable. All that we can do now is to look ahead. Although you have not had to pay for board and lodging in Mannheim, you have spent quite enough money; and as you will now be spending far more, you really must think things out, for you will not be able to earn another farthing there. The parcel of music will no doubt have reached you by this time. You know what our circumstances are and you have ample reason to watch every farthing, for never yet have I been in such a predicament! I pray God that He may send Wolfgang better luck in Paris. Believe me, everything will depend on the skill with which you manage your affairs, wherever you are placed—and you should throw your whole heart into this. It is lucky for Wolfgang that Herr von Grimm is in Paris. He should place complete trust in him and do whatever he advises. Thus must Time be taken by the forelock.

Baron Grimm may be ordered away again soon and may have to undertake some journey in the spring. If so, you would again be left high and dry. If things were to go on in this way, we should be hopelessly in debt and suddenly find ourselves destitute, so that in the end one of us could no longer help the other. In all my letters I have tried to tell you the unvarnished truth; but apparently you have just glanced through them rapidly with half an eye and have then thrown them away. In Heaven's name, I implore you to read them through several times both carefully and attentively; *and in future to consult your own interests only and not always those of other people and to give up being at everybody's beck and call.* Otherwise I swear that you will suddenly be faced with the necessity of having to pawn or even sell your possessions. I have sent a reply to Baron Grimm, explaining fully why Wolfgang did not accompany Wendling to Paris, and telling him that he had to give him some other excuse. Perhaps you will have had a letter from Wendling in the meantime. I mention this so that you may tell Grimm the whole truth. I have arranged for you to draw an extra five louis d'or in Mannheim, but you must be able to draw some louis d'or in Paris on your arrival, for people will not begin to shower money on you at once. So I shall send you a letter of introduction which you can present there. Therefore, as soon as you have moved into your lodgings, send me your new address. At the same time I must think out some other arrangement, so that you may not find yourselves in a fix. But first of all, as soon as you have settled in your new quarters, you must let me know exactly where you are living. Grimm will very probably not be able to put you up; so you should make enquiries from M. Mayer. Keep well. This is my last letter to Mannheim, *as you will surely leave on the 15th.* God keep you and grant you a happy journey. Nannerl and I kiss you millions of times and I remain, faithful unto death, your old

MZT

As a precaution I am sending you again the address of Baron de Grimm, which is:
Rue de la Chausee d'Antin, près le Boulevard.

(296) *Mozart to his Father*

[*Autograph in the Mozarteum, Salzburg*]

MONSIEUR　　　　　　　　　　　　　　　　[MANNHEIM, 7 *March* 1778]
MON TRÉS CHER PÉRE

We have had no letter from you today, but we hope that the only reason is that owing to the bad weather the post has not arrived punctually, or that you have not written at all. I have received your letter of February 26th. I am very much obliged to you for all the trouble you have taken about the arias. You are indeed punctilious about everything. *Next to God comes Papa* was my motto or axiom as a child, and I still cling to it. Certainly you are right when you say that *Learning comes before doing.* Indeed you must not regret all the bother and trouble this has caused you, for Mlle Weber well deserves your kindness. I only wish you could hear her sing my new aria[1] about which I wrote to you the other day; I say, hear her sing it, for it is absolutely made for her. A man like you who really understands what portamento singing is, would certainly find complete satisfaction in her performance. Once I am happily settled in Paris and, as I hope, our circumstances with God's help have improved and we are all more cheerful and in better spirits, I shall tell you my thoughts more fully and ask you for a great favour. But I must tell you that I was absolutely horrified and that tears came into my eyes when I read in your last letter that ⟨you have to go about so shabbily dressed.⟩ My very dearest Papa! That is certainly not my fault—you know it is not! We ⟨economize⟩ in every possible way here; food and lodging, wood and light ⟨have cost us nothing⟩, and what more can we want! As for dress, you surely know that in places where you are not known, it is out of the question ⟨to be badly dressed,⟩ for appearances must be kept up. I have now set all my hopes on Paris, for the German princes are all skinflints. I mean to work with all my strength so that I may soon have the happiness ⟨of helping you out of your present distressing circumstances.⟩ And now for our journey. A week today, that is, the 14th, we shall leave here. We have been unfortunate about the sale of the carriage, for so far no buyer has turned up. We shall have to be content if we get four louis d'or for it. If we cannot dispose of it, people here advise us to hire a driver and drive in it as far as Strassburg, where we could sell it more easily. However, as it is cheaper to travel by mail coach, I shall leave it here in charge of honest people. Now you must know that, as this is not a commercial town, no carriers go to Paris, and everything is sent by mail coach. I am told that from here to Strassburg the fare for each passenger is half a louis d'or, so I think it should not cost us more than fifteen gulden in all. Meanwhile

---

[1] K. 294, 'Non so d'onde viene'.

farewell. Let us put our trust in God, Who will certainly never forsake us. Before I leave I will write one more or even two more letters to you. If only I were in Paris, for I dislike the thought of that tiresome journey. Wendling writes that he was most horribly bored on the journey. Well, I must close so as to leave a little room for Mamma. Adieu. I kiss your hands 100000 times and remain your most obedient son

WOLFGANG MOZART

Mannheim, 7 March 1778.

(296a) *Mozart to his Sister*

[Autograph in the Mozarteum, Salzburg]

MA TRÈS CHERE SŒUR! [MANNHEIM, 7 *March* 1778]

You must imagine, dearest sister, and that too with a most powerful stretch, that I have written a separate letter to you.

I have turned up to thank you for the 50 gulden you so kindly lent me, and which indeed were very badly needed. And here I congratulate you and tell you how inexpressibly delighted I am that you have such a good heart. I am extremely sorry that I am obliged for some time to rob you of 50 gulden. But, as truly as I am your sincere brother, I shall not rest until I have repaid you for all you have done for me in the goodness of your heart. Happy is that brother who has such a good sister. Please trust me absolutely and never think that I shall forget you; but remember that things do not always turn out, or at least not always exactly, as one wishes. But all will be well in time. Go on practising and whilst scrambling through scores do not forget your galanterie performance, lest I be proved a liar, when people, to whom I have sung your praises, hear you play. For I have always told them that you play with greater precision than I do. Well, adieu, dear sister. I hope that soon we shall be able to embrace one another with joy. I put my trust in God. In my prayers I ask Him for what I believe will be most useful to me and all of us, but I always add: 'Lord, may Thy will be done in earth as it is in heaven'. We mortals often think it is evil and in the end—it turns out to be good. God always knows best how things ought to be. Adieu, my most beloved sister. I kiss you 100000 times and remain your faithful and sincere brother until death.

WOLFGANG AMADÉ MOZART

Now I am happy to set off for Paris because our good friend Grimm is there. I place all my confidence in him and will follow all the advice of such a good friend.[1]

---

[1] This postscript is written on the cover.

(296b) *Maria Anna Mozart to her Husband*

[*Autograph in the Mozarteum, Salzburg*]

MY DEAR HUSBAND,   [MANNHEIM, 7 *March* 1778]
    First of all I must tell you that we always receive your letters on Tuesdays and Saturdays. So next Saturday we shall not be able to get any more of them, as the mail coach leaves at six o'clock in the morning and the post only arrives about noon. But if you write next Monday, March 9th, they will forward your letter to Paris. We have not received the arias this week, so we shall expect them next week. The carriage is a great worry to us, for not a soul has turned up even to look at it. People here expect to get everything for a song and to be paid for everything at three times the usual price. I am infinitely delighted that Baron Grimm is in Paris; indeed it is the one thing that comforts me. We can certainly rely on him, as he is a sincere and true friend to us. Wolfgang will very soon do him honour and Grimm will never regret having taken an interest in him. I am frightfully busy this week, and until everything has been settled I shall not know whether I am standing on my head or on my heels. Everything comes on me and, as you may imagine, I have enough things to think about. But I hope that with God's help all will go off well and that we shall arrive in Paris safe and sound. True, this long journey will be very trying for us, but as God wills it, so must it be. Addio. Keep well, both of you. I kiss you both many 1000 times and remain your faithful wife

                                                        MARIA ANNA MOZART

    All sorts of messages to all our acquaintances, particularly to Monsieur Bullinger and Mlle Sallerl, likewise to Herr Deibl and many others.

(297) *Mozart to his Father*

[*Autograph in the Mozarteum, Salzburg*]

[MANNHEIM, 11 *March* 1778]

MONSIEUR MON TRÉS CHER PÉRE,
    I have received your letter of March 5th and am most delighted to hear that our good, kind friend, Baron Grimm, is in Paris.
    You are quite right; we are leaving here next Saturday, the 14th, but we have not yet settled whether we shall take the mail coach or whether we shall travel to Strassburg or Metz. However, everything will be fixed up tomorrow morning. Perhaps I shall even be able to send you definite information immediately, for the post doesn't leave until tomorrow

evening and before then we must come to some final decision. We are
having a horrible time trying to sell our chaise. But we must do so, no
matter how little we get for it. For if I were to leave it here, things would
just drag on and after having had the honour of paying storage at a gulden
a month, I might not in the end get more than four louis d'or for it. A
coachman called today and I made him raise his offer from 30 to 38 gulden;
perhaps I shall screw him up to 40. He says that the coach is still quite
good, but that he couldn't make any use of the chassis. He is coming again
tomorrow morning and if he offers me 40 gulden, then in God's name I
shall let him have it. He is the same man who is to drive us from here to
Paris via Metz (which, as you already know, is the shorter route) for
eleven louis d'or. If tomorrow he agrees to do this for ten louis d'or, I
shall certainly engage him, and perhaps even if he demands eleven. For in
any case it is cheaper, which is our chief consideration, and it is more
comfortable for us, as he will use our chaise, that is to say—he will fix the
body on a chassis of his own; and it will be infinitely more convenient for
us, as we have so many odd trifles, which we can easily stuff in our chaise,
but which we could not pack into the mail coach; again, we shall be alone
and able to talk about what we like. For I assure you that if after all I do
travel by mail coach, my only worry will be the boredom of not being
able to talk about what I like and find most convenient; and, because we
really must study economy now, I am very much inclined to do this.
The difference, it is true, will not be very great, but it will be something;
and of course the main thing is to be comfortable, and to this I pay
particular attention on account of my mother. Well, tomorrow I shall
probably be able to write more fully about everything. The difference
amounts to one louis d'or, or one and a half. For we should have to buy
another trunk and a couple of cushions, for people say that the mail coach
jolts you so; which is only natural, as there is a chaussée the whole way.
Please forgive me for writing so little today and so badly, but I have still
so many things to do that I do not know where to begin. Meanwhile
farewell. In about a fortnight's time, after you have read this letter, I trust
that you will have received my first one from Paris. I kiss your hands 1000
times and embrace my sister with all my heart and remain until death
your most obedient son

WOLFGANG AMADÉ MOZART

Mannheim, 11 March 1778.

PS.—A propos. Please send something which I asked you for a long
time ago, and that is, the alphabet, both capitals and small letters, in your
handwriting.[1] Please don't forget this. You asked me the other day to

---

[1] See letter 237a postscript, and p. 530. Mozart wanted to improve his handwriting, the
untidiness of which he continually deplored.

send you Herr Weber's address, so that you might let him have the other arias. If they have not been copied yet, then please have them copied on small paper, that is, if you still have some, so that the postal fee may not be too high.

À Monsieur fridelin Weber
à Mannheim

at the cabinet-maker's,
    opposite the lottery-house.

Adieu. My greetings to all our good friends and particularly to my best friend, Herr Bullinger.

We have just this minute come to an agreement with the coachman. He is going to drive us to Paris for eleven louis d'or in our own chaise, which he has bought for 40 gulden. Tomorrow I shall put it down in black and white that, as I have not made him pay me for the chaise, when we reach Paris, I shall only have to pay him seven louis d'or and four gulden.

FRAU ANNA MARIA MOZART (*c.* 1775)

From a portrait by an unknown artist
(Mozart Museum, Salzburg)

MARIA ANNA THEKLA MOZART, THE 'BÄSLE' (1778)

From a drawing by an unknown artist
(Mozart Museum, Salzburg)

FRIEDRICH MELCHIOR GRIMM (1778)

From a water-colour painting by Carmontelle
(Musée Condé, Chantilly)

POSTSCRIPT FROM FRAU MOZART TO HER HUSBAND (13 November 1777)

Autograph in the Library of the University of Prague

PORTION OF A LETTER FROM MOZART TO HIS COUSIN (10 May 1779)

Autograph in the Stefan Zweig Collection, British Library, London

THE MOZART FAMILY (1780–81)

From a portrait by Johann Nepomuk de la Croce

(Mozart Museum, Salzburg)

After their arrival in Paris on 23 March 1778, Mozart's prospects at first seemed favourable, but owing partly to the lack of patrons and partly to his own listlessness no commissions came. Further, after a short illness his mother died early in July; and Grimm, who offered him hospitality, discouraged any hopes he might still have cherished of making good in France. So, urged by his father to take up an appointment as Court Organist in Salzburg and thus help him to pay his debts, Mozart returned home by way of Nancy, Strassburg and Munich. During these ten months he composed few important works, among them a symphony, the flute and harp concerto, and keyboard sonatas (some with violin). Letters 298–355.

(298) *Leopold Mozart to his Wife and Son*

[*Extract*]   [*Autograph in the Mozarteum, Salzburg*]

SALZBURG, 16 *March* 1778

MY DEAR WIFE AND DEAR SON!

With God's help you will have arrived safe and sound in Paris. Ever since yesterday, the 15th, I have been very anxious, as we have had heavy snow and bitterly cold weather. I kept thinking all the time of Mamma on that journey, which must have been very chilly and tedious. As I have reckoned that you will not be bringing much money with you to Paris (particularly if you have not sold our chaise) and as I have not been able to make any arrangements for raising a further sum, because everyone at the Hagenauers has been exceptionally busy on account of the Lenten fair, I had a word today with Herr Franz Gschwendner,[1] whose brother is with the bankers Körman in Paris. Gschwendner is going to write to him by the post which goes on Thursday, the 19th, telling him to give you a few louis d'or on my account. I cannot write, or rather finish what I have ★ begun to write to Baron Grimm, before the 19th; for it is nothing less than a description of my whole life. I send him my most humble greetings and feel sure that when he hears exactly and circumstantially about all the oppression, persecution and tyranny which we people in Salzburg have had to endure for the last six years, his pity will be stirred and his heart moved to help us. For when he was in Russia he cannot have exchanged his tender heart for a Muscovite one. The King of Prussia has sent a very ★ sarcastic and impertinent letter to the Emperor on the subject of Austria's claim to the territories of the Bavarian Electorate.[2] I hope to have good ★ news from you soon. Nannerl and I kiss you millions of times and I am your old

MZT

M. de Voltaire is in Paris. But whether M. Noverre (who, as I see in the newspapers, has also received the Order from the Pope)[3] is there, I do not know for certain. If you are commissioned to write a piece of counterpoint or something similar for the Concert Spirituel, work it out with the greatest care and be sure to hear beforehand what is being

---

[1] Franz Xaver Gschwendner, an ironmonger in the Getreidegasse.
[2] i.e. the claim made by the Emperor of Austria to be allowed to succeed to the estates of the late Elector of Bavaria in exchange for the surrender of the distant Netherlands, his wife's inheritance. The question was eventually submitted to Catherine of Russia for arbitration and was settled by the Treaty of Teschen in 1779.
[3] The Order of the Golden Spur, which Mozart too had received.

composed in Paris and what people prefer. You will find their *bass singers* very powerful and excellent. Whatever you compose must be written out in full, for sometimes compositions are engraved in score. Addio.

★ Hagenauer, the architect, has left Salzburg with the Bishop of Gurk in order to make additions to the latter's residence there; *but he is not coming back.* For the Archbishop has treated him disgracefully, presenting him with ten thalers, as if he were a good-for-nothing. Hence for all the work he has done since he has been here, he has received *fourteen thalers and four ducats!*

★

(299) *Mozart to his Father*

[*Autograph in the Mozarteum, Salzburg*]

MON TRÉS CHER PÉRE,　　　　　　　PARIS, 24 *March* 1778

Yesterday, Monday the 23rd, at four o'clock in the afternoon we arrived here, thank God, both safe and sound, having been nine and a half days on our journey. We really thought that we should not be able to hold out; for never in all my life have I been so bored. You can easily imagine what it meant for us to leave Mannheim and so many dear, kind friends and then to have to spend nine and a half days, not only without these good friends, but without anyone, without a single soul with whom we could associate or converse. Well, thank Heaven! we are at our journey's end and I trust that with the help of God all will go well. Today we are going to take a fiacre and look up Grimm and Wendling. Tomorrow morning, however, I intend to call on the Minister of the Palatinate, Herr von Sickingen (a great connoisseur and passionate lover of music, for whom I have two letters from Herr von Gemmingen[1] and Mr. Cannabich). Before leaving Mannheim I had copies made for Herr von Gemmingen of the quartet[2] which I composed one evening at the inn at Lodi, and also of the quintet[3] and the variations on a theme by Fischer.[4] On receiving them he sent a most polite note, expressing his pleasure at the souvenir which I was leaving him and enclosing a letter for his intimate friend Herr von Sickingen with the words: 'I feel sure that you will be a greater recommendation for the letter than it can possibly be for you'. To cover the expenses of copying he sent me three louis d'or. He assured me of his friendship and asked me for mine. I must say that all the courtiers who

---

[1] Baron Otto Heinrich von Gemmingen-Homberg (1753–1836), who held a government post in Mannheim, was the author of *Mannheimische Dramaturgie*, 1779, and of a successful drama, *Der deutsche Hausvater*, 1780. In 1782 he moved to Vienna, where he became Grand Master of the Masonic Lodge 'Zur Wohltätigkeit'. It is thought that he encouraged Mozart to become a Freemason. He also introduced Mozart to Baron van Swieten. See C. Flaischlen, *Otto Heinrich von Gemmingen*, Stuttgart, 1890.

[2] K. 80 [73f], the first three movements of which were written in 1770, the last movement, a rondo, in 1773 or 1774.

[3] K. 174, composed in 1773.　　　　　　　[4] K. 179 [189a], composed in 1774.

knew me, Court Councillors, Chamberlains and other worthy people, as well as all the court musicians, were very reluctant and sorry to see me go. There is no doubt about that. We left on Saturday, the 14th and on the previous Thursday there was an afternoon concert at Cannabich's, where my concerto for three claviers[1] was played. Mlle Rosa Cannabich played the first, Mlle Weber the second and Mlle Pierron Serrarius, our house nymph, the third. We had three rehearsals of the concerto and it went off very well. Mlle Weber sang two arias of mine, the 'Aer tranquillo' from 'Il Rè pastore'[2] and my new one, 'Non so d'onde viene'.[3] With the latter my dear Mlle Weber did herself and me indescribable honour, for every-one said that no aria had ever affected them as did this one; but then she sang it as it ought to be sung. As soon as it was over, Cannabich called out loudly: 'Bravo! Bravissimo, maestro! Veramente scritta da maestro!'[4] It was the first time I had heard it with orchestral accompaniment and I wish you also could have heard it, exactly as it was performed and sung there with that accuracy in interpretation, piano and forte. Who knows, perhaps you may hear it yet—I hope so. The members of the orchestra never ceased praising the aria and talking about it. I have many good friends in Mannheim (people of position and means), who wished very much to keep me there. Well if they pay me decently, they can have me. Who knows, perhaps it will come off. I wish it would. And still I have a feeling and I still cherish the hope that it will. Cannabich is an honest, worthy man and my very good friend, but he has just one failing, which is, that, although no longer young, he is rather careless and absent-minded. If you are not perpetually after him, he forgets everything. But when it's a matter of helping a *real friend*, he roars like a bull and takes the deepest interest in him; and that means a great deal, for he has influence. But on the whole I can't say much of his courtesy and gratitude, for I must confess that, in spite of their poverty and obscurity, and although I did much less for them, the Webers have shown themselves far more grateful. For M. and Mme Cannabich did not say a word to me, nor did they even offer me the smallest keepsake, not even a bagatelle, to show their kindly feeling. They gave me nothing at all, they didn't even thank me, after I had spent so much time and trouble on their daughter. She can now perform before anyone, and for a girl of fourteen and an amateur she plays quite well; and it is thanks to me, as all Mannheim knows. She now has taste and can play trills; her time is good and her fingering is much better; formerly she had nothing of this. So in three months' time they will miss me sorely; for I fear she will soon be spoiled again and will spoil herself, because, unless she has a master constantly beside her, and one who knows his job, she will be no good, as she is still too childish and careless to practise seriously and

[1] K. 242, composed in 1776. [2] K. 208, composed in 1775.
[3] K. 294. [4] Really a masterpiece of composition!

to any purpose by herself. Mlle Weber out of the goodness of her heart has knitted me two pairs of mittens in filet, which she has given me as a remembrance and a small token of her gratitude. And Herr Weber copied out gratis whatever I required, supplied me with music paper and also made me a present of Molière's comedies (as he knew that I had not yet read them) with this inscription: Ricevi, amico, le opere del Molière in segno di gratitudine, e qualche volta ricordati di me.[1] And once, when alone with Mamma, he said: 'Indeed our best friend, our benefactor, is about to leave us. Yes, that is certain, we owe everything to your son. He has done a great deal for my daughter and has taken an interest in her and she can never be grateful enough to him.' The day before I left they wanted me to have supper with them, but I could not do so, as I had to be at home. All the same I had to spend two hours before supper at their house. They thanked me repeatedly, saying that they only wished they were in a position to show their gratitude; and when I left, they all wept. Forgive me, but my eyes fill with tears when I recall the scene. Herr Weber came downstairs with me, and remained standing at the door until I had turned the corner and called out after me—Adieu! The expenses of our journey, food and drink, lodging and tips, amounted to over four louis d'or, for the farther we penetrated into France, the dearer things became. This very moment I have received your letter of the 16th. Please don't worry, I will certainly make good. And I have one request to make, which is, to show in your letters a cheerful spirit. If war breaks out near Salzburg, come and join us. My greetings to all our good friends. I kiss your hands a thousand times and embrace my sister with all my heart and remain your most obedient son

WOLFGANG AMADÈ MOZART

(299a) *Maria Anna Mozart to her Husband*

[*Autograph in the Mozarteum, Salzburg*]

MY DEAR HUSBAND,   [PARIS, 24 *March* 1778[2]]

Praise and thanks be to God, we have arrived here safe and sound. We are lodging at Herr Mayer's, in the same house where Herr von Waldburg[3] lived. We don't know yet what we shall have to pay, but this we shall hear tomorrow. We called today on Baron Grimm, who was not at home; but we left a note, so that he may know that we have arrived. Tomorrow Wolfgang is going to drive to his house again and deliver his

---

[1] Accept, my friend, the works of Molière in token of gratitude and think of me sometimes.
[2] A postscript to Mozart's letter, written on the cover.
[3] The alias of Count Anton Willibald Wolfegg, canon of Salzburg Cathedral.

other letters of recommendation. On our journey we had the most beautiful weather for eight days, bitterly cold in the morning and warm in the afternoon. But during the last two days we were nearly choked by the wind and drowned by the rain, so that we both got soaking wet in the carriage and could scarcely breath. We managed to get through the customs examination all right except for Wolfgang's small music paper, for which we had to pay 38 sous; and in Paris we had no customs examination whatever. Wolfgang is bored, as he hasn't got a clavier yet. The weather has been so bad that he hasn't been able to see about one. Addio, take care of yourselves. I kiss you both 10,000 times and remain your faithful wife

FRAU MOZART

Give our greetings to all. We drank Herr Bullinger's health on St. Joseph's day,[1] when we were at Clermont.

(300) *Maria Anna Mozart to her Husband*

[*Autograph in the Mozarteum, Salzburg*]

MY DEAR HUSBAND, PARIS, *5 April* 1778[2]

Praise and thanks be to God, we are both well, and trust that you and Nannerl are in good health. If so, with God's help all will be well. Wolfgang has a terrible lot to do, as he has to compose for the Concert Spirituel in Holy Week a Miserere,[3] which must have three choruses, a fugue, a duet and everything else with a great many instruments. It must be finished by next Wednesday, so that it may be rehearsed. He is composing it at the house of Monsieur Le Gros,[4] the director of these concerts, and he generally lunches there. If he likes, he can lunch every day at Noverre's and also at Madame d'Épinay's. Then he has to write two concertos, one for the flute and one for the harp,[5] and in addition an act for an opera for the French theatre.[6] Besides all this he has a pupil,[7] who pays him six livres a lesson, that is, three louis d'or for twelve, though we shan't get the money until they are all finished. Thus we shan't pocket a kreuzer before Easter. Meanwhile our capital has become very small and won't go very

[1] 19 March.
[2] This letter and Mozart's were not sent off until 10 April. See p. 534.
[3] See p. 521, which corrects this statement.
[4] Jean Le Gros (1730–1793), operatic singer and composer, became in 1777 Director of the Concert Spirituel, which he managed until its dissolution in 1791.
[5] See p. 587, which corrects this statement. Mozart wrote a concerto for flute and harp K. 299 [297c], for the Duc de Guines, to whom Grimm introduced him.
[6] See p. 521, which corrects this statement.
[7] The daughter of the Duc de Guines, who a few months later married M. de Chartus, and died in 1780 in childbirth.

far, for we shall have to move into other rooms, as it is too far off here to walk and we have already spent a lot of money on drives. I shall be sorry to leave this house, for they are excellent folk with whom, moreover, I can chat in German. Madame d'Épinay has been on the look-out for another lodging for us. Send your letters to Herr Mayer, who will keep them for us, until I let you have another address. We have not yet looked up Herr Gschwendner, but if we need money, that is, if our capital comes to an end, we shall certainly ask him for an advance, although indeed we should much prefer (and it would be much better too) not to have to do this. Words fail me to tell you how famous and popular is our Wolfgang. Long before we arrived, Herr Wendling had made a great reputation for him and has now introduced him to his friends. He really is a true friend of humanity. Monsieur de Grimm too has urged Wendling to do his best to make Wolfgang known, as, being a musician, he has much more influence. As for my own life, it is not at all a pleasant one. I sit alone in our room the whole day long as if I were in gaol, and as the room is very dark and looks out on a little courtyard, I cannot see the sun all day long and I don't even know what the weather is like. With great difficulty I manage to knit a little by the daylight that struggles in. And for this room we have to pay thirty livres a month. The hall and the stairs are so narrow that it would be impossible to bring up a clavier. So Wolfgang can't compose at home, but has to go to the house of Monsieur Le Gros who has one. Thus I never see him all day long and shall forget altogether how to talk. The food which the traiteur sends in is perfectly magnificent. For a lunch which costs 15 sous I get three courses, first of all, soup with some butter which I detest, secondly, a little slice of very poor meat, thirdly, a slab of calf's foot in some dirty sauce, or a piece of liver as hard as a stone. In the evening we don't have any food sent in, but Frau Mayer buys us a couple of pounds of veal and has it roasted at the baker's. So we have it hot for the first time, and afterwards cold as long as it lasts, as is the custom in England. We have never had soup in the evenings. I simply cannot describe to you the fast days, which are positively unendurable. Everything here is half as dear again as it was the last time we were here twelve years ago. Today, the 10th, I have been packing all day long, for we are moving into another lodging where we shall only have to pay one louis d'or a month, where we shall have two rooms looking out on the street and where we shall be near the aristocracy and the theatres. I would have sent off this letter sooner, but we wanted to wait for one from you, so that we could reply to it. For each letter we post we have to pay 17 sous and for each we receive 24. Baron de Grimm came to see me yesterday and asked me to tell you not to worry so much, as everything will be all right in the end. We must just be a little bit patient. He will reply to your letter later on, but at the moment he has a great deal to do.

(300a) *Mozart to his Father*

[*Autograph in the Mozarteum, Salzburg*]

[PARIS, 5 *April* 1778]

Well, I must explain more clearly what my Mamma has been writing about, as it is a bit vague. Kapellmeister Holzbauer has sent a Miserere here, but as the choruses at Mannheim are weak and poor, whereas in Paris they are powerful and excellent, the choruses he has composed would not be effective. So M. Le Gros (Director of the Concert Spirituel) has asked me to compose others, Holzbauer's introductory chorus being retained. 'Quoniam iniquitatem meam', an Allegro, is my first one. The second, an Adagio, 'Ecce enim in iniquitatibus'. Then an Allegro. 'Ecce enim veritatem dilexisti' as far as 'ossa humiliata'. Then an Andante for soprano, tenor and bass soli. 'Cor mundum crea' and 'Redde mihi laetitiam', but allegro as far as 'ad te convertentur'. I have also composed a recitative for a bass singer, 'Libera me de sanguinibus'—because a bass aria by Holzbauer follows 'Dominus labia mea'. Now because 'Sacrificium Deo spiritus' is an aria andante for Raaff with an oboe and bassoon solo accompaniment, I have added a short recitative 'Quoniam si voluisses', also with oboe and bassoon obbligatos, for recitatives are now very popular here. 'Benigne fac' as far as 'Muri Jerusalem' is Andante moderato. A chorus. Then 'Tunc acceptabis' as far as 'Super altare tuum vitulos', Allegro and tenor solo (Le Gros) and a chorus all together.[1] Finis. I may say that I am very glad to have finished that hack-work, which becomes a curse when one cannot compose at home and when in addition one is pressed for time. Thanks and praise be to God, I have finished it and only trust that it will produce the desired effect. When he saw my first chorus, Mr. Gossec,[2] whom you doubtless know, said to M. Le Gros (I was not present) that it was charmant and would certainly produce a good effect, and that the words were well arranged and on the whole excellently set to music. He is a very good friend of mine and at the same time a very dull fellow. I am not simply going to compose an act for an opera,[3] but a whole opera en deux actes.[4] The poet has already written the first act. Noverre (at whose house I lunch as often as I like) arranged the whole thing and indeed suggested the idea. I think it is to be called 'Alexandre et Roxane'. Madame Jenomé[5] is also in Paris. I am now going to compose a

---

[1] There is no trace of this composition. See Köchel, p. 308.

[2] François Joseph Gossec (1734-1829), a Belgian by birth, became a famous operatic composer. He came to Paris in 1751 and in 1769 founded and directed until 1777 the Concert des Amateurs.

[3] Mozart means that he is not going to contribute to a *pasticcio*.

[4] This operatic plan was never carried out.

[5] Mlle Jeunehomme, a French clavier-player, for whom, while she was on a visit to Salzburg, Mozart wrote his clavier concerto K. 271 in January 1777.

sinfonia concertante[1] for flute, Wendling; oboe, Ramm; horn, Punto;[2] and bassoon, Ritter. Punto plays magnifique. I have this moment returned from the Concert Spirituel. Baron Grimm and I often give vent to our musical rage at the music here, I mean, between ourselves, of course. For in public we shout: Bravo, Bravissimo, and clap our hands until our fingers tingle. Now farewell. I kiss your hands a hundred times and remain

WOLFGANG AMADÈ MOZART

[*Autograph in the Staatsbibliothek Preussischer Kulturbesitz, West Berlin*]

5 April 1778[3]

M. Raaff is here. He is staying with M. Le Gros, so we meet almost every day. My dearest Papa, I must really beg you once more not to worry so much, not to be so anxious; for now you have no reason to be so. I am at last in a place where it is certainly possible to make money, though this requires a frightful amount of effort and work. But I am willing to do anything to please you. What annoys me most of all in this business is that our French gentlemen have only improved their *goût* to this extent that they can now listen to good stuff as well. But to expect them to realise that their own music is bad or at least to notice the difference—Heaven preserve us! And their singing! Good Lord! Let me never hear a Frenchwoman singing Italian arias. I can forgive her if she screeches out her French trash, but not if she ruins good music! It's simply unbearable.

Now for our new address:—

Rue Gros Chenet, vis à vis celle
du Croissant, à l'Hôtel des emont fils

You must add the number four, as it appears thus on the house.[4]

(301) *Leopold Mozart to his Wife and Son*

[*Extract*]   [*Autograph in the Mozarteum, Salzburg*]

SALZBURG, 6 *April* 1778

Today we had the most earnestly longed for pleasure of receiving your letter written on March 24th. I was all the more anxious about your journey, as at that very time we were having the most horrible weather and as I know only too well what it is to travel with a hired coachman.

---

[1] K. App. 9 [K. 297B]. Not preserved, at least in the original form. See Köchel, pp. 309 and 866.

[2] Giovanni Punto, or Johann Wenzel Stich (1746–1803), an eminent horn-player, who travelled widely and for whom Beethoven wrote his horn and piano sonata, op. 17.

[3] This postcript is written on the cover.   [4] i.e. des quatre fils Aymon.

Thank God that you have arrived safe and sound. I was worried too about your living expenses, for in Italy things are much easier to arrange, as you know what the price is *a pasto*; but in France you must make a previous arrangement (which they are not very willing to do), or else be fleeced unmercifully. I did not tell you anything about this, for I was assuming that you would certainly travel by mail coach, in which case one can do what the others do. Basta! Thank God you have both arrived safely. I now urge you very strongly to win, or rather to preserve *by a complete and childlike trust* the favour, affection and friendship of Baron Grimm, to consult him in all matters, not to act on your own judgment or preconceived ideas, and constantly to bear in mind your interest and in this way *our common interest*. The mode of living in Paris is very different from that in Germany and there is something quite peculiar and distinctive about the manner of expressing oneself politely in French, seeking patrons, introducing oneself, and so forth, so that during our stay there long ago Baron Grimm had to give me a few hints and tell me what I should say and how I should express myself. When you convey my most dutiful greetings to him, tell him that I have mentioned this to you and he will confirm the truth of my statement. I still have in my possession *some instructions* which he gave me as to how to leave notes on people of rank whom I could not see; and how often did I not write to M. Grimm by the petite poste to ask him for advice or send him word about something, when by reason of the great distance between the rue St. Antoine and the rue Neuve Luxembourg it was not possible for us to meet. In all matters of this sort I am sure that you will turn to this most trustworthy friend of ours. You will now have received my letter, addressed to Herr Mayer, informing you that I have asked Herr Gschwendner to tell his brother to assist you, should you be short of money. This is only a father's precaution, for indeed I hope and trust that you will not have to draw on him, for you know, in the first place, how we stand, that is, ⟨that I have enough debts already and don't know how I am going to pay them;⟩ and, secondly, that it attracts attention here, does you no honour and only draws contempt on me when it becomes known that ⟨I have to go on sending you money.⟩ If, however, you are in dire necessity, well, you will have to draw some, in which case you should tell everything to Baron Grimm, as I have informed him in two long letters of all our ⟨debts⟩ and difficulties, and have given him a full description of the persecution and the contempt which we have suffered at the hands of the ⟨Archbishop,⟩ adding that you will confirm my statements when you see him. I have also told him that the ⟨Archbishop⟩ only flattered you in a condescending manner when he wanted to get something out of you and that he never paid you a farthing for all your compositions; so you may give him a full account of my wretched situation. If, like Honnauer or the late Schobert, you could count on a monthly salary from some prince in Paris,[1] and, in addition, do some work occasionally for the theatre, the Concert Spirituel and the Concert des Amateurs, and now and then have something engraved par souscription, and if your sister and I could give lessons and she could play at concerts and musical entertainments, then we should certainly have enough to live on in comfort. *You would like me to be very cheerful in my letters.* My dear Wolfgang! You know *that honour is dearer to me than life itself.* Consider the whole course of events. Remember that although I hoped *with your help* to get out of ⟨debt⟩, so far I have only sunk deeper and deeper. As you know, my credit with everyone here stands high— but the moment I lose it, my honour will vanish too. Moreover, the kindness and goodwill of tradespeople lasts only as long as you keep on paying them; and if payment is delayed too long, well then, good-bye to the friendship of this world. And the ⟨Archbishop?⟩ Is he indeed to have the pleasure of hearing that things are going badly with us and of being able to laugh at us and mock us? *Rather than face this I would drop dead immediately.* When I received your letter and read it, *I was at once in the best of humours.* So to all, who have been making particular enquiries about you, we passed on the good news that you had arrived safe and sound in Paris, gave it to the Arco family, and Nannerl to the Hagenauers and the Mölks, all of whom send you their greetings.

As you know, it has ever been my habit to reflect and consider; and but for this I should not have got on as well as I have, for I never had anyone to advise me; and, as you are aware, from my youth up I have never confided wholly in anyone until I had definite proofs of his sincerity. Just look at my brothers and myself; when you consider the difference between us, you will realize how valuable has been my reflection and meditation. Well, since from my early youth I have been accustomed to think things over, how can you blame me if such an extremely important matter, affecting the prosperity of all my loved ones, is on my mind night and day? For it is a matter which concerns not only myself, but also those who are dearest to me in the whole world! You say that if war were to break out near home I ought to join you at once; and you advise me to do so even if there is no danger of war. But I must first be able to ⟨pay my debts,⟩ or else we should not have enough ⟨money⟩ for the journey. My good spirits depend, my dear son, on your circumstances, which indeed can restore me to health, as far as health is possible at my age. Yet I feel that your active endeavours and your anxiety to drag me out of this miserable situation are really bringing me back health and strength. Once you have made your father's happiness your first consideration, he will continue to think of your welfare and happiness and to stand by you as a

---

[1] Honnauer was in the service of Prince Louis de Rohan; Schobert, who died in 1767, had been attached to the Prince de Conti. See p. 37, n. 4 and n. 6.

loyal friend. I trust that you are doing so; and this trust revives me and makes me happy and cheerful. Why, I foretold in a previous letter what you have just written about Mr. ⟨*Cannabich's*⟩ lack of gratitude. Poor, but honourable people, are always more grateful than those who pride themselves on their rank and distinction, sacrifice their true honour to some other imagined honour of which they boast, consider every kindness done to them as their due and think perhaps that by giving you a few meals they have rewarded you. Do you know what M. von Grimm wrote to me when he sent you ⟨*Cannabich's*⟩ symphonies?

> C'est moi qui lui (he meant you) fais présent des symphonies de Cannabich. Imaginez que celui-ci envoie chez moi un exemplaire pour moi, un pour vous, et se fait payer tous les deux par le Baron Bagge pour mon Compte, et prend même six francs de plus et décampe.

You will remember that some time ago you had to give him free of charge your Paris, London and Dutch sonatas [1] and he promised to let you have his symphonies in return; but he took the money and cleared off. Now do you believe that such a wretched scribbler of symphonies would really like to see you appointed to the same service? Particularly as you are young and he is getting on in years? I don't for a moment believe it! To tell the truth, I never liked the Mannheim compositions. The orchestra there is good—and very powerful—but the interpretation is not in that true and delicate style which moves the hearer.

Write and tell me whether France has really declared war on England. [2] You will now see the American Minister, Dr. Franklin. [3] France recognises the independence of the thirteen American provinces and has concluded treaties with them.

Nannerl sends warm greetings to her Mamma and to her brother. We kiss you both millions of times and I remain your old

MZT

So my dear wife has seen Paris once again, and so have Madame d'Épinay's red satin gown and fan. Oh, if only we were with you! I shall send you soon the ABC you asked for. [4]

The castrato, [5] who comes to see us every day, sends you his greetings. He sings for us, while Nannerl accompanies him like a first-rate Kapellmeister.

[1] K. 6–9, 10–15, 26–31.
[2] On 6 February 1778, the French Government concluded with the United States an open treaty of amity and commerce and, at the same time, a secret treaty acknowledging the independence of the Thirteen Colonies and contracting with them a defensive alliance. The open treaty was communicated to the British Government on March 13th and the British Ambassador in Paris was at once recalled.
[3] Benjamin Franklin (1706–1790) arrived in Paris on 2 December 1776. It was as a result of his successful negotiations that France signed the treaty of amity and commerce.
[4] See Letter 273a postscript and p. 530.   [5] Francesco Ceccarelli.

(302) *Leopold Mozart to his Wife and Son*

[*Extract*]   [*Autograph in the Mozarteum, Salzburg*]

MY DEAR WIFE AND DEAR SON!   SALZBURG, 12 *April* 1778

By tomorrow's post I am hoping to hear that you are both well. In the meantime I write to say that we are performing the late Adlgasser's Litany today, Haydn's tomorrow and Wolfgang's[1] on Tuesday. In the last-named Signor Ceccarelli is singing all the solos and during the Golden Salve[2] the Regina Coeli, which Wolfgang composed for Frau Haydn.[3] He comes to our house every evening, unless there happens to be a big concert, and always brings with him an aria and a motet. I play the violin and Nannerl accompanies and plays the solo passages written for violas or wind-instruments. Then we play a clavier concerto or perhaps a violin trio, Ceccarelli playing the second violin; and indeed we sometimes get a good laugh, for it was in Salzburg that he began to learn the violin and he has only been playing it for six months. His time is up at the end of April. If he returns in the autumn or if he now stays on for good, the Archbishop is to give him 800 gulden a year for six years. He has agreed to stay for this salary, but only for two years, and provided the Archbishop will pay his travelling expenses as well. He is now waiting for a reply. If he returns to Salzburg, he will be back on November 1st. He is going to leave all his arias with us, only taking away a few. He much regrets that he has not met the two of you and is sorry that he did not make our acquaintance immediately after his arrival, for apart from us he
★ does not associate with anyone. Count Czernin is not content with fiddling at Court, and as he would like to do some conducting, he has collected an amateur orchestra who are to meet in Count Lodron's hall every Sunday after three o'clock. Count Sigmund Lodron came to invite Nannerl (as an amateur) to play the clavier and to ask me to keep the second violins in order. A week ago today, on the 5th, we had our first practice. There was Count Czernin, first violin, then Baron Babbius, Sigmund Lodron, young Wienrother, Kolb, Kolb's student from the Nonnberg, and a couple of young students whom I did not know. The second violins were myself, Sigmund Robinig, Cusetti, Count Altham, Cajetan Andretter, a student and Ceccarelli, la coda dei secondi.[4] The two violas were the two ex-Jesuits, Bullinger and Wishofer; the two oboes were Weiser, the lacquey, and Schulze's son, who acted in the Linz play. Two watchman's apprentices played the horns. The double basses were Cassl[5] and Count Wolfegg, with Ranftl doing duty occasionally. The cellos were the new young

---

[1] K. 243, composed in 1776.
[2] It is not known to which particular 'Salve' Leopold Mozart is referring.
[3] Probably K. 127, composed in 1772. See Abert, vol. i. p. 316, n. 3, and Köchel, p. 152.
[4] The tail of the second violins.   [5] See p. 337 n. 1.

canons, Count Zeill and Spaur, Court Councillor Mölk, Siegbert Andretter and Ranftl. Nannerl accompanied all the symphonies and she also accompanied Ceccarelli who sang an aria per l'apertura della accademia di dilettanti.[1] After the symphony Count Czernin played a beautifully written concerto by Sirmen[2] alla Brunetti, and dopo una altra sinfonia[3] Count Altham played a horrible trio, no one being able to say whether it was scraped or fiddled—whether it was in ¾ or common time, or perhaps even in some newly invented and hitherto unknown tempo. Nannerl was to have played a concerto, but as the Countess wouldn't let them have her good harpsichord (which is Casus reservatus pro summo Pontifice)[4], and only the Egedacher one with gilt legs was there, she didn't perform. In the end the two Lodron girls had to play. It had never been suggested beforehand that they should do so. But since I have been teaching them they are always quite well able to perform. So on this occasion too they both did me credit.

Monday, 13 *April* [1778]

Well, we have had no letter from you today. The postman did call—and brought one from Mysliwecek, who writes to say that instead of the twenty-five or thirty ducats he was expecting for the six concertones, which he rewrote at the Archbishop's order, he has only received twelve *a titolo per il viaggio*,[5] and that he is leaving Munich on Maundy Thursday and so forth. In every single letter (and he has written very often asking for my assistance) he has made some excuse about the scrittura for Naples, which he is expecting to receive, he says, by every post. Thus he now informs me that: 'Finora da Napoli non ebbi la scrittura; ma spero di finir quest' affare alla mia venuta, per ove partirò giovedi santo; frattanto sono a pregarla d'una grazia, (otherwise he wouldn't have written to me), cioè di mandarmi gli sei concerti di Bach, etc. Io sono stato pregato dal Signor Hamm per questa finezza, etc. Non ardiscono loro stessi di scriver a Vostra Signoria, etc.'[6] That I can well believe. For Herr Hamm was *so polite* as to send me no reply whatever to my letter of six months ago, in which I asked only 200 gulden a year for his daughter's *full board and*

[1] For the opening of the amateur concert.
[2] Maddalena Sirmen, *née* Lombardini (*c.* 1735– ?), born in Venice, was a distinguished eighteenth-century violinist and composer, a pupil of Tartini and a rival of Nardini. She performed constantly in London, but after 1772 abandoned her career as a violinist and took up singing with considerably less success.   [3] After another symphony, etc.
[4] i.e. Sacred to Her Holiness. Mozart makes a sarcastic comparison to cases reserved, by canon law, for Papal judgment.
[5] To meet the expenses of his journey.
[6] So far I have not received the scrittura from Naples, but I hope to settle the affair on my arrival. I am leaving for Naples on Maundy Thursday. Meanwhile I must ask a favour of you, . . . and that is to send me Bach's six concertos, etc. Herr Hamm has asked me to do him this kindness. They (he and his daughter) do not dare to write to you themselves, etc.

lodging, including her instruction. So Mysliwecek had to ask on his behalf for the concertos. Well, he can wait for them and I shall write and tell Mysliwecek the reason. On Palm Sunday, the 12th, we had our second amateur concert. On both occasions symphonies by Stamitz[1] were performed, which are very much liked, as they are very noisy. Baron Babbius, who is having lessons from Pinzger,[2] played a very easy violin concerto, but at least in strict time and not at all out of tune. Then Herr Kolb played your Cassation,[3] which provoked the most extraordinary applause. Count Czernin, who had neither heard Kolb play the fiddle nor your Cassation, stood sometimes behind and sometimes beside him, and turned over for him with fixed attention. He praised it to the skies and, on hearing that it was your composition, he asked me most eagerly three or four times: 'Why, when did he compose it? I can't have been here!' and, with the flaming red face and quivering voice which you know so well, he never ceased expressing his admiration for your composition and for Kolb's performance. Everyone listened in absolute silence, and after each movement Counts Wolfegg, Zeill, Spaur and the rest called out: *Bravo il Maestro e bravo il Signor Kolb!* The Countesses Lodron, Lützow and all the rest listened with delight. It was only the variations, which you had had so often to play for her, which led the Countess to recognize that it was that Cassation which you had dedicated to her.[4] She ran up to me in great excitement to tell me so—for I was playing the second violin, Kolb's pupil the viola, Cassel the double bass, and the two watchmen who had often played it at Kolb's, the French horns. To end up, the two Kletzl girls[5] gave a wretched performance on the clavier, the elder unspeakably badly. It would have driven you away, for it was really unendurable, even worse than the way in which the two sang in Kühnburg's play. On Easter Sunday the two Lodron girls are to sing or croak, I don't know which, for I haven't heard them for a long time. Nannerl has already been asked to accompany them. *On the 16th.* Still no letter from you. We hope that you are well and we realize that just at first you will have a lot to do looking up people, making new acquaintances and renewing our old ones. A violoncellist, Xavier Pietragrua by name, has arrived here with his wife. He plays exceedingly well; he has already performed at Court for the sum of ten ducats, *which was agreed upon beforehand,* and he is giving a concert on the 21st. He and his wife (who sings, but how I do not know) send their greetings to you, although they haven't met you. They have been to our house three times and are coming to shoot with us tomorrow, for I am writing this on Sunday, the 19th.

---

[1] Either Carl Stamitz (1745–1801), viola-player and composer, or Anton Stamitz (1754–1809), violinist and composer. They were both sons of the Mannheim composer Johann Stamitz.   [2] See p. 281, n. 3.

[3] K. 287 [271H], composed in 1777.   [4] The Countess Lodron.

[5] Eleonore and Franziska, daughters of Count Christoph Josef Kletzl.

Monday, 20 [April 1778]

We had another amateur concert yesterday, but only a very short one, as it began after the Regina Coeli in the Cathedral, in which the castrato sang most excellently. When I got home from the Cathedral your letter of the 5th was awaiting me. I am surprised that it has arrived so late. Surely you must have posted it later than the 5th, because a letter from Paris can get here in nine days. I suggest that you direct your letters—Par Strassbourg, Augsbourg—for your first letter also arrived late and, what is more, by the roundabout route through Mannheim. There are several Salzburgs. Remember to add these words at the side

   Par Strassbourg etc.
    Augsbourg
     à Salzbourg.

My dear Wolfgang, I am absolutely delighted that you have got work already and I am only sorry that you have had to hurry so much with the composition of the choruses, which is a work which assuredly requires considerable time, if you want to do yourself credit. I hope and trust that it will win applause. I assume that when composing your opera *you will be guided by the French taste*. If you can only *win applause and get a decent sum of money*, let the devil take the rest. If your opera is a success, there will soon be something in the papers. That indeed I should be delighted to see, if only to spite the Archbishop. I should also love to hear your sinfonia concertante performed by those good players. If you could find in Paris a good clavichord, such as we have, you would no doubt prefer it and it would suit you better than a harpsichord. I am sorry to hear that the French have not yet altered their taste completely; but, believe me, they will do so gradually, for it is no easy matter to remould a whole nation. It is already a sufficiently good sign that they can listen to what is good; for by degrees they too will notice the difference. I implore you, before you write for the French stage, to listen to their operas and find out what above all pleases them. Well, you will now become a thorough Frenchman and you will endeavour, I hope, to acquire the correct accent. Thank God, Nannerl and I are well, and I am now free from all worry and thoroughly happy, knowing that our excellent friend Baron de Grimm is taking an interest in you and that you are in the one place which, if you are industrious, as you are by nature, can give you a great reputation throughout the world. As long as I am not anxious about you, I am well. And you must know me, how I value honour and glory above all else. You won a great reputation as a child—and you must continue to do so, for this always was and still is my object. You must turn the coming years to account both for your own sake and for that of us all. God keep you both in good health. Give warm greetings from Nannerl and myself to

Baron de Grimm, M. and Mme de Noverre, Madame Jenomé, Madame d'Épinay, M. Wendling, M. Raaff, M. Gossec and the rest. I have 100000 greetings to send you both from our whole household, from the whole orchestra, from Bullinger (who thanks you for having drunk his health at Clermont), Sallerl, Katherl Gilowsky, the Hagenauers, Herr Deibl and so ★ forth. My dear wife! I am very sorry that you are having such a bad time with your food. Would it not be possible to find someone who cooks in our German way? You must try and find some better fare, even if it means paying a little more. I have been anxious about this for a long time. And you cannot cook for yourself either, can you? You will have in the end to make some other arrangement, as you are not in Paris for just a few months—seeing that Paris is at the moment the safest place to live in, both ★ from the money point of view and because it is untouched by fear of war.

★   You will probably have received my reply to your first letter and Baron Grimm will have had my two exceedingly long letters.[1] Wolfgang wants an ABC,[2] but he won't have much time to spend on it. Here is something for him to go on with.

ABCDEFGHIJKLMNOPQRSTUVWXYZ
a b c d e f g h i j k l m n o p q r s t u v w x y z

I can't write a good hand today, for my pen is no good; and I have to hurry off to Vespers, as the Italians are to be there too. We kiss you both a million times and I am your old faithful

                                                                                MZT

    Addio. *Keep well.*
    Pimperl is in good form. She stands on the table and scratches the rolls very gingerly with her paw as a hint that she should be given one. She also scratches the knife to suggest that a slice should be cut for her. And when there are four or five snuff-boxes on the table, she scratches at the one containing Spanish snuff, by which she means that someone should take a pinch, and then let her lick the snuff off his fingers.

(303) *Mozart to his Father*

[*Autograph in the Mozarteum, Salzburg*]

MON TRÉS CHER PÉRE!   PARIS, 1 *May* 1778
    We have received your letter of April 12th. I waited for it and that is the reason why it is so long since I wrote. Please do not take it amiss if now and then I leave you for a long time without a letter, but postal fees are very heavy here and, unless one has something absolutely necessary to

---

[1] This passage is written on the cover.   [2] See Letter 273a postscript.

say, it is not worth while spending twenty-four sous and sometimes more. I had intended to postpone writing until I had news and could tell you more about our circumstances. But now I feel compelled to give you an account of a few matters which are still in doubt. The little violoncellist Zygmontofscky and his worthless father are here. Perhaps I have told you this already—but I merely mention it en passant, as I have just remembered that I met him at a place about which I now want to tell you, I mean, at the house of Madame la Duchesse de Chabot.[1] M. Grimm gave me a letter to her, so I drove there. The main object of this letter was to recommend me to the Duchesse de Bourbon[2] (who was in a convent the last time I was here[3]), to introduce me to her again and to recall me to her mind. Well, a week went by without any news. However, as she had asked me to call on her after a week had elapsed, I kept my word and went. I had to wait for half an hour in a large ice-cold, unheated room, which hadn't even a fireplace. At last the Duchesse de Chabot appeared. She was very polite and asked me to make the best of the clavier in the room, as none of her own were in good condition. Would I perhaps try it? I said that I would be delighted to play something, but that it was impossible at the moment, as my fingers were numb with cold; and I asked her to have me taken at least to a room where there was a fire. 'Oh oui, Monsieur, vous avez raison', was all the reply I got. She then sat down and began to draw and continued to do so for a whole hour, having as company some gentlemen, who all sat in a circle round a big table, while I had the honour to wait. The windows and doors were open and not only my hands but my whole body and my feet were frozen and my head began to ache. There was *altum silentium*[4] and I did not know what to do for cold, headache and boredom. I kept on thinking: 'If it were not for M. Grimm, I would leave this house at once'. At last, to cut my story short, I played on that miserable, wretched pianoforte. But what vexed me most of all was that Madame and all her gentlemen never interrupted their drawing for a moment, but went on intently, so that I had to play to the chairs, tables and walls. Under these detestable conditions I lost my patience. I therefore began to play the Fischer variations[5] and after playing half of them I stood up. Whereupon I received a shower of éloges. Upon which I said the only thing I had to say, which was, that I could not do myself justice on that clavier; and that I should very much like to fix some other day to play, when a better instrument would be available. But, as the Duchess would not hear of my going, I had to wait for another half hour, until her husband came in. He

---

[1] A daughter of the Earl of Stafford, married Guy, Conte de Rohan Chabot.
[2] A daughter of the Duc d'Orléans and the sister of the Duc de Chartres, who was later Philippe Égalité.
[3] On the occasion of the Mozart's first visit to Paris in 1764. The Duchess at the age of fifteen had entered a convent, where she remained for some years. See p. 471 f.
[4] profound silence. [5] K. 179 [189a].

sat down beside me and listened with the greatest attention and I—I forgot the cold and my headache and in spite of the wretched clavier, I played—as I play when I am in good spirits. Give me the best clavier in Europe with an audience who understand nothing, or don't want to understand and who do not feel with me in what I am playing, and I shall cease to feel any pleasure. I told Grimm all about it afterwards. You say that I ought to pay a good many calls in order to make new acquaintances and revive the old ones. That, however, is out of the question. The distances are too great for walking—or the roads too muddy—for really the mud in Paris is beyond all description. To take a carriage—means that you have the honour of spending four to five livres a day, and all for nothing. People pay plenty of compliments, it is true, but there it ends. They arrange for me to come on such and such a day. I play and hear them exclaim: 'Oh, c'est un prodige, c'est inconcevable, c'est étonnant!', and then it is—Adieu. At first I spent a lot of money driving about—often to no purpose, for the people were not at home. Those who do not live in Paris cannot imagine how annoying this is. Besides, Paris is greatly changed; the French are not nearly so polite as they were fifteen years ago; their manners now border on rudeness and they are detestably self-conceited. Well, I must give you an account of the Concert Spirituel—which reminds me that I must tell you briefly that my work on those choruses turned out in fact to be useless, for Holzbauer's Miserere[1] in itself was too long and did not please. Thus they only performed two of my choruses instead of four, and left out the best. But that was of no consequence, for few people knew that I had composed some of the music and many knew nothing at all about me. However, there was great applause at the rehearsal and I myself (for I attach little value to Parisian praises) am very well satisfied with my choruses. There appears, however, to be a hitch with regard to the sinfonia concertante,[2] and I think that something is going on behind the scenes and that doubtless here too I have enemies. Where, indeed, have I not had them?—But that is a good sign. I had to write the sinfonia in a great hurry and I worked very hard at it. The four performers were and still are quite in love with it. Le Gros kept it for four days to have it copied, but I always found it lying in the same place. The day before yesterday I couldn't find it—I searched carefully among the music—and discovered it hidden away. I pretended not to notice it, but just said to Le Gros: 'A propos. Have you given the sinfonia concertante to be copied?' 'No', he replied, 'I forgot all about it.' As of course I could not command him to have it copied and performed, I said nothing; but when I went to the concert on the two days when it should have been performed, Ramm and Punto came up to me greatly enraged to ask me why my sinfonia concertante was not being played. 'I really don't know', I replied. 'It's the

[1] See p. 521.　　　　　　　　　　　　[2] K. App. 9 [K. 297B]. See p. 522.

first I've heard of it. I know nothing about it.' Ramm flew into a passion and in the music-room he cursed Le Gros in French, saying it was a dirty trick and so forth. What annoys me most in the whole affair is that Le Gros never said a word to me about it—I alone was to be kept in the dark. If he had even made an excuse—that the time was too short or something of the kind—but to say nothing at all! I believe, however, that Cambini,[1] an Italian maestro here, is at the bottom of the business. For in all innocence I swept the floor with him at our first meeting at Le Gros's house. He has composed some quartets, one of which I heard at Mannheim. They were quite pretty. I praised them to him and played the beginning of the one I had heard. But Ritter, Ramm and Punto, who were there, gave me no peace, urging me to go on and telling me that what I could not remember I myself could supply. This I did, so that Cambini was quite beside himself and could not help saying: 'Questa è una gran testa!'[2] But I am convinced that he did not enjoy it. If this were a place where people had ears to hear, hearts to feel and some measure of understanding of and taste for music, these things would only make me laugh heartily; but, as it is (so far as music is concerned), I am surrounded by mere brute beasts. How can it be otherwise? For in all their actions, emotions and passions they are just the same. There is no place in the world like Paris. You must not think that I exaggerate when I talk thus of the music here. Ask anyone you like—provided he is not a Frenchman born —and, if he knows anything at all of the matter, he will say exactly the same. Well, I am here. I must endure it for your sake. But I shall thank Almighty God if I escape with my taste unspoiled. I pray to God daily to give me grace to hold out here with fortitude and to do such honour to myself and to the whole German nation as will redound to His greater honour and glory; and that He will enable me to prosper and make a great deal of money, so that I may help you out of your present difficulties; and that He will permit us to meet again soon, so that we may all live together in happiness and contentment. For the rest, may His will be done on earth as it is in heaven. But I entreat you, dearest Papa, in the meantime, to do your best so that I may soon revisit Italy, where after this experience I may revive. Do me this favour, I beg you. And now I implore you to keep up your spirits. I shall hack my way through here as best I can, and I hope to get out without any bones broken! Adieu. I kiss your hands a thousand times and embrace my sister with all my heart and remain your most obedient son

WOLFGANG AMADÈ MOZART

---

[1] Giuseppe Maria Cambini (1746–1825), a pupil of Tartini and Padre Martini, was a violinist and a prolific composer. He had been in Paris since 1770 and was a protégé of Gossec, who performed his symphonies at the Concert Spirituel.
[2] What a head!

(303a) *Maria Anna Mozart to her Husband*

[*Autograph in the Mozarteum, Salzburg*[1]]

MY DEAR HUSBAND,   [PARIS, 1 *May* 1778]

I trust that you and Nannerl are well. All this long while, about three weeks, I have been plagued with toothache, sore throat and earache, but now, thank God, I am better. I don't get out much, it is true, and the rooms are cold, even when a fire is burning. You have just to get used to it. If by any chance Count Wolfegg is coming to Paris and could bring me a black powder and a digestive one, I should be very glad, for I have almost come to an end of our supply. Remember me to all my acquaintances. Monsieur Heina and his wife also send their greetings. He often comes to see me. Addio. Keep well, both of you. I kiss you many 100000 times and remain your faithful wife

MARIA ANNA MOZART

(304) *Leopold Mozart to his Wife and Son*

[*Extract*]   [*Autograph in the Mozarteum, Salzburg*]

SALZBURG, *Wednesday* 6 [*May* 1778[2]]

MY DEAR WIFE AND DEAR SON!

★   We have not had any letter from you since your second one despatched from Paris on April 10th, but which Mamma began to write on
★ April 5th. The Archbishop is now trying to get Bertoni[3] to be Kapellmeister here for a time. Did not Herr Raaff tell Wolfgang that Padre Martini of Bologna had written to him on his behalf? As long ago as February 14th Padre Martini wrote to me saying that he had received Wolfgang's portrait and adding the following remarks about what he had written to Mannheim: 'Le vicende della Baviera e della partenza di S.A. Elettorale Palatina da Mannheim forse impediranno che non possino avere tutto il buon effetto appresso la sua Altezza Elettorale; tuttavia se tarderanno, non mancheranno'.[4] I have a new pupil, Count Perusa, whom I shall be charging a ducat just to go to his house for twelve lessons, as he is a com-
★ plete ass. I hear that if war breaks out (about which there is hardly any doubt) Herr Duschek and his wife will go off to Paris.
★

---

[1] This postscript is on the cover.
[2] The opening of this letter, which has been omitted here, is dated 29 April 1778.
[3] Bertoni did not accept the invitation, but went to Paris and later to London. See p. 494, n. 3.
[4] Matters connected with Bavaria and the departure of the Elector Palatine from Mannheim may perhaps prevent my recommendations from having much influence with His Electoral Highness. However, though they may be delayed, they will certainly reach him in due course.

Monday, May 11th. I have received this very moment your letter of May 1st, and gather from your having addressed it *par Strassbourg, Augsbourg* that, although you only mention my first letter, my second sent off, if I am not mistaken, on April 20th, and addressed to your present lodging, must have reached you. My dear Wolfgang! I shall now reply to all your points. I know by experience that in Paris you have to pay a hundred calls for nothing and indeed I told you this long ago. Further, I am well aware that the French pay people in compliments. Moreover, it is an undeniable fact that everywhere you will have enemies, inasmuch as all men of great talent have them. For all those who have made a name for themselves in Paris and have dug themselves in, refuse to be driven out of their trenches, and are doubtless fearful lest their reputation, on which their interests depend, should suffer. Not only Cambini but Stamitz[1] too—and Piccinni and others are bound to become jealous of you. *Is Piccinni still in Paris?* And will not Grétry envy you? So Wendling has told you that the music has undergone a change. I don't believe it. Perhaps it is true of their *instrumental music*, for that was improving in my time. But their *vocal music* will not have improved so quickly. But you must not let yourself be discouraged or unnerved by those who envy you; for it is the same everywhere. Remember Italy and your first opera, and your third opera too, and d'Ettore and so forth; likewise the intrigues of De Amicis and all the rest. You will have to fight your way through. If only you and Mamma have enough to live on, I shall be quite happy; and in the meantime we must wait and see what the situation in Germany is going to be. The whole country is full of soldiers, and there is no talk of anything but the delivery of horses and the transport of food. In Prussia and Austria people are being whipped off the streets and pulled out of their beds to be turned into soldiers. You must realize that I cannot help you with money— and that without money Mamma cannot come home nor can you go to Italy. If with the little bit of money which I still have ⟨I now pay our debts,⟩ then your Mamma and your sister would not ⟨have a farthing *after my death*⟩ and, further, I could not assist you in any way. So we must just wait and see how things turn out. Meanwhile you are both in a safe spot. For Heaven's sake, use patience and exert yourself! Who knows what we may not be able to do with the Elector of Mannheim, when things are going smoothly again? But if you are to get to Italy, you simply must have money, and that too even if I succeed in wangling a *scrittura* for you; for a journey means money. Do you imagine that I am in a position ⟨to pay our debts⟩ and at the same time to provide you with money, even with such a small sum as three or four hundred gulden, for a journey to Italy? Cheer up, resign yourself to circumstances, and, since you tell me that you have been commissioned to compose an opera, follow my advice

---

[1] Anton Stamitz. See p. 528, n. 1.

and remember that *your whole reputation depends on your first work*. Before you write it, listen to what the French people like and ponder upon it, I mean, hear and see their operas. I know your capabilities. You can imitate anything. *Don't compose in a hurry*, for no man in his senses does that. Discuss the text beforehand with Baron Grimm and Noverre and make schizzi[1] and let them hear them. Everybody does that. Why, Voltaire reads out his poems to his friends, listens to their verdict and makes alteratious accordingly. Your object is to make a name for yourself and to get money; and then, when we can afford to do so, we shall go to Italy again. If you compose something which is to be engraved, make it easy, suitable for amateurs and *rather popular*. Don't write in a hurry! Strike out what doesn't satisfy you. Don't do anything gratis; be sure and get paid for everything. We are all well. Farewell, we kiss you both 1000 times and I am your old

MZT

My dear wife, do not forget *to be bled*. Remember that you are away from home. And you, my dear Wolfgang, do take care of your health. Have you a clavier in your lodging? Since you left, Nannerl has been working extremely hard at galanterie-playing, interpretation, expression and accompanying. Ceccarelli, who sends you his greetings, and is leaving on the 18th, brought us a violin solo without the bass, which he wanted me to fill in for him. As I was not at home that morning, Nannerl wrote it in for him, as she now very often does for me. Addio. Farewell. I quite understand that you cannot write very often, as letters are so expensive. Baron de Grimm has written to me and I shall reply by the next post.

Cornet Andretter spent a short time with us yesterday. He sends you his greetings. Count Colloredo, Archbishop of Olmütz, is to be consecrated here next Sunday and Rust's serenata is to be performed on the occasion. I shall find out whether Count Wolfegg is going off to Paris again. Perhaps you can get the black powder at some chemist's shop. It is called *Pulvis epilepticus niger*. Bullinger has been on the verge of a bad attack of jaundice and has been ill for a fortnight: but he has now been allowed to eat a little meat again. He and all our friends send their greetings—in short the whole of Salzburg do so!

(305) *Maria Anna Mozart to her Husband*

[Autograph in the Mozarteum, Salzburg]

MY DEAR HUSBAND,   PARIS, 14 *May* 1778

Praise and thanks be to God, we are both well and we trust that you too are in good health. To hear this is our only pleasure. As for our circum-

---

[1] sketches.

stances we ought to be quite satisfied just now, as it is the slack season. Wolfgang has got hold of a good family. He has to teach composition for two hours daily to a mademoiselle, the daughter of the Duc de Guines, who pays handsomely and is the Queen's favourite. He is immensely fond of Wolfgang. At the moment Wolfgang has three pupils and could have many more, but he cannot take them on account of the distances. Besides, he really hasn't the time until our affairs are more settled. When winter comes he will have so much to do that he will not know whether he is standing on his head or his heels—at least everyone tells him this. We think too (and all our good friends are giving us this advice) that when the summer is over, we ought to rent a few rooms, buy our own furniture, which is easily found here, and cook for ourselves. In this way one can live for half the cost. We are going to do this as soon as we have made more money. What I should like to hear is something about the war, for there is a rumour here that peace has been concluded between the Emperor and Prussia. War between France and England has not yet been declared, but great preparations are being made. The Queen is pregnant; this too is not yet public property, but there is no doubt about it; and the French are absolutely delighted.[1] Please give our greetings to Herr Ceccarelli (if he is still in Salzburg). We are sorry that we have not had the honour of making his acquaintance. How is Frau Adlgasser? Is little Victoria still with her? And how are Barbara Eberlin and Berantzky? Do they still come to our house sometimes? Does Nannerl go to Andretter's every week as usual? Is young Andretter still in Neu-Ötting,[2] I mean, since all these changes have taken place in Bavaria? Do Fräulein von Schiedenhofen and Nannerl Kranach still come to shoot? Herr von Schiedenhofen must be very proud of himself with such a rich wife, and will probably not condescend to come to our house, though indeed it doesn't matter much. Otherwise I trust that Salzburg is still in the same old spot. Things have changed very much in Paris since we were here last. It is much bigger and is so spread out that I simply cannot describe it. For instance, the Chaussée D'Antin, where Monsieur Grimm lives, is a completely new suburb and there are many other fine wide streets like it. True, I haven't seen many of them, but I have a new map of the town, which is quite different from our old one. Here is something for Nannerl. The 'mode' here is to wear no earrings, nothing round your neck, no jewelled pins in your hair, in fact, no sparkling jewels, either real or imitation. The frisure they wear is extraordinarily high, not a heart-shaped toupee, but the same height all round, more than a foot. The cap, which is even higher than the toupee, is worn on top, and behind is the plait or chignon which is worn right

---

[1] In December 1778 Marie-Antoinette gave birth to a daughter, Marie-Thérèse-Charlotte, afterwards Duchesse d'Angoulême.
[2] A small town near Alt-Ötting, the oldest and most famous place of pilgrimage in Bavaria.

down low into the neck with lots of curls on either side. The toupee, however, consists entirely of crêpe, not of smooth hair. They have been wearing this frisure even higher, so that at one time the roofs of the carriages had to be raised, because no woman could sit upright in them. But they have now lowered them again. The Bolognesi are extremely fashionable and most beautifully made. The corselets worn by spinsters are smooth round the waist in front and have no folds. Nannerl will now know enough about the 'mode' for some time and I must leave some room for Wolfgang. Keep well, both of you. I kiss you both 100000 times. My greetings to all our good friends, Monsieur Bullinger, Sallerl, Deibl, Jungfer Mitzerl and all the others. I remain your faithful wife

MARIANNA MOZART

I send greetings to Theresa and a kiss to Bimperl. Is the warbler still alive?

(305a) *Mozart to his Father*

[Autograph in the Mozarteum, Salzburg]

[PARIS, 14 May 1778]

I have so much to do already, that I wonder what it will be like in winter! I think I told you in my last letter that the Duc de Guines, whose daughter is my pupil in composition, plays the flute extremely well, and that she plays the harp magnifique. She has a great deal of talent and even genius, and in particular a marvellous memory, so that she can play all her pieces, actually about two hundred, by heart. She is, however, extremely doubtful as to whether she has any talent for composition, especially as regards invention or ideas. But her father who, between ourselves, is somewhat too infatuated with her, declares that she certainly has ideas and that it is only that she is too bashful and has too little self-confidence. Well, we shall see. If she gets no inspirations or ideas (for at present she really has none whatever), then it is to no purpose, for—God knows—I can't give her any. Her father's intention is not to make a great composer of her. 'She is not', he said, 'to compose operas, arias, concertos, symphonies, but only grand sonatas for her instrument and mine.' I gave her her fourth lesson today and, so far as the rules of composition and harmony are concerned, I am fairly well satisfied with her. She filled in quite a good bass for the first minuet, the melody of which I had given her, and she has already begun to write in three parts. But she very soon gets bored, and I am unable to help her; for as yet I cannot proceed more quickly. It is too soon, even if there really were genius there, but unfortunately there is none. Everything has to be done by rule. She has no ideas whatever—nothing comes. I have tried her in every possible way. Among other things I hit on the idea of writing down a very simple minuet, in order to

538

see whether she could not compose a variation on it. It was useless. 'Well', I thought, 'she probably does not know how she ought to begin.' So I started to write a variation on the first bar and told her to go on in the same way and to keep to the idea. In the end it went fairly well. When it was finished, I told her to begin something of her own,—only the treble part, the melody. Well, she thought and thought for a whole quarter of an hour and nothing came. So I wrote down four bars of a minuet and said to her: 'See what an ass I am! I have begun a minuet and cannot even finish the melody. Please be so kind as to finish it for me.' She was positive she couldn't, but at last with great difficulty—something came, and indeed I was only too glad to see something for once. I then told her to finish the minuet, I mean, the treble only. But for *home work* all I asked her to do was to alter my four bars and compose something of her own. She was to find a new beginning, use, if necessary, the same harmony, provided that the melody should be different. Well, I shall see tomorrow what she has done. I shall soon, I believe, get the libretto for my opera en deux actes. Then I must first present it to the Director M. de Vismes,[1] to see if he will accept it, though there is no doubt about that, for Noverre suggested it and De Vismes owes his appointment to him. Noverre is also going to arrange a new ballet for which I am going to compose the music.[2] Rodolphe[3] (who plays the French horn) is in the Royal service here and is a very good friend of mine; he understands composition thoroughly and writes well. He has offered me the post of organist at Versailles, if I will accept it. The salary is 2000 livres a year, but I should have to spend six months at Versailles and the other six in Paris, or wherever I like. I do not think that I shall accept it, but I have yet to hear the advice of some good friends on the subject. After all, 2000 livres is not such a big sum. It would be so in Germany money, I admit, but here it is not. It amounts to 83 louis d'or, 8 livres a year—that is, to 915 gulden, 45 kreuzer in our money (a considerable sum, I admit), but here worth only 333 thalers, 2 livres— which is not much. It is frightful how quickly a thaler disappears here. I am not at all surprised that so little is thought of a louis d'or in Paris, for it really does not go far. Four of these thalers or one louis d'or, which is the same thing, are spent in no time. Well, adieu. Farewell. I kiss your hands a thousand times and embrace my sister with all my heart and remain your most obedient son

WOLFGANG AMADÈ MOZART

My greetings to all our good friends, and especially to Herr Bullinger.

---

[1] De Vismes, Director-General of the Paris Académie Royale de Musique.
[2] Mozart's ballet music *Les Petits Riens*, K. App. 10 [K. 299b], performed on 11 June 1778.
[3] Jean Joseph Rodolphe (1730–1812), born at Strassburg, studied the horn and violin in France and Italy. In 1767 he entered the service of Prince Conti, became solo horn at the Opéra in 1769 and member of the Royal Chapel in 1773. He composed several operas and ballets and wrote two valuable works on the theory of music.

(306) *Leopold Mozart to his Wife and Son*

[*Extract*]   [*Portion of autograph in the Mozarteum, Salzburg*]

MY DEAR WIFE AND DEAR SON!   SALZBURG, 28 *May* 1778

I received on the 25th your letter of the 14th and I trust that in the meantime you will have received mine which I sent off on the 11th. I am absolutely delighted that you are both in good health and that things are going well for you this season. Remember what I told you about Paris and how I kept on urging you to go there. Do have patience; things are sure to improve. Here's a piece of news! Ceccarelli, who left for Italy on the night of the 18th by the ordinary post-chaise, is to be back here on November 1st. He has signed a contract for three years at 800 gulden a
★ year, with an addition of forty ducats for his journey there and back. He has been as kind to Bimperl as Bullinger; and I have never come across such a good and sincere Italian, not to mention a castrato, as he is. The whole town are delighted that he is returning.
★ The famous Carl Besozzi [1] has been here and has played twice at Court, each time two concertos of his own composition. His writing, although it smacks a little of the older style, is neatly and soundly worked out and has something in common with that of our Haydn. But indeed his oboe-playing is all that is to be desired and I found it absolutely different from what it was when I heard him play in Vienna. In short, he has everything! Words fail me to describe his precision and the extremely pure tone he preserves in the most rapid runs and jumps. What is particularly remarkable is his ability to sustain his notes and his power to increase and decrease their volume, without introducing even the very slightest quiver into his very pure tone. But this *messa di voce* was too frequent for my taste and has the same melancholy effect on me as the tones of the harmonica, for it produces almost the same kind of sound. Besozzi sends you his greetings. He is still in the service of Saxony [2] and is only going to Turin because the King has conferred on him the rights of citizenship. Otherwise, as he was born in Naples, he could not claim the right to inherit from his two uncles, [3] one of whom, the bassoon-player, has just died. I have given him your sincere greetings [4] and have asked him to convey our compliments to Abbate Gasparini. Our Archbishop has given him twenty ducats. The Archbishop of Olmütz [5] was consecrated on the 17th. If you had not had so much to do for other people at Mannheim, you might have finished

[1] Carlo Besozzi (1738–after 1798), son of Antonio Besozzi (1714–1781) of Turin. They were both famous oboists.   [2] He was attached to the Dresden Court from 1755 until 1792.
[3] Alessandro Besozzi (1702–1793), and, probably, Paolo Girolamo Besozzi (1704–1778). See p. 455, n. 4.
[4] The surviving portion of the autograph breaks off here. The remainder, including the address, is now lost. A complete copy of the letter is in the Staatsbibliothek Preussischer Kulturbesitz, West Berlin.
[5] Count Colloredo, cousin of the Archbishop of Salzburg.

your mass[1] and sent it to me. For at our practices Brunetti was always chattering about who should compose the Consecration mass, and was hoping to arrange for Haydn to get the commission from the Archbishop. But the latter never replied; nor did Counts Czernin and Starhemberg who were approached by Brunetti and Frau Haydn. I therefore produced Wolfgang's mass with the organ solo,[2] taking the Kyrie from the Spaur mass.[3] I had them copied and received six ducats for my pains. In addition the Prince of Olmütz contributed thirty ducats for the occasional music and the Serenata, and the Archbishop sent this sum to me to distribute. I apportioned it, drew up the list and sent it to him for his approval; for in order to save myself from malicious criticism, I was determined that he should see that I had not included myself. I then distributed the money. By the way, he removed Abbate Varesco's name from the list. Wolf, the new Archbishop's physician, also came over from Olmütz. It was for his little daughter that Wolfgang composed his aria[4] at Olmütz long ago. ★ Thank God, we are in good health. I believe I have already suggested that it might be more economical for you to do your own cooking, as you would then save a good deal. My dear son! I beg you to try and keep the friendship of the Duc de Guines and to win his favour. I have often read about him in the papers. He is all-powerful at the French Court. As the Queen is pregnant, there will surely *be great festivities later on*, and you might get something to do which would make your fortune. For on such occasions *whatever the Queen demands* is carried out. In your letter today you say that you have given the Duke's daughter her fourth lesson and you seem to expect her to be able to invent melodies. Do you think that everyone has got your genius? Let her alone. It will come in time! She has a good memory. Eh bien! Let her steal or—to put it more politely— apply what she has learnt. Nothing goes well at first until one gets self-confidence. You have started her off on the right path by giving her variations; so, carry on! If Monsieur le Duc but hears some little composition by his daughter, he will be beside himself with delight. Why, you now have a very fortunate acquaintanceship! As for the opera which you have been commissioned to write, I sent you a few suggestions the other day. I remind you once more to *think over the subject carefully, read through the text with Baron de Grimm and come to an understanding with Noverre as to how the emotions are to be expressed, and follow the French taste in singing*, which your talent for modulation and for writing for voices will raise and distinguish from the work of others. So Rodolphe has offered

---

[1] Mozart wrote the Kyrie of this mass, K. 322 [296a]. See pp. 482 and 499.

[2] K. 259, which has an organ solo during the Benedictus. This mass was composed in December 1776.

[3] Probably K. 262 [246a], composed in 1775, apparently for the consecration of Count Friedrich Franz Joseph Spaur.

[4] Perhaps K. 53 [47e], a song with clavier accompaniment, 'Freude, Königin der Weisen', composed in autumn 1768.

you the post of organist at Versailles? Does the appointment rest with him? If so, he will surely help you to get it! You must not throw that away so lightly. You should bear in mind that *you would be earning 83 louis d'or in six months—and that you would have another six months in which to make money in other ways.* Further, it is probably *a life appointment,* I mean, that you hold it whether you are well or ill—and, moreover, that *you can always resign it.* You should remember too that you *would be at Court,* that is, constantly in the presence of the King and Queen; that when there is a vacancy, *you might obtain one of the two posts of Kapellmeister; that in due course, if there should be a Royal family, you would become clavier-teacher to the young princes, which would be a very remunerative post; that nobody could prevent you from composing for the theatre and the Concert Spirituel and so forth, from having music engraved and dedicating it to your patrons,* since, during the summer at least, a great many ministers stay at Versailles; *that Versailles is a small town in itself and has many distinguished residents,* among whom you would surely find one or two pupils—and finally that an appointment of this kind *would be the surest way to win the protection of the Queen* and make yourself popular. Read what I say to Baron Grimm and get his

★ opinion. If our dear Wolfgang comes across some good pieces for the clavier, he might put a few together and send them to us by mail coach; for we need them for our pupils. Do this as soon as you have an opportunity!

Where are your rooms! *In which district?* I can't find the Rue du Gros

★ Chenet. I keep on looking round the Palais Royal, where the theatre is.

★ Nannerl was delighted to hear all about the latest 'modes'. She kisses your
★ hands and thanks you. We kiss you millions of times and I am your old

MZT

(307) *Maria Anna Mozart to her Husband*

[*Autograph in the Mozarteum, Salzburg*]

MY DEAR HUSBAND,   PARIS, 29 *May* 1778

We have received your letter of May 11th and are delighted to hear that you and Nannerl are well. Your news amused me greatly. Indeed I pity Sandl Auer[1] from the bottom of my heart, and trust that in the meantime she has completely recovered her reason. As for Sigmund Haffner[2] I had a real good laugh, for I know the girl. She was a bosom friend of our Nannie,[3] who let us down so; she used to come and see her

---

[1] Frau Mozart is referring to a story in her husband's letter of May 6th-11th, which for lack of space has had to be omitted.

[2] In the same letter Leopold Mozart discusses at length Sigmund Haffner's engagement. For lack of space this portion of the letter has had to be omitted.

[3] A former servant of the Mozarts. See p. 95.

very often and is still very friendly with her. She is the daughter of a brewer of Uttendorf[1] and she can't be more than twenty-six; she looks older, but only because she was worked to death at the colonel's. If he has married her, he has made a charming match, God bless him. He won't have any reason to be jealous of her, for certainly nobody would fall in love with her. We don't hear very much about a war. I can well believe what you say, that is, that the King of Prussia is trying to form alliances, but it will not be easy, because Russia cannot very well come in on account of the Turks, and the Turks are determined to have a war. Nor is it possible for the Swedes to do so, for the King of France has auxiliaries from them amounting to 30,000 men and pays them 12 million livres a year. And there is nothing doing in Denmark, whose entire man-power is about 30,000 men. Why, the whole country would be empty. Besides, don't you think that they are scared of France, who spends her time abusing the King of Prussia to all the other Powers? That's why he doesn't attack. Otherwise he wouldn't wait, for he has always been aggressive and has never hesitated so long. The whole town here is wholeheartedly for the Emperor, save perhaps the Lutherans—and not even all of them, for some too are for the Emperor, who made himself very popular during his stay in Paris. Here is something for Nannerl. Tell her she must get herself a pretty walking-stick, for the great fashion here is for all women (except serving-maids) to carry sticks to church, when visiting, walking, whether they go, in the streets, of course, but not when driving. No woman goes out walking without a stick because it is very slippery here under foot, particularly after the rain. It appears that some woman twisted her foot a while ago, and a doctor declared that it would be better if women carried walking-sticks; upon which it immediately became the fashion. Living is extremely expensive in Paris; a pound of good butter costs 30 to 40 sous, inferior butter, not fit to eat, 24 sous; a pound of beef 10 sous; veal 12 to 14 sous; a shoulder of lamb 3 livres, a young chicken 3 livres; wine is dear and very poor, as the innkeepers always adulterate it. It is even more expensive than it was in England, when we were there. You cannot do any more with a louis d'or in Paris than you can in Germany with a Bavarian thaler, and with a thaler you cannot do more than we can in Salzburg with 24 kreuzer. Everything is twice as dear as it used to be. But thanks and praise be to God, we are well and only wish that you were both with us. I will remember to be bled; only I must first look about for a good surgeon, for people in Paris are no longer bled as commonly as they used to be. Indeed, how fashions do change! We send greetings to Cornet Andretter. We are sorry that Bullinger has been ill and are delighted that he is well again. We send greetings to him and to my dear Sallerl. What is

---

[1] A small village in the Austrian Tyrol, about twelve miles from Zell am See.

she doing? Does she ever think of me? Wolfgang and I often talk about her. Ah, often and often do we talk about our friends in Salzburg when we sit at supper together in the evening. Addio. Keep well, both of you. I kiss you many 10000 times and remain your faithful wife

MARIANNA MOZART

All sorts of messages from us to all our good friends. I send greetings to Theresa.

(307a) *Mozart to his Father*

[Autograph in the Mozarteum, Salzburg]

[PARIS, 29 May 1778]

I am tolerably well, thank God, but I often wonder whether life is worth living—I am neither hot nor cold—and don't find much pleasure in anything. What, however, cheers me up most of all and keeps me in good spirits is the thought that you, dearest Papa, and my dear sister are well— that I am an honest German—and that, even if I may not always say what I like, I may at any rate think it. That, however, is all. Yesterday I went for the second time to see Count von Sickingen, Envoy of the Palatine Electorate (having already lunched there once with Wendling and Raaff). I do not remember whether I have already told you this—but he is a charming man, a passionate lover and a true connoisseur of music. I spent eight hours quite alone with him. We were at the clavier morning, after-noon and evening until ten o'clock, playing, praising, admiring, analysing, discussing and criticizing all kinds of music. He has nearly thirty operatic scores.

Well, I must not forget to tell you that I have had the honour of seeing your 'Violinschule' in a French translation, which, I think, appeared at least eight years ago.[1] I happened to be in a music shop buying a collection of sonatas by Schobert for a pupil and I mean to go there again soon and have a good look at the book in order to be able to send you more particulars. I had too little time the other day. Well, good-bye. I kiss your hands a thousand times and embrace my sister with all my heart. Mes compliments à tous mes amis, particulièrement à M. Bullinger.

WOAMOZART[2]

---

[1] Leopold Mozart's *Versuch einer gründlichen Violinschule*, which was published in 1756, appeared in 1770 in a French translation by a certain Valentin Roeser.
[2] The cover of this letter bears the following remark in Leopold Mozart's handwriting: 'Received on the evening of the 7th and answered on June 11th'.

(308) *Leopold Mozart to his Wife and Son*

[*Extract*]   [*Autograph formerly in the Mozarteum, Salzburg*[1]]

MY DEAR WIFE AND DEAR SON!   SALZBURG, 11 *June* 1778   ★
We still have our amateur concerts in Lodron's hall every Sunday.
The two Lodron girls have each played three times already and, what is
more, they have played some music which I gave them, for they could not
have managed one single piece of all the music which they learnt during
five years with the late Adlgasser. Leopold Arco too has played three times.
They all did themselves and myself great credit. Fräulein von Mölk
played once after Nannerl had given her several lessons on her piece. Well,
Mlle Villersi[2] was asked to perform. Countess von Lützow had had Wolfgang's concerto[3] copied for her some time ago and Spitzeder had taught
it to her. Thinking that she could play it very well, she tried it in her own
room with the violins. Bullinger was there too. They all told her, and
she agreed, that she played it abominably. So she came out to our house
in tears and begged us to coach her, postponing her performance for a
fortnight and ending by learning it so proficiently that she really did herself great credit. She now takes lessons with Nannerl and comes to our
house for that purpose, so that the maids at the Langer Hof may not know
anything about it, as Spitzeder still teaches her. Both the Count and
Countess know it, however, and the latter much regrets her own wilful-
ness and does not know what to do about her two girls, who in five whole
years have learnt absolutely nothing. On June 7th the Lodron girls performed again, the elder playing Lucchesi's concerto very well indeed.
Sigmund Robinig has played twice already; the first time Wolfgang's
piece in B♭ (I think) from the Finalmusik,[4] the second time some other
easy concerto. He did not play at all badly, but his cadenzas were detestably Pinzgerish.[5] We received your letter of May 29th on the evening of   ★
the 7th and are delighted that you are both in good health. Thank God,
we too are well, though indeed at times a melancholy feeling comes over
me when I think how far away we are from one another and wonder
whether—and when—I shall ever see you again! By self-control and
fortitude I will try to banish these sad thoughts and leave all to the will of
God. I am not at all surprised that everything is much dearer in Paris than
it used to be, because the same thing is happening everywhere from year
to year. It is generally the case that *where money is plentiful, everything is
dear, and where living is cheap, money will be scarce.* Nannerl is thinking of
starting here the fashion of walking-sticks for women next winter, because

---

[1] Copy in the Staatsbibliothek Preussischer Kulturbesitz, West Berlin.
[2] Daughter of the Archbishop's former tutor, Casimir Villersi, and governess to Count
Kühnburg's children.   [3] K. 246, written for Countess Lützow.
[4] Either K. 254, composed in 1776, or K. 287 [271H], composed in 1777.
[5] In the manner of Pinzger. See p. 281, n. 3.

the streets are so slippery for pedestrians. In winter fans are out of place and a woman generally likes to have something to carry. And the war? Well, what am I to say? Things are just as they were. Preparations to terrify us—and in the meantime one courier after another, indicating that negotiations are in progress. One day—reliable news of a compromise— the next day, further information, equally trustworthy, that no compro-
★ mise can be hoped for. God grant us peace! I told you some time ago that the Elector would not leave Munich so soon. God knows when the people of Mannheim will see him, for if peace prevails, it is quite certain that he will spend most, if not all of his time, in Bavaria.

My dear Wolfgang! Your remarks: *I am tolerably well—I often wonder whether life is worth living—I am neither hot nor cold—I don't find much pleasure in anything*—seem to me to indicate that you were *discontented* or annoyed at the time or that you were writing in a bad humour. I don't like it. But I can't say anything about it, as I don't know the cause of your displeasure. Indeed, earning your daily bread is a very different matter from being able to live without this anxiety and allow someone else to attend to it. *Experience is our only teacher.* Perhaps you will realise now the work, the efforts and the daily worries which I have had to cope with during *thirty years* of married life, in order to support a family, *worries* with which I shall be saddled until the hour of my death. There is no reason whatever why you should be unhappy. God has bestowed great talents upon you. You were desperately impatient to leave Salzburg. You have now found out that a great many things I prophesied have turned out to be true; otherwise, in your opinion, I myself ought to have cleared out of Salzburg long ago with all my belongings. At least you are in a city where, even though everything is exceptionally dear, a lot of money can be made. But pains and hard work are necessary! Nothing can be achieved without some effort! You are young! Whereas I in my *59th year* have to tear my hair over five pupils, and that too *for a wretched pittance*! If some things do not turn out as you wish, hope or imagine—if you have enemies—if you are persecuted—in short, if events do not shape themselves as you want and expect them to, remember that in this world it has always been and always will be thus, and that this is something to which everyone, from beggar to king, must submit. Was your sinfonia concertante[1] not per- formed at all? Were you paid for it? And did they not return your score? You do not say a word about the French opera—nor about your pupil in composition. In short! You still tell me at the moment of writing of the most recent events that have happened, and this last time you must have been very absent-minded indeed, for you even wrote the address par Augsbourg—Strassbourg, as if the letter were to go to Augsburg first and then to Strassburg. I replied to you on May 28th about the post of organist

[1] K. App. 9 [K. 297B]. See p. 522.

at Versailles. I regard the whole affair as a *pious wish* on the part of ★
Rodolphe. But it has given rise to the following incident here. The
Countess[1] asked me a few days ago (when we met on the stairs) how you
both were and what news I had had. I told her quite coolly and rather
hastily (for I was hurrying back to lunch) that you were both in good
health and that, if you chose, you might perhaps have one of the two posts
of Royal organist, in a word, exactly what you told me in your letter.
Bullinger came to see us yesterday at the usual hour and burst out at once
with a piece of news, namely, that Abbé Henri had made a point of going
and telling him what I had told her. She said that she was extremely sorry
that she was away when your affair took place; that she would like to
know whether I wished to have you back in Salzburg; that she would
make sure that *later on you should certainly become Kapellmeister*, but that this
was at the moment out of the question, seeing that you had resigned from
the Prince's service; that you could, however, be appointed Konzertmeister and organist (which would only mean performing on the big
organ and accompanying at Court) at fifty gulden a month. She commissioned Abbé Henri to ask Herr Bullinger whether he could give him
some information about my views or intentions. Bullinger replied that
however delighted I might be to have my wife and son at home again, he
was quite sure that when I told the story about the post of organist at
Versailles I had no such intention, and that Abbé Henri ought to discuss
the matter quite frankly with me, and I would surely give my candid
opinion both to him and to the Countess. I have been watching this bit
of fun for a long time. But I wanted to keep out of the whole business;
and, although we must have another organist, I said nothing, so that
people should not think that I have anything in my mind. You can well
imagine how bad things are, for since Adlgasser's death Lipp[2] has been
accompanying at Court. Whenever Ceccarelli has been singing, he has
cursed aloud in public. I am in no hurry to discuss the matter with Abbé
Henri, so that they may see that I am not particularly keen on their
proposal. As soon as I have spoken to him, I will let you know how things
are going. The Archbishop has been sending off letters to all the towns in
Italy, but he cannot find a Kapellmeister. He has written to Vienna,
Prague and Königgrätz, yet he cannot get a decent organist and clavierist.
Nor can he arrive at an arrangement with Bertoni about the post of
Kapellmeister—and—you will laugh! *Luigi Gatti*[3] *of Mantua* (you will re-
member him, for he copied out your mass[4] there), whom the Archbishop

---

[1] Maria Franziska, Countess von Wallis (1746–1795), a sister of the Archbishop, who held her
own court in a wing of the archiepiscopal residence opposite the cathedral.
[2] Franz Ignaz Lipp was second organist in Salzburg cathedral.
[3] Abbate Luigi Gatti (1740–1817), a native of Mantua, was appointed in 1783 Kapellmeister
at Salzburg, where he remained until his death. See Constantin Schneider, *Geschichte der
Musik in Salzburg*, 1935, p. 142.
[4] Probably K. 66, the Dominicus mass, composed in October 1769.

of Olmütz had recommended as an eminent clavierist and to whom he himself had written, has refused to leave his native town for more than two or three months. Ceccarelli too has been commissioned to find a Kapellmeister and a tenor, which reminds me that Meisner has not been singing for the last three months—he is finished! Hasse of Königgrätz would never come as clavierist, nor would he be asked to do so, since our good lady Theresa Arco has been spreading the news that he is one of the finest swillers and jokers. There is no longer any thought of promoting Haydn. The whole affair has acquired the most dirty connection since Brunetti's Judith was delivered on the vigil of St. Joseph and the child was baptized in the Cathedral at half past six in the evening, being christened Josepha Antonia. The girl was always at Haydn's, so that before her confinement he had to send her home to her father, or the Abbot of St. Peter's would have turned him out of his quarters. No one is saying anything, and why? Because this is the second Brunetti affair. So people are now awaiting the third, when they will report it to the Court Council and have the contract annulled, as was done in the case of Marini. If Count Czernin leaves, Brunetti will be off too! Now for my 'Violinschule'. *If it has my name on it, try to get a copy at a reduced price and send it to me by mail coach*, for, as I have the Dutch translation,[1] I should like to have the French one too. I told you the other day that if you can find *some pleasing clavier pieces, suitable for pupils*, you might send them to me when you have an opportunity, and perhaps you could do this when you send me the French translation. But there is really no hurry and we can easily wait until Wolfgang sends us something of his own composition, even if it is only little trifles for the clavier for his sister, that is to say, if he has time to do so. I hear that Vogler at Mannheim has brought out a book,[2] which the Government of the Palatinate has prescribed for the use *of all clavier teachers in the country, both for singing and composition*. I must see this book and I have already ordered it. There must be some sound stuff in it, for he could copy the clavier method from Bach's[3] book, the outlines of a singing method from Tosi[4] and Agricola,[5] and rules for composition and

---

[1] The Dutch translation was published in 1766 during the Mozarts' visit to Holland. See p. 64.

[2] *Kurpfälzische Tonschule* (Mannheim, 1778), which embodies an earlier work, *Stimmbildungskunst* (Mannheim, 1776).

[3] Carl Philipp Emanuel Bach's *Versuch über die wahre Art das Klavier zu spielen*, which was published at Berlin in two parts in 1753 and 1762.

[4] Pier Francesco Tosi (*c.* 1653–1732) spent the majority of his life in London, where he won renown as a teacher of singing. In 1723 he published his treatise on singing, *Opinioni de' cantori antichi e moderni, o sieno osservazioni sopra il canto figurato*, which was translated into English by Galliard and into German by Agricola.

[5] Johann Friedrich Agricola (1720–1774), organist and composer of operas and church music. He became in 1751 court composer to Frederick the Great and established a good reputation as a teacher of singing. He translated Tosi's treatise on singing.

harmony from Fux,[1] Riepel,[2] Marpurg,[3] Mattheson,[2] Spiess,[5] Scheibe,[6] d'Alembert,[7] Rameau[8] and a host of others, and then boil them down into a shorter system, such as I have long had in mind. Thus I am anxious to see whether his ideas accord with mine. You ought to have the book, for such works are useful when giving lessons. As a teacher one is led by experience to adopt certain good methods of dealing with this or that problem, and these good methods do not come to one all at once. You know well—but indeed, *that suddenly reminds me!* The day after tomorrow is the Feast of St. Anthony and you are away! Who will arrange the serenade for the Countess?[9] Who?—Why, la compagnie des amateurs. Count Czernin and Kolb are the two violini principali. They have astounding solos to play, their work being made up as follows—an Allegro and Adagio by Hafeneder, and a minuet with three trios by Czernin—*all new compositions.* The march is by Hafeneder, wretched pilfered stuff which sounds like chop-sticks, all screeching and *out of tune* —like the world! Will Mamma please tell me in her next letter *what* ★ *wages Theresa should get*? For she has been paid nothing since you left: and neither of us can remember when we last paid her. All that we can find is a note jotted down in February 1777—15 gulden 20 kreuzer for five quarters. All our friends send their greetings to you, especially ★ Bullinger and Sallerl, who are always thinking of you and talking about you, Mitzerl, Theresa, dear Pimperl—Andretter—Hagenauer and so forth, and we kiss you millions of times and I am your old

MZT

Nannerl gets up every morning at half past five—goes to half past six Mass and then carries on her work methodically the whole day long.

[1] Johann Joseph Fux (1660–1741) was Kapellmeister to the Imperial court of Vienna and wrote a famous treatise on contrapuntal composition, *Gradus ad Parnassum*, which was translated into four languages. The original, in Latin, appeared in 1725, the German edition in 1742 and the Italian edition in 1761.

[2] Joseph Riepel (1709–1782), music director to Prince Taxis at Regensburg, published several works on the theory of music.

[3] Friedrich Wilhelm Marpurg (1718–1795) was an eminent writer on music. From 1750 until 1790 he published several treatises, the most important being his great work in five volumes, *Historisch-Kritische Beyträge* (Berlin, 1754–1778).

[4] Johann Mattheson (1681–1764), a famous organist and a writer of numerous works on music which appeared from 1713 until 1739.

[5] Meinrad Spiess (1683–1761), musical director and abbot of the monastery of Yrsee, Swabia. He composed a great deal of church music and wrote works on the theory of music.

[6] Johann Adolf Scheibe (1708–1776) became in 1744 director of the court opera at Copenhagen. He was a prolific composer of church and chamber music, and wrote several works on the theory of music.

[7] Between the years 1747 and 1765 d'Alembert wrote several treatises on acoustics, which were published in the *Proceedings* of the Paris and Berlin Academies, and also some general works on music, such as *Éléments de musique théorique et pratique suivant les principes de M. Rameau*, 1752.

[8] Rameau's first work on music was his *Traité de l'harmonie*, which appeared in 1722. From that time onwards he published a number treatises on harmony and accompaniment.

[9] The Countess Antonia Lodron.

(309) *Maria Anna Mozart to her Husband*

[*Autograph in the Mozarteum, Salzburg*]

MY DEAR HUSBAND,   PARIS, 12 *June* 1778

We received on June 9th your letter of May 28th and were delighted to hear that you were both in good health. Thank God, Wolfgang and I are quite well. I was bled yesterday, so I shan't be able to write much today. Wolfgang is not at home, as he is lunching with Herr Raaff at Count Sickingen's, where they go at least once a week, for Sickingen is devoted to Wolfgang and is himself a great connoisseur of music and composes too. Herr Raaff comes to see us almost every day. He calls me 'Mother', is very fond of us and often spends two or three hours with us. One day he came especially to sing to me and sang three arias, which gave me great pleasure. And now whenever he comes to see us he always sings something to me, for I am quite in love with his singing. He is a most honourable man and sincerity itself; if you knew him, you would love him with all your heart. You want to know where we are lodging? First of all, find the rue Montmartre and then the rue Cléry. It is the first street on the left, if you enter the rue Cléry from the rue Montmartre. It is a fine street, inhabited almost entirely by the upper classes, very clean, fairly near the Boulevards, and the air is healthy. The owners of the house are good, honest folk and not out to make money, which is unusual in Paris. I lunched at Herr Heina's the day before yesterday and after lunch I went for a walk in the Luxembourg gardens; then I went into the Palace to see the fine picture gallery and was frightfully tired when I got home. I was all alone, as Wolfgang was lunching with Raaff at Monsieur Grimm's. Herr Heina saw me home. He often comes to see us. His wife too has been to see us twice with her daughter who is already married. You do not say how the Serenata went off, whether it was beautiful and whether the Archbishop was pleased with it. Which Colloredo is the Bishop of Olmütz? Is he a brother or a cousin of our Prince? A propos. How is Lenerl Martinelli? Where has she gone to? To her cousins or to the lieutenant of the guards? As for the lightning conductor I can't find out what people here think about it, as I don't know the language. But I have not seen any. In Mannheim, however, it cropped up once in conversation. They don't think much of it there, for they say that it attracts storms, when there would otherwise be none at all, and that where there are many conductors, the storm settles in that particular spot until everything is smashed to pieces and all the crops destroyed. It is far better to let nature take its course than to force it. For God can find anybody he wants to and no lightning conductor can save him. When the Kapuzinerberg collapsed, people were indeed very lucky, for there might have been a great disaster.

Truly mountains are not safe when houses are built so near them. Why, the Neues Tor may also collapse some day. We are having the most glorious summer here—very pleasant weather and, thank God, no storms up to the present. When Wolfgang lunches at home he and I get a meal for 15 sous. In the evening we buy four pasties for four sous. That you may know what these are, let me tell you that they are a kind of pastry which the French call 'plaisirs' and which we call 'Holehiper'. Please give our compliments to all our good friends. Every day we talk about our friends in Salzburg and wish that they could be with us. Many of them would stare and gape if they saw the things we see here. Addio. Keep well, both of you. I kiss you several thousand times and remain your faithful wife

FRAU MOZART

I must stop, for my arm and eyes are aching.

(309a) *Mozart to his Father*

[Autograph in the Mozarteum, Salzburg]

[PARIS, 12 *June* 1778]

I must now say something about our Raaff. You will remember, no doubt, that I did not write too favourably about him from Mannheim, and was by no means pleased with his singing—enfin, that I did not like him at all. The reason, however, was that I scarcely heard him properly, as it were, at Mannheim. I heard him for the first time in the rehearsal of Holzbauer's 'Günther', when he was in his everyday clothes, with his hat on and a stick in his hand. When he was not singing he stood there like a child at stool: when he began to sing the first recitative, it went quite tolerably, but every now and then he gave a kind of shout, which I could not bear. He sang the arias in a way so obviously careless—and some notes he sang with too much emphasis—which did not appeal to me. This has been a constant habit of his—and perhaps it is a characteristic of the Bernacchi school—for he was a pupil of Bernacchi's.[1] At Court, too, he always sang arias which, in my opinion, by no means suited his voice; so that I did not like him at all. But when he made his début here in the Concert Spirituel, he sang Bach's scena 'Non so d'onde viene', which, by the way, is a favourite of mine[2]—and then for the first time I really heard him sing—and he pleased me—that is, in his particular style of

---

[1] Antonio Bernacchi (1685–1756), a successful singer and teacher, founded in 1736 his famous school of singing at Bologna.

[2] Johann Christian Bach's aria in his opera *Alessandro nell' Indie*, produced at Naples in 1762. Bach introduced it, altering it to ¾-time, into the pasticcio *Ezio* which was performed in London in November 1764. See p. 54, n. 7. This is therefore the setting which Mozart knew. See C. S. Terry, *John Christian Bach*, p. 55.

singing, although the style itself—the Bernacchi school—is not to my taste. Raaff is too much inclined to drop into the cantabile. I admit that when he was young and in his prime, this must have been very effective and have taken people by surprise. I admit also that I like it. But he over-does it and so to me it often seems ridiculous. What I do like is when he sings short pieces, as, for example, some andantinos; and he has also certain arias, which he renders in his peculiar style. Well, each in his own way. I fancy that his forte was bravura singing—and, so far as his age permits, you can still tell this from his manner; he has a good chest and long breath; and then—these andantinos. His voice is beautiful and very pleasant. If I shut my eyes and listen to him, he reminds me very much of Meisner, only that Raaff's voice seems to me even more pleasing. I am talking about their voices as they are at present, for I have never heard them in their prime. So all that I can discuss is their style or method of singing, which a singer always retains. Meisner, as you know, has the bad habit of making his voice tremble at times, turning a note that should be sustained into distinct crotchets, or even quavers—and this I never could endure in him. And really it is a detestable habit and one which is quite contrary to nature. The human voice trembles naturally—but in its own way—and only to such a degree that the effect is beautiful. Such is the nature of the voice; and people imitate it not only on wind-instruments, but on stringed instruments too and even on the clavier. But the moment the proper limit is overstepped, it is no longer beautiful—because it is contrary to nature. It reminds me then of the organ when the bellows are puffing. Now Raaff never does this—in fact, he cannot bear it. Yet, so far as real cantabile is concerned, I prefer Meisner to Raaff (though not quite unconditionally, for he too has his mannerisms). In bravura singing, long passages and roulades, Raaff is absolute master and he has moreover an excellent, clear diction, which is very beautiful; and as I have already said, his andantinos or little canzonette are charming. He has composed four German songs, which are perfectly lovely. He likes me very much and we are very intimate. He comes almost every day to see us. I have lunched at least six times with Count Sickingen, Minister of the Palatinate—where people always stay from one to ten in the evening. But the time flies so quickly in his company that you simply don't notice it. He is very fond of me and I like being with him; he is such a friendly sensible person with such excellent judgment and he has a real insight into music. I was there again today with Raaff. I took some of my own compositions, as the Count had asked me long ago to do so. I brought along the new sym-phony [1] which I have just finished and with which the Concert Spirituel will open at Corpus Christi. They both liked it very much and I too am quite pleased with it. But I cannot say whether it will be popular—and, to

---

[1] K. 297 [300a].

tell the truth, I care very little, for who will not like it? I can answer for its pleasing the few intelligent French people who may be there—and as for the stupid ones, I shall not consider it a great misfortune if they are not pleased. I still hope, however, that even asses will find something in it to admire—and, moreover, I have been careful not to neglect *le premier coup d'archet* [1]—and that is quite sufficient. What a fuss the oxen here make of this trick! The devil take me if I can see any difference! They all begin together, just as they do in other places. It is really too much of a joke. Raaff told me a story of Abaco's [2] about this. He was asked by a Frenchman at Munich or somewhere—'Monsieur, vous avez été à Paris?' 'Oui.' 'Est-ce que vous étiez au Concert Spirituel?' 'Oui.' 'Que dites-vous du premier coup d'archet? Avez-vous entendu le premier coup d'archet?' 'Oui, j'ai entendu le premier et le dernier.' 'Comment, le dernier? Que veut dire cela?' 'Mais oui, le premier et le dernier—et le dernier même m'a donné plus de plaisir.' Now I must close. Please give my greetings to all my good friends, and particularly to Herr Bullinger. I kiss your hands a thousand times and embrace my sister with all my heart and remain your most obedient son

WOLFGANG AMADÈ MOZART

(310) *Leopold Mozart to his Wife and Son*

[Extract]   [Autograph in the Mozarteum, Salzburg]

MY DEAR WIFE, MY DEAR SON!   SALZBURG, 29 *June* 1778

We trust that you are well. We are both in excellent health! You will have received my letter of June 11th. On Holy Trinity Sunday I lunched, as usual, at the priests' house. In the afternoon Haydn played the organ during the Litany and the Te Deum, the Archbishop being present, and he played so abominably that we were all terrified and thought he was going the way of Adlgasser of pious memory. [3] But it was only a slight tipsiness, which made his head and his hands refuse to agree. Since Adlgasser's accident I have never heard anything like it. After the Litany Count Starhemberg asked me to go and see him on the morrow, saying that there was something which he would like to discuss with me. I went and found no one there but his brother, a Major in the Imperial Army, who is living with him here and is trying to cure himself in Salzburg of his fear of Prussian powder and lead. He told me that an organist had been recommended to him, but that he didn't want to take up the matter without first knowing whether he was any good. He wanted therefore to find

---

[1] The opening of a symphony with a powerful *tutti* passage, generally in unison.

[2] Giuseppe Clemens Ferdinand Dall' Abaco (1710–1805) of Verona. In 1738 he became director of music to the Elector of Bonn. He composed some music, chiefly for the violoncello.

[3] Adlgasser, while playing the organ in the cathedral, had had a fatal stroke.

out from me whether I knew him. He said that his name was Mandl or something—but that he was not quite sure. I thought to myself: '*Oh—you clumsy rascal!* Someone in Vienna has been commissioned or requested to recommend an organist and has forgotten to send the name of the candidate.' I was not supposed to notice, of course, that his opening was to induce me to talk about my son. And what did I say? Not a syllable! I said—that I hadn't the honour of knowing the candidate and that in any case I should never dare to recommend anyone to the Prince, as it was always difficult to find a person who would be sure to suit him permanently. 'Yes,' he said, 'I too should not recommend anyone. It is far too difficult! Your son ought to be here!' I thought to myself: 'Bravo! I've caught you out. *What a pity this man is not a great statesman or ambassador!*' I then said: '*Do let us talk quite frankly*'. I asked him whether people had not done everything in their power to drive you out of Salzburg? I went back to the beginning and omitted nothing and I told him everything that had happened, so that his brother was absolutely amazed and he himself could not but admit that it was the plain truth. We then began to talk about all sorts of things connected with the Court music. I explained everything most frankly and he agreed that what I said was perfectly true. Finally he turned to his brother and observed that there was nothing which strangers who had come to the Salzburg Court *had admired so much as young Mozart's performances*. He tried to persuade me to send the proposal to my son. But I told him that I really couldn't do it, for it would be a waste of effort, as my son would laugh at such an offer. It would only be possible if I could mention at the same time the salary he would have, for I could not hope for a reply if it were a case of Adlgasser's salary, and that even if His Grace decided to give him fifty gulden a month, it was extremely doubtful whether he would accept it. We all three left his house together—for they were going off to the riding-school and I walked along with them. We continued to talk on the same subject, *I for my part holding firmly to what I had said already, while he maintained that he was only interested in my son*. We remarked that Haydn's wife [1] would soon be giving up—that Meisner had done so already—that Haydn would drink himself into dropsy in a few years, or, at any rate, as he is now too lazy for anything, would go on getting lazier and lazier. Finally I pointed out once again that I could not say anything to you—without knowing whether I could mention the likelihood of a decent salary, and with this I let him go off! Well, I must tell you that the Prince is not going to get a good organist who is also a first-rate clavierist and that he is now saying (but only to his favourites) that Beecke is a quack and a joker, and that Mozart far surpasses them all, and that he himself would much prefer to

[1] Maria Magdalena, daughter of the second cathedral organist, Franz Ignaz Lipp, and an excellent soprano.

have someone whose ability he knows about rather than pay a large salary to someone of whom he has had no experience. If the Prince wants to offer a smaller salary, he cannot promise anyone an income from giving lessons, for there are very few pupils to be had. I have most of them already and besides I enjoy the reputation of being the best teacher. So there's the rub! But I am not writing all this, my dear Wolfgang, in order to persuade you to return to Salzburg—for I do not rely to the slightest degree on the words of the Archbishop. Further I have not said a word to the Countess [1] and I rather avoid any occasion of meeting her; for she might interpret my slightest word as obsequiousness and solicitation. They must come to me—and, before I agree to anything, the conditions they offer must be very favourable and advantageous—all of which is extremely unlikely. Well, we must wait and see. Don't say anything about this too soon except 'biting off your nose'.[2]   ★

As I was asked to do so, *I had your two Litanies De Venerabili*[3] *copied and sent to the Holy Cross Monastery in Augsburg, where they were performed with great success on May the 10th and 11th, when they have their great Procession there.* The good old Abbot sent me his thanks and reminded me on behalf of himself and of the whole monastery that if ever I should go to Augsburg with my daughter we must stay with them. Soon afterwards, however, he fell ill and died.

I only received on the 26th your letter of June 12th. I trust that my last ★ one of the 11th has now reached you. Your whole letter deals with M. Raaff, who must be very charming and whom I should like to meet. *I am absolutely delighted that my dear son enjoys the respect and friendship of such a distinguished man, to whom I send my most humble greetings.* I am glad that ★ Wolfgang does not always wonder *whether life is worth living.* True indeed, one cannot always be in a good humour. But you say nothing more about *your pupil in composition*—nothing about *Noverre's ballet*—and nothing about *your opera.* I haven't heard whether Wendling is still in Paris? Whether Wolfgang has seen Baron Bagge? Whether Piccinni is still there? Whether Wolfgang has met the two Stamitzes?[4] Whether he has seen Grétry? Whether the players at the Concert Spirituel are any good, and what the performances are like? I should be delighted to hear something about all these matters; but you need not cover whole pages with them. ★ My dear son can easily imagine that it is a sort of torture for me to know that he has been composing a great deal—and that I, alas! cannot hear any of his compositions, which used formerly to give me the greatest pleasure. Patience is the counsel of a coward! Rust's Serenata (as you ask about it) was not a success. It was just the same old ding-dong. Colloredo, the ★

---

[1] The Countess von Wallis. See p. 547, n. 1.
[2] 'Als das Nasenabbeisen', a Viennese idiom.
[3] K. 125, composed in 1772, and K. 243, composed in 1776.   [4] See p. 528, n. 1.

Archbishop of Olmütz, we all met at Podstatzky's[1] when we were in Vienna, for he was then canon of the cathedral. He is a rather stout, but handsome man, with a fat fresh-coloured face, a very fine-looking fellow! He is only a cousin of our Archbishop.

★   As soon as you described your whereabouts to me, I found the street in which you are living and where the air, I am glad to hear, is very good. After hearing how you are living I really do not know whether you would gain so much by changing, especially as you are with very kind people. I hope that Wolfgang's symphony[2] for the Concert Spirituel was a success. To judge by the Stamitz symphonies which have been engraved in Paris, the Parisians must be fond of noisy music. For these are nothing but noise. Apart from this they are a hodge-podge, with here and there a good idea, but introduced very awkwardly and in quite the wrong place. So Voltaire is dead too! and died just as he lived; he ought to have done something better for the sake of his reputation with posterity.[3]

★   Nannerl and I, together with Bimperl, kiss and lick you both, but not your arses, a million times, and I am, with all our congratulations ad primas vesperas,[4]

your old

MZT

Mme Duschek has sent me a letter of introduction to a certain virtuoso on the clarinet, M. Joseph Beer,[5] who is in the service of the Prince de Lambesc, Chief Equerry to the King of France. Tell me whether I am to send it to you. Try to see M. Beer.

(311) *Mozart to his Father*

[*Autograph in the Mozarteum, Salzburg*]

MONSIEUR   PARIS, 3 *July* 1778
     MON TRÉS CHER PÉRE!

I have very sad and distressing news to give you, which is, indeed, the reason why I have been unable to reply sooner to your letter of June 11th. My dear mother is very ill.[6] She has been bled, as in the past, and it was very necessary too. She felt quite well afterwards, but a few days later she complained of shivering and feverishness, accompanied by diarrhoea and headache. At first we only used home remedies—antispasmodic

---

[1] See p. 75, n. 6.   [2] K. 297 [300a].
[3] In Leopold Mozart's opinion Voltaire was an atheist.
[4] Frau Mozart's name-day was 26 July.
   [5] Joseph Beer (1744–1812), of Czech extraction, was a remarkable clarinet-player. He served as trumpeter in the French army during the Seven Years' War. In 1771 he settled in Paris, where he became a proficient player on the clarinet. On 4 March 1791, Beer gave a concert at Vienna, at which Mozart played his piano concerto in B flat, K. 595.
   [6] Mozart's mother had died at ten o'clock that night. He wrote this letter afterwards.

powders; we would gladly have tried the black powder too, but we had none and could not get it here, where it is not known even by the name of *pulvis epilepticus*. As she got worse and worse (she could hardly speak and had lost her hearing, so that one had to shout to make oneself understood), Baron Grimm sent us his doctor. But she is still very weak and is feverish and delirious. They give me hope—but I have not much. For a long time now I have been hovering day and night between hope and fear—but I have resigned myself wholly to the will of God—and trust that you and my dear sister will do the same. How else can we manage to be calm or, I should say, calmer, for we cannot be perfectly calm! Come what may, I am resigned—for I know that God, Who orders all things for our good, however strange they may seem to us, wills it thus. Moreover I believe (and no one will persuade me to the contrary) that no doctor, no man living, no misfortune and no chance can give a man his life or take it away. None can do so but God alone. These are only the instruments which He usually employs, though not always. For we see people around us swoon, fall down and die. Once our hour has come, all means are useless; they rather hasten death than delay it. This we saw in the case of our late friend Hefner. I do not mean to say that my mother will and must die, or that all hope is lost. She may recover health and strength, but only if God wills it. After praying to Him with all my might for health and life for my dear mother, I like to indulge in these consoling thoughts, because they hearten, soothe and comfort me; and you may easily imagine that I need comfort! Now let us turn to something else. Let us banish these sad thoughts; let us hope, but not too much; let us put our trust in God and console ourselves with the thought that all is well, if it is in accordance with the will of the Almighty, as He knows best what is profitable and beneficial to our temporal happiness and our eternal salvation.

I have had to compose a symphony [1] for the opening of the Concert Spirituel. It was performed on Corpus Christi day with great applause, and I hear, too, that there was a notice about it in the *Courier de L'Europe*, —so it has given great satisfaction. I was very nervous at the rehearsal, for never in my life have I heard a worse performance. You have no idea how they twice scraped and scrambled through it. I was really in a terrible way and would gladly have had it rehearsed again, but as there was so much else to rehearse, there was no time left. So I had to go to bed with an aching heart and in a discontented and angry frame of mind. I decided next morning not to go to the concert at all; but in the evening, the weather being fine, I at last made up my mind to go, determined that if my symphony went as badly as it did at the rehearsal, I would certainly make

---

[1] Mozart's symphony, K. 297 [300a], was performed on 18 June. The notice in the *Courier de l'Europe* appeared on the 26th.

my way into the orchestra, snatch the fiddle out of the hands of Lahoussaye,[1] the first violin, and conduct myself! I prayed God that it might go
well, for it is all to His greater honour and glory; and behold—the
symphony began. Raaff was standing beside me, and just in the middle of
the first Allegro there was a passage which I felt sure must please. The
audience were quite carried away—and there was a tremendous burst of
applause. But as I knew, when I wrote it, what effect it would surely
produce, I had introduced the passage again at the close—when there were
shouts of 'Da capo'. The Andante also found favour, but particularly the
last Allegro, because, having observed that all last as well as first Allegros
begin here with all the instruments playing together and generally unisono,
I began mine with two violins only, piano for the first eight bars—followed instantly by a forte; the audience, as I expected, said 'hush' at the
soft beginning, and when they heard the forte, began at once to clap their
hands. I was so happy that as soon as the symphony was over, I went off to
the Palais Royal, where I had a large ice, said the Rosary as I had vowed to
do—and went home—for I always am and always will be happiest there,
or else in the company of some good, true, honest German who, if he is a
bachelor, lives alone like a good Christian, or, if married, loves his wife
and brings up his children properly. Now I have a piece of news for you
which you may have heard already, namely, that that godless arch-rascal
Voltaire[2] has pegged out like a dog, like a beast! That is his reward! You
are quite right, we owe Theresa wages for five quarters. That I do not like
being here, you must long ago have noticed. I have very many reasons,
but, as I am here, it is useless to go into them. It is not my fault, however,
that I dislike Paris and it never shall be, for I will do my very best. Well,
God will make all things right! I have a project in my mind for the success
of which I daily pray to Him. If it is His divine will, it will succeed, and if
not, then I am content also—at least I shall have done my part. When all
this has been set going and if all turns out as I wish, you too must do your
part, or the whole work would be incomplete—I trust to your kindness
to do so. Only don't indulge in unnecessary conjectures now. I only
wanted to beg one favour of you beforehand, which is, not to ask me to
reveal my thoughts more clearly, until it is time to do so.

As for the opera, matters are as follows. It is very difficult to find a good
libretto. The old ones, which are the best, are not adapted to the modern
style and the new ones are all quite useless. For poetry, the only thing of
which the French have had reason to be proud, becomes worse every day

---

[1] Pierre Lahoussaye (1735–1818) had his early training as a violinist in Paris, toured in Italy
and may then have been leader at the Italian opera in London. In 1776 he returned to
Paris and became first violin at the Concert Spirituel, and later a professor at the Conservatoire.

[2] Voltaire died on 30 May 1778. No doubt Mozart had heard the infamous stories circulated at the time by Voltaire's Catholic opponents. See Desnoiresterres, *Voltaire et la société
française au dix-huitième siècle*, 2nd ed., 1876, vol. VIII, p. 370 f.

—and yet the poetry is the one thing which must be good here, for they do not understand music. There are now two operas in aria which I might compose. One en deux actes, and the other en trois. The one en deux is 'Alexandre et Roxane'—but the poet who is writing the libretto is still in the country; the one en trois is a translation of Demofoonte (by Metastasio) interlarded with choruses and dances and altogether adapted to the French stage.[1] Of this one too I have not yet been able to get a glimpse.

Write and tell me whether you have Schröter's[2] concertos in Salzburg —and Hüllmandel's[3] sonatas? If not, I should like to buy them and send them to you. Both works are very fine. As for Versailles, I never thought of going there. I asked Baron Grimm and some other good friends for their advice and they all thought as I did. The salary is small and I should have to pine for six months of the year in a place where nothing else can be earned and where my talent would be buried. Whoever enters the King's service, is forgotten in Paris—and then, to be an organist! I should very much like a good appointment, but it must be a Kapellmeister's and a well-paid one too. Now, farewell. Take care of your health; put your trust in God—it is there you will find consolation. My dear mother is in the hands of the Almighty. If He still spares her, as I hope He will, we shall thank Him for this blessing. But if it is His will to take her to Himself, all our fears and sorrows and all our despair can be of no avail. Let us rather resign ourselves with fortitude to His divine will, fully convinced that it will be for our good—for He does nothing without a cause. Farewell, then, dearest Papa, take care of your health for my sake. I kiss your hands a thousand times and embrace my sister with all my heart and remain your most obedient son

WOLFGANG AMADÈ MOZART

(312) *Mozart to the Abbé Bullinger, Salzburg*

[Autograph formerly in the Mozarteum, Salzburg]

MOST BELOVED FRIEND! PARIS, 3 *July* 1778
For you alone.

Mourn with me, my friend! This has been the saddest day of my life— I am writing this at two o'clock in the morning.[4] I have to tell you that

---

[1] Mozart did not compose this opera, but both Cherubini in 1788 and Johann Christoph Vogel in 1789 wrote a *Démophon.*

[2] Johann Samuel Schröter (1752–1788), a brother of the famous singer, Corona Schröter, became a well-known clavier-player and composer. He came to London in 1772 and remained in England until his death. The work to which Mozart refers is *Six concertos for the harpsichord with an accompaniment for two violins and bass, Op. 3,* which were published in London about 1774. Mozart wrote cadenzas for three of these concertos. See Köchel, p. 734, 735.

[3] Nikolaus Joseph Hüllmandel (1751–1823), born at Strassburg, was trained by C. P. E. Bach. He came to London in 1771, and after spending some time in France, settled in England as clavier-player and teacher. He composed a large number of sonatas for the harpsichord with and without violin accompaniment. [4] 4 July.

my mother, my dear mother, is no more! God has called her to Himself. It was His will to take her, that I saw clearly—so I resigned myself to His will. He gave her to me, so He was able to take her away from me. Only think of all my anxiety, the fears and sorrows I have had to endure for the last fortnight. She was quite unconscious at the time of her death—her life flickered out like a candle. Three days before her death she made her confession, partook of the Sacrament and received Extreme Unction. During the last three days, however, she was constantly delirious, and today at twenty-one minutes past five the death agony began and she at once lost all sensation and consciousness. I pressed her hand and spoke to her—but she did not see me, she did not hear me, and all feeling was gone. She lay thus until she expired five hours later at twenty-one minutes past ten. No one was present but myself, Herr Heina (a kind friend whom my father knows) and the nurse. It is quite impossible for me to describe today the whole course of her illness, but I am firmly convinced that she was bound to die and that God had so ordained it. All I ask of you at present is to act the part of a true friend, by preparing my poor father very gently for this sad news. I have written to him by this post, but only to say that she is seriously ill; and now I shall wait for his answer and be guided by it. May God give him strength and courage! O my friend! Not only am I now comforted, but I have been comforted for some time. By the mercy of God I have borne it all with fortitude and composure. When her illness became dangerous, I prayed to God for two things only—a happy death for her, and strength and courage for myself; and God in His goodness heard my prayer and gave me those two blessings in the richest measure. I beg you, therefore, most beloved friend, watch over my father for me and try to give him courage so that, when he hears the worst, he may not take it too hardly. I commend my sister to you also with all my heart. Go to them both at once, I implore you—but do not tell them yet that she is dead—just prepare them for it. Do what you think best—use every means to comfort them—but so act that my mind may be relieved—and that I may not have to dread another blow. Watch over my dear father and my dear sister for me. Send me a reply at once, I entreat you. Adieu. I remain your most obedient and grateful servant

WOLFGANG AMADÈ MOZART

As a precaution I send you my address:
    rue du gros chenet,
        vis à vis celle du croissant
            à l'Hôtel des quatre fils aimont.

(313) *Mozart to his Father*

[*Autograph in the Mozarteum, Salzburg*]

MONSIEUR MON TRÉS CHER PÉRE!   PARIS, 9 *July* 1778

I hope that you are now prepared to hear with fortitude one of the saddest and most painful stories; indeed my last letter of the 3rd will have told you that no good news could be hoped for. On that very same day, the 3rd, at twenty-one minutes past ten at night my mother fell asleep peacefully in the Lord; indeed, when I wrote to you, she was already enjoying the blessings of Heaven—for all was then over. I wrote to you during that night and I hope that you and my dear sister will forgive me for this slight but very necessary deception; for as I judged from my own grief and sorrow what yours would be, I could not indeed bring myself suddenly to shock you with this dreadful news! But I hope that you have now summoned up courage to hear the worst, and that after you have at first given way to natural, and only too well justified tears and anguish, you will eventually resign yourself to the will of God and worship His unsearchable, unfathomable and all-wise providence. You will easily conceive what I have had to bear—what courage and fortitude I have needed to endure calmly as things grew gradually and steadily worse. And yet God in His goodness gave me grace to do so. I have, indeed, suffered and wept enough—but what did it avail? So I have tried to console myself: and please do so too, my dear father, my dear sister! Weep, weep your fill, but take comfort at last. Remember that Almighty God willed it thus—and how can we rebel against Him? Let us rather pray to Him, and thank Him for His goodness, for she died a very happy death. In those distressing moments, there were three things that consoled me—my entire and steadfast submission to the will of God, and the sight of her very easy and beautiful death which made me feel that in a moment she had become so happy; for how much happier is she now than we are! Indeed I wished at that moment to depart with her. From this wish and longing proceeded finally my third source of consolation—the thought that she is not lost to us for ever—that we shall see her again—that we shall live together far more happily and blissfully than ever in this world. We do not yet know when it will be—but that does not disturb me; when God wills it, I am ready. Well, His heavenly and most holy will has been fulfilled. Let us therefore say a devout Paternoster for her soul and turn our thoughts to other matters, for all things have their appropriate time. I am writing this in the house of Madame d'Épinay and M. Grimm, with whom I am now living. I have a pretty little room with a very pleasant view and, so far as my condition permits, I am happy. It will be a great help to restoring my tranquillity to hear that my dear father and sister are

submitting wholly and with calmness and fortitude to the will of God—
are trusting Him with their whole heart in the firm belief that He orders
all things for the best. My dearest father! Do not give way! Dearest sister!
Be firm! You do not yet know your brother's good heart—for he has not
yet been able to prove it. My two loved ones! Take care of your health.
Remember that you have a son, a brother, who is doing his utmost to
make you happy—knowing well that one day you will not refuse to
grant him his desire and his happiness—which certainly does him honour,
and that you also will do everything in your power to make him happy.
Oh, then we shall live together as peacefully, honourably and contentedly
as is possible in this world—and in the end, when God wills it, we shall
all meet again in Heaven—for which purpose we were destined and
created.

I have received your last letter of the 29th and see with pleasure that you
are both, thank God, in good health. I had to laugh heartily about Haydn's
tipsy fit. If I had been there, I should certainly have whispered in his ear
'*Adlgasser!*' It is really disgraceful that such an able man should through
his own fault render himself incapable of performing his duties—at a
service instituted in honour of God—in the presence of the Archbishop
too and the whole Court—and with the church full of people. How
disgusting! That is one of my chief reasons for detesting Salzburg—those
coarse, slovenly, dissolute court musicians. Why, no honest man, of good
breeding, could possibly live with them! Indeed, instead of wanting to
associate with them, he would feel ashamed of them. It is probably for
this very reason that musicians are neither popular nor respected among
us. Ah, if only the orchestra were organized as they are at Mannheim.
Indeed I would like you to see the discipline which prevails there and the
authority which Cannabich wields. There everything is done seriously.
Cannabich, who is the best conductor I have ever seen, is both beloved
and feared by his subordinates. Moreover he is respected by the whole
town and so are his soldiers. But certainly they behave quite differently
from ours. They have good manners, are well dressed and do not go to
public houses and swill.[1] This can never be the case in Salzburg, unless the
Prince will trust you or me and give us full authority *as far as the music is
concerned*—otherwise it's no good. In Salzburg everyone—or rather no
one—bothers about the music. If I were to undertake it, I should have to
have complete freedom of action. The Chief Steward should have nothing
to say to me in musical matters, or on any point relating to music. For a
courtier can't do the work of a Kapellmeister, but a Kapellmeister can well
be a courtier. A propos, the Elector is back in Mannheim. Madame Cannabich and her husband too correspond with me. If what I dread does not

[1] During the Mozarts' first visit to Mannheim in 1763 Leopold Mozart expressed the same
appreciation of the Mannheim orchestra. Cp. p. 25.

happen—and it would be a thousand pities if it did—if, I mean, the orchestra is not to be considerably reduced—I still cherish some hope. You know that there is nothing I desire more than a good appointment, good in its standing and good in money—no matter where—provided it be in a Catholic country. You acted most skilfully, indeed like Ulysses, throughout the whole affair with Count Starnbock;[1] only continue as you have begun and do not allow yourself to be hoodwinked—and be especially on your guard, should you by any chance have to talk to that crested goose.[2] I know her, and, believe me, she has pepper in her head and heart, even though she has sugar and honey in her mug. It is quite natural ⟨that the whole affair should still be in an unsettled state, and many points must be conceded before I could accept the offer; while, even if they were, I should still prefer to be anywhere than in Salzburg.⟩ But I need not worry, for it is ⟨highly improbable that all I ask will be granted, as I am asking a great deal.⟩ Yet nothing is impossible; and ⟨if everything were properly organized, I should no longer hesitate⟩—if only to have the happiness ⟨of being with you. If the people of Salzburg want to have me, then they must fall in with all my wishes—or they will certainly never get me.⟩ So the Abbot of Baumburg has died the usual abbot's death! I had not heard that the Abbot of the Holy Cross Monastery was also dead. I am very sorry to hear it. He was a good, honest fellow. So you did not think that Dean Zeschinger would be made abbot? Upon my honour I never imagined anything else; indeed, I do not know who else could have got it; and for music what better abbot could they have? So the young lady's daily walk with her faithful lacquey did lead to something after all? They lost no time indeed and have not been idle. Idleness is the mother of all vices. So amateur theatricals have been started? How long will they last, I wonder?[3] Countess Lodron, I daresay, will never again ask for such concerts. Why, Czernin is but a young puppy and Brunetti a thoroughly ill-bred fellow. My friend Raaff is leaving here tomorrow. He is going via Brussels to Aix-la-Chapelle and Spa—and thence to Mannheim, when he is immediately to inform me of his arrival, for we mean to correspond. He sends his greetings to you and my sister, although he does not know you. You say that you have heard nothing more for a long time about my pupil in composition; that is so, but what am I to say about her? She will never be a composer—all my trouble is in vain, for she is not only thoroughly stupid, but also thoroughly lazy. In my last letter I replied about the opera. As for Noverre's ballet, all that I ever told you was that he might perhaps design a new one. He only needed half a ballet and for this I composed the music. Six pieces in it are composed by others and are

[1] Count Josef Starhemberg, canon of Salzburg cathedral. See p. 553.
[2] The Countess von Wallis. See p. 547, n. 1.
[3] These comments refer to passages in his father's letter of 29 June, which for lack of space have had to be omitted.

made up entirely of wretched old French airs, while the overture and contredanses, about twelve pieces in all, have been contributed by me.[1] This ballet has already been performed four times[2] with the greatest applause. But I am now determined not to compose anything more, unless I know beforehand what I am going to get for it; for what I did was only an act of friendship to Noverre. Herr Wendling left Paris on the last day of May. If I were to see Baron Bagge, I should have to have very good eyes, for he is not here, but in London. Is it possible that I have not told you this already? You will find that in future I shall answer all your letters very accurately. It is said that Baron Bagge will soon return. I should be glad of that—for many reasons—but especially because his house will always afford an opportunity of trying over some really good music. Kapellmeister[3] Bach too will be here soon. I believe he is going to compose an opera. The French are and always will be asses, and as they can do nothing themselves, they are obliged to have recourse to foreigners. I spoke to Piccinni at the Concert Spirituel. He is most polite to me and I to him when—by chance—we do meet. Otherwise I do not seek acquaintanceship, either with him or with any other composer. I understand my job—and so do they—and that is enough. I told you already that my symphony at the Concert Spirituel was a tremendous success. If I am commissioned to compose an opera, I shall have annoyance in plenty, but that I shall not mind very much, for I am pretty well inured to it; if only that confounded French tongue were not so detestable for music. It really is hopeless; even German is divine in comparison. And then the men and women singers! Indeed they hardly deserve the name, for they don't sing —they yell—howl—and that too with all their might, through their noses and throats. For next Lent I have to compose a French oratorio[4] which is to be performed at the Concert Spirituel. Monsieur le Gros, the Director, is amazingly taken with me. You must know that, although I used to be with him every day, I have not been near him since Easter; I felt so indignant at his not having performed my sinfonia concertante. I often went to the same house to visit Monsieur Raaff and each time I had to pass his rooms. His servants and maids often saw me and I always sent him my compliments. It is really a pity that he did not perform it, as it would have made a great hit—but now he no longer has an opportunity of doing so, for where could four such players be found to perform it? One day, when

---

[1] K. App. 10 [K. 299b]. Mozart wrote the music for the ballet *Les petits riens* which was introduced into Piccinni's opera *Le finte gemelle*, performed on 11 June 1778. Noverre, the designer of the ballet, was quoted as the composer. The autograph was found by Victor Wilder in 1872 in the Library of the Paris Opéra. See Köchel, p. 314.

[2] It was performed six times during June and July.

[3] Johann Christian Bach. His opera *Amadis de Gaule* was produced in Paris on 14 December 1779.

[4] There is no trace of this work. Probably this plan, like those for two French operas, was never carried out.

I went to call on Raaff, I was told that he was out but would certainly be home very soon and I therefore waited. M. Le Gros came into the room and said: 'It is really quite wonderful to have the pleasure of seeing you again'. 'Yes, I have a great deal to do.' 'I hope you will stay to lunch with us today?' 'I am very sorry but I am already engaged.' 'M. Mozart, we really must spend a day together again soon.' 'That will give me much pleasure.' A long pause; at length, 'A propos. Will you not write a grand symphony for me for Corpus Christi?' 'Why not?' 'Can I then rely on this?' 'Oh yes, if I may rely with certainty on its being performed, and that it will not have the same fate as my sinfonia concertante.' Then the dance began. He excused himself as well as he could but did not find much to say. In short, the symphony was highly approved of—and Le Gros is so pleased with it that he says it is his very best symphony. But the Andante has not had the good fortune to win his approval; he declares that it has too many modulations and that it is too long. He derives this opinion, however, from the fact that the audience forgot to clap their hands as loudly and to shout as much as they did at the end of the first and last movements. For indeed the Andante is a great favourite with myself and with all connoisseurs, lovers of music and the majority of those who have heard it. It is just the reverse of what Le Gros says—for it is quite simple and short. But in order to satisfy him (and, as he maintains, some others) I have composed a fresh Andante—each is good in its own way—for each has a different character. But the last pleases me even more.[1] On the first possible occasion I shall send you this symphony and also the 'Violinschule',[2] some pieces for the clavier, and Vogler's book *Tonwissenschaft und Tonsezkunst*;[3] I shall then want to hear what you think of them. On August 15th, the Feast of the Assumption, my symphony with the new Andante is to be performed for the second time. The symphony is in Re, and the Andante in Sol, for here you must not say D or G. Le Gros is now heart and soul for me. Well, it is time for me to think of closing this letter. When you write, perhaps it would be better to address your letter: *Chez M. le Baron de Grimm, Chaussée d'Antin, près le Boulevard.* M. Grimm is writing to you very soon. He and Madame d'Épinay send their greetings to you both as well as their heartfelt condolences. They feel sure, however, that you will be able to face calmly an event which cannot be altered. Take comfort and pray without ceasing—that is the only resource which is left to us. Oh yes! I wanted to ask you to have Holy Masses said at Maria-Plain and Loreto. I have made arrangements here. As for the letter of recommendation

---

[1] The autograph score of the Paris symphony, K. 297 [300a] contain as 6/8 Andantino, preceded by an unfinished version which Mozart cancelled. The first edition, printed by Sieber, in parts, in 1779, has a different movement in 3/4 marked Andante which is now rarely heard. See A. Tyson, *The Musical Times*, cxxii (1981), p. 17 ff.

[2] The French translation of Leopold Mozart's *Violinschule*. See p. 544, n. 1.

[3] See p. 442, n. 1.

to Herr Beer.[1] I don't think it is necessary to send it to me; so far I have not made his acquaintance; I only know that he is an excellent clarinet player, but in other respects a dissolute sort of fellow. I really do not like to associate with such people, as it does one no credit; and, frankly, I should not like to give him a letter of recommendation—indeed I should feel positively ashamed to do so—even if he could do something for me! But, as it is, he is by no means respected here—and a great many people do not know him at all. Of the two Stamitz brothers only the younger one is here, the elder (the real composer à la Hafeneder) is in London.[2] They indeed are two wretched scribblers, gamblers, swillers and adulterers—not the kind of people for me. The one who is here has scarcely a decent coat to his back. A propos, if by any chance Brunetti were to be dismissed, I should very much like to recommend a good friend of mine to the Archbishop as first violin; he is a most worthy fellow, and very steady. I should take him to be forty, and he is a widower. Rothfischer[3] is his name. He is Konzertmeister at Kirchheim-Bolanden in the service of the Princess of Nassau-Weilburg. Between ourselves, he is dissatisfied—for the Prince does not like him, or rather, does not like *his* music. He has urged me most earnestly to do something for him—and indeed it would give me real pleasure to help him. For he is one of the best fellows. Adieu. I kiss your hands 100000 times and embrace my sister with all my heart and remain your most obedient son

WOLFGANG AMADÈ MOZART

(314) *Leopold Mozart to his Wife and Son*

[Extract]   [Autograph in the Mozarteum, Salzburg]

MY DEAR WIFE AND MY DEAR SON!   SALZBURG, 13 *July* 1778

I am writing today so that my letter may reach you a few days before my dear wife's name-day.[4] I wish her millions of happinesses and congratulate her on being able to celebrate it once more, and I pray to Almighty God that He may send her many happy returns with good health and as much good fortune as is possible on this changeable stage of the world. I am absolutely convinced that if she is to be really happy she must have her husband and her daughter. God in His unsearchable wisdom and His most holy providence will order all things for our good. Would you have thought a year ago that you would be spending your next name-day in Paris? However incredible this would then have seemed to many, though indeed not to ourselves, it is just as possible that before we expect it,

---

[1] See p. 556, n. 5.   [2] See p. 535, n. 1.
[3] Paul Rothfischer. See p. 460, n. 1.   [4] 26 July.

we may all with God's help be reunited; for it is only this separation which gnaws at my heart, I mean, to be separated from you, *and to be living so very far off*. Otherwise, thank God, we are well. We both kiss you and Wolfgang millions of times and implore you to take the very greatest care of your health.

I wrote the above yesterday, July 12th, and today, the 13th, this very moment, shortly before ten o'clock in the morning, I have received your distressing letter of July 3rd. You can imagine what we are both feeling like. We wept so bitterly that we could scarcely read the letter—and your sister! Great God in Thy mercy! Thy most holy will be done! My dear son! Though I am resigning myself as far as possible to the will of God, you will surely find it quite human and natural that my tears almost prevent me from writing. And after all, what conclusion am I to draw? Why none other than this, that this very moment as I write, she is probably gone—or that she has recovered, for you wrote to me on the 3rd, and today is the 13th. You say that after the blood-letting she felt quite well, but that a few days later she complained of shivering and feverishness. The last letter from both of you was dated June 12th and in it your mother said: '*I was bled yesterday*'. So that was on the 11th—and why was it done on a Saturday?—on a fast day? Well, I assume that she had eaten some meat. She waited far too long to be bled. Knowing her as I do, I am aware that she likes to postpone everything from one day to the next, and especially in a strange place, where she would have first to make enquiries about a surgeon. Well, it has been done—and there is no help for it now. I have complete confidence in your filial love, and know that you have taken all possible care of your *devoted* mother, and if God still spares her, you will always do so; for she is a *good* mother and *you were the apple of her eye*. She was immensely attached to you, she was inordinately proud of you and (I know this better than you do) was absolutely bound up in your welfare. But if all our hopes are vain! If we have lost her!—Great God! *Then, indeed, you do need friends, honest friends!* Otherwise you will be ruined as far as your possessions are concerned—what with the funeral expenses, and so forth. Great Heavens! There are innumerable expenses about which you know absolutely nothing. People deceive, overcharge, delude a stranger, lure him into unnecessary extravagance and, if he has no honest friends, squeeze him dry. You can have no conception of it. If this misfortune has befallen you, ask Baron Grimm to let you bring all your mother's effects to him to keep, so that you may not have so many things to look after; or else lock up everything carefully, for, since for whole days at a time you are not at home, people might easily break into your room and rob you. God grant that all my precaution is unnecessary; but here you will recognize your father. My dear wife! my dear son! As she fell ill a few days after the blood-letting, she must have been suffering

since June 16th or 17th. Surely you waited too long. She hoped to cure herself by resting in bed—by dieting—by treating herself. I know how it is.
★ One hopes and postpones from day to day. Almighty God! We are in Thy hands.

I congratulate you on having got through the Concert Spirituel so successfully with your symphony. I can imagine your nervousness. Your determination to dash into the orchestra if the performance had not gone off well, was surely only a wild idea. God forbid! You must put all such fancies out of your head, for they are wholly injudicious. Such a step might cost you your life, which no man in his senses risks for a symphony. Such an insult—and, what is more, a public insult, not only a *Frenchman*, but everyone who values his honour would and ought to avenge, sword in hand. An Italian would say nothing; he would lie in wait for you at a
★ street corner and shoot you dead. I began this letter with my wishes—and Nannerl wanted to close it with hers. But, as you can imagine, she is incapable of writing a single word. For it is like this; when she tries to write —each stroke, each letter brings tears to her eyes. You, her dear brother, must take her place, if you can still do so, as we hope and trust you can. Alas, you cannot do so any longer! Your mother has passed away! You try too earnestly to console me. No one does that so zealously if he is not driven to do so by the loss of all human hope or by the event itself. I am now going to lunch, but indeed I have very little appetite.

I am writing this at half past three in the afternoon. I know now that my dear wife is in heaven. I write with tears in my eyes, but in complete submission to the will of God! As the church consecration took place at Holy Trinity yesterday, our usual shooting was postponed until today. I couldn't and didn't want to cancel it at such a late hour. We ate very little. Nannerl, who before lunch had wept copiously, had to vomit; she started a dreadful headache and afterwards lay down on her bed. Bullinger found us in the most distressing state, as did all the others. Without a word I gave him your letter to read; he acted his part very well and asked me what I thought. I replied that I was convinced that my dear wife had died already. He said that indeed he was inclined to think so himself; he urged me to take comfort, and being a true friend, he told me all that I had already *thought to myself.* I tried hard to be cheerful, and to resign myself to God's most holy will. We finished our shooting and all our friends went away feeling very sad. Bullinger stayed with me, and asked me quietly whether I thought that there was any hope for her in the condition which you had described. I replied that I was convinced not only that she was now dead but that she had died on the day you wrote to me, that I was submitting to the will of God and must remember that *I still had two children, who I hoped would continue to love me, seeing that I lived only for their sakes;* that I was so firmly persuaded that she was gone that I had even sent off a letter to you, reminding you and urging you to take care of her possessions and so forth. Whereupon he said: '*Yes, she is dead*'. As he said this, the scales fell from my eyes. So you had doubtless written the truth to Bullinger at the same time as I was reading your letter to me, which had really stunned me. At first I was too dejected to be able to collect my thoughts; and even now I do not know what to say. You may be quite easy in your mind about me; I shall play the man. But do not forget how tenderly loving was your mother—and you will only realize now how she cared for you—just as later on when I am gone you will love me more and more. If you love me, *as I do not doubt you do*, take care of your health. *On yours depends my life* and the future support of your excellent sister who loves you with all her heart. It is mysteriously sad when death severs a very happy marriage —you have to experience it before you can realize it. *Tell me everything in detail.* Perhaps she wasn't bled sufficiently? It is quite certain that she trusted too much to her strength and called in the doctor much too late. In the meantime the internal inflammation must have gained the upper hand. *Take care of your health!* If you do not, you will make us all unhappy! Nannerl doesn't know yet about Bullinger's letter. But I have prepared her so that she now suspects that her most beloved mother is dead. Write to me soon—tell me everything—what day she was buried—where? Great God! To think that I shall have to go to Paris to see her grave![1] We both embrace you with all our heart. I must close. The post is going.

Your honest and grievously distressed father

MOZART

Make sure that none of your possessions are lost.

(315) *Mozart to his Father*

[*Autograph in the Mozarteum, Salzburg*]

MONSIEUR MON TRÉS CHER PÉRE! PARIS, 18 *July* 1778

I hope you have safely received my last two letters. We will not talk any more about their chief contents. It is all over now; and were we to cover whole pages, we couldn't alter it! The principal object of this letter is to congratulate my dear sister on her name-day. But first of all, I must have a little chat with you. A fine style this, isn't it? But, patience—I am not in the mood today to write more elegantly. You will have to be satisfied if you succeed in more or less understanding what I am trying to say. I think I told you already that M. Raaff had left Paris; but that he is my true and very special friend, on whose friendship I can absolutely

---

[1] Frau Mozart was buried in the cemetery of St.-Eustache. For her death certificate see Abert, vol. ii., p. 905, and *MDB*, p. 176.

rely, this I can't possibly have told you, for I myself didn't know that his affection for me was so deep. Now, to tell a tale properly, one ought to roll it off from the beginning. You must know, therefore, that Raaff lodged with M. Le Gros. Why, that reminds me, you do know this already! [1] But what am I to do? It's written, and I simply can't begin this letter over again; so let's get on. When he arrived we all happened to be at table. This, too, has nothing to do with the case; it is only to let you know that in Paris too we sit down to table as we do elsewhere; and, after all, the midday meal at Le Gros's is much more relevant to my tale of friendship than the coffee-houses and drummers to a description of a musical journey. [2] When I went there the following day there was a letter for me from Herr Weber, which Raaff had brought. Now if I wished to deserve the name of historian, I ought to insert here the contents of this letter; and I may say that I am very reluctant to keep them back. But I must not be too long-winded. Brevity is most admirable, as you can see by my letter! The third day I found Raaff at home and thanked him; for, to be sure, it's a good thing to be polite! I have forgotten what we talked about. That historian must be a very clumsy fellow who cannot forthwith supply some falsehood—I mean, romance a bit. Well, we chatted about—the fine weather; and when we had talked ourselves out, we were silent—and I went off. A few days later—I forget which day it was—anyhow, on some day of the week, I happened to be seated at the clavier—at the clavier, I say—and Ritter, our good wood-biter, was sitting beside me. Now, what is to be deduced from that? A great deal. Raaff had never heard me play at Mannheim, except at the concert, where the noise and uproar was so great that nothing could be heard—and he himself has such a miserable clavier that I could not have done myself justice on it. Here, however, at Le Gros's the chopping-board is good; and I saw Raaff sitting opposite me, quite lost in thought. So, as you may imagine, I preluded in the manner of Fischietti, [3] played off a galanterie sonata in the style and with the fire, spirit and precision of Haydn, [4] and then played fugues with all the skill of a Lipp, Hülber and Aman. [5] My fugal playing has won me everywhere the greatest reputation! Well, when I had finished playing (while Raaff kept on shouting 'Bravo' and showing by his expression his true and sincere delight) I dropped into conversation with Ritter and among other things said that I was not very happy here; and I added: 'The chief reason is, of course, the music. Besides, I can find no soulage-

---

[1] See p. 564.

[2] Possibly a reference to Charles Burney, whose musical travels, with their constant references to military band performances and occasional notes on taverns, had been translated into German in 1772–1773 by Ebeling and Bode (*Tagebuch einer musikalischen Reise*).

[3] Domenico Fischietti (*c.* 1725–*c.* 1810), born in Naples, was Kapellmeister in Dresden from 1765 until 1772, when he was appointed Kapellmeister in Salzburg, a post which he held until 1783. He composed a good deal of church music and some operas.

[4] Michael Haydn.   [5] This sentence is ironical.

ment here, no recreation, no pleasant and sociable intercourse with anyone, especially with women, for most of them are prostitutes and the few who are not, have no savoir vivre.' Ritter could not deny that I was right. Raaff then said with a smile: 'Yes, I can quite believe it—for Herr Mozart is only *partly* here—that is, when it comes to admiring all the Parisian beauties. One half of him is elsewhere—where I have just come from.' This of course gave rise to much laughing and joking. In the end Raaff became quite serious and said: 'But you are right and I cannot blame you. She deserves it, for she is a charming, pretty, honourable girl and has excellent manners; besides, she is clever and is really very talented.' This gave me an excellent opportunity to recommend to him with all my heart my beloved Mlle Weber; but it was really not necessary for me to say much, as he was already very much taken with her. He promised, as soon as he returned to Mannheim, to give her lessons and to take an interest in her. I ought, by rights, to insert something at this point, but I really must finish my tale of friendship; if there is still room, I may do so. Well, in my eyes Raaff was still only an everyday acquaintance and nothing more; but I often went to see him in his room and I began gradually to confide in him more and more. I told him my whole story about Mannheim and how I had been led by the nose, adding every time that perhaps I might still get an appointment there. He said neither yes nor no and, whenever I mentioned the matter, he always seemed to be more indifferent than interested. At last, however, I thought I noticed more cordiality in his manner, and indeed he often began to talk about my affair himself. I introduced him to M. Grimm and Madame d'Épinay. On one occasion he came and told me that he and I were to lunch on such and such a day with Count Sickingen, and added: 'The Count and I were talking together, and I said to him: "A propos, has Your Excellency heard our Herr Mozart?" "No, but I should very much like both to see and hear him, for people have been writing most astonishings things about him from Mannheim." "Well, when Your Excellency does hear him, you will realize that what has been written to you is not too much, but too little." "Is it possible?" "Yes, most certainly, Your Excellency." ' Well, this was the first time that I noticed that Raaff was really interested in me. Then we became more friendly, and one day I brought him back to my room; after that he often came of his own accord—and finally he came every day. The morning after his departure a handsome man came to my room with a picture and said, 'Monsieur, je viens de la part de ce monsieur'—and showed me a portrait of Raaff, an excellent likeness. Presently he began to talk German; and it turned out that he was a painter of the Elector's, whom Raaff had often mentioned to me, but to whose house he had always forgotten to take me; and his name—I believe you know him, for he must be the very person whom Mademoiselle Ursprünger of Mainz spoke of in her letter, as he says that he saw us all at the Ursprüngers [1]—his name is Kymli.[2] He is a most kind and amiable man, upright, honourable and a good Christian, the best proof of which is his friendship with Raaff. Now comes the main evidence that Raaff is fond of me and is really interested in me—inasmuch as he discloses his real intentions rather to those whom he can trust than to the person immediately concerned, since he is slow to promise anything unless he is sure of a happy issue. For that is what Kymli told me. Raaff had asked him to call on me and to show me his portrait. He was to come and see me very often, to assist me in every way, and to establish an intimate friendship with me. It seems that Raaff used to go to Kymli every morning and that he said repeatedly: 'I was at our Herr Mozart's again yesterday evening. He really is a devilishly clever little fellow—quite a phenomenon——' and that he never ceased praising me. He told Kymli all, my whole Mannheim story—everything in fact. So now you see, people who are high-principled, religious and well-conducted always like each other. Kymli says I may rest assured that I am in good hands. 'Raaff', he tells me, 'will certainly do his best for you; and he is a wise man, who will manage things cleverly; he won't say that you want it, but rather that the Mannheim people should do so. Moreover he is on very good terms with the Chief Equerry. Depend upon it, he'll never give in, so just let him go ahead.'

A propos, there is one thing more. Padre Martini's letter to Raaff, in which he praises me, must have gone astray; for Raaff has not heard from him for a long time, and in none of his previous letters was I ever mentioned. Possibly it is still lying in Mannheim, but this is unlikely, as I know for a positive fact that during his stay in Paris all his letters were forwarded to him regularly. Now since the Elector rightly thinks a lot of the Padre Maestro's opinion, I believe it would be a very good thing if you would be so kind as to ask him to send another letter about me to Raaff. It would surely be of use; and good Padre Martini would not hesitate to do me this kindness twice over, as he knows well that in so doing he might make my fortune. It is to be hoped that he will write in such a manner that Raaff can show the letter, if need be, to the Elector. Enough of this. I trust that all will turn out well, so that I may soon have the joy of embracing my dear father and my dear sister. Oh, how happily and contentedly we shall live together! With all my strength I pray to God to grant me this favour! Sometime, please God, things must take a different turn. Meanwhile in the fond hope that the day will come—and the sooner the better—when

---

[1] The Mozart family passed through Mainz in August 1763. Leopold Mozart's *Reiseaufzeichnungen*, p. 23, mentions the Ursprünger family. Franziska Ursprünger was the prima donna at Mainz.

[2] Franz Peter Joseph Kymli (*c.* 1748–*c.* 1813), a native of Mannheim. Helped by the Elector Karl Theodor he went to Paris in 1775 to study painting and on his return was appointed court painter at Mannheim. During the years 1779–1787 he exhibited his portraits and miniatures in Paris. Most of his works are to be found at Nuremberg, Stuttgart and Mannheim.

we shall all be happy, I intend, in God's name, to persevere in my life *here*, which is totally opposed to my genius, inclinations, knowledge and sympathies. Believe me, this is only too true. I am telling you nothing but the truth. If I were to give you all my reasons, I should write my fingers crooked, and it would do no good. For here I am and I must just do my best. God grant only that I may not impair my talents by staying here; but I hope that it won't last long enough for that. God grant it!

A propos, an ecclesiastic came to see me the other day. He used to be choir-master at St. Peter's in Salzburg, and knows you very well. His name is Lendorff. You will probably have forgotten him. He gives clavier lessons here—in Paris. By the way, you will soon shudder at the very mention of Paris, won't you? I strongly recommend him to the Archbishop as organist. He says he would be satisfied with 300 gulden.

Now farewell. Take care of your health. Keep up your good spirits. Just think that perhaps you will soon have the pleasure of tossing off a good glass of Rhine wine with your son—your truly happy son. Adieu. I kiss your hands a thousand times and embrace my dear sister with all my heart and remain as long as I breathe your most obedient son

WOLFGANG AMADÈ MOZART

All sorts of messages to my best friend Bullinger.

(315a) *Mozart to his Father*

[Autograph in the Library of the University of Prague]

[PARIS], 20 July [1778]

Please forgive me for being so late in sending my congratulations. But I wanted to present my sister with a little Preambulum.[1] The manner of playing it I leave to her own feeling. This is not the kind of Prelude which passes from one key into another, but only a sort of Capriccio, with which to test a clavier. My sonatas[2] will soon be engraved. Up to the present everyone has refused to give me what I asked for them, so in the end I shall have to give in and let them go for fifteen louis d'or. It is the best way too to make my name known here. As soon as they are ready, I shall send them to you by some carefully thought out means (and as economically as possible), together with your 'Violinschule',[3] Vogler's book on composition,[4] Hüllmandel's sonatas,[5] Schröter's concertos,[6] a few of my clavier sonatas,[7] the symphony I composed for the Concert Spirituel,[8] my

---

[1] Possibly K. 395 [300g]. See Saint-Foix, vol. iii. p. 98 f. But compare Köchel, pp. 323, 324.
[2] Mozart's violin sonatas, K. 301–306 [293a–c, 300c, 293d, 300l]. They were engraved by Sieber.   [3] See p. 544, n. 1.   [4] See p. 442, n. 1.   [5] See p. 559, n. 3.
[6] See p. 559, n. 2.   [7] These were previously thought to be K. 330–332 [300h, i, k], which however were not yet composed. Mozart is evidently referring to earlier sonatas, perhaps K. 309–311 [284b, 300d, 284c].   [8] K. 297 [300a].

sinfonia concertante,[1] two flute quartets[2] and my concerto for harp and flute.[3]

Well, what are you hearing about the war? For the last three days I have been dreadfully sad and depressed. True, it doesn't really concern me, but I am so sensitive, that I immediately feel interested in any matter. I hear that the ⟨Emperor⟩ has been defeated. First of all, it was reported that the ⟨King of Prussia⟩ had surprised ⟨him⟩, or rather that he had surprised the troops commanded by the ⟨Archduke Maximilian;⟩ that two thousand had fallen on the ⟨Austrian⟩ side; that fortunately the ⟨Emperor⟩ had come to his assistance with forty thousand men, but had been forced to retreat. Secondly, it was said that ⟨the King⟩ had attacked the ⟨Emperor⟩ and completely surrounded him and that if General ⟨Laudon⟩[4] had not come to his rescue with eighteen hundred cuirassiers, he would have been taken prisoner; that sixteen hundred cuirassiers had been killed and ⟨Laudon⟩ himself shot dead. But I have not seen this in any newspaper. Today, however, I was told that the ⟨Emperor⟩ had invaded Saxony with forty thousand men; but I don't know whether this is true. A nice scrawl this, isn't it? I haven't the patience to write a beautiful hand; and as long as you can read it, it'll do. A propos, I saw in the papers that in a skirmish between the Saxons and Croats a Saxon Captain of Grenadiers, Hopfgarten by name, had lost his life and was deeply mourned. Can this be our good, kind Baron Hopfgarten, whom we knew in Paris with Herr von Bose?[5] I should be very sorry if it were, although indeed I would much rather that he died such a glorious death, than a shameful one—in Paris in bed, for instance, as most young men do in this place. It is almost impossible to find anyone here who has not suffered two or three times—or is not suffering at the moment—from one of these nice diseases. Why, in Paris children are born with them. But this is no news to you. You know it already, but believe me, it is now worse than ever. Adieu.

NB.—I hope that you will be able to decipher the end of the prelude. As a precaution I am adding a short explanation. In the bass octave C, c, d, f, a, and b are kept down with the left hand, until the right hand comes in. The last two notes[6] in the bass are c, g and octave c and a crotchet f and a once accented E. You need not be very particular about the time. This is a peculiar kind of piece. It's the kind of thing that may be played as you feel inclined. Adieu.

Please congratulate Jungfer Mitzerl from me. Give my greetings to the whole company of marksmen. I should like to give that miserable flunkey twenty-five stripes on his back for not marrying our nice Katherl. Nothing

---

[1] See p. 522, n. 1.   [2] K. 285 and 285a.   [3] K. 299 [297c].
[4] Ernst Gideon, Baron von Laudon (1717–1790), who together with Daun retrieved Maria Theresia's losses in 1757 and restored the prestige of the Austrian Empire.
[5] See p. 42 f.   [6] Possibly Mozart means 'chords'.

is more shameful, in my opinion, than to make a fool of an honest girl—
or perhaps seduce her! But he hasn't done that, I hope! If I were her
father, I would soon put a stop to the whole affair.[1]

(315b) *Mozart to his Sister*

[*Autograph in the Mozarteum, Salzburg*]

DEAREST SISTER!   [PARIS, 20 *July* 1778]
    Your name-day has arrived! I know that you, like myself, do not
care about a lot of words and that you realize that not only today but
every day I wish you with all my heart all the happiness you desire—and
that too as sincerely as is to be expected from a true brother, who loves
his sister.
    I am sorry not to be able to send you a present of a musical composition,
such as I did a few years ago. But let us hope that the happy future is not
far off when a brother and sister, so united and affectionate, will be able
to talk to one another and tell one another all their most intimate thoughts
and feelings. Meanwhile farewell—and love me, as I do you. I embrace
you with all my heart, with all my soul, and ever remain your sincere—
your true brother
                                                    W. MOZART[2]

(316) *Leopold Mozart to his Son*

[*Extract*]   [*Autograph in the Mozarteum, Salzburg*]

MY DEAR SON!   SALZBURG, 20 *July* 1778
    I am very anxious about your health; and now I shall have to wait
until I get a letter from you, for no doubt you will not write until you
have received mine of the 13th. Herr Bullinger couldn't write to you that
day, as the post always goes at five o'clock. So I could only finish my
letter, which will have told you that he carried out his commission very
well. He is going to write to you some time soon. You should really have ★
written to me sooner; we are all very anxious on your account. The
sorrow and sympathy of the whole town I simply cannot describe. Your
dear departed mother was known everywhere from her childhood and
was loved by all, for she was friendly to everyone and never offended a
soul. Your sister cheers me up, but I now feel very anxious for you. You ★
see that I am sending you some *black powders*. God grant that they may
find you in good health. Write and tell me *how much you have had to pay*

---

[1] Mozart refers to a story in his father's letter of 29 June, which for lack of space has had
to be omitted.   [2] The postscript is on the cover.

★ *for them.* Where are you now? In the house of Baron de Grimm, I presume.
I trust that you have kept safely all your dear Mamma's *clothes and linen
—her watch—her ring and her other jewelry.* Later on you will have to pack
★ these carefully in some chest or box and send them home. You can then
put in Schröter's concertos (of which I know *only* one, in E♭) and Hüllmandel's sonatas (which I do not know at all) and also my 'Violinschule'
in French. If you can give us the pleasure of sending us some of your own
compositions ah, do so! For when will such a convenient opportunity
turn up again of sending us something? In that case we should prefer to
★ wait a little. We both kiss you and I am your honest father

                                                            MZT

(317) *Mozart to Fridolin Weber, Mannheim*

[*Autograph in the Goethe- und Schiller-Archiv, Weimar*[1]]

MONSIEUR MON TRÉS CHER ET PLUS CHER AMY!   PARIS, 29 *July* 1778
     I have this moment received your letter of July 15th, for which I had
been waiting with such longing and about which I had thought so much!
Basta! Well, your esteemed letter has restored my peace of mind—save
for its chief contents which made my blood boil—so that—but I will stop
—you know me, my friend—so you will understand all that I felt when I
read it through. I cannot omit to do so—I must reply at once, for I think
it is most necessary. Yet I must ask you whether you too received my
letter of June 29th? I sent you three—one after another—one dated the
27th, addressed to you direct—one of the 29th sent to Herr Heckmann,
and one of the 3rd to the same address.[2] Now to the point. Didn't I always
tell you that the Elector would make his residence in Munich? I have
heard already that Count Seeau has been appointed Intendant both for
Munich and Mannheim! Well, I have something really important to tell
you, which, however, I cannot possibly express in German. You will soon
find it out. Meanwhile I hope that, whether the Court moves to Munich
or remains in Mannheim, your salary will be increased and your daughter
will get a good one—so that you may pay off all your debts and may all
breathe a little more freely. Things must improve in time. If not, well then
—our present circumstances are so favourable that we can afford to be
patient, to wait for a suitable time, and then settle down *somewhere else*, in
better surroundings. My friend, if I had the money which many a man,
who does not earn it, squanders so disgracefully—how gladly would I
then help you! But unfortunately—he who can does not want to and he
who wants to cannot! Well, listen. I wanted to use my influence (and

---

[1] According to Blümml, p. 118, Friedrich Rochlitz, who had long been collecting material
for a biography of Mozart, presented Goethe with this and the following letters.
[2] There is no trace of these three letters.

perhaps not altogether in vain) to bring you and your daughter to Paris this winter. But the position is as follows: M. Le Gros, Director of the Concert Spirituel, to whom I have already spoken about my friend, your daughter, can't have her here this winter—because he has already engaged Madame Le Brun [1] for the season—and *at the moment* he is not in such a fortunate position as to be able to pay two such singers as they deserve (and I shall *not agree to any other arrangement*). So there is no money to be made here—but this plan will be quite practicable during the following winter. I only wanted to tell you that if you really can't endure it any longer—I say, not any longer—you can come to Paris. The journey, food, lodging, wood and light will cost you nothing. However, that is not enough. For allowing that you manage to get through the winter—as there are private concerts and I might perhaps arrange something for you at the Concert des Amateurs—what would you do in the summer? Indeed I am not nervous about the following winter, when you would certainly get an engagement for the Concert Spirituel. Basta, send me your views about this—I shall then undertake to do all I can. Most beloved friend! I am almost ashamed to make you such a proposal—which, even if you were to accept, would still be uncertain—and not so advantageous as you deserve and as I desire! But—just remember that my intention is good—the will is there. I would gladly help but—I look in every direction to see whether something cannot be arranged and whether it cannot be managed. Wait. I shall see. If what I now have in mind succeeds—but patience—we should never hurry up a thing too much—if so, it goes wrong or does not work out at all. In the meantime press as hard as you can to have your own salary raised and to get a good one for your daughter. Apply frequently in writing—and mind, if our heroine is to sing at Court —and meanwhile you have received no reply, or at least no favourable one to your application—then just don't let her sing—make the excuse of some slight indisposition—do it often—I beg you—and when you have often done so, then all of a sudden let her sing again—and you will see how effective that dodge will be. But you must do it with great subtlety and cunning. You must seem to be extremely sorry that Louisa [2] should be indisposed just when she has to perform. Of course, if you do this three or four times in succession, people will begin to see the joke! and that is just what I want—and when she does sing again, then, of course, you must make it quite clear that she is only doing it to oblige! She must still be slightly indisposed—she is only doing her best to please the Elector—you understand—and, at the same time, she must sing with great passion, with all her heart and soul; and meanwhile you must continue to make known to the world, both verbally and in writing, your complaints,

which are only too well justified; and if the Intendant perhaps (or someone else who you know gossips about it) enquires about your daughter's
health—tell him as a great secret that it's no wonder—the poor girl suffers
from hypochondria, a disease which can hardly be cured in Mannheim—
that she has devoted herself to singing with great zest and industry and
has really made progress—which nobody can deny—and that unfortunately she now realizes that all her trouble and hard work have been in
vain and that her eagerness and delight to be able to serve His Highness
the Elector have been frustrated—and that she would have lost all her love
of music too, have neglected herself and really given up singing—had you
not said to her: 'My daughter, your trouble and hard work have not been
in vain. If you are not rewarded here, people will reward you elsewhere—
and that too is what I intend. I cannot stand it any longer—I cannot any
longer let my child make such well-justified reproaches to me.' And then
—suppose he asks you, 'Where are you off to?'—tell him, 'I don't know
yet. Put that in your pipe and smoke it.' But only do this if you think that
all hope is lost—which I cannot possibly believe: because the Elector
really cannot keep her dangling any longer—for, when he sees that he
can't get anything out of your daughter, without tossing a salary at her,
he will just have to pay her—for he must have her—he really needs her.
After all, whom has he got at Mannheim? Franziska Danzi?[1] As sure as I'm
writing this, she won't stay. And in Munich? Why, there he will certainly
not find someone at once. For I know Munich in and out; I have been
there five times. So he must have her—he cannot let her go—and as for
you, your chief complaint must always be—your debts. But now, so that
you may not be made a fool of, if it should happen that nothing can be
done (which I truly hope will not be the case), you would do well to look
about in secret for something permanent, of course, at some court. Rest
assured that I too shall do all I can. My idea for yourself is that you should
apply privately to Mainz. Why, you were there quite recently. You will
at any rate know someone who can—who really can—do something.
But for God's sake don't mention that Seyler company[2] to me—I couldn't
bear to think that your daughter—or even if she were not your daughter
—even if she were only a foundling—I should be very sorry indeed that
she with her talent should fall among players—which would mean that
she is only good enough to be a stop-gap—for the main thing with the
Seylers, indeed with all theatrical companies, is always the play—the
singspiel is just put in to give occasional relief to the players now and then
—indeed, very often in order to give the actors time and room to change
—and generally as a diversion. You must always think of your reputation.

[1] Madame Le Brun. See p. 374, n. 3.
[2] One of the leading theatrical companies in Germany, who gave performances in Mainz,
Frankfurt and, from 1779 onwards, in Mannheim.

I at least always think of mine. Well, there you have my very candid opinion—perhaps you won't like it, but with my friends it is my custom to be sincere. Besides, you can do what you like—I shall never take the liberty of prescribing anything. I shall just advise you as a true friend. You see that I am not entêté that you should remain in Mannheim—I should be quite pleased if you were to go to Mainz—but provided it is with honour and reputation. By Heaven, my joy at going to Mainz would be considerably lessened if I should have to look up your daughter amongst the players—which might easily happen. It is not at all impossible, of course, between ourselves, that I may go to Mainz, I need hardly add, under contract. Only to you, my friend, do I tell my affairs, just as you tell me yours. One thing more. Could you, my friend, bear to have your daughter acting with players in that very same place where Mlle Hellmuth [1] (who cannot be compared with her) has an engagement at Court? —and would consequently take precedence of her? Dearest friend—let this be my last, my most drastic argument for preventing it. Well, I am going briefly to sum up all this. You seem to me (but you must not take this remark amiss) to get very easily depressed—you lose all your courage at a go—you give up hope too quickly—you cannot deny this, for I know your circumstances—they are distressing, it is true, but not at all as distressing as you think. I know how pained and hurt is an honest man when he is forced to run up debts—I know it from experience. But let us look at things in the right way—who is running up these debts? You? No— the Elector is.—If you were to leave today and stay away—and never pay your debts—you could not do anything which could more easily be justified,—and no one, not even the Elector himself, would say a word— but—you need not do this—you will certainly find yourself in a position —to be able to pay those debts. I advise you, therefore, to be patient until the winter after next—and meanwhile to do your best to improve your position in Mannheim—and at the same time to try to get another appointment. If either of these alternatives comes off, so much the better; if they do not, then come to Paris the winter after next. By that time I guarantee that you will be able to earn sixty louis d'or at least. At the same time Louisa will have improved in her singing and especially in her acting. In the meantime I shall look about for an opera for her in Italy. When she has sung in one opera there—then she will be launched. If in the meantime Madame Le Brun should come to Mannheim—both of you should make friends with her. For she might be useful to you for London. She is coming here this winter—and when she does, I shall immediately press

---

[1] Josepha Hellmuth, *née* Heist, a native of Munich, was a famous singer in her day. She was first a member of the Seyler theatrical company, but after her marriage to Friedrich Hellmuth, tenor and composer at Mainz, she had engagements at Weimar and Gotha and from 1778 onwards held an appointment as singer at the Elector's court at Mainz.

your case. Although, as I am sure you do not doubt, I should prefer to see
you here today—rather than tomorrow, yet as a true friend I must dissuade you from coming here—even this winter—in the way I suggested
(the only possible way at the moment). First of all, it would be a little
uncertain—and then it would not be good for your reputation to come
here without an engagement. Besides, it is not very pleasant to have to be
supported by someone else. But indeed, if I were in the fortunate position
of being able to entertain you absolutely free of charge, then you could
certainly come without the slightest fear that such a procedure would be
bad for your reputation—for I swear to you on my honour—that not a
soul should know it. Well, I have given my views, my opinions and my
advice. Do what you think best. But please do not imagine that I am
trying to prevent you from setting out on your travels and to persuade
you to stay in Mannheim or to get some engagement in Mainz, simply
because I have hopes of getting work in one of these places—I mean, in
order to have the pleasure of embracing you very soon. Not at all—it is
just because I am convinced that for many reasons it would be advisable
for you to wait a little longer. Indeed, most beloved friend, if I could
arrange for us to live together in the same place joyfully and happily—
that is what I should certainly like best of all—that is what I should prefer
—but rest assured that I value your happiness more than my own well-
being and pleasure—and that I would sacrifice all my pleasure just to know
that you are all happy and cheerful. I have absolute confidence in God
Who will surely grant me once more the joy of seeing those whom I love
so dearly with all my heart and soul, and perhaps—even of being able to
live with them. Be patient, therefore, dearest, most beloved friend—and
meanwhile keep on looking out for an engagement. I must now tell you
something about my own affairs. You have no idea what a dreadful time
I am having here. Everything goes so slowly; and until one is well known
—nothing can be done in the matter of composition. In my previous
letters I told you how difficult it is to find a good libretto. From my description of the music here you may have gathered that I am not very
happy, and that (between ourselves) I am trying to get away as quickly as
possible. Unfortunately Herr Raaff will not be in Mannheim until the end
of August. But he is then going to do his best for me, so that perhaps we
may hope that something will turn up. If not, I shall very probably go to
Mainz. Count Sickingen (at whose house I was yesterday and to whom I
said a great deal about you) has a brother there—and the Count himself
suggested that this brother might do something for me. So I think that
things may move a bit. Now you know my prospects, which have been
kept a secret from everyone except the Count and yourself. But, sad as
my present position is, I am infinitely more disappointed to think that I
am not able to serve you—as I should like to do, and this I swear to you

on my honour. Adieu, most beloved friend, farewell. Write to me soon—reply to all my questions—and to my previous letters, I beg you. Give my best greetings to your wife, and to all your loved ones; and rest assured that I shall use every effort to help you to improve your position. If I hadn't a father and a sister, to whom I must sacrifice everything and whom I must try to support, I would completely renounce my own interests with the greatest pleasure—and consult your interests only. For your welfare—your pleasure—your happiness are the very foundation of mine. Farewell, your constant

MOZART

(318) *Mozart to Aloysia Weber, Mannheim*

[Autograph in the Goethe- und Schiller-Archiv, Weimar]

DEAREST FRIEND!   PARIS, 30 *July* 1778 [1]

Please forgive me for not sending you this time the variations I have composed on the aria which you sent me.[2] But I have thought it so necessary to reply as quickly as possible to your father's letter that I have not had time to copy them and therefore cannot let you have them. But you shall certainly have them in my next letter. I am hoping that my sonatas[3] will be engraved very soon—and I shall send in the same parcel the 'Popoli di Tessaglia', which is already half finished.[4] If you are as pleased with it as I am, I shall be delighted. Meanwhile until I have the pleasure of hearing from you whether you really like this scena—for, since I have composed it for you alone,—I desire no other praise than yours—I can only say that of all my compositions of this kind—this scena is the best I have ever composed. I shall be delighted if you will set to work as hard as you can at my Andromeda scena 'Ah, lo previdi',[5] for I assure you that it will suit you admirably—and that you will do yourself great credit with it. I advise you to watch the expression marks—to think carefully of the meaning and the force of the words—to put yourself in all seriousness into Andromeda's situation and position!—and to imagine that you really are that very person. With your beautiful voice and your fine method of producing it you will undoubtedly soon become an excellent singer, if you continue to work in this way. The greater part of the next

---

[1] This letter is in Italian.

[2] Probably the coloratura passages for the closing bars of the aria 'Non so d' onde viene', K. 294.

[3] Mozart's violin sonatas, K. 301-306 [293a-c, 300c, 293d, 300l].

[4] K. 316 [300b], a recitative and aria composed to words taken from Gluck's *Alceste*. The autograph bears the date 8 January, 1779, obviously the day on which Mozart handed it to Aloysia Weber.

[5] K. 272, a recitative and aria composed to words taken from Paisiello's *Andromeda*. Mozart wrote this scena for Madame Duschek. See p. 280, n. 4.

letter which I shall have the honour of sending you will consist of a short explanation of the manner in which I should like you to sing and act this scene. At the same time I urge you to work at it for a little by yourself—and then you will see the difference—which will be a very useful lesson for you—although indeed I am quite sure that there won't be very much to correct or alter—and that you will sing my passages in the way I desire —for you know by experience how I like my compositions to be sung.— In the aria 'Non so d'onde viene',[1] which you learnt by yourself, I found nothing to criticize or correct—you sang it to me with the interpretation, with the method and the expression which I desired. So I have reason to have every confidence in your ability and knowledge. In short, you are capable—most capable—so that all that I ask you (and this I do beg you most earnestly to do) is to be so good as to re-read my letters now and then and to follow my advice—resting assured and convinced that my sole object when I say and when I used to say all these things, is, and always will be, to do as much for you as I possibly can.

Dearest friend! I hope that you are in excellent health—I beg you to take great care of it—for good health is the best thing in the world. Thank God, I am very well, as far as my health is concerned, because I watch it. But my mind is not at rest—nor will it be until I have heard (and what a comfort that will be) that your merits have received their just reward. Yet my condition and my situation will be the happiest on that day when I shall have the infinite pleasure of serving you again and embracing you with all my heart. This too is all that I can long for and desire, and my only consolation and my sole comfort lie in this hope and desire. Please write to me very often. You have no idea how much pleasure your letters afford me. Please write to me whenever you have been to see Herr Marchand[2] —and tell me something about your study of stage acting—to which I urge you most warmly to apply yourself. Basta, you know that everything that concerns you interests me very greatly. By the way, I have a thousand compliments to deliver from a gentleman—who is the only friend I care about here, and of whom I am very fond, because he is a great friend of your family and had the good fortune and the pleasure of carrying you about in his arms and kissing you hundreds of times when you were still a tiny child. He is Herr Kymli—painter to the Elector. For this friendship I have to thank Raaff who is now my intimate friend, and therefore yours and also the friend of the whole Weber family, knowing, as he does, that he could not be my friend, unless he were yours also. Herr Kymli, who has a great regard for you all, is never tired of talking about

---

[1] K. 294. See p. 497, n. 3.

[2] Theobald Marchand (1746–1800) had been since May 1777 manager of the 'Churfürstliche Deutsche Schaubühne' in Mannheim. He became later a theatrical manager in Munich. His gifted children, Margarete, an operatic singer, and Heinrich, a violinist, were trained by Leopold Mozart.

you, and I—I never stop talking about you. Hence my sole pleasure is to converse with him; and he, who is a true friend of your whole household and who has heard from Herr Raaff that the greatest kindness he can render me is to talk about you, is for ever doing so. Addio, for the present, dearest friend! I am very anxious to get a letter from you. So please do not keep me waiting and do not make me suffer too long. In the hope of having news from you very soon, I kiss your hands, I embrace you with all my heart, and am, and ever shall be, your true and sincere friend

WAMozart

Please embrace your dear mother and all your sisters for me.

(319) *Mozart to his Father*

[Autograph in the Mozarteum, Salzburg]

Monsieur mon trés cher Pére!   Paris, 31 *July* 1778

I hope you have received my two letters—I think of the 11th and 18th. Meanwhile I have received yours of the 13th and 20th. The first brought tears of sorrow to my eyes—because I was reminded of the sad death of my dear departed mother—and everything came back to me so vividly. As long as I live I shall never forget it. You know that I had never seen anyone die, although I had often wished to. How cruel that my first experience should be the death of my mother! I dreaded that moment most of all, and I prayed earnestly to God for strength. My prayer was heard and strength was given to me. Sad as your letter made me, yet I was beside myself with joy when I heard that you had taken it all as it should be taken—and that thus I need have no fears for my most beloved father and my dearest sister. As soon as I had read your letter through, I fell on my knees and thanked our gracious God with all my heart for this blessing. I am quite calm now, for I know that I have nothing to fear for the two persons who are dearest to me in this world. Had it been otherwise, it would have been the greatest misfortune for me—and would have certainly crushed me. Do take care, both of you, of your health, which is so precious to me, and grant to him who flatters himself that he is now the dearest thing in the world to you, the happiness, the joy and the bliss of folding you soon in his arms. Your last letter drew tears of joy from me, for it convinced me completely of your true fatherly love and care. I shall strive with all my might to deserve still more your fatherly affection. I kiss your hand in tender gratitude for sending me the powders, and am sure you will be glad to know that I do not need them. Once during my dear departed mother's illness a dose was almost necessary—but now, thank God, I am perfectly well and healthy. From time to time I have fits of melancholy—but I find that the best way to get rid of them is to write or receive letters, which invariably cheer me up again. But, believe me, there is always a cause for these sad feelings. Would you like to know how much I had to pay for your last letter containing the powders? Forty-five sous. You would like to have a short account of her illness and of all its circumstances? You shall have it, but I must ask you to let it be short—and I shall only allude to the main facts, since it is all over now and, unfortunately, cannot be undone—and I need room to write about things which have to do with our present situation. First of all, I must tell you that my dear departed mother *had to die*. No doctor in the world could have saved her this time—for it was clearly the will of God; her time had come—and God wanted to take her to Himself. You think she put off being bled until it was too late? That may be. She did postpone it a little. But I rather agree with the people here who tried to dissuade her from being bled—and to persuade her to take a lavement. She would not, however, have this—and I did not venture to say anything, as I do not understand these things and consequently should have been to blame if it had not suited her. If it had been my own case, I should have consented at once—for this treatment is very popular here—whoever has an inflammation takes a lavement—and the cause of my mother's illness was nothing but an internal inflammation—or at least was diagnosed as such. I cannot tell you accurately how much blood she was let, for it is measured here not by the ounce but by the plate; they took a little less than two platefuls. The surgeon said that it was very necessary—but it was so terribly hot that day that he did not dare to bleed her any more. For a few days she was all right. Then diarrhoea started—but no one paid much attention to it, as foreigners who drink a good deal of water commonly find it a laxative. And that is true. I had it myself when I first came to Paris, but since I have given up drinking plain water and always add a little wine, I have been free of this trouble, though indeed, as I cannot altogether do without drinking plain water, I purify it with ice and drink it en glace—and take two tumblerfuls before going to bed. Well, to continue. On the 19th she complained of headache, and for the first time she had to spend the day in bed; she was up for the last time on the 18th. On the 20th she complained of shivers—and then fever—so that I gave her an antispasmodic powder. All this time I was very anxious to send for a doctor, but she would not consent; and when I urged her very strongly, she said she had no confidence in a French physician. So I looked about for a German—but as of course I could not go out and leave her, I waited anxiously for M. Heina, who was in the habit of coming regularly every day to see us—but, needless to say, on this occasion he had to stay away for two days! At last he came, but as the doctor was prevented from coming the following day, we could not consult him. Thus he did not come until the 24th. On the previous day, when I had wanted him so badly, I had a great fright—for all of a sudden she lost her hearing. The doctor (an old German of about seventy) gave her a rhubarb powder in wine. I cannot understand that, for people usually say that wine is heating. But when I said so, they all exclaimed: 'How on earth can you say so? Wine is not heating, but strengthening—water is heating'—and meanwhile the poor patient was longing for a drink of fresh water. How gladly would I have given it to her! Most beloved father, you cannot imagine what I endured. But there was no help for it, for by Heaven I had to leave her in the hands of the doctor. All I could do with a good conscience was to pray to God without ceasing that He would order all things for her good. I went as if I was bereft of my reason. I had ample leisure then for composing, but I could not have written a single note. On the 25th the doctor did not come. On the 26th he visited her again. Imagine my feelings when he said to me quite unexpectedly: 'I fear she will not last out the night. If she is taken with pains and has to go to the night-stool, she may die at any moment. You had better see that she makes her confession.' So I ran out to the end of the Chaussée d'Antin, well beyond the Barrière, to find Heina, who I knew was at a concert at the house of a certain Count. He told me he would bring a German priest next day. On my way back, as I was passing, I went in for a moment to see Grimm and Mme d'Épinay. They were distressed that I had not told them sooner, for they would have sent their own doctor at once. I had not said anything to them before, because my mother would not have a French doctor—but now I was at my wit's end. They said therefore that they would send their doctor that very evening. When I got home, I told my mother that I had met Herr Heina with a German priest who had heard a great deal about me and was longing to hear me play, and that they were coming on the morrow to pay me a visit. She was quite satisfied, and as I thought that she seemed better (although I am no doctor), I said nothing more. I see now that it is impossible for me to tell a thing briefly. I like to write about everything in detail and I think that you too will prefer it. So, as I have more urgent matters to write about, I shall continue this story in my next letter. Meanwhile you must have seen from my last letters where I am living and that all my possessions and those of my beloved mother are in good order. When I come to this point I shall explain fully how this was arranged. Heina and I did everything. Clothes, linen, jewels, indeed everything belonging to her I shall send to Salzburg at the first opportunity and with every precaution. I shall arrange all that with Gschwendner. Now for our own affairs. But first of all I must beg you again not to worry at all about what I told you in my letter of the 3rd, in which I asked you not to insist on my disclosing my ideas until the time should be ripe.[1] I cannot tell you about it yet, for indeed it

---

[1] Mozart's letter to Fridolin Weber, p. 576 ff., explains more fully his state of mind at that time.

is not yet time—and, if I did, I should do more harm than good. But for your peace of mind let me say that it *only concerns myself.* It will not affect your circumstances either for better or for worse and I shall not think about it until I see you in a better position. But when we are happily re-united and can live somewhere together (which is my sole ambition)—when that happy time comes—and God grant it may be soon!—then the moment will have arrived and the rest will depend on you. So do not worry about it now—and rest assured that in all matters where I know that your peace and happiness are involved, I shall always put my trust in you, my most beloved father and my truest friend, and shall tell you everything in detail. If I have not always done so hitherto—it has not been entirely my fault. M. Grimm said to me the other day: 'What am I to write to your father? What course do you intend to pursue? Are you staying here or going to Mannheim?' I really could not help laughing. 'What could I do in Mannheim now?' I said, 'would that I had never come to Paris—but so it is. Here I am and I must use every effort to make my way.' 'Well,' he said, 'I hardly think that you will make a success of things in Paris.' 'Why?' I asked. 'I see a crowd of miserable bunglers here who are able to get on, and with my talents should I not be able to do so?—I assure you that I liked being at Mannheim—and should be glad to have an appointment there—but it must be an honourable and reputable one. I must be certain how I stand before I move a step.' 'Well, I am afraid', said he, 'that you have not been sufficiently active here—you do not go about enough.' 'Well,' I replied, 'that is just what I find most difficult to do here.' After all, during my mother's long illness I couldn't go anywhere —and two of my pupils are in the country—and the third (the daughter of the Duc de Guines)[1] is getting married—and (what is no great loss to my reputation) will not continue her studies. Moreover I shall lose no money, for he only pays me what everyone else does. Just imagine, the Duc de Guines, to whose house I have had to go daily for two hours, let me give twenty-four lessons and (although it is the custom to pay after every twelve) went off into the country and came back after ten days without letting me know a word about it, so that had I not enquired out of mere curiosity—I should not have known that they were here! And when I did go, the housekeeper pulled out a purse and said: 'Pray forgive me if I only pay you for twelve lessons this time, but I haven't enough money'. There's noble treatment for you! She paid me three louis d'or, adding: 'I hope you will be satisfied—if not, please let me know'. So M. le Duc hasn't a spark of honour and must have thought, 'After all, he's a young man and a stupid German into the bargain—(for all French-men talk like this about the Germans)—so he'll be quite glad of it'.—But

[1] See p. 519, n. 5.

the stupid German was not at all glad of it, in fact he didn't take it. It amounted to this, that the Duke wanted to pay me for one hour instead of two—and that from égard. For he has already had, for the last four months, a concerto of mine for flute and harp,[1] for which he has not yet paid me. So I am only waiting until the wedding is over and then I shall go the housekeeper and demand my money. What annoys me most of all here is that these stupid Frenchmen seem to think I am still seven years old, because that was my age when they first saw me. This is perfectly true. Mme d'Épinay said as much to me quite seriously. They treat me here as a beginner—except, of course, the real musicians, who think differently. But it is the majority that counts. After my conversation with Grimm I went the very next day to Count Sickingen. He was entirely of my opinion —that I should have patience and wait for the arrival of Raaff, who will do everything in his power to help me. Then, if that is no use, Count Sickingen himself has offered to get me an appointment at Mainz. So that is my prospect at present. Meanwhile I shall do my utmost to get along here by teaching and to earn as much money as possible, which I am now doing in the fond hope that my circumstances may soon change; for I cannot deny, and must indeed confess, that I shall be delighted to be released from this place. For giving lessons here is no joke. Unless you wear yourself out by taking a *large number of pupils*, you cannot make much money. You must not think that this is laziness on my part. No, indeed! It just goes utterly against my genius and my manner of life. You know that I am, so to speak, soaked in music, that I am immersed in it all day long and that I love to plan works, study and meditate. Well, I am prevented from all this by my way of life here. I shall have a few free hours, it is true, but these few hours I shall need more for rest than for work. I told you in my last letter about the opera. I cannot help it—I must write a grand opera or none at all; if I write a small one, I shall get very little for it (for everything is taxed here). And should it have the misfortune not to please these stupid Frenchmen, all would be over—I should never get another commission to compose—I should have gained nothing by it— and my reputation would have suffered. If, on the other hand, I write a grand opera—the remuneration will be better—I shall be doing the work in which I delight—and I shall have better hopes of success, for with a big work you have a better chance of making your name. I assure you that if I am commissioned to write an opera, I shall have no fears whatever. True, the devil himself must certainly have invented the language of these people—and I fully realize the difficulties with which all composers have had to contend. But in spite of this I feel I am as well able to overcome them as anyone else. Au contraire, when I fancy, as I often do, that I have

---

[1] K. 299 [297c].

got the commission, my whole body seems to be on fire and I tremble from head to foot with eagerness to teach the French more thoroughly to know, appreciate and fear the Germans. For why is a grand opera never entrusted to a Frenchman? Why must it always be a foreigner? For me the most detestable part of the business would be the singers. Well, I am ready—I wish to avoid quarrels—but if I am challenged, I shall know how to defend myself. But I should prefer to avoid a duel, for I do not care to wrestle with dwarfs. God grant that a change may come soon! Meanwhile I shall certainly not fall short in industry, pains and labour. My hopes are centred on the winter, when everyone returns from the country. Meanwhile farewell—and continue to love me. My heart leaps up when I think of the happy day when I shall have the joy of seeing you again and embracing you with all my heart. Adieu. I kiss your hands 100000 times, embrace my sister in brotherly fashion and remain your most obedient son

WOLFGANG AMADÈ MOZART

Another rigmarole for you!

[Autograph in the Staatsbibliothek Preussischer Kulturbesitz, West Berlin]

[PARIS, 31 July 1778]

You say in your letter that Count Seeau has been appointed Intendant both at Munich and at Mannheim.[1] This seems to me so incredible that I really wouldn't believe it if a letter from Mannheim had not convinced me that it must be true. The day before yesterday my dear friend Weber wrote to me, among other things, that the very day after the Elector's arrival it was publicly announced that he would take up his residence in Munich, a message which fell upon all Mannheim like a thunderbolt and completely extinguished, as it were, the joy which the inhabitants had expressed on the previous day by a general illumination. Moreover all the Court musicians were notified of it with the supplementary information that each was at liberty to follow the Court to Munich or to remain in Mannheim at the same salary; and that in four days each was to hand in to the Intendant[2] his decision written and sealed. Weber, who, as you know, is undoubtedly in the most wretched circumstances, sent in the following statement: 'I anxiously desire to follow my gracious lord to Munich, but my shattered affairs prevent me from doing so'. Before this occurred, there had been a grand concert at Court, at which my poor Mlle Weber was made to feel the fangs of her enemies. For this time she did not sing. Nobody knows who was at the bottom of this. Afterwards, however,

---

[1] Mozart refers to a statement in his father's letter of 13 July, a large portion of which for lack of space has had to be omitted.   [2] Count Savioli.

there was a concert at Herr von Gemmingen's, and Count Seeau was present. She sang two of my arias and had the good fortune to please, in spite of those Italian blackguards, those infamous scoundrels, who keep on spreading the report that her singing is definitely going off. But when her arias were over, Cannabich said to her: 'Mademoiselle, I hope that your singing will always continue to go off in this way. Tomorrow I shall write to Herr Mozart and praise you.' Well, the main thing is that if war had not already broken out, the Court would by this time have moved to Munich. Count Seeau, who is absolument determined to have Mlle Weber, would have made the greatest effort to have her taken too. So there might have been some hope of the whole family being placed in better circumstances. But nothing more is being said about the Munich journey; and these poor people may have to wait for a long time, while their debts become heavier every day. If only I could help them! Dearest father! I commend them to you with all my heart. If only they could enjoy an income of a thousand gulden even for a few years!

Now for some war news! Let me think! Since the information I sent you in my last letter all that I have heard is that the King of Prussia for the time being has had to retreat. It is even rumoured that General Wunsch and 15000 men have been taken prisoner. But I don't believe a word of it, although ⟨I wish it with all my heart.⟩ If only ⟨the Prussian would get a good thrashing!⟩ I daren't say such a thing in this house. Adieu.

My greetings to the whole of Salzburg, and especially to Bullinger and to the whole high and mighty company of marksmen.

(319a) *Mozart to his Sister*

[Autograph in the Staatsbibliothek Preussischer Kulturbesitz, West Berlin]

MA TRÉS CHERE SOEUR! [PARIS, 31 *July* 1778]

I trust that you will be quite satisfied with my little prelude.[1] It isn't exactly what you asked for, I admit,—I mean, a prelude modulating from one key into the next and in which the performer can stop when he likes. But I hadn't sufficient time to write a prelude of that kind, for that sort of composition requires more work. As soon as I have time, I shall present you with one. At the same time when I send home Mamma's belongings, I shall despatch this new prelude with Schröter's concertos, Hüllmandel's sonatas, the 'Violinschule', and a few other sonatas of my own composition.[2] Adieu, farewell. I will not awaken sad memories. Resign yourself to the will of God and trust in Him. Remember that you have a brother,

---

[1] Possibly K. 395 [300g]. [2] See p. 573, n. 7.

who loves you with all his heart and will always think of your welfare and happiness. Adieu, love me. I kiss you most tenderly and am ever your faithful and sincere brother

WOLFGANG . MOZART

My greetings to all, especially to Cornet Andretter, if he is still in Salzburg. No doubt it's better to be in Salzburg than in Bohemia, where one is in greater danger of losing one's head.

(320) *Leopold Mozart to his Son*

[*Extract*]   [*Autograph in the Mozarteum, Salzburg*]

★ MY DEAR SON!   SALZBURG, 3 *August* 1778

I wish your last letter had contained some details about your dear mother's fatal illness and particularly about her burial and the difficulties you must have had to contend with. Your next letter will, I hope, tell me something. Surely you will have had to seek the assistance of Herr Heina or of some other friend, to whom (whoever he may be) I send my heartfelt thanks and greetings. As for the illness itself, I am sure that my dear departed wife neglected herself and on that account was neglected by others. For she was extremely economical, she would put off doing things from one day to the next and therefore would not call in a doctor, as she was convinced that she would get stronger in time. Her chronic *constipation*, her *high colour*, which was really *far too beautiful* for an old woman, her frequent *attacks of catarrh* and her *peculiar cough* were sure signs that some internal inflammation might at any time develop. I told you in May that she ought not to postpone being bled, as the climate of Paris was warmer than that of Salzburg. Yet she put it off until June 11th and even then she would probably not have had it done, if she hadn't felt that it was absolutely necessary. The day before this treatment she took far too violent exercise, and got home exhausted and overheated; she was probably bled too little; and finally the doctor was called in far too late, for as her feverishness and shivering were accompanied by diarrhoea, she was already in danger. Doubtless she did not say much, but just stayed quiet, hoping that things would right themselves. You had your engagements, you were away all day, and as she didn't make a fuss, you treated her condition lightly. All this time her illness became more serious, in fact mortal—and only then was a doctor called in, when of course it was too late. If she had not had such an excellent constitution, she could not have lasted a fortnight. Well, it is all over. God willed it. The unbreakable chain of Divine Providence preserved your mother's life when you were born, though indeed she was in very great danger and though we almost thought that she was gone. But she was fated to sacrifice herself for her son in a different way. She readily agreed to leave Salzburg with you. When I was hoping to have her back from Mannheim and was urging you to make your arrangements and had already written to my brother in Augsburg, I received a letter from you which caused me astonishment, bewilderment and distress. In that very letter she wrote to me (without your knowledge) that, for certain reasons and out of love for you, she wanted to travel with you to Paris. So all this was fore-ordained to happen, because in accordance with Divine Providence her days were numbered and her sands had then run out.

Now for a piece of news! Ferlendis resigned three days ago, having left ★ the service at the end of June. This has been the more unexpected and up-setting as during the last two months whenever Ferlendis played a con-certo, the Archbishop had been in the habit of giving him one or two ducats. Moreover he was the favourite in the orchestra and since Besozzi's [1] arrival in Salzburg had learnt a good deal from him. Now for another story *which I alone know about.* Ferrari is going to leave at the end of August. These two events will mean the ruin of Brunetti. The Italians are losing their good name. Everyone is going for them now, Count Arco, Countess Lodron, the two Starhembergs, the Bishop of Königgrätz and others. I shrug my shoulders and say nothing. Ferlendis professes that the air doesn't please his wife.

I shall now have to try and find a player on the French horn, an oboist, a tenor, a cellist, a violinist and—no—not an organist. They are still waiting for me to make a move; but they are waiting in vain. You may rest assured, my dearest son, that if you stay away, I shall die much sooner, and that if I could have the joy of having you with me, I should live several years longer. All this is quite certain, for—apart from my fits of melancholy—I am in very good health. But matters would have to be arranged properly, advantageously and honourably. If they were, then this place—as a centre between Munich, Vienna and Italy—would always have certain advantages. For Mannheim has been superseded. Seeau has been introduced to the Mannheim people and the court is returning to Munich very soon, I think that we shall be *laying new foundations here with male and female singers and instrumentalists.* The Archbishop has already given me a few commissions. Tell me something about Rothfischer, but truthfully and impartially. Your sister kisses you a million times. She is working excessively hard, and indeed looks after me very well. Give our best greetings to Baron Grimm and Mme d'Épinay. I thank them most humbly for all the kindnesses you are enjoying in their house. My son, take care of your health. I must close, for the post is going.

MZT

[1] See p. 540, n. 1.

You need not send me Vogler's book, as we can get it here. Are Eckardt and Honnauer still alive?

On July 4th Kolb performed your Lodron Cassation[1] in the street in front of the Andretters' house.

On July 9th Kolb gave a Nachtmusik in front of Herr von Mayer's house, which took the form of a Finalmusik of your composition[2] and the concerto you wrote for Kolb.[3] We listened to it across the water. It sounded charming. We hadn't heard a word about it.

(321) *Leopold Mozart to the Court Council of Salzburg*

[*Autograph sold by J. A. Stargardt, Marburg, 1–2 June 1976*]

SALZBURG, 7 *August* 1778

MOST WORTHY AND MOST LEARNED MEMBERS OF THE COURT COUNCIL OF SALZBURG,

PRESIDENT OF THE COURT COUNCIL, COURT CHANCELLOR AND COURT COUNCILLORS!

The unexpected and distressing death of my late wife in Paris has necessitated the application of the usual customs ban on certain articles under seal. As, however, my late wife at the time of our marriage had no property whatever, as, in view of my small salary, there was not the slightest prospect of her ever having any, and as, apart from the clothes which she took away with her, she had no effects whatsoever, I most humbly beg you graciously to remove the ban and to exempt me from any expenses connected therewith. If, however, there is any just claim for payment against me, I shall willingly fulfil it.

I remain, most worthy Court Councillors,
your most humble and obedient servant
LEOPOLD MOZART
Deputy-Kapellmeister to His Grace the Prince

(322) *Mozart to the Abbé Bullinger, Salzburg*

[*Autograph in the Mozarteum, Salzburg*]

DEAREST FRIEND!   PARIS, 7 *August* 1778

Allow me above all to thank you most warmly for the new proof of friendship you have given me by your kind interest in my dear father—

---

[1] K. 287 [271H], composed in 1777.
[2] Possibly K. 250 [248b], Mozart's Haffner serenade, composed in 1776.
[3] One of the five violin concertos which Mozart composed in 1775.

first in preparing him for his loss and then in consoling him so sympatheti-cally. You played your part most admirably—these are my father's own words. Most beloved friend, how can I thank you sufficiently? You have saved my dear father for me; I have you to thank that I still have him. Permit me to say no more on this subject and not to attempt to express my gratitude, for indeed I feel far too weak, too incompetent—too weary to do so. Most beloved friend! I am always your debtor. But patience! On my honour I am not yet in a position to repay what I owe you—but do not doubt me, for God will grant me the opportunity of showing by deeds what I am unable to express in words. Such is my hope. Meanwhile until that happy time arrives, allow me to beg you to continue your most precious and valued friendship towards me—and at the same time to accept mine afresh, both now and for ever, to which I pledge myself in all sincerity of heart. I know that it will not be of much use to you, but it will be none the less genuine and lasting. You know well that the best and truest of all friends are the poor. The wealthy do not know what friend-ship means, especially those who are born to riches; and even those whom fate enriches often become spoilt by their good fortune. But when a man is placed in favourable circumstances not by blind fate but by reasonable good fortune and merit, that is, a man who during his early and less prosperous days never lost courage, remained faithful to his religion and his God, was an honest man and a good Christian and knew how to value his true friends—in short, one who really deserved better luck— from such a man no ingratitude need be feared!

I will now reply to your letter. You will all be in no further anxiety about my health, for by this time you will have received three letters from me. The first, containing the sad news of my mother's death, was enclosed to you, most beloved friend. I know that you will forgive my silence on the subject, but my thoughts are ever returning to it. You say that I should now think only of my father and that I should disclose all my thoughts to him with entire frankness and put my trust in him. How unhappy should I be if I needed the reminder! It was expedient that you should suggest it, but I am glad to say (and you will be glad to hear it) that I do not need this advice. In my last letter to my dear father I told him what I myself knew up to the time, assuring him that I should always report everything to him very fully and inform him candidly of my views, because I placed my entire confidence in him and trusted completely to his fatherly care, love and goodness. I feel sure that *some day* he will not deny me a request on which the whole happiness and peace of my life depend and which will certainly be quite fair and reasonable, for he cannot expect anything else from me. Dearest friend, do not let my father read this. You know him. He would only worry, and *quite unnecessarily*.

Now for our Salzburg story. You, most beloved friend, are well aware how I detest Salzburg—and not only on account of the injustices which my dear father and I have endured there, which in themselves would be enough to make us wish to forget such a place and blot it out of our memory for ever! But let us set that aside, if only we can arrange things so as to be able to live there respectably. To live respectably and to live happily are two very different things, and the latter I could not do without having recourse to witchcraft—indeed if I did, there would have to be something supernatural about it—and that is impossible, for in these days there are no longer any witches. But, stop, I have an idea. There are certain people born in Salzburg—indeed the town swarms with them—you would only have to alter the first letter of their true name and then they could help me.[1] Well, happen what may, it will always be the greatest pleasure to me to embrace my very dear father and sister, and the sooner the better. Yet I cannot deny that my joy and delight would be doubled if I could do so elsewhere, for I have far more hope of living pleasantly and happily in any other place. Perhaps you will misunderstand me and think that Salzburg is too small for me? If so, you are greatly mistaken. I have already given some of my reasons to my father. In the meantime, content yourself with this one, that Salzburg is no place for my talent. In the first place, professional musicians there are not held in much consideration; and, secondly, one hears nothing, there is no theatre, no opera; and even if they really wanted one, who is there to sing? For the last five or six years the Salzburg orchestra has always been rich in what is useless and superfluous, but very poor in what is necessary, and absolutely destitute of what is indispensable; and such is the case at the present moment. Those cruel French are the cause of the orchestra having no Kapellmeister.[2] I feel assured, therefore, that quiet and order are now reigning there! That, of course, is the result of not making provision in time. Half a dozen Kapellmeisters should always be held in readiness, so that if one drops out, another can instantly be substituted. But where, at present, can they get even one? Yet the danger is pressing! It will not do to allow order, peace and intelligence to gain the upper hand in the orchestra, or the mischief will spread still further and in the long run become irremediable. Are there really no ancient periwigs with asses' ears, no lousy heads available, who could restore the concern to its former disabled condition? I shall certainly do my best in the matter. Tomorrow I intend to hire a carriage for the day and drive round to all the hospitals and infirmaries and see if I can't find some Kapellmeister for them.[3] Why were they so careless as to let Mysliwecek give them the slip?—and he was so near too! He would

---

[1] The point of Mozart's remarks is lost in translation. He means that by altering the first letter, 'Fexen' (idiots) can become 'Hexen' (witches).

[2] The Archbishop had tried to secure Ferdinando Giuseppe Bertoni, who, however, preferred to accept an invitation to Paris. See p. 534, n. 2.

[3] This comment on the Salzburg orchestra is, of course, ironical.

have been a fat morsel for them. It would not be easy to get someone like him and someone moreover who has just been discharged from the Duke Clemens Conservatorio.[1] He would have been the man to terrify the whole Court orchestra by his presence.[2] Well we need not be uneasy—where there is money, there are always plenty of people to be had. Only my opinion is that they should not postpone action too long, not because I am so foolish as to be afraid that they might not get anyone at all,—I know only too well that all these gentlemen are longing for a Kapellmeister as eagerly and hopefully as the Jews are awaiting their Messiah—but simply because in the present circumstances things are unendurable. It would be more useful and profitable, therefore, to look around for a Kapellmeister, as they really have *none* at present, rather than to be writing in all directions (as I have been told they are doing) in order to secure a good female singer. But I can scarcely believe this! A female singer! When we have so many already! And all admirable singers! If it were a tenor, I could more easily understand it, though we do not require one either. But a prima donna! When we now have a castrato! It is true that Mme Haydn is in poor health. She has overdone her austere mode of living. There are few of whom this can be said. I am surprised that she has not lost her voice long ago by her perpetual scourgings and flagellations, her hair-shirt and her unnatural fasts and night prayers! But she will long retain her powers and, instead of becoming worse, her voice will improve daily. When at last God places her among the number of His saints, we shall still have five singers left, each of whom can dispute the palm with the other. So you see how superfluous a new singer is! But just let me argue from an extreme case. Suppose that, apart from our weeping Magdalene,[3] we had no other female singer, which, of course, is not the case; but suppose that one were suddenly confined, the second were imprisoned, the third were whipped to death, the fourth had her head chopped off and the fifth were perhaps whisked off by the devil, what would happen? Nothing!—For we have a castrato.[4] You know what sort of animal he is? He can sing high treble and can thus take a woman's part to perfection. The Chapter would interfere, of course. But, all the same, interference is better than intercourse; and they wouldn't worry him to any great extent. Meanwhile let Ceccarelli be sometimes man, sometimes woman. Finally, because I know that in Salzburg people like variety, changes and innovations, I see before me a wide field, the cultivation of which may make history. As children, my sister and I worked at

[1] Mozart means the Hospital in Munich, where Mysliwecek had been undergoing treatment for his disease.
[2] Mysliwecek's face was greatly disfigured.
[3] Michael Haydn's wife was Maria Magdalena Lipp.
[4] Francesco Ceccarelli.

it a little bit, and what would not grown-ups be able to do? Why, if one is généreux, one can get anything. I have no doubt (and I would even undertake to arrange it) that we could get Metastasio to come over from Vienna, or that we could at least make him an offer to write a few dozen opera texts in which the primo uomo and the prima donna would never meet. In this way the castrato could play the parts of both the lover and his mistress and the story would be even more interesting—for people would be able to admire that virtue of the lovers which is so absolute that they purposely avoid any occasion of speaking to one another in public. There is the opinion of a true patriot for you! Do your best to find an arse for the orchestra, for that is what they need most of all! They have a head indeed, but that is just their misfortune! Until a change has been made in this respect, I shall not go to Salzburg. When it has been made, I am willing to come and to turn over the page whenever I see V.S.[1]

Now for the war. As far as I know we shall soon have peace in Germany. The King of Prussia is rather alarmed, it seems. I have read in the papers that the Prussians surprised an Imperial detachment, but that the Croats and two regiments of cuirassiers were in the neighbourhood and, hearing the tumult, came at once to their rescue and attacked the Prussians, placing them between two fires and capturing five cannon. The route by which the Prussians entered Bohemia is now entirely cut up and destroyed, so that they cannot retreat. The Bohemian peasants are making it as hot as they can for the Prussians, who are suffering moreover from constant desertions among their troops. But these are matters of which you must have had earlier and more accurate news than ourselves. But I must now send you some of our news here. The French have forced the English to retreat, but it was not a very hot fight.[2] The most remarkable thing is that of friends and foes, only a hundred men were killed. Nevertheless there is tremendous jubilation here and nothing else is talked of. It is also reported that we shall soon have peace. It is all the same to me as far as this country is concerned. But I should be very glad indeed for many reasons if we were soon to have peace in Germany. Now farewell, dearest friend! Forgive my bad writing, but my pen is no good. Give my compliments to the whole of Salzburg, and above all give my respects to your Count, my greetings to Count Leopold,[3] and a long, long compliment in verse to dear Sallerl. And to my dear father and sister say all that a son and a brother would say if he were lucky enough to be able to speak to them himself. Adieu. I beg you to continue your valuable friendship, and I

[1] *volti subito.*

[2] Probably one of the numerous engagements which took place at the end of June between the French forces under the Marquis de la Fayette and the first column of the British Army under General Knyphausen, after Sir Henry Clinton's evacuation of Philadelphia.

[3] Count Leopold Arco, son of the Chief Chamberlain to the Archbishop. The Abbé Bullinger had been his tutor.

assure you that I shall ever be your true friend and most grateful servant

WOLFGANG ROMATZ

(323) *Leopold Mozart to his Son*

[*Extract*]   [*Autograph in the Mozarteum, Salzburg*]

MON TRES CHER FILS!   SALZBURG, 13 *August* 1778

At last I have received two letters from you at once, dated July 20th and 31st, both of which only arrived on the 11th. Baron Grimm sent off to me on July 27th a letter which both *pleases* and *displeases* me. It *pleases* me, because he tells me that you are well—that you fulfilled most punctiliously (which I never doubted you would) your filial duty to your dear departed mother. At the same time his letter *displeases* me, because he very much doubts (expressing himself in the same way as he did to you) whether you are going to get on in Paris or make your fortune or even, as he suggests, earn a bare living for yourself. He says: He is *too good-natured*, peu actif, trop aisé à attraper, trop peu occupé des moyens qui peuvent conduire à la fortune. Ici, pour percer, il faut être retors, entreprenant, audacieux. Je lui voudrais pour sa fortune la moitié moins de talent et le double plus d'entregent, et je n'en serais pas embarrassé. Au reste, il ne peut tenter ici que deux chemins pour se faire un sort. Le premier, c'est de donner des Leçon de Clavecin; mais, sans compter qu'on n'a des écoliers qu'avec beaucoup d'activité et même de charlatanerie, je ne sais s'il aurait assez de santé pour soutenir ce métier, car c'est une chose très fatigante de courir les quatre coins de Paris et de s'épuiser à parler pour montrer. Et puis ce métier ne lui plaira pas, parce qu'il l'empêchera d'ecrire, ce qu'il aime par-dessus tout. Il pourrait donc s'y livrer tout à fait; mais en ce pays-ci le gros du public ne se connaît pas en musique. On donne par conséquent tout aux noms, et le mérite de l'ouvrage ne peut être jugé que par un très petit nombre. Le public est dans ce moment ci ridiculement partagé entre Piccinni et Gluck et tous les raisonnements qu'on entend sur la musique font pitié. Il est donc très difficile pour votre fils de réussir entre ces deux partis, etc. All that is quite true. But the last statement depends largely on luck and chance. *And just because there are two parties, a third party could hope for greater success than if the whole public were infatuated with one composer only.* For my part I think that the most difficult problem is how to get a commission to write an opera and that it is high time that you did so. Piccinni and Gluck will do everything to prevent it; and indeed I am very doubtful as to your prospects of getting one.

Noverre alone might have secured it for you. When I realized that at the moment you are earning nothing (for this must be near the truth, as your pupils are in the country, while in his letter Grimm adds: Vous voyez, mon cher maitre, que dans un pays où tant de musiciens médiocres et détestables même ont fait des fortunes immenses, je crains fort que Mr: votre fils ne se tire pas seulement d'affaires), a heavy load once more settled on my heart, and particularly when I came to the words: Je vous ai fait cet exposé fidele, non pour vous affliger, mais pour prendre ensemble le meillieur parti possible. Il est malheureux que la mort de l'Electeur de Baviere ait empesché M. votre fils d'être placé à Mannheim, etc. In my reply I told Grimm that people here would like to have you back, that the Elector is leaving Mannheim and going to Munich, that if you were in Salzburg you might easily obtain an appointment under the Elector and so forth. Grimm will probably have told you. Of course, the conditions which you are offered must be acceptable; and (if the arrangement does not work) you would have to be able to leave Salzburg again without being made to suffer for it. People are gossiping a good deal, but I say nothing. If the Countess [1] wanted to have me appointed, she would have said that she was going to do so. But so far there has not been a word —only perpetual questions—as to how you are—whether I have had letters from you—to which I keep on replying—very well—excellent. Old Lolli died on August 11th. We have buried him and we held a service for him yesterday at St. Sebastian. I am now *the only one* of the four Kapellmeisters who were on the original list.[2] Well, things will be set going again in Salzburg. I shall write to Padre Martini tomorrow. Time will show to what extent you can rely on your friends and what they are able to do for you. Experience (which you can only gain through misfortune) has quite convinced me that there is no true friend—using the word *in its fullest sense*—but a father. Even children are not *in the same degree* friends towards their own parents. Just reflect—think things out and face facts—and you will find enough examples in the world to persuade you of the truth of my dictum. It is for this reason too that God thought it necessary to lay down the commandment that children should honour their parents, and even to add a punishment, whereas he did not think it necessary to enjoin upon parents any such commandment. Mysliwecek's letters have cost me a fortune and they all say that your scrittura for Naples is ready, fixed and absolutely certain. After I had helped him to obtain thirty-seven ducats,[3] he left Munich before Easter, and I haven't had a line from him since. I trust that you have now sold those compositions[4] to your engraver for fifteen louis d'or.

[1] The Countess von Wallis. See p. 547, n. 1.   [2] See p. 10, n. 1.
[3] From the Archbishop of Salzburg.
[4] Mozart's violin sonatas, K. 301-306 [293a-c, 300c, 293d, 300l].

If you have not got any pupils, well then compose something more. Even if you have to let your work go for a smaller sum, why, at any rate this will help to make you known in Paris. But let it be something short, easy and popular. Discuss the matter with some engraver and find out what he would best like to have—perhaps some easy quartets for two violins, viola and cello. Do you imagine that you would be doing work unworthy of you? If so, you are very much mistaken. Did Bach,[1] when he was in London, ever publish anything but similar trifles? *What is slight can still be great*, if it is written in a natural, flowing and easy style—and at the same time bears the marks of sound composition. Such works are more difficult to compose than all those harmonic progressions, *which the majority of people cannot fathom*, or pieces which have pleasing melodies, but which are *difficult to perform*. Did Bach lower himself by such work? Not at all. Good composition, sound construction, il filo—these distinguish the master from the bungler—even in trifles. If I were you I should compose in advance something of that kind and then move Heaven and earth to get a commission for an opera. You must try to sell a work or two to some engraver or other. You must have money in order to live. And if your pupils are in the country, what other way is there for you to make money? You really must do something! I have never told you anything about Madame d'Épinay's circumstances; but now that you are living in her house and, I presume, are taking your meals with her, it is time I told you more about her. She is not as well off as you may think. When we were in Paris long ago, she only had the small sum to live on, which her husband, a Parisian libertine, was obliged to allow her. So I cannot let you be an expense to her as far as your food and drink are concerned; and I am sure that Baron Grimm is paying her out of his own pocket. At the same time I strongly suspect that he too is not in very opulent circumstances, for a little Court, like that of Saxe-Gotha, cannot make large payments. I can read between the lines in the following passage from his letter: Je voudrais que ma position me permit de le secourir efficacement. Si j'avais deux ou trois mille livres à lui donner tous les ans, je ne vous en parlerais seulement pas, et je vous épargnerais tous les soins: mais vous m'avez vu pendant votre séjour à Paris dans un état beaucoup plus obscur, et cependant j'étais plus riche alors que je ne le suis aujourd'hui que ma place m'oblige à une infinité de depenses que je n'avais pas alors. Depuis trente ans, que je suis en France,[2] je n'ai jamais été dans un état aussi gêné que cette année qu'il a fallu faire avec un revenu très modique mon établissement de ministre, après avoir voyagé de Paris par Naples à Petersbourg et de Petersbourg par Stockholm à Paris, ce qui m'a mangé un argent incroyable.' Naturally he will conceal his financial difficulties by

---

[1] Johann Christian Bach.
[2] Grimm had come to Paris from Germany in 1749. See p. 43, n. 4.

pretending to be quite comfortably off. So, if he allows you to lunch at her house, you must ask him to permit you to pay him, for to be invited to a meal a few times is one thing, but to be constantly lunching in the same house is quite another. Such behaviour would be most indiscreet. Wherever you are, you will have to pay. Surely this is the most sensible and advantageous course and one which will bring you more honour if you are able to stay with Baron Grimm. You cannot expect to do this for nothing, since to do so would be to abuse the kindness of a friend who, far from being well-to-do, has debts to pay off. Again, I should like to know, and I must know, whether you owe him anything? Has he lent you any cash? If so, I want to hear exactly how much it is. From his letter I suspect something of this kind. I have already told him that in this case I shall refund him. I have implored him to look after you, if he can possibly do so. If you owe him money, be sure that you repay it even in small sums. Do not pay him off with empty words, as, for example, that you are going to sell your sonatas for fifteen louis d'or. Sell them and see that they are engraved soon. Now that you are alone, I trust that you will be able to live without running up debts. Let me know at once *whether you owe* Baron Grimm anything and, if so, *how much*. He has rendered us so many kindnesses that we really must show him our gratitude. If he has given you money, it is money which he needs to meet his own expenses. Besides, I remember that when we were in Paris, Madame d'Épinay was already a delicate woman, and she is probably so today. I am sorry for her. The remaining portion of Baron Grimm's letter is an expression of his care and desire for your happiness. He points out that you have been in Paris for four months and even longer and adds: Et il est presqu'aussi peu avancé que le premier jour, ayant pourtant mangé près de mille livres. Well, either you have earned that sum—or you owe it. He wishes that I were with you. Yes, indeed, if I were, things would take a different turn. He says: Un malheur à ajouter à tous les autres, c'est, que je suis si accablé d'affaires que je n'en puis faire que la moitié; par conséquent il ne me reste aucun moyen de m'occuper de Mr. votre fils ou de lui chercher des ressources. Yes, and you
★ yourself are not at all anxious, or only a trifle so. Your sister thanks you for the praeambulum, which is excellent, and she is going to write to you herself. It arrived at four o'clock. I got home after five and she told me that she had made up something and would write it down if I liked it. She began to play the first page of your prelude by heart. I stared at her and exclaimed: 'Where the devil have you got those ideas from?' She laughed and pulled the letters out of her pocket. Bullinger and all our good friends,
★ and particularly the company of marksmen, send their greetings. Addio. The post is going. I remain
your honest father

MZT

(324) *Leopold Mozart to Hieronymus Colloredo, Archbishop of Salzburg*

[*Autograph in the Landesarchiv, Salzburg*]

YOUR GRACE!　　　[SALZBURG, *between* 11 *and* 27 *August* 1778]
MOST WORTHY PRINCE OF THE HOLY ROMAN EMPIRE!

Seeing that Kapellmeister Lolli[1] has passed over into eternity, that he only drew the salary of a Deputy-Kapellmeister, that, as Your Grace is aware, I have been serving this worthy Archbishopric for thirty-eight years, and that since the year 1763, that is, for fifteen years, I have been performing and still perform without reproach as Deputy-Kapellmeister most of the services required, and indeed nearly all of them, I humbly beseech Your Grace to allow me to recommend myself to you and to remain with the deepest homage

your most obedient servant

LEOPOLD MOZART[2]

(325) *Leopold Mozart to Padre Martini, Bologna*

[*Autograph in the Nationalbibliothek, Vienna*]

MOST REVEREND PADRE MAESTRO!　　　[SALZBURG, 21 *August* 1778[3]]
MOST ESTEEMED FATHER,

I should not have failed to send you, most Reverend Father, my portrait, as you desired to possess it, if the painter had not left our country and we had no other artist. But as another has at length arrived in our town and has already by some portraits given proof of his skill, I hope to be able to carry out your wish on the occasion of the St. Andrew's Fair at Bozen. For the painter, who is the only good one we have, has a great deal to do. Moreover I can think of no better opportunity of sending my portrait safely and gratis than that of the coming fair.

I now ask you, most Reverend Father, to favour my son with a very strong recommendation to the Mannheim Court. You were good enough to say in your letter 'I shall not fail to write to Signor Raaff, urging him to recommend your son on my behalf to His Highness the Elector', and subsequently in your letter acknowledging the receipt of my son's portrait: 'Matters connected with Bavaria and the departure of the Elector Palatine from Mannheim may perhaps prevent my recommendations from having much influence with His Electoral Highness. However, though they may

---

[1] Giuseppe Francesco Lolli had died on 11 August.
[2] Leopold Mozart's application was unsuccessful. Domenico Fischietti was appointed Kapellmeister.　　　[3] This letter is in Italian.

be delayed, they will certainly reach him in due course.'[1] You must know, however, most dear and esteemed Padre Maestro, that M. Raaff never received your letter.

My son and his mother reached Paris on March 23rd and Signor Raaff arrived soon afterwards. He and my son struck up such an intimate friendship that Raaff came to see him almost every day, used to stay for two or three hours, used to call my wife his dear mother and longed most ardently to see my son appointed to the service of the Elector of the Palatinate. Alas, what a tragedy! Fate willed it that my dear wife should fall sick and die after a fortnight's illness. Great God! What a blow! I ask you, most Reverend Father, to imagine my condition and that of my poor daughter, and the situation of my son, all alone and bereaved in Paris. As soon as the Elector returned to Mannheim, Raaff left Paris after assuring my son of his sincere friendship and of his great interest and adding that his one desire was to have a letter of recommendation from our most beloved Padre Maestro. The fact is that (as you may perhaps know already) His Highness the Elector only has performances of operas in the German language. *Therefore he now wants a German maestro.* Count Seeau, who is in charge of the music at Munich, has now been established in his new appointment and at the moment is at Mannheim sorting out the two musical organisations, one for Munich and the other for Mannheim. In due course the Court will return to Munich where in future the Elector will reside.

Most beloved and esteemed Padre Maestro! You have heard that my young son aged twenty-two is all by himself in Paris, a most dangerous city! And you—you by putting in a favourable word are in a position to save the soul and to build up the fortune of a talented youth. By a letter addressed to His Highness the Elector, or at least by a letter of recommendation to Signor Raaff and another one to Count Seeau testifying to my son's talent, you can do a good work, further the prospects of a youth who is well educated but is now exposed to a thousand dangers, and help forward a particularly talented young man, who is only seeking an opportunity to make his way and whose whole time is spent in study and composition. Finally you can soothe the anxious heart and save the life of a father. Forgive my cries of anguish! The death of an excellent wife and mother and the position of so gifted a son have almost driven me crazy. I rely wholly on your kind heart, I commend my son and myself to your favour and remain with the deepest homage

your most humble, devoted and
obedient servant

LEOPOLD MOZART
Kapellmeister to His Grace the Archbishop

[1] See p. 534, n. 3.

If, as I hope, you will do me this kindness, I entreat you not to lose time and to write forthwith to Mannheim.

Prince Henry of Prussia made an attempt to join forces with the King, but General Laudon prevented this move and the Prince had to withdraw to Leipa. General Laudon is at the moment at Tornau. For the last seven weeks the King has not been able to move.

(326) *Leopold Mozart to his Son*

[*Extract*]   [*Autograph in the Mozarteum, Salzburg*]

MY DEAR SON!   SALZBURG, 27 *August* 1778

You will have received my letter of the 13th in which I promised to reply very soon to your two letters which arrived together. The first, which you wrote between July 18th and 20th, told me a good deal about the beginning and the deepening of your valuable friendship with Herr Raaff, whose efforts on your behalf, on which you place such reliance, have, I hope, had a good effect. I remember, however, that in a letter from Mannheim you both mentioned that Raaff was a very honourable, excellent old man, but that *he would never be able to do anything for you.* To tell the truth, I found it difficult to believe this. For a man of his standing has surely a very high reputation, although on account of his age he may not be such a good singer as he once was. I have written to Padre Martini and we must now await the result. Your second letter of July 31st gives me   ★ an account of the illness of your most beloved mother. That she should have been the first person whose death you had to witness was a special ordering of God. Indeed I made that very remark to those who were present when I received the news. My dear son! Fate provided the occasion for another remark. Your dear mother was only too glad to take you away from Salzburg. She was to have returned home from Mannheim. It was only after your acquaintanceship and your trip with those Webers that you began to think seriously and decided not to travel to Paris with Wendling. You sent off that letter so late that before my reply could reach you, Wendling had already taken his departure. I had worked everything out quite accurately, otherwise you would not have remained behind. I had therefore to write and tell you to be off to Paris as soon as possible, as the season was coming to an end. Your dear mother saw it all, but she wished to spare me every anxiety and wrote at the end of your letter:[1] 'My dear husband, you will have seen from this letter that when Wolfgang makes new acquaintances, he immediately wants to give his life and property for them. True, she sings exceedingly well; still, we must

---

[1] See p. 463 f.

not lose sight of our own interests. I never liked his being in the company of Wendling and Ramm, but I never ventured to raise any objections, nor would he ever have listened to me. But as soon as he got to know the Webers, he immediately changed his mind. In short, he prefers other people to me, for I remonstrate with him about this and that, and about things which I do not like; and he objects to this. I do not consider his journey to Paris with Wendling at all advisable. I would rather accompany him myself later on. Perhaps you will still get a reply from Herr Grimm.' This, my dear son, is the sole postscript which your dear departed mother wrote to me in confidence about you during the whole period of your absence. And although she might have written more explicitly and called things by their right names, she loved both of us too dearly to speak more plainly. If your mother had returned home from Mannheim, she would not have died. But as Divine Providence had fixed the hour of her death for July 3rd, she had to leave home with you and, owing to your
★ new friendship, her return had to be abandoned. I am delighted that Count Sickingen has offered to help you to obtain a post in Mainz. But do not imagine that it is a foregone conclusion that you will get one. All that his offer means is that he will make an effort on your behalf. Whether he will succeed is another matter. There is an old Kapellmesiter in Mainz called Schmid, who has seen better days. Kreusser[1] went there at the right time, that is, just after Jacobi,[2] the Konzertmeister, had died. His easy symphonies, which are pleasant to listen to, were a success, so that he was immediately appointed Konzertmeister. At present he is working hard to fit himself for the post of Kapellmeister. I cannot forgive you for having neglected, during your very long stay in Mannheim, *to go to Mainz*. If you consider everything impartially, you will have to acknowledge that you have very seldom followed my advice and precepts. A journey to Mainz would have been of more use to you than that stupid trip of yours to Kirchheim-Bolanden, for Mainz is after all a Court where there are some prospects and where you would find many acquaintances amongst the nobility and several other friends. You see, then, that at present *all your planning must be directed solely to making your way successfully in Paris*. As for all the rest about Mannheim, Mainz or Salzburg, you must wait and see and not engage your thoughts with mere idle dreams which only render
★ you incapable of dealing with our present necessary arrangements. You are forever writing about the embarrassed circumstances of the Weber family. But tell me, how, if you have any common sense, can you entertain the idea that you could be the person capable of making the fortune

---

[1] Georg Anton Kreusser (1746–1810), a famous violinist who studied in Italy, returned to Germany in 1773 and became Konzertmeister to the Elector of Mainz. He composed a great many orchestral works.

[2] Father of the violinist and composer Konrad Jacobi (1756–1811).

of these people? You have now learnt by degrees (or so I hope) *how much money a single man needs to keep himself in decency*. We may of course make ★ an effort to assist Mlle Weber as far as possible and even achieve in due course all you desire; but are our resources sufficient to succour a family with six children? Who can do this?—I?—You? You, who have not yet been able to help your family? How can you help others before you have helped yourself? You write: *'Dearest father! I commend them to you with all my heart. If only they could enjoy an income of a thousand gulden even for a few years.'*[1] My dearest son! When I read that, could I help fearing for your reason? Great God! I am to help them to get a thousand gulden for a few years! If I could do so, I would first of all help *you and myself and your dear sister, who is already twenty-seven years of age and is not provided for, while I am growing old*. Where, pray, are the Courts, where is there a single Court, which will give a thousand gulden to a singer? In Munich they get five, six or at most seven hundred gulden, and do you imagine that someone is going to give a thousand gulden forthwith to a young person, who is considered a beginner? That you will never find, even if you think about it day and night and imagine it half done or quite easy to arrange; more particularly since, *as you yourself are constantly hearing and seeing*, one must make a name for oneself and obtain a certain reputation, before one can take longer strides towards one's fortune in this world. If you spend the whole day pondering and dreaming of a hundred thousand imaginary possibilities, not only will the miracle not happen, but unless you turn your present circumstances to profit and advantage to yourself, you will spend your life in effectiveness, remain unknown and poor, ruin yourself and me and thus help nobody. You must write to Cannabich and Raaff and ask them to propose you to the Elector and to Count Seeau as a composer for the German opera. Count Sickingen must write in the same strain to Gemmingen and others. You should also write a letter in French to the same effect to the Imperial Ambassador, Baron Lehrbach. *Grimm could draft one for you*. In short, you should write to everyone who may have any influence with the Elector, for in the future German operas will always be performed in Munich.[2] On St. Charles's day, November 4th, the opera by Wieland and Schweitzer[3] is to be performed and will probably be continued throughout the carnival: I shall also approach Count Seeau from here. Even if you were to get only six hundred gulden, it would be something. When did Gluck, when did Piccinni, when did all the others first come to the fore? Gluck must be at least sixty,[4] and it is only twenty-six or twenty-seven years since people began to talk about

---

[1] See p. 589.
[2] The Electoral Court was transferred from Mannheim to Munich in September 1778.
[3] *Rosemunde*, which was to have been performed in Mannheim on 11 January 1778.
[4] Gluck was sixty-four.

him; and you want the French public, or perhaps only the theatrical managers, to be convinced already of your ability in composition, although they have never yet heard anything of yours, and only know of you from your childhood as a remarkable clavier-player and an outstanding genius. You must therefore make an effort to get on and to make yourself known as a composer of all kinds of music. And for this you must look out for opportunities, seek out friends indefatigably, spur them on relentlessly, wake them up when they seem to be going to sleep, and not believe that what they promised has already been done. I myself would have written long ago to M. de Noverre, if I had had his address. In the meantime your friends and I will work hard for you in Munich. All your thoughts and cares for Herr Weber, and mine too, are absolutely futile until you are in a better position; and that must now be your main object.

Your sister and I kiss you a million times with all our hearts. She has not been able to write to you, as I have more than filled the paper. She will do so next time. For Heaven's sake, take care of your health, or we shall both come to grief. I am your true friend and honest father

MZT.

(327) *Mozart to his Father*

[*Autograph in the Mozarteum, Salzburg*]

MON TRÉS CHER PÉRE!   ST. GERMAIN, 27 *August* 1778

I am writing to you in the greatest haste. You will see that I am not in Paris. Mr. Bach[1] from London has been here for the last fortnight. He is going to write a French opera, and has only come to hear the singers. He will then go back to London and compose the opera, after which he will return here to see it staged.[2] You can easily imagine his delight and mine at meeting again; perhaps his delight may not have been quite as sincere as mine—but one must admit that he is an honourable man and willing to do justice to others. I love him (as you know) and respect him with all my heart; and as for him, there is no doubt but that he has praised me warmly, not only to my face, but to others also, and in all seriousness—not in the exaggerated manner which some affect. Tenducci[3] is here too. He is Bach's bosom friend. He also was greatly delighted to see me again.[4] I must now tell you how I happen to be at St. Germain. As you already know (for I

---

[1] Johann Christian Bach.
[2] Bach's opera *Amadis de Gaule* had its first performance in Paris on 14 December 1779.
[3] Giustino Ferdinando Tenducci (1736–1790), a celebrated male soprano, who came to London in 1758 and remained in England and Ireland until 1791. He then returned to Italy. His portrait was painted by Gainsborough.
[4] The Mozarts had met Tenducci during their visit to London. See Leopold Mozart's *Reiseaufzeichnungen*, p. 35. and MBA, No. 99.

am told that I was taken *here* fifteen years ago,[1] though I don't remember it), the Maréchal de Noailles lives here. Tenducci is a great favourite of his, and because Tenducci is *very* fond of me, he was anxious to procure me this acquaintance. I shall not gain anything here, save perhaps a trifling present; at the same time I shall not lose anything, for this visit is costing me nothing; and even if I do not get anything, I shall still have made a very useful acquaintance. Well, I must make haste, for I am composing a scena for Tenducci,[2] which is to be performed on Sunday; it is for pianoforte, oboe, horn and bassoon, the performers being the Maréchal's own people —Germans, who play very well. I should like to have written to you long ago, but just as I had started a letter (which is now lying in Paris) I was obliged to drive to St. Germain, intending to return the same day. But I have now been here a week. I shall return to Paris as soon as possible, though I shall not lose much there by my absence, for I have now only one pupil, the others being in the country. I could not write to you before from here either, as we have been obliged to wait patiently for an opportunity to send a letter to Paris. Thank God, I am quite well, and I trust that both of you are the same. You must have patience—everything goes very slowly. I must make friends—France is rather like Germany in feeding people with praises. Yet there is some hope that by means of your friends you can make your fortune. The best part of the business is ⟨that food and lodging cost me nothing. When you write to the friends with whom I am staying,[3] don't be too obsequious in your thanks. There are reasons for this of which I shall tell you some other time.⟩ The rest of the story of my mother's illness will follow in the next letter. You really want a portrait of Rothfischer? He is an intelligent, hardworking conductor— not a great genius. But I was delighted with him—and, best of all, he is the kindest fellow, with whom you can do anything—of course, if you know how to set about it. He conducts better than Brunetti, but is not so good at solo-playing. He has better execution, and plays well in his way (a little bit in the old-fashioned Tartini manner)—but Brunetti's style is more pleasing. The concertos which he writes for himself are pretty— for playing now and then. They are always pleasant to listen to—and who can tell whether he may not please? Of course he plays ten million times better than Pinzger; and, as I have already said, he is a good conductor and very hardworking. I recommend him to you heartily, for he is the best fellow in the world. Adieu. I shall write a great deal more next time. A thousand compliments from Mr. Tenducci. A propos. M. Follard and his wife, a native of Munich, are here. He was French Ambassador in

---

[1] During the Mozart's first visit to Paris, from November 1763 to April 1764.
[2] There is no trace of this composition. Tenducci appears to have taken it to London, as Burney speaks very highly of it. See Barrington's *Miscellanies*, p. 289, and C. F. Pohl, *Mozart und Haydn in London*, vol. i. p. 121, and C. B. Oldman, 'Mozart's Scena for Tenducci', *Music and Letters*, Jan. 1961. [3] Grimm and Madame d' Épinay.

Munich and they met us there. When she heard my name she recognised me at once. But I cannot remember her. Adieu. Farewell. I kiss your hands a thousand times and embrace my dear sister with all my heart and remain your most obedient son

WOLFGANG MOZART

My compliments to Mr. Bullinger and to all my good friends.

(328) *Leopold Mozart to his Son*

[*Extract*]   [*Autograph in the Mozarteum, Salzburg*]

MY DEAR SON,   SALZBURG, 31 *August* 1778
    Since the two letters which I received together, the second being dated July 31st, I have not had a line from you, although I have written to you twice. You do not like being in Paris and on the whole I cannot
★ blame you. Well, thanks to my brave perseverance, not only have I got my way, that is, not only has the Archbishop agreed to everything, both for me and for you (you are to have five hundred gulden),[1] but he has even apologized for not being able at the present moment to appoint you Kapellmeister; you are, however, to take my place if I am tired or indisposed. And he mentioned that he had always intended that you should have a better salary, etc. In a word, I was astonished—but more particularly at the very polite apology. That reminds me, he has raised Paris's[2] salary by five gulden, so that he is to be responsible for most of the services; and you will be appointed Konzertmeister as before. So together we shall receive *an official salary* of a thousand gulden a year, as I have already told you. Everything now depends on whether you believe that I am still in possession of my mental faculties, whether you think that I have served your best interests, and whether you want to see me dead or alive. I have thought out everything. The Archbishop has declared that he will give you leave to travel where you like for the purpose of composing an opera. To excuse himself for having refused us leave last year, he said that he could not tolerate people going about the world begging. In Salzburg you will be midway between Munich, Vienna and Italy. It will be easier for you to get a commission for an opera in Munich than to get an appointment there, for where are German composers to be found? And
★ how many? My next letter will tell you that you are to leave. Your sister and I already kiss and embrace you in thought. Take care of your health.

    [1] Actually, according to his certificate of appointment, Mozart received 450 gulden. See Abert, vol. ii. p. 906.
    [2] Anton Paris (1739–1809), third organist to the Salzburg court.

We can hardly await the hour and the moment when we shall see you. I shall revive when you are here. I remain your honest father

MZT

Stick to Baron Grimm, for he will make arrangements for your journey. I write in haste, as it was only this morning that the matter of your appointment was settled.

(329) *Leopold Mozart to his Son*

[*Extract*]   [*Autograph in the Mozarteum, Salzburg*]

MY DEAR SON!   SALZBURG, 3 *September* 1778
    I hope that all my letters have reached you. I wrote to you on August 3rd, 13th and 27th, and enclosed a short note for you in a letter to Baron Grimm.[1] Yet since your letter of July 31st I have not had a line from you; and this makes my heart, which is already depressed, even more anxious. As the Elector and his Court are expected in Munich on September 15th, ★ you may be able, when you are travelling through, to speak to your friends, to Count Seeau and perhaps to the Elector himself. You might say that your father wished to have you back in Salzburg and that the Prince had offered you a salary of seven or eight hundred gulden as his Konzertmeister (for you should add two or three hundred gulden, though it is a lie), which salary you had accepted out of filial respect for your father, *although indeed he would prefer to see you in the service of the Elector.* But that is all; you should not say a word more! ★
    As for Mlle Weber, you should not think that I would be opposed to this acquaintance. All young people must learn by experience.[2] You can continue your exchange of letters as hitherto; I will not ask you about it, still less will I hanker after reading anything. Moreover, I will give you some advice—here you have enough people whom you know well and can have your Weber letters addressed to someone else and kept secret if you feel you are not safe against my curiosity. I should prefer you to ★ speak to the Imperial Ambassador, Baron Lörbach, who will be in Munich, and tell him that you are only applying for a commission to compose an opera in order to show what you can do. How, in Heaven's name, is the Elector to make up his mind to appoint you his Court Composer when he has never heard any of your compositions? You must arrange the business from here. It will be all the easier for you to get a commission, since the Italians can no longer push themselves forward.

---

[1] Letter 328.
[2] i.e. am Narrnseil laufen—a Viennese idiom—'run on a fool's string'.

Then things will move of their own accord. And finally I swear to you most solemnly that, as you yourself must know, I only remained tied to Salzburg in order that, whatever happened, your poor mother might have been sure of a pension. Well, that is all over now, the pension is no longer needed, and so we shall not stand any tyranny but be up and away. In your last letter you say '*My heart leaps up when I think of the happy day when I shall have the joy of seeing you again and embracing you with all my heart!*'[1] Well, my dear son, that day is now approaching; and I hope that God will let me live to see it. You will scarcely know your poor father. On the two occasions when I was summoned to the Archbishop, he was so shocked at my appearance that he spoke of it to everyone. I was ill when you left a year ago, and what have I not had to experience during this year? I must have a constitution of iron, or I should be dead already. If, when you return, you do not lift this heavy burden from my heart, it will crush me utterly. All heart-strengthening medicines are powerless to cure a distressed soul. You alone can save me from death. And no one will help you more loyally than your father who blesses, loves and kisses you with all his heart and who desires to fold you in his arms and who will use every effort which is humanly possible to achieve your happiness.

MOZART

★ I send my most obedient greetings to Baron von Grimm.

(330) *Leopold Mozart to his Son*

[Extract]   [Autograph in the Mozarteum, Salzburg]

MY DEAR SON!   SALZBURG, 10 *September* [1778]
  Indeed I cannot tell you how anxious I have been at not hearing from you for a whole month. I received two letters on August 11th, and one from St. Germain arrived today, September 10th. So four letters from me will have been awaiting you in Paris. One thing only I beg of you, and that is to read them carefully and think over my plans for you calmly ★ and setting aside all minor considerations. Are you going to remain in Paris? If you do, all your hopes for Munich are in vain, as are also your hopes for Italy. You are too far away. You will, of course, become better known in Paris, but you will be completely forgotten in Munich and Italy. You should move nearer to the centre at which you are aiming. I have explained everything with absolute clearness in my last letters. And what fortifies me in my plans for you is the following list of the Mannheim musicians who are going to Munich:

[1] See p. 588.

Female singers	*Flutes*
Madame Wendling *née* Sarselli	Wendling
„ Danzy	Metzger
„ Strasser	
	Oboes
Male singers	Ramm, Le Brun and Hieber
Signor Giorgetti, soprano	
„ Raff, tenor	*Violoncellos*
„ Hartig, tenor	Danzy and Schwarz
„ Zoncka, bass	
„ Weber, bass	*Double basses*
	Marconi and Bohrer
Violins	
Signor Cannabich	*Bassoons*
„ Toeschi	Ritter and Holzbauer
„ Jean Toeschi	
„ Fränzel	*Horns*
„ Wendling	Lang, Eck, Dimler and Lang
„ Ritschel	Junior
„ Winter	
„ Danner Junior	*Clarinets*
„ Schönge	Hampel, Tausch and Tausch
„ Sepp	Junior
„ Falgara	
„ Eck	*But no Kapellmeister*
„ Hampèl	This is the list which Becke [1]
„ Strasser	has sent me

and they are trying to get three more.

In this list I have found neither a *clavier* player nor an *organist* nor a *Kapellmeister*! So you see that you can do a great deal on your way through Munich, where the Court is to arrive on the 25th. I will tell you more about this by the next post or at the latest in a week, when I shall have received your certificate of appointment with the Archbishop's signature. I will tell you too how to arrange your journey to Donaueschingen, through which the diligence passes, and your visit to Prince von Fürstenberg; and I will send you a money order for Strassburg. By the ★ way, you may rest assured that the Archbishop has now great respect for you and that he will show it. No doubt he used to adopt that high and mighty attitude of his, in part to prevent us from putting forward our requests and in part because he never believed that you would really leave

[1] Johann Baptist Becke, flautist in the Munich court orchestra. He corresponded regularly with Leopold Mozart.

Salzburg. But he has had proofs to the contrary. He wishes to see you conduct from the harpsichord, and he has already handed over all the rest of the work to me. So he does not require any more Italian Kapellmeisters, and indeed he has been bamboozled far too much. I have nothing more to tell you, save that I can hardly contain myself for joy when I think that soon I shall fold you in my arms.

Your honest father

MZT

(331) *Mozart to his Father*

[*Autograph in the Mozarteum, Salzburg*]

MON TRÉS CHER PÉRE!   PARIS, 11 *September* 1778

I have received your three letters of August 13th, 27th and 31st, but I shall only reply to the last one, as it is the most important. When I read it through (M. Heina, who sends his compliments to you both, was with me), I trembled with joy, for I fancied myself already in your arms. It is true (and you will confess this yourself) that no great fortune is awaiting me in Salzburg. Yet, when I think of once more embracing you and my dear sister with all my heart, I care for no other advantage. This indeed is the only real excuse I can make to the people here who keep on shouting in my ears that I must remain in Paris: for I always reply at once: 'What do you mean? I am satisfied, and that settles it. There is one place where I can say I am at home, where I can live in peace and quiet with my most beloved father and my dearest sister, where I can do as I like, where apart from the duties of my appointment I am my own master, and where I have a permanent income and yet can go off when I like, and travel every second year. What more can I desire?' To tell you my real feelings, the only thing that disgusts me about Salzburg is the impossibility of mixing freely with the people and the low estimation in which the musicians are held there—and—that the Archbishop has no confidence in the experience of intelligent people, who have seen the world. For I assure you that people who do not travel (I mean those who cultivate the arts and learning) are indeed miserable creatures; and I protest that unless the Archbishop allows me to travel every second year, I can't possibly accept the engagement. A fellow of mediocre talent will remain a mediocrity, whether he travels or not; but one of superior talent (which without impiety I cannot deny that I possess) will go to seed, if he always remains in the same place. If the Archbishop would only trust me, I should soon make his orchestra famous; of this there can be no doubt. I can assure you that this journey has not been unprofitable to me, I mean from the point of view of composition, for, as for the clavier, I play it as well as I ever shall. But there is one thing more I must settle about Salzburg and that is that I shall not be kept to the violin, as I used to be. I will no longer be a fiddler. I want to conduct at the clavier and accompany arias. It would indeed have been a good thing if I could have obtained a written agreement regarding the post of Kapellmeister, for otherwise it may be that I shall have the honour of filling two posts and being paid for one—and in the end the Archbishop may again promote some stranger over my head. Dearest father! I must confess that were it not for the pleasure of seeing you both again, I really could not decide to accept. And yet I am glad to get away from Paris, which I detest, although my affairs here are beginning to improve steadily and I do not doubt that if I could make up my mind to hold out here for a few years, I should certainly get on very well. For I am now fairly well known, or—rather, people know me, even if I don't know *them*. I have made quite a name for myself by my two symphonies,[1] the second of which was performed on the 8th. Now that I have said that I am going away I could easily get a commission for an opera; but I have told Noverre; 'If you will guarantee that *it will be performed* as soon as it is finished, and will tell me exactly what I am going to get for it, I will stay on for another three months and compose it'. For I could not reject the offer at once, or people would have thought that I distrusted myself. Noverre could not agree to these terms (and I knew beforehand that he couldn't), for they are not the terms which are ordinarily offered here. What happens in Paris, as you probably know, is this:—When the opera is finished, it is rehearsed and if these stupid Frenchmen do not like it, it is not performed —and the composer has had all his trouble for nothing. If they think it good, it is produced and paid for in proportion to its success with the public. There is no certainty whatever. However, I am saving up these matters to discuss when we meet. I must tell you candidly that my own affairs are now beginning to prosper. It is no use trying to hurry matters— chi va piano, va sano.[2] My complaisance has won me both friends and patrons; if I were to tell you all, my fingers would ache! Well, I shall be able to relate all this by word of mouth and make it plain to you that M. Grimm may be able to help *children*, but not grown-up people—and— but no, I had better not write anything—and yet I must. Do not imagine that he—is the same as he was. Were it not for Madame d'Épinay, I should not be in this house. And he need not be so proud of his hospitality—for there are four houses where I could have had both board and lodging. The good fellow doesn't know that, *if I had remained in Paris*, I should have cleared out of his house next month and gone to a less boorish and stupid household, where people can do you a kindness without constantly casting it in your teeth. Such conduct is enough to make me *forget* a benefit. But I will be more generous than he is—I am only sorry that I am

---

[1] K. 297 [300a] is one of these symphonies. The other was probably an earlier work. See N. Zaslaw, *The Musical Times*, cxix (1978), p. 753 ff. [2] Slow and sure wins the race.

not remaining here, for I would show him that I do not need him—and that I can do as well as his Piccinni [1]—although I am only a German. The greatest kindness he has shown me has taken the form of fifteen louis d'or, which he lent me bit by bit during my mother's illness and death.—Is he afraid of losing them, I wonder? If he has any doubts about it, he really deserves to be kicked, for in that case he is distrusting my honesty (which is the only thing which is capable of driving me into a rage) and also my talents—but I know that he distrusts the latter, for he himself once said to me that he did not believe I was capable of composing a French opera. When I leave I shall return the fifteen louis d'or with thanks and I shall say a few very polite words. My poor mother often said to me: 'I don't know how it is, to me he seems to be quite changed'. But I always took his part, though secretly I was convinced that he was changed. He spoke about me to no one—or if he did, it was always done very stupidly and awkwardly or disparagingly. He was always wanting me to run off to see Piccinni, and Caribaldi [2] also—for they have a miserable opera buffa here now—but I invariably said: 'No, I shan't go a single step to see them' and so on. In a word, he is of the Italian faction—he is false and is even trying to down me. This seems incredible, does it not? But it is true, and here is the proof: I opened my whole heart to him as a true friend—and good use he has made of it! He always gave me bad advice, supposing that I should be stupid enough to follow it; but he was only successful two or three times, for latterly I have never consulted him—and when he has offered me advice, I have not taken it, although I have always said yes, so that I might not have to swallow more insults from him.

Well, enough of this. We can talk it over when we meet. At all events Madame d'Épinay has a better heart. The room I am living in belongs to her and not to him. It is the sick-room—that is, if anyone in the house is ill, he is put up there; it has nothing to recommend it, except the view: only four bare walls; no cupboard or anything. So now you may judge whether I could have stood it any longer. I would have told you this long ago, but I was afraid that you would not believe me. But, whether you believe me or not, I cannot keep silence any longer—and yet I feel sure that you do believe me, for I have still sufficient credit with you to convince you that I tell the truth. I take my meals too with Madame d'Épinay; but you must not suppose that he pays her anything, for indeed I cost her next to nothing. They have the same meals whether I am there or not, for as they never know when I am going to be in, they can't consider me; and in the evening I eat fruit and drink a glass of wine. All the time I have been in their house, which is now more than two months, I have not lunched with them more than fourteen times at most. So, with the exception of

---

[1] In the Gluck-Piccinni rivalry Grimm actively sided with the Piccinnists.
[2] Caribaldi was an opera buffa tenor whom the Mozarts had heard in Vienna. See p. 83.

the fifteen louis d'or, which I mean to repay with thanks, Grimm has been put to no expense whatever on my account save for candles; and I should really be ashamed of myself more than of him, were I to offer to supply my own; in fact, I could not bring myself to say such a thing—on my honour, I couldn't. I am like that. When he spoke to me the other day rather harshly, boorishly and stupidly, I hadn't the courage to say, as I was afraid of offending him, that he need not worry about his fifteen louis d'or. I just put up with it—and asked him whether he had said all that he wished. I then replied, 'Your obedient servant', and went off. He makes out that I must leave Paris in a week—*he is in such a hurry.* I have told him that this is impossible—and have given him my reasons. 'Oh,' he said, 'that doesn't matter; it is your father's wish.' 'Excuse me, in his last letter he said that he would let me know in his next when I was to leave.' 'Well, get ready for the journey anyhow.' But I must tell you plainly that it will be impossible for me to leave before the beginning of next month—or at the earliest the end of the present one, for I have still six trios to compose,[1] for which I shall be well paid. Moreover I must first get my money from Le Gros and the Duc de Guines—and, further, as the Court goes to Munich at the end of this month, I should like to be there at the same time to present my sonatas[2] to the Electress[3] in person, which might perhaps bring me a present. I shall pack my things and talk to Gschwendner, and send them off immediately or as soon as possible. I see that it is not adviseable to leave things behind with Grimm. As for my three concertos, the one written for Mlle Jeunehomme, the one for Countess Lützow and the one in B♭,[4] I shall sell them to the man who engraved my sonatas, provided he pays cash for them. And, if I can, I shall do the same with my six difficult sonatas.[5] Even if I don't get much—it will be surely better than nothing. On a journey one needs money. As for the symphonies,[6] most of them are not in the Parisian taste. If I have time, I shall rearrange some of my violin concertos,[7] and shorten them. In Germany we rather like length, but after all it is better to be short and good. In your next letter I shall no doubt find some instructions for my journey. I only hope that you have sent them to me alone, as I would rather have nothing more to do with Grimm. I trust that you have done so, and it would be better too —for on the whole a Gschwendner and a Heina can arrange these things better than this upstart Baron. Indeed I owe Heina more than I owe him, if you will but look at it by the light of a farthing candle. Well, I shall

[1] There is no trace of these works.   [2] K. 301-306 [293a-c, 300c, 293d, 300l].
[3] Marie Elizabeth, wife of the Elector Karl Theodor.
[4] K. 271, written in January 1777 for Mlle Jeunehomme; K. 246, written in 1776 for the Countess Lützow; K. 238, written in 1776.
[5] K. 279-284 [189d-h, 205b], the six clavier sonatas which Mozart composed in 1775.
[6] Mozart means his earlier symphonies, written in Salzburg.
[7] Mozart is referring to the five violin concertos which he composed in 1775.

expect an early reply to this letter and I shall not leave Paris until it comes. I have already worked out the times. You will get this letter on September 22nd; you will reply immediately; the post leaves on Friday the 25th and I shall have your answer on October 3rd. I can then leave on the 6th, for I am not in a hurry; nor is my stay here vain or fruitless, as I shut myself up and work in order to make as much money as possible. But there is one thing I want to ask you. I don't know yet how you want me to travel. As I shall not have a lot of extra luggage with me (for when I get an opportunity, I shall send in advance what I do not require), I could perhaps purchase a pretty cabriolet, of the type which is now very popular here. That's what Wendling did. After Strassburg you can travel as you like, with the mail coach or with a vetturino. The cabriolets here are different from what they used to be, for they are now closed and have glass windows. But they have two wheels and will take two persons who are not too stout. Well, I shall arrange all that when you have replied to this letter. I have another request which I trust you will not refuse. If it should happen, though I hope and believe it is not so, that the Webers have not gone to Munich, but are still at Mannheim, I should like to have the pleasure of going there to visit them. I know that this would take me a little out of my way, but it would not be much—or at all events it would not seem much to me. But I don't think that, after all, it will be necessary, for I'm sure I shall find them in Munich. I hope to be assured of this tomorrow by a letter. But, if that should not be the case, I am already convinced that you will not deny me this pleasure. Most beloved father! If the Archbishop wants a new singer, by Heaven I do not know of a better one. He will never get a Teiber or a De Amicis; and the rest are certainly worse. I am only sorry that when the Salzburg people flock to Mannheim for the next carnival and 'Rosemunde' is given, poor Mlle Weber will probably not please, or at least that they will not be able to judge her as she deserves —for she has a miserable part—almost that of a *persona muta*—and has only to sing a few lines between the choruses. She has one aria where something good might be expected from the ritornello, but the voice part is alla Schweitzer, as if dogs were yelping. She has only one song, a sort of rondo in the second act, where she has an opportunity of sustaining her voice a little and showing what she can do. Yes, unhappy indeed is the singer, male or female, who falls into Schweitzer's hands, for as long as he lives he will never learn how to write for the voice! When I return to Salzburg, I shall certainly not fail to plead with great enthusiasm for my dear friend. Meanwhile, please do all you can for her, for you cannot give your son greater pleasure. I think of nothing now but the delight of embracing you very soon. Please see that everything the Archbishop has promised you is absolutely assured—and also what I asked you for, that is, that my place should be at the clavier. My greetings to all my good friends, and particularly to Herr Bullinger. Oh, what fun we shall have together! I see it all in thought already—it is all before my eyes. Adieu.

I kiss your hands 100000 times and embrace my sister with all my heart. Hoping to have a reply at once, so that I may leave immediately, I remain your most obedient son

WOLFGANG AMADÈ MOZART

[PARIS, 11 *September* 1778] [1]

A propos. You will know from my last letter that I have been to St. Germain, where I was given a commission. Madame Follard, wife of a former French Ambassador in Munich, who is a bosom friend of the Bishop of Chiemsee, would like to know whether by any chance he has not received the letters which she sent him? For she has had no reply. So please do her this kindness, for she pressed me most earnestly to find out. Adieu. I await your reply, and I shall not leave until I get it. Do not appear to know anything about what I have told you concerning a certain gentleman. I like to reward people of his type with courtesy—which hurts them far more, for then they can't retort. Adieu.

(332) *Leopold Mozart to his Son*

[*Extract*]   [*Autograph in the Mozarteum, Salzburg*]

MY DEAR SON!   SALZBURG, 17 *September* 1778

I have been expecting a letter from you for two post-days, as I gathered from your last one of August 27th from St. Germain that you would be back in Paris at the end of August or the beginning of September and that you would have read my letters and thought over my plans. Well, either you must get settled in Munich or return for the time being to Salzburg, where you will enjoy a great reputation, a large salary and more consideration and responsibility. If you were here, it would be easier to further your prospects in Munich either by getting an appointment there or by writing operas. That I have pressed the matter earnestly to Padre Martini you can judge from the following reply which I received from him yesterday:

Ho piacere grande, etc.—Ritornato a Mannheim il Signor Raaff le ho scritto raccomandandole con tutta l'efficacia il di lei figlio, avendo ancora io grande premura che sia collocato decorosamente e vantaggiosamente: ma perchè il

Signor Raaff non rispose a una mia di somma premura, replico in quest'ordinario, e le raccomando l'affare quanto mai so e posso. Sento poi con rammarico la perdita della sua degna consorte, etc.—S'assicuri che ho tutta la premura possibile perchè ella venga consolata, e spero in Dio che obtenga il di lui contento, etc. Bologna 6 settembre.[1]

So you see that I am making every possible effort to get you an appointment in Munich. Everyone is longing to see you again! The Chief Steward offers you his horses and Dr. Prex his fine little bay; Louisa Robinig her love; I my health—long life—and all the good things which you would like your father to have; your sister her sisterly friendship, love and service; our maid Theresa all the thirteen capons which she has bought for you; and Bimperl several thousand licks. What more can you ask? Indeed the capons, which have been ordered in advance to celebrate your return, are already awaiting you. The players are to arrive this evening, and on Sunday we shall have the first play. *Look after your things and send off with your poor Mamma's belongings what you will not require for your journey. Take care of your possessions and make friends with no one when travelling. Sell the copies of all your music,* of which you or I have the original scores. *Bring back the addresses of the music dealers,* so that you may be able to correspond with them. And relieve me at last of all my worries which are causing me sleepless nights; and see to it that I may soon embrace you with the most inexpressible delight.

Your loving honest father

MZT

Bullinger and all our friends send their greetings and Nannerl and I kiss you a million times. Take care of your health!

(333) *Leopold Mozart to his Son*

[Extract]   [Autograph in the Mozarteum, Salzburg]

MY DEAR SON!   SALZBURG, 24 September 1778
    I have read your letter of the 11th with the greatest pleasure. ⟨I am not very much surprised at all you tell me about our mutual friend, for his letters have always struck me as rather suspicious.⟩ It would have been much better if you had told me all this long ago. ⟨I am not writing to him

[1] I am delighted, etc. On his return to Mannheim I wrote to Signor Raaff recommending your son to him very strongly, as I too am particularly anxious that he should have a suitable and profitable appointment. As Signor Raaff has not replied to my letter immediately, I am writing again by this post and urging him as far as I can to take up the matter. I am grieved to hear of the loss of your gracious wife, etc. Rest assured that it is my most earnest wish that you should be comforted, and I hope that God will grant you consolation, etc. Bologna, September 6th.

today, as I sent him a letter by the last post-day but one.⟩ You will now have received my letter of the 17th. Well, I must tell you that Baron von Grimm wrote to say that he would make arrangements for your journey to Strassburg, and from his letter I gathered that he must have advanced you money. So I replied that I wanted to pay everything and asked him to give me a letter of credit to Augsburg. Great Heavens! I had to write it, for how could I leave you high and dry? He replied, however: 'Je ne veux pas entendre parler de remboursement dans ce moment-ci. Quand vous serez plus à votre aise, nous solderons nos comptes. Je vous l'ai dit, je voudrais être en état de faire une pension à votre fils, etc.' My dear son, why, that is very polite, and you see that he has complete confidence in us. He goes on to say: 'Ne vous inquiétez pas de m'envoyer de l'argent, mais tracez à votre fils tout ce qu'il doit faire pendant sa route. Je vous le livrerai jusqu'à Strassbourg, si vous lui faites trouver là de l'argent pour continuer sa route par Augsbourg et Salzbourg, etc.' Such remarks, far from showing distrust of me, suggest that he has complete confidence in me. This was a great relief, for Grimm, who has travelled a good deal, must know best how you can get from Paris to Strassburg most safely and conveniently and without much expense. He knows the route, which I do not, and he will be responsible for the expenses of the journey. His letter ★ closes with these words: 'Employez donc l'argent que vous voulez m'envoyer, à son voyage depuis Strassbourg à Salzbourg, etc.' You may judge from this remark whether your suspicions were not too hasty. I do ★ not think that you should leave anything behind. But, if you can, you should sell some of your music at once. It is better that whatever does you no honour, should not be given to the public. That is the reason why I have not given any of your symphonies to be copied, because I suspect that when you are older and have more insight, you will be glad that no one has got hold of them, though at the time you composed them you were quite pleased with them. One gradually becomes more and more fastidious. Your idea of going to Mannheim is absolutely impracticable, because by the end of the month everyone who is not already at Munich will be going off there. Your desire that the Webers should have a thousand gulden a year has been fulfilled, for a letter from Munich of September 15th informs me that Count Seeau has engaged Mlle Weber for the German theatre at six hundred gulden. So if you add her father's four hundred they will have a thousand. I must now urge you most insistently to abandon all your high-flown ideas which are too exalted for our Salzburg orchestra. You think that I ought to have demanded for you a written promise of the post of Kapellmeister? But do you think that I attach such importance to this post?—Not at all! If you are at a small Court like ours, will you not always be perfectly free to leave? Again, you say—'*I will no longer be a fiddler*'. Why, formerly you were nothing but a *fiddler* and also incidentally *Konzertmeister*. But now you are Konzertmeister and Court Organist and your main duty will be to *accompany at the clavier*. As a lover of music you will not consider it beneath you to play the violin in the first symphony any more than does the Archbishop himself[1] and also the courtiers who play with us. You would surely not deny to Haydn certain achievements in music? Has he, a Konzertmeister, become a court viola-player, because he plays that instrument in the chamber music concerts? Why, one does it for one's own amusement; and as the concert is short and only consists of four items, believe me that to play is a pleasant recreation, as one doesn't know what to do with oneself in the evenings. If something more important turns up, eh bien! one stays away—as others have done. And I wager that rather than let your own composition be bungled—you will prefer to take part in the performance. It does not follow, however, that you will be regarded as a fiddler, while others enjoy themselves, and that you will have to play their trios and quartets. Not at all! My chief satisfaction in this arrangement is that your salary and my improved one will enable us to pay ⟨our debts⟩ and live in comfort. You are returning ⟨with a great reputation.⟩ Everyone knows that ⟨the Archbishop has invited you to return⟩ and the whole town is delighted that you have decided to come home and help your father who is now a widower and give him the necessary support in his old age. God keep you in good health and grant you a pleasant journey! It is a long one! Take care of yourself! Do not strike up an intimate friendship with anyone on the journey! Trust no one! Keep your medicines in your night-bag, in case you should need them. Look after your luggage when you get in and out

★ of the coach. Give my compliments to Baron von Grimm and ⟨*be sure not to play any impudent prank on him.*⟩ I shall write to him when I hear that you have left. We are counting the days until we can embrace you. That idiot of a maid Theresa has bought six more capons and Nannerl ironed

★ for you yesterday a most beautiful pair of *lace cuffs*. She and I kiss you a million times and I remain your father who is hoping to see you soon.

MZT

(334) *Leopold Mozart to his Son*

[*Extract*]   [*Autograph in the Mozarteum, Salzburg*]

SALZBURG, 1 *October* 1778

I am very much annoyed with Grimm for the way in which he has hurried up your departure from Paris. I received on September 29th his letter of the 11th, in which he informed me that you were leaving on the 26th par les carosses de Strassbourg; and my reply to your letter will not

---

[1] The Archbishop frequently played the violin in his orchestra. For an account of these performances see Abert, vol. i. p. 323.

arrive until October 3rd. He said that your journey would take ten days
and that you would arrive in Strassburg on October 5th or 6th. If you ★
cannot give a concert in Strassburg or make money quickly in some other
way, then hurry off and do not waste your time and substance. Scherz is to
give you just as much money as he thinks you require, for you will get
some more from my brother at Augsburg, to whom I am writing. I hope ★
to hear from you from Strassburg *what route you have chosen*, so that I may
make arrangements accordingly. I wish you a pleasant journey. Nannerl,
Bullinger and I are praying God to grant you this. I remain your honest
father, who awaits you,

MOZART

Nannerl and I kiss you a million times.

(335) *Mozart to his Father*

[Autograph in the Mozarteum, Salzburg]

MON TRÉS CHER PÉRE,   NANCY, 3 *October* 1778
     Please forgive me for not having informed you of my departure
before leaving Paris, but I simply cannot describe it to you, on account of
the way in which the whole business was hurried up, contrary to my
plans, hopes and wishes. At the last moment I wanted to send my luggage
to Count Sickingen's instead of to the Bureau des Diligences, and stay on
in Paris for a few days longer—and on my honour I would have done so,
had I not—thought of you—for I did not wish to cause you any anxiety.
We shall be able to go into all this more satisfactorily in Salzburg. But one
thing more. Just imagine, M. Grimm actually deceived me, when he said
that if I went by the diligence I should arrive in Strassburg in five days. It
was not until the last day that I found out that it was quite another coach,
which goes at a snail's pace, never changes horses and takes ten days! So
you may easily conceive my rage; but I only expressed my feelings to my
intimate friends—to him I pretended to be quite happy and contented.
When I got into the carriage, I heard the pleasant news that we should be
twelve days on the road. So you can see the great wisdom of Herr Baron
von Grimm. He sent me off by this slow conveyance simply to save
money, without ever considering that, as I should have continually to
be making use of inns, my expenses would be just the same. Well, it
is all over now; but what annoyed me most in the whole affair was his
not being straightforward with me. Of course it was his own money
which he saved, and not mine, as he paid for my journey, but not for my
keep; whereas, had I stayed eight or ten days longer in Paris, I should have
been able to arrange for my journey myself and much more comfortably.

Well, I endured a week in that carriage, but any longer I could not stand —not on account of fatigue, for the carriage was well sprung, but for want of sleep. We were off every morning at four o'clock, so we had to get up at three; and twice I had the honour of getting up at one o'clock, as the carriage was to leave at two. You know that I cannot sleep in a coach; so it was impossible for me to go on in this way without endangering my health. Moreover, one of our fellow-travellers was badly afflicted with the French disease—and didn't deny it either—which in itself was enough to make me prefer, should it come to the point, to travel by post-chaise. But that is not necessary, for I have had the good fortune to fall in with a man whom I like—a German merchant who lives in Paris and deals in English wares. Before getting into the coach we exchanged a few words, and from that moment we remained together. We did not take our meals with the other passengers, but in our own room, where we also slept. I am glad I met this man, for he has travelled a great deal and therefore understands the business. As he too has got bored with that coach, we have both left it and tomorrow we are proceeding to Strassburg by a good conveyance which does not cost us much. There I hope to find a letter from you and to learn from it something about my further journey. I hope you have received all my letters. Yours have reached me safely. Please forgive me for not writing much, but I am never in a good humour when I am in a town where I am quite unknown; though I believe that, if I had friends here, I should like to stay on, for it is indeed a charming place with hand-some houses, fine broad streets and superb squares. I have one thing more to ask you, which is to put a large chest in my room, so that I may have all my belongings beside me. I should also like to have beside my writing-desk the little clavier which Fischietti and Rust had, as it suits me better than Stein's small one.[1] I am not bringing you many new compositions, for I haven't composed very much. I have not got the three quartets[2] and the flute concerto[3] for M. De Jean, for, when he went to Paris, he packed them into the wrong trunk and so they remained in Mannheim. But he has promised to send them to me as soon as he returns to Mannheim, and I shall ask Wendling to forward them. I am therefore bringing no finished work with me except my sonatas[4]—for Le Gros purchased from me the two overtures[5] and the sinfonia concertante.[6] He thinks that he alone has them, but he is wrong, for they are still fresh in my mind and, as soon as I get home, I shall write them down again. The Munich players must now be giving performances. Are they popular? Do people go to see them?

[1] The portable clavier which Leopold Mozart purchased from Stein during the Mozarts, stay in Augsburg in 1763. See p. 22, n. 4.
[2] See p. 481, n. 2.   [3] K. 313 [285c] or K. 314 [285d].
[4] The clavier and violin sonatas K. 301–306 [293a–c, 300c, 293d, 300l].
[5] Another name for symphonies. See p. 613, n. 1.
[6] K. App. 9 [K. 297B]. See p. 522, n. 1.

I suppose that Piccinni's "Fishermaiden" (La pescatrice) or Sacchini's[1] "Peasant girl at court" (La contadina in corte) will be the first of the Singspiele to be given. The prima donna will be Mlle Kaiser, the girl I wrote to you about from Munich. I do not know her—I have only heard her sing. It was then her third appearance on the stage and she had only been learning music for three weeks. Well, good-bye. I shall not have one quiet hour until I see again all those I love in this world. I embrace my dear sister with all my heart and I kiss your hands a thousand times and remain your most obedient son

Wolfgang Amadè Mozart

My greetings to all my good friends, and especially to our true, dear friend Bullinger.

(336) *Mozart to his Father*

[Autograph in the Mozarteum, Salzburg]

Monsieur   Strassburg, 15 *October* 1778
   mon trés cher Père!

I have received your three letters of September 17th and 24th and October 1st, but it has been quite impossible to answer them sooner. I hope that you got my last letter from Nancy. I am most delighted that, thank God, you are both in good health. I too, thank God, am well—very well. I now want to reply as far as I can to the most important points in your three letters. What you have told me about M. Grimm I, of course, know better than you do. He was all courtesy and civility—that I know well. Had he been anything else, I should certainly not have stood on such ceremony with him. All that I owe M. Grimm, is fifteen louis d'or, and it is his own fault that I have not repaid them—and I have told him so. But what is the use of this rigmarole? We can talk it all over in Salzburg. I am very much obliged to you for having put my case so strongly before Padre Martini, and also for having written about me to Mr. Raaff. But I never doubted that you would do so, for I know that you like to see your son happy and contented and that you are aware that there is no place where I could be happier than in Munich, because, as it is so near Salzburg, I could often visit you. That Mlle Weber, or rather my dear Mlle Weber, is now receiving a salary, and that justice has at last been done to her merits, delights me as much as is to be expected from one who is deeply interested in her affairs. I commend her once more to you most warmly; though I

---

[1] Antonio Maria Gasparo Sacchini (1730–1786), a popular operatic composer in his day, whose operas were performed on nearly all the stages of Europe.

must now, alas! give up all hope of what I so desired—that is, that she should get an appointment in Salzburg—for the Archbishop would never give her the salary she is now drawing. At most she might come for a time to Salzburg to sing in an opera. I have had a letter from her father, written in great haste the day before their departure for Munich, in which he also mentions this piece of news. The poor things had all been in the greatest anxiety about me. They thought I was dead, as they had not heard from me for a whole month, for my last letter but one had gone astray—and they were further confirmed in this fear as it was being said in Mannheim that my poor mother had died of some contagious disease. So they had all been praying for my soul, and the poor girl had gone every day to the Capuchin Church to do so. Perhaps you will laugh? But I don't. I am touched and I cannot help it. Well, to proceed. I think I shall certainly go to Augsburg by way of Stuttgart, as, judging from your letters, there is nothing or generally not much to be made in Donaue- schingen. But you will hear all this in a letter which I shall send you before I leave Strassburg.

Dearest father! I assure you that were it not for the joy of embracing you so soon, I should certainly not return to Salzburg. For, apart from this praiseworthy and really delightful reason, I am truly committing the greatest folly in the world. Rest assured that these are my very own thoughts and have not been borrowed from other people. Of course, when people heard of my intention to leave Paris, they opposed it with strong argu- ments, against which my only effective weapon was my true and tender affection for my most beloved father, for which naturally people could not but praise me, adding, however, that if my father knew of my present circumstances and excellent prospects (and had not received different and false information from a certain good friend),[1] he would surely not have written to me in such a strain that resistance to his wish was out of the question. And I thought to myself that if I had not had to put up with so much vexation in the house where I was staying, and if matters had not developed into a series of thunderclaps, leaving me no time to consider the question coolly, I should have earnestly besought you to have had patience for a time and to have left me for a little longer in Paris, where I assure you I should have gained honour, reputation and wealth and should most certainly have removed the burden of your debts. But now the thing is done, and you must not for a moment suppose that I regret it, for you alone, dearest father, can sweeten for me the bitterness of Salzburg; and that you will do so, I feel convinced. Still, I must frankly confess that I should arrive in Salzburg with a lighter heart, did I not remember that I am to be in the service of the Court. It is that thought which is intolerable to me. Consider it yourself—put yourself in my place! At Salzburg I

[1] Grimm.

never know how I stand. I am to be everything—and yet—sometimes—nothing! Nor do I ask *so much* nor *so little*—I just want something—I mean to be something! In any other place I should know what my duties were. Everywhere else, whoever undertakes the violin, sticks to it, and it is the same with the clavier, etc. But no doubt all this can be arranged. Well, I trust that everything will turn out fortunately and happily for me. I rely wholly on you. Things here are in a poor state, but the day after tomorrow, Saturday the 17th, I am giving a subscription concert *all by myself* (for the sake of economy) to please some kind friends, amateurs and connoisseurs. If I engaged an orchestra, it would cost me, with lighting, over three louis d'or, and who knows whether I shall make that sum? I am obliged to you for having made such excellent arrangements about money for my journey. I do not think I shall need it—even if I do not give a concert. But I shall draw a few louis d'or either here or in Augsburg as a precaution, for one never can tell what may happen. Meanwhile, farewell. I shall tell you more in my next letter. My sonatas[1] cannot have been engraved yet, although they were promised for the end of September. That is what happens if you cannot see to a thing yourself. And that again is due to Grimm's obstinacy. They will very likely be full of mistakes, because I have not been able to revise them myself, but have had to get someone else to do so. And I shall probably have to go to Munich without these sonatas. These seemingly trivial matters may often bring success, honour and wealth or, on the other hand, disgrace. Well, adieu. I embrace my dearest sister with all my heart and you, my most beloved father, I kiss in the flattering hope of soon being able to embrace you and kiss your hand myself. I remain your most obedient son

WOLFGANG AMADÈ MOZART

My greetings to all Salzburg, and particulary to our dear and true friend Bullinger.

(337) *Leopold Mozart to his Son*

[*Extract*]   [*Autograph in the Mozarteum, Salzburg*]

MON TRES CHER FILS!   SALZBURG, 19 *October* 1778
    I received your letter from Nancy on October 13th. After reading it ★ I was more angry than ever with Baron Grimm. I cannot understand what his object was in hurrying you off so inconsiderately; and it would have been a good thing, provided that Count Sickingen could have taken you in, if you had remained a few days longer in Paris and waited for my last

---

[1] K. 301–306 [293a–c, 300c, 293d, 300l].

letter, that is, of course, if you had been sure of making some more money. I am annoyed with Grimm for other reasons too, which I shall reserve for our conversation. Now for a blow! *A most frightful blow!* I had written to the brothers Frank at Strassburg on October 1st, telling them of your arrival and of the money order on Herr Scherz. They replied on the 9th, saying *that you had not yet arrived, that the conductor of the coach had told them that you had stayed behind in Nancy with some travelling companions and so forth.* But you wrote to me from Nancy about the 3rd, saying that *you and that merchant had left the coach at Nancy and that you were both going off on the following morning to Strassburg by a good conveyance which would not cost much.* Well, seeing that six days later you had not reached Strassburg, must we not all think that *you have fallen ill?—or that the merchant in question was perhaps a robber or a knave?* And I am still in this dreadful state of anxiety, as today, October 19th, I have still had no letter from you. I await one with longing and yet I tremble, and so do we all, at sight of the postman, for I fear some frightful news. Whenever Bullinger appears, I watch his features with the greatest attention, lest he should be bringing my sentence of death. I have now spent four sleepless nights—*such ghastly nights, my son!* I dread them; and I am glad when the day breaks, which unfortunately is very late now. One single shimmer of hope still shines and soothes me when I turn to that passage in your letter where you say: '*Though I believe that, if I had friends here, I should like to stay on, for it is indeed a charming place with handsome houses, fine broad streets and superb squares*'.[1] As Abbé Henri has told me that Nancy has a theatre and a concert hall and as I feel sure that in such an important town you will have called on *some Kapellmeister, conductor or organist and tried one of the organs*, I am hoping that you have made acquaintances and found an opportunity of remaining for a few days and resting. You will remember that on our travels long ago we used to do this and at least went to see the organs in the churches. God grant that this may be so! I will gladly endure this dreadful agony, if there has been no ground for it. I have confessed and received Communion together with your sister and I have prayed God most earnestly to preserve you. Our excellent Bullinger prays daily for you at Holy Mass. I implore you to travel to Munich by the safest possible conveyance, for only three days ago two French merchants turned up here, who had been attacked near Plattling in Bavaria by nine robbers on a moonlight night and had lost a trunk. Take care of your health. Nannerl and I kiss you millions of times. I can hardly await the hour when I shall see you. I remain your very anxious father

MOZART

[1] See p. 622.

(338) *Mozart to his Father*

[*Autograph in the Mozarteum, Salzburg*]

Mon trés cher Pére!   Strassburg, 26 *October* 1778

As you see, I am still here and that too on the advice of Herr Frank
and some other Strassburg bigwigs; but I am leaving tomorrow. In my
last letter, which I hope you have received safely, I told you that on
Saturday the 17th I was giving a concert of sorts, for to give a concert here
is an even worse undertaking than in Salzburg. That, of course, is over
now—I played quite alone and I engaged no musicians, so that at least I
might lose nothing. Briefly, I took in three louis d'or in all. The chief
receipts consisted in the shouts of "Bravo! and Bravissimo!" which
echoed on all sides. Prince Max von Zweibrücken too honoured the
concert with his presence. I need not tell you that everyone was pleased.
I wanted to leave Strassburg at once, but they advised me to stay on until
the following Saturday and give a grand concert in the theatre. I did so
and to the surprise, indignation and disgrace of all the people of Strassburg,
my receipts were exactly the same. The Director, M. Villeneuve, cursed
the inhabitants of this really detestable town in a way that was delightful
to listen to. I took in a little more money certainly, but the cost of the
orchestra (who are very bad but demand to be paid handsomely), the
lighting, the guard, the printing, the crowds of attendants at the entrances and so forth made up a considerable sum. Still I must tell you that
the applause and clapping of hands made my ears ache as much as if the
whole theatre had been full. All who were present loudly and publicly
abused their fellow-citizens—and I told them all, that if I could have
reasonably supposed that so few people would have come, I should gladly
have given the concert gratis merely for the pleasure of seeing the theatre
well filled. And indeed I should have preferred it, for upon my word
there is nothing more depressing than a large T-shaped table laid for
eighty with only three at dinner. Besides, it was so cold—though indeed
I soon warmed myself, for, in order to show these gentlemen of Strassburg
how little I cared, I played a very long time for my own amusement,
giving one more concerto than I had promised—and, in the end, extemporizing for quite a while. Well, that is over—and at least I have won
honour and glory. I have drawn eight louis d'or from Herr Scherz simply
by way of precaution, for one can never know what may happen on a
journey; and a bird in the hand is always worth two in the bush. I have
read the fatherly, well-meaning letter which you sent to Mr. Frank, when
you were so anxious about me. Of course you could not know what I did
not know myself when I wrote to you from Nancy, that is, that I should
have to wait so long for a good opportunity. Your mind may be quite at

ease about the merchant with whom I am travelling. He is the most upright man in the world, takes more care of me than of himself, and, just to please me, is coming to Augsburg and Munich, and possibly even to Salzburg. We constantly shed tears when we think that we shall have to part. He is not a learned man, but a man of experience; and we live together like children. When he thinks of his wife and children, whom he has left in Paris, I try to console him; and when I think of my own people, he endeavours to comfort me.

November 2nd. On October 31st, my worthy name-day, I amused myself, or rather, I amused others for a couple of hours. At the repeated requests of Herr Frank, De Beyer and others, I gave another concert at which, after paying the expenses (which this time were not heavy), I actually cleared one louis d'or. Now you see what Strassburg is! I said at the beginning of this letter that I would leave on the 27th or 28th. But it has proved impossible, owing to sudden floods which have caused a great deal of damage. No doubt you will read about them in the papers. Travelling was thus out of the question, and that was the only reason which induced me to consent to give another concert, as I had to stay on in any case. Tomorrow I am leaving by the diligence and travelling through Mannheim. Do not be startled at this. In foreign countries it is expedient to follow the advice of those whom experience has taught better. Most of the strangers who travel to Stuttgart (I mean, by the diligence) think nothing of this détour of eight hours, for the road is better and the mail coach too. Well, all that I have to do now is to congratulate you, most beloved father, with all my heart on your approaching name-day.

Most beloved father! With all my heart I wish you all that a son can wish for his dear father, for whom he has great respect and real affection. I thank God Almighty that He has permitted you again to pass this day in excellent health, and I only ask Him for this grace that all my life long (and I hope to live for a good many years to come) I may be able to congratulate you every year. However strange and perhaps ridiculous this wish may seem to you, I assure you that it is both sincere and genuine.

I trust that you received my last letter of October 15th from Strassburg. I don't want to run down M. Grimm any more; but I cannot help saying that it is entirely due to his stupidity in hurrying up my departure that my sonatas [1] have not yet been engraved, or have not appeared—or at any rate that I have not yet received them. And when they do come, I shall probably find them full of mistakes. If I had only stayed three days longer in Paris, I could have corrected them myself and brought them with me. The engraver was in despair when I told him that I should not be able to revise them myself, but should have to commission someone else to do so.

---

[1] K. 301-306 [293a-c, 300c, 293d, 300l].

Why? Because, when I told Grimm that, as I could not spend three more days in his house, I was going to stay with Count Sickingen for the sake of the sonatas, he replied, his eyes sparkling with rage: 'Look here. If you leave my house before you leave Paris, I shall never look at you again as long as I live. In that case you must never come near me, for I shall be your worst enemy.' Well, self-control was indeed very necessary. Had it not been for you, who knew nothing about the whole affair, I should certainly have replied: 'Well, be my enemy; be so by all means. You are my enemy as it is, or you would not be preventing me from putting my affairs in order here—from doing what I have promised to do—and thereby preserving my honour and reputation—from making money and perhaps even my fortune. For if I present my sonatas to the Electress when I go to Munich, I shall be keeping my promise, I shall get a present—or even make my fortune.' But, as it was, I only bowed and went off without saying a word. Before I left Paris, however, I did say all this to him—but he answered me like an idiot—or like some wicked fellow who now and then prefers to behave like one. I have written twice to M. Heina, but have got no reply. The sonatas ought to have appeared by the end of September and M. Grimm was to have forwarded the promised copies to me at once. So I expected to find them in Strassburg. M. Grimm says in a letter that he has not seen or heard anything of them, but that he will forward them to me as soon as he gets them. I hope I shall have them soon. Strassburg is loth to let me go! You cannot think how much they esteem and love me here. They say that everything about me is so distinguished—that I am so composed—and polite—and have such excellent manners. Everyone knows me. As soon as they heard my name, the two Herren Silbermann[1] and Herr Hepp,[2] the organist, came to call on me, and also Kapellmeister Richter.[3] The latter now lives very economically, for instead of forty bottles of wine a day he only swills about twenty. I have played here in public on the two best organs built by Silbermann, which are in the Lutheran churches—the New Church and St. Thomas's Church. If the Cardinal[4] (who was very ill when I arrived) had died, I might have got a good appointment, for Richter is seventy-eight. Now, farewell! Be cheerful

[1] Johann Andreas Silbermann (1712–1783) belonged to a famous family of organ-builders. He built 54 organs, including the organ of the Dominican Church at Strassburg. He also wrote a history of Strassburg which was published in 1775. His younger brother, Johann Heinrich Silbermann (1727–1799), also an organ-builder, was living in Strassburg at that time. They were both sons of Andreas Silbermann (1678–1734), who built the Strassburg Cathedral organ.

[2] Sixtus Hepp (1732–1806).

[3] Franz Xaver Richter (1709–1789) was at first bass singer at the Mannheim court. In 1769 he left Mannheim for Strassburg, where he became Kapellmeister at the cathedral and where he remained until his death. He composed 64 symphonies in the style of the Mannheim school and an enormous amount of church music.

[4] Louis Constantin de Rohan (1697–1779), who in 1756 became bishop of Strassburg and in 1761 cardinal. His successor was the famous Cardinal de Rohan.

and in good spirits. Remember that your son, praise and thanks be to God, is in good health and is delighted that his happiness daily draws nearer. My greetings to all my good friends, and particularly to Herr Bullinger. I embrace my dearest sister with all my heart, and kiss your hands a thousand times and remain your most obedient son

WOLFGANG MOZART

Last Sunday I heard in the Minster a new mass by Richter, which is charmingly written.

(339) *Mozart to his Father*

[*Autograph in the Mozarteum, Salzburg*]

MON TRÉS CHER PÉRE!   MANNHEIM, 12 *November* 1778
I arrived here safely on the 6th and pleasantly surprised all my good friends. God be praised that I am back again in my beloved Mannheim! I assure you, if you were here, you would say the same. I am staying with Madame Cannabich, who, with her family and all my good friends here, was almost beside herself with joy at seeing me again. We have not finished talking yet, for she is telling me of all the events and changes which have taken place during my absence. Since I came here I have not been able to lunch at home once, as there is a regular scramble to have me. In a word, Mannheim loves me as much as I love Mannheim. And I am not positive, but I believe that I may yet obtain an appointment here— here, not in Munich; for my belief is that the Elector ⟨will be glad to have his residence again in Mannheim, as he will not be long able to stand the insolence of those Bavarian gentry!⟩ You know that the Mannheim company is in Munich. Well, the Bavarians have already hissed there the two best actresses, Madame Toscani and Madame Urban, and there was such an uproar that ⟨the Elector himself⟩ leaned over his ⟨box⟩ and called out—'Sh'—and when nobody took the slightest notice, he sent someone down to put a stop to it—and ⟨Count Seeau,⟩ who had asked certain officers not to make such a noise, as ⟨the Elector⟩ did not like it, got the reply ⟨that they had paid to come in and would take orders from no one.⟩ But, what a fool I am! You must have heard this long ago from our—[1] Now for something important. I have a chance of making forty louis d'or here! To be sure, I should have to stay six weeks, or at most two months in Mannheim. The Seyler company are here, whom no doubt you already know by reputation; Herr von Dalberg is their manager. He

---

[1] Mozart omits the name. The reference is to Johann Baptist Becke, flautist in the Munich Court orchestra, who corresponded regularly with Leopold Mozart.

refuses to let me go until I have composed a duodrama for him; and indeed it did not take me long to make up my mind, for I have always wanted to write a drama of this kind.[1] I cannot remember whether I told you anything about this type of drama the first time I was here? On that occasion I saw a piece of this kind performed twice and was absolutely delighted. Indeed, nothing has ever surprised me so much, for I had always imagined that such a piece would be quite ineffective! You know, of course, that there is no singing in it, only recitation, to which the music is like a sort of obbligato accompaniment to a recitative. Now and then words are spoken while the music goes on, and this produces the finest effect. The piece I saw was Benda's[2] 'Medea'. He has composed another one, 'Ariadne auf Naxos', and both are really excellent.[3] You know that of all the Lutheran Kapellmeisters Benda has always been my favourite, and I like those two works of his so much that I carry them about with me. Well, imagine my joy at having to compose just the kind of work I have so much desired! Do you know what I think? I think that most operatic recitatives should be treated in this way—and only sung occasionally, when the words *can be perfectly expressed by the music*. An Académie des Amateurs, like the one in Paris, is about to be started here. Herr Fränzl is to lead the violins. So at the moment I am composing a concerto for violin and clavier.[4] I found my dear friend Raaff still here—but he left on the 8th. He has been singing my praises and has been using his influence on my behalf. I hope he will do the same in Munich. Do you know what that ⟨confounded rascal Seeau⟩ has been saying here? That my opera buffa[5] was hissed off the boards in Munich! Unfortunately for him he said it at a place where I am very well known! But what annoys me is his impudence, for when people go to Munich, they will hear the exact opposite! There is a whole regiment of Bavarians here, including Fräulein de Pauli (I don't know her present name). But I have been to see her already, for she sent for me at once. Oh! what a difference there is between the Palatines and the Bavarians! What a language Bavarian is! So coarse!—as is their whole manner of living too! I really get scared when I think that I shall have to listen to their 'hoben' and 'olles mit einonder' and their 'gestrenger Herr'.[6] Well, good-bye, and write to me soon. Just put my name on the cover, for they know at the post office

---

[1] Mozart was to compose the music for *Semiramis*, a drama by Otto Heinrich von Gemmingen. See p. 638, n. 2.   [2] See p. 444, n. 2.

[3] *Ariadne auf Naxos* had its first performance on 27 January 1775, and *Medea* on 1 May 1775. Both duodramas were produced at Gotha, where Georg Benda was Kapellmeister.

[4] K. App. 56 [K. 315f.]. This work was never completed. The fragment consists of 120 bars. Saint-Foix adds to his discussion of this unfinished concerto (vol. iii. ךp. 122-124) the following remark: 'On est tenté de penser, lorsqu'on a étudié les projets musicaux de Mozart, que ses œuvres inachevées sont parfois les plus belles, et eussent été les plus achevées'.

[5] *La finta giardiniera*, written for the 1775 carnival in Munich.

[6] Mozart gives examples of the Bavarian dialect.

where I am! I will give you one instance which proves how well my name
is known here and that it is indeed quite impossible that a letter for me
could go astray. My cousin [1] wrote to me, addressing the letter 'Fränkischer
Hof' instead of 'Pfälzischer Hof'. The landlord sent it immediately to
Privy Court Councillor Serrarius, where I lodged the last time I was here.
I am writing to my cousin by this post [2] to tell her to forward the letters
which are waiting for me at their house.

What delights me most of all in the Mannheim and Munich story is
that Weber has feathered his nest so well. They will now have 1600
gulden—for the daughter alone has 1000 and her father 400 with an
additional 200 as prompter. This is due mainly to Cannabich—but it's a
long story. As for ⟨Count Seeau,⟩ well, if you don't know that story
already, I shall tell it to you in my next letter.

Meanwhile, farewell, my dearest, most beloved father. I kiss your hands
a thousand times and embrace my dear sister with all my heart and remain
your most obedient son

WOLFGANG AMADÈ MOZART

I beg you, dearest father, to make use of this affair [3] at Salzburg and to
speak so strongly and emphatically that the Archbishop may be led to
think that perhaps I shall not come after all, so that he may thus be induced
to give me a better salary; for I declare that I cannot think of the whole
business with composure. Indeed the Archbishop cannot pay me enough
for that slavery in Salzburg! As I said before, I feel the greatest pleasure at
the thought of paying you a visit—but only annoyance and anxiety when
I see myself back at that beggarly Court! The Archbishop had better not
begin to play the high and mighty with me as he used to—for it is not at all
unlikely that I shall pull a long nose at him! Indeed it is quite likely; and
I am sure that you too will share the pleasure which I shall have in so doing.
Adieu. I say, if you would like to save me ten kreuzers, always address
your letters to Mannheim thus:

> à Monsieur
> 　　Monsieur Heckmann, Registrateur
> 　　　　de la chambre des finances de S:A:S:
> 　　　　　　Élect: Palatine
> 　　　　　　　à Mannheim.

Well, adieu—farewell. Take care of your health which is so precious
to me.

My greetings to all my good friends, and especially to our true friend
Bullinger.

[1] Maria Anna Thekla Mozart, the 'Bäsle'.
[2] If Mozart did so, the letter has disappeared.
[3] His commission to write a duodrama for Dalberg.

(340) *Leopold Mozart to his Son*

[*Extract*]   [*Autograph in the Mozarteum, Salzburg*]

MON TRÈS CHER FILS!   SALZBURG, 19 *November* 1778

Really, I don't know what to say to you. I shall go mad or die of a decline. The very recollection of all the projects which since your departure from Salzburg you have formed and communicated to me is enough to drive me crazy. They have all amounted to proposals, empty words ending in *nothing whatever*. And now, having cherished since September 26th the comforting hope of seeing you in Salzburg *on your name-day*,[1] I have had to endure *my first taste of mortal agony*, for on the 3rd you wrote from Nancy that you were going to Strassburg the following day, while on the 9th the brothers Frank wrote to say that you had not yet arrived there. Then you did not write to me from Strassburg until the 14th. So during your stay in Nancy you were playing ducks and drakes with your money, when, instead of frittering it away, you might have spent it in hiring a conveyance of your own and thus making your way more quickly to Strassburg. Then you sat down in Strassburg until the heavy rains began, although I had previously told you that, if there was no profit to be made, you should leave at once and not throw your money away; and although you yourself had told me that things there were in a poor state and that you would leave at once after the little concert you were giving on the 17th. But people praised you!—*and that is always enough for you!* There you sat without writing me a line, and thus you gave me *my second taste of mortal agony* (for we too had rain and floods here), and only on November 10th was the burden of anxiety lifted by your letter sent off on November 2nd. Had you left Strassburg on the 19th or 20th after your concert on the 17th, you would have arrived in Augsburg before the floods, we should have been relieved of our anxiety, and the wasted money would have been still in your pocket. Then Herr Scherz wrote to say that you were leaving on the 5th. So I kept on hoping every post-day for news from Augsburg that you had arrived. But it was always 'He is not here yet', and a letter of November 13th actually stated that you were not coming at all. And so, having had no word from you until today, the 19th, I was naturally in *my third state of agony*, as I could not possibly entertain the mad supposition that you would stay at Mannheim, where there is no longer a court, and consequently thought that you must have arrived at Augsburg on the 10th at the very latest. Why, I believed this with the greater certainty as I thought you would lose no time in getting to Munich, where, as I imagined, the moment you left Nancy you would apply for work in connection with the Festival of St. Charles.[2] So you only

---

[1] October 31st.   [2] November 4th.

drew eight louis d'or in Strassburg as a precaution and simply in order to sit about in Mannheim? You hope to get an appointment there? An appointment? What does that mean? You must not take an appointment at present either in Mannheim or anywhere else in the world. I will not hear the word *appointment*. If the Elector were to die today, a whole battalion of musicians in Munich and Mannheim would have to go about the world begging their bread, for the Duke of Zweibrücken has an orchestra of thirty-six, and the present orchestra of the Bavarian Electorate and Mannheim costs 80,000 gulden a year.

★

The main thing is that *you should now return to Salzburg*. I do not want to hear anything more about the forty louis d'or which *perhaps* you may be able to earn. Your whole intention seems to be to ruin me, simply in order to go on building your castles in the air. When you left Paris, you
had *more than fifteen louis d'or* in your pocket, that is   165 gulden
According to your statement you made
at least seven louis d'or in Strassburg   77 gulden
You drew eight louis d'or from Herr Scherz   88 gulden
_____
330 gulden

The carriage from Paris was paid for. So that is a nice sum for a single person—seeing that when travelling by the diligence the expenses are small—à proportion, of course.

In short, I am *absolutely determined* not to remain covered with disgrace and deep in debt on your account; and still less to leave your poor sister destitute. Neither you nor I know how long God will permit you to live. If I were to write and tell Madame Cannabich that

on your departure from Salzburg I provided   300 gulden
that I arranged for you to draw in Mannheim   200 gulden
that I paid for money which you drew from
Gschwendner in Paris   110 gulden
that I owe Baron Grimm fifteen louis d'or   165 gulden
that you drew eight louis d'or in Strassburg   88 gulden
so that in fourteen months *you have plunged
    me into debt to the extent of*   863 gulden
_____

if I were to ask her *to give this information to all who are advising you to remain in Mannheim and to tell them that I am asking you to come to Salzburg to take an appointment for a couple of years, as then I might have some prospect of paying off these debts*, they would not say one word to hold you back and they would make quite different faces. In short, up to the present I have written to you not only as a father, but also as a friend. I trust therefore that when you receive this letter you will hasten your journey home and so arrange your affairs that I shall be able to receive you with joy and not have to meet you with reproaches. I hope to have a letter from you ★ shortly, telling me that you have left. God grant you a pleasant journey. I kiss you a million times and remain your father, who awaits you,

MZT ★

(341) *Leopold Mozart to his Son*

[*Extract*]   [*Autograph in the Mozarteum, Salzburg*]

MON CHER FILS!   SALZBURG, 23 *November* 1778

I hope that this letter will no longer find you in Mannheim and, as you will have received my reply of the 19th, I trust that, if you are still there, you will leave by the very first mail coach. Two things seem to be ★ turning your head and altogether preventing you from thinking out matters sensibly. The first and chief one is your love for Mlle Weber, to which I am not at all opposed. I was not against it when her father was poor, so why should I be so now, *when she can make your happiness—* though you cannot make hers? I assume that her father knows about this love, as everyone in Mannheim knows about it. Fiala heard about it there. Bullinger, who is tutor in Count Lodron's house, told us that when the Count was driving with the Mannheim musicians in the mail coach from Ellwangen (where he was on holiday), they talked to him of nothing but your skill, your talent for composition and your love for Mlle Weber. Well, I told you long ago that by entering the Archbishop's service you will have the advantage of being nearer Munich, which you can reach in eighteen hours, where we can hear about everything, even the smallest matter, whither we can take a trip as easily as to Seeon,[1] and whence Herr Weber and his daughter can visit us and even stay with us. Further, by ★ entering the Archbishop's service (which, however, is the *second thing* which seems to be turning your head) you will have the one and only opportunity of getting to Italy again, a plan which attracts me most of all. Yesterday Herr Fiala was with the Archbishop, who questioned him ★ about the Mannheim musicians and especially about their compositions. Fiala told him that the best music in Mannheim was Mozart's, that at the very first concert, there being one every Monday in the Kaisersaal, apart from Cannabich's symphony everything else was Mozart's, and that immediately after the symphony Mlle Weber had sung an aria by Mozart,[2] the like of which he had never heard in his life. Then he had to give an exact account to the Archbishop, who wanted to have full details about each of the players who had performed your concertos, and displayed

---

[1] A famous Benedictine monastery on an island in the Klostersee, near the Chiemsee.
[2] K. 294, a recitative and aria 'Non so d'onde viene', written for Aloysia Weber. See p. 497, n. 3.

great satisfaction. Then he had to give him full particulars about Mlle Weber, her singing, her age and so forth. My dear Wolfgang, I am inclined to think that Herr Weber is a man like most of his type, who make capital out of their poverty and, when they become prosperous, lose their heads completely. He flattered you when he needed you—perhaps he would not even admit now that you had shown her or taught her anything. Those who have been poor generally become very haughty when ★ their circumstances improve. I have had a useful chest made for your room in which you can lay your clothes on shelves. It has no drawers, only two doors. The clavichord has been under your writing-table for a very ★ long time. Do not delay your arrival any longer, if you are in Mannheim, that is, if you want me to believe that you love me and wish to keep me alive. I kiss you a million times and remain your honest father

MZT

Your sister embraces you with all her heart. Ceccarelli can hardly await the moment when he will meet you. Bullinger, Fiala and his wife, Feiner,[1] Rüscherl Gilowsky,[2] all the Robinigs, Andretters, Mölks, Hagenauers and Kolbs send their greetings. I have found rooms for Fiala in Hagenauer's house three flights up, where you and your sister were born. I trust you will leave at once. If not, I shall write to Madame Cannabich. If it is God's will, I want to live a few years longer, pay my debts—and then, if you care to do so, you may have your own obstinate way. But, no! you have too good a heart! You have no vices. You are just thoughtless! You will be all right in time!

(342) *Mozart to Heribert von Dalberg*[3]

[Autograph in the Staatsbibliothek, Munich]

MONSIEUR LE BARON!   MANNHEIM, 24 *November* 1778

I have called on you twice to pay my respects, but have not had the good fortune to find you at home. Yesterday you were in the house, it seems, but I could not see you! So I hope that you will forgive me for troubling you with these few lines, for it is very important to me to explain myself fully. Herr Baron, you are well aware that I am not a self-interested person, particularly when I know that it is in my power to

---

[1] Joseph Feiner, second oboist in the Salzburg orchestra.   [2] Katherl Gilowsky.

[3] Baron Wolfgang Heribert von Dalberg (1750–1806) had obtained from the Elector Karl Theodor a charter dated 1 September 1778, allowing the establishment of a Mannheim National Theatre under the management of Dalberg and with a subsidy of 500 gulden from the Court. From 1779 onwards this theatre prospered and attracted some of the leading German actors, including Iffland, and the best dramatists, particularly Schiller. See F. Walter, *Geschichte des Theaters und der Musik am Kurpfälzischen Hofe* (Leipzig, 1898), and J. H. Meyer, *Die bühnen-schriftstellerische Tätigkeit des Freiherrn Wolfgang Heribert von Dalberg* (Heidelberg, 1904).

render a service to so great a lover and so true a connoisseur of music as yourself. At the same time I am convinced that certainly you would not wish that I should be a loser here. I therefore take the liberty of stating my final conditions, as it is quite impossible for me to remain here any longer in uncertainty. I undertake to compose a monodrama for the sum of twenty-five louis d'or, to stay on here for another two months, to make all the arrangements which will be necessary in connexion with it, to attend all the rehearsals and so forth, but on this condition that, whatever happens I, shall be paid by the end of January. In addition I shall of course expect free admission to the theatre. You see, my dear Baron, that this is all I can do! If you consider it carefully, you will admit that I am certainly acting with great discretion. In regard to your opera[1] I assure you that I should be delighted to compose the music for it; but you yourself must agree that I could not undertake this work for twenty-five louis d'or, as (reckoned at its lowest) it would be twice the labour of writing a mono-drama. Again, what would deter me most would be the fact that Gluck and Schweitzer, as you yourself told me, are already composing the music. Yet, even assuming that you were willing to give me fifty louis d'or, I should still as an honest man most certainly dissuade you from the under-taking. An opera without male and female singers! What an extra-ordinary idea! Still, if in the meantime there is a prospect of its being per-formed, I shall not refuse to undertake the work to oblige you—but it would be no light task, that I swear to you on my honour. Well, I have now set forth my ideas clearly and candidly and I request your decision as soon as possible. If I might have it today, I should be the better pleased, as I hear that someone is travelling alone to Munich next Thursday and I should very much like to take advantage of this opportunity. Meanwhile I have the honour to remain with the greatest respect—

> Monsieur Le Baron!
>   your most obedient servant
>   WOLFGANG AMADÈ MOZART

ce mercredi le 24 novembre
       1778.

(343) *Mozart to his Father*

[*Autograph in the Mozarteum, Salzburg*]

MONSIEUR   MANNHEIM, 3 *December* 1778
   MON TRÉS CHER PÉRE!

I must ask your forgiveness for two things—firstly, that I have not written to you for so long—and secondly, that this time also I must be

---

[1] Dalberg had written *Cora, ein musikalisches Drama* and was negotiating with Gluck and Schweitzer with a view to having it set to music. The plan was dropped. *Cora* was published in a *Beitrag zur pfälzischen Schaubühne* (Mannheim, 1780).

brief. My not having answered you sooner is the fault of no one but yourself, and of your first letter to me at Mannheim.[1] Really I never could have believed—but peace! I will say no more about it. For it is all over now. Next Wednesday, December 9th, I am leaving Mannheim. I could not do so any sooner, for, thinking that I was going to be here for a couple of months, I took some pupils; and of course I wanted to make up my twelve lessons. I assure you that you have no idea what good and true friends I have here. Time will certainly prove it. Why must I be brief? Because I am up to the eyes in work! To please Herr von Gemmingen and myself I am now composing the first act of the declaimed opera (which I was commissioned to write) and I am also doing this *for nothing*; I shall bring it with me and finish it at home.[2] You see how strong is my liking for this kind of composition. Herr von Gemmingen is the poet, of course—and the duodrama is called 'Semiramis'.

I have received your last letter of November 23rd. I am setting off next Wednesday, and do you know how I am travelling? With the worthy Imperial Abbot of Kaysersheim. When a kind friend of mine spoke to him about me, he at once recognized my name and said what a pleasure it would be to him to have me as a travelling companion. Although he is a priest and a prelate, he is a most amiable man. So I am travelling through Kaysersheim and not through Stuttgart; but it is all the same to me, and indeed I am very lucky in being able to spare my rather slender purse a little on the journey. Do answer the following questions. What do people in Salzburg think of the players? Is not the girl who sings called Kaiser? Does Herr Feiner play the cor anglais as well? Ah, if only we had clarinets too! You cannot imagine the glorious effect of a symphony with flutes, oboes and clarinets. I shall have much that is new to tell the Archbishop at my first audience and I shall make some suggestions as well. Ah, how much finer and better our orchestra might be, if only the Archbishop desired it. Probably the chief reason why it is not better is because there are far too many performances. I have no objection to the chamber music, but only to the concerts on a larger scale. A propos—you do not mention it, but I assume that you have received the trunk; if not Herr von Grimm is responsible. You will find in it the aria I wrote for Mlle Weber.[3] You have no idea what an effect it produces with instruments; you cannot judge of it by the score, for it must be rendered by a singer like Mlle Weber. Please do not give it to anyone, for that would be the greatest injustice, as it is written solely for her and fits her like a well-tailored garment. Now farewell, dearest, most beloved father. I embrace my dear sister with all my heart. Please give all sorts of messages to our dear friend Bullinger, and my greetings to Ceccarelli, Fiala, his wife and Herr Feiner and to all

---

[1] Leopold Mozart's letter of 19th November (Letter 340).
[2] There is no trace of this composition.   [3] K. 294, 'Non so d'onde viene'.

those people of Salzburg who have some idea what life is like outside their native district. Adieu. I kiss your hands a thousand times and—remain your most obedient son

WOLGANG AMADÈ MOZART

(344) *Leopold Mozart to his Son*

[*Extract*]   [*Autograph in the Mozarteum, Salzburg*]

MON TRÉS CHER FILS!   SALZBURG, 10 *December* 1778

After waiting so long for it I was delighted to receive today your letter of December 3rd, to which I am replying at once. I daresay my letter will still reach you at Kaysersheim, though indeed I hope that you will not prolong your stay there unduly. You want to know what Salz- ★
burg thinks of the players? Up to the present I have been in no humour to write to you about such trifles. Well, on the whole the company is a rather poor one, but two of them, Herr Heigel and his wife,[1] *are excellent*. Mlle Kaiser is not with the company, because the Dowager Duchess Clemens, who gives her a salary and her keep, has refused to let her come. So they have had to bring another singer, who is of good family and acts under the name of Mlle Ballo.[2] Her only asset is a very powerful chest voice, which, however, is quite untrained. Well, I have no idea, in fact I cannot really imagine, what a declaimed duodrama, as you describe it, really is. I suppose that in this type of opera a great deal more depends on declamation and action than on fine singing, or rather than on a first-class voice. Herr Heigel and his wife would certainly do it to perfection, as both of them sing in operettas and are such good actors that one forgets how poor their voices are. Your trunk has arrived. Everything was very care- ★ ★
fully packed. As well as a few oddments the following articles are missing: —two new caps of Brussels lace, a length of gold lace and the little amethyst ring which Madame d'Épinay gave your mother a long time ago. And where is your mother's *gold watch*? Has it been pawned?

Signor Ceccarelli has come in this very moment. He again sends you his greetings and asks me to tell you that he is longing to meet you. He has just sat down at the clavier and is learning Schröter's first concerto in F[3] with your sister. Herr Bullinger too sends his greetings. He is delighted that we have heard from you at last, that, thank God, you have started on your homeward journey and that from September 26th to December 9th you have covered such a distance so rapidly.[4]

[1] Franz Xaver Heigel and Caroline Reiner. They had given a farewell performance of *Romeo and Juliet* at Munich on 15 September 1778, and possibly repeated it at Salzburg.
[2] Franziska Ballo, who afterwards married Marschhauser, the actor.
[3] Op. III, no. 1. For the first movement of this concerto Mozart wrote a cadenza. See Köchel, p. 735.
[4] The last paragraph (p. 640) is written on the cover.

I have actually set up music engraving here, as I have found someone whom I have trained. On your arrival you will find here your variations on Salieri's arioso [1] engraved on seven sheets. I only wish you had not made them so well known, for then I could sell more copies. [2] They are beautifully engraved, far more clearly than Schröter's concerto. You must compose something new as soon as possible and have it engraved. Your variations were finished today.

★

(345) Mozart to his Father

[Autograph in the Mozarteum, Salzburg]

MON TRÉS CHER PÉRE!   KAYSERSHEIM, 18 December 1778

Thank God, I arrived here safely on Sunday, the 13th. I travelled in the most agreeable way and had, moreover, the indescribable pleasure of finding a letter from you waiting for me. The reason why I did not reply to you at once was because I wanted to send you the most certain and precise information about my departure from here, for which I myself had not fixed any definite date. But I have at last decided—as the Abbot is going to Munich on the 26th or 27th, to accompany him again. I must tell you, however, that he is not travelling by way of Augsburg. I shan't lose anything by this; but if you have anything to arrange or transact where my presence might be necessary, I can always, if you wish it, take a short trip there from Munich, as it is very near. My journey from Mannheim to Kaysersheim would have been certainly most pleasant to a man who was leaving a town with a light heart. The prelate and his chancellor, a very honest, worthy and amiable fellow, drove in one carriage; and Father Daniel, the cellarer, Brother Anton, the secretary, and I, always drove ahead by half an hour—and sometimes an hour. But for me, to whom nothing has ever been more painful than leaving Mannheim, this journey was only partly agreeable, and would not have been at all pleasant, but indeed very boring, if from my youth up I had not been so much accustomed to leave people, countries and cities, and with no great hope of soon, or ever again, seeing the kind friends whom I had left behind. I cannot deny, but must at once admit, that not only myself, but all my intimate friends, and particularly the Cannabichs, were in the most pitiable distress during the last few days, when the time of my sad departure had been finally settled. We really believed that it would not be possible for us

---

[1] K. 180 [173c], composed in 1773, six clavier variations on 'Mio caro Adone' from Antonio Salieri's opera La fiera di Venezia, which Mozart may have seen in Vienna during the summer of 1773.

[2] Evidently Leopold Mozart did not know that his son had already sold these variations to the Paris music publisher, Madame Heina. No copies of a Salzburg edition are known to survive.

to part. I set off at half past eight in the morning, but Madame Cannabich did not get up—she simply would not and could not say good-bye. I too did not wish to distress her, so I left the house without seeing her. Dearest father! I assure you that she is one of my best and truest friends, for I only call those friends who are so in every situation, who day and night think of nothing else but how they can best serve the interests of their friend, and who make use of their influential acquaintances and work hard themselves to secure his happiness. Well, that is the faithful portrait of Madame Cannabich. Of course, there may be some self-interest in this; but where does anything take place, indeed how can anything be done in this world without some self-interest? And what I like best about Madame Cannabich is that she never attempts to deny it. I shall tell you when we meet in what way she told me so. For, when we are alone, which, I regret to say, is very seldom, we become quite confidential. Of all the intimate friends who frequent her house I am the only one who possesses her entire confidence, who knows all her domestic and family troubles, affairs, secrets and circumstances. We did not get to know one another nearly so well the first time I was here (we have agreed on this point), nor did we understand one another so thoroughly; but living in the same house affords greater facilities for getting to know a person. It was when I was in Paris that I first began to realize fully how sincere was the friendship of the Cannabichs, having heard from a trustworthy source the interest which both of them were taking in me. I am saving up a good many things to tell you and discuss with you, for since my return from Paris the scene has undergone some remarkable changes, though not in all respects.

Now for my cloistered life. The monastery itself has made no great impression on me, for once you have seen the Abbey of Kremsmünster,[1] well. . . . !—But of course I am only speaking about the exterior and what they call here the court—for I have yet to see the most famous part. What appears to me truly ridiculous is *the formidable military organization* —I should like to know of what use it is. At night I hear perpetual shouts of 'Who goes there?' and I invariably reply 'Guess!' You know what a good, kind man the Abbot is, but you do not know that I am classed among his favourites, which, I think, will do me neither good nor harm. However, it is always helpful to have one more friend in the world. I do not know either Mlle Ballo or Herr Heigel and his wife. With regard to the monodrama or duodrama, a voice part is by no means necessary, as not a single note is sung; everything is spoken. In short, it is a recitative with instruments, only the actor speaks his words instead of singing them. If you could but hear it once, even with the clavier, it could not fail to

---

[1] A famous Benedictine abbey on the river Krems, about twenty miles south of Linz. It was founded in 777.

please you; and if you could hear it performed, you would be swept off your feet, I warrant you. At the same time it requires a good actor or actress. Well, I shall feel quite ashamed if I arrive in Munich without my sonatas.[1] I cannot understand the delay. It was a stupid trick of Grimm's and I have written to tell him so, adding that he will now see that he was in rather too great a hurry. Nothing up to the present has ever provoked me so much. Consider the matter. I know that my sonatas were published at the beginning of November—and I, the author have not yet received them—and therefore cannot present them to the Electress, to whom they are dedicated. Meanwhile, however, I have made arrangements which will ensure my getting them. I hope that my cousin in Augsburg has received them or that they are lying there at Joseph Killian's. I have therefore written to tell her to send them to me at once.[2] Until I come myself I commend to your kindness an organist,—who is at the same time a good clavierist, Herr Demmler from Augsburg.[3] I had entirely forgotten him and was very glad when I heard of him here. He is very talented, and an appointment in Salzburg might be extremely useful in promoting his further success, for all he needs is a good guide in music—and there I know of no one better than you, my dearest father; it would be really a pity if he were to leave the right path.

Well, that melancholy 'Alceste' by Schweitzer[4] is now being performed in Munich. The best part (besides some of the openings, middle passages and the finales of a few arias) is the beginning of the recitative 'O Jugendzeit'[5]—and it was Raaff's contribution which *made this a success*; for he phrased it for Hartig[6] (who sings the part of Admet) and by so doing introduced the *true expression* into the aria. But the worst part of all (though most of it is bad) is undoubtedly the overture. As for the trifles which have disappeared from the trunk, it is quite natural that in such circumstances something should have been lost, or even stolen. The little amethyst ring I felt I ought to give to the nurse who attended my dear mother, for otherwise she would have kept her wedding-ring. The ink-bottle is too full and I am too hasty in dipping in my pen, as you will perceive. As for the watch, you guessed rightly. I pawned it, but I only got five louis d'or for it, and that on account of the works, which were in good order—for the shape, as you know, was out of date and completely out of fashion. Talking of watches, I must tell you that I am bringing with me one for myself—*a real Parisian one*. You know the sort of thing my jewelled watch was—how inferior the little stones were, how clumsy and

---

[1] Mozart's violin sonatas, K. 301-306 [293a-c, 300c, 293d, 300], which he was proposing to present to the Electress Marie Elizabeth.
[2] This letter, if Mozart ever wrote it, has disappeared.   [3] See p. 340, n. 2.
[4] Anton Schweitzer composed *Alceste* on a text by Wieland for the Ducal Theatre at Weimar, where it was produced in 1773. It was performed at Mannheim in 1775.
[5] *Alceste*, Act IV, Scene 2.   [6] See p. 451, n. 2.

awkward its shape; but I would not have minded all that, had I not been obliged to spend so much money on having it repaired and regulated; yet in spite of that the watch would one day gain and the next day lose an hour or two. The watch the Elector gave me did just the same and, moreover, the works were even worse and more fragile. I exchanged these two watches and their chains for a Parisian one worth twenty louis d'or. So now at last I know what the time is—which I never managed to do with my five watches. At present, out of four watches I have at least one on which I can rely. Now farewell, dearest father. As soon as I reach Munich, I shall inform you of my arrival. Meanwhile I kiss your hands a thousand times and embrace my dear sister with all my heart and remain your most obedient son

WOLFGANG AMADÈ MOZART

My greetings to all our good friends, and particularly to our dear Bullinger. Heina's address is—
A Monsieur
   Monsieur Heina, rue de Seine.
     feauxbourg St. Germain, à l'Hôtel de Lille
      à
        Paris.

(346) *Mozart to his Cousin, Maria Anna Thekla Mozart, Augsburg*

[*Autograph in the Stefan Zweig Collection, British Library, London*]

MA TRÉS CHER COUSINE!   KAYSERSHEIM, 23 *December* 1778
   In the greatest haste and with the most profound regret and sorrow and with fixed determination I now write to inform you that tomorrow I am leaving for Munich. Dearest coz, don't be a fuz. I would gladly have gone to Augsburg, I assure you, but the Imperial Abbot wouldn't let me go and I can't blame him, you know, for that would be contrary to God's and Nature's law and whoever doubts this is a wh—e. Well, that's how things are at the moment. Perhaps I shall take a trip from Munich to Augsburg. But I am not sure about this. So if it really gives you pleasure to see me, come to Munich, that fine town. Make a point of being there before the New Year, mind, and I shall take a good look at you in front and behind; I shall take you round the town and, if necessary, wash you down. The only thing I regret is that I can't give you a shake-down, because I shall not be staying at an inn, but shall be living—where do you think? I should love to know where. Well, j-o-o-o-king apart! That is

just the reason why it is very necessary that you should come and stay, perhaps you will have a great part to play. So come for a bit or else I'll shit. If you do, this high and mighty person will think you very kind, will give you a smack behind, will kiss your hands, my dear, shoot off a gun in the rear, embrace you warmly, mind, and wash your front and your behind, pay you all his debts to the uttermost groat, and shoot off one with a rousing note, perhaps even let something drop from his boat.

Adieu, my angel, my sweetheart.

I am aching to see you.

Do send me a nice little letter of 24 pages to Munich, Poste Restante; but do not say where you will be staying, so that I may not find you, nor you me.

Votre sincère co[1]

W: A[1]

PS.—Shit-Dibitari, the parson at Rodampl, licked his cook's arse, to others as an example.

vivat vivat.

(347) *Leopold Mozart to his Son*

[*Extract*]   [*Autograph in the Mozarteum, Salzburg*]

MON CHER FILS!   SALZBURG, 28 *December* [1778]

While I am writing this letter you will probably have arrived in Munich. I have told you repeatedly that our interests and my prospects demand that you should return to Salzburg. I assumed that you would be guided by your common sense and that you would have more confidence in your father's judgment, which you know to be sound, than in your own futile wishes. So I felt sure that by the New Year at latest you would be home in Salzburg. But, when I was least expecting it and was already hoping to get a letter from you from Augsburg, you acquaint me with the fact that you are not travelling to Munich with the Abbot until the 26th or 27th. Good! The occasion excuses you. Please do not think, ★ however, that you are going to sit about in Munich. But what is the use of my saying anything? You yourself, if you will think over everything impartially and set all your gay dreams aside, will have to admit that I am right; and it is hardly necessary for me to take the trouble to justify my opinion to you, the more so as I am heartily sick of composing these long letters and during the last fifteen months have almost written ★ myself blind. You left Paris on September 26th. If you had travelled

---

[1] A corner has been torn off the letter.

straight to Salzburg, I should have paid, or rather I *could have paid off* one hundred gulden of our debts. So I command you to leave at once, for your conduct is disgraceful and I am heartily ashamed of having assured everyone that you would quite certainly be home by Christmas or by the New Year at the very latest. Good God! How often have you made a liar of me! The sonatas[1] for the Electress must not prevent this. If you have them, you may present them. If you have not, you may commission Cannabich to do so and correspond with him about it. The devil may wait for them! It is ridiculous that you should be acting thus. Who knows what is now concealed behind this pretty arrangement! If the sonatas are not there and turn up later, I shall consider what ought to be done. I think that I have now made myself quite clear—or am I to take the mail coach myself and fetch you? Surely my son will not let things reach such a pitch! There was a great turn-out at our shooting yesterday, in fact, a whole crowd of us. Everyone sends their greetings to you and particularly Ceccarelli and Bullinger. Nannerl and I kiss you several 100000 times and I remain your father who is still awaiting you.

MZT

(348) *Mozart to his Father*

[Autograph in the Mozarteum, Salzburg]

MON TRÉS CHER PÉRE!   [MUNICH, 29 *December* 1778]

I am writing this letter at Herr Becke's house. Thank God, I arrived here safely on the 25th, but until now it has been impossible for me to write to you. I am saving up everything until our happy and joyous meeting, for today I can only weep.[2] I have far too sensitive a heart. Meanwhile, I must tell you that the day before I left Kaysersheim I received my sonatas; so I shall be able to present them myself to the Electress. I shall only wait on here until after the first performance of the opera,[3] when I intend to leave immediately, unless I find that it would be very useful and profitable to me to remain here for some time longer, in which case I feel certain, nay, quite assured, that you would not only be satisfied that I should do so, but would yourself advise it. I have naturally a bad handwriting, as you know, for I never learnt to write; but all my life I have never written anything worse than this letter; for I really cannot write—my heart is too full of tears. I hope you will write to me soon and comfort me. Address your letter, Poste Restante, and then I can fetch it myself. I am staying with the Webers. I think that after all it

---

[1] K. 301-306 [293a-c, 300c, 293d, 300l].
[2] Mozart is referring to the cool reception he has had from Aloysia Weber. See Nissen, pp. 414-415.
[3] Schweitzer's *Alceste*. See p. 642, n. 4.

would be better, far better, to address your letters to our dear friend Becke. I am going to compose a mass [1] here (I am just telling you this as a tremendous secret). All my good friends are advising me to do so. I cannot tell you what good friends Cannabich and Raaff have been to me! Now farewell, most beloved, dearest father! Write to me soon. I kiss your hands a thousand times and embrace my dear sister with all my heart and remain until death

your

A Happy New Year! I cannot manage anything more today—

most obedient son

WOLFGANG AMADÈ MOZT

MUNICH, 29 *December* 1778

My greetings to all my good friends. I hope to see Frau von Robinig here.

(349) *Leopold Mozart to his Son*

[Extract]   [Autograph in the Mozarteum, Salzburg]

SALZBURG, 31 December 1778

MY DEAR SON!   For the last time 1778

I was very much surprised to read your and Mr. Becke's letters. If your tears, your sadness and heart-felt anxiety have no other reason but that you doubt my love and tenderness for you, then you may sleep peacefully—eat and drink peacefully and return home still more peacefully. For I now realize that you do not really know your father. From our friend's letter [2] this seems to be the main cause of your sadness; and oh! I trust there is no other! If this is really so, then you have no reason to fear a cool reception or disagreeable days in the company of your sister and

★ myself. But what plunges me into a state of anxiety and is bound to worry me is your prolonged absence. As it is already four months since I received your provisional certificate of appointment [3]—as people know that you left Paris on September 26th—as they know that I have been for ever telling you that you should come—for our friends expected to see you here on my name-day, [4] then at Christmas, and finally by the New Year for certain, you will understand me when I tell you that people are saying to my face that you are treating the Prince—and, what is worse, your own

---

[1] There is no trace of this composition.

[2] *MBA*, No. 514 prints Becke's letter to Leopold Mozart, in which he assures him that Mozart has the best heart in the world, but is afraid of a chilly welcome from his father.

[3] As Mozart's certificate of appointment as court organist is dated 17 January 1779 (see Abert, vol. ii. p. 906 and *MDB*, pp. 181–182), Leopold Mozart must refer to some earlier document, signed by the Archbishop, which has not been preserved.

[4] November 15th.

father, as a fool; and that I could not say anything if the Prince were to
take back his certificate. You have been in Munich since the 25th. When ★
you wrote to me on the 29th you had not yet presented the sonatas.[1] Well,
I suppose that during the holidays it was difficult to get them bound. I
assume that in the meantime you will have done all this. You say that
I ought to comfort you, while I say, *come and console me.* I shall embrace you
most joyfully. As I write this letter I am almost going crazy, for it is New
Year's Eve, and, although the door is closed, the bell is ringing the whole
time, Bimperl is barking, Ceccarelli is shouting and chattering, and people
are deafening me with wishes for a Happy New Year, although they see
that I am writing and that I am in a hurry, for the post is going off. Mlle ★
Mellin left for Munich this morning in her own carriage, a two-seated
coach with glass windows. The driver is bringing you a letter from me
and he can wait a couple of days, if you should prefer to return with him
in this very comfortable carriage instead of in the jolting mail coach. We ★
wish you from our hearts a Happy New Year. Oh, would that you were
here already, how peacefully then would I sleep! God grant you a pleasant
journey. We kiss you a million times and I look forward to telling you
soon that I am your father who loves you with all his heart.

MZT

(350) *Mozart to his Father*

[*Autograph in the Mozarteum, Salzburg*]

MON TRÉS CHER PÉRE!   MUNICH, 31 *December* 1778

I have this moment received your letter through our friend Becke.
I wrote to you from his house the day before yesterday—a letter such as I
never wrote before; for this friend talked to me so much about your tender
paternal love, your indulgence towards me and your complaisance and
discretion when it is a question of furthering my future happiness, that my
heart melted within me! But from your letter of the 28th I see only too
clearly that Herr Becke in his conversation with me was inclined to
exaggerate. Well, let's be frank and plain. As soon as the opera (Alceste)[2]
has been performed, I shall leave, whether the mail coach goes off the day
after the opera or the same night. If only you had spoken to Frau von
Robinig, I might have travelled home with her! Well, be that as it may.
The opera is to be given on the 11th; and (if the diligence leaves) I shall set
off on the 12th. It would be to my interest to remain here a little longer,
but I will sacrifice that for your sake and in the hope that I shall be doubly
rewarded for it in Salzburg. As for the sonatas,[3] your idea is not a very
happy one! Do you think that, if I do not get them, I ought still to leave
at once? Or that I ought not to appear at Court at all? I really could not

[1] K. 301-306 [293a-c, 300c, 293d, 300l].   [2] See p. 642, n. 4.   [3] See n. 1.

do this, as I am so well known here. But do not worry. I received my sonatas at Kaysersheim and, as soon as they are bound, I shall present them to the Electress. A propos, what do you mean by 'gay dreams'? I do not mind the reference to dreaming, for there is no mortal on the face of this earth who does not sometimes dream! But *gay dreams*! Peaceful dreams, refreshing, sweet dreams! That is what they are—dreams which, if realized would make my life, which is more sad than cheerful, more endurable. This moment, January 1st, I have received, through a Salzburg *vetturino*, a letter from you, which, at first reading, truly staggers me. For Heaven's sake, tell me, do you really think that I can fix a day for my departure now? Or is it your belief that I would rather not come at all? Now that I am so very near home, I should have thought that you might be more at ease on that point. When the fellow had fully explained his route to me, a great desire came over me to go off with him; but I cannot do so yet. I shall not be able to present my sonatas to the Electress until tomorrow or the next day, and then (no matter how much I hurry up these people) I shall probably have to wait a few days for a present. I give you my word of honour that to please you I shall make up my mind not to see the opera at all, but to leave the very day after I receive the present; though I confess it will be a great disappointment. However, if a few days more or less make such a difference to you, so be it! Send me a reply at once on this point. I am writing like a pig, because I have to hurry so, for the fellow is leaving this very moment.

January 2nd. I am looking forward to talking to you, for then you will hear everything in detail, and particularly how my affairs stand here. You must not distrust or be annoyed with Raaff. He is the most honourable man in the world, though, I admit, he does not like writing letters. But the chief cause of his silence is that he is unwilling to make premature promises and yet likes to hold out hopes. At the same time he (like Cannabich) has worked for me relentlessly. Well, good-bye. My greetings to all my good friends. I embrace my dear sister with all my heart, and you, dearest father, and your hands I kiss a thousand times and remain until death

your most obedient son
WOLFGANG AMADÈ MZT

(351) *Mozart to his Father*

[*Autograph in the Mozarteum, Salzburg*]

MON TRÉS CHER PÈRE!   MUNICH, 8 *January* 1779
      I hope you received my last letter, which I meant to give to the hired coachman but which, as I missed him, I entrusted to the post. I have received all your letters, and your last one of December 31st through Herr

Becke. I let him read my letter and he also showed me his.

I assure you, my dearest father, that I am looking forward with all my heart to returning to *you* (but not to Salzburg), as your last letter convinces me that you know me better than formerly! There never was any other reason than this doubt for my long delay in returning home—for the sadness which in the end I could no longer conceal and so opened my heart completely to my friend Becke. What other reason could I possibly have? As far as I know, I have done nothing to cause me to fear your reproaches. I am guilty of no fault (by fault I mean something which does not become a Christian and a man of honour). In short, I rejoice at the thought of seeing you and I am looking forward to the pleasantest and happiest days—but only in the company of yourself and my very dear sister.

I swear to you on my honour that I cannot bear Salzburg or its inhabitants (I mean, the natives of Salzburg). Their language—their manners are quite intolerable to me. You have no idea what I suffered during Madame Robinig's visit here, for indeed it is a long time since I met such a fool; and, to annoy me still more, that idiotic and deadly dull Mosmayer was with her! Well, let's talk about something else. I went yesterday with my dear friend Cannabich to the Electress and presented my sonatas.[1] Her apartments here are exactly what I should like mine to be one day,—just like those of a private individual, very charming and pretty rooms, except for the view which is abominable. We spent over half an hour with her and she was very gracious. So that I may be paid soon, I have managed to let her know that I am leaving here in a few days. You need not be uneasy about Count Seeau, for I don't believe that the matter will go through his hands, and, even if it does, he dare not put a spoke in my wheel. Well, to sum up. Please believe that I have the most aching longing to embrace you and my dear sister once more. If only it were not in Salzburg! But as I can't see you without going to Salzburg, I do so gladly. Well, I must make haste, for the post is going. My little cousin is here—and why? Well, to please me, her cousin! That indeed is the ostensible reason. But—well, we shall talk about this in Salzburg—and on this account I should very much like ⟨her to⟩ come home with me! You will find a few lines in her own handwriting nailed to the fourth page of this letter. She would like to come. So, if it would really give you pleasure to have her in your house, be so kind as to write at once to your brother, saying that it is all right. When you see her and get to know her, you will certainly like her, for she is a favourite with everyone. Well, good-bye, dearest, most beloved father. I kiss your hands a thousand times and embrace my dear sister with all my heart and ever remain your most obedient son

W A Mozart

___

[1] K. 301-306 [293a-c, 300c, 293d, 300l].

Madame Hepp, née Tosson, died yesterday in childbirth. She too has been done in by these doctors.

(351a) *Maria Anna Thekla Mozart, the 'Bäsle', to her Uncle*

[Autograph in the Mozarteum, Salzburg]

MONSIEUR MON TRÉS CHÉR ONCLE   [MUNICH, 8 *January* 1779[1]]
I trust that you and Mlle my cousin are well. I have had the honour of finding my cousin, your son, in Munich and in excellent health. He wants me to travel with him to Salzburg, but I don't know yet whether I shall have the honour of seeing you.

(351b) *Mozart resumes writing*[2]

●

A portrait of my cousin, who is writing in shirt-sleeves!

(351c) *The 'Bäsle' resumes writing*

Indeed my cousin is a first-rate fool, as you can see. I wish you all the best, mon cher oncle, and I send a thousand compliments to Mademoiselle ma cousine. Je suis de tout mon coeur

FRÄULEIN MOZART
Munich the 8 je moi
1779

(351d) *Mozart resumes writing*

Monsieur
where the latter has not yet shit—votre invariable cochon.

(352) *Leopold Mozart to his Son*

[Extract]   *[Autograph in the Mozarteum, Salzburg]*

MON TRÉS CHER FILS!   SALZBURG, 11 *January* 1779
From the letter which I sent off to Mr. Becke on the 7th, enclosing a note for Herr Gschwendner and just a few lines for you, as I did not wish to overweight it, you will have gathered that I want you to make an effort to leave with Herr Gschwendner, as I have suggested it to him, and

---

[1] A postscript to Mozart's letter.
[2] The autograph has a large ink-blot, which Mozart proceeds to explain away.

as you could not find a more convenient means or one more advantageous for your purse. In your last letter you tell me that *my niece is in Munich and that you would like her to accompany you to Salzburg, that she would like to come and that if I should care to have her I ought to write about this to my brother.* I have often invited my niece already, but I have reminded her also that the winter in Salzburg is not as pleasant as the summer. She too has written to say that she could come, because the Munich mail coach, *through the good offices of a friend,* was always at her service. But you cannot stay on in Munich just to wait for a reply from my brother about this, *for I am determined that you shall leave with Herr Gschwendner.* If my niece wants to honour me with a visit, *she can follow on the 20th by the mail coach.* The Electress's present cannot delay you, as the sonatas[1] were handed to her on the 7th. So, if matters *can only be hurried up,* everything ought to be settled within a week. You have, therefore, no excuse. You have seen the opera, and so you have done everything you wanted to do. I am expecting you to arrive with Herr Gschwendner without fail. Your sister and I kiss you a million times, and I remain your loving father

MZT

(353) *Mozart to Hieronymus Colloredo, Archbishop of Salzburg*

[MS in the Landesarchiv, Salzburg[2]]

YOUR GRACE,   [SALZBURG, *January* 1779]
MOST WORTHY PRINCE OF THE HOLY ROMAN EMPIRE! MOST GRACIOUS
    PRINCE AND LORD!
After the decease of Cajetan Adlgasser Your Grace was so good as to take me into your service. I therefore humbly beseech you to grant me a certificate of my appointment as Court Organist.
    I remain,
        Your Grace's most humble and obedient servant,

WOLFGANG AMADÉ MOZART[3]

(354) *Mozart to his Cousin, Maria Anna Thekla Mozart, Augsburg*

[Autograph in the Stefan Zweig Collection, British Library, London]

SALZBURG, 10 May 1709[4]
Blow into my behind.
It's splendid food,
May it do you good.

---

[1] K. 301-306 [293a-c, 300c, 293d, 300l].
[2] Mozart's certificate of appointment was signed on 17 January 1779. See *MDB*, p. 181 f.
[3] Written by Leopold Mozart.   [4] 10 May 1779.

Dearest, most beloved,
most beautiful, most amiable,
    most charming
        little bass [1]
            or
        little cello,
whom a worthless cousin
        has enraged!

Whether I, Joannes Chrisostomus Sigismundus Amadeus Wolfgangus Mozartus, shall be able to quell, assuage or soften the anger which doubtless enhances your fascinating beauty (visibilia and invisibilia) by a full slipper-heel, is a question which I cannot answer. Soften means to carry someone softly in a soft chair. By nature I am very soft, and I like mustard too, particularly with beef. So it is all right about Leipzig, although Mr. Feigelrapée insists on recapitulating or rather decapitating that nothing will come of the pastel. Well, I simply cannot believe this. Why, it wouldn't be worth my while to stoop down and pick it up. If it were a purse full of Convention-farthings, then one might after all scoop it up, gather it up or reach out for it. As I say, I shan't let it go for less; it's my lowest price. I refuse to bargain, for I am not a woman; so that's that. Yes, my dear little cello, it's the way of the world, I'm told. Tom has the purse and Dick has the gold; and whoever has neither, has nothing, and nothing is equal to very little, and little is not much; therefore nothing is still less than little, and little is still more than not much, and much is still more than little and—so it is, was and ever shall be. Finish the letter, close it and despatch it to its destination—Feigele,

        Your most obedient,
            most humble slave, but please,
            my arse indeed is no Viennese.
Please turn over, volti subito.

PS.—Have Böhm's [2] company left yet? Do tell me, my beloved, I beg you for the love of Heaven! Ah! No doubt they are rehearsing now? Do set my mind at rest about this, I implore you by all that is sacred. The gods know that it is my sincere desire. Is the 'Thüremichele' [3] still whole? Blow into my hole. How has Vogt [4] got on with his spouse? Have they not yet had any rows?

    [1] Here Mozart puns on the word 'Bäschen', which can mean either 'little cousin' or 'little bass'. The whole letter is full of puns of this kind.
    [2] Johannes Böhm, manager of a theatrical company, which gave performances in Salzburg in 1779 and 1780. For a good account of his company, which was succeeded in Salzburg by Emanuel Schikaneder's, see Hans Georg Fellmann, Die Böhmsche Theatertruppe und ihre Zeit (Leipzig, 1928).
    [3] A figure of St. Michael, constructed by Christof Murmann in 1616, which appeared at Michaelmas in the belfry of the Perlach-Tower and marked the hours from 6 A.M. to 6 P.M. by piercing the dragon with his sword.
    [4] Peter Vogt (Voigt) was master of the ballet in Böhm's theatrical company.

A heap of questions for you.
A tender ode![1]
Thy picture sweet, O cousin,
Is e'er before my eyes.
Yet weep I must, forsooth,
That thou'rt not here thyself.
I see thee when the evening
Darkens and when the moon
Shines forth. Alas! I weep
That thou'rt not here thyself.
By all the flowering blossoms
Which I would strew for thee,
By all the myrtle branches
Which I would twine for thee,
I conjure thee, fair spirit,
Appear, transform thyself,
Transform thyself, fair spirit,
And be—my little coz!

Finis Coronat Opus   S. V.[2]
The Honourable Pig's Tail   P. T.[3]

and I promise that it shall be something very sensible and important,
[4] and we must just be content with that until further notice. Adieu—

Adieu—Angel—

I shall write more by the next ordinary post—

---

[1] Mozart translates one of Klopstock's odes, *Edone* (published in 1773), making slight changes in two lines.   [2] Salva verecundia: with modesty preserved.
[3] Pleno titulo: i.e. with full title.
[4] For the sketch of his cousin, which fills this space in the autograph, see facsimile facing this page.

Greetings from myself and from us all to your father and mother who produced you, I mean, to him who made the effort to do so, and to her who submitted to it. Adieu—Adieu—Angel. My father gives you his avuncular blessing and my sister gives you a thousand cousinly kisses; and your cousin gives you what he may not give you.
Adieu—Adieu—Angel.

(355) *Mozart to his Cousin, Maria Anna Thekla Mozart, Augsburg*

[*Autograph in a private collection*]

MA TRÈS CHÈRE COUSINE!   SALZBURG, 24 *April* 1780
You answered my last letter so beautifully that I really don't know where I shall find words to express my thanks and at the same time to tell you once more how very much I am
your most obedient servant and
sincere cousin
WOLFGANG AMADÉ MOZART

I wanted to write more but, as you see, the space
is
too   adieu! adieu!
small.

Well, jest and earnest. You must really forgive me this time for not replying word for word, as it deserves, to your most charming letter, and you will permit me to say only what is necessary. The next time I shall endeavour to make up as far as possible for my shortcomings.

It is now a fortnight since I replied to M. Böhm and I should just like to know whether my letter has not perhaps gone astray, for which I should be very sorry. For I know only too well that M. Böhm is exceedingly busy every day. However that may be, I beg you in any case, my pretty face, to give him a thousand greetings. Tell him that as soon as I get a sign from him, he shall have his aria.[1]

I hear that Munschhauser[2] is also laid up. Is that so? That would be very awkward for M. Böhm. Well, my dear, you too are probably going to the theatre every day, hail, rain and sunshine, the more so as you have free entry. I have no news to send you except that unfortunately Joseph

---

[1] Perhaps an aria to replace one of the original arias in *La finta giardiniera*, which Böhm was producing (in a German translation by the actor Franz Xaver Stierle) in Southern Germany, or possibly an aria to be inserted in some play. For Mozart's association with Böhm's company (*La finta giardiniera*, *Thamos* and *Zaide*) see Köchel, pp. 223, 224, 351–356.

[2] Marschauser, an actor in Böhm's company. See p. 639, n. 2.

Hagenauer, in whose bow-window you and my sister and I drank chocolate, has died, which is a great loss for his father. His brother Johannes (the one who is married), who, because he could rely absolutely on his late brother, became more or less of an idler, must now buckle to, a thing which he finds rather difficult to do.

Well, my dearest, most beloved, most beautiful, most charming and most amiable cousin, hurry up and write to me! Please do. And send me all the news at home and elsewhere. And give to all the people who sent greetings to me, twice as many in return. Adieu. The next time I shall cover a whole sheet. But please, sweetheart, do you send me a whole reamful. Adieu. All sorts of messages from my Papa and my sister Zizibe; and to your parents from us three, two boys and a girl, 12345678987654321 greetings, and to all our good friends from myself 624, from my father 100, and from my sister 150, that is a total of 1774, and summa summarum 12345678987656095 compliments.

In the autumn of 1780 Mozart was commissioned to compose for the Munich carnival season an opera seria Idomeneo, rè di Creta, based on a libretto chosen by the Court. After writing some of the music in collaboration with his librettist, Abbate Varesco, Court Chaplain of Salzburg, Mozart proceeded to Munich early in November. The ensuing correspondence with his father, who acted as intermediary between his son and Varesco, throws much light on Mozart's method of dealing with his opera texts and adjusting them to the shortcomings of the singers. Letters 356–392.

(356) *Mozart to his Father*

[*Autograph in the Mozarteum, Salzburg*]

MON TRÉS CHER PÉRE!   MUNICH, 8 *November* 1780 [1]

My arrival here was happy and pleasant—happy, because no mishap occurred during the journey; and pleasant, because we could hardly wait for the moment to reach our destination, on account of our drive, which though short was most uncomfortable. Indeed, I assure you that none of us managed to sleep for a moment the whole night through. Why, that carriage jolted the very souls out of our bodies—and the seats were as hard as stone! After we left Wasserburg I really believed that I should never bring my behind to Munich intact. It became quite sore and no doubt was fiery red. For two whole stages I sat with my hands dug into the upholstery and my behind suspended in the air. But enough of this; it is all over now, though it will serve me as a warning rather to go on foot than to drive in a mail coach.

Now for Munich. We arrived here at one o'clock in the afternoon and on the very same evening I called on Count Seeau, for whom, as he was not at home, I left a note. On the following morning I went there with Becke, who sends his greetings to you all. Seeau has been moulded like wax by the Mannheim people. With regard to the libretto [2] the Count says that Abbate Varesco need not copy it out again before sending it—for it is to be printed here—but I think that he ought to finish writing the text, and not forget *the little notes*,[3] and send it to us with the synopsis as quickly as possible. As for the names of the singers, that is of no importance whatever, for these can be added most conveniently here. Some slight alterations will have to be made here and there, and the recitatives will have to be shortened a bit. But *everything will be printed*. I have just one request to make of the Abbate. Ilia's aria in Act II, Scene 2, should be altered slightly to suit what I require. 'Se il padre perdei, in te lo ritrovo'; this verse could not be better. But now comes what has always seemed unnatural to me—I mean, in an aria—and that is, *a spoken aside*. In a dialogue all these things are quite natural, for a few words can be spoken aside hurriedly; but in an aria where the words have to be repeated, it has a bad

[1] Mozart left Salzburg on November 5th. See p. 690, where Mozart states that on Monday, 18 December he will have been away from Salzburg for six weeks.

[2] The Munich court had chosen an old French libretto written by Danchet and set to music by Campra, which had been performed in Paris in 1712 and 1731. Mozart asked Abbate Varesco, who since 1766 had been Court Chaplain in Salzburg, to write an Italian text for this opera seria. Varesco finished his libretto early in October and Mozart began immediately to set it to music. In the course of composition Varesco's text had to undergo numerous alterations, which are the subject of the letters exchanged between Mozart and his father. See D. Heartz, *Mozart-Jahrbuch 1967*, p. 150 ff.

[3] Presumably stage directions, which would be written in a smaller hand.

effect, and even if this were not the case, I should prefer an uninterrupted aria. The beginning may stand, if it suits him, for the poem is charming and, as it is absolutely natural and flowing and therefore as I have not got to contend with difficulties arising from the words, I can go on composing quite easily; for we have agreed to introduce here an aria andantino with obbligatos for four wind-instruments, that is, a flute, oboe, horn and bassoon. I beg you therefore to let me have the text as soon as possible. Now for a sorry story. I have not, it is true, the honour of being acquainted with the hero dal Prato;[1] but from the description I have been given of him I should say that Ceccarelli is almost the better of the two; for often in the middle of an aria his breath gives out; and, mark you, he has never been on any stage—and Raaff[2] is like a statue. Well, just picture to yourself the scene in Act I. Now for a cheerful story. Madame Dorothea Wendling[3] is *arcicontentissima*[4] with her scene and insisted on hearing it played three times in succession. The Grand Master of the Teutonic Order arrived yesterday. 'Essex'[5] was given at the Court Theatre, followed by a magnificent ballet. The whole theatre was illuminated. They began with an overture by Cannabich, which, as it is one of his latest, I did not know. I am sure, if you had heard it, you would have been as much pleased and excited as I was; and if you had not previously known it, you would never have believed that it was by Cannabich. Do come soon, and hear and admire the orchestra. I have nothing more to write about. There is to be a grand concert this evening, at which Mara[6] is singing three arias. Is it snowing as heavily in Salzburg as it is here? My greetings to Herr Schikaneder[7] and ask him to forgive me for not yet sending him the aria,[8] but I have not been able to finish it completely.

[1] Vincenzo dal Prato (1756–1828), a castrato. He had been chosen for the part of Idamante.
[2] Raaff sang the part of Idomeneo.
[3] Dorothea Spurni (1737–1811), the wife of J. B. Wendling, the Mannheim flautist. She was an operatic singer and a successful teacher. She sang the part of Ilia in Mozart's *Idomeneo*.
[4] Highly content.
[5] *Die Gunst der Fürsten*, the German version by Christian Heinrich Schmidt of *The Unhappy Favourite*, a tragedy on the fate of the Earl of Essex, written and produced in 1681 by John Banks.
[6] Gertrud Elisabeth Mara (1749–1833), one of the greatest sopranos of the eighteenth century. She was the daughter of Schmeling, a poor musician in Cassel, and studied in Vienna and Leipzig. Frederick the Great gave her an appointment at his Court, but disapproved of her marriage in 1773 to J. B. Mara, the Munich cellist. Her greatest successes were in London from 1784 onwards. Burney, who heard her in Berlin in October 1772, gives an entertaining description of her singing powers. See Burney, *op. cit.* vol. ii. pp. 108 ff.
[7] Emanuel Schikaneder (1751–1812), a famous actor-manager and playwright. After Böhm's theatrical company left Salzburg in 1780, Schikaneder, who since 1778 had had a successful tour with his company in Stuttgart, Nuremberg, Laibach, Klagenfurt and Linz, arrived there in September 1780. For an interesting account of Schikaneder's career see Egon v. Komorzynski, *Emanuel Schikaneder* (Vienna, 1951), and Blümml, pp. 90–103 and 140–162.
[8] There is no trace of this aria, which Mozart composed for Schikaneder's production of the German translation by J. G. Dyk of Carlo Gozzi's drama *Le due notti affannose*. The performance of *Peter der Grausame oder Die zwei schlaflosen Nächte* took place in Salzburg on 1 December 1780. See Köchel, p. 365.

I kiss your hands a thousand times and embrace my sister with all my heart and remain,

> mon trés chér pére,
>> your most obedient son
>>> WOLF: AMDÈ MOZART

Cannabich and Wendl: send you a thousand compliments and hope soon to have the pleasure of making your and my sister's acquaintance. Adieu.[1]

(357) *Leopold Mozart to his Son*

[*Extract*]   [*Autograph in the Mozarteum, Salzburg*]

MON TRÈS CHER FILS,   SALZBURG, 11 *November* 1780

I am writing in great haste at half past nine in the evening, as I have had no time all day. Varesco brought me the libretto very late and Count Sepperl Überacker[2] was with us from five o'clock until now.

I am returning the libretto and the draft, so that His Excellency Count Seeau may see that everything has been carried out to order. In about a week a complete copy of the text will follow by the mail coach, showing exactly how Abbate Varesco wants it to be printed. It will also include the necessary notes. Here is the aria, which is, I think, quite suitable. If not, let me know at once. What you say about the singers ⟨is really distressing.⟩ Well, ⟨your musical composition⟩ will have to ⟨make up for their deficiencies.⟩ I wish I could have heard Madame Mara. Do tell me how she sings. You can imagine that I am looking forward with childish delight to hearing that excellent orchestra. I only wish that I could get away soon. But I shall certainly not travel by mail coach, for I am rather careful of my two damson stones. Well, I must close, for it is time, first to say the Rosary and then to sleep. Your sister's eyes are drowsy. She kisses you. Pimperl is snoring. I remain your faithful father

> LEOPOLD MOZART

Our compliments to the Cannabichs, to the two Wendling families,[3] to Figlio Becke and to all who know us or would like to.

[1] The autograph has a short postscript in Italian by J. B. Becke, first published in *MM*, November 1920, p. 32. See also *MBA*, No. 535.

[2] Count Wolf Joseph Überacker (1743–1809), son of Count Wolf Leopold Überacker, court councillor in Salzburg.

[3] The families of the brothers Johann Baptist Wendling, flautist, and Franz Anton Wendling, violinist in the Mannheim orchestra, which had been transferred to Munich.

(358) *Mozart to his Father*

[*Autograph in the Mozarteum, Salzburg*]

MON TRÈS CHER PÈRE,   MUNICH, 13 *November* 1780

I write in the greatest haste, for I am not yet dressed and must be off to Count Seeau's. Cannabich, Quaglio[1] and Le Grand, master of the ballet, are lunching there too in order to make the necessary arrangements for the opera. Cannabich and I lunched yesterday with Countess Baumgarten, née Lerchenfeld. My friend is positively worshipped by her family and now I am too. It is the best and most useful house for me here, for owing to their kindness all has gone well with me and, God willing, will continue to do so. It is she who has a fox's tail sticking out of her arse and, oh vanity, an odd-looking watch-chain hanging under her ear and a fine ring; I have seen it myself, though death should take me, unfortunate fellow, without a nasal extremity,[2] sapienti pauca.

Well, I must get dressed. But I must not omit the chief point and indeed the principal object of my letter, which is, to wish you, my dearest and kindest father, every possible good on this your name-day. Further, I commend myself to your fatherly love and assure you of my eternal obedience. Countess La Rosée sends her greetings to you and my sister, and so do all the Cannabichs, the two Wendling families, Ramm, Eck,[3] father and son, Becke and Dal Prato † † † who happens to be with me. † † † Yesterday Count Seeau presented me to the Elector, who was very gracious. If you were to speak to Count Seeau now, you would scarcely recognize him, so completely have the Mannheimers transformed him.

The second duet is to be omitted altogether—and indeed with more profit than loss to the opera. For, when you read through the scene, you will see that it obviously becomes limp and cold by the addition of an aria or a duet, and very gênant for the other actors who must stand by doing nothing; and, besides, the noble struggle between Ilia and Idamante would be too long and thus lose its whole force.

A propos! I forgot to tell you the other day that Herr Wegscheider only sent 118 gulden instead of 120, so that M. Grandville could not give me a formal receipt. He has probably written to him about it. Madame de Fosman and her sister send their most cordial greetings to Madame Maresquelle;[4] and so does her mother. Baron Götz sends his best regards

---

[1] Lorenzo Quaglio had been stage designer in Munich since 1778.

[2] The underlined initial letters spell out the word 'favourite'. Mozart is alluding to the Countess's position at the Elector's court.

[3] Georg Eck was a horn-player in the Munich orchestra from 1778. His son, Friedrich Johann Eck (1767–1838), born in Mannheim, became an excellent violinist, and from 1778 until 1788 was a member of the Munich orchestra.

[4] An actress and dancer in Schikaneder's theatrical company. She took part in the Mozarts' shooting matches and used Mozart's gun during his absence in Munich.

to Herr Gilowsky and Herr Berantzky. Indeed he is an amiable fellow! Well, although I have a lot to tell you, I really must close. I kiss your hands a thousand times and embrace my sister most cordially and ever remain,

mon trés cher pére,

your most obedient son,

WOLF AMD MOZART

Ex commissione of His Excellency I ought to reply in his name to Abbate Varesco; but I have no time and was not born to be a secretary. To Act I, Scene 8, Quaglio has made the same objection that we made originally—I mean, that it is not fitting that the king should be quite alone in the ship. If the Abbé thinks that he can be reasonably represented in the terrible storm, forsaken by everyone, without a ship, quite alone and exposed to the greatest peril, then let it stand; but please cut out the ship, for he cannot be alone in one; but if the other situation is adopted, a few generals, who are in his confidence, must land with him. Then he must address a few words to his people and desire them to leave him alone, which in his present melancholy situation is quite natural. A propos. Shall I soon have the aria for Madame Wendling?

Mara has not had the good fortune to please me. She has not the art to equal a Bastardella [1] (for this is her peculiar style)—and has too much to touch the heart like a Weber [2]—or any sensible singer.

PS.—My compliments to all our good friends. A propos. As translations are so badly done here, Count Seeau would like to have the opera translated in Salzburg.[3] Only the arias need be in verse. He says that I ought to make a contract. In that case payments would be made simultaneously to the poet and to the translator. Send me a reply about this soon. Adieu. What about the family portrait?[4] Is it a good likeness of you? Has the painter started on my sister yet? The first performance of the opera will not be until January 20th.[5] Be so kind as to send me the scores of the two masses[6] which I brought away with me—and also the mass in Bb [7] for Count Seeau will be telling the Elector something about them shortly. I should also like people to hear some of my compositions in this style. I have heard only one mass by Grua.[8] Things like this one could easily turn

---

[1] Lucrezia Agujari. See p. 120, n. 4. [2] Aloysia Weber.

[3] The German translation of *Idomeneo* was done by Mozart's friend, Johann Andreas Schachtner. See F. Lehrndorfer's article in *MMB*, no. 38, 1919, p. 204 ff. In a letter to Breitkopf of 10 August 1781 (Letter 420), Leopold Mozart points out that *Idomeneo* is wholly a product of Salzburg.

[4] The painter of this family portrait, which is in the Mozart Museum, Salzburg, was Johann Nepomuk della Croce (1736–1819). Mozart had been painted during the summer and the portrait was finished during the winter. See illustration no. 10.

[5] The first performance of *Idomeneo* took place on 29 January 1781.

[6] Probably K. 317, composed in 1779, and K. 337, composed in 1780.

[7] K. 275 [272b], composed in 1777.

[8] Paul Grua (1754–1833), a member of a large family of Italian musicians. He studied under Padre Martini, became a member of the Mannheim orchestra and in 1784 succeeded Bernasconi

out at the rate of half a dozen a day. If I had known that this castrato[1] was
so bad, I should certainly have recommended Ceccarelli!

(359) *Mozart to his Father*

[*Autograph in the Mozarteum, Salzburg*]

MON TRÉS CHER PÉRE!   MUNICH, 15 *November* 1780
    I have received your letter or rather the whole parcel. Many thanks
for the money order. So far I have not lunched once at home—and consequently have had no expenses save for friseur, barber and laundress—and
breakfast. The aria is excellent now, but there is still one more alteration,
for which Raaff is responsible. He is right, however,—and even if he were
not, some courtesy ought to be shown to his grey hairs.[2] He was with me
yesterday. I ran through his first aria for him and he was very well pleased
with it. Well—the man is old and can no longer show off in such an aria
as that in Act II—'Fuor del mar ho un mar nel seno'. So, as he has no aria
in Act III and as his aria in Act I, owing to the expression of the words,
cannot be as cantabile as he would like, he wishes to have a pretty one to
sing (instead of the quartet) after his last speech, 'O Creta fortunata! O me
felice!' Thus too a useless piece will be got rid of—and Act III will be far
more effective. In the last scene of Act II Idomeneo has an aria or rather a
sort of cavatina between the choruses. Here it will be *better* to have a mere
recitative, well supported by the instruments. For in this scene which will
be the finest in the whole opera (on account of the action and grouping
which were settled recently with Le Grand), there will be so much noise
and confusion on the stage that an aria at this particular point would cut
a poor figure—and moreover there is the thunderstorm, which is not
likely to subside during Herr Raaff's aria, is it? The effect, therefore, of a
recitative between the choruses will be infinitely better. Lisel Wendling[3]
has also sung through her two arias half a dozen times and is delighted
with them. I have it from a third party that the two Wendlings praised
their arias very highly; and as for Raaff, he is my best and dearest friend!
    But to my molto amato castrato dal Prato I shall have to teach the
whole opera. He has no notion how to sing a cadenza effectively, and his
voice is so uneven! He is only engaged for a year and at the end of that
time, next September, Count Seeau will get somebody else. Ceccarelli
might then have a chance—sérieusement.
    I had almost forgotten my best news. Last Sunday after the service
Count Seeau presented me en passant to His Highness the Elector, who

as Kapellmeister to the Munich court. He wrote a great deal of church music, and one opera,
Telemacco, for the Munich carnival, 1780.
    [1] dal Prato.   [2] Raaff was sixty-six.
    [3] Elizabeth, wife of Franz Anton Wendling. See p. 374, n. 2. She took the part of Elettra.

was very gracious to me and said: '*I am glad to see you here again*'. On my replying that I would do my best to retain the good opinion of His Highness, he clapped me on the shoulder and said: '*Oh, I have no doubt whatever that all will go well*'. A piano piano, si va lontano.[1]

Please do not forget to reply to all points which concern the opera, as, for instance, my remark in my last letter about the translator. For I have been asked to make a contract.

The deuce take it! Again I cannot write all that I should like to. Raaff has just been to see me. He sends you his greetings, and so do the whole Cannabich household, the two Wendling familes and Ramm also. And now farewell. I kiss your hands a thousand times. The driver is just going off. Adieu. I embrace my sister.

I remain ever your most obedient son

WOLF AM: MOZART

My sister must not be lazy, but practise hard, for people are already looking forward to hearing her play. My lodging is in the Burggasse at M. Fiat's. But it is not at all necessary to add the address, for at the post office they know me—and know too where I am living. Adieu.

Eck and his son and Becke send their compliments.

(360) *Leopold Mozart to his Son*

[*Extract*]   [*Autograph in the Mozarteum, Salzburg*]

MON CHER FILS!   SALZBURG, 18 *November* 1780

What on earth are you thinking of? The way you are treating Herr Schikaneder[2] is really shameful. On my name-day,[3] when we had our shooting, I said to him: '*The aria will certainly be here tomorrow*'. With what I knew, was there anything else I could tell him? A week before I had had to inform him that *you had not been able to finish it*. Indeed I was absolutely certain that you would send it a week later by the mail coach, the more so as he is going to produce only twelve more comedies. I really do not know what story I shall tell him when he comes to our shooting tomorrow. As you know, I am not much good at telling lies. All that I can say is that *you missed the mail coach, that the extra postage fee was too heavy for you, and that the aria will certainly come by the next one*. But I refuse to tell another lie. And indeed it is no small compliment for three of us to have free passes to all the seats in the theatre over such a long period.

I am now replying to your two letters, the first of which I received by post on Thursday and the second on Friday.

---

[1] Slow and sure wins the race.   [2] See p. 660, n. 7.   [3] November 15th.

Idomeneo must land from the ship with his retinue. Then follow the words which he speaks to them, upon which they withdraw. You will remember that I sent off this objection to Munich; but your reply was that thunderstorms and seas pay no attention to the laws of etiquette. This, I admit, would be true, if a shipwreck were to take place. But the vow has released them. This landing will produce a very fine effect. For a long time Varesco refused to touch the duet 'Deh soffri in pace, o cara'. But I have persuaded him. Idamante and Ilia have still a very short discussion consisting of a few words in recitative, which is interrupted, *as it were*, by a subterranean rumbling, and then the utterance of a subterranean voice is heard. This voice and its accompaniment must be moving, terrifying and altogether unusual; and it can be a masterpiece of harmony. I enclose the alteration which has already been made.

First of all, there is an alteration in Act I, Scene 1, no. 1, where Ilia in her recitative must say Achiva instead of Argiva. This occurs again in Act II, Scene 2, no. 4, as you will see on the other side of Varesco's page above. The reason is that Achivo is a word which can be used of any Greek, but Argivo can only be used of the Greeks of Argos. But you must not be confused when you find the word Argivo in another place. There it is perfectly correct. But in the two places I have marked, it ought to be Achivo, because the reference is to Greece as a whole. Now for alteration no. 2. This is in Idomeneo's speech to his retinue, after they have left the ships, and when he dismisses them. There you will find at the end the words, e al ciel natío etc. This natío, which stands for nativo, has an accent on the i, which is long. The verse shows this.

Alteration no. 3 is a very necessary one, and the idea of it only came to me after I had read the text very carefully. Idamante must not say (as Varesco makes him do) that he has witnessed the glory of his father; he must say the exact opposite, that is, that *he regrets not to have been able to witness the great deeds and the glory of his father*. You must note all these points in your copy immediately, so that when you are composing the music, none of them may be overlooked.

Alteration no. 4 is what I have said above about Achivo.

Alteration no. 5 is to substitute for the duet a recitative, which should be sung at the end in a very lively manner, when Ilia runs to the altar, while Idamante holds her back. Then she turns to the priest with great eagerness, throws herself on her knees and before she has finished her speech and during the words 'a te, sacro ministro'—the subterranean rumbling prevents her from saying anything more and fills everyone with amazement and terror. If this rumbling is properly reproduced, one peal of thunder following another, it will have a tremendous effect on the audience, especially as *the subterranean voice* is heard immediately afterwards. Then follows the alteration to which you refer in your second letter.

Signor Raaff, to whom your sister and I send our greetings, will be well served with his new aria. His former one, between the choruses, will now be altered to a spirited recitative, which can be accompanied, if necessary, by thunder and lightning. Up to the present Varesco has just adhered to the prescribed draft, which was returned to you with the libretto. My eyes are aching and I really cannot write any more, except to add that the two scores will follow. You will probably need them in order to add parts for wind-instruments.

Am I to send you the original score of the mass in Bb [1] by itself—or add a copy? I have not yet found the original.

Farewell. I am your old father and friend   ★

L. MOZART

★

One more important point. If there is anything else to be altered, you must let me know by the next post. For Varesco cannot go on copying the text for the printer as he has been doing and then have to throw it aside and start afresh. So you must carefully consider whether it can now stand as it is, particularly as the German translation ought to be done in Salzburg. That it should stand would be the best solution. I have spoken to Schachtner,[2] but he wants to leave the arrangements to me. I told him that he could not expect more than *forty gulden, or eight ducats*. He thinks that I ought to suggest *ten ducats*. But compared with Varesco's remuneration this figure to me seems too high. I think, however, that he deserves to get *eight ducats* for his work, as the arias and choruses will have to be translated into verse; and that indeed will be no joke, as 27 numbers will have to be translated into verse, including some long choruses. I am certain that for a smooth prose translation Count Seeau cannot offer less than *six ducats* and that in fact *eight ducats* will certainly not be too much. Further, I shall arrange that the copy sent to Munich shall be sufficiently neat that it can be handed straight to the printers. Reply at once. There is no time to be lost. Addio.

Oh my poor eyes!

Our greetings to the whole Cannabich household, the two Wendling families, Becke, Ramm, Lang, Eck, in fact to all who love us.

Poor eyes!

Half past seven in the evening and no spectacles. ⟨If you think that Count Seeau is likely to give Schachtner ten ducats,⟩ try to arrange it.

---

[1] K. 275 [272b].
[2] Johann Andreas Schachtner, the Salzburg court trumpeter and poet. See p. 663, n. 3.

(361) *Leopold Mozart to his Son*

[*Extract*]   [*Autograph in the Mozarteum, Salzburg*]

MON TRÉS CHER FILS!   SALZBURG, 20 *November* 1780

You will have received the parcel, which I sent off yesterday by the mail coach. I now hope to receive without fail and by the same means *the aria for Schikaneder.* If you have not yet posted it, do so at once and he will pay all expenses. I am really ashamed. Why, that honest fellow ran after the mail coach in order to say good-bye to you when you left. You are very wise ⟨*to ingratiate yourself with Countess von Baumgarten.*⟩ No doubt you will call on ⟨*Count Sensheim*⟩ and ⟨*the 'Presidentess'.*[1]⟩ If you do not manage to call in the forenoon, but have to do so after luncheon, no one will take it amiss, as people know that you are up to the eyes in work. Many thanks for your good wishes. In return I wish you *good luck* and trust that ⟨*your opera may be a great success.*⟩ Your whole future depends on this.

★   Is it really true that Madame Mara was annoyed because her husband[2] was not allowed to accompany her? That she addressed the orchestra on the subject? That Cannabich and her husband exchanged some heated words about it? I think Fiala heard all this from his father-in-law.

You ask how the family portrait[3] is turning out? So far nothing more has been done to it. Either I have had no time to sit, or the painter could not arrange a sitting; and now your sister is laid up with a cold and cannot leave the house.

★   Send me a reply soon about Schachtner and let me know whether any further alterations will have to be made.

★   Your sister kisses you a million times and I am your honest old father and friend

L. MOZART

We send our greetings to all.

I am now off to Vespers and the Litany. *Tomorrow is the anniversary of my wedding-day,*[4] which is now but a sad memory—a thing you will not understand—at least, not now!

(362) *Mozart to his Father*

[*Autograph in the Mozarteum, Salzburg*]

MON TRÉS CHER PÉRE!   MUNICH, 22 *November* 1780

At last I am sending you the long-promised aria[5] for Herr Schikaneder. During the first week I couldn't get it finished on account of the business

---

[1] See p. 284, n. 2.
[2] Johann Baptist Mara (1744–1808), cellist in the Munich orchestra.
[3] See p. 663, n. 2.   [4] 21 November 1747.   [5] See p. 660, n. 8.

for which, after all, I came here—and the other day Le Grand, master of the ballet, a terrible talker and seccatore,[1] happened to be with me and by his chattering made me lose the mail coach. I hope that my sister is quite well. I have a cold at the moment, which in this weather is quite the fashion here. I hope and trust, however, that it will soon leave me, for the two light cuirassier regiments, cough and phlegm, are gradually disappearing. In your last letter you say repeatedly: 'Oh! my poor eyes!—I do not wish to write myself blind—half past seven in the evening and no spectacles.' But why do you write in the evening? And why without spectacles? That I cannot understand. I have not yet had an opportunity of speaking to Count Seeau, but I hope to do so today and I shall send you an account of our conversation by the next post. For the moment everything will probably remain as it is. Herr Raaff came to see me yesterday morning and I gave him your regards, which pleased him immensely. He too sends you his greetings. He is indeed a worthy and thoroughly honest fellow! The day before yesterday dal Prato sang at the concert—most disgracefully. I bet you that fellow will never get through the rehearsals, still less the opera. Why, the rascal is rotten to the core.—Come in! Why, it's Herr Panzacchi,[2] who has already paid me three visits and has just invited me to lunch on Sunday. I hope I shall not have the same experience as the two of us had with the coffee. He has enquired very meekly whether instead of 'se la sa' he may not sing 'se co la'—Well, why not 'ut re mi fa sol la'?

I am delighted whenever you send me long letters, but please do not write in the evening—and still less without spectacles. You must, however, forgive me if I do not send you much in return, for every minute is precious; and, as it is, I can generally only compose in the evenings, as the mornings are so dark; then I have to dress—and the merchant's servant at the Weiser sometimes lets in a troublesome visitor. When the castrato comes, I have to sing with him, for I have to teach him his whole part as if he were a child. He has not got a farthing's worth of method.

I shall write more fully next time.

How is the family portrait getting on?

My sister, if she has nothing better to do, might jot down on paper the titles of the best comedies that have been performed during my absence. Is Schikaneder still getting good receipts?

My greetings to all our good friends and to Katherl Gilowsky's arse. Give Bimperl a pinch of Spanish tobacco, a good wine-sop, and three kisses. Do you not miss me at all? A thousand compliments from all—to

---

[1] A boring person.
[2] Domenico de Panzacchi (1733–1805), who took the part of Arbace.

all—all. Adieu. I kiss your hands a thousand times and embrace my sister most cordially and hope that she will soon recover. Adieu.

Your most obedient son

WOLFGANG AMADÈ MOZART

(363) *Mozart to his Father*

[*Autograph in the Mozarteum, Salzburg*]

MON TRÉS CHER PÉRE!   MUNICH, 24 *November* 1780

I have received the parcel and your letter of November 20th. Herr Schachtner is to get *ten ducats* for his efforts. I trust that in the meantime you have received the aria for Herr Schikaneder.

Please give my most humble respects to Mlle Catherina Gilowsky de Urazowa—and wish her in my name every possible happiness on her name-day; above all I hope that this may be the last time that she will be congratulated as Mademoiselle. What you reminded me to do with regard to Count ⟨Sensheim⟩, I have done long ago—these things are all links in the one chain. I have already lunched with him once, twice with ⟨Baumgarten⟩ and once with ⟨Lerchenfeld,⟩ father of Countess ⟨Baumgarten.⟩ —Not a single day passes without one of these people at least coming to Cannabich's. Do not worry, dearest father, ⟨about my opera.⟩ I trust that all will go well. No doubt it will be attacked by ⟨a small cabal,⟩ who in all probability will be covered with ridicule; for ⟨the most distinguished and influential families of the nobility⟩ are in my favour, and ⟨the leading musicians⟩ are one and all for me. I cannot tell you what ⟨a good friend Cannabich is⟩—how ⟨active⟩ and ⟨successful!⟩ Why, he is a real ⟨watchdog,⟩ when it is a case of ⟨doing someone a good turn.⟩

I want to tell you the whole story about Mara. I did not write about it, as I thought that, if you knew nothing about it, you would hear all the particulars in Munich, while if you knew something, there was plenty of time to tell you the whole truth; for probably additions have been made to the story—at least, in this town it has been told in several different ways. But no one can know it better than I do, as I was present and therefore saw and heard the whole affair. When the first symphony was over, it was Madame Mara's turn to sing and I saw her husband come creeping up behind her with his violoncello. I thought that she was going to sing an aria with a cello obbligato. Old Danzi[1] is first violoncello here and accompanies very well. All at once old Toeschi[2] (who also conducts, but has no authority when Cannabich is present) said to Danzi, who is, by the

---

[1] Innocenz Danzi, father of the greater Franz Danzi (1763–1826), joined the Mannheim orchestra as cellist in 1754.   [2] See p. 370, n. 3.

way, his son-in-law, 'Stand up, and give Mara your place'. When Cannabich heard this, he called out, 'Danzi, stay where you are. The Elector prefers that his own people should play the accompaniments.' Then the aria began, Giovanni Mara standing behind his wife, looking very sheepish and still holding his big fiddle. The moment they entered the hall, I had taken a dislike to both of them, for really you could not find two more insolent-looking people; and of this the sequel will convince you. The aria has a second part. Madame Mara, however, did not think it necessary to let the orchestra know beforehand that she was going to stop, but, after the last ritornello, came down into the room with her usual air d'effronterie to pay respects to their Highnesses. In the meantime her husband literally attacked Cannabich—I cannot tell you every detail, for it would take too long; but, in a word, he insulted both the orchestra and Cannabich's character. Cannabich naturally got angry, gripped his arm and said: 'This is not the place to, answer you'. Mara wished to reply, but Cannabich threatened that if he did not hold his tongue, he would have him removed by force. Everyone was indignant at Mara's impertinence. A concerto by Ramm was then given, during which this charming couple proceeded to lay their complaint before Count Seeau; but from him also, as well as from every-one else, they heard that they were in the wrong. At last Madame Mara committed the sottise of speaking to the Elector himself on the subject, her husband in the meantime saying in an arrogant tone, 'My wife is this very moment complaining to the Elector—it will mean the ruin of Cannabich. I am sorry for him.' But people only burst out laughing in his face. The Elector, replying to Madame Mara's complaint, said: 'Madame, you sang like an angel, although your husband did not accompany you'. And when she wished to press her grievance, he said: 'Well, that is Count Seeau's affair, not mine'. When they saw that nothing could be done, they left the hall, although she had still two arias to sing. In our tongue that is called insulting the Elector; and I know for certain that if the Archduke and a number of other strangers had not been present, they would have been treated very differently. But in the circumstances Count Seeau simply got very nervous; he sent after them at once—and they came back. She sang her two arias, but was not accompanied by her husband. During the last one (and I shall always believe that Herr Mara did this on purpose) three bars were missing —but only in the copy, mark you, from which Cannabich was playing. When they reached this point, Mara seized Cannabich's arm. The latter found his place directly, but hit the stand with his bow, exclaiming audibly, 'This copy is all wrong'. When the aria was over, he said: 'Herr Mara, I want to give you a piece of advice, and I hope you will profit by it. Never seize the arm of the conductor of an orchestra—for, if you do, you may have to reckon with getting at least half a dozen boxes on the ear.' Mara's tone was now, however, entirely lowered. He begged to be forgiven, and excused himself as best he could. The most disgraceful part of the whole affair was that Mara (a wretched violoncellist, as they all declare) would never have been heard at Court at all but for Cannabich, who had used his influence on his behalf. At the first concert before my arrival he played a concerto and accompanied his wife, taking Danzi's place without saying a word either to Danzi or to anyone else. All this was overlooked. The Elector was not at all pleased with his manner of accompanying and said that he preferred to hear his own people. Cannabich, who knew this, told Count Seeau before the concert began that he had no objection to Mara's playing on the other side, but that Danzi must also play. When Mara came, he was told as much, and yet he was guilty of this insolence. If you only knew these people, you would at once see conceit, arrogance and unblushing *effronterie* written on their faces.

I hope that my sister is now quite well again. Pray do not write any more melancholy letters to me, for I really need at the moment a cheerful spirit, a clear head and an inclination to work, and one cannot have these when one is sad at heart. I know and, God knows, I deeply feel how much you deserve rest and peace, but am I the obstacle?—I would not willingly be so and yet—alas! I fear I am. But—if I ⟨attain my object⟩—if I succeed in ⟨getting a good appointment here,⟩ then you must ⟨leave Salzburg immediately.⟩ You will say—that will never be. At all events, ⟨industry and effort will⟩ not be wanting on my part. Do try and come to Munich soon. If only the *ass who smashes a ring, and by so doing cuts himself a hiatus in his behind so that I hear him shit like a castrato with horns, and with his long ear offers to caress the fox's posterior*,[1] were not so . . . Why, we can all live together. I have a large alcove in my bedroom which has two beds. These would do capitally for you and me. As for my sister, all we need do is to get a stove put in the other room, which will only be a matter of four or five gulden; for, even if we were to heat the stove in my room until it is red-hot and leave the doors open into the bargain—yet the room would not be endurable, for it is bitterly cold there.

Do ask Abbate Varesco if we may not break off at the chorus in Act II, 'Placido è il mar', after Elettra's first verse when the chorus has been repeated—or, failing that, after the second, for it is really far too long! By the next mail coach I hope to receive the recitative and aria for Herr Raaff. I have now stayed at home for two days on account of my cold—and, luckily for me, I have very little appetite, for in the long run it would be inconvenient to have to pay for meals. But I have written a note to the Count on the subject, and have received a reply that he will discuss the matter with me shortly. By God! I shall not pay a single kreuzer. He ought to be thoroughly ashamed of himself. Well, adieu. Give my greetings to

[1] The underlined initial letters spell out the word 'archbishop'.

all my good friends, and a thousand compliments from everyone in Munich. I kiss your hands a thousand times and embrace my sister most cordially and wish her a speedy recovery. I am ever

your most obedient son

WOLFGANG AMADÈ MOZART

(364) *Leopold Mozart to his Son*

[*Extract*]   [*Autograph in the Mozarteum, Salzburg*]

MON TRÉS CHER FILS!   SALZBURG, 25 *November* 1780

Written at half past nine in the evening with spectacles. I have been ★ busy all day in the cathedral and giving lessons. Your sister has not yet recovered, but she is somewhat better, though indeed she still has a nasty cough.   ★

Here is Abbate Varesco's alteration. I do not agree that in the first line of Herr Raaff's aria the words *ed era* should be made to belong to the following line. True, this combination is often to be found in Metastasio, where, however, its treatment depends on the skill of the composer. Many Italian asses have set to music 'Il cor languiva, ed era' and added some other disconnected melody to 'gelida massa in petto'. Take care of your health, and do not go to bed too late. Young people, particularly when they are engaged in mental work, must have their proper amount of sleep. Otherwise their nerves become weak, their stomach gets out of order and they fall into a decline.

If people come in and settle on you in the morning, just stop it. That sort of thing is no joke, for in the end you will have to compose until you are half dead; and how can you know how much you may not have to alter? As soon as your sister is better, she will write to you about all kinds of matters. I received today a letter from Ceccarelli's father. He begs me 'a fargli la consolazione di dargli qualche avviso della dimora del suo figlio'.[1] His son, it seems, has not written to him for a long time and has probably told him some story to the effect that when he went on that journey, he left Salzburg for good; he may have deceived him in this way, because he does not want to help his poor father and prefers to spend his money on an unnecessary number of clothes and, as you know, on all kinds of silly trifles. Farewell. I shall tell you more in my next letter. Take care of your health! Your sister and I kiss you.

L. MZT.

Send me a reply about Schachtner!
Foot-baths are an excellent remedy for a cold!

---

[1] To comfort him by sending him some information as to the whereabouts of his son.

(365) *Mozart to his Father*

[*From Nissen, pp.* 421-422[1]]

MUNICH, 29 *November* 1780

The aria for Raaff which you have sent me pleases neither him nor myself. I shall not say anything about *era*, for in an aria of this kind that is always a mistake. Metastasio makes it sometimes, but very rarely, and, moreover, those particular arias are not his best; and is there any necessity for it? Besides, the aria is not at all what we wished it to be; I mean, it ought to express peace and contentment, and this it indicates only in the second part: for we have seen, heard and felt sufficiently throughout the whole opera all the misfortune which Idomeneo has had to endure; but he can certainly talk about his present condition. Nor do we need a second part—which is all the better. In the opera 'Achille in Sciro',[2] for which Metastasio wrote the text—there is an aria of this kind in the style which Raaff would have liked:

> Or che mio figlio sei,
> sfido il destin nemico;
> sento degli anni miei
> il peso alleggerir.

Tell me, don't you think that the speech of the subterranean voice is too long? Consider it carefully. Picture to yourself the theatre, and remember that the voice must be terrifying—must penetrate—that the audience must believe that it really exists. Well, how can this effect be produced if the speech is too long, for in this case the listeners will become more and more convinced that it means nothing. If the speech of the Ghost in Hamlet[3] were not so long, it would be far more effective. It is quite easy to shorten the speech of the subterranean voice and it will gain thereby more than it will lose.

For the march in Act II, which is heard in the distance, I require mutes for the trumpets and horns, which it is impossible to get here. Will you send me one of each by the next mail coach, so that I may have them copied?

---

[1] The autograph of this letter was sold by Puttick & Simpson on 18 December 1848 as Lot No. 548.

[2] The opera by Pietro Pompeo Sales, which was produced at Munich in 1774. See p. 255, n. 5.

[3] Schikaneder's company had performed in Salzburg on 13 October 1780, F. W. L. Schröder's translation and adaptation of Shakespeare's *Hamlet*. It is probable that Mozart saw this performance.

(366) *Nannerl Mozart to her Brother*

[*Extract*]   [*Autograph in the Mozarteum, Salzburg*]

DEAREST BROTHER!   [SALZBURG,] 30 *November* 1780

Thank you for remembering to enquire after my health. I have not quite recovered yet, but with God's help I shall gradually do so. And you, dearest brother! How is your cold? Is it really on the mend? I hope and trust that it may not be so persistent as mine is and that this letter may find you in perfect health.

You want to know about the plays which have been performed since you left Salzburg. Well, I am sending you a list.[1]   ★

On the 27th we had the 43rd play, a brand new comedy in four acts, which had never been performed in Salzburg. It was entitled 'Rache für Rache'[2] and was announced in the following way.

Notice

Today we hope to win the reputation of having produced the finest of all character-plays. Each character is new and flavoured with the best comic salt; so that my gracious patrons will not have to digest either tasteless or warmed up stuff, of which there is unfortunately a great deal about, but will certainly leave our theatre thoroughly delighted. To this play, my gracious patrons, you are invited by

your obedient servant

SCHIKANEDER, Manager

Latterly I had not set foot outside the house; but since Madame Maresquelle had all along been urging me to see this play, if it was performed, as it was such an excellent piece, I decided to do so without consulting the doctor and went off to see it. Katherl had also been saving up for this play, as she wanted to celebrate her name-day with me at the theatre. By praising up his production to the skies Herr Schikaneder had persuaded the Archbishop to go and see it. In short, people were so eager to attend that there was not an empty seat in the theatre. The actors played their parts most admirably; but the play itself, which lasted fully four hours, was so wretched that if it had been written on purpose to drive people out of the theatre and to incite them to hiss it off the stage, it could not have been more successful. You can imagine how distressed we felt on poor Schikaneder's account. During the third act the Archbishop went out; and so, by degrees, did a number of people. We ourselves did not want to be present if Schikaneder was going to be insulted; so we left

---

[1] The portion of this letter which is omitted is a list of the plays performed by Schikaneder's company from November 5th to the 26th inclusive.

[2] The author of this comedy was Johann Karl Wezel, a minor poet and playwright.

during the last scene. And we heard on the following day that when the play was over the audience clapped, hissed, banged the floor with their sticks and very sarcastically shouted out 'fuori'. So Herr Schikaneder, we fear, has lost a great deal of his reputation. If he produces a new play, no one will ever believe that it is going to be a good one.

On the 28th we had the 44th play, 'Trau, schau, wem?,[1] with an absolutely new ballet, describing the battle at sea between Turks and Moors.

Well, my dear brother, I have done what you wanted. Six more plays in all will still be performed, and you will hear later on what they are. Herr Schikaneder is delighted with your aria, and the singer[2] who is learning it at our house would have thoroughly mastered it, but unfortunately the time is too short, as the play in which she has to sing it is being performed tomorrow. You probably know already that the Empress is so ill that at any moment she may play us a pretty prank. If she dies now, your opera may still be performed; but if she dies later, my whole pleasure may be spoiled.[3] Farewell, dearest brother. If it is God's will, I hope to see you in Munich.

(366a) *Leopold Mozart to his Son*

[*Autograph in the Mozarteum, Salzburg*]

MON CHER FILS!   [SALZBURG, 30 *November* 1780[4]]

I hope that your cold will get better soon and have no consequences; perhaps it is gone already. Herr Schachtner has now begun the translation. As for ⟨*intrigues,*⟩ the best way to make people feel ashamed of themselves is to be extremely ⟨*friendly and polite to those who are your enemies*⟩; for then they become so confused and abashed that they lose a great deal ⟨*of their courage and their power to harm*⟩. You ask me not to send you any melancholy news. Why, all I said was that your sister was ill, and surely I had to tell you that. Well, be honest and do not worry about me. But should you fall ill, *which God forbid*, do not hide it from me, so that I may come at once and look after you. If I had been with your mother during her illness, she might still be alive; but no doubt her hour had come and so I had to be absent. Here we see the hand of God, which, however, we recognize only in our hours of necessity and lose sight of at other times. I do not ask you to spend your time writing letters; but I must hear from you or M. Becke whether you are in good health or not, if only to set my mind at rest. As for the chorus 'Placido è il mar', you may stop where you

---

[1] *Der Gasthof* or *Trau, schau, wem?*, a comedy by Johann Christian Brandes.
[2] According to Blümml, p. 145, this singer was Mademoiselle Adelheit.
[3] Maria Theresia had died on the previous day.
[4] A postscript to his daughter's letter, written on the cover.

like; but remember that everything must be printed in the libretto. Farewell. I am your honest father

MZT

(367) *Mozart to his Father*

[Autograph in the Mozarteum, Salzburg]

MON TRÉS CHÉR PÉRE!   MUNICH, 1 *December* 1780

The rehearsal went off extremely well. There were only six violins in all, but we had the requisite wind-instruments. No listeners were admitted except Count Seeau's sister and young Count Sensheim. This day week we are to have another rehearsal, when we shall have twelve fiddlers for the first act (which I am having copied for double forces in the meantime), and when the second act will be rehearsed (like the first on the previous occasion). I cannot tell you how delighted and surprised they all were. But indeed I never expected anything else, for I assure you I went to that rehearsal with as easy a mind as if I were going to a lunch party somewhere. Count Sensheim said to me: '*I assure you that though I expected a great deal from you, I really did not expect that*'. The Cannabichs and all who frequent their house are really true friends of mine. When I walked home with Cannabich to his house after the rehearsal (for we still had much to talk over with the Count), Madame Cannabich came out to meet us and embraced me, delighted that the rehearsal had gone off so well. For Ramm and Lang had gone to her house, simply beside themselves with joy. The good lady—a true friend of mine—who had been alone in the house with her sick daughter Rosa, had been absorbed in a thousand anxieties on my account. Ramm said to me—now when you meet him, you will call him a true German—for he tells you to your face exactly what he thinks: '*I must honestly confess that no music has ever made such an impression on me, and I can assure you that I thought fifty times of your father and of what his delight will be when he hears this opera*'.

But enough of this. My cold has become somewhat worse owing to the rehearsal—for, when honour and glory are at stake, you naturally get excited—however cool you may be at first. I have used all the remedies you prescribed, but it is a slow business and very inconvenient for me at the moment, for composing does not stop a cold; and yet I must compose. I have begun to take fig-syrup and a little almond-oil today, and already I feel some relief; and I have stayed indoors again for two days.

Yesterday morning Mr. Raaff came to see me again in order to hear the aria in Act II. The fellow is as infatuated with it as a young and ardent lover might be with his fair one, for he sings it at night before going to sleep and in the morning when he awakes. As I heard first from a reliable source and now from his own lips, he said to Herr von Viereck, Chief Equerry, and to Herr von Castel: 'Hitherto both in recitatives and arias I have always been accustomed to alter my parts to suit me, but here everything remains as it was written, for I cannot find a note which does not suit me, etc.'. Enfin, he is as happy as a king. At the same time he would like, as I should, to alter slightly the aria which you have sent me. He too objects to the era—and then—we should like at this point to have a peaceful quiet aria. Even if it has only one part—so much the better; in every aria the second part must always be kept for the middle section—and often indeed it gets in my way.[1] In 'Achille in Sciro'[2] there is an aria of this kind—

> Or che mio figlio sei
> sfido il destin nemico;
> sento degli anni miei
> il peso alleggerir.

Meanwhile Herr Sieger will have been to see you and will have brought you a letter[3] from me. Please send the mutes for the horns and trumpets soon.

Many thanks to my sister for the list of plays she sent me. It is very strange about the comedy 'Rache für Rache.' For it has often been performed here with great success—and quite recently too, though I was not there myself.

My most devoted greetings to Fräulein Therese von Barisani.[4] If I had a brother I should ask him to kiss her hands with the deepest respect, but as I have a sister, it is even better. So I ask her to embrace her most affectionately for me.

Please give my greetings to Fräulein Babette von Mölk and, as she is now convinced that I am really very busy, she will surely forgive me for not having yet written to her as I promised. I congratulate her most cordially on her name-day. Well, adieu. I kiss your hands a thousand times and embrace my sister with all my heart and am ever your

most obedient son

WOLFGANG AMADÈ MOZART

PS.—Please send me the recipe for cooking sago—for a good friend. A thousand compliments from all—all.

A propos. Do write to Cannabich some time. He deserves it, and a letter from you will give him immense pleasure. What does it matter,

---

[1] Mozart probably means that in the end he finds that he does not need a second part at all.

[2] A drama by Metastasio, which was first set to music in 1767 by Johann Gottlieb Naumann (1741–1801) and in 1774 by Pietro Pompeo Sales (c. 1729–1797).

[3] Letter 365.

[4] Daughter of the Archbishop's physician, Dr. Sylvester von Barisani.

after all, if he does not reply? He does not mean to be what he appears to be. He is the same with everyone—you must just get to know him.

(368) *Leopold Mozart to his Son*

[*Extract*]　　　　　　　　　　　　　　[*Autograph in the Mozarteum, Salzburg*]

MON TRÉS CHÉR FILS!　　　　　　　　SALZBURG, 2 *December* 1780

If today were post-day, this would be one of the many letters informing Munich of the death of the Empress;[1] for the courier brought the news today, Saturday, December 2nd, at half past three in the morning. But as my letter cannot reach you before Monday, December 4th, her death will no longer be news to you. I do not know what effect it will have on the Munich opera. Here it has stopped for the time being the journey of the Archbishop. For I must tell you that full preparations for a visit to Vienna had been made very quietly. No one was to know anything about it; yet everyone knew. Wenzl, *that reliable and most courteous new cook*, was sent off to Vienna two days ago and he must now retrace his steps. You can imagine how glad I should have been if this journey had come off. The Empress's death will save Schikaneder the expense of a journey to Laibach and, as plays have been stopped there for a time, he will thank God if he can stay on in Salzburg.[2]

The play for which you composed your aria was performed yesterday.[3] The play itself was excellent, the house was full, the Archbishop too was present, your aria was well performed and the singer[4] sang it well—as well, that is to say, as it was possible, seeing how short a time she had in which to learn it. For she too, like Mlle Ballo, is inclined to be lazy. In spite of the fact that the play went on until half past nine, the audience left the theatre absolutely delighted. Now for another piece of news. A *61-year-old* bridegroom (but not myself) and a *19-year-old* bride—well, who are they? Count Lodron,[5] the fat Court Marshal, is to marry Countess Louise Lodron,[6] who is staying with Count Arco. So we shall get a clavier player and a lover of music and the Archbishop another arch-cuckold. I ★ am very anxious about the Munich opera. Basta! Accidents must happen! I am waiting most impatiently to hear how it goes off. Give our greetings to all our friends; and whenever you receive a letter from me, please remember that I should have to use a separate sheet of paper if I were to enclose all the compliments and greetings which people ask me to send

---

[1] Maria Theresia had died on 29 November.
[2] Schikaneder's company continued to give performances in Salzburg until Lent, 1781. They then moved on to Graz.
[3] See p. 660, n. 8.　　　　[4] See p. 676, n. 2.　　　　[5] Count Nikolaus Sebastian Lodron.
[6] One of the two daughters of the Countess Lodron, sister of the Archbishop. Both daughters since the death of Adlgasser in 1777 had been Leopold Mozart's pupils. .

you. You will have received my letter with the enclosure from your sister. The continuation of her list of plays will follow shortly. We both kiss you millions of times and in the comforting hope that you are feeling better, I am your sincere father

MZT

Pimperl sends her compliments to you and so does Theresa. At first, whenever she heard the hall door open, she used to think that you were coming. She would run to the door, prick up her ears and often look for you in the rooms. By the way, do send us a message occasionally for Theresa, or else she will be dreadfully disappointed. The creature is an idiot!

PS.—Fräulein Barisani had a lesson from your sister this morning. She is going to come three times a week. She says that she prefers to have her lessons in our house, as it is quieter than in her own home. Farewell! Herr Schikaneder thanks you for the aria. I shall have to have the aria 'Dentro il mio petto io sento' from the opera buffa[1] copied for him too. He has bought himself a very fine popgun which we are going to christen at our shooting tomorrow. Katherl Gilowsky thanks you for your congratulations on her name-day.

★

(369) *Leopold Mozart to his Son*

[*Extract*]   [*Autograph in the Mozarteum, Salzburg*]

MON TRÉS CHER FILS!   SALZBURG, 4 *December* 1780

I only received yesterday, December 3rd, at noon your letter of November 29th, and that was when Professor Döhl and Herr Sieger came to call on me. My first enquiry was—for your health, and as he completely reassured me, I was perfectly happy. At the same moment, just about half past eleven, Herr von Edelbach and three strangers came into the room. So I put the letter in my pocket without reading it. Your sister had to play a short piece on the pianoforte for them, after which they all promised to return at a more convenient time. Herr Sieger is spending a few days in Salzburg and is living with Herr Döhl, who will show him all the sights. If I had received your letter on Saturday, December 2nd, the mutes would now be in Munich. As it is, they will arrive this day week by the next mail coach. I have just been to see Varesco. As your letter of December 1st arrived while I was out, your sister read it, looked up the

---

[1] A tenor aria sung by the Podestà in Act I of *La finta giardiniera*, composed for the Munich carnival, 1775. See Köchel, p. 223, 224.

passage in Metastasio, and sent the letter and the book after me to Varesco's. All that you have pointed out shall be done. You know that *I too thought the subterranean speech too long.* I have given Varesco my candid opinion and it will now be made as short as possible. We are delighted to hear that the rehearsal went so well. I have no doubt whatever nor am I the slightest bit anxious about your work, provided the production is good, I mean, *provided there are good people to perform it*—and that is the case in Munich. So I am not at all nervous; but when your music is performed by a mediocre orchestra, it will always be the loser, because it is composed with so much discernment for the various instruments and is far from being commonplace, as, on the whole, Italian music is. That your cold should have become worse after the rehearsal is only natural, for, owing to the concentration upon hearing and seeing, all the nerves of the head become excited and strained, and eagerness and attention extends this tension to the chest also.

A proposito of compliments. Madame Maresquelle came to congratulate me on my name-day, rattled off her French wishes and while so doing kept on lowering to my face her right pock-marked cheek. I did not suspect anything, nor did I think that there was any devilment on her part. At last she came so close that I awoke from my stupidity and understood that I was to enjoy this favour and kiss her, which I did with the greatest embarrassment. Whereupon she turned her left cheek and I had to kiss that one too. I looked at myself at once in the mirror, for I felt as bashful as I did in my youth when I kissed a woman for the first time, or when after the ball in Amsterdam the women forced me to kiss them. I think it would be a good idea to have her in the room when my portrait is being painted, for my colour would be far more vivid. Ah! I see that the paper is at an end. We kiss you and wish you a quick recovery. Be patient! Take care! *Rest now and then when you are composing!* Go to bed early! Do not catch cold! Perspire a little every morning! Be careful with your diet! Good night! I am your faithful honest father

L MZT

(370) *Mozart to his Father*

[Autograph in the Mozarteum, Salzburg]

MON TRÉS CHER PÉRE!   MUNICH, 5 *December* 1780
    The death of the Empress does not affect my opera in the least, for none of the theatres have been closed and plays are being performed as usual. The entire mourning is not to last longer than six weeks and my opera will not be performed before January 20th. I beg you to have my *black suit* thoroughly brushed, shaken out, done up as well as possible and

sent to me by the next mail coach—for next week everyone will be in mourning—and I, who have always to be about, *must also weep* with the others. In your last letter I cannot find any mention of a certain Herr Sieger, who travelled by the last mail coach to Salzburg, and still less of a letter which I gave him for you.[1] I had a cold at the time and stayed indoors for two days. On account of his affairs Sieger could not call on me again. My letter was ready, but I, not intending to go out, was not dressed. So I sent it to the post, from where the coach starts, and attached a note bearing the name of Sieger and the instruction that if a traveller of that name were to appear, the letter should be given to him. I am inclined to think that this fellow, who has several commissions for Salzburg, has perhaps not been able to call on you. I am very much disappointed, because in that particular letter I asked you for something which I urgently require for my opera— and that is—to send me a *trumpet mute*—of the kind we had made in Vienna—and also one *for the horn*—which you can get from the watchmen. I need them for the march in Act II. Please send them soon. In regard to the *ultima aria* for Raaff, I mentioned that we both wished to have more pleasing and gentle words. The *era* is forced. The beginning would do quite well, but *gelida massa*—again is hard. In short, far-fetched or unusual words are always unsuitable in an aria which ought to be pleasing.

Then again I should like the aria to express only peace and contentment —and even if it had only one part—it would do quite well—in fact, I should almost prefer it. I also wrote about Panzacchi; we must do what we can to oblige this worthy old fellow. He would like to have his recitative in Act III lengthened by a couple of lines, which owing to the *chiaro e oscuro* and his being a good actor will have a capital effect. For example, after the verse: 'Sei la città del pianto, e questa reggia quella del duol' there is a slight glimmering of hope, and then! (How foolish I am! Whither does my grief lead me?) 'Ah Creta tutta io vedo, etc.!' But Abbate Varesco need not rewrite the act on account of these points, for the alterations can easily be added. I mentioned too that both I and others think the subterranean speech far too long to be effective. Just think it over. Well, I must close, as I have a terrible lot of writing to do. I have not seen Baron Lehrbach[2]—and do not know whether he is still here or not; as I have no time to run about, I may very well *not know* whether he is here, but he must know positively that I am. No doubt if I were a girl, he would have come to see me long ago. I am very sorry that the dear, young, beautiful, clever and sensible Fräulein Louise Lodron has fallen into the clutches of such a pot-belly.[3] She will manage to play with him the beginning of the *second part* of the minuet which I learnt from Bach,[4] for I

---

[1] Letter 365.   [2] Imperial envoy to the Munich court.   [3] See p. 679, n. 5.

[4] Johann Christian Bach. In Einstein's opinion this is a missing trio or coda to the eighth minuet of a series of clavier minuets (K. 315a [315g]); however, he assumed a date of 1779 for these minuets, and they are now believed to date from 1773. See Köchel, p. 334.

daresay he will not be able to make much of the conclusion—or at least he will be very clumsy. I send greetings to Pepperl Lodron and most

cordial condolences in her grief at seeing her sister snap up that nice tit-bit. Well, adieu—a thousand compliments from everyone in Munich. My greetings to all my good friends. I have this moment received your letter of December 4th. You must accustom yourself a little to kissing. You could practise in the meantime on Madame Maresquelle. For here whenever you call at Dorothea Wendling's (where everything is rather in the French style) you will have to embrace both mother and daughter—but on the chin, of course, so that their rouge may not become blue. But more of this next time. Adieu. I kiss your hands a thousand times and embrace my sister with all my heart and am ever your most obedient son

WOLFG. AMADÈ MOZART

PS.—Do not forget about my black suit; I must have it, or I shall be laughed at, which is never very pleasant.

(371) *Leopold Mozart to his Son*

[*Extract*]   [*Autograph in the Mozarteum, Salzburg*]

MON TRES CHER FILS,   SALZBURG, 7 *December* 1780

The two trumpet mutes will certainly arrive by the mail coach. But the horn mutes belong to the two watchman's apprentices, who at the moment are not in Salzburg. I hope that your cold is no worse. God grant ★ it. Thank God, we are well. Ceccarelli came into my room this morning with a stranger, whose face I recognized, but whose name I could not recall. It was Herr Esser,[1] whom we met in Mainz eighteen years ago[2] and whose playing you criticized by telling him that *he played well, but that he added too many notes and that he ought to play music as it was written.* He comes from Vienna and the card on his door describes him as: Herr Esser, Knight of the Golden Spur. Schiavo, Signor Collega![3] He makes a point of wearing his order and I do not doubt but that he will display *his spur* to

[1] Karl Michael, Ritter von Esser (1737– ?), a famous violinist, was born in Aix-la-chapelle, and in 1761 became Konzertmeister at Kassel. He later toured Europe and had much success in London and Paris. Many of his symphonies and violin duets were published during his lifetime. See p. 27, n. 6.

[2] In August 1763. Mozart was then seven years old.

[3] Your slave, my colleague!

the whole world with the greatest advantage together with his violin, his viola d'amore and the rest, and indulge the other extraordinary exercises of his art. For I hear that he plays a whole concerto of his own composition on a tuned-up G-string only. At the same time he may be an excellent violinist, who cloaks his real merits in the tricks of a charlatan. Basta! Sentiremo![1] He has just come from Vienna, where he gave a concert in the theatre, which I read about in the newspaper. Ceccarelli knew him in Italy. Why, Herr Esser has come in this very moment and is to accompany your sister in your clavier sonatas. So I must close if I am not to miss the post. I have just got home from Vespers and the Litany. I enclose Varesco's whole text with the exception of the last aria for Raaff. You will find a few more notes, which you must jot down and correct at once, so that nothing may be forgotten. Your sister and I kiss you. Addio.

Your honest father

MZT

Give our greetings to everyone.

(372) *Leopold Mozart to his Son*

[*Extract*]　　　　　　　　　　　　　　　[*Autograph in the Mozarteum, Salzburg*]

[SALZBURG, 9 December 1780]

Here is the suit, such as it is. I had to have it patched quickly, for the whole taffeta lining of the waistcoat was in rags. I am writing this letter on Saturday, December 9th, at half past nine in the evening. Herr Esser gave a concert in the theatre today and actually made a profit of forty gulden. He will arrive in Munich by this diligence and will call on you at once. He is a jolly old fool of a fellow. But he plays (when he plays *seriously*) with the *surest and most astounding execution*. At the same time he has *a beautiful adagio*, which few good allegro-players possess. But when he starts playing the fool, he plays on the G-string only and with the greatest skill and technique. By striking his strings with a wooden pencil he performs whole pieces with amazing rapidity and precision. He plays the viola d'amore charmingly. But what touched me and struck me at first as rather childish was his *whistling*. He whistles recitatives and arias as competently as any singer and with the most perfect expression, introducing portamento, flourishes, trills and so forth, most admirably, and all the time accompanying himself pizzicato on the violin. He came to see us every day ⟨*and drank like a fish*⟩. This great talent of his brings him in a good deal of money—⟨*and yet he never has any cash*⟩.

---

[1] Well, we shall hear!

Addio. We both kiss you. I shall write to you again on Monday. Farewell. I am your faithful father

MZT

You will find the two trumpet mutes packed with the suit.

★

(373) *Leopold Mozart to his Son*

[Extract]   [Autograph in the Mozarteum, Salzburg]

MON TRES CHER FILS!   SALZBURG, 11 *December* 1780

You will have received your black suit by the mail coach. Herr Esser, ★
who is probably staying at Albert's, will have called on you by now.

As for Schachtner's drama[1] it is impossible to do anything *at the moment*, ★
for the theatres are closed and there is nothing to be got out of the
Emperor, who usually interests himself in everything connected with the
stage. It is better to let things be, as the music is not finished. Besides, who
knows but that this opera may later give you an opportunity of getting to
Vienna?

I enclose a note from Varesco and also the aria.[2] Act I with the translation and possibly Act II will arrive in Munich next week by the mail
coach. I trust that you are well. I advise you when composing to consider
not only the musical, but also *the unmusical public*. You must remember
that to every *ten real connoisseurs* there are a *hundred ignoramuses*. So do not
neglect the so-called *popular* style, which tickles *long ears*. What about the
score? Are you not going to have it copied? You must think over what
you are going to do and ⟨*you must make some sensible arrangement*⟩. The
remuneration you are getting ⟨*is so small that you really cannot leave your
score behind*⟩. Farewell. Give our greetings to all, just as all here send their
greetings to you. We kiss you millions of times and I am your honest old
father

L. MZT.

Do not hurry over Act III. You will certainly be ready in time.
All's well that ends well!

[1] Mozart's unfinished opera *Zaide*, for which Schachtner wrote the libretto. Mozart began
it in the autumn of 1779, probably with a view to its being performed by Böhm's company.
The subject resembles that of *Die Entführung aus dem Serail* and the method of composition
shows the marked influence of Benda's duodramas. Evidently Mozart had been trying to
arrange for its performance in Vienna.
[2] For Raaff. See p. 682.

(374) Mozart to his Father

[Autograph in the Mozarteum, Salzburg]

MON TRÉS CHER PÉRE!   MUNICH, 13 December 1780

I have received your last letter with the alterations and the scena for Panzacchi, and also the suit and the trumpet mutes. I am now hoping to have the aria for Raaff very soon. Herr Esser has not yet been to see me. He will not be able to find out my lodging so easily. He spoke to Cannabich at the play. Your last two letters seemed to me far too short, so I searched all the pockets in my black suit to see if I could not find something more. Well, in Vienna and in all the Imperial dominions the theatres are to be reopened six weeks hence—a very sensible arrangement, for mourning, if unduly prolonged, does not do the dead lord or lady half as much good as it does harm to numbers of other people. Is Herr Schikaneder going to remain in Salzburg? If so, he may still see and hear my opera. People in Munich cannot understand (and rightly so) why this mourning should last for three months, while that for our late Elector[1] only lasted six weeks. The theatre, however, goes on as usual.

You do not say how Herr Esser accompanied my sonatas. Badly? Or very well?

The comedy 'Wie man sich die Sache denkt' or 'Die zwei schlaflosen Nächte'[2] is charming. I saw it here—no, no, I did not see it, I only read it, for it has not yet been performed; besides, I have only been to the theatre once, as I have no time, since the evening is always my favourite time for working.

If Her Grace, the most sensible and gracious Frau von Robinig, does not this time condescend to postpone for a little her journey to Munich, then she will not be able to hear a note of my opera. I am of the opinion, however, that her Grace in her supreme wisdom will deign to oblige your excellent son and stay on here a little longer.

I suppose that your part of the portrait is now begun, and doubtless my sister's also? What is it like? Have you received any answer yet from our plenipotentiary at Wetzlar? I have forgotten his name—Fuchs, I think—I mean, about the duets for two claviers. It is always satisfactory to explain a thing distinctly—and the arias in Aesop's hand are, I suppose, still lying on the table?[3] Send them to me by the mail coach, so that I may give them myself to Herr von Dummhoff, who will then forward them post-free. To whom? Why, to Heckmann—a charming fellow, is he not? And a passionate lover of music. Ah, Herr Sieger. All the time today the chief topics keep on turning up at the end—I can't help it. The other day

---

[1] Maximilian III of Bavaria.   [2] See p. 660, n. 8.
[3] A rather obscure passage. Obviously Aesop was the nickname of a Salzburg copyist. See p. 696.

after lunching at Lisel Wendling's I drove with Le Grand to Cannabich's (as it was snowing heavily). Looking out of the window they thought it was you and really believed that we had come together. I could not understand, until it was explained to me upstairs, why both Karl[1] and the children came running downstairs to meet us—and why, when they saw Le Grand, they did not say a word, and looked very much disappointed. Well, I shall not write anything more, because you have written so little to me. I shall just add that M. Eck, who this very moment has crept into the room to fetch his sword, which he left behind him the last time he was here, sends thousands of greetings to Theresa, Bimperl, Jungfer Mitzerl, Katherl Gilowsky, my sister, and, last of all, to yourself. His son and heir filled his bed last night with spitting, pissing and shitting. *Non plus ultra.*[2]

Please give my compliments to everyone—and I have greetings to deliver to you from everyone in Munich. Well, I must stop, or else I shall have to ride after the mail coach with the letter in my hand. Adieu. I kiss your hands a thousand times and embrace my sister with all my heart and am ever your

most obedient son

WOLFGANG MOZART

Kiss Theresa, but if you really can't do so, the hatter[3] can do it. A thousand kisses to Bimperl. Adieu.

(375) *Leopold Mozart to his Son*

[*Extract*]　　　　　　　　　　　　[*Autograph in a private collection, U.S.A.*]

MON TRÈS CHER FILS,　　　　　　SALZBURG, 15 *December* 1780

You say that my letters are too short; but really what news can I send you from Salzburg? You will now have received the aria for Mr. Raaff, to whom we send our greetings. I sent it off by the post last Monday, so it must have reached you on Tuesday evening or Wednesday morning.

It is impossible to obtain mutes for the horns. Herr Fiala, however, tells me that his father-in-law, Herr Proschalka, has a couple. Fiala has just been to see me and has shown me a letter from Herr Becke, full of praises of your music to Act I. He said that *tears of joy and delight came into his eyes when he heard it, and that all the performers maintained that this was the most*

---

[1] Cannabich's eldest son (1771–1806), who in 1800 succeeded his father as conductor at Munich. He was a good violinist but a mediocre composer.
[2] Nothing more.
[3] Or possibly Paul Hutterer, a violinist in the Salzburg court orchestra. See Hammerle, *op. cit.* p. 34.

beautiful music they had ever heard, that it was all new and strange and so forth —that they were now about to rehearse Act II—that he would then write to me —that I must forgive him for not having written before, as he had been rather indisposed, etc. Well, thank God, everything is going well. *Knowing your work as I do,* I am perfectly certain that these statements are not empty compliments, for I am convinced that your composition, if it is adequately performed, is bound to be effective.

Yesterday Herr Sieger went off by himself to visit the salt mines at Hallein, whence he will travel to Vienna. He is not only a lover of music, but a very good performer on the violin, and the day before yesterday he accompanied your sister, who played your engraved sonatas[1] in the presence of M. d'Yppold[2] and Herr Schikaneder. Further, he plays the clavier a little, is a most competent lawyer and is going to practise in Vienna at the Imperial Court Council. Herr Esser, apart from making some grimaces which are peculiar to people of his type, and playing in a cut and dried manner, accompanied your sonatas rather well. You know, of course, that players of this kind cannot render anything naturally. Oh, how few play as I like! In regard to the mourning for the late Empress, people here have followed the Munich Court—that is, Court mourning for three months. The plays are to go on. Schikaneder has cut his engagement at Laibach, is staying on here and is absolutely determined to hear
★ your opera. No further progress has been made with the family portrait, the reason being that when the days were long and bright, your sister was ill and that I myself had a heavy cold and rather bad rheumatism at that time. I did not tell you about it, as I did not want to make you anxious.
★ Besides, as you are aware, I always look after myself.

Meanwhile I have had a letter from Madame Duschek enclosing a text for an aria. I have already sent her a reply to the effect that nothing can be done before the New Year. She mentioned that she was still in your debt for the last aria.[3] Well, as she seemed to be in a hurry, I had to make it quite clear to her, as politely as I could, that it was impossible for you to compose anything for her now.
★ Well, I have no more news. We both kiss you and I am your honest old father

L MZT

I am sending you a pair of socks by the mail coach conductor.

---

[1] The series of violin and clavier sonatas, K. 301-306 [293a–c, 300c, 293d, 300l].

[2] Franz d'Yppold (*c.* 1730–*c.* 1790), tutor to the Salzburg Court pages and a member of the war council, was an admirer, but unsuccessful suitor of Nannerl.

[3] K. 272, composed in 1777.

(376) *Mozart to his Father*

[*Autograph in the Mozarteum, Salzburg*]

MON TRÉS CHER PÉRE!   MUNICH, 16 *December* 1780

Herr Esser came to see me yesterday for the first time. When he was in Salzburg, did he go about on foot or did he always drive around in a carriage as he does here? I think the bit of money he made there will not long remain in his purse. We are lunching together on Sunday at Cannabich's, where he is to let us hear his solos, both serious and crazy. He says that he will not give a concert here; nor will he perform at Court. He is not making any effort to do so. He says that if the Elector wishes to hear him, '*Eh bien—here I am—it will be a pleasure—but—I shall not announce myself*'. Well, after all, he may be an honest fool—the devil take it!— knight, I meant to say. He asked me why I did not wear my spur?[1] I said I had one in my head which was quite difficult enough to carry. He was kind enough to brush my coat a little for me, saying: 'One knight must serve another'. Nevertheless on the afternoon when he came to Cannabich's, *forgetfulness*, I suppose, had caused him to leave at home his spur (I mean, the outward and visible one) or, alternatively, he had contrived to conceal it so well that not a trace of it was to be seen. Well, I must be quick, lest I forget it again—I must tell you that owing to the air and water here Madame and Mlle Cannabich are both becoming rather fat about the throat; which in the end may turn to goitre. Heaven forbid! They are taking a certain powder, now what on earth is it? No, that's not the name. In any case it's not doing them any good. So I have taken the liberty of recommending what we call goitre pills, pretending, in order to enhance their value, that my sister had three goitres, each larger than the last, and yet in the end, thanks to those splendid pills, got rid of them entirely. If they can be made up here, please send me the prescription. But if they are only to be had in Salzburg—please send me a few hundredweight of them by the next mail coach, cash on delivery. You know my address. That story about the Electress is a first-rate lie. Because the Empress has died, people think that one great lady after another must suffer the same fate. The death of the Margrave of Anspach has already been announced, and the Emperor is supposed to have had a fall—and to be suffering from some internal trouble. I will readily admit that he is slightly indisposed, perhaps too for political reasons, I mean, on account of the church services. Herr Bergopzoomer[2] and his wife, formerly Mlle Schindler, may come to Munich, for Count Seeau told me yesterday that he had had letters from

---

[1] Esser, like Mozart, was a Knight of the Golden Spur.
[2] Johann Baptist Bergopzoomer (1742–1804), an actor-manager in Vienna. He married in 1777 Katharina Leithner-Schindler (1755–1788), a well-known singer at the Italian opera in Vienna.

him, asking whether he would be able to give a concert here and, if so, whether it would be worth his while. But I don't know if he will come when he gets the Count's reply. Acts I and II are being rehearsed again this afternoon in the Count's apartments; then we shall have a chamber rehearsal of Act III only, and afterwards go straight to the theatre. The rehearsal has been put off again and again on account of the copyist— which has made Count Sensheim devilishly furious. As to having my score copied, it has not been necessary for me to beat about the bush. I have simply been quite frank with the Count. It was always the custom in Mannheim (in a case where the Kapellmeister has been well paid) that the original score should be returned to him; and the reason why in my case the copying has been done even more quickly than usual (for Act I has been copied already) is that Danzi, the cellist, who is getting on in years, would not be able to read my small notes at night. As for what is called the popular taste, do not be uneasy, for there is music in my opera for all kinds of people, but not for the long-eared. A propos, what about ⟨the Archbishop?⟩ Next Monday[1] I ⟨shall have been away from Salzburg for six weeks.⟩ You know, my dear father, that ⟨it is only to please you⟩ that I am staying on there, since, by Heaven, if I had followed my inclination, ⟨before leaving⟩ the other day ⟨I would have wiped my behind with my last contract,⟩ for I swear to you on my honour that it is not Salzburg itself but the ⟨Prince⟩ and ⟨his conceited nobility⟩ who become every day more intolerable to me. Thus I should be delighted, were he to send me word in writing that he ⟨no longer required my services;⟩ for with ⟨the great patronage which I now have here, both my present and future position⟩ would be sufficiently ⟨safeguarded—save for deaths⟩—which ⟨no one⟩ can guard against, but which ⟨are no great misfortune to a man of talent who is single.⟩ But I would do anything in the world to please you. Yet it would be less trying to me, if I could occasionally clear out for a short time, just to draw breath. You know how difficult it was ⟨to get away this time:⟩ and without some ⟨very urgent cause,⟩ there would ⟨not be the slightest chance⟩ of such a thing happening again. ⟨To think of it is enough to make one weep.⟩ So away with the thought. Adieu!—I kiss your hands a thousand times and embrace my sister with all my heart and am ever your most obedient son

WOLFGANG AMADÉ MOZART

Join me in Munich soon—and hear my opera—and then tell me whether ⟨it is wrong of me to be sad when I think of Salzburg!⟩ Adieu—my compliments to all my good friends and greetings from everyone here, and especially from the Cannabichs.

[1] 18 December.

(377) *Nannerl Mozart to her Brother*

[*Extract*]   [*Autograph in the Mozarteum, Salzburg*]

DEAREST BROTHER!   [SALZBURG, 18 *December* 1780]

I am absolutely delighted that you are well again and that, as far as I have gathered from your letter, you are in good spirits. I now finish the list of the plays which were performed before Advent.[1]   ★

Last Thursday, December 14th, we started to wear mourning for the late Empress and it will last three months as in Munich.

If the Archbishop really goes to Vienna, as I have heard it suggested again, a great many people from Salzburg may pay a visit to Munich to hear your opera. M. Fiala and young Weinrother have made up their minds to do so.   ★

Keep well until the time comes, very soon, I hope, when we shall join you in Munich.

I am your sincere and loving sister

MARIE ANNE MOZART

Katherl Gilowsky would very much like to come with us to Munich, if she could only find free board and lodging somewhere. But it would be too expensive for us, if we had to put her up too.

(377a) *Leopold Mozart to his Son*

[*Autograph in the Mozarteum, Salzburg*]

[SALZBURG, 18 *December* 1780[2]]

I have this moment received your letter of December 16th. When he was in Salzburg Herr Esser went about *on foot* and wore his *black cloth suit with his spur attached*, which, if I remember rightly, was his *whole wardrobe*, although, as I know for certain, he made a good deal of money in Vienna. Further, he must have made seventy gulden here over and above his living expenses. He is indeed a jolly fellow, but an idiotic fool as far as the management of money is concerned. He has real merits; but he conceals them with the tricks of a charlatan and wins admiration from and makes money out of the ignorant.

The goitre pills will arrive by mail coach. Your sister thanks you for your charming recommendation based on her three goitres. She would be quite willing to appear as a typical native of Salzburg with a small goitre which is our true national mark—of beauty. As to the *six weeks'*

---

[1] The long list of plays performed in Salzburg by Schikaneder's company has been omitted.
[2] Postscript to his daughter's letter.

leave of absence I shall reply by the next post. At the moment I have too little time. Keep well. We both kiss you most cordially and I am your faithful old father

MZT

The whole opera copied out ready for printing with the Italian and German texts side by side will follow by the next mail coach. I have been paying out so much money in letters and mail coach fees for His Excellency Count Seeau that I do not know exactly how much it amounts to. But I hope that he will make it up to me. I have said in my earlier letters and now repeat that I do not doubt the soundness and excellence of your composition, and its success, particularly if you have a good orchestra; which you have. Questo basta![1] I hope that the second rehearsal went as satisfactorily as the first; and Act III likewise. Finis coronat opus. Oh! Oh! Finis Corona Topus. Farewell!

(378) *Mozart to his Father*

[*Autograph in the Mozarteum, Salzburg*]

MON TRÉS CHER PÉRE!   MUNICH, 19 *December* 1780

I have received safely the last aria for Raaff (who sends greetings to you), the two trumpet mutes, your letter of the 15th, and the pair of socks. The second rehearsal went off as well as the first. The orchestra and the whole audience discovered to their delight that the second act was actually more expressive and original than the first. Next Saturday both acts are to be rehearsed again. But this time the rehearsal is to be held in a large hall at Court, and this I have long wished for, because there is not nearly room enough at Count Seeau's. The Elector is to listen incognito in an adjoining room. Well, as Cannabich said to me, 'We shall have to rehearse like the deuce.' At the last rehearsal he was dripping with perspiration. A propos, speaking of sweating, I am inclined to think that at that play both causes must have worked together.[2] Has my sister delivered those compliments?

Herr Esser also heard my rehearsal. He was to have lunched at Cannabich's on Sunday. But he found an opportunity of getting to Augsburg—so off he went! Bon voyage! He came to say good-bye to me, or so they tell me, but I was not at home; I was at Countess Baumgarten's.

Herr Director Cannabich, whose name-day it is today, and who happens to be here at the moment, and sends you very friendly greetings, has

---

[1] That is sufficient!
[2] Mozart refers to a story in Leopold Mozart's letter of 15 December, which for lack of space has had to be omitted.

scolded me for not going on with my letter—and has now left, so that I may do so.

As for Madame Duschek,[1] the thing, of course, is impossible at the moment—but when my opera is finished, it will be a pleasure for me to compose an aria for her. Meanwhile please send her my compliments. And as for the debt, we were to settle that when she next came to Salzburg. What I should like best would be if I could have a few worthy gentlemen like old Czernin—that would be a little help yearly—but it would have to be not less than a hundred gulden a year, in which case they might have any kind of music they liked.

I hope you are now, please God, quite well again? Yes, it cannot well be otherwise if you are having good frictions given to you by someone like Theresa Barisani. You will have noticed from my letters that I am well and happy. One is indeed glad to be rid of such a great and laborious task—and—that too, with honour and glory. For the work is almost finished. Only three arias, the last chorus of Act III, the overture and the ballet are still lacking—and then—adieu partie! As for those arias for Heckmann, which have no words, there are only two which you do not know. The rest include one from 'Ascanio in Alba'—or rather, I mean, two—and the aria for Madame Duschek,[2] which you can send me without the words, as I have them here and can write them in myself. There is also one by Anfossi[3] and one by Salieri[4] with oboe solo—both belonging to Madame Haydn. I forgot to copy the words, as I did not think I should have to leave in such a hurry. I do not know them by heart.

A propos—now for the most important thing of all—for I must hurry. I hope to receive by the next mail coach the first act at least, together with the translation. The scene between father and son in Act I and the first scene in Act II between Idomeneo and Arbace are both too long. They would certainly bore the audience, particularly as in the first scene both the actors are bad, and in the second, one of them is; besides, they only contain a narrative of what the spectators have already seen with their own eyes. These scenes are being printed as they stand. But I should like the Abbate to indicate how they may be shortened—and as drastically as possible,—for otherwise I shall have to shorten them myself. These two scenes cannot remain as they are—I mean, when set to music.

I have just received your letter which, as my sister began it, is of course without a date. A thousand compliments to Theresa, my future upper and

---

[1] See p. 688.   [2] K. 272.
[3] Pasquale Anfossi (1727–?1797) of Naples. He first studied the violin and then took lessons in harmony and composition from Piccinni. From 1758 onwards he composed several operas, which were very successful. From 1792 until 1797 he was maestro di cappella to the Lateran.
[4] Antonio Salieri (1750–1825). He was trained by Gassmann, in 1774 became Court composer in Vienna, and on Bonno's death in 1788 Court Kapellmeister. In addition he was director of the Viennese Opera from 1774 until 1790. He was on most cordial terms with Haydn and Beethoven, but Mozart suspected him of intrigue.

lower nurse-maid. I can well believe that Katherl would like to come to Munich, if (apart from the journey) you could let her take my place at table. Eh bien—I can easily manage it. She can share a room with my sister. A propos. Please let me know at least a week beforehand when you will be arriving, so that I may have a stove put in the other room. Adieu. What beautiful handwriting! I kiss your hands a hundred times and embrace my sister with all my heart and am ever your most obedient son

WOLF. AMDE: MZT

Mes compliments à tous nos amis et amies.
A longer and more legible letter next time.

(379) *Leopold Mozart to his Son*

[*Autograph in the Rudolf Nydahl Collection, Stiftelsen Musikkulturens*
[*Extract*]   *Främjande, Stockholm*]

MON TRÈS CHER FILS!   SALZBURG, 22 *December* 1780

I must write in haste, for the mail coach is leaving tomorrow morning, that is, a day earlier than usual.

★   Here are the three acts copied out for the printer. Space has been left for the insertion of the names of the singers, the particulars of the ballets, the ballet music and so forth. What he has inserted before each principal change of scene can easily be altered in the final text, if at any point Herr Quaglio has to do so. For example, in Act I, sc. 8, it is stated: *Nettuno esce, etc.* and then: *Nel fondo della prospettiva si vede Idomeneo che si sforza arrampicarsi sopra quei dirupi, etc.* Well, you will have to give the announcement and description of these scenes, exactly as it is intended to produce them, I mean, according to whether Idomeneo is to remain in his ship, or is not to be shipwrecked, but, on being made aware of the danger, is to leave the ship with his people and save himself on the rocks. In short, it all depends upon the manner of the production. This, I suppose, will be left to Herr Quaglio, who is intelligent and experienced. But there must be disabled ships about, for in his recitative in scene 10 Idamante says: '*Vedo fra quegli avanzi di fracassate navi su quel lido sconosciuto guerrier*'. Well, let's get on! You insisted on having two recitatives shortened. I sent for Varesco at once, for I received your letter only at five o'clock this evening, and the mail coach leaves tomorrow morning. We have considered the first recitative in all its bearings and we both find no occasion to shorten it. It is translated from the French, according to the draft which was arranged. What is more, if you consult the draft, you will see that it was suggested that this recitative should be lengthened a little, so that father and son should not recognize one another too quickly. And now you want to make it ridiculous by making them recognize one another after they have exchanged only a few words. Let me explain my point. Idamante must surely say why he is there. Then he sees the stranger and offers him his services. Idomeneo goes so far as to mention his own sufferings. At the same time he must return his greetings. Upon which Idamante will tell him that he can sympathize with the unfortunate, as he himself has experienced misfortune. Idomeneo's reply must be a question. Idamante now describes the king's misfortune and Idomeneo by his mysterious words '*Uom più di questo*' gives Idamante a ray of hope. The latter then asks eagerly '*Dimmi, amico, dimmi dov'è?*' This eagerness makes Idomeneo ask '*Ma d' onde, etc.*' Surely Idamante must explain things at this point in such a way as to describe himself as a son worthy of his father and to awaken in Idomeneo admiration, respect and longing to hear who this youth is? Moreover, when he does recognize his son, the whole story becomes far more interesting! But if something has *par force* to be omitted, I have come to the conclusion that it should be after the recitative of Idamante: '*Che favelli? vive egli ancor? etc.*,' which closes with: '*Dove quel dolce aspetto vita mi renderà?*' Idomeneo: '*Ma d'onde nasce questa, che per lui nutri tenerezza d'amor?*' From this point you might jump to: '*Perchè quel tuo parlar sì mi conturba?*' Idamante: '*E qual mi sento anch' io*' and then continue. At page 32 in Varesco's copy, one and a half pages will thus be omitted—that is, the beautiful description of Idamante's heroic deed, I mean, where he begins: '*Potessi almeno io, etc.*' In this way the recitative will be shortened by a *minute*, yes, in puncto, by a whole minute. Great gain, forsooth! Or do you want to make father and son run up and recognise one another just as Harlequin and Brigella, who are disguised as servants in a foreign country, meet, recognize and embrace each other immediately? Remember that this is one of *the finest scenes in the whole opera*, nay, *the principal scene*, on which the entire remaining story depends. Further, this scene cannot weary the audience, *as it is in the first act*.

Nothing more can be cut in Act II, save a portion of Idomeneo's second speech. Idomeneo. '*Un sol consiglio or mi fa d'uopo. Ascolta. Tu sai quanto a' Troiani fu il mio brando fatal.*' Arbace. '*Tutto m' è noto, etc.*' Then the dialogue continues, and not a single word can be omitted without destroying the sense. Besides, the whole recitative cannot last long, because several passages must be spoken eagerly and rapidly. And if you were to cut it, you would only gain *half a minute*! Great gain, forsooth! Nor can this recitative weary a single soul, as it is the *first scene* in Act II. What you might possibly omit is a passage after the recitative of Arbace: '*male s'usurpa un rè, etc.*'; when Idomeneo immediately rejoins: '*Il voto è ingiusto.*' Then you could leave out Idomeneo: '*Intendo, Arbace, etc.*' and Arbace: '*Medica mano, etc.*' The question is whether it is worth while to make an alteration by which you will gain at most two and a half minutes. I am not at all sure, especially as these recitatives are so placed that they cannot weary the audience. Everyone is patient during the first act of any opera and, further, the first recitative in a second act can never weary anyone. I think the whole thing is rather ridiculous. It is true that at a rehearsal where the eye has nothing to engage it, a recitative immediately becomes boring; but at the performance, where between the stage and the audience there are so many objects to entertain the eye, a recitative like this is over before the listeners are aware of it. You may tell the whole world that from me. However, if in spite of all, something has to be omitted, I insist that the passages shall be printed in full. Varesco knows nothing of what I have written to you. If Schachtner has not done his part as perfectly as you would wish, you must remember that he had very little time. Here are all the arias which Aesop[1] has copied and also a letter from Schachtner, who with Varesco sends his greetings to you. We wish you luck and trust that the opera may be a success. More news next post-day. Addio. I have written the whole of this letter by candle-light and with spectacles. We send our greetings to all, we kiss you millions of times and I am your faithful old father

L. MOZART

(380) *Leopold Mozart to his Son*

[*From Nissen, pp.* 427-430]

SALZBURG, 25 *December* 1780

The whole town is talking about the excellence of your opera. Baron Lehrbach spread the first report. The Court Chancellor's wife tells me that he told her that your opera was being praised to the skies. The second report was set going by Herr Becke's letter to Fiala, which the latter made everyone read. I should like Act III to produce the same effect. I feel certain that it will, the more so as in this act great passions are expressed and the subterranean voice will undoubtedly astonish and terrify. Basta, I trust that people will say: *Finis coronat opus.* But do your best to keep the whole orchestra in good humour; flatter them, and, by praising them, keep them all well-disposed towards you. For I know your style of composition—it requires unusually close attention from the players of every type of instrument; and to keep the whole orchestra at such a pitch of industry and alertness for at least three hours is no joke. Each performer, even the most inferior viola-player, is deeply touched by personal praise and becomes much more zealous and attentive, while a little courtesy of this kind only costs you a word or two. However—you know all this yourself—I am just mentioning it, because rehearsals afford few opportuni-

[1] See p. 686, n. 3.

ties to do this, and so it is forgotten; and when the opera is staged, one really needs the cordial friendship and the keenness of the whole orchestra. Their position is then quite different, and the attention of every single performer must be strained even further. You know that you cannot count on the goodwill of everyone, for there is always *an undercurrent of doubt and questioning*. People wondered whether Act II would be as original and excellent as Act I. As this doubt has now been removed, few will have any doubts as to Act III. But I will wager my head that there are some who are wondering whether *your music will produce the same effect in a theatre as it does in a room*. And here you really need the greatest keenness and goodwill on the part of the whole body of players.

In regard to your *six weeks' leave of absence* I have made up my mind not to make any move or to say anything. But if I am questioned, I have decided to reply that we had understood that *you would be allowed to stay on in Munich for six weeks after composing the opera in order to attend the rehearsals and the performance, as I could hardly think that His Grace the Prince could expect an opera of this kind to be composed, copied and performed in the space of six weeks.*

Herr Esser has written to me and also to Ferrari from Augsburg. He praised very highly the two acts which he had heard and said that the opera was being rehearsed from five to eight. Herr Becke, to whom we send our greetings, has written to say that the storm chorus in Act II is so powerful that even in the heat of midsummer it would make anyone feel as cold as ice. He has praised very highly Dorothea Wendling's aria with solo instruments in Act II[1] and so forth. In short, it would take too long to tell you how much he has praised your work.

Herr Ferrari sends you his congratulations on the general approval of your opera. He showed me the letter he had received from Esser, who sent his thanks to our orchestra for accompanying him at the concert he gave in Salzburg, and also to all at Court, especially to Haydn, Brunetti, Hafeneder and the rest. So we read too that he had heard the two acts of your opera, and che abbia sentito una musica ottima e particolare, universalmente applaudita.[2]

(381) *Mozart to his Father*

[*Autograph in the Mozarteum, Salzburg*]

MON TRÉS CHER PÉRE!   MUNICH, 27 *December* 1780

I have received the whole text, Schachtner's letter, your note and the pills. In regard to the two scenes which are to be shortened, it was not my suggestion, but one to which I have consented—my reason being that

---

[1] Ilia's aria *Se il padre perdei*, with flute, oboe, bassoon and horn obbligato accompaniment.
[2] That he had listened to excellent and original music, which was unanimously applauded.

Raaff and dal Prato spoil the recitative by singing it without any spirit or fire, and *so* monotonously. They are the most wretched actors that ever walked on a stage. I had a desperate row the other day with Seeau about the inexpediency, inconvenience and the practical impossibility of omitting anything. However, everything is to be printed as it is, to which he at first refused *absolument* to agree; but in the end, as I scolded him roundly, he gave in. The last rehearsal was splendid. It took place in a spacious room at Court. The Elector was there too. This time we rehearsed with the whole orchestra (I mean, of course, with as many players as can be accommodated in the opera house). After the first act the Elector called out to me quite loudly, Bravo! When I went up to kiss his hand he said: '*This opera will be charming and cannot fail to do you honour*'. As he was not sure whether he could remain much longer, we had to perform the aria with obbligatos for wind-instruments[1] and the thunderstorm at the beginning of Act II, when he again expressed his approval in the kindest manner and said with a laugh: '*Who would believe that such great things could be hidden in so small a head?*' And the next day at the levée too he praised my opera very highly. The next rehearsal will probably be in the theatre. A propos. Becke told me a few days ago that he had written to you after the last rehearsal but one and among other things had mentioned that Raaff's aria in Act II did not suit the rhythm of the words. '*So I am told,*' he said, '*but I know too little Italian to be able to judge. Is it so?*' I replied, 'If you had only asked me first and written about it afterwards! I should like to tell you that whoever said such a thing knows very little Italian.' The aria is very well adapted to the words. You hear the *mare* and the *mare funesto* and the musical passages suit *minacciar*, for they entirely express *minacciar* (threatening). On the whole it is the most superb aria in the opera and has also won universal approval. Is it true that the Emperor is ill? Is it true that the Archbishop is coming to Munich? To return, Raaff is the best and most honest fellow in the world, but so tied to old-fashioned routine that flesh and blood cannot stand it. Consequently, it is very difficult to compose for him, but very easy if you choose to compose commonplace arias, as, for instance, the first one, '*Vedrommi intorno*'. When you hear it, you will say that it is good and beautiful—but if I had written it for Zonca,[2] it would have suited the words much better. Raaff is too fond of everything which is cut and dried, and he pays no attention to expression. I have just had a bad time with him over the quartet. The

---

[1] Ilia's aria in Act II, 'Se il padre perdei'.
[2] Giovanni Battista Zonca (1728–1809) was born at Brescia and trained in Italy. In 1763 he became bass singer to the Mannheim court, which he followed to Munich in 1778. He retired in 1788. Evidently Mozart would have preferred to write the part of Idomeneo for a bass voice. Indeed he intended to rewrite it later for a performance in Vienna in which J. I. L. Fischer, the famous bass singer, was to take this part. Mozart's plan was never carried out. See p. 765.

more I think of this quartet, as it will be performed on the stage, the more effective I consider it; and it has pleased all those who have heard it played on the clavier. Raaff alone thinks it will produce no effect whatever. He said to me when we were by ourselves: 'Non c' è da spianar la voce.[1] It gives me no scope.[1] As if in a quartet the words should not be spoken much more than sung. That kind of thing he does not understand at all. All I said was: 'My very dear friend, if I knew of one single note which ought to be altered in this quartet, I would alter it at once. But so far there is nothing in my opera with which I am so pleased as with this quartet; and when you have once heard it sung as a whole, you will talk very differently. I have taken great pains to serve you well in your two arias; I shall do the same with your third one—and shall hope to succeed. But as far as trios and quartets are concerned, the composer must have a free hand.' Where-upon he said that he was satisfied. The other day he was very much annoyed about some words in his last aria—*rinvigorir*—and *ringiovenir*
—and especially *vienmi a rinvigorir*[2]—five *i*'s!—It is true that at the end of an aria this is very unpleasant. Well, I most close, for the mail coach is starting this very moment.

I have had my black suit turned, for it was really very shabby. Now it looks quite presentable. Adieu. My greetings to all my good friends, and particularly to your beautiful and clever pupil.[3] I embrace my sister with all my heart and kiss your hands a thousand times and am ever your most obedient son

WOLFG: AMD: MOZART

(382) *Leopold Mozart to his Son*

[*Extract*]   [*Autograph in the possession of Elisabeth Firestone Willis, New York*]

A Happy New Year!   SALZBURG, 29 *December* 1780

I absolutely insist that everything that Varesco has written shall be printed. The omissions amount to only a few lines. In 'Telemacco'[4] too everything was printed, although in the music a few lines of the recitative were left out. I wish we could correct the proofs together in Salzburg. There is nothing more objectionable than to find in a book a number of misprints, which often make the sense quite unintelligible. It would be a good thing if you yourself would undertake to read through the revised proofs before the final printing, even if it has to be done at the printer's. Further, I hope

---

[1] You can't let yourself go in it.

[2] In the autograph the *i*'s are numbered in Mozart's handwriting. Varesco had to write a third version, 'Torna la pace al cor'. At the first performance on 29 January 1781, this aria and that of Idamante, 'No, la morte io non pavento', both in Act III, were omitted. See p. 708.

[3] Perhaps Therese von Barisani.

[4] An opera by Paul Grua, composed for the Munich carnival, 1780. See p. 663, n. 8.

that Count Seeau will not object to sending Varesco and Schachtner *at least a dozen copies in all.*

In regard to *'vienmi a rinvigorir'* it is true that there are five *i*'s, but it is also true that I can pronounce the phrase twenty times without any inconvenience, in fact with the greatest rapidity and ease. In the aria from Metastasio's 'Achille in Sciro' which you sent me as a model, the closing lines, *'il peso alleggerir'* and *'lo vede rinfiorir'*, especially the *'rinfiorir'* (on account of the initial *r*), are certainly far more inconvenient. Basta! To please everyone the devil himself may go on altering and altering. Signor Raaff is far too pernickety. I need not say anything about the quartets, and so forth, for which declamation and action are far more essential than great singing ability or his everlasting *'spianar la voce'*.[1] In this case action and diction are the necessary qualities.

God be praised that His Highness is satisfied with the first two acts, or rather is thoroughly delighted. I daresay that when your opera is staged, you will have many more points to raise, particularly in Act III, where there is so much action.

I assume that you will choose very deep wind-instruments to accompany the subterranean voice. How would it be if after the slight subterranean rumble the instruments *sustained, or rather began to sustain, their notes piano and then made a crescendo such as might almost inspire terror, while after this and during the decrescendo the voice would begin to sing?* And there might be a terrifying crescendo at *every phrase uttered by the voice.* Owing to the rumble, which must be short, and rather like the shock of a thunderbolt, which sends up the figure of Neptune, the attention of the audience is aroused; and this attention is intensified by the introduction of a quiet, prolonged and then swelling and very alarming wind-instrument passage, and finally becomes strained to the utmost when, behold! *a voice* is heard. Why, I seem to see and hear it.

It was a good thing to have your suit turned. Now that we are discussing clothes, *I suppose I can save myself the trouble of bringing my braided suit. You know that I do not care about dressing up.* Please let me know about this. We both kiss you most cordially and I am your honest old father

L. Mozart

Salzburg, 30 *December* 1780

★ While taking dessert after lunch yesterday, December 29th, the Archbishop cut his finger very badly.

★ The Emperor is not laid up; but *old Papa Colloredo*[2] is dangerously ill. Otherwise the Archbishop would have gone to Vienna. If Colloredo dies, he will not go at all. I have not heard a syllable about the Archbishop going to Munich.

★

---

[1] Letting himself go. See p. 699.
[2] Prince Rudolf Colloredo, father of the Salzburg Archbishop.

(382a) *Nannerl Mozart to her Brother*

[*Extract*]   [*Autograph in the possession of Elisabeth Firestone Willis, New York*]

SALZBURG, 30 *December* 1780[1]

I wish you a Happy New Year, constant good health and prosperity! Please continue to give me *your brotherly affection*. Above all I hope that your opera, when staged, will win universal applause and will bring you great honour and glory. All my hopes and wishes are centred on this. I am writing to you with an erection on my head and I am very much afraid of burning my hair. The reason why the Mölks' maid has dressed my hair is that tomorrow for the first time I am sitting for the painter.[2]

Again I wish you a Happy New Year, and so do thousands of all our good friends. I have delivered your message to my beautiful pupil, who sends you her greetings in return.[3]

(383) *Mozart to his Father*

[*Autograph in the Mozarteum, Salzburg*]

MON TRÉS CHER PÉRE!   MUNICH, 30 *December* 1780

A Happy New Year! Forgive me for not writing much this time, but I am up to the eyes in work. I have not quite finished the third act, and, as there is no extra ballet, but only an appropriate divertissement in the opera, I have the honour of composing the music for that as well; but I am glad of it, for now all the music will be by the same composer. The third act will turn out to be *at least* as good as the first two—in fact, I believe, infinitely better—and I think that it may be said with truth, *finis coronat opus*. The Elector was so pleased at the rehearsal that, as I wrote to you the other day, he praised my opera most highly at his levée on the following morning—and again at Court in the evening. I have heard too from a very good source that on the same evening after the rehearsal he spoke of my music to everyone with whom he conversed, saying: '*I was quite surprised. No music has ever made such an impression on me. It is magnificent music.*' The day before yesterday we had a rehearsal of recitatives at Wendling's and we went through the quartet together. We repeated it six times and now it goes well. The stumbling-block was dal Prato; the fellow is utterly useless. His voice would not be so bad if he did not produce it in his throat and larynx. But he has no intonation, no method, no feeling, but sings—well, like the best of the boys who come to be tested in the hope of getting a place in the chapel choir. Raaff is delighted

---

[1] Postscript to her father's letter.
[2] For the family portrait. See p. 663, n. 2.   [3] See p. 699, n. 3.

that he was mistaken about the quartet and no longer doubts its effect. I am now in a difficulty in regard to his last aria, and you must help me out of it. He cannot stomach the '*rinvigorir*' and '*ringiovenir*'—and these two words make the whole aria distasteful to him. It is true that *mostrami* and *vienmi* are also not good, but the two final words are the worst of all. To avoid the shake on the *i* in the first *rinvigorir*, I really ought to transfer it to the *o*. In 'Natal di Giove',[1] which is, I admit, very little known, Raaff has now found, I believe, an aria which is admirably suited to this situation. I think it is the '*aria di licenza*'[2]—

> Bell' alme al ciel dilette,
> si, ah! respirate ormai,
> già palpitaste assai;
> è tempo di goder.
> Creta non oda intorno,
> non vegga in sì bel giorno,
> che accenti di contento,
> che oggetti di piacer.

Well, he wants me to set this to music. 'No one knows the words,' he says, 'and we can keep quiet about it.' He fully realizes that we cannot expect the Abbate to alter this aria a third time, and he will not sing it as it stands. I beg you to reply immediately. I hope to hear from you on Wednesday—and then I shall have plenty of time to compose his aria. Well, I must close, for I must now write at break-neck speed. Everything has been composed, but not yet written down. Please give my greetings to all my good friends and my New Year wishes too. I drew the fifteen gulden yesterday. I shall not have very much left, for there are a hundred trifles which made inroads on my money; and I certainly do not spend it unnecessarily. Why, it cost me seven gulden, twenty-four kreuzer, just to have my black coat turned, a new damask lining put in, and a sleeve of my brown costume patched. So I must ask you to send me another draft. It is just as well to have something in hand, as I really can't go about in a penniless condition. Adieu. I kiss your hands a thousand times and embrace my sister with all my heart and am ever your most obedient son

WOLFGANG AMADÈ MOZART

My compliments to dear Theresa. The maid who waits on me here is also a Theresa—but Heavens! how different from our Theresa from Linz, in beauty, virtue, charms—and a thousand other merits! You probably know that the worthy castrato Marchesi,[3] or *Marquesius*

---

[1] A drama by Metastasio.

[2] An aria generally inserted in an opera as an epilogue or an address to some distinguished guest.

[3] See p. 303, n.3 . There was no truth in this sensational story. Marchesi lived until 1829.

di Milano, has been poisoned at Naples. And how? He was in love with a duchess, whose rightful lover became jealous and sent three or four fellows to give him his choice, either to drink poison out of a cup or to be assassinated. He chose the former, but being an Italian coward, he died *alone*, and allowed his murderers to live on in peace and quiet. Had it been myself and had it been absolutely necessary for me to die, I should have taken at least a couple with me into the next world. Such an excellent singer is a great loss.—Adieu.

(384) *Mozart to his Father*

[Autograph formerly in the Mozarteum, Salzburg]

MON TRÉS CHER PÉRE! MUNICH, 3 *January* 1781

My head and my hands are so full of Act III that it would be no wonder if I were to turn into a third act myself. This fact alone has cost me more trouble than a whole opera, for there is hardly a scene in it which is not extremely interesting. The accompaniment to the subterranean voice consists of five instruments only, that is, three trombones and two French horns, which are placed in the same quarter as that from which the voice proceeds. At this point the whole orchestra is silent. The dress rehearsal will take place *for certain* on January 20th and the first performance on the 22nd.[1] All you will both require and all that you need bring with you is one black dress—and another, for everyday wear—when you are just visiting intimate friends, where there is no standing on ceremony —so that you may save your black one a little; and, if you like, a more elegant dress to wear at the ball and the académie masquée. I shall tell you about the stove next post-day. I shall probably have to send this letter too by the post. I have told the conductor a hundred times always to send for my letters at eleven o'clock. The coach goes at half past eleven. I never dress before half past twelve, as I have to compose. So I can't go out. I can't send him the letter, for he takes it by private arrangement, as they don't like my doing this at the post office. Herr von Robinig is already here and sends greetings to you both. I hear that the two Barisanis are also coming to Munich. Is this true? Thank God that the cut in the Archbishop's finger was of no consequence. Heavens! How frightened I was at first. Cannabich thanks you for your charming letter, and the whole family send their greetings. He told me that you had written very humorously. You also must have been in good spirits.

No doubt we shall have a good many points to raise in Act III, when it is staged. For example, in Scene 6, after Arbace's aria, I see that Varesco has

---

[1] In the end the first performance did not take place until 29 January.

Idomeneo, Arbace, etc. How can the latter reappear immediately? Fortunately he can stay away altogether. But for safety's sake I have composed a somewhat longer introduction to the High Priest's recitative. After the mourning chorus the king and all his people go away; and in the following scene the directions are, 'Idomeneo in ginocchione nel tempio'. That is quite impossible. He must come in with his whole suite. A march must be introduced here, and I have therefore composed a very simple one for two violins, viola, cello and two oboes, to be played a mezza voce. While it is going on, the King appears and the priests prepare the offerings for the sacrifice. Then the King kneels down and begins the prayer.

In Elettra's recitative, after the subterranean voice has spoken, there ought to be an indication—Partono. I forgot to look at the copy which has been made for the printer to see whether there is one and, if so, where it comes. It seems to me very silly that they should hurry away so quickly for no better reason than to allow Madame Elettra to be alone. I have this moment received your five lines of January 1st.

When I opened the letter I happened to hold it in such a way that nothing but a blank sheet met my eyes. At last I found the writing.

I am delighted to have the aria for Raaff, for he was absolutely determined that I should set to music the words he had found. With a man like Raaff I could not possibly have arranged it in any other way than by having Varesco's aria printed and Raaff's sung. Well, I must close, or I shall waste too much time. I thank my sister most warmly for her New Year wishes, which I cordially return. I hope that we shall soon be able to have some fun together. Adieu. I kiss your hands a thousand times and embrace my sister with all my heart and am ever your most obedient son

WOLFG: AMAD: MOZART

My greetings to all my good friends—and please do not forget Rüscherl. Young Eck sends her a little kiss—a sugary one, of course.

(385) Leopold Mozart to his Son

[Extract]   [Autograph in the University Library, Prague]

MON TRÈS CHER FILS!   SALZBURG, 4 January 1781

I received your letter of December 30th at nine o'clock, just as I was going to the service. After Church I did my New Year seccature[1] and then went to see Varesco at half past ten. He was horribly angry and said the most foolish things, as Italians or half-Italians do. He mentioned among other things that he had written a few days ago to Count Seeau, asking him to see that there would be no misprints in the text; good! that he

---

[1] The Italian 'seccare' means 'to bore'. Leopold Mozart obviously refers to his New Year calls.

would like to have twelve copies; basta! that he hoped to receive a few more ducats in recognition of the fact that he had copied the text four times and subsequently had had to make a good many alterations: and that, if he had known beforehand, he would not have agreed to write the text for the small remuneration of twenty ducats. *As far as I am concerned, it was a good move.* But I immediately began to think that the godless Italian idea might occur to Varesco that *we had made a better bargain and were keeping the money.* The reasons for my supposition are that he is only *half-Italian, peggio del Italiano vero*;[1] that I was unable to give him Count Seeau's letter about his contract, but only read it out, as he was not to know about certain other matters; that when he sent Act III to you through Count Seeau and the latter did not reply, you wrote to me saying that the Count had commissioned you to do so. All this may have aroused his suspicion that there are in the world more people *of his own type.* He will probably have judged us after his own pattern. Well, to continue. I listened to him with absolute calmness and when at last I got tired of his railing and his silly chatter, I said to him: '*The only reply I want is whether or not I am to write today to say that next post-day, January 4th, another aria will be sent to Munich. For reply I must! The rest does not concern me in the very least.*' He then said: '*I will see whether anything occurs to me*'. So I went off to finish my New Year *seccature.* You can gather from the remarks he has jotted down beside the aria what else he said and how enraged he was. I shall tell you all about it when we meet. But do see that Count Seeau *pays him and Schachtner* as soon as possible. Just give the money to Gschwendner. It is much the quickest way. You know that I am a lover of peace and an honest fellow, who desires to spare everyone any annoyance. You will see from Varesco's minute that he has written another aria to be sung, but wants to have an aria '*Sazio è il destin, etc.*' printed. It would be ridiculous to have one aria in the text and another sung. The best solution would be to print both arias, but to put brackets at the end of every line of '*Sazio è il destin*', to show that it is not being sung. In this way all unpleasantness would be avoided—and it would only be a question of printing a few more lines. Let me know when the dress rehearsal is to take ★ place.

I am your old father

MZT ★

(386) *Leopold Mozart to his Son*

[*Extract*]   [*Autograph in the Mozarteum, Salzburg*]

Mon très cher Fils!   Salzburg, 8 *January* 1781
    Instead of going to the ball we went yesterday to Herr Hagenauer's. They all send you their greetings. Your sister has sat twice to the painter.

---

[1] Worse than a pure Italian.

It's a good likeness and, if it is not spoilt in the painting, the head will be charming.

★   Your sister has decided to have a new black dress made, which will cost her altogether about seventy gulden. She hopes that ⟨*the Elector will be obliged to pay for it!*⟩ We kiss you a million times and I am your faithful and honest old father

MOZART

★

(387) *Mozart to his Father*

[*Autograph in the Mozarteum, Salzburg*]

MON TRÉS CHER PÉRE!   MUNICH, 10 *and* 11 *January* 1781

The latest news is that the opera has been postponed again for a week. The dress rehearsal will not take place until the 27th—my birthday, mark you—and the first performance on the 29th. Why? Presumably in order that Count Seeau may save a few hundred gulden. But I am delighted, as it will give us an opportunity of further and more careful rehearsals. The Robinigs pulled long faces when I gave them this piece of news. Louise and Sigmund are delighted to stay on, and it would be easy enough to persuade Mamma to do so. But Lisa[1]—*that miserable specimen of humanity*—has such a stupid Salzburg tongue—that she really drives me crazy. Perhaps they will stay on. I hope so for Louise's sake. In addition to many other minor rows with Count Seeau I have had a desperate fight with him about the trombones. I call it a desperate fight, because I had to be rude to him, or I should never have got my way. Next Saturday the three acts are to be rehearsed in private. I have received your letter of January 8th and read it with the greatest delight. I like the burlesque very much.[2]

Forgive me if this time too I write very little and must now close. First of all, as you see, my pen and ink are no good, and, secondly, I have still a few arias to compose for the ballet—but—I hope that you will never again send me such a letter as your last one of three or four lines.

My congratulations to Madame Fiala on her scabies. Well, she has something that few people have. So she can say: '*It's mine*'. But someone else ought to try to get it in order to be able to say the same thing. Herr Proschalka tells me that Katherl Gilowsky is coming to Munich. Is it true? Please tell the Barisanis that my opera has been postponed, so that they may make their arrangements accordingly.

Well, I can't think of any more news to send you, save that through the hunchbacked brother of Madame Zimmerl (the famous remover of

---

[1] Elizabeth Robinig (1749–1792), Frau von Robinig's eldest daughter.
[2] Mozart alludes to a long story in Leopold Mozart's letter of 8 January, which for lack of space has had to be omitted.

grease spots), who is here with Madame Ludwig of Salzburg, and is living with her as her husband, I have heard, and that too as a certainty, that the Storchenfelds have left Böhm[1] and that Murschhauser[2] has left as well—that Peter Vogt[3] left him long ago—and that Elias[4] has deserted his wife and decamped—that Böhm is in Mainz and that the Zimmerls and Müllers had also left him, but that they joined him again as soon as he got there. If I had had time, I would have written to him long ago, just to get some news from him. Well adieu. How is Schikaneder? I hope to see him here during the carnival. Please give him my regards. I kiss your hands a thousand times and embrace my sister with all my heart and am ever your most obedient son

WOLF: AMD: MOZART

(388) *Leopold Mozart to his Son*

[*Extract*]   [*Autograph in the Mozarteum, Salzburg*]

MON TRES CHER FILS!   SALZBURG, 11 *January* 1781

We intend to leave here on Thursday, January 18th, and to arrive in Munich on Friday, January 19th. But up to the present I have not said anything definite. I hope to let you know for certain on Monday, January 15th. No one knows when the Archbishop is going to Vienna, doubtless because he himself, as usual, does not know.

I am expecting to have a letter from you tomorrow by the post or possibly today by the mail coach. It has just occurred to me that it is really not necessary to put a stove in the other room. Can't a bed be put in the room where you have been composing? There are two beds already in the alcove. True, I do not know the rooms. But surely we can put up with a little discomfort, especially for such a short time. As it is, we shall be in your rooms very little. Your sister and I can sleep in the alcove and you can sleep outside. Why, we can live like gypsies and soldiers. That will be no new experience for us. Surely we can't expect it to be like home? I only hope we can get something to eat *in your rooms or near by*. Well, just make as good arrangements as you can. I have no more news to send you; and it is old news that we both kiss you and that I am your honest old father

L MOZART

---

[1] Johannes Böhm, manager of a theatrical company, which had given several performances at Salzburg in 1779 and 1780.
[2] Marschhauser, an actor, who married the singer Franziska Ballo.
[3] Peter Vogt was master of the ballet in Böhm's theatrical company during their visit to Salzburg in 1779.
[4] Elias Vogt, brother of Peter Vogt.

(389) *Leopold Mozart to his Son*

[*Extract*]   [*Autograph formerly in the Mozarteum, Salzburg*[1]]

MON TRES CHER FILS!   SALZBURG, 13 *January* 1781

⋆ So the opera has been postponed. Well, then, I shall wait until the Archbishop leaves, which will be on the 20th or the 22nd at latest. I trust that the rehearsal of the three acts which took place today, January 13th, went very well. It will have been a long one, the more so if Act III was rehearsed for the first time. Act III ought to have been rehearsed by itself ⋆ or at least at the beginning, before the orchestra got tired.

We both kiss you and hope to see you soon. Keep well. I am your honest old father

⋆   L. MOZT

(390) *Mozart to his Father*

[*Autograph in the Mozarteum, Salzburg*]

MON TRÉS CHER PÉRE!   MUNICH, 18 *January* 1781

I have received your letter of the 11th—and your last one of the 13th, sent through Herr Fiala. Please forgive a short letter, but I must be off to the rehearsal this very moment (it is almost ten o'clock—in the morning, of course). For the first time we are having a rehearsal of recitatives today in the theatre. I have not been able to write until now, as my time has been taken up with those confounded dances. Laus Deo—I have got rid of them at last! But I can only send you my most important news. The rehearsal of Act III went off splendidly. It was considered much superior to the first two acts. But the libretto is too long and consequently the music also (an opinion which I have always held). Therefore Idamante's aria, 'No, la morte io non pavento', is to be omitted; in any case it is out of place there. But those who have heard it with the music deplore this. The omission of Raaff's last aria too is even more regretted; but we must make a virtue of necessity. The speech of the oracle is still far too long and I have therefore shortened it; but Varesco need not know anything of this, because it will all be printed just as he wrote it. Frau von Robinig will bring back with her the money due to him and to Schachtner. Gschwendner refused to take any money with him. Meanwhile tell Varesco from me that he will not get a farthing more out of Count Seeau than was agreed upon—for all the alterations were made, not for the Count, but for *me*; and he ought to be obliged to me into the bargain, for they were made for the sake of his own reputation. There is a good deal that might still be altered; and I assure him that he would not have come off so well with any other composer. I have spared no trouble in defending him.

[1] Copy in the Staatsbibliothek Preussischer Kulturbesitz, West Berlin.

A stove is out of the question, for it costs too much. I shall have another bed put in the room where the alcove is. We shall just have to manage as best we can.

Do not forget to bring my little watch with you. I hope we shall go over to Augsburg, where we can have the enamel repaired. I should like you to bring Schachtner's operetta[1] too. There are some people who come to the Cannabichs, who might just as well hear a thing of this kind. Now I must be off to the rehearsal. Adieu. I kiss your hands a thousand times and embrace my sister with all my heart, and remain your obedient son

                                                                W: A: MZT

More news the next time—and still more when we meet. All sorts of messages from the Cannabichs.

(391) *Leopold Mozart to his Son*

[*Extract*]   [*Autograph in the Mozarteum, Salzburg*]

MON TRÉS CHER FILS!   SALZBURG, 22 *January* 1781

Varesco has this moment been to see me. The greedy, money-grubbing fool simply can't wait for his money. But I told him that he will have to be patient until the return of Madame von Robinig, who is to bring it with her. In spite of his good income the fellow is hopelessly in debt. He said that his money could easily have been sent to him by the mail coach; and he tried to make out that Schachtner had spoken to him about it, though indeed the latter has not only never approached me, but on the contrary, when I mentioned it to him, told me that he was astonished at Varesco's importunity, and that he himself had never counted on receiving the money before our return from Munich. Have you not yet handed the   ★ money to Frau von Robinig? You must not keep it so long. Suppose it were stolen from you! Count Seeau has written to Varesco *che abbia consegnato la cambiale al Signor maestro di cappella*.[2] The word *cambiale* means a bill of exchange. Well, if it is a draft, you ought to have enclosed it in a letter, so that I might get it cashed here and give each his share. But, as you have not done this, I must assume that it is in cash. If so, the currency question comes in. Basta! When I am in Munich, I shall see that each gets his share. *Varesco mi ha seccato i coglioni*.[3] Well, we have fixed on Thursday, January 25th, for our departure. But should some *extraordinary accident*,   ★ such as I cannot foresee, prevent it, you will have a letter by the Salzburg post which reaches Munich on Friday, the very day we ought to arrive.   ★

[1] *Zaide*. See p. 685, n. 1.
[2] That he has delivered the bill of exchange to the Kapellmeister.
[3] Varesco has worn me to a shred.

Give our greetings to everyone. We both kiss you and I am your honest father

L MOZART

(392) *Leopold Mozart to Breitkopf and Son, Leipzig*

[*Extract*]   [*Copy in the Staatsbibliothek Preussischer Kulturbesitz, West Berlin*][1]

MUNICH, 12 *February* 1781

I have been wishing for a long time that you would print some of my son's compositions. Surely you will not judge him by the clavier sonatas which he wrote as a child?[2] True, you will not have seen a note of what he has been composing for the last few years, save perhaps the six sonatas for clavier and violin which he had engraved in Paris with a dedication to the present Electress of the Bavarian Palatinate.[3] *For we only allow very little to be published.* You might try what you can do with a couple of symphonies or clavier sonatas, or even quartets, trios and so forth. You need only give us a few copies. I should very much like you to see my son's style of composition. But far be it from me to persuade you to anything. The idea, however, has often occurred to me, because I see works engraved and printed which really arouse my pity.[4]

[1] Autograph in the Universitätsbibliothek, Bonn.
[2] K. 6-7, Œuvre I, dedicated to Madame Victoire; K. 8-9, Œuvre II, dedicated to the Comtesse de Tessé; K. 10-15, Œuvre III, dedicated to Queen Charlotte; K. 26-31, Œuvre IV, dedicated to Princess Caroline of Nassau-Weilburg, and perhaps the lost sonatas of 1766, K. App. 199–202 [K. 33 d–g].
[3] K. 301-306 [293a–c, 300c, 293d, 300l]. The series was published in November 1778 by Sieber in Paris.
[4] See Leopold Mozart's letters to J. G. I. Breitkopf of 7 February 1772, and 6 October 1775. These applications met with no response. It was only after Mozart's death that his widow succeeded in persuading this publishing firm to bring out in 1793 a piano arrangement of *Der Schauspieldirektor* by Siegfried Schmiedt.

Early in March 1781 Mozart, as a member of the Arch-bishop's household, was summoned by his master to Vienna, where he was to spend the remaining ten years of his life. The first months were marked by his breach with the Archbishop and the renewal of his friendship with the Weber family, which eventually led to his marriage to Constanze Weber. This is the period of Mozart's masterpieces, his piano con-certos, his operas, his symphonies and his finest contributions to chamber music. Letters 393-616.

(393) *Mozart to his Father*

[*Autograph in the Mozarteum, Salzburg*]

MON TRÈS CHER AMY!   VIENNA, 17 *March* 1780 [1781]

Yesterday, the 16th, I arrived here,[1] thank God, all by myself in a post chaise—at nine o'clock in the morning—I was nearly forgetting to mention the hour. I travelled in the mail coach as far as Unterhaag—but by that time I was so sore in my behind and its surrounding parts that I could endure it no longer. So I was intending to proceed by the ordinaire, but Herr Escherich, a government official, had had enough of the mail coach too and gave me his company as far as Kemmelbach. There I was proposing to wait for the ordinaire, but the postmaster assured me that he could not possibly allow me to travel by it, as there was no head office there. So I was obliged to proceed *by extra post*, reached St. Pölten on Thursday, the 15th, at seven o'clock in the evening, as tired as a dog, slept until two in the morning and then drove on straight to Vienna. Where do you think I am writing this letter? In the Mesmers' garden in the Landstrasse. The old lady is not at home, but Fräulein Franzl, who is now Frau von Bosch,[2] is here and asks me to send a thousand greetings to you and my sister. Well, upon my honour, I hardly recognized her, she has grown so plump and fat. She has three children, two young ladies and a young gentleman. The eldest young lady, who is called Nannerl, is four years old, but you would swear that she was six; the young gentleman is three, but you would swear that he was seven; and the infant of nine months you would take to be two years old, they are all so strong and robust. Now for the Archbishop. I have a charming room in the very same house where he is staying. Brunetti and Ceccarelli are lodging in another. *Che distinzione!*[3] My neighbour is Herr von Kleinmayr[4]—who loaded me on my arrival with all sorts of kindnesses. He is indeed a charming man. We lunch about twelve o'clock, unfortunately somewhat too early for me. Our party consists of the two valets, that is, the body and soul attendants of His Worship, the contrôleur, Herr Zetti,[5] the confectioner,[6] the two cooks, Ceccarelli, Brunetti and—my insignificant self. By the way, the two valets[7] sit at the top of the table, but at least I

[1] Mozart left Munich on 12 March, having been summoned to Vienna by the Archbishop, who had gone there at the end of January, probably in connection with the death of the Empress.
[2] Fräulein Franzl (Franciska von Osterling), whom Dr. Mesmer had cured, had married his stepson, Franz de Paula von Bosch.
[3] What a distinction!
[4] Private secretary to the Archbishop and chairman of the Court Council.
[5] Zetti was 'Kammerfourier', or Private Messenger, to the Archbishop.
[6] E. M. Kölnberger.   [7] Franz Schlauka, and J. U. Angerbauer. See p. 717, n. 2.

have the honour of being placed above the cooks.[1] Well, I almost believe myself back in Salzburg! A good deal of silly, coarse joking goes on at table, but no one cracks jokes with me, for I never say a word, or, *if I have to speak*, I always do so with the utmost gravity; and as soon as I have finished my lunch, I get up and go off. We do not meet for supper, but we each receive three ducats—which goes a long way! The Archbishop is so kind as to add to his lustre by his household, robs them of their chance of earning and pays them nothing. We had a concert yesterday at four o'clock, and at least twenty persons of the highest rank were present. Ceccarelli has already had to sing at Count Palffy's. Today we are to go to Prince Galitzin,[2] who was at the Archbishop's yesterday. Well, I must wait and see whether I shall get anything. If I get nothing, I shall go to the Archbishop and tell him with absolute frankness that if he will not allow me to earn anything, then he must pay me, for I cannot live at my own expense. Well, I must close this letter which I shall hand in at the post office on my way, for I must be off to Prince Galitzin's. I kiss your hands a thousand times and embrace my sister with all my heart and am ever your most obedient son

WOLFGANG AMADÉ MOZART

PS.—Rossi,[3] the buffo singer, is here. I have been to see the Fischers—I cannot describe how delighted they were to see me—the whole household send you their greetings. I hear that concerts are being given in Salzburg. Goodness, just think what I am missing! Adieu! My address is:

Im Deutschen Hause,
Singerstrasse.[4]

(394) *Mozart to his Father*

[Autograph in the Mozarteum, Salzburg]

[VIENNA, before 24 March 1781]

Copie du billet autographe de Sa Majesté l'Empereur au Prince de Kaunitz-Rittberg dans une boîte de tous les portraits de la famille Impériale du 14 mars 1781:

MON CHER PRINCE,

Je n'ai pas pu résister à l'envie de vous envoyer cette tabatière, que je viens de recevoir de Bruxelles et qui avait été donnée par feue Sa Majesté au

---

[1] It was customary in the eighteenth century for Court musicians to be treated in the same way as other servants in the retinue of a Prince Archbishop or any other great lord.

[2] Russian Ambassador to the Viennese Court since 1763.

[3] Rossi, a tenor, had probably taken the part of the Podestà in the Munich production of *La finta giardiniera*, 1775. See Köchel, p. 223.

[4] Mozart was allotted quarters in the Deutsches Ordenshaus, the headquarters of the Teutonic Order, in the Singerstrasse no. 856 (at present no. 7). For a full list of Mozart's many residences in Vienna during the last ten years of his life, see Abert, vol. ii. p. 1035 f.

Prince Charles.[1] Quelque vilaine incommode qu'elle soit, il m'a paru qu'elle était faite uniquement pour séjourner sur votre table et pour vous rappeler parfois les physionomies de personnes, qui toutes ensemble et chacune en particulier vous doivent beaucoup de reconnaissance pour les services essentiels que vous leur avez rendus. Je n'en fais qu'une partie, mais je ne crains point d'être leur interprète, assuré qu'ils pensent tous comme moi à ce sujet. Adieu. Pardonnez cette folie à l'amitié raisonnée que vous me connaissez inviolablement pour vous.

JOSEPH

Réponse du Prince Kaunitz-Rittberg!

Par les expressions du billet autographe dont Votre Majesté Impériale a eu la bonté d'accompagner la boîte qu'elle a daigné m'envoyer, et qui contient le précieux receuil des portraits de toute la famille Impériale, elle vient de recompenser de la façon du monde qui pourrait être la plus agréable à mon cœur les services que j'eu pu avoir le bonheur de rendre à son auguste maison depuis quarante ans. Il ne me reste à désirer que de les voir honorer des sentiments que Votre Majesté veut bien leur accorder, et il ne manque plus rien moyennant cela à mon entière satisfaction, qui est d'autant plus vive que les traits de ce genre ne peuvent manquer de transmettre les noms de Votre Majesté à la postérité dans le sens de ceux de Trajan, de Marc-Aurèle et de Henri Quatre, dont jusqu'à nos jours on a béni la mémoire et prononcé encore les noms avec autant de vénération que d'attendrissement. Je ne puis en témoigner ma reconnaissance à Votre Majesté Impériale qu'en continuant et en redoublant même, s'il est possible, de zèle pour son service et d'attachement pour sa personne. J'y prends bien plus d'intérêt qu'à moi-même et comme je crois qu'il ne se trouvera peut-être jamais l'occasion plus propre à donner de Votre Majesté Impériale l'opinion que je désire que toute la terre puisse prendre d'elle que ne l'est le contenu de son gracieux billet, que je ne saurais lui cacher que je désirais fort qu'elle trouvât bon qu'il ne reste pas ignoré. Je ne ferai cependant rien à cet égard avant d'en avoir obtenu la permission, si ce n'est un fidé-commis dans ma famille de la boîte ainsi que de ce respectable billet. Je supplie Votre Majesté Impériale de vouloir bien accueillir en attendant avec bonté l'assurance respectueuse de ma vive reconnaissance et de mon attachement sans bornes pour sa personne qui ne finira pas qu'avec moi.

KAUNITZ

As I have just had the opportunity at Madame Lamotte's of copying out these two delightful billets, I thought I ought to do so. Mademoiselle Lamotte[2] is no longer living with the Countess Schönborn.[3] She has

---

[1] Brother of the Emperor Francis I and Governor of the Austrian Netherlands. He died in 1780.

[2] The mother and sister of Franz Lamotte, a famous violinist who had been in the service of the Empress Maria Theresia. See p. 146, n. 2.

[3] A sister of the Archbishop of Salzburg.

written to us and, moreover, has replied to all the points about Count Rosenberg¹ and Baron Kleinmayr. She swears that she has done so. Further, she and her mamma send a thousand greetings to you both; and so does Herr von Vogter, who was at Milan and who is to leave shortly for Klagenfurt with the Archduchess Maria Anna.² I kiss your hands a thousand times, embrace my sister most cordially and remain³

(395) Mozart to his Father

[Autograph in the Mozarteum, Salzburg]

MON TRÈS CHER PÈRE!   VIENNA, 24 March 1781

I have received your letter of the 20th and am delighted to hear that both of you have reached home⁴ safely and are in very good health. You must put it down to my pen and this wretched ink, if you have to spell out this letter rather than read it. Basta! It must be written—and the gentleman who cuts my pens, Herr von Lirzer, has let me down this time. You probably know him better than I do. I cannot describe him more appropriately than by saying that he is, I believe, a native of Salzburg and that up to the present I have never seen him except once or twice at the Robinigs' so-called eleven o'clock music. He, however, called on me at once and seems to be a very pleasant and (since he has been cutting my pens for me) a very civil fellow. I take him to be a secretary. I have also had a surprise visit from Gilowsky, Katherl's brother.⁵ Why a surprise visit?—Well, because I had entirely forgotten that he was in Vienna. How quickly a foreign city can improve a man! Gilowsky will certainly become an upright, honest fellow, both in his métier and in his demeanour. Meanwhile you will have received the letters exchanged between the Emperor and Prince Kaunitz.⁶ What you say about the ⟨Archbishop⟩ is to a certain extent perfectly true—I mean, as to the manner in which I tickle his ⟨ambition⟩. But of what use is all this to me? I can't subsist on it. Believe me, I am right in saying that he acts as a *screen* to keep me from the notice of others. What ⟨distinction,⟩ pray, does he confer upon me? Herr von Kleinmayr and Bönike⁷ have ⟨a separate table⟩ with the illustri-

¹ Franz Xaver Wolf Orsini-Rosenberg (1723–1796), who had been appointed in 1779 Chief Chamberlain and Director of the Court Theatre in Vienna.
² The Archduchess Maria Anna (1738–1789) was the second child of the Empress Maria Theresia.
³ The signature and date have been cut off the autograph.
⁴ Mozart's father and sister had remained on in Munich after he had been summoned by the Archbishop to Vienna.
⁵ Franz Wenzel Gilowsky (1757–1816), who became a doctor in Vienna. He was best man at Mozart's marriage to Constanze Weber in 1782.
⁶ See Letter 394.
⁷ Johann Michael Bönike was private secretary to the Archbishop and a member of the Ecclesiastical Council.

ous Count ⟨Arco⟩.¹ It would be some distinction if ⟨I sat at that table,⟩ but there is none in sitting ⟨with the valets,⟩ who, when they are not occupying the best seats ⟨at table,⟩ have to light the chandeliers, open the doors and wait in the anteroom (*when I am within*)—and with the cooks too! Moreover, when we are summoned to a house where there is a concert, Herr Angerbauer² has to watch outside until the Salzburg gentlemen arrive, when he sends a lackey to show them the way in. On hearing Brunetti tell this in the course of a conversation, I thought to myself, 'Just wait till I come along!'. So the other day when we were to go to Prince Galitzin's Brunetti said to me in his usual polite manner: 'Tu, bisogna che sii qui stasera alle sette per andare insieme dal Principe Galitzin. L'Angerbauer ci condurrà.' Ho risposto: 'Va bene—ma—se in caso mai non fossi qui alle sette in punto, ci andate pure, non serve aspettarmi—so bene dove sta, e ci verrò sicuro'³—I went there alone on purpose, because I really feel ashamed to go anywhere with them. When I got upstairs, I found Angerbauer standing there to direct the lackey to show me in. But I took no notice, either of the valet or the lackey, but walked straight on through the rooms into the music room, for all the doors were open,—and went straight up to the Prince, paid him my respects and stood there talking to him. I had completely forgotten my friends Ceccarelli and Brunetti, for they were not to be seen. They were leaning against the wall behind the orchestra, not daring to come forward a single step. If a lady or a gentleman speaks to Ceccarelli, he always laughs: and if anyone at all addresses Brunetti, he colours and gives the dullest answers. Oh, I could cover whole sheets if I were to describe all the scenes which have taken place between the ⟨Archbishop⟩ and the two of them since I have been here and indeed before I came. I am only surprised that he is not ashamed of Brunetti. Why, I am ashamed on his account. And how the fellow hates being here! The whole place is *far too grand* for him, I really think he spends his happiest hours at table. Prince Galitzin asked Ceccarelli to sing today. Next time it will be my turn to perform. I am going this evening with Herr von Kleinmayr to Court Councillor Braun, a good friend of his, who is supposed to be one of the greatest enthusiasts for the clavier. I have lunched twice with Countess Thun⁴ and go there almost every day. She is the most charming and most lovable lady I have ever met; and I

---

¹ Count Karl Arco (1743–1830), one of the principal members of the Archbishop's household. He was the son of Count Georg Anton Felix Arco, Chief Chamberlain to the Archbishop.
² Johann Ulrich Angerbauer, one of the Archbishop's private valets.
³ 'You must be here at seven o'clock this evening, so that we may go together to Prince Galitzin's. Angerbauer will take us there.' I replied: 'All right. But if I'm not here at seven o'clock sharp, just go ahead. You need not wait for me. I know where he lives and I will be sure to be there.'
⁴ Countess Wilhelmine Thun (1747–1800), wife of Count Franz Josef Thun (1734–1788), and the mother of three beautiful daughters. She had been a pupil of Haydn and was later a friend of Beethoven.

am very high in her favour. Her husband is still the same peculiar, but well-meaning and honourable gentleman. I have also lunched with Count Cobenzl.[1] I owe this to his aunt, the Countess von Rumbeck,[2] sister of the Cobenzl in the Pagerie, who was at Salzburg with her husband. Well, my chief object here is to introduce myself to ⟨the Emperor⟩ in some becoming way, for I am absolutely determined that he shall *get to know me*. I should love to run through my opera[3] for him and then play a lot of fugues, for that is what he likes. Oh, had I but known that I should be in Vienna during Lent, I would have written a short oratorio and produced it in the theatre for my benefit, as they all do here. I could easily have written it beforehand, for I know all the voices. How gladly would I give a public concert, as is the custom here. But I know for certain that I should never get permission to do so—for just listen to this! You know that there is a society in Vienna which gives concerts for the benefit of the widows of musicians,[4] at which every professional musician plays gratis. The orchestra is a hundred and eighty strong.[5] No virtuoso who has any love for his neighbour, refuses to give his services, if the society asks him to do so. Besides, in this way he can win the favour both of the Emperor and of the public. Starzer was commissioned to invite me and I agreed at once, adding, however, that I must first obtain the consent of my Prince, which I had not the slightest doubt that he would give—as it was a matter of charity, or at any rate a good work, for which I should get no fee. *He would not permit me to take part.* All the nobility in Vienna have made a grievance of it. I am only sorry for the following reason. I should not have played a concerto, but (as the Emperor sits in the proscenium box) I should have extemporized and played a fugue and then the variations on 'Je suis Lindor'[6] on Countess Thun's beautiful Stein pianoforte, which she would have lent me. Whenever I have played this programme in public, I have always won the greatest applause—because the items set one another off so well, and because everyone has something to his taste. But pazienza!

Fiala has risen two thousand times higher in my estimation for refusing to play for less than a ducat. Has not my sister been asked to play yet? I hope she will *demand* two ducats. For, as we have always been utterly different *in every way* from the other court musicians, I trust we shall be different in this respect too. If they won't pay, they can do without her—

[1] Count Johann Philipp von Cobenzl, Court and State Chancellor in Vienna.
[2] Countess Maria Karoline Thiennes de Rumbeke (1755–1812).
[3] *Idomeneo*.
[4] The Wiener Tonkünstlersozietät, which was founded in 1771 by Florian Gassmann. Since 1862 it has been the Haydnverein. Mozart, who wished to join this society in 1785 and who had several times performed gratis for its benefit, was refused admission because he could not produce a certificate of baptism. See Pohl, *Haydn*, vol. ii. p. 134 f., and Hanslick, *Geschichte des Konzertwesens in Wien*, 1869, p. 6 ff.
[5] This figure includes, of course, the choir.
[6] K. 354 [299a]. Twelve clavier variations, composed in Paris in 1778, on 'Je suis Lindor', an arietta in Beaumarchais's *Le Barbier de Séville*.

but if they want her, then, by Heaven, let them pay.

I shall go to Madame Rosa one of these days and you will certainly be pleased with your clever diplomat.[1] I shall handle the matter as tactfully as did Weiser,[2] when the bell was tolled for his wife's mother.

Herr von Zetti offered immediately after my arrival to deliver my letters. He will send them off with the parcel. I do not require the two quartets[3] nor the Baumgarten aria.[4] A propos. What about ⟨the Elector's present?⟩ Has anything ⟨been sent yet?⟩ Did you call on ⟨the Countess Baumgarten⟩ before you left Munich?

Please give my greetings to all my good friends, and especially to Katherl, Schachtner and Fiala. Herr von Kleinmayr, Zetti, Ceccarelli, Brunetti, the contrôleur, the two valets, Leutgeb[5] and Ramm, who leaves on Sunday, send their compliments to all. A propos, Peter Vogt is here. Well, goodbye. I kiss your hands a thousand times and embrace my sister most cordially and am ever your most obedient son

WOLFG: AMADÈ MOZART

Rossi, the buffo singer, is here too.

March 28th. I could not finish this letter, because Herr von Kleinmayr fetched me in his carriage to go to a concert at Baron Braun's. So I can now add that ⟨the Archbishop has given me permission to play at the concert for the widows.⟩ For Starzer went to the concert at ⟨Galitzin's⟩ and he and ⟨all the nobility worried the Archbishop until he gave his consent.⟩ *I am so glad.* Since I have been here I have lunched at home only four times. The hour is too early for me—and the food is wretched. Only when the weather is very bad, as today, *par exemple*, I stay at home.

Do write and tell me what is going on in Salzburg, for I have been plagued with questions. These gentlemen are far more anxious for news of Salzburg than I am. Madame Mara is here and gave a concert in the theatre last Tuesday. Her husband dared not let himself be seen, or the orchestra would not have accompanied her; for he published in the newspapers that there was no one in all Vienna fit to do this. Adieu. Herr von Moll paid me a visit today and I am to breakfast with him tomorrow or the day after and bring my opera[6] with me. He sends greetings to you both. As soon as the weather improves, I shall call on Herr von

---

[1] Mozart hoped to obtain from Rosa Barducci a portrait which she had painted of his mother about 1765 and taken to Vienna. The portrait has since disappeared. See Letter 413.

[2] A former mayor of Salzburg.

[3] Possibly one of these quartets is K. 370 [368b], an oboe quartet composed at Munich early in 1781 for Mozart's friend Ramm.

[4] K. 369, 'Misera, dove son!', written for the Countess Baumgarten on 8 March 1781.

[5] Joseph Leutgeb, horn-player in the Salzburg court orchestra, had opened a cheese-monger's shop in a suburb of Vienna with the half of a money loan from Leopold Mozart. He continued to play in public and he and Mozart became fast friends. Mozart's horn concertos, K. 417, 447, and 495, composed between the years 1783 and 1787, were written for Leutgeb.

[6] *Idomeneo.*

Auernhammer and his fat daughter.[1] From these remarks you will see that I have received your last letter of the 24th. Old Prince Colloredo[2] (at whose house we held a concert) gave each of us five ducats. Countess Rumbeck is now my pupil. Herr von Mesmer (the school inspector) and his wife and son send you their greetings. His son plays magnifique, but, as he imagines that he knows quite enough already, he is lazy. He has also considerable talent for composition, but is too indolent to devote himself to it, which vexes his father. Adieu.

(396) *Mozart to his Father*

[*Autograph in the Mozarteum, Salzburg*]

MON TRÉS CHER PÉRE!   VIENNA, 4 *April* 1781

My letter today must be very short, but Brunetti returns to Salzburg on Sunday and then I shall be able to write you a longer one.

You want to know how we are getting on in Vienna—or rather, I hope, how I am getting on; for the other two I do not count as having anything to do with me. I told you in a recent letter that ⟨the Archbishop⟩ is a great hindrance to me here, for he has done me out of at least a hundred ducats, which I could certainly have made by giving ⟨a concert in the theatre.⟩ Why, the ladies themselves offered *of their own accord* to distribute the tickets. I can say with truth that I was very well pleased with the Viennese public yesterday, when I played at the concert for the widows[3] in the Kärtnerthor Theatre. I had to begin all over again, because there was no end to the applause. Well, how much do you suppose I should make if I were to give a concert of my own, now that the public has got to know me? But this ⟨arch-booby⟩ of ours will not allow it. He does not want his people to have any profit—only loss. Still, he will not be able to achieve this in my case, for if I have two pupils I am better off in Vienna than in Salzburg. Nor do I need his board and lodging. Now listen to this. Brunetti said today at table that Arco had told him on behalf of the Archbishop that he (Brunetti) *was to inform us* that we were to receive the money for our mail coach fares and to leave before Sunday. On the other hand, whoever wanted to stay on (*oh, how judicious!*) could do so, but would have to live at his own expense, as he would no longer get board and lodging from the Archbishop. Brunetti, qui ne demande pas mieux,

---

[1] Fräulein Josepha Auernhammer (1758–1820) became Mozart's pupil on the clavier, and he wrote for her his sonata for two pianos, K. 448 [375a]. She married in 1786 and, as Frau Bessenig, was still performing in public in 1813. She herself composed several series of pianoforte variations.

[2] Prince Rudolf Colloredo, father of the Archbishop of Salzburg.

[3] See p. 718, n. 4. Mozart played a piano concerto and one of his symphonies, possibly K. 297 [300a], was performed. See E. Hanslick, *Geschichte des Konzertwesens in Wien*, p. 32.

smacked his lips. Ceccarelli, *who would like to remain*, but who is not so well known as I am and does not know his way about so well as I do, is going to make a push to get something. If he does not succeed, well, in God's name, he must be off, for there is not a house in Vienna where he can get either a meal or a room without paying for it. When they asked me what I intended to do, I replied: '*I do not know as yet that I have to leave, for until Count Arco tells me so himself, I shall not believe it. When he does, I shall then disclose my intentions. Put that in your pipe and smoke it.*' Bönike was present and grinned. Oh indeed, ⟨I shall certainly fool the Archbishop to the top of his bent and how I shall enjoy doing it!⟩ I shall do it with the greatest politesse—⟨and he will not be able to dodge me.⟩ Enough of this. In my next letter I shall be able to tell you more. Rest assured that unless I am in a good position and can see clearly that it is to my advantage to do so, I shall certainly not remain in Vienna. But if it is to my advantage, why should I not profit by it? Meanwhile, ⟨you are drawing two salaries and have not got to feed me.⟩ If I stay here, I can promise you that I shall soon ⟨be able to send home some money.⟩ I am speaking seriously, and if things turn out otherwise, I shall return to Salzburg. Well, adieu. You shall have the full story in my next letter. I kiss your hands a thousand times and embrace my sister with all my heart, and I hope that she has replied to Mlle Hepp. Adieu, ever your most obedient son

WOLFG AMADÈ MOZART

My compliments to all—all—all.

PS.—I assure you that this is a splendid place—and for my métier the best one in the world. Everyone will tell you the same. Moreover, I like being here and therefore I am making all the profit out of it that I can. Believe me, my sole purpose is to make as much money as possible; for after good health it is the best thing to have. Think no more of my follies, of which I have repented long ago from the bottom of my heart. Misfortune brings wisdom, and my thoughts now turn in a very different direction. Adieu. You will have a full account in my next letter.

Adieu.

(397) *Mozart to his Father*

[*Autograph in the Mozarteum, Salzburg*]

MON TRÉS CHER PÉRE! VIENNA, 8 *April* 1780 [1781]

⟨I began a longer and more interesting letter to you, but I wrote too much about Brunetti in it, and was afraid that his curiosity might tempt him to open the letter, because Ceccarelli is with me.⟩ I shall send it by the

next post and in it I shall write more fully than I can today. Meanwhile
you will have received my other letter.[1] I told you about the applause in
the theatre, but I must add that what delighted and surprised me most of
all was the amazing silence—and also the cries of 'Bravo!' while I was
playing. This is certainly honour enough in Vienna, where there are such
numbers and numbers of good pianists. Today (for I am writing at eleven
o'clock at night) we had a concert, where three of my compositions were
performed—new ones, of course; a rondo for a concerto for Brunetti;[2] a
sonata with violin accompaniment for myself,[3] which I composed last
night between eleven and twelve (but in order to be able to finish it, I only
wrote out the accompaniment for Brunetti and retained my own part in
my head); and then a rondo for Ceccarelli,[4] which he had to repeat. I must
now beg you to send me a letter as soon as possible and to give me your
fatherly and most friendly advice on the following matter. ⟨It is said that
we are to return to Salzburg in a fortnight. I can stay on here, and that too
not to my loss, but to my advantage.⟩ So I am ⟨thinking of asking the
Archbishop to allow me to remain in Vienna.⟩ Dearest father, ⟨I love you
dearly; that you must realize from the fact that for your sake I renounce
all my wishes and desires. For, were it not for you, I swear to you on my
honour that⟩ I should not hesitate for a moment ⟨to leave the Archbishop's
service.⟩ I should ⟨give a grand concert, take four pupils, and in a year I
should have got on so well in Vienna that I could make at least a thousand
thalers a year.⟩ I assure you that I often ⟨find it difficult to throw away
my luck as I am doing.⟩ As you say, I am still ⟨young.⟩ True—but ⟨to
waste one's youth in inactivity in such a beggarly place is really very sad—
and it is such a loss.⟩ I should like to have your kind and fatherly advice
about this, and very soon,—for I must tell him what I am going to do.
But do have confidence in me, for I am more prudent now. Farewell. I
kiss your hands a thousand times and embrace my sister with all my heart
and am ever your most obedient

W. A: MOZART

(398) *Mozart to his Father*

[*Autograph in the Mozarteum, Salzburg*]

MON TRÈS CHER PÈRE!   VIENNA, 11 *April* 1781

Te Deum Laudamus that at last that coarse and dirty Brunetti has left,
who is a disgrace to his master, to himself and to the whole orchestra—or

---

[1] Letter 396.   [2] K. 373. Rondo for violin and orchestra in C major.
[3] Probably K. 379 [373a]. See Köchel, p. 383.
[4] K. 374. A recitative and aria, 'A questo seno deh vieni'.

so say Ceccarelli and I. There is not a word of truth in all the Vienna news which you have heard, except that Ceccarelli is to sing in the opera at Venice during the next carnival. Great Heavens! A thousand devils! I hope that this is not swearing, for if so, I must at once go and confess again. For I have just returned from confession, because tomorrow (Maundy Thursday) the Archbishop in his sublime person is to feed[1] the whole Court Personnel. Ceccarelli and I went off today after lunch to the Theatines[2] to find Father Froschauer, who can speak Italian. A pater or frater, who happened to be standing on the altar and trimming the lights, assured us, however, that the Father and another one who knows Italian had not lunched at home and would not return until four o'clock. So this time I went on alone and was shown upstairs into a room where there was a priest; while Ceccarelli waited for me below in the courtyard. What did please me was that when I told the reverend chandelier-cleaner that eight years ago[3] I had played a violin concerto in that very choir, he immediately mentioned my name. But now to return to my swearing, I must tell you that it is only a pendant to my last letter, to which I hope to receive a reply by the next post. In short, next Sunday week, April 22nd, Ceccarelli and I are to go home. When I think that I must leave Vienna without bringing home *at least* a thousand gulden, my heart is sore indeed. So, for the sake of a ⟨malevolent Prince⟩ who ⟨plagues me⟩ every day and only pays me a ⟨lousy salary of four hundred gulden,⟩ I am to ⟨kick away a thousand?⟩ For I should ⟨certainly⟩ make that sum if I ⟨were to give a concert.⟩ When we had our first grand concert in this house, ⟨the Archbishop sent each of us four ducats.⟩ At the last concert for which I composed ⟨a new rondo for Brunetti,⟩[4] a ⟨new sonata⟩ for myself,[5] and ⟨also a new rondo for Ceccarelli,⟩[6] I received ⟨nothing⟩. But what made me almost ⟨desperate⟩ was that the very same ⟨evening⟩ we had this ⟨foul⟩ concert I was invited to Countess Thun's, but of course could not go; and who should be there but ⟨*the Emperor!*⟩ Adamberger[7] and Madame Weigl[8] were there and received fifty ducats each! Besides, what an opportunity! I cannot, of course, arrange for ⟨the Emperor to be told that if he wishes to hear me he must hurry up,⟩ as ⟨I am leaving⟩ Vienna in a few days. One has to ⟨wait for⟩ things like that. Besides, I ⟨neither can nor will remain here unless I give a concert.⟩ Still, even if I have only

[1] Intentionally irreverent for 'administer the sacrament'.
[2] The order of the Theatines or Cajetans was dissolved in Vienna in 1784.
[3] During the Mozarts' visit to Vienna in the summer of 1773.
[4] K. 373.   [5] See p. 722, n. 3.   [6] K. 374.
[7] Johann Valentin Adamberger (1740–1804), famous tenor and a successful teacher. He was born in Munich, studied under Valesi in Italy, where he assumed the name of Adamonti, and made his first appearance at the German National Theatre in Vienna in 1780.
[8] Madame Weigl, the prima donna of the German National Theatre, was the wife of Joseph Weigl (1749–1820), cellist in Prince Esterházy's orchestra at Eisenstadt and later in the Court orchestra in Vienna. Her son, Joseph Weigl (1766–1846), became a famous operatic composer.

two 〈pupils,〉 I am better off here than in Salzburg. But if I had 1000 or 1200 gulden 〈in my pocket, I should be a little more solicited〉 and therefore 〈exact better terms.〉 That is what he 〈will not allow, the inhuman villain.〉 I must 〈call him that, for he is a villain and all the nobility call him so.〉 But enough of this. Oh, how I hope to hear by the next post whether I am to go on 〈burying my youth and my talents in Salzburg, or whether I may make my fortune as best I can, and not wait until it is too late.〉 It is true 〈that I cannot make my fortune〉 in a fortnight or three weeks, any more than I 〈can make it in a thousand years in Salzburg.〉 Still, it is more pleasant to wait 〈with a thousand gulden a year〉 than with 〈four hundred.〉[1] For if I wish to do so, I am quite certain of making that sum—〈I have only to say that I am staying on here〉—and I am not 〈including in my calculations what I may compose.〉 Besides, think of the contrast—〈Vienna and Salzburg!〉 When 〈Bonno dies, Salieri will be Kapellmeister,〉[2] and then 〈Starzer〉 will take the place of 〈Salieri〉 in conducting the practices; and so far 〈no one〉 has been mentioned to take the place of 〈Starzer.〉 Basta;—I leave it entirely to you, my most beloved father!—You ask whether I have been to see Bonno? Why, it was at his house that we went through my symphony[3] for the second time. I forgot to tell you the other day that at the concert the symphony[4] went magnifique and had the greatest success. There were forty violins, the wind-instruments were all doubled, there were ten violas, ten double basses, eight violoncellos and six bassoons.

The whole Bonno household send their greetings to you. They are truly delighted to see me again. He is just the same worthy and honourable man. Fräulein Nanette is married and I have lunched with her twice. She lives near me. A thousand compliments from the Fischers, on whom I called on my way home from the Theatines. Farewell; and remember that your son's sole object is *to establish himself permanently*—for—〈he can get four hundred gulden anywhere.〉 Adieu. I kiss your hands a thousand times and embrace my dear sister with all my heart and am ever your most obedient son

W. A: MZT

PS.—Be so kind as to tell M. d'Yppold that I shall answer his letter by the next post and that I have duly received the letter of his good friend.—Adieu.

My compliments to all who are not too dreadfully 〈Salzburgish.〉 Court Councillor Gilowsky too has played a Salzburg trick on Katherl.

[1] Mozart's yearly salary as Court organist in Salzburg was 450 gulden.
[2] This did happen. Salieri succeeded Bonno on the latter's death in 1788.
[3] Possibly K. 297 (300a), the 'Paris' symphony of 1778.
[4] No doubt the same symphony.

(399) Mozart to his Father

[Autograph in the Mozarteum, Salzburg]

MON TRÉS CHER PÉRE!   VIENNA, 18 *April* 1781

I can't write much today either, as it is almost six o'clock and I must give this letter to Zetti directly. I have just come from Herr, Frau and Fräulein von Auernhammer, with whom I have been lunching and where we all drank your health. In regard to your long letter (you know the one I mean) I can only say that you are both right and wrong; but the points where you are right far outweigh the points where you are wrong. Therefore I shall certainly return and with the greatest pleasure, too, as I am fully convinced that you will never prevent me from making my fortune. Up to this moment I have not heard a word about the date of my departure. I shall certainly not leave on Sunday, for from the very first I declared that I would not travel by the mail coach. For my part I shall travel by the ordinaire. If Ceccarelli wants to bear me company, it will be all the pleasanter for me, for then we can take an extra post-chaise. The whole difference, ⟨so small as to be laughable⟩, consists in a few gulden; for I should travel day and night, and thus spend very little on the road. I have noticed that it is almost dearer by the diligence, or at all events about the same, as one has to pay all the expenses of the conductor. There is no hope of doing anything in Linz, for Ceccarelli told me that he only scraped together forty gulden and had to give more than thirty to the orchestra. Moreover it would not be ⟨*creditable*⟩ to perform ⟨in such a small town,⟩ nor would it be worth the trouble for such a ⟨*bagatelle*⟩— much better for me to go straight home, unless ⟨the nobility⟩ were to get up something to make it worth while. Still, you can get me some ⟨addresses⟩ there. Well, I must close, or else I shall miss the parcel. ⟨As for Schachtner's operetta,[1]⟩ there is nothing to be done—for the same reason which I have often mentioned. Stephanie junior[2] is going to give me a new libretto, a good one, as he says; and, if in the meantime I have left Vienna, he is to send it to me. I could not contradict ⟨Stephanie.⟩ I merely said that save for the long dialogues, which could easily be altered, the piece[3] was very good, but not suitable for Vienna, where people prefer comic pieces. Farewell. I am ever your most obedient son

W. A. MZT

I embrace my sister with all my heart and send my greetings to all my good friends.

[1] *Zaide.*

[2] Gottlieb Stephanie (1741–1800) first served in the army and then went on the stage, and finally became stage-manager of the German Opera in Vienna. He arranged the text of Mozart's opera *Die Entführung aus dem Serail*, 1782, and wrote the libretto for his one-act opera *Der Schauspieldirektor*, 1786. His elder brother was Christian Gottlob Stephanie, an actor in Vienna.   [3] *Zaide.*

(400) *Mozart to his Father*

[*Autograph in the Mozarteum, Salzburg*]

MON TRÉS CHER PÉRE!   VIENNA, 28 *April* 1781

You are looking forward to my return with great joy, my dearest father! That is the only thing that can make me decide to leave Vienna. I am writing all this in our plain language,[1] *because the whole world knows and should know that the Archbishop of Salzburg has only you to thank, my most beloved father, that he did not lose me yesterday for ever (I mean, as far as he himself is concerned).* We had a grand concert here yesterday, probably the last of them. It was a great success, and in spite of all the obstacles put in my way by His Archiepiscopal Grace, I still had a better orchestra than Brunetti. Ceccarelli will tell you about it. I had a great deal of worry over arranging this. Oh, it is far easier to talk than to write about it. If, however, anything similar should happen again, which I hope may not be the case, I can assure you that I shall lose all patience; and certainly you will forgive me for doing so. And I beg you, dearest father, to allow me to return to Vienna during Lent towards the end of the next carnival. This depends on you alone and not on the Archbishop. For if he does not grant me permission, I shall go all the same; and this visit will certainly not do me any harm! Oh, if he could only read this, I should be delighted. But what I ask, you must promise me in your next letter, for it is only on this condition that I shall return to Salzburg; *but it must be a definite promise*, so that I may give my word to the ladies here. Stephanie is going to give me a German opera to compose. So I await your reply. Up to the present Gilowsky has not brought me any fichu. If he does, I shall not fail to lay it nice and flat among the linen in the trunk, so that it may not be crushed or spoilt. And I shall not forget the ribbons.

I cannot yet say when I shall leave or how. It is really very tiresome that no information can ever be got out of these people. All of a sudden we shall be told, 'Allons, off with you!' One moment we are told that a carriage is being got ready in which the contrôleur, Ceccarelli and I are to travel home; the next moment we are told that we are to return by the diligence; and again we are told that each will be given the diligence fare and may travel as he likes—an arrangement which indeed I should much prefer. One moment we are told that we are to leave in a week; the next moment it is in a fortnight or three weeks; and then again, even sooner. Good God! We don't know what to believe; we simply can't make any plans. But by the next post I hope to be able to let you know—*à peu près.* Well, I must close, for I must be off to the Countess Schönborn. After the concert yesterday the ladies kept me at the piano for a whole hour. I

---

[1] Mozart means that he is not using cypher.

believe that if I had not stolen away I should be sitting there still. I thought I had really played enough *for nothing*. Adieu. I kiss your hands a thousand times and embrace my sister with all my heart and am ever your most obedient son

W: A: MOZART

PS.—My greetings to all my good friends. I embrace young Marchand[1] most cordially. Please ask my sister, when she happens to be writing to Mlle Hepp, to be so good as to give her a thousand compliments from me and to tell her that the reason why I have not written to her for so long is that I should have had to tell her not to reply until I wrote to her again. Thus, as I could not say anything else in my second letter, I should never have received a letter from her in Vienna—(my future plans being so uncertain)—and that would have been intolerable to me. Whereas, as things are, I have no right to expect one. I shall write to her before I leave. Adieu.

(401) *Mozart to his Father*

[*Autograph in the Mozarteum, Salzburg*]

MON TRÉS CHER PÉRE!   VIENNA, 9 *May* 1781

I am still seething with rage! And you, my dearest and most beloved father, are doubtless in the same condition. My patience has been so long tried that at last it has given out. I am no longer so unfortunate as to be in Salzburg service. Today is a happy day for me. Just listen.

Twice already that—I don't know what to call him—has said to my face the greatest *sottises* and *impertinences*, which I have not repeated to you, as I wished to spare your feelings, and for which I only refrained from taking my revenge on the spot because you, my most beloved father, were ever before my eyes. He called me a ⟨rascal⟩ and a ⟨dissolute fellow⟩ and told me to be off. And I—endured it all, although I felt that not only my honour but yours also was being attacked. But, as you would have it so, I was silent. Now listen to this. A week ago the footman came up unexpectedly and told me to clear out that very instant. All the others had been informed of the day of their departure, but not I. Well, I shoved everything into my trunk in haste, and old Madame Weber[2] has been good

---

[1] Heinrich Marchand (1770– ?), son of Theobald Marchand (1741–1800), theatrical manager in Munich. In 1781 Leopold Mozart took him and his sister Margarete, aged fourteen, into his house and gave them their musical education. Margarete, who in 1790 married Franz Danzi (1763–1826), the cellist and composer, became an excellent operatic singer at Munich. Heinrich became a fine violinist and clavier-player and later obtained an appointment at Regensburg.

[2] The widow of Fridolin Weber. Her second daughter Aloysia had obtained in September 1779 an appointment at the German Opera in Vienna, and the whole family had migrated from Munich to the Imperial capital. Fridolin Weber died during the following month, and

enough to take me into her house, where I have a pretty room. Moreover, I am living with people who are obliging and who supply me with all the things which one often requires in a hurry and which one cannot have when one is living alone. I decided to travel home by the ordinaire on Wednesday, that is, today. May 9th. But as I could not collect the money still due to me within that time, I postponed my departure until Saturday. When I presented myself today, the valets informed me that the Archbishop wanted to give me a parcel to take charge of. I asked whether it was urgent. They told me, 'Yes, it is of the greatest importance'. 'Well,' said I, 'I am sorry that I cannot have the privilege of serving His Grace, for (on account of the reason mentioned above) I cannot leave before Saturday. I have left this house, and must live at my own expense. So it is evident that I cannot leave Vienna until I am in a position to do so. For surely no one will ask me to ruin myself.' Kleinmayr, Moll, Bönike and the two valets, all said that I was perfectly right. When I went in to the Archbishop—that reminds me, I must tell you first of all that ⟨Schlauka[1]⟩ advised me to ⟨make the excuse⟩ that the ⟨ordinaire was already full,⟩ a reason which would carry more weight with him than if I gave him the true one,—well, when I entered the room, his first words were:—*Archbishop*: 'Well, young fellow, when are you going off?' *I*: 'I intended to go tonight, but all the seats were already engaged.' Then he rushed full steam ahead, without pausing for breath—I was the ⟨most dissolute fellow he knew—no one⟩ served him so badly as I did—I had better leave today or else he would write home and have my ⟨salary⟩ stopped. I couldn't get a word in edgeways, for he blazed away like a fire. I listened to it all very calmly. He lied to my face that my salary was five hundred gulden,[2] called me ⟨a scoundrel, a rascal, a vagabond.⟩ Oh, I really cannot tell you all he said. At last my blood began to boil, I could no longer contain myself and I said, 'So Your Grace is not satisfied with me?' 'What, you dare to threaten me—you ⟨scoundrel?⟩ There is the ⟨door!⟩ Look out, for I will have nothing more to do with such ⟨a miserable wretch.⟩' At last I said: 'Nor I with you!' 'Well, be off!'[3] When leaving the room, I said, 'This is final. You shall have it tomorrow in writing.' Tell me now, most beloved father, did I not say the word too late rather than too soon? Just listen for a moment. My honour is more precious to me than anything

Aloysia in 1780 married the actor Josef Lange. Frau Weber, who had moved with her family to a house Am Peter, called the 'Auge Gottes', where they occupied the second floor, decided to let some vacant rooms to lodgers. Mozart went to live there on 2 May 1781. For a detailed account of Frau Weber's life and Mozart's relations with her, see Blümml, pp. 10-20. See also a short article in *MM*, November 1918, pp. 9-12, and an excellent character-study by Arthur Schurig, *Konstanze Mozart*, 1922, p. xxi ff.

[1] One of the Archbishop's valets.

[2] According to Mozart's certificate of appointment as court organist his salary was 450 gulden. See Abert, vol. ii. p. 906.

[3] Throughout this conversation, as reported by Mozart, the Archbishop used the contemptuous form of address 'Er'.

else and I know that it is so to you also. Do not be the least bit anxious about me. I am so sure of my success in Vienna that I would have resigned even without the slightest reason; and now that I have a very good reason —and that too thrice over—I cannot make a virtue of it. Au contraire, I had twice played the coward and I could not do so a third time.

As long as ⟨the Archbishop⟩ remains here, I shall not ⟨give a concert.⟩ You are altogether mistaken if you think that I shall ⟨get a bad name with the Emperor and the nobility,⟩ for ⟨the Archbishop⟩ is detested here and ⟨most of all by the Emperor.⟩ In fact, he is furious because the Emperor did not invite him to Laxenburg. By the next post I shall send you a little ⟨money⟩ to show you that I am not starving. Now please be cheerful, for my good luck is just beginning, and I trust that my good luck will be yours also. Write to me ⟨in cypher⟩ that you are pleased—and indeed you may well be so—⟨but in public rail at me as much as you like, so that none of the blame may fall on you. But if, in spite of this, the Archbishop should be the slightest bit impertinent to you,⟩ come at once with my ⟨sister to Vienna, for I give you my word of honour that there is enough for all three of us to live on.⟩ Still, I should prefer it if you could ⟨hold out⟩ for another year. Do not send any more letters to the Deutsches Haus,[1] nor enclose them in their parcels—I want to hear nothing more about Salzburg. I hate the Archbishop to madness.

Adieu. I kiss your hands a thousand times and embrace my dear sister with all my heart and am ever your obedient son

W: A: MOZART

    Just address your letters:

To be delivered Auf dem Peter, im Auge Gottes,
2nd Floor.[2]

⟨Please inform me soon of your approval, for that is the only thing which is still wanting to my present happiness.⟩ Adieu.

(402) *Mozart to his Father*

[Autograph in the Mozarteum, Salzburg]

MON TRÉS CHER PÉRE!   VIENNA, 12 *May* 1781
    You will know from my last letter that I have asked the Prince for my discharge, because he himself has told me to go.[3] For already in the

---

[1] Mozart's quarters while he was in the Archbishop's service.

[2] Frau Weber's apartments, where she let vacant rooms to lodgers. This house 'Zum Auge Gottes', which no longer exists, stood at Am Peter No. 11. See Abert, vol. ii. p. 1035.

[3] For a good study of the reign of Archbishop Hieronymus Colloredo, who, despite the autocratic and somewhat ruthless methods he adopted to carry out his reforms, appears to have had certain redeeming qualities, see Hans Widmann, *Geschichte Salzburgs*, Gotha, 1914, vol. iii. pp. 460-556. For an account of the Mozarts' relations with the Archbishop, see Abert, vol. i. p. 357 f.

two previous audiences he said to me: '*Clear out of this, if you will not serve me properly*'. He will deny it, of course, but all the same it is as true as that God is in His Heaven. Is it any wonder then if, after being roused to fury by 'knave' scoundrel, rascal, dissolute fellow', and other similar dignified expressions uttered by a Prince, I at last took '*Clear out of this*' in its literal sense? On the following day I gave Count Arco a petition to present to His Grace, and I returned my travelling expenses, which consisted of fifteen gulden, forty kreuzer for the diligence, and two ducats for my keep. He refused to take either and assured me that I could not resign without your consent, my father. 'That is your duty,' said he. I retorted that I knew my duty to my father as well as he did and possibly better, and that I should be very sorry if I had to learn it first from him. 'Very well,' he replied, 'if he is satisfied, you can ask for your discharge; if not, you can ask for it all the same.' A pretty distinction! All the edifying things which the Archbishop said to me during my three audiences, particularly during the last one, all the subsequent remarks which this fine servant of God made to me, had such an excellent effect on my health that in the evening I was obliged to leave the opera in the middle of the first act and go home and lie down. For I was very feverish, I was trembling in every limb, and I was staggering along the street like a drunkard. I also stayed at home the following day, yesterday, and spent the morning in bed, as I had taken tamarind water.

The Count has also been so kind as to write very flattering things about me to his father,[1] all of which you will probably have had to swallow by now. They will certainly contain some astounding passages. But whoever writes a comedy and wants to win applause, must exaggerate a little and not stick too closely to the truth. Besides, you must remember how very anxious these gentlemen are to serve the Archbishop.

Well, without losing my temper (for my health and my life are very precious to me and I am only sorry when circumstances force me to get angry) I just want to set down the chief accusation which was brought against me in respect of my service. I did not know that I was a valet— and that was the last straw. I ought to have idled away a couple of hours every morning in the antechamber. True, I was often told that I ought to present myself, but I could never remember that this was part of my duty, and I only turned up punctually whenever the Archbishop sent for me.

I will now confide to you very briefly my inflexible determination, but so that the whole world may hear it. If I were offered a salary of 2000 gulden by the Archbishop of Salzburg and only 1000 gulden somewhere else, I should still take the second offer. For instead of the extra 1000 gulden I should enjoy good health and peace of mind. I trust, therefore,

[1] Count Georg Anton Felix Arco, Chief Chamberlain to the Archbishop.

by all the fatherly love which you have lavished on me so richly from my childhood and for which I can never thank you enough (though indeed I can show it least of all in Salzburg), that, if you wish to see your son well and happy, you will say nothing to me about this affair and that you will bury it in the deepest oblivion. For one word about it would suffice to embitter me again and—if you will only admit it—to fill you too with bitterness.

Now farewell, and be glad that your son is no coward. I kiss your hands a thousand times, embrace my sister with all my heart and am ever your most obedient son

WOLFGANG AMADÈ MOZART

(403) *Mozart to his Father*

[*Autograph in the Mozarteum, Salzburg*]

MON TRÉS CHER PÉRE!　　　　　　　　VIENNA, 12 *May* 1781

In the letter you received by post I spoke to you as ⟨if we were in the presence of the Archbishop, but now I am going to talk to you, my dearest father, as if we were quite alone.⟩ I shall say nothing whatever about all the injustice with which the Archbishop has treated me from the very beginning of his reign[1] until now, of the incessant abuse, of all the *impertinences* and *sottises* which he has uttered to my face, of my undeniable right to leave him—for that cannot be disputed. I shall only speak of what would have induced me to leave him even without any cause of offence. I have here the finest and most useful acquaintances in the world. I am liked and respected by the greatest families. All possible honour is shown me and I am paid into the bargain. So why should I pine away in Salzburg for the sake of 400 gulden,[2] linger on without remuneration or encouragement and be of no use to you in any way, when I can certainly help you here? What would be the end of it? Always the same. I should have to endure one insult after another or go away again. I need say no more, for you know it yourself. But this I must tell you, ⟨that everyone in Vienna has already heard my story. All the nobility are urging me not to let myself be made a fool of.⟩ Dearest father, people ⟨will come to you with fair words, but they are serpents and vipers.⟩ All base people are thus —disgustingly proud and haughty, ⟨yet always ready to crawl.⟩ How horrible! The two ⟨private valets have seen through the whole swinishness⟩, and Schlauka in particular said to someone: 'As for me, ⟨I really cannot think that Mozart is wrong—in fact, I think he is quite right. I should like to have seen the Archbishop treat me in the same way. Why,

---

[1] April 1772.　　　　[2] See p. 728, n. 2.

he spoke to him as if he were some beggarly fellow.⟩ I heard him—
⟨infamous it was!' The Archbishop acknowledges that he has been unjust,⟩
but he has not had frequent occasion to ⟨acknowledge it?⟩ Has he ⟨re-
formed?⟩ Not a bit. So let us have done with him. If I had ⟨not been
afraid of injuring you,⟩ things would have been ⟨on a very different
footing⟩ long ago. But after all what can he ⟨do to you?—Nothing.
Once you know that all is going well with me, you can easily dispense
with the Archbishop's favour. He cannot deprive you of your salary, and
besides you always do your duty.⟩ I pledge myself ⟨to succeed.⟩ Otherwise I ⟨should never have taken this step,⟩ although I must confess that
after that insult, I should have gone off even if I had had to beg. For who
will let himself be bullied, especially when he can do far better? So, if you
⟨are afraid, pretend to be angry with me, scold me roundly in your letters,
provided that we two know how things really are between us. But do not
let yourself be won over by flatteries—and be on your guard.⟩ Adieu. I
kiss your hands a thousand times and embrace my dear sister with all my
heart. By the next occasion I shall send you the portrait,[1] the ribbons, the
fichu and everything else. Adieu. I am ever your most obedient son

WOLFGANG AMADÈ MOZART

My compliments to all Salzburg, and especially to Katherl and March-
and.

(404) *Mozart to his Father*

[*Autograph in the Mozarteum, Salzburg*]

MON TRÉS CHER PÉRE!　　　　　　　　　　VIENNA, 16 *May* 1781

I could hardly have supposed otherwise than that in the heat of the
moment you would have written just such a letter as I have been obliged
to read, for the event must have taken you by surprise (especially as you
were actually expecting my arrival). But by this time you must have
considered the matter more carefully and, as a man of honour, you must
feel the insult more strongly, and must know and realize that ⟨what you
have thought likely to happen, has happened already. It is always more
difficult to get away in Salzburg, for there he is lord and master, but here
he is—a nobody, an underling, just as I am in his eyes.⟩ Besides, pray
believe me when I say that I know you and know ⟨the strength of my
affection⟩ for you. Even if ⟨the Archbishop had given me another two
hundred gulden,⟩—and I—I had agreed—we should have had the ⟨same
old story⟩ over again. Believe me, most beloved father, I need all my
manliness to write to you what common sense dictates. God knows how

---

[1] See p. 719, n. 1.

hard it is for me to leave you; but, even if I had to beg, I could never serve such a master again; for, as long as I live, I shall never forget what has happened. I implore you, I adjure you, by all you hold dear in this world, to strengthen me in this resolution instead of trying to dissuade me from it, for if you do you will only make me unproductive. ⟨My desire and my hope is to gain honour, fame and money,⟩ and I have every confidence that I shall be ⟨more useful to you in Vienna than if I were to return to Salzburg. The road to Prague⟩[1] is now less closed to me than ⟨if I were at Salzburg.⟩ What you ⟨say about the Webers,⟩ I do assure you is not true. I was a fool, I admit, about Aloysia Lange,[2] but what does not a man do ⟨when he is in love?⟩ Indeed I loved her truly, and even now I feel that she is not a matter of indifference to me. It is, therefore, a good thing for me that her husband is a jealous fool and lets her go nowhere, so that I seldom have an opportunity of seeing her. Believe me when I say that ⟨old Madame Weber is a very obliging woman⟩ and that I cannot do enough for her in return for her kindness, as unfortunately I have no time to do so. Well, I am longing for a letter from you, my dearest and most beloved father. Cheer up your son, for it is only the thought of displeasing you that can make him unhappy in his very promising circumstances. Adieu. A thousand farewells. I am ever, and I kiss your hands a thousand times as, your most obedient son

W: A: MZT

PS.—If you should imagine that I am staying here merely out of hatred for Salzburg and an *unreasonable* love for Vienna, then make enquiries. Herr von ⟨Strack,[3]⟩ a very good friend of mine, will, as a man of honour, certainly tell you the truth.

(405) *Mozart to his Father*

[*Autograph in the Mozarteum, Salzburg*]

MON TRÉS CHER PÉRE!　　　　　　　　　　VIENNA, 19 *May* 1781

I too do not know how to begin this letter,[4] my dearest father, for I have not yet recovered from my astonishment and shall never be able to do so, if you continue to think and to write as you do. I must confess that there is not a single touch in your letter by which I recognize my father!

---

[1] Through his friendship with the Duscheks Mozart had already established a connection with Prague, which was renowned for its musical activities.

[2] Aloysia Weber had married in October 1780 Josef Lange (1751–1831), an excellent actor and a talented portrait-painter. For an interesting account of Lange's connection with the Webers, see Blümml, p. 21 f.

[3] Johann Kilian Strack, an influential valet of the Emperor Joseph II.

[4] Mozart is obviously quoting the opening sentence of his father's last letter.

I see a father, indeed, but not that most beloved and most loving father, who cares for his own honour and for that of his children—in short, not *my* father. But it must have been a dream. You are awake now and need no reply from me to your points in order to be fully convinced that—*now more than ever*—I can never abandon my resolve. Yet, because in certain passages my honour and my character are most cruelly assailed, I must reply to these points. You say that you can never approve of my having tendered my resignation while I was in Vienna.[1] I should have thought that if I wished to do so (although at the time I did not, or I should have done so on the first occasion) the most sensible thing was to do it in a place where I had a good standing and the finest prospects in the world. It is possible that you will not approve this in the presence of the Archbishop, but to me you cannot but applaud my action. You say that the only way to save my honour is to abandon my resolve. How can you perpetrate such a contradiction! When you wrote this you surely did not bear in mind that such a recantation would prove me to be the basest fellow in the world. All Vienna knows that I have left the Archbishop, and all Vienna knows the reason! Everyone knows that it was because my honour was insulted—and, what is more, insulted three times. And am I publicly to prove the contrary? Am I to make myself out to be a cowardly sneak and the Archbishop a worthy prince? No one would like to do the former, and I least of all; and the latter God alone can accomplish, if it be His will to enlighten him. You say that I have never shown you any affection and therefore ought now to show it for the first time. Can you really say this? You add that I will never sacrifice any of my pleasures for your sake. But what pleasures have I here? The pleasure of taking trouble and pains to fill my purse? You seem to think that I am revelling in pleasures and amusements. Oh, how you deceive yourself indeed! That is, as to the present—for at present I have only just as much money as I need. But the subscription for my six sonatas[2] has been started and then I shall have some money. It is all right, too, about the opera,[3] and in Advent I am to give a concert; then things will continue to improve, for in the winter season a fine sum can be made here. If you call it *pleasure* to be rid of a prince, who does not pay a fellow and bullies him to death, then it is true that my pleasure is great. If I were to do nothing but think and work from early morning till late at night, I would gladly do so, rather than

---

[1] From now on Mozart, feeling that he has completely shaken off the Archbishop's fetters, ceases to use cypher, except on very rare occasions. That the Archbishop still continued to read his letters is evident from occasional references in Leopold Mozart's letters to Nannerl after her marriage in 1784. See Deutsch-Paumgartner: *Leopold Mozarts Briefe an seine Tochter*, 1936, p. 241 f.

[2] K. 296, written in 1778 at Mannheim for Mozart's pupil Therese Pierron Serrarius, and K. 376–380 [374d, e, 317d, 373a, 374f], four of which were written in 1781. These are violin and clavier sonatas, which Mozart subsequently dedicated to his pupil Josephine Auernhammer. They were published in November 1781 by Artaria and Co.   [3] See p. 726.

depend upon the favour of such a—I dare not call him by his right name. I have been forced to take this step, so I cannot deviate from my course by a hair's breadth—it is quite impossible! All that I can say to you is this, that on your account—but solely on your account, my father—I am very sorry that I was driven to take this step, and that I wish that the Archbishop had acted more judiciously, if only in order that I might have been able to devote my whole life to you. To please you, my most beloved father, I would sacrifice my happiness, my health and my life. But my honour—*that* I prize, and you too must prize it, above everything. You may show this to Count Arco and to all Salzburg too. After that insult, that threefold insult, were the Archbishop to offer me 1200 gulden in person, I would not accept them. I am no skunk, no rascal; and, had it not been for you, I would not have awaited for him to say to me for the third time, '*Clear out of this*', without taking him at his word! What am I saying? Waited! Why, *I* should have said it, and not *he*! I am only surprised that the Archbishop would have behaved with so little discretion, particularly in a place like Vienna! Well, he will see that he has made a mistake. Prince Breuner and Count Arco need the Archbishop, but I do not; and if the worst comes to the worst and he forgets all the duties of a prince—of a *spiritual prince*—then come and join me in Vienna. You can get four hundred gulden anywhere. Just imagine how he would disgrace himself in the eyes of the Emperor, who already hates him, if he were to do that! My sister too would get on much better in Vienna than in Salzburg. There are many distinguished families here who hesitate to engage a male teacher, but would give handsome terms to a woman. Well, all these things may happen some day. By the next occasion, it may be when Herr von Kleinmayr, Bönike or Zetti go to Salzburg, I shall send you a sum with which to pay the debt to which you refer. The contrôleur, who left today, will bring the lawn for my sister. Dearest, most beloved father, ask of me what you will, only not that—anything but that—the mere thought of it makes me tremble with rage. Adieu. I kiss your hands a thousand times and embrace my sister with all my heart and am ever your most obedient son

WOLFGANG AMADÈ MOZART

(406) *Mozart to his Father*

[*Autograph in the Mozarteum, Salzburg*]

MON TRÈS CHER PÈRE!   VIENNA, 26 *May.* VIENNA, 6 *May* 1781 [1]

You are quite right, and I am quite right too, my dearest father! I know and am aware of all my faults; but—is it impossible for a man to reform? May he not have reformed already? The more I consider the

---

[1] The double dating of the autograph is explained by the fact that Mozart used a sheet of paper on which he had begun a letter to his father on May 6th.

whole question, the more I realize that the best way for me to serve myself and you, my most beloved father, as well as my dear sister, is to stay in Vienna. It seems as if good fortune is about to welcome me here, and now I feel that I *must* stay. Indeed, I felt that when I left Munich. Without knowing why, I looked forward most eagerly to Vienna. You must be patient for a little while longer and then I shall be able to prove to you how useful Vienna is going to be to us all. Believe me when I say that I have changed completely. Apart from my health I now think that there is nothing so indispensable as money. I am certainly no skinflint and it would be very difficult for me to become one. Yet people here think that I am more disposed to be mean than to spend freely—and surely that is enough to begin with. As for pupils, I can have as many as I want, but I do not choose to take many. I intend to be paid better than others, and so I prefer to have fewer pupils. It is advisable to get on your high horse a little at first, otherwise you are done for and must follow the common highway with the rest. The subscription[1] is going on well; and as for the opera I don't know why I should hesitate. Count Rosenberg,[2] on the two occasions when I called on him, received me most politely; and he heard my opera[3] at Countess Thun's, when Van Swieten[4] and Herr von Sonnenfels[5] were also present. And as ⟨Stephanie⟩ is a good friend of mine, everything is progressing satisfactorily. Believe me when I say that I do not like to be idle but to work. I confess that in Salzburg work was a burden to me and that I could hardly ever settle down to it. But why? Because I was never happy. You yourself must admit that in Salzburg— for me at least—there is not a farthing's worth of entertainment. *I refuse to associate with a good many people there*—and most of the others do not think me good enough. Besides, there is no stimulus for my talent! When I play or when any of my compositions are performed, it is just as if the audience were all tables and chairs. If only there were even a tolerably good theatre in Salzburg! For in Vienna my sole amusement is the theatre. It is true that in Munich, without wishing to do so, I put myself in a false light as far as you were concerned, for I amused myself too much. But I swear

---

[1] For his violin and clavier sonatas. See p. 734, n. 2.
[2] See p. 716, n. 1.   [3] *Idomeneo.*
[4] Baron Gottfried van Swieten (1733–1803), son of the Empress Maria Theresia's famous private physician Gerhard van Swieten, was born in Leyden and taken to Vienna in 1745. He underwent a long period of training in the Austrian diplomatic service and held posts in Brussels, Paris and Warsaw, and was from 1770 to 1777 Imperial Ambassador in Berlin, where he had ample opportunity of indulging his great love of music. In 1778 he returned to Vienna and was made Prefect of the Imperial Library, and in 1781 President of the Court Commission on Education. His house was the meeting-place of writers, artists and musicians, and it was there that Mozart deepened his knowledge particularly of Handel and Johann Sebastian Bach. See Abert, vol. ii, p. 86, and an article by R. Bernhardt in *Der Bär*, 1929–1930, pp. 74–166.
[5] Josef von Sonnenfels (1733–1817), Professor at the University of Vienna, was a well-known dramatist and writer and a leader of the 'Aufklärung' in Austria. He is commonly known as the 'Austrian Lessing'.

to you on my honour that until the first performance of my opera [1] I had never been to a theatre, or gone anywhere but to the Cannabichs'. It is true that during the last few days I had to compose the greater and most difficult part of my opera; yet this was not from laziness or negligence—but because I had spent a fortnight without writing a note, simply because I found it *impossible to do so*. Of course I composed a lot, but wrote down nothing. I admit that I lost a great deal of time in this way, but I do not regret it. That I was afterwards too gay was only due to youthful folly. I thought to myself, where are you going to? To Salzburg! Well, you must have a good time. It is quite certain that when I am in Salzburg I long for a hundred amusements, but here not for a single one. For just to be in Vienna is in itself entertainment enough. Do have confidence in me; I am no longer a fool, and still less can you believe that I am either godless or an ungrateful son. So rely absolutely on my brains and my good heart, and you will never regret it. Why, where could I have learnt the value of money, when up to the present I have had so little to handle? All I know is that once when I had twenty ducats, I considered myself wealthy. Necessity alone teaches one to value money.

Farewell, dearest, most beloved father! My duty now is to make good and to replace by my care and industry what you think you have lost by this affair. This I shall certainly do and with a thousand thrills of delight. Adieu. I kiss your hands a thousand times and embrace my sister with all my heart, and am ever your most obedient son

WOLFGANG AMADÈ MOZART

PS.—So soon as one of the Archbishop's people goes to Salzburg, I shall send the portrait. Hò fatto fare la soprascritta da un altro espressamente, perchè non si può sapere [2]—for who would trust a knave?

My greetings to all my acquaintances.

(407) *Mozart to his Father*

[*Autograph in the Mozarteum, Salzburg*]

MON TRÉS CHER PÉRE!   [VIENNA, *between* 26 *May and* 2 *June* 1781]
    The day before yesterday Count Arco sent me a message to call on him at noon, saying that he would expect me at that hour. He has often sent me this kind of message, and so has Schlauka. But as I detest discussions, in which every word to which I have to listen is a lie, I have always

---

[1] *Idomeneo*, the first performance of which was on 29 January 1781.
[2] I have got somebody else to write the address on purpose, for you never can tell.

avoided going. And this time too I should have done the same, if he had not added that he had had a letter from you. I therefore went. It would be impossible to repeat the whole conversation, which was conducted in a very calm tone and, at my urgent request, without irritation on either side. In short, he put everything before me in so friendly a manner that really I could have sworn that what he said came altogether from his heart. I think, however, that he would not be prepared to swear that the same was true of myself. In answer to his plausible speeches I told him the whole truth with all possible calmness and courtesy and in the most charming manner in the world; and he could not find a word to say against it. The result was that I tried to make him take my memorandum and my travelling expenses, both of which I had brought with me. But he assured me that it would be too distressing for him to interfere in this matter and that I had better give the document to one of the valets; and as for the money, he would not take it until the whole affair was settled. The Archbishop runs me down to everyone here and has not the sense to see that such a proceeding does him no credit; for I am more highly respected in Vienna than he is. He is only known as a presumptuous, conceited ecclesiastic, who despises everyone here, whereas I am considered a very amiable person. It is true that I become proud when I see that someone is trying to treat me with contempt and *en bagatelle*; and that is the way in which the Archbishop invariably treats me; whereas by kind words he could have made me do as he pleased. I told this too to the Count and added among other things that the Archbishop did not deserve the good opinion you had of him. And towards the end I said: 'Besides, what good would it do, if I were to go home now? In a few months' time and even if I did not receive any fresh insult, I should still ask for my discharge, for I cannot and will not serve any longer for such a salary.' 'And pray why not?' 'Because', said I, 'I could never live happily and contentedly in a place where I am so badly paid that I am constantly thinking, 'Ah, if only I were there! or there!' But if I were paid such a salary that I should not be tempted to think of other places, then I should be perfectly satisfied. And if the Archbishop chooses to pay me that salary, well, then, I am ready to set off today.' But how delighted I am that the Archbishop does not take me at my word! For there is no doubt, as you will see, that my being here is both to your advantage and to my own. Now farewell, my dearest, most beloved father. All will go well yet. I am not writing in a dream, for my own welfare also depends on it. Adieu.

I kiss your hands a thousand times and embrace my dearest sister most cordially and am ever your most obedient son

WOLFGANG AMADÈ MOZART

PS.—My compliments to all my good friends.

(408) *Mozart to his Father*

[*Autograph in the Mozarteum, Salzburg*]

MON TRÈS CHER PÈRE! VIENNA, 2 *June* 1781

You will have gathered from my last letter that I have spoken to Count Arco himself. Praise and thanks be to God that everything has passed off so well! Do not be anxious; you have nothing whatever ⟨to fear⟩ from ⟨the Archbishop,⟩ for Count Arco did not say a single word to suggest that I ought to take care or that *the affair ⟨might injure you.⟩* When he told me that you had written to him and had complained bitterly about me, I immediately interrupted him and said: *'And have I not heard from him too? He has written to me in such a strain that I have often thought I should go crazy. But, however much I reflect, I simply cannot, etc.'* Upon which he said: 'Believe me, you allow yourself to be far too easily dazzled in Vienna. A man's reputation here lasts a very short time. At first, it is true, you are overwhelmed with praises and make a great deal of money into the bargain—but how long does that last? After a few months the Viennese want something new.' 'You are right, Count,' I replied. 'But do you suppose that I mean to settle in Vienna? Not at all. I know where I shall go. That this affair should have occurred in Vienna is the Archbishop's fault and not mine. If he knew how to treat people of talent, it would never have happened. I am the best-tempered fellow in the world, Count Arco, provided that people are the same with me.' 'Well,' he said, 'the Archbishop considers you a dreadfully conceited person.' 'I daresay he does,' I rejoined, 'and indeed I am so towards him. I treat people as they treat me. When I see that someone despizes me and treats me with contempt, I can be as proud as a peacock.' Among other things he asked me whether I did not think that he too often had to swallow very disagreeable words. I shrugged my shoulders and said: 'You no doubt have your reasons for putting up with it, and I—have my reasons for refusing to do so'. All the rest you will know from my last letter. Do not doubt, dearest and most beloved father, that everything will certainly turn out for my good and consequently for yours also. It is perfectly true that the Viennese are apt to change their affections, *but only in the theatre*; and my special line is too popular not to enable me to support myself. Vienna is certainly the land of the clavier! And, even granted that they do get tired of me, they will not do so for a few years, certainly not before then. In the meantime I shall have gained both honour and money. There are many other places; and who can tell what opportunities may not occur before then? Through Herr von Zetti, to whom I have already spoken, I am sending you a small sum. You must be content with very little this time, for I cannot let you have more than thirty ducats. Had I foreseen this event, I should have taken the pupils who wanted to come to me. But at that time I thought I should be leaving in a week, and now they are in the country. The portrait will also follow.[1] If Zetti cannot take it, I shall send it by the mail coach. Now farewell, dearest, most beloved father. I kiss your hands a thousand times and embrace my sister with all my heart and am ever your most obedient son

WOLFGANG AMADÈ MOZART

My greetings to all my good friends. I shall reply to Ceccarelli shortly.

(409) *Mozart to his Father*

[*Autograph in the Mozarteum, Salzburg*]

MON TRÉS CHER PÈRE!   VIENNA, 9 *June* 1781

Well, Count Arco has made a nice mess of things! So that is the way to persuade people and to attract them! To refuse petitions from innate stupidity, not to say a word to your master from lack of courage and love of toadyism, to keep a fellow dangling about for four weeks, and finally, when he is obliged to present the petition in person, instead of *at least* granting him admittance, to throw him out of the room and give him a kick on his behind—that is the Count, who, according to your last letter, has my interest so much at heart—and that is the court where I ought to go on serving—the place where whoever wants to make a written application, instead of having its delivery facilitated, is treated in this fashion! The scene took place in the antechamber. So the only thing to do was to decamp and take to my heels—for, although Arco had already done so, I did not wish to show disrespect to the Prince's apartments. I have written three memoranda, which I have handed in five times; and each time they have been thrown back at me. I have carefully preserved them, and whoever wishes to read them may do so and convince himself that they do not contain the slightest personal remark. When at last I was handed back my memorandum in the evening through Herr von Kleinmayr (for that is his office), I was beside myself with rage, for the Archbishop's departure was fixed for the following day. I could not let him leave thus and, as I had heard from Arco (or so at least he had told me) that the Prince knew nothing about it, I realized how angry he would be with me for staying on so long and then at the very last moment appearing with a petition of this kind. I therefore wrote another memorandum, in which I explained to the Archbishop that it was now four weeks since I had drawn up a petition, but, finding myself for some unknown reason always put off, I was now obliged to present it to him in person, though at the very last moment.

[1] See p. 732, n. 1.

This memorandum procured me my dismissal from his service in the most pleasant way imaginable. For who knows whether the whole thing was not done at the command of the Archbishop himself? If Herr von Kleinmayr still wishes to maintain the character of an honest man, he can testify as can also the Archbishop's servants, that his command was carried out. So now I need not send in any petition, for the affair is at an end. I do not want to write anything more on the subject, and if the Archbishop were to offer me a salary of 1200 gulden, I would not accept it after such treatment. How easy it would have been to persuade me to remain! By kindness, but not by insolence and rudeness. I sent a message to Count Arco saying *that I had nothing more to say to him.* For he went for me so rudely when I first saw him and treated me as if I were a rogue, which he had no right to do. And—by Heaven! as I have already told you, I would not have gone to him the last time, if in his message he had not added that he had had a letter from you. Well, that will be the last time. What is it to him if I wish to get my discharge? And if he was really so well disposed towards me, he ought to have reasoned quietly with me—or have let things take their course, rather than throw such words about as 'clown' and 'knave' and hoof a fellow out of the room with a kick on his arse; but I am forgetting that this was probably done by order of our worthy Prince Archbishop.

I shall reply very briefly to your letter, for I am so sick of the whole affair that I never want to hear anything more about it. In view of the original *cause* of my leaving (which you know well), no father would dream of being angry with his son; on the contrary, he would be angry if his son *had not left.* Still less ought you to have been angry, ⟨*as you knew that even without any particular cause I definitely wanted to leave.* Really, you cannot be in earnest;⟩ and I am therefore led to suppose that ⟨you are driven to adopt this attitude on account of the Court.⟩ But I beg you, most beloved father, ⟨not to cringe too much; for the Archbishop cannot do you any harm.⟩ Let him try! I almost wish he would; for that would be a deed, a fresh deed, ⟨which would ruin him completely with the Emperor, who, as it is, not only does not like him, but positively detests him.⟩ If after ⟨such treatment you were to come to Vienna and tell the story to the Emperor,⟩ you would at all events receive ⟨from him the salary you are drawing at present,⟩ for in such cases ⟨the Emperor⟩ behaves most admirably. Your comparison of me to Madame Lange [1] positively amazed me and made me feel distressed for the rest of the day. That girl lived on her parents as long as she could earn nothing for herself. But as soon as the time came when she could show them her gratitude (remember that her father died before she had earned anything

[1] Aloysia Weber. See p. 733, n. 2.

in Vienna),[1] she deserted her poor mother, attached herself to an actor and married him—and her mother has never had *a farthing* from her. Good God! *He* knows that my sole aim is to help you and to help us all. Must I repeat it a hundred times that I can be of more use to you here than in Salzburg? I implore you, dearest, most beloved father, for the future to spare me such letters. I entreat you to do so, for they only irritate my mind and disturb my heart and spirit; and I, who must now keep on composing, need a cheerful mind and a calm disposition. The Emperor is not here, nor is Count Rosenberg. The latter has commissioned Schröder[2] (the eminent actor) to look around for a good libretto and to give it to me to compose.

Herr von Zetti has had to leave unexpectedly by command and has set off so very early that I can neither send the portrait, nor the ribbons for my sister, nor *the other thing you know of*[3] until tomorrow week by the mail coach.

Now farewell, dearest, most beloved father! I kiss your hands a thousand times and embrace my dear sister most cordially and am ever your most obedient son

Wolfgang Amadè Mozart

(410) *Mozart to his Father*

[Autograph in the Mozarteum, Salzburg]

Mon trés cher Pére!   Vienna, 13 *June* 1781

Most beloved of all fathers! How gladly would I not continue to sacrifice my best years to you in a place where I am so badly paid—if my salary were the only drawback! But to be badly paid and to be scoffed at, despised and bullied into the bargain—is really too much. For the Archbishop's concert I composed a sonata for myself, a rondo for Brunetti and one for Ceccarelli.[4] At each concert I played twice and the last time when the concert was over I went on playing variations[5] (for which the Archbishop gave me the theme) for a whole hour and with such general applause that if the Archbishop had any vestige of humanity, he must have felt delighted. But, instead of showing me—or not showing me, for all I care—his pleasure and satisfaction, he treats me like a street urchin and tells me to my face to clear out, adding that he can get hundreds to serve him better than I—and why? Just because I could not set off from Vienna on *the very day* which he had chosen. I had to leave his house, live at my

---

[1] See p. 727, n. 2.
[2] Friedrich Ludwig Schröder (1744-1816), the famous Viennese actor, who translated, adapted and produced Shakespeare's plays.
[3] The thirty ducats. See p. 739.   [4] K. 379 [373a], 373 and 374. See p. 722 f.
[5] During the summer of 1781 Mozart wrote three sets of clavier variations K. 359, 360 and 352, [374a–c], the first two with violin accompaniment. Possibly it was the theme of one of these that the Archbishop suggested.

own expense and yet not be at liberty to delay my departure until my purse should permit me to travel. Besides, I was not needed in Salzburg and the whole difference was a matter of two days. The Archbishop on two occasions said the most insulting things to me and I never said a word in reply. Nay, what is more, I played at his concert with the same zeal and assiduity as if nothing had happened; and instead of acknowledging my readiness to serve him and my endeavour to please him, he behaves for the third time, and at the very moment when I am expecting something quite different, in the most disgraceful way imaginable; and, moreover, that I should not be in the wrong, but absolutely in the right, he acts as if he were resolved to get rid of me by force. Well, if he does not want me, that is exactly what I wish. Instead of taking my petition or procuring me an audience or advising me to send in the document later or persuading me to let the matter lie and to consider things more carefully, —enfin, whatever he wanted—Count Arco hurls me out of the room and gives me a kick on my behind. Well, that means in our language that Salzburg is no longer the place for me, except to give me a favourable opportunity of returning the Count's kick, even if it should have to be in the public street. I am not demanding any satisfaction from the Archbishop, for he cannot procure it for me in the way in which I intend to obtain it myself. But one of these days I shall write to the Count and tell him what he may confidently expect from me, as soon as my good fortune allows me to meet him, wherever it may be,—provided it is not in a place that I am bound to respect. Do not be anxious, most beloved father, about the welfare of my soul. I am as liable to err as any young man, but for my own consolation I could wish that all were as free from sin as I am. Probably you believe things of me of which I am not guilty. My chief fault is that—*judging by appearances*—I do not always act as I should. It is not true that I boasted of eating meat on all fast-days; but I did say that I did not scruple to do so or consider it a sin, for I take fasting to mean abstaining, that is, eating less than usual. I attend Mass every Sunday and every Holy day and, if I can manage it, on weekdays also, and that you know, my father. The only association which I had with the person of ill repute was at the ball, and I talked to her long before I knew what she was, and solely because I wanted to be sure of having a partner for the contredanse. Afterwards I could not desert her all at once without giving her the reason; and who would say such a thing to a person's face? But in the end did I not on several occasions leave her in the lurch and dance with others? On this account too I was positively delighted when the carnival was over. Moreover, no one, unless he is a liar, can say that I ever saw her anywhere else, or went to her house. Do rest assured that I really hold to my religion; and should I ever have the misfortune (which God forbid!) to fall into evil courses, I shall absolve you, my most beloved father, from all responsibility. For in that case I alone should be the villain, as I have you to thank for all good things and for both my temporal and spiritual welfare and salvation. Well, I must close, or I shall miss the post. I kiss your hands a thousand times and embrace my sister most cordially and am ever your most obedient son

WOLFGANG AMADÈ MOZART

PS.—My greetings to young Marchand, to Katherl and to all my good friends.

(411) *Mozart to his Father*

[Autograph in the Mozarteum, Salzburg]

MON TRÉS CHER PÉRE!   VIENNA, 16 *June* 1781

Tomorrow the portrait and the ribbons for my sister will sail off to Salzburg. I do not know whether the ribbons will be to her taste; but I assure her that they are in the latest fashion. If she would like to have some more or perhaps some which are not painted, she has only to let me know, and if there is anything else which she thinks can be got better in Vienna, she has only to write to me. I hope that she did not pay for the fichu, as it was paid for already. I forgot to mention this when writing, probably because I had so much to tell you about that accursed affair. I shall remit the money in the way you have directed.

Well, at last I can tell you something more about Vienna. Up to the present I have had to fill my letters with that swinish story. Thank God, it is over. The present season is, as you know, the worst for anyone who wants to make money. The most distinguished families are in the country. So all I can do is to work hard in preparation for the winter, when I shall have less time to compose. As soon as the sonatas are finished,[1] I shall look about for a short Italian cantata and set it to music,[2] so that it may be produced at the theatre in Advent—for my benefit, of course. There is a little cunning in this, for then I can give it twice and make the same profit each time, since, when it is performed for the second time, I shall play something on a pianoforte. At present I have only one pupil, Countess Rumbeck,[3] Cobenzl's cousin. I could have many more, it is true, if I chose to lower my terms, but by doing so, I should lose repute. My terms are six ducats for twelve lessons and even then I make it clearly understood that I am giving them as a favour. I would rather have three pupils who pay me well than six who pay badly. With this one pupil I can just make

---

[1] K. 376, 377 and 380 [374d–f]. See p. 734, n. 2.
[2] According to Mozart's letter of 1 August 1781 (see p. 754), Rossi provided the words for this cantata. Nothing more is known for certain of this composition. See Köchel, p. 401.
[3] See p. 718.

both ends meet, and that is enough for the present. I simply mention this in order that you may not think me guilty of selfishness in sending you only thirty ducats. Believe me, I would gladly deprive myself of everything, if only I had it! But things are bound to improve. We must never let people know how we really stand financially.

Well, let us talk about the theatre. I think I mentioned the other day that before his departure Count Rosenberg commissioned Schröder to hunt up a libretto for me. It has now been found, and Stephanie junior, who is manager of the opera, has got it. Bergopzoomer, a really good friend of Schröder's and of mine, gave me the hint at once. So off I went to Stephanie, *en forme de visite*. For we thought it possible that his partiality for Umlauf[1] might make him play me false. This suspicion proved, however, quite unfounded. For I heard afterwards that he had commissioned someone to ask me to go and see him, as there was something he wished to discuss with me. And the moment I entered his room, he said: 'Ah, you are just the very person I wanted to see.' The opera is in four acts; and he tells me that the first act is exceedingly fine, but that the rest is on a much lower level. If Schröder allows us to alter it as we think advisable, a good libretto can be made out of it. He does not want to give it to the management in its present state, that is, until he has discussed it with Schröder, as he knows in advance that it would be rejected. So the two of them can settle the matter between them. After what Stephanie told me, I did not express any desire to read it. For, if I do not like it, I must say so plainly, or I should be the victim. Besides, I do not want to lose the favour of Schröder, who has the greatest respect for me. Therefore I can always make the excuse that I have not read it.

Well, I must now explain why we were suspicious of Stephanie. I regret to say that the fellow has the worst reputation in Vienna, for he is said to be rude, false and slanderous and to treat people most unfairly. But I pay no attention to these reports. There may be some truth in them, for everyone abuses him. On the other hand, he is in great favour with the Emperor. He was most friendly to me the very first time we met, and said: 'We are old friends already and I shall be delighted if it be in my power to render you any service'. I believe and hope too that he himself may write an opera libretto for me. Whether he has written his plays alone or with the help of others, whether he has plagiarised or created, he still understands the stage, and his plays are invariably popular. I have only seen two new pieces of his, and these are certainly excellent, the first being 'Das Loch in der Türe',[2] and the second 'Der Oberamtmann und die

---

[1] Ignaz Umlauf (1746–1796), a popular operatic composer. In 1772 he joined the Vienna court orchestra as viola-player and in 1778, after the great success of his light opera *Die Bergknappen*, he was made Kapellmeister of the new National Singspiel Theatre. By 1782 he had become deputy to Salieri as conductor of the Vienna court orchestra.

[2] A comedy by Gottlieb Stephanie.

Soldaten'.[1] Meanwhile I am going to set the cantata to music; for even if I had a libretto, I would not put pen to paper, since Count Rosenberg is not here; and if at the last moment he did not approve of it, I should have had the honour of composing for nothing. None of that for me, thank you! I have not the slightest doubt about the success of the opera, provided the text is a good one. For do you really suppose that I should write an opéra comique in the same style as an opera seria? In an opera seria there should be as little frivolity and as much seriousness and solidity, as in an opera buffa there should be little seriousness and all the more frivolity and gaiety. That people like to have a little comic music in an opera seria, I cannot help. But in Vienna they make the proper distinction on this point. I do certainly find that in music the Merry Andrew has not yet been banished, and in this respect the French are right. I hope to receive my clothes safely by the next mail coach. I do not know when it goes, but as I think this letter will reach you first, I beg you to keep the stick for me. People carry sticks here, but for what purpose? To walk with, and for that purpose any little stick will do. So please use the stick instead of me, and always carry it if you can. Who knows whether in your hand it may not avenge its former master on Arco? I mean, of course, *accidentaliter*, or by chance. That arrogant jackass will certainly get a very palpable reply from me, even if he has to wait twenty years for it. For to see him and to return his kick will be one and the same thing, unless I am so unlucky as to meet him first in some sacred place.

Well, adieu. Farewell. I kiss your hands a thousand times and embrace my sister with all my heart and am ever your most obedient son

W: A: MZT

My greetings everywhere.

(412) *Mozart to his Father*

[*Autograph in the Mozarteum, Salzburg*]

MON TRÉS CHER PÉRE!   VIENNA, 20 *June* 1781

I have received the parcel, and hope that by now you have got the portrait and the ribbons. I do not know why you did not pack everything together in a trunk or a chest, for it costs more to send things one by one, since you have to pay for each article separately, than to send one big package. I can well believe that the Court flunkeys are eyeing you askance, but why should you worry about such miserable menials? The more hostile these people are to you, the more proudly and contemptuously you must treat them.

[1] *Der Oberamtmann und die Soldaten* was a free adaptation by Gottlieb Stephanie of a similar piece by Calderon. It was set to music later by Umlauf and performed in 1782.

As for Arco, I have but to consult my own feelings and judgment and therefore do not need the advice of a lady or a person of rank to help me to do what is right and fitting, and neither too much nor too little. It is the heart that ennobles a man; and though I am no count, yet I have probably more honour in me than many a count. Whether a man be count or valet, the moment he insults me, he is a scoundrel. I intend at first to tell him quite reasonably how badly and clumsily he has played his part. But in conclusion I shall feel bound to assure him in writing that he may confidently expect from me a kick on his behind and a few boxes on the ear in addition. For when I am insulted, I must have my revenge; and if I do no more than was done to me, I shall only be getting even with him and not punishing him. Besides, I should be placing myself on a level with him, and really I am too proud to measure myself with such a stupid booby.

Unless I have something particularly important to tell you, I shall only write to you once a week, as I am very busy just now. I must close this letter, as I have some variations to finish for my pupil.[1] Adieu. I kiss your hands a thousand times and embrace my sister with all my heart and am ever[2]

(413) *Mozart to his Father*

[*Autograph in the Mozarteum, Salzburg*]

MON TRÉS CHER PÉRE!   VIENNA, 27 *June* 1781

As for Madame Rosa I must tell you that I called on her three times until at last I had the good fortune to find her at home. You would hardly recognize her, she has got so thin. When I asked her about the portrait, she offered to make me a present of it, adding that she did not require it and that she would send it to me on the following day. But three weeks went by and no portrait came. Again I went to her house three times in vain. Finally, however, I went there one day very early in the morning when she and her plebeian spouse were still at breakfast. Well, instead of wanting to give me the portrait *free*, she had suddenly decided *not to let me have it at all*. Thereupon it occurred to me that in such cases the best way to treat Italians is to be extremely rude. So I told her that she was as cracked as ever, but that, just to pander to her ingrained failings, I did not choose to play in my father's eyes the part of a fool, who says black one day and white the next; and that I could assure her that I did not require the portrait. Whereupon she spoke very civilly and promised to send it the next day, which she did. You must, however, return it *in due course*.

---

[1] Countess Thiennes de Rumbeke. The variations to which Mozart refers are one of the sets K. 359, 360, 352 [374a–c], which were composed in the summer of 1781.
[2] The signature has been cut off the autograph.

I have this moment come from Herr von Hippe, Prince Kaunitz's private secretary, who is an extremely amiable man and a very good friend of mine. He first came to visit me, and I then played to him. We have two harpsichords in the house where I am lodging, one for galanterie playing and the other an instrument which is strung with the low octave throughout, like the one we had in London, and consequently sounds like an organ. So on this one I improvised and played fugues. I go to Herr von Auernhammer almost every afternoon. The young lady is a fright, but plays enchantingly, though in cantabile playing she has not got the real delicate singing style. She clips everything. She has told me (as a great secret) of her plan, which is to work hard for two or three years more and then go to Paris and make music her profession. She said: '*I am no beauty— au contraire*, I am ugly. I have no desire to marry some chancery official with an income of three or four hundred gulden and I have no chance of getting anyone else. So I prefer to remain as I am and to live by my talent.' And there she is right. She begged me to assist her in carrying out her project, which she prefers not to mention beforehand to anyone else.

I shall send you the opera[1] as soon as possible. Countess Thun still has it and at present she is in the country. Please have the sonata in B♭ à quatre mains[2] and the two concertos for two claviers[3] copied for me and send them to me as soon as possible. I should be very glad, too, to receive my masses[4] by degrees.

Gluck has had a stroke and his health is in a very precarious state.[5] Tell me whether it is true that Becke was almost bitten to death by a dog in Munich? Well, I must close, for I must go off to lunch with the Auernhammers. Adieu. I kiss your hands a thousand times and embrace my dear sister with all my heart and am ever your most obedient son

WOLFG. AMADÉ MOZART

Madame Bernasconi[6] is here and is drawing a salary of five hundred ducats because she sings all her arias a good comma higher than others. This is really a great achievement, for she always keeps in tune. She has now promised to sing a quarter of a tone higher still, but on condition that she is paid twice as much. Adieu.

[1] *Idomeneo.*   [2] K. 358 [186c], composed in 1773–1774.
[3] K. 365 [316a], composed in 1779, and K. 242, a concerto for three claviers, composed in 1776, which Mozart himself had arranged for two. See Köchel, p. 251.
[4] Probably K. 275 [272b], composed in 1777, K. 317, composed in 1779, and K. 337, composed in 1780.
[5] Gluck had had several apoplectic seizures in 1779 and again in May 1781.
[6] Antonia Bernasconi, who had sung in Mozart's *Mitridate*, produced at Milan, December 1770.

(414) *Mozart to his Father*

[*Autograph in the Mozarteum, Salzburg*]

MON TRÉS CHER PÉRE!   VIENNA, 4 *July* 1781

I have not written to Count Arco and shall not do so, since you ask me to desist for the sake of your peace of mind. It is just as I suspected. You really are too timid, and yet you have nothing whatever to fear; for you—you yourself are as much insulted as I am. I do not ask you to make a row or even to put forward the slightest complaint. But the Archbishop and the whole pack of them must be afraid of speaking to you on the subject. For you, my father, need have no scruples in saying boldly (if you are driven to it) that you would be ashamed of having brought up a son who would allow himself to be so grossly insulted by such an infamous scoundrel as Arco; and you may assure them all that if I had the good fortune to meet him today, I should treat him as he deserves and he would certainly remember me as long as he lived. All I insist on, and nothing else, is that you should show the whole world that you are not afraid. Be silent, if you choose; but when necessary, speak—and speak in such a way that people will remember it. The Archbishop secretly offered 1000 gulden to Kozeluch,[1] who, however, has declined, saying that he was better off in Vienna and that unless he could improve his position, he would never leave. But to his friends he added: 'What deters me most of all is that affair with Mozart. If the Archbishop lets such a man go, what on earth would he not do to me?' So you see how he knows me and appreciates my talents. I have received the chest with the clothes. If M. Marchall or the Syndic of the Chapter comes to Vienna, I should be delighted if you would send me my favourite watch. I will return yours, if you will let me have the small one too, which I should particularly like to have. I wrote to you the other day about the masses.[2] I badly need the three cassations[3] —those in F and B♭ would do me for the time being—but you might have the one in D copied for me some time and sent on later, for the charge for copying is so very heavy in Vienna; in addition to which they copy most atrociously. Well, although I am in a great hurry, I must say a few words about Marchand,[4] as far as I know him. When his father corrected the younger boy at table, he took up a knife and said: 'Look

---

[1] Leopold Kozeluch (1747–1818), a Czech, was trained in Prague, and in 1778 went to Vienna as clavier teacher to the Archduchess Elizabeth. He soon gained a reputation as a clavier-player and composer of grand operas, symphonies and clavier music. He succeeded Mozart in 1792 in his post of chamber composer to the Emperor at almost twice the salary which his predecessor had received.

[2] See p. 748, n. 4.

[3] Probably K. 247 and 287 [271H], written in 1766 and 1777, and K. 334 [320b], written in 1779–80.

[4] Theobald Marchand, theatrical manager in Munich and father of Margarete (singer), Heinrich (violinist) and David (cellist) Marchand.

here, Papa. If you say another word, I shall cut off my finger at the joint and then I shall be a cripple on your hands and you will have to feed me.' Both boys have frequently run down their father to other people. You will no doubt remember Mlle Boudet[1] who lives in their house? Well, old Marchand being rather partial to her, these rascals made infamous remarks about it. When Hennerle[2] was eight years old he said to a certain girl: 'Indeed I would far sooner sleep in your arms than find myself hugging the pillow when I wake up'. He also made her a formal declaration of love and a proposal of marriage, adding: 'I cannot exactly marry you at present, but when my father dies, I shall have money, for he is not absolutely destitute and, then we shall live together very comfortably. Meanwhile let us love one another and enjoy our love to the full. For what you allow me to do now, you will not be able to permit later on.' I know too that in Mannheim no one ever allowed their boys to go where the Marchands were. For they were caught—helping one another. Well, it is a great pity for the lad himself; but you, my father, will be able to reform him completely, of that I am quite sure. As their father and mother are on the stage, they hear nothing all day long (and nothing else is ever read out to them) but tales of love, despair, murder and death. Besides, the father has too little stability for his age. So they have no good examples at home. Well, I must stop, or my letter will reach Peisser too late. Farewell. I kiss your hands a thousand times and am ever your most obedient son

WOLFGANG AMADÈ MOZART

PS.—My greetings to all my good friends. Do tell me the story about my sister's cap. You mentioned something about it in a letter. Adieu.

(415) *Mozart to his Sister*

[*Copy in the Staatsbibliothek Preussischer Kulturbesitz, West Berlin*]

MA TRÈS CHÈRE SOEUR!   VIENNA, 4 *July* 1781
    I am delighted that the ribbons are to your taste. I shall find out the price of the ribbons, both the painted and the unpainted ones. At present I do not know it, for Frau von Auernhammer, who was so kind as to procure them for me, refused to take any payment, but begged me to send you all sorts of nice messages, although she does not know you, and to tell you that she will be very glad at any time to be able to do you a kindness. I have already conveyed to her your greetings in return. Dearest sister! I wrote the other day to our dear father that if there is anything in

[1] Marianne Boudet, who in 1782 married Martin Lang (1755–1819), horn-player in the Munich Court orchestra.   [2] Little Heinrich.

Vienna which you would like to have, whatever it may be, I should be delighted to do this service for you.[1] I now repeat this, adding that it would distress me very greatly if I were to hear that you were commissioning someone else in Vienna. I am heartily glad when you are well. Praise and thanks be to God, I too am in good health and in excellent spirits. My sole entertainment is the theatre. How I wish that you could see a tragedy acted here! Generally speaking, I do not know of any theatre where all kinds of plays are *really well* performed. But they are here. Every part, even the most unimportant and poorest part, is well cast and understudied. I should very much like to know how things are progressing between you and a certain good friend, you know whom I mean.[2] Do write to me about this! Or have I lost your confidence in this matter? In any case, please write to me often, I mean, when you have nothing better to do, for I should dearly love to hear some news occasionally—and you are the living chronicle of Salzburg, for you write down every single thing that occurs; so, to please me, you might write it down a second time. But you must not be angry with me, if now and then I keep you waiting a long time for a reply.

As for something new for the clavier I may tell you that I am having four sonatas engraved. Those in C and B♭ are among them[3] and only the other two[4] are new. Then I have written variations on three airs,[5] which I could send you, of course; but I think it is hardly worth the trouble and I would rather wait until I have more to send. Well, I suppose the marksmen's feast will soon be held? I beg you *solemniter* to drink the health of a loyal marksman. When it is my turn again to provide the target, please let me know and I shall have one painted. Now farewell, dearest, most beloved sister, and rest assured that I shall ever remain your true friend and sincere brother

WOLFGANG AMADÈ MOZART

(416) *Mozart to his Father*

[*Autograph in the Mozarteum, Salzburg*]

MON TRÉS CHER PÉRE!   [REISENBERG, *near* VIENNA], 13 *July* 1781

I cannot write very much, for Count Cobenzl is driving off to town this very moment and I must give him this letter if I wish it to be posted. I am writing to you at an hour's distance from Vienna, at a place called Reisenberg. I once spent a night here, and now I am staying for a few days. The little house is nothing much, but the country—the forest—in which

---

[1] See p. 744 f.   [2] Franz d'Yppold. See p. 688, n. 2.
[3] The violin and clavier sonatas, K. 296 in C major, composed in 1778, and K. 378 [317a] in B , composed in 1779 or early in 1781.
[4] K. 376 [374d] and 379 [373a].   [5] K. 359, 360, 352 [274a–c].

my host has built a grotto which looks just as if Nature herself had fash-
ioned it! Indeed the surroundings are magnificent and very delightful. I
have received your last letter. I have long been intending to leave the
Webers and I shall certainly do so. But I swear to you that I have not heard
a word about going to live with Herr von Auernhammer. It is true that I
might have lodged with Mesmer, the writing-master, but really I prefer
to stay with the Webers. Mesmer has Righini[1] (formerly opera buffa
singer and now a composer) in his house and is his great friend and protector; but Frau Mesmer is still more so. Until I find a good, cheap and
comfortable lodging I shall not leave my present one; and even then I
shall have to make up some story to tell the good woman, for really I have
no reason to leave. Herr von ⟨Moll⟩ has, I know not why, a very malicious tongue, which particularly surprises me in his case. He says that he
hopes that I shall think better of it and soon return to Salzburg, for I shall
hardly find things so easy here as I do there, and he declares that, as it is,
I am here only on account of the Viennese women. Fräulein von Auernhammer repeated this to me. But everywhere he gets very strange replies
on this point. I can pretty well guess why he talks in this strain. He is a very
strong supporter of Kozeluch. Oh! how silly it all is!

The story about Herr von Mölk greatly astonished me. I have always
thought him capable of anything,—but I never could have believed he
was a scoundrel. I pity the poor family from my heart. Write to me soon
and send me lots of news. I must stop, as the Count is going off. Farewell.
I kiss your hands a thousand times and embrace my dear sister with all my
heart and am ever your most obedient son

WOLFGANG AMADÈ MOZART

(417) *Mozart to his Father*

[Autograph in the Mozarteum, Salzburg]

MON TRÉS CHER PÉRE!   VIENNA, 25 *July* 1780 [1781]

I repeat that I have long been thinking of moving to another lodging,
and that too solely because people are gossiping. I am very sorry that I am
obliged to do this on account of silly talk, in which there is not a word of
truth. I should very much like to know what pleasure certain people can
find in spreading entirely groundless reports. Because I am living with
them,[2] therefore I am going to marry the daughter.[3] There has been no
talk of our being in love. They have skipped that stage. No, I just take

---

[1] Vincenzo Righini (1756–1812), born at Bologna, first became a singer and may later have
studied composition under Padre Martini. He was a prolific composer of operas and church
music. One of his operas, *Il convitato di pietra*, a forerunner of Mozart's *Don Giovanni*, was
produced in Vienna in 1777.

[2] i.e. Frau Weber and her daughters.   [3] Constanze Weber.

rooms in the house and *marry*. If ever there was a time when I thought less of getting married, it is most certainly now! For (although the last thing I want is a rich wife) even if I could now make my fortune by a marriage, I could not possibly pay court to anyone, for my mind is running on very different matters. God has not given me my talent that I might attach it to a wife and waste my youth in idleness. I am just beginning to live, and am I to embitter my own life? To be sure, I have nothing against matrimony, but at the moment it would be a misfortune for me. Well, there is no other way; although it is absolutely untrue, I must at least avoid even the appearance of such a thing—even though this appearance rests on nothing but the fact that I am living here. People who do not come to the house cannot even tell whether I associate with her as much as with the rest of God's creatures, for the children seldom go out; indeed they go nowhere except to the theatre, where I never accompany them, as I am generally not at home when the play begins. We went to the Prater a few times, but the mother came too, and, as I was in the house, I could not refuse to accompany them. Nor had I at that time heard anything of these foolish rumours. I must also tell you that I was only allowed to pay *my own share*. Further, when the mother heard this talk herself and also heard it from me, she herself, let me tell you, objected to our going about together and advised me to move to another house in order to avoid further unpleasantness. For she said that she would not like to be the innocent cause of any misfortune to me. So this is the only reason why for some little time (since people began to gossip) I have been intending to leave. So far as truth goes, I have no reason, but these chattering tongues are driving me away. Were it not for these rumours, I should hardly think of leaving, for, although I could easily get a nicer room, I could hardly find such comfort and such friendly and obliging people. I will not say that, living in the same house with the Mademoiselle to whom people have already married me, I am ill-bred and do not speak to her; but I am not in love with her. I fool about and have fun with her when time permits (which is only in the evening when I take supper at home, for in the morning I write in my room and in the afternoon I am rarely in the house) and—that is all. If I had to marry all those with whom I have jested, I should have two hundred wives at least. Now for the money question. My pupil[1] remained three weeks in the country, so I made nothing, while my own expenses went on. Therefore I could not send you thirty ducats—only twenty. But as I was very hopeful about the subscriptions, I thought I would wait until I should be able to send you the promised sum. Countess Thun, however, has just told me that it is useless to think of subscriptions before the autumn, because all the people with money are in the country. So far she has only found ten subscribers and my pupil only seven. In the meantime I am

[1] Countess Rumbeke.

having six sonatas engraved. Artaria, the music engraver, has already discussed the matter with me.[1] As soon as they are sold and I get some money, I shall send it to you. I must beg my dear sister to forgive me for not having sent her a letter of congratulation on her name-day. A letter I began is lying on my desk. After I had begun it on Saturday, Countess Rumbeck sent her servant to say that they were all going to the country and would I not go with them? So, because I do not like to refuse anything to Cobenzl, I left the letter lying there, hastily put my things together and went with them. I thought to myself—my sister will not make a grievance of it. I now wish her in the octave of her name-day[2] every possible good and every blessing which a sincere and loving brother can wish his sister with his whole heart; and I kiss her most tenderly. I drove into Vienna today with the Count and tomorrow I am driving out with him again. Now farewell, dearest, most beloved father. Believe and trust your son, who cherishes the most kindly feelings towards all right-minded people. Why then should he not cherish them towards his dear father and sister? Believe in him and rely on him more than on certain individuals, who have nothing better to do than to slander honest folk. Well, adieu. I kiss your hands a thousand times and am ever your most obedient son

WOLFGANG AMADÈ MOZART

(418) Mozart to his Father

[Autograph in the Mozarteum, Salzburg]

MON TRÉS CHER PÉRE!   VIENNA, 1 *August* 1781

I fetched the sonata for four hands at once,[3] for Frau von Schindl lives just opposite the 'Auge Gottes'. If Madame Duschek happens to be in Salzburg, please give her my most friendly greetings and ask her whether, before she left Prague, a gentleman called on her and brought her a letter from me. If not, I shall write to him at once and tell him to forward it to Salzburg. This was Rossi of Munich, who asked me to help him with a letter of introduction. He took with him from here some excellent letters to Prague. If my letter only concerned his introduction, I should certainly let him dispose of it; but in it I also asked Mme Duschek to assist me in the matter of subscriptions for my six sonatas.[4] I was particularly glad to render this service to Rossi, as he has written the poem for the cantata which I want to produce for my benefit in Advent.[5]

Well, the day before yesterday Stephanie junior gave me a libretto to

---

[1] See p. 734, n. 2. They were published by Artaria and Co. in November 1781.
[2] 26 July.   [3] K. 358 [186c], composed in 1773–1774.
[4] See p. 734, n. 2.   [5] See p. 744, n. 2.

compose.[1] I must confess that, however badly he may treat other people, about which I know nothing, he is an excellent friend to me. The libretto is quite good. The subject is Turkish[2] and the title is: *Belmonte und Konstanze*, or *Die Verführung aus dem Serail*. I intend to write the overture, the chorus in Act I and the final chorus in the style of Turkish music. Mlle Cavalieri,[3] Mlle Teiber,[4] M. Fischer,[5] M. Adamberger,[6] M. Dauer[7] and M. Walter[8] are to sing in it. I am so delighted at having to compose this opera that I have already finished Cavalieri's first aria, Adamberger's aria and the trio which closes Act I. The time is short, it is true, for it is to be performed in the middle of September;[9] but the circumstances connected with the date of performance and, in general, all my other prospects stimulate me to such a degree that I rush to my desk with the greatest eagerness and remain seated there with the greatest delight. The Grand Duke of Russia[10] is coming here, and that is why Stephanie entreated me, if possible, to compose the opera in this short space of time. For the Emperor and Count Rosenberg are to return soon and their first question will be whether anything new is being prepared? Stephanie will then have the satisfaction of being able to say that Umlauf's opera,[11] on which he has been engaged for a long time, will soon be ready and that I am composing one for the occasion. And he will certainly count it a merit on my part to have undertaken to compose it for this purpose in so short a time. No one but Adamberger and Fischer knows anything about it yet, for Stephanie begged us to say nothing, as Count Rosenberg is still absent and any disclosure might easily lead to all kinds of gossip. Stephanie does not even wish to be regarded as too good a friend of mine; but he wants it to be

---

[1] The original text was by Christoph Friedrich Bretzner (1748–1807), a Leipzig merchant, whose light-opera libretti were very popular, several having been collected and published in 1779. *Belmonte und Constanze* was written in 1780, set to music by the successful operatic composer Johann André (1741–1799), and performed in May 1781 at the Döbbelin Theatre in Berlin. Gottlieb Stephanie, chiefly at Mozart's instigation, made considerable alterations and additions to this text. For a full discussion of this revision see Abert, vol. i. pp. 931 ff.

[2] Bretzner's text was not by any means an original work. Several opera libretti had already been written on subjects connected with life in a Turkish seraglio, notably Dancourt's *Pilgrimme von Mekka* (set to music by Gluck, 1764), Martinelli's *La schiava liberata* (set to music by Jommelli, 1768, and Schuster, 1777) and Grossmann's *Adelheid von Veltheim*, which appeared in 1780 and was set to music in 1780 by Neefe, who was Beethoven's teacher at Bonn.

[3] Katharina Cavalieri (1755–1801), an Austrian by birth, was trained in Vienna by Salieri. She made her first appearance in Italian opera in 1775. She took the part of Constanze.

[4] Therese Teiber (1760–1830), a daughter of the violinist Matthäus Teiber. She married Ferdinand Arnold, a well-known tenor. She took the part of Blonde.

[5] Johann Ignaz Ludwig Fischer (1745–1825), one of the finest bass singers of his day, who married the singer Barbara Strasser in 1779. He created the part of Osmin.

[6] See p. 723, n. 7. Adamberger took the part of Belmonte.

[7] Johann Ernst Dauer (1746–1812), a fine tenor and an excellent actor. He took the part of Pedrillo.

[8] Walter is not listed in the cast given in Letter 425★★.

[9] The first performance of the opera was on 16 July 1782.

[10] The Grand Duke Paul Petrovitch, afterwards Paul I.

[11] Probably *Das Irrlicht*, on C. F. Bretzner's libretto. This opera was performed in 1782. See *MM*, February 1919, p. 8.

thought that he is doing all this because Count Rosenberg desires it; and indeed the Count on his departure did actually order him to look around for a libretto, but no more.

Well, I have nothing more to tell you, for I have heard no news. The room into which I am moving is being got ready.[1] I am now going off to hire a clavier, for until there is one in my room, I cannot live in it, because I have so much to compose and not a minute must be lost. Indeed I shall miss a great many comforts in my new lodging—particularly in regard to meals. For whenever I had anything very urgent to finish, the Webers always delayed the meal for me as long as I chose; and I could go on writing *without dressing* and just go to table in the next room, both for lunch and supper; whereas now, when I wish to avoid spending money on having a meal brought to my room, I waste at least an hour dressing (which up to the present I have postponed until the afternoon) and must go out—particularly in the evening. You know that usually I go on composing until I am hungry. Well, the kind friends with whom I take supper sit down to table as early as eight or half past eight at latest. At the Webers' we never did so before ten o'clock. Well, adieu. I must close, for I must go out and find a clavier. Farewell. I kiss your hands a thousand times and embrace my dear sister with all my heart and am ever your most obedient son

WOLF: AMADÈ: MOZART

PS.—My greetings to all Salzburg.

(419) *Mozart to his Father*

[*Autograph in the Mozarteum, Salzburg*]

MON TRÈS CHER PÈRE!   VIENNA, 8 *August* 1781
I must write in haste, for I have only this very instant finished the Janissary chorus[2] and it is past twelve o'clock and I have promised to drive out at two o'clock sharp with the Auernhammers and Mlle Cavalieri to Mingendorf near Laxenburg, where the camp now is. Adamberger, Mlle Cavalieri and Fischer are exceedingly pleased with their arias. I lunched yesterday with Countess Thun and am to do so again tomorrow. I played to her what I have finished composing and she told me afterwards that she would venture her life that what I have so far written cannot fail to please. But on this point I pay no attention whatever to *anybody's praise or blame*—I mean, until people have heard and seen the work *as a whole*. I simply follow *my own feelings*. All the same you may judge from this how pleased she must have been to express herself so emphatically.

---

[1] This was not Am Graben no. 1175 (now no. 8), the lodging into which Mozart moved early in September, but a room in the house of Herr Auernhammer. See p. 759.
[2] In Act I.

As I have nothing of any consequence to write about, I will just tell you a shocking story; but perhaps you have heard it already. In Vienna it is called the Tyrolese tale. It particularly interests me, because when I was in Munich I knew intimately the unfortunate man concerned in it, who, moreover, used to come to see us here every day. His name is Herr von Wiedmer, and he is a nobleman. Whether it was owing to misfortunes or to a natural inclination for the stage, I know not, but some months ago he formed a theatrical company with whom he went to Innsbruck. One Sunday morning at about twelve o'clock this good fellow was strolling along the street very leisurely and some gentlemen were walking close behind him. One of them, Baron Buffa by name, kept on abusing the impresario, saying 'That idiot ought to teach his dancer to walk before he lets her go on the stage', using at the same time all sorts of epithets. Herr von Wiedmer, after listening to this for a while, naturally looked round at last, upon which Buffa asked him why he was looking at him. Wiedmer replied very good-humouredly: 'Why, you are looking at me as well. *The street is free, anyone can look round if he pleases*', and continued to walk ahead. Baron Buffa, however, went on abusing him, which in the end proved too much for the good man's patience, so that he asked Buffa for whom these remarks were intended. 'For you, you contemptible cur!' was the reply, accompanied by a violent box on the ear, which Herr von Wiedmer instantly returned with interest. Neither had a sword, or Wiedmer would certainly not have paid him back in his own coin. My friend went home very quietly in order to arrange his hair (for Baron Buffa had seized him by the hair as well) and he intended to bring the case before the President, Count Wolkenstein. But he found his house filled with soldiers, who took him off to the guard-room. Say what he would, it was of no avail and he was condemned to receive twenty-five lashes on his behind. At last he said: 'I am a nobleman and I will not submit to be beaten when I am innocent. I would rather enlist as a soldier in order to have my revenge.' For in Innsbruck the stupid Tyrolese custom evidently is that no one may hit a nobleman, no matter what right he may have to do so. Whereupon he was taken to gaol, where he had to receive not twenty-five, but fifty lashes. Before he lay down on the bench, he cried out: 'I am innocent and I appeal publicly to the Emperor'. But the corporal answered him with a sneer: 'Perhaps the gentleman will first take his fifty lashes and after that the gentleman can appeal'. It was all over in two hours—that is to say, at about two o'clock. After the fifth lash his breeches were torn already. I am amazed that he was able to stand it; and indeed he was carried away unconscious and was confined to bed for three weeks. As soon as he was cured, he came post-haste to Vienna, where he is anxiously awaiting the arrival of the Emperor, who has already been informed of the whole affair, not only by people here, but by his sister, the

Archduchess Elizabeth,[1] who is at Innsbruck. Wiedmer himself has a letter from her to the Emperor. On the day before this occurred the President had received orders to punish no one, whoever he might be, without first informing the authorities in Vienna—which makes the case still worse. The President must indeed be a very stupid and malicious dolt. But how can this man ever obtain adequate compensation? The lashes must always remain. If I were Wiedmer, I would demand the following satisfaction from the Emperor—that the President should receive fifty lashes on the same place and in my presence and, in addition, pay me 6000 ducats. And if I could not obtain this satisfaction I would accept no other; but at the very first opportunity I would run my sword through his heart. By the way, Wiedmer has already been offered 3000 ducats to stay away from Vienna and to hush up the affair. The people of Innsbruck speak of him as 'He who was scourged for us and who will also redeem us'. No one can bear the President, and his house has had to be guarded the whole time. There is a regular gospel about him in Vienna. Nothing else is being talked of. I feel very sorry for poor Wiedmer, for he is never well now and is always complaining of headaches and bad pains in his chest.

Now, farewell. I kiss your hands a thousand times and embrace my dear sister with all my heart and am ever your most obedient son

W. A: MZT

My greetings to the Duscheks, whom I hope to see in Vienna. Adieu.

(420) *Leopold Mozart to Breitkopf and Son, Leipzig*

[Extract]   [Autograph in the Staatsbibliothek Preussischer Kulturbesitz, West Berlin]

SALZBURG, 10 *August* 1781

★

As for my son, he is no longer in service in Salzburg. When we were in Munich, the Prince,[2] who was then in Vienna, commanded him to join him there. So he left Munich on March 12th and my daughter and I returned to Salzburg on the 14th. As His Grace the Prince treated my son extremely badly in Vienna and as, on the other hand, all the great noble families marked him out for their special favours, he was easily persuaded to resign a service to which a miserable salary was attached, and to remain in Vienna. As far as I know, six sonatas[3] for clavier and violin are being engraved in Vienna. Further, my son has been asked to compose an operetta which is to be performed in the middle of September. He has undertaken to do this, as the operetta is to celebrate the arrival of the Grand Duke of Russia.

[1] Archduchess Elizabeth (1743–1808), Maria Theresia's sixth child.
[2] i.e. the Archbishop of Salzburg.   [3] See p. 734, n. 2.

The six sonatas dedicated to Her Highness the Electress of the Bavarian Palatinate have been published by Herr Sieber [1] in Paris and can be bought from him. His address is: rue St. Honoré, à l'Hôtel d'Aligre, Ancien Grand Conseil. He took them from my son and gave him 15 louis d'or, thirty copies and full liberty in regard to their dedication. The opera my son wrote for Munich was 'Idomeneo'. The strange thing about it was that it was manufactured entirely by Salzburg people. The libretto was written by the Salzburg Court chaplain, Abbate Varesco, the music by my son, and Herr Schachtner did the German translation. People tried hard to persuade us to have the opera printed or engraved, the whole score or possibly a clavier arrangement. Subscribers, among whom was Prince Max von Zweibrücken and so forth, put down their names for about twenty copies. But my son's departure for Vienna and other attendant circumstances obliged us to postpone everything. I should add that 'Trois Airs Variés pour le clavecin ou le fortepiano' were also published in Paris by Herr Heina, rue de Seine, Faubourg St. Germain, à l'Hôtel de Lille, at the price of four livres. [2] But we haven't any copies left. Perhaps I ought to mention that my son never gives any compositions to be engraved or printed which are already in other hands. For we are very particular about having only one set of copies of every work; for this reason very little by him is known.   ★

(421) *Mozart to his Father*

[*Autograph in the Mozarteum, Salzburg*]

MON TRÉS CHER PÉRE!   VIENNA, 22 *August* 1781
    I cannot let you know the address of my new lodging, as I have not yet got one. [3] But I am bargaining about the prices of two, one of which I shall certainly take, as I cannot stay here next month and so must move out. It appears that Herr von Auernhammer wrote and told you that I had actually found a lodging! I had one, it is true, but what a habitation! fit for rats and mice, but not for human beings. At noon I had to look for the stairs with a lantern. The room was a little closet and to get to it I had to pass through the kitchen. In the door there was a tiny window and although they promised me to put up a curtain inside, they asked me at the same time to draw it back as soon as I was dressed, for otherwise they would not be able to see anything either in the kitchen or in the adjoining rooms. The owner's wife [4] herself called the house the rats' nest—in short,

----

[1] Jean Georges Sieber (1734–1822), the famous Paris publisher, who issued the six violin sonatas K. 301–306 [293a–c, 300c, 293d, 300l] as Opus I.
[2] The first edition of K. 180 [173c] (six variations on 'Mio caro Adone', composed in 1773), K. 179 [189a] (twelve variations on Fischer's minuet, composed in 1774) and K. 354 [299a] (twelve variations on 'Je suis Lindor', composed in 1778).   [3] See p. 756, n. 1.
[4] Frau Auernhammer.

it was a dreadful place to look at. Ah, what a splendid dwelling for me indeed, who have to receive visits from various distinguished people. The good man, of course, was only thinking of himself and his daughter, who is the greatest *seccatrice* I have ever met. As your last letter contains such a eulogy à la Count Daun of this family, I must really give you some account of them. I would have passed over in silence all you are going to read, regarding it as a matter of indifference and only as a private and personal *seccatura*, but, as your letter indicates that you place reliance on this family, I think myself bound to tell you frankly about their good and bad points. Well, he is the best-tempered fellow in the world—indeed, too much so, for his wife, the most stupid, ridiculous gossip imaginable, so rules the roost, that when she opens her mouth, he does not dare to say a word. As we have often gone out walking together, he has begged me not to mention before his wife that we had taken a fiacre or drunk a glass of beer. Well, I simply cannot have any confidence in a man who is so utterly insignificant in his own family. He is quite a good fellow and a very kind friend; and I could often lunch at his house. But it is not my habit to allow people to pay me for *my favours*—though indeed a midday plate of soup at lunch would be no payment. But people of that type think that it is! I do not go to their house for my own advantage, but *for theirs*, for I can see no profit for myself; and I have never yet met a single person there who would be worth mentioning in this letter. In short—they are decent people, but nothing more—people who have sense enough to see how useful an acquaintance with me is to their daughter who, as everyone says who heard her play before, has entirely changed since I have been teaching her. I will not attempt to describe the mother. Suffice it to say that when I am at table it is all I can do not to burst out laughing. Basta! You know Frau Adlgasser? Well, this *meuble* is even more aggravating, for she is *médisante* into the bargain—I mean, she is both stupid and malicious. Now for the daughter. If a painter wanted to portray the devil to the life, he would have to choose her face. She is as fat as a farm-wench, perspires so that you feel inclined to vomit, and goes about so scantily clad that really you can read as plain as print: '*Pray, do look here*'. True, there is enough to see, in fact, quite enough to strike one blind; but—one is thoroughly well punished for the rest of the day if one is unlucky enough to let one's eyes wander in that direction—tartar is the only remedy! So loathsome, dirty and horrible! Faugh, the devil! Well, I have told you how she plays, and also why she begged me to assist her. I am delighted to do people favours, provided they do not plague me incessantly. But she is not content if I spend a couple of hours with her every day. She wants me to sit there the whole day long—and, what is more, she tries to be attractive. But, what is worse still, she is *sérieusement* in love with me! I thought at first it was a joke, but now I know it to be a fact. When I noticed it—for

she took liberties with me—for example, she made me tender reproaches
if I came somewhat later than usual or could not stay so long, and more
nonsense of the same kind—I was obliged, not to make a fool of the girl,
to tell her the truth very politely. But that was no use: she became more
loving than ever. In the end I was always very polite to her except when
she started her nonsense—and then I was very rude. Whereupon she took
my hand and said: '*Dear Mozart, please don't be so cross. You may say what
you like, I am really very fond of you.*' Throughout the town people are
saying that we are to be married, and they are very much surprised at me,
I mean, that I have chosen such a face. She told me that when anything of
the kind was said to her, she always laughed at it; but I know from a
certain person that she confirmed the rumour, adding that we would then
travel together. That enraged me. So the other day I gave her my mind
pretty plainly and warned her not to abuse my kindness. Now I no longer
go there every day, but only every other day, and I shall gradually drop
it altogether. She is nothing but an amorous fool. For before she got to
know me, she once said in the theatre, on hearing me play: 'He is coming
to see me tomorrow and I shall play his variations to him in the very same
style'. On this account I did not go, because it was not only a conceited
speech, but a downright lie, as I had never heard a word about calling on
her the next day. Well, adieu, my paper is full. I have now finished the
first act of my opera.[1] I kiss your hands a thousand times and embrace my
sister with all my heart and am ever your obedient son

W: A: Mozart

(422) *Mozart to his Father*

[*Autograph in the Mozarteum, Salzburg*]

Mon très cher Père!   Vienna, 29 *August* 1781
    I will now reply to your questions. Herr von Asee is Herr von
Moll.[2] Madame Bernasconi gets 500 ducats from the management or, for
all I can tell, from the Emperor, but only for one year. I should add that
she grumbles and wishes she had left long ago; but that is only a *furberia
italiana*[3]—and just because she is grumbling, she is going to remain here.
Otherwise she would hardly have left London to come to Vienna.[4] For
one fine day she turned up, no one knows how or why. I believe that
Count Dietrichstein (Master of the Horse), who is her protector, knew
something about it beforehand, and that Gluck (who wanted to have his
French operas performed in German) also lent a hand. What is certain is

---

[1] *Die Entführung aus dem Serail.*
[2] See p. 752. Evidently Leopold Mozart had not realised that the word was in cypher.
[3] A piece of Italian knavery.
[4] Antonia Bernasconi (1741-1803) had been singing at the Italian Opera in London from
1778 until 1781.

that she was really forced on the Emperor. The great herd of the nobility are very much taken with her, but in his heart of hearts not the Emperor, who in fact is as little taken with her as he is with Gluck. Nor is she a favourite with the public. It is true that in great tragic parts she will always remain Bernasconi, but in operettas she is a total failure, as they no longer suit her. Moreover, as she herself admits, she is more Italian than German, and her accent on the stage is as thoroughly Viennese as it is in ordinary conversation. So now you can picture her to yourself. And when she occasionally tries to correct her accent, it is just as if you were to hear a princess declaim in a puppet-show. Her singing too is now so bad that no one will compose for her.[1] But that she may not draw her 500 ducats for nothing, the Emperor (with some difficulty) has been induced to have Gluck's 'Iphigenie' and 'Alceste' performed—the former in German, the latter in Italian.[2] I know nothing of Signor Righini's success. He makes a good deal of money by teaching, and last Easter he was successful with his cantata,[3] which was performed twice in succession and had good receipts on both occasions. He composes *very charmingly* and he is not by any means superficial; but he is a monstrous thief. He offers his stolen goods in such superfluity, in such profusion, that people can hardly digest them. As for the Dorotheans,[4] it is only gossip that is going round—nothing has happened—perhaps it will. The Emperor went off again for a fortnight, but has now returned.

We have had hardly any thunderstorms. At the most there were two, and they were very slight. But we have had terrible heat, so that everyone has been saying that never in his life has he endured anything like it.

The Grand Duke of Russia[5] is not coming until November, so I can write my opera more at leisure. I am delighted. I shall not have it performed before All Saints' Day, for that is the best time, as everyone returns from the country then.

I have now taken a very prettily furnished room in the Graben and shall be living there when you read this letter.[6] I purposely chose one not looking on the street in order to be quiet. Continue to address your letters to Peisser, for I shall always get them. But, if you do not send them through Hagenauer, you must enclose them in a cover and put his address on it. For I have all my letters addressed to him. As for Herr Duschek, I have already mentioned in a letter to his wife the price of the sonatas, which is three ducats.[7]

[1] Antonia Bernasconi was well past her prime.
[2] Gluck's *Iphigenie in Tauris* was given in German on 23 October 1781, and was followed by further performances of *Alceste* on 3 December and *Orfeo* in Italian on 31 December.
[3] *La Sorpresa Amorosa.*
[4] The Dorotheerkloster in Vienna, founded by Duke Albrecht II in the 14th century, was occupied from 1414 onwards by the Augustinerchorherren, and incorporated with Klosterneuburg in 1782.
[5] See p. 755, n. 10.   [6] See p. 756, n. 1.   [7] See p. 734, n. 2.

Well, adieu. I have no more news. I kiss your hands a thousand times and embrace my sister with all my heart and am ever your most obedient son

WOLFGANG AMADÈ MOZART

(423) Mozart to his Father

[*Autograph in the Mozarteum, Salzburg*]

MON TRÉS CHER PÈRE!   VIENNA, 5 *September* 1781

I am now writing to you in my *new room in the Graben, No. 1175, 3rd floor*. From the way in which you have taken my last letter—as if I were an arch-scoundrel or a blockhead or both!—I am sorry to see that you rely more on the gossip and scribblings of other people than you do on me—and that in fact you have no trust in me whatever. But I assure you that all this does not disturb me; people may write themselves blind —and you may believe them as much as you please—but I shall not alter by a hair's breadth; I shall remain the same honest fellow as ever. And I swear to you that if you had not wanted me to move into another lodging, I would not have left the Webers; for I feel just like a person who has left his own comfortable travelling carriage for a post-chaise. But not another word on the subject. It is really no use talking about it. For the nonsense which God knows who puts into your head always outweighs any reasons of mine. But one thing I do beg of you. When you write to me about something I have done, of which you disapprove or which you think might have been done better, and in reply I send you my ideas on the subject, please regard the whole matter as one between father and son alone, a secret, I mean, and something which is not to be told to others, as I myself always regard it. I therefore entreat you to leave it at that and not to apply to other people, for, by God, I will not give the smallest account to others of what I do or leave undone, no, not even to the Emperor himself. Do trust me always, for indeed I deserve it. I have trouble and worry enough here to support myself, and it therefore does not help me in the very least to read unpleasant letters. From the first moment I came here I have had to live entirely on my own means, that is, on what I could make by my own efforts. The others always drew their pay. Ceccarelli made more money than I did, but blew every penny of it in Vienna. If I had done the same, I should never have been in a position to quit the service. It is certainly not my fault, my dearest father, that you have not yet had any money from me; it is due to the present bad season. Only have patience—I, too, have to cultivate it. God knows that I shall never forget you! At the time of my affair with the Archbishop I wrote to you for clothes, for I had nothing with me but my black suit. The mourning was over, the weather was hot and my clothes did not arrive. So I had to have some made, as I could not go about Vienna like a tramp, particularly in the circumstances. My linen was a pitiful sight; no house-porter in Vienna wore shirts of such coarse linen as mine, which in a man is certainly the most objectionable thing. That meant more expense. I had only one pupil—and she stayed away for three weeks, which was a further loss for me. One must not make oneself cheap here—that is a cardinal point—or else one is done. Whoever is *most impertinent* has the best chance. From all your letters I gather that you believe that I do nothing but amuse myself. Well, you are most dreadfully mistaken. I can truthfully say that I have no pleasure—none whatever—save that of being away from Salzburg. I hope that all will go well in winter; and then, my most beloved father, I shall certainly not forget you. If I see that it is to my advantage, I shall remain here. If not, I am thinking of going straight to Paris—and I should like to have your opinion about this. Now farewell. I kiss your hands a thousand times and embrace my dear sister with all my heart and am ever your most obedient son

W: A: MZT

PS.—My compliments to the Duscheks. Please send me too when you can the aria I composed for Countess Baumgarten, the rondo for Mme Duschek and the one for Ceccarelli.[1] Adieu.

(424) *Mozart to his Father*

[Autograph in the Mozarteum, Salzburg]

MON TRÉS CHER PÉRE!   VIENNA, 12 *September* 1781

I have received your two letters, the one of the 5th through M. Marchall and the one of the 7th through the post—and, what is more, that of the 7th reached me before that of the 5th. Rust's serenade must have sounded very effective in the Rock Theatre,[2] particularly as the singers were seated and sang from their music, which would not have been practicable in a room or a hall. Really I have to laugh. People are always talking here about concerts to be given in honour of the Grand Duke[3] and—one fine day the Grand Duke will arrive—and we shall have no

---

[1] K. 369, 272 and 374.
[2] A natural grotto in the park of Schloss Hellbrunn, the summer residence of the Arch-bishop, about half an hour's drive from Salzburg.
[3] The Grand Duke Paul Petrovitch of Russia. See p. 755, n. 10.

Rock Theatre for him. Herr Lipp must have cut a nice figure before the great dignitaries, a little worse even than Haydn, if that were possible. The pluck which the latter displayed in the hospital grounds was of no little benefit to my health![1] I am dreadfully sorry for the poor unfortunate sufferers in Radstadt. Speaking of fire, I must tell you that the Magdalen Chapel in St. Stephen's Church has been blazing away the whole night. The smoke wakened the watchman at five o'clock in the morning, but until half past five not a soul came to extinguish it, and it was six o'clock and the fire was raging most fiercely before they brought water and hoses. The whole altar with all its decorations, and the chairs and everything in the chapel were burnt to ashes. They were obliged to drive the people with blows to assist in putting out the fire and, as scarcely anyone wanted to help, people in laced coats and embroidered waistcoats were seen lending a hand. It is said that no such disgraceful lack of organization has ever been seen since Vienna was a city. The Emperor is not here, of course. If only Daubrawaick[2] would come soon, so that I could have my music. Fräulein von Auernhammer is worrying me to death about the two double concertos.[3] We are now having one rehearsal after another in the theatre.[4] The ballet-master Antoine has been summoned from Munich, and supers are being recruited throughout Vienna and all its suburbs. There is still a sorry remnant of Noverre's ballet,[5] who, however, have not moved a leg for the last eight years and most of whom are like sticks. I think I mentioned the other day that Gluck's 'Iphigenie' is to be given in German and his 'Alceste' in Italian.[6] If only one of the two were to be performed, I should not mind, but both—that is very annoying for me. I will tell you why. The translator of 'Iphigenie' into German is an excellent poet,[7] and I would gladly have given him my Munich opera to translate.[8] I would have altered the part of Idomeneo completely and changed it to a bass part for Fischer.[9] In addition I would have made several other alterations and arranged it more in the French style. Mme Bernasconi, Adamberger and Fischer would have been delighted to sing it, but, as they now have two operas to study, and such exhausting ones, I am obliged to excuse them. Besides, a third opera would be too much.

I must now hurry off to Marchall (for I have promised to introduce him to Count Cobenzl), or I shall be too late. Now farewell. I kiss your hands

---

[1] i.e. made me laugh heartily.
[2] Johann Anton Daubrawa von Daubrawaick, Court Councillor in Salzburg.
[3] See p. 748, n. 3.
[4] For Mozart's opera Die Entführung aus dem Serail.
[5] Noverre had left Vienna for good in 1774 to take up his appointment as maître des ballets en chef to the Paris Opéra. Hence Mozart's statement is a slight exaggeration.
[6] See p. 762.
[7] Johann Baptist von Alxinger (1755–1797), a young Viennese poet. Gluck helped with the translation.
[8] Evidently Mozart was not altogether satisfied with Schachtner's translation of his Idomeneo.
[9] See p. 698, n 2.

a thousand times and embrace my sister with all my heart and am ever your most obedient son

W: A: Mozart

PS.—My greetings to all my good friends. A kiss to Marchand.

(425) *Mozart to his Sister*

[*Autograph in the Mozarteum, Salzburg*]

MA TRES CHERE SOEUR!   VIENNA, 19 *September* 1781

I gather from our dear father's last letter that you are ill, which causes me no little sorrow and anxiety. I see that for a fortnight you have been drinking waters, so you must have been ill for a long time—and yet I never heard a word about it. Well, I am going to be quite frank with you about your constantly recurring indispositions. Believe me, dearest sister, that I am quite serious when I say that the best cure for you would be a husband—and if only because marriage would have such a profound influence on your health, I wish with all my heart that you could marry soon. In your last letter you scolded me, but not as much as I deserved. I am ashamed when I think of it—and the only excuse I can offer is that I started to write to you the moment I received your last letter but one, and then—left it unfinished! In the end I tore it up. For the time has not yet arrived for me to be able to give you *more definite and comforting news*, although I hope to be able to do so soon. Now listen to my suggestions. You know that I am composing an opera. Those portions which I have finished have won extraordinary applause on all sides. I know this nation —and I have reason to think that my opera will be a success. If it is, then I shall be as popular in Vienna as a composer as I am on the clavier. Well, when I have got through this winter, I shall know better how I stand, and I have no doubt that my circumstances will be favourable. For you and d'Yppold there are scarcely any—indeed, I may say with certainty—no prospects in Salzburg. But could not d'Yppold manage to get something *here*? I suppose he is not *absolutely* penniless? Ask him about it—and if he thinks the project at all practicable, he has only to tell me what steps to take, and I will certainly do my utmost, for I take the greatest interest in this affair. If this were accomplished, you could certainly marry; for, believe me, you could earn a great deal of money in Vienna for example, by playing at private concerts and by giving lessons. You would be very much in demand—and you would be well paid. In that case my father would have to resign his post and come too—and we could live very happily together again. I see no other solution—and even before I knew that your affair with d'Yppold was serious, I had something like this in mind for you. Our dear father was the only difficulty, for I wanted him to enjoy his rest and not to have to worry and torment himself. But I think that in this way it might be arranged. For with your husband's earnings, your own and mine, we can easily manage, and enable our father to live in peace and comfort. Do talk this over soon with d'Yppold and let me know at once what you would like me to do, for the sooner I begin to arrange matters, the better. I can do most through the Cobenzls—but d'Yppold must write and let me know how and what.

M. Marchall sends his greetings to you—and particularly to M. d'Yppold, whom he thanks most warmly for his great kindness to him on his departure. Well, I must close, for I have still to write to Papa. Farewell, dearest sister! I hope to have better news of your health in Papa's next letter—and to have it confirmed soon by your own hand. Adieu. I kiss you a thousand times and am ever your brother who will always love you with all his heart

W. A. MOZART

You will probably have not been able to read this letter, for my pen is a wretched one. Please give my most cordial greetings to M. d'Yppold and tell him to count on my true friendship. My greetings to Katherl and all my good friends. Adieu. I have asked you to address your letters to Peisser. But, if you do, you will have to put each letter into a separate cover and then it will immediately cost sixteen kreuzers. So perhaps you had better direct them as usual: *Auf dem Peter, im Auge Gottes; 2nd floor.* This address is so well known at the post office that even when a letter has arrived in Vienna with only my name on it, it has been delivered to me. If you do this, I shall certainly receive your letters. Adieu.

PS.—My greetings to all Salzburg.[1]

(425*) *Mozart to his Father*

[*Autograph in a private collection*[2]]

MON TRÉS CHER PÉRE!   [VIENNA, *before 26 September* 1781]
Forgive me if you have to pay a little more for the letter this time. But I wanted to give you some idea at least of the first act, so that you may judge what the whole opera will be like—and I could not have done it with less. I hope that your fits of dizziness will soon cease. You gave me rather a fright about my sister, because it was so unexpected. I do hope that she is better now. I kiss her a thousand times and kiss your hands a hundred times and am ever your most obedient son

W. A. MZT

---

[1] This postscript was previously thought to belong to Letter 422.
[2] The verso of the sheet bears a copy in Constanze Weber's handwriting of Constanze's aria in *Die Entführung* 'Ach, ich liebte, war so glücklich'.

(425**) Mozart to his Father

[*Autograph in the possession of the late S. L. Courtauld, Southern Rhodesia*]

[VIENNA, *before* 26 *September* 1781 [1]]

I am sending you a little foretaste of the opera, as I have nothing new and urgent to write about—The characters are:

	An Actor
Bassa Selim—Herr Jautz	He has nothing to sing
Konstanze, beloved by Belmont.	Mlle Cavalieri
Blonde, maid to Konstanze.	Mlle Teiber.
Belmont.—	Herr Adamberger
Pedrillo, servant to Belmont and steward of the Pasha's gardens.	Herr Dauer.
Osmin, steward of the Pasha's country house.	Herr Fischer.
A rude fellow.	*Bass*

Please send the concertos soon.

(426) Mozart to his Father

[*Autograph in the Koch Collection, Basel*]

MON TRÉS CHER PÉRE!   VIENNA, 26 *September* 1781

Forgive me for having made you pay an extra heavy postage fee the other day. But I happened to have nothing important to tell you and thought that it would afford you pleasure if I gave you some idea of my opera. As the original text began with a monologue,[2] I asked Herr Stephanie to make a little arietta out of it—and then to put in a duet instead of making the two chatter together after Osmin's short song.[3] As we have given the part of Osmin to Herr Fischer, who certainly has an excellent bass voice (in spite of the fact that the Archbishop told me that he sang too low for a bass and that I assured him that he would sing higher next time), we must take advantage of it, particularly as he has the whole Viennese public on his side. But in the original libretto Osmin has only this short song and nothing else to sing, except in the trio and the finale; so he has been given an aria in Act I, and he is to have another in Act II. I have explained to Stephanie the words I require for the aria[4]—indeed I

---

[1] The date on this autograph has been added in a later hand. See *Music and Letters*, vol. xxxv, April 1954, where this letter was first published with commentary by Emily Anderson.

[2] In the original text by C. F. Bretzner. See p. 755, n. 1.

[3] It is worthy of note that the part of Osmin, which in Bretzner's libretto is negligible, was transformed by Mozart in collaboration with Stephanie into the towering figure in *Die Entführung*. Possibly Mozart was encouraged to do this as he was composing for a magnificent singer.

[4] 'Solche hergelaufne Laffen' in Act I.

had finished composing most of the music for it before Stephanie knew anything whatever about it. I am enclosing only the beginning and the end, which is bound to have a good effect. Osmin's rage is rendered comical by the use of the Turkish music. In working out the aria I have (in spite of our Salzburg Midas)[1] allowed Fischer's beautiful deep notes to glow. The passage 'Drum beim Barte des Propheten' is indeed in the same tempo, but with quick notes; and as Osmin's rage gradually increases, there comes (just when the aria seems to be at an end) the allegro assai, which is in a totally different metre and in a different key; this is bound to be very effective. For just as a man in such a towering rage oversteps all the bounds of order, moderation and propriety and completely forgets himself, so must the music too forget itself. But since passions, whether violent or not, must never be expressed to the point of exciting disgust, and as music, even in the most terrible situations, must never offend the ear, but must please the listener, or in other words must never cease to be *music*, so I have not chosen a key foreign to F (in which the aria is written) but one related to it—not the nearest, D minor, but the more remote A minor. Let me now turn to Belmonte's aria in A major, 'O wie ängstlich, o wie feurig'. Would you like to know how I have expressed it—and even in-dicated his throbbing heart? By the two violins playing octaves. This is the favourite aria of all those who have heard it, and it is mine also. I wrote it expressly to suit Adamberger's voice. You see the trembling—the faltering—you see how his throbbing breast begins to swell; this I have expressed by a crescendo. You hear the whispering and the sighing—which I have indicated by the first violins with mutes and a flute playing in unison.

The Janissary chorus is, as such, all that can be desired, that is, short, lively and written to please the Viennese. I have sacrificed Constanze's aria a little to the flexible throat of Mlle Cavalieri, 'Trennung war mein banges Los und nun schwimmt mein Aug' in Tränen'. I have tried to express her feelings, as far as an Italian bravura aria will allow it. I have changed the 'Hui' to 'schnell', so it now runs thus—'Doch wie schnell schwand meine Freude'. I really don't know what our German poets are thinking of. Even if they do not understand the theatre, or at all events operas, yet they should not make their characters talk as if they were addressing a herd of swine. Hui, sow!

Now for the trio at the close of Act I. Pedrillo has passed off his master as an architect—to give him an opportunity of meeting his Constanze in the garden. Bassa Selim has taken him into his service. Osmin, the steward, knows nothing of this, and being a rude churl and a sworn foe to all strangers, is impertinent and refuses to let them into the garden. It opens quite abruptly—and because the words lend themselves to it, I have made

[1] i.e. the Archbishop.

it a fairly respectable piece of real three-part writing. Then the major key begins at once pianissimo—it must go very quickly—and wind up with a great deal of noise, which is always appropriate at the end of an act. The more noise the better, and the shorter the better, so that the audience may not have time to cool down with their applause.

I have sent you only fourteen bars of the overture, which is very short with alternate fortes and pianos, the Turkish music always coming in at the fortes. The overture modulates through different keys; and I doubt whether anyone, even if his previous night has been a sleepless one, could go to sleep over it. Now comes the rub! The first act was finished more than three weeks ago, as was also one aria in Act II and the drunken duet [1] (*per i signori viennesi*) which consists entirely of *my Turkish tattoo*. But I cannot compose any more, because the whole story is being altered —and, to tell the truth, at my own request. At the beginning of Act III there is a charming quintet or rather finale, but I should prefer to have it at the end of Act II.[2] In order to make this practicable, great changes must be made, in fact an entirely new plot must be introduced—and Stephanie is up to the eyes in other work. So we must have a little patience. Everyone abuses Stephanie. It may be that in my case he is only very friendly to my face. But after all he is arranging the libretto for me—and, what is more, as I want it—exactly—and, by Heaven, I do not ask anything more of him. Well, how I have been chattering to you about my opera! But I cannot help it. Please send me the march[3] which I mentioned the other day.[4] Gilowsky says that Daubrawaick will soon be here. Fräulein von Auernhammer and I are longing to have the two double concertos.[5] I hope we shall not wait as vainly as the Jews for their Messiah. Well, adieu. Farewell. I kiss your hands a thousand times and embrace with all my heart my dear sister, whose health, I hope, is improving, and am ever your most obedient son

W: A: MOZART

(427) *Mozart to his Father*

[*Autograph in the Mozarteum, Salzburg*]

MON TRÉS CHER PÉRE!   VIENNA, 6 *October* 1781

I have so far always received your letters on Mondays and have been accustomed to reply to them on Wednesdays; but the other day I did not receive your letter until Wednesday and, what is more, it arrived so late

[1] The duet between Pedrillo and Osmin, 'Vivat Bacchus, Bacchus lebe'.
[2] This is the quartet at the end of Act II, 'Ach Belmonte! ach— mein Leben!'
[3] Possibly K. 249, written in 1776 for the wedding of Elizabeth Haffner to F. X. Späth, for which Mozart also composed K. 250 [248b], the Haffner serenade.
[4] The letter in which Mozart made this request has unfortunately been lost.
[5] See p. 748, n. 3.

in the afternoon that I hadn't time to write to you. Meanwhile you will have received the description of the music of my opera. The day after I got your letter I went to see Herr von Scharf himself at the Post Office, had a word with him and gave him my address, so that he should send me the music at once. For I simply cannot bring myself to walk out to Leopoldstadt or spend a zwanziger[1] to drive out there just to please young Herr von Mayer. However, he has not yet arrived. Moreover, Herr von Scharf too knows nothing whatever about the arrival of his father-in-law, which is supposed to be so imminent. There was a rumour that the Archbishop intended to come here this month (with a numerous suite, too), but people are now contradicting it. As for Ceccarelli, I am quite sure that he will be appointed, for indeed I don't know where the Archbishop could find a better castrato *for the money*. Perhaps you already know what happened to the Alumni who were travelling to Strassburg—on their arrival there? Why, they were actually refused permission to pass through the gates of the town, because they looked not only like beggars but scamps. Herr von Auernhammer told me that he heard this from the cousin of the person to whom they had an introduction, adding that he said to them: 'Well, my dear young men, you will have to stay in my house for four or five days, so that first of all I may have you decently dressed. For you cannot go out as you are, without running the risk of having street-urchins running after you and pelting you with mud.' A nice testimonial to His Grace the Prince! I must now carry out a commission and put a question to you, exactly as it was put to me:—Who were the Counts von Klessheim? *And what has become of them?* Schmidt, my cousin's[2] poor, unfortunate adorateur, who is now in Trattner's[3] bookshop, begged me most urgently to obtain some information for him on the point.

Well, I am beginning to lose patience at not being able to go on writing my opera. True, I am composing other things in the meantime—yet—all my enthusiasm is for my opera, and what would at other times require fourteen days to write I could now do in four. I composed in one day Adamberger's aria in A, Cavalieri's in B♭ and the trio, and copied them out in a day and a half.[4] At the same time nothing would be gained if the whole opera were finished, for it would have to lie there until Gluck's two

---

[1] i.e. twenty pfennigs.

[2] Maria Anna Thekla Mozart, the 'Bäsle'.

[3] Johann Thomas Edler von Trattner (1717–1798) owned an important printing and bookselling business in Vienna and other cities. His second wife, Therese Edle von Trattner (1758–1793), was an excellent clavier-player. She became a pupil and an intimate friend of Mozart, who dedicated to her his clavier sonata in C minor, K. 457, written in 1784, and his clavier Fantasia in the same key, K. 475, written in 1785. Nottebohm, p. 131, quotes a statement of Constanze Mozart according to which Mozart is supposed to have written to Frau von Trattner 'two interesting letters about music'. Niemetschek, p. 59, mentions one letter. There is no trace of these valuable documents.

[4] All in Act I.

operas [1] were ready—and there is still an enormous amount in them which the singers have to study. Moreover, Umlauf has been obliged to wait with his opera,[2] which is ready and which took him a whole year to write. But (between ourselves) you must not believe that the opera is any good, just because it took him a whole year. I should have thought (again between ourselves) that it was the work of fourteen or fifteen days, particularly as the fellow must have learnt so many operas *by heart*, and all he had to do was to sit down—and that is precisely how he composed it—you notice it at once when you hear it! That reminds me, I must tell you that he invited me to his house in the most polite manner (*c'est-à-dire*, in his own manner) that I might hear his opera, adding: 'You must not think that it is worth your while to hear it—I have not got as far as you have, but indeed I do my best'. I heard afterwards that he said: 'It's quite certain that Mozart has a devil in his head, his limbs and his fingers—why, he played off my opera (which I have written out so disgracefully that I myself can hardly read it) as if he had composed it himself.' Well, adieu. I hope that my dear sister, whom I embrace with all my heart, will gradually recover. And you, my dear father—get some cart-grease, wrap it in a bit of paper and wear it on your chest. Take the bone of a leg of veal and wrap it up in paper with a kreuzer's worth of leopard's bane and carry it in your pocket. I am sure that this will cure you. Farewell. I kiss your hands a thousand times and am ever your most obedient son

W. A. Mozart

(428) *Mozart to his Father*

[Autograph in the Mozarteum, Salzburg]

Mon très cher Père!   Vienna, 13 *October* 1781
    Fräulein von Auernhammer and I thank you for the concertos.[3] M. Marchall brought young Herr von Mayer to my room yesterday morning and in the afternoon I drove out and fetched my things. M. Marchall has hopes of becoming tutor in the family of Count Jean Esterházy; Count Cobenzl has given him a written recommendation to the Count. He said to me: 'J'ai donné une lettre à Monsieur votre protégé', and when he saw Marchall again, he said to him: 'D'abord que j'aurai de réponse, je le dirai à M. Mozart, votre protecteur'.
    Now as to the libretto of the opera. You are quite right so far as Stephanie's work is concerned. Still, the poetry is perfectly in keeping with the character of stupid, surly, malicious Osmin. I am well aware that

---

[1] *Iphigenie in Tauris* and *Alceste*.   [2] Probably *Das Irrlicht*. See p. 755, n. 11.
[3] See p. 748, n. 4.

the verse is not of the best, but it fitted in and it agreed so well with the musical ideas which already were buzzing in my head, that it could not fail to please me; and I would like to wager that when it is performed, no deficiencies will be found. As for the poetry which was there originally, I really have nothing to say against it. Belmonte's aria 'O wie ängstlich' could hardly be better written for music. Except for 'Hui' and 'Kummer ruht in meinem Schoss' (for sorrow—cannot rest), the aria too is not bad, particularly the first part. Besides, I should say that in an opera the poetry must be altogether the obedient daughter of the music. Why do Italian comic operas please everywhere—in spite of their miserable libretti— even in Paris, where I myself witnessed their success? Just because there the music reigns supreme and when one listens to it all else is forgotten. Why, an opera is sure of success when the plot is well worked out, the words written solely for the music and not shoved in here and there to suit some miserable rhyme (which, God knows, never enhances the value of any theatrical performance, be it what it may, but rather detracts from it)—I mean, words or even entire verses which ruin the composer's whole idea. Verses are indeed the most indispensable element for music—but rhymes—solely for the sake of rhyming—the most detrimental. Those high and mighty people who set to work in this pedantic fashion will always come to grief, both they and their music. The best thing of all is when a good composer, who understands the stage and is talented enough to make sound suggestions, meets an able poet, that true phoenix; in that case no fears need be entertained as to the applause even of the ignorant. Poets almost remind me of trumpeters with their professional tricks! If we composers were always to stick so faithfully to our rules (which were very good at a time when no one knew better), we should be concocting music as unpalatable as their libretti.

Well, I think I have chattered enough nonsense to you; so I must now enquire about what interests me most of all, and that is, your health, my most beloved father! In my last letter I suggested two remedies for giddiness, which, if you do not know them, you will probably not think any good. But I have been assured that they would certainly have a splendid effect; and the pleasure of thinking that you might recover made me believe this assurance so entirely that I could not refrain from suggesting them with my heart's wishes and with the sincere desire that you may not need them—but that if you do use them, you will recover completely. I trust that my sister is improving daily. I kiss her with all my heart and, my dearest, most beloved father, I kiss your hands a thousand times and am ever your most obedient son

W. A. MOZART

As soon as I receive the watch, I shall return yours. Adieu.

(429) *Mozart to his Cousin, Maria Anna Thekla Mozart, Augsburg*

[Autograph formerly in the possession of Richard Strauss]

MA TRÈS CHÈRE COUSINE!   [VIENNA, 23 *October* 1781]

I had been hungering all this long time for a letter from you, dearest cousin—wondering what it would be like—and it proved to be exactly what I had imagined. For after once letting three months elapse, I should never have written again—even if the executioner had stood behind me with his naked sword. For I should not have known how, when, where, why and what? I simply had to wait for your letter.

As you doubtless know, several important things have happened to me in the meantime, in connexion with which I have had to do a good deal of thinking and have had a great amount of vexation, worry, trouble and anxiety, which indeed may serve to excuse my long silence. As for all the other things, let me tell you that the gossip which people have been so kind as to circulate about me, is partly true and partly false. That is all I can say at the moment. But let me add, in order to set your mind at rest, that I never do anything without a reason—and, what is more, without a well-founded reason. If you had shown more confidence and friendship and had applied to me direct (and not to others—and what is more . . . !). But silence. If you had addressed yourself direct to me, you would certainly have heard more than everyone else—and, possibly, more than —I myself! But—Well, I was nearly forgetting. Be so kind, dearest, most beloved cousin, as to deliver immediately, in person, the enclosed letter to Herr Stein,[1] and ask him to answer it at once or at any rate to tell you what you should write to me about it. For I hope that our correspondence, dear little cousin, will now start off again! That is, if our letters do not cost you too much! If, as I hope, you honour me with a reply, be so gracious as to address your letter as you did the other day, namely, *Auf dem Peter, im Auge Gottes, 2nd floor*. True, I no longer live there, but the address is so well known at the post office, that when a letter is addressed to my new lodging, it is held up for a day or two.

Now farewell, dearest, most beloved cousin! Keep me in your friendship which is so precious to me. Be completely assured of my friendship. I am ever, ma trés chére cousine, your most sincere cousin and friend,

WOLFGANG AMADÈ MOZART

My greetings to your father and mother and also to Fräulein Juliana.[2] Mme Weber and her three daughters[3] send their greetings to you—

[1] Johann Andreas Stein (see p. 274, n.1.). There is no trace of this letter.
[2] Probably Maria Juliana Creszentia Mozart, a cousin of the 'Bäsle'.
[3] Josefa, Constanze and Sophie.

and she asks you to do her a favour. Herr Bartholomei, the bookseller (whom no doubt you know), asked for the portrait of Aloysia,[1] who is now Mme Lange, in order to have an engraving made. Well, it will be two years next March and we have heard nothing either about the portrait or about the payment for it—and its return was promised for last March. So Mme Weber requests you to make a few enquiries, as she would like to know what she ought to do. I should add that it is the same portrait which Baron Götz had in Munich. I think that you too have seen it. So it is very bad of him to have given it into strange hands without saying a word about it. Adieu, ma chère, write to me soon.
Vienna, 23 October 1781

(430) *Mozart to his Father*

[*Autograph in the Mozarteum, Salzburg*]

MON TRÉS CHER PÉRE!   VIENNA, 24 *October* 1781
    I have had no letter from you today, most beloved father—and my only consolation is the thought that probably you have had no time to write. Many thanks for the two divertimenti[2] and the cuffs, which I have received safely. I was not at home when young Daubrawaick called, and he would not entrust the watch to the people in the house. I shall fetch it myself some day soon and at the same time give him yours in exchange. I hear that Daubrawaick is staying here for two months, but this time he is not lodging in Trattner's house. I can't write very much to you at the moment, as I have still to write to my cousin and to Herr Stein at Augsburg; for Count Czernin has asked me to order a pianoforte for his wife. A propos, do you know that Count Czernin . . . I wish . . . I should not like . . .[3] The first performance of 'Iphigenie'[4] took place yesterday, but I wasn't there, for whoever wanted to get a seat in the parterre had to be at the theatre by four o'clock, so I preferred to stay away. I tried to get a reserved seat in the third circle six days beforehand, but they were all gone. However, I was at nearly all the rehearsals. Well, I must close. I trust that both you, my most beloved father, and my dear sister are in good health. Praise and thanks be to God, I am too. I kiss your hands a thousand times and embrace my sister with all my heart and am ever, mon trés cher pére, your most obedient son

                                                    W: A: MOZART

[1] There is no trace of this portrait.
[2] Probably K. 247 and 287 [271H]. See p. 749, n. 3.
[3] In the first case two lines, in the second and third cases several words have been blotted out, probably by Leopold Mozart.
[4] Gluck's *Iphigenie in Tauris.*

(431) *Mozart to his Father*

[*Autograph in the Mozarteum, Salzburg*]

MON TRÈS CHER PÈRE!   VIENNA, 3 *November* 1781

Please forgive me for not having acknowledged by the last post the receipt of the cadenzas,[1] for which I thank you most submissively. It happened to be my name-day,[2] so I performed my devotions in the morning, and just as I was going to write to you, a whole crowd of congratulating friends literally besieged me. At twelve o'clock I drove out to Baroness Waldstädten[3] at Leopoldstadt, where I spent my name-day. At eleven o'clock at night I was treated to a serenade performed by two clarinets, two horns and two bassoons—and that too of my own composition[4]—for I wrote it for St. Theresa's Day,[5] for Frau von Hickel's sister, or rather the sister-in-law of Herr von Hickel, Court Painter,[6] at whose house it was performed for the first time. The six gentlemen who executed it are poor beggars who, however, play quite well together, particularly the first clarinet and the two horns. But the chief reason why I composed it was in order to let Herr von Strack, who goes there every day, hear something of my composition; so I wrote it rather carefully. It has won great applause too and on St. Theresa's Night it was performed in three different places; for as soon as they finished playing it in one place, they were taken off somewhere else and paid to play it. Well, these musicians asked that the street door might be opened and, placing themselves in the centre of the courtyard, surprised me, just as I was about to undress, in the most pleasant fashion imaginable with the first chord in Eb. I shall add the second piano part to the cadenzas and return them to you.

It would be a very good thing if my opera were ready, for Umlauf cannot produce his at present, because both Mme Weiss and Mlle Schindler are ill. I must go off to Stephanie at once, for he has sent word at last that he has something ready for me.

I have no news whatever to give you, for small matters are not likely to interest you and important ones you surely know quite as well as we Viennese. There is now a Dauphin[7]—a small thing, I admit, until it becomes a big one—I am telling you this so that the Duc d'Artois may

---

[1] Probably the cadenzas for K. 365 [316a], Mozart's concerto for two claviers. See p. 748, n. 3.   [2] October 31st.

[3] Martha Elizabeth, Baroness von Waldstädten, *née* von Schäfer (1744–1811). She was separated from her husband and lived at Leopoldstadt, no. 360. She was an excellent performer on the clavier and became a friend and patroness of Mozart.

[4] K. 375, a serenade composed in October 1781.   [5] October 15th.

[6] Joseph Hickel (1736–1807) studied in Vienna and in 1768 was sent to Italy by the Empress Maria Theresia. On his return he did a portrait of Joseph II and was appointed in 1772 Court Painter to the Emperor.

[7] Louis Joseph Xavier François, born on 22 October 1781. He died on 4 June 1789.

not have all the credit of a bon mot. For when during her pregnancy the Queen complained one day that the Dauphin was causing her great inconvenience and said: 'Il me donne de grands coups de pied au ventre', the Duke replied: 'O Madame, laissez-le venir dehors; qu'il me donnera de grands coups de pied au cul'. Well, the day the news arrived all the theatres and shows in Vienna were free.

It is striking three, so I must hurry off to Stephanie, or I may miss him and then have to wait again. I hope that every day you will feel better and my dear sister too, whom I embrace with all my heart. Farewell. I kiss your hands a thousand times and am ever your most obedient son

W: A: MOZART

(432) *Mozart to his Father*

[Autograph in the Mozarteum, Salzburg]

MON TRÉS CHER PÉRE! VIENNA, 10 *November* 1781

I thank you a thousand times for your congratulations on my name-day, and send you mine for St. Leopold's Day.[1] Dearest, most beloved father! I wish you every imaginable good that one can possibly wish. Nay rather, I wish nothing for you, but everything for myself. So I wish for my own sake that you may continue to enjoy good health, and that you may live many, many years for my happiness and my infinite pleasure. I wish for my own sake that everything I do and undertake may be in accordance with your desire and pleasure, or rather that I may never do anything which may not cause you the very greatest joy. I hope it may be so, for whatever contributes to your son's happiness must naturally be agreeable to you.

Herr von Auernhammer, in whose house I am writing, his wife and the two young ladies also send you their congratulations.

At the play the other day I was talking to Gschwendner, who told me that Frau Späth[2] has died. I hope that I may perhaps hear from you tomorrow whether this news is true or false.

The Duke of Wurtemberg[3] is expected today, so tomorrow there is to be a Redoute and on the 25th there is to be a public Redoute at Schönbrunn. But people are extremely embarrassed about this, for, according to general report, the Grand Duke will only stay ten days, and the festival of St. Catherine, which the ball is to celebrate, falls according to the Greek

[1] November 15th.
[2] Marie Elizabeth Haffner, daughter of Sigmund Haffner, merchant and burgomaster of Salzburg, for whose marriage to F. X. Späth, 22 July 1776, Mozart composed a march, K. 249, and a serenade, K. 250 [248b].
[3] The visitors were Duke Friedrich Eugen of Wurtemberg and his wife, his daughter Princess Elizabeth, who was betrothed to the Archduke Francis, and his son Prince Ferdinand. They arrived in Vienna on November 11th.

calendar on December 6th. So no one knows yet what will be done. Now for another comical tale. The Emperor commanded each of the actors to select a part in which to appear before the Grand Duke. Lange[1] applied for that of Hamlet, but Count Rosenberg, who does not like Lange, said that this could not be, because Brockmann[2] had been playing that part for ages. When this was repeated to Brockmann, he went to Rosenberg and told him that he could not appear in the part and that the play could not be performed at all. And why? *Because the Grand Duke himself was Hamlet.*[3] The Emperor (it is said—it is said—it is said) on hearing this sent Brockmann fifty ducats. Now I have no more news. I thank you again a thousand times and renew my wishes. I shall write to my sister very soon. I kiss your hands a thousand times and embrace my dear sister with all my heart and am ever your most obedient son

W: A: Mozart

PS.—My thanks and greetings to all who sent me their congratulations. A propos. Is it true that the Elector of Bavaria is dying?[4] Adieu.

(433) *Mozart to his Father*

[Autograph in the Mozarteum, Salzburg]

Mon très cher Père!   Vienna, 17 *November* 1781

I have received your letter of the 6th. In regard to Ceccarelli, it is quite impossible even for a single night; for I have only one room, which is not large and is so crammed already with my wardrobe, table and clavier that really I do not know where I could put another bed—and as for sleeping in one bed—that I shall only do with my future wife. But I shall look about for as cheap a lodging as possible, provided I know precisely when he is to arrive. I have not seen Countess Schönborn at all this time. I had not the heart to call and I still feel just the same. *I know her through and through.* She would most certainly say something which I should probably not swallow without retorting, and it is always better to avoid such incidents. In any case she knows that I am here; and if she wants to see me, she can send for me. Czernin could not get the hang of the Mölk affair and asked him at a public dinner whether he had any news of his brother, the Court Councillor? Mölk was taken aback and could not reply. I would certainly have given him some answer. He was corrupted

---

[1] Josef Lange, who had married as his second wife Aloysia Weber. See p. 733, n. 2.

[2] Hieronymus Brockmann, a popular actor.

[3] A popular comparison at the time. After the death of his father, Peter III, and the establishment of his mother, Catherine, as sole ruler of Russia, the Grand Duke Paul, feeling that his rights had been usurped and that he had no part to play in the government of his country, fell into a state of melancholy.

[4] The Elector of Bavaria lived until 1799.

in a house which you frequented a great deal.[1] I shall look up the Kletzl family as soon as possible. Well, I have at last got something to work at for my opera. Indeed, if we were always to trust and believe tale-bearers, how often should we injure ourselves! I simply cannot tell you how people abused Stephanie junior to me. I really became quite uneasy about him, and if I had acted as I was advised, I should have transformed a good friend into an enemy who might have done me a great deal of harm; and all this without any just cause.

Yesterday at three o'clock in the afternoon the Archduke Maximilian[2] sent for me. When I went in, he was standing near the stove in the first room and was waiting for me. He came up to me at once and asked me if I had anything particular to do that day. I replied: 'Nothing whatever, your Royal Highness; and if I had, I should still consider it a favour to be allowed to wait on your Royal Highness'. 'No, no,' he said, 'I refuse to inconvenience anyone.' He then told me that he was intending to give a concert that very evening to the visitors from Wurtemberg[3] and suggested that I should play and accompany the arias, adding that I was to come back at six o'clock when all the guests would be assembled. So I played there yesterday. When God gives a man a sacred office, He generally gives him understanding; and so it is, I trust, in the case of the ⟨Archduke.⟩ But before he became a priest, he was far more witty and intelligent and talked less, but more sensibly. You should see him now! ⟨Stupidity⟩ oozes out of his eyes. He talks and holds forth incessantly and always in falsetto— and he has started a goitre. In short, the fellow seems to have changed completely. The Duke of Wurtemberg, however, is a charming person and so are the Duchess and the Princess. But the Prince, who is eighteen, is a regular stick and an out-and-out calf.

Well, I must close. Farewell and be as cheerful as possible! I kiss your hands a thousand times and embrace my dear sister with all my heart and am ever your most obedient son

W: A: MOZART

(434) *Mozart to his Father*

[Autograph in the Mozarteum, Salzburg]

MON TRÉS CHER PÉRE!   VIENNA, 24 *November* 1781

I happened to be at Auernhammer's concert yesterday, when Ceccarelli brought your letter to my lodging. So, as he did not find me in, he left it with the Webers, who at once sent it on to me. At the concert there were Countess Thun (whom I had invited), Baron van Swieten,

---

[1] This obscure passage is probably connected with the passages in Letter 430 which have been obliterated.
[2] The Archduke Maximilian (1756–1801) was the Emperor's youngest brother. He was Archbishop of Cologne.   [3] See p. 777, n. 3.

Baron Godenus, the rich converted Jew Wetzlar,[1] Count Firmian, Herr von Daubrawaick and his son. We played the concerto a due[2] and a sonata for two claviers,[3] which I had composed expressly for the occasion and which was a great success. I shall send you this sonata by Herr von Daubrawaick, who said he would be proud to have it lying in his trunk. The son told me this and, mark you, he is a native of Salzburg. The father, however, when he was leaving, said aloud to me: 'I am proud of being your countryman. You are doing Salzburg great credit. I hope the times will change so that we shall have you back again, and then most certainly we shall not let you go.' My reply was: 'My own country will always have the first claim upon me'. I have seen Herr Gschwendner once at the theatre and once at the Redoute. As soon as I meet him again, I shall ask him when he is leaving. Kerschbaumer, the king of the Moors, is also in Vienna; and when I went to see Mme Contrarini (who is living in this house and also on the third floor), in order to borrow a domino from her, who should walk in but Freysauf[4] and Atzwanger.[5] One damned Salzburger after another!

The Grand Duke,[6] the big noise, has arrived. Tomorrow 'Alceste'[7] is to be given (in Italian) at Schönbrunn, followed by a free Redoute. I have been looking about for Russian popular songs, so as to be able to play variations on them.[8]

My sonatas[9] have been published and I shall send them to you as soon as I get a chance.

No doubt Ceccarelli will want to give a concert with me. But he won't succeed, for I don't care about going shares with people. All that I can do, as I intend to give a concert in Lent, is to let him sing at it and then to play for him gratis at his own.

Well, I must close, for I must be off to Frau von Trattner.[10] Some time during the next few days I shall reply to my dear sister, whom I embrace with all my heart. Dearest, most beloved father, I kiss your hands a thousand times and am ever your most obedient son

W: A: MOZART

[1] Baron Karl Abraham Wetzlar von Plankenstern (1716–1799). His eldest son, Raimund, became Mozart's landlord in 1782. See p. 838, n. 1.
[2] K. 365 [316a], concerto in E♭ for two claviers, composed in 1779.
[3] Probably K. 448 [375a], sonata in D major for two claviers.
[4] Either Anton Freysauf or his brother Franz. The brothers kept a shop in the Judengasse.
[5] Raimund Felix Atzwanger (1742–1814), a tax-collector and town councillor of Salzburg.
[6] The Grand Duke Paul Petrovitch of Russia.
[7] Gluck's Alceste was not performed until December 3rd.
[8] There is no trace of these compositions, if Mozart ever wrote them down.
[9] The six violin and clavier sonatas, K. 296 and 376–380 [374d, e, 317d, 373a, 374f], published by Artaria. They were dedicated to Mozart's pupil, Josephine Auernhammer.
[10] See p. 771, n. 3.

(435) *Mozart to his Father*

[*Autograph in the Mozarteum, Salzburg*]

MON TRÉS CHER PÉRE!   VIENNA, 5 *December* 1781

I have had no letter from you today, so I shall send you all the news I have heard, which is, indeed, little enough and most of it made up. That is just the reason why I never send you any, because I am afraid of disgracing myself. For example, General Laudon was positively dead—and is now risen again, fortunately for the house of Austria![1] The Grand Duke is to remain here until the New Year and the Emperor is wondering how he is going to entertain him for such a long time. But to avoid racking his brains too much—he is not entertaining him at all. It is quite enough, he thinks, if he looks after ⟨the Grand Duchess,⟩ and for this ⟨he himself suffices.⟩ There was horrible confusion at the Schönbrunn ball. As the admirable arrangements made it perfectly easy to foresee what would happen, Herr Ego did not put in an appearance, for he is no lover of crushes, digs in the ribs and blows, even if they happen to be ⟨Imperial⟩ ones! Strobel, the Court messenger, had to distribute the tickets, and three thousand people were expected. It was publicly announced that everyone could be entered on the list by applying to Strobel. So they all went, and Strobel took down their names, and all they had to do was to send for their tickets. A few very eminent persons had theirs sent to their houses, this commission being entrusted to any scamp who chanced to be loitering about. Well, it happened that a fellow asked someone he met on the stairs whether his name was so-and-so, and for a joke he said it was and thus secured the ticket. I know of two families who owing to this lack of organization got no tickets. They were on the list, but when they sent for their tickets, Strobel replied that he had despatched them long ago. In this way the ball was full of friseurs and housemaids. But now for the most amusing part of the story, which has greatly incensed ⟨the nobility. The Emperor⟩ walked about the whole time with ⟨the Grand Duchess⟩ on his arm. The nobility had arranged two sets of contredanses—Romans and Tartars. Into one of these sets the Viennese mob, who are never particularly civil, pushed themselves so roughly that they forced ⟨the Grand Duchess to let go⟩ the ⟨Emperor's⟩ arm, and shoved her forward among the dancers. ⟨The Emperor⟩ began to stamp furiously, cursed like a lazzarone, pushed back a crowd of people and dealt blows right and left. Some of the Hungarian Guards wanted to support him and help him to clear a space, but he sent them off. All I can say is that it serves him right. For what else can you expect from a mob? I have this moment received your letter of November 27th. It is quite true that, out of love for the Princess, ⟨the

---

[1] Laudon lived until 1790. He had been in poor health for some time.

Emperor⟩ drove out to meet the Duke of Wurtemberg. This affair is an open secret in Vienna, but no one knows whether she is going to be a morsel for himself or for some Tuscan prince. Probably the latter. All the same ⟨the Emperor⟩ is far too ⟨loving⟩ with her for my taste. He is always kissing her hands, first one and then the other, and often both at once. I am really astonished, because she is, you might say, still a child. But if it be true, and what people predict does happen, then I shall begin to believe that in his case charity begins at home. For she is to remain here in a convent for two years—and—probably—if there is no hitch—she will become my pupil on the clavier.

I know the bassoon-player well whom they want to foist on the Archbishop. He plays second to Ritter at the opera. You say that I must not forget you! That you rejoice to think that I do not, gives me the greatest pleasure. But if you could believe it possible that I should forget you, that indeed would pain me dreadfully. You say that I must remember that I have an immortal soul. Not only do I think it, but I firmly believe it. If it were not so, wherein would consist the difference between men and beasts? Just because I both know and most firmly believe this, I have not been able to carry out all your wishes exactly in the way you expected. Now farewell. I kiss your hands a thousand times and embrace my sister with all my heart and am ever your most obedient son

W: A: Mozart

(436) *Mozart to his Father*

[*Autograph in the Mozarteum, Salzburg*]

Mon très cher Père!   Vienna, 15 *December* 1781

I have this moment received your letter of the 12th. Herr von Daubrawaick will bring you this letter, the watch, the Munich opera,[1] the six engraved sonatas,[2] the sonata for two claviers[3] and the cadenzas.[4] As for the Princess of Wurtemberg and myself, all is over. The Emperor has spoilt everything, for he cares for no one but Salieri. The Archduke Maximilian recommended *me* to her and she replied that had it rested with her, she would never have engaged anyone else, but that on account of her singing the Emperor had suggested Salieri. She added that she was extremely sorry. What you tell me about the House of Wurtemberg and yourself may possibly prove useful to me.

Dearest father! You demand an explanation of the words in the closing sentence of my last letter! Oh, how gladly would I have opened my heart to you long ago, but I was deterred by the reproaches you might have made to me for *thinking of such a thing at an unseasonable time*—although indeed thinking can never be unseasonable. Meanwhile I am very anxious

---

[1] *Idomeneo*.   [2] See p. 780, n. 9.
[3] Probably K. 448 [375a], composed in November 1781.   [4] See p. 776, n. 1.

to secure here a small but *certain* income, which, together with what chance may provide, will enable me to live here quite comfortably—and then—to marry! You are horrified at the idea? But I entreat you, dearest, most beloved father, to listen to me. I have been obliged to reveal my intentions to you. You must, therefore, allow me to disclose to you my reasons, which, moreover, are very well founded. The voice of nature speaks as loud in me as in others, louder, perhaps, than in many a big strong lout of a fellow. I simply cannot live as most young men do in these days. In the first place, I have too much religion; in the second place, I have too great a love of my neighbour and too high a feeling of honour to seduce an innocent girl; and, in the third place, I have too much horror and disgust, too much dread and fear of diseases and too much care for my health to fool about with whores. So I can swear that I have never had relations of that sort with any woman. Besides, if such a thing had occurred, I should not have concealed it from you; for, after all, to err is natural enough in a man, and to err *once* would be mere weakness—although indeed I should not undertake to promise that if I had erred once in this way, I should stop short at one slip. However, I stake my life on the truth of what I have told you. I am well aware that this reason (powerful as it is) is not urgent enough. But owing to my disposition, which is more inclined to a peaceful and domesticated existence than to revelry, I who from my youth up have never been accustomed to look after my own belongings, linen, clothes and so forth, cannot think of anything more necessary to me than a wife. I assure you that I am often obliged to spend unnecessarily, simply because I do not pay attention to things. I am absolutely convinced that I should manage better with a wife (on the same income which I have now) than I do by myself. And how many useless expenses would be avoided! True, other expenses would have to be met, but—one knows what they are and can be prepared for them—in short, one leads a well-ordered existence. A bachelor, in my opinion, is only half alive. Such are my views and I cannot help it. I have thought the matter over and reflected sufficiently, and I shall not change my mind. But who is the object of my love? Do not be horrified again, I entreat you. Surely not one of the Webers? Yes, one of the Webers—but not Josefa,[1] nor Sophie,[2] but Constanze,[3] the middle one. In no other family have I ever

[1] Josefa Weber (1758–1819), the eldest daughter. She became a singer and took the part of the 'Königin der Nacht' in the first performances of *Die Zauberflöte* in Vienna. She married in 1788 Franz de Paula Hofer (1755–1796), an excellent violinist, and, after his death, Friedrich Sebastian Mayer (1773–1835), a well-known actor. See Blümml, pp. 119 ff.

[2] Maria Sophie Weber (*c.* 1763–1846), the youngest daughter. She married in 1806 the composer Jakob Haibel (1762–1826), who occasionally sang in Schikaneder's productions in Vienna.

[3] Constanze Weber (1762–1842), the third daughter. The best account of Constanze's life and character is to be found in A. Schurig, *Konstanze Mozart*, Dresden, 1922. See also Farmer and Smith, *New Mozartiana*, Glasgow, 1935, pp. 29–52.

come across such differences of character. The eldest is a lazy, gross perfidious woman, and as cunning as a fox. Mme Lange [1] is a false, malicious person and a coquette. The youngest—is still too young to be anything in particular—she is just a good-natured, but feather-headed creature! May God protect her from seduction! But the middle one, my good, dear Constanze, is the martyr of the family and, probably for that very reason, is the kindest-hearted, the cleverest and, in short, the best of them all. She makes herself responsible for the whole household and yet in their opinion she does nothing right. Oh, my most beloved father, I could fill whole sheets with descriptions of all the scenes that I have witnessed in that house. If you want to read them, I shall do so in my next letter. But before I cease to plague you with my chatter, I must make you better acquainted with the character of my dear Constanze. She is not ugly, but at the same time far from beautiful. Her whole beauty consists in two little black eyes and a pretty figure. She has no wit, but she has enough common sense to enable her to fulfil her duties as a wife and mother. It is a downright lie that she is inclined to be extravagant. On the contrary, she is accustomed to be shabbily dressed, for the little that her mother has been able to do for her children, she has done for the two others, but never for Constanze. True, she would like to be neatly and cleanly dressed, but not smartly, and most things that a woman needs she is able to make for herself; and she dresses her own hair every day. Moreover she understands housekeeping and has the kindest heart in the world. I love her and she loves me with all her heart. Tell me whether I could wish myself a better wife?

One thing more I must tell you, which is that when I resigned the Archbishop's service, our love had not yet begun. It was born of her tender care and attentions when I was living in their house.

Accordingly, all that I desire is to have a small assured income (of which, thank God, I have good hopes), and then I shall never cease entreating you to allow me to save this poor girl—and to make myself and her—and, if I may say so, all of us very happy. For you surely are happy when I am? And you are to enjoy one half of *my fixed income*. My dearest father, I have opened my heart to you and explained my remarks. It is now my turn to beg you to explain yours in your last letter. You say that I cannot imagine that you were aware of *a proposal which had been made to me and to which I, at the time when you heard of it, had not yet replied*. I do not understand one word of this—I know of no such proposal. Please take pity on your son! I kiss your hands a thousand times and am ever your most obedient son

W: A: Mozart

[1] Aloysia Weber (c. 1760–1839), the second daughter.

(436a) *Mozart to his Sister*

[From Ludwig Nohl, Mozarts Briefe, 2nd edition, p. 322]

MA TRÉS CHERE SŒUR! VIENNA, 15 *December* 1781 [1]

Here are the six engraved sonatas [2] and the sonata for two claviers. [3] I hope you will like them. Only four will be new to you. [4] The copyist was not able to finish the variations, [5] which I shall send you in my next letter.

Dear sister! I have beside me a letter which I began to you, [6] but as I have written a long letter to Papa, I have not been able to go on with yours. So please be content this time with this cover, and I shall write to you by the next post. Addio, farewell. I kiss you a thousand times and am ever your sincere brother

W. A. MOZART.

(437) *Mozart to his Sister*

[Autograph in the Mozarteum, Salzburg]

MA TRÉS CHÉRE SŒUR! VIENNA, 15 *December* 1781 [7]

I thank you for all the news you have sent me. Here are my six sonatas. Only four of them will be new to you. It is not possible to let you have the variations, as the copyists are too busy. But as soon as I can, I shall send them to you.

December 22nd. Meanwhile you will have received the cover, [8] in which I sent a letter to my father. Herr von Daubrawaick has returned the opera, [9] so I must look about for some other opportunity of sending it to Salzburg Indeed Ceccarelli would have been taken aback, had you accepted his offer, for when I spoke to him about it, he quickly replied: 'Certo, l'avrei presa meco subito'. [10] And when I asked him why he had not done so, he had no better reason to give than '*Where could I have put her here?*' 'Oh—as to that,' I replied, 'there would have been no difficulty, for I know plenty of houses where they would have been delighted to put her up.' And, indeed, it is quite true. If you find a good opportunity of coming to Vienna for a time, just write and let me know beforehand.

---

[1] A postscript written on the cover of the letter to his father.
[2] K. 296, 376-380 [374d, e, 317d, 373a, 374f].   [3] Probably K. 448 [375a].
[4] K. 296 and 378 [317d] were earlier works. See p. 751, n. 3.
[5] Probably K. 359, 360, 352 [374a–c], mentioned in Letter 415.
[6] The following letter (Letter 437), begun on the 15th and finished on the 22nd of December.
[7] The beginning of this letter was written before the postscript to Letter 436. Mozart continued the letter on December 22nd.
[8] See Letter 436a.   [9] *Idomeneo.*
[10] Certainly, I would have taken her with me at once.

Do you not think that 'Das Loch in der Thür'[1] is a good comedy? But you ought to see it performed here. 'Die Gefahren der Verführung'[2] is also a capital piece. 'Das öffentliche Geheimnis'[3] is only endurable if one remembers that it is an Italian play, for the Princess's condescension to her servant is really too indecent and unnatural. The best part of this play is—the public secret itself—I mean, the way in which the two lovers, though preserving their secret, still contrive to communicate with one another publicly. What is the name of the acrobat? Elias Vogt is with Böhm and little Peter[4] is in Berlin. It was real news to me that Feigele has gone home and that Andretter is back in Salzburg.

I cannot send you any news, my dear sister, because at the moment I have none. In regard to our old acquaintances I must tell you that I have only been out once to see Frau von Mesmer.[5] The house is no longer what it was. If I want to get a free meal, I need not drive out to the Landstrasse for it, for there are plenty of houses in town to which I can go on foot. The Fischers are living in the Tiefer Graben where I scarcely ever happen to go; but if my way does take me in that direction, I pay them a visit of a few minutes, since I really cannot endure for longer their tiny, over-heated room and the wine on the table. I am well aware that people of their class consider this to be the greatest possible compliment, but I am no lover of such compliments and still less of people of that type. I have not yet seen a single one of the Breans. I have talked quite often to Grill (who is now married) and to Heufeld. As for my shooting fund, I do not know either what is to be done. Surely there is some money there, some interest, I mean, on the hundred gulden? Why, you will just have to take some of it. Perhaps I shall be more fortunate next year. What about the target?

Good God! I have received this very moment a letter from my dearest and most beloved father! How can there be such monsters in the shape of men? But patience! my rage and fury are such that I cannot write any more; but do tell him that I shall reply to his letter by the next post and that I shall convince him that there are men who are worse—than devils. In the meantime let him be easy in his mind. Say that his son is possibly more worthy of him than he thinks. Adieu. I kiss my dearest, most beloved father's hands a thousand times and embrace you, my dearest sister, with all my heart and am ever your sincere brother

W: A: MOZART

A thousand compliments to M. d'Yppold. Adieu.

[1] See p. 745, n. 2.
[2] A German adaptation of Georg Lillo's George Barnwell.
[3] A German translation of Carlo Gozzi's Il pubblico segreto, which was an adaptation of Calderón's El secreto á voces. Gozzi's comedy was first performed at Modena on 20 May 1769.
[4] See p. 707, nn. 3, 4.
[5] The wife of Dr. Franz Anton Mesmer, who in the meantime had settled in Paris.

(438) *Mozart to his Father*

[*Autograph in the Mozarteum, Salzburg*]

MON TRÉS CHER PÉRE!   VIENNA, 22 *December* 1781

I am still full of rage and fury at the disgraceful lies of that arch-villain Winter [1]—and yet I am calm and composed, because they do not affect me—and delighted and contented with my most inestimable, most dear and most beloved father. But I could never have expected anything else from your good sense, and your love and kindness to me. No doubt by this time you will have received my letter with the confession of my love and my intentions, and you will have gathered from it that I shall not be so foolish as to marry rashly in my twenty-sixth year without having some certain income—and that I have very well founded reasons for getting married as soon as possible—and that, from the description of her which I gave you, my girl will be a very suitable wife for me. For she is just as I have described her, not one whit better or worse. As for the marriage contract, I want to make the most frank confession, fully convinced as I am that you will forgive me for taking this step; for had you been in my place, you would most certainly have done the same thing. But for one thing alone I ask your pardon—and that is, that I did not tell you all about this long ago. In my last letter I apologized to you for my delay and gave you the reason which deterred me. So I hope that you will forgive me, particularly as no one has suffered more by it than I have—and even if you had not provided the occasion for doing so in your last letter, I should have written to you and disclosed everything. For, by Heaven, I could not have stood it—much—much longer.

Well, let's come to the marriage contract, or rather to the written assurance of my honourable intentions towards the girl. You know, of course, that as the father is no longer alive (unhappily for the whole family as well as for my Constanze and myself) a guardian [2] has taken his place. Certain busybodies and impudent gentlemen like Herr Winter must have shouted in the ears of this person (who doesn't know me at all) all sorts of stories about me—as, for example, that he should beware of me—that I have no settled income—that I was far too intimate with her—that I should probably jilt her—and that the girl would then be ruined, and so forth. All this made him smell a rat—for the mother who knows me and knows

---

[1] Peter von Winter (1754–1825), born in Mannheim, joined the Mannheim orchestra as violinist in 1775. In 1787 he became Deputy-Kapellmeister to the Munich Court orchestra, and in 1798 Kapellmeister. From 1793 to 1797 he had nine operas performed at the Burgtheater and Schikaneder's theatre in Vienna. He also composed a great deal of church music. He was in Vienna during the winter of 1781 for the production of three ballets, for which he had written the music.

[2] Johann von Thorwart (1737–1813). From 1776 to 1791 he was in charge of the financial affairs of the National Theatre in Vienna, and was Count Rosenberg's right hand. For a full study of Thorwart's strange career see Blümml, pp. 54 ff.

that I am honourable, let things take their course and said nothing to him about the matter. For my whole association with her consisted in my lodging with the family and later in my going to their house every day. No one ever saw me with her outside the house. But the guardian kept on pestering the mother with his representations until she told me about them and asked me to speak to him myself, adding that he would come some day to her house. He came—and we had a talk—with the result (as I did not explain myself as clearly as he desired) that he told the mother to forbid me to associate with her daughter until I had come to a written agreement with him. The mother replied: 'Why, his whole association with her consists in his coming to my house, and—I cannot forbid him my house. He is too good a friend—and one to whom I owe a great deal. I am quite satisfied. I trust him. You must settle it with him yourself.' So he forbade me to have anything more to do with Constanze, unless I would give him a written undertaking. What other course was open to me? I had either to give him a written contract or—to desert the girl. What man who loves sincerely and honestly can forsake his beloved? Would not the mother, would not my loved one herself place the worst interpretation upon such conduct? That was my predicament. So I drew up a document to the effect *that I bound myself to marry Mlle Constanze Weber within the space of three years and that if it should prove impossible for me to do so owing to my changing my mind, she should be entitled to claim from me three hundred gulden a year.* Nothing in the world could have been easier for me to write. For I knew that I should never have to pay these three hundred gulden, because I should never forsake her, and that even should I be so unfortunate as to change my mind, I should only be too glad to get rid of her for three hundred gulden, while Constanze, as I knew her, would be too proud to let herself be sold. But what did the angelic girl do when the guardian was gone? She asked her mother for the document, and said to me: '*Dear Mozart? I need no written assurance from you. I believe what you say*', and tore up the paper. This action made my dear Constanze yet more precious to me, and the document having been destroyed and the guardian having given his *parole d'honneur* to keep the matter to himself, I was to a certain extent easy in my mind on your account, my most beloved father. For I had no fear but that ultimately you would give your consent to our marriage (since the girl has everything but money), because I know your sensible ideas on this subject. Will you forgive me? Indeed I hope so! Nor do I doubt it for a moment. Well, now I want to talk about those blackguards (however repulsive it may be to me). I believe that Herr Reiner's only disease was that he was not quite right in the head. I happened to meet him in the theatre, where he gave me a letter from Ramm. I asked him where he was lodging, but he could neither tell me the street nor the house, and he cursed the day when he had let himself be persuaded to come here.

I offered to present him to the Countess [1] and to introduce him wherever I had the entrée; and I assured him that if he found he could not give a concert, I would certainly take him to the Grand Duke.[2] All he said was: 'Pooh! There is nothing to be done here. I shall go off at once.' 'Do but have a little patience,' I said, 'and since you cannot tell me where you lodge, I shall give you my address, which is easy to find.' However, I saw nothing more of him. I made enquiries, but by the time I had found out where he was living, he had left. So much for that gentleman. As for Winter, if he deserves to be called a man (for he is married) or at least a human being, I may say that on account of Vogler he has always been my worst enemy.[3] Since, however, he is a beast in his way of living and a child in the rest of his conduct and actions, I should be ashamed to write a single word about him. For he thoroughly deserves the contempt of every man of honour. So I shall not tell infamous truths about him in return for the infamous lies he has told about me, but—give you instead some account of my own manner of life.

Every morning at six o'clock my friseur arrives and wakes me, and by seven I have finished dressing. I compose until ten, when I give a lesson to Frau von Trattner and at eleven to the Countess Rumbeck,[4] each of whom pays me six ducats for twelve lessons and to whom I go *every day*, unless they put me off, which I do not like at all. I have arranged with the Countess that she is never to put me off, I mean that, if I do not find her at home, I am at least to get my fee; but Frau von Trattner is too economical for that. I do not owe a single kreuzer to any man. I have not heard a word about any amateur concert where two persons played very finely on the clavier. And I must tell you candidly that I do not think it worth the trouble to reply to all the filth which such a lousy cad and miserable bungler may have said. He only makes himself ridiculous by doing so. If you really believe that I am detested at Court and by the old and new aristocracy, just write to Herr von Strack, Countess Thun, Countess Rumbeck, Baroness Waldstädten, Herr von Sonnenfels, Frau von Trattner, *enfin*, to anyone you choose. Meanwhile let me tell you that at table the other day the Emperor gave me the very highest praise, accompanied by the words: '*C'est un talent, décidé!*' and that the day before yesterday, December 24th, I played at Court.[5] Another clavier-player, an Italian called Clementi,[6] has arrived here. He too had been invited to Court. I

---

[1] Countess Thun.   [2] The Grand Duke Paul Petrovitch of Russia.
[3] Peter von Winter was one of Abt Vogler's most loyal friends and supporters.
[4] See p. 718, n. 2.
[5] Mozart did not finish this letter, begun on December 22nd, until December 26th.
[6] Muzio Clementi (1752–1832), a famous composer for the pianoforte. He was born in Rome, where Peter Beckford, cousin of William Beckford, the author of *Vathek*, discovered him in 1766 and took him to England, where he was trained to be a musician. Clementi was 'conductor' (from the keyboard) at the Italian Opera in London in the late 1770s. In 1780 he began his travels to the various capitals of Europe and returned to England in 1785, where he

was sent fifty ducats yesterday for my playing, and indeed I need them very badly at the moment.

My dearest, most beloved father, you will see that little by little circumstances will improve. Of what use is a great sensation—and rapid success? It never lasts. *Chi va piano, va sano.*[1] One must just cut one's coat according to one's cloth. Of all the mean things which Winter said, the only one which enrages me is that he called my dear Constanze a slut. I have described her to you exactly as she is. If you wish to have the opinion of others, write to Herr von Auernhammer, to whose house she has been a few times and where she has lunched once. Write to Baroness Waldstädten, who had her at her house, though, unfortunately, for a month only, because she, the Baroness, fell ill. Now Constanze's mother refuses to part with her and let her go back. God grant that I may soon be able to marry her.

Ceccarelli sends you his greetings. He sang at Court yesterday. There is one thing more I must tell you about Winter. Among other things he once said to me: 'You are a fool to get married. Keep a mistress. You are earning enough money, you can afford it. What prevents you from doing so? Some damned religious scruple?' Believe now what you will. Adieu. I kiss your hands a thousand times and embrace my dear sister with all my heart and am ever your most obedient son

W: A: Mzt

The address of the Baroness is
   A Madame La Baronne de Waldstädten
      née de Schäfer
        à Vienne
Leopoldstadt no. 360.

(439) *Mozart to his Father*

[*Autograph in the Mozarteum, Salzburg*]

Mon trés cher Pére!   Vienna, 9 *January* 1782

I have not yet received a reply to my last letter, which accounts for my not having written to you by the last post. I do hope I shall have a letter from you today. As in my last letter, though without being aware of it, I partly replied in advance to yours of December 28th, I must first await your reply.

Meanwhile I must inform you that the Pope is supposed to be coming

---

remained until 1802. He then spent eight years touring as a performer on the pianoforte, and again returned to England, where he remained until his death. He taught J. B. Cramer and John Field.

[1] Slow and steady wins the race.

to Vienna.[1] The whole town is talking about it. But I do not believe it, for Count Cobenzl told me that the Emperor will decline his visit. The Russian Royalties left on the 5th. Well, I have just been to Peisser's myself to see whether there was a letter from you, and I have sent again; it is almost five o'clock. I cannot understand why I do not hear from you! Can it be that you are so angry with me? You may be annoyed with me for having so long concealed the affair from you, and no doubt you are right. But if you have read my apology, surely you can forgive me. And surely you cannot be vexed with me for wishing to marry? I believe that in my wishing to do so you will have been able to recognize what is best of all, my religion and my honourable feelings. Oh, I could say a great deal more in reply to your last letter and make many remonstrances, but my maxim is: what does not affect me I do not consider it worth while to discuss. I cannot help it—such is my nature. I am really shy of defending myself, when I am falsely accused. I always think that the truth will come out some day. Well—I cannot write anything more to you on the subject, because I have not yet received a reply to my last letter. I have no news. So farewell. Once more I ask your forgiveness and implore you to be indulgent and compassionate to me. I never can be happy and contented without my dearest Constanze, and without your approval I shall only be so in part. So make me altogether happy, my dearest, most beloved father! I entreat you to do so. I am ever your most obedient son

W. A. MOZART

PS.—I kiss my dearest sister a thousand times with all my heart. Fräulein von Auernhammer played the treble in the sonata for two claviers.[2]

(440) *Mozart to his Father*

[Autograph in the Mozarteum, Salzburg]

MON TRÉS CHER PÉRE! VIENNA, 12 *January* 1782

I have begun a reply to your last letter of January 7th, but I cannot possibly finish it, as a servant of Countess Rumbeck has just come with an invitation to a small musical party at her house. Well, I must first have my hair dressed and I must change all my clothes. So, although I do not wish to leave you entirely without any news of me, I cannot write very much.

---

[1] Pius VI (1717–1799), formerly Cardinal Braschi, who succeeded Clement XIV in 1775. He visited Vienna in order to obtain from the Emperor a promise that the latter's ecclesiastical reforms would not contain any violation of Catholic dogmas nor compromise the dignity of the Pope. Though magnificently received, his mission on the whole proved a failure.
[2] K. 448 [375a].

Clementi plays well, so far as execution with the right hand goes. His greatest strength lies in his passages in thirds. Apart from this, he has not a kreuzer's worth of taste or feeling—in short he is simply a *mechanicus*.

The friseur has arrived, so I must close. In my next letter I shall tell you more about Clementi. I entreat you to make me happy by giving me your approval—I implore you to do so. I am convinced that you will learn to love my dear Constanze. I kiss your hands a thousand times and am ever your most obedient son

W: A: MOZART

I embrace my dear sister with all my heart.

(441) *Mozart to his Father*

[*Autograph in the Mozarteum, Salzburg*]

MON TRÉS CHER PÉRE! VIENNA, 16 *January* 1782

I thank you for your kind and affectionate letter. If I were to give you detailed replies to every point, I should have to fill a quire of paper. As this is impossible, I shall deal only with the most important of them. The guardian's name is Herr von Thorwart; he is Inspector of theatrical properties, that is to say, everything connected with the theatre has to pass through his hands; the Emperor's fifty ducats were sent to me through him; I applied to him too about my concert in the theatre, since most matters of this kind depend on him and because he has much influence with Count Rosenberg and Baron Kienmayr.[1] I must confess that I myself thought that he would disclose the whole affair to you without saying a word to me on the subject. This he has not done. But (notwithstanding his word of honour) he has told the story to the whole town of Vienna, which has very much shaken the good opinion I once had of him. I quite agree with you in thinking that Madame Weber and Herr von Thorwart have been to blame in showing too much regard for their own interests, though the Madame is no longer her own mistress and has to leave everything, particularly all matters of this kind, to the guardian, who (as he has never made my acquaintance) is by no means bound to trust me. But that he was too hasty in demanding from me a written undertaking is undeniable, especially as I told him that as yet you knew nothing about the affair and that at the moment I could not possibly disclose it to you. I asked him to have patience for a short time until my circumstances should take another turn, when I would give you a full account of everything and then the whole matter would be settled. However, it is all over now; and love must be my excuse. Herr von Thorwart did not behave well, but not so

[1] Johann Michael, Baron von Kienmayr (1727–1792), assistant-manager of the Vienna Court theatre.

badly that he and Madame Weber 'should be put in chains, made to sweep streets and have boards hung round their necks with the words *"seducers of youth"* '. That too is an exaggeration. And even if what you say were true, that in order to catch me she opened her house, let me have the run of it, gave me every opportunity, etc., even so the punishment would be rather severe. But I need hardly tell you that it is not true. And it hurts me very much to think that you could believe that your son could frequent a house where such things went on. Let me only say that you should believe precisely the opposite of all you have been told. But enough of this. Now a word about Clementi. He is an excellent cembalo-player, but that is all. He has great facility with his right hand. His star passages are thirds. Apart from this, he has not a farthing's worth of taste or feeling; he is a mere *mechanicus*.

After we had stood on ceremony long enough, the Emperor declared that Clementi ought to begin. 'La Santa Chiesa Cattolica', he said, Clementi being a Roman. He improvised and then played a sonata.[1] The Emperor then turned to me: 'Allons, fire away'. I improvised and played variations. The Grand Duchess produced some sonatas by Paisiello[2] (wretchedly written out in his own hand), of which I had to play the Allegros and Clementi the Andantes and Rondos. We then selected a theme from them and developed it on two pianofortes. The funny thing was that although I had borrowed Countess Thun's pianoforte, I only played on it when I played alone; such was the Emperor's desire—and, by the way, the other instrument was out of tune and three of the keys were stuck. 'Never mind', said the Emperor. Well, I put the best construction on it I could, that is, that the Emperor, already knowing my skill and my knowledge of music, merely wanted to show especial courtesy to a foreigner. Besides, I have it from a very good source that he was extremely pleased with me.[3] He was very gracious, said a great deal to me privately, and even mentioned my marriage. Who knows? Perhaps—what do you think? At any rate I might make the attempt. More of this in my next letter. Farewell. I kiss your hands a thousand times and embrace my dear sister with all my heart and am ever your most obedient son

W: A: MOZART.

[1] In the next edition which was published of this sonata, in B flat, op. 24 n. 2. Clementi headed it with the remark:' Cette sonate, avec la toccata qui la suit, a été jouée par l'auteur devant Sa Majesté Joseph II en 1781, Mozart étant présent'. It is frequently stated but without justification that the first movement of Clementi's sonata gave Mozart the idea for the theme of the opening allegro in his overture to *Die Zauberflöte*. Cf. A. Hyatt King, *Mozart in Retrospect*. London, 1955, pp. 143, 144.

[2] Giovanni Paisiello (1740–1816), an eminent composer of the Neapolitan school and a rival of Piccinni, who wrote over a hundred operas and many other works. During the years 1776 to 1784 he lived in St. Petersburg and dedicated some clavier compositions to the Grand Duchess.

[3] Bridi in his *Brevi notizie*, pp. 51 ff., when describing this competition, states that the Emperor had laid a wager with the Grand Duchess that Mozart would excel, and won it.

(442) *Mozart to his Father*

[*Autograph in the Mozarteum, Salzburg*]

MON TRÉS CHER PÉRE!   VIENNA, 23 *January* 1782

There is nothing more disagreeable than to be obliged to live in uncertainty, not knowing what is happening. Such is my case at the moment with regard to my concert; and it is the same with everyone who wishes to give one. Last year the Emperor intended to continue the plays throughout Lent; perhaps he may do so this year. Basta! At all events I have secured the day (if there is no play), namely, the third Sunday in Lent. If I know a fortnight ahead, I shall be satisfied; otherwise my whole plan will be upset, or I shall be obliged to incur expenses for nothing. Countess Thun, Adamberger and other good friends of mine are advising me to select the best scenes from my Munich opera[1] and have them performed in the theatre, and myself to play only one concerto[2] and to improvise at the close. I too had thought of this and I have now quite decided to do so, particularly as Clementi is also giving a concert. So I shall have a slight advantage over him, the more so as I shall probably be able to give mine twice.

I have enquired at Peisser's, but no letter has arrived. Well, I want to give you my opinion as to my prospects of a small permanent income. I have my eye here on three sources. The first is not certain, and, even if it were, would probably not be much; the second would be the best, but God knows whether it will ever come to pass; and the third is not to be despised, but the pity is that it concerns the future and not the present. The first is young Prince Liechtenstein,[3] who would like to collect a wind-instrument band (though he does not yet want it to be known), for which I should write the music. This would not bring in very much, it is true, but it would be at least something certain, and I should not sign the contract unless it were to be for life. The second (in my estimation, however, it is the first) is the Emperor himself. Who knows? I intend to talk to Herr von Strack about it and I am certain that he will do all he can, for he has proved to be a very good friend of mine; though indeed these court flunkeys are never to be trusted. The manner in which the Emperor has spoken to me has given me some hope. Great lords do not like to hear these speeches, and, needless to say, they themselves do not make them; for they must always expect a stab in the back and are great adepts in avoiding it. The third is the Archduke Maximilian. Now of him I can say that he thinks the world of me. He shoves me forward on every occasion, and I might almost say with certainty that if at this moment he were

---

[1] *Idomeneo.*

[2] K. 175, composed in 1773, with a new finale, the rondo K. 382. See p. 798, n. 3.

[3] Prince Alois Josef, nephew of Prince Karl Borromäus Josef Liechtenstein (1730–1789), Imperial Field-Marshal.

Elector of Cologne, I should be his Kapellmeister. It is, indeed, a pity that these great gentlemen refuse to make arrangements beforehand. I could easily manage to extract a simple promise from him, but of what use would that be to me now? Cash would be more acceptable. Dearest, most beloved father! If I could have it in writing from God Almighty that I shall keep in good health and not get ill, ah! then I would marry my dear faithful girl this very day. I have three pupils now,[1] which brings me in eighteen ducats a month; for I no longer charge for twelve lessons, but monthly. I learnt to my cost that my pupils often dropped out for weeks at a time; so now, whether they learn or not, each of them must pay me six ducats. I shall get several more on these terms, but I really need only one more, because four pupils are quite enough. With four I should have twenty-four ducats, or 102 gulden, 24 kreuzer. With this sum a man and his wife can manage in Vienna if they live quietly and in the retired way which we desire; but, of course, if I were to fall ill, we should not make a farthing. I can write, it is true, at least one opera a year, give a concert annually and have some things engraved and published by subscription. There are other concerts too where one can make money, particularly if one has been living in a place for a long time and has a good reputation. But I should prefer not to count on such takings but rather to regard them as windfalls. However, if the bow will not bend, it must break, and I will rather take the risk than go on waiting indefinitely. My affairs cannot get worse; on the contrary, they must continue to improve. And my reason for not wishing to wait any longer is not so much on my account as on hers. I must rescue her as soon as possible. I shall tell you about this in my next letter. Now farewell. I kiss your hands a thousand times and embrace my dear sister with all my heart and am ever your most obedient son

W: A: MOZART

(443) *Mozart to his Father*

[*Autograph in the Mozarteum, Salzburg*]

MON TRÉS CHER PÉRE! VIENNA, 30 *January* 1782

I am writing to you in a great hurry, and at half past ten at night, as I had really intended to postpone writing until Saturday. But I have an urgent request to make. I hope that you will not take it amiss if I send you such a short letter. Will you please send me, when you next write, a libretto of 'Idomeneo', with or without the German translation? I lent one copy to Countess Thun, who has now moved into another house, and cannot find it. Probably it is lost. Fräulein Auernhammer had my other copy, which she has looked for but has not yet found. Perhaps she

[1] Countess Thiennes de Rumbeke, Frau von Trattner and Fräulein Josephine Auernhammer.

will find it. But if she doesn't, I shall be left high and dry and at the very moment when I really require it. In order therefore to be on the safe side, please let me have it at once, whatever the cost may be, for I need it immediately in order that I may arrange the programme of my concert, which is to take place on the third Sunday in Lent. Please send it off to me directly. I shall forward the sonatas [1] by the next mail coach. My opera [2] has not gone to sleep, but—has suffered a setback on account of Gluck's big operas [3] and owing to many very necessary alterations which have to be made in the text. It is to be performed, however, immediately after Easter. [4]

Well, I must close. Just one thing more (for if I did not say it I could not sleep in peace). Please do not suspect my dear Constanze of harbouring such evil thoughts. Believe me, if she had such a disposition, I could not possibly love her. Both she and I long ago observed her mother's designs. But the latter is very much mistaken, for she wishes us (when we marry) to live with her, as she has apartments to let. That is out of the question, for on no account would I consent to it, and my Constanze still less. Au contraire, she intends to see very little of her mother and I shall do my best to stop it altogether, for we know her too well. Dearest, most beloved father, my only wish is that we may soon meet, so that you may see her and—love her, for you love those who have kind hearts—that I know. Now farewell, dearest, most beloved father. I kiss your hands a thousand times and am ever your most obedient son

W: A: Mozart

I embrace my dear sister with all my heart. I shall not forget the variations. [5]

(444) *Mozart to his Sister*

[Autograph in the Mozarteum, Salzburg]

MA TRÉS CHÉRE SŒUR!　　　　　VIENNA, 13 *February* 1782

Thank you for sending me the libretto, [6] for which indeed I have been waiting with the greatest longing! I hope that by the time you receive this letter, you will have our dearest, most beloved father with you again. You must not gather from my not replying, that you and your letters are a nuisance to me! I shall always be delighted, dear sister, to have the honour of receiving a letter from you. If the necessary business of earning my living did not prevent me, God knows that I would answer your letters at once! And have I never sent you a reply? Well, then—forgetfulness it cannot be—nor negligence, either; therefore it is entirely due to

---

[1] K. 296 and 376-380 [374d, e, 317d, 373a, 374f].
[2] *Die Entführung aus dem Serail.*　　　　[3] *Iphigenie in Tauris, Alceste* and *Orfeo.*
[4] The first performance took place on 16 July 1782.
[5] Probably K. 359, 360, 352 [374a-c].　　　　[6] The text of *Idomeneo.*

positive hindrances—to genuine impossibility. Do I not write little enough to my father? And very wrong, too, you will say! But, in Heaven's name, you both know what Vienna is. In such a place has not a man (who has not a kreuzer of assured income) enough to think about and to work at day and night? Our father, when he has finished his duties in church, and you, when you have done with your few pupils, can both do what you like for the rest of the day and write letters containing whole litanies. But it is not so with me. I described my manner of life the other day to my father and I will repeat it to you. My hair is always done by six o'clock in the morning and by seven I am fully dressed. I then compose until nine. From nine to one I give lessons. Then I lunch, unless I am invited to some house where they lunch at two or even three o'clock, as, for example, today and tomorrow at Countess Zichy's[1] and Countess Thun's. I can never work before five or six o'clock in the evening, and even then I am often prevented by a concert. If I am not prevented, I compose until nine. I then go to my dear Constanze, though the joy of seeing one another is nearly always spoilt by her mother's bitter remarks. I shall explain this in my next letter to my father. For that is the reason why I am longing to be able to set her free and to rescue her as soon as possible. At half past ten or eleven I come home—it depends on her mother's darts and on my capacity to endure them! As I cannot rely on being able to compose in the evening owing to the concerts which are taking place and also to the uncertainty as to whether I may not be summoned now here and now there, it is my custom (especially if I get home early) to compose a little before going to bed. I often go on writing until one—and am up again at six. Dearest sister! If you imagine that I can ever forget my dearest, most beloved father and you, then—but I shall say no more. God knows all about me and that is consolation enough. May He punish me, if I can ever forget you. Adieu. I am ever your sincere brother

W. A: MOZART

PS.—If my dearest father is back in Salzburg,[2] tell him that I kiss his hands a thousand times.

(445) *Mozart to his Father*

[Autograph in the Mozarteum, Salzburg]

MON TRÉS CHER PÉRE!   VIENNA, 23 *March* 1782

I am very sorry that I heard only yesterday that a son of Leutgeb's was going to Salzburg by the mail coach, which would have been a

---

[1] Countess Anna Maria Antonia, *née* Khevenhüller-Metsch (1759–1809), the wife of Count Karl Zichy (1753–1826), Court Councillor in Vienna.
[2] Leopold Mozart had gone to stay with the Marchands in Munich. See p. 749, n. 4.

capital opportunity of sending you a whole lot of things free of charge. But as it was impossible to copy out the variations[1] in these two days, I have only been able to give him the two copies of my sonatas.[2] I am sending you at the same time *the last rondo*[3] which I composed for my concerto in D major and which is making such a furore in Vienna. But I beg you to guard it like a *jewel*—and not to give it to a soul to play—not even to Marchand and his sister.[4] I composed it *specially* for myself—and no one else but my dear sister must play it. I also take the liberty of presenting you with a snuff-box and a few watch-ribbons. The snuff-box is quite pretty; the painting represents an English scene. The watch-ribbons are of no great value, but are now very much in fashion. I am sending my dear sister two caps in the latest Viennese mode. Both are the handiwork of my dear Constanze. She sends her most devoted greetings to you and kisses your hands and also embraces my sister most affectionately and asks her to forgive her if the caps are not as becoming as she would have wished, but the time was too short. Please return the bandbox by the next mail coach, for I borrowed it. But that the poor fool may not travel all alone, be so good as to put the rondo in again (after you have had it copied)—and also, if possible, the last scena I composed for Countess Baumgarten[5]—and the scores of a few of my masses[6]—enfin—whatever you may find and may think might be useful to me. Well, I must close. But I must tell you that the Pope arrived in Vienna yesterday afternoon at half past three—a pleasant piece of news.[7] And now for a sad one. Frau von Auernhammer has at last worried her poor dear husband to death. He died yesterday evening at half past six. He had been poorly for some time, but his death was not expected so soon. It was all over in a moment. May God have mercy on his soul. He was a good, kind man. Well, I must close, for Leutgeb is waiting for my letter. I really recommend the lad to you, my dear father. His father would like to get him into a business house or into the Salzburg printing firm. Please lend him a helping hand. My dear Constanze has surprised me this very moment and has just asked me whether she might dare to send my sister a little souvenir? At the same time I am to apologize for her, and to say that, as she is a poor girl, she has nothing to give—and that she hopes that my sister will take the will for the deed. The little cross is of no great value, but it is all the fashion in Vienna. But the little heart pierced by an arrow is something like my sister's *heart with the arrow*—and will please her better on that account. Now farewell. I kiss

---

[1] K. 359, 360, 352 [374a–c].   [2] K. 296 and 376–380 [374d, e, 317d, 373a, 374f].

[3] K. 382, a rondo written for K. 175, clavier concerto in D major, composed in 1773. This is the rondo which Mozart sent to the Baroness von Waldstädten. See p. 824.

[4] Heinrich and Margarete Marchand, who had gone to live with Leopold Mozart. Heinrich, then aged twelve, became an excellent violinist, and Margarete, then aged fourteen, a fine operatic singer.   [5] K. 369.

[6] Perhaps K. 317, composed in 1779, and K. 337, composed in 1780.

[7] See p. 791, n. 1.

your hands a thousand times and embrace my dear sister with all my heart and am ever your [1]

(446) *Mozart to his Father*

[*Autograph in the Mozarteum, Salzburg*]

MON TRÉS CHER PÉRE! VIENNA, 10 *April* 1782

I see from your letter of April 2nd that you have received everything safely. I am glad that you are so pleased with the watch-ribbons and the snuff-box and my sister with the two caps. I did not buy either the snuff-box or the watch-ribbons, for Count Zapara made me a present of them. I have delivered greetings from you both to my dear Constanze, who kisses your hands in return, my father, and embraces my sister most cordially and hopes that she will be her friend. She was absolutely de-lighted when I told her that my sister was very much pleased with the two caps, so greatly did she desire to give her pleasure. Your postscript about her mother is justified only in so far as she likes wine, and more so, I admit, than a woman ought to. Still, I have never yet seen her drunk and it would be a lie if I were to say so. The children only drink water—and, although their mother almost forces wine upon them, she cannot induce them to touch it. This often leads to a lot of wrangling—can you imagine a mother quarrelling with her children about such a matter?

I have said nothing to you about the rumour you mention of my being certainly taken into the Emperor's service, because I myself know nothing about it. It is true that here too the whole town is ringing with it and that a number of people have already congratulated me. I am quite ready to believe that it has been discussed with the Emperor and that perhaps he is contemplating it. But up to this moment I have no definite information. At all events things are so far advanced that the Emperor is considering it, and that too without my having taken a single step. I have been a few times to see Herr von Strack (who is certainly a very good friend of mine) in order to let myself be seen and because I like his company, but I have not gone often, because I do not wish to become a nuisance to him, or to let him think that I have ulterior motives. As a man of honour he is bound to state that he has never heard me say a word which would give him reason to think that I should like to stay in Vienna, let alone enter the Emperor's service. We have only discussed music. Therefore it must have been quite spontaneously and entirely without self-interest that he has been speaking so favourably of me to the Emperor. If things have gone so far without any effort on my part, they can now proceed to their conclusion in the same way. For if one makes any move oneself, one immediately receives less pay, because, as it is, the Emperor is a niggard. If he wants me,

[1] The signature has been cut off.

he must pay me, for the honour alone of serving him is not enough. Indeed, if he were to offer me 1000 gulden and some Count 2000, I should decline the former proposal with thanks and go to the Count—that is, of course, if it were a permanent arrangement. A propos, I have been intending to ask you, when you return the rondo,[1] to enclose with it Handel's six fugues[2] and Eberlin's toccatas and fugues. I go every Sunday at twelve o'clock to the Baron van Swieten, where nothing is played but Handel and Bach. I am collecting at the moment the fugues of Bach—not only of Sebastian, but also of Emanuel[3] and Friedemann.[4] I am also collecting Handel's and should like to have the six I mentioned. I should like the Baron to hear Eberlin's too. I suppose you have heard that the English Bach[5] is dead? What a loss to the musical world! Now, farewell. I kiss your hands a thousand times and embrace my dear sister with all my heart and am ever your most obedient son

W: A: Mozart

PS.—May I also ask you to send me when you can (but the sooner the better) my concerto in C major, written for Countess Lützow?[6]

(447) *Mozart to his Sister*

[*Autograph in the Mozarteum, Salzburg*]

Dearest Sister!　　　　　　　　　　　Vienna, 20 *April* 1782

My dear Constanze has at last summoned up courage to follow the impulse of her kind heart—and that is, to write to you, my dear sister! Should you be willing to favour her with a reply (and indeed I hope you will, so that I may see the sweet creature's delight reflected on her face), may I beg you to enclose your letter to me? I only mention this as a precaution and so that you may know that her mother and sisters are not aware that she has written to you. I send you herewith a prelude and a three-part fugue.[7] The reason why I did not reply to your letter at once was that on account of the wearisome labour of writing these small notes, I could not finish the composition any sooner. And, even so, it is awkwardly done, for the prelude ought to come first and the fugue to follow. But I composed the fugue first and wrote it down while I was thinking out the prelude. I only hope that you will be able to read it, for it is written

---

[1] See p. 798, n. 3.
[2] Probably the six fugues for the clavecin, composed in 1735.
[3] Carl Philipp Emanuel Bach (1714–1788), J. S. Bach's second son.
[4] Wilhelm Friedemann Bach (1710–1784), J. S. Bach's eldest son.
[5] Johann Christian Bach, J. S. Bach's youngest son, died on 1 January 1782. For the last twenty years of his life he had lived almost entirely in England.
[6] K. 246, written in 1776.　　　　　[7] K. 394 [383a], Fantasy and Fugue in C major.

so very small; and I hope further that you will like it. Another time I will send you something better for the clavier. My dear Constanze is really the cause of this fugue's coming into the world. The Baron van Swieten, to whom I go every Sunday, gave me all the works of Handel and Sebastian Bach to take home with me (after I had played them to him). When Constanze heard the fugues, she absolutely fell in love with them. Now she will listen to nothing but fugues, and particularly (in this kind of composition) the works of Handel and Bach. Well, as she had often heard me play fugues out of my head, she asked me if I had ever written any down, and when I said I had not, she scolded me roundly for not recording some of my compositions in this most artistic and beautiful of all musical forms, and never ceased to entreat me until I wrote down a fugue for her. So that is its origin. I have purposely written above it *Andante Maestoso*, as it must not be played too fast. For if a fugue is not played slowly, the ear cannot clearly distinguish the theme when it comes in and consequently the effect is entirely missed. In time, and when I have a favourable opportunity, I intend to compose five [1] more and then present them to the Baron van Swieten, whose collection of good music, though small in quantity, is great in quality. And for that very reason I beg you to keep your promise not to show this composition to a soul. Learn it by heart and play it. It is not so easy to pick up a fugue by ear. If Papa has not yet had those works by Eberlin copied, so much the better, for in the meantime I have got hold of them and now I see (for I had forgotten them) that they are unfortunately far too trivial to deserve a place beside Handel and Bach. With due respect for his four-part composition I may say that his clavier fugues are nothing but long-drawn-out voluntaries. Now farewell. I am glad that the two caps suit you. I kiss you a thousand times and remain your sincere brother

W. A: Mozart

Tell Papa I kiss his hand. I received no letter today.

(447a) *Constanze Weber to Nannerl Mozart*

[Autograph in the Mozarteum, Salzburg]

Most honoured and valued Friend! [Vienna, 20 *April* 1782]
    I should never have been so bold as to follow the dictates of my heart and to write to you, most esteemed friend, had not your brother assured me that you would not be offended by this step which I am taking solely from an earnest longing to communicate, if only in writing, with a person

---

[1] K. App. 39 [K. 383d] unfinished, was probably Mozart's attempt to carry out this plan. See Köchel, pp. 402 ff.

who, though unknown to me, is yet very precious, as she bears the name of Mozart. Surely you will not be angry if I venture to tell you that though I have not the honour of knowing you personally I esteem you most highly, as the sister of so excellent a brother, and that I love you and even venture to ask you for your friendship. Without undue pride I may say that I partly deserve it and shall endeavour to do so wholly! May I in exchange offer you mine, which, indeed, has long been yours in the secrecy of my heart? Ah! I trust you will accept it, and in this hope I remain, most honoured and valued friend, your most obedient servant and friend

CONSTANZE WEBER

Please tell your Papa that I kiss his hand.

(448) *Mozart to Constanze Weber*

[*Autograph formerly in the possession of Frau Jähns*]

DEAREST, MOST BELOVED FRIEND!   [VIENNA], 29 *April* 1782
    Surely you will still allow me to address you by this name? Surely you do not hate me so much that I may be your friend no longer, and you —no longer mine? And even if you will not be my friend any longer, yet you cannot forbid me to wish you well, my friend, since it has become very natural for me to do so. Do think over what you said to me today. In spite of all my entreaties you have thrown me over three times and told me to my face that you intend to have nothing more to do with me. I (to whom it means more than it does to you to lose the object of my love) am not so hot-tempered, so rash and so senseless as to accept my dismissal. I love you far too well to do so. I entreat you, therefore, to ponder and reflect upon the cause of all this unpleasantness, which arose from my being annoyed that you were so impudently inconsiderate as to say to your sisters—and, be it noted, in my presence—that you had let a *chapeau* [1] measure the calves of your legs. No woman who cares for her honour can do such a thing. It is quite a good maxim to do as one's company does. At the same time there are many other factors to be considered—as, for example, whether only intimate friends and acquaintances are present— whether I am a child or a *marriageable* girl—more particularly, whether I am already betrothed—but, above all, whether only people of my own social standing or my social inferiors—or, what is even more important, my social superiors are in the company? If it be true that the Baroness [2] herself allowed it to be done to her, the case is still quite different, for she is already past her prime and cannot possibly attract any longer—and besides,

---

[1] A young gallant.   [2] The Baroness von Waldstädten.

she is inclined to be promiscuous with her favours. I hope, dearest friend, that, even if you do not wish to become my wife, you will never lead a life like hers. If it was quite impossible for you to resist the desire to take part in the game (although it is not always wise for a man to do so, and still less for a woman), then why in the name of Heaven did you not take the ribbon and measure your own calves *yourself* (as *all self-respecting women* have done on similar occasions in my presence) and not allow a *chapeau* to do so?—Why, I myself *in the presence of others* would never have done such a thing to you. I should have handed you the ribbon myself. Still less, then, should you have allowed it to be done to you by a stranger—a man about whom I know nothing. But it is all over now; and the least acknowledgment of your somewhat thoughtless behaviour on that occasion would have made everything all right again; and if you will not make a grievance of it, dearest friend, everything will still be all right. You realise now how much I love you. *I do not fly into a passion as you do.* I think, I reflect and I feel. *If you will but surrender to your feelings,* then I know that this very day I shall be able to say with absolute confidence that Constanze is the virtuous, honourable, prudent and loyal sweetheart of her honest and devoted

MOZART

(449) *Leopold Mozart to Breitkopf's Son and Co., Leipzig*

[*Extract*]   [*Autograph in the Universitätsbibliothek, Bonn*]

SALZBURG, 29 *April* 1782 ★

My son is in Vienna and is remaining there. Herr Artaria has published some of his clavier sonatas.[1]

Meanwhile I am having a pleasant time with two pupils, the twelve-year-old son and the fourteen-year-old daughter of Herr Marchand,[2] theatrical manager in Munich, whom I am instructing. I hope to make a great violinist and clavier-player out of the boy and a good singer and excellent clavier-player out of the girl.

(450) *Mozart to his Father*

[*Autograph in the Mozarteum, Salzburg*]

MON TRÉS CHER PÉRE!   VIENNA, 8 *May* 1782

I have received your last letter of April 30th and yesterday too my sister's letter with the enclosure for my dear Constanze, to whom I gave it

---

[1] K. 296 and 376–380 [374d, e, 317d, 373a, 374f], the violin and clavier sonatas dedicated to Fräulein Auernhammer.

[2] Heinrich and Margarete Marchand.

at once. It caused her sincere pleasure and she will take the liberty of writing to her again very soon. Meanwhile (as I cannot possibly find time to write to my sister today) I must put a question to you on behalf of Constanze, which is, whether *fringes* are being worn in Salzburg? Whether my sister is wearing them already? Whether she can make them herself? Constanze has just trimmed two piqué dresses with them, for they are all the fashion in Vienna. As she can make them herself now, she would like to send some to my sister, if the latter will tell her which shade she prefers. For they are worn in all colours, white, black, green, blue, puce, etc. A satin or gros de turc silk dress must be trimmed, of course, with silk fringes, and Constanze has a dress of this kind. An ordinary dress of pretty Saxon piqué, trimmed with cotton fringes (which, unless you feel them, can hardly be distinguished from silk), looks very well; and the advantage of such a combination is that the fringes can be washed on the dress.

Please write and tell me how Salieri's opera[1] in Munich went off. I am sure that you managed to hear it, but, if not, you are certain to know how it was received. I called twice on Count Daun,[2] but each time he was not at home. However, I sent for the music. Indeed he is only at home in the mornings, when not only do I never go out, but I do not even dress, as I have such a lot of composing to do. All the same I shall try to see him next Sunday. Perhaps he will be able to take my Munich opera[3] as well as the variations.[4]

I was at Countess Thun's yesterday and played through my second act[5] to her, with which she seems no less pleased than she was with the first. I have had Raaff's aria[6] copied long ago and have given it to Fischer, whom he had commissioned to get it. You said once in a letter that you would like to have the Robinig music.[7] Who has it? I haven't. I think Eck gave it back to you. I asked you for it in my letter as well as for the Cassations in F and B♭.[8] Do please send me soon the scena I composed for Countess Baumgarten.[9] This summer there is to be a concert every Sunday in the Augarten.[10] A certain Martin[11] organized last winter a series of amateur concerts, which took place every Friday in the Mehlgrube.[12] You know that there are a great many amateurs in Vienna, and some very good ones too, both men and women. But so far these concerts have not been

---

[1] Salieri's *Semiramide*, performed during the Munich carnival season, 1782.
[2] Count Daun, a canon of Salzburg Cathedral.
[3] *Idomeneo*.   [4] K. 359, 360, 352 [374a–c].
[5] Of his opera *Die Entführung aus dem Serail*.   [6] K. 295, composed in 1778.
[7] A divertimento, K. 334 [320h], and a march, K. 445 [320c], composed in 1779–80.
[8] K. 247, composed in 1776, and K. 287 [271H], composed in 1777.   [9] K. 369.
[10] A well-known public garden in the Leopoldstadt suburb of Vienna, where, as at Vauxhall and Ranelagh, public concerts were held. It was opened in 1775 by the Emperor Joseph II.
[11] Philipp Martin of Regensburg.
[12] A very old building in the Neuer Markt, to which a flour warehouse in the basement gave its name. It was then an inn with a large hall, where balls and concerts were held. The Hotel Ambassador (Kranz) now occupies the site.

properly arranged. Well, this Martin has now got permission from the Emperor under charter (with the promise too of his gracious patronage) to give twelve concerts in the Augarten and four grand serenades in the finest open places of the city. The subscription for the whole summer is two ducats. So you can imagine that we shall have plenty of subscribers, the more so as I am taking an interest in it and am associated with it. Assuming that we get only a hundred subscribers, then each of us will have a profit of three hundred gulden (even if the costs amount to two hundred gulden, which is most unlikely). The Baron van Swieten and Countess Thun are very much interested in it. The orchestra consists entirely of amateurs, with the exception of the bassoon-players, the trumpeters and drummers. I hear that Clementi is leaving Vienna tomorrow. Have you seen his sonatas?

Please have a little patience with poor Leutgeb. If you knew his circumstances and saw how he has to muddle along, you would certainly feel sorry for him. I shall have a word with him and I feel sure that he will pay you, at any rate by instalments. Now farewell. I kiss your hands a thousand times and am ever your most obedient son

W: A: Mzt

PS.—I kiss my dear sister a thousand times. My remembrances to Katherl and a greeting to Thresel—and tell her that she is to be my nursery-maid, but that she will have to practise her singing hard. Adieu. A pinch of Spanish snuff for Bimperl.

(451) *Mozart to his Father*

[*Autograph in the Mozarteum, Salzburg*]

Mon trés cher Pére!   Vienna, 25 *May* 1782

This time I must really steal a moment, so that you may not wait too long for a letter. For tomorrow our first concert takes place in the Augarten and at half past eight Martin is fetching me in a carriage and we have still six visits to pay, which I must finish off by eleven o'clock, as I then have to go to Countess Rumbeck. Afterwards I am lunching with Countess Thun and, I should add, in her garden. In the evening we are having the rehearsal of the concert. A symphony by Van Swieten and one of mine [1] are being performed; an amateur singer, Mlle Berger, is going to sing; a boy of the name of Türk is playing a violin concerto; and Fräulein Auernhammer and I are playing my E♭ concerto for two pianos. [2]

---

[1] Probably K. 338, composed in 1780.   [2] K. 365 [316a], composed in 1779.

(451a) *Constanze Weber to Leopold Mozart*

[*Autograph in the Mozarteum, Salzburg*]

[VIENNA, 25 *May* 1782]

Your dear son has been summoned this very moment to Countess Thun's and hasn't time to finish this letter to his dear father, which he much regrets. He has commissioned me to let you know this, for, as today is post-day, he does not wish you to be without a letter from him. He will write more to his dear father the next time. Please forgive me for writing to you. These few lines cannot be as agreeable to you as those which your son would have written.

I am ever your faithful servant and friend

CONSTANZE WEBER

Please give my compliments to your amiable daughter.

(452) *Mozart to his Father*

[*Autograph in the Mozarteum, Salzburg*]

MON TRÉS CHER PÉRE!   VIENNA, 29 *May* 1782

I was positively prevented the other day from finishing my letter and therefore asked my dear Constanze to make my apologies to you. She hesitated for some time, fearing that you might laugh at her spelling and style; and she is giving me no peace until I write to you and convey her excuses.

The first amateur concert went off tolerably well. The Archduke Maximilian was there, Countess Thun, Wallenstein, the Baron van Swieten and a whole crowd of other people. I am earnestly longing for the arrival of the next mail coach, which is to bring me some music. In regard to the Robinig music [1] I can assure you most faithfully that I never took it with me—and that Eck must still have it, for he had not returned it when I left Munich. The organizer of these amateur concerts, M. Martin, knows Abbé Bullinger very well, for he was a pupil at the Munich seminary in his day. He is a very worthy young man, who is trying to make his way by his music, by his elegant writing and generally by his ability, intelligence and sound judgment. When he came to Vienna, he had a hard struggle—and had to manage for a fortnight on half a gulden. Adamberger, who knew him in Munich, has been very kind to him. He is a native of Regensburg and his father was private physician to Prince

---

[1] See p. 804, n. 7.

Taxis. My dear Constanze and I are lunching tomorrow with Countess Thun and I am to play over my third act [1] to her. At the moment I have nothing but very tiresome work—that is, correcting. We are to have our first rehearsal next Monday. I must confess that I am looking forward with much pleasure to this opera. A propos. A few days ago I had a letter—from whom? From Herr von Feigele. And the contents—that he is in love—and with whom? With my sister? Not at all—with my cousin! [2] Well, he will have to wait a long time before getting an answer from me; for you know how little time I have for writing. But I am rather curious to see how long his infatuation will last.

Now for something that I heard quite by accident and which makes me very much annoyed with Count Kühnburg. Fräulein von Auernhammer told me yesterday that Herr von Moll has asked her whether she would be willing to enter a nobleman's family in Salzburg at a salary of three hundred gulden a year. The name was Kühnburg. What do you think of that? So it seems that my sister's services count for nothing! Make your own use of this information. He was only here for a day, but if he returns, I shall find an opportunity of speaking to him on the subject. Now farewell. I kiss your hands a thousand times and embrace my dear sister with all my heart. I also send to Mlle Marchand (with my dear Constanze's permission) a few kisses, and I am ever your most obedient son

W: A: Mozart

PS.—My dear Constanze kisses your hands and embraces my sister as her true friend and future sister-in-law.

(453) *Mozart to his Father*

[*Autograph in the Mozarteum, Salzburg*]

Mon trés cher Pére! VIENNA, *20 July* 1782

I hope that you received safely my last letter informing you of the good reception of my opera.[3] It was given yesterday for the second time. Can you really believe it, but yesterday there was an even stronger cabal against it than on the first evening! The whole first act was accompanied by hissing. But indeed they could not prevent the loud shouts of 'bravo' during the arias. I was relying on the closing trio,[4] but, as ill-luck would have it, Fischer went wrong, which made Dauer (Pedrillo) go wrong too; and Adamberger alone could not sustain the trio, with the result that the

---

[1] Of *Die Entführung aus dem Serail*.
[2] Maria Anna Thekla Mozart, the 'Bäsle'. She died in 1841 at the age of eighty-two. According to Schurig, vol. i. p. 455, descendants of her illegitimate daughter, Marianne Viktoria Mozart (1793–1857), were living in Vienna in 1923.
[3] *Die Entführung aus dem Serail* was performed on 16 July. The letter to which Mozart refers is unfortunately lost. [4] 'Marsch, marsch, marsch!', the last number of Act I.

whole effect was lost and that this time *it was not repeated*. I was in such a rage (and so was Adamberger) that I was simply beside myself and said at once that I would not let the opera be given again without having a short rehearsal for the singers. In the second act both duets were repeated as on the first night, and in addition Belmonte's rondo 'Wenn der Freude Tränen fliessen'. The theatre was almost more crowded than on the first night and on the preceding day no reserved seats were to be had, either in the stalls or in the third circle, and not a single box. My opera has brought in 1200 gulden in the two days. I send you herewith the original score and two copies of the libretto. You will see that I have cut out several passages. I knew that here the practice is for the score to be copied at once; but I first gave free rein to my ideas and then made my alterations and cuts at the last moment. The opera was performed just as you now have it; but here and there the parts for trumpets, drums, flutes, and clarinets, and the Turkish music are missing, because I could not get any music paper with so many lines. Those parts were written out on extra sheets, which the copyist has probably lost, for he could not find them. The first act, when I was sending it somewhere or other—I forget where, unfortunately fell in the mud, which explains why it is so dirty.

Well, I am up to the eyes in work, for by Sunday week I have to arrange my opera for wind-instruments. If I don't, someone will anticipate me and secure the profits. And now you ask me to write a new symphony![1] How on earth can I do so? You have no idea how difficult it is to arrange a work of this kind for wind-instruments, so that it suits these instruments and yet loses none of its effect. Well, I must just spend the night over it, for that is the only way; and to you, dearest father, I sacrifice it. You may rely on having something from me by every post. I shall work as fast as possible and, as far as haste permits, I shall turn out good work.

Count Zichy[2] has this moment sent me a message inviting me to drive with him to Laxenburg, so that he may present me to Prince Kaunitz. So I must close this letter and dress. For when I have no intention of going out I always remain en négligé. The copyist has just sent me the remaining parts. Adieu. I kiss your hands a thousand times and embrace my dear sister with all my heart and am ever your most obedient son

W. A. MOZART

PS.—My dear Constanze sends greetings to you both.

[1] K. 385, the 'Haffner' symphony in D major. Mozart had already written a march (K. 249) and a serenade (K. 250 [248b]) for the wedding of Elise Haffner, daughter of Sigmund Haffner, merchant and burgomaster of Salzburg. According to Deutsch-Paumgartner, *op. cit.* p. 533, the symphony was commissioned to celebrate the granting of a title of nobility to young Sigmund Haffner (1756–1787). See also Köchel, p. 416.

[2] His wife, Countess Zichy, was Mozart's pupil on the clavier.

(454) *Mozart to his Sister*

[*Autograph in the Koch Collection, Basel*]

[VIENNA, 24 July 1782]

Forgive me, dear sister, for not sending you a formal letter of congratulation, but I really have no time. Besides you know that, as it is, I wish you daily every good thing. It was impossible for me to find a moment today to write to my father. But I shall certainly do so next post-day. Adieu. Farewell. My opera is to be performed in your honour on your name-day.[1] I kiss my dear father's hands and I kiss you a thousand times and am ever your sincere brother

Vienna, 24 July 1782   W: A: MOZART

(454a) *Constanze Weber to Nannerl Mozart*

[*Autograph in the Koch Collection, Basel*]

MOST PRECIOUS FRIEND!   [VIENNA, 24 July 1782]

Forgive me for taking the liberty of worrying you again with my scrawl. Your approaching name-day must be my excuse! And if my good wishes are a nuisance to you, as indeed all congratulations are, my consolation must be that already I am not the only one who is bothering you in this way. All that I deserve is that for the love of God you should suffer me as you do all the others. Yet could you but see into my heart and read what is there, perhaps I might be exempted from your general complaint; that at least. Possibly, nay assuredly, among the exempted I should even be given some preference. So I wish with all my heart that you will be, and not only become, very happy, and that you will really be as happy as I am confident that I shall be in the future. If you are, then . . .[2]

(455) *Mozart to his Father*

[*Autograph in the Mozarteum, Salzburg*]

MON TRÉS CHER PÉRE!   VIENNA, 27 July 1782

You will be surprised and disappointed to find that this contains only the first Allegro;[3] but it has been quite impossible to do more for you, for I have had to compose in a great hurry a serenade,[4] but only for wind-instruments (otherwise I could have used it for you too). On Wednesday

---

[1] 26 July.   [2] The autograph breaks off here.
[3] Of his new symphony for the Haffner family, K. 385.   [4] K. 375 or 388 [384a].

the 31st I shall send the two minuets, the Andante and the last movement.[1] If I can manage to do so, I shall send a march too.[2] If not, you will just have to use the one[3] in the Haffner music, which hardly anyone knows—

I have composed my symphony in D major, because you prefer that key.

My opera was given yesterday for the third time in honour of all the Nannerls[4] and won the greatest applause; and again, in spite of the frightful heat, the theatre was packed. It was to be given again next Friday, but I have protested against this, for I do not want it to become hackneyed. I may say that people are absolutely infatuated with this opera. Indeed it does one good to win such approbation. I hope that you have safely received the original score. Dearest, most beloved father, I implore you by all you hold dear in the world to give your consent to my marriage with my dear Constanze. Do not suppose that it is just for the sake of getting married. If that were the only reason, I would gladly wait. But I realize that it is absolutely necessary for my own honour and for that of my girl, and for the sake of my health and spirits. My heart is restless and my head confused; in such a condition how can one think and work to any good purpose? And why am I in this state? Well, because most people think that we are already married. Her mother gets very much annoyed when she hears these rumours, and, as for the poor girl and myself, we are tormented to death. This state of affairs can be remedied so easily. Believe me, it is just as easy to live in expensive Vienna as anywhere else. It all depends on economy and good management, which cannot be expected from a young fellow, particularly if he is in love. Whoever gets a wife like my Constanze will certainly be a happy man. We intend to live very modestly and quietly and yet we shall be happy. Do not be uneasy, for, if I were to fall ill today, which God forbid, I would wager that the leading nobles would stand by me manfully and the more so if I were married. I can say this with entire confidence. I know what Prince Kaunitz has said about me to the Emperor and to the Archduke Maximilian. Most beloved father, I am longing to have your consent. I feel sure that you will give it, for my honour and my peace of mind depend upon it. Do not postpone too long the joy of embracing your son and his wife. I kiss your hands a thousand times and am ever your

obedient son

W. A. Mozart

---

[1] Of his new symphony, K. 385. One minuet seems to have been lost. See Köchel, p. 416.
[2] K. 408, No. 2 [385a].   [3] K. 249, composed in 1776.   [4] 26 July, St. Anne's Day.

PS.—I embrace my dear sister most cordially. My dear Constanze sends her kind regards to you both. Adieu.

(456) *Mozart to his Father*

[Autograph formerly in the Mozarteum, Salzburg]

MON TRÉS CHER PÉRE!   VIENNA, 31 *July* 1782

You see that my intentions are good—only what one cannot do one cannot! I am really unable to scribble off inferior stuff. So I cannot send you the whole symphony[1] until next post-day. I could have let you have the last movement, but I prefer to despatch it all together, for then it will cost only one postage. What I have sent you has already cost me three gulden. I received today your letter of the 26th, but a cold, indifferent letter, such as I could never have expected in reply to my news of the good reception of my opera.[2] I thought (judging by my own feelings) that you would hardly be able to open the parcel for excitement and eagerness to see your son's work, which, far from merely pleasing, is making such a sensation in Vienna that people refuse to hear anything else, so that the theatre is always packed. It was given yesterday for the fourth time and is to be repeated on Friday. But you—have not had the time. So the whole world declares that by my boasting and criticising I have made enemies of the professors of music and of many others! *What* world pray? Presumably the world of Salzburg, for everyone in Vienna can see and hear enough to be convinced of the contrary. And that must be my reply. In the meantime you will have received my last letter; and I feel confident that your next will contain your consent to my marriage. You can have no objection whatever to raise—and indeed you do not raise any. Your letters show me that. For Constanze is a respectable honest girl of good parentage, and I am able *to support her*. We love each other—and want each other. All that you have written and may possibly write to me on the subject can only be *well-meaning advice* which, however fine and good it may be, is no longer applicable to a man who has gone so far with a girl. In such a case nothing can be postponed. It is better for him to put his affairs in order and act like an honest fellow! God will ever reward that. I mean to have nothing with which to reproach myself.

Now farewell. I kiss your hands a thousand times and am ever your most obedient son

W: A. MOZART

PS.—I embrace my dear sister with all my heart. Adieu.

---

[1] K. 385.   [2] *Die Entführung aus dem Serail.*

(457) *Mozart to the Baroness von Waldstädten*

[Autograph in a private collection, London]

[VIENNA, *shortly before* 4 *August* 1782[1]]

MOST HIGHLY ESTEEMED BARONESS!

Madame Weber's maid-servant has brought me my music, for which I have had to give her a written receipt. She has also told me something in confidence which, although I do not believe it could happen, since it would be a disgrace to the whole family, yet seems possible when one remembers Madame Weber's stupidity; and which consequently causes me anxiety. It appears that Sophie[2] went to the maid-servant in tears and when the latter asked her what was the matter, she said: 'Do tell Mozart in secret to arrange for Constanze to go home, for my mother is absolutely determined to have her fetched by the police'. Are the police in Vienna allowed to go into any house? Perhaps the whole thing is only a trap to make her return home. But if it could be done, then the best plan I can think of is to marry Constanze tomorrow morning—or even today, if that is possible. For I should not like to expose my beloved one to this scandal—and there could not be one, if she were my wife. One thing more. Thorwart has been summoned to the Webers today. I entreat you, dear Baroness, to let me have your friendly advice and to assist us poor creatures. I shall be at home all day. I kiss your hands a thousand times and am your most grateful servant

W: A: MOZART

In the greatest haste. Constanze knows *nothing* of this as yet. Has Herr von Thorwart been to see you? Is it necessary for the two of us to visit him after lunch today?

(458) *Mozart to his Father*

[Autograph in the Mozarteum, Salzburg]

MON TRÉS CHER PÉRE!   VIENNA, 7 *August* 1782

You are very much mistaken in your son if you can suppose him capable of acting dishonestly. My dear Constanze—now, thank God, at last my wife[3]—knew my circumstances and heard from me long ago all that I had to expect from you. But her affection and her love for me were so great that she willingly and joyfully sacrificed her whole future to share

---

[1] The autograph is undated.   [2] Sophie, Frau Weber's youngest daughter.
[3] The marriage took place on 4 August 1782.

my fate. I kiss your hands and thank you with all the tenderness which a son has ever felt for a father, for your kind consent and fatherly blessing. But indeed I could safely rely on it. For you know that I myself could not but see only too clearly all the objections that could be raised against such a step. At the same time you also know that I could not act otherwise without injury to my conscience and my honour. Consequently I could certainly rely on having your consent. So it was that having waited two post-days in vain for a reply and the ceremony having been fixed for a day by which I was certain to have received it, I was married by the blessing of God to my beloved Constanze. I was quite assured of your consent and was therefore comforted. The following day I received your two letters at once—Well, it is over! I only ask your forgiveness for my too hasty trust in your fatherly love. In this frank confession you have a fresh proof of my love of truth and hatred of a lie. Next post-day my dear wife will ask her dearest, most beloved Papa-in-law for his fatherly blessing and her beloved sister-in-law for the continuance of her most valued friendship. No one was present at the wedding save her mother and her youngest sister, Herr von Thorwart as guardian and witness for both of us, Herr von Cetto, district councillor, who gave away the bride, and Gilowsky as my best man.[1] When we had been joined together, both my wife and I began to weep. All present, even the priest, were deeply touched and all wept to see how much our hearts were moved. Our whole wedding feast consisted of a supper given for us by the Baroness von Waldstädten, which indeed was more princely than baronial. My dear Constanze is now looking forward a hundred times more to a visit to Salzburg, and I wager—I wager—that you will rejoice in my happiness when you get to know her, that is, if you agree with me that a right-minded, honest, virtuous and amiable wife is a blessing to her husband.

I send you herewith a short march.[2] I only hope that all will reach you in good time, and be to your taste. The first Allegro[3] must be played with great fire, the last—as fast as possible. My opera was given again yesterday—and that too at Gluck's request. He has been very complimentary to me about it. I am lunching with him tomorrow. You see by my writing how I must hurry. Adieu. My dear wife and I kiss your hands a thousand times and we both embrace our dear sister with all our hearts and I am ever your most obedient son

W. A. Mozart

---

[1] For Mozart's certificate of marriage, see Abert, vol. ii. p. 907, and *MDB*, p. 203 f.
[2] K. 408, No. 2 [385a], the promised addition to K. 385, the 'Haffner' symphony.
[3] i.e. of the 'Haffner' symphony.

(459) *Mozart to his Father*

[*Autograph in the Mozarteum, Salzburg*]

MON TRÉS CHER PÉRE!   VIENNA, 17 *August* 1782

I forgot to tell you the other day that on the Day of Portiuncula [1] my wife and I performed our devotions together at the Theatines. Even if a sense of piety had not moved us to do so, we should have had to do it on account of the banns, without which we could not have been married. Indeed for a considerable time before we were married we had always attended Mass and gone to confession and received Communion together; and I found that I never prayed so fervently or confessed and received Communion so devoutly as by her side; and she felt the same. In short, we are made for each other; and God who orders all things and consequently has ordained this also, will not forsake us. We both thank you most submissively for your fatherly blessing. I hope you have now received my wife's letter.

In regard to Gluck, my ideas are precisely the same as yours, my dearest father. But I should like to add something. The Viennese gentry, and in particular the ⟨Emperor,⟩ must not imagine that I am on this earth solely for the sake of Vienna. There is no monarch in the world whom I should be more glad to serve than the Emperor, but I refuse to beg for any post. I believe that I am capable of doing credit to any court. If Germany, my beloved fatherland, of which, as you know, I am proud, will not accept me, then in God's name let France or England become the richer by another talented German, to the disgrace of the German nation. You know well that it is the Germans who have always excelled in almost all the arts. [2] But where did they make their fortune and their reputation? Certainly not in Germany! Take even the case of Gluck. Has Germany made him the great man he is? Alas no! Countess Thun, Count Zichy, the Baron van Swieten, even Prince Kaunitz, are all very much displeased with the Emperor, because he does not value men of talent more, and allows them to leave his dominions. Kaunitz said the other day to the Archduke Maximilian, when the conversation turned on myself, that '*such people only come into the world once in a hundred years and must not be driven out of Germany, particularly when we are fortunate enough to have them in the capital.*' You cannot imagine how kind and courteous Prince Kaunitz was to me when I visited him. When I took my leave, he said: '*I am much*

---

[1] 2 August. In 1223 Pope Honorius III, at the request of St. Francis, granted an annual indulgence to anyone who should visit the Portiuncula chapel in the Church of St. Mary of the Angels at Assisi on August 2nd. Gregory XV in 1622 extended it to all churches of the Observant Franciscans; in 1856 it was further extended to all churches where the Third Order of St. Francis was canonically established, and in 1910 to all Catholic churches and chapels.

[2] For an interesting article on Mozart's patriotism as revealed in his letters, see *MM*, November 1918, pp. 14-18.

obliged to you, my dear Mozart, for having taken the trouble to visit me.' You would scarcely believe what efforts Countess Thun, the Baron van Swieten and other eminent people are making to keep me here. But I cannot afford to wait indefinitely, and indeed I refuse to remain hanging on here at their mercy. Moreover, I think that even though he *is* the Emperor, I am not so desperately in need of his favour. My idea is to go to Paris next Lent, but of course not simply on chance. I have already written to Le Gros about this and am awaiting his reply. I have mentioned it here too—particularly to *people of position*—just in the course of conversation. For you know that often in conversation you can throw out a hint and that this is more effective than if the same thing were announced in the tones of a dictator. I might be able to get engagements for the Concert Spirituel and the Concert des Amateurs—and besides, I should have plenty of pupils—and now that I have a wife I could superintend them more easily and more attentively—and then with the help of compositions and so forth—but indeed I should rely chiefly on opera commissions. Latterly I have been practising my French daily and have already taken three lessons in English. In three months I hope to be able to read and understand English books fairly easily. Now farewell. My wife and I kiss your hands a thousand times and I-am ever your most obedient son

W: A: Mozart

PS.—*What does Luigi Gatti*[1] *say?*

My compliments to Perwein.[2] I hope my dear sister's indisposition will not have serious consequences. My dear wife and I kiss her a thousand times and hope that she is now quite well again. Adieu.

(460) *Leopold Mozart to the Baroness von Waldstädten, Vienna*

[*Copy in the Staatsbibliothek Preussischer Kulturbesitz, West Berlin*]

HIGHLY BORN AND GRACIOUS LADY! [SALZBURG, 23 *August* 1782]
    I thank your Ladyship most warmly for the very special interest you take in my circumstances and for your extraordinary kindness in celebrating my son's wedding day with such liberality. When I was a young fellow I used to think that philosophers were people who said little, seldom laughed and turned a sulky face upon the world in general. But my own experiences have completely persuaded me that without knowing it I must be a philosopher. For having done my duty as a father, having in countless letters made the clearest and most lucid representations to

---

[1] See p. 547, n. 3. Abbate Luigi Gatti was appointed Kapellmeister at Salzburg in February 1783.

[2] The oboist Markus Perwein, who had recently left Wallerstein and returned to Salzburg.

Wolfgang on every point and being convinced that he knows my trying circumstances, which are extremely grievous to a man of my age, and that he is aware of the degradations I am suffering in Salzburg, since he must realize that both morally and materially I am being punished for his conduct, all that I can now do is to leave him to his own resources (as he evidently wishes) and pray God to bestow on him His paternal blessing and not withdraw from him His Divine grace. For my part I shall not abandon the cheerfulness which is natural to me and which in spite of my advancing years I still possess; and I shall continue to hope for the best. On the whole, I should feel quite easy in my mind, were it not that I have detected in my son an outstanding fault, which is, that he is far too *patient* or rather *easy-going*, too *indolent*, perhaps even too *proud*, in short, that he has the sum total of all those traits which render a man *inactive*; on the other hand, he is too *impatient*, too *hasty* and will not bide his time. Two opposing elements rule his nature, I mean, there is either too *much* or too *little*, never the golden mean. If he is not actually in want, then he is immediately satisfied and becomes *indolent* and *lazy*. If he has to bestir himself, then he realizes his worth and *wants to make his fortune at once.* Nothing must stand in his way; yet it is unfortunately the most capable people and those who possess outstanding genius who have the greatest obstacles to face. Who will prevent him from pursuing his present career in Vienna if he only has a little patience? Kapellmeister Bonno is a very old man. After his death Salieri[1] will be promoted and will make room for someone else. And is not Gluck too an old man? My dear lady, please instil a little patience into my son. And may I ask you to let me have your opinion of his circumstances? My daughter sends you her most respectful regards and both she and I wish that we had the good fortune to be able to kiss your Ladyship's hands. She is very much touched at being honoured quite undeservedly with a remembrance from your Ladyship. Ah, if only we were not so far away from Vienna! How delightful it would be to devote ourselves together to music! May Hope, sole consolation of our desires, soothe my spirit! Perhaps I may yet be happy enough to be able to assure your Ladyship in person not only of my friendship, which, though it may be of little advantage to you, is heartfelt and true, but also of my deepest esteem and regard. I am indeed your most humble and obedient servant

LEOPOLD MOZART

Salzburg, 23 August 1782

My son wrote to me some time ago saying that, when he married, he would not live with his wife's mother. I trust that by now he has left that house. If not, he is storing up trouble for himself and his wife.

[1] After the death of Bonno in 1788 Salieri was appointed Kapellmeister to the Viennese Court.

(461) *Mozart to his Father*

[*Autograph in the Mozarteum, Salzburg*]

MON TRÉS CHER PÉRE!   VIENNA, 24 *August* 1782

You have only imagined what I was really intending and still intend to do. I must likewise confess the truth to you, which is, that my wife and I have been waiting from day to day for some *certain* information about the arrival of the Russian visitors, in order to decide whether to undertake or to postpone the journey we have planned; and as we have heard nothing definite up to this moment, I have not been able to write to you on the subject. Some say they are to arrive on September 7th, others again that they are not coming at all. If the latter be the truth, we shall be in Salzburg by the beginning of October. If, however, they do come, then, according to the advice of my good friends, it is not only very necessary that I should be here, but my absence would be a real triumph for my enemies and consequently highly detrimental to me. If I am appointed music master to the Princess of Wurtemberg, which is extremely probable, I can easily obtain leave of absence for a time in order to visit my father. If our project has to be postponed, no one will be more disappointed than my dear wife and I, for we can hardly await the moment to embrace our dearest, most beloved father and our dearest sister.

You are perfectly right about France and England! It is a step which I can always take, and it is better for me to remain in Vienna a little longer. Besides, times may change too in those countries. Last Tuesday (after, thank Heaven! an interval of a fortnight) my opera was again performed with great success.

I am delighted that the symphony [1] is to your taste. A propos, you have no idea (but perhaps you have?) where I am living. Where do you think? In the same house where we lodged fourteen years ago, on the Hohe Brücke, in Grünwald's house. But now it is called Grosshaupt's house, No. 387. [2] Stephanie junior arrived yesterday and I went to see him today. Elizabeth Wendling is also here. Well, you must forgive me if I close this letter already, but I have been wasting my time gossiping to Herr von Strack. I wish with all my heart that those Russian people may not come, so that I may soon have the pleasure of kissing your hands. My wife sheds tears of joy when she thinks of our journey to Salzburg. Farewell. We kiss your hands a thousand times and embrace our dear sister with all our hearts and are ever your most obedient children

W. A. MOZART
Man and wife
Are one life.

[1] K. 385.
[2] Now Wipplingerstrasse no. 19. The Mozarts took rooms in this house on their return to Vienna from Olmütz in 1768.

(462) *Mozart to his Father*

[*Autograph in the Mozarteum, Salzburg*]

MON TRÉS CHER PÉRE!   VIENNA, 31 *August* 1782

You wonder how I can flatter myself that I shall be maestro to the Princess?[1] Why, Salieri is not capable of teaching her the clavier! All he can do is to try to injure me in this matter by recommending someone else, which quite possibly he is doing! On the other hand the Emperor knows me; and the last time she was in Vienna the Princess would gladly have taken lessons from me. Moreover, I know that my name is in the book which contains the names of all those who have been chosen for her service. Le Chevalier Hypolity has not put in an appearance yet. You say that I have never told you on what floor we are living? That in truth must have stuck in my pen! Well, I am telling you now—that we are living on the second floor. But I cannot understand how you got the idea that my highly honoured mother-in-law is living here too. For indeed I did not marry my sweetheart in such a hurry in order to live a life of vexations and quarrels, but to enjoy peace and happiness; and the only way to ensure this was to cut ourselves off from that house. Since our marriage we have paid her two visits, but on the second occasion quarrelling and wrangling began again, so that my poor wife started to cry. I put a stop to the bickering at once by saying to Constanze that it was time for us to go. We have not been there since and do not intend to go until we have to celebrate the birthday or name-day of the mother or of one of the two sisters. You say too that I have never told you on what day we got married. I must indeed beg your pardon—but either your memory has deceived you this time, in which case you need only take the trouble to look among my letters for that of August 7th, where you will find it stated clearly and distinctly that we confessed on Friday, the Day of Portiuncula, and were married on the following Sunday, August 4th—or you never received that letter, which, however, is not very likely, as you got the march[2] which was enclosed with it and also replied to various points in the letter. I now have a request to make. The Baroness Waldstädten is leaving here and would like to have a good small pianoforte. As I have forgotten the name of the pianoforte maker at Zweibrücken, I should like to ask you to order one from him. It must, however, be ready within a month or six weeks at the latest and the price should be the same as that of the Archbishop's. May I also ask you to send me some Salzburg tongues either by some acquaintance or by mail coach (if the customs duty does not make it impossible)? I am under great obligations to the Baroness and when the conversation one day turned on tongues and she said she would very much

---

[1] Princess Elizabeth of Wurtemberg.   [2] See p. 813, n. 2.

like to try a Salzburg one, I offered to get one for her. If you can think of any other delicacy for her and will send it to me, I shall indeed be very much obliged to you. I am particularly anxious to give her some such pleasure. I can refund the cost through Peisser or give it to you when we meet.

Can you send me some Schwarzreuter?[1] Now farewell. My wife and I kiss your hands a thousand times and we embrace our dear sister with all our hearts and are ever

your   most obedient daughter
most obedient son
WOLFGANG and CONSTANZE MOZART[2]

PS.—Should you be writing to my cousin,[3] please give her kind regards from us both. Addio.

(463) *Mozart to his Father*

[*Autograph in the Mozarteum, Salzburg*]

MON TRÉS CHER PÉRE!   VIENNA, 11 *September* 1782

Many thanks for the tongues. I gave two to the Baroness and kept the other two for myself; and we are to sample them tomorrow. Please be so good as to tell me how you wish the payment to be made. If you can also obtain some Schwarzreuter for me, you will indeed give me much pleasure. The Jewess Eskeles[4] has no doubt proved a very good and useful tool for breaking up the friendship between the Emperor and the Russian court, for the day before yesterday *she was taken to Berlin* in order that the King might have the pleasure of her company. She is indeed a sow of the first order. Moreover, she was the whole cause of Günther's misfortune, if indeed it be a misfortune to be imprisoned for two months in a beautiful room (with permission to have all his books, his pianoforte and so forth) and to lose his former post, but to be appointed to another at a salary of 1200 gulden; for yesterday he left for Hermannstadt. Yet an experience of that kind always injures an honest man and nothing in the world can compensate him for it. I just want you to realize that he has not committed a great crime. His conduct was due entirely to étourderie, or thoughtlessness, and consequently lack of discretion, which in a Privy

---

[1] A kind of trout (*Salmo salvelinis*) found in the Salzkammergut lakes.
[2] After his marriage to Constanze Weber, Mozarts' letters to his father and to his sister bear, almost without exception, this double signature.
[3] Maria Anna Thekla Mozart, the 'Bäsle'.
[4] For a full account of the Günther-Eskeles *cause célèbre*, which vindicates the honour of Eleonore Fliess-Eskeles, see *MM*, February–May 1921, pp. 41 ff.

Councillor is certainly a serious fault. Although he never divulged any-thing of importance, yet his enemies, chief of whom is the former Stadt-holder, the Count von Herberstein, managed to play their cards so cleverly that the Emperor who formerly had such immense confidence in Günther that he would walk up and down the room arm in arm with him for hours, now began to distrust him with an equal intensity. To make matters worse, who should appear on the scene but that sow Eskeles (a former mistress of Günther's), who accused him in the most violent terms. But when the matter was investigated, these gentlemen cut a very poor figure. However, the affair had already caused terrific commotion; and great people never like to admit that they have been in the wrong. Hence the fate of poor Günther, whom I pity from my heart, as he was a very good friend of mine and, if things had remained as they were, might have rendered me good service with the Emperor. You can imagine what a shock and how unexpected it was to me and how very much upset I was; for Stephanie, Adamberger and I had supper with him one evening and on the morrow he was arrested. Well, I must close, for I may miss the post. My dear wife and I kiss your hands a thousand times and embrace our dear sister with all our hearts and are ever your most obedient children

CONSTANZE and MOZART

My wife is almost ninety-one.[1]

(464) *Leopold Mozart to the Baroness von Waldstädten, Vienna*

[*Copy in the Staatsbibliothek Preussischer Kulturbesitz, West Berlin*]

[SALZBURG, 13 *September* 1782]

HIGHLY BORN AND GRACIOUS LADY!

It is impossible for me to describe to your Ladyship my heartfelt pleasure on reading your charming and flattering letter. It reminded me, as I read it, of Wieland's Sympathies.[2] It is undoubtedly true that many people are blessed with a higher plane of thought and unconsciously dwell together in a secret spiritual union before they have ever seen or spoken to one another. Good books and music are your Ladyship's occupation and entertainment. They are also mine. Your Ladyship has withdrawn herself from social functions; and for several months I too have not appeared at Court and only do so when I am obliged to. I live quietly

---

[1] Apparently a numerical joke of Mozart's, though Constanze was now twenty.
[2] Wieland's *Sympathien*, published in 1756, was one of his earliest prose writings.

with my daughter and have a few friends who come to see me. Reading, music and an occasional walk are our recreation and in bad weather a very humble game of taroc or tresette and occasionally a game of chess. Further, your Ladyship feels that *sorrow has greatly saddened you* and refuses when out of humour to be a burden to anyone. I for my part have had so much to endure from unmerited persecutions and have become so closely acquainted with envy, falseness, deception, malice and all the many other fine qualities of human nature that I purposely avoid large social functions in order not to become completely *out of humour* and to retain that modicum of cheerfulness which I still possess. Hence it is naturally my most ardent wish to have the privilege of meeting your Ladyship, as I feel certain that your Ladyship's outlook entirely agrees with mine, and that we should chatter away to our hearts' content. I regard it indeed as a great compliment that your Ladyship should consider me worthy of your invaluable friendship and quite undeserved esteem; and as I see no means of deserving it—of really deserving it, I hope at least, without saying anything ridiculous or improper, to find suitable words to express the feeling of great regard which I cherish towards a lady of such worth.

Your Ladyship has been so gracious as to offer me a lodging, should I come to Vienna. Indeed I am quite overcome! It would be most daring of me to avail myself of this gracious invitation; but my first outing in Vienna will certainly be to kiss your Ladyship's hands. Who can tell? Perhaps I may still have the good fortune to do so!

I beg your Ladyship to take care of your health and well-being. I was grievously distressed when I read that, owing to much sorrow and suffering, your Ladyship had lost your health and peace of mind. May God in His goodness watch over you! I am profoundly affected! After receiving my letter my son to some extent abandoned his resolve to leave Vienna; and, as he is coming to visit me in Salzburg, I shall make further very necessary and weighty representations to him. I am delighted to hear that his wife does not take after the Webers. If she did, he would indeed be unhappy. Your Ladyship assures me that she is a good soul—and that is enough for me!

My daughter kisses your Ladyship's hands and like myself is disappointed that we are so far from Vienna. Meanwhile I console myself with the thought that although mountains and valleys cannot meet, people can do so; that your Ladyship will continue to think me worthy of your favour and esteem; and that I, through my son, shall always continue to have news of the health and happiness of so kind a lady. I hope to be able to prove that with the greatest esteem, regard and devotion I am your Ladyship's most humble and obedient servant

LEOPOLD MOZART

Salzburg, 13 September 1782

(465) *Mozart to his Father*

[*Autograph in the Mozarteum, Salzburg*]

MON TRÉS CHER PÉRE!   VIENNA, 25 *September* 1782

I have received your last letter of September 20th and hope that you got my four lines [1], which only said that we were in good health. Now for a really comical event! But who can prevent possible coincidences and developments? Herr Gabel, who arrived here some days ago, is actually with me and is waiting for me to finish this letter in order to accompany my sonatas on the violin, which, if he is to be believed, he must play well. He has already played to me on the horn and could really do nothing on it. But what I can do for him I will; it is enough that I am your son. He sends his compliments to you both. It was news to me to hear that the paintings in the churches which serve no useful purpose, the many votive tablets and the instrumental music and so forth, which are to be done away with in Vienna, have already been abolished in Salzburg. No doubt ⟨the Archbishop⟩ hopes *by doing this* to ingratiate himself with ⟨the Emperor;⟩ but I can hardly believe that this policy of his will be of much service to him. Well, I can't bear to see anyone waiting for me; and I dislike to be kept waiting myself. So I must reserve for my next letter my description of the Baroness von Waldstädten and merely ask you to do me a most urgent favour. But I beg you, on account of the place where I am, not to divulge what I am about to say. The Prussian Ambassador, Riedesel, has informed me that he has been commissioned by the Berlin court to send my opera 'Die Entführung aus dem Serail' to Berlin and has asked me to have it copied, adding that the remuneration for the music will follow in due course. I promised at once to have this done. Now, as I have not got the opera myself, I should have to borrow it from the copyist, which would be very inconvenient, for I could not be *sure* of keeping it for three days in succession, because the Emperor often sends for it (he did so only yesterday) and, moreover, the opera is very often given. Why, since August 16th it has been performed ten times. So my idea is to have it copied in Salzburg, where it could be done more secretly and more cheaply! I beg you, therefore, to have the score copied out at once—and as quickly as possible. If, when you send me the copy, you will let me know the cost, I shall remit the amount at once through Herr Peisser. Now farewell. My wife and I kiss your hands a thousand times and embrace our dear sister with all our hearts and we are your most obedient children

W: A: and M: C: MOZART

[1] This letter is missing.

(466) *Mozart to the Baroness von Waldstädten*

[Autograph in the Koch Collection, Basel]

DEAREST BARONESS!   VIENNA, 28 *September* 1782

When your Ladyship was so gracious yesterday as to invite me to lunch with you tomorrow, Sunday, I had forgotten that a week ago I had made an engagement to lunch on that day in the Augarten.

Martin, the little angel, who fancies himself under an obligation to me in several ways, absolutely insists on treating me to a dînée. I thought yesterday that I could arrange and accommodate the matter in accordance with my wishes; but it has proved impossible, for the little angel has already ordered and arranged everything, and consequently would be put to useless expense. Therefore on this account your Ladyship will kindly excuse me this time, and with your Ladyship's permission we shall both have the honour of waiting upon you next Tuesday to deliver our *congratulations* and to give Fräulein von Auernhammer,[1] some *purgations*, if she must let us see her toilet *operations*. But now, joking apart, I really do not want to let the concerto [2] which I played in the theatre go for less than six ducats. On the other hand I should undertake to pay for the copying. As for the beautiful red coat, which attracts me enormously, please, please let me know *where it is to be had and how much it costs*—for that I have completely forgotten, as I was so captivated by its splendour that I did not take note of its price. I must have a coat like that, for it is one that will really do justice to certain buttons which I have long been hankering after. I saw them once, when I was choosing some for a suit. They were in Brandau's button factory in the Kohlmarkt, opposite the Milano. They are mother-of-pearl with a few white stones round the edge and a fine yellow stone in the centre. I should like all my things to be of good quality, genuine and beautiful. Why is it, I wonder, that those who cannot afford it, would like to spend a fortune on such articles and those who can, do not do so? Well, I think it is long past the time for me to stop this scribbling. j kiss your hands, and hoping to see you in good health the Tuesday j am your most humble servant[3]

MOZART

Constanze, my better half, kisses your Ladyship's hands a thousand times and gives that Auernhammer girl a kiss. But I am not supposed to know about this, for the very thought makes me shudder.

[1] Since her father's death Fräulein Auernhammer had been living with the Baroness von Waldstädten.
[2] Probably K. 175, which Mozart played at his concert on 23 March 1783. See p. 843.
[3] In the autograph this sentence is in English.

(467) Mozart to the Baroness von Waldstädten

[Copy in the Staatsbibliothek Preussischer Kulturbesitz, West Berlin]

DEAREST, BEST AND LOVELIEST OF ALL,   [VIENNA, 2 October 1782]
GILT, SILVERED AND SUGARED,
 MOST VALUED AND HONOURED
  GRACIOUS LADY
   BARONESS!

Herewith I have the honour to send your Ladyship the rondo[1] in question, the two volumes of plays and the little book of stories. I committed a terrible blunder yesterday! I felt all the time that I had something more to say and yet I could cudgel nothing out of my stupid skull. But it was to thank your Ladyship for having at once taken so much trouble about the beautiful coat, and for your goodness in promising to give me one like it. But it never occurred to me, which is what usually happens with me. It is my constant regret that I did not study architecture instead of music, for I have often heard it said that he is the best architect to whom nothing ever occurs.[2] I can say with truth that I am a very happy and a very unhappy man—unhappy since the night when I saw your Ladyship at the ball with your hair so beautifully dressed—for—gone is my peace of mind! Nothing but sighs and groans! During the rest of the time I spent at the ball I did not dance—I skipped. Supper was already ordered, but I did not eat—I gobbled. During the night instead of slumbering softly and sweetly—I slept like a dormouse and snored like a bear and (without undue presumption) I should almost be prepared to wager that your Ladyship had the same experience *à proportion*! You smile! you blush! Ah, yes—I am indeed happy. My fortune is made! But alas! Who taps me on the shoulder? Who peeps into my letter? Alas, alas, alas! My wife! Well, well, in the name of Heaven, I have taken her and must keep her! What is to be done? I must praise her—and imagine that what I say is true! How happy I am that I need no Fräulein Auernhammer as a pretext for writing to your Ladyship, like Herr von Taisen or whatever his name is! (how I wish he had no name!), for I myself had something to send to your Ladyship. Moreover, apart from this, I should have had occasion to write to your Ladyship, though indeed I do not dare to mention it. Yet why not? Well then, courage! I should like to ask your Ladyship to—Faugh, the devil—that would be too gross! A propos. Does not your Ladyship know the little rhyme?

  A woman and a jug of beer,
  How can they rhyme together?

---

[1] Probably K. 382. See p. 798 n. 3.
[2] Mozart is punning on the word 'einfallen', which means 'to collapse' and 'to occur.'

The woman has a cask of beer
Of which she sends a jugful here.
Why, then they rhyme together.

I brought that in very neatly, didn't I? But now, *senza burle*.[1] If your Ladyship could sent me a jugful this evening, you would be doing me a great favour. For my wife is—is—is—and has longings—but only for beer prepared in the English way! Well done, little wife! I see at last that you are really good for something. My wife, who is an angel of a woman, and I, who am a model husband, both kiss your Ladyship's hands a thousand times and are ever your

faithful vassals,

MOZART magnus, corpore parvus,

et

CONSTANTIA, omnium uxorum pulcherrima
et prudentissima.

Vienna, 2 October 1782.

Please give my kind regards to that Auernhammer girl.

(468) *Leopold Mozart to Breitkopf's Son and Co., Leipzig*

[Autograph formerly in the possession of Dr. E. Prieger, Bonn]

[SALZBURG, 4 *October* 1782[2]]

My son will probably remain in Vienna for good. He has written a German opera, 'Die Entführung aus dem Scrail'. It is in three acts and is a free adaptation of Bretzner's libretto and has been arranged for the Imperial National Theatre. That it has won applause I gather from the fact that it has already been performed sixteen times.

(469) *Mozart to his Father*

[Autograph in the Mozarteum, Salzburg]

MON TRÉS CHER PÉRE!   VIENNA, 5 *October* 1782

I can only reply to the chief points of your letter, as I have just this moment received it. Unfortunately I have had to read the exact reverse of what I expected. I went myself to see the Baron von Riedesel, who is a charming man, and as I was fully confident that my opera was already being copied, I promised to let him have it at the end of this month or the

---

[1] Joking apart.   [2] Only this fragment of this letter survives.

beginning of November at latest. I therefore beg you to make sure that I shall have it by that time. But in order to relieve you of all care and anxiety on the subject (which, however, I most gratefully regard as a proof of your fatherly love), I can say nothing more convincing than that I am extremely grateful to the Baron for having ordered the copy from me and not from the copyist, from whom he could have got it at any time by paying cash. Besides, it would mortify me very much, if my talent was such that it could be remunerated once and for all—and with a hundred ducats too! At the moment I shall say nothing to anyone, simply because it is unnecessary. If my opera is given in Berlin,[1] of which there seems no doubt (which is to me the most pleasing feature of the affair), people will certainly hear about it. And, what is more, my enemies will not mock me, nor treat me like a contemptible fellow, but will only be too glad to give me an opera to compose if I choose—though very likely I shall not choose. What I mean is that I am willing to write an opera, but not to look on with a hundred ducats in my pocket and see the theatre making four times as much in a fortnight.[2] I intend to produce my opera at my own expense, I shall clear at least 1200 gulden by three performances and then the management may have it for fifty ducats. If they refuse to take it, I shall have made some money and can produce the opera any-where. Well, I hope that hitherto you have not detected the least sign of an inclination on my part to act shabbily. No man ought to be mean, but neither ought he to be such a simpleton as to let other people take the profits from his work, which has cost him so much study and labour, by renouncing all further claims upon it.

The Grand Duke arrived yesterday. Well, the distinguished clavier teacher for the Princess has at last been appointed. I need only mention his pay and you will easily estimate the competence of this master—400 gulden. His name is Summer.[3] Even if I were disappointed, I should do my best not to let it be seen. But as things are, I need not, thank God, make any pretence, for the only thing which would have mortified me would have been my appointment, which, of course, I should have had to decline—always an unpleasant proceeding, when one is in the unfortunate position of having to refuse a great lord. I must urge you once mcre to hurry up as much as possible the copying of my opera. And while I kiss your hands a thousand times I am ever your most obedient son

W: A: MOZART

---

[1] *Die Entführung aus dem Serail* was not performed in Berlin until 1788. It was given in Prague, Mannheim, Frankfurt, Bonn and Leipzig in 1783, Salzburg in 1784, Kassel in 1785, and Breslau and Coblenz in 1787.

[2] According to a letter from Schröder to Dalberg of 22 May 1784 (quoted in Abert, vol. i. p. 896, n. 3), Mozart received 50 ducats for his opera, but the account books of the theatre show that he actually received 100 ducats.

[3] Georg Summer (1742–1809) was appointed in 1781 instructor on the clavier to the Imperial Court. From 1791 until his death he was organist in the Vienna Court Chapel.

My dear wife kisses your hands and we both embrace our dear sister with all our hearts. We saw the cross which my sister received from the Baroness Waldstädten the day before she sent it to her. I despatched by the mail coach today five quires of ruled paper with twelve staves to a page.

We do not yet know—nor indeed does the Baroness herself—when she is going into the country. But as soon as I hear, I shall write and tell you. Adieu.

(470) Mozart to his Father

[Autograph in the Mozarteum, Salzburg]

MON TRÉS CHER PÉRE!   VIENNA, 12 October 1782

If I could have foreseen that the copyists in Salzburg would have so much to do, I should have decided to have the opera copied here in spite of the extra expense. Well, I must go off to the Ambassador and explain the real reason to him. But please do your very best to have it sent to me soon, and the sooner the better. You think that I should not have got it in a shorter time from a Vienna copyist? Why, I could have got it from the theatrical copyist here within a week or at most ten days. The fact that that *ass Gatti* asked the Archbishop to be allowed to compose a serenade, alone renders him worthy of the name and makes me surmise that it is equally applicable to his learning in music.

You say that 400 gulden a year as an *assured salary* are not to be despised. What you say would be true if in addition I could work myself into a good position and could treat these 400 gulden simply as an extra. But unfortunately that is not the case. I should have to consider the 400 gulden as my chief income and everything I could earn besides as a windfall, the amount of which would be very uncertain and consequently in all probability very meagre. For you can easily understand that you cannot act as independently towards a pupil who is a Princess[1] as towards other ladies. If a Princess does not feel inclined to take a lesson, why, you have the honour of waiting until she does. She is living with the Salesians auf der Wieden, so that if you do not care to walk, you have the honour of paying at least a zwanziger[2] to drive there and back. Thus of my pay only 304 gulden would remain, I mean, if I were only to give three lessons a week; and if I were obliged to wait, I should be neglecting in the meantime my other pupils or other work (by which I might easily make more than 400 gulden). If I wanted to come in to Vienna, I should have to pay double, as I should be obliged to drive out again. If I stayed auf der Wieden and were giving my lesson in the morning, as no doubt I should be doing, I should have to go at lunchtime to some inn, take a wretched meal and pay

---

[1] Princess Elizabeth of Wurtemberg.
[2] See p. 771, n. 1.

extravagantly for it. Moreover, by neglecting my other pupils, I might lose them altogether—for everyone considers that his money is just as good as that of a Princess. At the same time I should be losing the time and inclination to earn more money by composition. To serve a great lord (be the office what it may) a man should be paid a sufficient income to enable him to *serve his patron alone*, without being obliged to seek additional earnings in order to avoid penury. A man must provide against want. Please do not think that I am so stupid as to tell all this to anyone else. But believe me, ⟨the Emperor⟩ himself is well aware of his own meanness and has passed me over solely on that account. No doubt, if I had applied for the appointment I should certainly have got it, but with more than 400 gulden, though probably with a less salary than would have been fair and just. I am not looking for pupils, for I can have as many as I please; and from two of them, without causing me the slightest hindrance or inconvenience, I get as much as the Princess gives her master, who has thus no better prospect than that of avoiding starvation for the rest of his life. You know well how services are generally rewarded by great lords. Well, I must close, for the post is going. We kiss your hands a thousand times and embrace our dear sister with all our hearts and are ever your most obedient children

W: ET C: MOZART

More the next time.

(471) *Mozart to his Father*

[*Autograph in the Mozarteum, Salzburg*]

MON TRÉS CHER PÉRE!   VIENNA, 19 *October* 1782

I must again write in a hurry. I do not understand how it is, but formerly I always used to get a letter from you on Friday after lunch; but now, send as I will, I never get it until Saturday evening. I am very sorry that you have had so much trouble over my opera. Indeed I have heard about England's victories[1] and am greatly delighted too, for you know that I am an out-and-out Englishman.

The Russian Royalties left Vienna today. My opera was performed for them the other day, and on this occasion I thought it advisable to resume my place at the clavier and conduct it. I did so partly in order to rouse the orchestra who had gone to sleep a little, partly (since I happen to be in Vienna) in order to appear before the royal guests as the father of my child.

My dearest father, I must confess that I have the most impatient longing to see you again and to kiss your hands; and for this reason I wanted to be

---

[1] The relief of Gibraltar by Lord Howe and Sir Edward Hughes's crushing defeat of the French navy off Trincomalee.

in Salzburg on November 15th, which is your name-day. But the most profitable season in Vienna is now beginning. The nobility are returning from the country and are taking lessons. Moreover, concerts are starting again. I should have to be back in Vienna by the beginning of December. How hard it would be for my wife and myself to be obliged to leave you so soon! For we would much rather enjoy for a longer period the company of our dear father and our dear sister. So it depends on you—whether you prefer to have me for a longer or shorter time. We are thinking of going to you in the spring. If I only mention Salzburg to my dear wife, she is already beside herself with joy. The barber of Salzburg[1] (not of Seville) called on me and delivered kind messages from you, from my sister and from Katherl. Now farewell. We both kiss your hands a thousand times and embrace my dear sister with all our hearts and are ever your most obedient children

M: C: ET W: A: MOZART

(472) *Mozart to his Father*

[Autograph in the Mozarteum, Salzburg]

MON TRÉS CHER PÉRE!   VIENNA, 26 *October* [1782]

How gladly would we take the post-chaise and alla Wolfgang Mozart fly to Salzburg! But this is quite out of the question, because I cannot get away from here before November 3rd without ruining someone, as Fräulein von Auernhammer (whom I have placed with the Baroness von Waldstädten, who gives her board and lodging) is giving a concert in the theatre on that day and I have promised to play with her. My wife's boundless desire and my own to kiss your hands and to embrace our dear sister will make us do all in our power to enjoy this happiness and pleasure as soon as possible. Enough! All I can say as yet is that the month of November is not favourable to those natives of Salzburg who may not be able to tolerate my presence. I have many things too to discuss with you, my dearest father, on the subject of music. It is all the same to me whether the opera is stitched together or bound; I should have it bound in blue paper. You will see by my writing that I am in a desperate hurry. It is now seven o'clock and in spite of all my enquiries I have only this moment received your letter. Well, adieu. My dear wife and I kiss your hands a thousand times and embrace our dear sister with all our hearts and are ever your most obedient children

W AND C. MOZART

[1] Wenzel Andreä Gilowsky.

(473) Mozart to his Father

[Autograph in the Mozarteum, Salzburg]

MON TRÉS CHER PÉRE!   VIENNA, 13 November 1782

We are in considerable perplexity. I did not write to you last Saturday, because I thought we were certain to leave Vienna on Monday. But on Sunday the weather became so dreadful that carriages could scarcely make their way through the town. I still wished to set off on Monday afternoon, but I was told at the post that not only would each stage take four or five hours, but we should not be able to get much beyond the first and should have to turn back. The mail coach with eight horses did not even reach the first stage and has returned to Vienna. I then intended to leave tomorrow, but my wife has such a severe headache today that, althought she insists on setting out, I dare not allow her to run such a risk in this odious weather. So I am waiting for another letter from you (I trust that in the meantime road conditions will have improved) and then we shall be off. For the pleasure of embracing you again, my dearest father, outweighs all other considerations. My pupils can quite well wait for me for three or four weeks. For although the Countesses Zichy and Rumbeck have returned from the country and have already sent for me, it is not at all likely that they will engage another master in the meantime. Well, as I have not been so fortunate as to be able to congratulate you in person, I now do so in writing and send you the wishes of my wife and your future grandson or granddaughter. *We wish you a long and happy life, health and contentment and whatever you wish for yourself.* We kiss your hands a thousand times and embrace our dear sister with all our hearts and are ever your most obedient children.

W: et C: MOZART

(474) Mozart to his Father

[Autograph in the Mozarteum, Salzburg]

MON TRÉS CHER PÉRE!   VIENNA, 20 November [1782]

I see alas! that the pleasure of embracing you must be postponed until the spring, for my pupils positively refuse to let me go, and indeed the weather is at present far too cold for my wife. Everyone implores me not to take the risk. In the spring then (for I call March, or the beginning of April at latest spring, as I reckon it according to my circumstances), we can certainly travel to Salzburg, for my wife is not expecting her confinement before the month of June. So I am unpacking our trunks today, as I left everything packed until I heard from you. For had you desired us to come, we should have been off at once without telling a soul, just to show you that we were not to blame in the matter. M. and Mme Fischer and the old lady (who all send their greetings) can best tell you how sorry I am not to be able to make the journey at present. Yesterday Princess Elizabeth (as it was her name-day) received from the Emperor a present of 90,000 gulden as well as a gold watch set with brilliants. She was also proclaimed an Archduchess of Austria, so she now has the title of Royal Highness. The Emperor has had another attack of fever. ⟨I fear that he will not live long⟩ and only hope that I am mistaken.

Madame Heisig, née De Luca, who visited Salzburg with her husband and played the psaltery in the theatre, is in Vienna and is giving a strumming recital. She sent me a written invitation and begged me to speak well of her, adding that she attached great value to my friendship. Well, I must close. My wife and I kiss your hands a thousand times and embrace our dear sister with all our hearts and are ever your most obedient children

W: et C: MOZART

(475) *Mozart to his Father*

[*Autograph in the Mozarteum, Salzburg*]

MON TRÉS CHER PÉRE!   VIENNA, 21 *December* 1782

Passionate as was my longing to get a letter from you again after a silence of three weeks, I was none the less amazed at its contents. In short, we have both been in the same state of anxiety. You must know that I replied to your last letter on December 4th[1] and expected an answer from you in eight days. Nothing came. Well, I thought that perhaps you had not had time to write; and from a rather pleasant hint in your previous letter, we almost thought that you would arrive yourself. The next post again brought us nothing. All the same I intended to write, but was unexpectedly summoned to Countess Thun and consequently was prevented from doing so. Then our anxiety began. We consoled ourselves, however, with the thought that if anything had been wrong, one of you would have written. At last your letter came today, by which I perceive that you never received my last letter. I can scarcely think that it was lost in the post, so no doubt the maid must have pocketed the money. But, by Heaven! I would far rather have made a present of six kreuzers to such a brute than have lost my letter so *mal à propos*; and yet it is not always possible to post the letter oneself. We have now got another maid, whom I have lectured well on the subject. What annoys me most of all is that it has caused you so much anxiety and also that I can no longer remember exactly what I wrote. I know that I was at a concert at Galitzin's that same evening and

---

[1] This letter is missing.

that I mentioned among other things that my poor little wife was obliged to content herself for the present with a little silhouette portrait of yourself, which she always carries about in her bag and kisses more than twenty times a day. I also asked you to send me by the first opportunity which presents itself the new symphony which I composed for Haffner at your request.[1] I should like to have it for certain before Lent, for I should very much like to have it performed at my concert. I asked you too whether you would like to know to what little silhouette portrait I was referring? Ah! Yes! I added that I was most anxious to know what very urgent matter you wished to discuss with me. And then about our visit in the spring! That is all that I can remember. Confound the creature! For how can I know whether that letter did not contain something which I should be very sorry to see falling into other hands? But I do not think that it did and I trust that it didn't; and I am only pleased and happy to hear that you are both in good health. My wife and I, thank God, are very well.

Is it true that the Archbishop is coming to Vienna after the New Year? Countess Lützow has been here for three weeks and I only heard of her arrival yesterday. Prince Galitzin told me of it. I am engaged for all his concerts. I am always fetched in his coach and brought to his house and treated there most magnificently. On the 10th my opera was performed again with the greatest applause. It was the fourteenth time and the theatre was as full as on the first night, or rather it was as packed as it has invariably been. Count Rosenberg himself spoke to me at Prince Galitzin's and suggested that I should write an Italian opera. I have already commissioned someone to procure for me from Italy the latest opere buffe texts to choose from, but as yet I have not received any, although I myself wrote to Ignaz Hagenauer about it. Some Italian male and female singers are coming here at Easter. Please send me Lugiati's address at Verona, for I should like to try that channel too.

A new opera, or rather a comedy with ariettas by Umlauf, entitled 'Welche ist die beste Nation?' was performed the other day[2]—a wretched piece which I could have set to music, but which I refused to undertake, adding that whoever should compose music for it without altering it completely would run the risk of being hooted off the stage; had it not been Umlauf's, it would certainly have been hooted; but, being his, it was only hissed. Indeed it was no wonder, for even with the finest music no one could have tolerated such a piece. But, what is more, the music is so bad that I do not know whether the poet or the composer will carry off the prize for inanity. To its disgrace it was performed a second time; but I think we may now say, *Punctum satis.*

[1] K. 385.   [2] On December 13th.

MOZART (1782)
From an unfinished portrait by Josef Lange
(Mozart Museum, Salzburg)

Vienne ce 4 de Mars
1783

Mon très cher Pere !

LETTER FROM MOZART TO HIS FATHER (4 January 1783)

[Autograph in the Staatsbibliothek Preussischer Kulturbesitz, West Berlin]

CONSTANZE MOZART, *NÉE* WEBER (1782)

From a portrait by Josef Lange
(Hunterian Museum, University of Glasgow)

MARIANNE MOZART, FREIFRAU VON BERCHTOLD ZU
SONNENBURG (1785)

From a portrait by an unknown artist
(Mozart Museum, Salzburg)

LORENZO DA PONTE

From a water-colour painting by an unknown artist
(Formerly in the possession of Signor Riccardo Rossi, Vittorio Veneto)

MOZART (1789)

From a silver point drawing by Dora Stock
(City Music Library, Leipzig)

EMANUEL SCHIKANEDER

From an engraving by Löschenkohl
(Gesellschaft der Musikfreunde, Vienna)

Well, I must close, or I shall miss the post. My dear wife and I kiss your hands a thousand times and embrace our dear sister with all our hearts and are ever your most obedient children

W: et C: MOZART

(476) *Mozart to his Father*

[Autograph in the Mozarteum, Salzburg]

MON TRÉS CHER PÉRE!   VIENNA, 28 *December* 1782

I must write in the greatest haste, as it is already half past five and I have asked some people to come here at six for a little concert. Altogether I have so much to do that often I do not know whether I am on my head or my heels. I spend the whole forenoon giving lessons until two o'clock, when we have lunch. After the meal I must give my poor stomach an hour for digestion. The evening is therefore the only time I have for composing and of that I can never be sure, as I am often asked to perform at concerts. There are still two concertos wanting to make up the series of subscription concertos.[1] These concertos are a happy medium between what is too easy and too difficult; they are very brilliant, pleasing to the ear, and natural, without being vapid. There are passages here and there from which the connoisseurs alone can derive satisfaction; but these passages are written in such a way that the less learned cannot fail to be pleased, though without knowing why. I am distributing the tickets at six ducats apiece. I am now finishing too the piano arrangement[2] of my opera, which is about to be published; and at the same time I am engaged in a very difficult task, the music for a bard's song by Denis[3] about Gibraltar. But this is a secret, for a Hungarian lady wishes to pay this compliment to Denis. The ode is sublime, beautiful, anything you like, but too exaggerated and pompous for my fastidious ears. But what is to be done? The golden mean of truth in all things is no longer either known or appreciated. In order to win applause one must write stuff which is so inane that a coachman could sing it, or so unintelligible that it pleases precisely because no sensible man can understand it. This is not what I have been wanting to discuss with you; but I should like to write a book, a short introduction to music, illustrated by examples, but, I need hardly add, not under my own name.

I send you an enclosure from the Baroness Waldstädten, who fears that her second letter may have gone astray. You cannot have received her last

---

[1] K. 414 [385p], composed in 1782, and K. 413 and 415 [387a–b], composed in 1782–1783. Mozart announced a subscription publication of these three works in January 1783. See p. 837.
[2] *Die Entführung aus dem Serail*. See p. 895, Letter 535.
[3] An ode entitled 'Gibraltar' by J. N. C. Michael Denis (1729–1800), Jesuit priest and poet. The poem was written in the style of Klopstock. Mozart's setting was never finished. The fragment 'O Calpe!' K. App. 25 [K386d], consists of 58 bars.

letter, for you have not mentioned it. I asked you about it in the letter which was lost. Well, adieu. More shortly. My little wife and I kiss your hands a thousand times and embrace our dear sister with all our hearts and are ever your most obedient children

W: et C: MZT

(476*) Mozart to his Wife

[From Nissen, p. 687]

[VIENNA, ? 1782]

Good-morning dear little wife! I hope that you have slept well, that nothing disturbed you, that you haven't got up too hastily, that you are not catching cold, that you are not bending or stretching, that you are not angry with your servants, that you don't fall over the threshold in the next room. Spare yourself household worries until I return. Only may nothing happen to you! I am coming at—o'clock etc.

(477) Mozart to his Father

[Autograph in the Staatsbibliothek Preussischer Kulturbesitz, West Berlin]

MON TRÉS CHER PÉRE!   VIENNA, 4 *January* 1783

It is impossible for me to write very much, as we have just got home from Baroness Waldstädten's and I have to change all my clothes, as I am invited to a concert at Court Councillor Spielmann's. We both thank you for your New Year wishes and confess of our own accord that we were absolute owls to have forgotten our duty so completely. So, laggards as we are, we are sending you, not our New Year wishes, but our general everyday wishes; and we must leave it at that. It is quite true about my moral obligation and indeed I let the word flow from my pen on purpose. I made the promise in my heart of hearts and hope to be able to keep it. When I made it, my wife was still single; yet, as I was absolutely determined to marry her soon after her recovery, it was easy for me to make it —but, as you yourself are aware, time and other circumstances made our journey impossible. The score of half of a mass,[1] which is still lying here waiting to be finished, is the best proof that I really made the promise.

I got a new pupil today, the elder Countess Pálffy, the daughter of ⟨the Archbishop's sister.⟩ But please keep this news to yourself for the present, for I am not quite sure whether her family would like it to be

---

[1] K. 427 [417a], Mozart's mass in C minor, at which he worked during the years 1782 and 1783 and which he left unfinished. It was performed in St. Peter's Church in Salzburg on 26 October, Constanze singing the soprano part. Mozart used portions of this mass for his cantata *Davidde penitente*, written in 1785.

known. It is all the same to me whether you send me the symphony of
the last Haffner music [1] which I composed in Vienna, in the original score
or copied out, for, as it is, I shall have to have several copies made for my
concert. I should like to have the following symphonies as soon as possible.

Then there are a few counterpoint works by Eberlin copied out on small
paper and bound in blue,[6] and some things of Haydn,[7] which I should like

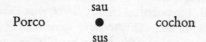

Porco   sau ● sus   cochon

to have for the Baron van Swieten, to whose house I go every Sunday
from twelve to two. Tell me, are there any really good fugues in Haydn's
last mass or vesper music, or possibly in both? If so, I should be very much
obliged to you if you would have them both scored for me bit by bit.
Well, I must close. You will have received my last letter with the enclosure from the Baroness. She did not tell me what she had written to
you; she just said that she had asked you about something to do with
music. But the next time I go to see her, she will certainly tell me all about

[1] K. 385.
[3] K. 201 [186a], composed in 1774.
[5] K. 183 [173dB], composed in 1773.
[7] Michael Haydn.

[2] K. 204 [213a], a serenade, composed in 1775.
[4] K. 182 [173dA], composed in 1773.
[6] See p. 322 n. 1.

it, as she knows that I am not at all inquisitive. Indeed she is a dreadful chatterbox. I have it, however, from a third party that she would like to have someone for herself, as she is leaving Vienna. Well, I just want to warn you that, if this is the case, you should be a little bit on your guard, as she is as *changeable* as the wind. Besides, I feel sure that however much she may imagine that she is going to leave Vienna, she will hardly do so; for as long as I have had the honour of her acquaintance, she has always been on the point of leaving. Well, adieu. We kiss your hands a thousand times and embrace our dear sister with all our hearts and are ever your obedient children

W. et C: Mozart

PS.—Only three concertos[1] are being published and the price is four ducats.

(478) *Mozart to his Father*

[*Autograph in the Mozarteum, Salzburg*]

Mon très cher Père!   Vienna, 8 *January* [1783]

Were it not on account of poor Finck,[2] I should really have to ask you to excuse me today and put off writing until next post-day, as I have to finish a rondo[3] this evening for my sister-in-law Aloysia Lange, which she is to sing on Saturday at a big concert in the Mehlgrube. Meanwhile you will have received my last letter and you will have seen from it that I knew nothing whatever about the Baroness's commission, that I guessed what it might be and had heard about it privately from another quarter, upon which, as I know this lady only too well, I warned you to be a little bit on your guard. First of all, I must tell you that Finck would not be at all suitable for her, as she wants to have someone for herself and not for her children.[4] You see, therefore, that what is important is that he should play with taste, feeling and brilliancy; and that a knowledge of thorough bass and extemporising in the style of the organ would be of no use to him whatever. Further, I should like you to realize that the words which I used, '*herself*'—'*for herself*', imply a good deal. She has often had someone of the kind in her house, but the arrangement has never lasted very long. You may put whatever construction you like on this. Suffice it to say that the result of these scenes is that people speak very lightly about her. She is weak; but I shall say no more—and the little I have said is only for your-

---

[1] K. 413–415 [387a, 385p, 387b]. See p. 833, n. 1.
[2] Ignaz Finck, court trumpeter in Salzburg. Evidently he had offered to take a letter to Mozart's father.
[3] K. 416. Recitative 'Mia speranza adorata'; rondo 'Ah, non sai, qual pena'. Aloysia sang this aria too at Mozart's concert on 23 March. See p. 843.
[4] The Baroness had three sons.

self; for I have received a great many kindnesses from her and so it is my duty to defend her so far as possible, or at least to say nothing. Well, she is talking of going off in a few days to Pressburg and of staying there. My opinion is that she may do so—or that she may not. If I were in your place, I should politely decline to have anything to do with the whole business. Well, I must close or my aria will never be finished. My opera was given again yesterday in a crowded theatre and with the greatest applause. Do not forget my symphonies.[1] Adieu. My little wife who is quite plump (but only about the belly) and I both kiss your hands a thousand times and embrace our dear sister with all our hearts and are ever your most obedient children

W et C Mozart

(479) Mozart to his Father

[Autograph in the Mozarteum, Salzburg]

Mon très cher Pére!   Vienna, 22 January 1783

You need have no fear that the three concertos[2] are too dear. I think after all that I deserve a ducat for each concerto—and besides—I should like to know who could get them copied for a ducat! They cannot be copied, as I shall not let them out of my hands until I have secured a certain number of subscribers. They have been advertised three times in the Wiener Diarium;[3] and subscription tickets at four ducats each have been on sale since the 20th at my house, where the concertos can be obtained during the month of April.

I shall send the cadenzas and lead-ins[4] to my dear sister at the first opportunity. I have not yet altered the lead-ins in the rondo,[5] for whenever I play this concerto, I always play whatever occurs to me at the moment. Please send me the symphonies[6] I asked for as soon as possible, for I really need them. And now, one more request, for my wife is giving me no peace on the subject. You are doubtless aware that this is carnival time and that there is as much dancing here as in Salzburg and Munich. Well, I should very much like to go as Harlequin (but not a soul must know about it)—because here there are so many—indeed nothing but—silly asses at the Redoutes. So I should like you to send me your Harlequin costume. But please do so very soon, for we shall not attend the Redoutes until I have it, although they are now in full swing. We prefer private balls. Last week I gave a ball in my own rooms, but of course the chapeaux each paid two gulden. We began at six o'clock in the evening and kept on until seven. What! Only an hour? Of course not. I meant, until seven

---

[1] See p. 835.   [2] K. 413-415 [387a, 385p, 387b].
[3] For the announcement, which actually appeared in the Wiener Zeitung, see MDB, p. 212.
[4] The German term is 'Eingänge'. See p. 840, n. 2.
[5] K. 382. See p. 798, n. 3.   [6] See p. 835.

o'clock next morning. You will wonder how I had so much room? Why, that reminds me that I have always forgotten to tell you that for the last six weeks I have been living in a new lodging—but still on the Hohe Brücke, and only a few houses off. We are now in the small Herberstein house, No. 412, on the third floor.[1] The house belongs to Herr von Wetzlar—a rich Jew. Well, I have a room there—1000 feet long and one foot wide[2]—and a bedroom, an anteroom and a fine large kitchen. Then there are two other fine big rooms adjoining ours, which are still empty and which I used for this private ball. Baron Wetzlar and his wife were there, the Baroness Waldstädten, Herr von Edelbach, that gasbag Gilowsky,[3] Stephanie junior et uxor, Adamberger and his wife, Lange and his, and so forth. It would be impossible to name them all. Well, I must close, as I still have a letter to write to Madame Wendling at Mannheim about my concertos. Please remind that ever ready operatic composer,[4] Gatti, about the opera libretti.[5] I do wish I had them already. Well, adieu. We kiss your hands a thousand times and embrace our dear sister with all our hearts and are ever your most obedient children

W: et C: MOZART

(480) Mozart to his Father

[Autograph in the Mozarteum, Salzburg]

MON TRÉS CHER PÉRE!   VIENNA, 5 February 1783

I have received your last letter and trust that in the meantime you have also received my last one with my request for the Harlequin costume. I now repeat it, begging you at the same time to be so very kind as to dispatch it with all possible speed. And please send the symphonies,[6] especially the *last one*,[7] as soon as possible, for my concert is to take place on the third Sunday in Lent, that is, on March 23rd, and I must have several duplicate parts made. I think therefore, that if it is not copied already, it would be better to send me back the original score just as I sent it to you; and remember to put in the minuets.[8]

Is Ceccarelli no longer at Salzburg? Or was he not given a part in

---

[1] This was Mozart's fourth move since his arrival in Vienna. He and his wife lived in this house (now Wipplingerstrasse no. 14) from December 1782 until March 1783. Their landlord, Baron Raimund Wetzlar von Plankenstern (1752–1810), was godfather to their first child, Raimund Leopold, and appears to have helped them financially.

[2] A favourite joke of the Mozart family. See p. 8.

[3] Franz Wenzel Gilowsky von Urazowa (1757–1816), brother of Katherl Gilowsky. He was now a young surgeon in Vienna and had been best man at Mozart's wedding.

[4] Einstein suggests an allusion to Johann P. Kirnberger's *Der allezeit fertige Polonaisen- und Menuettenkomponist*, Berlin, 1757.

[5] Mozart hoped that through Gatti (see p. 547 n. 3) he might find a suitable Italian text for an opera buffa.   [6] See p. 835.   [7] K. 385.

[8] See p. 810, n. 1.

Gatti's cantata? This I ask, as you do not mention him among the squabblers and wranglers.

My opera was performed yesterday for the seventeenth time with the usual applause and to a full house.

On Friday, the day after tomorrow, a new opera is to be given, the music of which, a *galimatias*, is by a young Viennese, a pupil of Wagenseil, who is called *gallus cantans, in arbore sedens, gigirigi faciens*.[1] It will probably not be a success. Still, it is better stuff than its predecessor, an old opera by Gassmann, 'La notte critica', in German 'Die unruhige Nacht',[2] which with difficulty survived three performances. This in its turn had been preceded by that execrable opera of Umlauf,[3] about which I wrote to you and which never got so far as a third performance. It really seems as if they wished to kill off before its time the German opera, which in any case is to come to an end after Easter; and Germans themselves are doing this—shame upon them!

I asked you in my last letter to keep on reminding Gatti about the Italian opera libretti and I again repeat my request. Let me now tell you of my plan. I do not believe that the Italian opera will keep going for long, and besides, I hold with the Germans. I prefer German opera, even though it means more trouble for me. Every nation has its own opera and why not Germany? Is not German as singable as French and English? Is it not more so than Russian? Very well then! I am now writing a German opera for myself. I have chosen Goldoni's comedy 'Il servitore di due padroni', and the whole of the first act has now been translated. Baron Binder is the translator. But we are keeping it a secret until it is quite finished.[4] Well, what do you think of this scheme? Do you not think that I shall make a good thing of it? Now I must close. Fischer, the bass singer, is with me and has just asked me to write about him to Le Gros in Paris, as he is going off there in Lent. The Viennese are making the foolish mistake of letting a man go who can never be replaced. My wife and I kiss your hands a thousand times and embrace our dear sister with all our hearts and are ever your most obedient children

W: et C: MOZART

Gaetano Majorano (Caffarelli)
   Amphion Thebas
   Ego Domum.[5]

---

[1] Johann Mederitsch (1752–1835), called Gallus. His opera *Rose, oder Pflicht und Liebe im Streit* was performed on 9 February 1783. He wrote a number of other works for the stage.
[2] Gassmann's opera *La notte critica* was performed on 10 January 1783.
[3] Umlauf's opera *Welche ist die beste Nation?*. See p. 832.
[4] This plan was never carried out. Saint-Foix, vol. iii. p. 389, n., suggests that the arias K.433, 435 [416c, b], composed for bass and tenor respectively, have some connection with this project. See also Köchel, pp. 422, 443.
[5] These words are written on the cover of the letter.
   Gaetano Majorano (1710–1783), a famous castrato, who took the name of Caffarelli from

(481) Mozart to his Father

[Autograph in the Mozarteum, Salzburg]

Mon trés cher Père!   VIENNA, 15 February 1783

Most heartfelt thanks for the music you have sent me. I am extremely sorry that I shall not be able to use the music of 'Thamos',[1] but this piece, which failed to please here, is now among the rejected works which are no longer performed. For the sake of the music alone it might possibly be given again, but that is not likely. Certainly it is a pity! Herewith I send my sister the three cadenzas for the concerto in D and the two lead-ins for the one in Eb.[2] Please send me at once the little book which contains the oboe concerto[3] I wrote for Ramm, or rather for Ferlendis. Prince Esterházy's oboist is giving me three ducats for it and has offered me six, if I will compose a new concerto for him.[4] But if you have already gone to Munich, well then, by Heaven, there is nothing to be done; for the only person to whom in that case we could apply, I mean, Ramm himself, is not there either. I should like to have sat in a corner at Strassburg —but indeed not—for I don't think I should have spent a peaceful night.[5] My new Haffner symphony[6] has positively amazed me, for I had forgotten every single note of it. It must surely produce a good effect. I think that during the last carnival days we shall collect a company of masqueraders and perform a small pantomime. But please do not betray us. I have at last been fortunate enough to meet the Chevalier Hypolity, who had never been able to find me. He is a charming person. He has been to see me once and he is to come again soon and bring an aria so that I may hear him. I must close, as I am off to the theatre. My little wife and I kiss your hands a thousand times and embrace our dear sister with all our hearts and are ever your most obedient children

W: A: MOZART

his friend and patron, Pasquale Caffaro, the Neapolitan composer, studied under Porpora and in 1724 made his first appearance in Rome. In 1738 he sang in London and then returned to Italy. When he was 65 he had amassed an immense fortune and built a palace near Naples, over the door of which was the inscription 'Amphion Thebas, ego domum', referring to the classical legend of Amphion, who is said to have built the walls of Thebes by the magic strains of his lute.

Caffarelli is not mentioned previously in the letters, but his name appears in Leopold Mozart's *Reiseaufzeichnungen*, p. 53, in the handwriting of Mozart himself, who adds the remark: 'Musico ricchissimo, va nelle chiese per chiappare qualche denaro' (a very rich castrato, who goes and sings in churches in order to scrape up a few coins). See *MBA*, No. 192. Caffarelli died on 1 February 1783.

[1] K. 345 [336a], Mozart's incidental music to Baron von Gebler's drama *Thamos, König von Ägypten*, composed during the years 1773 to 1779. See Köchel, pp. 352, 353.

[2] Cadenzas for K. 175, composed in 1773, and lead-ins for K. 271, composed in 1777.

[3] Probably K. 314 [285d]. See p. 320, n. 1.

[4] Possibly K. 293 [416f], a fragment, 61 bars, of an oboe concerto.

[5] Mozart may be referring to a performance at Strassburg of his *Die Entführung aus dem Serail*.   [6] K. 385.

(482) *Mozart to the Baroness von Waldstädten*

[*Autograph sold by Artaria and Co., Vienna, 22 March* 1934, *No.* 636]

MOST HIGHLY ESTEEMED BARONESS! [VIENNA, 15 *February* 1783]

Here I am in a fine dilemma! Herr von Trattner and I discussed the matter the other day and agreed to ask for an extension of a fortnight. As every merchant does this, unless he is the most disobliging man in the world, my mind was quite at ease and I hoped that by that time, if I were not in the position to pay the sum myself, I should be able to borrow it. Well, Herr von Trattner now informs me that the person in question absolutely refuses to wait and that if I do not pay the sum before tomorrow, he will *bring an action against me*. Only think, your Ladyship, what an unpleasant business this would be for me! At the moment I cannot pay —not even half the sum! If I could have foreseen that the subscriptions for my concertos[1] would come in so slowly, I should have raised the money on a longer time-limit. I entreat your Ladyship for Heaven's sake to help me to keep my honour and my good name!

My poor little wife is slightly indisposed, so I cannot leave her; otherwise I should have come to you myself to ask in person for your Ladyship's assistance. We kiss your Ladyship's hands a thousand times and are both your Ladyship's most obedient children

W. A. and C. MOZART

At home, 15 February 1783.

(483) *Mozart to his Father*

[*Autograph in the Mozarteum, Salzburg*]

MON TRÉS CHER PÉRE! VIENNA, 12 *March* 1783

I hope that you have not been uneasy but have guessed the cause of my silence, which was that, as I did not know for certain how long you would stay in Munich,[2] I delayed writing until now, when I am almost sure that my letter will find you in Salzburg. My sister-in-law, Madame Lange, gave her concert yesterday in the theatre and I played a concerto.[3] The theatre was very full and I was received again by the Viennese public so cordially that I really ought to feel delighted. I had already left the platform, but the audience would not stop clapping and so I had to repeat the rondo; upon which there was a regular torrent of applause. It is a good advertisement for my concert which I am giving on Sunday, March 23rd.

---

[1] K. 413-415 [387a, 385p, 387b].
[2] Leopold Mozart had been to Munich on one of his frequent visits to the family of Theobald Marchand.
[3] K. 175 with the rondo K. 382. See p. 798, n. 3.

I added my symphony which I composed for the Concert Spirituel.[1] My sister-in-law sang the aria 'Non so d'onde viene'.[2] Gluck had a box beside the Langes, in which my wife was sitting. He was loud in his praises of the symphony and the aria and invited us all four to lunch with him next Sunday. It is possible that the German opera may be continued, but no one knows what will happen. One thing is certain, and that is, that Fischer is off to Paris in a week. I entreat you most earnestly to send me the oboe concerto[3] I gave to Ramm—and as soon as possible. When doing so, you might put in something else, for example, the original scores of my masses[4] and of my two vesper compositions.[5] This is solely with a view to the Baron van Swieten hearing them. He sings treble, I sing alto (and play at the same time), Starzer sings tenor and young Teiber[6] from Italy sings bass. Send me in the meantime the 'Tres sunt' by Haydn, which will do until you can let me have something else of his. Indeed I should very much like them to hear the 'Lauda Sion'. The full score of the 'Tres sunt' copied out *in my own handwriting* must be somewhere at home.[7] The fugue 'In te Domine speravi' has won great applause and so have the 'Ave Maria' and the 'Tenebrae' and so forth. I beg you to enliven our Sunday music practices[8] with something soon.

On Carnival Monday our company of masqueraders went to the Redoute, where we performed a pantomime which exactly filled the half hour when there is a pause in the dancing. My sister-in-law was Columbine, I Harlequin, my brother-in-law Pierrot, an old dancing master (Merk) Pantaloon, and a painter (Grassi) the doctor. Both the plot and the music of the pantomime were mine.[9] Merk, the dancing master, was so kind as to coach us, and I must say that we played it charmingly. I am enclosing the programme which was distributed to the company by a mask, dressed as a local postman. The verses, although only doggerel, might have been done better. I had nothing to do with them. Müller,[10] the actor, dashed them off. Well, I must close, for I am going to a concert at Count Esterházy's. Meanwhile farewell. Please do not forget about the music. My wife and I kiss your hands a thousand times and embrace our dear sister with all our hearts and I am ever your most obedient son

W: A: et C: Mozart

[1] K. 297 [300a], composed in 1778.   [2] K. 294, composed in 1778.
[3] See p. 320, n. 1.   [4] Probably K. 275 [272b], 317 and 337.
[5] Probably K. 321, composed in 1779, and K. 339, composed in 1780.
[6] Anton Teiber (1756–1822), a brother of the famous singers, Elizabeth and Therese Teiber.
[7] See p. 322, n. 1. Haydn's 'Tres sunt' and 'Lauda Sion', once believed lost, have been rediscovered and edited by Karl Pfannhausen (Doblinger, c. 1960).
[8] At the house of the Baron van Swieten.
[9] K. 446 [416d]. The autograph, a fragment, has only the first violin part. See Köchel, pp. 443, 444.
[10] Johann Heinrich Friedrich Müller (1738–1815), an actor at the National Theatre in Vienna, who was particularly successful in comic parts. See R. Payer von Thurn, *Joseph II als Theaterdirektor*, Vienna, 1920, *passim*.

(484) *Mozart to his Father*

[*Autograph in the Mozarteum, Salzburg*]

MON TRÉS CHER PÉRE!   VIENNA, 29 *March* 1783

I need not tell you very much about the success of my concert,[1] for no doubt you have already heard of it. Suffice it to say that the theatre could not have been more crowded and that every box was full. But what pleased me most of all was that His Majesty the Emperor was present and, goodness!—how delighted he was and how he applauded me! It is his custom to send the money to the box-office before going to the theatre; otherwise I should have been fully justified in counting on a larger sum, for really his delight was beyond all bounds. He sent twenty-five ducats. Our programme was as follows:

(1) The new Haffner symphony.[2]

(2) Madame Lange sang the aria 'Se il padre perdei' from my Munich opera, accompanied by four instruments.[3]

(3) I played the third of my subscription concertos.[4]

(4) Adamberger sang the scena which I composed for Countess Baumgarten.[5]

(5) The short concertante symphonie from my last Finalmusik.[6]

(6) I played my concerto in D major, which is such a favourite here, and of which I sent you the rondo with variations.[7]

(7) Mlle Teiber sang the scena 'Parto, m'affretto' out of my last Milan opera.[8]

(8) I played alone a short fugue (because the Emperor was present) and then variations on an air from an opera called 'Die Philosophen' which were encored. So I played variations on the air 'Unser dummer Pöbel meint' from Gluck's 'Pilgrimme von Mekka'.[9]

(9) Madame Lange sang my new rondo.[10]

(10) The last movement of the first symphony.[11]

Mlle Teiber[12] is giving a concert tomorrow, at which I am going to play. Von Daubrawaick and Gilowsky are off to Salzburg next Thursday and will bring you my Munich opera,[13] the two copies of my sonatas,[14] some variations for my sister and also the money which I owe you for

---

[1] On March 23rd.   [2] K. 385.
[3] Ilia's aria in Act II of *Idomeneo*, with flute, oboe, bassoon and horn obbligatos. It was written originally for Dorothea Wendling.
[4] K. 415 [387b].   [5] K. 369.   [6] K. 320, composed in 1779.
[7] K. 175, for which Mozart wrote the rondo K. 382.
[8] Aria no. 16 in *Lucio Silla*, composed in 1772.
[9] The first set of variations is K. 398 [416e], six variations on 'Salve tu, Domine' from Paisiello's *I filosofi immaginarii*, which was performed in Vienna in 1781 as *Die eingebildeten Philosophen*. The second set is K. 455, ten variations on 'Unser dummer Pöbel meint'.
[10] K. 416.   [11] The 'Haffner' symphony, K. 385.   [12] Therese Teiber.
[13] *Idomeneo*.   [14] K. 296 and 376-380 [374d, e, 317d, 373a, 374f].

having my opera[1] copied. I have received the parcel of music and thank you for it. Please do not forget about the 'Lauda Sion';[2] and what we should like to have as well, my dearest father, is some of your best church music, for we like to amuse ourselves with all kinds of masters, ancient and modern. So I beg you to send us very soon some of your own compositions. Well, I must close. My wife and I kiss your hands a thousand times and embrace our dear sister with all our hearts and are ever your most obedient children

W: A: Mozart

(485) *Mozart to his Father*

[*Autograph in the Mozarteum, Salzburg*]

Mon trés cher Pére!   Vienna, 3 *April* 1783

I send you herewith my Munich opera[3] and the two copies of my sonatas![4] The variations[5] I promised will be sent to you by the first opportunity, for the copyist could not finish them in time. The two portraits[6] will follow too. I only hope that you will be pleased with them. I think they are both good likenesses and all who have seen them are of the same opinion. Well, I am afraid you have read a lie at the beginning of my letter—I mean, about the two copies of my sonatas. But it is not my fault. When I went to buy them, I was told that there was not a single copy left, but that I could have them tomorrow or the day after. It is too late to get them off now, so I shall send them along with the variations. I enclose the sum I owe for the copying of my opera and I only hope that the balance may be of some use to you. I cannot spare any more at present, as I foresee many expenses in connexion with my wife's confinement, which will probably take place towards the end of May or the beginning of June. Well, I must close, as Von Daubrawaick is leaving very early in the morning and I must send him the letter. My wife and I kiss your hands a thousand times and embrace our dear sister with all our hearts and are ever your most obedient children

W: A: et C: Mozart

---

[1] *Die Entführung aus dem Serail.*   [2] Michael Haydn's composition. See p. 322.
[3] *Idomeneo.*   [4] K. 296 and 376-380 [374d, e, 317d 373a, 374f].
[5] K. 359, 360, 352 [374a–c].

[6] Two small pastel portraits which had been painted of Mozart and his wife. Constanze sent Mozart's portrait to Breitkopf and Härtel in 1804; both have now disappeared.

(486) *Mozart to his Father*

[*Autograph in the Mozarteum, Salzburg*]

MON TRÉS CHER PÉRE!   VIENNA, 12 *April* 1783

I received this morning your last letter of the 8th and see from it that you have got everything which I entrusted to Daubrawaick. I am sorry to say that the mail coach does not leave until this day week, so I cannot send you the two copies of my sonatas[1] until then. But you shall also have the voice part with variations of the aria 'Non so d'onde viene'.[2] The next time you send me a parcel, please let the rondo for an alto voice which I composed for the castrato who was with the Italian company in Salzburg[3] and the one which I composed for Ceccarelli *in Vienna*[4] take the same trip. When the weather gets warmer, please make a search in the attic under the roof and send us some of your own church music. You have no reason whatever to be ashamed of it. Baron van Swieten and Starzer know as well as you and I that musical taste is continually changing —and, *what is more*, that this extends even to church music, which ought not to be the case. Hence it is that true church music is to be found *only* in attics and in a worm-eaten condition. When I come to Salzburg with my wife in July, as I hope to do, we shall discuss this point at greater length. When Daubrawaick went off, I really could scarcely hold back my wife, who insisted *absolument* on our following him to Salzburg. She thought that we might even get there first. And had it not been for the very short time we could have stayed—what am I saying—why, she might have had to be confined in Salzburg—which made this plan impossible, our most ardent wish to embrace you, most beloved father, and my dearest sister would by this time have been fulfilled; for, as far as my wife is concerned, I should have had no fears about this short journey. She is in such excellent health and has become so robust that all women should thank God if they are so fortunate in their pregnancy. As soon as my wife has sufficiently recovered from her confinement, we shall certainly go off to Salzburg at once. You will have seen from my last letter that I was to play at another concert, that is, at Mlle Teiber's. The Emperor was there too. I played my first concerto which I played at my concert.[5] I was asked to repeat the rondo. So I sat down again; but instead of repeating it I had the conductor's rostrum removed and played alone. You should have heard how delighted the public were with this little surprise. They not only clapped but shouted 'bravo' and 'bravissimo'. The Emperor too stayed to hear me to the end and as soon as I left the piano he left his box;

---

[1] K. 296 and 376–380 [374d, e, 317d, 373a, 374f].   [2] K. 294.
[3] K. 255, a recitative and aria, 'Ombra felice', composed in 1776 for Francesco Fortini, a member of a company under Pietro Rosa, who were performing comic operas at Salzburg and Innsbruck.   [4] K. 374.   [5] K. 415 [387b].

evidently he had only remained to listen to me. Please send me, if possible, *the reports* about my concert. I rejoice with my whole heart that the small sum which I was able to send has been so useful to you. I have a great deal more to write about, but I am afraid that the post may ride off without this letter, as it is a quarter to eight. So goodbye for the present. My dear little wife and I kiss your hands a thousand times and embrace our dear sister with all our hearts and are ever your most obedient children

W: et C: MOZART

Our compliments to the whole of Salzburg. Adieu.

(487) *Mozart to J. G. Sieber, Paris*

[*From the 'Bulletin de la Société française de musicologie', July* 1921]

MONSIEUR!   VIENNA, 26 *April* 1783

I have now been in Vienna for two years. You have probably heard about my pianoforte sonatas with accompaniment for one violin [1] which I have had engraved here by Artaria and Co. I am not very well pleased, however, with the way in which works are engraved in Vienna and, even if I were, I should like some of my compositions once more to find their way into the hands of my fellow-countrymen in Paris. Well, this letter is to inform you that I have three piano concertos [2] ready, which can be performed with full orchestra, or with oboes and horns, or merely a quattro. Artaria wants to engrave them. But I give you, my friend, the first refusal. And in order to avoid delay, I shall quote my lowest terms to you. If you give me thirty louis d'or for them, the matter is settled. Since I wrote those piano concertos, I have been composing six quartets for two violins, viola and cello.[3] If you would like to engrave these too, I will gladly let you have them. But I cannot allow these to go so cheaply; I mean that I cannot let you have these six quartets under fifty louis d'or. If you can and will make a deal with me on these conditions, I shall send you an address in Paris where you will be handed my compositions in exchange for the sums I have quoted. Meanwhile, I remain your most obedient servant

WOLFGANG AMADÈ MOZART

[1] K. 296 and 376-380 [374d, e, 373a, 374f], published by Artaria and Co. in November 1781.

[2] K. 413-415 [387a, 385p, 387b]. They were published by Artaria and Co. in March 1785.

[3] K. 387, 421 [417b], 428 [421b], 458, 464, 465, the six quartets which Mozart dedicated in September 1785 to Joseph Haydn. K. 387 was composed in 1782, K. 421 [417b] and 428 [421b] in 1783. They were published by Artaria and Co. in October 1785.

(488) Mozart to his Father

[Autograph in the Bibliothèque Municipale, Nantes]

Mon très cher Père!   Vienna, in the Prater, 3 May 1783

I simply cannot make up my mind to drive back into town so early. The weather is far too lovely and it is far too delightful in the Prater today. We have taken our lunch out of doors and shall stay on until eight or nine in the evening. My whole company consists of my little wife who is pregnant, and hers consists of her little husband, who is not pregnant, but fat and flourishing. I went straight to Herr Peisser, got from him the address of the banker Scheffler and then went off to the said banker. But he knew nothing whatever about a merchant's son called Rosa, who might have an introduction to him. For safety's sake I left my address with him. I shall now wait and see what happens. I must ask you to wait patiently for a longer letter and the aria with variations [1]—for, of course, I cannot finish them in the Prater; and for the sake of my dear little wife I cannot miss this fine weather. Exercise is good for her. So today I am only sending you a short letter to say that, thank God, we are both well and have received your last letter. Now farewell. We kiss your hands a thousand times and embrace our dear sister with all our hearts and are ever your obedient children

W. A: and C: Mozart

(489) Mozart to his Father

[Autograph in the Mozarteum, Salzburg]

Mon très cher Père!   [Vienna, 7 May 1783]

Another short letter! I intended to postpone writing until next Saturday, as I have to go to a concert today; but as I have something to say which is of considerable importance to myself, I must steal time in order to write at least a few lines. I have not yet received the music I wanted, nor do I know what has happened. Well, the Italian opera buffa has started again here and is very popular. The buffo is particularly good— his name is Benucci.[2] I have looked through at least a hundred libretti and more, but I have hardly found a single one with which I am satisfied; that is to say, so many alterations would have to be made here and there, that even if a poet would undertake to make them, it would be easier for him to write a completely new text—which indeed it is always best to do.

---

[1] K. 294.

[2] Francesco Benucci, a basso buffo, who was the original Figaro in Mozart's opera, which had its first performance on 1 May 1786. Benucci first sang in Venice, 1778–1779, and after the re-establishment of Italian opera by the Emperor Joseph II, was summoned to Vienna in 1783. In 1788 he sang in London, but with little success.

Our poet here is now a certain Abbate da Ponte.[1] He has an enormous amount to do in revising pieces for the theatre and he has to write *per obbligo* an entirely new libretto for Salieri,[2] which will take him two months. He has promised after that to write a new libretto for me. But who knows whether he will be able to keep his word—or will want to? For, as you are aware, these Italian gentlemen are very civil to your face. Enough, we know them! If he is in league with Salieri, I shall never get anything out of him. But indeed I should dearly love to show what I can do in an Italian opera! So I have been thinking that unless Varesco is still very much annoyed with us about the Munich opera,[3] he might write me a new libretto for seven characters. Basta! You will know best if this can be arranged. In the meantime he could jot down a few ideas, and when I come to Salzburg we could then work them out together. The most essential thing is that on the whole the story should be really *comic*; and, if possible, he ought to introduce *two equally good female parts*, one of these to be *seria*, the other *mezzo carattere*, but both parts equal *in importance and excellence*. The third female *character*, however, may be entirely buffa, and so may all the male ones, if necessary. If you think that something can be got out of Varesco, please discuss it with him soon. But you must not tell him that I am coming to Salzburg in July, or he will do no work; for I should very much like to have some of it while I am still in Vienna. Tell him too that his share will certainly amount to 400 or 500 gulden, for the custom here is that the poet gets the takings of the third performance.

Well, I must close, for I am not yet fully dressed. Meanwhile, farewell. My wife and I kiss your hands a thousand times and embrace our dear sister with all our hearts and are ever your most obedient children

W: A: MOZART

Vienna, 7 May 1783.

(490) *Mozart to his Father*

[*Autograph in the Mozarteum, Salzburg*]

MON TRÉS CHER PÉRE!   VIENNA, 21 *May* 1783

I made enquiries the other day from the banker Scheffler about a person of the name of Rosa as well as Rossi. Meanwhile he himself has

---

[1] Lorenzo da Ponte (1749–1838), the famous librettist of Mozart's *Figaro, Don Giovanni, Così fan tutte*, and probably of his unfinished *Lo sposo deluso*. After an adventurous youth da Ponte was appointed poet to the Imperial Theatres in Vienna, but left in 1791 on the death of Joseph II. He then lived for a time in London, where he tried to sell Italian books. Owing to money difficulties he was forced to leave England, and fled in 1805 to New York where he settled for the rest of his life, and where he wrote his well-known memoirs which began to appear in 1823. For the best accounts of da Ponte's life see E. J. Dent, *Mozart's Operas* (London, 1913), p. 146 ff, J. L. Russo, *Lorenzo Da Ponte* (New York, 1922), and the introduction to *Memoirs of Lorenzo Da Ponte* edited by L. A. Sheppard (London, 1929).

[2] Salieri's *Il ricco d' un giorno*, performed on 6 December 1784.

[3] *Idomeneo*, for which Abbate Varesco had written the libretto.

been to see me, so that at last I have received the music. I have also received Ceccarelli's rondo[1] from Gilowsky, for which I thank you. I am now sending you the voice part with variations of 'Non so d'onde viene'[2] and only hope that you may be able to read it. I am heartily sorry to hear about poor dear Frau von Robinig.[3] My wife and I almost lost an honest friend, Baron Raimund Wetzlar, in whose house we used to live. That reminds me, we have been living in another house for some time and have not yet told you. Baron Wetzlar has taken a lady into his home; so, to oblige him, we moved before the time to a wretched lodging in the Kohlmarkt,[4] in return for which he refused to take any rent for the three months we had lived in his house, and also paid the expenses of our removal. Meanwhile we looked round for decent quarters and at last found them in the Judenplatz, where we are now living. Wetzlar paid for us too when we were in the Kohlmarkt. Our new address is: 'Auf dem Judenplatz, im Burgischen Hause, No. 244. First floor'.[5] Now our sole desire is to have the happiness of embracing you both soon. But do you think that this will be in ⟨Salzburg?⟩ I ⟨hardly⟩ think so, unfortunately! An idea has been worrying me for a long time, but as it never seemed to occur to you, my dearest father, I banished it from my mind. Herr von Edelbach and Baron Wetzlar, however, have confirmed ⟨my suspicion, which is that when I come to Salzburg, the Archbishop may have me arrested⟩ or at least— Basta!—What chiefly makes me ⟨dread⟩ this, is the fact that I have not yet received my formal ⟨dismissal.⟩ Perhaps he has ⟨purposely held it back, in order to catch me later.⟩ Well, you are the best judge; and, if your opinion is to the contrary, then ⟨we shall certainly come;⟩ but if you agree with me, then we must choose a third ⟨place⟩ for our meeting— perhaps ⟨Munich. For a priest⟩ is capable of anything. A propos, have you heard about the famous quarrel between the ⟨Archbishop and Count Daun⟩ and that ⟨the Archbishop received an infamous letter from the chapter of Passau?⟩ Please keep on reminding Varesco about the matter you know of. The chief thing must be the comic element, for I know the taste of the Viennese. Meanwhile farewell. My wife and I kiss your hands a thousand times and embrace our dear sister with all our hearts and are ever your most obedient children

W. et C: MOZART

[1] K. 374.
[2] K. 294. See p. 497, n. 3. No doubt Leopold Mozart was proposing to teach these coloratura passages to his pupil, Margarete Marchand.
[3] Frau von Robinig died on 24 April 1783.
[4] Now Kohlmarkt no. 7. The Mozarts spent three months here.
[5] Now no. 3, where the Mozarts' first child was born.

849

(491) *Mozart to his Father*

[*Autograph in the Staatsbibliothek Preussischer Kulturbesitz, West Berlin*]

MON TRÉS CHER PÉRE!   VIENNA, 7 *June* 1783

Praise and thanks be to God, I am quite well again! But my illness has left me a cold as a remembrance, which was very charming of it! I have received my dear sister's letter. My wife's name-day is neither in March nor in May, but on February 16th; and is not to be found in any calendar. She thanks you both, however, most cordially for your kind good wishes, which are always acceptable, even though it is not her name-day. She wanted to write to my sister herself, but in her present condition she must be excused if she is a little bit commode—or, as we say, indolent. According to the midwife's examination she ought to have had her confinement on the 4th, but I do not think that the event will take place before the 15th or 16th. She is longing for it to happen as soon as possible, particularly that she may have the happiness of embracing you and my dear sister in Salzburg. As I did not think that this would happen so soon, I kept on postponing going down on my knees, folding my hands and entreating you most submissively, my dearest father, to be godfather! As there is still time, I am doing so now. Meanwhile, (in the confident hope that you will not refuse) I have already arranged (I mean, since the midwife took stock of the *visum repertum*) that someone shall present the child in your name, whether is it *generis masculini* or *feminini!* So we are going to call it Leopold or Leopoldine.

Well, I have a few words to say to my sister about Clementi's sonatas. Everyone who either hears them or plays them must feel that as compositions they are worthless. They contain no remarkable or striking passages except those in sixths and octaves. And I implore my sister not to practise those passages too much, so that she may not spoil her quiet, even touch and that her hand may not lose its natural lightness, flexibility and smooth rapidity. For after all what is to be gained by it? Supposing that you do play sixths and octaves with the utmost velocity (which no one can accomplish, not even Clementi) you only produce an atrocious chopping effect and nothing else whatever. Clementi is a *ciarlatano*, like all Italians. He writes *Presto* over a sonata or even *Prestissimo* and *Alla breve*, and plays it himself *Allegro* in $\frac{4}{4}$ time. I know this is the case, for I have heard him do so. What he really does well are his passages in thirds; but he sweated over them day and night in London. Apart from this, he can do nothing, absolutely nothing, for he has not the slightest expression or taste, still less, feeling.

Now for Herr von Amann. Herr von Fichtl told me that Court Councillor Amann has been locked up, as he is supposed to be quite mad.

I was not at all surprised to hear this, for he always went about with a morose expression. I always used to say that study was not the cause of it; upon which Herr von Fichtl used to laugh heartily. But I am very sorry for Basilius Amann. And indeed I should never have thought it of him. I would sooner have thought that he would become saner. Well, perhaps he will take me into his service when I come to Salzburg? I shall certainly go and see him. If you can get hold of some German song which he has written, be so kind as to send it to me, so that I may have something to make me laugh. I shall set it to music. No, no! I know a fool here who will do the job.

Have you heard anything yet from Varesco? Please do not forget what I asked you. When I am in Salzburg we should have such an admirable opportunity of working together, if in the meantime we had thought out a plan.

Now farewell. My wife and I kiss your hands a thousand times and embrace our dear sister with all our hearts and are ever your most obedient children

W: et C: MOZART

PS.—I trust that you received the voice part with variations of the aria 'Non so d'onde viene'? [1]

(492) *Mozart to his Father*

[*Autograph in the Pierpont Morgan Library, New York City*]

MON TRÉS CHER PÉRE!   VIENNA, 18 *June* 1783

Congratulations, you are a grandpapa! Yesterday, the 17th, at half past six in the morning my dear wife was safely delivered of a fine sturdy boy,[2] as round as a ball. Her pains began at half past one in the morning, so that night we both lost our rest and sleep. At four o'clock I sent for my mother-in-law—and then for the midwife. At six o'clock the child began to appear and at half past six the trouble was all over. My mother-in-law by her great kindness to her daughter has made full amends for all the harm she did her *before her marriage*. She spends the whole day with her.

My dear wife, who kisses your hands and embraces my dear sister most affectionately, is as well as she can be in the circumstances. I trust with God's help that, as she is taking good care of herself, she will make a complete recovery from her confinement. From the condition of her breasts I am rather afraid of milk-fever. And now the child has been given

[1] K. 294.
[2] Raimund Leopold, who died on August 21st during his parents' visit to Salzburg. For a full account of Mozart's six children see Blümml, pp. 1-9.

to a foster-nurse against my will, or rather, at my wish! For I was quite determined that whether she should be able to do so or not, my wife was never to feed her child. Yet I was equally determined that my child was never to take the milk of a stranger! I wanted the child to be brought up on water, like my sister and myself. However, the midwife, my mother-in-law and most people here have begged and implored me not to allow it, if only for the reason that most children here who are brought up on water do not survive, as the people here don't know how to do it properly. That induced me to give in, for I should not like to have anything to reproach myself with.

Now for the godfather question. Let me tell you what has happened. After my wife's safe delivery I immediately sent a message to Baron Wetzlar, who is a good and true friend of mine. He came to see us at once and offered to stand godfather. I could not refuse him and thought to myself: 'After all, my boy can still be called Leopold'. But while I was turning this round in my mind, the Baron said very cheerfully: 'Ah, now you have a little Raimund'—and kissed the child. What was I to do? Well, I have had the child christened Raimund Leopold. I must frankly confess that if you had not sent me in a letter your opinion on the matter, I should have been very much embarrassed, and I am not at all sure that I should not have refused his offer! But your letter has comforted me with the assurance that you will not disapprove of my action! After all, Leopold is one of his names. Well, I must close. My newly confined wife and I kiss your hands a thousand times and embrace our dear sister a thousand times and are ever your most obedient children

W: A: C. Mozart

(493) *Mozart to his Father*

[*Autograph in the Library of Congress, Washington*]

Mon trés cher Pére!   Vienna, 21 *June* 1783

This will have to be a very short letter. I must only tell you what is absolutely necessary, as I have far too much to do. For a new Italian opera is being produced,[1] in which for the first time two German singers are appearing, Madame Lange, my sister-in-law, and Adamberger, and I have to compose two arias for her[2] and a rondo for him.[3] I hope you received my last letter of rejoicing. Thank God, my wife has now survived the two critical days, yesterday and the day before, and in the circumstances is very well. We now hope that all will go well. The child too is quite strong and healthy and has a tremendous number of things to do,

---

1 Anfossi's *Il curioso indiscreto*. It was performed on 30 June 1783.
2 K. 418, 'Vorrei spiegarvi, oh Dio' and K. 419, 'No, no, che non sei capace'.
3 K. 420, 'Per pietà, non ricercate'.

I mean, drinking, sleeping, yelling, pissing, shitting, dribbling and so forth. He kisses the hands of his grandpapa and of his aunt. Now for Varesco. I like his plan quite well.[1] But I must speak to Count Rosenberg at once, so as to make sure that the poet will get his reward. Why, I consider it a great insult to myself that Herr Varesco is doubtful about the success of the opera. Of one thing he may be sure and that is, that his libretto will certainly not go down if the music is no good. For in the opera the chief thing is the music. If then the opera is to be a success and Varesco hopes to be rewarded, he must alter and recast the libretto as much and as often as I wish and he must not follow his own inclinations, for he has not the slightest knowledge or experience of the theatre. You may even give him to understand that it doesn't much matter whether he writes the opera or not. I know the story now; and therefore anyone can write it as well as he can. Besides, I am expecting today four of the latest and best libretti from Italy among which there will surely be one which will be some good. So there is plenty of time. Well, I must close. My newly confined wife and I kiss your hands, most beloved father, and embrace our dear sister with all our hearts and are ever your most obedient children

W: A et C: Mozart

Herr von Gilowsky sends his greetings to both of you and thanks to his father and sister for never writing to him—although they must know that he is laid up with a fever.

(494) *Mozart to his Father*

[*Autograph in the Stadtarchiv, Bratislava*]

Mon très cher Père!   Vienna, 2 *July* 1783

My head was so full last post-day that I completely forgot to write. Madame Lange was at our house to try over her two arias and we were discussing how we could be cleverer than our enemies—for I have plenty of them—and Madame Lange too has enough to do with this *new singer*, Mlle Storace.[2] Only when I was alone did I remember that it was post-day and then of course it was too late. Anfossi's opera 'Il curioso indiscreto,' in which Madame Lange and Adamberger appeared for the first time, was performed the day before yesterday, Monday, for the first time. It

[1] Varesco's plan for the opera *L' oca del Cairo.*

[2] Anna (Nancy) Storace (1765–1817), a famous English soprano. She was born in London, her mother being English and her father Italian. She studied under Rauzzini in Italy, where she made her first appearance in Venice in 1780. She came to Vienna in 1783, and was the original Susanna in Mozart's *Figaro.* In March 1787 she returned to England and continued to sing in public until 1808. When in Vienna she married the English violinist John Abraham Fisher (1744–1806).

failed completely with the exception of my two arias,[1] the second of which, a bravura, had to be repeated. Well, I should like you to know that my friends were malicious enough to spread the report beforehand that '*Mozart wanted to improve on Anfossi's opera*'. I heard of this and sent a message to Count Rosenberg that I would not hand over my arias unless the following statement were printed in the copies of the libretto, both in German and in Italian.

Avvertimento

Le due arie a carta 36 e a carta 102 sono state messe in musica dal Signor Maestro Mozart, per compiacere alla Signora Lange, non essendo quelle state scritte dal Signor Maestro Anfossi secondo la di lei abilità, ma per altro soggetto. Questo si vuole far noto perchè ne vada l'onore a chi conviene, senza che rimanga in alcuna parte pregiudicata la riputazione e la fama del già molto cognito Napolitano.[2]

Well, the statement was inserted and I handed out my arias, which did inexpressible honour both to my sister-in-law and to myself. So my enemies were quite confounded! And now for a trick of Salieri's, which has injured poor Adamberger more than me. I think I told you that I had composed a rondo for Adamberger.[3] During a short rehearsal, before the rondo had been copied, Salieri took Adamberger aside and told him that Count Rosenberg would not be pleased if he put in an aria and that he advised him as his good friend not to do so. Adamberger, provoked by Rosenberg's objection and not knowing how to retaliate, was stupid enough to say, with ill-timed pride, '*All right. But to prove that Adamberger has already made his reputation in Vienna and does not need to make a name for himself by singing music expressly written for him, he will only sing what is in the opera and will never again, as long as he lives, introduce any aria.*' What was the result? Why, that he was a complete failure, as was only to be expected! Now he is sorry, but it is too late. For if he were to ask me this very day to give him the rondo, I should refuse. I can easily find a place for it in one of my own operas. But the most annoying part of the whole affair is that his wife's prophecy and mine have come true, that is, that Count Rosenberg and the management *know nothing whatever about it*, so that it was only a ruse on the part of Salieri. Thank God, my wife is quite well again, save for a slight cold. We and our little Raimund, aged a fortnight, kiss your hands

---

[1] K. 418 and 419.

[2] The two arias on p. 36 and p. 102 have been set to music by Signor Maestro Mozart to suit Signora Lange, because the arias of Signor Maestro Anfossi were not written for her voice, but for another singer. It is necessary that this should be pointed out so that honour may be given to whom it is due and so that the reputation and the name of the most famous Neapolitan may not suffer in any way whatsoever.   [3] K. 420.

and embrace our dear sister with all our hearts and are ever your most
obedient children

W: A: C: Mozart

(495) *Mozart to his Father*

[*Autograph in the Koch Collection, Basel*]

MON TRÉS CHER PÉRE, VIENNA, 5 *July* 1783

We both thank you for the prayer you made to God for the safe
delivery of my wife. Little Raimund is so like me that everyone immediately remarks it. It is just as if my face had been copied. My dear little wife
is absolutely delighted, as this is what she had always desired. He will
be three weeks old next Tuesday and he has grown in an astonishing
manner. As for the opera[1] you have given me a piece of advice which I
had already given myself. But as I prefer to work slowly and with deliberation, I thought that I could not begin too soon. An Italian poet here has
now brought me a libretto[2] which I shall perhaps adopt, if he agrees to
trim and adjust it in accordance with my wishes. I feel sure that we shall
be able to set out in September; and indeed you can well imagine that
our most ardent longing is to embrace you both. Yet I cannot conceal
from you, but must confess quite frankly that many people here are
alarming me to such an extent that I cannot describe it. *You already know
what it is all about.*[3] However much I protest I am told: '*Well, you will see,
you will ⟨never get away again.⟩ You have no idea of what ⟨that wicked
malevolent Prince is capable of!⟩ And you ⟨cannot⟩ conceive what ⟨low tricks⟩
are resorted to in affairs of this kind. Take my advice and ⟨meet your father⟩ in
some third place.*' This, you see, is what has been worrying my wife and me
up to the present and what is still perturbing us. I often say to myself:
'Nonsense, it's quite impossible!' But the next moment it occurs to me
that after all it might be possible and that it would not be the ⟨first
injustice⟩ which he has ⟨committed.⟩ Basta! In this matter no one can
comfort me but you, my most beloved father! And so far as I am concerned, whatever happened would not worry me very much, for I can
now adapt myself to any circumstances. But when I think of my wife and
my little Raimund, then my indifference ceases. Think it over. If you can
give me an assurance that I shall be ⟨running no risk,⟩ we shall both be
overjoyed. If not, then we must hit on some plan; and there is one which
I should prefer above all others! As soon as I receive your reply, I shall tell

[1] *L'oca del Cairo.*
[2] Probably the Italian poet is da Ponte and the libretto that of *Lo sposo deluso*, Mozart's
unfinished opera buffa. For a discussion of the evidence for this theory see *Music and Letters*,
April 1937, p. 131 f. where the translation of this letter was first published.
[3] See p. 849.

you about it. I am convinced that if one is to enjoy a great pleasure, one must forgo something. Why! In the greatest happiness there is always something lacking. Meanwhile, farewell. Take care of your health. We both kiss your hands and embrace our dear sister with all our hearts and are ever your most obedient children

W: C: MOZART

PS.—This does not mean that you are to give up prodding Varesco. Who knows whether I shall like the opera of the Italian poet?

Adieu

(496) Mozart to his Father

[Autograph in the Universitätsbibliothek, Basel]

MON TRÉS CHER PÉRE!   VIENNA, 12 July 1783

I have received your letter of the 8th and am delighted to hear that, thank God, you are both well. If you insist on calling what are real obstacles mere humbug, I cannot prevent you from doing so. Anyone may call a thing by a wrong name if he pleases; but whether it is right to do so, is a very different matter. Have I ever given you the impression that I had no desire or longing to see you? Most certainly never! But assuredly you will have observed that I have no desire whatever to see Salzburg or the Archbishop. So, if we were to meet in a third place, who would then be humbugged? Why, the Archbishop, and not you. I suppose I need not repeat that I care very little for Salzburg and not at all for the Archbishop, that I shit on both of them and that it would never enter my head voluntarily to make a journey thither, were it not that you and my sister lived there. So the whole business was due solely to the well-meant caution of my good friends, who surely are not devoid of sound common sense. And I did not think that I was acting unreasonably if I made some enquiries from you on the subject and then followed your advice. My friends' anxiety amounted to this, that, as I have never been discharged, the Archbishop might have me arrested. But you have now set my mind completely at rest and we shall come in August, or certainly in September at the latest. Herr von Babbius met me in the street and walked home with me; he went off today and if he had not had another engagement he would have lunched with us yesterday.

Dear father! You must not suppose that because it is summer I have nothing to do. Everyone has not gone into the country and I still have a few pupils to look after. Just now I have one for composition, who will make a nice face when I tell him of my journey. Well, I must close, as I have a good deal to write. Meanwhile, arrange the bowling-green in the garden, for my wife is a great lover of the game. She is always a little bit nervous lest you should not like her, because she is not pretty. But I console her as well as I can by telling her that my dearest father thinks more of inward than of outward beauty. Now farewell. My wife and I kiss your hands a thousand times and embrace our dear sister with all our hearts and are ever your most obedient children

W: A: C: Mozart

(497) *Constanze Mozart to Nannerl Mozart*

[Autograph in the Gesellschaft der Musikfreunde, Vienna]

Vienna, 19 July 1783

Most precious and dearest Mademoiselle Sister-in-law!

My dear husband has received your letter and both he and I are delighted that you are looking forward so much to seeing us. But he was a little annoyed by your suspicion that we were not so very anxious to see you; and indeed I myself felt rather hurt. To prove, however, that everything is all right again, let me tell you that we always intended to go to you in August; and so we wanted to give you a little surprise, which will no longer be one for you, but will be so at any rate for our dear beloved father—that is, if you can keep it quiet, which we beg you to do; for only on this condition are we telling you the truth. Well, you have dragged our secret out of us by your naughty letter; and we shall be quite content if only we give this unexpected pleasure to our dear father. So—please do not mention our plan. Well, about August 1st I shall have the joy and happiness of embracing you. Until then I remain with the deepest respect, my dearest sister-in-law, yours sincerely,

Maria Constanza Mozart

Vienna, 19 July 1783

(497a) *Constanze Mozart to Margarete Marchand*[1]

[Autograph in the Gesellschaft der Musikfreunde, Vienna]

Dearest Mademoiselle Marchand!   [Vienna, 19 *July* 1783]

I am delighted that you still remember me and have taken the trouble to write to me. Believe me, I am just as much longing to see Salzburg and to have the joy and happiness of meeting personally my dear papa-in-law and my dear sister-in-law and showing them my devotion as you can possibly be longing for an opportunity of seeing your own beloved parents again. And then the pleasure of embracing my dear

[1] See p. 582 n 2.

Mademoiselle Marguérite, whom I knew in Mannheim and Munich as a very clever young woman and who in the meantime has had plenty of opportunity of perfecting her gifts! How delighted I shall be to see her again, kiss her and admire her talents. God willing, I shall be able to do so on August 1st. Meanwhile I urge you to observe the strictest silence and I remain your most devoted servant and friend

MARIA CONSTANZA MOZART

(497b) Mozart to Margarete Marchand and his Sister

[Autograph in the Gesellschaft der Musikfreunde, Vienna]

[VIENNA, 19 July 1783 [1]]

MOST BELOVED MLLE MARCHAND AND DEAREST SISTER!

Neither of you should believe a word of what my wife has scrawled up above. How can we be in Salzburg on August 1st if we must be here on the 26th? But if it is not necessary for me to be here on the 26th, we shall certainly be with you on August 1st. I shall congratulate you then in person on your name-day,[2] my sister! and I shall be able to congratulate you also in the octave.[3] Meanwhile farewell, dear sister, and you too, dear Mlle Marchand. I hope soon to hear you sing and play on the clavier. We must celebrate my sister's name-day with a concert. Farewell to both of you. Dearest sister, I kiss you most cordially and am ever your sincere brother

W: A: MOZART

(498) Mozart to his Sister

[From Otto Jahn, W. A. Mozart, 2nd edition, vol. ii. p. 559 f.[4]]

[SALZBURG, 31 July 1783]

Here's to you
In a fine punch-brew!
Today I went out shopping, and why, you'd never guess,
But now that I must tell you, the reason was no less
Than with some trifling gift my sister to delight,
For her to please I'd strive with all my main and might.
Alas! I'm not quite sure if punch you like to drink?
Ah! Please do not say no, or else the seal will stink.
But to myself I thought, she loves the English faces.
For if she favoured Paris, I'd give her pretty laces,

---

[1] A postscript to his wife's letters.   [2] 26 July.   [3] i.e. during the following week.
[4] Copy in the Landesmuseum, Linz.

A bouquet of fine flowers or perhaps some perfume rare.
But you, my dearest sister, are no coquette, I swear.
So from your brother take this punch (it's very strong and choice)
And may repeated draughts of it your heart and soul rejoice.

W. A. Mozart
Poet-laureate of the marksmen

Salzburg, 31 July 1783.

(499) Mozart to his Father

[Autograph in the Nationalbibliothek, Vienna; cover in the Stadtbibliothek, Vienna]

Linz, 31 October 1783,[1]

We arrived here safely yesterday morning at nine o'clock. We spent the first night in Vöcklabruck and reached Lambach next morning, where I arrived just in time to accompany the 'Agnus Dei' on the organ. The abbot[2] was absolutely delighted to see me again and told me the anecdote about you and himself in Salzburg. We spent the whole day there and I played both on the organ and on a clavichord. I heard that an opera was to be given next day at Ebelsberg at the house of the Prefect Steurer (whose wife is a sister of Frau von Barisani) and that almost all Linz was to be asembled. I resolved therefore to be present and we drove there. Young Count Thun (brother of the Thun in Vienna) called on me immediately and said that his father had been expecting me for a fortnight and would I please drive to his house at once for I was to stay with him. I told him that I could easily put up at an inn. But when we reached the gates of Linz on the following day, we found a servant waiting there to drive us to old Count Thun's, at whose house we are now staying. I really cannot tell you what kindnesses the family are showering on us. On Tuesday, November 4th, I am giving a concert in the theatre here and, as I have not a single symphony with me, I am writing a new one[3] at breakneck speed, which must be finished by that time. Well, I must close, because I really must set to work. My wife and I kiss your hands, ask you to forgive us for inconveniencing you for so long and thank you once more very much for all the kindnesses we have received. So farewell. We send cordial greetings to little Greta,[4] to Heinrich[5] (about whom I have already said a great deal here) and Hanni.[6] Please give a

---

[1] Owing to the visit of Mozart and his wife to Salzburg during the months of August, September and October there is a gap in his letters to his father.
[2] Amandus Schickmayr, whom Mozart had met in 1767.
[3] K. 425, the 'Linz' symphony in C major.
[4] Margarete Marchand.   [5] Heinrich Marchand.
[6] Maria Johanna Brochard, the eight-year-old cousin of Heinrich and Margarete Marchand, had also become a pupil of Leopold Mozart, in whose house she was living. In 1790 she joined the Munich court theatre and subsequently married the dancer Franz Renner.

special message to little Greta, and tell her that when she sings she must not be so arch and coy; for cajolings and kissings are not always palatable —in fact only silly asses are taken in by such devices. I for one would rather have a country lout, who does not hesitate to shit and piss in my presence, than let myself be humbugged by such false toadyings, which after all are so exaggerated that anyone can easily see through them. Well, adieu. We kiss our dear sister most cordially. I am ever your most grateful son

W: A: Mozart

(500) *Mozart to his Father*

[Autograph in the Mozarteum, Salzburg]

Mon trés cher Pére!   Vienna, 6 *December* 1783

As I had no idea that you would write to me at Vienna until I had informed you of my arrival, I only went to Peisser today to ask for letters and found your letter of November 21st, which had been lying there for twelve days. I trust that you have received my letter from Vienna. And now I have a request to make. No doubt you remember that when you came to Munich while I was composing my grand opera,[1] you reproached me with the debt of twelve louis d'or which I had drawn from Herr Scherz in Strassburg, adding these words, *'What annoys me is your lack of confidence in me. Well, at all events I now have the honour of paying twelve louis d'or for you.'* I went off to Vienna and you returned to Salzburg. From what you said I assumed that I need not give the matter another thought. Moreover, I presumed that if you had not paid my debt, you would have written to me or told me of it when we were together lately. So imagine my embarrassment and my surprise when the day before yesterday a clerk of the banker Herr Öchser brought me a letter from Herr Haffner in Salzburg, which contained an enclosure from Herr Scherz. As the transaction took place five years ago, he is demanding interest on the sum. On hearing this I said quite frankly that any such payment was out of the question and added that legally I was not bound to pay a farthing, as the bill was payable six weeks from the date and consequently had expired; still, in consideration of Herr Scherz's friendship I should pay the original sum, but, no interest being named, I was not liable for anything more. All that I ask of you, dearest father, is to be good enough to go security for me with Haffner, or rather Triendl, just for a month. As a man of experience you can easily imagine that just now it would be very inconvenient for me to be left short of money. Herr Öscher's clerk had to admit that I was right, but contented himself with saying that he would

[1] *Idomeneo.*

tell Herr Haffner. What annoys me most about the whole business is that Herr Scherz will not have a very good opinion of me—a proof that chance, coincidence, circumstances, a misunderstanding and Heaven knows what may rob an innocent man of his good name! Why did Herr Scherz never mention the transaction all this long while? Surely my name is not so obscure! My opera[1] which was performed at Strassburg must at least have given him some idea that I was in Vienna! And then his connection with Haffner in Salzburg. If he had reminded me during the first year, I should have paid him on the spot with pleasure. I mean to pay it still, but at the moment I am not in a position to do so. Perhaps he thought that he had to do with some simpleton, who would pay what he does not owe? Well, then, let him keep the title for himself.

Now let us talk of something else. I have only three more arias to compose and then the first act of my opera[2] will be finished. I can really say that I am quite satisfied with the aria buffa, the quartet and the finale and am looking forward to their performance. I should therefore be sorry to have written this music to no purpose, I mean, if what is absolutely necessary doesn't take place. Neither you nor Abbate Varesco nor I have noticed that it will have a very bad effect and even cause the entire failure of the opera if neither of the two principal female singers appear on the stage until the very last moment, but keep on walking about on the bastions or on the ramparts of the fortress. The patience of the audience might hold out for one act, but certainly not for a second one—that is quite out of the question. This first occurred to me at Linz, and it seems to me that the only solution is to contrive that some of the scenes in the second act shall take place in the fortress—*camera della fortezza*. The scene could be so arranged that when Don Pippo gives orders for the goose to be brought into the fortress, the stage should represent a room where Celidora and Lavina are. Pantea comes in with the goose and Biondello slips out. They hear Don Pippo coming and Biondello again becomes a goose. At this point a good quintet would be very suitable, which would be the more comic as the goose would be singing along with the others. I must tell you, however, that my only reason for not objecting to this goose story altogether was because two people of greater insight and judgment than myself have not disapproved of it, I mean yourself and Varesco. But there is still time to think of other arrangements. Biondello has vowed to make his way into the tower; how he manages to do so, whether in the form of a goose or by some other ruse, does not really matter. I should have thought that effects far more natural and amusing might be produced, if he were to remain in human form. For example, the news that in despair at not being able to make his way into the fortress he has thrown himself into the sea, could be brought in at the very

---

[1] *Die Entführung aus dem Serail*. See p. 840, n. 5.   [2] *L'oca del Cairo*.

beginning of Act II. He might then disguise himself as a Turk or anyone he chose and bring Pantea with him as a slave (a Moorish girl, of course). Don Pippo is willing to purchase the slave for his bride. Therefore the slave-dealer and the Moorish girl must enter the fortress in order to be inspected. In this way Pantea has an opportunity of bullying her husband and addressing all sorts of impertinent remarks to him, which would greatly improve her part, for the more comic an Italian opera is the better. Well, I entreat you to expound my views very clearly to Abbate Varesco and to tell him that I implore him to go ahead. I have worked hard enough in this short time. Why, I should have finished the whole of Act I, if I did not require some alterations in the words of some of the arias. *But say nothing of this to him at present.* My German opera 'Die Entführung aus dem Serail' has been performed both in Prague and Leipzig excellently and with the greatest applause. I have heard both these facts from people who saw the performances. I shall make a point of looking up Herr von Deckelmann [1] and shall give him *the cadenzas, the concerto* and the four ducats. Please send me as soon as possible my 'Idomeneo', the two violin duets [2] and Sebastian Bach's fugues. [3] I require 'Idomeneo' because during Lent I am going to give as well as my concert in the theatre six subscription concerts, at which I should like to produce this opera. Further, will you please ask Tomaselli to let us have the prescription for that eczema ointment, which has done us excellent service. One never knows when one may need it again either for oneself or to hand on to someone else. A bird in the hand is always worth two in the bush. Well, adieu. My wife and I kiss your hands a thousand times and embrace our dear sister with all our hearts and are ever your most obedient children

W: et C: Mozart

PS.—Please give Varesco a good talking to and hurry him up. Do send the music soon. We kiss Greta, Heinrich and Hanni; I shall write to Greta one of these days. Tell Heinrich from me that both here and in Linz I have already said many things in his favour. Tell him too that he ought to concentrate hard on staccato-playing, for it is just in this particular that the Viennese cannot forget Lamotte. [4] Adieu.

---

[1] Bernard Freiherr von Deglmann, whose name also appears on p. 870 as 'Bar: Tögel-man'.

[2] K. 423 and 424, duets for violin and viola, which Mozart composed during the summer at Salzburg for Michael Haydn, who owing to an indisposition could not carry out a commission from the Archbishop.

[3] Mozart had arranged for string quartet, five fugues (No. 2, 5, 7, 8 and 9) from Book 2 of the '48' (K. 405).

[4] Franz Lamotte, an excellent violinist, had been since 1772 in the service of the Viennese Court. He died in 1781.

(501) *Mozart to his Father*

[*Copy in the Staatsbibliothek Preussischer Kulturbesitz, West Berlin*][1]

MON TRÉS CHER PÉRE!   VIENNA, 10 *December* 1783

I am writing in the greatest haste to tell you that I have already bought the opera 'Der Rauchfangkehrer'[2] for six ducats and have it at home. If the mail coach leaves for Salzburg next Sunday, I shall send it along with the two concertos; if not, well then it shall go by letter post. As for the money, just please deduct the four ducats which you were good enough to advance me. There is no German translation of the opera 'Fra due litiganti';[3] and judging by your letter you seem to think that 'Der Rauchfangkehrer' is an Italian opera! Not at all. It is a German and, what is more, a wretched work, the author of which is Doctor Auernszucker[4] in Vienna. You will remember that I told you about it and of how Herr Fischer publicly damned it in the theatre. Herr Kühne has probably got the charming little libretto. Please give many compliments from us both to him and to his wife. As for Herr Lange and his wife, the truth is that he has obtained permission from His Majesty to travel for a few months and that before their departure they are going to perform an opera for their own benefit and that this opera will be my 'Entführung aus dem Serail'. There is not a word of truth in the story about Herr Schröder.

Meanwhile you will have received my last letter. Do your very best to make my libretto a success. I wish that in Act I some arrangement could be made to let the two women come down from the bastion when they have to sing their arias; in this case I would gladly consent to their singing the whole finale up above. We are both very sad about our poor, bonny, fat, darling little boy.[5] Well, I must close. Dearest, most beloved father! We both kiss your hands and embrace our dear sister with all our hearts and are ever your most obedient children

W: et C: MOZART

1000,000,000 kisses to Greta, Heinrich and little Hanni. Adieu.

PS.—We both send Nannerl
     (1) a couple of boxes on the ear
     (2) a couple of slaps on the face
     (3) a couple of raps on the cheek
     (4) a couple of whacks on the jaw

[1] Autograph in the Bibliothèque Nationale, Paris. The two postscripts are missing in this source and were probably written on the cover, which is lost.

[2] The libretto of *Der Rauchfangkehrer*, which was performed in 1781, was by Dr. Auenbrugger, the music by Salieri.

[3] *Fra i due litiganti*, by Giuseppe Sarti (1729–1802), a famous operatic composer of the eighteenth century.

[4] Dr. Auenbrugger.   [5] See p. 851, n. 2.

(5) a couple of smacks on the jowl
(6) a couple of cuffs on the mug.

PS.—Please do not forget about Tomaselli. That reminds me, will you please send us, when you have time, a couple of images of the infant Jesus of Loreto. By the way, I must not forget about little Lisa, Theresa's cousin who often came to your house. If she wants to come to Vienna, we shall take her at once.[1] Well, *adieu, really adieu* this time.

(502) *Mozart to his Father*

[*Autograph in the Nationalbibliothek, Vienna*]

MON TRÉS CHER PÈRE!   VIENNA, 24 *December* 1783

I have received your last letter of the 19th enclosing a portion of the opera. Well, let me deal with this, which is the most urgent matter. Abbate Varesco has written in the margin beside Lavina's cavatina: 'a cui servià la musica della cavatina antecedente',[2] that is, Celidora's cavatina. But that is out of the question, for in Celidora's cavatina the words are very disconsolate and despairing, whereas in Lavina's they are most comforting and hopeful. Besides, for one singer to echo the song of another is a practice which is quite out of date and is hardly ever made use of. It can only be tolerated in the case of a soubrette and her amant, that is, in the *ultime parti*.[3] My opinion is that the scene should start with a fine duet, which might very well begin with the same words and with a short *aggiunta* for the coda. After the duet the conversation can be resumed. *E quando s'ode il campanello della custode*,[4] Mlle Lavina, not Celidora, will be so good as to remove herself, so that the latter, as a prima donna, may have an opportunity of singing a fine bravura aria. Some arrangement of this kind would suit much better the composer, the singer, the spectators and the audience, and the whole scene would undoubtedly become far more interesting. Further, the audience would hardly be able to tolerate *the same aria* from the second singer, after having heard it sung by the first. In the next place, I do not know what you are both driving at by the following arrangement. At the end of the newly inserted scene between the two women in Act I, the Abbate writes: Segue la scena VIII che prima era la VII e così cangiansi di mano in mano i numeri.[5] From this description I am to suppose that, contrary to my wish, the scene after the quartet

---

[1] Lisa Schwemmer whom later Mozart and his wife employed as their maid, a kindness which they had cause to regret. See Letter 514.
[2] For which the music of the preceding cavatina will do.
[3] i.e. secondary characters. Mozart himself did this in *La finta giardiniera*, composed in 1775, that is to say, in nos. 9a and 9b of Act I.
[4] And when the duenna's bell is heard.
[5] Scene VIII, formerly Scene VII, then follows, and thus the numbers are correspondingly altered.

in which both women sing their little tunes in turn at the window, is to remain; but that is impossible. For not only would the act be very much lengthened, and to no purpose, but it would become very tedious. It always seemed to me very ridiculous to read:—

CELIDORA: Tu qui m' attendi, amica. Alla custode farmi veder vogl' io; ci andrai tu poi.
LAVINA: Si, dolce amica, addio. (Celidora parte.)[1]

Lavina sings her aria. Celidora comes in again and says: Eccomi, or vanne, etc.[2] Now it is Lavina's turn to go and Celidora sings her aria. They relieve each other like soldiers on guard. Moreover, as in the quartet they all agree to carry out their proposed scheme, it is far more natural that the men should go off and beat up the people required for this purpose and that the two women should betake themselves quietly to their apartments. The most they could still be allowed is a few lines of recitative. Indeed, I have not the smallest doubt that it was never intended that the scene should be retained, and that Varesco simply forgot to indicate that it was to be omitted. I am very curious to see how you carry out your capital idea of bringing Biondello into the tower. Provided it is diverting, I shall raise no objection, even if it is a little unnatural. I am not at all alarmed at the notion of a few fireworks, for the arrangements of the Viennese fire brigade are so excellent that there is no cause for uneasiness about having fireworks on the stage. Thus 'Medea' is often performed here, at the end of which one half of the palace collapses, while the other half goes up in flames. Tomorrow I shall look round for copies of the libretto of the 'Rauchfangkehrer'.[3] I have not yet been able to find the 'Contessina' (or the 'Countess').[4] If it is not to be had, would any of the following be suitable, 'Das Irrlicht' by Umlauf, 'Die schöne Schusterin' by the same,[5] or 'Die Pilgrimme von Mekka'?[6] The two latter operas especially would be very easy to perform. Kühne probably has them already. Please deliver greetings from both of us to him and to his wife. I trust that you received my last short letter. Let me remind you once more to send me the two duets, Bach's fugues and, *above all*, 'Idomeneo'—you will know the reason. I am particularly anxious to go through this opera on the clavier with Count Sickingen. If you could have Emanuel Bach's fugues (there are six of them, I think) copied and sent to me some time, you would be

---

[1] Celidora: Wait for me here, my friend. I wish to show myself to the duenna. You may go later.
Lavina: Yes, sweet friend, good-bye. (Exit Celidora.)
[2] Here I am, now you may go, etc.
[3] See p. 863, n. 1. Evidently Leopold Mozart was looking for operas suitable for performance at Salzburg.
[4] By Florian Leopold Gassmann (1729–1774).
[5] *Das Irrlicht* was produced in 1782, *Die schöne Schusterin* in 1779, both at the Burgtheater in Vienna.
[6] Gluck's opera *Die Pilgrimme von Mekka* was produced in 1764.

doing me a great kindness. I forgot to ask you to do this when I was at Salzburg. Meanwhile, farewell. The day before yesterday, Monday, we had another grand concert of the society,[1] when I played a concerto and Adamberger sang a rondo of my composition.[2] The concert was repeated yesterday, but a violinist played a concerto in my place. The day before yesterday the theatre was full. Yesterday it was empty. I should add that it was the violinist's first performance. Well, adieu. I kiss your hands a thousand times and we are both your most obedient children

W: et C: MOZART

A thousand smacks to my sister and to all. Adieu.

(503) *Mozart to his Father*

[*Autograph in a private collection, New York*]

MON TRÉS CHER PÉRE!   VIENNA, 10 *February* 1784

How very stupid of Artaria! He thought that they would not take the parcel at the Post Office and instead of returning it to me at once, he kept it back until it was time for the mail coach to leave, without telling me a word about the arrangement! This time I have had no letter from you. I really do not understand Peisser. These people are about *three yards* away from our house (I have measured the distance). Sometimes I myself ask whether any letters have arrived, but usually my maid does so. They bawl out 'No' in the most impertinent manner, and when the *asses* (I mean, the gentlemen) have a look, why, they suddenly find one after all. Again, if a letter happens to come at some odd time, they prefer to leave it lying for a fortnight rather than send it to me by the shopboy, which I have often asked them to do. So I beg you to write direct to my address. I have already received three letters from different countries. Just address it 'Im Trattnerischen Hause, Zweite Stiege, im Dritten Stock'.[3] Besides, I think that Herr Peisser makes a small profit on my letters.

In my last letter I wrote to you about Varesco and my opera.[4] At present I haven't the slightest intention of producing it. I have works to compose[5] which *at the moment* are bringing in money, but will not do so later. The opera will always bring in some; and besides, the more time I take, the better it will be. As it is, the impression I have gained from Varesco's text is that he has hurried too much, and I hope that in time he will realize this

---

[1] The Wiener Tonkünstlersozietät.   [2] Probably K. 431 [425b], composed in 1783.

[3] The Mozarts had moved into new lodgings in a house belonging to J. T. von Trattner, am Graben no. 591 (now no. 29). See p. 771, n. 3.

[4] *L'oca del Cairo*, which Mozart never finished.

[5] Probably his clavier concertos, six of which (K. 449, 450, 451, 453, 456, 459) were composed in 1784. From 1784 to 1786 Mozart was the most popular and successful clavier-player in Vienna. See p. 869 f.

himself. That is why I should like to see the opera *as a whole* (he need only jot it down in rough and ready fashion). Then we can make drastic alterations. For by Heaven there is no need to hurry. If you were to hear what I have composed, then you would wish, as I do, that my work should not be spoilt! And that is so easily done—and so often. What I have composed has been put away safely. I guarantee that in all the operas which are to be performed until mine is finished, not a single idea will resemble one of mine. Well, I must close, for I must really compose. I spend the whole morning giving lessons, so I have only the evening for my beloved task— composition. I have just one more question to ask, and that is, whether you are now having in Salzburg such unbearably cold weather as we are having here? Herr Freyhold[1] of Mainz wanted to call on me and sent up a servant with the letter, he himself remaining below—probably in the coach. But as I had to go out immediately I took the letter and asked him to come some afternoon, when I am always at home. I have been wanting to go along one of these days (for he has not turned up), but have not had the time. Well, adieu. My wife and I kiss your hands a thousand times and embrace our dear sister with all our hearts and are ever your most obedient children

W: and C: MOZART

(504) *Mozart to his Father*

[*Autograph in the Rudolf Nydahl Collection, Stiftelsen Musikkulturens Främjande, Stockholm*]

MON TRÉS CHER PÉRE!   VIENNA, 20 *February* 1784

I have received your last letter. Yesterday I was fortunate enough to hear Herr Freyhold play a concerto of his own wretched composition.[2] I found very little to admire in his performance and missed a great deal. His whole tour de force consists in double-tonguing. Otherwise there is nothing whatever to listen to. I was delighted that the Adagio, which by the way he played at your house, was very short. For at first the players who accompanied him could not get the hang of it, as, although the movement was written in common time, he played it Alla Breve. And, when I thereupon noted down Alla Breve with my own hand, he admitted that my Papa in Salzburg had also made a fuss. The rondo ought to be jolly, but it was the silliest stuff in the world. As soon as I heard the first Allegro, I realized that if Herr Freyhold would only learn composition properly, he would not be a bad composer. I am very sorry that Herr

---

[1] Johann Philipp Freyhold, who had been flautist in the service of the Margrave of Baden-Durlach. He gave concerts in 1776 and 1779 at Frankfurt-am-Main, and on 30 March 1784 in the Burgtheater at Vienna. He described himself as a musician of the Elector of Mainz.

[2] The autograph has 'scomposition', one of Mozart's favourite devices for expressing contempt.

Hafeneder has died so prematurely, and particularly because you will now be saddled with that *seccatura*. Yet I must admit that the Prince is right. In his place I should have made the arrangement long before Hafeneder's death. But I should have accompanied my command with an increase of salary, and arranged that the boys should go to your house or that you should have free quarters in the Kapellhaus. Well, two gentlemen, a deputy-contrôleur and a cook, are going off to Salzburg in a few days, and I shall probably ask them to take with them a sonata,[1] a symphony,[2] and a new concerto.[3] The symphony is in the original score, which you might arrange to have copied some time. You can then send it back to me or even give it away or have it performed anywhere you like. The concerto is also in the original score and this too you may have copied; but have it done as quickly as possible and return it to me. Remember, do not show it to a *single soul*, for I composed it for Fräulein Ployer,[4] who paid me handsomely. But the sonata you may keep for good. Well, I must ask you something about which I know nothing whatever. If I have some work printed or engraved at my own expense, how can I protect myself from being cheated by the engraver? For surely he can print off as many copies as he likes and therefore swindle me. The only way to prevent this would be to keep a sharp eye on him. Yet that was impossible in your own case, when you had your book printed, for you were at Salzburg and the printer was at Augsburg.[5] Why, I almost feel inclined not to sell any more of my compositions to any engraver, but to have them printed or engraved by subscription at my own expense, as most people do and in this way make good profits. I am not nervous about getting subscribers. For I have already had subscription offers from Paris and Warsaw. So please let me know what you think about this. Now I have another request to make. Would it be possible to let me have a copy of my certificate of baptism? They all swear here that the first time I came to Vienna I must have been at least ten years old.[6] The Emperor himself contradicted me to my face last year in the Augarten. Herr von Strack now believes *my statement*. If I showed them my certificate of baptism I could shut them all up at one go. Now farewell. My wife and I kiss your hands a thousand

---

1 Possibly K. 448 [375a], sonata for two claviers, composed in 1781.

2 K. 425, the 'Linz' symphony, composed in 1783.

3 K. 449, composed for Barbara Ployer. This is the first entry in Mozart's *Verzeichnis aller meiner Werke*—the thematic list of his composition which he kept from 9 February 1784 until his death. A facsimile edition of this list, with an introduction by O. E. Deutsch, was published by Herbert Reichner, Vienna, 1938 (English edition 1956). The entries are also included in *MBA*.

4 Barbara, daughter of Franz Cajetan Ployer, who was a friend of Mozart and a cousin of Court Councillor Gottfried Ignaz von Ployer, since 1780 agent of the Salzburg Court in Vienna. She was Mozart's pupil on the clavier and in composition, and for her he composed his clavier concertos K. 449 and K. 453.

5 Mozart is referring to his father's *Violinschule*, which was published in 1756 by J. J. Lotter.

6 Mozart's first visit to Vienna was in 1762, when he was six.

times and embrace our dear sister with all our hearts and are ever your
most obedient children

W: et C: Mozart

(505) *Mozart to his Father*

[*Autograph in the possession of the Metropolitan Opera Guild Inc., New York*]

MON TRÉS CHER PÉRE! VIENNA, 3 *March* 1784[1]
 I have received your letter of February 24th. It is much better for you
always to send your letters through the post. I received on Monday your
letter which, if you had sent it through Peisser, I should not have had until
Tuesday or Wednesday. I have not yet received the concertos, but I shall
ask Artaria about them at once.[2] You must forgive me if I don't write very
much, but it is impossible to find time to do so, as I am giving three subscription concerts in Trattner's room on the last three Wednesdays of
Lent, beginning on March 17th. I have a hundred subscribers already and
shall easily get another thirty. The price for the three concerts is six gulden.
I shall probably give two concerts in the theatre this year. Well, as you
may imagine, I must play some new works—and therefore I must compose. The whole morning is taken up with pupils and almost every evening I have to play. Below you will find a list of all the concerts at which I
am playing. But I must tell you quickly how it has come about that all of
a sudden I am giving private concerts. Richter,[3] the clavier virtuoso, is
giving six Saturday concerts in the said room. The nobility subscribed,
but remarked that they really did not care much about going unless I
played. So Richter asked me to do so. I promised to play three times and
then arranged three concerts for myself, to which they all subscribed.

Thursday, February 26th, at Galitzin's
Monday, March 1st, at Johann Esterházy's
Thursday, March 4th, at Galitzin's
Friday March 5th, at Esterházy's
Monday 8th, at Esterházy's
Thursday 11th, at Galitzin's
Friday 12th, at Esterházy's
Monday 15th, at Esterházy's
Wednesday 17th, my first *private* concert
Thursday 18th, at Galitzin's
Friday 19th, at Esterházy's
Saturday 20th, at Richter's

[1] Nissen, pp. 479-480, throws together this letter and the following one of March 20th
thereby producing a strange confusion in dates.
[2] K. 413-415 [387a, 385p, 387b], which were published early in 1785 by Artaria and Co.
[3] Georg Friedrich Richter, a popular clavier-player and teacher.

Sunday 21st, my first concert *in the theatre*
Monday 22nd, at Esterházy's
Wednesday 24th, my second *private* concert
Thursday 25th, at Galitzin's
Friday 26th, at Esterházy's
Saturday 27th, at Richter's
Monday 29th, at Esterházy's
Wednesday 31st, my third *private* concert
Thursday April 1st, my second concert *in the theatre*
Saturday 3rd, at Richter's

Well, haven't I enough to do? I don't think that in this way I can possibly get out of practice. Adieu. We both kiss your hands and embrace our dear sister with all our hearts and are ever your most obedient children

W: A: MOZART

(506) *Mozart to his Father*

[*Autograph in the Nationalbibliothek, Vienna*][1]

[VIENNA, 20 *March* 1784]

Princesse d'Auersperg
Prince Charles d'Auersperg
Comte Nadasty Général
L'Ambassadeur d'Espagne
Comte Joseph Seilern
Comte de Soldyk
Madame de Trattner
De Grezmüller maj.
Madame de Hess née Baronin de
 Kannegiesser
Comte de Würm
Madame de Margelique
Bar: Gondar
Waseige
Mr. de Lamezan
Comtesse Kevenhüller
Bar: van Suiten
Comtesse Sauer
de Sonnenfels
Lewenau
Comte Charles d'Auersperg
Gotek

C. Aug. Seilern
Comte d'Herberstein
De Fichtl Agent
Princesse Palm
Prince Palm
Comte de Nimptsch
Conseiller Greiner
Ployer Agent
Madame de Hess née de Leporini
L'evecque d'Herberstein
Comte de Rottenhan
Comte Jos: d'Herberstein
Jacomini
Madame de Stökel
Comte Gundacker Sternberg
Bar: Tögelman
Mr. de Käs
Raab
Mr. de Jahn
D'Edlenbach
Comtesse Schafgotsch née Kollnitsch

[1] The first page of the autograph is a torn sheet. The beginning of the letter has been lost. The names of Mozart's subscribers have been left in their original spelling.

Comte de Sauer
D'Härring
Comte Wilhelm d'Auersperg
Prince Joseph Lobkowitz
E. Würm
Comte de Banffi
Prince Adam d'Auersperg
P. J. Schwab
Pentzenstein
de Rosty
Baronin de Waldstätten
Isdenizy
Bedekovich
Névery
de Hönikstein
Paszthory
de Grezmüller Jun.
Comtesse Staremberg née Neiperg
Comtesse Althan née Batiany
Comtesse Passowitz
Comte Nep: d'Herberstein
Comte Joseph Potztatzky
Comte Paar
Joseph Palfy
Comte Koller
d'Arensteiner
Bar: Wetzlar Père
Comtesse Nimptsch
de Braun
de Luerewald
de Hentschl
Bar: de Ditmar
Bar: de Gebsattel
Comtesse Esterhazy
Comte Jean Esterhazy
Joseph Dietrichstein
Bar: de Brandau
Bar: de Stockmayer
Bar: d'Hochstätter
Comtesse Sauer
Prince Louis Lichtenstein
de Meyenberg
Comte Sallabourg

Bar: de Mandelsloh
Louis Würben
Ernest Harrach
Le Comte Keplowitz
Le comte Fries
de Schleinitz
de Puthon
de Madruce
de Jacobi
de Lutz
Comtesse Thun née d'Ulfeld
Jos: de Weinbremes
de Smitmer
Urmeny
Bar: de Martini
de Born
Prince Gallizin
Bar: Vockel
Comte Ladislaus d'Ertödy
Comte Hugart
Comte Kollnitsch
Leopold Hoyos
Comte Czernin
Comte Neiperg
Comte Antoine Batiany
Prince de Würtemberg
Grenieri Envoyé de Sardaigne
Comte Kluschofsky
Joh: Adam Bienenfeld
Bar: Wezlar Raymond
de Drostik
Strurrewitz
Arenfeld
Madame Türkheim
Madame de Poncet
Dominic Kaunitz
Comte d'Ötting
Comte de Kuffstein
Bar: Winkler
Reichshof: von Wölkern
Bar: de Braun
Prince de Paar
Comte d'Oeynhausen

Le Comte de Dzierzanowschy
de Knecht
Comte Sternberg
Comte Waldstein
Comte George Waldstein
Le Comte Harrach l'ainé
Bar: Zois
von Ott
Le Comte de Nostiz
De Nostiz général
Bar: Jungwirth
Hofrat Bötti
Madame d'Engelsbourg
Comte Marchal
Hofrath Müller
Bar: Brandau
Comte Wolscheck
Comtesse Waldstein née d'Ulfeld
Mylord Morton
Madame de Puffendorf
Chevalier Hall
Madame de Neuhold
Comte Adam Sternberg

Comte Etienne Zitchi
Lord Stopford
Princess Lignowsky
de Sonnenfeld
Madame de Burkart
Prince de Schwarzenberg
Madame d'Eichelbourg
Comte Zinzendorf
de Hartenstein
Bar: Burkardt
Comte Bergen
Bar: de Dalberg
Madame Betty
Bar: de Gleichen
Mr. de Techenbach
Bar: Findak
Comtesse Apumoni
Comte Charles Zitchi
Comte François d'Esterhazy
Bar: d'Engelstrom
Prince de Meklenbourg
Comtesse de Hazfeld
Comte Montecuculi

I am sending you the list of all my subscribers. I alone have thirty more than Richter [1] and Fischer [2] together. The first concert on March 17th went off very well. The hall was full to overflowing; and the new concerto [3] I played won extraordinary applause. Everywhere I go I hear praises of that concert.

My first concert in the theatre was to have been tomorrow. But Prince Louis Liechtenstein is producing an opera in his own house, and has not only run off with the cream of the nobility, but has bribed and seduced the best players in the orchestra. So I have postponed my concert until April 1st and have had a notice printed to this effect. Well, I must close, as I must go off to Count Zichy's concert. You must have patience with me until Lent is over. We both kiss your hands and embrace our dear sister with all our hearts and are ever your most obedient children

W: A. MOZART

Vienna, 20 March 1784.
I have safely received your last letter.

[1] See p. 869, n. 3.
[2] Either John Abraham Fisher (1744–1806), the English violinist and composer who married in 1784 in Vienna Nancy Storace, or the bass singer J. I. L. Fischer.
[3] Probably K. 449. See Köchel, p. 483.

(507) *Leopold Mozart to Sebastian Winter, Donaueschingen*[1]

[Autograph in the Fürstlich Fürstenbergische Hofbibliothek, Donaueschingen]

DEAR HERR WINTER,   SALZBURG, 3 *April* 1784

I write in haste just to send you the four concertos[2] which, as I informed you, are the latest and cost four ducats each. I still have six sonatas[3] for the clavier only, which no one knows about, as my son composed them for us alone. If His Highness, to whom we send our most respectful greetings, would care to have these too, he has only to let me know. Farewell. I must close, as four people have just turned up from Munich to fetch young Marchand,[4] now fifteen years old, whom I have been teaching for three years and who is now returning as an excellent violinist and performer on the clavier and also a proficient composer. At the same time he has not neglected his Latin, although as his chief sideline he has been learning Italian and French, in which he has made good progress. Addio!

I ever remain your honest old friend

MOZART

(508) *Mozart to his Father*

[Autograph in the Library of the Paris Conservatoire]

MON TRÉS CHER PÉRE!   VIENNA, 10 *April* 1784

Please don't be vexed that I haven't written to you for so long. Surely you realise how much I have to do in the meantime! I have done myself great credit with my three subscription concerts, and the concert I gave in the theatre was most successful. I composed two grand concertos[5] and then a quintet,[6] which called forth the very greatest applause: I myself consider it to be the best work I have ever composed. It is written for one oboe, one clarinet, one horn, one bassoon and the pianoforte. How I wish you could have heard it! And how beautifully it was performed! Well, to tell the truth I was really worn out in the end after playing so much—and it is greatly to my credit that my listeners never got tired.

I now have a commission for you. Old Baron Beine du Pain,[7] who has all kinds of music, good and bad, would like to have the following compositions: Gatti's rondo and duet. Recitative. Ah! Non sdegnarti, o cara.

---

[1] Sebastian Winter, formerly the Mozarts' friseur, had been since 1764 valet and friseur to the Prince von Fürstenberg at Donaueschingen.

[2] Leopold Mozart means the series of three clavier concertos, K. 413-415 [387a, 385p, 387b]. See p. 874.

[3] Probably K. 279-284 [189d-h, 205b], composed in 1775. See W. Plath, *Acta Mozartiana*, xxi (1974), p. 26 ff.

[4] Heinrich Marchand, Leopold Mozart's pupil.

[5] K. 450, finished on 15 March, and K. 451, finished on 22 March.

[6] K. 452, finished on 30 March.   [7] Baron de Beine de Malchamp, probably the 'Baron Dupin' whom the Mozarts met in 1771. See pp. 201, 204.

Rondo. Nel lasciarti in questo istante. Duet. Nei giorni tuoi felici.¹ So I should be very much obliged if you could procure these two works for me as soon as possible. I shall send you the money for having them copied in due course through Herr Peisser. I have finished today another new concerto for Fräulein Ployer.² At the moment I am almost dressed to go to Prince Kaunitz. Yesterday I played at Leopold Palffy's. Tomorrow I am playing at the concert which Mlle Bayer is giving. One thing more. As Hafeneder has died, Herr von Ployer has been commissioned to find a violinist. I recommended to him a certain Menzel,³ a handsome and clever young fellow. But I asked him not to say anything about me, as otherwise it might not work. He is now awaiting the decision. I think he has asked for and is to get four hundred gulden—and a suit of clothes. I have already scolded him about the suit of clothes—for it is a beggarly request. If anything comes of this, I shall give him a letter for you and the music too. You will think him a charming violinist, and he is also a very good sight-reader. So far no one in Vienna has played my quartets⁴ so well at sight as he has. Moreover he is the kindest fellow in the world, and he will be delighted to play at your house whenever you want him to. I had him in the orchestra at my concert. Well, I must close. My wife and I kiss your hands two thousand times and embrace our dear sister with all our hearts and are ever your obedient children

MOZART

(509) *Leopold Mozart to Sebastian Winter, Donaueschingen*

[*Autograph in the Fürstlich Fürstenbergische Hofbibliothek, Donaueschingen*]

DEAREST HERR WINTER,   SALZBURG, 22 *April* 1784

Your letter of the 17th has made things rather difficult for me, as on the afternoon of April 3rd I packed the three concertos⁵ in waterproof cloth and handed the parcel to the mail coach, which left here *on the 4th at eight o'clock in the morning*. You wrote to me exactly a fortnight later, when the concertos must long since have arrived at Donaueschingen. I addressed the parcel: *To Herr Sebastian Winter, valet to His Highness, etc.* If it has not reached you, please ask the postmaster to make urgent enquiries and investigations and I shall do the same both here and in Munich. Meanwhile I trust that I shall soon hear from you and be relieved of all anxiety. I write in great haste. We send our compliments to His Highness and I am ever your most devoted

MOZART

¹ On a text by Metastasio.   ² K. 453, finished on April 12th.
³ Zeno Franz Menzel (1756–1823), who in 1787 became violinist in the Vienna Court orchestra.
⁴ Probably K. 387, 421 [417b], 428 [421b].   ⁵ K. 413–415 [387a, 385p, 387b].

(510) *Mozart to his Father*

[*From Nissen*, p. 481]

VIENNA, 24 *April* [1784]

We now have here the famous Strinasacchi[1] from Mantua, a very good violinist. She has a great deal of taste and feeling in her playing. I am this moment composing a sonata[2] which we are going to play together on Thursday at her concert in the theatre.[3] I must tell you that some quartets have just appeared, composed by a certain Pleyel,[4] a pupil of Joseph Haydn. If you do not know them, do try and get hold of them; you will find them worth the trouble. They are very well written and most pleasing to listen to. You will also see at once who was his master. Well, it will be a lucky day for music if later on Pleyel should be able to replace Haydn.

(511) *Mozart to his Father*

[*Autograph in Harvard University Library, Locker Lamson Collection*]

MON TRÉS CHER PÉRE,   VIENNA, 28 *April* 1784

I must write in a hurry. Herr Richter, the clavier-player, is making a tour on his way back to Holland, his native country. I have given him a letter to Countess Thun[5] at Linz. As he would like to visit Salzburg too, I have given him just four lines for you, dearest father. So I am now writing to say that he will turn up soon after you receive this letter. He plays well so far as execution goes, but, as you will discover when you hear him, he is too rough and laboured and entirely devoid of taste and feeling. Otherwise he is the best fellow in the world and is not the slightest bit conceited. When I played to him he stared all the time at my fingers and kept on saying: 'Good God! How hard I work and sweat—and yet win no applause—and to you, my friend, it is all child's play.' 'Yes,' I replied, 'I too had to work hard, so as not to have to work hard any longer.' Enfin, he is a fellow who may be included among our good clavier-players and I trust that the Archbishop will be more inclined to hear him, because he is a

---

[1] Regina Strinasacchi (1764–1823), a distinguished violinist and guitar player. She was trained in Venice and Paris, toured Italy in 1780–1783, and in 1784 came to Vienna. She married later Johann Conrad Schlick (1759–1825), an excellent violoncellist in the orchestra of the Duke of Gotha.

[2] K. 454.   [3] 29 April.

[4] Ignaz Joseph Pleyel (1757–1831), a most prolific instrumental composer. He was trained in Vienna by Vanhal. His patron was Count Erdödy, who had Pleyel taught by Haydn and who probably appointed him his Kapellmeister. In 1783 he became deputy Kapellmeister and in 1789 Kapellmeister to Strassburg Cathedral. In 1791 he was invited to London to take charge of the Professional Concerts. Four years later he settled as a music-publisher in Paris, where he founded in 1807 the Pleyel pianoforte factory and where he remained until his death.

[5] Elizabeth, the fourth wife of Count Johann Josef Anton Thun (1711–1788), father of Countess Wilhelmine Thun's husband.

clavierist—*en dépit de moi*—and I shall be very glad to incur that spite. It is all settled about Menzel the violinist, and he will probably clear out on Sunday. You will have some music from me too which he is taking. Now, farewell. We both kiss your hands and embrace our dear sister with all our hearts and am ever your obedient children

W. C: MOZART

(512) *Mozart to his Father*

[*Autograph in the possession of Maurice Lehmann, Paris*]

MON TRÈS CHER PÈRE!   VIENNA, 8 *May* 1784

Menzel went off at a moment's notice and didn't find me at home, so I could not give him a letter for you. But I hope that he has already been to see you. I purposely did not give him the music I promised you, because I did not like to entrust it to him, being far too particular about it. I prefer to send it by the mail coach. Perhaps my good friend Richter is now at your house. If so, please give him our greetings. Well, I must go down to the first floor to a concert at Frau von Trattner's. She has commissioned me to make the necessary arrangements. So I cannot write any more, beyond saying that we are both well and trust that you two are in good health also. Paisiello is in Vienna at the moment on his way back from Russia. He is going to write an opera[1] here. Sarti is expected here any day on his way through to Russia. I am looking forward to the shoe buckles. Farewell. We both kiss your hands and embrace our dear sister with all our hearts and are ever your obedient children

W. A. MOZART

(513) *Mozart to his Father*

[*Autograph in the Musikhistorisches Museum von W. Heyer, Cologne*]

MON TRÉS CHER PÉRE!   VIENNA, 15 *May* 1784

I gave to the mail coach today the symphony[2] which I composed at Linz for old Count Thun and also four concertos.[3] I am not particular about the symphony, but I do ask you to have the four concertos copied at home, for the Salzburg copyists are as little to be trusted as the Viennese. I know for a positive fact that Hofstetter made two copies of Haydn's music.[4] For example, I *really* possess the last three symphonies he wrote.[5] And as no one but myself possesses these new concertos in B♭ and D,[6] and no one but *myself* and Fräulein von Ployer (for whom I composed

---

[1] *Il Re Teodoro in Venezia*, performed on 23 August, 1784.
[2] K. 425.   [3] K. 449-451 and 453.   [4] Compositions of Joseph Haydn.
[5] Perhaps Haydn's symphonies Nos. 76, 77, and 78.
[6] K. 450 and 451.

them) those in Eb and G,[1] the only way in which they could fall into other hands is by that kind of cheating. I myself have everything copied in my room and in my presence. After careful consideration I decided not to entrust the music to Menzel. Further, I formed the opinion, which I still hold, that the music would not be of much use to you, because except for the Eb concerto, which can be performed a quattro without wind-instruments, the other three concertos all have wind-instrument accompaniment; and you very rarely have wind-instrument players at your house. Well, I don't know what it was that you were thinking about and did not want to mention in your letter; and therefore to avoid all misunderstanding, I am sending you herewith all my new compositions. I have no news to give you save that the Emperor intended to leave for Budapest today but was prevented from doing so by a stye in his eye. Praise and thanks be to God, we are both well and trust that you are all in good health. We kiss your hands a thousand times and embrace our dear sister with all our hearts and are ever your obedient children

                                                    W. & C. MOZART

Please give my kind regards to Menzel. He knows all four concertos very well.

(514) *Mozart to his Father*

[*Autograph in the Rudolf Nydahl Collection, Stiftelsen Musikkulturens Främjande, Stockholm*]

MON TRÈS CHER PÉRE!   VIENNA, 26 *May* 1784

Your last letter tells me that you have received my letter and the music. I thank my sister for her letter and, so soon as time permits, I will certainly write to her. Meanwhile please tell her that either Herr Richter is mistaken about the key of the concerto or else I have misread a letter in her writing. The concerto Herr Richter praised to her so warmly is the one in Bb,[2] the first one I composed and which he praised so highly to me at the time. I really cannot choose between the two of them, but I regard them both as concertos which are bound to make the performer perspire. From the point of view of difficulty the Bb concerto beats the one in D.[3] Well, I am very curious to hear which of the three in Bb, D and G[4] you and my sister prefer. The one in Eb[5] does not belong at all to the same category. It is one of a quite peculiar kind, composed rather for a small orchestra than for a large one. So it is really only a question of the three grand concertos. I am longing to hear whether your judgment will coincide with the *general opinion* in Vienna and with *my own view*. Of course it is necessary to hear all three well performed and with all the

---

[1] K. 449 and 453.   [2] K. 450.   [3] K. 451.   [4] K. 453.   [5] K. 449.

parts. I am quite willing to wait patiently until I get them back, so long as no one else is allowed to get hold of them. Only today I could have got twenty-four ducats for one of them, but I think that it will be more profitable for me to hold on to them for a few years more and then have them engraved and published.

Well, I have something to tell you about Liserl Schwemmer.[1] She wrote a letter to her mother and as the address was so quaint that the Post Office would hardly have accepted the letter, for it was as follows:

> Dieser Brief zueku-
> men meiner vilgeliebtisten
> Frau Mutter in Salzburg
> barbarü schbemerin
> abzugeben in der
> Jüdengasen in Kauf
> man eberl haus
> in dritten Stock

I told her that I would write another address for her. Out of curiosity and with a view to reading some more of this amazing composition rather than with that of prying into her secrets, I broke the seal of the letter. She complains that she gets to bed too late and has to get up too early—though I should have thought that one would get enough sleep between eleven and six, which is after all seven hours! We ourselves do not go to bed until midnight and we get up at half past five or even five, as we go to the Augarten almost every morning. Then she complains about the food and that too in the most impertinent fashion. She says she has to starve and that the four of us, that is, my wife, myself, the cook and she do not get as much to eat as she and her mother used to have between the two of them. You know that I took this girl at the time purely out of pity and to help her when she was a stranger in Vienna. We promised her twelve gulden a year, and she was quite satisfied, though in her letter she complains about this. And what has she to do? To clear the table, hand round the dishes and take them away and help my wife to dress and undress. Moreover, apart from her sewing she is the clumsiest and stupidest creature in the world. She cannot even light a fire, let alone make coffee, things which a girl who pretends to be a parlour-maid should be able to do. We gave her a gulden and the very next day she was asking for more money. I insisted on her giving me an account of how she had spent her money and I found that most of it had gone on beer. A certain Herr Johannes who travelled with her to Vienna had better not put his nose inside my door again. *Twice* when we were out, he came to our quarters, ordered in *wine*, and

---

[1] See p. 864, n. 1.

the girl, who is not accustomed to drinking it, swilled so heavily, that she couldn't walk without support and the second time she was sick all over her bed. I should like to know who would keep a creature who carries on in this way?

I would have contented myself with the lecture I gave her when it happened and would have said nothing to you, but her impertinent letter to her mother has driven me to it. So will you please send for her mother and tell her that I shall put up with her daughter for a little while longer, but that she must look about for another place. Were it not that I hate to make people unhappy I should get rid of her on the spot. She says something too, in her letter, about a certain Herr Antoni—a future husband, perhaps!

Well, I must close. My wife thanks you both for your congratulations on her pregnancy and coming confinement, which will probably take place during the first days of October.[1] We both kiss your hands and embrace our dear sister with all our hearts and are ever your most obedient children

W. et C. Mozart

PS.—We have not yet been able to do anything about the fichu in lawn or muslin, because my wife doesn't know whether my sister would prefer it untrimmed. Untrimmed fichus cost about a ducat each, but are not worn very much. Those with a little pretty trimming cost at least seven ducats apiece in Viennese currency. So we are waiting for the next letter and as soon as we know, my sister shall have what she requires. Addio.

PS.—Please send me the buckles by the next mail coach. I am simply longing to see them.

(515) *Mozart to his Father*

[*Autograph formerly in the possession of Landgerichtsdirektor A. Zahn, Landau*]

MON TRÉS CHER PÉRE!   VIENNA, 9 *June* 1784

No doubt you have received my last letter. I have received the buckles and also your letter of June 1st. The buckles are very handsome, but far too large. However, I shall try to dispose of them.

Next Friday the court goes to Laxenburg for two or perhaps three months. I went to Baden last week with His Excellency Count Thun to visit his father, who had come over from Linz to take the cure. On our way home we drove through Laxenburg, where we visited Leemann, who is now the governor of the castle. His daughter was not at home, but he and

[1] Karl Thomas (1784–1858), the Mozarts' second child, was born on September 21st.

his wife were absolutely delighted to see me again. They both send greetings to both of you.

June 12th. As visitors came in, I was prevented from finishing this letter. In the meantime I have received your letter of the 8th. My wife sends her love to my sister and will despatch a smart fichu by the next mail coach. But she is going to make it herself, as it will thus be somewhat cheaper and much prettier. Please tell my sister that there is no adagio in any of these concertos[1]—only andantes. She is quite right in saying that there is something missing in the solo passage in C in the Andante of the concerto in D.[2] I will supply the deficiency as soon as possible and send it with the cadenzas.[3] Tomorrow Herr Ployer, the agent, is giving a concert in the country at Döbling, where Fräulein Babette is playing her new concerto in G,[4] and I am performing the quintet;[5] we are then playing together the grand sonata for two claviers.[6] I am fetching Paisiello in my carriage, as I want him to hear both my pupil and my compositions. If Maestro Sarti had not had to leave Vienna today, he too would have come with me. Sarti is a good honest fellow! I have played a great deal to him and have composed variations on an air of his,[7] which pleased him exceedingly. Menzel is, and always will be an ass. The whole affair is as follows: Herr von Ployer asked me whether I knew of a violinist. I spoke to Menzel, who was much gratified. You can imagine that I as an honest man advised him not to accept anything but a permanent post. But he never came to see me until the last moment and Herr von Ployer told me that he was going off to Salzburg on trial for 400 gulden and, mark you, *a suit of clothes.* But Menzel declared to me and to everyone here that he had actually been appointed. Further, it now seems that he is married, of which no one here knew anything. His wife has been three or four times at von Ployer's. I have now given Artaria, to engrave, the three sonatas for clavier only, which I once sent to my sister, the first in C, the second in A, and the third in F.[8] I have given three others to Torricella, the last of which is the one in D, which I composed for Dürnitz in Munich.[9] Further, I am giving three of my six symphonies to be engraved, and these I shall dedicate to Prince von Fürstenberg.[10] Well, I must close. My wife and I kiss your hands a thousand times and embrace our dear sister with all our hearts and are ever your obedient children

W. et C. Mozart

[1] K. 449–451 and K. 453.　　　　　　　　　　　　　　　[2] K. 451.

[3] Mozart sent her these cadenzas. See Köchel, p. 486, 487.

[4] K. 453.　　　　　　　　[5] K. 452.　　　　　　　　[6] K. 448 [375a].

[7] Probably K. 460 [454a], variations on 'Come un' agnello' from Sarti's *Fra i due litiganti.*

[8] K. 330–332 [300h, i, k]. See p. 589, n. 2. For particulars of this first edition, which was advertised in the *Wiener Zeitung* on 25 August 1784, see Köchel, p. 325.

[9] K. 284 [205b]. For particulars of this first edition, which included the sonatas K. 333 [315c] and K. 454, see Köchel, p. 229.

[10] Josef Maria Benedikt, Prince von Fürstenberg, Donaueschingen. Mozart did not carry out this plan.

(516) *Mozart to his Sister*

[Autograph in the Staatsbibliothek Preussischer Kulturbesitz, West Berlin]

DEAREST SISTER! VIENNA, 21 *July* 1784

My wife and I wish you much happiness on your name-day.[1] She would have written to you herself, but she finds it difficult to remain seated for long, because our future son and heir gives her no peace. She therefore joins me in wishing you all possible joy and happiness and we ask you to keep us ever in your sisterly affection. Old Hampel[2] and his son from Munich have been here for a week and are leaving for Russia the day after tomorrow. They are lunching with us tomorrow and in the evening we are going to have a little concert. I hope that in the meantime you will have received everything by the mail coach. I would gladly have sent you the cadenzas for the other concertos, but you have no idea how much I have to do! As soon as I have a little time to myself, I shall certainly devote it to you. When you have tried over the three grand concertos,[3] I shall be most anxious to hear which of them you like best. I beg Papa not to forget to send me by the next mail coach what I asked him for. I should be delighted if he could send me my old oratorio 'La Betulia liberata'[4] too. I have to compose the same oratorio for the Society[5] in Vienna and possibly I might use bits of it here and there. Please give my greetings to Gretl[6] and tell her that perhaps I shall reply myself, but I cannot promise to do so, for I fear that I may not be able to keep my promise, as I am far too busy. As for the aria[7] she must exercise a little patience. But what I do advise her to do, if she wants to have the aria soon and without fail, is to choose a text which suits her and send it to me, as it is impossible for me to find time to wade through all sorts of operas. Well, I must close, as I have to go off at once to give a lesson. My wife and I kiss you a thousand times and ask you to kiss Papa's hands for us. We are ever your sincere

W: A: C: MOZART

(517) *Mozart to his Sister*

[Autograph in the possession of the Historical Society of Pennsylvania, Philadelphia]

MA TRÉS CHERE SŒUR! VIENNA, 18 *August* 1784

Potz Sapperment! It is high time I wrote to you if I want my letter to find you still a vestal virgin! A few days more and—it is gone! My wife and I wish you all joy and happiness in your change of state and are only

[1] 26 July.
[2] Thaddäus Hampel, whose son was a violinist, was himself a clarinet-player in the Munich Court orchestra. [3] K. 450, 451, 453.
[4] K. 118 [74c], *La betulia liberata*, an oratorio on a text by Metastasio, composed in 1771.
[5] The Wiener Tonkünstlersozietät. [6] Margarete Marchand.
[7] Perhaps 'Der Liebe himmlisches Gefühl', K. 119 [382h], composed in 1782.

heartily sorry that we cannot have the pleasure of being present at your wedding. But we hope to embrace you as Frau von Sonnenburg[1] and your husband also next spring both at Salzburg and at St. Gilgen. Our only regrets are for our dear father, who will now be left so utterly alone! True, you will not be far away from him and he can often drive out and see you—but he is tied to that accursed Kapellhaus again! If I were in his place, I should do as follows:—Seeing that I have served the Archbishop for so many years I should ask him to allow me to retire, and then, on receiving my pension, I should go to my daughter at St. Gilgen and live there in peace and quiet. If the Archbishop refused my request, I should apply for my discharge and join my son in Vienna. And what I chiefly want to ask you is—to do your best to persuade him to do this. I have suggested the same thing in my letter to him today. And now I send you a thousand good wishes from Vienna to Salzburg, and hope particularly that you two will live together as harmoniously as—we two! So take a little piece of advice from my poetical brainbox! Listen:

Wedlock will show you many things
Which still a mystery remain;
Experience soon will teach to you
What Eve herself once had to do
Before she could give birth to Cain.
But all these duties are so light
You will perform them with delight.
Yet no state is an unmixed joy
And marriage has its own alloy,
Lest us its bliss perchance should cloy.
So when your husband shows reserve
Or wrath which you do not deserve
And perhaps a nasty temper too,
Think, sister, 'tis a man's queer way.
Say: 'Lord, thy will be done by day,
But mine at night you'll do'.[2]

Your sincere brother

W. A. MOZART

[1] Nannerl Mozart was married on 23 August 1784, to Johann Baptist von Berchtold zu Sonnenburg, magistrate at St. Gilgen, her mother's birthplace, then about six hours' drive from Salzburg. Her husband was a widower with five children. He died in 1801, and Nannerl returned to Salzburg with her son and stepchildren. For a study of Nannerl Mozart, see W. Hummel, *Nannerl, Wolfgang Arnadeus Mozarts Schwester*, Zürich, 1952.

[2] C. B. Oldman has pointed out the resemblances between the concluding lines of Mozart's poem and a verse in Playford's *Wit and Mirth; or, Pills to Purge Melancholy*, 3rd edition, 1707, vol. i. p. 150.

(518) *Leopold Mozart to his Daughter* [1]

[*Extract*]   [*Autograph in the Mozarteum, Salzburg*]

SALZBURG, 14 *September* 1784

My son has been very ill in Vienna. At a performance of Paisiello's new opera [2] he perspired so profusely that his clothes were drenched and in the cold night air he had to try to find his servant who had his overcoat, as in the meantime an order had been given that no servant was to be allowed into the theatre by the ordinary entrance. So not only my son, but a number of other people caught rheumatic fever, which became septic when not taken in hand at once. My son writes as follows: [3] 'Four days running at the very same hour I had a fearful attack of colic, which ended each time in violent vomiting. I have therefore to be extremely careful. My doctor is Sigmund Barisani, who since his arrival in Vienna has been almost daily at my rooms. People here praise him very highly. He is very clever too and you will find that in a short time he will make his way. When you write to St. Gilgen, please send millions of kisses to our brother-in-law and to my sister, etc.'

(519) *Leopold Mozart to his Daughter*

[*Extract*]   [*Autograph in the Mozarteum, Salzburg*]

SALZBURG, 17 *September* 1784

On the following day [4] we had a big concert at Barisani's, where your brother's new and excellent symphony [5] was performed under my direction. There too the leading actor, who knows Joseph Barisani, was introduced to me. When he heard my name, he was beside himself with delight. He is called Schmidt and is the Schmidt who took the part of Pedrillo at the performance in Vienna of the 'Entführung aus dem Serail'. [6] He therefore knows your brother very well. There is thus every hope that these people will give an excellent performance of your brother's opera, for Schmidt himself took a part in Vienna and later produced the opera in Prague [7] more than a dozen times. Moreover, Herr Brandl, [8] that excellent actor and singer, is in the company.

[1] After Nannerl's marriage to Berchtold zu Sonnenburg at St. Gilgen, Leopold Mozart wrote long letters to her about once a week, giving her a full account of everything that was happening in Salzburg. Nearly all these letters, which cover the years 1784 to 1787, that is, from Nannerl's departure until Leopold Mozart's death, have been preserved and they were first edited by Otto Erich Deutsch and Bernhard Paumgartner, *Leopold Mozarts Briefe an seine Tochter*, Salzburg, Leipzig, 1936. They appear complete in *MBA*.
[2] *Il Re Teodoro in Venezia*, which was performed on 23 August 1784.
[3] This letter is missing.   [4] 15 September.   [5] K. 425, the 'Linz' symphony.
[6] Ludwig Schmidt, who was originally an operatic singer, was manager of a theatrical company. He had taken the place of Dauer, the original Pedrillo in the Vienna production of *Die Entführung aus dem Serail*.
[7] *Die Entführung aus dem Serail* was performed in Prague in 1783.
[8] He was leading bass singer in the Salzburg company.

(520) *Leopold Mozart to his Daughter*

[*Autograph in the Rudolf Nydahl Collection, Stiftelsen Musikkulturens Främjande, Stockholm*]

[*Extract*]   SALZBURG, 19 *November* 1784

My son gave a small musical party on his name-day,[1] at which his pupils performed and, what is more, Baron Bagge from Paris amused the company by playing a violin concerto. 'We simply howled with laughter', my son writes, adding 'I have received my sister's letter and hope that in the meantime she has received mine'. He probably means the letter to me.

'Die Entführung aus dem Serail' was performed fairly well on the 17th with the greatest applause, and three numbers had to be repeated. At five o'clock there was no more room in the lower part of the theatre and at a quarter past five it was quite full up above. It is being performed again on Sunday, the 21st. After that it will probably be dropped for five weeks. The whole town is delighted with it. Even the Archbishop was gracious enough to say: 'Really it wasn't at all bad'. I hear that they took 191 gulden. The aria with the solo instruments[2] was performed by Stadler[3] (violin, the part being an easy one), Feiner (oboe), Reiner (flute) and Fiala (cello) and they played very well together. Herr Kassel, who had been asked to play the flute, came to the first rehearsal. But the following day he told Stadler that he would not turn up any more, that they should get hold of someone else, as he found rehearsing too boring. Everyone is very much annoyed with him, even the nobles. On the other hand Herr Fiala not only played, but even refused to take a fee, saying that he was doing it to please Herr Schmidt and particularly Herr Mozart.

(521) *Leopold Mozart to his Daughter*

[*Extract*]   [*Copy in the Staatsbibliothek Preussischer Kulturbesitz, West Berlin*]

SALZBURG, [*after* 21] *November* 1784

The opera[5] was performed here again on Sunday with the greatest applause. Indeed the opera is becoming such a favourite that the whole town praises it and calls it a very fine work. Michael Haydn sat in the orchestra behind the clavier. Of course everyone asked him for his opinion and he said that all that this opera needed was an orchestra of sixty to seventy players and the necessary intermediate instruments, that is, clarinets and a cor anglais, whose parts have to be taken here by violas. Only then, he declared, could one really hear what an excellent piece of work it was. He was delighted beyond measure. Well, the opera is now to

---

[1] 31 October.   [2] Constanze's aria 'Martern aller Arten'.
[3] Matthias Stadler, a violinist in the Salzburg court orchestra.
[4] Autograph in a private collection.   [5] *Die Entführung aus dem Serail.*

have a rest until Christmas, when it will be performed again twice. Blonde's duet with her Pedrillo and her aria [1] were again repeated. The drinking song in the second act 'Vivat Bacchus!' had even to be sung three times. All who have seen the opera in Vienna are unanimous in declaring that the acting here is far better, more lively and more natural, and the whole production more thorough than in Vienna. This is the opinion too of the Count von Ehlss and of the two Barons von Fechenbach, who saw the opera performed in Berlin, Mainz and Mannheim.

(522) *Leopold Mozart to his Daughter*

[*Extract*]   [*Autograph in the Mozarteum, Salzburg*]

SALZBURG, 22 *January* 1785

I have this moment received ten lines from your brother, who says that his first subscription concert will take place on Friday, February 11th,[2] and that he is to give the remaining concerts on successive Fridays. He adds that during the first week in Lent he will certainly have a box for this concert in the theatre for Heinrich and that I ought to come soon. He adds that last Saturday he performed his six quartets[3] for his dear friend Haydn[4] and other good friends, and that he has sold them to Artaria for a hundred ducats. At the end of his letter he says: 'Now I must get on with the composition of the concerto[5] which I have just begun. Adieu!'

(523) *Leopold Mozart to his Daughter*

[*Extract*]   [*From Ludwig Nohl, Neue Zeitschrift für Musik,* 1870, *no.* 40[6]]

[VIENNA, 16 *February* 1785]

We arrived at the Schulerstrasse No. 846, first floor,[7] at one o'clock on Friday. That your brother has very fine quarters with all the necessary furniture you may gather from the fact that his rent is 460 gulden. On the same evening we drove to his first subscription concert, at which a great many members of the aristocracy were present. Each person pays a souverain d'or or three ducats for these Lenten concerts. Your brother is

---

[1] Probably 'Durch Zärtlichkeit und Schmeicheln'.

[2] In a letter written from Munich, dated 2 February 1785, Leopold Mozart adds: 'Heinrich (Marchand) and I will probably leave for Vienna on Carnival Sunday in Herr Marchand's carriage in order to be present at your brother's concert on Friday, February 11th, as I have had a letter from him suggesting this. Herr Le Brun and his wife will follow us to Vienna on the 5th.'

[3] The six string quartets K. 387, 421 [417b], 428 [421b], 458, 464, 465, which Mozart dedicated to Joseph Haydn, were published by Artaria and Co. in October 1785. See p. 846, n. 3.

[4] Joseph Haydn.   [5] K. 466, clavier concerto in D minor.

[6] Autograph in the possession of Otto Kallir, New York.

[7] The Mozarts had moved on 29 September 1784 to these rooms, now Schulerstrasse no. 8.

giving them at the Mehlgrube and only pays half a souverain d'or each time for the hall. The concert was magnificent and the orchestra played splendidly. In addition to the symphonies a female singer of the Italian theatre sang two arias. Then we had a new and very fine concerto[1] by Wolfgang, which the copyist was still copying when we arrived, and the rondo of which your brother did not even have time to play through, as he had to supervise the copying. You can well imagine that I met many acquaintances there who all came up to speak to me. I was also introduced to several other people.

On Saturday evening Herr Joseph Haydn[2] and the two Barons Tinti[3] came to see us and the new quartets were performed, or rather, the three new ones[4] which Wolfgang has added to the other three which we have already. The new ones are somewhat easier, but at the same time excellent compositions. Haydn said to me: 'Before God and as an honest man I tell you that your son is the greatest composer known to me either in person or by name. He has taste and, what is more, the most profound knowledge of composition.'

On Sunday evening the Italian singer, Madame Laschi,[5] who is leaving for Italy, gave a concert in the theatre, at which she sang two arias. A cello concerto was performed, a tenor and a bass each sang an aria and your brother played a glorious concerto,[6] which he composed for Mlle Paradis[7] for Paris. I was sitting only two boxes away from the very beautiful Princess of Wurtemberg[8] and had the great pleasure of hearing so clearly all the interplay of the instruments that for sheer delight tears came into my eyes. When your brother left the platform the Emperor waved his hat and called out 'Bravo, Mozart!' And when he came on to play, there was a great deal of clapping.

★ We were not at the theatre yesterday, for every day there is a concert. This evening there is another one in the theatre, at which your brother is
★ again playing a concerto. I shall bring back several of his new compositions. Little Karl[9] is the picture of him. He seems very healthy, but now

[1] K. 466, clavier concerto in D minor.
[2] On the previous day Haydn had joined the Freemasons' Lodge, 'Zur wahren Eintracht'. Mozart had been a member of the Lodge 'Zur Wohltätigkeit' since December 1784, and his father joined both lodges on the occasion of his visit to Vienna. See Otto Erich Deutsch, *Mozart und die Wiener Logen*, Vienna, 1932.
[3] They were members of the Masonic Lodge 'Zur wahren Eintracht'.
[4] K. 458, 464 and 465.
[5] Luisa Laschi made her first appearance in Vienna in 1784, and was the original Countess in *Le nozze di Figaro*. In 1787 she married the tenor Domenico Francesco Mombelli (1751–1835).
[6] Probably K. 456, in B , finished on 30 September 1784. See Hermann Ullrich, 'Maria Theresia Paradis and Mozart', *Music and Letters*, vol. xxvii, 1946, pp. 224–33.
[7] Maria Theresia Paradis (1759–1824), a blind pianist of Vienna. In 1783 she had begun a grand tour of the European capitals.
[8] Elizabeth (1767–1790), the eighth child of Duke Friedrich Eugen of Wurtemberg. She was married in 1788 to the Archduke Francis of Austria.
[9] Mozart's second child, Karl Thomas (1784–1858), who was born on 21 September 1784.

and then, of course, children have trouble with their teeth. On the whole ★ the child is charming, for he is extremely friendly and laughs when spoken to. I have only seen him cry once and the next moment he started to laugh.

Yesterday, the 15th, there was again a recital in the theatre given by a girl[1] who sings charmingly. Your brother played his new grand concerto in D minor[2] most magnificently. Today we are going to a concert given at the house of the Salzburg agent, Herr von Ployer. ★

Your brother, your sister-in-law, Marchand and I kiss you millions of times and I am your faithful father

MOZART

(524) *Leopold Mozart to his Daughter*

[*Extract*] [*Autograph in the Stadtarchiv, Augsburg*]

VIENNA, *Monday,* 21 *February* 1785

You will have received my first letter. I thought that I had completely shaken off the cold I caught on my journey. But yesterday evening I had pains in my left thigh and before going to bed I discovered that I really had rheumatism. So I drank some burr root tea in bed this morning and did not get up until half past one, just in time for lunch, at which I had the company of your sister-in-law's youngest sister Sophie.[3] She is still with me now at eight o'clock in the evening, for your brother, his wife and Heinrich lunched today with Herr von Trattner, an invitation which unfortunately I had to refuse; and this evening your brother is performing at a big concert at Count Zichy's, at which Herr Le Brun and his wife are appearing for the first time. But your sister-in-law and Marchand have gone to the concert at Herr von Ployer's, our agent. As usual, it will probably be one o'clock before we get to bed. We lunched on Thursday, the 17th, with your brother's mother-in-law, Frau Weber. There were just the four of us, Frau Weber and her daughter Sophie, since the eldest daughter[4] is in Graz. I must tell you that the meal, which was neither too lavish nor too stingy, was cooked to perfection. The roast was a fine plump pheasant; and everything was excellently well prepared. We lunched on Friday, the 18th, with Stephanie junior, just the four of us and Herr Le Brun, his wife, Karl Cannabich and a priest. Let me tell you at once that there was no thought of a fast-day. We were only offered meat dishes. A pheasant as an additional dish was served in cabbage and the rest

[1] Elizabeth Distler (1769–1790), operatic singer, who belonged to a large family of Viennese musicians. She sang in the two performances of Mozart's *Davidde penitente* on 13 and 17 March 1785, given for the benefit of the Tonkünstlersozietät. [2] K. 466.
[3] Sophie Weber (1763–1846) became in 1780 an actress at the Burgtheater in Vienna. She married in 1807 the musician and composer Jakob Haibel (1762–1826), and some time after his death went to live in Salzburg with her elder sister Constanze, who had survived both Mozart and her second husband, Georg Nikolaus von Nissen.
[4] Josefa Weber. See p. 783, n 1.

was fit for a prince. Finally we had oysters, most delicious glacé fruits and (I must not forget to mention this) several bottles of champagne. I need hardly add that everywhere coffee is served. From Stephanie's we drove to your brother's second concert at the Mehlgrube at seven o'clock. This concert too was a splendid success. Heinrich played a violin concerto. Stephanie asked for you the moment he saw us and we went on talking about the old days. Up to the present I have never been offered any fast dishes. Yesterday, the 20th, we were at a lunch given to twenty-one people by Herr Müller, the actor. It was a splendid affair, but not exaggeratedly lavish. He must have a very large apartment, as he has eight children and pays a yearly rent of seven hundred gulden. Herr Stephanie has a small apartment, which costs him, however, five hundred gulden, as it is in the Michaelerplatz close to the theatre. The two concerts which Herr Le Brun and his wife are giving in the theatre are on Wednesday, the 23rd, and Monday, the 28th. All the boxes for the first concert were sold out on the 18th. These people are going to make an enormous amount of money.

★

(525) *Leopold Mozart to his Daughter*

[*Extract*]   [*Autograph in the Gesellschaft der Musikfreunde, Vienna*]

★   VIENNA, 12 *March* 1785

Your brother made 559 gulden at his concert, which we never expected, as he is giving six subscription concerts at the Mehlgrube to over 150 people, each of whom pays a souverain d'or for the six. Besides, as a favour he has been playing frequently at other concerts in the theatre. As for the clavier arrangement of the 'Entführung aus dem Serail', all that I can tell you is that a certain Torricella [1] is engraving it. Your brother is arranging it, but it isn't quite finished yet. He may have only completed Act I. I shall find out. Torricella has also engraved three sonatas, only one of which has a violin accompaniment. [2] Well, I shall buy everything that has been published.

★

We never get to bed before one o'clock and I never get up before nine. We lunch at two or half past. The weather is horrible. Every day there are concerts; and the whole time is given up to teaching, music, composing and so forth. I feel rather out of it all. If only the concerts were over! It is impossible for me to describe the rush and bustle. Since my arrival your brother's fortepiano has been taken at least a dozen times to the theatre or to

[1] Christoph Torricella, a music publisher in Vienna and a member of the Masonic Lodge 'Zur Beständigkeit'. In May 1784 he had opened in Cramer's *Magazin der Musik* a subscription list for Mozart's clavier arrangement of *Die Entführung aus dem Serail*. The overture and first act were engraved and Mozart was at work on the second act, when another clavier arrangement of the whole opera was published. See p. 895.

[2] K. 333 [315c], 284 [205b] and 454. See p. 880, n. 9.

some other house. He has had a large fortepiano pedal made, which stands under the instrument and is about two feet longer and extremely heavy. It is taken to the Mehlgrube every Friday and has also been taken to Count Zichy's and to Prince Kaunitz's.[1]

(526) *Leopold Mozart to his Daughter*

[*Extract*]   [*Copy in the Staatsbibliothek Preussischer Kulturbesitz, West Berlin*[2]]

VIENNA, 25-26 *March* 1785

Well, I have twice heard Madame Lange sing five or six arias at the clavier in her own house, and this she did most readily. That she sings with the greatest expression cannot be denied. I had often questioned people about her and I now understand why some said that she had a very weak voice and others that she had a very powerful one. Both statements are true. Her held notes and those she emphasizes are astonishingly loud, her tender phrases, passages and grace notes and high notes are very delicate, so that in my opinion there is too much discrepancy between the two renderings. In a room her loud notes offend the ear and in a theatre her delicate passages demand great silence and attention on the part of the audience. I shall tell you more about this when we meet.

Madame Lange's husband is a fine painter. He did a sketch of me yesterday evening on a sheet of red paper.[3]

(527) *Leopold Mozart to his Daughter*

[*Extract*]   [*Autograph in the Mozarteum, Salzburg*]

VIENNA, 16 *April* 1785

The Baroness von Waldstädten is sending us her horses on Tuesday and we are to drive out to see her at Klosterneuburg, her present headquarters, lunch with her and return in the evening. I am very anxious to meet this woman of my heart, since I, *invisus*,[4] have been the man of her heart.[5]

---

[1] Another letter from Leopold Mozart to his daughter sent from Vienna and dated 19 March 1785, contains this interesting statement: 'If my son *has no debts to pay*, I think that he can now lodge two thousand gulden in the bank. Certainly the money is there, and so far as eating and drinking is concerned, the housekeeping is extremely economical.'
[2] Autograph in a private collection.
[3] This sketch of Leopold Mozart has unfortunately been lost.   [4] i.e. unseen.
[5] See pp. 820, 821.

(528) Mozart to Professor Anton Klein, Mannheim [1]

[*Autograph formerly in the possession of the heirs of Stefan Zweig*]

MOST HIGHLY ESTEEMED PRIVY COUNCILLOR!   [VIENNA, 21 May 1785]

It was very wrong of me, I must confess, not to have informed you at once of the safe arrival of your letter and the parcel which you sent along with it. You presume that in the meantime I have received two more letters from you; but this is not the case. The first would have instantly aroused me from my slumber and I should have replied, as I am now doing. No, I received last post-day your two letters together. Well, I have already acknowledged my guilt in not replying immediately. But as for the opera, I should have been able to say as little then as I can now. Dear Privy Councillor! My hands are so full that I scarcely ever find a minute I can call my own. A man of such great insight and experience as yourself will know even better than I that a libretto of this kind has to be read through with all possible attention and deliberation, and not once only, but several times. So far I have not had time to read it through even once without interruption. All that I can say at the moment is that I should not like to part with it yet. So I beg you to leave the play with me for a little longer. If I should feel inclined to set it to music, I should like to know beforehand whether its production has actually been arranged for a particular place; since a work of this kind, from the point of view both of the poetry and of the music, deserves a better fate than to be composed to no purpose. I trust that you will clear up this point.

At the moment I cannot send you any news about the coming German operatic stage, for at present, apart from the building operations at the Kärtnerthor theatre, which has been set apart for this purpose, things are progressing very slowly. They say that it is to be opened early in October. I for my part have no great hopes of its success. To judge by the preparations which have been made up to the present, it looks as if they were trying altogether to ruin German opera, which is probably only suffering a temporary eclipse, rather than to help to put it on its legs again and keep it going. My sister-in-law Madame Lange is the only singer who is to join the German opera. Madame Cavalieri, Adamberger, Mlle Teiber, all Germans of whom Germany may well be proud, have to stay at the Italian opera—and compete against their own countrymen! At present it is easy to count up the German singers, male and female; and even if there really are as good singers as the ones I have mentioned, or even better ones, which I very much doubt, yet I am inclined to think that the

---

[1] Professor Anton Klein (1748–1810), an ex-Jesuit, was a lecturer on philosophy and aesthetics and a popular dramatist. He wrote the text of Holzbauer's successful opera *Günther von Schwarzburg* and in 1780 a drama *Kaiser Rudolf von Habsburg*, which he sent to Mozart with the suggestion that the latter should set it to music.

directors of our theatre are too niggardly and too little patriotically-minded to offer large sums of money to strangers, when they have on the spot better singers, or at least equally good ones, whom they can rope in for nothing. For the Italian company does not need them—so far as numbers go. The company can fill all the parts themselves. The idea at present is to carry on the German opera with actors and actresses, who only sing when they must. Most unfortunately the directors of the theatre and those of the orchestra have all been retained, and it is they who owing to their ignorance and slackness are chiefly responsible for the failure of their own enterprise. Were there but one good patriot in charge—things would take a different turn. But then, perhaps, the German national theatre which is sprouting so vigorously would actually begin to flower; and of course that would be an everlasting blot on Germany, if we Germans were seriously to begin to think as Germans, to act as Germans, to speak German and, Heaven help us, to sing in German!!

Dear Privy Councillor, do not take it amiss if in my zeal I have perhaps gone too far! Completely convinced as I am that I am talking to a *true German*, I have given rein to my tongue, a thing which unfortunately is so seldom possible in these days that after such an out-pouring of the heart one might boldly drink oneself tipsy without running the risk of endangering one's health.

I remain, with the deepest respect, most esteemed Privy Councillor your most obedient servant

W. A. MOZART

Vienna, 21 May 1785.

(529) *Mozart to Joseph Haydn*[1]

[VIENNA, 1 September 1785]

To my dear friend Haydn.

A father who had decided to send out his sons into the great world, thought it his duty to entrust them to the protection and guidance of a man who was very celebrated at the time and who, moreover, happened to be his best friend.

In like manner I send my six sons to you, most celebrated and very dear friend. They are, indeed, the fruit of a long and laborious study; but the hope which many friends have given me that this toil will be in some degree rewarded, encourages me and flatters me with the thought that these children may one day prove a source of consolation to me.

---

[1] A dedication, in Italian, published in Artaria's first edition of the six string quartets K. 387, 421 [417b], 428 [421b], 458, 464 and 465, which Mozart had composed during the years 1782 to 1785.

During your last stay in this capital you yourself, my very dear friend, expressed to me your approval of these compositions. Your good opinion encourages me to offer them to you and leads me to hope that you will not consider them wholly unworthy of your favour. Please then receive them kindly and be to them a father, guide and friend! From this moment I surrender to you all my rights over them. I entreat you, however, to be indulgent to those faults which may have escaped a father's partial eye, and, in spite of them, to continue your generous friendship towards one who so highly appreciates it. Meanwhile I remain with all my heart, dearest friend, your most sincere friend

W. A. MOZART

Vienna, 1 September 1785.

(530) *Leopold Mozart to his Daughter*

[*Extract*]   [*Autograph in the Mozarteum, Salzburg*]

SALZBURG, 16 *September* 1785

It will be four weeks tomorrow since I had a letter from your brother. Hs is probably in the country. I do hope that I shall have a letter tomorrow, as I have written to him twice. Or perhaps he is going to come himself?

September 17th, in the morning

I have this moment received a letter from your brother. He says that he had already written, telling me the story about Lange,[1] which was made known to the public in the *Wiener Courant*. He adds that the Emperor said to your sister-in-law: 'What a difference it makes to have a good husband!' Your brother has dedicated his quartets to Herr Joseph Haydn with an Italian dedication. I am to have them by the next mail coach. Your brother kisses you and your husband most cordially. He says that I ought to send Fiala to Vienna and that he will take him at once to the Count von Kuffstein,[2] so that he may obtain an appointment without delay.

(531) *Leopold Mozart to his Daughter*

[*Extract*]   [*Autograph in the Mozarteum, Salzburg*]

SALZBURG, 3 *November* 1785

I haven't had a single line from your brother. His last letter was dated September 14th and the quartets were to have come by the next mail

---

[1] Josef Lange, the husband of Aloysia Weber, who was known to be exceedingly jealous.
[2] Johann Ferdinand, Count von Küfstein (1752–1818), was Court Councillor in Vienna and an amateur violinist and composer. He was one of Mozart's patrons, and in 1784 subscribed to his concerts.

coach.[1] If he were ill, Herr Artaria would have informed me in his letter of September 28th. The journalist[2] met me a few days ago and said: 'It is really astonishing to see what a number of compositions your son is publishing.[3] In all the announcements of musical works I see nothing but Mozart. The Berlin announcements, when quoting the quartets, merely add the following words: "It is quite unnecessary to recommend these quartets to the public. Suffice it to say that they are the work of Herr Mozart." ' I had nothing to say as I knew nothing, for it was more than six weeks since I had had a letter from your brother. My informant said something too about a new opera.[4] Basta! I daresay we shall hear about it.

(532) *Leopold Mozart to his Daughter*

[Extract]   *[Autograph in the Mozarteum, Salzburg]*

SALZBURG, 11 *November* 1785

At last I have received a letter of twelve lines from your brother, dated November 2nd. He begs to be forgiven, as he is up to the eyes in work at his opera 'Le Nozze di Figaro'. He thanks me and both of you for our good wishes and asks me particularly to make his excuses to you and to tell you with his love that he hasn't time to answer your letter at once. He adds that in order to keep the morning free for composing, he is now taking all his pupils in the afternoon, etc. I know the piece; it is a very tiresome play and the translation from the French will certainly have to be altered very freely, if it is to be effective as an opera.[5] God grant that the text may be a success. I have no doubt about the music. But there will be a lot of running about and discussions before he gets the libretto so adjusted as to suit his purpose exactly. And no doubt according to his charming habit he has kept on postponing matters and has let the time slip by. So now he must set to work seriously, for Count Rosenberg is prodding him.

---

[1] See p. 892.

[2] Professor Lorenz Hübner of Munich, who since the previous year had been editor of the *Salzburger Zeitung*, later *Oberdeutsche Staatszeitung*.

[3] Artaria had published in 1785 the symphonies K. 385 and 319, the six quartets dedicated to Haydn, the three clavier concertos K. 413-415 [387a, 385p, 387b], the fantasia and sonata for clavier K. 475 and 457, while Torricella and Hoffmeister each had printed a few minor works.

[4] *Le nozze di Figaro*.

[5] Beaumarchais' comedy *Le mariage de Figaro, ou La folle journée* was first produced in Paris on 27 April 1784, and was repeated sixty-eight times. Two German translations by Johann Rautenstrauch and Johann Friedrich Unger were printed immediately, although the play itself was forbidden in Vienna. Da Ponte used Beaumarchais' comedy as the basis for his libretto.

(533) Mozart to Franz Anton Hoffmeister[1]

[Autograph in the Gesellschaft der Musikfreunde, Vienna]

DEAREST HOFFMEISTER!   [VIENNA, 20 November 1785]

I turn to you in my distress and beg you to help me out with some money, which I need very badly at the moment. Further, I entreat you to endeavour to procure for me as soon as possible the thing you know about. Forgive me for constantly worrying you, but as you know me and are aware how anxious I am that your business should succeed, I am convinced that you will not take my importunity amiss and that you will help me as readily as I shall help you.

MZT.

20 November 1785.

(534) Leopold Mozart to his Daughter

[Extract]   [Autograph in the Mozarteum, Salzburg]

SALZBURG, 2 December 1785

★   At last the messenger brought me yesterday from the mail coach a carefully packed parcel containing the six quartets[2] and three scores, that is, a quartet for piano, violin, viola and cello obbligato[3] and the two grand new piano concertos.[4] The piano quartet was only finished on October 16th and your brother has sent me printed copies of the violin and viola parts, which have already been engraved. I was feeling horribly bored. Fortunately young Preymann[5] turned up at five o'clock and, although my eyes were rather tired as I had been writing during the morning and the afternoon an astonishingly long letter to Marchand which I had just taken to the post, yet it was refreshing to work carefully through three of the new quartets with Preymann as I did until eight o'clock. We can now perform them some time, as I shall coach two people in the second violin and cello parts and play the viola myself. The copyist at the moment has

---

[1] Franz Anton Hoffmeister (1754–1812), composer and music publisher. Probably this request refers to his publication of Mozart's piano quartet K. 478. Hoffmeister noted on the envelope 'two ducats'.

[2] The quartets dedicated to Haydn. See p. 892, n. 1.

[3] K. 478, piano quartet in G minor, composed in 1785 and published by Franz Anton Hoffmeister.

[4] K. 466 in D minor and K. 467 in C major, both composed in 1785. In a letter of 14 January 1786, Leopold Mozart makes the following interesting remarks about the concerto in C major: 'Indeed the new concerto is astonishingly difficult. But I very much doubt whether there are any mistakes, as the copyist has checked it. Several passages may not harmonise unless one hears all the instruments playing together. But of course it is quite possible that the copyist may have read a ♯ for ♭ in the score or something of the kind, for if so it cannot be right. I shall get to the bottom of it all when I see the original score.'

[5] Anton Preymann (1762–1841), a student at Salzburg university, was a violinist who subsequently joined Prince Liechtenstein's orchestra in Vienna and frequently performed at the Burgtheater.

enough to copy and it will be slow work. I am letting him do the clavier parts first of all, for the concertos will require a great deal of practice.

(535) *Leopold Mozart to his Daughter*

[*Extract*] [*Autograph in the Mozarteum, Salzburg*]

SALZBURG, 16 *December* 1785

Well, what I told my son long ago has now happened, and a clavier arrangement of the 'Entführung' has been published by the Augsburg bookseller Stage at the price of seven gulden and I forget how many kreuzer. Canonicus Stark has arranged it for the clavier. It has been engraved at Mainz and has been trumpeted forth in the Augsburg papers with many laudatory remarks about the famous Herr von Mozart.[1] If Torricella has already engraved a large portion of your brother's own arrangement, he will lose considerably.[2] And your brother will have wasted his time arranging two acts, which, I think, he had already finished.

(536) *Leopold Mozart to his Daughter*

[*Extract*] [*Autograph in the Mozarteum, Salzburg*]

SALZBURG, 13 *January* 1786

I received a command from the Archbishop to write to your brother about André, who is living with him. So is Fiala. If André will undertake to serve the Archbishop for fifteen gulden a month, he will be appointed. Another nice commission for me! I wrote at once. Meanwhile to two letters of mine I have had only one reply from your brother, dated December 28th, in which he said that he gave without much preparation three subscription concerts to 120 subscribers, that he composed for this purpose a new piano concerto in Eb,[4] in which (a rather unusual occurrence!) he had to repeat the Andante, and that he had taken Fiala in at once. He did not mention André, but Norman[5] wrote about this to Brunetti. Your brother added that he had already made three separate

---

[1] This unauthorised vocal score of Mozart's opera by the choirmaster Starck was published in Mainz by Schott. Evidently the Augsburg bookseller Stage was selling copies. On the title page Starck is described as 'Abbé'.

[2] Torricella had already engraved the overture and the first act of Mozart's arrangement.

[3] A young oboist who was visiting Vienna with Fiala, his teacher.

[4] K. 482.

[5] Norman is mentioned in a letter from Leopold Mozart to his daughter of 30 August 1784 (see Deutsch-Paumgartner, *Leopold Mozarts Briefe an seine Tochter*, 1936, p. 7), as the new fiddler who had performed before the Archbishop. Evidently Norman had moved on to Vienna. See *MBA*, No. 803.

attempts to find some means by which Fiala might earn a living and that he would send me by the mail coach a new clavier sonata.[1]

(536*) Mozart to ?Count Wenzel Paar

[From Schiedermair, vol. II, pp. 363, 364]

DEAR BROTHER!   [VIENNA, 14 January 1786?]

It is an hour since I came home—afflicted with acute headache and cramp in the stomach. I went on hoping for improvement but unfortunately am experiencing the reverse so that I realize that I am not destined to attend our first ceremony today and so I beg you dear Brother to apologize kindly for me on the very spot. No one loses more than I do in this matter.

I am always your truest brother

MOZART

Your Lordship's——
Oh Yes of course. . . .

(537) Leopold Mozart to his Daughter

[Extract]   [Autograph in the British Library, London]

MUNICH, [15] February 1786

★ I really think that Heinrich must have practised extremely hard, for you will be surprised when you hear him play your brother's Fantasia and Sonata,[2] which I sent you and which he too possesses, and also Clementi's sonatas. He played them on Herr von Hofstetten's[3] fortepiano so excellently that I was thrilled.

★

(538) Leopold Mozart to his Daughter

[Extract]   [Autograph in the Mozarteum, Salzburg]

SALZBURG, 23 March 1786

★ We had our concert yesterday. Marchand[4] performed the concerto in D minor,[5] which I sent to you the other day. As you have the clavier part, he played it from the score and Haydn[6] turned over the pages for him

---

[1] K. 457, sonata in C minor, and the fantasia in the same key, K. 475, which Mozart composed for his pupil Frau von Trattner, and which were published in December 1785 by Artaria.
[2] K. 475 and 457.   [3] An amateur musician and copyist of Munich.
[4] Heinrich Marchand, Leopold Mozart's pupil, who was not only a good violinist but also an excellent clavier-player.   [5] K. 466.   [6] Michael Haydn.

and at the same time had the pleasure of seeing with what art it is composed, how delightfully the parts are interwoven and what a difficult concerto it is. I chose this one, since you have the clavier parts of all the others and I still possessed the score of this one. We rehearsed it in the morning and had to practise the rondo three times before the orchestra could manage it, for Marchand took it rather quickly. This time too there was a great crowd and all the Ecclesiastical Councillors and University Professors were present. Madame Schlauka [1] made a good deal of money, for during the interval the members of the orchestra have a rest and come down into the hall, where the majority hasten to take some refreshments, which are very daintily and liberally served. In short, the Emperor might have been there. The Archbishop remained until nine o'clock.

★

(539) *Leopold Mozart to his Daughter*

[*Extract*]   [*From Otto Jahn, W. A. Mozart, vol. iv.* p. 189, 1856]

SALZBURG, 28 *April* 1786 ★

'Le Nozze di Figaro' is being performed on the 28th for the first time. [3] It will be surprising if it is a success, for I know that very powerful cabals have ranged themselves against your brother. Salieri and all his supporters will again try to move heaven and earth to down his opera. Herr & Mme Duschek told me recently that it is on account of the very great reputation which your brother's exceptional talent and ability have won for him that so many people are plotting against him.

★

(540) *Mozart to Sebastian Winter, Donaueschingen*

[*Autograph in the Fürstlich Fürstenbergische Hofbibliothek, Donaueschingen*]

[VIENNA, 8 *August* 1786]

DEAREST FRIEND! COMPANION OF MY YOUTH!

I was particularly delighted to receive your letter and nothing but business which could not be postponed has prevented me from replying sooner. I am very glad that you have applied to me in person. I should long ago have sent some specimens of my poor work to your highly respected Prince [4] (to whom I beg you to convey my homage and my thanks for the present he has sent me), if I had known whether or not my

---

[1] The wife of one of the Archbishop's valets.   [2] Autograph in a private collection.
[3] The first performance of *Le nozze di Figaro* took place on 1 May 1786.
[4] Josef Maria Benedikt, Prince von Fürstenberg, who in 1764 had taken into his household Sebastian Winter, the Mozarts' valet and friseur.

father had already sent him something and, if so, what he had sent. I am therefore jotting down at the end of my letter a list of my latest compositions from which His Highness has only to choose, so that I may hasten to serve him. If His Highness should so desire, I shall send him in future all the new works which I compose. Further, I venture to make a little musical proposal to His Highness which I beg you, my friend, to put before him. As His Highness possesses an orchestra, he might like to have works composed by me *for performance solely at his court*, a thing which in my humble opinion would be very gratifying. If His Highness would be so gracious as to order from me every year a certain number of symphonies, quartets, concertos for different instruments, or any other compositions which he fancies, and to promise me a fixed yearly salary, then His Highness would be served more quickly and more satisfactorily, and I, being sure of that commission, should work with greater peace of mind. I do trust that His Highness will not take my proposal amiss, if it does not suit him, for it is indeed prompted by an impulse of genuine anxiety to serve His Highness diligently, which in such a situation as mine is only possible if one can be sure of at least some support and can afford to give up less important tasks.

Awaiting an early reply with the order from your most worthy Prince, I ever remain your true friend and servant

WOLFGANG AMADÈ MOZART

Vienna, 8 August 1786.

SINFONIA[1]

di WOLFGANGO AMADEO MOZART

[1] K. 425 (1783), K. 385 (1782), K. 319 (1779), K. 338 (1780).

CONCERTI PER CEMBALO[1]

SONATA PER CEMBALO CON VIOLINO[2]

TERZETTO: CEMBALO, VIOLINO E VIOLONCELLO[3]

[1] K. 453 (1784), K. 456 (1784), K. 451 (1784), K. 459 (1784), K. 488 (1786).
[2] K. 481 (1785).   [3] K. 496 (1786).

QUARTETTO: CEMBALO, VIOLINO, VIOLA
E VIOLONCELLO[1]

(541) *Mozart to Sebastian Winter, Donaueschingen*

[Autograph in the Fürstlich Fürstenbergische Hofbibliothek, Donaueschingen]

DEAREST FRIEND!   [VIENNA, 30 *September* 1786]

The music you asked for is being sent off tomorrow by the mail coach.[2] You will find at the end of this letter the amount due to me for the copies. It is quite natural that some of my compositions should be sent abroad, but those which I do send are deliberately chosen. I only sent you the themes, because it is quite possible that these works have not reached you. But the compositions which I keep for myself or for a small circle of music-lovers and connoisseurs (who promise not to let them out of their hands) cannot possibly be known elsewhere, as they are not even known in Vienna. And this is the case with the three concertos which I have the honour of sending to His Highness. But here I have been obliged to add to the cost of copying a small additional fee of six ducats for each concerto; and I must ask His Highness not to let them out of his hands. There are two clarinets in the A major concerto.[3] Should His Highness not have any clarinets at his court, a competent copyist might transpose the parts into the suitable keys, in which case the first part should be played by a violin and the second by a viola. As for the proposal which I took the liberty of making to your worthy Prince, I should have to be exactly informed, first of all, as to what kinds of composition His Highness might require or prefer and, secondly, as to how many of each kind he would like to have every year, in order to be able to make my calculations. I wish to offer my homage to His Highness, and I request you to make known to him my desire. And now, dearest friend! Companion of my youth! As I have often been in Ricken[4] during these many years and yet

---

[1] K. 478 (1785). The incipits of all these works are given as they appear in the autograph of the letter. In some cases they differ from the generally accepted versions.

[2] On the autograph of Letter 540 the incipits of K. 385, 453, 465, 481, 496 and 478 have been crossed out. A note by Winter indicates that the remaining works were chosen by the Prince.

[3] K. 488.

[4] This is the word in the autograph. It may have some connection with an anecdote which Mozart's sister sent in November 1799 to Breitkopf and Härtel (see Nottebohm, p. 137, n. 1), describing how during their early travels her brother imagined a Kingdom called Rücken, of which he was to be King and for which their servant, Sebastian Winter, had to sketch a map. See *MBA*, No. 1268.

have never had the pleasure of meeting you, my dearest wish indeed would be that you should visit me in Vienna or that I should visit you at Donaueschingen. The latter I should almost prefer, for in addition to the pleasure of embracing you I should have the privilege of paying my respects to your most gracious Prince, and I should be more forcibly reminded of the many favours which in my younger years I enjoyed at his court, favours which I shall never forget as long as I live. Awaiting an early reply and in the flattering hope of meeting you once more in this world, I am ever your most devoted friend and servant

WOLFGANG AMADÈ MOZART

Vienna, 30 September 1786.

Account	Gulden	Kreuzer
Three concertos without the piano parts		
109 sheets @ 8 kreuzer	14	32
Three piano parts		
33½ sheets @ 10 kreuzer	5	35
Fee for the three concertos		
18 ducats @ 4 gulden, 30 kreuzer	81	..
Three symphonies		
116½ sheets @ 8 kreuzer	15	32
Customs fee and postage	3	..
TOTAL	119	39 [1]

(542) *Leopold Mozart to his Daughter*

[Extract]   [Autograph in the Mozarteum, Salzburg]

SALZBURG, 17 *November* 1786 ★

I had to reply today to a letter from your brother, and this took me a considerable time. So I cannot write very much to you. Moreover it is late and I want to go to the play today, as I have a free pass, and have only just finished that letter to Vienna. You can easily imagine that I had to express myself very emphatically, as your brother actually suggested that I should take charge of his two children,[2] because he was proposing to undertake a journey through Germany to England in the middle of next carnival. I wrote therefore very fully and added that I would send him the continuation of my letter by the next post. Herr Müller, that good

---

[1] The autograph has a note by Sebastian Winter, stating that the letter was received on 11 October, the music on 14 October, and that the sum of 143¼ gulden was sent to Mozart on 8 November.

[2] Karl Thomas, born on 21 September 1784, and Johann Thomas Leopold, born on 18 October 1786. The latter died on 15 November 1786.

and honest maker of silhouettes,[1] had said a lot of nice things about little Leopold[2] to your brother, who heard in this way that the child is living with me. I had never told your brother. So that is how the brilliant idea occurred to him or perhaps to his wife. Not at all a bad arrangement! They could go off and travel—they might even die—or remain in England —and I should have to run off after them with the children. As for the payment which he offers me for the children and for maids to look after them, well—Basta! If he cares to do so, he will find my excuse very clear and instructive.

(543) Leopold Mozart to his Daughter

[Extract]   [Autograph in the Mozarteum, Salzburg]

SALZBURG, 12 January 1787

Your brother and his wife must be in Prague by this time, for he wrote to say that he was leaving Vienna last Monday.[3] His opera 'Le Nozze di Figaro' was performed there with such success that the orchestra and a company of distinguished connoisseurs and lovers of music sent him letters inviting him to Prague and also a poem which was composed in his honour.[4] I heard this from your brother, and Count Starhemberg heard about it from Prague. I shall send you the poem by the next courier. Madame Duschek is off to Berlin. I am still receiving from Vienna, Prague and Munich reports which confirm the rumour that your brother is going to England.

(544) Mozart to Baron Gottfried von Jacquin,[5] Vienna

[Facsimile in catalogue of the Alfred Morrison Collection, vol. iv. p. 324[6]]

DEAREST FRIEND!   PRAGUE, 15 January 1787

At last I have found a moment to write to you. I resolved immediately after my arrival to write four letters to Vienna, but in vain! I was only able to manage one (to my mother-in-law) and then only half of it. My wife

---

[1] Possibly Franz Xaver Müller (1756–1837), a well-known copper-engraver in Vienna.

[2] Leopold Mozart had taken entire charge of Nannerl's son Leopold, who was born at Salzburg in June 1785.

[3] Mozart and his wife arrived in Prague on 11 January 1787.

[4] Le nozze di Figaro had been frequently performed in Prague since December 1786 by Pasquale Bondini's theatrical company with Johann Josef Strobach as conductor. The poem composed in honour of Mozart by A. D. Breicha is quoted in R. Procházka, Mozart in Prag, 1892, p. 28, and translated in MDB, p. 282 f.

[5] Gottfried von Jacquin (1767–1792) was the second son of the famous botanist, Professor Nicolaus Josef, Baron von Jacquin (1727–1817). He and his sister Franziska (1769–1853) were pupils of Mozart.

[6] Copy in the Staatsbibliothek Preussischer Kulturbesitz, West Berlin.

and Hofer[1] had to finish it. Immediately after our arrival at noon on Thursday, the 11th, we had a dreadful rush to get ready for lunch at one o'clock. After the meal old Count Thun[2] entertained us with some music, performed by his own people, which lasted about an hour and a half. This kind of *real entertainment* I could enjoy every day. At six o'clock I drove with Count Canal[3] to the so-called Breitfeld[4] ball, where the cream of the beauties of Prague is wont to gather. Why—*you* ought to have been there, my friend! I fancy I see you running, or rather, limping after all those pretty girls and women! I neither danced nor flirted with any of them, the former, because I was too tired, and the latter owing to my natural bashfulness. I looked on, however, with the greatest pleasure while all these people flew about in sheer delight to the music of my 'Figaro', arranged for contredanses and German dances. For here they talk about nothing but 'Figaro'. Nothing is played, sung or whistled but 'Figaro'. No opera is drawing like 'Figaro'. Nothing, nothing but 'Figaro'. Certainly a great honour for me! Well, to return to my order of the day. As I got home very late from the ball and moreover was tired and sleepy after my journey, nothing in the world could be more natural than that I should sleep it out next morning; which was just what I did. So the whole of the next morning was spent *sine linea.*[5] After lunch the Count's music must always be listened to, and as on that very day an excellent pianoforte had been put in my room, you may readily suppose that I did not leave it unused and untouched for the whole evening; and that as a matter of course we performed amongst ourselves a little *Quatuor in caritatis camera*[6] ('und das schöne Bandl hammera')[7] and in this way the whole evening was again spent *sine linea*; and so it actually was. Well, you must scold not me but Morpheus, for that deity is very attentive to us in Prague. What the cause may have been I know not; at any rate we slept it out. Still, we managed to be at Father Unger's at eleven o'clock and made a *thorough* inspection of the Imperial Library and the General Theological Seminary. When we had almost stared our

---

[1] Franz de Paula Hofer (1755–1796), Court violinist in Vienna. He married, in July 1788, Frau Weber's eldest daughter Josefa.

[2] As Madame Duschek was in Berlin, the Mozarts stayed with Count Thun.

[3] Josef Emanuel, Count Canal von Malabaila (1745–1826), botanist and lover of music, lived in Prague and had a private orchestra.

[4] Baron Breitfeld, a wealthy member of the Bohemian aristocracy, gave famous balls.

[5] i.e. without writing a line.

[6] We performed a little quartet for ourselves. This was probably the piano quartet K. 493.

[7] K. 441, called the Bandl-Terzett, a humorous three-part song for soprano, tenor and bass, which Mozart composed in 1783, and dedicated to Gottfried von Jacquin. Mozart and his wife and Jacquin were out walking one day when Constanze happened to lose a ribbon which her husband had given her and exlaimed, using the Viennese dialect: 'Liebes Mandl, wo is's Bandl?' Jacquin, a tall fellow, picked up the ribbon and refused to let her have it until she or her little husband should catch it. Upon which Mozart wrote the poem which he afterwards set to music. 'Und das schöne Bandl hammera' means 'und das schöne Bändchen haben wir auch'. See Jahn, vol. ii, p. 58.

eyes out, we thought that we heard a little stomach-aria in our insides and that it would be just as well to drive to Count Canal's for lunch. The evening surprised us sooner than you might perhaps believe. Well, it was soon time to go to the opera. We heard 'Le gare generose'.[1] In regard to the performance of this opera I can give no definite opinion because I talked a lot; but that quite contrary to my usual custom I chattered so much may have been due to . . . Well, never mind! that evening too was frittered away *al solito*. Today I have at last been so fortunate as to find a moment to enquire after the health of your dear parents and the whole Jacquin family. I hope and trust with all my heart that you are all as well as we are. I must frankly admit that, although I meet with all possible courtesies and honours here and although Prague is indeed a very beautiful and pleasant place, I long most ardently to be back in Vienna; and believe me, the chief cause of this homesickness is certainly *your* family. When I remember that after my return I shall enjoy only for a short while the pleasure of your valued society and shall then have to forgo this happiness for such a long time, perhaps for ever, then indeed I realize the extent of the friendship and regard which I cherish for your whole family.[2] Now farewell, dearest friend, dearest Hinkiti Honky! That is your name, so that you know. We all invented names for ourselves on the journey. Here they are. I am Punkititi. My wife is Schabla Pumfa. Hofer is Rozka-Pumpa. Stadler[3] is Natschibinitschibi. My servant Joseph is Sagadaratà. My dog Gauckerl is Schamanuzky. Madame Quallenberg is Runzifunzi. Mlle Crux.[4] PS. Ramlo is Schurimuri. Freistädtler[5] is Gaulimauli. Be so kind as to tell him his name. Well, adieu. My concert is to take place in the theatre on Friday, the 19th, and I shall probably have to give a second one, which unfortunately will prolong my stay here. Please give my kind regards to your worthy parents and embrace your brother (who by the way could be christened Blatterrizi) a thousand times for me; and I kiss your sister's hands (her name is Signora Diniminimi) a hundred thousand times and urge her to practise hard on her new pianoforte.[6] But this admonition is really unnecessary, for I must confess that I have never yet had a female pupil who was so diligent and who showed so much zeal—and indeed I am looking forward to giving her lessons again according to my small ability. A propos. If she wants to come tomorrow, I shall certainly be at home at eleven o'clock. But surely it is high time to close, is it not? You will have been thinking so for a long time.

[1] Giovanni Paisiello's *Le gare generose* was first produced at Naples in 1786.
[2] Mozart was planning to go to England. See p. 901.   [3] Anton Stadler. See p. 937, n. 3.
[4] Marianne, daughter of Peter Crux, master of the ballet at the Vienna opera. She was a singer and also a successful performer on the violin and clavier.
[5] Franz Jakob Freistädtler (1761–1841), a pupil of Mozart, who composed for him K. 232 [509a], a canon for four voices on the words 'Lieber Freistädtler, lieber Gaulimauli'. Friestädtler composed a collection of songs, dedicated to Josephine Auernhammer.
[6] Gottfried von Jacquin's sister Franziska was one of Mozart's pupils.

Farewell, beloved friend! Keep me in your precious friendship. Write to me soon—very soon—and if perchance you are too lazy to do so, send for Satmann and dictate a letter to him, though indeed no letter comes as much from the heart as it does when one writes oneself. Well, I shall see whether you are as truly my friend as I am entirely yours and ever shall be.

MOZART

PS.—Address the letter which you will possibly write to me 'At Count Thun's palace'.

My wife sends her kindest regards to the whole Jacquin family, and so does Hofer.

NB.—On Wednesday I am to see and hear 'Figaro' in Prague, if I have not become deaf and blind before then. Possibly I may not become so until after the opera.[1]

(545) *Leopold Mozart to his Daughter*

[*Extract*]   [*Autograph in the Mozarteum, Salzburg*]

SALZBURG, 1 March 1787 ★

At half past six o'clock on Monday evening I received from Madame Storace, the Vienna opera singer, a note saying that she had arrived at the Trinkstube. I found her mother with her, who is an Englishwoman (the daughter was born in England), the Vienna opera tenor O'Kelly,[2] who is an Englishman by birth, another Englishman whom I did not know but who is probably cicisbeo to the mother and daughter, her brother, Maestro Storace,[3] and a little Englishman called Attwood,[4] who was sent to Vienna two years ago for the sole purpose of taking lessons from your brother. As Madame Storace had a letter of introduction from Countess Guntacker Colloredo, the Archbishop was obliged to hear her sing and to give her a handsome present. After a year's stay in London she is returning to the Vienna opera.[5] I galloped round the town with them on Tuesday

---

[1] For an excellent account of Mozart's four visits to Prague in 1787, 1789 and 1791, see R. Procházka, *Mozart in Prag*, 1892 (revised by P. Nettl as *Mozart in Böhmen*, 1938).

[2] Michael Kelly (1762–1826), who in Mozart's catalogue of his own works appears as 'Occhelly', was born in Dublin. He went to Naples in 1779 to be trained as an operatic tenor, and four years later came to Vienna where he enjoyed the intimate friendship of Mozart. Kelly took the parts of Basilio and Don Curzio in the first performance of *Le nozze di Figaro*. He also composed songs which were popular. His *Reminiscences* in two volumes, written by Theodore Hook with the help of material supplied by Kelly, appeared in 1826. They contain accounts of Mozart which are both interesting and important.

[3] Stephen Storace (1762–1796) had studied at Naples and is best known for his operas, of which he wrote about a dozen. Two of them were composed in Vienna. His last opera *Mahmoud* was completed by Kelly and Nancy Storace.

[4] Thomas Attwood (1765–1838) first studied music at Naples from 1783 until 1785, and then went to Vienna to learn composition under Mozart. His exercise books are printed in W. A. Mozart: *Neue Ausgabe sämtlicher Werke*, x/30/1 (Kassel, 1965). In 1796 he was appointed organist of St. Paul's Cathedral. In later life Attwood wrote many successful operas and became a close friend of Mendelssohn.

[5] Nancy Storace never returned to Vienna.

from ten to two in order to show them a few sights. We lunched at two
o'clock. In the evening she sang three arias and they left for Munich at
midnight. They had two carriages, each with four post-horses. A servant
rode in advance as courier to arrange for the changing of eight horses.
Goodness, what luggage they had! This journey must have cost them a
fortune. They all spoke English, far more than Italian. A funny thing is
that my son sent a letter for me to the house where his pupil Attwood was
staying. Attwood had gone out and Madame Storace's mother took the
letter and was stupid enough to pack it in some trunk or maybe to lose it.
Basta! the letter was not to be found. I shall write to your brother about it
tomorrow.

March 2nd. As for your brother I hear that he is back in Vienna. I had
no reply to the letter I sent to him at Prague. The English company told me
that he made a thousand gulden there, that little Leopold, his last boy, has
died,[1] and that, as I had gathered, he wants to travel to England, but that
his pupil[2] is first going to procure a definite engagement for him in London, I mean, a contract to compose an opera or a subscription concert, etc.
Probably Madame Storace and the whole company had filled him with
stories to the same effect and these people and his pupil must have been the
first to give him the idea of accompanying them to England. But no doubt
after I sent him a fatherly letter, saying that he would gain nothing by a
journey in summer, as he would arrive in England at the wrong time, that
he ought to have at least two thousand gulden in his pocket before undertaking such an expedition, and finally that, unless he had procured in
advance some definite engagement in London, he would have to be prepared, no matter how clever he was, to be hard up at first at any rate, he
has probably lost courage, particularly as Madame Storace's brother will
of course write the opera for the next season.[3]

★

(546) *Mozart to his Father*

[*Autograph formerly in the Musikhistorisches Museum von W. Heyer, Cologne*[4]]

MON TRÉS CHER PÈRE!   [VIENNA, 4 *April* 1787]
    I am very much annoyed that owing to the stupidity of Madame
Storace my letter never reached you. Amongst other things it contained,
I expressed the hope that you had received my last letter; but as you do
not mention this particular one, I mean, my second letter from Prague,
I do not know what to think. It is quite likely that some servant of Count

---

[1] Mozart's third child, Johann Thomas Leopold, died on 15 November 1786.
[2] Thomas Attwood.
[3] Stephen Storace's *La cameriera astuta* was performed on 4 March 1788, at the King's Theatre
in the Haymarket.
[4] Copy in the Staatsbibliothek Preussischer Kulturbesitz, West Berlin.

Thun's[1] had the brilliant idea of pocketing the postage money. Indeed I would rather pay double postage than suspect that my letters have fallen into the wrong hands. Ramm and the two Fischers, the bass singer[2] and the oboist from London,[3] came here this Lent. If the latter when we knew him in Holland[4] played no better than he does now, he certainly does not deserve the reputation he enjoys. *But this is between ourselves.* In those days I was not competent to form an opinion. All that I remember is that I liked his playing immensely, as indeed everyone did. This is quite understandable, of course, on the assumption that taste can undergo remarkable changes. Possibly he plays in some old-fashioned style? Not at all! The long and short of it is that he plays like a bad beginner. Young André, who took some lessons from Fiala, plays a thousand times better. And then his concertos! His own compositions! Why, each ritornello lasts a quarter of an hour; and then our hero comes in, lifts up one leaden foot after the other and stamps on the floor with each in turn. His tone is entirely nasal, and his held notes like the tremulant on the organ. Would you ever have thought that his playing is like this? Yet it is nothing but the truth, though a truth which I should only tell to *you.*

This very moment I have received a piece of news which greatly distresses me, the more so as I gathered from your last letter that, thank God, you were very well indeed. But now I hear that you are really ill. I need hardly tell you how greatly I am longing to receive some reassuring news from yourself. And I still expect it; although I have now made a habit of being prepared in all affairs of life for the worst. As death, when we come to consider it closely, is the true goal of our existence, I have formed during the last few years such close relations with this best and truest friend of mankind, that his image is not only no longer terrifying to me, but is indeed very soothing and consoling! And I thank my God for graciously granting me the opportunity (you know what I mean) of learning that death is the *key* which unlocks the door to our true happiness. I never lie down at night without reflecting that—young as I am—I may not live to see another day. Yet no one of all my acquaintances could say that in company I am morose or disgruntled. For this blessing I daily thank my Creator and wish with all my heart that each one of my fellow-creatures could enjoy it. In the letter which Madame Storace took away with her,

---

[1] The Mozarts during their stay in Prague were the guests of Count Thun. See p. 903.

[2] J. I. Ludwig Fischer (1745–1825), who took the part of Osmin in the original production of *Die Entführung aus dem Serail.*

[3] Johann Christian Fischer (1733–1800), a famous oboist in his day. He held an appointment at the Dresden Court from 1764 until 1771, and then more or less settled in London, where he was a frequent performer at the Bach-Abel concerts. He married the daughter of Gainsborough, who painted his portrait. It was on his minuet that Mozart composed in 1774 his popular Fischer variations (K. 179 [189a]).

[4] The Mozart family met J. C. Fischer at The Hague in 1765. See Leopold Mozart's *Reiseaufzeichnungen*, p. 42, and *MBA*, No. 105.

I expressed my views to you on this point, in connexion with the sad death of my dearest and most beloved friend, the Count von Hatzfeld.[1] He was just thirty-one, my own age. I do not feel sorry for him, but I pity most sincerely both myself and all who knew him as well as I did. I hope and trust that while I am writing this, you are feeling better. But if, contrary to all expectation, you are not recovering, I implore you by . . . not to hide it from me, but to tell me the whole truth or get someone to write it to me, so that as quickly as is humanly possible I may come to your arms. I entreat you by all that is sacred—to both of us. Nevertheless I trust that I shall soon have a reassuring letter from you; and cherishing this pleasant hope, I and my wife and our little Karl[2] kiss your hands a thousand times and I am ever

your most obedient son

W: A: MOZART

(547) *Mozart to Baron Gottfried von Jacquin*

[*Copy in the Deutsche Staatsbibliothek, East Berlin*[3]]

DEAREST FRIEND!   [VIENNA?, *end of May* 1787]

Please tell Herr Exner to come at nine o'clock tomorrow morning to bleed my wife.

I send you herewith your Amynt and the sacred song. Please be so good as to give the sonata[4] to your sister with my compliments and tell her to tackle it at once, for it is rather difficult. Adieu. Your true friend

MOZART

I inform you that on returning home today I received the sad news of my most beloved father's death.[5] You can imagine the state I am in.

---

[1] The Count August von Hatzfeld (1754–1787), an excellent amateur violinist and an intimate friend of Mozart's.

[2] Mozart's son, Karl Thomas, born on 21 September 1784.

[3] Autograph in the Geigy-Hagenbach Collection, Basel.

[4] K. 521, sonata in C major for four hands, composed in 1787, which Mozart dedicated later to two sisters, Babette and Marianne (Nanette) Natorp, the former of whom subsequently married Jacquin's brother.

[5] Leopold Mozart died on 28 May 1787. The last letter of his which is preserved is addressed to his daughter, is dated May 10th–11th, and contains the following remark about his son: 'Your brother is now living in the Landstrasse no. 224. He does not say why he has moved. Not a word. But unfortunately I can guess the reason.' Mozart and his family, for the sake of economy, had moved at the end of April into a cheaper house, the yearly rent of which was about fifty gulden. They left this house at the end of the year.

(547*) *Mozart to his Sister*

[*From Neues Mozart-Jahrbuch, III, p. 87 ff. Regensburg, G. Bosse.* 1943][1]

DEAREST SISTER! [VIENNA, 2 *June* 1787]

You can easily imagine, as our loss is equally great, how pained I was by the sad news of the sudden death of our dearest father. Since at the moment it is impossible for me to leave Vienna (which I would the more gladly do to have the pleasure of embracing you) and since it would be hardly worth my while to do so for the sake of our late father's estate, I must confess that I too am entirely of your opinion about having a public auction. But before it takes place I should like to see the inventory, so as to be able to choose some personal effects. But if, as Herr d'Yppold has written to tell me, there is a dispositio paterna inter liberos, then, of course, I must be informed of this dispositio beforehand, so as to be able to make further arrangements;—hence I am now expecting an accurate copy of it and after a rapid perusal of its contents I shall let you have my opinion at once—Please see that the enclosed letter is handed to our kind and sincere friend Herr d'Yppold. As he has already proved his friendship to our family on so many occasions, I trust that he will again be a friend to me also and act for me in any necessary events. Farewell, dearest sister! I am ever your faithful brother

W. A. MOZART

PS.—My wife wishes to be remembered to you and your husband, and so do I.

Vienna, 2 June 1787

(548) *Mozart to his Sister*

[*From Nissen,* pp. 525-526]

DEAREST, MOST BELOVED SISTER! VIENNA, 16 *June* 1787

I was not at all surprised, as I could easily guess the reason, that you yourself did not inform me of the sad death of our most dear father, which to me was quite unexpected. May God take him to Himself! Rest assured my dear, that if you desire a kind brother to love and protect you, you will find one in me on every occasion. My dearest, most beloved sister! If you were still unprovided for, all this would be quite unnecessary, for as I have already said and thought a thousand times, I should leave everything to you with the greatest delight. But as the property would really be of no use to you, while, on the contrary, it would be a considerable help to me, I think it my duty to consider my wife and child.

[1] From the autograph then in the Archiepiscopal Archives at Erlau, Hungary. It was noted in 1971 as being in the estate of Johann Ladislaus Pyrker.

(549) *Mozart to his Sister*

[*Autograph in the Koch Collection, Basel*]

DEAREST, MOST BELOVED SISTER!   [VIENNA, 1 *August* 1787]
     At the moment I am simply replying to your letter, so I am writing very little and in great haste, as I really have far too much to do. As both your husband, my dear brother-in-law, whom I ask you to kiss a thousand times for me, and I are particularly anxious to wind up the whole business as soon as possible, I am accepting his offer, on the understanding, however, that the thousand gulden shall be paid to me not in Imperial but in Viennese currency and, moreover, as a bill of exchange. Next post-day I shall send your husband the draft of an agreement or rather of a contract between us. Then two original copies of it will follow, one signed by me, the other to be signed by him. I will send you as soon as possible some new compositions of mine for the clavier. Please do not forget about my *scores*. A thousand farewells to you. I must close. My wife and our Karl send a thousand greetings to you and your husband, and I am ever your brother who loves you sincerely,

                                                                    W. A. MOZART

The Landstrasse,[1] 1 August 1787.

(549*) *Mozart to his Brother-in-Law, Baron von Berchtold zu Sonnenburg, St. Gilgen*

[*Autograph in possession of Michael George Schnitzler, Vienna*]

DEAREST BROTHER!   [VIENNA, 29 *September* 1787]
     In great haste. I am delighted with our good arrangement. When you send me the bill of exchange, please address it to Herr Michael Puchberg —at the house of Count Walsegg in the Hohe Markt because he has instructions to take charge of the money since I am leaving for Prague very early on Monday. Goodbye. Kiss our dear sister a thousand times on behalf of both of us and be assured I shall ever be your sincerest brother

                                                                    W. A. MOZART

Vienna, 29 September 1787

---

[1] Mozart lived here (Hauptstrasse 224, now Landstrasser Hauptstrasse 75) from spring 1787 until about the end of the year. See p. 908, n. 4.

(550) *Mozart to Baron Gottfried von Jacquin, Vienna*

[*Autograph in the Gräflich Czernisches Archiv, Neuhaus*]

DEAREST FRIEND!   PRAGUE, 15 *October* 1787

You probably think that my opera [1] is over by now. If so, you are a little mistaken. In the first place, the stage personnel here are not as smart as those in Vienna, when it comes to mastering an opera of this kind in a very short time. Secondly, I found on my arrival that so few preparations and arrangements had been made that it would have been absolutely impossible to produce it on the 14th, that is, yesterday. So yesterday my 'Figaro' was performed in a fully lighted theatre and I myself conducted.

In this connexion I have a good joke to tell you. A few of the leading ladies here, and in particular one very high and mighty one, were kind enough to find it very ridiculous, unsuitable, and Heaven knows what else that the Princess [2] should be entertained with a performance of Figaro, the 'Crazy Day', [3] as the management were pleased to call it. It never occurred to them that no opera in the world, unless it is written specially for it, can be exactly suitable for such an occasion and that therefore it was of absolutely no consequence whether this or that opera were given, provided that it was a good opera and one which the Princess did not know; and 'Figaro' at least fulfilled this last condition. In short by her persuasive tongue the ringleader brought things to such a pitch that the government forbade the impresario to produce this opera on that night. So she was triumphant! '*Ho vinto*', [4] she called out one evening from her box. No doubt she never suspected that the *ho* might be changed to a *sono*. But the following day Le Noble appeared, bearing a command from His Majesty to the effect that if the new opera could not be given, 'Figaro' was to be performed! My friend, if only you had seen the handsome, magnificent nose of this lady! Oh, it would have amused you as much as it did me! 'Don Giovanni' has now been fixed for the 24th.

October 21*st*. It was fixed for the 24th, but a further postponement has been caused by the illness of one of the singers. As the company is so small, the impresario is in a perpetual state of anxiety and has to spare his people as much as possible, lest some unexpected indisposition should plunge him

---

[1] During his first visit to Prague in January 1787 Mozart was asked to compose an opera buffa for the autumn season, and signed a contract to this effect with the theatrical manager Bondini. He was to receive the usual fee of 100 ducats. There is no evidence to show exactly when Mozart and Constanze arrived in Prague but they left Vienna on 1 October. See Letter 549*. *Don Giovanni*, for which da Ponte wrote the libretto, was performed on 29 October.

[2] Prince Anton of Saxony and his bride, the Archduchess Maria Theresa, a niece of the Emperor Joseph II, spent a few days in Prague during their honeymoon.

[3] The sub-title of Beaumarchais' comedy *Le mariage de Figaro* is *La folle journée*.

[4] I have conquered.

into the most awkward of all situations, that of not being able to produce any show whatsoever!

So everything dawdles along here because the singers, who are lazy, refuse to rehearse on opera days and the manager, who is anxious and timid, will not force them. But what is this?—Is it possible? What vision meets my ears, what sound bombards my eyes? A letter from——I am almost rubbing my eyes sore—Why, it is—The devil take me † God protect us † It actually is from you—indeed! If winter were not upon us, I would smash the stove in good earnest. But as I frequently use it now and intend to use it more often in future, you will allow me to express my surprise in a somewhat more moderate fashion and merely tell you in a few words that I am extraordinarily pleased to have news from you and your most precious family.

October 25th. Today is the eleventh day that I have been scrawling this letter. You will see from this that my intentions are good. Whenever I can snatch a moment, I daub in another little piece. But indeed I cannot spend much time over it, because I am far too much at the disposal of other people and far too little at my own. I need hardly tell you, as we are such old friends, that this is not the kind of life I prefer.

My opera is to be performed for the first time next Monday, October 29th. You shall have an account of it from me a day or two later. As for the aria,[1] it is absolutely impossible to send it to you for reasons which I shall give you when we meet. I am delighted to hear what you say about Katherl,[2] that is, that she commands the respect of cats and knows how to retain the friendship of dogs. If your Papa, to whom I send most cordial greetings, likes to keep her, well, let us pretend that she never belonged to me. Now, farewell. Please kiss your gracious Mamma's hands for me, give my best greetings to your sister and your brother and rest assured that I shall ever be your true friend and servant

W: A: Mozart

(551) *Mozart to Baron Gottfried von Jacquin, Vienna*

[*Autograph in the Nationalbibliothek, Vienna*]

Dearest, most beloved Friend!   Prague, 4 *November* 1787

I hope you received my letter. My opera 'Don Giovanni' had its first performance on October 29th and was received with the greatest applause. It was performed yesterday for the fourth time, for my benefit. I am

---

[1] There is no trace of this composition, if it was an aria written specially for Jacquin. Einstein suggests Masetto's aria in *Don Giovanni*, Act I, 'Ho capito, Signor, sì'.
[2] Mozart's dog.

thinking of leaving here on the 12th or 13th. When I return, you shall have the aria[1] at once, remember, *between ourselves*. How I wish that my good friends, particularly you and Bridi,[2] were here just for one evening in order to share my pleasure! But perhaps my opera will be performed in Vienna after all! I hope so.[3] People here are doing their best to persuade me to remain on for a couple of months and write another one. But I cannot accept this proposal, however flattering it may be. Well, dearest friend, how are you? I trust that you *all* are as fit and well as we are. You cannot fail to be happy, dearest friend, for you possess everything that you can wish for *at your age and in your position*, particularly as you now seem to be entirely giving up your former rather *restless way of living*. Surely you are becoming every day more convinced of the truth of the little lectures I used to inflict upon you? Surely the pleasure of a transient, capricious infatuation is as far removed as heaven from earth from the blessed happiness of a deep and true affection? Surely in your heart of hearts you often feel grateful to me for my admonitions? You will end up by making me quite conceited. But, jesting apart, you do owe me some thanks after all, if you have become worthy of Fräulein N——,[4] for I certainly played no insignificant part in your reform or conversion. My great-grandfather used to say to his wife, my great-grandmother, who in turn told her daughter, my grandmother, who repeated it to her daughter, my mother, who used to remind her daughter, my own sister, that to talk well and eloquently was a very great art, but that an equally great one was to know the right moment to stop. So I shall follow the advice of my sister, thanks to our mother, grandmother and great-grandmother, and put a stop not only to my moral digression but to my whole letter.

November 9th. It has been a most pleasant surprise to receive your second letter. If the song in question is necessary to prove my friendship for you, you have no further cause to doubt it, for here it is.[5] But I trust that even *without this song* you are convinced of my true friendship, and in this hope I remain ever your most sincere friend

W: A: MOZART

PS.—That neither your dear parents nor your brother and sister should have sent me any remembrances, I really cannot understand. I put it down, my friend, to *your* forgetfulness and flatter myself that I am not mistaken. Now I must explain the double seal. The red wax was no good, so I put black wax on the top of it. And I had left my usual seal behind me in Vienna.

Adieu. I hope to embrace you soon.

[1] See p. 912, n. 1.   [2] Probably Giuseppe Antonio Bridi. See p. 170, n. 2.
[3] *Don Giovanni* was performed in Vienna on 7 May 1788.
[4] Marianne von Natorp, to whom Gottfried von Jacquin dedicated some songs.
[5] K. 530, 'Wo bist du, Bild', written for Gottfried von Jacquin.

We both send our compliments to your whole family and to the Natorps.[1]

(552) *Mozart to his Sister*

[*Autograph in the British Library, London*]

DEAREST SISTER,   VIENNA, 19 *December* 1787
I most humbly beg your pardon for having left you so long without an answer. Of my writing 'Don Giovanni' for Prague and of the opera's triumphant success you may have heard already, but that His Majesty the Emperor has now taken me into his service [2] will probably be news to you. I am sure you will be pleased to hear it. Will you please send me the box with my scores as soon as possible? As for recent clavier music of my own, will you please note down the themes of the pieces I have sent you from Vienna and send them to me, so that I may not send you anything twice over? This will be to your advantage as well as to mine.

Well, good-bye, dear sister. Write to me frequently. If I don't always answer promptly, put it down not to any negligence on my part, but simply to stress of work. Adieu. I embrace you with all my heart and am ever your sincerely affectionate brother

W: A: MOZART

A thousand kisses from my wife, who is expecting to be confined any moment.[3] All sorts of messages to your dear husband from us both.

(553) *Mozart to Michael Puchberg*[4]

[*From Nottebohm, Mozartiana, p. 55*][5]

DEAREST BROTHER![6]   [VIENNA, *June* 1788]
Your true friendship and brotherly love embolden me to ask a great favour of you. I still owe you eight ducats. Apart from the fact that at the

---

[1] See p. 908, n. 3. For a full account of the Natorp family and their connection with the Jacquins and Mozart see Deutsch–Oldman, *ZMW*, xiv., and Hedwig Kraus, *ZMW*, xv.

[2] Mozart's appointment as Kammerkomponist to the Emperor Joseph II dated from 7 December 1787. His yearly income was 800 gulden. Gluck, his predecessor, had received 2000 gulden.

[3] The Mozarts' fourth child, a daughter christened Theresia, was born on December 27th. She died six months later, on 29 June 1788.

[4] Michael Puchberg was a wealthy merchant of Vienna and a talented musician. He was closely connected with several Masonic Lodges, though not with the particular Lodge 'Zur Wohltätigkeit', of which Mozart had become a member in December 1784. For a very full account of Mozart's connections with the leading Freemasons in Vienna and the works he composed for their festive occasions, see Otto Erich Deutsch, *Mozart und die Wiener Logen*, Vienna, 1932.

[5] The earliest source for most of Mozart's letters to Puchberg is Nottebohm's *Mozartiana*, Leipzig, 1880, which, however, rarely quotes any dates. The present arrangement of these letters follows that of Ludwig Schiedermair, which is based on Spitta's article, 'Zur Herausgabe der Briefe Mozarts', in the *AMZ*, 1880, p. 402 f. The letters appear complete in *MBA*.

[6] i.e. Brother Freemason.

moment I am not in a position to pay you back this sum, my confidence in you is so boundless that I dare to implore you to help me out with a hundred gulden until next week, when my concerts in the Casino are to begin. By that time I shall certainly have received my subscription money[1] and shall then be able quite easily to pay you back 136 gulden with my warmest thanks.

I take the liberty of sending you two tickets which, as a brother, I beg you to accept without payment, seeing that, as it is, I shall never be able adequately to return the friendship which you have shown me.

Once more I ask your forgiveness for my importunity and with greetings to your esteemed wife I remain in true friendship and fraternal love, your most devoted brother

W. A. MOZART[2]

(554) *Mozart to Michael Puchberg*

[Autograph in the Koch Collection, Basel]

[VIENNA, before 17 June 1788]

MOST HONOURABLE BROTHER OF THE ORDER,[3]

DEAREST, MOST BELOVED FRIEND!

The conviction that you are *indeed my friend* and that you know me to be *a man of honour* encourages me to open my heart to you completely and to make you the following request. In accordance with my natural frankness I shall go straight to the point without affectation.

If you have sufficient regard and friendship for me to assist me for a year or two with one or two thousand gulden, at a suitable rate of interest, you will help me enormously! You yourself will surely admit *the sense and truth* of my statement when I say that it is difficult, nay impossible, to live when one has to wait for various odd sums. If one has not at least *a minimum of capital* behind one, it is impossible to keep one's affairs in order. *Nothing* can be done with nothing. If you will do me this kindness then, *primo*, as I shall have some money to go on with, I can meet necessary expenses *whenever they occur*, and therefore *more easily*, whereas now I have to *postpone* payments and then often *at the most awkward time* have to spend *all I receive at one go*; *secondo*, I can work with a mind *more free* from care and *with a lighter heart*, and thus *earn more*. As to security I do not suppose that you will have any doubts. You know more or less how I stand and you know *my principles*. You need not be anxious about the subscription:

---

[1] Mozart refers to his three string quintets, K. 406 [516b], 515, 516 of which copies were first offered on subscription in April 1788, the offer being later extended to January 1789. Tickets were on sale to subscribers at Puchberg's house.

[2] Puchberg noted on this letter, 'sent 100 gulden'.

[3] i.e. of Freemasons.

I am now extending the time by a few months.[1] I have hopes of finding more patrons *abroad* than *here*.

I have now opened my *whole* heart to you in a matter which is of the utmost importance to me; that is, I have acted as a *true brother*. But it is only with a *true brother* that one can be *perfectly* frank. And now I look forward eagerly to your reply, which I do hope will be *favourable*. I do not know, but I take you to be *a man* who, provided he can do so, will like *myself* certainly assist a friend, if he be a *true* friend, or his brother, if he be *indeed a brother*. If you should find it inconvenient to part with so large a sum at once, then I beg you to lend me until tomorrow *at least a couple of hundred gulden*, for my landlord in the Landstrasse has been so importunate that in order to avoid an unpleasant incident I have had to pay him on the spot, and this has made things very awkward for me! We are sleeping tonight, for the first time, in our new quarters, where we shall remain both summer and winter.[2] On the whole the change is all the same to me, in fact I prefer it. As it is, I have very little to do in town and, as I am not exposed to so many visitors, I shall have more time for work. If I have to go to town on business, which will certainly not be very often, any fiacre will take me there for ten kreuzer. Moreover our rooms are cheaper and during the spring, summer and autumn *more pleasant*, as I have a garden too. The address is Währingergasse, bei den Drei Sternen, No. 135.[3] Pray regard this letter as a real proof of my complete confidence in you and remain ever my friend and brother as I shall be until the grave, your true, most devoted friend and brother

W. A. MOZART[4]

PS.—When are we to have a little musical party at your house again? I have composed a new trio![5]

(555) *Mozart to Michael Puchberg*

[*Copy in the Staatsbibliothek Preussischer Kulturbesitz, West Berlin*]

MOST HONOURABLE B.O.,[6]   [VIENNA, 27 *June* 1788]
DEAREST, MOST BELOVED FRIEND!

I have been expecting to go to town myself one of these days and to be able to thank you in person for the kindness you have shown me. But

---

[1] Cf p. 915, n. 1.
[2] The Mozarts had left the Landstrasse early in December 1787, as their fourth child was born on 27 December in a house 'Unter den Tuchlauben 281' (now no. 27). They moved again into a house in a street somewhat outside the town.
[3] Now Währingerstrasse no. 16.
[4] Puchberg noted on this letter, 'sent 200 gulden on 17 June 1788'.
[5] K. 542, piano trio in E major.   [6] i.e. Brother of the Order.

now I should not even have the courage to appear before you, as I am obliged to tell you frankly that it is impossible for me to pay back so soon the money you have lent me and that I must beg you to be patient with me! I am very much distressed that your circumstances at the moment prevent you from assisting me as much as I could wish, for my position is so serious that I am unavoidably obliged to raise money somehow. But, good God, in whom can I confide? In no one but you, my best friend! If you would only be so kind as to get the money for me through some other channel! I shall willingly pay the interest and whoever lends it to me will, I believe, have sufficient security in my character and my income.[1] I am only grieved to be in such an extremity; but that is the very reason why I should like a *fairly substantial* sum for a *somewhat longer period*, I mean, in order to be able to prevent a recurrence of this state of affairs. If you, my most worthy brother, do not help me in this predicament, I shall lose my honour and my *credit*, which of all things I wish to preserve. I rely entirely on your genuine friendship and brotherly love and confidently expect that you will stand by me in word and deed. If my wish is fulfilled, I can breathe freely again, because I shall then be able to put my affairs in order and *keep them so*. Do come and see me. I am always at home. During the ten days since I came to live here I have done more work than in two months in my former quarters, and if such black thoughts did not come to me so often, thoughts which I banish by a tremendous effort, things would be even better, for my rooms are pleasant—comfortable—and— *cheap*. I shall not detain you any longer with my drivel but shall *stop talking*—and *hope*.

Ever your grateful servant, true friend and B.O.

W. A. Mozart

27 June 1788.

(556) *Mozart to Michael Puchberg*

[*Copy in the Staatsbibliothek Preussischer Kulturbesitz, West Berlin*]

Dearest Friend and B.O.,   [Vienna, *beginning of July*, 1788]

Owing to great difficulties and complications my affairs have become so involved that it is of the utmost importance to raise some money on these two pawnbroker's tickets. In the name of our friendship I implore you to do me this favour; but you must do it immediately. Forgive my importunity, but you know my situation. Ah! If only you had done what I asked you! Do it even now—then everything will be as I desire.

Ever your

Mozart

(557) Mozart to his Sister

[From Ludwig Nohl, Mozarts Briefe, 2nd edition, p. 431[1]]

DEAREST SISTER!　　　　　　　　　　　　[VIENNA, 2 August 1788]

Indeed you have every reason to be vexed with me! But will you really be so, when you receive by this mail coach my very latest compositions for the clavier?[2] Surely not! This, I hope, will make everything all right again.

As you must be convinced that every day I wish you every possible happiness, you will forgive me for limping along rather behind with my congratulations on your name-day.[3] Dearest sister, with my whole heart and soul I wish you all that you believe is most advantageous to yourself. So now *Punctum*.

Dear sister! You must realize that I have a great deal to do. Besides, you know very well that I am rather lazy about letter-writing. So do not take it amiss, if I *seldom* write to you. But this must not prevent you from writing very often to *me*. Indeed, though I detest writing letters, I love getting them. Moreover you have far more to write about than I have, for Salzburg affairs interest me more than what is happening in Vienna can interest you.

Well, I have a request to make. I should very much like Haydn[4] to lend me for a short time his two Tutti-masses and the Graduale which he has composed, all of them in the original scores. Tell him that I shall return them with many thanks. It is now exactly a year since I wrote to him and invited him to come and stay with me; but he has not replied. As a matter of fact, as far as answering letters is concerned, he seems, don't you think, to have a good deal in common with myself. So I urge you to arrange this for me in the following way. Invite him to your house at St. Gilgen and play to him some of my latest compositions. I am sure he will like the Trio and the Quartet.[5] Adieu, dearest sister! As soon as I can collect some new music again, I shall send it to you. I am ever your sincere brother

W: A: MOZART

PS.—My wife sends her love to you and we both send ours to our dear brother-in-law.

PS.—In reply to your question about my appointment, I must tell you that the Emperor has taken me into his household. I now have therefore a permanent appointment, but *for the time being* at a salary of only 800 gulden. However, no one else in the household is drawing *so large a sum*. The notice which was printed at the time when my Prague opera 'Don

---

[1] Autograph in the Kestner Collection, Stadtbibliothek, Hannover.
[2] Perhaps K. 540, adagio in B minor, K. 545, sonata in C major, and K. 547, clavier and violin sonata in F major.　　　　　[3] 26 July.　　　　　[4] Michael Haydn.
[5] Probably K. 542, piano trio in E major, and K. 493, piano quartet in E♭. See Köchel, p. 615.

Giovanni' (which by the way is being given again today) was performed and on which there are certainly not *too many* particulars about me, for the management of the Imperial Theatre were responsible for it, stated:— 'The music is by Herr Mozart, duly-appointed Kapellmeister to His Imperial Majesty'.

(558) *Mozart to Franz Hofdemel*[1]

[*Autograph sold by Leo Liepmannssohn, Berlin, 16 November, 1928, Catalogue 52*]

DEAREST FRIEND!   [VIENNA, *end of March*, 1789]

I am taking the liberty of asking you without any hesitation for a favour. I should be very much obliged to you if you could and would lend me a hundred gulden until the 20th of next month. On that day I receive the quarterly instalment of my salary and shall then repay the loan with thanks. I have relied too much on a sum of a hundred ducats due to me from abroad. Up to the present I have not yet received it, although I am expecting it daily. Meanwhile I have left myself too short of cash, so that *at the moment* I greatly need some ready money and have[2] therefore appealed to your goodness, for I am absolutely convinced of your friendship.

Well, we shall soon be able to call one another by *a more delightful name!* For your novitiate is very nearly at an end![3]

MOZART[4]

(559) *Mozart to his Wife*

[*From Nottebohm, Mozartiana, p. 83*[5]]

DEAREST LITTLE WIFE!   BUDWITZ [8 *April* 1789]

While the Prince[6] is busy bargaining about horses, I am delighted to seize this opportunity to write a few lines to you, dearest little wife of my heart. How are you? I wonder whether you think of me as often as I think of you? Every other moment I look at your portrait—and weep partly for

---

[1] Franz Hofdemel, private secretary to a certain Count Seilern, held later as 'Justizkanzlist' an appointment in the Vienna Law Courts. He married Magdalene Pokorny, the daughter of Kapellmeister Gotthard Pokorny and a pupil of Mozart's. Shortly after the latter's death Hofdemel in a fit of jealousy attempted to murder his wife, an incident which gave rise to a rumour that she had been Mozart's mistress.

[2] Prince Karl Lichnowsky had offered to take Mozart to Berlin and introduce him to King Frederick William II. Evidently Mozart needed money for this journey.

[3] Hofdemel had joined the Order of Freemasons.

[4] Hofdemel acceded to Mozart's request and Mozart sent him a receipt dated 2 April 1789, and a promise to repay the sum within four months.

[5] Portion of autograph in a private collection, Switzerland.

[6] Prince Karl Lichnowsky, a son-in-law of Countess Wilhelmine Thun, was a pupil and friend of Mozart's.

joy, partly for sorrow. Look after your health which is so precious to me and fare well, my darling! Do not worry about me, for I am not suffering any discomforts or any annoyance on this journey—apart from your *absence*—which, as it can't be helped, can't be remedied. I write this note with eyes full of tears. Adieu. I shall write a longer and more legible letter to you from Prague, for then I shan't have to hurry so much. Adieu. I kiss you millions of times most tenderly and am ever yours, true till death

stu—stu—

MOZART

Kiss Karl for me and give all sorts of messages to Herr and Frau von Puchberg. More very soon.

(560) *Mozart to his Wife*

[Copy in the Staatsbibliothek Preussischer Kulturbesitz, West Berlin]

PRAGUE, Good Friday, 10 April 1789

DEAREST, MOST BELOVED LITTLE WIFE!

We arrived here safely today at half past one in the afternoon. Meanwhile I trust that you have received my little note from Budwitz. Now for my account of Prague. We alighted at the 'Unicorn' and after I had been shaved, had my hair done and got dressed, I drove out to Canal's[1] on the chance of having a meal with him. But as my drive took me past the Duscheks', I called there first and was told that Madame had left yesterday for Dresden! So I shall meet her there. Duschek was lunching at Leliborn's, where I too used often to lunch. So I drove straight there. I sent in a message to Duschek, just as if someone or other wished to speak to him, and asked him to come out. You can just imagine our delight. So I lunched at Leliborn's. After it was over I drove off to Canal and Pachta,[2] but they were both out. So I went on to Guardasoni,[3] who has practically arranged to give me 200 ducats next autumn for the opera and 50 ducats for travelling expenses.[4] Then I came home to write all this to my dear little wife. That reminds me. Only a week ago Ramm left Prague to return home. He came from Berlin and said that the King[5] had frequently and insistently enquired whether it was certain that I was coming to Berlin, as I had not yet appeared. He had said a second time: 'I fear that

---

[1] Count Canal. See p. 903, n. 3.
[2] Count Johann von Pachta. See p. 304, n. 1.
[3] Domenico Guardasoni had been manager of the National Theatre at Prague since 1788. In 1789 he went to Warsaw to organise theatrical productions there, and only returned to Prague in 1791.   [4] This commission was never carried out.
[5] King Frederick William II, who was an excellent performer on the violoncello and a great lover and active patron of music.

he will not come at all'. Ramm became very uneasy and tried to convince him that I really was coming. Judging by this, my affairs ought to be fairly successful. I am now taking the Prince[1] to see Duschek, who is expecting us, and at nine o'clock we are starting off for Dresden, where we hope to arrive tomorrow evening. Dearest little wife! I am simply aching for news of you. Perhaps I shall find a letter at Dresden! Great God, fulfil my wishes! When you receive this letter you must write to me at Leipzig—Poste Restante, of course. Adieu, my love, I must close, or I shall miss the post. Kiss our Karl a thousand times and I, who kiss you most ardently,

remain ever your faithful

MOZART

PS.—All sorts of messages to Herr and Frau von Puchberg. I must wait until I get to Berlin to write and thank him.

Adieu, aimez-moi et gardez votre sante si chere et precieuse a votre epaux.

(561) *Mozart to his Wife*

[Copy in the Staatsbibliothek Preussischer Kulturbesitz, West Berlin[2]]

DRESDEN, 13 April 1789
At seven o'clock in the morning

DEAREST, MOST BELOVED LITTLE WIFE!

We expected to reach Dresden after dinner on Saturday, but we did not arrive until yesterday, Sunday, at two o'clock in the afternoon, because the roads were so bad. All the same I went yesterday to the Neumanns,[3] where Madame Duschek is staying, in order to deliver her husband's letter. Her room is on the third floor beside the corridor and from it you can see anyone who is coming to the house. When I arrived at the door, Herr Neumann was already there and asked me to whom he had the honour to speak. 'That I shall tell you in a moment,' I replied, 'but please be so kind as to call Madame Duschek, so that my joke may not be spoilt.' But at the same moment Madame Duschek stood before me for she had recognized me from the window and had said at once: 'Why here comes someone who is very like Mozart'. Well, we were all delighted. There was a large party, consisting entirely of ugly women, who by their charm, however, made up for their lack of beauty. The Prince and I are going to breakfast there today; we shall then see Naumann[4] and then the

---

[1] Prince Karl Lichnowsky.
[2] Autograph in the Pierpont Morgan Library, New York City.
[3] Johann Leopold Neumann, secretary to the Saxon War Council, wrote and translated opera texts. His wife was an excellent pianist.
[4] Johann Gottlieb Naumann (1741–1801), a prolific composer of operas and church music. He studied in Italy under Tartini and Padre Martini, and in 1776 was appointed Kapellmeister

chapel. Tomorrow or the day after we shall leave for Leipzig. After receiving this letter you must write to Berlin, Poste Restante. I trust that you got my letter from Prague. All the Neumanns and the Duscheks send their greetings to you and also to my brother-in-law Lange and his wife. Dearest little wife, if only I had a letter from you! If I were to tell you all the things I do with your dear portrait, I think that you would often laugh. For instance, when I take it out of its case, I say, 'Good-day, Stanzerl!—Good-day, little rascal, pussy-pussy, little turned-up nose, little bagatelle, Schluck und Druck', and when I put it away again, I let it slip in very slowly, saying all the time, 'Nu—Nu—Nu—Nu!' with the peculiar *emphasis* which this word so full of meaning demands, and then just at the last, quickly, 'Good night, little mouse, sleep well'. Well, I suppose I have been writing something very foolish (to the world at all events); but to us who love each other so dearly, it is not foolish at all. Today is the sixth day since I left you and by Heaven! it seems a year. I expect you will have some difficulty here and there in reading my letter, because I am writing in a hurry and therefore rather badly. Adieu, my only love! The carriage is waiting. This time I do not say: 'Hurrah—the carriage has come at last', but *'male'*.[1] Farewell, and love me for ever as I love you. I kiss you a million times most lovingly and am ever your husband who loves you tenderly

W: A: MOZART

PS.—How is our Karl behaving? Well, I hope. Kiss him for me. All sorts of kind messages to Herr and Frau von Puchberg. Remember, you must not regulate the length of your letters by that of mine. Mine are rather short, but only because I am in a hurry. If I were not, I should cover a whole sheet. But you have more leisure. Adieu.

(562) *Mozart to his Wife*

[Copy in the Deutsche Staatsbibliothek, Berlin]

DRESDEN, 16 *April* 1789
DEAREST, MOST BELOVED LITTLE WIFE!   Half past eleven at night
What? Still in Dresden? Yes, my love. Well, I shall tell you everything as minutely as possible. On Monday, April 13th, after breakfasting with the Neumanns we all went to the Court chapel. The mass was by Naumann, who conducted it himself, and very poor stuff it was. We

and in 1786 Oberkapellmeister to the Dresden Court. During a stay in Stockholm, from 1777, he produced two of his best works *Amphion* and *Cora*, the Swedish texts of which were subsequently translated into German by J. L. Neumann.   [1] i.e. Confound it!

were in an oratory opposite the orchestra. All of a sudden Neumann nudged me and introduced me to Herr von König, who is the Directeur des Plaisirs (of the melancholy plaisirs of the Elector). He was extremely nice and when he asked me whether I should like His Highness to hear me, I replied that it would indeed be a great privilege, but that, as I was not travelling alone, I could not prolong my stay. So we left it at that. My princely travelling companion invited the Neumanns and Madame Duschek to lunch. While we were at table a message came that I was to play at court on the following day, Tuesday, April 14th, at half past five in the evening. That is something quite out of the ordinary for Dresden, for it is usually very difficult to get a hearing, and you know that I never thought of performing at Court here. We had arranged a quartet among ourselves at the Hôtel de Pologne. So we performed it in the Chapel with Anton Teiber (who, as you know, is organist here) and with Herr Kraft,[1] Prince Esterházy's cellist, who is here with his son.[2] At this little concert I introduced the trio[3] which I wrote for Herr von Puchberg and it was played quite decently. Madame Duschek sang a number of arias from 'Figaro' and 'Don Giovanni'. The next day I played at Court my new concerto in D,[4] and on the following morning, Wednesday, April 15th, I received a very handsome snuff-box. Then we lunched at the Russian Ambassador's, where I played a great deal. After lunch we agreed to have some organ playing and drove to the church at four o'clock— Naumann was there too. At this point you must know that a certain Hässler,[5] who is organist at Erfurt, is in Dresden. Well, he too was there. He is a pupil of a pupil[6] of Bach's. His forte is the organ and the clavier (clavichord). Now people here think that because I come from Vienna, I am quite unacquainted with this style and mode of playing. Well, I sat down at the organ and played. Prince Lichnowsky, who knows Hässler very well, after some difficulty persuaded him to play also. This Hässler's chief excellence on the organ consists in his foot-work, which, since the pedals are graded here, is not so very wonderful. Moreover, he has done no more than commit to memory the harmony and modulations of old Sebastian Bach and is not capable of executing a fugue properly; and his

[1] Anton Kraft (1749–1820), a distinguished cellist. He studied in Vienna, where Haydn secured him for the orchestra of Prince Esterházy. On the latter's death in 1790 Kraft became chamber musician to Prince Grassalkowics, and in 1795 to Prince Lobkowitz, in whose service he died. He composed several works for his instrument.

[2] Nicolaus Kraft (1778–1853), son of Anton Kraft. He early became proficient on the cello, accompanied his father on concert tours and in 1790 settled with him in Vienna, where he was one of Prince Karl Lichnowsky's famous quartet. He was a more gifted composer than his father.

[3] K. 563, a divertimento for violin, viola and cello, composed in 1788.

[4] K. 537, clavier concerto in D major, composed in 1788.

[5] Johann Wilhelm Hässler (1747–1822), who enjoyed a great reputation as an organist and had already won success by his performances at Dresden in 1788.

[6] Johann Christian Kittel (1732–1809), one of the last pupils of Johann Sebastian Bach. He was organist first at Langensalza and later at the Dominican Church in Erfurt, his native town.

playing is not thorough. Thus he is far from being an Albrechtsberger.[1] After that we decided to go back to the Russian Ambassador's, so that Hässler might hear me on the fortepiano. He played too. I consider Mlle Auernhammer as good a player on the fortepiano as he is, so you can imagine that he has begun to sink very considerably in my estimation. After that we went to the opera, which is truly wretched. Do you know who one of the singers is? Why—Rosa Manservisi.[2] You can picture her delight at seeing me. But the leading woman singer, Madame Allegranti,[3] is far better than Madame Ferraresi,[4] which, I admit, is not saying very much. When the opera was over we went home. Then came the happiest of all moments for me. I found a letter from you, that letter which I had longed for so ardently, my darling, my beloved! Madame Duschek and the Neumanns were with me as usual. I immediately went off in triumph to my room, kissed the letter countless times before breaking the seal, and then devoured it rather than read it. I stayed in my room a long time; for I could not read it or kiss it often enough. When I rejoined the company, the Neumanns asked me whether I had had a letter from you, and when I said that I had, they all congratulated me most heartily—for every day I had been lamenting that I had not yet had any news. They are delightful people. Now for your dear letter. For you shall receive shortly an account of what will have taken place here up to the time of our departure.

Dear little wife, I have a number of requests to make.

(1) I beg you not to be melancholy,

(2) *to take care of your health* and *to beware of* the spring breezes,

(3) not to go out walking alone—and preferably not to *go out walking* at all,

(4) to feel absolutely assured of my love. Up to the present I have not written a single letter to you without placing your dear portrait before me.

(5) I beg you in your conduct not only to be careful of *your honour* and *mine*, but also to consider *appearances*. Do not be angry with me for asking this. You ought to love me even more for thus valuing our honour.

---

[1] Johann Georg Albrechtsberger (1736–1809), organist and composer. He was appointed in 1772 Court organist at Vienna and in 1791 assistant to the Kapellmeister at St. Stephen's, Leopold Hofmann. He was also a famous teacher and the author of a great theoretical work, *Grundliche Anweisung zur Composition*, Leipzig, 1790.

[2] Rosa Manservisi took the part of Sandrina in Mozart's *La finta giardiniera*, which was performed at Munich in 1775.

[3] Maddalena Allegranti, a famous soprano singer of the eighteenth century. She studied under Holzbauer at Mannheim and made her first appearance in Venice in 1770, and from that time sang frequently in Italy. She performed in England in 1781.

[4] Adriana Ferraresi del Bene first appeared in Vienna in 1788 in Martin's *L'arbore di Diana*. For the revival of *Le nozze di Figaro* in August 1789 Mozart composed for her the rondo 'Al desio di chi t'adora' and the aria 'Un moto di gioia', sung by Susanna. He also wrote for her the part of Fiordiligi in *Cosi fan tutte*, which was performed on 26 January 1790.

(6) and lastly I beg you to send me more details in your letters. I should very much like to know whether our brother-in-law Hofer came to see us the day after my departure? Whether he comes very often, as he promised me he would? Whether the Langes come sometimes? Whether progress is being made with the portrait?[1] What sort of life you are leading? All these things are naturally of great interest to me.

Now farewell, dearest, most beloved! Please remember that every night before going to bed I talk to your portrait for a good half hour and do the same when I awake. We are leaving on the 18th, the day after tomorrow. *So continue to write to Berlin, Poste Restante.*

O Stru! Stri! I kiss and squeeze you 1095060437082 times (now you can practise your pronunciation) and am ever your most faithful husband and friend.

                                                             W. A. Mozart

The account of the rest of our Dresden visit will follow shortly. Good night!

(563) *Mozart to his Wife*

[*Autograph in the possession of Baron Peter Hatvany, London*]

Leipzig, 16 *May* 1789

Dearest, most beloved little Wife of my Heart!

What? Still in Leipzig?[2] My last letter, dated May 8th or 9th, told you, it is true, that I was leaving at two o'clock that night; but the insistent requests of my friends persuaded me not to make the whole of Leipzig suffer for the shortcomings of one or two persons, but to give a concert on Tuesday, the 12th. From the point of view of applause and glory this concert was absolutely magnificent, but the profits were wretchedly meagre. Madame Duschek, who happens to be in Leipzig, sang at it. The Neumanns of Dresden are all here too. The pleasure of being as long as possible in the company of these dear good people, who all send their best greetings to you, has up to the present delayed my journey. I wanted to get away yesterday, but could find no horses. I am having the same difficulty today. For at the present moment everyone is trying to get off, and the number of travellers is simply enormous. But we shall be on the road tomorrow at five o'clock. My love! I am very sorry and yet perhaps a little glad that you are in the same state as I have been. No, no! I would rather that you had never been in the same sad situation

---

[1] Possibly a lost portrait of Constanze.
[2] This letter was written during Mozart's second visit to Leipzig, whither he made a trip from Potsdam.

and I hope and trust that at the time I am writing this letter, you will have received at least *one* of mine. God knows what the cause may be! I received in Leipzig on April 21st your letter of April 13th. Then I spent seventeen days in Potsdam *without any letters*. Not until May 8th did I receive your letter of April 24th, while apart from this I have not received any, with the exception of one dated May 5th, which came yesterday. For my part I wrote to you from Leipzig on April 22nd, from Potsdam on the 28th, again from Potsdam on May 5th, from Leipzig on the 9th, and now I am writing on the 16th. The strangest thing of all is that we both found ourselves *at the same time in the same sad situation*. I was very anxious from April 24th until May 8th, and to judge from your letter this was also the time when you were worried. But I trust that by now you will have got over this. And my consolation is that soon letters will no longer be necessary, for we shall be able to talk to each other and kiss and press each other to our hearts. In my last letter I told you not to write to me any more; and that is the safest course. But I am now asking you to send a reply to this letter, and to address it to Duschek at Prague. You must put it in a proper *couvert* and ask him to keep it until my arrival. I shall probably *have* to spend at least a week in Berlin. So I shall not be able to reach Vienna before June 5th or 6th—that is, ten or twelve days after you receive this letter. One thing more about the loss of our letters. I also wrote to our dear friend Puchberg on April 28th. Please give him a thousand greetings from me and thank him on my behalf. I had no idea that Schmidt[1] was ill. You probably told me this in the letter which I did not receive. A thousand thanks for the account of Seydelmann's opera.[2] Indeed a more suitable name for him would be Maasmann. But if you knew him personally, as I do, you would probably call him Bluzermann, or at any rate, Zimmentmann.[3] Farewell, dear little wife. *Please do all the things I have asked you to do in my letters, for what prompted me was love—real, true love; and love me as much as I do you.* I am ever

your only true friend and faithful husband

W: A: Mozart

---

[1] Dr. Anton Schmith, a friend of Mozart's.

[2] Franz Seydelmann (1748–1806), a native of Dresden and a pupil of J. G. Naumann. After studying in Italy he was appointed in 1772 church composer in Dresden and in 1787 Kapellmeister. His opera *Il Turco in Italia*, produced at Dresden in 1788, was performed in Vienna on 28 April 1787. Evidently Constanze had seen it.

[3] The words 'Seidel, Maas, Bluzer, Zimment' are expressions in the Viennese dialect for drinking-measures. Mozart alludes, of course, to Seydelmann's tendency to drink.

(564) *Mozart to his Wife*

[*From Nottebohm, Mozartiana,* p. 33]

BERLIN, 19 *May* 1789[1]

DEAREST, MOST BELOVED LITTLE WIFE OF MY HEART!

Well, I trust that you will by now have received some letters from me, for they can't all have been lost. This time I can't write very much to you, as I have to pay some calls and I am only sending you this to announce my arrival. I shall probably be able to leave by the 25th; at least I shall do my best to do so. But I shall let you know definitely before then. I shall quite certainly get away by the 27th. Oh, how glad I shall be to be with you again, my darling! But the first thing I shall do is to take you by your front curls; for how on earth could you think, or even imagine, that I had forgotten you? How could I possibly do so? For even *supposing* such a thing, you will get on the very first night a thorough spanking on your dear little kissable arse, and this you may count upon.

Adieu.

Ever your only friend and your husband
who loves you with all his heart

W. A. MOZART

(565) *Mozart to his Wife*

[*Autograph in the Koch Collection, Basel*]

BERLIN, 23 *May* 1789

DEAREST, MOST BELOVED, MOST PRECIOUS LITTLE WIFE!

I was above measure delighted to receive here your dear letter of May 13th, and only this very moment your previous one of the 9th, which had to find its way from Leipzig to Berlin. Well, the first thing I am going to do is to make a list of all the letters which I sent you and then a list of the letters which I have received from you.

I wrote to you on April 8th from the post-stage Budwitz

On April 10th from Prague
On April 13th
and 17th } from Dresden
On April 22nd (in French) from Leipzig
On April 28th
and May 5th } from Potsdam

---

[1] For an account of Mozart's visit to Berlin, see an article by Ernst Friedländer, 'Mozart-Beziehungen zu Berlin', in *MMB*, April 1897.

On May 9th⎫
and 16th⎭ from Leipzig

On May 19th from Berlin

and I am now writing on the 23rd.[1]

That makes eleven letters.

I received your letter of April 8th on April 15th in Dresden
     „   „   of April 13th „ April 21st in Leipzig
     „   „   of April 24th „ May 8th in Leipzig ⎫ on my
     „   „   of May 5th   „ May 14th in Leipzig ⎭ retrn
     „   „   of May 13th „ May 20th in Berlin
     „   „   of May 9th „ May 22nd in Berlin

That makes six letters.

You see that there is a gap between April 13th and 24th. So one of your letters must have gone astray and thus I was without a letter for seventeen days. So if you too had to spend seventeen days in the same condition, one of my letters must have been lost. Thank God, we shall soon have got over these mischances. *In your arms* I shall be able to tell you all, all that I felt at that time. But you know how I love you. Well, where do you think I am writing this letter? In my room at the inn? Not at all. In a restaurant in the Tiergarten (in a summer-house with a lovely view) where I lunched today *all by myself*, in order to devote myself wholly to you. The Queen wants to hear me play on Tuesday, *but I shan't make much money*. I only announced my arrival because such is the custom here, and because she would have taken it amiss had I not done so. First of all, my darling little wife, when I return you must be more delighted with having me back than with the money I shall bring. A hundred friedrichs d'or are not nine hundred gulden but seven hundred—at least that is what they have told me here. Secondly, Lichnowsky (as he was in a hurry) left me here, and so I have had to pay for my keep in Potsdam, which is an expensive place. Thirdly, I had to lend him a hundred gulden, as his purse was getting empty. I could not well refuse him: you will know why. Fourthly, my concert at Leipig was a failure, as I always said it would be, so I had a journey of sixty-four miles there and back almost for nothing. Lichnowsky alone is to blame for this, for he gave me no peace but insisted on my returning to Leipzig. I shall tell you more about this when we meet. But (1) if I gave a concert here I should not make much out of it and (2) the King would not care for me to give one. So you must just be satisfied *as I am with this*, that I am fortunate enough to be enjoying the King's favour. What I have just written to you is for ourselves alone. On Thursday, the 28th, I shall leave for Dresden, where I shall spend the night. On June 1st

[1] Mozart's four letters written between April 22nd and May 9th have unfortunately been lost.

I intend to sleep in Prague, and on the 4th—the 4th—with my darling little wife. Arrange your dear sweet nest very daintily, for my little fellow deserves it indeed, he has really behaved himself very well and is only longing to possess your sweetest. . . .[1] Just picture to yourself that rascal; as I write he crawls on to the table and looks at me questioningly. I, however, box his ears properly—but the rogue is simply . . .[1] and now the knave burns only more fiercely and can hardly be restrained. Surely you will drive out to the first post-stage to meet me? I shall get there at noon on the 4th. I hope that Hofer, whom I embrace a thousand times, will be with you. If Herr and Frau von Puchberg drive out with you too, then all the friends I want to see will be together. Don't forget to bring our Karl. But the most important thing of all is that you should have with you someone you can rely on (Satmann or someone else), who can drive off to the customs in my carriage with my luggage, so that *I* may not have to face that unnecessary seccatura, but can drive home with all you dear people. Now remember this.

Well, adieu. I kiss you millions of times and am ever your most faithful husband

W. A. MOZART[2]

(566) *Mozart to his Wife*

[*Autograph in the Nationalbibliothek, Vienna*]

DARLING, MOST BELOVED LITTLE WIFE!   PRAGUE, 31 *May* 1789

I have just arrived this very moment. I hope that you received my last letter of the 23rd. Well, the arrangement still stands. I shall arrive on Thursday, June 4th, between eleven and twelve o'clock at the last, or rather the first post-stage, where I hope to find you all. Do not forget to bring someone with you, who can drive to the customs instead of me. Adieu. Good God, how delighted I am to be seeing you again! In haste.

MOZART

(567) *Mozart to Michael Puchberg*

[*From Nottebohm, Mozartiana, pp. 12–14*]

[VIENNA] 12 *July* 1789

DEAREST, MOST BELOVED FRIEND AND MOST HONOURABLE B.O.

Great God! I would not wish my worst enemy to be in my present position. And if you, most beloved friend and brother, forsake me, we

---

[1] Each dotted passage represents a word which has been blotted out in the autograph.

[2] The autograph of this letter has the address 'Auf dem Hohen Markt, im Walseckischen Hause, bei Herrn von Puchberg'. This house belonged to Count Franz Walsegg-Stuppach for whom Mozart was to compose the Requiem in 1791. Puchberg had moved into this house at Hohe Markt 522 (now no. 1) in 1784. Probably Mozart's wife and child were living with the Puchbergs during his absence in Germany.

are altogether lost, *both my unfortunate and blameless self* and my poor sick wife and child. Only the other day when I was with you I was longing to open my heart to you, but I had not the courage to do so—and indeed I should still not have the courage—for, as it is, I only dare to write and I tremble as I do so—and I should not even dare to write, were I not certain that you know me, that you are aware of my circumstances, and that you are wholly convinced of my *innocence* so far as my unfortunate and most distressing situation is concerned. Good God! I am coming to you not with thanks but with fresh entreaties! Instead of paying my debts I am asking for more money! If you really know me, you must sympathize with my anguish at having to do so. I need not tell you once more that owing to my unfortunate illness I have been prevented from earning anything. But I must mention that in spite of my wretched condition I decided to give subscription concerts at home in order to be able to meet at least my present great and frequent expenses, for I was absolutely convinced of your friendly assistance. But even this has failed. Unfortunately Fate is so much against me, *though only in Vienna*, that even when I want to, I cannot make any money. A fortnight ago I sent round a list for subscribers and so far the only name on it is that of the Baron van Swieten! Now that (on the 13th) my dear little wife seems to be improving every day, I should be able to set to work again, if this blow, this heavy blow, had not come. At any rate, people are consoling me by telling me that she is better—although the night before last she was suffering so much—and I on her account—that I was stunned and despairing. But last night (the 14th), she slept so well and has felt so much easier all the morning that I am very hopeful; and at last I am beginning to feel inclined for work. I am now faced, however, with misfortunes of another kind, though it is true, only for the moment. Dearest, most beloved friend and brother—you know *my present circumstances*, but you also know *my prospects*. So let things remain as we arranged; that is, *thus or thus*, you understand what I mean. Meanwhile I am composing six easy clavier sonatas for Princess Friederike [1] and six quartets for the King,[2] all of which Kozeluch is engraving at my expense. At the same time the two dedications will bring me in something. In a month or two my fate must be decided *in every detail*. Therefore, most beloved friend, you will not be risking anything so far as I am concerned. So it all depends, my only friend, upon whether you will or can lend me another 500 gulden. Until my affairs are settled, I undertake to pay back ten gulden a month; and then, as this is bound to happen in a few months, I shall pay back the whole sum with whatever interest you may demand,

---

[1] Princess Friederike, the eldest daughter of King Frederick William II of Prussia. Mozart appears to have finished only one of these sonatas, K. 576, in D major, his last clavier sonata.
[2] Mozart finished three quartets, K. 575, composed in 1789, and K. 589 and 590, composed in 1790. K. 590 was Mozart's last string quartet. Kozeluch did not engrave these works, which were published by Artaria immediately after Mozart's death.

and at the same time acknowledge myself to be your debtor for life. That, alas, I shall have to remain, for I shall never be able to thank you sufficiently for your friendship and affection. Thank God, that is over. Now you know all. Do not be offended by my confiding in you and remember that unless you help me, the honour, the peace of mind, and perhaps the very life of your friend and brother Mason will be ruined.

Ever your most grateful servant, true

friend and brother

W. A. MOZART

At home, 14 July 1789.

O God!—I can hardly bring myself to despatch this letter!—and yet I must! If this illness had not befallen me, I should not have been obliged to beg so shamelessly from my only friend. Yet I hope for your forgiveness, for you know both the good *and the bad prospects of my situation*. The bad is temporary; the good will certainly persist, once the momentary evil has been alleviated. Adieu. For God's sake forgive me, only forgive me!— and—Adieu!

(568) *Mozart to Michael Puchberg*

[*Autograph formerly in the Musikhistorisches Museum von W. Heyer, Cologne*[1]]

DEAREST, MOST BELOVED FRIEND [VIENNA] 17 *July* 1789
AND MOST HONOURABLE B.O.

I fear you are angry with me, for you are not sending me a reply! When I compare the proofs of your friendship with my present demands upon it, I cannot but admit that you are perfectly right. But when I compare my misfortunes (for which I am not to blame) with your kindly disposition towards me, then I do find that there is some excuse for me. As in my last letter to you, my dear friend, I told you quite frankly everything that was burdening my heart, I can only repeat today what I said then. But I must still add that (1) I should not require such a considerable sum if I did not anticipate very heavy expenses in connexion with the cure my wife may have to take, particularly if she has to go to Baden.[2] (2) As I am positive that in a short time I shall be in better circumstances, the amount of the sum I shall have to repay is a matter of indifference to me. Nevertheless at the present moment I should prefer it to be a large sum, which would make me feel safer. (3) I entreat you, if it is quite impossible for you to assist me this time with such a large sum, to show your friendship and brotherly affection *by helping me at once with as much as you can spare*, for I am really in very great need. You certainly cannot doubt my

---

[1] Copy in the Staatsbibliothek Preussischer Kulturbesitz, West Berlin.
[2] A watering-place and health resort about seventeen miles south of Vienna.

integrity, for you know me too well for that. Nor can you distrust my assurances, my behaviour or my mode of life, as you are well acquainted with my manner of living and my conduct. Consequently forgive me for thus confiding in you, for I am absolutely convinced that only the *impossibility* of doing so will prevent you from helping your friend. If you can and if you will *entirely* relieve me, I shall return thanks to you as my saviour even beyond the grave, for you will be enabling me to enjoy further happiness on earth. But if you cannot do this, then I beg and implore you, in God's name, *for whatever temporary assistance you can give me* and also for your advice and comforting sympathy.

Ever your most grateful servant

MOZART

PS.—My wife was wretchedly ill again yesterday. Today leeches were applied and she is, thank God, somewhat better. I am indeed most unhappy, and am forever hovering between hope and fear! Dr. Closset came to see her again yesterday.[1]

(569) *Mozart to Michael Puchberg*

[*From Nottebohm, Mozartiana, p. 85*]

DEAREST FRIEND AND BROTHER!   [VIENNA, *second half of July*, 1789]
Since the time when you rendered me that great and friendly service, I have been living in such *misery*, that for very grief not only have I not been able to go out, but I could not even write.

At the moment she is easier, and if *she had not contracted bed-sores*, which make her condition most wretched, she would be able to sleep. The only fear is that the bone may be affected. She is extraordinarily resigned and awaits recovery or death with true philosophic calm. My tears flow as I write. Come and see us, most beloved friend, if you can; and, *if you can*, give me your advice and help *in the matter you know of*.

MOZART

(570) *Mozart to his Wife at Baden*[2]

[*From Nottebohm, Mozartiana, p. 35*]

DEAREST LITTLE WIFE!   [VIENNA, *first half of August,* 1789]
I was delighted to get your dear letter—and I trust that you received yesterday my second one together with the infusion, the electuaries and

---

[1] Puchberg noted on this letter, 'answered the same day, 17 July 1789, and sent 150 gulden.'
[2] This and the following letters to Constanze are addressed to her at Baden, where she had gone for her health.

the ants' eggs. I shall sail off to you at five o'clock tomorrow morning. Were it not for the joy of seeing you again and embracing you, I should not drive out to Baden just yet, for 'Figaro' is going to be performed very soon,[1] and as I have some alterations to make, my presence will be required at the rehearsals. I shall probably have to be back here by the 19th. But to stay here until the 19th *without you* would be quite impossible. Dear little wife! I want to talk to you quite frankly. You have no reason whatever to be unhappy. You have a husband who loves you and does all he possibly can for you. As for your foot, you must just be patient and it will surely get well again. I am glad indeed when you have some fun—of course I am—but I do wish that you would not sometimes make yourself so cheap. In my opinion you are too free and easy with N.N.[2] ... and it was the same with N.N., when he was still at Baden. Now please remember that N.N. are not half so familiar with other women, whom they perhaps know more intimately, as they are with you. Why, N.N. who is usually a well-conducted fellow and particularly respectful to women, must have been misled by your behaviour into writing the most disgusting and most impertinent sottises which he put into his letter. A woman must always make herself respected, or else people will begin to talk about her. My love! Forgive me for being so frank, but my peace of mind demands it as well as our mutual happiness. Remember that you yourself once admitted to me that you were inclined to *comply too easily*. You know the consequences of that. Remember too the promise you gave to me. Oh, God, do try, my love! Be merry and happy and charming to me. Do not torment yourself and me with unnecessary jealousy. Believe in my love, for surely you have proofs of it, and you will see how happy we shall be. Rest assured that it is only by her prudent behaviour that a wife can enchain her husband. Adieu. Tomorrow I shall kiss you most tenderly.

MOZART

(571) *Mozart to his Wife at Baden*

[From Nottebohm, Mozartiana, p. 27]

DEAREST LITTLE WIFE!   [VIENNA, ?19 *August*, 1789]

I arrived here safely at a quarter to eight[3] and when I knocked at my *door*—Hofer has written this, who happens to be here and sends you greetings—I found it closed, because the servant was not at home. I waited in vain for about a quarter of an hour, then I drove to Hofer's, imagined I was at home and finished dressing there. The little aria, which I composed

---

[1] See p. 924, n. 4.
[2] In this and the following letters to his wife certain names have been crossed out by a later hand.
[3] Mozart had been staying with his wife at Baden.

for Madame Ferraresi,[1] ought, I think, to be a success, provided she is able to sing it in an artless manner, which, however, I very much doubt. She herself liked it very much. I have just lunched at her house. I think that 'Figaro' will be performed on Sunday for certain, but I shall let you know beforehand. How delighted I am when we hear it together! I am off this very moment to see whether any change has possibly been made in the arrangements. If it is not going to be performed before Saturday, I shall be with you today. Adieu, my love! *Never* go out walking alone. The very thought of this terrifies me.

Ever your loving

MOZART

(572) *Mozart to Michael Puchberg*

[*From Nottebohm, Mozartiana*, p. 63]

MOST HONOURABLE FRIEND AND B.O.   [VIENNA, *December* 1789]

Do not be alarmed at the contents of this letter. Only to you, most beloved friend, who know everything about me and my circumstances, have I the courage to open my heart completely. According to the present arrangement I am to receive from the management next month 200 ducats for my opera.[2] If you can and will lend me 400 gulden until then, you will be rescuing your friend from the greatest embarrassment; and I give you my word of honour that by that time you will have the money back in full and with many thanks. In spite of the great expenses I have to incur daily, I should try to hold out until then, were it not the New Year, when I really must pay off the chemists and doctors, whom I am no longer employing, unless I wish to lose my good name. We have in particular alienated Hundschowsky[3] (for certain reasons) in a rather unfriendly fashion, so that I am doubly anxious to settle accounts with him. Beloved friend and brother!—I know only too well how much I owe you! I beg you to be patient a little longer in regard to my old debts. I shall certainly repay you, that I promise on my honour. Once more I beg you, rescue me just this time from my horrible situation. As soon as I get the money for my opera, you shall have the 400 gulden back for certain. And this summer, thanks to my work for the King of Prussia,[4] I hope to be able to convince you completely of my honesty. Contrary to our arrangement we cannot have any music at our house tomorrow—I have too much work. By the way,

---

[1] K. 579. See Köchel p. 654.
[2] *Così fan tutte*, performed on 26 January 1790.
[3] Johann Nepomuk Hunczowsky (1752–1798), Doctor and Professor at the military hospital at Gumpendorf, a suburb of Vienna. He was also a Freemason.
[4] See p. 930, n. 2.

if you see Zistler,[1] you might tell him this. But I invite you, you alone, to come along on Thursday at 10 o'clock in the morning to hear a short rehearsal of my opera.[2] I am only inviting Haydn and yourself. I shall tell you when we meet about Salieri's plots, which, however, have completely failed already. Adieu.

Ever your grateful friend and brother,

W. A. Mozart[3]

(573) *Mozart to Michael Puchberg*

[*From Nottebohm, Mozartiana, p. 57*]

Dearest Friend!   [Vienna, 20 *January* 1790]

They forgot to deliver at the proper time your last kind note. So I could not reply to it sooner. I am very much touched by your friendship and kindness. If you can and will send an extra hundred gulden, you will oblige me very greatly.

We are having the first instrumental rehearsal in the theatre tomorrow.[4] Haydn is coming with me. If your business allows you to do so and if you care to hear the rehearsal, all you need do is to be so kind as to turn up at my quarters at ten o'clock tomorrow morning and then we shall all go there together.

Your most grateful friend

W. A. Mozart[5]

20 January, 1790.

(574) *Mozart to Michael Puchberg*

[*From Nottebohm, Mozartiana, p. 56*]

Dearest Friend!   [Vienna, 20 *February* 1790]

Had I known that your supply of beer had almost run out, I should certainly never have ventured to rob you of it; I therefore take the liberty of returning herewith the second measure, as today I am already provided with wine. I thank you heartily for the first one, and the next time you have a supply of beer, pray send me a little of it. You know how much I like it. I beg you, most beloved friend, to lend me a few ducats just for a few days *if you can do so*, as I have to settle a matter at once which cannot

---

[1] Nottebohm, p. 64, n. 2, suggests the violinist, Joseph Zistler, who in 1782 became Konzertmeister at Pressburg.   [2] *Così fan tutte.*
[3] Puchberg noted on this letter, 'sent 300 gulden'.   [4] *Così fan tutte.*
[5] Puchberg noted on this letter, 'sent on the same day 100 gulden'.

be postponed. Forgive my importunity, which is prompted by my complete confidence in your friendship.

Ever your

MOZART [1]

(575) *Mozart to Michael Puchberg*

[From Nottebohm, Mozartiana, p. 87]

[VIENNA, *end of March or beginning of April,* 1790]
Herewith, dearest friend, I am sending you Handel's life.[2] When I got home from my visit to you the other day, I found the enclosed note from the Baron van Swieten.[3] You will gather from it, as I did, that my prospects are now better than ever.[4] I now stand on the threshold of my fortune; but the opportunity will be lost for ever, if this time I cannot make use of it. My present circumstances, however, are such that in spite of my excellent prospects I must abandon all hope of furthering my fortunes unless I can count on the help of a staunch friend. For some time you must have noticed my constant sadness—and only the very many kindnesses which you have already rendered me, have prevented me from speaking out. Now, however—once more, but for the last time—I call upon you to stand by me to the utmost of your power in this most urgent matter which is going to determine my whole happiness. You know how my present circumstances, were they to become known, would damage the chances of my application to the Court, and how necessary it is that they should remain a secret; for unfortunately at Court they do not judge by circumstances, but solely by appearances. You know, and I am sure you are convinced that if, as I may now confidently hope, my application is successful, you will certainly lose nothing. How delighted I shall be to discharge my debts to you! How glad I shall be to thank you and, in addition, to confess myself eternally your debtor! What a pleasant sensation it is to reach one's goal at last—and what a blessed feeling it is when one has helped another to do so! Tears prevent me from completing the picture! In short!—my whole future happiness is in your hands. Act according to the dictates of your noble heart! Do what you can and re-

---

[1] Puchberg noted on this letter, 'sent on 20 February 1790, 25 gulden'.
[2] Most probably John Mainwaring's *Memoirs of the Life of the late G. F. Handel*, 1760, which had appeared in 1761 in a German translation by Johann Mattheson.
[3] The Baron van Swieten was endeavouring to introduce Handel's oratorios to the Viennese public and had already given some performances in the large hall of the Hofbibliothek under the management of Joseph Starzer. On the latter's death in 1787 Mozart was entrusted with the organisation of these performances, and for this purpose reorchestrated Handel's *Acis and Galatea* in 1788, his *Messiah* in 1789, and his *Alexander's Feast* and *Ode on St. Cecilia's Day* in 1790. See also p. 736, n. 3.
[4] Since the death of Emperor Joseph II and the accession of Emperor Leopold II Mozart had greater hopes of being appointed Kapellmeister to the Viennese Court.

member that you are dealing with a right-minded and eternally grateful man, whose situation pains him even more on your account than on his own.

MOZART[1]

(576) *Mozart to Michael Puchberg*

[Copy in the Staatsbibliothek Preussischer Kulturbesitz, West Berlin[2]]

[VIENNA, *on or before* 8 *April* 1790]

You are right, dearest friend, not to honour me with a reply! My importunity is too great. I only beg you to consider my position from every point of view, to remember my cordial friendship and my confidence in you and to forgive me! But if you can and will extricate me from a temporary embarrassment, then, for the love of God, do so! Whatever you can easily spare will be welcome. If possible, forget my importunity and forgive me.

Tomorrow, Friday, Count Hadik[3] has invited me to perform for him Stadler's quintet[4] and the trio I composed for you.[5] Hering[6] is going to play. I would have gone to see you myself in order to have a chat with you, but my head is covered with bandages due to rheumatic pains, which make me feel my situation still more keenly. Again I beg you to help me as much as you can *just for this once*; and forgive me.

Ever your

MOZART[7]

(577) *Mozart to Michael Puchberg*

[From Nottebohm, Mozartiana, p. 57]

DEAREST FRIEND AND BROTHER,   [VIENNA, *on or before* 23 *April* 1790]

If you can send me something, even though it be only the small sum you sent me last time, you will greatly oblige your ever grateful friend and brother

MOZART[8]

---

[1] Puchberg noted on this letter, 'sent 150 gulden'.
[2] Autograph in a private collection.
[3] Count Johann Karl Hadik, Councillor to the Hungarian Exchequer.
[4] K. 581, quintet in A major for clarinet and strings, composed in 1789 for Anton Stadler (1753–1812), an excellent clarinettist for whom Mozart also wrote in 1791 his clarinet concerto in A major, K. 622.
[5] K. 563, divertimento in E♭ for violin, viola and violoncello, composed in 1788.
[6] A banker and amateur violinist.
[7] Puchberg noted on this letter, 'sent on 8 April 1790, 25 gulden in banknotes'.
[7] Puchberg noted on this letter, 'sent on 23 April, 25 gulden'.

(578) Mozart to Michael Puchberg

[From Nottebohm, Mozartiana, p. 62]

[VIENNA, *beginning of May*, 1790]

DEAREST, MOST BELOVED FRIEND AND BROTHER!

I am very sorry that I cannot go out and have a talk with you myself but my toothache and headache are still too painful and altogether I still feel very unwell. I share your view about getting some good pupils, but I thought of waiting until I should be in our new quarters,[1] as I intended to give lessons at home. In the meantime I beg you to tell people about this plan of mine. I am also thinking of giving subscription concerts at home during the three months of June, July and August. So it is only my present situation which is oppressing me. When I move out of these quarters, I shall have to pay 275 gulden towards my new home. But I must have something to live on until I have arranged my concerts and until the quartets[2] on which I am working have been sent to be engraved. So if only I had in hand 600 gulden at least, I should be able to compose with a fairly easy mind. And ah! I must have peace of mind. But what worries me dreadfully at the moment is a debt to the haberdasher in the Stock im Eisen,[3] who, although he at first saw my difficulty and said that he was content to wait, is now demanding payment urgently and impatiently. The debt amounts to 100 gulden. I wish with all my heart that I were rid of this unpleasant business. Well, I have made frank confession to you and I entreat you to do the utmost that your means and true friendship permit.

Ever your

MOZART[4]

(579) Mozart to Archduke Francis[5]

[Autograph in the Mozarteum, Salzburg]

YOUR ROYAL HIGHNESS,   [VIENNA, *during the first half of May*, 1790]

I make so bold as to beg your Royal Highness very respectfully to use your most gracious influence with His Majesty the King with regard to my most humble petition to His Majesty. Prompted by a desire for fame, by a love of work and by a conviction of my wide knowledge, I venture to apply for the post of second Kapellmeister, particularly as Salieri,[6] that

---

[1] The Mozarts moved on 30 September 1790 to the first floor of a house in the Rauhensteingasse 970 (now no. 8). It was here that Mozart died.

[2] K. 589 and 590. They were not engraved during Mozart's lifetime. See p. 930, n. 2.

[3] A small square adjoining the Stefansplatz in Vienna.

[4] Puchberg noted on this letter, 'sent 100 gulden'.

[5] This is the unfinished draft of a petition to the Archduke Francis to use his influence with his father, King Leopold II, who had succeeded to the throne on 13 March, 1790, and was crowned Holy Roman Emperor on 9 October.

[6] Salieri had been appointed Court Kapellmeister in 1788.

very gifted Kapellmeister, has never devoted himself to church music, whereas from my youth up I have made myself completely familiar with this style. The slight reputation which I have acquired in the world by my pianoforte playing, has encouraged me to ask His Majesty for the favour of being entrusted with the musical education of the Royal Family. In the sure conviction that I have applied to the most worthy mediators who, moreover, are particularly gracious to me, I am full of confidence and[1] . . .

(580) *Mozart to Michael Puchberg*

[*Copy in the Staatsbibliothek Preussischer Kulturbesitz, West Berlin*]

DEAREST FRIEND AND B.O.   [VIENNA, *on or before* 17 *May* 1790]

You will have heard, no doubt, from your household that I called on you yesterday, uninvited, as you had given me permission to do. You know how things are with me; in short, as I can find no true friends to help me, I am obliged to resort to moneylenders; but as it takes time to seek out the most Christian among this un-Christian class of people, I am at the moment so destitute that I must beg you, dearest friend, in the name of all that is sacred, to assist me with whatever you can spare. If, as I hope to do, I get the money in a week or a fortnight, I shall at once repay what you lend me now. Alas, I must still ask you to wait patiently for the sums I have already been owing you for such a long time. If you only knew what grief and worry all this causes me. It has prevented me all this time from finishing my quartets.[2] I now have great hopes of an appointment at court, for I have reliable information that the Emperor has not sent back my petition with a favourable or damning remark, as he has the others, but has retained it. That is a good sign. Next Saturday I intend to perform my quartets at home, and request the pleasure of your company and that of your wife. Dearest, most beloved friend and brother, do not withdraw your friendship because of my importunity, but stand by me. I rely wholly on you and am ever your most grateful

MOZART

PS.—I now have two pupils and should very much like to raise the number to eight. Do your best to spread the news that I am willing to give lessons.[3]

---

[1] The remainder of the autograph is increasingly illegible.
[2] See p. 938, n. 2.
[3] Puchberg noted on this letter, 'sent, on 17 May, 150 gulden'.

(581) *Mozart to his Wife at Baden*

[*From Nottebohm, Mozartiana*, p. 75]

[VIENNA,? 2 *June* 1790]

DEAREST LITTLE WIFE!   *Wednesday*

I trust that you have received my letter. Well, I must scold you a little, my love! Even if it is not possible for you to get a letter from me, you could write all the same; for must all your letters be *replies* to mine? I was most certainly expecting a letter from my dear little wife—but unfortunately I was mistaken. Well, you must make amends and I advise you to do so, otherwise I shall never, never forgive you. Yesterday I was at the second part of 'Cosa rara',¹ but I did not like it as much as 'Die Antons'.² If you return to Vienna on Saturday, you will be able to spend Sunday morning here. We have been invited to a service and to lunch at Schwechat.³ Adieu—Take care of your health. A propos. N.N. (you know whom I mean) is a cad. He is very pleasant to my face, but he runs down 'Figaro' in public—and has treated me most abominably in the matters you know of—*I know it for certain*.

Your husband, who loves you with all his heart,

MOZART

(582) *Mozart to Michael Puchberg*

[*From Nottebohm, Mozartiana*, p. 85]

DEAREST FRIEND AND B.O.,   [VIENNA, *on or before* 12 *June* 1790]

I have returned to town in order to conduct my opera.⁴ My wife is slightly better. She already feels some relief, but she will have to take the baths sixty times—and later on in the year she will have to go out there again. God grant that it may do her good. Dearest friend, if you can help me to meet my present urgent expenses, oh, do so! For economy's sake I am staying at Baden and only come into town when it is absolutely necessary. I have now been obliged to give away my quartets⁵ (those very difficult works) for a mere song, simply in order to have cash in hand to meet my present difficulties. And for the same reason I am now composing

---

¹ *Una cosa rara*, an opera composed by Vicente Martín y Soler (1754–1806), which, on its production in Vienna in November 1786, completely threw Mozart's *Figaro* into the shade. According to the monograph by O. E. Deutsch, *Das Wiener Freihaustheater*, Vienna, 1937, p. 16, the second part of this opera, *Der Fall ist noch weit seltner*, by Schikaneder and Schack, was first performed on 10 May 1790. Hence Mozart's letter must have been written after that date.
² *Der dumme Gärtner oder Die zween Anton*, an operetta by Benedict Schack (1758–1826), a Czech, who in 1784 had joined Schikaneder's theatre in Vienna. He was an excellent flautist, possessed a good tenor voice, and created the part of Tamino in Mozart's *Die Zauberflöte*.
³ A small village near Vienna, where Mozart's friend Joseph Eybler lived.
⁴ *Così fan tutte*.   ⁵ See p. 930, n. 2.

some clavier sonatas.[1] Adieu. Send me what you can most easily spare. One of my masses[2] is being performed tomorrow at Baden. Adieu. About ten o'clock.

Ever your

MOZART

PS.—Please send me the viola as well.[3]

(583) *Mozart to Michael Puchberg*

[*From Nottebohm, Mozartiana, p. 53*[4]]

DEAREST FRIEND AND BROTHER,   [VIENNA, 14 *August* 1790]

Whereas I felt tolerably well yesterday, I am absolutely wretched today. I could not sleep all night for pain. I must have got overheated yesterday from walking so much and then without knowing it have caught a chill. Picture to yourself my condition—ill and consumed by worries and anxieties. Such a state quite definitely prevents me from recovering. In a week or a fortnight I shall be better off—certainly—but at present I am in want! Can you not help me out with a trifle? The *smallest* sum would be very welcome just now. You would, for the moment at least, bring peace of mind to your true friend, servant and brother

W. A. MOZART[5]

(584) *Mozart to his Wife*[6]

[*Autograph in the Jewish National and University Library, Jerusalem*]

FRANKFURT AM MAIN, 28 *September* 1790

DEAREST, MOST BELOVED LITTLE WIFE OF MY HEART!

We have this moment arrived, that is, at one o'clock in the afternoon; so the journey has only taken us six days. We could have done it still more quickly, if on three occasions we had not rested a little at night. Well, we have just alighted at an inn in the suburb of Sachsenhausen, and are in the seventh heaven of delight at having secured a room. So far we do not yet know what our fate will be, I mean, whether we shall be together or be separated. If I cannot get a room anywhere for nothing, but if I find the

---

[1] Mozart's last complete clavier sonata was K. 576, composed in 1789, but the fragments K. App. 29, 30, 37 [590a–c] and the sonata movement K. 312 [590d] were probably intended for this set.

[2] Probably K. 317. See p. 950, n. 3.

[3] Puchberg noted on this letter, 'sent, on 12 June, 25 gulden'.

[4] Autograph formerly in the possession of Fritz Donebauer, Prague.

[5] Puchberg noted on this letter, 'sent, on 14 August 1790, 10 gulden'.

[6] This and the following letters were written from Frankfurt am Main, which Mozart visited in the hope of getting work in connection with the coronation of the Holy Roman Emperor Leopold II on 9 October. He took as his companion his wife's brother-in-law Franz de Paula Hofer. They left Vienna on September 23rd.

inns not too expensive, I shall certainly stay on here. I hope that you received my letter from Efferding.[1] I could not write more to you during our journey, as we stopped seldom and then only to rest. The journey was very pleasant, and we had fine weather except on one day; and even this one day caused us no discomfort, for my carriage (I should like to give it a kiss!) is splendid. At Regensburg we lunched magnificently to the accompaniment of divine music, we had angelic cooking and some glorious Moselle wine. We breakfasted at Nuremberg, a hideous town. At Würzburg, a fine, magnificent town, we fortified our precious stomachs with coffee. The food was tolerable everywhere, but at Aschaffenburg, two and a half stages from here, mine host was kind enough to fleece us disgracefully.

I am longing for news of you, of your health, our affairs and so forth. I am firmly resolved to make as much money as I can here and then return to you with great joy. What a glorious life we shall have then! I will work—work so hard—that no unforeseen accidents shall ever reduce us to such desperate straits again. I should like you to get Stadler to send N.N. to you about that matter. His last suggestion was that the money should be advanced on Hoffmeister's draft alone, that is, 1000 gulden in cash and the remainder in cloth. Then everything could be paid off, we should have a little over, and on my return I should have nothing to do but work. The whole business could be settled by a friend with carte blanche from me. Adieu. I kiss you a thousand times.

Ever your

Mzt

(585) *Mozart to his Wife*

[*Autograph formerly in the possession of Arturo Toscanini*[1]]

[Frankfurt am Main, 30 *September* 1790]
Dearest little Wife of my Heart!

If only I had a letter from you, all would be well. I hope that you have received mine from Efferding and Frankfurt. In my last one I told you to speak to Redcurrant Face.[2] For safety's sake I should very much like to raise 2000 gulden on Hoffmeister's draft. But you will have to give some other reason; you may say, for example, that I am making some speculation about which you know nothing. My love, there is no doubt whatever that I shall make something in this place, but certainly not as much as you and some of my friends expect. That I am both known and respected here is undeniable. Well, we shall see. But as in every case I

---

[1] There is no trace of this letter, which must have been sent off on 23 September.
[2] Copy in the Staatsbibliothek Preussischer Kulturbesitz, West Berlin.
[3] Probably Mozart's nickname for Anton Stadler.

prefer to play for safety. I should like to make that deal with H——,[1] as I shall thus obtain some money and not have to pay anything; all I shall have to do is to work and that I shall willingly do for the sake of my dear little wife. When you write to me, always address your letters, Poste Restante. Where do you think I am living? In the same house as Böhm,[2] and Hofer is with me too. We pay thirty gulden a month, which is wonderfully cheap, and we also take our meals there. And whom do you think I have come across? The girl who so often played hide-and-seek with us in the Auge Gottes. I think her name was Buchner. She is now Madame Porsch[3] and this is her second marriage. She asks me to send you all sorts of kind messages. As I do not know whether you are at Baden or Vienna, I am addressing this letter again to Madame Hofer.[4] I am as excited as a child at the thought of seeing you again. If people could see into my heart, I should almost feel ashamed. To me everything is cold— cold as ice. Perhaps if you were with me I might possibly take more pleasure in the kindness of those I meet here. But, as it is, everything seems so empty. Adieu, my love. I am ever your husband, who loves you with all his soul,

MOZART

Frankfurt am Main, 30 September 1790.

(586) *Mozart to his Wife*

[*From Nottebohm, Mozartiana*, p. 44]

FRANKFURT AM MAIN, 3 October 1790

DEAREST, MOST BELOVED LITTLE WIFE! *Sunday*

At last I feel comforted and happy. First of all, because I have had news from you, my love, news for which I was simply aching; and, secondly, on account of the reassuring information about my affairs. I have now made up my mind to compose at once the Adagio for the clockmaker[5] and then to slip a few ducats into the hand of my dear little wife. And this I have done; but as it is a kind of composition which I detest, I have unfortunately not been able to finish it. I compose a bit of it

---

[1] Hoffmeister.

[2] Johannes Böhm's theatrical company had been giving performances in Frankfurt since 1780. On 12 and 22 October they produced Mozart's *Die Entführung aus dem Serail* and *La finta giardiniera*, the latter in a German translation. Böhm was living in the Kalbächergasse near the theatre.

[3] Porsch was an actor at the Frankfurt National Theatre.

[4] Josefa, Constanze's eldest sister, who since 1788 had been married to Hofer.

[5] Probably K. 594, Adagio and Allegro in F minor and major for a mechanical organ, composed for Count Josef Deym, owner of the Müller waxworks, on the occasion of the exhibition of the effigy of the late Field-Marshal Laudon, who had died on 14 July 1790. For the same instrument Mozart wrote in 1791 K. 608, Fantasy in F minor, and K. 616, Andante in F major. See A. Hyatt King, *Mozart in Retrospect*, London 1956, pp. 198–215.

every day—but I have to break off now and then, as I get bored. And indeed I would give the whole thing up, if I had not such an important *reason to go on with it*. But I still hope that I shall be able to force myself gradually to finish it. If it were for a large instrument and the work would sound like an organ piece, then I might get some fun out of it. But, as it is, the works consist solely of little pipes, which sound too high-pitched and too childish for my taste.

Up to the present I have been living here altogether in retirement. Every morning I stay indoors in my hole of a bedroom and compose. My sole recreation is the theatre, where I meet several acquaintances from Vienna, Munich, Mannheim and even Salzburg. Franz Lang, the horn player, and Gres, the Treasurer, are here—and old Wendling too with his Dorothea. This is the way I should like best of all to go on living—but— I fear that it will soon come to an end and that I am in for a restless life. Already I am being invited everywhere—and however tiresome it may be to let myself be on view, I see nevertheless how necessary it is. So in God's name I submit to it. Well, it is probable that my concert may not be a failure. I wish it were over, if only to be nearer the time when I shall once more embrace my love! On Tuesday the theatrical company of the Elector of Mainz are performing 'Don Giovanni' in my honour.[1] Fare- well, my love. Give my greetings to the few friends who wish me well. Take care of your health which is so precious to me and be ever my Constanze as I shall ever be your

MOZART

Remember, keep on writing to me even though you only send me a few lines.

PS.—I lunched yesterday with Herr Schweitzer, the wealthiest banker in all Frankfurt. Mlle Crux is here too. I have not yet seen the girl, but Madame Quallenberg tells me that she has grown so tall and buxom that I shan't recognize her. Adieu.

The state entry takes place tomorrow—Monday, and the coronation a week later.[2]

(587) *Mozart to his Wife*

[Autograph in the Koch Collection, Basel]

[FRANKFURT AM MAIN, 8 October 1790]

DEAREST, MOST BELOVED LITTLE WIFE!

I have now had three letters from you, my love. That of September 28th has this moment arrived. I have not yet received the one you sent by

---

[1] This performance did not take place. But *Figaro* was performed during Mozart's stay at Frankfurt.
[2] The coronation took place on 9 October.

Herr von Alt, but I shall make enquiries about it at once at Le Noble's. You must now have had four letters from me.[1] This is the fifth. You will not be able to write to me any more, for in all probability when you read this letter I shall no longer be here, as I intend to give my concert on Wednesday or Thursday and then on Friday forthwith—tschiri-tschitschi —seek safety in flight! Dearest little wife! I trust that you have dealt with the business about which I wrote to you, and are still dealing with it. I shall certainly not make enough money here to be able to pay back 800 or 1000 gulden immediately on my return. But if the business with Hoffmeister is at least so far advanced that *only my presence* is required, then, after deducting interest at the rate of 20%, I shall have 1600 out of 2000 gulden. I can then pay out 1000 gulden and shall have 600 left. Well, I shall begin to give little quartet subscription concerts in Advent and I shall also take pupils. I need never repay the sum, *as I am composing* for Hoffmeister—so everything will be quite in order. But please settle the affair with Hoffmeister, that is, if you really want me to return. If you could only look into my heart. There a struggle is going on between my yearning and longing to see and embrace you once more and my desire to bring home a large sum of money. I have often thought of travelling *farther afield*, but whenever I tried to bring myself to take the decision, the thought always came to me, how bitterly I should regret it, if I were to separate myself from my beloved wife for *such an uncertain prospect, perhaps even to no purpose whatever.* I feel as if I had left you years ago. Believe me, my love, if you were with me I might perhaps decide more easily, but I am too much accustomed to you and I love you too dearly to endure being separated from you for long. Besides, all this talk about the Imperial towns is mere misleading chatter. True, I am famous, admired and popular here; on the other hand, the Frankfurt people are even more stingy than the Viennese. If my concert is at all successful, it will be thanks to *my name*, to Countess Hatzfeldt and the Schweitzer family who are working hard on my behalf. But I shall be glad when it is over. If I work very hard in Vienna and take pupils, we can live very happily; and nothing but a *good engagement at some court* can make me abandon this plan. But do your best with the help of *Red-currant Face*[2] or someone *else to conclude that business with Hoffmeister and to make known generally* my intention to take pupils. Then we shall certainly have enough to live on. Adieu, my love. You will still get a few more letters from me. But I, alas! can get no more from you.

Ever love your own

MOZART

Frankfurt am Main, 8 October 1790.

---

[1] See p. 942, n. 1.   [2] See p. 942, n. 2.

The Coronation is tomorrow.
Take care of your health—and be careful when you go out *walking*.
Adieu.

(588) *Mozart to his Wife*

[*From Nottebohm, Mozartiana,* p. 84]

[FRANKFURT AM MAIN, 15 *October* 1790]
DEAREST LITTLE WIFE OF MY HEART!
I have not yet received a reply to any of my letters from Frankfurt,
which makes me rather anxious. My concert took place at eleven o'clock
this morning.[1] It was a splendid success from the point of view of honour
and glory, but a failure as far as money was concerned. Unfortunately
some Prince was giving a big déjeuner and the Hessian troops were holding
a grand manœuvre. But in any case some obstacle has arisen on every day
during my stay here. You can't imagine how—.[2] But in spite of all these
difficulties I was in such good form and people were so delighted with me
that they implored me to give another concert next Sunday. I shall therefore leave on Monday. I must close this letter, or I shall miss the post. I
gather from your letters that you have not yet received any from me from
Frankfurt. Yet I sent you four. Moreover I seem to notice that you doubt
my punctuality or rather my eagerness to write to you, and this pains me
bitterly. Surely you ought to know me better. Good God! Only love me
half as much as I love you, and I shall be content. Ever your

Frankfurt, 15 October 1790.   MOZART

(589) *Mozart to his Wife*

[*Copy in the Staatsbibliothek Preussischer Kulturbesitz, West Berlin*[3]]

[MAINZ, 17 *October* 1790][4]
PS.—While I was writing the last page, tear after tear fell on the paper.
But I must cheer up—catch!—An astonishing number of kisses are flying
about—The deuce!—I see a whole crowd of them! Ha! Ha! . . . I have
just caught three—They are delicious!—You can still answer this letter,
but you must address your reply to Linz, Poste Restante—That is the
safest course. As I do not yet know for certain whether I shall go to

---

[1] Mozart played his piano concertos K. 459 and K. 537, the so-called Coronation Concerto.
A Mozart symphony was played also, probably K. 297 [300a], 319 or 385. See *MDB*, pp. 373 f.
[2] Nottebohm, the only source for this letter, omits the word or words. According to
Einstein they may be about the wretched performance of Margarete Schick (*née* Hampel),
who sang an aria and a duet with Ceccarelli.
[3] Autograph in the Brasch–Waksel Collection, Leningrad Public Library.
[4] The letter to which this is a postscript has unfortunately been lost.

Regensburg, I can't tell you anything definite. Just write on the cover that the letter is to be kept until called for. Adieu—Dearest, most beloved little wife—Take care of your health—and don't think of walking into town. Do write and tell me how you like our new quarters[1]—Adieu. I kiss you millions of times.

(590) *Mozart to his Wife*

[*From Nottebohm, Mozartiana*, p. 29]

MANNHEIM, 23 *October* 1790

DEAREST, MOST BELOVED LITTLE WIFE OF MY HEART!

We are going to Schwetzingen tomorrow to see the gardens. In the evening 'Figaro' will be given here for the first time. We shall leave the day after tomorrow. It is 'Figaro' which is responsible for my being here still, for the whole cast implored me to stay on and help them with the rehearsals. 'Figaro' too is the reason why I cannot write as much to you as I should like to, for it is just the time for the dress rehearsal. Why, the first act at least will already be over. I trust that you received my letter of the 17th from Mainz. The day before my departure I played before the Elector, but only received the meagre sum of fifteen carolins. Get things going so that that affair with Hoffmeister may be concluded. I now hope to embrace you for certain in a fortnight, that is, six or seven days after you receive this letter. But you will still get letters from me from Augsburg, Munich and Linz. You, however, cannot send any more letters to me. All the same if you write immediately after receiving this letter, I can still get your reply at Linz. Do try to do this. Now, farewell, dearest little wife! I kiss you a thousand times and am ever and unchangingly your faithful husband

MOZART

(591) *Mozart to his Wife*

[*Copy in the Staatsbibliothek Preussischer Kulturbesitz, West Berlin*]

[MUNICH, *before* 4 *November* 1790]

DEAREST, MOST BELOVED LITTLE WIFE OF MY HEART!

You have no idea how much it pains me that I have to wait until I get to Linz before I can have news from you. Patience; for if one does not know how long one is going to stay in a place, it is impossible to make better arrangements. Though I would have gladly prolonged my stay with my old Mannheim friends, I only wanted to spend a day here; but now I am obliged to remain until the 5th or 6th, for the Elector has asked me to perform at a concert which he is giving for the King of Naples. It is

[1] See p. 938, n. 1.

greatly to the credit of the Viennese Court that the King has to hear me in a foreign country.[1] You can well imagine that I have had a good time with the Cannabichs, Herr Le Brun, Ramm, Marchand and Brochard, and that we have talked a great deal about you, my love. I am looking forward to seeing you, for I have a great deal to discuss with you. I am thinking of taking this very same journey with you, my love, at the end of next summer, so that you may try some other waters. At the same time the company, the exercise and the change of air will do you good, for it has agreed very well with me. I am greatly looking forward to this, and so are all my friends.

Forgive me for not writing as much as I should like to, but you cannot conceive what a fuss they are making of me. I must now be off to Cannabich's, where a concerto is being rehearsed. Adieu, dear little wife. According to my calculation I cannot expect an answer to this letter. Farewell, my love, I kiss you millions of times and am ever, until death, your loving husband

MOZART

PS.—Gretl[2] is now married to Madame Le Brun's[3] brother, so her name is Madame Danzi. Little Hannah Brochard[4] is now sixteen and alas! her looks have been spoilt by smallpox. What a pity! She never stops talking about you. She plays the clavier very nicely.

(592) *Mozart to Michael Puchberg*

[From Nottebohm, Mozartiana, p. 52[5]]

MOST VALUED FRIEND AND BROTHER!   [VIENNA, 13 *April* 1791]

I shall be drawing my quarterly pay on April 20th, that is, in a week, If you can and will lend me until then about twenty gulden, you will oblige me very much, most beloved friend, and you will have it back with very many thanks on the 20th, as soon as I draw my money. I am anxiously awaiting the sum. Ever your most grateful friend

MOZART[6]

13 April 1791.

[1] Mozart is alluding to the visit to Vienna in September 1790 of King Ferdinand and Queen Caroline of Naples for the celebration of the double wedding of their daughters, Maria Theresa and Louisa, to the Archdukes Francis and Ferdinand. The festivities consisted of performances of operas by Salieri and Weigl and a concert at which works by Haydn and other composers were rendered. Mozart was entirely neglected.

[2] Margarete Marchand, Leopold Mozart's former pupil, married in 1790 Franz Danzi (1763–1826), cellist in the Munich Court orchestra.

[3] Franziska Danzi, daughter of the Mannheim cellist, Innocenz Danzi, had married in 1778 the Mannheim oboist, Ludwig August Le Brun.

[4] Maria Johanna Brochard, cousin of Heinrich and Margarete Marchand, had been Leopold Mozart's pupil.

[5] Autograph in the possession of Heinrich Eisemann, London.

[6] Puchberg noted on this letter, 'sent, on 13 April 1791, 30 gulden'.

(593) *Mozart to Michael Puchberg*

[*Autograph in the Germanische Nationalmuseum, Nuremberg*]

[VIENNA, *between* 21 *and* 27 *April* 1791]

I trust that Orsler[1] has returned the keys. It was not my fault. Further I hope that on my behalf he has asked you in advance to lend me for today a violin and two violas. They are for a quartet at Greiner's.[2] You know already that I am very anxious to have them. If you should care to come to our little concert in the evening, both he and I most politely invite you to do so.

MOZART

PS.—Please forgive me for not having repaid, as I promised to do, the sum you know of. But Stadler, who was to have gone to the pay office for me, because I have so much to do, altogether forgot about the 20th. So I must wait for another week.

(594) *Mozart to the Municipal Council of Vienna*

[*Autograph in the Koch Collection, Basel*]

[VIENNA, *c.* 25 *April*, 1791]

MOST HONOURABLE AND MOST LEARNED MUNICIPAL COUNCILLORS OF VIENNA!

MOST WORTHY GENTLEMEN!

When Kapellmeister Hofmann[3] was ill, I thought of venturing to apply for his post, seeing that my musical talents, my works and my skill in composition are well known in foreign countries, my name is treated everywhere with some respect, and I myself have the honour to be employed as composer to the Court of Vienna. I trusted therefore that I was not unworthy of this post and that I deserved the favourable consideration of our enlightened municipal council.

Kapellmeister Hofmann, however, has recovered his health and in the circumstances—for I wish him from my heart a long life—it has occurred to me that it might perhaps be of service to the Cathedral and, most worthy gentlemen, to your advantage, if I were to be attached for the time being as unpaid assistant to this ageing Kapellmeister and were to have the opportunity of helping this worthy man in his office, thus gaining

---

[1] Probably Josef Orsler, a cellist in the Vienna Court orchestra from 1772 to 1806.

[2] Court Councillor von Greiner (1732–1798), the father of Caroline Pichler, writer and musician. For an excellent account of her connection with Mozart, see Blümml, pp. 104–118.

[3] Leopold Hofmann (1738–1793), Kapellmeister at St. Stephen's Cathedral in Vienna.

the approbation of our learned municipal council by the actual performance of services which I may justly consider myself peculiarly fitted to
render on account of my thorough knowledge of both the secular and
ecclesiastical styles of music.

Your most humble servant,

WOLFGANG AMADÉ MOZART
Royal and Imperial Court Composer[1]

(595) *Mozart to Choir Master Stoll*[2] *at Baden*

[Copy in the Deutsche Staatsbibliothek, Berlin][3]

DEAR OLD STOLL!   [VIENNA, *end of May,* 1791]
Don't be a poll!

Primo. I should like to know whether Stadler called on you yesterday
and asked you for this mass:[4]

Did he? Well then, I hope that I shall get it today. If not, please be so
kind as to send it to me at once and, remember, with all the parts. I shall
return it very soon.

Secondo. Will you please find a small apartment for my wife? She only
needs two rooms, or one room and a dressing-room. But the main thing is
that they should be on the ground floor. The rooms I should prefer are
those which Goldhahn[5] used to occupy on the grond floor at the butcher's.
Please enquire there first; perhaps they are still to let. My wife is going out
to Baden on Saturday, or Monday, at latest. If we cannot have these
rooms, then you must look for something fairly near the baths; but the
important point is that they should be on the ground floor. The ground
floor at the town notary's, where Dr. Alt stayed,[6] would do very well, but
the rooms at the butcher's would be best of all.

Terzo. I should like to know whether the theatre in Baden is open yet?

Please reply as quickly as possible and send me information on these
three points.

MOZART

[1] The Municipal Council of Vienna granted Mozart's request, but Kapellmeister Hofmann
outlived the petitioner. His successor was Johann Georg Albrechtsberger.

[2] Anton Stoll (1747–1805), school teacher and choir-master of Baden near Vienna. Mozart
wrote for him on 17 June 1791, his motet K. 618, 'Ave, verum corpus' for four voices, strings
and organ.

[3] Autograph sold by J. A. Stargardt, Marburg, 25–26 February 1975.

[4] K. 317, composed in 1779, Mozart's so-called Coronation Mass.

[5] Josef Odilo Goldhahn was one of Mozart's acquaintances in Vienna.

[6] Stoll took these rooms in the Renngasse for Constanze. See *MM.* May 1920, pp. 109-112.

PS.—My address is: In the Rauhensteingasse, in the Kaiserhaus, No. 970, first floor.

PS.—This is the silliest letter I have ever written in my life; but it is just the very thing for you.

(596) *Mozart to his Wife at Baden*

[*From Nottebohm, Mozartiana*, p. 24]

MA TRÈS CHERE EPOUSE!   [VIENNA, 5 *June* 1791]

I hope that on alighting from the carriage my letter handed you Sabinde and that after you read Sabinde, you were very glad that I let it go off for a drive to Baden. It slept with me last night and I wrote Sabinde early this morning—ss—ss—a. A whole crowd of people were made fools of today in St. Stephan. Madame Schwingenschuh and Lisette called on me very early in the morning and I told them so. Then I sent Lorl[1] to church to tell Jacquin and Schäfer at once. They both came to see me immediately. I then sent another message, for they had seen Hofmann go to the choir. I shall fly to you on Wednesday in the company of the Schwingenschuhs. I am sleeping tonight at Leutgeb's—and the whole time I am thinking that I have given Lorl the *consilium abeundi*.[2] I am looking forward to reading a letter from you soon. Adieu, my love. Ever your husband

MOZART

(597) *Mozart to his Wife at Baden*

[*Autograph in the Mozarteum, Salzburg*]

MA TRÉS CHER EPOUSE!   [VIENNA, 6 *June* 1791]

J'écris cette lettre dans la petite chambre au jardin chez Leutgeb ou j'ai couché cette nuit excellement—et j'espere que ma chere epouse aura passée cette nuit aussi bien que moi. J'y passerai cette nuit aussi, puisque j'ai congedié Leonore et je serais tout seul à la maison, ce qui n'est pas agreable.

J'attends avec beaucoup d'impatience une lettre qui m'apprendra comme vous avés passée le jour d'hier. Je tremble quand je pense au bain de Saint Antoin, car je crains toujours le risque de tomber sur l'escalier en sortant—et je me trouve entre l'esperance et la crainte—une situation bien desagreable! Si vous n'etiés pas grosse, je craignerais moins.[3] Mais

---

[1] Leonore, the Mozart's maidservant.   [2] i.e. her dismissal.
[3] The Mozarts' sixth child, Franz Xaver Wolfgang, was born on 26 July 1791. He became a professional pianist and died at Karlsbad in 1844.

abandonnons cette idee triste! Le ciel aura eu certainement soin de ma chère Stanzi-Marini.[1]

Madame de Schwingenschuh m'a priée de leur procurer une loge pour ce soir au theatre de Wieden,[2] ou l'on donnera la cinquiemè partie d'Antoin,[3] et j'etais si heureux de pouvoir les servir. J'aurai donc le plaisir de voir cet opera dans leur compagnie.

I have this moment received your dear letter and am delighted to see that you are well and in good spirits. Madame Leutgeb has laundered my neck-tie today, but I should like you to see it! Good God! I kept on telling her, *Do let me show you how she (my wife) does them!*'—But it was no use. I am delighted that you have a good appetite—but whoever gorges a lot, must also shit a lot—no, walk a lot, I mean. But I should not like you to take *long walks* without me. I entreat you to follow my advice exactly, for it comes from my heart. Adieu—my love—my only one. Do catch them in the air—those 2999½ little kisses from me which are flying about, waiting for someone to snap them up. Listen, I want to whisper something in your ear—and you in mine—and now we open and close our mouths—again—again and again—at last we say: 'It is all about Plumpi—Strumpi——' Well, you can think what you like—that is just why it's so convenient. Adieu. A thousand tender kisses. Ever your

MOZART

6 June 1791.

(598) *Mozart to his Wife at Baden*

[From Nottebohm, Mozartiana, p. 11]

BADEN,[4] 7 *June* 1791

N.B—Since you headed your letter Vienna, I must head mine Baden.

DEAREST, MOST BELOVED LITTLE WIFE!

I simply cannot describe my delight at receiving your last letter of the 6th, which told me that you are well and in good health, and that, very sensibly, you are not taking baths every day. Heavens! How delighted I should have been if you had come to me with the Wildburgs! Indeed I was wild with myself for not telling you to drive into town—but I was afraid of the expense. Yet it would have been *charmant* if you had done so. At five o'clock tomorrow morning, we are all driving out, three carriage-fuls of us, and so between nine and ten I expect to find in your arms all the joy which only a man can feel who loves his wife as I do! It is only a pity that I can't take with me either the clavier or the bird! That is why I would

[1] One of Mozart's pet-names for Constanze.   [2] Schikaneder's theatre.
[3] *Anton bei Hofe*, an opera by Benedict Schack.
[4] Mozart was writing from Vienna.

rather have gone out alone; but, as it is, I can't get out of the arrangement without offending the company.

I lunched yesterday with Süssmayr [1] at the 'Ungarische Krone',[2] as I still had business in town at one o'clock,—as S——[3] has to lunch early and Mme S——, who wanted me very much to lunch with them one of these days, had an engagement at Schönbrunn. Today I am lunching with Schikaneder, for you know, you too were invited.

So far I have had no letter from Mme Duschek; but I shall enquire again today. I can't find out anything about your dress, as I have not seen the Wildburgs since. If it is at all possible, I shall certainly bring your hat with me. Adieu, my little sweetheart. I simply cannot tell you how I am looking forward to tomorrow. Ever your

MOZART

(599) *Mozart to his Wife at Baden*

[*From Nottebohm, Mozartiana, p. 46*]

MA TRÉS CHERE EPOUSE!   [VIENNA, 11 *June* 1791]

Criés avec moi contre mon mauvais sort! Mlle. Kirchgessner [4] ne donne pas son academie lundi! [5] Par consequent j'aurais pu vous posseder, ma chère, tout ce jour de dimanche. Mercredi je viendrai sûrement.

I must hurry, as it is already a quarter to seven—and the coach leaves at seven. When you are bathing, do take care not to slip and never stay in alone. If I were you I should occasionally omit a day in order not to do the cure too violently. I trust that someone slept with you last night. I cannot tell you what I would not give to be with you at Baden instead of being stuck here. From sheer boredom I composed today an aria for my opera.[6] I got up as early as half past four. Wonderful to relate, I have got back my watch—but—as I have no key, I have unfortunately not been able to wind it. What a nuisance! Schlumbla! That is a word to ponder on. Well, I wound *our big clock* instead. Adieu—my love! I am lunching today with

---

[1] Franz Xaver Süssmayr (1766–1803), born at Schwanenstadt in Upper Austria, became a pupil of Mozart in composition. He accompanied Mozart and Constanze to Prague in August 1791, and was probably responsible for the recitatives of Mozart's opera *La Clemenza di Tito*. He completed Mozart's Requiem after the composer's death. See Abert, vol. ii. p. 850 ff.

[2] A restaurant in the Himmelpfortgasse, which no longer exists.

[3] Possibly Benedict Schack, who had married a contralto singer.

[4] Marianne Kirchgessner (1769–1808) was a blind performer on the armonica. She undertook numerous successful concert tours. Mozart composed for her in May 1791 K. 617, an adagio and rondo in C minor and major for armonica, flute, oboe, viola and violoncello.

[5] She gave a concert on 10 June in the National Theatre but the concert apparently intended for 13 June was postponed until 19 August, when K. 617 was performed.

[6] *Die Zauberflöte*, which Schikaneder had commissioned Mozart to write for performance at his theatre Auf der Wieden.

Puchberg. I kiss you a thousand times and say with you in thought: 'Death and despair were his reward!'[1]
Ever your loving husband

W. A. MOZART

See that Karl behaves himself. Give him kisses from me.
Take an electuary if you are constipated—not otherwise. Take care of yourself in the morning and evening, if it is chilly.

(600) *Mozart to his Wife at Baden*

[*From Nottebohm, Mozartiana,* pp. 27-29]

DEAREST, MOST BELOVED LITTLE WIFE!   [VIENNA, 12 *June* 1791]
Now why did I not get a letter from you last night? So that you might keep me even longer in anxiety about your baths? This and something else spoilt the whole of yesterday for me. I went to see N.N. in the morning, who promised me, parole d'honneur, to call on me between twelve and one in order to settle up everything. So I could not lunch with Puchberg, but had to wait at home. Well, I waited until half past two. He never came, so I sent a note to his father by our servant. Meanwhile I went off to the 'Ungarische Krone', as it was too late to get lunch anywhere else; even there I had to take my meal *alone*, as all the guests had already left. You can imagine the sort of lunch I had, worried as I was about you and annoyed with N.N. If only I had had someone to console me a little. It is not at all good for me to be alone, when I have something on my mind. At half past three I was at home again. The servant had not yet returned. I waited and waited until half past six when she turned up with a note. Waiting is always disagreeable, to be sure, but even more so when the result is not what you expect. The note only contained apologies for not having been able to get some definite information, and assurances that he would not forget me and would certainly keep his word. To cheer myself up I then went to the Kasperle Theatre to see the new opera 'Der Fagottist',[2] which is making such a sensation, but which is shoddy stuff. When passing the coffee-house I looked in to see whether Loibl[3] was there, but there was not a sign of him. In the evening I again took a meal at the 'Krone' simply in order not to be alone, and there at least I had a chance to talk. Then I went straight to bed. I was up again at five o'clock, got dressed at once, went to see Montecuculi[4]—whom I found at home—then

[1] A quotation from *Die Zauberflöte.*
[2] *Kaspar der Fagottist*, by Wenzel Müller (1767-1835), who was conductor at Marinelli's Theatre in Vienna. The first performance of this opera was on 8 June 1791.
[3] Probably Johann Martin Loibl, a notary, a lover of music and like Mozart a freemason.
[4] Ludwig Franz, Marchese di Montecuculi, was an amateur musician and perhaps a pupil of Mozart's.

went off to N.N., who however, had already decamped. I am only sorry that *on account of that business, which has not yet been settled,* I was not able to write to you this morning. How I should have liked to write!

I am off now to the Rehbergs, that is, to the *great banquet which they are giving to their friends.* If I had not made a solemn promise to turn up and if it were not extremely rude of me to stay away, I should not go at all. But what good would that do me? Well, tomorrow I am driving out to Baden and to you! If only my affairs were settled! Who will now keep on prodding N.N. on my behalf? For if he is not prodded, he becomes lukewarm. I have had to look him up every morning, otherwise he would not have done even what he *has* done. Please do not go to the Casino today even if Mme Schwingenschuh should go out to Baden. Save it up for when I am with you. If only I had news from you! Well, it is half past ten now and the Rehbergs lunch at noon. Why, it is striking eleven! So I can't wait any longer! Adieu, dear little wife, love me as I do you. I kiss you 2000 times in thought. Ever your

MOZART

Sunday.

(601) *Mozart to his Wife at Baden*

[Autograph formerly in the possession of Richard Strauss]

MA TRÉS CHERE EPOUSE! [VIENNA, ?*June* 1791][1]

. . .[2] has this moment gone off to Baden. It is now nine o'clock in the evening and I have been with him since three. I think he will keep his word this time. He promised to call on you, so I urge you to go for him hard. But please do not go to the Casino.

Primo, the company[3] is—*you understand what I mean*—and
Secondo, you can't dance, as things are—and to look on?—

Why, you can do that more easily when your little husband is with you.

I must close, as I have still to go and see Montecuculi. I just wanted to dash off this piece of news to you. You will have a proper letter tomorrow. Adieu—do what I have told you about the *baths* and love me as much as I love and shall ever love you.

Ever your

MOZART

My greetings to your court jester![4]

---

[1] This letter is undated.   [2] A name has been deleted.
[3] Probably the Schwingenschuhs, of whom Mozart disapproved.
[4] Perhaps Süssmayr.

(602) *Mozart to his Wife at Baden*

[*From Nottebohm, Mozartiana*, p. 35[1]]

DEAREST, MOST BELOVED LITTLE WIFE!   [VIENNA, 24 or 25 June 1791]
These are only a few lines written to you in haste, as I am going to give Leutgeb a surprise by going out to breakfast with him. It is now half past five. After lunch I shall write more. And I am hoping that by then I shall have had a letter from you. Adieu—I only wanted to say good morning. Take care of yourself, particularly when you are taking the baths. If you feel the slightest weakness, stop them at once. Adieu! Two thousand kisses.

MOZART

An arse full of compliments to Snai[2] and tell him to pester N.N. unmercifully.

[*Autograph in the possession of Heinrich Eisemann, London*]

MA TRÉS CHERE ÉPOUSE!   [VIENNA, 25 June 1791]
I have this moment received your letter, which has given me extraordinary pleasure. I am now longing for a second one to tell me how the baths are affecting you. I too am sorry not to have been present yesterday at your fine concert, not on account of the music, but because I should have been so happy to be with you. I gave . . .[3] a surprise today. First of all I went to the Rehbergs. Well, Frau Rehberg sent one of her daughters upstairs to tell him that a dear old friend had come from Rome and had searched all the houses in the town without being able to find him. He sent down a message to say, would I please wait for a few minutes. Meanwhile the poor fellow put on his Sunday best, his finest clothes, and turned up with his hair most elaborately dressed. You can imagine how we made fun of him. I can never resist making a fool of someone—if it is not ..., then it must be ... or Snai. And where did I sleep? At home, of course. And I slept very well, save that the mice kept me most excellent company. Why, I had a first-rate argument with them. I was up before five o'clock. A propos, I advise you not to go to Mass tomorrow. Those peasant louts are too cheeky for my taste. True, you have a rough *compagnon*, but the peasants don't respect him, *perdunt respectum*, as they see at once that he is a silly ass—Snai!
I shall give a verbal reply to Süssmayr. I would rather not waste paper on him.

---

[1] Autograph in the Pierpont Morgan Library, New York City.
[2] Abert, vol. ii. p. 753, n. 2, suggests that Snai was one of Mozart's nicknames for Süssmayr who was then at Baden.
[3] A name, probably Leutgeb, has been crossed out.

Tell Krügel or Klüsel that you would like to have better food. Perhaps, when you are passing, you could speak to him yourself. That would be even better. He is a good fellow in other ways and respects me.

Tomorrow I shall join the procession to the Josefstadt, holding a candle in my hand!—Snai!

Do not forget my warnings about the morning and evening air and about bathing too long. My kind regards to Count and Countess Wagensperg. Adieu. I kiss you one thousand times in thought and am ever your

MOZART

Vienna, 25 June 1791.

PS.—Perhaps after all it would be well to give Karl a little rhubarb. Why did you not send me that long letter? Here is a letter for him—I should like to have an answer. Catch—Catch——bis—bis—bs—bs—kisses are flying about for you—bs—why, another one is staggering after the rest!

I have this moment received your second letter. Beware of the baths! And do sleep more—and not so irregularly, or I shall worry—I am a little anxious as it is.

Adieu.

(603) *Mozart to Michael Puchberg*

[*Copy in the Staatsbibliothek Preussischer Kulturbesitz, West Berlin*[1]]

DEAREST, MOST BELOVED FRIEND!   [VIENNA,] *25 June 1791*
MOST HONOURABLE BROTHER!

Business has prevented me from having the pleasure of calling on you today. I have a request to make. My wife writes to say that she can see that, although they are not expecting it, the people with whom she is living would be glad to receive some payment for her board and lodging and she begs me to send her some money. I had intended to settle everything when it was time for her to leave and I now find myself in very great embarrassment. I should not like to expose her to any unpleasantness; yet at the moment I cannot leave myself short of money. If you, most beloved friend, can assist me with a small sum, which I can send to her at once, you will oblige me exceedingly. I require the loan only for a few days, when you will receive 2000 gulden in my name, from which you can then refund yourself.

Ever your

MOZART[2]

[1] Autograph (discovered in 1971) in the Pierpont Morgan Library, New York City.
[2] Puchberg noted on this letter, 'sent on same day 25 gulden'.

(604) *Mozart to his Wife at Baden*

[*From Nottebohm, Mozartiana, p. 34*]

DEAREST LITTLE WIFE!   [VIENNA, *end of June or beginning of July*, 1791]
I have just this moment arrived and have already called on Puchberg
and Montecuculi. The latter was not at home—so I shall call again at half
past nine. I am now going to look up N.N. You will have received a
letter for me from Montecuculi. As I think it probable that instead of
spending Sunday with you I shall have to spend it in Vienna, please send
me the two summer suits, white and brown, with their trousers. I entreat
you to take the baths only every other day, and only for an hour. But if
you want me to feel quite easy in my mind, do not take them at all, until I
am with you again. Adieu. I kiss you a thousand times and am ever your
MOZART

NB.—My greetings to Snai and tell him that I should like to know how
he is—probably as tough as an ox. Tell him to keep on writing until I get
my belongings. Adieu.
I am sealing this letter in the presence of that good fellow Primus.[1]

(605) *Mozart to his Wife at Baden*

[*Autograph in the Pierpont Morgan Library, New York City*]

MA TRÉS CHERE EPOUSE!   [VIENNA, 2 *July* 1791]
I trust that you are very well. I have just remembered that you have
very seldom been upset during pregnancy. Perhaps the baths are having a
too laxative effect? I should not wait for *certain proofs*, which would be too
unpleasant. My advice is that you should stop them now! Then I should
feel quite easy in my mind. Today is the day when you are not supposed
to take one and yet I wager that that little wife of mine has been to the
baths? *Seriously*—I had much rather you would prolong your cure well
into the autumn. I hope that you got my first little note.
Please tell that idiotic fellow Süssmayr to send me my score of the first
act, from the introduction to the finale, so that I may orchestrate it.[2]
It would be a good thing if he could put it together today and dispatch it
by the first coach tomorrow, for I should then have it at noon. I have just
had a visit from a couple of Englishmen who refused to leave Vienna
without making my acquaintance. But of course the real truth is that they

---

[1] Possibly Mozart's nickname for a waiter at the 'Goldene Schlange', an eating-house and
beer-shop in the Kärntnerstrasse, where Mozart not infrequently lunched.
[2] Mozart was composing *Die Zauberflöte*.

wanted to meet that great fellow Süssmayr and only came to see me in order to find out where he lived, as they had heard that I was fortunate enough to enjoy his favour. I told them to go to the 'Ungarische Krone' and to wait there until he should return from Baden![1] Snai! They want to engage him to clean the lamps. I am longing most ardently for news of you. It is half past twelve already and I have heard nothing. I shall wait a little longer before sealing my letter. . . . Nothing has come, so I must close it! Farewell, dearest, most beloved little wife! Take care of your health, for as long as you are well and are kind to me, I don't care a fig if everything else goes wrong. Follow the advice I gave you at the beginning of this letter and farewell. Adieu—a thousand kisses for you and a thousand boxes on the ear for Lacci Bacci. Ever your

MOZART

Vienna, Saturday, 2 July 1791.

(606) *Mozart to his Wife at Baden*

[*Autograph in the Mozarteum, Salzburg*]

[VIENNA, 3 *July* 1791]

DEAREST, MOST BELOVED LITTLE WIFE OF MY HEART!

I received your letter together with Montecucoli's and am delighted to hear that you are well and in good spirits. I thought as much. If you take the baths twice in succession, you will be thoroughly spanked when I come out to you again! Thanks for the finale you sent and my clothes, but I cannot understand why you did not put in a letter. I searched all the pockets in the coat and trousers. Well, perhaps the post-woman is still carrying it about in her pocket! I am only delighted that you are in good health, my dear little wife. I rely on your following my advice. If you do, I can feel a little calmer! As for my health, I feel pretty well. I trust that my affairs will improve as rapidly as possible. Until they are settled I cannot be quite easy in my mind. But I hope to be so soon.

I trust that Süssmayer will not forget to copy out at once what I left for him; and I am counting on receiving today those portions of my score for which I asked. I see from . . . 's Latin letter that neither of you is drinking any wine. I don't like that. Have a word with your supervisor, who no doubt will only be too delighted to give you some on my account. It is a wholesome wine and not expensive, whereas the water is horrid. I lunched yesterday at Schikaneder's with the Lieutenant-Colonel, who is also taking the Antony baths. Today I am lunching with Puchberg. Adieu, little sweetheart. Dear Stanzi Marini, I must close in haste, for I have just

---

[1] Mozart is punning on the word 'baden', which means 'to bathe'.

heard one o'clock strike; and you know that Puchberg likes to lunch early. Adieu. Ever your

MOZART

Sunday, 3 July 1791.

Lots of kisses for Karl—and whippings for . . .[1]

(607) *Mozart to his Wife at Baden*

[*From Nottebohm, Mozartiana*, p. 34]

DEAREST LITTLE WIFE!   [VIENNA, 4 *July* 1791]
    I must be brief. It is half past one and I have not yet had any lunch. I wish I could send you more money. Meanwhile, here are three gulden. You will get some more tomorrow at noon. Cheer up and keep up your spirits. All will be well yet. I kiss you a thousand times. I am weak for want of food. Adieu.

Ever your

MOZART.

I have waited until now in the hope of being able to send you more money!

(608) *Mozart to his Wife at Baden*

[*Autograph in the Royal Library, Copenhagen*]

DEAREST, MOST BELOVED LITTLE WIFE!   [VIENNA, 5 *July* 1791]
    Here are twenty-five gulden. Settle the account for your baths. When I come we shall pay for everything. Tell Süssmayer to send me Nos. 4 and 5 of my manuscript—and the other things I asked for and tell him he must lick my arse—. I must hurry off to Wetzlar[2] or I shall miss him. Adieu. I kiss you one thousand times and am

ever your

MOZART

Vienna, 5 July 1791.

    PS.—Didn't you laugh when you got my three gulden? But I thought it would be better than nothing. Have a good time, little sweetheart, and be ever my Stanzi Marini.

---

[1] Probably Süssmayr.   [2] See p. 780, n. 1.

(609) *Mozart to his Wife at Baden*

[*From Nottebohm, Mozartiana,* p. 31[1]]

DEAREST, MOST BELOVED LITTLE WIFE!   [VIENNA, 5 *July* 1791]
    Do not be melancholy, I beg you! I hope you received the money.
It is surely better for your foot that you should stay on at Baden, for there
you can go out more easily. I hope to hold you in my arms on Saturday,
perhaps sooner. As soon as my business here is over, I shall be with you,
for I mean to take a rest in your arms; and indeed I shall need it, for
this mental worry and anxiety and all the running about connected with it
is really exhausting me. I received safely the last parcel and thank you for
it. I am more delighted than I can express that you are not taking any
more baths. In a word, all I need now is your presence. Sometimes I think
I cannot wait for it any longer. True, when my business is over I could
have you back for good—but—I should
like to spend a few more delightful days
with you at Baden. N.N. is with me at
the moment and tells me that I ought to
do this to you. He has a penchant for you
and is perfectly certain that you must have
noticed it.

    And what is my second fool doing now? I find it hard to choose
between the two fools! When I turned in at the 'Krone' yesterday evening,
I found the English lord lying there quite exhausted, as he was still waiting
for Snai.[2] On my way to Wetzlar's today I saw a couple of oxen yoked to
a waggon and when they began to pull, they moved their heads exactly
like our idiotic N.N. Snai!

    If you need anything, little sweetheart, let me know quite frankly, for
I shall indeed be delighted to try to satisfy in every way my Stanzi
Marini—

Ever your

MOZART.

Vienna, 5 July 1791.

    Karl must be a good boy. Then perhaps I shall answer his letter. Adieu.

---

[1] Autograph in the Royal Library, Copenhagen.
[2] Süssmayr. See p. 956, n. 1.

(609*) *Mozart to Michael Puchberg*[1]

[*From Schiedermair*, vol. II, p. 364]

DEAREST FRIEND!   [VIENNA, ? *Summer* 1791]

Thank you very much for what you have sent. Since you insist that I am to be frank, I shall be, but on condition that you make no mention of it to Herr Deyerkauf if you think that my frankness could offend him; in this you must know your friend better than I do.

The total value of the musical items is 120 ducats—that is 540 fl,—I think if I reduce it by two thirds it is still quite honourable—then I should get altogether 180 fl. I am frank because you wish it and I beg you again to make no use of my observation if you should suspect that my proposal would offend Herr Deyerkauf.

I am entirely your

MOZART

(610) *Mozart to his Wife at Baden*

[*From Nottebohm, Mozartiana*, p. 81[2]]

DEAREST, MOST BELOVED LITTLE WIFE!   [VIENNA, 6 *July* 1791]

With indescribable pleasure I received the news that you got the money safely. I can't remember, but I'm sure I never told you to settle up *everything*. Now, how could I, a sensible person, have written such nonsense? Well, if I did, I must have been completely out of my mind! Which is quite possible, as at the moment I have so many important things to think about. I only meant that you should pay *for your baths* and use the rest yourself. All other debts, the amount of which I have more or less reckoned up, I shall settle myself when I come. This very moment Blanchard[3] is either going up in his balloon—or else will fool the Viennese for the third time. That this should be taking place today is most inconvenient for me, for it is preventing me from settling up my business. N.N. promised to come and see me before going out there, but he hasn't turned up. Perhaps he will when the fun is over. I shall wait until two o'clock, then I shall stuff down a little food and go off and hunt him up. Our life is not at all a pleasant one. But patience! Things are bound to improve. And then I shall rest in your arms!

I thank you for your advice not to rely entirely on N.N. But in such cases *you are obliged to deal with only one person*. If you turn to two or three, and the affair becomes common property, others, with whom you cannot

---

[1] This letter was formerly thought to have been to Baron Raimund Wetzlar.
[2] Autograph sold by J. A. Stargardt, Marburg, 20–21 February 1979.
[3] Blanchard went up in his balloon Montgolfière on 6 July 1791, starting from the Prater and coming down in the neighbourhood of Vienna.

deal, regard you as a fool or an unreliable fellow. But the greatest pleasure of all you can give me is to be happy and jolly. *And if I know for certain that you have everything you want*, then all my trouble is a joy and a delight. Indeed the most difficult and complicated situation, in which I can possibly find myself, becomes a trifle, if only I know that *you are well and in good spirits*. And now, farewell. Make good use of your table-fool. Think of me and talk about me very often, both of you. Love me for ever as I do you and be always my Stanzi Marini, as I shall always be your

Stu! Knaller Praller
Schnip-Schnap-Schnur
Schnepeperl—
Snai!—

Give N.N. a box on the ear and tell him that you simply must kill a fly which I have spied on his face! Adieu—Look there! Catch them—bi—bi—bi—three kisses, as sweet as sugar, are flying over to you!

Wednesday, Vienna, 6 July 1791.

(611) *Mozart to his Wife at Baden*

[*From Nottebohm, Mozartiana*, p. 21]

DEAREST, MOST BELOVED LITTLE WIFE!   [VIENNA, 7 *July* 1791]
    You will forgive me, I know, for only sending you *one letter* a day. The reason is that I must keep hold of N.N. and not let him escape. I am at his house every day at seven o'clock in the morning.
    I hope that you got my letter yesterday. I did not go to see the balloon, for it is the sort of thing which one can imagine. Besides, I thought that this time too nothing would come of it. But goodness! How the Viennese are rejoicing! They are as full of his praises now as they have been up to the present of abuses.
    There is something in your letter which I cannot read and something I cannot understand. You say: 'I am certain that my—little husband will be in the Prater today in a numerous com. etc.' I cannot read the adjective before 'little husband'. I presume that 'com.' stands for 'company'—but what you mean by 'numerous company' I cannot think.
    Tell Sauermayer[1] from me that I have not had time to be for ever running off to his Primus and that whenever I did go he was never at home. Just give him the three gulden, so that he may not cry.
    My one wish now is that my affairs should be settled, so that I can be with you again. You cannot imagine how I have been aching for you all this long while. I can't describe what I have been feeling—a kind of

---

[1] A pun of Mozart's on the name Süssmayr ('süss' means sweet; 'sauer' means sour).

emptiness, which hurts me dreadfully—a kind of longing, which is never satisfied, which never ceases, and which persists, nay rather increases daily. When I think how merry we were together at Baden—like children— and what sad, weary hours I am spending here! Even my work gives me no pleasure, because I am accustomed to stop working now and then and exchange a few words with you. Alas! this pleasure is no longer possible. If I go to the piano and sing something out of my opera,[1] I have to stop at once, for this stirs my emotions too deeply. Basta! The very hour after I finish this business I shall be off and away from here. I have no news to tell you. The illuminations at Baden were, I daresay, a little premature—as the truth is precisely to the contrary. I shall enquire at the Court chemist's, where the electuary may perhaps be obtained. If so, I shall send it to you at once. Meanwhile, if it is necessary, I should advise you to take *tartar* rather than *brandy*. Adieu, dearest little wife,

Ever your

MOZART.

Vienna, 7 July 1791.

(612) *Mozart to his Wife at Baden*

[Copy in the Staatsbibliothek Preussischer Kulturbesitz, West Berlin]

DEAREST, MOST BELOVED LITTLE WIFE!   [VIENNA, 9 *July* 1791]
I have received your letter of the 7th together with the receipt for the correct payment. But for your own sake I should like to have seen the signature of a witness. For if N.N. chooses to be dishonest, he may make things rather unpleasant for you in regard to *genuineness* and *short weight*. As the document simply says 'box on the ear', he can suddenly send you a legal summons for a heavy or a violent or even a gentle box on the ear. What will you do then? You will have to pay him at once, which is not always convenient! I should advise you to come to a friendly understanding with your opponent and give him two heavy and three violent boxes on the ear followed by one gentle one, and even more, if he is not satisfied. For I maintain that kindness cures everything, that magnanimous and forbearing conduct has often reconciled the bitterest enemies and that if you are not in a position to pay the whole debt, you still have acquaintances who can. No doubt, if you ask Madame N., she will make herself responsible for the payment in cash, if not of the whole, at any rate of part of the debt.

Dearest little wife, I hope you received my letter of yesterday. The time, the happy time of our reunion is drawing ever nearer. Have patience

---

[1] *Die Zauberflöte.*

and be as cheerful as possible. Your letter of yesterday made me feel so depressed that I almost made up my mind to let that business slide and drive out to you. But what good would it have done? I should only have had to drive in again at once or, instead of being happy, I should have been most dreadfully worried. The affair must be concluded in a few days, for Z's promises were really serious and solemn. Then I shall go straight to you. But if you prefer it, I shall send you the money you need and you can then pay everything and return to Vienna. There is nothing I should like better. At the same time I do think that in this fine weather Baden must be very pleasant for you and most beneficial to your health, as there are such glorious walks there. You yourself must feel this more than anyone. So if you find that the air and exercise thoroughly agree with you, stay a little longer. I shall come and fetch you or, if you like, spend a few days with you. But, as I have already said, if you would rather do so, return to Vienna tomorrow. Tell me quite frankly which you prefer. Now farewell, dearest Stanzi Marie. I kiss you millions of times and am ever your

MOZART

Vienna, 9 July 1791.

PS.—Give the following message to N.N. from me:—

What does he say? Does he like it? Not particularly, I daresay. They are difficult expressions and rather hard to understand. Adieu.

(613) *Mozart to Choir-master Stoll at Baden*

[*Autograph formerly in the possession of Hofrat Viktor Keldorfer*]

[VIENNA, 12 *July* 1791]

Stoll, my dear,
You're a little bit queer
And an ass, I fear.
You've been swilling some beer!
The minor, I hear,
Is what tickles your ear!

I have a request to make, and that is, that you would be so kind as to send me by the first mail coach tomorrow my mass in B♭[1] which we

---

[1] Probably K. 275 [272b], composed in 1777.

performed last Sunday, and Michael Haydn's Graduale in B♭, 'Pax Vobis', which we also performed. I mean, of course, the parts, not the scores. I have been asked to conduct a mass in a church. Please do not think that this is an excuse to get back my mass. If I were not quite satisfied that you should have it, I should never have given it to you. On the contrary, I am delighted to be able to do you a kindness. I rely entirely on you, for I have given a promise.

                                                                    MOZART

Vienna, 12 July 1791.

[on the verso, in a feigned hand]

BELOVED HERR VON SCHROLL!   [VIENNA, 12 *July* 1791]
     Do not let us down or we shall be landed in the gutter. My beautiful delicate handwriting testifies to the truth of what Herr von Mozart has said, that is—the mass and Michael Haydn's Graduale—or no news of his opera.
     We shall return them at once.
     By the way, be so kind as to kiss the hand of my dear Theresa for me. If you don't, I swear eternal enmity. Your handwriting must testify to it, as mine is doing now. Then you will get back Michael Haydn's mass about which I have already written to my father.
     Remember, a man keeps his word!
     I am
                              your sincere friend
                                                        FRANZ SÜSSMAYR
                                                             Muckshitter
Shitting-house, July 12th.

(614) *Mozart to his Wife at Baden*

[Autograph in the Geigy-Hagenbach Collection, Basel]

[VIENNA, 7–8 *October* 1791 [1]]
Friday, half past ten at night
DEAREST, MOST BELOVED LITTLE WIFE!
     I have this moment returned from the opera, which was as full as ever.[2] As usual the duet 'Mann und Weib' and Papageno's glockenspiel in

---

     [1] The non-existence of any letters from Mozart between the middle of July and the beginning of October 1791 is partly due to Mozart's and Constanze's visit to Prague for the performance of his *Clemenza di Tito*, the opera which he had been commissioned to compose for the coronation on 6 September of the Emperor Leopold II as King of Bohemia. Süssmayr accompanied the Mozarts.
     [2] The first performance of *Die Zauberflöte* took place on 30 September 1791, Mozart himself conducting from the clavier. Schikaneder took the part of Papageno. Josefa Hofer was the Queen of Night.

Act I had to be repeated and also the trio of the boys in Act II. But what always gives me most pleasure is the *silent approval*! You can see how this opera is becoming more and more esteemed. Now for an account of my own doings. Immediately after your departure I played two games of billiards with Herr von Mozart, the fellow who wrote the opera which is running at Schikaneder's theatre; then I sold my nag for fourteen ducats; then I told Joseph[1] to get Primus to fetch me some black coffee, with which I smoked a splendid pipe of tobacco; and then I orchestrated almost the whole of Stadler's rondo.[2] Meanwhile I have had a letter which Stadler[3] has sent me from Prague. All the Duscheks are well. I really think that she cannot have received a single one of your letters—and yet I can hardly believe it. Well, they have all heard already about the splendid reception of my German opera.[4] And the strangest thing of all is that on the very evening when my new opera was performed for the first time with such success, 'Tito' was given in Prague for the last time with tremendous applause. Bedini[5] sang better than ever. The little duet in A major which the two maidens sing was repeated;[6] and had not the audience wished to spare Madame Marchetti,[7] a repetition of the rondo would have been very welcome.[8] Cries of 'Bravo' were shouted at Stodla[9] from the parterre and even from the orchestra—'What a miracle for Bohemia!' he writes, 'but indeed I *did my very best*'. Stodla writes too that Süssmayr[10] .... but I now see that he is an ass— ...., I mean, not Stodla, who is only a bit of an ass—but .... ,[11] why, he is a full-blown ass. At half past five I left my room and took my favourite walk by the Glacis to the theatre. But what do I see? What do I smell? Why, here is Don Primus with the cutlets! Che gusto![12] Now I am eating to your health! It is just striking eleven. Perhaps you are already asleep? St! St! St! I won't wake you.

Saturday, the 8th. You should have seen me at supper yesterday! I couldn't find the old tablecloth, so I fished out one as white as a snowdrop, and put in front of me the double candlestick with wax candles. According to Stadler's letter the Italians are done for in Vienna. Further, Madame Duschek must have got *one* letter from you, for he says: 'The lady was very well pleased with Mathies' postscript. She said: "I like the ASS, or A-S-S, as he is".' Do urge .... ,[11] to write something for .... ,[11] for he has begged me very earnestly to see to this. As I write, no doubt you will be

---

[1] Probably Joseph Preisinger, landlord of the 'Goldene Schlange'.
[2] The rondo of K. 622, clarinet concerto in A major, one of Mozart's last compositions.
[3] Anton Stadler, who had taken part in the performance of *La Clemenza di Tito*, had stayed on in Prague.
[4] *Die Zauberflöte.*   [5] Bedini took the part of Sesto.
[6] No. 7, 'Ah, perdona al primo affetto'.
[7] Signora Marchetti-Fantozzi, the prima donna, took the part of Vitellia.
[8] No. 19, 'Deh per questo istante solo'.
[9] Anton Stadler, the clarinettist. Mozart is probably imitating his dialect.
[10] Half a line has been deleted here.   [11] A name has been deleted here.
[12] What a delicious taste!

having a good swim. The friseur came punctually at six o'clock. At half
past five Primus had lit the fire and he then woke me up at a quarter to six.
Why must it rain just now? I did so much hope that you would have
lovely weather. Do keep very warm, so that you may not catch a cold.
I hope that these baths will help you to keep well during the winter. For
only the desire to see you in good health made me urge you to go to
Baden. I already feel lonely without you. I knew I should. If I had had
nothing to do, I should have gone off at once to spend the week with you;
but I have *no facilities for working at Baden*, and I am anxious, as far as
possible, to avoid all risk of *money difficulties*. For the most pleasant thing
of all is to have a mind at peace. To achieve this, however, one must work
hard; and I like hard work. Give . . . .¹ a few sound boxes on the ear from
me, and I ask . . .¹, whom I kiss a thousand times, to give him a couple too.
For Heaven's sake do not let him starve in this respect. The last thing in
the world I could wish would be his reproach that you had not treated or
looked after him properly. Rather give him too many blows than too few.
It would be a good thing if you were to leave a bump on his nose, or
knock out an eye, or inflict some other visible injury, so that the fellow
may never be able to deny that he has got something from you.

Adieu, dear little wife! The coach is just going. I trust that I shall have a
letter from you today and in this sweet hope I kiss you a thousand times
and am ever

your loving husband

W. A. MOZART

(615) *Mozart to his Wife at Baden*

[Portions of autograph in the Zavertal Collection, University of Glasgow
and in the Mozarteum, Salzburg]

[VIENNA, 8-9 October² 1791]
Saturday night at half past ten o'clock

DEAREST, MOST BELOVED LITTLE WIFE,

I was exceedingly delighted and overjoyed to find your letter on my
return from the opera. Although Saturday, as it is post-day, is always a
bad night, the opera was performed to a full house and with the usual
applause and repetition of numbers. It will be given again tomorrow, but
there will be no performance on Monday. So Süssmayr must bring Stoll
in on *Tuesday* when it will be given again *for the first time*. I say *for the first
time*, because it will probably be performed again several times in
succession. I have just swallowed a delicious slice of sturgeon which Don

---

¹ A name has been deleted here.
² The autograph of this letter, which bears no date, has been published by Farmer and
Smith, *New Mozartiana*, pp. 65-75, 123-127. The editors maintain that his letter was written
after the letter dated 14 October, but do not provide sufficient evidence to upset the traditional order of Mozart's last letters.

Primus (who is my faithful valet) has brought me; and as I have a rather voracious appetite today, I have sent him off again to fetch some more if he can. So during this interval I shall go on writing to you. This morning I worked so hard at my composition that I went on until half past one. So I dashed off in great haste to Hofer, simply in order not to lunch alone, where I found Mamma[1] too. After lunch I went home at once and composed again until it was time to go to the opera. Leutgeb begged me to take him a second time and I did so. I am taking *Mamma* tomorrow. Hofer has already given her the libretto to read. In her case what will probably happen will be that she will *see* the opera, but not *hear* it. The ....[2] had a box this evening ....[3] applauded *everything* most heartily. But he, the know-all, showed himself to be such a thorough *Bavarian* that I could not remain or I should have had to call him an ass. Unfortunately I was there just when the second act began, that is, at the solemn scene. He laughed at everything. At first I was patient enough to draw his attention to a few passages. But he laughed at everything. Well, I could stand it no longer. I called him a Papageno and cleared out. But I don't think that the idiot understood my remark. So I went into another box where *Flamm*[4] and his wife happened to be. There everything was very pleasant and I stayed to the end. But during Papageno's aria with the glockenspiel I went behind the scenes, as I felt a sort of impulse today to play it myself. Well, just for fun, at the point where Schikaneder has a pause, I played an arpeggio. He was startled, looked behind the wings and saw me. When he had his next pause, I played no arpeggio. This time he stopped and refused to go on. I guessed what he was thinking and again played a chord. He then struck the glockenspiel and said '*Shut up*'. Whereupon everyone laughed. I am inclined to think that this joke taught many of the audience for the first time that Papageno does not play the instrument himself. By the way, you have no idea how charming the music sounds when you hear it from a box close to the orchestra—it sounds much better than from the gallery. As soon as you return—you must try this for yourself.

Sunday, at seven o'clock in the morning. I have slept very well and hope that you too have done the same. I have just enjoyed thoroughly my half of a capon which friend Primus has brought back with him. I am going to the service at the Piarists at ten o'clock, for Leutgeb has told me that I can then have a word with the Director;[5] and I shall stay to lunch.

Primus told me last night that a great many people in Baden are ill. Is this true? Do take care and don't trust the weather. Well, Primus has just returned with the tiresome news that the coach left today before seven

---

[1] Frau Weber.   [2] A name has been deleted.   [3] Part of a line has been deleted.
[4] Franz Xaver Flamm was a clerk of Chancery to the Vienna Magistrat in 1785. His daughter Antonie afterwards became a famous singer.
[5] Mozart was thinking of removing his little son Karl from his school at Perchtoldsdorf, a village near Vienna, and placing him at a Christian Brothers' seminary.

o'clock and that there won't be another one until the afternoon. So all my writing at night and in the early morning has been to no purpose and you will not get my letter until this evening, which is very annoying. I shall certainly come out next Sunday, when we shall all visit the Casino and come home together on Monday. Lechleitner was again at the opera. Though he is no connoisseur, he is at any rate a genuine lover of music, which N.N.[1] is not. He is really a nonentity and much prefers a dinée. Farewell, my love—I kiss you millions of times and am ever your

MOZART

PS.—Kiss Sophie for me. I send Süssmayr a few good *nose-pulls* and a proper *hair-tug* and Stoll a thousand greetings. Adieu. The hour is striking —Farewell—We shall meet again.[2]

NB—You probably sent the two pairs of yellow winter stockings for the boots to the laundry, for Joseph and I have hunted for them in vain! *Adieu.*

(616) *Mozart to his Wife at Baden*

[Copy in the Staatsbibliothek Preussischer Kulturbesitz, West Berlin]

DEAREST, MOST BELOVED LITTLE WIFE,   [VIENNA, 14 *October* 1791]
    Hofer drove out with me yesterday, Thursday the 13th, to see our Karl.[3] We lunched there and then we all drove back to Vienna. At six o'clock I called in the carriage for Salieri and Madame Cavalieri—and drove them to my box. Then I drove back quickly to fetch Mamma and Karl, whom I had left at Hofer's. You can hardly imagine how charming they were and how much they liked not only my music, but the libretto and everything. They both said that it was an *operone*,[4] worthy to be performed for the grandest festival and before the greatest monarch, and that they would often go to see it, as they had never seen a more beautiful or delightful show. Salieri listened and watched most attentively and from the overture to the last chorus there was not a single number that did not call forth from him a bravo! or bello! It seemed as if they could not thank me enough for my kindness. They had intended in any case to go to the opera yesterday. But they would have had to be in their places by four o'clock. As it was, they saw and heard everything in comfort in my box. When it was over I drove them home and then had supper at Hofer's with Karl. Then I drove him home and we both slept soundly. Karl was absolutely delighted at being taken to the opera. He is looking splendid. As far as health is concerned, he could not be in a better place, but every-

---

[1] A name has been deleted here.   [2] A quotation from *Die Zauberflöte.*
[3] Karl Mozart was at school in Perchtoldsdorf, a suburb of Vienna.
[4] A 'grand opera'.

thing else there is wretched, alas! All they can do is to turn out a good peasant into the world. But enough of this. As his serious studies (God help them!) do not begin until Monday, I have arranged to keep him until after lunch on Sunday. I told them that you would like to see him. So tomorrow, Saturday, I shall drive out with Karl to see you. You can then keep him, or I shall take him back to Heeger's[1] after lunch. Think it over. A month can hardly do him much harm. In the meantime the arrangement with the Piarists, which is now under discussion, may come to something. On the whole, Karl is no worse; but at the same time he is not one whit better than he was. He still has his old bad manners; he never stops chattering just as he used to do in the past; and he is, if anything, *less inclined to learn than before*, for out there [at Perchtoldsdorf] all he does is to wander about in the garden for five hours in the morning and five hours in the afternoon, as he has himself confessed. In short, the children do nothing but eat, drink, sleep and go for walks. Leutgeb and Hofer are with me at the moment. The former is staying to supper with me. I have sent out my faithful comrade Primus to fetch some food from the Bürgerspital. I am quite satisfied with the fellow. He has only let me down once, when I was obliged to sleep at Hofer's, which annoyed me intensely, as they sleep far too long there. I am happiest at home, for I am accustomed to my own hours. This one occasion put me in a very bad humour. Yesterday the whole day was taken up with that trip to Bernstorf,[2] so I could not write to you. But that you have not written to me for two days, is really unforgivable. I hope that I shall certainly have a letter from you today, and that tomorrow I shall talk to you and embrace you with all my heart.

Farewell. Ever your

MOZART

14 October 1791.

I kiss Sophie a thousand times. Do what you like with N.N. Adieu.

[1] Wenzel Bernhard Heeger (1740–1807), headmaster of the school at Perchtoldsdorf.
[2] i.e. Perchtoldsdorf.

A letter, written many years later, which describes the last days of Mozart:

Sophie Haibel to Georg Nikolaus von Nissen, Salzburg[1]

[Extract]   [Autograph in the Gesellschaft der Musikfreunde, Vienna]

D[IAKOVAR],[2] 7 April 1825

Now I must tell you about Mozart's last days. Well, Mozart became
fonder and fonder of our dear departed mother[3] and she of him. Indeed
he often came running along in great haste to the Wieden (where she and
I were lodging at the Goldner Pflug), carrying under his arm a little bag
containing coffee and sugar, which he would hand to our good mother,
saying, 'Here, mother dear, now you can have a little "Jause" '.[4] She used
to be as delighted as a child. He did this very often. In short, Mozart in the
end never came to see us without bringing something.

Now when Mozart fell ill, we both made him a night-jacket which he
could put on frontways, since on account of his swollen condition he was
unable to turn in bed. Then, as we didn't know how seriously ill he was,
we also made him a quilted dressing-gown (though indeed his dear wife,
my sister, had given us the materials for both garments), so that when he
got up he should have everything he needed. We often visited him
and he was really delighted with the dressing-gown. I used to go into
town every day to see him. Well, one Saturday when I was with him,
Mozart said to me: 'Dear Sophie, do tell Mamma that I am fairly well
and that I shall be able to go and congratulate her in the octave of her
name-day'. Who could have been more delighted than I to bring such
cheerful news to my mother, when she could barely expect the news?
I hurried home therefore to comfort her, the more so as he himself really
seemed to be bright and happy. The following day was a Sunday.
I was young then and rather vain, I confess, and liked to dress up. But
I never cared to go out walking from our suburb into town in my fine
clothes, and I had no money for a drive. So I said to our good mother:
'Dear Mamma, I'm not going to see Mozart today. He was so well
yesterday that surely he will be even better today, and one day
more or less won't make much difference.' Well, my mother said:
'Listen to this. Make me a cup of coffee and then I'll tell you what you
ought to do.' She was rather inclined to keep me at home; and indeed my

---

[1] Mozart, who had been in poor health for some time, became very ill early in November
and bedridden about a fortnight before his death on 5 December 1791. A vivid and moving
account of his last days is given in the above letter written many years later by Sophie Haibel
to her elder sister Constanze's second husband, Georg Nikolaus von Nissen, formerly Counsellor at the Danish Legation in Vienna, who at the time was collecting materials for his biography
of Mozart. See Nissen, p. 573 ff. and p. 687 ff. The letter was first published in full in *MM*,
November 1918, pp. 21–23.

[2] Sophie Weber's husband, Jakob Haibel (1761–1826), musician and composer, was choir-
master at Diakovar.

[3] Frau Cäcilie Weber, who died on 22 August 1793.   [4] i.e. afternoon coffee.

sister knows how much I had to be with her. I went into the kitchen. The fire was out. I had to light the lamp and make a fire. All the time I was thinking of Mozart. I had made the coffee and the lamp was still burning. Then I noticed how wasteful I had been with my lamp, I mean, that I had burned so much wax. It was still burning brightly. I stared into the flame and thought to myself, 'How I should love to know how Mozart is'. While I was thinking and gazing at the flame, it went out, as completely as if the lamp had never been burning. Not a spark remained on the big wick and yet there wasn't the slightest draught—that I can swear to. A horrible feeling came over me. I ran to our mother and told her all. She said: 'Well, take off your fine clothes and go into town and bring me back news of him at once. But be sure not to delay.' I hurried along as fast as I could. Alas, how frightened I was when my sister, who was almost despairing and yet trying to keep calm, came out to me, saying: 'Thank God that you have come, dear Sophie. Last night he was so ill that I thought he would not be alive this morning. Do stay with me today, for if he has another bad turn, he will pass away tonight. Go in to him for a little while and see how he is.' I tried to control myself and went to his bedside. He immediately called me to him and said: 'Ah, dear Sophie, how glad I am that you have come. You must stay here tonight and see me die.' I tried hard to be brave and to persuade him to the contrary. But to all my attempts he only replied: 'Why, I have already the taste of death on my tongue.' And, 'if you do not stay, who will support my dearest Constanze if you don't stay here?' 'Yes, yes, dear Mozart,' I assured him, 'but I must first go back to our mother and tell her that you would like me to stay with you today. Otherwise she will think that some misfortune has befallen you.' 'Yes, do so,' said Mozart, 'but be sure and come back soon.' Good God, how distressed I felt! My poor sister followed me to the door and begged me for Heaven's sake to go to the priests at St. Peter's and implore one of them to come to Mozart—a chance call, as it were. I did so, but for a long time they refused to come and I had a great deal of trouble to persuade one of those clerical brutes to go to him. Then I ran off to my mother who was anxiously awaiting me. It was already dark. Poor soul, how shocked she was! I persuaded her to go and spend the night with her eldest daughter, the late Josefa Hofer.[1] I then ran back as fast as I could to my distracted sister. Süssmayr was at Mozart's bedside. The well-known Requiem[2] lay on the quilt and Mozart was explaining to

---

[1] Josefa Weber-Hofer, who in 1797 had married as her second husband the actor and singer Friedrich Sebastian Mayer (1773–1835), died on 29 December 1819.

[2] K. 626. Six months previously Mozart had been commissioned by Count Franz Walsegg-Stuppach (see p. 929, n. 2) to compose this work, which, however, had been delayed by his journey to Prague early in September for the production of *La Clemenza di Tito*, and by his work on *Die Zauberflöte*, first performed on 30 September. For a discussion of Süssmayr's share in the composition of the *Requiem* see Köchel, p. 728 ff.

him how, in his opinion, he ought to finish it, when he was gone. Further, he urged his wife to keep his death a secret until she should have informed Albrechtsberger, for the post should be his before God and the world.[1] A long search was made for Dr. Closset, who was found at the theatre, but who had to wait for the end of the play. He came and ordered *cold* poultices to be placed on Mozart's burning head, which, however, affected him to such an extent that he became unconscious and remained so until he died.[2] His last movement was an attempt to express with his mouth the drum passages in the Requiem. That I can still hear. Müller[3] from the Art Gallery came and took a cast of his pale, dead face. Words fail me, dearest brother, to describe how his devoted wife in her utter misery threw herself on her knees and implored the Almighty for His aid. She simply could not tear herself away from Mozart, however much I begged her to do so. If it was possible to increase her sorrow, this was done on the day after that dreadful night, when crowds of people passed by and wept and wailed for him. All my life I have never seen Mozart in a temper, still less, angry.[4]

---

[1] As Mozart intended, Albrechtsberger, the court organist, succeeded him as assistant to the Kapellmeister at St. Stephen's Cathedral, Leopold Hofmann.

[2] Mozart died at 55 minutes past midnight on 5 December.

[3] Count Josef Deym von Střítež (1752–1804), alias Müller, was the owner of a collection of wax-works, casts from the antique, and miscellaneous attractions which from 1797 onwards was housed in a building on the Danube canal. Mozart's death-mask has disappeared. According to Nohl (*Mozart nach den Schilderungen seiner Zeitgenossen*, p. 393) Constanze, one day while cleaning, smashed the copy in her possession. She is said to have remarked that 'she was glad that the ugly old thing was broken' (A. Schurig, *Leopold Mozarts Reiseaufzeichnungen*, p. 92).

[4] For the final passage of this letter, describing an instance of Mozart's attentiveness to Constanze, see *MDB*, p. 526.

BIBLIOGRAPHY

Allgemeine musikalische Zeitung (Leipzig, 1798/9–1848) [*AMZ*]

F. X. Niemetschek: *Leben des k.k. kapellmeisters Wolfgang Gottlieb Mozart nach Originalquellen beschrieben* (Prague, 1798, enlarged 2/1808; Eng. trans., 1956) [p. refs. to 1798 edn.]

G. N. Nissen: *Biographie W. A. Mozarts nach Originalbriefen* (Leipzig, 1828/R1964 and 1972)

O. Jahn: *W. A. Mozart* (Leipzig, 1856, 2/1867; ed. H. Deiters, 3/1889–91, 4/1905–7; Eng. trans., 1882) [p. refs. to 1856 edn.]

L. von Köchel: *Chronologisch-thematisches Verzeichnis sämtlicher Tonwerke Wolfgang Amade Mozarts* (Leipzig, 1862; 2/1905 ed. P. Graf von Waldersee; 3/1937 ed. A. Einstein, repr. 4/1958, 5/1963, with suppl. 3/1947; 6/1964 ed. F. Giegling, A. Weinmann and G. Sievers, repr. 7/1965) [p. refs. to 1964 edn.]

L. Nohl: *Mozarts Briefe* (Salzburg, 1865, 2/1877; Eng. trans., 1865) [p. refs. to 1877 edn.]

G. Nottebohm: *Mozartiana* (Leipzig, 1880/R1972)

Mitteilungen für die Mozartgemeinde in Berlin (1895–1925) [*MMB*]

E. von Komorzynski: *Emanuel Schikaneder: ein Beitrag zur Geschichte des deutschen Theaters* (Berlin, 1901, rev. 2/1951)

T. de Wyzewa and G. de Saint-Foix: *Wolfgang Amédée Mozart: sa vie musicale et son oeuvre* (Paris, 1912–46/R1979) [iii–v by Saint-Foix alone] [WSF]

A. Schurig: *Wolfgang Amadeus Mozart: sein Leben und sein Werk* (Leipzig, 1913, 2/1923)

L. Schiedermair, ed.: *Die Briefe W. A. Mozarts und seiner Familie: erste kritische Gesamtausgabe* (Munich and Leipzig, 1914)

Mozarteums-Mitteilungen (1918–21) [*MM*]

Zeitschrift für Musikwissenschaft (Leipzig, 1918/19–1935) [*ZMW*]

H. Abert: *W. A. Mozart: neu bearbeitete und erweiterte Ausgabe von Otto Jahns 'Mozart'* (Leipzig, 1919–21, 3/1955–66) [p. refs. to 1923–4 edn.]

A. Schurig: *Leopold Mozarts Reiseaufzeichnungen 1763–1771* (Dresden, 1920)

E. K. Blümml: *Aus Mozarts Freundes- und Familienkreis* (Leipzig, 1923)

Mozart-Jahrbuch, i–iii (1923–9)

A. Leitzmann: *Wolfgang Amadeus Mozarts Leben in seinen Briefen und Berichten der Zeitgenossen* (Leipzig, 1926)

C. Girdlestone: *Mozart et ses concertos pour piano* (Paris, 1939; Eng. trans., 1958)

Neues Mozart-Jahrbuch, i–iii (1941–3)

E. Müller von Asow, ed.: *Gesamtausgabe der Briefe und Aufzeichnungen der Familie Mozart* (Berlin, 1942)

A. Einstein: *Mozart: his Character, his Work* (Eng. trans., New York, 1945; Ger. orig., 1947, 4/1960)

I. Hoesli: *Wolfgang Amadeus Mozart: Briefstil eines Musikgenies* (Zürich, 1948)

E. von Komorzynski: *Der Vater der Zauberflöte: Emanuel Schikaneders Leben* (Vienna, 1948)

A. Hutchings: *A Companion to Mozart's Piano Concertos* (London, 1948, 2/1950, rev. 1980)

H. and E. Müller von Asow, eds.: *Wolfgang Amadeus Mozart: Briefwechsel und Aufzeichnungen* (Lindau in Bodensee, 1949)

Mozart-Jahrbuch 1950– [with annual bibliography up to 1975]

H. Dennerlein: *Der unbekannte Mozart: die Welt seiner Klavierwerke* (Leipzig, 1951)

Mitteilungen der Internationalen Stiftung Mozarteum (1952–)

Acta Mozartiana, Mitteilungen der Deutschen Mozart-Gesellschaft (1954–)

N. Medici di Marignano and R. Hughes: *A Mozart Pilgrimage: Being the Travel Diaries of Vincent and Mary Novello in the Year 1829* (London, 1955/R1975)

E. Schenk: *Wolfgang Amadeus Mozart: eine Biographie* (Vienna and Zurich, 1955, rev. 2/1975; Eng. trans., abridged, 1960 as *Mozart and his Times*)

Kongressbericht: Wien Mozartjahr 1956

H. C. R. Landon and D. Mitchell, eds.: *The Mozart Companion* (London, 1956, 2/1965)

E. and P. Badura-Skoda: *Mozart-Interpretation* (Vienna, 1957; Eng. trans., 1962)

W. Hummel, ed.: *Nannerl Mozarts Tagebuchblätter, mit Eintragungen ihres Bruders Wolfgang Amadeus* (Stuttgart, 1958)

O. E. Deutsch: *Mozart und seine Welt in zeitgenössischen Bildern* (Kassel, 1961) [in Ger. and Eng.]

O. E. Deutsch: *Mozart: die Dokumente seines Lebens, gesammelt und erläutert* (Kassel, 1961; Eng. trans., 1965, 2/1966; suppl. 1978) [*MDB*; p. refs. to Eng. edn.]

W. A. Bauer, O. E. Deutsch and J. H. Eibl, eds.: *Mozart: Briefe und Aufzeichnungen* (Kassel, 1962–75) [*MBA*] [complete edn.; for supplementary material see J. H. Eibl in *Mozart-Jahrbuch 1976–7*, 289 and *Mozart-Jahrbuch 1980–83*, 318; for later discoveries see G. Croll, *Mozart-Jahrbuch 1967*, 12, and R. Angermüller and S. Dahms-Schneider, *Mozart-Jahrbuch 1968–70*, 211–41]

O. Schneider and A. Algatzy: *Mozart-Handbuch: Chronik, Werk, Bibliographie* (Vienna, 1962)

W. Hildesheimer: *Mozart* (Frankfurt am Main, 1977; Eng. trans., 1982)

S. Sadie: *Mozart* [The New Grove] (London, 1982, 2/1984)

INDEX OF PERSONS

Where there are several entries under one name, the main biographical note is indicated by bold type.
German surnames which contain in the first syllable a vowel marked with an umlaut are entered as if spelt out fully, e.g. Hässler precedes Hafeneder.

A

Abel, Karl Friedrich, **47 n. 3**
Adamberger, Frau, 838
— Johann Valentin, 290 n. 3, **723 n. 7**, 755, 756, 765, 768, 769, 771, 794, 806, 807, 808, 820, 838, 843, 852, 853, 854, 866, 890
Adélaïde, Princess, of France, 35 n. 2
Adelheit, Mlle, 676 n. 2
Adlgasser, Anton Cajetan, **26 n. 3**, 56, 63, 78 n. 1, 83, 100, 184, 192, 218, 219, 265, 377, 391, 431, 436, 437, 441, 449, 495, 526, 545, 547, 553, 554, 562, 651, 679 n. 6
— Maria Anna, 377, 384, 391, 436 n. 1, 438, 537, 760
— Victoria, 279, 296, 377, 391, 438, 495, 537
Aesop(us), 686, 696
Afferi, Signor, 105
Affligio, Giuseppe, **82 n. 2**, 88, 90, 93
Agricola, Johann Friedrich, **548 n. 5**
Agujari, Lucrezia, **120 n. 4**, 121 n. 5, 494 n. 4, 663 n. 1
Aichelburg, Régine Josepha, 872
Aiguillon, Duchess d', 43, 472
Albert (innkeeper), 273, 275, 276, 277, 282, 284, 290, 293, 294, 295, 297, 299, 307, 308, 320, 331, 406, 415, 425, 685
Albert, Duke of Saxe-Teschen, **79 n. 5**
Albrecht II, Duke of Austria, 762 n. 4
Albrechtsberger, Johann Georg, **924 n. 1**, 950 n. 1, 977
Alembert, Jean le Rond d', 472 n. 1, 493, **549 n. 7**
Alfonso, Brother, 109, 114 n. 1
Allegranti, Maddalena, **924 n. 3**
Allegri, Gregorio, 127 n. 1
Alphen, Eusebius Johann, **207 n. 2**
Alt, Herr von, 945, 950
Altemps, Duke di, *see* Attems, Duke di
Alterdinger, Rochus, 86 n. 3
Altham, Count, 526, 527
Althann, Countess Eleonore, 871

Alxinger, Johann Baptist von, **765 n. 7**
Amadori, Signor, 146
Amalia, Princess of Prussia, 30 n. 2
Aman, Herr, 570
Amann, Basilius, **116 n. 3**, 117, 121, 218, 850, 851
— Franz Anton von, 116 n. 3
Ambassador, Dutch, in London, 46, 57
French, in The Hague, 62
in Munich, 293, 607
in Naples, 142, 143
in Vienna, *see* Châtelet-Lomont, Count Florent Louis Marie
Neapolitan, in The Hague, 62
Portuguese, in The Hague, 62
Russian, in Dresden, *see* Belovselsky-Beloserky, Prince Alexander
Sardinian, in Vienna, *see* Graneri, Count Peter Josef
Spanish, in The Hague, 62
Spanish, in Vienna, *see* Yriarte, Don Domingo
Swedish, in London, 132
Viennese, in Brussels, 43
in The Hague, 62
in Munich, 255
in Paris, *see* Starhemberg, Count Georg Anton
in Venice, *see* Durazzo, Count
Amelli, Signor, 105 n. 3
Amicis, Anna de, *see* De Amicis
Amman (tailor), 458
André, Herr, **895 n. 3**, 907
— Johann, 755 n. 1
— Johann Anton, xii n. 4
Andretter family, 377, 391, 395, 415, 636
— Fräulein, 263
— Cajetan, 275, 376, 526, 549
— Johann Ernst von, 236 n. 1, 259, 446, 537, 592
— Siegbert, 527
— Sigmund (Cornet), 259, 445, 536, 537, 543, 590, 786

CLASSIFIED INDEX OF WORKS

The traditional order has been retained as far as possible. Numbers given in square brackets are those of the sixth edition of Köchel's catalogue, Wiesbaden, 1964

Unfinished works are marked ★
Lost works are marked †

MASSES

- Missa brevis in G (K. 49 [47d], 1768), 95 n. 5
- Missa brevis in D minor (K. 65[61a], 1769), 95 n. 2, n. 5
- Missa (Pater Dominicus Mass) in C (K. 66, 1769), 52 n. 5, 95 n. 5, 237 n. 2, 430 n. 1, 547 n. 4
- Missa solemnis in C minor (K. 139[47a], 1768), 94 n.1, 95 n.2
- Missa brevis in F (K. 192 [186f], 1774), 262 n. 2, 337 n. 4, 378 n. 2
- Missa brevis in D (K. 194 [186h], 1774), 262 n. 2
- Missa brevis in C (K. 220 [196b], 1775–6), 337 n. 4, 378 n. 2
- Missa (Credo Mass) in C (K. 257, 1776), 266 n. 3
- Missa brevis in C (K. 258, 1776), 266 n. 3
- Missa brevis in C (K. 259, 1776), 266 n. 3, 541 n. 1
- Missa longa in C (K. 262 [246a], 1775), 541 n. 2
- Missa brevis in B♭ (K. 275 [272b], 1777), 431 n. 2, 663 n. 5, 667 n. 1, 748 n. 4, 842 n. 4, 965 n. 1, 966
- Missa (Coronation Mass) in C (K. 317, 1779), 663 n. 6, 748 n. 4, 798 n. 6, 842 n. 4, 941 n. 2, 950 n. 4
- Missa solemnis in C (K. 337, 1780), 663 n. 6, 748 n. 4, 798 n. 6, 842 n. 4
- ★Mass in C minor (K. 427 [417a], 1782–3), 834 n. 1
- ★Requiem (K. 626, 1791), 929 n. 2, 976–7

MISCELLANEOUS CHURCH MUSIC

- Antiphon, 'Quaerite primum regnum Dei' (K. 86 [73v], 1770), 166 n. 1
- Offertory, 'Benedictus sit Deus' (K. 117 [66a], 1769), 94 n. 2, 153 n. 5
- Litaniae de venerabili altaris sacramento (K. 125, 1772), 250 n. 1, 253 n. 1, 555 n. 3
- 'Regina Coeli' (K. 127, 1772), 526 n. 3
- †Eight pieces in a 'Miserere' by I. Holzbauer (K. [297a], 1778), 521 n. 1
- Vesperae solemnes de confessore (K. 339, 1780), 842 n. 5
- Motet, 'Ave, verum corpus' (K. 618, 1791), 950 n. 2
- Motet, 'Exsultate, jubilate' (K. 165 [158a], 1773), 226 n. 2
- Offertorium de tempore, 'Misericordias Domini' (K. 222 [205a], 1775), 266 n. 1, 378 n. 2, 402 n. 2, 418 n. 1, 432 n. 5, 466 n. 3
- Litaniae de venerabili altaris sacramento (K. 243, 1776), 266 n. 3, 379 n. 1, 526 n. 1, 555 n. 3
- Vesperae de Dominica (K. 321, 1779), 842 n. 5
- ★Kyrie in E♭ (K. 322 [296a], 1778), 482 n. 2, 540 n. 6

SACRED CHORAL WORKS

● *La betulia liberata*, azione sacra (K. 118 [74c], 1771), 97, 185 n. 2, 881 n. 4
❢ *Davidde penitente*, cantata (K. 469, 1785), 834 n. 1, 887 n. 1

OPERAS

❢ *Bastien und Bastienne*, Singspiel in one act (K. 50 [46b], 1768), 71
● *La finta semplice*, opera buffa (K. 51 [46a], 1768), 71, 82, 88–93, 101 n. 2, 105,
    119–21, 123–4, 180 n. 4, 181 n. 3
❢ *Mitridate, rè di Ponto*, opera seria (K. 87 [74a], 1770), 83 n. 4, 97, 151, 163, 166,
    169–80, 184, 748 n. 6
● *Ascanio in Alba*, serenata teatrale (K. 111, 1771), 114 n. 2, 189, 193-204, 209,
    693
＊ *Il sogno di Scipione*, serenata drammatica (K. 126, 1772), 209 n. 1
● *Lucio Silla*, dramma per musica (K. 135, 1772), 27 n. 6, 211, 216 n. 1, 220-6,
    370 n. 1, 448 n. 3, 470 n. 1, 482 n. 9, 486 n. 2, 494 n. 1, 843 n. 8
❢ *La finta giardiniera*, opera buffa (K. 196, 1774–5), 247, 249 n. 3, n. 5, 253–61, 265,
    331 n. 5, 362 n. 2, 631 n. 5, 654 n. 1, 680 n. 1, 714 n. 3, 864 n. 3, 924 n. 2,
    943 n. 2
❢ *Il rè pastore*, dramma per musica (K. 208, 1775), 54 n. 6, 253 n. 2, 275 n. 8,
    306 n. 3, 470 n. 3, 482, 517 n. 2
● ＊*Zaide*, Singspiel (K. 344 [336b], 1779–80), 48 n. 2, 654 n. 1, 685 n. 1, 709 n. 1,
    725 n. 1, 725 n. 3
❢ *Idomeneo, rè di Creta*, opera seria (K. 366, 1780–1), 333 n. 1, 418 n. 4, 657, 659–
    690, 691–709, 718–19, 748 n. 1, 759, 765 n. 8, 782 n. 1, 785 n. 9, 794 n. 1,
    796 n. 6, 804 n. 3, 843 n. 3, n. 13, 844 n. 3, 848 n. 3, 860 n. 1, 865
❢ *Die Entführung aus dem Serail*, Komisches Singspiel (K. 384, 1781–2), 375 n. 1,
    685 n. 1, 725 n. 2, 754-6, 761 n. 1, 765 n. 2, 766–73, 776–7, 779, 796 n. 2,
    804 n. 5, 807, 811 n. 2, 817, 825–6, 828, 832, 833 n. 2, 837, 839, 840 n. 5,
    844, 861 n. 1, 862, 863, 883–5, 888, 895, 907 n. 2, 943 n. 2
†'German opera' (K. 416a, 1783), 839 n. 4
● ＊*L'oca del Cairo*, opera buffa (K. 422, 1783), 418 n. 4, 453 n. 1, 855 n. 1, 861-7
● ＊*Lo sposo deluso*, opera buffa (K. 430 [424a], 1783), 848 n. 1, 855 n. 2
● *Der Schauspieldirektor*, Komödie mit Musik (one act) (K. 486, 1786), 710 n. 3,
    725 n. 2
❢ *Le nozze di Figaro*, opera buffa (K. 492, 1785–6), 847 n. 2, 848 n. 1, 853 n. 2,
    893 n. 4, 897, 902–3, 905, 911, 923, 924 n. 4, 933, 934 n. 1, 940 n. 1,
    944 n. 1, 947
● *Don Giovanni*, dramma giocoso (K. 527, 1787), 752 n. 1, 848, 911-14, 919, 923,
    944
❢ *Così fan tutte*, opera buffa (K. 588, 1789–90), 848 n. 1, 924 n. 4, 934 n. 2, 935 n. 2,
    n. 4
❢ *Die Zauberflöte*, Deutsche Oper (K. 620, 1791), 216 n. 1, 783 n. 1, 793 n. 1,
    930 n. 2, 953 n. 6, 954 n. 1, 958 n. 2, 964 n. 1, 966 n. 2, 967 n. 4, 968-70,
    976 n. 2
❢ *La clemenza di Tito*, opera seria (K. 621, 1791), 953 n. 1, 966 n. 1, 967 n. 6, n. 8

MUSIC FOR PLAYS AND BALLETS

*★*Thamos, König in Ägypten, 'heroic drama', chorus and incidental music (K. 345 [336a], 1773–1779), 246 n. 1, 654 n. 1, 840 n. 1
● ★Music for a pantomime (K. 446 [416d], 1783), 842 n. 9
● Ballet music for the pantomime Les Petits Riens (K. App. 10 [299b], 1778) 74 n. 3, 539 n. 2, 564 n. 1
†Semiramis, music for the melodrama by Otto Freiherr von Gemmingen (K. App. 11 [315e], 1778), 631 n. 1
★Le gelosie del serraglio, ballet music (K. App. 109 [135a], 1772), 222 n. 1

ARIAS

SOPRANO
● Recitative and aria, 'Misero me', 'Misero pargoletto' (K. 77 [73e], 1770), 118 n. 1, 153 n. 4
● Aria, 'Per pietà, bell' idol mio' (K. 78 [73b], c. 1766), 153 n. 4
● Recitative and aria, 'O temerario Arbace', 'Per quel paterno amplesso' (K. 79 [73d], c. 1766), 153 n. 4
● Aria, 'Se ardire, e speranza' (K. 82 [73 o], 1770), 131 n. 3, n. 6, 153 n. 4
● Aria, 'Fra cento affani' (K. 88 [73c], 1770), 118 n. 1, 153 n. 4
● Aria, 'Der Liebe himmlisches Gefühl' (K. 119 [382h], 1782), 881 n. 7
● Recitative and aria, 'Ah, lo previdi', 'Ah, t'invola agl' occhi miei' (K. 272, 1777), 280 n. 4, 282 n. 1, 470 n. 2, 581 n. 5, 688 n. 3, 693 n. 2, 764 n. 1
● Recitative and aria, 'Alcandro, lo confesso', 'Non so d'onde viene' (K. 294, 1778), 497 n. 3, 506 n. 1, 517 n. 3, 581 n. 2, 582 n. 1, 635 n. 2, 638 n. 3, 842 n. 2, 845 n. 2, 847 n. 1, 849 n. 2, 851 n. 1
● Recitative and aria, 'Popoli di Tessaglia', 'Io non chiedo, eterni dei' (K. 316 [300b], 1778–9), 581 n. 4
● Scena and aria, 'Misera, dove son!' 'Ah! non son' io che parlo' (K. 369, 1781), 719 n. 4, 764 n. 1, 798 n. 5, 804 n. 9, 843 n. 5
● Recitative and aria, 'A questo seno deh vieni', 'Or che il ciel' (K. 374, 1781), 722 n. 4, 723 n. 6, 742 n. 3, 764 n. 1, 845 n. 4, 849 n. 1
● Scena and rondo, 'Mia speranza adorata', 'Ah, non sai, qual pena' (K. 416, 1783), 836 n. 3, 843 n. 10
● Recitative and aria, 'Vorrei spiegarvi, Oh Dio!' 'Ah conte, partite' (K. 418, 1783), 852 n. 2, 854 n. 1
● Aria, 'No, no, che non sei capace' (K. 419, 1783), 852 n. 2, 854 n. 1
● Recitative and aria, 'Basta, vincesti', 'Ah, non lasciarmi, no' (K. 486A [295a], 1778), 498 n. 1
● Rondo, 'Al desio, di chi t'adoro' (K. 577, 1789), 924 n. 4
● Aria, 'Un moto di gioia mi sento' (K. 579, 1789), 924 n. 4, 934 n. 1
†Aria, 'Misero tu non sei' (K. App. 2 [73A], 1770), 118 n. 1

ALTO
● Recitative and aria, 'Ombra felice', 'Io ti lascio' (K. 255, 1776), 845 n. 3

TENOR
● Aria, 'Va, dal furor portata' (K. 21 [19c], 1765), 54 n. 7

CLASSIFIED INDEX OF WORKS

♦ Recitative and aria, 'Se al labbro mio non credi', 'Il cor dolente' (K. 295, 1778), 496 n. 2, 804 n. 6
● Aria, 'Per pietà, non ricercate' (K. 420, 1783), 852 n. 3, 854 n. 3
● Recitative and aria, 'Misero! o sogno!', 'Aura, che intorno' (K. 431 [425b], 1783), 866 n. 2
● Aria, 'Müsst' ich auch durch tausend Drachen' (K. 435 [416b], 1783), 839 n. 4

BASS

● Aria, 'Männer suchen stets zu naschen' (K. 433 [416c], ?1783), 839 n. 4
● Recitative and aria, 'Alcandro, lo confesso', 'Non so d'onde viene' (K. 512, 1787), 497 n. 2

SONGS WITH PIANO ACCOMPANIMENT

● 'Freude, Königin der Weisen' (K. 53 [47e], 1768), 541 n. 3
● Arietta, 'Oiseaux, si tous les ans' (K. 307 [284d], 1777–8), 468 n. 1, 482 n. 10, 483 n. 1
● Arietta, 'Dans un bois solitaire' (K. 308 [295b], 1777–8), 498 n. 2
● 'Wo bist du, Bild' (K. 530, 1787), 913 n. 5
●*Denis's ode on Gibraltar. Recitative, 'O Calpe!' (K. App. 25 [368d], 1782), 833 n. 3

MISCELLANEOUS WORKS FOR VOICES

● Canon for four voices, 'Lieber Freistädtler, lieber Gaulimauli' (K. 232 [509a], 1787), 904 n. 5
● Nineteen coloratura cadenzas for three operatic arias by J. C. Bach (K. 293e, 1772–3), 482 n. 3, 494 n. 2
● Trio for soprano, tenor and bass voices, 'Liebes Mandl, wo is's Bandl?' (K. 441, ?1783), 903 n. 7

SYMPHONIES

● E♭ (K. 16, 1764–5), 50 n. 3, 55 n. 5
● D (K. 19, 1765), 50 n. 3, 55 n. 5
● B♭ (K. 22, 1765), 64 n. 2
● C (K. 73, 1772), 131 n. 5
● D (K. 81 [73l], 1770), 131 n. 5, 153 n. 3
● D (K. 84 [73q], 1770), 153 n. 3
● D (K. 95 [73n], 1770), 131 n. 5, 153 n. 3
● D (K. 97 [73m], 1770), 131 n. 5, 153 n. 1
● B♭ (K. 182 [173dA], 1773), 835 n. 4
● G minor (K. 183 [173dB], 1773), 835 n. 5
● A (K. 201 [186a], 1774), 835 n. 3
● D, 'Paris' (K. 297 [300a], 1778), 552 n. 1, 556 n. 2, 557 n. 1, 565 n. 1, 573 n. 8, 613 n. 1, 622, 720 n. 3, 724 n. 3, n. 4, 842 n. 1, 946 n. 1
● B♭ (K. 319, 1779), 893 n. 3, 898 n. 1, 900 n. 2, 946 n. 1
● C (K. 338, 1780), 805 n. 1, 898 n. 1, 900 n. 2

1018

MISCELLANEOUS WORKS FOR ORCHESTRA

CONCERTOS FOR PIANO

SERENADES FOR WIND INSTRUMENTS

- E♭ (K. 375, 1781), 776 n. 4, 809 n. 4
- C minor (K. 388 [384a], 1782 or 1783), 809 n. 4

STRING QUINTETS

- B♭ (K. 174, 1773), 516 n. 3
- C (K. 515, 1787), 915 n. 1, 916 n. 1
- C minor (K. 406 [516b], 1788), 915 n. 1, 916 n. 1
- G minor (K. 516, 1787), 915 n. 1, 916 n. 1
- E♭ (K. 614, 1791), xix n. 5

STRING QUARTETS

- G (K. 80 [73f], 1770 and 1773 or 1774), 118 n. 1, 119 n. 3, 516 n. 2
- D (K. 155 [134a], 1772), 213 n. 3
- C (K. 157, 1772 or 1773), 213 n. 3, 229 n. 2
- F (K. 158, 1772 or 1773), 229 n. 2
- B♭ (K. 172, 1773), 246 n. 1
- G (K. 387, 1782), 846 n. 3, 874 n. 4, 885 n. 3, 891-2, 893 n. 3
- D minor (K. 421 [417b], 1783), 846 n. 3, 874 n. 4, 885 n. 3, 891-2, 893 n. 3
- E♭ (K. 428 [421b], 1783), 846 n. 3, 874 n. 4, 885 n. 3, 891-2, 893 n. 3
- B♭ (K. 458, 1784), 846 n. 3, 885 n. 3, 886 n. 4, 891-2, 893 n. 3
- A (K. 464, 1785), 846 n. 3, 885 n. 3, 886 n. 4, 891-2, 893 n. 3
- C (K. 465, 1785), 846 n. 3, 885 n. 3, 886 n. 4, 891-2, 893 n. 3
- D (K. 575, 1789), 930 n. 2, 940
- B♭ (K. 589, 1790), 930 n. 2, 938 n. 2, 940
- F (K. 590, 1790), 930 n. 2, 938 n. 2, 940

Five four-part fugues arranged from J. S. Bach's '48', Book 2, nos. 2, 5, 7, 8, 9 (K. 405, 1782), 862 n. 3

MISCELLANEOUS CHAMBER MUSIC

QUINTETS
- E♭, for piano and wind instruments (K. 452, 1784), 873 n. 6, 880 n. 5
- A, for clarinet and strings (K. 581, 1789), 937 n. 4
- C minor-major, Adagio and Rondo for armonica, flute, oboe, viola, violoncello (K. 617, 1791), 953 n. 4, n. 5

QUARTETS
Flute and strings
- D (K. 285, 1777), 428 n. 1, 457 n. 1, 481 n. 2, 574 n. 2, 622 n. 2
- ★G (K. 285a, 1778), 457 n. 1, 482 n. 2, 574 n. 2, 622 n. 2
- C (K. App. 171 [285b], 1781-2), 481 n. 2, 490

Oboe and strings
● F (K. 370 [368b], 1781), 719 n. 3
Piano and strings
● G minor (K. 478, 1785), 894 n. 1, n. 3, 900 n. 1
●E♭ (K. 493, 1786), 903 n. 6, 918 n. 5

TRIOS
Piano and strings
● B♭ (K. 254, 1776), 300 n. 4, 453 n. 6, 545 n. 4
● G (K. 496, 1786), 899 n. 3
● E (K. 542, 1788), 916 n. 5, 918 n. 5
Violin, viola, and violoncello
● E♭ (K. 563, 1788), xix n. 5, 923 n. 3, 937 n. 5

DUOS
Violin and viola
● G (K. 423, 1783), 862 n. 2, 865
● B♭ (K. 424, 1783), 862 n. 2, 865

PIANO AND VIOLIN SONATAS AND VARIATIONS

● C (K. 6, 1762–4), 37 n. 5, n. 10, 40 n. 2, 53 n. 5, 55 n. 2, 77 n. 7, 433 n. 1,
    525 n. 1, 710 n. 2
● D (K. 7, 1763–4), 37 n. 10, 38 n. 2, 40 n. 2, 53 n. 5, 55 n. 2, 77 n. 7, 433 n. 1,
    525 n. 1, 710 n. 2
● B♭ (K. 8, 1763–4), 37 n. 5, n. 10, 40 n. 3, 53 n. 5, 55 n. 2, 77 n. 7, 525 n. 1,
    710 n. 2
●G (K. 9, 1764), 37 n. 10, 40 n. 3, 53 n. 5, n. 6, 55 n. 2, 77 n. 7, 525 n. 1, 710 n. 2
●B♭ (K. 10,[1] 1764), 52 n. 4, 56, 77 n. 7, 434 n. 1, 525 n. 1, 710 n. 2
●G (K. 11, 1764), 52 n. 4, 56, 77 n. 7, 434 n. 1, 525 n. 1, 710 n. 2
●A (K. 12, 1764), 52 n. 4, 56, 77 n. 7, 434 n. 1, 525 n. 1, 710 n. 2
●F (K. 13, 1764), 52 n. 4, 56, 77 n. 7, 434 n. 1, 525 n. 1, 710 n. 2
●C (K. 14, 1764), 52 n. 4, 56, 77 n. 7, 434 n. 1, 525 n. 1, 710 n. 2
●B♭ (K. 15, 1764), 52 n. 4, 56, 77 n. 7, 434 n. 1, 525 n. 1, 710 n. 2
●E♭ (K. 26, 1766), 64 n. 4, 77 n. 7, 391 n. 3, 405 n. 1, 434 n. 2, 525 n. 1, 710 n. 2
●G (K. 27, 1766), 64 n. 4, 77 n. 7, 391 n. 3, 405 n. 1, 434 n. 2, 525 n. 1, 710 n. 2
●C (K. 28, 1766), 64 n. 4, 77 n. 7, 391 n. 3, 405 n. 1, 434 n. 2, 525 n. 1, 710 n. 2
● D (K. 29, 1766), 64 n. 4, 77 n. 7, 391 n. 3, 405 n. 1, 434 n. 2, 525 n. 1, 710 n. 2
● F (K. 30, 1766), 64 n. 4, 77 n. 7, 391 n. 3, 405 n. 1, 434 n. 2, 525 n. 1, 710 n. 2
●B♭ (K. 31, 1766), 64 n. 4, 77 n. 7, 391 n. 3, 405 n. 1, 434 n. 2, 525 n. 1, 710 n. 2
  C (K. 296, 1778), 300 n. 8, 734 n. 2, 751 n. 8, 780 n. 9, 785 n. 2, 796 n. 1, 798 n. 2,
    803 n. 1, 843 n. 14, 844 n. 4, 845 n. 1, 846 n. 1
  G (K. 301 [293a], 1778), 300 n. 8, 445 n. 1, 482 n. 1, 498 n. 3, 573 n. 2, 581 n. 3,
    598 n. 4, 615 n. 2, 622 n. 4, 625 n. 1, 628 n. 1, 642 n. 1, 645 n. 1, 647 n. 1,
    649 n. 1, 651 n. 1, 688 n. 1, 710 n. 3, 759 n. 2
  E♭ (K. 302 [293b], 1778), 300 n. 8, 445 n. 1, 482 n. 1, 498 n. 3, 573 n. 2, 581 n. 3,
    598 n. 4, 615 n. 2, 622 n. 4, 625 n. 1, 628 n. 1, 642 n. 1, 645 n. 1, 647 n. 1,

---

[1] The sonatas K.10–K.15 have flute as an alternative to violin and an 'ad libitum' violoncello part.

649 n. 1, 651 n. 1, 688 n. 1, 710 n. 3, 759 n. 2
- C (K. 303 [293c], 1778), 300 n. 8, 445 n. 1, 482 n. 1, 498 n. 2, 573 n. 2, 581 n. 3, 598 n. 4, 615 n. 2, 622 n. 4, 625 n. 1, 628 n. 1, 642 n. 1, 645 n. 1, 647 n. 1, 649 n. 1, 651 n. 1, 688 n. 1, 710 n. 3, 759 n. 2
- E minor (K. 304 [300c], 1778), 445 n. 1, 482 n. 1, 498 n. 3, 573 n. 2, 581 n. 3, 598 n. 4, 615 n. 2, 622 n. 4, 625 n. 1, 628 n. 1, 642 n. 1, 645 n. 1, 647 n. 1, 649 n. 1, 651 n. 1, 688 n. 1, 710 n. 3, 759 n. 2
- A (K. 305 [293d], 1778), 300 n. 8, 445 n. 1, 482 n. 1, 498 n. 3, 573 n. 2, 581 n. 3, 598 n. 4, 615 n. 2, 622 n. 4, 625 n. 1, 628 n. 1, 642 n. 1, 645 n. 1, 647 n. 1, 649 n. 1, 651 n. 1, 688 n. 1, 710 n. 3, 759 n. 2
- D (K. 306 [300l], 1778), 445 n. 1, 482 n. 1, 498 n. 3, 573 n. 2, 581 n. 3, 598 n. 4, 615 n. 2, 622 n. 4, 625 n. 1, 628 n. 1, 642 n. 1, 645 n. 1, 647 n. 1, 649 n. 1, 651 n. 1, 688 n. 1, 710 n. 3, 759 n. 2
- F (K. 376 [374d], 1781), 734 n. 2, 736 n. 1, 744 n. 1, 754, 762, 780 n. 9, 785 n. 2, 796 n. 1, 798 n. 2, 800 n. 1, 843 n. 14, 844 n. 4, 845 n. 1, 846 n. 1
- F (K. 377 [374e], 1781), 734 n. 2, 736 n. 1, 744 n. 1, 754, 762, 780 n. 9, 785 n. 2, 796 n. 1, 798 n. 2, 803 n. 1, 843 n. 14, 844 n. 4, 845 n. 1, 846 n. 1
- B♭ (K. 378 [317d], 1779 or 1781), 734 n. 2, 736 n. 1, 751 n. 3, 754, 762, 780 n. 9, 785 n. 2, 796 n. 1, 798 n. 2, 803 n. 1, 843 n. 14, 844 n. 4, 845 n. 1, 846 n. 1
- G major-minor (K. 379 [373a], 1781), 722 n. 3, 723 n. 5, 734 n. 2, 736 n. 1, 754, 762, 780 n. 9, 785 n. 2, 796 n. 1, 798 n. 2, 803 n. 1, 843 n. 14, 844 n. 4, 845 n. 1, 846 n. 1
- E♭ (K. 380 [374f], 1781), 734 n. 2, 736 n. 1, 744 n. 1, 754, 762, 780 n. 9, 785 n. 2, 796 n. 1, 798 n. 2, 803 n. 1, 834 n. 14, 844 n. 4, 845 n. 1, 846 n. 1
- B♭ (K. 454, 1784), 875 n. 2, 880 n. 9, 888 n. 2
- E♭ (K. 481, 1785), 899 n. 2
- F (K. 547, 1778), 918 n. 2

VARIATIONS

- Twelve, on 'La Bergère Célimène' (K. 359 [374a], 1781), 742 n. 4, 747 n. 1, 751 n. 4, 785 n. 5, 796 n. 6, 798 n. 1, 804 n. 4, 844 n. 5
- Six, on 'Hélas, j'ai perdu mon amant' (K. 360 [374b], 1781), 742 n. 4, 747 n. 1, 751 n. 4, 785 n. 2, 796 n. 5, 798 n. 1, 804 n. 4, 844 n. 5

WORKS FOR TWO PIANOS AND PIANO DUETS

- Sonata for four hands in B♭ (K. 358 [186c], 1773–4), 412 n. 2, 448 n. 4, 453 n. 1, 466 n. 4, 470, 748 n. 2, 754 n. 3
- Sonata for four hands in D (K. 381 [123a], 1772), 412 n. 2, 448 n. 4, 453 n. 1, 466 n. 4, 470
- Sonata for two pianos in D (K. 448 [375a], 1781), 720 n. 1, 780 n. 3, 782 n. 3, 785 n. 3, 791 n. 2, 868 n. 1, 880 n. 6
- Sonata for four hands in C (K. 521, 1787), 908 n. 4

PIANO SONATAS

● C (K. 279 [189d],, 1775), 252 n. 2, 329 n. 1, 339 n. 1, 355 n. 7, 376 n. 1, 448 n. 8, 460 n. 2, 615 n. 5, 873 n. 3

● F (K. 280 [189e], 1775), 252 n. 2, 329 n. 1, 339 n. 1, 355 n. 7, 376 n. 1, 448 n. 8, 460 n. 2, 615 n. 5, 873 n. 3

● B♭ (K. 281 [189f], 1775), 252 n. 2, 329 n. 1, 339 n. 1, 355 n. 7, 368 n. 2, 448 n. 8, 460 n. 2, 615 n. 5, 873 n. 3

● E♭ (K. 282 [189g], 1775), 252 n. 2, 329 n. 1, 339 n. 1, 355 n. 7, 448 n. 8, 460 n. 2, 615 n. 5, 873 n. 3

● G (K. 283 (189h], 1775), 252 n. 2, 326 n. 1, 329 n. 1, n. 2, 339 n. 1, 355 n. 7, 448 n. 8, 460 n. 2, 615 n. 5, 873 n. 3

● D (K. 284 [205b], 1775), 287 n. 4, 320 n. 3, 329 n. 1, n. 3, 339 n. 1, 340 n. 3, 355 n. 7, 368 n. 2, 399 n. 1, 448 n. 8, 460 n. 2, 615 n. 5, 873 n. 3, 880 n. 9, 888 n. 2

● C (K. 309 [284b], 1777), 355 n. 2, 361, 363, 373, 397, 401, 402, 408, 414, 416 n. 1, 417, 432 n. 1, 446 n. 2, 451, 453 n. 5, 466 n. 4, 476, 573 n. 7

● A minor (K. 310 [300d], 1778), 573 n. 7, 873 n. 3

● D (K. 311 [284c], 1777), 359 n. 1, 403, 573 n. 7

● ★Allegro, G minor (K. 312 [590d], 1789–90), 941 n. 1

● C (K. 330 [300h], 1781–3), 573 n. 7, 880 n. 8

● A (K. 331 [300i], 1781–3), 573 n. 7, 880 n. 8

● F (K. 332 [300k], 1781–3), 573 n. 7, 880 n. 8

● B♭ (K. 333 [315c], 1783–4), 622 n. 4, 880 n. 9, 888 n. 2

● C minor (K. 457, 1784), xvii n. 2, 771 n. 3, 893 n. 3, 896 n. 1, n. 2

● C (K. 545, 1788), 918 n. 2

● D (K. 576, 1789), 930 n. 1, 941 n. 1

†G, B♭, C, F (K. App. 199–202 [K. 33d–g], 1766), 252 n. 2, 710 n. 2

● ★Fragments, F (K. App. 29, 30, 37 [K. 590 a–c], 1789–90), 941 n. 1

PIANO VARIATIONS

Eight, on a Dutch song (K. 24, 1766), 64 n. 5

Seven, on 'Willem van Nassau' (K. 25, 1766), 64 n. 6

Twelve, on a minuet by J. C. Fischer (K. 179 [189a], 1774), 252 n. 3, 256 n. 5, 339 n. 2, 397 n. 1, 401, 418, 421, 448 n. 5, 453 n. 2, 456, 466, 470, 516 n. 4, 531 n. 5, 759 n. 2, 907 n. 3

Six, on 'Mio caro Adone' (K. 180 [173c], 1773), 252 n. 3, 640 n. 1, 759

Eight, on the march in Grétry's 'Les Mariages samnites' (K. 352 [374c], 1781), 742 n. 2, 747 n. 1, 751 n. 4, 785 n. 5, 796 n. 5, 798 n. 1, 804 n. 4, 844 n. 5

Twelve, on 'Je suis Lindor' (K. 354 [299a], 1778), 718 n. 6, 759 n. 2

Six, on 'Salve tu, Domine' (K. 398 [416e], 1783), 843 n. 9

Ten, on 'Unser dummer Pöbel meint' (K. 455, 1784), 843 n. 9

Eight, on 'Come un' agnello' (K. 460 [454a], 1784), 880 n. 7

CLASSIFIED INDEX OF WORKS

MISCELLANEOUS WORKS FOR PIANO

Eight minuets with trios (K. 315a [315g], 1773), 682 n. 4
Fantasia and Fugue in C (K. 394 [383a], 1782), xix n. 2, 800 n. 7
Capriccio in C (K. 395 [300g], 1777), 573 n. 1, 589 n. 1, 600
Fantasia in C minor (K. 475, 1785), xvii n. 2, 771 n. 3, 893 n. 3, 896 n. 1, n. 2
Adagio in B minor (K. 540, 1788), 918 n. 2
*Fugue in E♭ (K. App. 39 [383d], 1782), 801 n. 1

WORKS FOR A MECHANICAL ORGAN

Adagio and Allegro in F minor-major (K. 594, 1790), 943 n. 5
Fantasy in F minor (K. 608, 1791), 943 n. 5
Andante in F major (K. 616, 1791), 943 n. 5

Copies of church works by Michael Haydn and Ernst Eberlin (K. App. 109vi
[App A. 13-15, 71-88], 1773), 322 n. 1, 343, 835, 842 n. 7

INDEX OF WORKS ARRANGED
ACCORDING TO KÖCHEL NUMBERS

The traditional order has been retained as far as possible. Numbers given in square brackets are those of the sixth edition of Köchel's catalogue, Wiesbaden, 1964

Unfinished works are marked ★
Lost works are marked †

K. 6 (Piano and violin sonata in C, 1762–4), 37 n. 5, n. 10, 40 n. 2, 53 n. 5, 55 n. 2, 77 n. 7, 433 n. 1, 525 n. 1, 710 n. 2

K. 7 (Piano and violin sonata in D, 1763–4), 37 n. 10, 38 n. 2, 40 n. 2, 53 n. 5, 55 n. 2, 77 n. 7, 433 n. 1, 525 n. 1, 710 n. 2

K. 8 (Piano and violin sonata in B♭, 1763–4), 37 n. 5, n. 10, 40 n. 3, 53 n. 5, 55 n. 2, 77 n. 7, 525 n. 1, 710 n. 2

K. 9 (Piano and violin sonata in G, 1764), 37 n. 10, 40 n. 3, 53 n. 5, n. 6, 55 n. 2, 77 n. 7, 525 n. 1, 710 n. 2

K. 10 (Piano, violin (or flute), and violoncello sonata in B♭, 1764), 52 n. 4, 56, 77 n. 7, 434 n. 1, 525 n. 1, 710 n. 2

K. 11 (Piano, violin (or flute), and violoncello sonata in G, 1764), 52 n. 4, 56, 77 n. 7, 434 n. 1, 525 n. 1, 710 n. 2

K. 12 (Piano, violin (or flute), and violoncello sonata in A, 1764), 52 n. 4, 56, 77 n. 7, 434 n. 1, 525 n. 1, 710 n. 2

K. 13 (Piano, violin (or flute), and violoncello sonata in F, 1764), 52 n. 4, 56, 77 n. 7, 434 n. 1, 525 n. 1, 710 n. 2

K. 14 (Piano, violin (or flute), and violoncello sonata in C, 1764), 52 n. 4, 56, 77 n. 7, 434 n. 1, 525 n. 1, 710 n. 2

K. 15 (Piano, violin (or flute), and violoncello sonata in B♭, 1764), 52 n. 4, 56, 77 n. 7, 434 n. 1, 525 n. 1, 710 n. 2

K. 16 (Symphony in E♭, 1764–5), 50 n. 3, 55 n. 5

†K. 16a [App. 220] (Symphony in A minor, 1765), 55 n. 5

K. 19 (Symphony in D, 1765), 50 n. 3, 55 n. 5

K. 19a [App. 223] (Symphony in F, 1765), 50 n. 3, 55 n. 5

†K. 19b [App. 222] (Symphony in C, 1765), 50 n. 3, 55 n. 5

K. [19c] = K. 21

K. 21 [19c] (Tenor aria, 'Va, dal furor portata', 1765), 54 n. 7

K. 22 (Symphony in B♭, 1765), 64 n. 2, 74 n. 5, 77

K. 24 (Eight piano variations on a Dutch song, 1766), 64 n. 5

K. 25 (Seven piano variations on 'Willem van Nassau', 1766), 64 n. 6

K. 26 (Piano and violin sonata in E♭, 1766), 64 n. 4, 77 n. 7, 391 n. 3, 405 n. 1, 434 n. 2, 525 n. 1, 710 n. 2

K. 27 (Piano and violin sonata in G, 1766), 64 n. 4, 77 n. 7, 391 n. 3, 405 n. 1, 434 n. 2, 525 n. 1, 710 n. 2

K. 28 (Piano and violin sonata in C, 1766), 64 n. 4, 77 n. 7, 391 n. 3, 405 n. 1, 434 n. 2, 525 n. 1, 710 n. 2

K. 29 (Piano and violin sonata in D, 1766), 64 n. 4, 77 n. 7, 391 n. 3, 405 n. 1, 434 n. 2, 525 n. 1, 710 n. 2

K. 258 (Missa brevis in C, 1776), 266 n. 3
K. 259 (Missa brevis in C, 1776), 266 n. 3, 541 n. 1
K. 261 (Adagio for violin and orchestra in E, 1776), 275 n. 2, 302 n. 1
K. [261a] = K. 269
K. 262 [246a] (Missa longa in C, 1775), 451 n. 2
K. 269 [261a] (Rondo concertante for violin and orchestra in B♭, 1776), 275 n. 2
K. 271 (Piano concerto in E♭, 1777), 300 n. 2, 456 n. 2, 521 n. 5, 615 n. 4, 840 n. 2
K. [271H] = K. 287
K. 272 (Recitative and aria for soprano, 'Ah, lo previdi', 'Ah, t'invola agl' occhi miei', 1777), 280 n. 4, 282 n. 1, 470 n. 2, 581 n. 5, 688 n. 3, 693 n. 2, 764 n. 1
K. [272b] = K. 275
K. 275 [272b] (Missa brevis in B♭, 1777), 431 n. 2, 663 n. 7, 667 n. 1, 748 n. 4, 842 n. 4, 965 n. 1, 966
K. 279 [189d] (Piano sonata in C, 1775), 252 n. 2, 329 n. 1, 339 n. 1, 355 n. 7, 377 n. 1, 448 n. 8, 460 n. 2, 615 n. 5, 873 n. 2
K. 280 [189e] (Piano sonata in F, 1775), 252 n. 2, 329 n. 1, 339 n. 1, 355 n. 7, 377 n. 1, 448 n. 8, 460 n. 2, 615 n. 5, 873 n. 2
K. 281 [189f] (Piano sonata in B♭, 1775), 252 n. 2, 329 n. 1, 339 n. 1, 355 n. 7, 368 n. 2, 448 n. 8, 460 n. 2, 615 n. 5, 873 n. 2
K. 282 [189g] (Piano sonata in E♭, 1775), 252 n. 2, 329 n. 1, 339 n. 1, 355 n. 7, 448 n. 8, 460 n. 2, 615 n. 5, 873 n. 2
K. 283 [189h] (Piano sonata in G, 1775), 252 n. 2, 326 n. 1, 329 n. 1, n. 2, 339 n. 1, 355 n. 7, 448 n. 8, 460 n. 2, 615 n. 5, 873 n. 2
K. 284 [205b] (Piano sonata in D, 1775), 287 n. 4, 320 n. 3, 329 n. 1, n. 3, 339 n. 1, 340 n. 3, 355 n. 7, 368 n. 2, 399 n. 1, 448 n. 8, 460 n. 2, 615 n. 5, 873 n. 2, 880 n. 9, 888 n.2
K. [284b] = K. 309
K. [284c] = K. 311
K. [284d] = K. 307
K. 285 (Quartet for flute and strings in D, 1777), 428 n. 1, 457 n. 1, 481 n. 2, 574 n. 2, 622 n. 2
★K. 285a (Quartet for flute and strings in G, 1778), 457 n. 1, 481 n. 2, 574 n. 2, 622 n. 2
K. [285b] = K. App. 171
K. [285c] = K. 313
K. [285d] = K. 314
K. 287 [271H] (Divertimento in B♭, 1777), 289 n. 2, 300 n. 5, 417 n. 5, 528 n. 3, 545 n. 4, 592 n. 1, 749 n. 3, 775 n. 2, 804 n. 8
★K. 293 [416f] (Oboe concerto in F, ?1783), 840 n. 4
K. [293a] = K. 301
K. [293b] = K. 302
K. [293c] = K. 303
K. [293d] = K. 305
K. 293e (Nineteen coloratura cadenzas for three operatic arias by J. C. Bach, 1772–3), 482 n. 3, 494 n. 2
K. 294 (Recitative and aria for soprano, 'Alcandro lo confesso', 'Non so d'onde viene', 1778), 497 n. 3, 506 n. 1, 517 n. 3, 581 n. 2, 582 n. 1, 635 n. 2, 638 n. 3, 842 n. 2, 845 n. 2, 847 n. 1, 849 n. 2, 851 n. 1

K. 295 (Recitative and aria for tenor, 'Se al labbro mio non credi', 'Il cor dolente', 1778), 496 n. 2, 804 n. 6

K. [295a] = K. 486a

K. [295b] = K. 308

K. 296 (Piano and violin sonata in C, 1778), 300 n. 8, 734 n. 2, 751 n. 2, 780 n. 9, 785 n. 2, 796 n. 1, 798 n. 2, 803 n. 1, 843 n. 14, 844 n. 4, 845 n. 1, 846 n. 1

K. [296a] = K. 322

K. 297 [300a] ('Paris' Symphony in D, 1778), 552 n. 1, 556 n. 2, 557 n. 1, 565 n. 1, 573 n. 8, 613 n. 1, 622 n. 5, 724 n. 3, 842 n. 1, 946 n. 1

†K. [297a] (Eight pieces in a 'Miserere' by I. Holzbauer, 1778), 521 n. 1

K. [297B] = K. App. 9

K. [297c] = K. 299

K. 299 [297c] (Concerto for flute and harp in C, 1778), 519 n. 5, 574 n. 3, 587 n. 1

K. [299a] = K. 354

K. [299b] = K. App. 10

K. [300a] = K. 297

K. [300b] = K. 316

K. [300c] = K. 304

K. [300d] = K. 310

K. [300g] = K. 395

K. [300h] = K. 330

K. [300i] = K. 331

K. [300k] = K. 332

K. [300l] = K. 306

K. 301 [293a] (Piano and violin sonata in G, 1778), 300 n. 8, 445 n. 1, 482 n. 1, 498 n. 3, 573 n. 2, 581 n. 3, 598 n. 4, 615 n. 2, 622 n. 4, 625 n. 1, 628 n. 1, 642 n. 1, 645 n. 1, 647 n. 1, 649 n. 1, 651 n. 1, 688 n. 1, 710 n. 3, 759 n. 2

K. 302 [293b] (Piano and violin sonata in E♭, 1778), 300 n. 8, 445 n. 1, 482 n. 1, 498 n. 3, 573 n. 2, 581 n. 3, 598 n. 4, 615 n. 2, 622 n. 4, 625 n. 1, 628 n. 1, 642 n. 1, 645 n. 1, 647 n. 1, 649 n. 1, 651 n. 1, 688 n. 1, 710 n. 3, 759 n. 2

K. 303 [293c] (Piano and violin sonata in C, 1778) 300 n. 8 445 n. 1, 482 n. 1, 498 n. 3, 573 n. 2, 581 n. 3, 598 n. 4, 615 n. 2, 622 n. 4, 625 n. 1, 628 n. 1, 642 n. 1, 645 n. 1, 647 n. 1, 649 n. 1, 651 n. 1, 688 n. 1, 710 n. 3, 759 n. 2

K. 304 [300c] (Piano and violin sonata in E minor, 1778), 445 n. 1, 482 n. 1, 498 n. 3, 573 n. 2, 581 n. 3, 598 n. 4, 615 n. 2, 622 n. 4, 625 n. 1, 628 n. 1, 642 n. 1, 645 n. 1, 647 n. 1, 649 n. 1, 651 n. 1, 688 n. 1, 710 n. 3, 759 n. 2

K. 305 [293d] (Piano and violin sonata in A, 1778), 300 n. 8, 445 n. 1, 482 n. 1, 498 n. 3, 573 n. 2, 581 n. 3, 598 n. 4, 615 n. 2, 622 n. 4, 625 n. 1, 628 n. 1, 642 n. 1, 645 n. 1, 647 n. 1, 649 n. 1, 651 n. 1 688 n. 1 710 n. 3, 759 n. 2

K. 306 [300l] (Piano and violin sonata in D, 1778), 445 n. 1, 482 n. 1, 498 n. 3, 573 n. 2, 581 n. 3, 598 n. 4, 615 n. 2, 622 n. 4, 625 n. 1, 628 n. 1, 642 n. 1, 645 n. 1, 647 n. 1, 649 n. 1, 651 n. 1, 688 n. 1, 710 n. 3, 759 n. 2

K. 307 [284d] (Arietta, 'Oiseaux, si tous les ans', 1777–8), 468 n. 1, 482 n. 10, 483 n. 1

K. 308 [295b] (Arietta, 'Dans un bois solitaire', 1777–8), 498 n. 2

K. 309 [284b] (Piano sonata in C, 1777), 355 n. 2, 361, 364, 370, 374, 397, 401, 402, 408, 414, 417, 432 n. 1, 446 n. 2, 451, 453 n. 5, 466 n. 4, 476

K. 310 [300d] (Piano sonata in A minor, 1778), 573 n. 7, 873 n. 3

K. 311 [284c] (Piano sonata in D, 1777), 359 n. 1, 403, 573 n. 7

WORKS ARRANGED ACCORDING TO KÖCHEL NUMBERS

K. [311A] = K. App. 8

K. 312 [590d] [Allegro in G minor, 1789–90), 941 n. 1

K. 313 [285c] (Flute concerto in G, 1778), 457 n. 2, 481 n. 1, 490, 622 n. 3

K. 314 [285d] (Flute concerto in D, 1778), 320 n. 1, 355 n. 5, 457 n. 2, 481 n. 1, 482 n. 6, 490, 622 n. 3, 840 n. 3

K. 315a [315g] (Eight minuets with trios for piano, 1773), 682 n. 4

K. [315c] = K. 333

K. [315e] = K. App. 11

K. [315f] = K. App. 56

K. [315g] = K. 315a

K. 316 [300b] (Recitative and aria for soprano, 'Popoli di Tessaglia', 'Io non chiedo, eterni dei', 1778, 1779), 581 n. 4

K. [316a] = K. 365

K. 317 (Mass (Coronation Mass) in C, 1779), 663 n. 6, 748 n. 4, 798 n. 6, 842 n. 4, 941 n. 2, 950 n. 4

K. [317d] = K. 378

K. 319 (Symphony in B♭ 1779), 893 n. 3, 898 n. 1, 900 n. 2

K. 320 (Serenade in D, 1779), 843 n. 6

K. [320b] = K. 334

K. [320c] = K. 445

K. 321 (Vesperae de Dominica, 1779), 842 n. 5

★K. 322 [296a] (Kyrie in E♭, 1778), 482 n. 2, 540 n. 6

K. 330 [300h] (Piano sonata in C,1781–3),573 n. 7, 589 n. 2, 622 n. 4, 873 n. 3,

K. 331 [300i] (Piano sonata in A, 1781–3), 573 n. 7, 880 n. 8

K. 332 [300k] (Piano sonata in F, 1781–3), 573 n. 7, 880 n. 8

K. 333 [315c] (Piano sonata in B♭, 1783–4), 622 n. 4, 873 n. 3, 880 n. 9, 888 n. 2

K. 334 [320b] (Divertimento in D, 1779–80), 749 n. 3, 804 n. 7

K. [336a] = K. 345

K. [336b] = K. 344

K. 337 (Missa solemnis in C, 1780), 663 n. 6, 748 n. 4, 798 n. 6, 842 n. 4

K. 338 (Symphony in C, 1780), 720 n. 3, 724 n. 3, n. 4, 805 n. 1, 898 n. 1, 900 n. 2

K. 339 (Vesperae solemnes de confessore, 1780), 842 n. 5

★K. 344 [336b] (Zaide, Singspiel, 1779–80), 48 n. 2, 654 n. 1, 685 n. 1, 709 n. 1, 725 n. 1, n. 3

★K. 345 [336a] (Choruses and incidental music for Thamos, König in Ägypten, 1773, 1779), 246 n. 1, 654 n. 1, 840 n. 1

K. 352 [374c] (Eight piano variations on the march in Grétry's 'Les Mariages samnites', 1781), 742 n. 2, 747 n. 1, 751 n. 4, 785 n. 5, 796 n. 5, 798 n. 1, 804 n. 4, 844 n. 5

K. 354 [299a] (Twelve piano variations on 'Je suis Lindor', 1778), 718 n. 6, 759 n. 2

K. 358 [186c] (Piano sonata for four hands in B♭, 1773–4), 412 n. 2, 448 n. 4, 453 n. 1, 466 n. 4, 470, 748 n. 2, 754 n. 3

K. 359 [374a] (Twelve variations for piano and violin on 'La Bergère Célimène', 1781), 742 n. 4, 747 n. 1, 751 n. 4, 785 n. 5, 796 n. 5, 798 n. 1, 804 n. 4, 844 n. 5

K. 360 [374b] (Six variations for piano and violin on 'Hélas, j'ai perdu mon amant', 1781), 742 n. 4, 747 n. 1, 751 n. 4, 785 n. 2, 796 n. 5, 798 n. 1, 804 n. 4, 844 n. 5

K. 365 [316a] (Concerto for two pianos in E♭, 1779), 748 n. 3, 765, 770, 772,

776 n. 1, 780 n. 2, 805 n. 2

K. 366 (*Idomeneo, rè di Creta*, opera seria, 1780–1), 333 n. 1, 418 n. 4, 657, 659–690, 691–709, 718–19, 748 n. 1, 759, 765 n. 8, 782 n. 1, 785 n. 9, 794 n. 1, 796 n. 6, 804 n. 3, 843 n. 3, n. 13, 844 n. 3, 848 n. 3, 860 n. 1, 862, 865

K. [368b] =K. 370

K. 369 (Scena and aria for soprano, 'Misera, dove son!', 'Ah! non son' io che parlo', 1781), 719 n. 4, 764 n. 1, 798 n. 5, 804 n. 9, 843 n. 5

K. 370 [368b] (Quartet for oboe and strings in F, 1781), 719 n. 3

K. 373 (Rondo for violin and orchestra in C, 1781), 722 n. 2, 723 n. 4, 742 n. 3

K. [373a] =K. 379

K. 374 (Recitative and aria for soprano, 'A questo seno deh vieni', 'Or che il ciel', 1781), 722 n. 4, 723 n. 6, 742 n. 3, 764 n. 1, 845 n. 4, 849 n. 1

K. [374a] =K. 359

K. [374b] =K. 360

K. [374c] =K. 352

K. [374d] =K. 376

K. [374e] =K. 377

K. [374f] =K. 380

K. 375 (Serenade for wind instruments in E♭, 1781), 776 n. 4, 809 n. 4

K. [375a] =K. 448

K. 376 [374d] (Sonata for piano and violin in F, 1781), 734 n. 2, 736 n. 1, 744 n. 1, 754, 762, 780 n. 9, 785 n. 2, 796 n. 1, 798 n. 2, 803 n. 1, 843 n. 14, 844 n. 4, 845 n. 1, 846 n. 1

K. 377 [374e] (Sonata for piano and violin in F, 1781), 734 n. 2, 736 n. 1, 744 n. 1, 754, 762, 780 n. 9, 785 n. 2, 796 n. 1, 798 n. 2, 803 n. 1, 843 n. 14, 844 n. 4, 845 n. 1, 846 n. 1

K. 378 [317d] (Sonata for piano and violin in B♭, 1779 or 1781), 734 n. 2, 736 n. 1, 751 n. 3, 754, 762, 780 n. 9, 785 n. 2, 796 n. 1, 798 n. 2, 803 n. 1, 843 n. 14, 844 n. 4, 845 n. 1, 846 n. 1

K. 379 [373a] (Sonata for piano and violin in G minor-major, 1781), 722 n. 3, 723 n. 5, 734 n. 2, 736 n. 1, 742 n. 3, 754, 762, 780 n. 9, 785 n. 2, 796 n. 1, 798 n. 2, 803 n. 1, 843 n. 14, 844 n. 4, 845 n. 1, 846 n. 1

K. 380 [374f] (Sonata for piano and violin in E♭, 1781), 734 n. 2, 736 n. 1, 744 n. 2, 754, 762, 780 n. 9, 785 n. 2, 796 n. 1, 798 n. 2, 803 n. 1, 843 n. 14, 844 n. 4, 845 n. 1, 846 n. 1

K. 381 [123a] (Piano sonata for four hands in D, 1772), 412 n. 2, 448 n. 4, 453 n. 1, 466 n. 4, 470

K. 382 (Rondo for piano and orchestra in D, 1782), 794 n. 2, 798 n. 3, 800, 824 n. 1, 837 n. 5, 841 n. 3, 843 n. 7

K. [382h] = K. 119

K. [383a] =K. 394

K. [383b] =K. App. 33 and K. App. 40

K. [383d] =K. App. 39

K. 384 (*Die Entführung aus dem Serail*, komisches Singspiel, 1781–2), 375 n. 1, 685 n. 1, 725 n. 2, 754–6, 761 n. 1, 765 n. 2, 766–73, 776–7, 779, 796 n. 2, 804 n. 5, 807, 811 n. 2, 817, 825–6, 828, 832, 833 n. 2, 837, 839, 840 n. 5, 844, 861 n. 1, 862, 863, 883–5, 888, 895, 907 n. 2, 943 n. 2

K. [384a] =K. 388

K. 385 ('Haffner' Symphony in D, 1782), 808 n. 1, 809 n. 3, 810 n. 1, 811 n. 1, 813 n. 2, 817 n. 1, 832 n. 1, 835 n. 1, 838 n. 7, 840 n. 6, 843 n. 2, 843 n. 11,

893 n. 3, 898 n. 1

K. [385a] =K. 408 no. 2

K. [385p] =K. 414

K. [386b] =K. 412 and 514

K. [386d] =K. App. 25

K. 387 (String quartet in G, 1782), 846 n. 3, 874 n. 4, 885 n. 3, 891-2, 893 n. 3

K. [387a] =K. 413

K. [387b] =K. 415

K. 388 [384a] (Serenade for wind instruments in C minor, 1782 or 1783), 809 n. 4

K. 394 [383a] (Fantasia and fugue for piano in C, 1782), xix n. 2, 800 n. 7

K. 395 [300g] (Capriccio for piano in C, 1777), 573 n. 1, 589 n. 1, 600

K. 398 [416e] (Six piano variations on 'Salve tu, Domine', 1783), 843 n. 9

K. 405 (Five four-part fugues arranged for string quartet from J. S. Bach's '48', Book 2, nos. 2, 5, 7, 8, 9, 1782), 862 n. 3

K. 406 [516b] (String quintet in C minor, 1788), 915 n. 1, 916 n. 1

K. 408 no. 2 [385a] (March in D for the 'Haffner' Symphony, K. 385, 1782), 810 n. 2, 813 n. 2, 818

K. 413 [387a] (Piano concerto in F, 1782-3), 833 n. 1, 836 n. 1, 837 n. 2, 841 n. 1, 846 n. 2, 869 n. 2, 873 n. 2, 874 n. 5, 893 n. 3

K. 414 [385p] (Piano concerto in A, 1782), 833 n. 1, 836 n. 1, 837 n. 2, 841 n. 1, 846 n. 2, 869 n. 2, 873 n. 2, 874 n. 5, 893 n. 3

K. 415 [387b] (Piano concerto in C, 1782-3), 833 n. 1, 836 n. 1, 837 n. 2, 841 n. 1, 843 n. 4, 845 n. 5, 846 n. 2, 869 n. 2, 873 n. 2, 874 n. 5, 893 n. 3

K. 416 (Scena and rondo for soprano, 'Mia speranza adorata', 'Ah, non sai, qual pena', 1783), 836 n. 3, 843 n. 10

†K. 416a (German opera, 1783), 839 n. 4

K. [416b] =K. 435

K. [416c] =K. 433

K. [416d] =K. 446

K. [416e] =K. 398

K. [416f] =K. 293

K. 417 (Horn concerto in E♭, 1783), 719 n. 5

K. 417a =K. 427

K. 417b =K. 421

K. 418 (Recitative and aria for soprano, 'Vorrei spiegarvi, oh Dio!' 'Ah conte, partite', 1783), 852 n. 2, 854 n. 1

K. 419 (Aria for soprano, 'No, no, che non sei capace', 1783), 852 n. 2, 854 n. 1

K. 420 (Aria for tenor, 'Per pietà, non ricercate', 1783), 852 n. 3, 854 n. 3

K. 421 [417b] (String quartet in D minor, 1783), 846 n. 3, 874 n. 4, 885 n. 3, 891-2, 893 n. 3

K. [421b] =K. 428

*K. 422 (L'oca del Cairo, opera buffa, 1783), 418 n. 4, 453 n. 1, 855 n. 1, 861-7

K. 423 (Duo for violin and viola in G, 1783), 862 n. 2, 865

K. 424 (Duo for violin and viola in B♭, 1783), 862 n. 2, 865

K. [424a] =K. 430

K. 425 ('Linz' Symphony in C, 1783), 859 n. 3, 868 n. 2, 876 n. 2, 883 n. 5, 898 n. 1, 900 n. 2

K. [425b] =K. 431

*K. 427 [417a] (Mass in C minor, 1782-3), 834 n. 1

K. 428 [421b] (String quartet in E♭, 1783), 846 n. 3, 874 n. 4, 885 n. 3, 891-2
893 n. 3

K. 430 [424a] (*Lo sposo deluso*, opera buffa, 1783), 848 n. 1, 855 n. 2

K. 431 [425b] (Recitative and aria for tenor, 'Misero! o sogno!', 'Aura, che
intorno', 1783), 866 n. 2

K. 433 [416c] (Aria for a bass voice, 'Männer suchen stets zu naschen', ?1783),
839 n. 4

K. 435 [416b] (Aria for tenor, 'Müsst' ich auch durch tausend Drachen', 1783),
839 n. 4

K. 441 (Trio for soprano, tenor and bass voices, 'Liebes Mandl, wo is's Bandl?',
?1783), 903 n. 7

K. 445 [320c] (March in D, 1780), 804 n. 7, 806

*K. 446 [416d] (Music for a pantomime, for two violins, viola and double bass,
1783), 842 n. 9

K. 447 (Horn concerto in E♭, ?1784-7), 719 n. 5

K. 448 [375a] (Sonata for two pianos in D, 1781), 720 n. 1, 780 n. 3, 782 n. 3,
785 n. 3, 791 n. 2, 868 n. 1, 880 n. 6

K. 449 (Piano concerto in E♭, 1784), 866 n. 5, 868 n. 3, 872 n. 3, 876 n. 3,
877 n. 1, n. 5, 880 n. 1, n. 9

K. 450 (Piano concerto in B♭, 1784), 866 n. 5, 873 n. 5, 876 n.3, n. 5, 877 n. 2,
880 n. 1, 881 n. 3

K. 451 (Piano concerto in D, 1784), 866 n. 5, 873 n. 5, 876 n. 3, n. 5, 877 n. 3,
880 n. 1, n. 2, 881 n. 3, 899 n. 1, 900 n. 2

K. 452 (Quintet for piano and wind instruments in E♭, 1784), 873 n. 6, 880 n. 5

K. 453 (Piano concerto in G, 1784), 866 n. 5, 874 n. 2, 876 n. 3, 877 n. 1, n. 4,
880 n. 1, n. 4, 881 n. 3, 899 n. 1

K. 454 (Sonata for piano and violin in B♭, 1784), 875 n. 2, 880 n. 9, 888 n. 2

K. [454a] = K. 460

K. 455 (Ten piano variations on 'Unser dummer Pöbel meint', 1784), 843 n. 9

K. 456 (Piano concerto in B♭, 1784), 866 n. 5, 886 n. 6, 899 n. 1

K. 457 (Piano sonata in C minor, 1784), xvii n. 2, 771 n. 3, 893 n. 3, 896 n. 1, n. 2

K. 458 (String quartet in B♭, 1784), 846 n. 3, 885 n. 3, 886 n. 4, 891-2, 893 n. 3

K. 459 (Piano concerto in F, 1784), 866 n. 5, 899 n. 1, 900 n. 2, 946 n. 1

K. 460 [454a] (Eight piano variations on 'Come un' agnello', 1784), 880 n. 7

K. 464 (String quartet in A, 1785), 846 n. 3, 885 n. 3, 886 n. 4, 891-2, 893 n. 3

K. 465 (String quartet in C, 1785), 846 n. 3, 885 n. 3, 886 n. 4, 891-2, 893 n. 3

K. 466 (Piano concerto in D minor, 1788), 885 n. 5, 886 n. 1, 887 n. 2, 894 n. 4,
896 n. 5

K. 467 (Piano concerto in C, 1785), 894 n. 4

K. 469 (*Davidde penitente*, cantata, 1785), 884 n. 1, 887 n. 1

K. 475 (Fantasia for piano in C minor, 1785), xvii n. 2, 771 n. 3, 893 n. 3,
896 n. 1, n. 2

K. 478 (Quartet for piano and strings in G minor, 1785), 894 n. 1, n. 3, 900 n. 1

K. 481 (Sonata for piano and violin in E♭, 1785), 899 n. 2

K. 482 (Piano concerto in E♭, 1785), 895 n. 4

K. 486 (*Der Schauspieldirektor*, Komödie mit Musik (one act), 1786), 710 n. 3,
725 n. 2

K. 486a [295a] (Recitative and aria for soprano, 'Basta, vincesti', 'Ah, non
lasciarmi no', 1778), 498 n. 1

K. 488 (Piano concerto in A, 1786), 899 n. 1, 900 n. 2, n. 3

K. 491 (Piano concerto in C minor, 1786), xix n. 5

K. 492 (*Le nozze di Figaro*, opera buffa, 1785–6), 847 n. 2, 848 n. 1, 853 n. 2, 893 n. 4, 897, 902–3, 905, 911, 923, 924 n. 4, 933, 934 n. 1, 940 n. 1, 944 n. 1, 947

K. 493 (Quartet for piano and strings in E♭, 1786), 903 n. 6, 918 n. 5

K. 495 (Horn concerto in E♭, 1786), 719 n. 5

K. 496 (Trio for piano, violin and violoncello in G, 1786), 899 n. 3

K. 509 (Six German dances for orchestra, 1787), 304 n. 1

K. [509a] = K. 232

K. 512 (Recitative and aria for a bass voice, 'Alcandro, lo confesso', 'Non so d'onde viene', 1787), 497 n. 2

K. 515 (String quintet in C major, 1787), 915 n. 1, 916 n. 1

K. 516 (String quintet in G minor, 1787), 915 n. 1, 916 n. 1

K. [516b] = 406

K. 521 (Piano sonata for four hands in C, 1787), 908 n. 4

K. 527 (*Don Giovanni*, dramma giocoso, 1787), 752 n. 1, 848, 911–14, 919, 923, 944

K. 530 (Song, 'Wo bist du, Bild', 1787), 913 n. 5

K. 537 (Piano concerto in D, 1788), 923 n. 4, 946 n. 1

K. 540 (Adagio for piano in B minor, 1788), 918 n.2

K. 542 (Trio for piano, violin, and violoncello in E, 1788), 916 n. 5, 918 n. 5

K. 545 (Piano sonata in C, 1788), 918 n. 2

K. 547 (Sonatina for piano and violin in F, 1788), 918 n. 2

K. 563 (Divertimento for violin, viola, and violoncello in E♭, 1788), xix n. 5, 923 n. 3, 937 n. 5

K. 575 (String quartet in D, 1789), 930 n. 2, 940

K. 576 (Piano sonata in D, 1789), 930 n. 1, 941 n. 1

K. 577 (Rondo for soprano, 'Al desio, di chi t'adora', 1789), 924 n. 4

K. 579 (Aria for soprano, 'Un moto di gioia mi sento', 1789), 924 n. 4, 934 n. 1

K. 581 (Quintet for clarinet and strings in A, 1789), 937 n. 4

K. 588 (*Così fan tutte*, opera buffa, 1789–90), 848 n. 1, 924 n. 4, 934 n. 2, 935 n. 2, n. 4

K. 589 (String quartet in B♭, 1790), 930 n. 2, 938 n. 2, 940

K. 590 (String quartet in F, 1790), 930 n. 2, 938 n. 2, 940

K. [590d] = K. 312

K. 594 (Adagio and Allegro for a mechanical organ in F minor-major, 1790), 943 n. 5

K. 595 (Piano concerto in B♭, 1791), 556 n. 5

K. 608 (Fantasy for a mechanical organ in F minor, 1791), 943 n. 5

K. 614 (String quintet in E♭, 1791), xix n. 5

K. 616 (Andante for a mechanical organ in F major, 1791), 943 n. 5

K. 617 (Adagio and Rondo for armonica, flute, oboe, viola, violoncello in C minor-major, 1791), 953 n. 4, n. 5

K. 618 (Motet, 'Ave, verum corpus', 1791), 950 n. 2

K. 620 (*Die Zauberflöte*, Deutsche Oper, 1791), 216 n. 1, 783 n. 1, 793 n. 1, 930 n. 2, 953 n. 6, 954 n. 1, 958 n. 2, 964 n. 1, 966 n. 2, 967 n. 4, 968–70, 976 n. 2

K. 621 (*La clemenza di Tito*, opera seria, 1791), 953 n. 1, 966 n. 1, 967 n. 6, n. 8

K. 622 (Clarinet concerto in A, 1791), 937 n. 4, 967 n. 2

*K. 626 (Requiem, 1791), 929 n. 2, 976–7

†K. App. 2 [73a] (Aria for soprano, 'Misero tu non sei', 1770), 118 n. 1

WORKS ARRANGED ACCORDING TO KÖCHEL NUMBERS

†K. App. 8 [311A] (Symphony in B♭, 1778) 613 n. 1, 622 n. 5

K. App. 9 [297B] (Sinfonia concertante for flute, oboe, horn, and bassoon in E♭, 1778), 522 n. 1, 529, 532 n. 2, 546, 564–5, 574 n. 1, 622 n. 6

K. App. 10 [299b] (Ballet music for the pantomime, *Les Petits Riens*, 1778), 74 n. 3, 539 n. 2, 564 n. 1

†K. App. 11 [315e] (Music for Otto Freiherr von Gemmingen's melodrama, *Semiramis*, 1778), 631 n. 1

K. [App. A 13–15] = K. App. 109 vi

★K. App. 25 [386d] (Denis's ode on Gibraltar. Recitative, 'O Calpe', 1782), 833 n. 3

★K. App. 39 [383d] (Fugue for piano in E♭, 1782), 801 n. 1

★K. App. 56 [315f] (Concerto for piano and violin in D, 1778), 631 n. 4

K. [App. 71–88] = K. App. 109 vi

★K. App. 109 [135a] (Ballet music, *Le gelosie del serraglio*, 1772), 222 n. 1

K. App. 109 vi [App. A 13–15, 71–88] (Copies made by Mozart of 19 church works by Michael Haydn and Ernst Eberlin, 1773), 322 n. 1, 343, 835, 842 n. 7

K. App. 171 [285b] (Quartet for flute and strings in C, 1781–2), 481 n. 2, 490

K. [App. C.11.01] = K. 166

†K. App. 199–202 [K. 33d–g] (Clavier sonatas in G, B♭, C and F, 1766), 252 n. 2, 710 n. 2